The Plate

The Plate

150 Years of Royal Tradition from Don Juan to Eye of the Leopard

LOUIS E. CAUZ
& BEVERLEY A. SMITH

Published by ECW PRESS
2120 Queen Street East, Suite 200, Toronto, Ontario, Canada M4E 1E2
416.694.3348 / info@ecwpress.com

LIBRARY AND ARCHIVES OF CANADA CATALOGUING IN PUBLICATION

Cauz, Louis, 1932-
The Plate : 150 years of royal tradition from Don Juan to
Eye of the Leopard / Louis E. Cauz and Beverley Smith.

ISBN 978-1-55022-894-6

1. Queen's Plate (Horse race)—History. 2. Horse racing—Ontario—
Toronto—History. I. Smith, Beverley, 1954– II. Title.

SF357.Q4C38 2009   798.4009713'541   C2009-902531-0

Design and typesetting: Greg Oliver and Paul Hodgson
Cover design: Rachel Ironstone
Printed and Bound in China by Shanghai Chenxi Printing
First printing, 2009

The Publication of *The Plate* has been generously supported by the OMDC Book Fund,
an initiative of the Ontario Media Development Corporation, and
by the Government of Canada through the Book Publishing Industry Development Program (BPIDP).

Canada

ECW PRESS
ecwpress.com

Contents

Foreword
By David S. Willmot

ormally, it is named "The Queen's Plate Stakes." Colloquially, it is referred to simply as "The Plate." By either name, it is one of the truly great Canadian sporting icons.

Certainly it is the oldest, inaugurated in 1860, seven years before Confederation, with a purse of "Fifty Guineas, the gift of Her Majesty Queen Victoria." The race has been run every year to this day and the tradition of the Reigning Monarch awarding fifty guineas to the winning owner has continued uninterrupted.

For Canadians past and present, this is the race they dream of winning with a thoroughbred foaled in this country, to be part of the continuing tradition, to celebrate the pageantry, and to win amongst their family, friends and peers.

The stories of the winners and participants in this unique event weave a thread through the colourful history of horse racing and sport in Canada and beyond, through the exploits and progeny of the truly greats such as *Northern Dancer* and *Dance Smartly*.

This book, detailing the first 150 years of The Queen's Plate, updates and expands upon the 1984 edition. It includes a golden era for Canadian horse racing when, after a lengthy drought without a Canadian Triple Crown winner, five were produced in a period of fourteen years. Their names will be remembered as some of the very best Canadian-breds of all time and isn't that what this wonderful book allows us to do, to look back, to remember, to compare and to drink in the pageantry of "The Plate" and the majesty of the thoroughbred.

DAVID S. WILLMOT.

Introduction
By Neil A. Campbell

The world has changed mightily since the first version of this book landed in all its handsome, glossy glory twenty-five years ago, not long after *Key to the Moon* bullied his way to victory over *Let's Go Blue*. An explosion of cheap and accessible computing power has forever altered our information habits. *Key to the Moon*'s year was a landmark in that it was the first time you could place a bet on the Queen's Plate at another racetrack. Now, of course, you can watch the whole Plate card on your computer from anywhere in the world while watching replays of Plate preps, studying online past performances, reading a live blog and tapping out whatever wager you feel like.

What hasn't changed a whit in twenty-five years is the irreplaceability of storytelling. The Internet can whet your Queen's Plate appetite in a high-level, mass-market way—videos of old Plates are on YouTube, the history of the race has its own page on Wikipedia, you can find endless links on Google. But nothing can match the incredible craftsmanship Louis Cauz brings to these pages. The original masterpiece wasn't enough. He burrowed tirelessly through more yellow newspaper clippings and more minutes of meetings. He kept tapping the greatest resource of all—asking questions of racetrack veterans who have a lifetime of colourful memories ready to be turned on like a tap. New information appears throughout the pages of the first 125 years.

For the new chapters, the past twenty-five years, Louis Cauz found a storytelling entry mate in Beverley Smith. Both honed their skills working for *The Globe and Mail*, and not just in horse racing. Both have won Sovereign Awards for their writing. But Beverley Smith brings a perspective that contrasts delightfully to Louis Cauz's professorial thoroughness. She began sketching horses as a child and still does so today, a hobby that colours her descriptive writing. *Woodcarver*, for example, is not just the 1999 Queen's Plate winner but "a fetching big grey with dark dapples scattered over his rump." *With Approval* won the 1989 Plate "by the bob of his pert roan nose." Beverley is the perfect guide for the past quarter-century. The lineup of stars we saw during those years was breathtaking.

The old dynasties were fading by the time *La Lorgnette* wore the storied Windfields Farm silks to victory in 1985. Jack Stafford and Conn Smythe were gone and despite *La Lorgnette*'s win the sun was beginning to set on the Windfields empire. New titans emerged. Sam-Son Farm was led by Ernie Samuel, a tall articulate, graceful man with an unquenchable thirst for winning. Bud Willmot, equally graceful, ran Kinghaven Farms along with his son David, who was bursting with intellect and energy. Frank Stronach came along, too, more ambitious than anyone and unwilling to be constrained by Canadian boundaries.

Their collective planning and investment yielded a parade of unforgettable champions. Kinghaven's *With Approval* swept Canada's Triple Crown in 1989, the first time in a generation it had happened. A year later Kinghaven's *Izvestia* also swept the Triple

Crown. In 1991 Sam-Son's *Dance Smartly*, a filly, won the Triple Crown, and then became the first Canadian to win a Breeders' Cup race. Kinghaven's *Alydeed* finished second in the Preakness in 1992 and then ran away with the Plate. Five years later Stronach sent an unknown colt named *Awesome Again* to win the Plate and the following season he completed an undefeated campaign by winning one of the greatest Breeders' Cup Classics. There was also *Peteski* in 1993 and *Wando* in 2003, Triple Crown winners both. Beverley Smith saw them all and brings them to life in an elegant recap of those remarkable years.

It's not just about the horses and the people, though. There are clues scattered throughout her chapters that tell of a changing landscape for horse racing in Ontario. There were new, convenient ways to bet, and this had a dampening effect on attendance. Woodbine itself had several dramatic facelifts during the twenty-five years. The old dirt track was moved inside a European-style, sweeping twelve-furlong grass course and was eventually replaced by an artificial surface. The building was overhauled to accommodate a casino, and the fences came down. Admission was free. Parking was free. No longer did you have to pay to watch the Queen's Plate.

And no longer was the Queen's Plate necessarily the biggest moment of the racing calendar for Canadians. A few months after *Key to the Moon*'s 1984 Plate win the Breeders' Cup was run for the first time, on an un-drenched November afternoon at Hollywood Park. Globalization had arrived in a big way at the track. Playing a part in this new international spectacle—competing against owners, trainers and jockeys from the United States, France, Ireland, England and beyond—became as appealing to some as basking in the Plate spotlight.

The Breeders' Cup didn't exist the first time this book was written. There was no casino at Woodbine. There was no Internet to allow bettors to watch and wager on races basically around the clock. It seems everything about the game has changed in twenty-five years, everything except for the Queen's Plate. It remains a mile and a quarter for Canadian-bred three-year-olds on a summer weekend at Woodbine, a comforting constant in a dizzying world.

And it remains a source of passion. It's there in Louis Cauz's newly fortified descriptions of the first 125 years of this remarkable Canadian institution. It's there in Beverley Smith's account of the past twenty-five years. It's there as well among those who are relatively new to the race.

Emma Jayne Wilson was a toddler when this book first appeared. She is a child of the Internet age, the racing age, the Breeders' Cup age. Yet when she had a chance to win her first Queen's Plate, in 2007, there she was, in the words of Beverley Smith, "scrubbing, pumping, pushing and urging . . . for all she was worth."

The horses, jockeys, owners and trainers come and go. But the magic of the Queen's Plate is seemingly forever. Enjoy this book for the treasure that it is.

Acknowledgements

Acknowledgments are authors ways of praising the people whose contributions to a book of this dimension and detail were of incredible assistance. They are personal and tend to interest only those whose names are recognized. I will salute these people in due time. First I prefer to recognize the people, horse men and the pioneer breeders who 150 years ago were indirectly involved in the 150th running of the Queen's Plate this past summer.

On 27 June 1860 a race was staged over a racecourse located in Carleton, a rural village northwest of Toronto. It was the opening day of the Toronto Turf Club's three-day meet and attracted a fashionable, gaily attired crowd of more than 2,500 to witness the Queen's Plate, a race that had never been contested before in Upper Canada (previously only in Quebec and Nova Scotia). It was regarded with interest for the novelty of the occasion, this being the first time that it had been offered for competition here. Racing in Toronto in the 1850s was at a low ebb. In an effort to rejuvenate it, the Club sought the patronage of the monarchy, sending a petition to Queen Victoria requesting a Plate worth the equivalent of Fifty Guineas. The Club hoped to renew interest in the sport, encourage breeders as well as provide prestige. In July 1859 Queen Victoria granted the Club's petition by donating Fifty Guineas for a race to be run annually in Upper Canada. Racing fans were curious about this newly inaugurated event that attracted eight provincial-bred maidens. There were two other races scheduled, one of which, the Toronto Cup, offered more money ($700) than the Plate.

An equine event that would continue uninterrupted for the next 150 years made its debut with little fanfare. Racing at this time didn't designate its historical context numerically. In fact, it wasn't until 1899 that the Ontario Jockey Club woke up to the fact and boasted that the 40th running of the Plate would be held. It would be safe to speculate that few, if any, on 27 June 1860 were aware if the historic significance unfolding on W.C. Keele's farm that summer afternoon, or suggest that Canada's most prestigious racing event might exist 150 years later.

Thus, my acknowledgments are directed to those fans making the six-mile trek in their carriages or passenger cars of the Grand Trunk Railway to the new track. Also to the racing officials and agricultural society's at fairs across the province who kept the Plate alive by maintaining the Plate's continuity at towns from London to Ottawa, Picton and Prescott, from Hamilton to St. Catharines, Barrie, Guelph and Woodstock. And the pioneering stalwarts of racing's upper crust—Denison, Grange, Gzowski, Hendrie, Howland, Boulton, Leys, Quetton St. George, Robinson, Heward and Dickson.

Also the brazen officials of the OJC in 1918 and 1919 who refused to buckle when the government banned all organized horse racing for the duration of the war in Europe. It took arbitrary steps to maintain the Plate's continuity, using the Toronto Hunt Club and the Red Cross as a shield to stage a non-betting, one-race program.

We would not have celebrated our 150th this summer except for these people.

The person who earns the lion's share of recognition is Beverley Smith, who collaborated with me in the writing of the manuscript. Seeking an author with a love and deep interest in horse racing, Ms Smith was a natural. I wanted a fresh outlook on the race's recent history, assigning her the stories of the next twenty five years following the celebration and publication of *The Plate: A Royal Tradition* in 1984. This allowed me to thoroughly research some of the untold stories of the race's history from 1860 to 1984, revising, adding new material and locating previously unpublished photos. Beverly was a studious running mate. We made a great literary entry. The complete contributions of others during the past four years would make the acknowledgments look like a page out of the telephone book.

To name a few—The staff at Woodbine Entertainment who put aside their own assignments to help answer my queries or direct me to "techies" who knew the science of computers. I'm talking about Adam Hickman, Christina Barth, John Siscos, Chris Lomon, Claudia Chavez, Andrew Faria, Jennifer Lym, Dione Hicks, Jennifer Knoch, the Ontario Arts Council and Jim Bannon. The two ladies at the Torstar photo syndicate service with their diligent research in locating photos from their archives. And Michael Burns and Dave Landry, opening up their photo archives. Also, Jim Ormiston, the former WEG executive who was always in my corner when I shouted help and was instrumental in coordinating the publishing contract with the men at ECW, David Caron and Jack David.

Finally, there are the people who put the book together: Greg Oliver, who toiled away on the production, Jim O'Leary who scanned countless photos and helped coordinate the move of this book into the electronic era, and Paul Hodgson for the initial design.

On a weekly basis it was my Girl Thursday, who delivered my cup of tea each morning and calmed me down on some of my stressful days when I would "lose it." And finally Miss Debbie, who each night listened to my moaning of "what had gone wrong" or boasting of another hurdle cleared toward the finish line.

— Louis E. Cauz

Origins: A Pair of Blacksmith's Bellows Against a Barrel of West Indian Molasses or $20 Cash

Organized race meetings under the auspices of regular turf clubs first became important in Upper Canada in the 1820s, when programs were held at Toronto, Cobourg, Kingston, Cornwall, Caledonia, Guelph, Hamilton, London and on the vast grassy plains around Fort George in the garrison town of Niagara. Contests, either trials of speed, one cavalry officer challenging another, or two farmers wagering livestock or produce to settle whose mare was the fastest, had been a form of an afternoon's entertainment long before the War of 1812–1814 between Upper and Lower Canada and the United States.

There are accounts of horse racing in 1797, in the *History of Niagara* which would indicate that in all garrison towns along the Governor's Road the amusement of racing had enthusiastic supporters.

Many of the old inhabitants tell of the three-days' races attended by crowds of visitors, and old Niagara papers contained advertisements. Not all places had such an extensive grass-grown plain for a racecourse, nor such a vantage-ground for a view as was afforded by the ramparts of Fort George. On 31 May, 1797, *Amicus* wrote advocating a racecourse, and the issue for 27 June, *Upper Canada Gazette*, read: 'Races will be run over the new course on the plains of Niagara.' In a later paper we learned that the races took place on 6, 7 and 8 July. One of the rules was: 'No one is to ride except in a short, round jacket. If caps are not to be had a black handkerchief to be worn as a substitute'. The letter of *Amicus* had recommended the establishment of the Turf Club to promote an intercourse of commerce, friendship and sociability between people of this province and those of the neighbouring parts of the United States.

In 1817, following the war that had engulfed the Niagara Peninsula, matches and sweepstakes were run over the course near Fort George. The 70th Regiment band played until "five in the morning after officers had given a dinner, ball and supper to a large party in their mess room." *The Gleaner* that year announced that a subscription of four dollars was needed from each member of the Niagara Turf Club to create a fund for purses. By 1826 newspapers were describing horses and the dress of jockeys; no dogs were allowed on the track and "persons riding about are warned to keep wide of the bushes which mark the track." Among the entrants for one of the races, to be decided by three one-mile heats, was Mr. Hamilton's strawberry mare, *Blind Hooky*; the rider's colours—yellow body and blue cap. In 1829 the planting of oak trees round the common was recommended to replace posts and to be an ornament to "our beautiful race course."

In T.C. Patteson's memoirs, printed in the *Toronto News* in 1905, he describes the Niagara course as "a grass one, as was sure to be the case where English officers held high carnival. There was no grandstand of more than ephemeral construction; but there was grand sport." He also told of the June afternoon in 1837 when Prince Louis Napoleon, who was visiting the American side of Niagara Falls, accepted an invitation for luncheon with the officers of the Niagara garrison. His source of information was the Honourable W.H. Dickson.

During the luncheon some discussion arose respecting the merits of a mare owned by Mr. Dickson and another animal, the property of an officer at the table. It was decided to run a match at once. Mr. Dickson's mare was sent for, and ridden in a harness bridle by a negro boy bareback, with one spur fastened to a naked foot. She "downed" the officer's nag. Few people know that the Emperor of the French was ever in Canada; fewer that he ever witnessed a race here.

Horse racing and the quality of the horses, most of which were half-breds sired by carriage horses, was of little account during this period. In *Five Years' Residence* Edward Talbot wrote of attending a race "about 1820" so that he might witness the speed of their sorry *chevaux* as they cantered over a quarter-of-a-mile course.

Four horses started for a bet of 10,000 *feet of boards*. The riders were clumsy-looking fellows, bootless and coatless. Before they started, every one seemed anxious to bet upon some one or other of the horses. Wagers were offered in every part of the field, and I was soon assailed by a host of fellows, requesting me to take their offers. The first who attracted my notice said he would bet me *a barrel of salt pork* that *Split-the-Wind* would win the day. When I refused to accept of this,

TORONTO TURF CLUB RACES.

Spring Meeting—Union Course.

TO COMMENCE

TUESDAY, 24th JUNE,

AND CONTINUE

WEDNESDAY, 25th June, and FRIDAY, 27th June, 1845,

Subject to the Rules and Regulations of the St. Leger Club, & under the management of the following Gentlemen, viz:

President—The Mayor of the City, W. H. BOULTON, Esq., M.P.P.
Vice-President—The Sheriff of the District, W. B. JARVIS, Esq.

STEWARDS:

Hon. H. SHERWOOD, M.P.P.   Dr. T. D. HUME, 82nd Regt.
R. P. CROOKS, Esq.   O. F. TIMMINS, Esq., 82nd Regt.

Treasurer—CHARLES THOMPSON, Esq.; Secretary—GEORGE D. WELLS, Esq.

FIRST DAY, TUESDAY, JUNE 24.

THE St. LEGER CUP, of Twenty Sovereigns, added to a Sweepstakes of Five Sovereigns each—two sovereigns forfeit—for foals dropped in Canada in 1842, and now 3 yrs old. One mile and three-quarters. Colts, 7st. 11lbs; Fillies, 7st. 7lbs. To name and forfeit paid to the Secretary, between the hours of 12 and 3 o'clock, of Saturday, 31st May 1845; and the rest of the entrance money to be paid on the day and time appointed for the closing of other stakes—run for at the meeting.

THE TURF CLUB PURSE, of £75, entrance £5 each—free for all horses. Turf Club Weights. Three mile heats.

THE LADIES' PURSE, of Ten Sovereigns, added to a Sweepstakes of Three Sovereigns each—free for all horses bona fide owned in Canada, 1st Jan, 1845. One mile and a quarter. Welter Weights, 2nd class. Gentlemen Riders.

SECOND DAY, WEDNESDAY, JUNE 25.

THE PROPRIETOR'S PURSE, of £25, (the gift of the Proprietor of the Course), added to a Sweepstakes of £6 5s. each—free for all horses. Two mile heats. Turf Club Weights. The winner of the Club Purse to carry 5lbs. extra.

THE MEMBERS' PURSE, of £25, added to a Sweepstakes of £2 10s. each—for horses bred in the United Province. Mile heats—best 3 in 5. Turf Club Weights. Maiden horses at time of entrance allowed 7lbs.

THE INNKEEPERS' PURSE, of £25, added to a Sweepstakes of £5 each—free for all horses—to carry 7st. 5lb. each without distinction. Two miles and a quarter—Heats.

THIRD DAY, FRIDAY, JUNE 27.

THE HURDLE RACE, of £20, added to a Sweepstakes of £5 each—free for all horses. Welter weights, first class. Two miles and a quarter—four hurdles (4 ft. high) in each mile. Gentlemen Riders.

THE CITY PURSE, of £25, added to a Sweepstakes of £2 10 each—free for all horses. Mile heats. Turf Club weights. The winner of the Club Purse 5lbs. extra—of the Proprietor's Purse 4lbs. extra—of both 7lbs. extra.

THE GOVERNOR GENERAL'S PURSE, of £25, added to a Sweepstakes of £5 each—free for all horses owned in Canada, 1st January, 1845. Two and three-quarter miles. Turf Club weights.

THE CONSOLATION STAKES, of —— added to a Handicap Sweepstakes of £2 10. St. Leger Distance.

N.B.—Horses imported into North America in 1845, and Province-bred Horses, allowed 10lbs., and Mares and Geldings allowed 3lbs. Second Horse, in all cases, to save his stakes.

TO START PRECISELY AT ONE O'CLOCK EACH DAY.

The Stewards' decisions, which are final, will be guided by the Rules and Regulations of the Club—and from such decision there can be no appeal whatever. All the above stakes will close at 3 o'clock, P.M., on Saturday, 31st June, 1845, on which day the Stewards will attend at Mr. McDonald's Hotel, from 12 to 3 o'clock, P.M., for the purpose of receiving entrances which will be required to be made in strict conformity with the Regulations. No person will be entitled to run, or train a horse on the Course, who is not a subscriber of at least £2 10s. to the Race Fund.

RICHARD TINNING, PROPRIETOR.

Toronto, 29th May, 1845.

another offered to bet me 3,000 *cedar shingles* that *Washington* would distance 'every damned scrape of them.' A third person tempted me with a wager of *50 lb. of pork sausages*, against *a cheese of similar weight*, that *Prince Edward* would be distanced. A fourth, who appeared to be a shoemaker, offered to stake *a raw ox-hide*, against half its weight in *tanned leather*, that *Columbus* would be either first or second. Five or six others, who seemed to be partners in *a pair of blacksmith's bellows*, expressed their willingness to wager them against *a barrel of West Indian molasses*, or twenty dollars in cash. In the whole course of my life, I never witnessed so ludicrous a scene.

In the early 1800s, a valuable horse was one that not only could draw a great load, but also could go at a good pace without injury to himself. The practice of importing high-spirited thoroughbreds from England and the United States did not take hold until the late 1840s.

In Patteson's memoirs, the former postmaster of Toronto and the man who was credited with founding the Ontario Jockey Club in 1881, referred to the incident at Niagara in 1837 and how breeding benefited by the presence of English officers at the garrison. "There is not one horse now in registration [1905] as a thorough-bred, who is descended from the horses who then raced over the Niagara Common. But the breed of horses in Ontario must be considerably indebted to the officers who used to buy horses down South and bring them into Canada for racing purposes. Especially useful was *Cademus*, who sowed his teeth widely over the Peninsula. He was a son of *American Eclipse*, who was himself by *Duroc* from a bona-fide *Messenger* mare. The grey horse, *Hamiltonian*, foaled about 1829 in Long Island, New York, was another useful sire in the counties of Welland and Lincoln . . . but Toronto was not idle. No doubt there were racehorses here very soon after the first officers were stationed at York."

There were, but as Richard L. Denison, a wealthy gentleman farmer of York, noted in 1858 in his address at the thirteenth annual exhibition of the Provincial Agricultural Association in Toronto, it was of little help. In 1838 the British Government had sent the Dragoon Guards to this country, both horses and men. The horses, which were chiefly geldings of a very superior class, were left behind when the Regiment returned to England. With a little consideration the Home Government might have thought to benefit this colony by sending mares in place of geldings.

The first course in York (it was not until 1834 that it officially was known as Toronto) was, strangely enough, on Toronto Island, the part of it known as "The Bend." It was a sandy neck of land that connected the central portion of the peninsula (the western tip of the peninsula at Gibraltar Point) with the main shore to the east. The course was not oval-shaped, but a long, straight level track. On 6 September 1793, Mrs. Elizabeth Simcoe, wife of Lieutenant Governor John Graves Simcoe, and Lieutenant Thomas Talbot, informally inaugurated horse racing on the peninsula. Contests, which were informal, were held periodically among military officers and local citizens. John Ross Robertson in *Landmarks of Toronto*, wrote of a letter he received from one of the city's oldest inhabitants. "After crossing the second bridge, the one on the 'Big Don,' as it was called, there was a plateau of smooth springy turf for half or three-quarters of a mile, extending southerly to the northernmost of the two ridges of sand forming the beautiful valley leading thence to the lighthouse at Gibraltar Point. The favourite resort for equestrians in those good old days was the Island, so long as the bridges lasted. The valley was mostly covered with grass, but it was rather heavy riding; the moment however the plateau was reached at either end there was a race to the other end. There was no 'regular' racecourse in the neighborhood of York at that time. Grooms would try their masters' horses at 'The Bend' but I never knew of a 'professional' race.

A LETTER FROM MEMBERS OF THE TORONTO TURF CLUB IN 1859 PETITIONING QUEEN VICTORIA TO GRANT A QUEEN'S PLATE TO BE RUN ANNUALLY AT THE CARLETON RACE COURSE "IN THE VICINITY OF THE CITY OF TORONTO."

The only public race I recollect in York in the early time was on Front Street, from 'Smalls Corner' to the Market Place. It was announced by placards posted throughout the town, the constable kept the course, and all York turned out to witness it." He added that "The Bend" was "also occasionally the scene of 'scratch' trotting matches between horses owned by people in or near the city. After the rebellion of 1837, this Island course was less and less used for pleasure, and not at all for racing purposes, even in the very mild form just described." The *British Colonist* noted that a great number of people viewed a race between *Deadnaught* and *Swift* on the peninsula race ground. The race ended with the saddle girth breaking on *Swift*. "Horse racing seems not to be the only amusement of the people of that town. With this they mix the more rational and beneficial employment, that of mending the roads."

Race meets in York began several years after the War of 1812–1814, along Front Street, from Small's Corner to Market Place, and in the late 1820s on a course that was laid out on the Garrison Common, between the Old and New Forts. The Upper Canada Turf Club grew out of a series of military races under the patronage of officers stationed at Fort York and at Niagara. During the mid 1830s a course was built on the property of John Scarlett, who lived in the Humber Valley above "The Old Mill." Scarlett's property, named "Runnymede," stretched north and east a considerable distance. Scarlett's Simcoe Chase Course was managed by the City of Toronto and the Home District Turf Club. It lay just north of Dundas Street, between Weston Road and the woods on the western bank of the Humber River. (It was near the present boundary of Lambton Golf Course, north of St Clair Avenue.) The inaugural meeting was 6 to 9 September 1837. A typical program in 1842 included the St. Leger Stakes for two pounds, ten shillings, with ten pounds added by the stewards, open to horses foaled in Canada 1839.

Later in the 1840s the St. Leger course was opened. It's 8, 9 and 10 June 1843 spring meeting featured the St. Leger Cup and the Cleaver Stakes "for horses bona fide owned by the butchers of this city, and to be ridden by butchers' boys in costume." There was also the Grand Provincial Garrison Plate for officers on full pay in Her Majesty's service in Canada and the Innkeepers' Purse of twenty-five pounds. About the same time in the fashionable Grange area of Toronto near the Cricket Grounds was the Union Course, better known as Boulton's St. Leger Race Course. Bill Boulton, who owned the property, was the manager. It occupied grounds bounded by Bloor Street, Baldwin and McCaul Streets and Spadina Avenue. A portion of the stands stood in 1888 according to John Ross Robertson in *Landmarks of Toronto*. This area is known today as *The Grange*. Several years later, from the 1850s until 1875, another course in the western section of the city existed, the Toronto Driving Park, a half-mile oval north of Queen Street, between Lisgar Street and Gladstone Avenue, and south of Dundas Street. In the 1840s, when Boulton's Union Course closed, horse racing moved eastwards to Kingston Road, east of the Don River. This track was Jack Maitland's course. It lay south of Queen Street and east of Broadview Avenue near the Don River. The locale is now the Cherry Street district.

Charles Gates, an innkeeper, opened the Newmarket course, just north of Danforth Road near Woodbine Avenue and the Don River in 1854. Three years later lawyer William C. Keele laid out the Carleton racetrack in an area later known as the West Toronto Junction—south of Dundas Street and north of High Park. It would be the home of the first running of the Queen's Plate in 1860, a race which was badly needed to encourage the breeding of a finer quality of racehorse than that already cluttering up tracks. Among the more practical encouragements given to horsemen with the royal gift of fifty "guineas" from Queen Victoria was the fact that the Plate would be contested by horses bred in Ontario which had never won a race, a condition that gave the sporting farmer an equal chance with wealthy stud owners. Horsemen needed a race that not only brought prestige, but was renewed on an annual basis.

In the mid-1850s racehorse breeding in the province was slowly being revolutionized. For the ordinary farmer, thoroughbreds derived their importance from the fact that they crossed with common horses to produce roadsters. Their preference for roadsters became increasingly pronounced in the 1850s for by this time there were plank or gravel roads, and the coming, actual or prospective, of the railway gave even farmers a taste for speed. Breeders in Hamilton, Niagara, Simcoe County, Toronto, London, Woodstock and Halton County were slowly bettering the pedigrees of their stock and clearing out the half-breds that infested every backroad and concession. However, there was a sharp difference in motivation between the period of the 1850s and the 1880s. In the 1850s Upper Canada farmers took much greater interest in improving their horses than their other livestock. Horsemen continued to bring thoroughbreds into the province from Kentucky and Virginia, as well as from England, but they made little effort to perpetuate the purity of the breed. There was so little demand for racehorses in Ontario, a consequence of the demoralization of the turf, that the leading Ontario breeder was selling almost all his young stock in the United States.

In 1860 breeders made significant gains as a direct result of the American Civil War. In pursuit of safety and better opportunities, large contingents of American horses were sent North, and a good

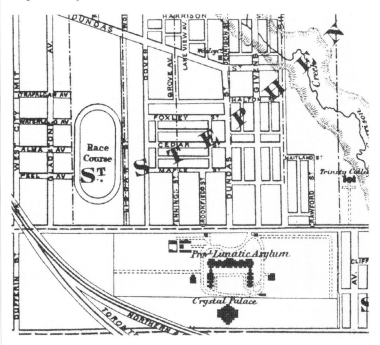

THE TORONTO DRIVING PARK COURSE WAS NORTH OF QUEEN STREET, BETWEEN LISGAR STREET AND GLADSTONE AVENUE.

number stayed to enrich stallion rosters. The climate of foreboding in the United States prompted R.A. Alexander, master of Woodburn Stud of Kentucky, to dispatch an agent with thirty-four horses to race and sell in Canada—the majority of them sired by the legendary *Lexington*. Alexander had been hard pressed by the increasing toll of his horses conscripted by the warring cavalries. The Woodburn blood bred on in Canada. The most prized acquisitions of this period were *Thunder*, a son of *Lexington*, and *Helmbold*, sired by **Australian*, names that cropped up in the pedigrees of early Plate winners. *Thunder* stood for a while in Quebec before moving to John Shedden's farm in Davenport, a hilly area that now overlooks Bloor Street in Toronto. **Sir Tatton Sykes* had been imported in the late 1840s by another Davenport farmer, George Cooper, and along with **Lapidist* and sons of **Yorkshire* dominated the sire lists in the 1860s. The prominent female lines came through **Mercer* and **Jordan*.

The Pioneering Years: The Early Plates, Ruled by the Whites of Halton, Farmers and Rural Horsemen

Landmarks are mileposts on the long road called Time, and they seem vital to man's sense of security as he makes his weary journey. If they do not exist in the form of a tree or a hill or a crumbling castle, man manufactures them, and calls them monuments. Lacking a monument, he may accept some existing feature of the landscape as a landmark, for he must have an object to point out as he says, 'Here it all began.'

DAVID ALEXANDER

More than a century before the American Revolution, "it all began" in 1665 at a racecourse called New Market, at Hempstead Plains on Long Island, New York—not too far from the present site of Belmont Park. In Lower Canada the first shipments of horses from France arrived in Quebec in July of the same year. Racing soon spread to Nova Scotia and Upper Canada, where English officers were garrisoned. In 1837, a petition from the Halifax Turf Club to King William IV for a King's Plate was rejected, but another petition for a Queen's Plate was sent to Queen Victoria in 1840 showing "That a Public Race Course was completed at Halifax in Your Majesty's Province of Nova Scotia in the year 1826. . . . That your Memorialists are aware of Your Majesty's solicitude to foster all sports which cultivate English habits and feelings in Your Colonies and rejoice that Royal patronage has been extended to the Races of the Canadas." The Halifax Queen's Plate received the monarch's blessing that same year.

In 1789 the Quebec Turf Club was formed, its track located on the historic Plains of Abraham. Public approval of this pastime soon caught on in Trois Rivières on the St. Lawrence River, about seventy miles from Montreal. Under the auspices of Lord Aylmer, Governor General of Lower Canada, the track earned the distinction of staging the first King's Plate race in the colonies in 1836. Authorized by William IV, on the advice of Lord Aylmer, the Plate carried a royal donation of fifty "guineas" and was restricted to horses bred in Lower Canada. This race, of two-mile heats, succeeded in "completely establishing the manly and interesting sport of racing in these hyperborean backwoods." In 1864 the Queen's Plate was run at the St. Maurice Course in Trois Rivières. The prize was fifty guineas and the race consisted of mile heats, won by *Emma Dale*. Her victory was protested because it was claimed she was not bred in Quebec. Quebec City also staged a race, called the Queen's Plate, at Victoria's Beacon Hill Park in 1868 and 1869, run in honour of the Queen's Birthday.

On 1 April 1859, the quest of royalty's recognition for a Queen's Plate to be staged in Upper Canada was formally initiated when a petition from members of the Toronto Turf Club was forwarded to Queen Victoria. The petition claimed that her patronage would "encourage the introduction of the best breed of horses into this section of the province in aid of agricultural improvement as well as to keep up one of the favourite national sports of our revered Mother County." The petitioners, noting that Her Majesty had "graciously patronized a royal bounty" to the Montreal Racecourse in Lower Canada, solicited a similar mark of royal favour on behalf of the Carleton Race Course in Upper Canada. "Your petitioners therefore most humbly pray that Your Majesty will be graciously pleased to order that a Queen's Plate be given annually to be run for on the Carleton Race Course by horses raised exclusively in Upper Canada and owned by resident proprietors therein." The petition was signed by club president, A. De Salabury, eight local Members of Provincial Parliament, as well as many of the prominent residents of Toronto, one of whom was Charles Littlefield, who would ride the first winner of the Plate a year later.

On 18 July a letter from Downing Street, signed by the Duke of Newcastle, was forwarded to Sir Edmund Head, Governor General of British North America. It said that he had laid the petition before the Queen and that Her Majesty "has been graciously pleased to grant the prayer of that petition and that a Plate of Fifty Guineas will be given by Her Majesty to be run for at Toronto or such other place in Upper Canada as Her Majesty may hereafter appoint." It wasn't until 5 August 1859 that a letter to the Toronto Turf Club and Lieutenant Colonel G.T. Denison was received from the Governor's secretary's office confirming Her Majesty's granting of the Toronto Turf Club petition.

Fifty guineas was the equivalent of fifty-two pounds, ten shillings. The minting of guineas was discontinued in 1813, during the reign of George III. It was George I who instituted the

THE HORSE RING—FAIR GROUNDS, TORONTO.

A PHOTO OF THE FIRST RACING CHARTER GRANTED IN ONTARIO, TO THE ONTARIO JOCKEY CLUB. THE ORIGINAL PETITIONERS WERE FREDERICK WILLIAM CUMBERLAND, THOMAS CHARLES PATTESON, ANDREW SMITH, HENRY QUETTON ST. GEORGE AND WILLIAM MULOCK OF TORONTO, AND WILLIAM HENDRIE OF HAMILTON. CAPITAL STOCK IN THE NEW COMPANY WAS $20,000 WITH SHARES SELLING FOR $100 APIECE.

gift of fifty guineas in racing. The word remained but the coins eventually became sovereigns, which were first minted in 1819. During the reign of Charles II (1649–1685), the Merry Monarch (as he was known at the track) gave the owners a little incentive by offering up a piece of royal silverware or plate for the winners. Queen Anne later replaced the plate with a cup. Today the value of the fifty sovereigns is issued in a bank draft drawn on Her Majesty's household allowance.

That spring, prior to the club's petition being sent to Her Majesty, The Patriot noted: "We also learn that a Jockey Club is to be formed in the course of this winter, founded on the Rules and Regulations of the Newmarket Club in England." Sir Edmund Head was absent at the historic first running of the Plate on 27 June 1860 and did not make the presentation of Her Majesty's royal donation to the owners of *Don Juan*, James and John White of Halton County. This function was likely carried out by Toronto Turf Club president Casimir S. Gzowski, the Polish-born engineer and railroad builder, who later would be the colonial aide-de-camp to Queen Victoria.

While there was no representative of royalty to present the fifty guineas, royalty was actually in Toronto in 1860, but unfortunately the arrival of Queen Victoria's eldest son, Albert Edward, the Prince of Wales, didn't occur until 11 September—almost three months after the first running of the Queen's Plate. The eighteen-year-old prince, who would become King Edward VII in 1901, was on a goodwill tour of Upper and Lower Canada. It was a royal tour that Canadians had been awaiting for years. There was a long-standing promise of a royal visit to honour Canada for the assistance it had given to British forces during the Crimean War. But both Victoria and Prince Albert suffered from seasickness and the long Atlantic voyage would not have been appropriate. The answer was obvious: Let Bertie do it. His arrival at the wharf at the foot of John Street was tumultuous. An enormous arch over John Street bore the words "Welcome to Toronto—Albert Edward." Three years later he married Princess Alexandra of Denmark. Their names existed in Toronto for years—the King Edward Hotel and the Royal Alexandria Theatre.

The first family to dominate the Queen's Plate, as well as racing and breeding in general in Ontario, was the White brothers, and later John's son-in-law, David Watson Campbell. James, whose home was Bronte, lived in the shadow of his brother John, a successful lumber merchant in Milton and a fiery politician for Halton County. Before he was bed-ridden in the 1870s as an invalid, it was James who operated Woodlands, breeding and training many of the twelve Plate winners raised at the family's 320-acre spread on the Bronte Side Road, just north of today's Queen Elizabeth Highway between Toronto and Hamilton.

The name of Irish-born John White was probably more widely known than that of any other prominent person of his time. He was the Liberal Member during the years of the "Perambulating Parliament," so called because it alternated between Quebec and Toronto. Born in Omagh, County Tyrone, in 1811, White came to Canada in 1823, settling first in Etobicoke, west of Toronto, and later in Halton. A lumberman who was recognized as a fearless and fluent speaker, White was the first reeve of the thriving community of Milton, a grist and sawmill town that was known for its "poor plank roads but good hotels"—Speed The Plough, Hampton's Inn, Farmer's Hotel and the Thompson House. He and his brother James owned seven farms in Halton and had sawmills in practically every part of the county, from Bronte to Acton and Nassagaweya; in Manitoulin to the north and in the state of Michigan.

John White was the first president of the Halton Agricultural Society. But it was his love for politics and horses that forever distinguished him, although by the twentieth century his deeds as a horseman would almost be forgotten because of the incredible string of victories by Joseph Seagram, the next dominant figure in Plate history. White was an outspoken opponent of "The Family Compact," a Liberal Whip for many years and a loyal supporter of William Lyon Mackenzie. After his defeat at the Battle of Montgomery's Tavern in the 1837 Rebellion, Mackenzie is said to have hidden for three days in Devil's Cave in the dense woods near the White brothers' Bronte farm of Woodlands before he escaped to the United States. White was also responsible for introducing a bill in the fourth Parliament of Upper Canada in 1853 that made Milton the county seat, instead of Oakville, when Halton separated from Wentworth County.

White was also acknowledged to have been the owner of the

THE FOUNDATION OF THE OLD BANK BARN AT THE WOODLANDS, HOME OF THE WHITE BROTHERS' PLATE WINNERS, WAS DESTROYED IN A 1983 FIRE.

first privately owned racetrack—Woodlands, an area later famous for its apple and cherry orchards. The racetrack was thoroughly equipped with stables and jockeys' quarters, and was located back of the breeding and foaling barns where the Whites housed a string of thoroughbreds they had imported from Tennessee.

In his memoirs, T.C. Patteson, who was largely responsible for the foundation of the Ontario Jockey Club and obtaining the first provincial racing charter in 1881, described the Whites as "the real pioneers" of breeding in the province, not only of racehorses but of all breeds. The foundation mare of their breeding operations was *Yellow Rose*, a Virginia-bred that had been brought into Canada in the early 1850s. She was the dam of Plate winners *Don Juan* and *Wild Rose*, but of more importance was *Liberty*, a filly she produced to the English stallion *Mercer*. From *Liberty* came Plate winners *Touchstone* and *Palermo* (the son of a trotting sire, *Royal George*) and *Lizzie Wright*, the dam of two more winners of the "guineas," *Amelia* and *Moss Rose*. There were also Plate-producing mares *Countess*, *Stolen Kisses* and *Nettie*, who not only was the dam of 1882 winner *Fanny Wiser*, but won it herself in 1868 at Toronto's Newmarket course.

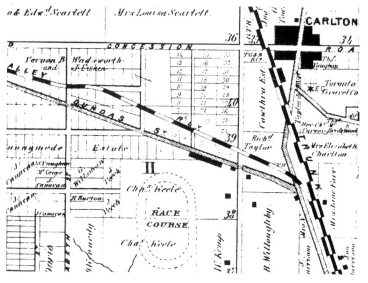

AN EARLY MAP OF YORK COUNTY SHOWS THE VILLAGE OF CARLTON [SIC] AND THE RACETRACK, TO THE SOUTH-WEST ON WILLIAM KEELE'S FARM.

The racehorses of the brothers White won no end of Plates, but did more for the improvement of the general breed of horses in Upper Canada than for the turf. They were well-to-do farmers, but had no access to sires good enough to be impressive. And it was some time before they had a really good racehorse in *Terror*. They were enterprising in their way, at one time sending the old mare *Liberty* all the way to Oak Ridges [north of Toronto], where Quetton St. George had the Levity stallion *Ruric*; but missing to him she was put to their own colt, *Terror*, a son of *Ruric*, then just two years old. From this marriage of May with December, *Emily* was the result. *Terror*'s dam, *Maratana*, they put to *Luther*, a big coarse son of the celebrated U.S. sire *Lexington*, whence came *Sharpcatcher*, whose foals used to dot the meadows between Milton and Guelph . . . the good old mare *Augusta*, they also put to *Ruric*, with 1874 Plate winner *The Swallow* as the result. *Annie Laurie*, another daughter of *Yellow Rose*, went to *Lexington*'s son *Copec*, a mating that gave the Whites *Stolen Kisses*, the dam of Plate winners *Vice Chancellor*, through *Terror*, and *Wild Rose*, by *Princeton*.

While the Whites got the early jump in the breeding of Plate winners, horsemen in London, Woodstock, Cobourg and in the counties south of Lake Simcoe soon were importing quality horseflesh from the United States. Successful were Dr. George Morton of Bradford, E.S. (Joe) Bilton, Colonel John (Squire) Peters, Thomas Hodgens, who gave London seven Plate winners, Roddy Pringle of Cobourg, Dr. Andrew Smith of Toronto and Woodstock horsemen Charles Boyle, Erastus (Ras) Burgess and John Forbes. The most prominent, however, was John Forbes, a bookmaker from Woodstock who owned the town's largest hotel and livery stable. While he and his bookmaking partners, Bill (The Major) Quimby and Ras Burgess, who was a splendid trainer as well, paid racetrack operators a fee to set up a book and set odds during race meets, Forbes was also an astute horse dealer, bringing in American mares *Maumee*, dam of Plate winner Harry Cooper, and *Bonnie Braes*, probably the finest mare to grace Ontario's turf. A daughter of **Balrownie*, she was the first winner of the Ladies' Handicap in New York, which still is the oldest stakes for mares on the continent. Forbes bred *Bonnie Braes* to *Judge Curtis*, who had won the second running of the Belmont Stakes under the name *Gen. Duke*, and was standing in Middlesex County. (It was not uncommon at the time for owners to change horse's names.) Subsequent matings produced Plate winners *Bonnie Bird* in 1880 and *Bonnie Duke* in 1887.

The 1860–1890 period was one that accomplished the original concepts laid down by Queen Victoria's royal donation, which was to encourage small breeders and owners. Of the thirty-one races staged during that period, only eight were captured by Toronto men, and only three were bred in the precincts of the expanding centre of commerce in the province. The Plate was basically the property of rural horsemen, who were even more encouraged when the race was celebrated at eleven different tracks—from Kingston, Prescott, Ottawa, Picton, Whitby, Barrie, Guelph, Hamilton, St. Catharines, London and Woodstock between 1864 and 1882. Three Toronto courses: Carleton in the West Toronto Junction played host for the first four years; Gates' Newmarket course out on the Danforth in 1868; and Woodbine Park, south of the hills of neighbouring Norway on Joseph Duggan's property close to the shores of Ashbridge's Bay and Lake Ontario, was the site in 1876 and 1881, the year the Ontario Jockey Club received its racing charter.

The Plate took one final road trip in 1882, back to London's Newmarket course, before finally settling at one of the most beautiful racetracks in North America—Woodbine. The 1883 visit to Woodbine of the Marquess of Lorne, Canada's fourth Governor General since Confederation, and Princess Louise, a daughter of Queen Victoria, which had been carefully scripted by Patteson and Gzowski, provided the royal sanctions the OJC directors hoped for, despite a stroke of bad luck. The vice-regal party was unable to visit Woodbine for the twenty-fourth running of the Plate, but did attend a program a week later and was suitably impressed with the hospitality proffered by Club president Colonel Gzowski and the long-range plans of Patteson and his associates, William Hendrie, J.H. Mead, the Honourable Frank Smith, Sir William Mulock, Dr. F.W. Strange, Dr. George Morton, William Christie, Sheriff J. Mercer, G.W. Torrance and Dr. Andrew Smith, to restore the public's faith in horse racing and rid it of the unsavoury practices that were common in its burgeoning years. When the royal party returned to England, word was soon received that the stability and the organization offered by the Ontario Jockey Club would be far

more beneficial than showcasing the race at tracks that lacked competent officials or as side attractions for agricultural fairs.

While the 1865 debacle at London's Newmarket course (a popular name, as St. Catharines and Toronto also had similarly named tracks) provided the most nefarious sequence of events—charges of an imported ringer from Michigan and a jockey weighing out after winning minus his saddle weights—there was hardly a Plate race held that did not provoke a rhubarb regarding the eligibility of the horses, or illegal riding tactics. *Willie Wonder*, ridden by the finest jockey of the period, Charles Littlefield, was disqualified in 1863, as was *Beacon* in 1865. Protests were also laid against *Wild Rose* in 1867, *John Bell* in 1870, and *Mignonette* in 1873, but were disallowed. The first running of the Plate at Woodbine in 1876 was also without incident as officials debated whether to allow horses who had won over the jumps (rules at the time stipulated a maiden was a horse who had not won on the flat) and then disqualified Francis Lowell's *Mary L.*, a mare from Galt, for interfering with Colonel Peters' mare from London, *Norah P.*

The Plate in its first thirty years was dominated by aged geldings or mares, thirteen of which won the "guineas." The most determined gelding in Plate history was *Fred Henry*, who went to the post five times (injuries kept him out on two other occasions) between 1884 and 1889. He was second three times, but when he finished last as a ten-year-old, his owner finally could not stand the embarrassment and retired him.

The imposing stallions of the period were *Terror*, a homebred of the Whites who sired four winners; the imported **Lapidist*, a son of St. Leger Stakes winner *Touchstone*, whose chief contributions to the improvement of the breed in Canada, besides three Plate winners, were through his half-bred son, *Clear Grit*, who founded one of the important Canadian trotting families; and *Jack the Barber*, an American stud who also sired three Plate champions.

Riders of note were Charles Littlefield, who later became one of North America's leading trainers; Richard (Red Dick) O'Leary from Port Credit and A.E. (Allie) Gates, a Toronto boy, who won the Plate three times. The respected trainers included O'Leary, who rode or trained five Plate winners, Ras Burgess and Charlie Boyle of Woodstock, Halton's James White and Jonathan Scott, Toronto's William Owen, Charlie Gates and Robert Davies, and Doc Hannon of Hamilton.

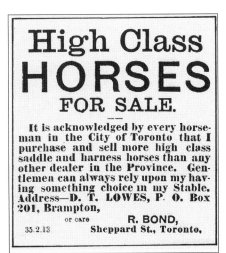

ROBERT BOND WON THE PLATE IN 1887.

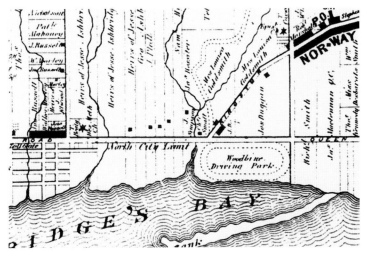

A TORONTO MAP OF THE 1870S LOCATES THE WOODBINE DRIVING PARK.

I n 1857 William Conroy Keele, an English-born lawyer who wrote legal manuals for the Upper Canada judiciary, laid out the Carleton racecourse on his farm he called Glenside, just south of today's Dundas and Keele Streets, an area northwest of Toronto that later became known as the West Toronto Junction. He bought the hundred-acre property in 1834 and added more land in 1840. In 1857 he created the Carleton racecourse. The tract of land was adjacent to Lambton Mills, Brockton, Seaton, and to Carleton, a village five-and-a-half miles from Toronto's Union Station. It was serviced by the Grand Trunk Railway. His son Charles later sold the racetrack in 1882 and after his death in 1884 the whole property was sold to land developers. The CPR terminal was opened in 1882 and the surrounding area began to be developed, with streets laid out and houses built.

Carleton, an oval course that was more than a mile round, had three low, wooden stands, weighing rooms for the jockeys and refreshment booths. Around the track were tall, stately trees and vast grassy paddocks. The most fashionable and gaily attired audiences visited the new course in their elegant carriages. In 1859 it became the new headquarters of the Toronto Turf Club, which had been in existence as early as 1843. Although Keele was apparently never an official of the Club, he was closely associated with its leading members, the elite of the Toronto business world, the unofficial aristocracy of Upper Canada—John Beverley Robinson, John and H.J. Boulton, Richard and George Denison, William Howland, John Ross, John Leys, George Grange. H. Quetton St. George, Richard Dempsey, Stephen Heward, Walter Dickson, Charles Douglas, Alexander Shaw and engineer Casimir Gzowski, who succeeded A. De Salabury as president in 1860.

JOHN WHITE (ABOVE) AND HIS BROTHER JAMES DOMINATED RACING IN UPPER CANADA FOR NEARLY THREE DECADES. THEY BRED THE FIRST PLATE WINNER *DON JUAN*.

The course that would host the first running of the Queen's Plate on 27 June 1860 was two hundred yards south of Dundas Street and west of what was then the concession line, but which is now Keele Street. To pinpoint it further: its northern and southern boundaries are Annette and Glenlake, streets that were built after the track had been subdivided into building lots in 1883.

Racing in Toronto in the 1850s was at a low ebb. In an effort to rejuvenate it, the Club sought the patronage of the monarchy. In 1836, during the reign of William IV, a King's Plate was run in Montreal, but it was discontinued fourteen years later. It would be renewed in 1861. A Queen's Plate, minus the "guineas," had also

been run in 1841 at Cobourg, Ontario, but it was a race that was simply named in Victoria's honour. Presenting prizes, royal plates or silver bells, had been a practice of several British monarchs in the fifteenth and sixteenth centuries—James I, Charles II and Queen Anne—but the practice was stopped by George I. However, by 1847 Queen's Plates were being awarded at most British racecourses and often carried the value of one-hundred "guineas."

In seeking the donation of a Plate worth the equivalent of fifty "guineas," the Toronto Turf Club hoped to renew interest in the sport as well as provide prestige; it communicated its wishes to Governor General Sir Edmund Head. On 1 April 1859, A. De Salabury, together with members of the Toronto Turf Club, "humbly prayed that her Most Gracious Majesty, Victoria, would order that a Queen's Plate be given annually to be run for on the Carleton Race Course." The petition to the Colonial Office was acknowledged on 18 July when the Duke of Newcastle informed Sir Edmund Head "that Her Majesty had been graciously pleased to grant the prayer of their petition, and that a Plate of Fifty 'Guineas' would be given to be run for in Toronto or such other place that Her Majesty might appoint."

After staging a three-day meet at the Newmarket course the week before, the Club carded races on 27, 28 and 29 June at Carleton, with the Plate race the opening-day feature. Fifty guineas was offered for horses bred in Upper Canada that had never won public money; three one-mile heats.

The Queen's Plate was the great attraction of the day, reported the U.S. sports journal *Wilkes' Spirit of the Times*: ". . . the race was regarded with the greatest interest, not only on account of the number of horses entered [eight], but also for the novelty of the occasion, this being the first time that it has been offered for competition." Reports on the attendance varied, from "considerably over 2,000," to "between 3,000 and 4,000," a sizeable number considering that Toronto's population was only 44,425. It was noted that people arrived by excursion train, carriage and on foot, and that the ladies' stand was filled. The scene presented a lively and interesting spectacle. All across the grounds there were carriages, both private and public, together with mounted equestrians. Betting was not very active; those inclined to invest evidently preferred holding back to see the result of the first heat. Shortly after two o'clock, preparations were made for the start, the riders weighing in and the different officers of the course taking their places. George Denison was the starter and John Boulton the clerk of the course.

When the blankets were removed from the horses, it was apparent that *Don Juan* was an exceedingly handsome specimen of horseflesh and he became the favourite among those disposed to bet. Yet there were few takers at the short odds. Newspaper coverage of the Plate was consistent, even though certain reports had the wrong Littlefield brother riding the winner, *Don Juan*, a five-year-old owned and bred by James and John White of Bronte in Halton Township. Both *The Daily Leader* of Toronto and the reporter for *Spirit of the Times* described how every horse got away in capital style, with the exception of Dr. Kirwin's grey colt *Paris*, which kicked and plunged savagely, and threw his rider, before he had gone a hundred yards. "The poor man was thrown violently in spite of all his efforts to retain his seat; the horse running over him and then joining in the race on his own account." The dismounted jockey, "Nelson" Littlefield (who was really Charles) was unhurt, and in subsequent races proved himself a most accomplished and skilful rider. A twenty-seven-year-old from Rochester, New York, Charles Littlefield had a seasonal residence in Toronto, and was one of the leading riders in North America. He had accompanied the famed Ten Broeck stable to England in 1857, riding *Prior*, *Prioress* and *Lecompte* for the gambler-horseman. Littlefield later rode Kentucky when it won the Inauguration Stakes at the opening of Jerome Park in New York.

Bob Marshall beat *Don Juan* by a length in the first heat. Wild Irishman was third and *Queen* "was an indifferent fourth." *Bob Marshall* was owned by John E. Ewart of Toronto, while *Highflier*, who was distanced in the first heat, was owned by William Weller and his brothers, Alonzo and Lorenzo, who were in the stage coach business, operating stables near the Gooderham & Worts buildings at the "Front of the Bay in St. Lawrence Ward," and lived on land owned by John Ewart. *Highflier* and the other three starters *Lady Carleton*, *Tom Sawyer* and *Paris* were eliminated from the second heat. President Gzowski, the wealthy Polish-born engineer who had built many of Ontario's railroads and bridges, allowed the horses twenty minutes to cool off before ringing a bell for the final heat. There was excitement and activity in the betting as Littlefield, the jockey thrown off *Paris* in the first heat, put on White's scarlet silks and was substituted for *Don Juan*'s unnamed former rider. It had probably been his brother, Nelson.

The second heat was a different story. Charles Littlefield displayed consummate skill; his beautiful riding brought out the full powers of the horse, giving it the heat without difficulty. Betting for the third heat was now all in favour

JOCKEY CHARLES LITTLEFIELD.

DON JUAN | 5-year-old bay gelding

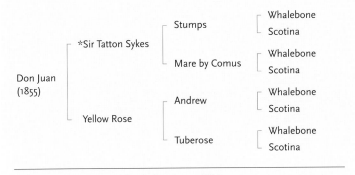

Owner: James White, Bronte; *Trainer:* James White
Jockey: Charles Littlefield; *Breeder:* White (James and John) Bros., Halton County

of *Don Juan*, 5 to 4 being offered. Gentlemen from Montreal, Prescott and Cobourg had large piles to wager, but experienced some difficulty in finding parties willing to accept their terms. *Don Juan* won the third heat handily and the Queen's Plate.

The first winner of the Plate was got by *Sir Tatton Sykes*, out of *Yellow Rose*, a famous mare belonging to the Whites—James of Bronte, who trained the winner, and John of Milton, the fearless and fluent Irish-born Member of Parliament for Halton County. Imported in the 1840s by George Cooper, *Sir Tatton Sykes* stood at his farm in the village of Davenport, a hilly area of apple orchards overlooking Toronto. The mare, bred by Thomas Watson of Virginia, was purchased by E.C. Jones of Toronto before the Whites bought her.

The day was judged a remarkable success even though the track was not as firm as the riders would have liked. The races were punctual and tolerably spirited, and the multitude preserved the best order. Everything apparently conspired to make this one of the most fashionable and interesting meetings that had taken place in and around Toronto for years. Booths supplied the crowd with all kinds of refreshments, and Mr. Gzowski entertained the ladies, stewards and other privileged parties at a substantial lunch.

1860 QUEEN'S PLATE STAKES

FIRST RACE
Toronto
Carleton Race Course
JUNE 27, 1860

THE QUEEN'S PLATE, 50 Guineas. Open to all horses bred in Upper Canada which have never won public money. Turf Club weights. Mile heats. Owners must pay $8 subscriber's fee to Toronto Turf club to enter horse.

Horse	A		Heat 1	Heat 2	Heat 3	Owner
DON JUAN	5	b.g.	2	1	1	James White
BOB MARSHALL	4	b.c.	1	2	2	J E Ewart
WILD IRISHMAN	7	ch.g.	3	3	3	George Henderson
QUEEN	5	ch.m.	4	4	Retired	George Palmer
HIGHFLIER	4	ch.g.	Dis.			William Weller
LADY CARLETON	4	b.f.	Dis.			William Byers
TOM SAYERS	3	b.c.	Dis.			Mr Alexander
PARIS	4	gr.c.	Lost rider			Dr Kirwin

Times—First heat: 1:58. Second heat: 2:05. Third heat: 1:58. Track fast. Dis. (Distanced).
Winner: Five-year-old bay gelding by *Sir Tatton Sykes*—Yellow Rose, by Andrew. Bred by James and John White, Halton. Trained by James White. Ridden by Charles Littlefield in heats two and three.
Betting on Don Juan: 100 to 80.
The start of the first heat was a splendid one—every horse getting away in capital style, with the exception of PARIS, which kicked and plunged savagely, throwing his rider, Charles Littlefield, close to the stands. The heat was strictly between BOB MARSHALL and DON JUAN, and after a long struggle, BOB MARSHALL came home the winner by a length. The second heat was a slightly different story as the rider of PARIS, Littlefield, was placed upon DON JUAN, and the jockey's skills brought out the full powers of the horse as DON JUAN won without difficulty, by two lengths over BOB MARSHALL. Only three horses contested the third heat and DON JUAN was headed only briefly by BOB MARSHALL before pulling away to win the Plate by a length.

CROWDS PACKED CARLETON RACE COURSE IN THE TORONTO JUNCTION TO WITNESS *WILD IRISHMAN'S* VICTORY FOR PORT HOPE'S GEORGE HENDERSON.

Toronto was in a festive mood in the early months of 1861, aware but not particularly frightened by the worsening news of the American Civil War. Accounts of skirmishes between Federal and Confederate forces were prominent in newspapers, which also carried advertisements from merchants in the United States eager to trade land and businesses for similar properties in Canada. Everything was under control, confided a Northern general in Virginia, who predicted that the rebellion would be defeated and the Union reconstructed.

In Canada citizens were more concerned with the visit of Prince Alfred, Queen Victoria's second son. Thousands sought a glimpse of the Royal entourage as it made its way by carriage to the Rossin House on Toronto's King Street after arriving by steamer from Hamilton. The Prince's arrival at the Custom House Wharf caused a furore as a crowd of more than six thousand, which had collected in front of Union Station to welcome him, dashed madly down York Street to the docks.

The following day the Royal suite and government officials attracted excited crowds as they toured the city, visiting the Parliament buildings, Osgoode Hall, the Normal School, the University of Toronto and the cricket grounds before departing in the evening. Regrettably, the second running of the Queen's Plate the following day was not on the Royal visitor's itinerary. Because of the Duchess of Kent's recent death, Queen Victoria requested that no public receptions be held for the Prince.

However, Her Majesty's donation of fifty "guineas" for the race named in her honour was again presented. One newspaper noted that the contest might some day rival the English Derby. "We bid to have our own Derby, in a small way, before many years. The munificence of Her Majesty the Queen in granting an annual plate of fifty "guineas," to be run under the direction of the Toronto Turf Club, has given a fresh impetus to horse racing in this section of the Province," said *The Leader*.

Getting to the racetrack in the village of Carleton was an adventure. The scene along Dundas Street was boisterous and carefree; all sorts of conveyances were used to carry the crowds. Cabs, carriages and the sulkies and dog carts of the fast young men churned up the dust. There had been little or no rain for some days and the journey was hot and uncomfortable. "The dust was an intolerable nuisance and had all its own way, flying about in clouds, blowing into your eyes, ears, nose and mouth, and adhering to your clothes in spite of every effort to shake it off."

The Grand Trunk Railway, which attracted the "less pretentious" sightseers, offered return trip tickets for twenty-five cents. Unfortunately, the "race special" returned to Toronto about an hour before the races finished, leaving hundreds stranded. "We trust some better arrangements will be made for today and tomorrow," said *The Leader*. "Especially for ladies. It is very unpleasant to have to 'foot' it some four or five miles along a railway track."

It was announced that the Queen's Plate would commence at 1:30 p.m. But races are rarely punctual and it was half past two before matters were got into anything like business order. The second running of the Plate brought together eight provincial-bred maidens and a collection of jockeys, described by *The Leader* as a "motley looking group." The clanging of a bell summoned the riders to the start; their mounts were described as presenting a

> . . . very pretty appearance. We cannot say ditto to their riders. They were dressed in every imaginable and unimaginable manner. There was a slight improvement on the previous year in this respect; but we think the Directors might, without injury to anybody, see that the jockeys be dressed with some nearer approach to uniformity in future.
>
> The best of order was preserved on the course throughout. There were a few tussles; they were not of a very serious nature, however; no one even received an 'Irishman's killing.'

Attendance was good but it was obvious that the Plate held scant importance since the crowd was larger the following day when the race program was less attractive. *The Leader* noted that on one side of the starting line were two stands, one reserved for the judges and another for the ladies. Club members, politicians and the press filled the first stand.

On the opposite side was a grandstand for the general public, which contained a large number of sightseers. Underneath these stands are the drinking booths. These, we must say, were well-patronized. Of course this is altogether to be accounted for by the great clouds of dust which would persist in obstructing people's throats.

Outside the stands are the gambling gentlemen, the thimble riggers, 'now you see, and now you don't class,' who dupe the thoughtless innocent, and the fool-hardy adventurer overburdened with dollars. Dice appeared to be the favourite game yesterday. There were numerous tables of this sort, and by the great array of 'quarters' which might be seen on these tables, there is no doubt that the proprietors succeeded in doing a lively business. The musical department seemed to be confined altogether to an enthusiastic bugler, who persisted in doing a little in this line on his own account. This is the same individual, to the music of whose instrument Prince Alfred doffed his beaver on his arrival in Toronto on Monday evening.

The Plate was captured by *Wild Irishman*, an eight-year-old chestnut gelding whose pedigree is traceable only on the sire's side. The gelding was by *Peter Pindar*, a son of the imported sire **Daghee*. According to Christine A. Matthes, who researches old bloodlines of early Canadian racehorses, the "nameless" dam of *Peter Pindar* was a daughter of another English stud, **Barefoot*, who was included in a shipment of horses to Massachusetts in 1828 by Admiral Sir Isaac Coffin, British Navy. **Daghee*, who was foaled in 1829, apparently was imported to the Maritimes by Commodore Sir Robert Barrie, and then exported to the United States in 1835, standing in New Jersey. Where **Daghee* stood during his stay in Canada is unknown, as well as where *Peter Pindar* was foaled in 1836. These questions to this day puzzle pedigree experts studying nineteenth-century breeding records.

WILD IRISHMAN | 8-year-old chestnut gelding

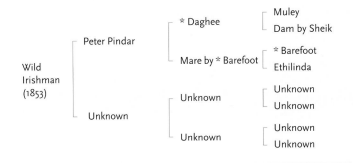

Owner: George Henderson, Port Hope; *Trainer:* George Henderson
Jockey: Ben Alcott; *Breeder:* Unknown

Wild Irishman, the third place finisher the year before, was beaten by *Belleville Lass* in the first heat but won the second and third heats. Later in his career the gelding went under harness and at the age of twelve was competing with trotters who had never bettered 3:00 in public. He was owned by George Henderson, who lived at 53 Hope Street North in Port Hope until his death in 1871. Henderson operated the Fancy Livery Stable on Queen Street and also owned a stagecoach line. It was said that Henderson's vehicles were the fastest and fanciest running coaches between the town and Toronto. Henderson's descendants continued to live in the Hope Street residence and his granddaughter, Mrs. Roy (Helen) Sanford Campbell, said in a letter dated 12 May 1971, "I have a picture [daguerreotype] of the horse with the jockey up. His name was Cameron." Later reports of the 1861 race attribute the trainer and jockey as Ben Alcott. She added, "The horse [*Wild Irishman*] was bred and born in a stable, which was behind the house I now live in."

According to author W. Arnold Craick, Henderson earlier in his career was heralded for his bravery on a wintry day in 1848 when he galloped into a seething surf on horseback to rescue two men after the schooner *Canada* wrecked in the vicinity of the Gull Rock Lighthouse.

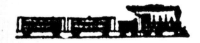

GRAND TRUNK RAILWAY.

CARLTON RACES.

SPECIAL TRAINS WILL LEAVE
Union Station for Carleton Races, on

Wednesday, the 26th, Thursday, the 27th and Friday, the 28th June, 1861,

AT ONE P.M. each day.

Returning leaves Carleton, at 6 00 P.M.; due in Toronto at 6 30 P.M.

FARE—11½ Down each way. If Tickets Are purchased at the Stations;

By Order.

Toronto, June 24, 1861.

1861 QUEEN'S PLATE STAKES

FIRST RACE
Toronto
Carleton Race Course
JUNE 26, 1861

THE QUEEN'S PLATE. 50 Guineas, gift of Her Majesty the Queen. For all horses bred in Upper Canada which have never won match, purse or subscription. One mile heats.

Horse	A		Heat 1	Heat 2	Heat 3	Owner
WILD IRISHMAN	8	ch.g.	2	1	1	George Henderson
BELLEVILLE LASS	6	m.	1	3	2	Mr Sterling
FLEETING MOMENTS	5	b.m.	4	2	3	Michael Dixon
MARION	6	b.m.	3	Lost rider		Mr Darby
BAY HORSE	4	b.c.	Dis.	Dis.		Charles Gates
KNOW NOTHING	6		Dis.			Mr Davidson
WILLY BELL	6		Dis.	Dis.		John Harrison
RATTLER	5		Dis.			William Weller

Times—First heat: 2:00. Second heat: none given. Third heat: 2:01. Track fast. Dis. (Distanced).
Winner: Eight-year-old chestnut gelding by Peter Pindar. Trained and ridden by Ben Alcott.
Betting odds on winner: 3 to 1.
After a false start MARION succeeded to get a good lead, closely followed by WILD IRISHMAN. About halfway around, BELLEVILLE LASS overhauled WILD IRISHMAN and won by a length over the gelding. MARION third. In the second heat a good start was affected. BELLEVILLE LASS led for half the course before being overtaken by WILD IRISHMAN and FLEETING MOMENTS. At this point MARION bolted, throwing her rider. A vigorous stretch duel developed between WILD IRISHMAN and FLEETING MOMENTS, who finished second by a head despite a badly gashed foreleg, which bled profusely. The third and deciding heat again saw BELLEVILLE LASS break on top. She was opening ground at the half but WILD IRISHMAN woke up in the stretch and won by a half length. FLEETING MOMENTS was third.

It isn't surprising that *Palermo*, the winner in the third running of the Plate at the Carleton course on William Keele's farm, was not a thoroughbred. He was a nondescript gelding; the breeding of racehorses before Confederation was at best a haphazard preoccupation by the settlers who developed the "Canadian-bred" thoroughbred. The main concern of these early racing bloodstock pioneers was to produce a stout-hearted, plodding racehorse rather than the spindly legged creature depicted by eighteenth-century artists.

Since English stud books were the only ones available in Canada, this deficiency abetted the proliferation of unauthenticated pedigrees in the ancestry of most horses in Upper Canada. Also, few farmers had access to quality imported sires from Britain and the United States and in most cases mares were bred to the best available stallion in the township.

The nine-year-old brown gelding *Palermo* was by *Royal George*, a popular trotting sire also known as *Field's* or *Doherty's Royal George*, and was a grandson of the famed *Tippoo*, an imposing progenitor of harness horses in the 1820s and 1830s. Bred by the White brothers of Halton County, *Palermo* inherited his running ability from the maternal branch of his family. It crops up in so many of the Plate winners of that period, who were bred in the Bronte and Milton area. His dam was *Liberty*, a sturdy granddaughter of English Derby winner *Emilius*, whose son **Mercer* was exported to North America. Bred to a trotter at the age of two, *Liberty* was an incredible producer for the Whites. She was also the dam of 1863 Plate winner *Touchstone* and dropped her last foal at the age of twenty-four.

Liberty, a half-sister to Plate winners *Don Juan* and *Wild Rose*, was out of *Yellow Rose*, the foundation mare of the White establishment. Imported from the United States by E.C. Jones of Church Street in Toronto, *Yellow Rose* went out to Halton and achieved unrivalled success: she mothered two Plate winners and was the grand-dam of four others.

Palermo's owner was probably George C. Chalmers of Hamilton, who leased him shortly before the 24 June race. Early accounts of the Plate are contradictory regarding ownership, some claiming he was leased by the "Chambers Bros." and others by a "Mr. Chalmers."

Because of his breeding, *Palermo* later posed a problem when he was shipped to St. Catharines. "What do you want him trained

JOCKEY CHARLES LITTLEFIELD HAD FEW EQUALS.

TRAINER CHARLIE BOYLE'S SON, KLONDIKE JOE, WOULD LATER BECOME A NATIONAL FOLK HERO.

for, to run or to trot?" inquired trainer James Pace. "For whatever he can do best," was the reply. *Palermo*'s efforts under harness were abysmal, prompting Pace to put the gelding into the running game. The experimenting undoubtedly confused *Palermo* and he was still a "maiden" at nine, a non-winner of a match, purse or a sweepstake and thus eligible for the Plate. However, he finally found a field he could conquer with his "trotting" stamina. After losing the first heat to the favoured *Lady Carleton*, he came back to win the next two heats, each at a mile. Third place was taken by *Palermo*'s much younger half-brother, *Touchstone*, who would win the Plate the following year. "Cute ones from Hamilton, who were better acquainted with the good qualities of this Wentworth horse [*Palermo*], bet liberally on him," reported *The Leader*.

There was nothing tainted, however, about *Palermo*'s handlers, two men of international repute. Charles Littlefield, a jockey from Rochester, New York, had few equals in the 1850s and 1860s and his services were eagerly in demand. The wily Littlefield had gained considerable fame in Europe while riding horses for the eccentric gambler Ten Broeck and later trained champion horses for the leading American stables. His craftiness gained him the enviable respect of horsemen. Littlefield, who rallied *Don Juan* to win the first Plate, had a third Plate win stripped away in 1863 when judges disqualified *Willie Wonder* because it had previously won public money.

Palermo's victory was largely due to Littlefield's skill said *The Leader*'s writer: ". . . He [*Palermo*] had the advantage, too, of being well-ridden by Littlefield. Baird rode the *Lady* well, too, but can't sit on a saddle to compare with Littlefield." For several years Littlefield lived on Boulton Street in Toronto and was the only "horse trainer" listed in the directory. Charles Boyle, who later became a partner of Littlefield's at major American tracks, prepped *Palermo* for the Plate win, his first of four Plate victories.

A horseman from Woodstock, Ontario, Boyle was as well known at tracks in New York, New Jersey and Maryland as in Canada; later he would play a major role in the success of the Seagram stable of Waterloo, winning two Plates (1897 and 1898) and one as owner and trainer of *Roddy Pringle* in 1883. Boyle's fame, however, was later transcended throughout the world by his son, Klondike Joe Boyle, a bigger-than-life character who to this day remains unheralded and virtually unknown in Canada. When he died in 1923 in England he was described as "Canada's greatest adventurer, hero and saviour of Roumania [sic]." A plaque in Woodstock, Ontario, entitled "The Firs," reads, "On this site stood 'The Firs', family home of Col. Joseph Whiteside Boyle, better known as 'Klondike Joe' Boyle, sportsman, prospector, Yukon entrepreneur and diplomat. During World War I, as an Allied agent in Russia, he reorganized the railway system, formed an espionage ring, saved the Roumanian [sic] crown jewels and became a friend and confidant of Queen Marie." The site of the plaque is now in front of a McDonald's Restaurant. Boyle and his brother Dave, won a huge bet on a horse called Destruction in 1894 and bought "The Firs," the longtime family home in Oxford Township, for his dad, the famed horse breeder and trainer Charles Boyle, and mother, Martha.

Early in his life Joe Boyle thought that he could find a place with his father at the racetrack, but soon learned that Charles Senior was adamant against permitting his own offspring to get into racing, prompting young Joe to head for the Yukon to prospect for gold.

Horse racing in the spring of 1862 in Toronto was an unrivalled sporting event, not only for the elite, but for the masses too. Cricket and lacrosse had a following, but racing was the major spectator sport. Before the Plate and the three-day Toronto Turf Club meeting at Carleton, a two-day card was staged at Charlie Gates' Newmarket course on The Danforth near the Don River. Although the Plate was the opening day feature, *The Leader*'s turf reporter wrote a lengthy philosophical article extolling the virtues of the sport before describing the race itself:

The races are out in the open air; the refreshing country air free to one and all; the fields are not barricaded; there are [sic] no barring of doors; no conventionalities shut out the mass; but everyone thinks of the races, goes to the races, and enjoys the races. For a little momentary occular indulgence and gratification to what

PALERMO | 9-year-old brown gelding

Owner: George C. Chalmers, Hamilton; *Trainer:* Charles Boyle
Jockey: Charles Littlefield; *Breeder:* White Brothers, Halton County
Note: Royal George was a trotting stallion descended from Messenger

trouble a few sporting men will go, what excitement they'll suffer, what risk they'll run, what sums of money they'll stake!

The great majority, nevertheless, go there for the purposes of being gratified, and very few indeed, return home disappointed. The usual quantity of differences, of course, take place, and the jockeys of losing horses quite naturally have a jealousy in unison with the chagrin of those who own the beaten animal. So it must be, and such is horse racing. The ugly feature of wrangling; quarreling and fighting is, happily, not so prominent in our races as it used to be, and they all now pass on orderly, and without the occurrence of anything either discreditable or offensive.

Considerable trouble ensued in getting the horses fairly started and a good many tricks were attempted by the cunning ones to gain advantages. The judges, however, were determined to have the start properly made, and there were five different efforts at starting. Some of the jockeys were young, green and inexperienced. At first there was a general skedaddle, and when the bell rung to come back, instead of returning, the six went round the Course, led by a foolish jockey, who seemed to go it the harder and louder the bell rang. Several times the horses went off this way, without the word being given, causing great annoyance and delay.

1862 QUEEN'S PLATE STAKES

FIRST RACE
Toronto
Carleton Race Course
JUNE 24, 1862

THE QUEEN'S PLATE. 50 Guineas, the gift of our Most Gracious Sovereign, Queen Victoria. Open to all horses bred in Upper Canada that have never won match, purse or sweepstakes. Mile heats; best two of three. Turf Club weights. Owners must pay $10 subscriber fee to Toronto Turf Club.

Horse	A		Heat 1	Heat 2	Heat 3	Owner
PALERMO	9	br.g.	2	1	1	George C. Chalmers
LADY CARLETON	6	b.m.	1	2	2	Mr Sherwood
TOUCHSTONE	3	br.c.	3	3	3	James White
WAIT-A-WHILE	4	ch.c.	4	4	—	P Langley
TYRANT	5	b.g.	—	—		Mr Stuart
DIANA	3	ch.f.	—	—		Mr Cunningham
MISCHIEF	4	b.c.	Dis.			John Davis

Times—First heat: 2:03. Second heat: 2:05. Third heat: 2:05¼. Track slow. Dis. (Distanced).
Winner: Nine-year-old brown gelding by Royal George—Liberty, by *Mercer. Bred by James and John White, Halton. Trained by Charles Boyle. Ridden by Charles Littlefield.** Betting 8 to 10 on Lady Carleton against field.

After six false starts and shenanigans by one "foolish" jockey who led the entire field around the course on one of the breaks, a fair and capital start was realized. LADY CARLETON took the lead over the tightly bunched field with PALERMO and TOUCHSTONE close behind at the half. In the stretch the bay mare pulled ahead to win by a length over PALERMO. The favored LADY CARLETON took the lead in the second heat in the early running but PALERMO took over at the half and won by a half length. The winners of the first two heats and TOUCHSTONE were the only starters in the final heat, which PALERMO won easily, pulling away to win by four lengths.

By 1863 the Queen's Plate was well established at the Toronto Turf Club's course in the village of Carleton and was a major event for the colonial horsemen of Upper Canada. The race, which carried the Monarch's approval as well as her gift of the dollar equivalent of fifty "guineas," had been won in its first three years by "out-of-towners" from Halton, Hamilton and Port Hope.

However, all was not well for the barristers and politicians who had gained the original petition from Her Majesty to stage the race. The club and its president, Colonel Casimir Gzowski, were confronted by hostile breeders and horsemen when it announced its three-day spring program. Letters to the editor were severely critical of purse monies being offered as well as

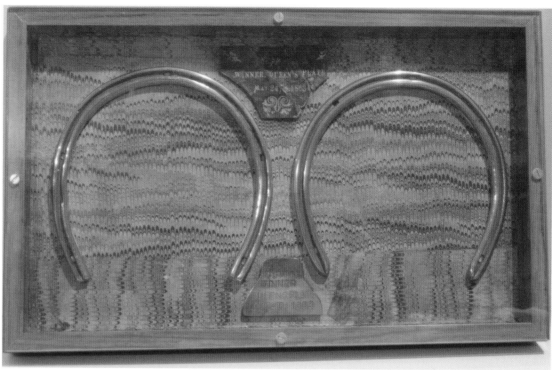

TROPHY AWARDED TO *TOUCHSTONE*'S JOCKEY WILLIAM SMALL.

changes in Plate rules. A gentleman who signed himself "Stockbreeder," said: "It is not only the worst bill ever got up in Canada, but it is the worst bill out this spring, and the meanest bill ever made for Carleton, and looks as though some of the makers, or their friends, just knew what these horses could do, and made the bill to suit them." He complained of offering a purse of $100 for horses which cost from $1,000 to $3,300 and the subscription fees of $30 to enter for a purse of $100. He also strenuously objected to the changing of Plate conditions by the Toronto Turf Club.

> In the first place, the Queen's Plate was intended by those who took the trouble to get it, for horses that never won a race of any kind; but this time the above departed from that rule. I suppose some of them have a horse that they want to ring in, as they call it; but that will be objected to, or instead of fourteen horses starting, that horse will start alone.
>
> Supposing a man has a good horse this spring, and he knows of a horse to run that can beat him, he will keep his [horse] over till next season, meanwhile running for all the Scurry Purses in the country, some of which are as valuable as the purse given this year at the Carleton Course for a two-mile race.

The amended Plate rules in 1863 stated that the race was open to horses bred in Upper Canada that had never won match, purse, or sweepstake, scurry excepted. The horseman bitterly added, "I

don't consider the present Club has any right to alter the rules by which it is to be governed; however, they may depend on it, their new idea will create considerable dissatisfaction, and that, with the rest of their one-sided arrangements, will tend shortly to bring racing to an end in Toronto." He also complained that for the first time an owner was required to pay a ten-dollar subscription

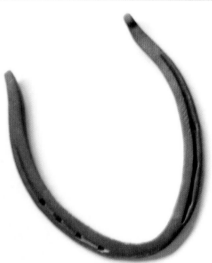

THE OLDEST EXISTING MEMENTO OF THE QUEEN'S PLATE, A SHOE WORN BY *TOUCHSTONE*.

fee to the Club to enter a horse. "There are the small towns of Whitby and St. Catharines, where much could not be expected, giving more money in one purse than our Club does altogether."

Three weeks after the stinging criticism of the arbitrary moves of the Toronto Turf Club, one of the most controversial Plate races was contested on the warm afternoon of 3 June. Again Charles Littlefield, unquestionably the quintessential jockey of that period, was involved and the final result of the race was not announced until two weeks later. Littlefield, who had made an unscheduled appearance on James White's *Don Juan* in deciding heats in the first Plate race, pulled the same trick on *Willie Wonder*. However, White, this time owner of runner-up *Touchstone*, protested that Littlefield's mount *Willie Wonder* was ineligible for the Plate because it had previously earned public money.

The horse, a seven-year-old bay gelding, had been partially maimed in one of his hind feet as a foal; in 1862 he had been sold for $60 because it was thought he was not worth putting into training. But a year later *Willie Wonder* was a Plate starter and finished second to *Touchstone* in the first heat. In the second heat he had a new jockey—Littlefield, who had been tossed off the back of *Shadow* at the half-mile post during the first heat. It was noted that some persons were uncharitable enough to say that the *rencontre* was not altogether accidental, "for Charley is a cute jockey." He pulled a good stroke in the next heat, winning it and the deciding heat and apparently the Plate.

Bets were still on, announced the judges, but because of the protest it would take several days to resolve the matter. Two weeks later Gzowski declared, with little elaboration, that *Willie Wonder* had been disqualified and that the horse from Halton, *Touchstone*, a half-brother to Plate winner *Palermo*, had been awarded the guineas. In an interview fifty years later with the *Canadian Sportsman*, Littlefield stated that *Willie Wonder* was one of his three Plate-winning mounts. So much for vivid recollections of the past! However, Littlefield's ability as a jockey certainly overshadowed his nefarious activities and his riding was the theme of universal commendation. "To succeed in getting him to ride a horse is about half the battle won. He is certainly the most finished and masterly rider in Canada," said *The Leader*.

Writers again were critical of the disorderly array of costumes worn by jockeys, chastising the Club for not enforcing its rules more rigidly. "Why, in the name of respectable racing, cannot jockeys be dressed [as] they ought to be?"

The practice of allowing horses to run under various names was also censured. Of the seven starters, two (Fusilier, formerly *Pluto*; and *Shadow*, the late *Beauregard*) had been renamed, while *Iago* (later *Paul Barnes*) and *Spring*, whose name would be *Beacon* when it won the Plate in 1866, would switch identities. The site of the Plate would also begin to perambulate.

TOUCHSTONE | 4-year-old brown gelding

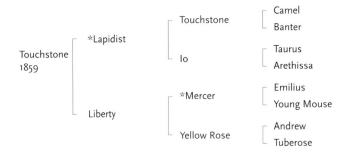

Owner: James and John White, Halton County; *Trainer:* James White
Jockey: William Small; *Breeder:* White Bros, Halton County

Only seven horses contested the Plate in 1863 and Club officials appeared to be losing their enthusiasm as the three-day meet finished with only a handful of horses. Racing deteriorated the second day when the Canadian Derby was cancelled for lack of entries and the weight of the day's officiating fell on treasurer Richard Denison, who acted as judge, starter, steward and in other assorted roles. It rained heavily on the final day, with Denison and H. Quetton St. George acting as judges while Major Green of the Thirtieth Regiment took over the position of starter.

"Thus ended the spring races, which toward the close might have given more satisfaction had a greater number of stewards taken an interest in it, instead of allowing the whole labor to devolve on one or two, who, however amiable, were liable to errors of judgment or other infirmities natural to man. *Mais assez*. A nod is as good as a wink to a blind horse," said *The Leader*.

The dire predictions by "Stockbreeder" of horse racing in Toronto and especially the fate of the Queen's Plate were unerringly precise. The Plate would be run in Toronto only twice in the next seventeen years (at the Newmarket track on the Danforth and at the newly renovated Woodbine Park by the lake) and it would be twenty years before the race would gain a permanent home within the city.

TWO WEEKS AFTER PLATE RACE SIR CASIMIR GZOWSKI ANNOUNCED THE WINNER.

1863 QUEEN'S PLATE STAKES

FIRST RACE
Toronto
Carleton Race Course
JUNE 3, 1863

THE QUEEN'S PLATE. 50 Guineas, the gift of our Most Gracious Sovereign. Open to all horses bred in Upper Canada that have never won match, purse or sweepstakes; scurry excepted. Mile heats; best two of three. Turf Club weights. Owners must pay $10 subscription fee to Club.

Horse	A		Heat 1	Heat 2	Heat 3	Owner
Ⓓ WILLIE WONDER	7	b.g.	2	1	1	Thomas Langley
TOUCHSTONE	4	br.c.	1	2	2	James White
IAGO	7	b.g.	3	4	3	John C M Davis
FUSILIER (late Pluto)	4	b.c.	4	3	4	Dennis Reedy
SPRING	5	br.h.	5	Lost rider		William Balkwill
PRINCE PATRICK	5	ch.g.	6	Dis.	—	Mr Power
SHADOW (late Beauregard)	5	b.g.	Lost rider	—		Nelson Littlefield

Ⓓ-Disqualified by judges. Touchstone awarded race by judges when his owner, Mr. White, protested that Willie Wonder had previously won purse money.

Times—First heat: 1:59½. Second heat: 2:00. Third heat: 2:05. Track good. Dis. (Distanced).

Winner: Four-year-old brown colt by *Lapidist—Liberty, by *Mercer. Bred by James and John White, Halton. Trained by James White.

Touchstone favorite in betting at 3 to 2; followed by Fusilier and Spring.

After two false starts, TOUCHSTONE jumped out in front. Strong and well-built, TOUCHSTONE's condition was apparent. He surrendered the lead briefly to IAGO and FUSILIER, but in the stretch regained the margin and held off WILLIE WONDER to win by a length. SHADOW, which also held the lead for a moment at the half-mile post, threw his jockey, Charles Littlefield, and was distanced. Littlefield climbed upon WILLIE WONDER for the second heat and his influence was apparent as WILLIE WONDER won the heat easily by six lengths over TOUCHSTONE. FUSILIER was third ahead of IAGO with PRINCE PATRICK distanced. WILLIE WONDER led throughout the final heat and pulled away from TOUCHSTONE to win by four lengths, IAGO third and FUSILIER fourth.

As far as one Guelph clergyman was concerned, horse racing was "ill suited to Canadian life." In a letter to John Comb Wilson on 20 July 1847, the Rev. Arthur Palmer of St. George's Anglican Church bitterly opposed the converting of leased parsonage grounds from a farm into a racecourse, saying it was "most painful and repugnant to my feelings."

Informal "pickup" matches between local favourites and widely advertised events sponsored by the Wellington District Turf Club had been held on parsonage grounds and were to continue, much to the cleric's dismay:

> I consider then, that any pleasure that may be derived from the trial of the speed of a few horses, of any supposed advantage in regard to the improvement of their breeds, is dearly purchased by the demoralizing effects produced by horse racing, in gambling, swearing and drunkenness that it generates, in the number of thoughtless and unprincipled persons it attracts to a place, and in the general spirit and habits which it diffuses; a spirit the very opposite of a sober or religious one, and habits specially ill suited to Canadian life.

Despite the Reverend Palmer's protests, a two-day meet took place in September. Seventeen years later, the bustling town of 5,500, with its log and stone homes, gravel roads and sidewalks of wooden planks, was host to the fifth running of the Plate on 5 July but at a different location. The race, which attracted its largest field ever—twelve Upper Canada-bred maidens—was run over a mile course near Gray's Inn and Bullfrog Pond on the Eramosa Road, property later known as the Newstead Farm. And for the first time, a filly, *Brunette,* won the fifty sovereigns. (This was the first time the Queen's gift was advertised as sovereigns instead of "guineas.")

A curious fact regarding the race at Guelph, and the one in London the next year, is that the prize of fifty guineas from Her Majesty is replaced by fifty sovereigns in the purse value and conditions of the race. This is the only time in the Plate's 150-year history that sovereigns are mentioned as Queen Victoria's gift. Patricia Morris, a resident of nearby Hanover, Ontario, owns an 1964 sovereign. Family descendants lived in Guelph at the time of the race and for many years afterward. Ms. Morris

WERE SOVEREIGNS PRESENTED INSTEAD OF GUINEAS?

believes the coin surfaced that year and was later passed down through various generations of the Coghlan, Smith and Morris families. Her grandfather, Pat Morris, was a Mount Forest blacksmith. His son and her father, Stan Morris, presented the family heirloom to his daughter in the 1960s.

Approval by the Governor General's office enabled the Guelph Turf Club to lure the race out of Toronto; as it turned out, it would be the only time the race was staged in the Royal City, which proudly boasts the white horse of Hanover on its escutcheon. The town, located north of Hamilton and west of Toronto, was accessible by the Grand Trunk and Grand Western Railways or dirt roads.

On Plate day, Guelph was alive as a steady stream of horse-drawn vehicles raised clouds of dust on the one-mile journey out of town to the track at Gray's Inn, which 140 years later was now called Freddie's Hairstyling. Pedestrians panted up hill and down dale and the whole picture showed a truthful representation of "the Derby," on as small a scale as possible to get up in Canada said the *Guelph Mercury:*

> It was a hot day and the crowd on the course and around the stands was motley enough. The fancy was well represented but we believe they did not reap a great harvest. Fast young men with turbans, the latest of peg tops and the latest of slang talk, were in abundance. There was quite a sprinkling of the older

1864 QUEEN'S PLATE STAKES

SECOND RACE
Guelph
Turf Club Course
JULY 5, 1864

THE QUEEN'S PLATE. 50 Sovereigns. Open to all horses bred in Upper Canada that have not won. The purse a gift from Her Majesty, Queen Victoria. Mile heats; best two out of three. Turf Club weights.

Horse	A		Heat 1	Heat 2	Heat 3	Owner
BRUNETTE	4	b.f.	4	1	1	Dr George D Morton
WAIT-A-WHILE	6	ch.h.	2	2	2	P Langley
SPRING	6	b.h.	3	3	3	William Balkwill
EDMONTON	5	b.h.	1	4	3	Joseph Grand
COLLEEN BAWN	6	b.m.	—	—	—	Mr Flannery
KITTY CLYDE	aged	b.m.	—	—	—	O Pooley
ANNIE LAURIE	5	ch.m.	—	—	—	James White
BEN OLCUTT	5	b.g.	—	—	—	George Henderson
BARNEY	4	b.g.	—	—	—	Dr O'Donnell
TORONTO LASS	5	ch.m.	—	—	—	Dennis Hayes
DISDAIN	aged	b.m.	—	—	—	Joseph Grand
IAGO	8	b.g.	—	—	—	J C M Davis

Times—First heat: 1:57. Second heat: 1:54¾. Third heat: 2:00. Track fast.

Winner: Four-year-old bay filly by *Lapidist—Belle of Scott, by Pilot. Trained by Dr. G. D. Morton. Bred by C. Wilson, Canada West.

EDMONTON led the field throughout the first heat, closely followed by WAIT-A-WHILE. SPRING and BRUNETTE were close behind. The start was uneven for the second heat. EDMONTON again went to the front but quickly fell out of contention as BRUNETTE took control and cut more than two seconds off the time of the first heat. The third heat was marred with confusion. The starter was absent at the break as three horses went round the course. Following the recall, SPRING joined in company and although this was much to the disadvantage of BRUNETTE, she took the third heat with the greatest ease.

sporting gents—veterans in horse racing—who only bet when they are sure to win and know, or pretend to know, much more about the horses than anybody else.

There was also a sprinkling of young ladies who seemed to have doubts in their own minds as to whether they should be there or not. Also a scattering of old dowagers who evidently felt that their presence was sufficient to make the affair fashionable. It was a grand collection of characters beginning at the lowest strata, and mounting up gradually to the honest man. One commendable feature was the entire absence of gamblers who ply their arts on the roulette table and make money out of the greenhorns by other knavish devices.

A few peep shows were on the grounds but they lacked customers. The drinking booths were well patronized. Attempts were made to get up a fight or two but they were nipped in the bud.

Prominently in attendance were local politicians; the Plate would soon become a "political plum." Race officials included the Hon. A.J. Fergusson Blair, the Hon. William Dickson, Mayor William Clarke, Sheriff George Grange, Judge J.J. Kingsmill and Arthur Hogg MPP.

It again took three heats to decide a winner, the four-year-old filly *Brunette*. There is not one account of the race which mentions her jockey, but after finishing a "decent" fourth in the first heat to Joseph Grand's *Edmonton*, *Brunette* came back to win the second and third heats over *Wait-a-While*. The deciding heat was greatly confusing. The field of three "got away" minus *Spring* (later *Beacon*, the 1866 winner) and an absent starter, C.E. Romaine, who belatedly rang his bell to recall the field. The false start did not bother *Brunette*, who outran the rested *Spring* and exhibited great stamina in winning for owner Dr. George Deane Morton of Bradford. The thirty-seven-year-old Irish-born physician, who was reeve and coroner of the Simcoe County town in 1866–1867, later became president of Bradford Flax Mill Company.

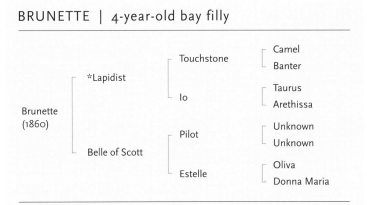

BRUNETTE | 4-year-old bay filly

Brunette (1860)			
	*Lapidist	Touchstone	Camel
			Banter
		Io	Taurus
			Arethissa
	Belle of Scott	Pilot	Unknown
			Unknown
		Estelle	Oliva
			Donna Maria

Owner: Dr. George D. Morton, Bradford; *Trainer:* Dr. G. D. Morton
Jockey: Unknown; *Breeder:* C. Wilson, Canada West (Ontario)

Dr. Morton, one of the leading breeders and horsemen of the 1860s, "set all Yonge Street agog to see so blue-blooded a patrician" when he imported *Antonio (by *Bay Middleton*), a full-brother to an English Derby winner, to stand at stud. Obscure breeding records of the era reveal that a Mr. C. Wilson of Canada West (Ontario) bred *Brunette*, who later won a sizeable number of races for her Bradford owner. She was by *Lapidist, leading sire of three Plate winners in the 1860s (*Touchstone* and *Wild Rose* were the others). Her dam was *Belle of Scott*, a mare of questionable pedigree. She is traced easily on her maternal side, but *Pilot*, her sire, would never qualify for the stud book. *Lapidist, sired by St. Leger winner *Touchstone* (a son of *Camel*, who sired three English Derby winners), was imported into Canada in 1858 by Tom Simpson of Holland Landing. *Lapidist's chief contributions to the improvement of the breed in Canada, however, were through his half-bred son, *Clear Grit*, who founded one of the important Canadian trotting families.

Like so many quality horses which gained an early reputation in Ontario, *Lapidist was sold to a breeder in New York at a relatively early age.

GUELPH ATTRACTED THE FOURTH RUNNING OF THE QUEEN'S PLATE ON A COURSE NEAR ERAMOSA ROAD. THE DRAWING IS OF THE ERAMOSA BRIDGE.

What actually transpired at Newmarket Racecourse on the eastern outskirts of London on 7 June 1865 is one of the most bizarre and inexplicable riddles in Plate history. Regrettably, the published accounts of that Wednesday afternoon—a humid, scorching day interrupted by winds of hurricane force and torrential rains—can never be substantiated. For more than one hundred years, researchers and authors periodically attempted to set the record straight, but without success. And so, the list of Plate winners will forever simply state:

1865, *Lady Norfolk*; owner and breeder, John Sheppard, Simcoe; jockey, unknown.

After a day of protests, disqualifications and weather delays, the judges and stewards of the London Turf Club tentatively awarded the Plate to Mr. Shepherd's [sic] bay mare, a decision which was reviewed by Governor General Viscount Monck's office before it was reportedly confirmed on 4 August in *The Leader*. The item said: "We are happy to learn that Mr. Shepherd [sic] of this town [there was no mention of Simcoe] has at last been awarded the Queen's Plate." Since then, Sheppard's name has been spelt in several ways. It is debatable whether he was from Simcoe in Norfolk County or Innisfil Township in Simcoe County since neither community has ever claimed him as a Plate winner.

Accounts of the 1865 Plate were glaringly inconsistent. Reports the following day in the London, Chatham, Toronto and Hamilton newspapers and subsequent historical articles in Toronto journals and Trent Frayne's *The Queen's Plate* have left the reader in a muddle about the race's result.

In defence of the press coverage, it should be stressed that newspapermen assigned to racing in this era had to cope with

LADY NORFOLK AND NORA CRIENA MET IN THE FINAL HEAT TO DECIDE THE WINNER.

unnumbered horses, jockeys wearing similar silks, and the skimpiest of information from the race officials. It is amazing that so much detail, however coloured or erroneous, was recorded of early years of the Queen's Plate.

Much of the confusion and the cause of howls of protest from various owners concerned four horses: an American-bred horse, incorrectly identified as *Stone Plover*, *Beacon* (formerly known as *Spring*), *Nora Criena* (possibly *Creina* or *Crena*) and *Lady Norfolk*, who was by Allendale, a stallion owned by Francis Lowell of Galt, Ontario.

Stone Plover won the first heat over *Nora Criena* and *Beacon*, who was making his third Plate appearance, while *Lady Norfolk* was distanced, failing to place among the top four finishers. Following the second heat, which was won by *Beacon* over *Stone Plover*, the judges were assailed with complaints regarding *Stone Plover*'s eligibility. The horse, entered by Henry Chappell of Sandwich, Ontario, near Windsor, was alleged to be an American-bred "ringer," owned by a resident of Detroit. He was subsequently disqualified.

The judges added to the turmoil by discounting the victory of the seven-year-old gelding *Beacon* because his jockey did not weigh out correctly after the race. It is unclear whether the rider dismounted before coming to the judges' stand for the weighing-out ceremony, which is contrary to racing rules, or whether he illegally jettisoned his lead saddle weights while seeking an advantage in the last quarter-mile.

Reports of what followed suggest that officials were in a state of disarray; there were claims that when the storm broke, they went home for supper before rendering a decision

1865 QUEEN'S PLATE STAKES

FIRST RACE
London
Newmarket Race Course
JUNE 7, 1865

THE QUEEN'S PLATE of 50 sovereigns, the gift of Her Most Gracious Majesty. Open to all horses bred and raised in the province that have never won a match, purse or sweepstake. Mile heats. Turf Club weights.

Horse	A		Heat 1	Heat 2	Heat 3	Owner
Ⓓ STONE PLOVER	3	ch.c.	1	2	—	Henry Chappell
LADY NORFOLK	3	b.f.	—	3	1	John Sheppard
NORA CRIENA	6	ch.m.	2	4	2	A Lepper
ⒹⒹ BEACON (late Spring)	7	br.h.	3	1	—	William Balkwill
PAUL BARNES (late Iago)	9	b.g.	4	—	—	J C M Davis
ANNIE LAURIE	6	ch.m.	—	—	—	James White
HECATE	6	ch.m.	D.n.f.	—	—	Joseph Grand
LETTIE BROWN	6	gr.m.	—	—	—	James Pace
CUMBERLAND MAID	4	b.f.	—	—	—	J Jackson

Ⓓ-Stone Plover disqualified as he was not a province-bred animal. ⒹⒹ-Beacon disqualified because jockey lost weights before weighing out.

Track fast and muddy. No times given for heats. D.n.f (Did not finish).

Winner: Three-year-old bay filly by Allendale—dam by Daniel Webster. Trained and bred by Mr. John Sheppard, Simcoe.

After a false start the field got away in uneven fashion. BEACON sprinted to the lead but surrendered it with a quarter-mile to go to STONE PLOVER and NORA CRIENA, who edged out the early leader for place. PAUL BARNES was fourth. LADY NORFOLK was unplaced and HECATE failed to finished because of an injury. The second heat was delayed by a thunderstorm. After three false starts the second heat finally got underway. STONE PLOVER and NORA CRIENA were troublesome prior to the break. BEACON again went to the lead and after a bitter struggle with STONE PLOVER, pulled away to win by two or three lengths. LADY NORFOLK and NORA CRIENA were close for third. A third heat was apparently awarded to LADY NORFOLK. Her victory was confirmed two months later by judges.

on the close finish between *Lady Norfolk* and *Nora Criena* for third place in the second heat. Furthermore, prolonged delays caused by numerous restarts and lengthy protest hearings prevented reporters from sending in their stories in time for the final editions.

Although it was published a week after the race, the *Weekly Spectator* of Hamilton still carried the headline, "*Stone Plover* Wins the Queen's Plate." In his account of the first day's results, the *Weekly*'s correspondent wrote:

> Since the race, however, objections have been raised as to the right of this horse [*Stone Plover*] to run at all for the Queen's Plate. It is said that the owner is not one of Her Majesty's subjects, and also that the horse itself was not bred in the Province. I trust that this matter will be rigidly inquired into by the judges. This race is established for the purpose of encouraging the breeding of good Canadian horses, and if foreign horses are admitted, the object of Her Majesty's gift is lost. Should *Stone Plover* be adjudged disqualified, the stakes will be handed to *Nora Creina* [*sic*], who was second. She was named after an Irish folk song.

The *Chatham Daily Planet* also suggested that the Plate should be awarded to *Nora Criena,* a mare owned by Toronto's Mr. A. Lepper, who lodged the protest against *Stone Plover:*

> . . . as his mare was third [*sic*] in the two heats, he sent her around the course alone for a third heat, and claimed the Plate. What decision has been come to I cannot yet tell, but it is too bad that the running for so important a prize should end in such a fizzle. The whole race has been far from a satisfactory one, and showed bad management somewhere.

The reporter for the *London Evening Advertiser,* who called the race the "London Derby," said: "If the protest holds good *Lady Norfolk* will get the Plate, if not *Stone Plover* will receive it. A third heat between *Lady Norfolk* and *Nora Crena* [*sic*] was won easily by the latter." Did he mean the "former"? After the third day of the meeting, this same reporter wrote: "In relation to the Queen's Purse we may mention that the case has been sent to His Excellency the Governor General for decision."

The opinion of the *London Free Press* was just as ambiguous. After reviewing the indiscretion of *Beacon*'s jockey and the ineligibility of *Stone Plover,* that paper's reporter wrote, "it was arranged that the competition should proceed between the next best, *Lady Norfolk* and *Nora Crena* [*sic*]." But he ended his article on a vague note, saying, "the running qualities of all four animals attracted general admiration." There was no mention of the final heat, or even if it took place.

Trent Frayne, in his book on the Plate's first one hundred years, states that *Nora Criena* led *Lady Norfolk* throughout the race and "to all intents, won the Plate." Years later a newspaper reported that *Nora Criena* had at one time

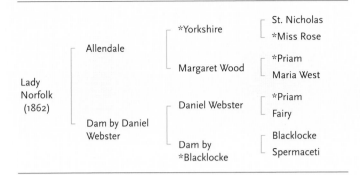

LADY NORFOLK | 3-year-old bay filly

Lady Norfolk (1862)
- Allendale
  - *Yorkshire
    - St. Nicholas
    - *Miss Rose
  - Margaret Wood
    - *Priam
    - Maria West
- Dam by Daniel Webster
  - Daniel Webster
    - *Priam
    - Fairy
  - Dam by *Blacklocke
    - Blacklocke
    - Spermaceti

Owner: John Sheppard, Simcoe; *Trainer:* John Sheppard
Jockey: Unknown; *Breeder:* John Sheppard

trained on the Winchester (Street) field, an area adjacent to Sackville Avenue (east of Parliament and north of Carlton Street).

If *Nora Criena* got "jobbed" that afternoon, her rider never complained. On the six-year-old mare in London was tiny, sixteen-year-old Robert Davies, who would go on to become one of Toronto's wealthiest citizens. Davies, who owned *Floss* and bred *Fearnaught,* both Plate winners, built Thorncliffe Stable, one of Canada's great racing and breeding establishments. He was vice-president of the Ontario Jockey Club and founded the Don and later Dominion Brewing Companies before establishing the Don Valley Paper Company and the Don Brick Works. He was also president of the Copland Brewing Company.

The judges' decision to disqualify *Stone Plover* was justified. He was a "ringer," probably *Free Press Boy* or perhaps *Limerick Boy,* a gelding who often raced in nearby Michigan. The "ringer's" sire was the real *Stone Plover.* As for Henry Chappell, who recalled racing horses over the ancient Lambton course on the banks of the Humber River in Etobicoke in the 1830s, his racing privileges were never denied. In 1904, at the age of ninety, he entered his last Plate starter at Woodbine Park.

RICHMOND STREET NEAR KING STREET IN LONDON, SCENE OF THE MOST CONTROVERSIAL PLATE OF ALL.

1866 | BEACON

Hamilton experienced the biggest, and perhaps the rowdiest, sporting event in its history the year before Confederation when the "great contest for the Queen's Plate of Fifty 'Guineas,'" was run for the first time on the monarch's birthday, 24 May. The site of the town's first Plate race was the new racecourse near the Delta Hotel in the city's east end—the Hamilton Riding and Driving Park, an elegant and spacious track owned by R.R. Waddell, a prominent local barrister.

Although the race had been plagued by crises and confusions in its sibling years, it appeared to be gaining substantially in popularity and stature and in 1866 eighteen entries were posted, including *Beacon* (formerly *Spring*), who was mounting his fourth bid for the Plate. The venerable brown horse, who was stabled at the Delta Hotel along with other out-of-town entrants, was the odds-on favourite, despite his losses at Carleton, Guelph and London. That spring hope had been rekindled when *Beacon* was put into training early by his new owner, Peter Duncan McKellar, a prominent businessman, county registrar and gentleman farmer from Chatham.

In all fairness, *Beacon*'s previous failures were not entirely his doing. His riders had to accept most of the blame. In 1863 the horse was disqualified for "losing" his rider and in the Queen's Plate race in London, after apparently winning the second heat, the judges ruled out his victory because his jockey failed to weigh out properly. A son of **Sir Tatton Sykes,* who sired *Don Juan,* the first Plate winner, *Beacon* was a London horse; he was bred there by Joseph Bilton, the brewer, and raced during much of his career for hotel owner William Balkwill before he was sold to McKellar.

On the holiday morning of the Plate, Hamilton awoke to the sounds of guns, pistols, miniature artillery and innumerable

CHATHAM'S PETER D. MCKELLAR OWNED *BEACON* WHEN THE GELDING WON THE PLATE ON HIS FOURTH ATTEMPT.

"crackers;" the city was festooned with flags and banners, gaily fluttering in the breeze. Meanwhile, *Beacon* was the centre of attention at the hotel's stables, which were within easy walking distance of the track. A crowd of citizens and horsemen assembled to get a look at him and *Eliza C.,* who had possibly been denied the Plate the year before at London when she raced under the name of *Nora Criena.*

The track site, later named Gage Park, had a one-mile oval with a soft, sandy loam surface, "easy on the horse's hooves, yet not too loose"; it was surrounded by a "conspicuous board fence." Perched inside were the grandstand, the ladies' stand and an open stand. The course was described as being "beyond all question the best adapted to its purpose within the province of Canada." Waddell, who opened the park the year before, leased the land to "certain gentlemen of Hamilton and vicinity . . . to encourage

THE ENTRANCE TO HAMILTON'S GORE PARK, CIRCA 1862, WAS THROUGH A TURNSTILE.

THE UBIQUITOUS ROBERT R. WADDELL, WHO BUILT A COURSE NEAR THE DELTA.

such lawful sports as will in their results give heartfelt recreation, and promote and sustain improvement in the breeding of Canadian horses."

Hamilton had been gearing up for the Plate since the previous summer when it was announced that the efforts of the Honourable Isaac Buchanan, the city's Member of Parliament, and Thomas Swinyard, general manager of the Great Western Railway, were largely responsible for the Plate's venue. In an editorial, the *Hamilton Spectator* noted that the race was being held to promote better bred horses and that a sum of one hundred "guineas" was sent annually from the Royal Treasury to Canada, through the Governor General. This sum was divided; half to Canada East, half to Canada West.

The Plate proved to be a frightful experience for both the track's proprietor and the *Spectator*'s reporter. At noon the elegant vehicles arrived carrying the fashionable elite of Hamilton society, along with the "thirsty souls" who came on foot and then crowded about the refreshment booths leased by several Hamilton taverns.

Problems quickly arose as Waddell, scurrying about on his mare *Sunbeam,* endeavoured to keep order on the track, in the stands and at the gates. Against his orders, however, gamblers gained access to the stands but were quickly evicted by Waddell, who declared, "I will keep the Park up to the highest point of respectability." He had spent $5,000 on its improvements and was determined that gamblers would not depreciate his property. About this point an exuberant holiday crowd of five thousand swirled into the exclusive space between the drawn gates, which had been reserved for the well-to-do.

During the ensuing melee, which involved three firemen "in tight blue uniforms," a racehorse lunged out and "as if indignant at the bad behaviour of the pugilists," struck one of them on the breast with his heels, causing blood to flow from the man's mouth. There was a pause, but the battle was renewed in front of the judges' stand as all sorts of intruders came over the rails, followed by Waddell on *Sunbeam,* striving vainly to maintain order.

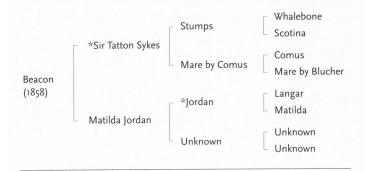

BEACON | 8-year-old brown horse

- Beacon (1858)
  - *Sir Tatton Sykes
    - Stumps
      - Whalebone
      - Scotina
    - Mare by Comus
      - Comus
      - Mare by Blucher
  - Matilda Jordan
    - *Jordan
      - Langar
      - Matilda
    - Unknown
      - Unknown
      - Unknown

Owner: Peter Duncan McKellar, Chatham; *Trainer:* Johnny Gagen
Jockey: Johnny Gagen; *Breeder:* Edward S. (Joe) Bilton, London

"Hamiltonians, it seems, always observe Her Monarch's birthday with unbridled enthusiasm. Liquor and beer on empty stomachs may have triggered the loutish behaviour. The absence of eatibles is a defect which operates against human happiness at these races very much indeed," said the *Spectator*. "Only some crackers and sandwiches were available."

The newspaper's reporter had other complaints too: "Only two of the nine jockeys wore the colours named in the official printed cards and some of these colours were in error." The newspaperman was told that neither the judges nor the starters knew the names of the horses and their jockeys. No record had been taken; consequently, none was preserved. "Very odd this, very singular indeed. The riders were weighed; was no name recorded with each man's weight?" the reporter inquired. Research reveals that John Gagen rode *Beacon* to successive heat victories. The only other rider to be identified was Nat Williams on *Pickpocket*.

The starter for Hamilton's first Plate was William Hendrie, who thirty-three years later would break Joseph Seagram's domination of the event with the bay filly *Butter Scotch*, winner of the Plate in 1899.

1866 QUEEN'S PLATE STAKES

FIRST RACE
Hamilton
Riding and Driving Park
MAY 24, 1866

THE QUEEN'S PLATE. 50 Guineas, the gift of Her Most Gracious Majesty, Queen Victoria. Open to all horses bred and raised in Upper Canada that have never won public money. Mile heats; best two in three. Time between heats 20 minutes. Eighteen entries. Nine started.

Horse	A		Heat 1	Heat 2	Jockeys	Owner
BEACON (late Spring)	8	br.h.	1	1	John Gagen	Peter D McKellar
PAUL BARNES (late Iago)	10	b.g.	4	2		J Williamson
BEESWING	aged	ch.m.	3	3		John Copeland
PICKPOCKET	6	ch.g.	2	4	N Williams	Thomas Grimshaw
CUMBERLAND MAID	5	b.m.	5	5		J Jackson
ROSE OF ALLANDALE	7	b.m.	Dis.	D.n.s.		P J Pilkney
PETROLIANA	aged	b.m.	Dis.	D.n.s.		J C M Davis
ELIZA C. (late Nora Criena)	7	ch.m.	Dis.	D.n.s.		Charles Gates

Times—First heat: 1:54. Second heat: 1:57½. Track fast. Dis. (Distanced). D.n.s. (Did not start).
Winner: Eight-year-old brown horse by *Sir Tatton Sykes—Matilda Jordan, by *Jordan. Bred by E. S. Bilton, London. Ridden by Johnny Gagen.
After three false starts, during which one starter retired, the first heat got away and was a fair race. BEACON led all the way with apparent ease despite the fact that his rider rode him fully around the course on the first false break. Favored ELIZA C. showed poorly and was distanced. Only PICKPOCKET challenged BEACON in the first heat. Five started for the second heat and BEACON prevailed and was therefore declared winner of the Queen's Plate.

Although he occasionally attended horse races, usually in the company of fellow politicians who owned prominent stables, Sir John A. Macdonald had more pressing duties in Ottawa on the afternoon of 18 June 1867. Confederation Day was less than two weeks away and the Dominion of Canada was poised to celebrate it. "A united British America, with its four millions of people, takes its place this day [1 July] among the nations of the world," proclaimed *The Globe* in Toronto. Upper (Ontario) and Lower (Quebec) Canada had united with New Brunswick and Nova Scotia, pushing the boundaries of Confederation from the Atlantic to the head waters of the Great Lakes. The confederation of equines, however, was still decades away as a field of nine galloped onto the oval of the St. Catharines Turf Club for the eighth running of the Queen's Plate.

The race was open only to horses owned and bred in Upper Canada that had never won a match, purse or sweepstake. Eligibility, however, was not the only bothersome issue. Horsemen had become irritable with St. Catharines' officials, who had decided to postpone the Plate for almost a month because of rainy weather and the lack of horses. The Plate originally was scheduled to "come off over the grounds of the Turf Club" on 24 May, Queen Victoria's birthday, and would be the main attraction of the club's four-day meet, which offered $1,700 in prizes, "the largest amount ever offered at a meeting in Upper Canada."

But two days before the meet was to open—on land recently leased from Colonel Thomas Adams—the *St. Catharines Daily Journal* observed that changes had been made in some of the races because of insufficient entries. On 22 May it was announced "that the state of the weather compelled the St. Catharines Turf Club to adjourn the races. The money was there for the horses to 'go for', but the elements were against the club. The weather was wet, murky and disagreeable, and the track was no better." The paper, however, disapproved of the club's decision, declaring that "it would have

HALTON POLITICIAN JOHN WHITE BRED AND OWNED TWO PLATE WINNERS NAMED *WILD ROSE*.

been more judicious to run the races. We believe a mistake was made in adjourning."

Instead of rescheduling the meeting and the Plate for a day or two, to placate horsemen who had travelled a long way to race and who had spent a considerable amount of money to ship their horses into the Niagara peninsula, the club postponed the meet until 18 June. The lengthy delay did not affect attendance and more than three thou-

1867 QUEEN'S PLATE STAKES

FIRST RACE

St. Catharines
Turf Club Grounds
JUNE 18, 1867

THE QUEEN'S PLATE. 50 Guineas, the gift of Her Most Gracious Majesty, Queen Victoria. Open to all horses owned and bred in Upper Canada that have never won match, purse nor sweepstake. Turf Club weights. No entrance fees. Mile heats. Fourteen entered May 15.

Horse	A		Heat 1	Heat 2		Owner
WILD ROSE	6	ch.m.	1	1		James White
COUNTRY MAID	7	b.m.	3	2		W B Flint
PRIDE OF ERIN	6	b.m.	2	4		A Lepper
IZEPPA	6	blk.h.	4	3		John Shedden
MARY ELLIOTT	4	b.f.	—	—		H J Middaugh
JENNIE ROBINSON	7	b.m.	—	—		Joshua Burtch
LADY AUGUSTA	3	b.f.	—	—		M Sinnett
JOHNNY SCHMOKER	6	b.g.	—	—		J P Eddy
ONTARIO BOY			—	—		Charles Gates

Times—First heat: 1:50½. Second heat: 1:51. Track fast.

Winner: Six-year-old chestnut mare by *Lapidist—Yellow Rose, by Andrew. Bred by James and John White, Halton. Trained by Mr. Fagan. Ridden by A. McLaughlin.

Following a fair start, WILD ROSE went to the lead but was collared by PRIDE OF ERIN at the quarter pole. The two ran neck-to-neck into the home stretch, where WILD ROSE pulled away to win by two lengths. In the second heat, which was delayed by three false starts, only eight started. WILD ROSE was challenged by COUNTRY MAID and IZEPPA in the early running and in the stretch a couple of blankets could have covered six of the horses in contention. WILD ROSE, however, prevailed, winning by a half-length over COUNTRY MAID. A protest against WILD ROSE stating that she had won public money the year before in Hamilton probably will not be sustained.

Scratched—Parasol, Fisherman, Country Boy and Isabella.

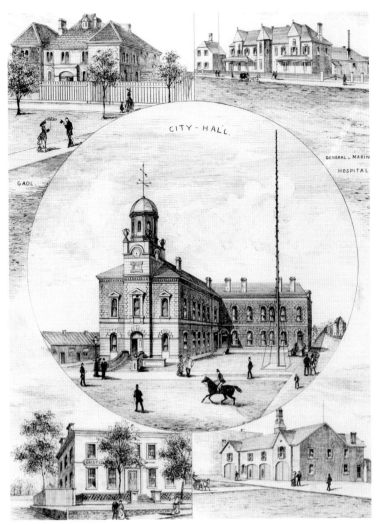

SKETCHES OF ST. CATHARINES SHORTLY AFTER CONFEDERATION.

WILD ROSE | 6-year-old chestnut mare

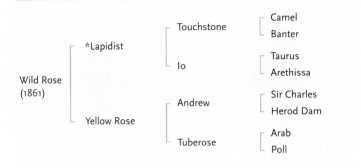

Wild Rose (1861)
- *Lapidist
  - Touchstone
    - Camel
    - Banter
  - Io
    - Taurus
    - Arethissa
- Yellow Rose
  - Andrew
    - Sir Charles
    - Herod Dam
  - Tuberose
    - Arab
    - Poll

Owner: James White, Bronte; *Trainer:* Mr. Fagan
Jockey: Alex McLaughlin; *Breeder:* White Bros., Halton County

AN ARTIST'S CONCEPTION OF JOCKEY ALEX MCLAUGHLIN.

sand people packed the course in ideal weather. However, the original field of fourteen dwindled to nine by Plate day. One of the runners was *Wild Rose,* a six-year-old chestnut mare, owned by the White brothers of Halton—James of Bronte and his influential brother, the Honourable John White of Milton.

Wild Rose was the favourite in the betting pools, but for a time there were fears that she might be declared ineligible because it was alleged she had won public money at Hamilton the year before. However, the protest was not sustained and the mare, with a "Mr. A. McLaughlin" in the saddle, easily won both mile heats and the Plate. She won the first heat in a record 1:50 1/2 and was only a half-second slower in coasting to a conclusive second heat triumph. The race was not without some excitement as *Wild Rose*'s trainer (or groom), a "Mr. Fagan," narrowly escaped with his life while urging

his mare onwards in the second heat. "A man named Fagan, trainer of *Wild Rose,*" said *The Evening Journal,* "ran into the track when the horses were nearing the judges' stand in order to tell the rider of *Wild Rose* to whip up. The horses came bowling along at full speed, and the man, not judging his distance correctly, was struck in the shoulder by *Country Maid,* who spun him round like a top into the ditch. He was somewhat stunned by the fall, but recovered sufficiently in a short time to feel that he had had a very narrow escape for his life."

Wild Rose was a half-sister to *Don Juan,* the Plate's first winner, and was the daughter of the imported English stud *Lapidist,* who sired three Plate winners in the space of four years. For the Whites of Trafalgar Township, the win marked the fourth time in seven years that they had either owned or bred the Plate winner.

1868 | NETTIE

Radical amendments to the rules and conditions of the Queen's Plate, as well as a new venue, occurred when the race again fell under the jurisdiction of the Toronto Turf Club. The distance was changed when one-mile heats, best two-of-three, were discarded in favour of a two-mile dash. More importantly, "winners" were allowed to compete. Still, there was a catch.

The Toronto Turf Club, which was controlled by English officers based in Canada and by the local militia, stipulated that horses which had won a steeplechase or a hurdle race were eligible. Horses were ineligible which had won a stakes on the flat at a public race meeting where money was awarded. The change of rules undoubtedly enlisted any number of aged chasers and "timber toppers" as the field swelled to fifteen, the largest ever. No three-year-olds were entered, and a change in weights also prompted several owners to ride their own animals. Old English customs still lingered, even though Canada was in its second year of Confederation. The Club's rules on weight allowances read: Three years, eight stone; four years, nine stone, seven pounds, and so on. In other words, 112 pounds for three-year-olds, 133 for four-year-olds. Six-year-olds and older carried 144 pounds.

Having been a touring roadshow for the previous four years, the Plate returned to the environs of the Queen City. The site in 1868, however, was the Newmarket Course, which was located just north of Danforth Road and east of the Don River, instead of Carleton, which had hosted the first four Plates. Built in 1854 and owned by innkeeper Charlie Gates, the Newmarket track was three-and-a-half miles east of Toronto, whose northern boundary in the 1860s was Bloor Street. It was served by a "good plank road," and the Grand Trunk Railway. To pinpoint it further in the 2000s, the track was situated north of Danforth Avenue, east of Gledhill Avenue and west of Main Street. The property reached almost up to Lumsden Avenue. Today several of the streets in this area where the ninth running of the Plate was staged are named after English race-tracks—Newmarket, naturally, Doncaster and Epsom.

The Daily Leader noted that the races attracted the "most intense interest, not only in Toronto, but all over the country," and "in the past ten days they have been the principal topic of conversation among sporting men and others heretofore not much interested in such sports." It was estimated that up to 12,000 people watched the Plate, the Dominion Plate and three other races, one of which was open only to riders on full pay in the army or navy, officers in the militia or volunteers quartered in Canada. Another was a three-quarter mile charge by the Eighteenth Hussars!

Getting to Newmarket posed considerable headaches. It was

POLICE RESTRAINED CROWDS EAGER TO WATCH NETTIE'S VICTORY BY A NECK AT THE NEWMARKET COURSE ON THE DANFORTH.

CHARLES GATES' HOTEL IN LITTLE YORK, 1870. A FAVOURITE PLACE FOR HORSEMEN, GATES' INN WAS LOCATED ON THE NORTH SIDE OF DANFORTH AVENUE. GATES ALSO OWNED AND BUILT THE NEWMARKET COURSE AND RAN A HORSE IN THE 1868 PLATE.

OWEN'S HOTEL, 1890. GATES' INN BECAME OWEN'S, AND IN THE REAR WAS THE NEWMARKET RACE COURSE.

reported that "despite the railways carrying extra passengers, all the available vehicles that could be obtained at the various livery stables were eagerly secured, and everything in the form of horseflesh was at a premium. Those who were fortunate enough to own a quadruped capable of reaching the track took it out for the occasion. Indeed, many poor things which should have been allowed to remain quietly at home were produced for the road. Parties were determined to reach the course, and it made little difference to them how they got there, so long as they succeeded in putting in an appearance.

"It has been said that horses that were never seen before always turn out upon Derby day, and one was forcibly struck with the remark upon examining into the character of the animals that were seen jogging along the Danforth road yesterday afternoon." Apparently, good humour was the order of the day, and the music of the Twenty-ninth Regiment's band enlivened proceedings. Between races the large crowd milled around the refreshment booths and on the track to inspect the horses.

Yet, when it came time to start the Plate, the spectators constituted a potential disruption of the event. Colonel John Jenyns came to the rescue, ordering eighteen or twenty of his mounted Hussars into a solid column to sweep the track clear of "all intruders without any apparent effort. The spectators fell back before the horses without a murmur. It was a beautiful spectacle to witness, the Hussars suddenly breaking in the centre of the column to allow the field to start off in a bunch at full speed. A spontaneous cheer burst from the spectators."

NETTIE | 5-year-old bay mare

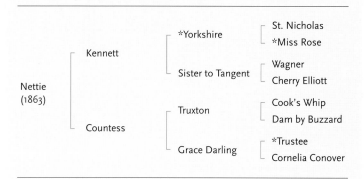

Owner: James and John White, Halton County; *Trainer:* Jonathan Scott
Jockey: Archie Fisher; *Breeder:* White Bros., Halton County

Twice around the one-mile oval they went, and *Nettie* began to pull away with half-a-mile to run. The five-year-old bay mare won by a neck over *Young Jack the Barber.* Owned and bred by the White brothers of Halton County, *Nettie* was *Nellie* on the day of her Plate win. Several weeks later she was racing as *Nettie,* the name under which she was registered in the stud books. There is also some question regarding the spelling of her sire—*Kennett* or *Kenneth.* In the *American Stud Book* and the 1868 racing records compiled in the United States, the sire's name is spelled *Kenneth.* However, this is undoubtedly a typo and the sire was *Kennett.* Her dam, *Countess,* is registered as also being the dam of both a *Nettie* and a *Nellie*—one foaled in 1863 (*Nettie*) and *Nellie* in 1867. However, *Nettie,* bred by R.R. Waddell, the man who built and owned the Hamilton racetrack, became the first Plate-winning mare to later produce a future champion (*Fanny Wiser,* 1882). She was a true Canadian-bred mare—her sire and dam were both foaled in Upper Canada. Contemporary newspapers listed Archie Fisher as *Nettie*'s owner. But he was her jockey and possibly a co-owner with James and John White, winners or breeders of their fifth Plate winner in nine years.

1868 QUEEN'S PLATE STAKES

THIRD RACE
Toronto
Newmarket Race Course
JUNE 17, 1868

HER MAJESTY'S PLATE of 50 Guineas for horses, geldings or mares bred, raised and trained in the Province of Ontario that have not previously won public money at any race meeting. Weights: three years, 8 stone; four years, 9 stone 7 lbs.; five years, 9 stone 13 lbs.; and six years and aged, 10 stone 5 lbs. The whole stakes to go to the winner. Two–mile dash.

Horse	A		Wt	Fin	Owner
NETTIE (late Nellie)	5	b.m.	139	1nk	James & John White
YOUNG JACK THE BARBER	4	b.c.	133	2	J Simpson
JOHN COLLINS	aged	ch.g.	144	3	M A Thomas
RATHOWEN	4	b.c.	133	4	Sheriff George Grange
ROSE OF ALLANDALE	9	b.m.	144	—	Dr G D Morton
BRICKBAT	aged	b.g.	144	—	John Copeland
ORLANDO	aged	b.g.	144	—	Mr Hodder
HIGHLAND MAID	4	b.f.	133	—	Charles Gates
WAIT-A-WHILE	5	b.g.	139	—	P Langley
TOM KEMBLE	5	b.h.	139	—	Joseph Grand
GLADIATEUR (late Dan)	6	b.g.	144	—	Joseph Grand
LOUISA	aged	b.m.	144	—	Mr Webb
BAREBONE (late Venture)	6	br.g.	144	—	R R Waddell
RIDGEWAY	5	ch.g.	139	—	D Van Eng
MEG MERILIES	aged	br.m.	144	—	Mr McIntosh

Time, 3:55. Track fast.

Winner: Five–year–old bay mare by Kennett—Countess, by Truxton. Trained by Jonathan Scott. Ridden by Archie Fisher. Bred by James and John White, Halton.

A galloping start behind the cavalry was orderly as eight horses were bunched for the first mile. RATHOWEN held a short lead over RIDGEWAY. NETTIE, back in the field, advanced steadily, moved to the lead with a half-mile to go and after engaging in a fierce duel with YOUNG JACK THE BARBER and JOHN COLLINS, inched away in the stretch to win by a neck over YOUNG JACK THE BARBER.

DUNDAS STREET, EAST OF TALBOT STREET, HAD WOOD-PLANKED SIDEWALKS IN THE EARLY 1870S.

Queen's Plate winner of '69 murdered . . . Poison, administered by a villain, kills *Bay Jack*, hero at London's Newmarket Race Course . . . Celebrated horse found dead in stall on 24 May 1872 in Strathroy . . . Feelings run high as townspeople mourn *Bay Jack*'s death . . . Crowd near state of lynching culprit . . . Coloured jockey charged with offense and sent to penitentiary.

Briefly, these are some of the details of the death of *Bay Jack*,

who coasted to a six-length triumph on 9 June 1869, an afternoon when London practically closed down. A handsome and spirited colt, *Bay Jack* was heavily supported and was the sentimental favourite for the tenth running of the Plate. Enormous amounts of money were staked on *Bay Jack*, co-owned by a prominent London physician, Dr. William Woodruff, and E.S. (Joe) Bilton, a soda pop manufacturer, who bred this four-year-old son of *Harper*.

Bay Jack had backers among all classes of the community, said the *London Free Press* and the *Daily Western Advertiser,* and many hundreds of dollars were wagered. "People who would be ashamed even to talk of horse racing at other times were caught by the confident predictions of his success." The Court, which was in full session, adjourned for the occasion. Those lawyers and merchants who could tear themselves away from their offices and stores, joined in the speculations upon the abilities of *Bay Jack,* who was a half-brother to the 1866 Plate winner *Beacon*. He was described as a "noble, beautiful looking animal, the finest of celebrated *Harper* stock. A

1869 QUEEN'S PLATE STAKES

		SECOND RACE

London

Newmarket Race Course
JUNE 9, 1869

THE QUEEN'S PLATE. 50 Guineas (Value $250), the Gift of Her Most Gracious Queen Victoria. Open to all horses bred and trained in the Province of Ontario that have never won public money. Turf Club weights. A dash of two miles. Entrance free.

Horse	A		Fin	Jockey	Owner
BAY JACK	4	b.c.	1⁶	A Robinson Jr	E S Bilton & Dr Wm Woodruff
KATE ALLAN (late Country Maid)	9	b.m.	2		J Henderson
LIBERTY (late Nelson)	4	ch.c.	3		Charles G Ray
JACK-ON-THE-GREEN	5	b.g.	4	A Fisher	John White & Archie Fisher

Time, 3:50. Track fast.

Winner: Four-year-old bay colt by Harper—Matilda Jordan, by *Jordan. Trained by James Berry. Bred by E. S. Bilton. Ridden by Abe Robinson Jr.

BAY JACK led with remarkable confidence and mettle from the outset, passing the grandstand the first time fully two lengths ahead of KATE ALLAN. The race was nip and tuck between them. LIBERTY and JACK-ON-THE-GREEN ran together 100 yards behind the leaders. KATE ALLAN pushed ahead momentarily but the winner soon regained the upper hand and came home six lengths ahead of the brown mare. LIBERTY and JACK-ON-THE-GREEN trailed badly, never threatening.

Scratched—Rapid Roan (late Roanoke).

model of equestrian grace and beauty."

Although *Bay Jack* faced only three other runners, a crowd of approximately four thousand was attracted from all parts of Canada "and the more sporting sections of the United States," to see him. "The Plate gives to our Canadian races the character of an English Derby. It is that to which most of our racing during the year leads up to," said the *London Free Press*.

The account of the race stated that "for some months he has been in training for Mr. James Berry, and his private efforts would seem to warrant great expectations. And creditably, *Bay Jack,* indeed, did fulfil the predictions and realize the expectations of his champions." His jockey was a "coloured lad from Kentucky, son of the celebrated horse trainer, 'Old Abe.'"

More than fifty years later, in a column entitled "Landmarks of London," E.J. Carty described the only landmark of the famous London racetrack, that still existed then—the home of Newmarket's caretaker at 1178 Trafalgar Street. He recalled receiving some old papers, documents and photographs of London's early racing history:

> After winning the Queen's "guineas," *Bay Jack* became a still more famous horse, and was toured all over the continent. He was entered for some big events at Toronto, but in the meantime was taken to Strathroy to race; Strathroy at that time being an important sporting centre. While there some person—one Jack Williams, a coloured jockey, was charged with the offense—gave him a dose of laudanum, intending to slow him up when he would be sent to Toronto the next day. But the dose was too great, and *Bay Jack* died of poisoning.
>
> Mr. Frank Butler of this city states that he was in Strathroy the day *Bay Jack* died, and the people of the town made it a day of general mourning. Had the man charged with administering the drug been caught he might have been lynched, so great was the feeling in the matter.

A second London historian, however, claimed that it was

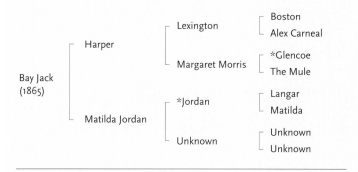

BAY JACK | 4-year-old bay colt

Bay Jack (1865)
- Harper
  - Lexington
    - Boston
    - Alex Carneal
  - Margaret Morris
    - *Glencoe
    - The Mule
- Matilda Jordan
  - *Jordan
    - Langar
    - Matilda
  - Unknown
    - Unknown
    - Unknown

Owner: Edward S. (Joe) Bilton and Dr. William Woodruff, London
Trainer: James Berry; *Jockey:* Abe Robinson; *Breeder:* E.S. Bilton

another jockey, not Williams, who administered the poison. Edwin Seaborn, in his *Reminiscences,* said *Bay Jack* "was ridden by a coloured boy named Robinson. This boy later poisoned the horse and was sent to penitentiary."

In his memoirs, Carty told of an incident that did little to resolve the identity of *Bay Jack*'s murderer: ". . . the other day a well-known citizen saw a little old man standing on Dundas Street, in front of the Sacred Heart Academy, gazing intently at the main building. As the citizen approached, the little man asked, 'Wasn't that the home of Police Magistrate Lawrason many years ago?'

"'Yes,' was the reply.

"The little man sighed. 'I remember it well, but I left here when a small boy to ride on the American tracks. Did you ever hear of *Bay Jack!* Joe Bilton and Doc Woodruff owned him. I rode him when he won some of his biggest cups.' Unfortunately the little man left without giving his name or address."

For years after *Bay Jack*'s death, stories of his slaying circulated at the tables of the White Ox Inn, Nelles' Tavern, Jim O'Leary's Tavern and the Newmarket Hotel, the neighbourhood drinking establishments near the old racetrack in London's east end.

London horse *Bay Jack*, hero of the Plate, was later poisoned in Strathroy.

WHITBY BUILT A NEW GRANDSTAND FOR THE EXPECTED ARRIVAL OF ROYALTY THE YEAR *JOHN BELL* WAS A SURPRISE WINNER.

Normally a placid little town, Whitby was under a state of "siege" in the warm weeks of May 1870. The fact that the Fenians were massing along the frontier between Canada and the United States and that raids by Irish-supported rebels were imminent was not about to spoil the biggest party in the town's history. More important matters were at hand. His Royal Highness Prince Arthur was coming to town, along with the much-heralded *Terror,* the overwhelming favourite for the eleventh running of the Queen's Plate on 24 May.

Preparations had been taking place ever since the Governor General had declared that Whitby had been awarded the race. By the eve of Queen Victoria's birthday, the prospering harbour community on the north shore of Lake Ontario was the "scene of unwonted animation" for the holiday. Flags and banners were displayed from almost every building and the detonation of explosives, firecrackers and sidearms kept up throughout the day.

Vast numbers of strangers flocked into town—by rail, boat and road. Hotels were crowded and there wasn't a bed to be had "for love or money." *The Globe* also noted that "those particularly unsatisfactory and uncomfortable arrangements, known as 'shakedowns,' were the only accommodations available to those who had not taken the wise precaution of bespeaking a bed a week or two ago." Private residents were besieged by "country cousins." Although hospitality and open houses were the order of the day, numbers of persons were glad to seek for the softest plank in any place of shelter, and "not a few permabulated the town throughout the entire night."

Whitby, a town formed when the villages of Windsor, Hamer's Corners and Perry's Corners were incorporated in 1855, was ecstatic that a member of the Royal Family had accepted an invitation to attend the race along with Governor General Baron Lisgar; Prime Minister Sir John A. Macdonald; Sir George Cartier, Quebec's father of Confederation; and Ontario's Lieutenant Governor Howland. To accommodate the royal party, a new grandstand had been erected at the town's racecourse, which had been built in 1858 under the management of the Ontario Turf Club. A special train was outfitted in regal fashion and the Grand Trunk Railway arranged for excursion trains out of Guelph, Belleville and Toronto, a city practically deserted on the afternoon when the royal entourage was expected to arrive in Whitby.

The town seethed with activity as workmen put the one-mile course, located on property owned by the Charles Lynde family (west of Lynde Creek where D'Hillier Street now runs), in excellent order. Besides the powerful *Terror* from the Halton stable of John White, the Plate attracted twenty-two other provincial-bred maidens. "Who has ever heretofore seen in this Dominion a field of twenty-three horses in one race?" asked the *Whitby Chronicle.* (Eventually only twelve started.)

Nearly every livery and hotel stable was fully occupied and each day spectators could catch a glimpse of the horses walking around and exercising on Dundas Street. The Robson House, headquarters for most of the owners, trainers and horses, along with "Major" Quimby, who was selling "pools" on the races, was packed like a sardine tin. "A stranger might fancy our fair town of Whitby a crack training place in the vicinity of Ascot or Doncaster, and to look at the horses, might see many to compare with those of the Old Sod," the *Chronicle* wrote.

On Plate day it was estimated that more than ten thousand people had been lured to the track for the anticipated appearance of the Queen's third son. But he was in St. Hyacinthe, Quebec, reviewing the troops. The only notable dignitary to attend was John Sandfield Macdonald, the provincial premier. *Terror,* who was heavily supported in the "pools," might as well have joined Prince Arthur; he went down to a thundering defeat.

Years later E. King Dodds, in his *Canadian Turf Recollections,* described the 1870 Plate in this manner: "Talk about a surprise party. There wasn't anything of the kind; it was a regular blizzard that flopped the knowing ones upside down, and turned their pockets inside out."

It was *John* (often called *Jack) Bell's* year. Dodds recalled how the horse's owner, Charlie Gates, who operated the Newmarket track on the Danforth near Toronto, had balked at accepting odds of 9-to-1 on his five-year-old and insisted that he belonged in the "field." Another who witnessed the upset by the rank outsider was George H. Ham, author of *Reminiscences of a Raconteur* and a close friend of Gates: "'Bet any one but *Jack Bell,'* advised Gates. Such is the perversity of youth that I immediately placed my money on *Jack . . .* that was one of the memorable races of the early days."

Dodds, summing up the misfortune suffered by the big bettors and the good fortune which befell those farmers who were willing to put up $5 on *John Bell,* said, "Oh, what a multitude of wallets were shrivelled up that memorable day. Yokels from 'away back' had won the price of a horse with a five-dollar note, and their breeches pockets were double-twisted to prevent the losers from coaxing it away from them the next day."

The two-mile Plate distance was not to *Terror's* liking and the huge throng was soon shouting, "*Terror* is beaten! The favourite is gone!" Indeed he was: the colt hung out the flag of distress after a mile. *John Bell* won by almost a length for jockey Jack Bennett, who was riding his first race in Canada. A "foul" claim against

"A MULTITUDE OF WALLETS WERE SHRIVELLED UP," AUTHOR E. KING DODDS RECALLED.

JOHN BELL | 5-year-old chestnut horse

```
                          ┌ Vandal        ┌ *Glencoe
          ┌ Jack the Barber │               └ Mare by *Tranby
          │               └ Nebraska      ┌ *Sovereign
John Bell │                               └ Mary Bowen's Dam
(1865)    │               ┌ Birmingham    ┌ *Hedgeford
          └ Country Maid  │               └ Miss Newbury
                          └ Mary Lisle    ┌ American Eclipse
                                          └ Dam by Sir Alfred
```

Owner: Charles Gates, Toronto; *Trainer:* Charles Gates
Jockey: John Bennett; *Breeder:* Charles Littlefield, Toronto

the winner was dismissed by the three judges, one of whom was Sheriff Nelson (Iron) Reynolds, one of the most flamboyant and controversial characters of his day.

Reynolds, elected to the Legislative Assembly at the age of twenty, was a patron of the Turf Club and one of Whitby's leading citizens. During the 1837 Rebellion, Reynolds remained loyal to the Crown but also criticized the Family Compact, the Toronto-based group that pretty well ran Upper Canada. He was wounded at Kingston, called a traitor, and fled to the United States but later returned, surrendered and stood trial for treason and conspiracy. The jury acquitted him without leaving their seats. His massive home in Whitby, which he named *Trafalgar* after Nelson's famous naval victory, boasted fifteen towers and was one of the most dramatic and ostentatious structures in Canada. It is now the Trafalgar Castle School, formerly the Ontario Ladies College.

The correspondent of *Wilkes' Spirit of the Times,* an American sports weekly, perhaps caught the ebullient proceedings of Whitby's Plate day perfectly when he said, "Notwithstanding the great excitement over the Fenian raid, and the fact that hundreds of our young men shouldered their muskets and went forth to do or die, the opening-day of our races was an unequivocal success."

1870 QUEEN'S PLATE STAKES

FIRST RACE
Whitby
Race Course
MAY 24, 1870

THE QUEEN'S PLATE. 50 Guineas. The gift of Her Gracious Majesty, Queen Victoria. Open to all horses bred, owned and trained in the Province of Ontario that have never won public money. Turf Club weights. A dash of two miles. Entrance free. A $5 membership in Ontario Turf Club required. Entries closed May 1 with 23 entered. Twelve to start.

Horse	A		Wt	Fin	Jockey	Owner
JOHN BELL	5	ch.h.	111	1¾	J Bennett	Charles N Gates
JACK-ON-THE-GREEN	6	b.g.	119	2		A Fisher & A Carson
RATHOWEN	6	b.h.	119	3		W A Bookless & Sheriff Grange
RAPID ROAN (late Roanoke)	6	ro.g.	119	4		C Boyle & J Duggan
TERROR	4	br.c.	101	5		John White
LIBERTY (late Nelson)	5	ch.h.	114	—		Charles Ray
GAIETY	5	ch.m.	111	—		Arthur Lepper
HIGHLAND MAID	6	b.m.	109	—		P Langley
KATE KENNETT	5	b.m.	111	—		William Robinson
LADY MAY	4	b.f.	101	—		Robert Davies
MAGGIE	4	ch.f.	101	—		J Simpson
NEW DOMINION	4	b.c.	101	—		A Dickson

Time, 3:54¼. Track fast.

Winner: Five-year-old chestnut horse by Jack the Barber—Country Maid, by Birmingham. Bred by Mr. Charles N. Gates. Ridden by John Bennett.

Betting—Terror overwhelming favorite; Rathowen was second choice.

After three false starts the field got away without further incident. The favored TERROR leaped into the lead and held it for the first half-mile. At the mile JACK-ON-THE-GREEN challenged TERROR with RATHOWEN and JOHN BELL not far behind. With a half-mile to go TERROR was in distress and fell completely out of contention. JOHN BELL and JACK-ON-THE-GREEN commenced their struggle to the wire as whip and spur were now brought into requisition. JOHN BELL won by almost a length. A protest against the winner was disallowed by the judges.

n 1871 the Queen's Plate journeyed to the head of Lake Ontario and Kingston's Cataraqui Course. The only fact about which turf historians are unanimous, however, is that the race occurred on 24 May, the Queen's birthday.

Ever since the Toronto newspapers began faithfully recording the details of each year's winner and the preceding champions as well (in the 1890s), the recipient of the 1871 Plate has been cited as *Floss,* although occasionally the mare's name was spelled *Flos* (as in the Township of Flos, north of Barrie). She was a bay in colour but her age is a moot point. *The Globe's* reporter in Kingston said *Floss* was a five-year-old. However, produce records of mares in the *American Stud Book (Vol. 3),* reveal that *Eclipse Mare,* a twenty-one-year-old broodmare, foaled a bay filly by *Jack the Barber* in 1865 that was later named *Floss.* So she likely was six.

The breeder apparently was Jack Stanton of Whitby, who leased *Floss* to twenty-two-year-old Robert T. Davies of Todmorden (now Toronto) before the race. At age sixteen, Davies had ridden *Nora Criena* in the disputed Plate of 1865. However, his connections with *Floss* have yet to be determined conclusively. Was he owner, trainer and jockey? In Trent Frayne's *The Queen's Plate,* it is emphatically stated that *Floss* was "owned, trained and ridden by Robert Davies of Toronto." But the *Kingston Weekly Whig's* reporter said that *Floss* was owned by (Archie) Fisher and Carson, who earlier in the day won the Hotel Keepers' Purse with *Sir Archibald. The Globe's* correspondent, commenting on the easy victory of *Floss,* said the mare was owned by "Mr. R. Davys." At the turn of the century, newspapers credited Davies as the owner, but the jockey was now a James Lee. Davies, who was born in Toronto on 19 May 1849, was one of Toronto's wealthiest citizens when he died at his home, Chester Park, on 22 March 1916; stories of his death included numerous references to *Floss.* But these, too, were contradictory.

The Toronto Daily News reported: "The late Mr. Davies was perhaps the only prominent Canadian owner to ever ride in the King's [*sic*] Plate. That was when he was in his teens. The race was run at London in 1865, and he rode *Nora Criena,* when *Lady Norfolk* was the winner. In 1871 he won the Guineas at Kingston with *Floss,*

ROBERT DAVIES OF TODMORDEN OWNED, TRAINED AND PERHAPS RODE *FLOSS.*

a filly he had leased from the late John Stanton of Whitby."

The Evening Telegram reporter also confused his facts when he noted, "In 1871 one of his horses, *Kingston,* won the Queen's Plate." He meant *Floss* not *Kingston,* site of the race. *The Mail's* correspondent also erred when he stated: Mr. Davies rode *Floss,* the winner of the Queen's Plate in 1871." *The Toronto World,* also uncertain of the race's outcome, carried these sentences: "One of his horses won the Queen's Plate at Kingston in 1871 when he was only 22 years of age. Unofficial records give Mr. Davies as the owner of *Floss,* but it is understood that he was the rider and not the owner."

Perhaps the most reliable version appeared in *The Toronto Daily Star* on 19 May 1900: it was written by Thomas Charles Patteson, the scholarly English gentleman who firmly established the Plate in Toronto in 1883. In a reference to Davies' attempt to win the Plate, Patteson asserted, "he has not only tried this before, but was successful, for he won the race of 1871 with *Jack the Barber's* mare, *Floss."* Jimmy Lee, who died at Saratoga six years ago, was the jockey.

So Davies was probably the owner and trainer, but not the jockey. However, there was no question of Robert Davies' future promi-

---

1871 QUEEN'S PLATE STAKES

THIRD RACE

Kingston
Cataraqui Course
MAY 24, 1871

THE QUEEN'S PLATE. 50 Guineas. The gift of Her Most Gracious Majesty. Entrance $10, to go with Plate. For province–bred and trained horses that have never won public money. Mile and three–quarter dash. Seven entries.

Horse	A	Wt	Fin	Jockey	Owner
FLOSS	6 b.m.	109	1	James Lee	Robert Davies
MURELLA	4 b.f.	101	2		H. Quetton St George
STYX	4 blk.f.	101	3		Mr Bolton
GIMCRACK	6 b.g.	116	4		Mr Connelly
MARIA PATON	5 b.m.	100	5		Mr Ewen

Time, 3:21. Track fast.

Winner: Six–year–old bay mare by Jack the Barber—Eclipse Mare, by American Eclipse. Bred by John Stanton, Whitby. **Owned and trained by Robert Davies.**

After a false start, the field broke cleanly with STYX on top, but she surrendered the lead to FLOSS, who immediately took command and left the rest of the field strung out to the home stretch. It was a "tail" race as FLOSS won by several lengths over her closest pursuers, MURELLA and STYX.

Scratched—Bog Oak and Young Rescue.

nence as a shrewd businessman and one of the leaders in horse racing in Canada. He was one of Toronto's wealthiest men when he died at age sixty-seven at his family residence, Chester Park, in Todmorden Mills. Davies owned the Don Valley Brick Works, which still can be seen today by motorists entering or exiting Toronto via the Parkway. He followed his English-born father into the brewery business, taking over the Don Brewing Company in 1872, and a year later founded Dominion Brewery. In the 1900s he bought the paper mill and brick yards owned by his wife's late father, George Taylor, which he incorporated as the Don Valley Paper Company. Later he presided over Copland Brewing Company. Davies succeeded with nearly everything he touched. He took hold of the Don Valley Brick Works and made it the biggest and best brick plant in Canada. Some of his success followed his marriage into the Taylor family in 1874. The Taylors had settled up the Don a hundred years ago and controlled over four thousand acres. Davies was able to acquire much of this land along the Don, later selling or renting parcels of it as its value soared when the city of Toronto expanded eastward.

Eminently successful in the racing and breeding of thoroughbreds and standardbreds, Davies' canary and black–coloured silks of Thorncliffe Stable were familiar sites in the winner's circle in Canada and the U.S. He was considered an excellent judge of a trotter and was familiar with the bloodlines of the best harness horses. Few amateurs ever excelled him as a reinsman. When road-riding was popular, Davies was considered one of the very best in Canada. After all, how many Plate owners had ridden in the race, finishing second as a sixteen-year-old in 1865, but had also trained and bred the winner. Thorncliffe Stable at times dominated the racing scene, winning numerous important stakes races, the Plate twice, Coronation Futurity four times and the Maple Leaf Stakes twice. The stable's success in the 1920s was largely due to Robert

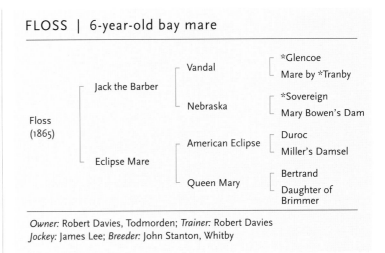

FLOSS | 6-year-old bay mare

Floss (1865)
- Jack the Barber
  - Vandal
    - *Glencoe
    - Mare by *Tranby
  - Nebraska
    - *Sovereign
    - Mary Bowen's Dam
- Eclipse Mare
  - American Eclipse
    - Duroc
    - Miller's Damsel
  - Queen Mary
    - Bertrand
    - Daughter of Brimmer

Owner: Robert Davies, Todmorden; *Trainer:* Robert Davies
Jockey: James Lee; *Breeder:* John Stanton, Whitby

Davies' acquisition of the Kentucky-bred filly, the swift *Southern Maid,* who would later produce two Plate winners, *South Shore* and *Shorelint,* for Davies' sons. Davies had six sons and three daughters.

Although a crowd of six thousand jammed the Cataraqui Course, often spilling onto the track, the Plate failed to attract a good field. That day Kingston was competing with the Ontario Turf Club's big meet at Whitby as well as a meeting in Ingersoll. But the crowd seemed to enjoy itself. "At the entrance to the course there was the bustle and life incident to a provincial exhibition on the grounds, Hindmarsh's Band enlivened the proceedings and three saloons added to the convenience and attraction—to many," said the *Weekly Whig's* reporter.

One noteworthy change in the conditions of the race was its distance. It was shortened to a mile and three-quarters from two miles.

Kingston in the 1870s—Queen's College.

"Pulling" or "yanking" a horse, thus allowing another to win, is one of the waggish practices that some horsemen have indulged in from time to time. It happened during a Plate race in Ottawa and, more than a century later the chicanery continues, despite the vigilant scrutiny of stewards, patrol judges and snooping cameras, and the threats of stiff fines and life suspensions for jockeys.

Accusations that a "job had been done" surfaced several years after the Plate was contested on 31 May 1872, at Ottawa's Mutchmor Driving Park. There was no question of who rode or owned the winner, but there were suggestions that *Fearnaught*'s victory for Alex Simpson, a Toronto hotel owner, and jockey Richard (Dick) O'Leary, who was also its trainer and was one of the most clever and skilful riders in Canadian horse racing, was tainted.

E. King Dodds stated that the race was not entirely on the "up and up" and that the favourite was involved in a bad case of "pulling":

> I once saw a Queen's Plate awarded to a horse, when to allow him to win, it was necessary to pull another horse all over the track, and though the pulling and yanking was done all down the stretch, everything went and the Governor General, who was present, was asked to award Her Majesty's guineas to the chap who got there first. I have seen some strong arm work in my racing days, but I never saw anything quite so barefaced as that Ottawa Plate, and I have often wondered whether the three judges on duty had condensed goggles on that only covered the radius in which the leading horse was travelling.

Dodd's comments were published in *Canadian Turf Recollections and Other Sketches*, but he mentioned no names.

Accounts of the race the following day varied. The reporter for the *Ottawa Daily Citizen* witnessed nothing untoward, but *The Globe*'s man was keenly disappointed: "Betting was even between Leary's stable and *Halton.*" He was likely referring to Tom Leary's

THE FIRST GOVERNOR GENERAL TO MAKE A PLATE PRESENTATION WAS LORD LISGAR.

Jack Vandal (not O'Leary's *Fearnaught*) and *Halton,* which had formerly run under the name of *Charles Douglas*. Although *Halton* was listed as being owned by Archie Jarvis, the official owner undoubtedly was John White, Member of Parliament for Halton County and the winner of several Plate races.

In his account of the race, which included a field of six running a mile-and-a-half (a quarter-mile shorter than in 1871), *The Globe* reporter said: "Mr. White's vaunted favourite thoroughly disgraced himself and his sire *Tester,* whose stock it is now evident are not calculated to stay. *Halton* could neither gallop fast nor far, and looked too wispy behind the saddle for a mile-and-a-half. It was a slow run race, and from start to finish all the way."

Two of the starters, *General Blacksmith* and *Bay Boston,* were eliminated during a poor start but there was no criticism of Charlie Wise, who

1872 QUEEN'S PLATE STAKES

THIRD RACE

Ottawa

Mutchmor Driving Park
MAY 31, 1872

THE QUEEN'S PLATE. 50 Guineas. The gift of Her Most Gracious Majesty. For horses bred, raised and trained in the Province of Ontario that have never won public money. Distance, one mile and a half. Turf Club weights. Entrance $10 p.p. to go with the Plate. The club will give $100 to second horse. Messrs. Young and Radford also will present a gold mounted whip to the rider of the winner.

Horse	A		Wt	Fin	Jockey	Owner
FEARNAUGHT	5	b.h.	118	1	R O'Leary	Alex Simpson
JACK VANDAL	5	b.g.	109	2	C Wise	Tom O'Leary
HALTON (late Chas. Douglas)	5	b.h.	112	3	N Williams	Archie Jarvis
ALZORA (late Gaiety)	7	ch.m.	115	4		Alex Simpson
BAY BOSTON	5	b.h.	112	5		John Copeland
GENERAL BLACKSMITH	4	blk.c.	104	Dis.		Archie Fisher

Time, 2:54½. Track fast. Dis. (Distanced).

Winner: Five–year–old bay horse by Jack the Barber—Daisy, by Prince Albert. Bred by Mr. Robert Davies, Toronto. Trained and ridden by Richard O'Leary.

Betting even between O'Leary Stable and Halton.

After numerous attempts to get the race started, the field got off very indifferently. The start eliminated the chances of BAY BOSTON and GENERAL BLACKSMITH and neither rider persevered with his mount. FEARNAUGHT took the lead immediately, followed by JACK VANDAL and the duo raced in that order throughout. HALTON, after a half-mile, fell out of contention.

rode *Jack Vandal* or Matt Williams, *Halton*'s rider. Following the race, O'Leary was presented with a gold-mounted whip and received a large ovation from the crowd when he brought *Fearnaught* over to Governor General Lisgar's box. "A compliment he well earned, not alone by his excellent riding, but by the condition of the horse, which proved him to be, as his friends assert, the best trainer in the Province."

Dodds' chapter on malfeasance concluded on a philosophical note: "Of course we hear a great deal about the naughty doings in those days, but page for page, the record then was just as clean as it is now. Those who race horses now are no improvement on those of twenty or thirty years ago. Crooked men will try to get in their dirty work and occasionally they succeed in getting away with the trick. So long as grass grows and water runs these jobs will be attempted, and the turfmen of today cannot successfully throw stones at their predecessors on the Canadian turf of thirty five years ago. That is my opinion . . ."

The spires of the Parliament Buildings glistened in the background as a large crowd made the mile trip to Mutchmor Park track,

FEARNAUGHT | 5-year-old bay horse

Fearnaught (1867)	Jack the Barber	Vandal	*Glencoe
			Mare by *Tranby
		Nebraska	*Sovereign
			Mary Bowen's Dam
	Daisy	Prince Albert	*Margrave
			Amanda
		Poppy	Unknown
			Unknown

Owner: Alex Simpson, Toronto; *Trainer:* Richard (Dick) O'Leary
Jockey: Richard (Dick) O'Leary; *Breeder:* Robert Davies, Todmorden

which was in excellent condition since rains earlier in the week had allowed workmen to roll the yellow sand. The times during the meet were considered fast, except for the leisurely paced Plate.

OTTAWA'S NEW POST OFFICE AND THE PARLIAMENT BUILDINGS.

"The Darkey" was the jockey aboard *Mignonette* at Barrie when she became the first three-year-old thoroughbred (1865 winner *Lady Norfolk* was a half-bred filly) to win the Queen's Plate. It was an era in which black jockeys outnumbered white riders throughout North America, and such a remark, which today would be termed racist and denigrating, was commonplace in the years following the Civil War. Black-skinned jockeys were in demand because they rode "light" (most weighed less than one hundred pounds) and mastered the craft of riding quicker than white jockeys. Black jockeys rode fifteen of the first twenty-eight Kentucky Derby winners and only one of the fifteen riders in the inaugural Derby in 1875 was white skinned. Owners clamoured for an Ike Murphy, Monk Overton, Willie Simms, Soup Perkins or Jimmy Winkfield to ride their horses.

Toronto's newspapers in 1873 had no compunction in describing Jacob (or perhaps Jason) Smith as "The Darkey," following his consummate victory on *Mignonette* at Barrie's racecourse near Kempenfeldt Bay on July 1. *The Toronto Daily Mail*, in its detailed account of the Dominion Day races, said: "The [Plate] race requires no description. Under a strong pull *Mignonette* lay in the ruck [the pack] till a mile had been run, the grey [*Lilly*] showing prominently thus far, but as soon as 'The Darkey' gave her his [*sic*] head the favourite put ten lengths between herself and her field." The summary stated that "Toby" was *Mignonette*'s rider. Miss Mary Morrison, daughter of the Honourable Angus Morrison MP, presented a handsome, gold-mounted whip with a commemorative inscription, "To the successful Negro boy who managed his horse well."

Mignonette, whose workouts over Barrie's brick-hard track (in the view of many it needed a little sprinkle of sand) "electrified the cognoscenti, who thought she bore a remarkable likeness, especially in the quarters, to John White's old race mare, *Nettie*." Betting men also liked her because she was assigned only eighty-seven pounds under prevailing weight-for-age conditions; it is possible that Smith got the "ride" because he could "do the weight." While Smith had little trouble with his filly, the crafty Dick O'Leary, who won the Plate the year before in Ottawa, was accused of deliberately running into

A LEADING HORSEMAN OF THE YEAR WAS RODDY PRINGLE, *MIGNONETTE*'S OWNER.

fourth-place finisher *Emily* with his mount *Charlotte R.,* at the first turn, "showing that, under no circumstance, if he can help it, will he slip an opportunity of proving his 'sort,'" wrote *The Mail*. O'Leary denied the accusation.

An accusing finger was also directed at R.R. (Roddy) Pringle of Cobourg, the proprietor of the Arlington House and *Mignonette*'s owner. Breeding records and past performances were practically unavailable in this era and losers frequently claimed that the winner was a "ringer." In this case a rumour quickly circulated that *Mignonette* was foreign bred and therefore ineligible for the Plate.

Pringle, a dedicated horseman and a pioneer in the growth of the burgeoning Canadian breeding industry, quickly squelched a possible scandal by expressing his willingness to take an oath that his filly had not been imported from the United States as a yearling and wagered $1,000 that no man could prove the allegation. His claim satisfied the judges, and records revealed that she was a daughter of *Kennett*, sire of 1868 Plate winner *Nettie*, and had been bred by Thomas Grimshaw, an Englishman living in Hamilton

1873 QUEEN'S PLATE STAKES

SECOND RACE
Barrie
Park Race Course
JULY 1, 1873

THE QUEEN'S PLATE. 50 Guineas. The gift of Her Most Gracious Majesty Queen Victoria. Entrance $10, which is to be added to the plate; second to receive $60 out of the stakes. For provincial–bred maidens. A dash of one and one–half miles. Twelve entered.

Horse	A		Wt	Fin	Jockey	Owner	Betting
MIGNONETTE	3	b.f.	87	1½	J Smith	R R Pringle	3-2
NORLANDER	4	b.c.	104	2¹	L Clarke	Charles Boyle	4-1
GOLDFINCH	4	ch.f.	107	3¹	W McBride	Dr G D Morton	
EMILY	4	br.f.	101	4	C Wise	T C Patteson	
LILLY	5	gr.m.	107	5	C Wright	S H Defries	
MINNIE LANGLEY	4	b.f.	101	6	W Image	Simon Langley	
BACHELOR	5	b.g.	107	7	H Croxon	D G Sutherland	
CHARLOTTE R.	aged	b.m.	113	8	R O'Leary	A E Talbot	
COLT BY FORREST	3	b.g.	87	9	Gray	George Gray	

Time, 2:57. Track fast. Start good.

Winner: Three–year–old bay filly by Kennett—Lily, by Peter Pindar. Bred by Thomas Grimshaw, Cobourg.

MIGNONETTE, racing under a hard pull by her jockey for the first mile, suddenly went to the front, opening up a 10-length lead. She came back to the field in the stretch but still had enough in reserve to beat back NORLANDER's challenge. LILLY set the early pace followed by BACHELOR. EMILY was interfered with by CHARLOTTE R. at the first turn. GOLDFINCH was in a tussle with NORLANDER for the place position.

CROWDS ARRIVED BY TRAIN AND STEAMBOAT TO SEE *MIGNONETTE* WIN THE PLATE.

Owner: R.R. (Roddy) Pringle, Cobourg; *Trainer:* Unknown
Jockey: Jacob Smith; *Breeder:* Thomas Grimshaw, Hamilton Township

Township near Cobourg.

Yet, despite the efforts of Pringle, Dr. Andrew Smith, Joe Bilton, Dr. George Morton and the Whites of Halton, Canadian breeding was still backward in the 1870s. In general, there "was too large a number of coarse, low-bred weeds." Years later, while eulogizing Pringle, E. King Dodds said:

> My old friend was among the handful of true sportsmen who kept the turf spirit alive in Ontario after the departure of the British troops and the advent of hard times which followed the American war.
>
> For at least twenty-five years the fate of Canadian flat racing and steeplechasing trembled in the balance. What, between the then greater popularity of the trotters, the scarcity of good thoroughbred horses, and the still greater lack of thoroughbred horsemen, it was a hard struggle to preserve the running turf from total eclipse. Had it not been for a faithful few, who manfully, for sheer love of the thoroughbred, and often at great personal and financial sacrifice, stood to their guns and kept the old spirit alive, the trotter would have had it all his own way, and the men of the present day would not have their Woodbine, nor would many of our modern Canadian breeding studs be in existence.

HORSE BREEDER DR. ANDREW SMITH FOUNDED TORONTO'S VETERINARY COLLEGE.

The nine Plate starters at Barrie were considered a rather undistinguished lot in comparison to those entered for the Canadian Derby the following day. It attracted twenty runners, including thirteen from Kentucky.

"The stimulus given by the Barrie [Canadian] Derby of the introduction into this Province of better horses than what we have, has been greater than a dozen Queen's Plates could have effected, and if this is the first and justifying principle of horse racing, the Barrie Association deserves the thanks of the community," wrote *The Mail*. "The Queen's Plate must be considered the criterion of success in province breeding; and viewed in that light, we must admit there is

still a great deal to be done before leaving off taxing foreigners half a stone [seven pounds] or thereabouts. The [Plate] lot were not a credit to Ontario, and before many years have passed we hope to see a great improvement."

Despite the sniping of the Toronto critics, Barrie was in its glory. A crowd of five thousand overflowed the sparkling stands and course, built the year before at a cost of $20,000. It was considered one of the finest in the Dominion and the four-day meet offered fifteen races for stakes worth more than $6,000. Yet although it was all a huge success, Barrie never again hosted the Plate. The track eventually became the training course for the Brookdale Stable, owned by the Dyment family, and later fell into the hands of William H. Wright, a horseman and mining executive who built *The Globe and Mail* building at King and York Streets in Toronto, and in 1939 was the breeder of King's Plate winner *Archworth*.

Charlie Boyle's horse racing career was a long, colourful and distinguished tableau, but one marred by a haunting, embarrassing episode. When he died in 1919 at The Firs, his long-time home in Woodstock, numerous articles recalled Boyle's exceptional training exploits and his Queen's Plate victories.

Invariably, however, an account of *Emily*'s defeat in the fifteenth running of the Plate in Hamilton was cited. Someone who was there that day was Judge Francis Nelson:

> To write the full story of Charlie Boyle's racing activities would be to cover the period of transition of the sport of turf from its days of little holiday gatherings of local horses, with no established authority and no permanence of organization, to the complete and well systematized racing of the present day. When I saw him first he was at the head of another Plater, T.C. Patteson's *Emily*, waiting for the fall of the flag from the hand of starter John Hendrie. This was the Plate won by Robert Thomson's *The Swallow* on the old Waddell track, now occupied by fine mansions in the east end of Hamilton. Charlie Wise was *Emily*'s rider and the experience of the late post-master's mare was unfortunate. She broke last, and though making up much ground, was not able to give away the advantage *The Swallow* had secured at the start. Second place was thus the best Mr. Patteson could reach in the event in which he was so anxious for victory.

Was Boyle at fault, inadvertently or otherwise? In his memoirs, written in 1907, but not released for publication by the Ontario Archives until 1980, Patteson was of the opinion that his trainer was at fault. A noted editor, horseman, politician, secretary of the Ontario Jockey Club and confidant of the Royal Family and its representatives, Patteson remained bitter about the incident until his death in 1907. "My mare should have won *The Swallow*'s Queen's Plate at Hamilton, if she had not lost hundred yards at the start. Boyle held her head after 'go' had been said. Her name would have

TRAINER CHARLES BOYLE. HIS FAULTY HANDLING OF *EMILY* AT THE START RESULTED IN HER DEFEAT CLAIMED OWNER T.C. PATTESON. WAS BOYLE AT FAULT, INADVERTENTLY OR OTHERWISE?

been on the scroll of Plate winners if her trainer had not wrongly thought a false start," contended Patteson. *Emily* was also a victim at Barrie a year earlier when a horse ridden by Dick O'Leary bumped her badly at the first turn.

When he died at age eighty-two in 1919 Nelson was extremely praiseworthy of Boyle's contributions to horse racing. "He was a master at his profession and was among the last of the old guard. He was a trainer with great faith in his horses and knew what they were capable of. They rarely failed to produce what he expected. Mr. Boyle was a robust character, out-spoken in the expression of his own clear-cut opinions, he conceding a similar liberty to others. He was intolerant only of humbug and pharisaism, and for these things his contempt was unlimited. He was 'square' in all his dealings, was a liberal purse giver and in his time accomplished much in stamping out crooked work, whether in the judges stand or on the course." For years Boyle acted as a racing official for the OJC.

The Dominion Day races on July 2 attracted a celebratory crowd. The *Spectator*'s man was annoyed because he had a poor view of the start, which was made at the half-mile

1874 QUEEN'S PLATE STAKES

SECOND RACE
Hamilton
Riding and Driving Park
JULY 2, 1874

THE QUEEN'S PLATE. 50 Guineas, the gift of Her Majesty Queen Victoria. Open to horses raised, bred, trained and owned in the Province of Ontario that have never won a match, purse or sweepstakes. Turf Club weights. Distance, one and one-half miles.

Horse	A			Fin	Jockey	Owner
THE SWALLOW	6	bl.m.		1	John Hazard	Robert Thomson, Hamilton
EMILY	5	br.m.		2	Charles Wise	T C Patteson, Toronto
FISHERWOMAN	3	b.f.		3	R O'Leary	Alex Simpson, Toronto
SON OF GILROY	3	b.c.		4	Blaylock	Francis Lowell, Galt
IRISH GIRL	6	b.m.		5	Jackson	W H Thomas, Toronto
SISTER TO VANDAL		b.m.		6	Wright	James O'Neill, Toronto
BELLE OF OTTAWA	4	ch.f.		7		Frank Gouin, Ottawa

Time, 2:51¾. Track fast.

Winner: Six-year-old black mare by Ruric—Augusta, by *Ainderby. Bred by John White, Milton. Trained by Doc Hannon.

The favored EMILY, who was led to the start by her trainer, Charles Boyle, got away slowly, napping at the drop of the starter's flag. She trailed the eight other starters badly as the field passed the judges' stand. THE SWALLOW was on the lead, followed by IRISH GIRL. At three-quarters EMILY moved up to challenge the leaders. IRISH GIRL backed off as THE SWALLOW and EMILY fought it out stride for stride in the stretch. EMILY gradually moved to THE SWALLOW's flank but the most vigorous application of the whip by Charlie Wise failed to bring her to front place, and the Hamilton-owned mare carried off the coveted prize by half a length.

pole on the far side of the course: "Complaint has been made that the start was not a fair one, but we are not in a position personally to say how the matter stands. From the reports of others, however, we have no doubt that the favourite, *Emily*, was placed at some little disadvantage either by the carelessness of her rider or by that of someone else. No intentional injustice is imputed by anyone, nor could any such charge be maintained."

Probably the most authentic account of the race came from Doc Hannon, who operated major stables in the United States and Canada, and was another of the pioneers of the Canadian turf. He was the trainer of *The Swallow*, a Hamilton-owned mare:

> I remember the race very well. In those days we were allowed to hold horses at the post. Boyle had hold of *Emily*'s head when Mr. Hendrie dropped the flag. 'Let go the mare,' said Mr. Hendrie to Mr. Boyle, 'It's a go.' The others got away in front, but *The Swallow* didn't get a much better start than *Emily*. My mare won by a length.

Hannon recalled that Boyle was dissatisfied with the race and "I offered to match *The Swallow* against *Emily* for $350 a side but he declined, saying he was going to Barrie with his mare."

The following day *Emily* won the Kempenfeldt Plate in Barrie, but two weeks later the two mares met at Carleton Park in Toronto and *The Swallow* won two of the three heats. "That proved *The Swallow*'s victory in the Plate was not a fluke," said Hannon.

Her Plate victory was gleefully received by Hamiltonians because she was owned by Robert Thomson, a lumber merchant from Scotland who was raised in Wellington Square (now Burlington) and Puslinch before moving to Hamilton not long before the race. A banker and gentleman farmer, Thomson was a close associate of Halton's White brothers, John and James. Like *Emily*, *The Swallow* was bred by the Whites, the province's major breeders.

A foal of 1868, *The Swallow* was by the good American sire *Ruric*, imported into Canada by H. Quetton St. George of Oak Ridges, and was out of the grand old Tennessee-bred mare *Augusta*. *Ruric* had gained immediate fame in Ontario with his son *Terror*, the sire of *Emily* and the sire of Plate winners *Victorious*, *Williams*, *Fanny Wiser*, and *Vice Chancellor*.

THE SWALLOW | 6-year-old black mare

			Emilius
		*Sovereign	Fleur-de-Lis
	Ruric		Trustee
The Swallow (1868)		Levity	Mare by *Tranby
		*Ainderby	Velocipede
	Augusta		Kate
		Princess Ann	*Leviathan
			Sally Kirby

Owner: Robert Thomson, Hamilton; *Trainer:* William H. (Doc) Hannon
Jockey: John Hazard; *Breeder:* John White, Milton

JUDGE FRANCIS NELSON.

OWNER ROBERT THOMSON.

TRAINER W.H. (DOC) HANNON.

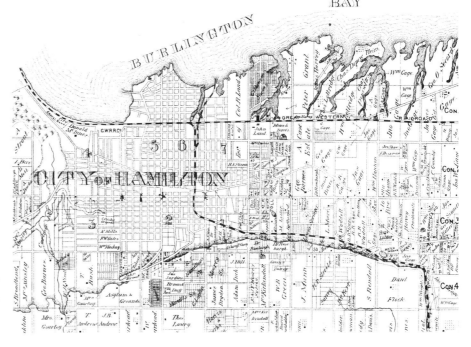

WADDELL'S TRACK NEAR GAGE PARK.

YOUNG TRUMPETER HAD SPENT YEARS AS A STUD BEFORE WINNING THE PLATE AT EIGHT YEARS OF AGE.

By the spring of 1875, a stallion known as *Young Trumpeter* had travelled most of the county and concession roads of Oxford, Middlesex and Kent, visiting the local livery stables and breeding sheds. He was advertised as a half-brother of *Bay Jack,* hero of the Queen's Plate of 1869 and the victim in the miscreant poisoning case at Strathroy in 1872.

Young Trumpeter was also a grandson of the famed imported sire **Glencoe,* but unfortunately he was just another stallion and his stud fee varied, "$15 or thereabouts," depending on the quality of mare and whether she "caught." Most of his mates were half-bloods or common livestock, bred to produce good roadsters for the dirt, plank and gravel roads of Ontario; they were not quality racehorses. Thus, when *Young Trumpeter*'s name appeared in the entries for the Plate in the 24 May holiday races at Woodstock's Driving Park, there were few in the crowd of four thousand who gave him the slightest chance of winning and he received little attention in the "betting pools."

THE THRIVING HORSE COMMUNITY OF WOODSTOCK, ABOVE AND AT RIGHT, PRODUCED GOOD HORSES AND GREAT HORSEMEN BEFORE THE TURN OF THE CENTURY.

The favourite was *Katie P.,* owned by Messrs. Fisher and Carson, but she was ruled ineligible after her owners unsuccessfully "attempted to palm her off as a province-bred." It took the judges nearly two hours to sort out the facts. Apparently it was the mare's appearance that gave her away. "She looked so well that she naturally challenged criticism, being of a cut not yet raised in the bitter cold of a Canadian February," said the *London Free Press.* To the chagrin of many, *Young Trumpeter* galloped home a winner by several lengths against his eight rivals and was described in the *Toronto Daily Mail* as a "despised outsider whom the best judges had calculated on running last."

Race fans and rival owners were not the only ones taken aback by *Young Trumpeter*'s stunning upset following his career at stud. His only previous track appearance was at London a year earlier when he finished up the track in mile heats for province breds. His trainer, Daniel Schoff, who operated a prominent public stable, was astonished. "I as much expected

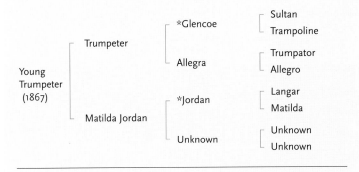

YOUNG TRUMPETER | 8-year-old chestnut horse

			Sultan
Young Trumpeter (1867)	Trumpeter	*Glencoe	Trampoline
		Allegra	Trumpator
			Allegro
	Matilda Jordan	*Jordan	Langar
			Matilda
		Unknown	Unknown
			Unknown

Owner: Robert Ellison and Charles Horton, St. Thomas; *Trainer:* Daniel Schoff
Jockey: Unknown; *Breeder:* E.S. (Joe) Bilton, London

to be shot as to see the race end that way," he said when the horse returned to the scales.

The result was as great a surprise as if the horse had dropped from the clouds. The way he came through his horses indicates not only great staying power but a considerable turn of speed. He's a chestnut horse, with four high white stockings and presents a striking appearance to [Joseph] Grand's old horse *Buford* . . . a corkey little horse, not more than fifteen hands high.

Young Trumpeter's owner was reported to be a Robert Ellison of St. Thomas, "who is highly elated with his success, and will no doubt pocket the Plate—fifty guineas plus entrance fee—with lively satisfaction," said the *Woodstock Weekly Review*. The following day all newspapers stated that Ellison was the owner. But thirty years later "official" records listed Charles Horton, also of St. Thomas, as the owner. T.C. Patteson, historian and secretary of the Ontario Jockey Club, added further doubt when he listed the Plate winner as a "Chatham horse." Research revealed that E.S. (Joe) Bilton of London was the breeder. He also bred his half-brother, *Bay Jack*.

As a two-year-old, *Young Trumpeter* was shown at the Bothwell Spring Show by Peter Duncan McKellar of Chatham, who won the Plate in 1866 with another Bilton-bred horse, *Beacon*. Census and directory records of the 1870s do not list Charles Horton as a resident of the St. Thomas area but there was a Robert Ellison in nearby Gosfield Township.

Who rode *Young Trumpeter* is a bigger mystery. Accounts of the race mention a Willie Taylor, who came to grief when his mount, *Wanderer*, fell and rolled over him. No other jockeys were cited. Ellison was possibly the rider, but OJC records and newspapers never gave him official credit in later years.

The Plate race was the biggest sporting spectacle in Woodstock's history; trains despatched crowds from Toronto, Hamilton, London and Ingersoll, while nearby county visitors travelled in by buggy. For years the racecourse along the Thames River near Admiral Street and the Credit Valley Railway tracks hosted meetings of runners and harness horses. But few ever held the puzzling aspects and unanswered questions of the Plate race on the Queen's birthday of 1875. First there was the mare that the judges deemed as too good looking to be a provincial-bred and declared her ineligible. Also, who was *Young Trumpeter's* owner or owners? And who did ride the winner? And could an eight-year-old horse whose career had been basically that of a stallion, and who had never shown any ability on a racecourse, suddenly gallop home the winner by several lengths?

It should be noted that another surprise race result occurred a week before the Plate when *Aristides,* also a small, compact chestnut horse, was the winner of the first running of the Kentucky Derby in Louisville.

1875 QUEEN'S PLATE STAKES

FIRST RACE
Woodstock
Driving Park
MAY 24, 1875

THE QUEEN'S PLATE. 50 Guineas, the gift of Her Majesty Queen Victoria. Open to horses bred and trained in the Province of Ontario which have never won public money. Weight for age. All entrance fees to be paid to winning owner plus the Guineas. A certificate signed by the stewards stating the winning owner and horse shall be forwarded to the Governor–General's secretary. Distance, one and one–half miles.

Horse	A	Fin	Owner
YOUNG TRUMPETER	8 ch.h.	1	Robert Ellison & Charles Horton
SON OF GILROY	4 b.g.	2	Francis Lowell
EMMA P.	5 br.m.	3	John White
PILOT (late Hippias)	4 ch.g.	4	F Martin
SAPPHO	4 br.f.	5	John White
HURRICANE	4 gr.g.	6	John White
FISHERWOMAN	4 b.f.	7	Alex Simpson
SHARPCATCHER	6 b.h.	8	W J Douglas
WANDERER	b.g.	Fell	F Golding

Time, 2:52½. Track fast.
Winner: Eight-year-old chestnut horse by Trumpeter—Matilda Jordan, by *Jordan. Bred by Edward S. Bilton, London. Trained by Daniel Schoff.
After one trifling break, the field got off to a tolerable start. SHARPCATCHER and FISHERWOMAN were last on their legs and were out of the race before a half-mile had been completed. WANDERER was also a casualty in the first mile as he fell. Jockey Willie Taylor escaped injury. PILOT was the early leader before EMMA P. replaced him in the backstretch. She did the mile in 1:50½. PILOT and EMMA P. continued to lead up the hill with YOUNG TRUMPETER and SON OF GILROY in close pursuit. In the stretch run down to the stands SON OF GILROY looked dangerous but when the longshot YOUNG TRUMPETER was once set into a drive the issue was never in doubt as he passed under the wire an easy winner by several lengths. The favored SAPPHO came in nowhere.
Scratched—Katie P. (Note: The mare was ruled ineligible because she was not a province–bred animal.)

A RESPLENDENT WOODBINE PARK ATTRACTED A LARGE THRONG ON PLATE DAY.

There wasn't an empty seat in Mrs. Morrison's Grand Opera House on King Street on 23 May as an enthusiastic audience awaited the debut of the great American tragedian, Edwin Booth, and his interpretation of the Prince of Denmark in *Hamlet*. About the same time, another "tragedy" was being enacted at the nearby Rossin House. After considerable debate, officials of the Woodbine Riding and Driving Park Association reluctantly agreed to postpone the Queen's Plate for a week.

The trotting and running track, which had opened the previous fall, was found to be too close to Ashbridge's Bay; the eroding waves of Lake Ontario, coupled with heavy spring rains, had turned the backstretch into a bog. It was a terrible blow to entrepreneurs Raymond Pardee and William Howell, who ran the Woodbine House on Yonge Street. They had acquired the site, just south of the corner of Kingston Road and Queen Street, from Joseph Duggan in 1874 and had built a road house on it. The origin of the track's name has often been debated. Was it named after Pardee and Howell's hotel on Yonge Street? Or after the Duggan's property that it stood on? In 2007 a distant relative of Duggan, a Joe Duggan, who lived in Hutton Cranswick, East Yorkshire, was researching his family's history and discovered that an uncle, grandfather and possibly great grandfather had Woodbine as their second Christian name. He said that Joseph Duggan originally owned the land on which the Old Woodbine course was established. The Duggan family had lived in northeast England but may originally have come from Ireland.

Across the street they had laid out a track and had built a spacious grandstand. In newspaper advertisements of the day, the Association proclaimed: "The Woodbine is second to none in America." It had been built at a cost of $40,000 and was just two-and-a-half miles from City Hall. It was easy to get to by streetcar or private conveyance, or even by water.

"Water!" *The Daily Leader* chastised the racetrack's management and predicted that it would run into similar problems every spring unless proper drainage was provided, a prophecy that would haunt the Ontario Jockey Club for the next century. The newspaper also blamed the Association for its failure to stage the race elsewhere, saying that Plate could have "come off over the Carleton course, which is in good condition. Fine racing on an old track like Carleton is preferable to bad racing and poor fields at The Woodbine."

Horsemen complained that the track's proximity to the lake made Woodbine a poor site for training horses in the early spring. They also suggested that, when granting the Plate to any association, the Governor General should stipulate that the contest not be held before 1 July, Dominion Day. The discontent over the Plate's early running, which was widely regarded as being harmful for young, green horses, would be raised frequently over the next hundred years.

The Mail, however, thought it was wise "not to imperil the hinds of young horses engaged in the contest for Her Majesty's Plate," stating that the four-day meet should wait until the sun came out and workmen could fill in the "thousands of holes and hoof cuts which could act as so many traps to break legs and bones." Confronted with a 24 May holiday crowd and the appearance of Toronto's fashionable upper class, including Lieutenant Governor John S. Macdonald, Woodbine officials neatly wriggled out of the predicament by carding some half-mile heats on a safe portion of the track and by holding steeplechase races on the inner course.

The program, which drew a small, dissatisfied crowd, provided ammunition for those anxious for a change in the rules governing horses' Plate eligibility. These rules stipulated that besides being bred in Ontario, horses must not have previously won public money.

On 31 May the track was fast, the weather delightful and a large crowd was in attendance at the "prettiest and most convenient course in America." *Grey Cloud* was among the nine Plate starters; *Boney* and *Ethel*, who were originally entered, were scratched. What happened in the race defies explanation. The Toronto dailies, *The Mail*, *The Daily Leader* and *The Globe*, reported the race slightly differently, not an unusual occurrence. However, they were in agreement that *Norah P.*, owned by Colonel John Peters of London, had won by half a head over *Sunnyside*. Less than twenty-five years later, however, one of these newspapers would claim that *Norah P.* had been declared the winner after *Mary L.* had been disqualified. This mare, owned by Francis Lowell of Galt—the man who guided Joseph E. Seagram into racing—had apparently won the race, but was disqualified for "clearly impeding" *Norah P.* and *Sunnyside* in the stretch.

In the ensuing years, whenever writers mentioned Lowell's name or the 1876 Plate, they invariably recalled that his mare, *Mary L.*, had been robbed of her victory because of a foul. *The Toronto Star*, in a full-page spread on 19 May 1900, reinforced this claim: "The mare [*Norah P.*] did not get home in front the year the Plate was first run at Woodbine. Francis Lowell's *Mary L.* finished first but was disqualified for fouling *Norah P.* and *Sunnyside*."

Was history being tampered with? On 1 June 1876, *The Globe* said nothing of *Mary L.*, stating simply that "the race proved an excellent one, especially at the finish, and was won by an outsider, *Norah B.* [*sic*], the favourite, *Sunbeam*, being nowhere." In its colourful account, *The Daily Leader* said that *Mary L.* fell back after three-quarters of a mile and that *Norah B.*'s [*sic*] rider "got his whip hand free and gave her a cut. She forged ahead and won the race by about a head over *Sunnyside*." Only *The Mail*, in a detailed account, referred to a foul, but it later contradicted itself, saying that *Mary L.* "hanging to the left, ran across the other two, clearly impeding them

NORAH P. | Aged brown mare

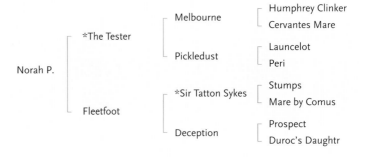

Owner: Colonel John (Squire) Peters, London; *Trainer:* Daniel Curtin
Jockey: Mr. Cook; *Breeder:* Colonel John Peters

within the meaning of the rule." The reporter concluded that "from this point on the three came on locked together. *Norah B.* [*sic*] getting up in the last stride and winning a splendid race by half a head from the Kentucky bred one."

Kentucky bred? How did she qualify? No mention was made of *Mary L.* at the finish, but the race summary showed her as last and disqualified. The winner was an aged brown mare, six or older, who had been sired by **The Tester*. Her name was either *Norah P.*, or *Nora P.*, not *Norah B./Nora B.*, as it had been reported in 1876.

One man who knew *Norah P.* well was blacksmith Louis Burns, who often "shoed her" along with Colonel Peters' other Plate winner, *King George*. In a 1925 article in the *London Advertiser*, Burns recalled: "She was a hard horse to train and had a bad habit of kicking and bucking every time a saddle was put on her back. Ralph Birrell and Dick Stilson finally managed to solve the problem. They led her down to the river [Thames] and up to her depth in water. Then they took turns riding her up and down the river. She couldn't kick and she couldn't buck, so she decided she was licked. They never had any trouble with the high-spirited mare after that."

Grand Inaugural Meeting.

WOODBINE
RIDING AND DRIVING PARK
Association,
TORONTO,
Wednesday, Thursday, Friday, and Saturday.

1876 QUEEN'S PLATE STAKES

THIRD RACE
Woodbine Park
MAY 31, 1876

THE QUEEN'S PLATE. 50 Guineas. The gift of Her Most Gracious Majesty, with an inside stake of $10 each, half forfeit, 50% of stake to go with plate, balance to second horse. For provincial bred horses which have never won a race on the flat. Distance, one and one half miles. Twelve entries.

Horse	A		Wt	Fin	Jockey	Owner
NORAH P.	5	br.m.	113	1hd	Cook	Col. John Peters
D MARY L.	5	b.m.	107	2nk	Blaylock	Francis Lowell
SUNNYSIDE (late Emma P.)	6	br.m.	107	3½	Charles Wise	Charles Boyle
GREY CLOUD (late Thunder colt)	5	gr.h	110	4	McLean	Jonathan Scott
SIR JOHN	4	ch.c	104	0	Ray	Charles G Ray
PILOT JR.	5	b.g	110	0	McAlpine	F McEwan
HARPER JR.	5	b.h	110	0	Ed Tiffin	Williamson & Middleton
FISHERWOMAN	5	b.m.	113	0	A E Gates	Alex Simpson
SUNBEAM	5	ch.m.	107	0	Robinson	Charles G Ray

D–Disqualified for interference in stretch and placed last.

Time, 2:52. Track fast. Start fair.

Winner: Five-year-old brown mare by **The Tester—Fleetfoot*, by **Sir Tatton Sykes*. Bred by owner. Trained by Daniel Curtin.

Betting pool—Sunbeam 5 to 1 against; 4 to 1 against Sunnyside and Grey Cloud. Remainder in field at 5 to 1 against.

There was a most annoying delay at the post caused by the repeated breaking away of SUNBEAM and PILOT JR., and the obstinacy of the grey (GREY CLOUD). Whatever chance SUNBEAM had was put out by a fall in one of the five false starts, and the mare who had sold at one time a prominent favorite was never formidable in the race. FISHERWOMAN was the first to show in front, but once in the straight MARY L. led her field a fair beat, with SUNNYSIDE being here, there and every where, and second when half the distance had been run. In the backstretch GREY CLOUD spurted and got on even terms with the leaders. Running to the outside pole in the home stretch, he let the three mares, MARY L., SUNNYSIDE and NORAH P., pass him on the inside. MARY L., hanging to the left, ran across the other two, clearly impeding them within the meaning of the rule. From this point the three came on locked together, NORAH P., getting up in the last stride and winning a splendid race by half a head. SUNNYSIDE was a neck back in third place with GREY CLOUD on her quarters on the extreme outside. The rest tailed off.

Scratched—Magnet, Boney and Ethel.

On the grassy slopes overlooking the St. Lawrence River was J.R. Wiser's town, Prescott. This "Fort Town" was acclaimed for its high-class whisky, the best bred and fed cattle in the country and the celebrated trotting horse *Rysdyk,* who reputedly had the action [stride] of *Hambletonian,* the endurance of *Lexington* and few equals upon the continent. The town's economic life thrived because of its distillery and Wiser's development of the cattle and horse-breeding industries. Wiser, a Member of Parliament, owned more than one hundred trotters, fifty thousand head of cattle, and huge stock farms and ranches in Kansas and Texas.

But Prescott was not a thoroughbred racing centre, a situation which distressed many horsemen when it was announced that the contest for Her Majesty's fifty "guineas" would be held at the South Grenville Fair Grounds on 2 July. In 1877 it was a long journey for a Plate candidate from Toronto or other southwestern Ontario centres to travel—Prescott was remote. The snaking, circuitous route along the dirt road that was Highway 2 was a burden for travellers and their horse-drawn carriages. The only other modes of travel to Prescott were via the Grand Trunk Railway or by one of the steamships that cruised the waters to the head of Lake Ontario.

It soon became obvious that the Queen's Plate was in a state of retrogression as horsemen began shipping their maiden prospects to courses in Whitby, Barrie, London and Toronto. The purses were as handsome as those being offered in Prescott and it was an ideal way for a trainer to prepare his horse, assuming that it did not win and so lose its "maiden" (*non*-winner on the flat) status and therefore its eligibility for the Plate.

This alarmed *The Mail* and its trenchant editor, T.C. Patteson,

whose influence on the future of the Plate was increasing because of his close ties with the Governor General's office (in this case Lord Dufferin) and with Prime Minister Sir John A. Macdonald. Patteson was concerned that the Prescott Plate would be "contested only by a lot of duffers that have been beaten all over the Province." To him, it was heresy. The honour of winning the Plate ought to be sufficient incentive to keep a youngster in the stable for the first five weeks of the summer campaign. Patteson feared that unless owners cooperated, the Governor General would intervene to see that "Her Majesty's gift is not made only a farce and delusion." Never one to mince words, Patteson proposed, "if the insignificant prize given is unable to 'draw,' then the two Plates now given respectively in Quebec and Ontario be amalgamated and run for in alternate years in Montreal and Toronto." (In 1836 the King's Plate was inaugurated in Lower Canada at a track near Montreal in honour of King William IV.)

Patteson's fears were well-founded; only four maidens were entered for Prescott, at ten dollars each for the right to earn "glamour, prestige and the 'guineas' [fifty-two pounds, ten shillings]." *Amelia,* a three-year-old filly, won handily over *Hurricane* and *Sir John,* a pair of aged geldings. All three had been "up the track" at Whitby on 24 May but *Amelia,* second a week later at The Woodbine, was the betting favourite. She was ridden by Charlie Phair, who more than thirty years later himself would train a Plate winner. The field's fourth starter was *Oakleaf,* but no indication of its age, sex, colour, jockey or owner was given.

In its account of the race, the *Brockville Recorder's* correspondent in Prescott said the day was "a gala one in our old town, the

PRESCOTT'S RYSDYK STOCK FARM WAS THE CENTRE OF STANDARDBRED BREEDING.

DANIEL'S HOTEL—THE YEAR THE PLATE WAS HELD IN PRESCOTT.

AMELIA | 3-year-old brown filly

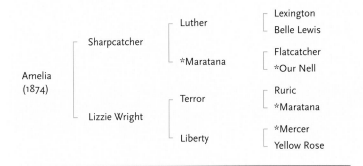

Owner: John White, Milton; *Trainer:* Jonathan Scott
Jockey: Charles Phair; *Breeder:* White Bros., Halton County

J.P. WISER OWNED THE BEST WHISKY, THE FINEST CATTLE AND TROTTING BLOODSTOCK IN EASTERN ONTARIO.

annual race for the Queen's Plate being the cause of the unusual excitement." An early morning rain somewhat dampened the ardour of sportsmen, but by nine o'clock "old sol" dispelled the vapours and made everything radiant for the rest of the day. The contest was particularly keen. *The Mail* paid little attention to the Plate, saying that the races were largely attended, the weather was propitious, the sport good, the track in excellent condition and that everything had passed off smoothly.

The White brothers of Halton and Trafalgar, especially John, the ebullient Member of Parliament from Milton, were delighted; the Plate win was the seventh for their breeding stock and its foundation mare, *Yellow Rose*. *Amelia* was out of *Yellow Rose*'s granddaughter, *Lizzie Wright*.

Whether the "Paris Mutuals" [sic] were used at South Grenville Fair Grounds on Plate day was never recorded. The new betting machines had been experimented with at Whitby for the first time on 24 May and had attracted a lot of attention. A couple of weeks later a Mr. Collins had them at The Woodbine, where they afforded fans an easier method of backing their fancy than the heavier (more costly) wagering of the ordinary auction pools, which were not generally liked. Prescott may not have had the "Paris Mutuals" [sic], but for one day in its history it was the hub of thoroughbred horse racing in the province.

1877 QUEEN'S PLATE STAKES

SECOND RACE
Prescott
South Grenville Fair Grounds
JULY 2, 1877

THE QUEEN'S PLATE. Valued at 50 Guineas, with a sweepstakes of $10 each added. Open to provincial breds which have never won a race on the flat. Dash of one and one-half miles. Turf Club weights. Four entries.

Horse	A		St	½	Str	Fin	Jockey	Owner
AMELIA	3	br.f.	4	2	1	1	C Phair	John White
HURRICANE	6	gr.g.	2	1	2	2		William Owen
SIR JOHN	5	ch.g.	1	3	3	3		Charles Ray
OAKLEAF			3	4	4	4		

Time, 2:56½. Track fast.
Winner: Three–year–old brown filly by Sharpcatcher—Lizzie Wright, by Terror. Bred by John White, Milton. Trained by Jonathan Scott. Ridden by Charles Phair.
SIR JOHN went to the front early and led for a mile. HURRICANE and OAKLEAF gave chase and AMELIA trailed. After a mile HURRICANE and AMELIA forged to the front and in the stretch AMELIA outgunned HURRICANE. SIR JOHN tired badly and was a distant third.

1878 | KING GEORGE

I n 1878 Louis Burns was seventeen years old, a burly apprentice in his father's blacksmith shop, when a horse he had shod, *King George,* won the Queen's Plate for Colonel John Peters, "The Squire of London." Young Louis had done his job well: the time for the mile-and-a-half race was 2:49 1/2, the fastest ever recorded in the race. "Those were the days that were worthwhile," said the "smitty," reminiscing in 1925. "My father [James] and I would go out to the track and plate eight or nine horses, before dinner, for the afternoon races. We would change the galloping shoes for the racing plates, which weighed about one and a half ounces. We got $2.50 for a set of plates, which were nailed right back to the heel to keep it from spreading. Trotting horses were just starting to come in about that time."

James and Louis Burns had also put the racing plates on Squire Peters' mare, *Norah P.,* before she was shipped to The Woodbine to win the Plate in 1876. "Both horses were shod by us at the Newmarket track. All our shoes were made by hand at that time and we got five shillings sixpence for a set of shoes. My father made the pattern for the first plate nails used. We looked after all the stage horses running in and out of the city and it kept us pretty busy. The planked roads were hard on shoes, as you may imagine."

On 5 June, the Newmarket Race Course was filled to capacity as an estimated twenty-five hundred travelled to the track east of Egerton Street, an area littered with hotels, saloons and livery stables. The large crowd was diverted on this warm afternoon by the playing of military bands and the occasional brawl. The *London Free Press* said that two or three fights broke out, temporarily distracting the crowd's attention from the pending delay of the Plate. The customary protests had to be dealt with before the "Off."

Hank Chappell of Sandwich, who had apparently entered a "ringer" in the 1865 Plate in London, was accused of making

GROSVENOR LODGE, A WHITE BRICK MANSION ON LONDON'S WESTERN ROAD, WAS THE PETERS'S FAMILY ESTATE.

COLONEL JOHN PETERS, THE SQUIRE OF PETERSVILLE, BRED TWO PLATE WINNERS.

another fraudulent entry. He stated that *Rankin* was a three-year-old; this would gain him a seventeen-pound advantage. After examining the horse's teeth, the judges said that it was a four-year-old, but Chappell insisted that his animal had been entered correctly, and that he could prove it. To settle the issue, the judges sought out Dr. Andrew Smith, a Toronto veterinary surgeon. But when he could not to be tracked down, they barred *Rankin,* much to Chappell's chagrin and the disappointment of a large number of punters who had backed his horse to win.

Strathmere, a grey mare owned by a Mr. Jones of Toronto, was also under protest. She had been conceived in England and then had been imported to Ontario, *in utero,* by a chap from Belleville. The judges allowed her to run because she was foaled in Ontario. Many thought *Strathmere* "was a winner," and if not her, then it was likely to be John White's strong entry of *Moss Rose* and *Exotic.* *Strathmere* did take command early in the race but her lack of conditioning was evident when she faded badly—"she had no bottom"—giving way to *King George,* who held off a late charge by *Moss Rose.* The winner was a local horse and a half-brother to Plate champion *Norah P.* His win surprised many since a substitute jockey, A.E. (Allie) Gates, "who was a complete stranger to the horse," was aboard. Richard (Dick) O'Leary, the crafty but respected rider who had won the Ottawa Plate on *Fearnaught,* was *King George*'s regular trainer and rider but was ailing and did not come to the track.

King George's victory was heralded by the London establishment since Colonel Peters was a son of one of the city's founding fathers, Samuel Peters Senior, a surveyor for the Canada Company since his arrival in Upper Canada, by wagon train, in 1835. The elder Peters, a distiller, grocer and abbatoir owner, surveyed the tracts of land around the "Forks of the Thames," and later built the elegant Grosvenor Lodge (now the Lawson Museum) on land just south of the University of Western Ontario; the area was then known as Petersville.

An artillery officer and Master of the Fox Hounds for the London Hunt Club, Colonel Peters was later Justice of the Peace and a long-time resident of Grosvenor Lodge, where he bred his Plate winners. Family tradition maintains that in 1880 the first reports of the grisly murders of the Donnelly clan, from nearby Lucan, were given to Colonel Peters when he was in the gazebo that served as his office.

KING GEORGE WAS ONE OF TRAINER RICHARD O'LEARY'S PLATE WINNERS.

KING GEORGE | Brown horse

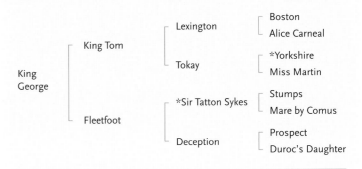

Owner: Colonel John (Squires) Peters, London; *Trainer:* Richard (Dick) O'Leary
Jockey: A.E. (Allie) Gates; *Breeder:* Colonel John Peters

1878 QUEEN'S PLATE STAKES

FIRST RACE

London

Newmarket Race Course
JUNE 5, 1878

THE QUEEN'S PLATE. 50 Guineas, the gift of Her Most Gracious Majesty, Queen Victoria. Open to all horses bred, raised and owned in the Province of Ontario that have never won a race. Dash of one and one-half miles. Entrance money $20. One half forfeit; two-thirds to second horse and one-third to third horse.

Horse	A	St		¾	Fin	Jockey	Owner
KING GEORGE	5	b.h.	6	3	1nk	A E Gates	Col. John Peters
MOSE ROSE	3	b.f.	3	4	2¹		John White
EXOTIC	5	b.m.	2	2	3		John White
STRATHMERE		gr.m.	1	1	4		Mr Jones
KING DODDS	3	b.c.	5	5	5		Bookless & Thomas
LADY HARPER		b.m.	4	6	6		Frank & Son

Time, 2:49½ (Record). Track fast.

Winner: Five-year-old bay gelding by King Tom—Fleetfoot, by *Sir Tatton Sykes. Bred by Col. John Peters, London. Trained by Richard O'Leary.

After two ineffectual starts, a good start was signalled. STRATHMERE broke on top followed closely by EXOTIC. After a quarter mile KING GEORGE and EXOTIC moved up on STRATHMERE and the three battled it out throughout the first mile before STRATHMERE began to back off. She showed lack of bottom. KING GEORGE assumed the lead and with a spurt in the stretch held off MOSS ROSE by a neck.

Scratched—Rankin.

(Note: RANKIN was debarred from running because he had been entered as a 3-year-old instead of four. STRATHMERE also protested against since she had been bred in England, but allowed to run regardless.)

WHEN THE RUNNERS LEFT PICTON, THE TROTTERS TOOK OVER AT THE OLD DRIVING PARK NEAR CENTRE STREET.

Thirteen days before the twentieth running of the Queen's Plate, a fire swept through John Allison's Picton Training Stable. Seven horses lost their lives in a conflagration that shocked the citizens of the small Bay of Quinte community.

Did the blaze kill several Queen's Plate candidates? Unfortunately, few details of the fire exist, and it just might be coincidental that only three horses, the smallest field in Plate history, paraded to the starting pole on 24 May at Picton's Driving Park. Actually there were four entries, but *King Tom* failed to make an appearance at the start. Perhaps the fire was one reason for the meagre field at the Prince Edward County racetrack, but this is unlikely. It was obvious to many that the peripatetic journey of the Plate was in a hopeless decline and its chances of survival were as bright as a horse attempting to sprint on sinking sand. A permanent home in a prosperous thoroughbred racing centre was essential if the race was going to prosper.

Picton was a pleasant place to grow apples, asparagus and strawberries, but it was not a thoroughbred breeding or racing region. Awarding the Queen's Plate to agricultural societies in small communities to boost attendance for holiday race programmes was retarding its growth. Towns the size of Picton were often alloted the race for Her Majesty's "guineas" as a reward to a local Member of Parliament. In four years it would settle at a permanent site—Toronto. However, in 1879 Picton was not about to turn up its nose at hosting the Plate. With the invitation in its possession, the Picton Driving Park Association a year earlier prepared for the event when it developed a racetrack on grounds where Queen Elizabeth School stood near Centre Street.

The Mail, in its brief report of the three-day holiday meet for Toronto readers, observed: "There was a much larger attendance at the races today [Saturday] than yesterday, the running for the Queen's Plate serving to attract a great many." The weather was ideal and the track seemed in excellent condition, but the race was hardly a spectacle. *Young Blenkiron,* one of the three starters, behaved poorly and bolted after the start.

The winner was *Moss Rose,* a formidable four-year-old bay filly by *Sharpcatcher* out of *Lizzie Wright,* who may have prompted the small field. Trainers of other Plate hopefuls possibly shied away from challenging the filly after her close finish to *King George* the previous year. An overwhelming favourite in the betting pools,

Moss Rose was described as a "beautiful bay mare," standing fifteen hands, two-and-a-half inches. She easily outran her only competitor, *King Dodds*.

Moss Rose was a full-sister to 1877 Plate winner *Amelia* and was the eighth winner of the "guineas" bred by the White brothers of Halton. All were from the family of *Yellow Rose*. Although *Moss Rose* ran under the name of David Watson Campbell of Bronte, she was owned by Campbell's father-in-law, John White. Riding the filly was Allie Gates, who was gaining the second of his three Plate victories. He was aware of her ability as he had been the jockey aboard *King George* in London the year before.

Picton became a trotting horse centre, before interest in horse racing dwindled in the 1950s. "For some years," said Phil Dodds, former editor of the *Picton Gazette,* "the Driving Club, which held races each 24 May, held the charter." Years ago agricultural societies had the sole right to hold race meets and were granted charters. However, as horse racing grew in popularity, and the demand from big cities for the charters increased, small communities began to sell them or to give them away. "Ours went to help get Rideau-Carleton started [in Ottawa]," said Dodds, who had been treasurer of the Prince Edward Agricultural Society for thirty years.

MOSS ROSE | 4-year-old bay filly

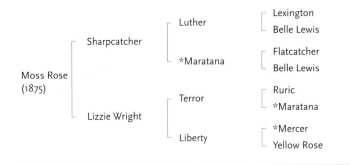

Owner: John White, Milton; *Trainer:* Jonathan Scott
Jockey: A.E. (Allie) Gates; *Breeder:* White Bros., Halton County

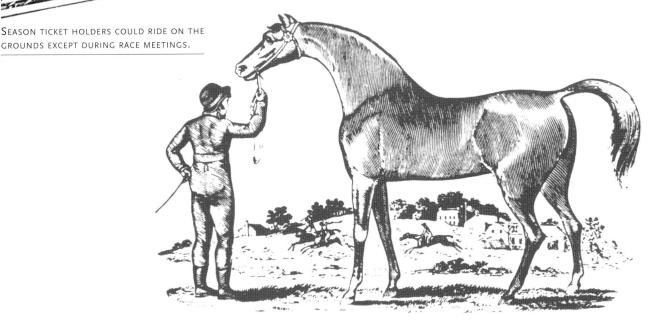

SEASON TICKET HOLDERS COULD RIDE ON THE
GROUNDS EXCEPT DURING RACE MEETINGS.

1879 QUEEN'S PLATE STAKES

FIRST RACE
Picton
Driving Park
MAY 24, 1879

THE QUEEN'S PLATE. 50 Guineas, the gift of Her Most Gracious Majesty the Queen. For horses bred, raised and owned in the Province of Ontario that have never won a race. Distance one and one–half miles. Turf club weights. Four entries, three started.

Horse	A		Fin	Jockey	Owner
MOSS ROSE	4	b.f.	1	A E Gates	John White
KING DODDS	4	b.g.	2		Messrs Bookless & Thomas
YOUNG BLENKIRON	3	b.g.	3		

Time, 2:54½. Track fast.

Winner: Four-year-old bay filly by Sharpcatcher—Lizzie Wright, by Terror. Trained by Jonathan Scott. Ridden by A. E. (Allie) Gates. Bred by John White, Milton.

MOSS ROSE was in command throughout, running the first mile in 1:49½. KING DODDS threatened in the last half-mile. YOUNG BLENKIRON acted badly and finally bolted.

Scratched—King Tom.

Moss Rose, ONE OF JOHN AND JAMES WHITE'S TWELVE PLATE WINNERS.

THE PARLIAMENT BUILDING'S CENTRE BLOCK FROM WELLINGTON STREET, OTTAWA.

There was a time in Ontario when bookmakers, the wily mathematicians of the turf, were as welcome as a warm spring day at a racetrack. They were "sporting chaps," gregarious and colourful characters such as Sam Page, Billy ("Major") Quimby and his sidekick, John Forbes—men with hardly a corrupt scheme up their natty sleeves.

Bookies have had a chequered history. They were considered quite acceptable by the British, but were suspected by the French, who implemented the pari-mutuels system. The earliest wagering in Canada was between owners or spectators, who set their own odds and sought takers, or indulged in "gentlemen's bets." The men who established the odds were assumed to be the lesser of two evils when the practice of the "pool box" was abolished in 1878. This change was lauded by the *London Free Press:* "Spectators require something more than a name to cause them to feel an interest in a race, and in that respect the pool box afforded them an opportunity. However, there is no denying the fact that it had its abuses, and placed the power in the hands of unscrupulous persons of selling races whenever a favourable chance presented itself."

And so, racing associations climbed into bed with the bookies, inviting them to bring their slate boards onto the premises and then exacted privilege fees from them. Astonishingly, there were no cries of collusion or conflict of interest in Ottawa in 1880 when the firm of Forbes and Burgess was allowed to set odds on races, which often included horses owned by them or their partners. This was the case in the nation's capital on 29 June as numerous cabinet ministers and their ladies gathered at debt-ridden Mutchmor Park. The track had recently come into the possession of the sheriff, W.F. Powell, whose colours were noted on two of the entries in the four-race card.

The winner of the Plate that day was a four-year-old filly, *Bonnie Bird,* who had a pedigree as lofty as that of Queen Victoria. *Bonnie Bird* carried Kentucky bloodlines and was of a quality rarely seen on Canadian turf. Her sire was *Lexington's* great son, *Judge Curtis,* who won the second renewal of the Belmont Stakes under the name

ARTIST'S CONCEPTION OF *BONNIE BIRD*, A FILLY, WHOSE PEDIGREE WAS "AS LOFTY AS THAT OF QUEEN VICTORIA."

BONNIE BIRD | 4-year-old bay filly

Owner: John Forbes, Woodstock; *Trainer:* Erastus (Ras) Burgess
Jockey: Richard (Dick) O'Leary; *Breeder:* John Forbes

Gen. Duke. Bonnie Braes was the dam, an imported daughter of *Balrownie* and the winner of the first Ladies' Handicap in New York, which is still the oldest stakes race for females on the continent. John Forbes was her owner; he operated a saloon and livery stable in Woodstock, and was a long-time associate of Billy Quimby's in the old pool-selling days. Forbes also bred *Bonnie Bird*. The filly's trainer was Erastus (Ras) Burgess, as clever and experienced a horseman ever to come out of Woodstock, which at one time was referred to as "the Newmarket of Canada."

Although Forbes and Burgess received the accolades and the Queen's fifty "guineas," there is speculation that they flopped as the "official bookmakers" of the Ottawa Racing Association. *The Daily Citizen* accused them of being too stingy with their odds: "The bookmakers lost on every race today, but they gave such small odds that they cannot be largely out of pocket." Curiously, *Bonnie Bird* was not the favourite in a small field, even though she had the services of veteran jockey, Richard O'Leary, who had won the Plate in 1872.

Bonnie Bird was second choice at 2-to-1, along with a future Plate winner, *Fanny Wiser. Roderick,* Roddy Pringle's three-year-old colt from Cobourg, was the favourite, even though he was rumoured to be lame and under protest as well. It was suggested that he was a year older and should be carrying ten more pounds than the ninety-seven he had been assigned.

Although he finished last after leading the field briefly, *Roderick* was pronounced a "magnificent specimen of thoroughbred," by *The Daily Citizen.* "In fact, it is doubtful whether a finer lot of horses ever competed for the Queen's Plate. All are exceptionally well bred." All except *Footstep.* Judges ousted the mare because she was owned by a Montrealer and had been raised in Quebec, not Ontario.

Despite a heavy track, *Bonnie Bird's* time for the mile-and-a-half was 2:47, a Plate record.

1880 QUEEN'S PLATE STAKES

SECOND RACE
Ottawa
Mutchmor Driving Park
JUNE 29, 1880

THE QUEEN'S PLATE. 50 Guineas, the gift of Her Majesty Queen Victoria. For provincial maidens bred, raised and owned in Ontario. A mile and a half dash. Second horse to receive $50. Weight for age. Six entries; five started. Value to winner $300.

Horse	A	Wt.	St	¼	½	Str	Fin	Jockey	Owner	Betting
BONNIE BIRD	4	107	5	5	5	1	1	R O'Leary	John Forbes	2-1
FANNY WISER	3	94	2	2	2	2	2	O'Hara	D W Campbell	2-1
KING TOM	4	110	3	3	3	3	3	Pierson	D W Campbell	5-1
LORD DUFFERIN	aged	121	4	4	4	4	4	A E Gates	J B Morrison	4-1
RODERICK	3	97	1	1	1	5	5	Lucas	R R Pringle	3-2

Time, 2:47. Track heavy.
Winner: Four-year-old bay filly by Judge Curtis—Bonnie Braes, by *Balrownie. Bred by Mr. John Forbes, Woodstock. Trained by Erastus (Ras) Burgess.

The favored RODERICK broke on top, setting a torrid pace, followed by FANNY WISER, KING TOM, LORD DUFFERIN and BONNIE BIRD. RODERICK led a merry drive but passing the half-mile pole the field began to bunch and just as the horses got out of sight RODERICK's bolt was shot and he quickly fell back to the rear of the field. BONNIE BIRD made a sudden move and swept to the lead followed by FANNY WISER and KING TOM. The trio was so close together that a small side show tent could have covered them. O'LEARY, however, hand rode the winner to the finish, needing neither whip nor spur to retain his margin over the Campbell twosome.

(Note: FOOTSTEP was withdrawn because it had not trained in the province. A protest against RODERICK was withdrawn after the race. It was claimed he was a 4-year-old and was carrying insuffient weight.)

WOODSTOCK BOOKMAKER AND LIVERY STABLE OWNER JOHN FORBES OWNED AND BRED *BONNIE BIRD.*

Thomas Charles Patteson was the gentleman who created the Ontario Jockey Club in 1881. An audacious and moralistic Englishman, it was Patteson who firmly grabbed horse racing by the scruff of its tarnished neck and directed it towards respectability. Although he maintained confidentially that he had to be coaxed into accepting this formidable task, nobody was more fitted for the role than the scholarly and distinguished forty-five-year-old former Etonian and Oxford graduate. He had been in Canada since 1858 and had witnessed the growth of racing as a young lawyer, politician, manager and editor of *The Mail*, postmaster (appointed by his friend Sir John A. Macdonald), and horse and cattle dealer.

Patteson was also Canada's and horse racing's "ambassador" to the Royal family and had close ties with the rich and powerful in the United States. He guided opinion and protected Canadian enterprises, but he was not without enemies. His merciless political attacks in *The Mail* prompted several libel actions; he is said to have carried brass knuckles in his pocket after twice being assaulted on the streets of Toronto.

In declaring that he would organize an Ontario Jockey Club, Patteson pledged to put down all nefarious practices with a strong hand while establishing such a "discipline" that would include owners, trainers, jockeys and the betting fraternity. He spoke with bitter experience of an earlier time when shameless practices had influenced him to sell out and have nothing more "to do with the game—sport, it could not be called." He had seen his mare *Emily* "pulled" in the 1874 Plate. Since then he had constantly criticized the decadent

THOMAS CHARLES PATTESON, THE ENGLISHMAN WHO CREATED THE ONTARIO JOCKEY CLUB.

state of horse racing in Canada through his column in *The Mail*: "When things get to the worst they mend, and nothing could be worse than the rottenness of the whole racing business in Canada. The open robberies committed through the pool box were notorious." Early in the spring of 1881 Patteson was anointed as The Saviour by The Deacon, one Joseph Duggan, proprietor of The Woodbine Race Course and hotel, when he convinced the postmaster, as he then was, to revive racing under respectable auspices and make a success of it. "At first I refused to fall in with his wishes," said Patteson, who immediately gained the support of Toronto's two major newspapers, *The Mail* and *The Globe*. By April he had the financial backing of William Hendrie, H. Quetton St. George, William Mulock, Colonel Frederick Cumberland, and Dr. Andrew Smith, and had orchestrated the granting of the club's original charter.

At a June meeting in the Queen's Hotel (later the Royal York Hotel) Patteson obtained the patronage and financial support of his old partner, Colonel Casimir Gzowski, who immediately put up $500 for five shares, along with most of the leading businessmen to "regenerate horse racing." An agreement between Duggan and the Ontario Jockey Club (OJC) was quickly negotiated (the rent was $2,000 per year for five years) and the Club agreed to keep the property in repair and to undertake renovations. Colonel Cumberland was elected the OJC's first president, but he died before he was able to take office and was replaced by Colonel Gzowski.

On 1 July the Queen's Plate was back in Toronto after a five-year absence. Patteson and Duggan, along with several prominent stockholders in the Club, were in charge of the two-day meet, which was advertised as being staged "under new management."

The OJC's first officially sanctioned meet, however, was not held until the middle of September 1881.

The Woodbine was glowing as an estimated crowd of five thousand pushed its way into the picturesque track by the shores of Lake Ontario. The stands were brightly painted, the fences had been whitewashed, the track levelled and generally improved and a top steeplechase course had been built. Platitudes soared.

In a word, The Woodbine July meeting, which opened yesterday, marks a new era in racing in Canada. . . . The spectators were treated to horse racing pure and simple, and too much credit cannot be given to the indefatigable promoters. . . . It is questionable if the history of the Canadian turf records a day's record which in all respects would bear favourable comparison with that witnessed yesterday. . . . There was no drunkenness, no howling at the judges, no gambling appliances in operation, in fact none of those objectionable practices that have hitherto done so much toward bringing horse racing into disrepute. . . . On the grandstand the spectacle was a very animated one. The ladies, caught in a high degree the excitement engendered by the struggles for victory of the 'noblest of animals,' forgot their wonted decorum and poised themselves on the backs of the benches.

But everything was not quite as rosy, as it had seemed at first. The roads leading to The Woodbine were unusually dusty and the tramway cars on the Kingston Road were overloaded. "The cars were dragged along by one poor horse, from whose flanks the trying exertion brought the perspiration in a stream. The headgear of passengers who had clambered aloft was threatened by overhanging branches of shade trees."

THE QUEEN'S PLATE ON JULY 1 WAS STAGED "UNDER NEW MANAGEMENT." THE PROGRAM ADVERTISED THE NEW ONTARIO JOCKEY CLUB'S SEPTEMBER MEETING.

VICE CHANCELLOR | 4-year-old bay gelding

Owner: John White, Milton; *Trainer:* Erastus (Ras) Burgess
Jockey: Mr. Brown; *Breeder:* John White, Milton

was the Halton lumberman and Member of Parliament who received the honour of being ushered to Sir John Beverley Robinson's box to receive "the highly prized certificate" from the Lieutenant Governor's wife, Lady Robinson. For the first time in its history, a Plate win was acknowledged by a presentation from one of Queen Victoria's representatives. Notification that White and his horse had qualified for the fifty "guineas" was forwarded by Patteson to the Marquis of Lorne, Canada's Governor General.

Vice Chancellor's win caught White by surprise:

> The general opinion was that though the little gelding had a fine turn of speed, he could never stay for a mile-and-a-half. In fact, as his owner, Mr. White, afterwards remarked, he was regarded as one of the culls [rejects] in his extensive stud, and had *Fanny Wiser* stayed in fix it is not at all likely that this fellow would have started.

White was lauded by the press, which said his victory would be "a popular one all over the country, as he is one of our oldest, pluckiest and most persistent breeders of racehorses."

At the end of the line, just over the Don Bridge, passengers "entered upon a mile and a half constitutional as the Kingston Tramway Company appeared to be unacquainted with the popular taste for race meetings."

Although there may not have been any garish displays of gambling appliances, considerable amounts of money changed hands. The ladies had their little fifty-cent pools, while "the bookmakers had their hands pretty full, and some of the more prominent sporting men of the city carried large rolls, using them freely to sustain their opinions regarding the respective merits of their favourites." John White's four-year-old bay gelding, *Vice Chancellor,* was not the favourite but it sprung an upset and it

1881 QUEEN'S PLATE STAKES

SECOND RACE
Woodbine Park
JULY 1, 1881

THE QUEEN'S PLATE. 50 Guineas, the gift of Her Majesty the Queen. Weight for age; entrance $10, to go with the plate to the first horse; $100 added from the fund for the second horse; the third to save his stake. For provincial bred maidens on the flat; distance, one and a half miles. Value to winner $340.

Horse	A	Wt.	Fin	Jockey	Owner	Betting
VICE CHANCELLOR	4	115	1¹	Brown	John White	16-4
JESSIE McCULLOCH	6	118	2½	C Gates	F Lowell	30-5
ATHLETE	6	119	3	A Gates	A W Godson	20-4
TOM MALONE	5	121	4	C Wise	H Chappell	3-2
ECHO	4	115	5	O'Leary	R O'Leary	16-4
RIENZI	3	103	6	Alexander	W F Powell	30-5
HELMBOLD colt	4	118	7	Warder	J Graham	30-5
LEXINGTON	5	121	8	Hayles	W Dickinson	35-5
JACK DAVIS	11	118	9	Robinson	J McKee	12-5

Start good. Time, 2:53. Track fast.

Winner: Four-year-old bay gelding by Terror—Stolen Kisses, by Copec. Bred by John White, Milton. Trained by E. Burgess.

There was little delay in getting the horses started and as the flag dropped VICE CHANCELLOR was the first to draw out of the ruck and cut the pace. JACK DAVIS and ATHLETE followed with the favored TOM MALONE moving up as the field swung around the clump of trees. When the dust cleared in the backstretch TOM MALONE had replaced JACK DAVIS and moved up to take VICE CHANCELLOR by the neck, and for a second or two those who had money on the favorite thought they had the race won. As they neared the half-mile pole the little son of Terror shook off the brown stallion and again drew out a length or two. TOM MALONE had run his race and backed off while JESSIE McCULLOCH drew up in the stretch to catch ATHLETE for place. The winner was a length in front of JESSIE McCULLOCH, who had almost a half lap on ATHLETE.

Scratched—Jonathan Scott, Tom Carlyle, Richard Foster.

ALLIE GATES WON HIS THIRD PLATE RACE ON THE FAVOURED *FANNY WISER*.

The final episode of the perambulating journey of the Queen's Plate occurred appropriately at London's Newmarket Race Course, the setting of numerous fiascos in the burgeoning years of the contest. London had hosted more Plates than any other centre, except for Toronto, and had seen its growth and maturation. The annual struggle over the site of the race, which had developed into an acrimonious rivalry among politicians who lobbied shamelessly to have the Plate allotted to their ridings, had finally been resolved. In a year it would become the permanent property of the fledgling Ontario Jockey Club at The Woodbine in Toronto.

Nevertheless, on 7 June 1882 the Plate was run for the fourth time at Newmarket, a course that would close down in a year or two. Fittingly, the last big act to play Newmarket was Colonel William F. Cody's "Buffalo Bill Wild West" show in 1883. "Wild" was what some of the early Plate races were in London. In 1865 *Lady Norfolk* was the mysterious victor, the year of a "ringer," a jockey jettisoning lead weights from his saddle and a reported empty judges' stand during the run-off heat. Then there was *Bay Jack*, the hero of 1869, who was later poisoned in Strathroy. In 1878 the judges ousted one entry because the owner had falsified its age, but they allowed a mare conceived in England to compete against *King George*, whose age was never stated at all. Perhaps it was a sign that the sport was growing up and gaining a vestige of respectability since the 1882 Plate was without incident or hint of chicanery.

A race which in the past had been dominated by rural and small town owners, the Plate was partially a "Toronto triumph," as *Fanny Wiser*, a five-year-old mare owned by Major Joseph H. Mead of Toronto, defeated future Plate winner *Williams*. Second by a neck in Ottawa in 1880 and the early favourite before being sidelined with an injury in 1881, *Fanny Wiser* was ridden by Toronto's Allie Gates, who thus became the first jockey to win three Plates.

Mead raced his horses under the pseudonym, "Mr. Arthur Abingdon," which was similar to the nom de plume used by George Alexander Baird, an extremely wealthy Scot who was reputed to be one of the three greatest amateur riders on the flat that England ever saw. Baird was known as "Mr. Abington" when he won the Derby at Epsom with *Merry Hampton* in 1887. Mead had been one of the founding fathers of the Ontario Jockey Club and had acquired the mare from her breeder, Halton County's John White.

Fanny Wiser was a true product of the Canadian turf since she was out of 1868 Plate winner *Nettie*, and was by White's formidable stallion *Terror*, the beaten favourite of the Whitby Plate in 1870. She was described in *The Mail* as a "mare of more than average size, without too much substance and a good deal of daylight underneath her. Of a fretful, nervous disposition, and delicate, her training is a matter of more than ordinary difficulty, but that she is a race nag was pretty well shown today." *Fanny Wiser*, who was eventually sold to a man attempting to break into the breeding business—Joseph Emm Seagram—was one of *Terror*'s four offspring

LONDON'S NEWMARKET RACE COURSE HAD MANY AN EXUBERANT RACING FAN DURING THE FOUR YEARS IT HOSTED THE PLATE.

FANNY WISER | 5-year-old bay mare

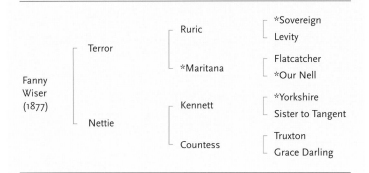

Owner: Arthur Abingdon Stable (Joseph H. Mead), Toronto
Trainer: W.E. Owen; *Jockey:* A.E. (Allie) Gates; *Breeder:* John White, Milton

to earn the guineas. She was White's tenth Plate victor. He hailed his string of victories by saying: "We should congratulate ourselves on the fact that we can raise stock able to compete with our American cousins, and I would hope soon to be able to compete with the Mother Country in the production of good stock. My only object as a breeder is to try and place this Province in the front rank."

Londoners thoroughly enjoyed a Plate race which would be the last ever staged outside of Toronto. It attracted a record twenty-three entries and more than five thousand people turned up, many in carriages, cabs and wagons, which ringed the course. The *London Advertiser* noted: "The old boilers belonging to the A.M. Ross Refinery, on the outside of the course, furnished a resting place for about one hundred and fifty men and boys, who all seemed happy and contented with the fact that they had saved the price of admittance." Courts in town adjourned at ten in the morning to allow lawyers, judges and jurymen to attend the Plate.

According to *The Mail*'s correspondent, the only unsettling fact of the day was the program. He said that management had erred in delegating their issue to some advertising men from Detroit, who sold them through the crowd at an exorbitant price of ten cents. "This might have been well enough had the publisher understood his duty, but there was an entire absence of information on what should have been a 'K'rect card.'" Even the owners' colours had been left out and some fanciful ribbons had been attributed instead of the conventional colours. Everything and everybody was mixed up and it was impossible to identify any of the runners.

1882 QUEEN'S PLATE STAKES

THIRD RACE
London
Newmarket Race Course
JUNE 7, 1882

THE QUEEN'S PLATE. 50 Guineas, with entrance money added, dash of one mile and a half. Open to horses bred, raised and owned in the Province of Ontario. $100 to second. Twenty–three entries. Value to winner $480.

Horse	A	Wt.	Fin	Jockey	Owner	Betting
FANNY WISER	5	117	1½	A E Gates	A Abingdon (J H Mead)	3–1
WILLIAMS	4	115	2	C Butler	D W Campbell	12–1
TULLAMORE	5	119	3		Ben Johnson	10–1
RODERICK	5	112	4	C Wise	R R Pringle	2–1
EASTER	3	96	5	Warder	Erastus Burgess	4–1
BONNIE VIC	3		6	W Jamieson	John Forbes	4–1
OLIVETTE			7		R Birrell	78–1
MARQUIS	3		8		D W Campbell	4–1
HARPER LEXINGTON	6		9		W Harper	14–1
GWENDOLINE	aged		10		R Birrell	12–1
DRIFTWOOD	5		11		G W Wilcox	20–1
FRANCIS L.	4		12		Francis Lowell	5–1
JONATHAN SCOTT	4		13		Robert Wilson	5–1
DUCHESS			14		G Watson	12–1

Track good. Time, 2:51.
Winner: Five–year–old bay mare by Terror—Nettie, by Kennett. Bred by John White, Milton. Trained by W. E. Owen. **Ridden by Allie Gates.**
After a poor start FANNY WISER took the lead from RODERICK. BONNIE VIC was with the leaders as well. FANNY WISER surrendered the lead going around the turn as RODERICK forged ahead by a length. WILLIAMS, TULLAMORE and EASTER moved up on the leaders and the six were closely bunched coming into the stretch. DUCHESS was also briefly in contention but faded. Gates shook up his mare, FANNY WISER, and won easily by a half-length over WILLIAMS.
Scratched—Inspector, Springbrook, Wild Daisy, Forsaken, Walter G., Orkney and Minnie.

PLATE WINNER FANNY WISER WAS OWNED BY TORONTO'S "MR. A. ABINGDON," A PSEUDONYM OF MAJOR J.H. MEAD.

The Queen's Plate was approaching its twenty-fourth birthday in 1883, a significant year for railways and businesses in North America as Standard Time was introduced. The idea of only twenty-four zones around the world was proposed by a Scottish-born engineer from Toronto, Sir Sandford Fleming (1827–1915). Some citizens disapproved, complaining about "tampering with God's time." Fleming's fascination with clocks and railway schedules resulted in the creation of an international unified standard for telling time. Fleming was motivated after missing a train in Ireland in 1876 when a misprint in his copy of *Irish Railroad Traveler's Guide* gave the train's departure time as 5:35 p.m. In fact, the train had left at 5:35 a.m., causing him to miss his connections to the ferry to England. Fleming was Canada's chief railway surveyor and construction engineer of the nineteenth century, and was chief engineer of the Canadian Pacific Railway. He was also the man who designed Canada's first postage

THE "RAILBIRDS" ON PLATE DAY OFTEN INCLUDED TORONTO'S MOST RECOGNIZABLE AND AFFLUENT CITIZENS.

stamp. When the colonial government took control of the post office in 1851, Fleming persuaded the postmaster-general to adopt a postage stamp system. The first Canadian stamp, Fleming's three-pence beaver, was issued 23 April 1851. The design included a beaver in the middle of a pond, surrounding vegetation and a waterfall in the foreground. A forty-seven-cent beaver stamp was reissued in 2001. A bronze plaque mounted on a pillar at 110 Yonge Street commemorates the location where Fleming designed the stamp.

Talk of horses was more of a concern for the people whose livelihoods depended on the equine. In California a horse called *Slippery Dick* upset the favoured but ancient *Chicago,* a twenty-four-year-old trotter, in four heats. Local breeders read that the average price of yearlings at a Kentucky auction was $549. Torontonians chuckled about the farmer from nearby Hamilton, whose horse suddenly disappeared into a municipal sewer while he was on his way to market. "The horse has not yet been extricated and it is supposed a law suit will result." In Toronto that spring there was a land boom as lots in The Junction (west of Keele, between Dundas and Bloor Streets) "were going cheap." Citizens were urged to inspect building lots on the "old Carleton Race Course, where the horses once ran for the Queen's Plate." To encourage prospective buyers, excursion trains ran daily from Queen and Yonge Streets. "Capitalists are sure of large and quick returns with low taxes and easy terms. Money to be made where money lost. No game of chance now. A sure thing," advertisements declared.

Toronto's most recent census indicated a population of eighty-four thousand, but the city was rapidly growing, even in the direction of the Toronto Islands, the home of Edward (Ned) Hanlan, illustrious world champion oarsman, who complained that he had been only granted a three-month licence for his popular hotel at the west point of Hanlan's Island. His resort attracted many families to build summer residences on the island and petitions suggested it would be a shame if the city lost the revenue it received in leasing the lots.

On 24 May the talk of two bridges was in Toronto newspapers. In New York City the Brooklyn

THE MARQUESS OF LORNE RECOMMENDED TO QUEEN VICTORIA THAT THE QUEEN'S PLATE BE RUN ANNUALLY AT THE WOODBINE.

Bridge, a towering steel structure spanning the East River, was opened. Here, the not-too-grandiose Don Bridge was massed with holidayers who converged on the passageway crossing the Don River. They were on their way to a horse race which would become a spring ritual. It was the Queen's birthday, a day to celebrate the twenty-fourth running of the Plate in its new home, The Woodbine.

Throngs of holidayers, some in fashionable carriages, others in less pretentious wagons and carts, still others on horseback and on foot, struggled over the bridge. Tram service halted at the bridge and, unless you were wealthy or willing to "club together" to hire a cab for ten or fifteen dollars for the afternoon, it was an arduous trip when the roads were dusty or muddy as the racecourse was nearly a two-mile hike from the bridge.

The Plate was an unquestionable success and a crowd of five thousand witnessed a stirring win by *Roddy Pringle,* a three-year-old gelding who had raced several times in the United States. Named after a hotel owner from Cobourg, the winner was owned by Charley Boyle of Woodstock, whose youngest son, Klondike Joe Boyle, would one day become a national folk hero. Most importantly, the race was organized for the first time by the Ontario Jockey Club's influential executive and stockholders. Yet it seems likely that officials viewed the day with mixed emotions. While more than $2,000 was collected at the gate, enough to cover the losses sustained at its 1882 meeting, the ojc was jilted by its royal guests, Princess Louise, fourth daughter of Queen Victoria, and the Marquess of Lorne, Canada's fourth Governor General.

Frenzied efforts by Colonel Casimir Gzowski, aide-de-camp to the Queen and president of the ojc, and Thomas Patteson, a close friend of royalty and the person most responsible for the founding of the Club, failed to alter the dates of the proposed vice regal visit to Toronto. A communique from Ottawa stated that Princess Louise "couldn't possibly witness the race for Her Majesty's "Guineas," and would not be in town before 28 May. There were suggestions that the ojc might postpone its 24 and 26 May holiday weekend meeting, since it was eager for royal patronage in the hope of securing the Queen's Plate on a permanent basis.

The Plate race was contested on schedule. But fate intervened, in the form of heavy winds and a steady downpour, and the Saturday program was postponed by the stewards until the following Saturday. *The Globe* reported that "even the horse owners, who had to stay over for that time at unexpected expense, did not find it in their hearts to grumble with the decision." Invitations were reissued and accepted. Royalty would attend the 2 June meet. *The Mail* commented: "It was an ill wind that blows nobody good. His

RODDY PRINGLE | 3-year-old brown gelding

```
                              ┌ *Australian ┌ West Australian
                  ┌ Helmbold ─┤             └ *Emilia
                  │           │
                  │           └ Lavender    ┌ Wagner
Roddy             │                         └ Alice Carneal
Pringle ──────────┤
(1880)            │           ┌ Zetland     ┌ Voltigeur
                  │           │             └ Merry Bird
                  └ *Castaway ┤
                              │             ┌ Lanercost
                              └ Castellan   └ Constance
```

Owner: Charles Boyle, Woodstock; *Trainer:* Charles Boyle
Jockey: Jacob Smith *Breeder:* Dr. Andrew Smith, Toronto

Excellency and Her Royal Highness are drawing cards."

The day turned out to be an incredible success, despite the fact that the program was delayed for more than thirty minutes by the tardy arrival of the vice-regal party, who were chauffeured to the track in Colonel Gzowski's landau. Her Royal Highness did have the courtesy to forward word to the track that her party would be late and to go ahead and run the first race without them. *The Mail* testily wrote that the visitors did not "maintain their reputation for punctuality, as they were conspicuous by their absence until after 3 o'clock."

Two weeks later at the ojc's annual meeting, Colonel Gzowski, who had entertained the Governor General and the Queen's daughter at dinner in his house on Bathurst Street, resigned the presidency on the grounds that "he was too busy to devote his full attention to the club's affairs." However, his ambitions, as well as Patteson's, had been fulfilled, as shareholders learned that Princess Louise and the Governor General had informed Buckingham Palace that they were impressed with the Ontario Jockey Club's efforts towards turf reform and the popularization of horse racing, and heartily endorsed the Club's petition—"The race for the Queen's Plate for Ontario should be run every year at this central point in the province."

MISSION ACCOMPLISHED, COL. CASIMIR GZOWSKI RESIGNED HIS PRESIDENCY OF THE OJC.

1883 QUEEN'S PLATE STAKES

SECOND RACE
Woodbine Park
MAY 24, 1883

THE QUEEN'S PLATE. 50 Guineas, and a sweepstake of $10 each with $50 added by the club for the second horse. For horses bred, owned and trained in Ontario that have never won a race. Entries closed 12th of May, 13 nominations. Distance 1¼ miles. Value to winner $420.

Horse	A	Wt.	Fin	Jockey	Owner	Betting
RODDY PRINGLE	3	97	1²	J Smith	Charles Boyle	2-1
WILLIAMS	5	123	2²	A Gates	A E Gates	4-1
PRINCESS LOUISE	3	95	3ⁿᵏ	W Jamieson	John Forbes	1-1
MARQUIS	4	118	4	C Butler	D W Campbell	7-1
ORKNEY	5	120	5	Kerr	D W Campbell	3-1
INSPECTOR	4	118	6	W Fuller	John Dyment	10-1
ATHLETE	8	121	7	Graves	R Crewe	100-1
HERCULES	4	118	8	Braithwaite	Mackie & Blute	10-1
WILD DEER	5	115	9	Warder	E Dickenson	100-1

Start poor. Time, 2:52¼. Track heavy.

Winner: Three-year-old brown gelding by Helmbold—*Castaway, by Zetland. Bred by Dr. Andrew Smith. Trained by Charles Boyle.

The field got off after a first attempt at a straggling start in which the favored PRINCESS LOUISE and ATHLETE got the worst. HERCULES shot to the front past the stand followed by WILLIAMS, RODDY PRINGLE, ORKNEY and INSPECTOR in that order. After a mile it was obvious that RODDY PRINGLE had the race in hand, bar accidents. HERCULES had shot his bolt and ATHLETE, WILD DEER and INSPECTOR were tolling hopelessly at the rear. Meanwhile PRINCESS LOUISE was working her way between horses and was fast gaining ground lost at the start. WILLIAMS tried to get at the leader and finished comfortably ahead of the fast-closing filly.

1884 | WILLIAMS

Despite its immaturity and rather limited exposure, horse racing was bounding with enthusiasm in Toronto during the spring of 1884. The Ontario Jockey Club's two-day meeting, with five races daily, attracted thousands of people to the brightly decorated Woodbine; if the Club had enough money in its coffers, there would be two days of racing in the fall, weather permitting. There were no autumn meets in 1882 or 1883. Today, in comparison, a spectator can witness as many races and twice the number of horses in a single day at Woodbine as he could in an entire season during the fledgling years of the Club.

A century ago newspapers reported extensively on horse racing, in Canada as well as in the United States, Britain and continental Europe. However, there was little brouhaha about the silver anniversary of the Queen's Plate. The race drew a record-equalling field of fifteen provincial-bred maidens, many of which were stabled at the Leslieville track in Little York (on the Danforth) or at hotels and livery stables of the nearby neighbourhood of Norway. Their owners had made nomination payments of five dollars each on 1 January and 12 May and fifteen dollars to start for a purse of $415; the horse finishing second would receive one hundred dollars from the Ontario Jockey Club.

In the saddling paddock at The Woodbine.

But the Plate attracted little more attention than the other four races on the holiday program. The names of the visiting dignitaries seemed to be of more vital interest to the newsmen than the identity of the winning jockey. *The Globe* did devote space to outline the pedigree of the Plate winner, *Williams*, a "genteel-looking bay gelding," who somehow had maintained his maiden status despite finishing second in the two previous Plate races. In earlier Plate starts *Williams* had run under the racing silks of David W. Campbell, son-in-law of John White, who had bred the gelding. *Williams* had also been raced under the name of *Micky Free*.

On this 24 May holiday, *Williams* had a new owner, John Halligan of Toronto. *The Mail* said: "There was considerable stir when little John Halligan struggled up the stairs leading to Lieutenant Governor John Robinson's box, where he was presented with a cheque for the amount of the prize won. John was profuse in his bows, and when he had descended to terra firma again, someone threw him a splendid bouquet, which he acknowledged gracefully."

Yet the newspapers failed to reveal who rode or trained the big

six-year-old gelding, who divided his time between flat racing and competing in steeplechase and hurdle events. It was noted that he had been "rather big in the spring but strong work had sufficiently rid him of superfluous flesh."

The only discordant note concerned the poor odds offered by John Forbes' bookmaking firm, which had a monopoly on the business and "figured things out to suit themselves, and when there was the slightest hope of any particular horse being dangerous, they immediately chalked him up at evens against the field." Most editors were beguiled with the colour and spectacle of The Woodbine course: its glistening coat of green paint and snowy whitewashed fences, the costumes and uniforms, the trials and tribulations of travelling to the course and the animated scenes inside Joe Duggan's horse palace by the lake. The account in the *Toronto News* was especially graphic:

> At one o'clock the enthusiastic, the penniless who had to walk all the way, and the selfish, with an eye towards the best seats, thronged in the same direction. Kingston Road from the bridge to the gates of Woodbine Park was thronged with pedestrians, cabs, tilburys, dog carts, coupes, express wagons, furniture vans, drays, donkey carts—everything that ran on wheels, and could be drawn by equines—good, bad and indifferent.
>
> The tide of humanity, on foot and on wheels, rolled on and

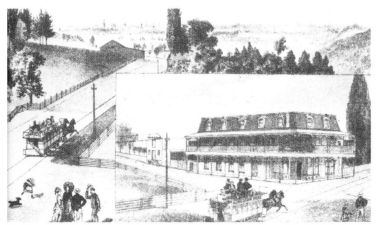

TORONTO COULD BE SEEN FROM THIS HOTEL ON THE KINGSTON ROAD AT WOODBINE IN THE NEIGHBOURING NORWAY, NORTH OF THE TRACK.

WILLIAMS | 6-year-old bay gelding

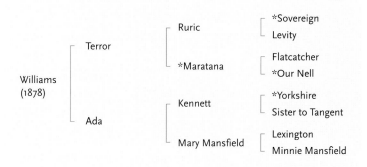

Williams (1878)			
	Terror	Ruric	*Sovereign
			Levity
		*Maratana	Flatcatcher
			*Our Nell
	Ada	Kennett	*Yorkshire
			Sister to Tangent
		Mary Mansfield	Lexington
			Minnie Mansfield

Owner: John Halligan, Toronto; *Trainer:* Mr. A. Martin
Jockey: Mr. A. Martin; *Breeder:* John White, Milton

sung and shouted and chaffed and locked wheels and swore and raised clouds of smoke and cracked whips and lost hats and yelled, and finally poured into the gates at The Woodbine with much chaffering and haggling and expostulations on the part of the uninitiated, when they discovered that a 50¢ ticket did not admit them to the judges' stand, nor on the track while a race was in progress. Over in the enclosure fifty horses were stamping about, blanketed (after the approved manner of the old school) and hooded, attended by fifty grooms and jockeys. The sportive element, i.e. the 'horsey' part of the sportive element, surged over to look at them and talk learnedly about this one being 'off her feed' and that one 'groggy'. Anxious owners conversed apart with optimistic grooms and ubiquitous jockeys as to the condition of their 'pets,' the 'boss' reiterating his instructions to the curved-back gentleman in stripes and spurs . . .

Summing up his thoughts of the Plate, the reporter left little doubt of his feelings: "This was the greatest race ever staged in Canada." A month later, at its annual meeting, the OJC presided over for the first time by president William Hendrie—the Hamilton merchant who originated the railway cartage business in Canada—received the news it had been expecting from Ottawa. A letter from Lord Meglund, secretary to the Governor General, the Marquess of Lansdowne, advised the Club that the race would be run in Toronto at such time as appears most suitable to the interests of racing. "I am also to inform you that until further notice from their office, the Queen's Plate will continue to be run for under the auspices of the Ontario Jockey Club."

A list of conditions, which had to be strictly observed, were included in the communique, as well as a request that a certificate signed by the stewards, stating which day the race had been run, the name of the owner of the winning horse, and the name of the horse, "shall be forwarded to me as soon as possible after the races are over. On receipt of this certificate the Governor General's Bill of Exchange on the Crown Agents for the Colonies for Fifty Guineas will be forwarded to the owner of the winning horse."

LIEUTENANT GOVERNOR JOHN B. ROBINSON.

1884 QUEEN'S PLATE STAKES

SECOND RACE
Woodbine Park
MAY 24, 1884

THE QUEEN'S PLATE. 50 Guineas, added to a conditional sweepstakes of $5 at the time of entrance (Jan. 1, 1884) and an additional $5, unless declared out, on or before the 12th of May. Entries made between Jan. 1 and 12th of May, when stake finally closes, $15 each p.p.; distance 1½ miles. For maiden horses bred, raised and trained in the province of Ontario. The club will give $100 to the second horse. Plate and stakes to winner. Value to winner $415. Twenty-two nominations.

Horse	A	Wt.	Fin	Jockey	Owner	Betting
WILLIAMS	6	121	1¹½	A Martin	John Halligan	15-5
MARQUIS	5	121	2ⁿᵏ	C Butler	D W Campbell	40-5
MODJESKA	5	118	3	Steeds	George Watson	15-5
J. P. WISER	7	121	4	Warder	D W Campbell	10-5
EDMONTON	4	115	5	W Jamieson	Ben Johnson	40-5
WILLIE W.	3	97	6	H Douglas	E Burgess	10-5
DRIFTWOOD	7	121	7	Balluna	G W Wilcox	20-5
FRED HENRY	5	123	8	Pierson	William Henry	50-5
MINNIE BYERS	5	118	9	Rowe	Dr Byers	50-5
CASTILENA	6	119	10	A Gates	James Simmons	60-5
DIRECTION	4	115	11	Graver	John Dyment	30-5
J. C. PATTERSON	6	124	12	Williams	W H Chappell	8-5
PACIFIC	5	118	13	C Gates	W H Chappell	20-5
GENERAL BUTLER	8	124	14	Walker	R Doyle	30-5
MISS BRUCE	6	124	15	Griffiths	J McCulloch	50-5

Time, 2:50¾. Track heavy.

Winner: Six-year-old bay gelding by Terror—Ada, by Kennett. Bred by John White, Milton. Trained by A. Martin.

After eight attempts to get the unwieldy field of 15 starters underway, DIRECTION, who had been one of the delinquents, broke on top while GENERAL BUTLER was left at the post. EDMONTON, MINNIE BYERS and DRIFTWOOD were closely bunched behind. After the first half-mile WILLIAMS challenged DIRECTION, who shortly afterwards had enough and backed off. At the mile it was J. C. PATTERSON, WILLIAMS and J. P. WISER in that order. It was anybody's race till they turned into the stretch where a lot of them began to catch the catgut heavily. PATTERSON gave it up with a furlong to run and WILLIAMS, with his full brother (J. P. WISER) on one flank and MARQUIS on the other, gradually pulled away to win a trifle within himself.

During the weeks leading up to the twenty-sixth running of the Queen's Plate the Ontario Jockey Club said that militia volunteers in uniform would be allowed into the races for free. It was a time for rejoicing in parts of Canada as Louis Riel, the fiery politician and leader of the Métis people of the prairies, and leader of the Red River Rebellion (1869–1870) and North-West Rebellion (1885), had been captured by the mounted police and government troops in the Battle of Batoche. Major-General F.G. Middleton was hailed in the Toronto newspapers, which daily carried the deaths of local soldiers at the battles of Fish Lake and Duck Lake, North-West Territories (Saskatchewan). Riel, the man considered by many as a folk hero in his fight to preserve Métis rights and culture and as the founder of the province of Manitoba, at age forty-one would be executed in Regina for high treason on 16 November 1885.

While the details of Riel's capture dominated the news pages, there was considerable consternation voiced by a *The Toronto World*'s reporter in an interview with the OJC's chairman regarding the inconvenience that race fans faced in attempting to reach Woodbine Park. Toll bars, interposed by the County of York, blocked carriages that had travelled three or four miles along South Park Street or Eastern Avenue from getting to the track's entrance. To avoid the pay tolls drivers were forced to divert seventy-five feet to Kingston Road, which was practically impassable because of sewer construction. "Such a state of things is disgraceful, and merely a wanton annoyance to the six or seven thousand people who will be at the ropes. I will make every effort to protect the public from this unscrupulous abuse of a questionable privilege." The reporter asked whether the chairman noticed that at Hamilton an obnoxious toll

FORMER RIDER HARVEY (DUP) DOUGLAS CHATS WITH JOCKEY FRANKIE MANN IN 1935.

bar was demolished. "Yes, and I trusted the incident would have some effect on public opinion, which once roused would insist the total abolition of turnpike gates. There is more money spent on the collection of tolls than on repairs to the road. It is a relic of barbarism long since abandoned in other civilized communities."

The toll bars may have had something to do with hundreds of vacant seats. The grandstand was not crowded and attendance was estimated at perhaps three thousand. *The Toronto World* observed that attendance was respectable, considering it was the day before a holiday and retail stores are particularly busy. "There were large numbers strolling about the grounds, a crowd more respectable looking and orderly than is usually found at race meetings. Management must be congratulated on the class of people who witnessed the race, many ladies, merchants, lawyers and respectable citizens and the Lieutenant-Governor's wife and party. The rougher element, evidently, had not enough money to pay admission, or had gone fishing."

A jockey who had ridden in the Plate a year earlier, Harvey (Dup) Douglas, recalled almost sixty years later the events of the 1884 Plate as

1885 QUEEN'S PLATE STAKES

SECOND RACE

Woodbine Park

MAY 23, 1885

THE QUEEN'S PLATE. 50 Guineas, for horses bred, raised, owned and trained in the province of Ontario, added to a conditional sweepstakes, payable $5 at the time of entrance (Jan. 1, 1885) and an additional $5 unless declared out on or before May 11. Entries made between Jan. 1 and May 11, when the stake finally closed, $15 each p.p. Distance 1½ miles. The club gives $100 to second horse. Plate and stakes to winner. Twenty–five entries, 13 starters. Value to winner $470.

Horse	A	Wt	Fin	Jockey	Owner	Betting
WILLIE W.	4	115	1¹	W Jamieson	E Burgess	Even
FRED HENRY	6	121	2³	Warder	William Henry	4-1
EDMONTON	5	120	3nk	C Butler	Ben Johnson	3-1
PAWNBROKER	5	120	4	Rowe	Robert Bond	5-1
FISHERMAN	4	115	5	R O'Leary	R Wilson	f-4-1
LUCY LIGHTFOOT	4	113	6	McLaughlin	John Dyment	f-4-1
AUNT ALICE	5	118	7	Cook	John Dyment	10-1
WILD ROSE	3	95	8	Bernard	D W Campbell	8-1
MINNIE A.	9	119	9	Moreland	H B B Alley	f-4-1
STATESMAN	4	118	10	R Hill	H Powley	f-4-1
BILLIE L.	4	118	11	Coughlin	S Leatherland	f-4-1
LADY DORA	3	95	12	Bennett	A Frank & Sons	f-4-1
BRAEWOOD	4	115	13	McLeod	Mr Richmond	f-4-1

f-Coupled in the field betting.

Track muddy. Time, 2:58.

Winner: Four–year–old bay gelding by Princeton—Roxaline, by Malcolm. Bred and trained by J. E. (Ras) Burgess, Woodstock.

It took four starts to get the field away and WILLIE W., who went on to win as he pleased, acted badly at the post and was last to get off. However, before a quarter-mile had been travelled, he forged ahead and never was headed off. FRED HENRY and EDMONTON were never far behind in the early going. BRAEWOOD, which had also been in contention, bolted to the outside fence near the three-quarter pole. EDMONTON showed signs of distress in the stretch and was fortunate to hold onto third place ahead of PAWNBROKER. WILLIE W. held off FRED HENRY's desperate attempts in the final hundred yards.

Scratched—Vanetta R., Prince Arthur, Jim Ferris, Ben Bolt and Fanny.

well as 1885 and its Plate winner *Willie W.,* which he had ridden as a seventeen-year-old skinny runt from Woodstock who weighed little more than ninety pounds. Unfortunately, he and his mount (*Willie W.*) were greener than a one dollar bill, and finished "in the ruck," a quaint racetrack expression of that era, meaning they were up the track with the also rans.

Willie W. was heavily backed that year, but the rangy, raw-boned gelding was immature and incapable of upsetting the more seasoned *Williams.*

The Globe boasted: "As we remarked before the race, that having never been brought up to racing pitch in his two-year-old form, and having had only a short season for preparation this year [1884], he could hardly be expected to be fit to go the trip." Equally ill-prepared was Douglas, a stablehand of Erastus (Ras) Burgess, the man who owned, bred and trained *Willie W.* In an interview fifty-nine years later, the dapper ex-jockey admitted that he had little riding experience, with the result that he did not get the mount on *Willie W.* the following year. William Jamieson, a cagey veteran, was in the irons in 1885 as *Willie W.* "so far outdistanced the others that from start to finish he led in the dance." The race was a rough contest and it was debatable who acted up more, *Willie W.* or Jamieson. The horse was one of the "worst actors in the party and on two or three occasions broke away by himself, causing a tedious delay." The riders were also criticized—"more than half were as green as the horses they were on." Jamieson's behaviour earned him a fine from starter John Stanton for disobeying orders; he was told that the next time he was complained about, he would have to "stand down" for the rest of the meeting. "He's a persistent obstructionist, and if he doesn't mend his ways is liable to earn a suspension before the season is far advanced," noted *The Canadian Sportsman.*

In an interview with *The Globe and Mail*'s Appas Tappas in 1943, Douglas recalled the archaic conditions of the 1880s—the large fields of inexperienced maidens, running on muddy and ploughed-up tracks that were often dangerous. "In those days there were no automobile ambulances to speed around the track to pick up injured riders. All we had was a horse-drawn buggy. I remember the year [1890] *Kitestring* won the Plate. I was on *Rose Maybud* and she was just making her move at the half-mile pole when she fell. She stepped into a hole and broke her hip." Douglas suffered a broken right leg and was left laying on the track until two steeplechase races had been run over the Woodbine infield. "That's how long it was before they carried me into the carriage and drove me back to the jockeys' quarters."

Douglas and *Willie W.* were reunited on many occasions after the four-year-old's Plate win, and often against *Williams,* but

WILLIE W. | 4-year-old bay gelding

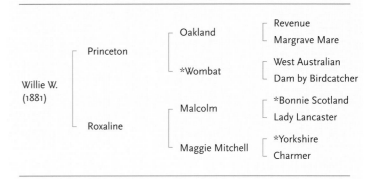

			Revenue
		Oakland	Margrave Mare
	Princeton		West Australian
		*Wombat	Dam by Birdcatcher
Willie W. (1881)			*Bonnie Scotland
		Malcolm	Lady Lancaster
	Roxaline		*Yorkshire
		Maggie Mitchell	Charmer

Owner: Erastus (Ras) Burgess, Woodstock; *Trainer:* E. Burgess
Jockey: William Jamieson; *Breeder:* Riverside Stud (E. Burgess), Woodstock

the Woodstock rider was never able to win the Plate before retiring at the turn of the century. As for *Willie W.,* he was running in claiming (selling) races at Saratoga Springs, New York, less than two months after the Plate triumph for "Ras" Burgess. *The Toronto World* observed that Mrs. J.B. Robinson, wife of Ontario's Lieutenant Governor, presented the certificate of victory in the Queen's Plate to Mr. Burgess on the day after the race and that the certificate would be sent to England by the next mail.

On Plate day *Willie W.* was described as possessing "a somewhat peacocky appearance. He presents the beau ideal of a non-stager and it may be inferred that the field behind him is anything but first class. His coat on Saturday shone like satin and his conditioning reflected the greatest credit on Mr. Burgess."

A great career was expected of *Willie W.* because of his breeding and his illustrious full-sister, *Princess,* nicknamed "the little giantess," after an incredible string of victories in the United States. But apart from the 1885 Plate, he never lived up to the great expectations. He was out of *Roxaline,* an Illinois-bred mare with impeccable bloodlines but deformed legs. *Roxaline* had been acquired cheaply by the senior Burgess, who once offered her for sale to a neighbour for sixty-five dollars (the offer was rejected) before he sold her to his son "Ras" for $125. In 1889, when "Ras" sold *Roxaline, The Canadian Sportsman* complained, saying the sale "takes out of Canada the most famous matron ever owned in it. It is only necessary to mention three of her get [offsprings] to prove her great superiority, viz. *Princess, Brait* and *Fred B.,* each one of the trio rank above the ordinary." The article made no mention at all of *Willie W.,* the Plate winner.

TRAINER ERASTUS (RAS) BURGESS, WHO FOUGHT IN THE FENIAN RAIDS OF THE 1860s, LATER RECEIVED A GOVERNMENT LAND GRANT OF 160 ACRES.

Wild Rose was the "last hurrah." It was 1 July, a day on which she would carry the flaming scarlet silks of the White family of Halton County into the winner's enclosure for yet another of their Queen's Plate victories. But it was their last win. Newspapers suggested that it was the thirteenth Plate win for John White, even though the filly did run in the name of his son-in-law, David W. Campbell. "But," said *The Globe,* "everyone knew that the victory added one more to the long list already scored by the veteran horseman from Milton." In truth, it was the twelfth Plate victory for the seventy-five-year-old warhorse of Halton politics and his crippled brother James, who managed the breeding farm in Bronte called "Woodlands." Their feat would be rivalled later by only two other men, Joseph Emm Seagram and Edward Plunket Taylor.

At Woodbine an exuberant throng milled about the grounds, celebrating Canada's nineteenth birthday and the much-anticipated racing season, which had been postponed since 22 May because the high waters of Lake Ontario had submerged the track's backstretch. On Plate day the track was quite dusty. *Wild Rose* won decisively when she made a bold, authoritative move in the stretch in excusing her rivals.

A big, raking chestnut filly, *Wild Rose* was described by *The World* as "being the best trained of the field and certainly the best ridden. She ran last year but was big and fat. On Thursday Charley Butler had her wound up to perfection." A daughter of *Stolen Kisses,* whose bloodlines would regrettably be allowed to leave the country, *Wild Rose* possessed the pedigree of numerous Plate winners, including an earlier *Wild Rose* of the same maternal family. She was the crowning bloom in a garland of Plate achievements for the prodigious old broodmare, *Yellow Rose.*

Yellow Rose played a prominent role in the foundation of Upper Canada's pioneer racing stock. She was a southern belle from Virginia, which at the time was the predominant horse racing state in the Union. Foaled in 1837, *Yellow Rose* took her first steps during a particularly tumultuous period in the history of Upper Canada. It was the year when William Lyon Mackenzie, a firebrand who had been the new city of Toronto's first mayor, led his unsuccessful revolt against the entrenched Tory government. Following his defeat at Montgomery's Tavern, Mackenzie fled towards the Niagara peninsula, stopping en route to take refuge in the densely treed backwoods along the Twelve Mile

WILD ROSE WAS THE "LAST HURRAH" OF THE PIONEERING WHITE FAMILY OF HALTON COUNTY. THE FILLY RAN UNDER THE NAME OF JOHN WHITE'S SON-IN-LAW, DAVID WATSON CAMPBELL.

Creek. For three days he hid in "Devil's Cave" on the 800-acre property of the White family near Bronte. A reward of a thousand pounds was posted on Mackenzie's head as loyalist troops scoured the area, which in a few years would be the site of Canada's first privately owned racetrack and the grazing meadows of herds of the best purebred cattle and more than sixty imported thoroughbreds. The breeding empire eventually succumbed to apple and cherry orchards and a major highway, The Queen Elizabeth Way. However, for a glorious period in Canadian racing, the paddocks and breeding sheds along the Bronte Side Road were the stomping grounds of White's *Terror,* the best provincially bred stallion of his era, winner of the Silver Medal as best thoroughbred at the 1876 World Exposition in Philadelphia, and the sire of four Plate winners. It was also the lair of *Yellow Rose.*

One hundred years after *Wild Rose*'s Plate victory, the Canadian Horse Racing Hall of Fame inducted her great-great grandmother, *Yellow Rose,* along with *Terror,* for their immense contributions to the growth of thoroughbred racing in Canada.

Don Juan, her son, won the first Queen's Plate in 1860. *Touchstone* followed in 1863, and in 1867 White's first *Wild Rose* won the Plate at St. Catharines. *Liberty,* a daughter, produced "guineas" victor *Palermo,* and two of *Yellow Rose*'s granddaughters, *Lizzie Wright* (*Amelia* and *Moss Rose*) and *Stolen Kisses* (*Vice Chancellor* and a second-hand *Wild Rose*) each foaled Plate champions. Eight of *Yellow Rose*'s progeny, an incredible achievement, won the fifty "guineas," a feat no mare has since come close to equalling. Among the intriguing sidelights of the mare's career is an incident involving her granddaughter, *Stolen Kisses* (*Copec*—*Annie Laurie,* by *Lapidist). She was whisked away to join the boudoir of mares owned by the revolutionary General Manuel Gonzalez, who enjoyed a short reign (1880–1884) as president of Mexico and was depicted as one of his country's greatest citizens and soldiers.

The silks of the Whites and David Campbell would appear in only one more Plate, on a pair of "also rans" in 1887. Dispersal sales, old age and tragedy would terminate the dynasty and by 1899 all three would be dead. Campbell, a leader in the Milton community and publisher of the local *Champion,* died on his kitchen table in 1896 at the age of forty-nine when physicians were unable to save his life after he suffered a ruptured appendix. A year later businesses closed for a day in Milton as the town mourned the death of its most

Ottawa
14th July 1886.

Sir,

I have the honour by desire of His Excellency the Governor General to forward to you herewith, First and Second of Exchange on the Crown Agents for the Colonies, for the sum of Fifty two pounds ten shillings, being the amount of the Queen's Plate won by "Wild Rose" at Toronto on the 1st Instant.

I have the honour to be
Sir,
Your obedient Servant

Henry Streatfield.

D. W. Campbell Esqre
Milton
Ontario

£52 "10 " 0

Governor General's Secretary

LETTER FROM THE GOVERNOR GENERAL'S SECRETARY ADVISING D.W. CAMPBELL THAT A CHEQUE HAD BEEN FORWARDED FOR THE SUM OF FIFTY-TWO POUNDS, TEN SHILLINGS—THE AMOUNT OF THE QUEEN'S PLATE WON BY *WILD ROSE*.

famous citizen, John White—farmer, lumber dealer, politician and horseman.

The Brandon Times, in observing his death:

No man in the Dominion has done more for the improvement

WILD ROSE | 4-year-old chestnut filly

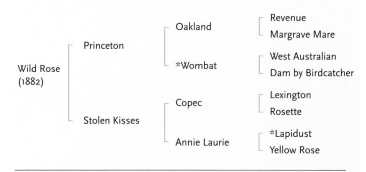

```
                           ┌─ Oakland    ┌─ Revenue
              ┌─ Princeton ─┤            └─ Margrave Mare
              │            └─ *Wombat    ┌─ West Australian
Wild Rose ────┤                          └─ Dam by Birdcatcher
(1882)        │            ┌─ Copec      ┌─ Lexington
              └─ Stolen    ─┤            └─ Rosette
                 Kisses    └─ Annie      ┌─ *Lapidust
                              Laurie     └─ Yellow Rose
```

Owner: David Watson Campbell, Milton; *Trainer:* Charles Butler
Jockey: Charles Butler; *Breeder:* John White, Milton

of Canadian thoroughbreds than John White, and though in late years he has not been so prominent as formerly in racing circles, his name stands as the owner of more Queen's Plate winners than any other horseman.

In its obituary, *The Milton Reformer* commented: "He was a man of great strength, both of body and mind, and very few cared to oppose him either in a physical or mental combat, as he generally came out the victor."

James White, who had been a bedridden invalid since 1872, died in 1899 at the age of ninety and was buried in nearby Palermo. A few years later T.C. Patteson, writing his memoirs for the *Toronto News,* recalled: "The days when James White of Bronte trained winners of the Queen's Plate in a forty-acre field as full of pine stumps as a man's hand is of fingers, are gone."

Today a historical plaque honours the Whites, *Yellow Rose* and her son *Don Juan* for the inaugural Plate victory. It stands about a hundred yards from James White's old homestead. The original stone structure of the barns that once housed *Terror* and *Yellow Rose* was destroyed by a fire in 1983. The racetrack, which used to attract curious schoolchildren as they watched the galloping horses train, is now covered with trees, and a distance away is "Devil's Cave" and the legends of William Lyon Mackenzie's perilous escape.

1886 QUEEN'S PLATE STAKES

SECOND RACE
Woodbine Park
JULY 1, 1886

THE QUEEN'S PLATE. 50 Guineas. For Province of Ontario horses, bred, raised, owned and trained. Payment of $5 at time of entry (Jan. 1, 1886) and an additional $5 on May 1 unless declared out. The club will give $100 to second owner and the third will save his stake. Plate and stakes to winner. Distance one and a half miles. Value to winner $490.

Horse	A	Wt	Fin	Jockey	Owner	Betting
WILD ROSE	4	113	1¾	C Butler	D W Campbell	20-5
FRED HENRY	7	122	2²	Warder	Wm Henry	20-5
WILD BRUCE	3	103	3¹	Pierson	Wm Hendrie	20-5
BEN BOLT	5	118	4	C Wise	Angus Allaster	40-5
AUNT ALICE	6	113	5	McLaughlin	John Dyment	50-5
BONNIE DUKE	4	115	6	Cowie	John Forbes	1-1
MAGGIE MAY	4	113	7	C Gates	John Dyment	20-5
BRAEWOOD	5	118	8	Johns	Shields Brothers	15-5
FISHERMAN	5	118	9	A Gates	Angus Allaster	20-5
DUKE OF WELLINGTON	4	115	10	Rowe	J Ward	50-5

Start good. Track fast. Time, 2:48¼.

Winner: Four-year-old chestnut filly by Princeton—Stolen Kisses, by Copec. Bred by John White, Milton. Trained by Charles Butler.

After a considerable delay the field broke cleanly. The delay was caused when BONNIE DUKE's saddle broke and he had to return to the paddock for repairs. Afterwards the favorite was never able to show better than fourth. The first surge of horses past the stand included BEN BOLT, DUKE OF WELLINGTON and FRED HENRY. AUNT ALICE and FISHERMAN were also in the first division. WILD ROSE was not far off in fifth place. Around the turn FRED HENRY replaced BEN BOLT on the lead while WILD ROSE moved up to third. Down the backstretch WILD ROSE moved up on the heels of FRED HENRY. Despite Warder's whipping FRED HENRY was beginning to lose ground to the filly at the top of the stretch. WILD ROSE gradually inched past the aging stallion and went under the wire an easy winner.

A PLAQUE ON BRONTE SIDE ROAD NEAR WHITE'S ORIGINAL BARN COMMEMORATES *YELLOW ROSE*, DAM OF THE FIRST PLATE WINNER, *DON JUAN*.

1887 | BONNIE DUKE

Although the Ontario Jockey Club was firmly in control of the Queen's Plate in 1887, amendments to the conditions and rules governing this burgeoning but parochial race occurred over a lengthy passage of time. Seventy years would elapse before the evolution of the rules that now exist. The race distance that year was shortened by two furlongs to a mile-and-a-quarter, which in 1957 would later become the permanent Plate distance.

On a balmy 21 May at Woodbine, *Bonnie Duke,* a five-year-old chestnut gelding and full-brother to Plate victor *Bonnie Bird,* took advantage of the shorter course to gain a head decision over the most persistent challenger in Plate history, the hapless and often ailing *Fred Henry.* Of the fourteen horses breaking from the wire that day, only *Harry Cooper,* a three-year-old colt, would have been eligible for the plate in 1939. A year later *Harry Cooper* romped home in front, but he would have been unable to compete under present-day rules because he was too old. It would be more than fifty years before a significant change would be introduced to rid the race of the same old faces—the *Fred Henrys* and the also rans from previous years. Unlike the Kentucky Derby or the Belmont Stakes, restricted to three-year-olds, horses of any age were eligible for the Plate, providing that they were provincially owned and bred maidens, which tended to diminish claims that the race was a classic.

Writers of the era loved to compare Woodbine Park and the Plate to Epsom on Derby Day or to Royal Ascot with its fashionably dressed crowds and dignitaries, and yet the calibre of horses in Toronto was plainly inferior to those in the British classics. Moreover, a three-year-old had only one chance to win the English and the Kentucky Derbys, while defeated Plate contenders would almost certainly be "put away" until the next contest for the fifty "guineas." A glaring example of this practice occurred in 1887 when almost half the field was made up of horses who had finished closest to *Wild Rose* the year before. The winner usually came out of this group the ensuing year and first-time starters seldom succeeded, exceptions in the 1880s being three-year-olds *Roddy Pringle* and *Colonist* and four-year-olds *Bonnie Bird* and *Vice Chancellor.*

However, the Ontario Jockey Club, under the direction of William Hendrie and its zealous executive chairman, T.C. Patteson, was slowly introducing minor revisions, some worthy, others so restrictive that they were later abolished. Shortly after the OJC was given royal assent to perpetuate the race at Woodbine, it introduced a five-dollar nomination payment for owners, payable in January and May, and a starting fee, which built up the stakes for the winner. It also put up money for the horses finishing second and third. The nomination fee was suggested as a method of "doing away with triflers." However, for a sum of twenty dollars, an owner who missed the 1 January payment could still enter before the draw for post positions. The Club hired a bugler in 1887 to announce the post parade, but they warned trainers that if they did not remove the warm-up blankets from their hopefuls, they would be reprimanded. Correct coloured silks were also mandatory.

Getting to the track was made a lot easier because the Club's requests for the city to complete the tramway on the Kingston Road, before the running of the Plate, proved successful, as *The World*'s reporter noted: "For the first time in the history of racing at Woodbine, the people who passed through the Kingston Road did so without being smothered with dust or having to furnish a 25¢ job to some of the industrious young men who make a livelihood on small salaries and fat tips at the hotels and restaurants by 'brushing you off.'" Although there was no dust to speak of, since Kingston Road was block-paved almost to the track, those who were compelled to take streetcars found them slow and bumpy.

In attendance to witness the triumph of Robert Bond's gelding *Bonnie Duke* were the Governor General and his wife, the Marquess and Marchioness of Lansdowne, along with the Canadian Pacific Railway vice-president William Van Horne. Bond, who ran the largest livery stable in

AT THE REINS OF HIS FAMILIAR TALLY-HO, *BONNIE DUKE*'S OWNER, ROBERT BOND.

ROBERT BOND, WHO OPERATED THE LARGEST LIVERY STABLE IN TORONTO, HIS SON HAROLD AND THE FAMILY SETTER.

BONNIE DUKE | 5-year-old chestnut gelding

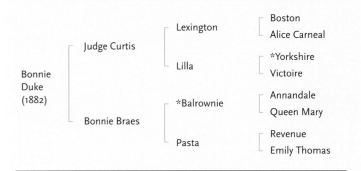

			Boston
		Lexington	Alice Carneal
	Judge Curtis		*Yorkshire
Bonnie		Lilla	Victoire
Duke			Annandale
(1882)		*Balrownie	Queen Mary
	Bonnie Braes		Revenue
		Pasta	Emily Thomas

Owner: Robert Bond, Toronto; *Trainer:* E. Owen
Jockey: Charlie Wise; *Breeder:* John Forbes, Woodstock

Government House officials were in his party. *Bonnie Duke* had been bred by John Forbes, the noted bookmaker and the man responsible for originating the Woodstock Stakes when he put up the purse for its first running in 1885. The horse possessed impressive bloodlines and proved that his Plate win was no fluke the following day when Charlie Wise rode the gelding to victory in the Dominion Handicap.

The Mail suggested that Wise's riding skills enabled *Bonnie Duke* to withstand *Fred Henry*'s stretch challenge: ". . . he showed that he had not forgotten all his cunning in the method of his riding. He was steered in a most masterly manner with splendid judgment, and to the trainer [William Owen] and jockey must be awarded much of the credit of the victory." *The Mail* raised a pertinent aside: "For the first time in the history of the race the distance this year was only a mile-and-a-quarter, a quarter, for some unexplained reason, having been chopped off, and any comparison in time, therefore, is out of the question." The time on a fast track was 2:19, slow even by standards of that era. Ten years later the winner would be six seconds quicker.

Toronto, arrived on Plate day in resplendent fashion, handling the reins of his familiar tally-ho coach with its pair of spanking bays in the wheels and two handsome, high-stepping browns on the lead.

CANADA'S GOVERNOR GENERAL, THE MARQUESS OF LANSDOWNE, ATTENDED THE QUEEN'S PLATE.

1887 QUEEN'S PLATE STAKES

SECOND RACE
Woodbine Park
MAY 21, 1887

THE QUEEN'S PLATE. 50 Guineas. For horses owned, bred, raised and trained in the Province of Ontario; added to a conditional sweepstakes payable $5 at the time of entry (Jan. 1, 1887), and an additional $5, unless declared out on or before May 1, 1887. The club will give $50 to the second horse and $25 to the third horse. Plate and stakes to winner. Twenty-two nominations. Mile and one quarter. Value to winner $357.

Horse	A	Wt.	Fin	Jockey	Owner	Betting
BONNIE DUKE	5	119	1hd	Charles Wise	Robert Bond	2-1
FRED HENRY	8	122	2½	Pierson	Wm Henry	3-1
AUNT ALICE	5	117	3	W Jamieson	Orkney Stable	12-1
FRED B.	4	118	4	H Douglas	E Burgess	10-1
AUGUSTA	5	117	5	Charles Butler	D W Campbell	4-1
BRIGHT STAR	4	113	6	Ed Whyte	William Hendrie	5-1
HARRY COOPER	3	102	7	C N Gates	J D Matheson	10-1
WILD BRUCE	4	118	8	McLaughlin	William Hendrie	3-1
MAGGIE MAY	6	117	9	Warder	Orkney Stable	3-1
BEN BOLT	6	119	10	Graham	Ben Johnson	6-1
GLENCAIRN	4	118	11	Steeds	T Bennett	9-1
D.W.C.	4	117	12	Hamilton	D W Campbell	20-1
BESSIE	6	117	13	Templeton	W Templeton	20-1
JIM FERRIS	6	119	14	A E Gates	R Wilson	10-1

Start good. Track fast. Time: 2:19.
Winner: Five-year-old chestnut gelding by Judge Curtis—Bonnie Braes, by *Balrownie. Bred by John Forbes, Woodstock. Trained by W. E. Owen.

First to show in front were FRED HENRY, MAGGIE MAY and BONNIE DUKE. The others were bunched with D.W.C. and AUGUSTA at the rear. FRED HENRY opened up a gap between himself and MAGGIE MAY at the stands and increased it to three lengths around the turn. MAGGIE MAY, along with BONNIE DUKE, HARRY COOPER and WILD BRUCE were close up. Going to the half AUNT ALICE and FRED B. closed up on the leaders. In the stretch FRED HENRY had the lead with BONNIE DUKE moving quickly on the outside along with AUNT ALICE and FRED B. BONNIE DUKE took the lead in the final hundred yards and held off FRED HENRY's challenge, winning by a narrow head. AUNT ALICE and FRED B. were less than a length back as all four horses hit the finish line in a group.

When a gambler has $2,000 riding on the outcome of a horse race, he often tends to abandon his scruples. In the 1888 Queen's Plate it meant purchasing one of the favourites and locking him up in his stall on the morning of the race. This manoeuvre was intended to save a substantial wager.

The horse in question was the venerable but somewhat tarnished *Fred Henry*, an aging chestnut who showed up in Plate nominations in the 1880s a record seven times. Unfortunately, old *Fred* had aching joints and made a habit of chasing winners across the finish line. Fans revelled in his courage and gallantry, but in five Plate starts he had five losses. Just why two players of the ponies would unleash their bankrolls on the nine-year-old maiden against *Harry Cooper*, a powerful colt who looked so good that the bookies refused to lay money against him, is what keeps racetracks in business.

There had been recurring rumours that *Fred Henry* was again aching and a trifle lame, but one of the papers optimistically reported: "*Fred Henry* will be hard to beat in the Plate, and a good many people think that he will be able to do what is asked in spite of his rumoured lameness." After three narrow defeats it was *Fred*'s turn, and undoubtedly the prospect of making a score on him overcame the high-rolling gamblers' better judgment. The early odds favoured J.D. Matheson's four-year-old colt *Harry Cooper*, which many punters claimed had been robbed by the judges the year before in the Woodstock Stakes, but if there was one horse in the field capable of upsetting him it was *War Cry*'s old son, *Fred Henry*.

The bookmakers eagerly accepted all wagers placed on *Fred Henry*. However, persistent comments of old *Fred*'s lameness were worrisome to the two intrepid gamblers. One of them had put up a bet of $1,600, but it was contingent upon *Fred Henry* being a starter. The other gambler, a Mr. C.J. Smith, who stood to lose $2,100 if *Harry Cooper* beat *Fred Henry*, had no intention of allowing owner William Henry to start a horse who was unfit to race, and wisely bought him for a reported sum of $500. Mr. Smith concluded that it would be cheaper to pay this much for the horse and keep him in the barn, than to have Henry suddenly change his mind and run *Fred Henry* on "three legs." As it turned out, the day was a great success for Mr. Smith, who "enjoyed such betting luck on the other races he was $100 to the good, besides being the owner of a thoroughbred."

FAVOURED *Harry Cooper* was ridden by Charles O'Leary instead of his father, Dick O'Leary.

There is some doubt about whether *Fred Henry* was even a thoroughbred of traceable pedigree. He was out of *Cheltenham Maid*, a mare that was never registered in official stud books of the period and that probably was a half-bred. Until the day he was unceremoniously acquired "to save a bet," *Fred Henry* was owned by William Henry of Cheltenham, a tiny village north of Georgetown, Ontario. Henry had bred the colt and entered him in the 1883 Plate as a fresh, eager four-year-old. But *Fred Henry* was scratched as being "too green." The following year he was a distant eighth to *Williams*. At the age of six he was beaten a length by *Willie W.* and in 1886 the filly *Wild Rose* squeezed past him—at the wire by a neck. Between Plate appointments, *Fred Henry* avoided encounters that might spoil his maiden status and eligibility; so he was stronger than ever in 1887, losing the race by only a head to *Bonnie Duke*.

In *The Queen's Plate,* by author Trent Frayne, it was stated that *Fred Henry* was owned by William Hendrie, president of the Ontario Jockey Club. *The Hendries and the Plate,* an

1888 QUEEN'S PLATE STAKES

SECOND RACE
Woodbine Park
MAY 24, 1888

THE QUEEN'S PLATE. 50 Guineas. For horses owned, bred, raised and trained in the Province of Ontario. Added to a conditional sweepstake, payable $5 at the time of entry (Jan. 1, 1888) and an additional $5 unless declared out on or before May 1, 1888; entries can be made between January 1 and May 1, on which day the stake finally closes, by the payment of $20 p.p. Distance about one mile and one quarter. To start from the head of the straight run in. The club will give $50 to the second horse and $25 to the third. Plate and stakes to winner. Nineteen nominations. Value to winner $487.

Horse	A	Wt.	Fin	Jockey	Owner	Betting
HARRY COOPER	4	118	1³	C O'Leary	J D Matheson	Out
EVANGELINE	4	113	2ⁿᵏ	A E Gates	Waverly Stable	12-5
CAST OFF	5	117	3	C Butler	J O'Rourke	20-5
BLACKBIRD	3	97	4	Coleman	Orkney Stable	75-5
GENESTA	5	117	5	Bowman	W T Bulmer	15-5
BONNIE BOY	5	122	6	Steeds	Col J Peters	100-5
BESSIE	7	117	7	Crowther	E A Brinkman	75-5

Start bad. Time: 2:18¼. Track fast.

Winner: Four-year-old bay colt by Long Taw—Maumee, by Revolver. Trained by Richard O'Leary. Bred by John Forbes, Woodstock.

BESSIE was left at the post as her rider was caught napping and she was never in contention. HARRY COOPER jumped out in front but allowed the speedy BLACKBIRD and EVANGELINE to take the lead going past the grandstand. BLACKBIRD continued to lead in the backstretch with the winner and EVANGELINE running together in second place. Rounding the turn young O'Leary on HARRY COOPER moved up quickly and in a twinkling he had cut down the leaders and was alone on the outside. BLACKBIRD fell back while EVANGELINE held second, three lengths back of HARRY COOPER. CAST OFF came up to get third.

Scratched—Fred Henry, Long Shot, Wild Bruce, Edmonton, D.W.C., Longspin, Vicino, Princess B., and Baffle.

Ontario = Jockey = Club.

WOODBINE PARK TORONTO.

* * * * * * *

MAY MEETING, 1888.

* * * * * *

President.
WM. HENDRIE, Hamilton.

Vice-Presidents.
HON. F. SMITH, T. C. PATTESON, Toronto.

Executive Committee.
G. W. TORRANCE, Chairman, A. SMITH,
HARTON WALKER.

L. OGDEN, Sec-Treasurer.
Box 447, Toronto, P. O.

HARRY COOPER | 4-year-old bay colt

Harry Cooper (1884)			
	*Long Taw	Longfellow	*Leamington
			Nantura
		Slipper	Planet
			Young Elssler
	Maumee	Revolver	Revenue
			Balloon
		Emily Peyton	Lexington
			Sally Roper

Owner: J.D. Matheson, Toronto; *Trainer:* Richard (Dick) O'Leary
Jockey: Charles O'Leary; *Breeder:* John Forbes, Woodstock

article by Michael Palethorpe, also emphatically claims that *Fred Henry* was Hendrie's horse. Thorough research of the 1883–1889 period reveals no connection between the horse and Hendrie. Hendrie and Henry often ran horses on the same program, and although Toronto newspapers frequently were guilty of misspelling horses and owners' names, there never was any suggestion that the two men were the same person. The only link between Hendrie and *Fred Henry* was that the colt was sired by a Hendrie-owned stallion, *War Cry.*

As for *Harry Cooper,* he was bred by John Forbes, the Woodstock bookmaker, and was named after a friend in Toronto. J.D. Matheson, a druggist, purchased the colt as a two-year-old. It was the third Plate winner that Forbes had bred. Trained by Richard (Dick) O'Leary, the cagey veteran of numerous Plate triumphs in the past, *Harry Cooper* was such a "sure thing" that the trainer put his young son Charley in the irons. The Plate was watched by an estimated crowd of eight thousand, the largest in Woodbine's history. It spilled out from the members' enclosure and grandstand, forcing officials to usher the overflow into the grassy inner course, which "became black as there were so many people milling about." *The Globe,* in a vehement attack, did not attribute the day's success to the Ontario Jockey Club: "It was not the Club's picayune advertising that brought the people, but the free notices of the press for the past six months, and in return the reporters who attended had to hustle for themselves. No quarters were reserved where they might do their work, and they were met at every step in obtaining information by all sorts of stupid regulations, which seemed to have no object but to cause confusion."

A HORSE-DRAWN STREETCAR PLODS ALONG FRONT STREET PAST THE QUEEN'S HOTEL, THE SITE OF TODAY'S FAIRMONT ROYAL YORK HOTEL.

By 1889, the year *Colonist* galloped home the length of the stretch in front of *Fred Henry,* the Queen's Plate had survived three decades. It was beginning to flourish and had become "the spectator sport" of late nineteenth-century Canada. Lest you forget, Lord Stanley and the Earl of Grey had yet to award their battered champagne buckets, and baseball was barely out of the Stone Age. Estimates of the 24 May holiday crowd at Woodbine in 1889 were as high as twenty thousand.

At the age of thirty the Plate was in a transitional period. A glance at the chart of the Plate and the results of the accompanying five races on the program was all anybody would need today to realize a hiatus was in the offing. The black jackets with yellow sashes of Joseph Emm Seagram, a distiller from Waterloo, appeared for the first time in Plate history. Two of his fillies, *Bonnie Ino* and *Vicino,* sisters to a future Seagram winner of the fifty "guineas," finished second and fifth respectively.

More familiar colours on the card were the brown jackets and yellow sleeves of OJC president William Hendrie. Horses from the Seagram, Hendrie and John Dyment stables dominated the two-day meeting, winning almost every contest, except for the prize that carried the greatest prestige, the Queen's Plate. The royal gift and purse, valued at $322.50, went to the former innkeeper, who was now proprietor, groundskeeper and "chief janitor" of Woodbine, Joseph (The Deacon) Duggan, and his partner, pharmacist J.D. Matheson, commonly known as "The Chemist."

Matheson, who had won the Plate in 1888, and Duggan acquired *Colonist* two months before the race for a paltry $400. The crowd lustily approved when Duggan proudly led the three-year-old bay gelding back to the scales "with as much pride as the Duke of Portland displays in leading back *Donovan* after winning $50,000,"

Ontario - Jockey - Club.

◁WOODBINE PARK. TORONTO▷

May Meeting, 1889

President :
WM. HENDRIE, HAMILTON.

Vice-Presidents :
HON. F. SMITH, T. C. PATTESON, TORONTO.

Executive Committee :
G. W. TORRANCE, Chairman, A. SMITH,
J. H. MEAD.
L. OGDEN, Secretary-Treasurer,
Box 447, TORONTO P.O.

RULES AND WEIGHTS.
Those of the American Jockey Club.

No objection, *after* a race, entertained till complainant lodges $5 with the Clerk of the Course, which will be forfeited if Executive Committee declare the objection to be frivolous or unfounded.

OWNERS ARE WARNED

That the strict letter of the Rule will be enforced in the case of all Jockeys whose colors are not declared to the Secretary in time for the day's Card, or whose colors differ from those announced.

Where foreign breds are not penalized, 5 lbs. allowed to Dominion breds.

Geldings allowed nothing.   Mares 5 lbs.

N.B.—The Committee reserve the right to change any Steeplechase into a Hurdle Race if the condition of the course renders that step necessary.

MAY WEIGHTS.

DISTANCE.	3 YRS.	4 YRS.	5 YRS.	6 & AGED.
¾ Mile	110	122	124	124
1 "	106	122	126	126
1½ "	104	122	127	128
2 "	102	122	128	129
2½ "	101	122	129	130

In races of intermediate lengths, the weights for the shorter distance are to be carried.

In races exclusively for 3 year old's, the weight is 122 lbs.

as *The Empire* reported. "The Chemist" was more retiring, *The World* wrote, and did not show himself before the stand until Duggan had made his way to receive the certificate for the Queen's Guineas from Miss Marjorie Campbell of Government House.

While acknowledging that *Colonist's* victory "exceeded in popularity anything that has ever been known in the history of the event," *The Empire* bemoaned the fact that "many people would have welcomed better luck to the Hendrie colours," and "would have rejoiced to see one of Mr. Seagram's horses carry off the blue ribbon." The newspaper criticized Hendrie's trainer, Mr. Alcock: "He does not take much stock in the Toronto meeting, and is disinclined to hurry the animals in his charge." In their view, he seemed more interested in preparing his horses for the American tracks because "two or three of those who appeared were palpably short of work, and were beaten." Alcock's services would shortly be terminated.

This Plate day belonged to *Colonist* and Dick O'Leary, who was reported to be the oldest jockey riding in America. According to *The World:* "He's in the neighbourhood of fifty five and as to his skill in the saddle, though probably not what it was a few years ago, he's still an excellent judge of pace. As a trainer, however, it is an undeniable fact that he has no equal in Canada." O'Leary was inducted into the Hall of Fame in the Legends category in 2000.

O'Leary was a Port Credit "boy" who had often skipped classes so that he could hang around the horses at the old Carleton course in The Junction. At fourteen or fifteen he ran away from home and was smuggled across the border to ride in the States. The 1889 race was O'Leary's fifth Plate win as either a jockey or trainer (and sometimes as both), but it was also his swan song. It was *Fred Henry's* farewell to Plate battles as well. Incredibly, he was now a non-

DICK O'LEARY HAD FLAMING RED HAIR AND DRESSED IN THE FANCIEST OF GARB.

COLONIST | 3-year-old brown gelding

Colonist (1886)
- Caligula
  - Enquirer
    - *Leamington
    - Lida
  - Clarina
    - *Australian
    - Flora G.
- Vanquish
  - Judge Curtis
    - Lexington
    - Lilla
  - Vanetta
    - Vandal
    - Dam by Boston

Owner: Joseph Duggan and J.D. Matheson, Toronto
Trainer: Richard (Dick) O'Leary; *Jockey:* Richard (Dick) O'Leary
Breeder: Thomas D. Hodgens, London

Plate winner *Blue Light.*

The winner, *Colonist,* who had been established as a heavy favourite by the "pencillers with their air-tight books and short odds," was the offspring of a mare whose previous two foals had been sired by the "coach horse." He had been raised by James Brady, a Glanworth farmer, and was bred by Thomas Hodgens, a former mayor of London and a man who would win the Plate the following year with another horse he had bred, called *Kitestring.* Interestingly, *Colonist* tried to win the Breeders' Stakes on Plate day, but was beaten a length by a Seagram filly who was carrying ten pounds less. The following day both Seagram and Hendrie horses beat *Colonist* in the Dominion Handicap.

The era of the sporting farmer and the small owner and breeder successfully competing for the Plate would forever be a losing struggle. The race's regulations were initially framed to give him a chance to challenge the big studs and stables, but the affluent establishments had already begun to assume control, and in two years they would dominate the Plate, winning it all but once during a twenty-year span. The black and yellow silks of Seagram would reign, along with those of William Hendrie and Nathaniel Dyment.

winner at the age of ten, creaking, tender and a trifle unsound in his joints. Charlie Wise, another veteran, was aboard but he could do little to prevent old *Fred* finishing last for his new owner, N.G.L. Marshall, the father of future OJC president K.R. Marshall, and owner of 1961

J.D. MATHESON, "THE DRUGGIST," OWNED A PHARMACY ON TORONTO'S KING STREET WEST.

1889 QUEEN'S PLATE STAKES

SECOND RACE
Woodbine Park
MAY 24, 1889

THE QUEEN'S PLATE. 50 Guineas. Added to a conditional sweepstake of $5 each at time of entry (Feb. 1, 1889) and an additional $5 unless declared out on or before (May 1). Entries can be made February 1 and May 1, on which day the stake finally closes by payment of $20 p.p. For all aged maidens, owned, bred and raised and trained in the Province of Ontario. Plate and stakes to winner. The club to give $75 to second horse and $50 to third.

Distance 1¼ miles. Value to winner $322.50.

Horse	A	Wt.	Fin	Jockey	Owner	Betting
COLONIST	3	106	1³	R O'Leary	J Duggan & J D Matheson	7-5
BONNIE INO	3	101	2¹	Coleman	J E Seagram	8-5
LONG SHOT	6	126	3hd	E Whyte	William Hendrie	3-1
EVANGELINE	5	121	4	A Gates	A E Gates	4-1
VICINO	4	117	5	Bowman	J E Seagram	6-1
CAST OFF	6	121	6	McIsaac	G A Forbes	4-1
AUNT ALICE	9	121	7	Jackson	Orkney Stable	8-1
FANNY CARTER	6	121	8	Hueston	R Wilson	15-1
AIDE-DE-CAMP	4	122	9	Brown	Col Milligan	20-1
FRED HENRY	10	126	10	C Wise	N G L Marshall	8-1

Start good. Track fast. Time: 2:16.
Winner: Three-year-old brown gelding by Caligula—Vanquish, by Judge Curtis. Bred by T. D. Hodgens, London. Trained by Richard O'Leary.

FANNY CARTER, VICINO and the aging FRED HENRY were the first to show. Past the grandstand for the first time BONNIE INO and LONG SHOT were close to the leaders. There was little change until the half-mile pole when COLONIST suddenly surged into third place behind the Seagram pair, BONNIE INO and VICINO. COLONIST duelled with BONNIE INO at the top of the stretch before the veteran jockey Dick O'Leary cut loose and came home the easiest type of winner by three lengths.

GOVERNOR GENERAL LORD STANLEY OF PRESTON.

LONDON MAYOR AND OIL PIONEER THOMAS HODGENS OWNED AND BRED FILLY *KITESTRING*.

Thomas Daniel Hodgens is regrettably one of the most neglected heroes in Queen's Plate history. He certainly deserves far greater recognition than the few, sparse facts that have been preserved in London, the city he served as a mayor, and which he represented in the Legislative Assembly. An Irish immigrant from Stadbally, Queen's County, Hodgens was also a livestock breeder and an oil merchant, who helped establish the Imperial Oil Company. However, it was a "gentleman's act" which earned him the fragment of distinction for which he is most remembered.

Hodgens' name appears on the distinguished scroll of Plate winners in 1890 because he honoured a widow's request and returned the twenty-five-dollar deposit her late husband had put up to bind the sale of *Kitestring* as a yearling. Accepting the Queen's fifty "guineas" was a memorable occasion for *Kitestring*'s owner: "A happier man than Mr. Hodgens was probably not to be found on the [Woodbine] course when he accepted the 'hearty congratulations' from the chief executive of the Dominion, Lord Stanley of Preston, the Earl of Derby." Four years later the Governor General would present a cup for hockey competition—the Stanley Cup.

Until Hodgens' death in 1899 at the age of sixty-two, nobody in Middlesex County bred better sheep, cattle or thoroughbreds. His horses won almost every major prize, including the first running of the Woodstock Cup in 1885, the second oldest horse race in Canada, the important Breeders' Stakes and two Queen's Plates. In some cases, however, they ran for other owners since Hodgens ran only horses he was unable to dispose of as yearlings or two-year-olds.

Breeding winners, rather than racing them, was Hodgens' hobby and he did it with a small band of broodmares. Among the first he acquired was *Tolima*, a Kentucky-bred mare by the imported English sire *Glen Athol*. She was bred to *Judge Curtis* from nearby Oxford County, and produced *Curtolima*, first winner of the Woodstock Stakes (now the Woodstock Cup). The following year Hodgens bred another good horse, *Colonist*, which won the Plate in 1889 under the colours of Joe Duggan and J.D. Matheson of Toronto. He sold them the Plate champion for four hundred dollars just two months before the race. Adhering to his policy of selling his young runners, Hodgens also attempted to rid himself of all stock that was eligible for the 1890 Plate. He did sell *La*

Blanche, an odds-on favourite who ran a disappointing second for owner Allie Gates, seeking his fourth Plate win.

Hodgens also made a deal to sell *Curtolima*'s first foal, a striking black filly named *Kitestring,* to trainer W.E. (Billy) Owen of Toronto for $300, accepting a downpayment of just $25. This left him with only one Plate candidate, *Countess,* a half-sister to *Curtolima,* who broke down while in training. However,

JUDGE A.S. POST (WITH BINOCULARS) AND T.C. PATTESON VIEW RUNNING OF PLATE RACE.

when the widow Mrs. Owen returned *Kitestring,* Hodgens suddenly had himself a Plate contender. The three-year-old was widely touted and received heavy support from bettors outside Toronto, despite the fact that she was unraced. Bookies rated her and *Rose Maybud* at 8-to-5 behind the favoured *La Blanche,* who, it was rumoured, reserved her serious training for "midnight workouts."

Despite a one-day postponement of the season and the Plate, a decision that was bitterly opposed by William Hendrie, president of the Ontario Jockey Club, a crowd of twelve thousand packed Woodbine Park on a cool, overcast and showery Saturday afternoon. The delay was caused by muddy track conditions and a steady downpour. Hendrie was the only member of the six-man executive committee to vote against postponement and was lauded by newspapers for his stand. Horsemen and spectators arrived at the track to find the doors closed. A day later only seven of the thirteen entries showed up for the Plate.

Before the field could get started, *Aide-de-Camp,* who was described as a "roguish brute," broke away and threw his rider, Charlie Butler. The jockey was knocked unconscious when his mount rolled over him, so a steeplechase rider, Jimmy Rowan, was summonsed to replace Butler. But Rowan was unable to control "the treacherous son *of Milesian,*" and never threatened the leaders. *Rose Maybud,* who was rumoured to be lame before the race, did make a challenge but she stumbled, suffering a broken hip, and had to be destroyed. Her jockey, Harvey (Dup) Douglas, was taken to hospital with a broken leg, but did receive some compensation when "the hat was passed around the paddock and about $130 was collected." The filly's owner, George Forbes, a bookmaker and brother of the celebrated Woodstock

KITESTRING | 3-year-old black filly

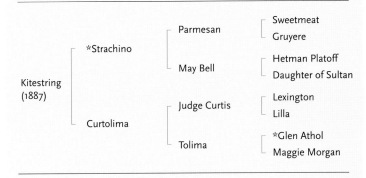

Kitestring (1887)	*Strachino	Parmesan	Sweetmeat
			Gruyere
		May Bell	Hetman Platoff
			Daughter of Sultan
	Curtolima	Judge Curtis	Lexington
			Lilla
		Tolima	*Glen Athol
			Maggie Morgan

Owner: Thomas D. Hodgens, London; *Trainer:* Daniel Curtain
Jockey: Fred Coleman; *Breeder:* T.D. Hodgens

AT THE WOODBINE.

LADIES INDULGED IN FIFTY CENT "HAT POOLS" IN AN ATTEMPT TO PICK A WINNER.

horseman John Forbes, was a victim of the mishap since he had *Rose Maybud* sold to a guest at the track, a Philadelphia millionaire.

1890 QUEEN'S PLATE STAKES

SECOND RACE
Woodbine Park
MAY 23, 1890

THE QUEEN'S PLATE. 50 Guineas. For all ages, for horses owned, bred, raised and trained in the Province of Ontario, that have never won public money, added to a conditional sweepstake, payable $5 at the time of entry, February 1, 1890, and an additional $5 unless declared out on or before May 1, 1890. Entries can be made between February 1 and May 1, on which day the stake finally closes, by payment of $20 p.p. The club will give $75 to the second horse and $25 to the third; plate and stakes to winner. About one mile and a quarter. Value to winner $327.

Horse	A	Wt.		Fin	Jockey	Owner	Betting
KITESTRING	3	105		1²	Coleman	T D Hodgens	8-5
LA BLANCHE	4	117		2²	A E Gates	A E Gates	3-5
FLIP FLAP	4	117		3	Gorman	Orkney Stable	8-1
DOM PEDRO	4	122		4	Harkley	John R Martin	12-1
AIDE-DE-CAMP	5	126		5	Rowan	Col Milligan	12-1
JOHNNY HUNTER	aged	131		6	Reardon	G Kennedy	20-1
ROSE MAYBUD	4	117	Broke down		H Douglas	H S Douglas	9-5

Start good. Time: 2:22. Track heavy.

Winner: Three-year-old black filly by *Strachino—Curtolima, by Judge Curtis. Owned and bred by T. D. Hodgens, London. Trained by Daniel Curtin.**

There was considerable delay at the post as AIDE-DE-CAMP was fractious and broke away, dropping in front of the stand and knocking jockey Charles Butler unconscious. Rowan, a steeplechase jockey, replaced Butler. ROSE MAYBUD, one of the early favorites, broke well but collapsed, landing on jockey Douglas, who suffered a broken leg. The mare died shortly afterwards. In the early running it was LA BLANCHE on top followed by KITESTRING and FLIP FLAP. The two pursued LA BLANCHE and in the backstretch KITESTRING took the lead and surrendered it briefly to FLIP FLAP. Coming into the stretch KITESTRING was in command but didn't edge away until the field straightened out. FLIP FLAP backed off the pace to finish third behind LA BLANCHE.

The Seagram Years: From *Victorious* to *Sally Fuller*— Iron Men Replace Pencillers, Continuity Threatened

He had a good sense of humour. Was gruff at times. I can recall the family Sunday dinners at his house in Waterloo when you would hear business, politics, local affairs, horses and the family discussed. What a pity things move so fast today that we do not seem to have the time for these family gatherings.

JOSEPH EDWARD FROWDE SEAGRAM, 1976

The man who revolutionized horse racing and breeding in Canada in the 1890s, winning eight successive Queen's Plates and fifteen before his death in 1919, was the son of Octavius Augustus Seagram and Amelia Stiles, both of whom came to Canada from Bratton, Wiltshire, England, in 1837; they were married at Fisher's Mills near the town of Galt. On 15 April 1841 the Seagrams celebrated the birth of their first son, Joseph Emm Seagram. His father gave him the middle name Emm in honour of the Emms, family friends from Wiltshire.

By the time he was twelve, Joseph and his brother Edward were orphans and were raised at Dr. Tassie's Boarding School in Galt.

Joseph later attended business college in Buffalo, New York, before trying his hand as a civil engineer and later running a tannery and mill in Stratford. Distilleries were subsidiaries of mills in those days, and it was not long before he was managing William Hespeler's Granite Mills and Distillery in Waterloo. Seagram, who married Stephanie Urbs, a niece of Hespeler, later bought out the part-owners of the distillery, George Randall and Mr. Roos, and in 1883 became sole proprietor of Joseph E. Seagram Distillers.

As a business entrepreneur, racing administrator, community leader and politician, Seagram was a powerful Canadian, but his greatest influence, perhaps because it was his fondest love, was as a breeder and proprietor of thoroughbred racehorses. His life is a definite study of success, and his stranglehold on Canada's most glamorous turf event was but one chord in his orchestration of achievements on the Canadian, indeed North American, turf. His steeds garnered every coveted prize offered in Canada and his stables regularly invaded the major courses of the United States with notable success. When his stable went to Saratoga Springs, New York, each

JOSEPH E. SEAGRAM

Year	Horse		Place
1889	Bonnie Ino		2nd
	Vicino		5th
1891	*Victorious*		**1st**
1892	*O'Donohue*		**1st**
	Martello		7th
1893	Martello		1st
	Athalo		2nd
1894	*Joe Miller*		**1st**
	Vicar of Wakefield		2nd
1895	*Bonniefield*		**1st**
	Millbrook		2nd
	Vicar of Wakefield		4th
	Confectioner		5th
1896	*Millbrook*		**1st**
	Springal		2nd
	Moorland		4th
1897	*Ferdinand*		**1st**
	Bon Ino		2nd
	Dalmoor		4th
1898	*Bon Ino*		**1st**
	Dalmoor		2nd
	The Tar		4th
1899	Dalmoor		2nd
	Curfew Bell		4th
	Terralta		5th
	Sardonyx		8th
1900	*Dalmoor*		**1st**
	Ottoman		11th
1901	*John Ruskin*		**1st**
	Oneiros		11th
	Juvencus		15th
1902	Fly-in-Amber		2nd
	Eastern Prince		**8th**
	Oneiros		10th
1903	War Medal		6th
	Perfect Dream		10th
	Fly-in-Amber	(Broke down)	15th
1904	Con Amore		6th
	Virtuoso		13th
1905	*Inferno*		**1st**
	Half Seas Over		**3rd**
1906	*Slaughter*		**1st**
	Haruko		**3rd**
1907	*Half a Crown*		**2nd**
	Sea Wall		**13th**
	Supper Dance		**15th**
1908	*Seismic*		**1st**
	Half a Crown		**3rd**
	Dog of War		**7th**

Year	Horse	Place
1909	Tollendal	2nd
	Courtier	5th
	Dog of War	6th
1910	Jane Shore	3rd
	Tollendal	7th
1911	Jane Shore	3rd
	Havrock	4th
1912	Rustling	3rd
	Havrock	7th
1913	Maid of Frome	2nd
	Voivode	4th
1914	Dark Rosaleen	2nd
	Sea Lord	3rd
	Froissart	7th
1915	Charon	8th
	Vastatio	10th
	Smithfield	12th
1916	*Mandarin*	**1st**
	Gala Water	2nd
	Gala Day	3rd
1917	*Belle Mahone*	**1st**
	Gala Dress	3rd
	Galley Head	5th
1918	Gold Galore	5th
	Sea Froth	8th
	Twelve Bells	9th
1919	Doleful	2nd
	Hong Kong	3rd
	Galway	8th

SEAGRAM STABLE

Year	Horse	Place
1920	Gallant Kitty	5th
	Crown of Gold	7th
1921	Crown of Gold	5th
1922	King's Court	9th
	Impersonator	10th
1923	*Flowerful*	**1st**
	Pelf	7th
	Floralia	12th
1924	Isoletta	4th
	Beau of the West	11th
1925	Duchess	2nd
	Goldlands	6th
	Tamarind	11th
1926	*Haplite*	**1st**
	Phanariot	6th
	Quartz-Sinter	10th
1927	Gems to let	3rd
	Gay Parisian	8th
	Quartzite	16th

Year	Horse	Place
1928	*Young Kitty*	**1st**
	Best Bonnet	4th
1929	Dance Circle	11th
	Circulet	14th
	Irish Sphere	15th
1930	Pandorus	9th
	Sphere of Beauty	12th
	Gilded Casino	18th
1931	Freethinker	8th
	Golader	9th
	Mythical Lore	10th
1932	King O'Connor	2nd
	Shady Well	4th
1933	*King O'Connor*	**1st**

EDWARD F. SEAGRAM

Year	Horse	Place
1934	Candy Feast	5th
1935	*Sally Fuller*	**1st**
	Gay Sympathy	3rd
1936	Samoan	5th
	Judge Pool	13th
1937	Poverty Struck	10th
	Gold Guard	11th

PHILIP SEAGRAM

Year	Horse	Place
1938	Tabhim	11th

J.E. FROWDE SEAGRAM

Year	Horse		Place
1939	Gold Fawn	(Broke down)	13th
1940	Silvos		6th
1941	Taffrail		4th
1945	Pattoy		14th
1946	Kanshore		7th
1947	Tregaron		9th
1948	Face Off		10th
1950	Roanite		13th
1952	Hielan Laddie		6th
	Flareday		19th
1953	Ballyray		11th
1954	Three Striper		8th
1955	Fair Shore		15th
1956	Lawday		7th
1959	Castleberry		14th
1968	Phelodie		4th
1970	Teddikus		7th
	King's Champion		13th

summer, the entourage included forty or fifty horses, two trainers, three jockeys, twenty grooms and exercise boys, and two cooks. The Seagram stable would set up its own personal dining hall and kitchen.

Seagram's interest in horses had developed while he was still a minor at boarding school before the first running of the Queen's Plate. Because he was a minor, and his affairs were in the hands of a guardian, his name did not appear on the transaction of the first horse he owned, in partnership with Francis Lowell of Galt, a leading horseman of the era. Entries were made in the name of Lowell, who owned both trotters and running horses. In the late 1880s the spark of his youth began to invade Seagram's pursuit of pleasure. He was fascinated by the components of a pedigree, intrigued by the physical mechanism of the racehorse and spurred by the prospect of success and pride in one's theories and systems being carried to the finish. In a space of ten years "Joe" developed the largest and the finest breeding and racing outfit in the first century of the Plate.

His racing silks soon became the most familiar in Canada, black with a yellow diagonal sash, representing his wife Stephanie's and his own favourite colours respectively. Seagram's first venture into the Plate came in 1889 when he ran an entry, *Bonnie Ino* and *Vicino*. A daughter of **Strachino*, *Bonnie Ino* finished second to *Colonist*, an auspicious debut but one that was the tip of the iceberg of what lay ahead. She later produced two Plate winners in matings to American-bred stallions, *Springfield* and *Marauder*, in *Bonniefield* (1895) and *Bon Ino* (1898). Seagram, however, was a firm believer in English bloodlines, and it was through the importation of mares carrying foals sired by English studs that he was able to create the dynasty at his breeding farms on Bridgeport Road in Waterloo. The catalyst was a bloodstock agent from Owen Sound, Edmund Haines, who purchased such mares as **Milley*, **Celandine*, **Counterscarp*, **Rusina* and **Lady Dalmeny*, dams of Seagram's early Plate winners.

Frowde Seagram, who later headed the distillery and maintained the stable and winning tradition as well as assuming a role in the operation of the Ontario Jockey Club as a trustee before his death in 1979, attested to his grandfather's interest in breeding: "I have all his stud books in which there are many notes that he wrote regarding certain horses and their lines. Physically, as I recall, he liked a good, straight hind leg, sloping shoulder, well sprung over the back, lots of lung power and good bone—a well-balanced horse."

Although born in Ontario, Seagram was a typical Englishman—reticent, insular and self-deprecating. He was a great supporter of The Jersey Act, a motion introduced in 1913 by Lord Jersey at a meeting of his fellow members of the English Jockey Club. It recommended that all future entries in the *General Stud Book* be confined to horses whose pedigrees could be traced without flaw to progenitors entered in previous volumes. The first edition of the *American Stud Book* had been published in 1868, not quite fifty years before the controversy broke out, thereby rendering most American-breds ineligible to the *English* or *General Stud Book*. Seagram advocated The Jersey Act, calling American-bred horses "half-breeds," and continued his importations of English stock. Ironically, both *Victorious*, Seagram's first Plate winner in 1891, and *Inferno* in 1905, undoubtedly the best horse bred by the Laird of Waterloo, were from American families. *Inferno* was by *Himyar*'s great son, *Havoc*, who sired four Plate winners between 1905 and 1916, while *Victorious* was out of *Bonnie Vic*, a dam of Kentucky bloodlines. When *Victorious* won in record time at Woodbine, he was entered by Seagram as simply the "Terror Colt." He earned himself a name that day as Governor General Lord Stanley suggested that Seagram name him "*Victorious*" during the Plate presentation of the scrip for fifty "guineas."

A diffident, reserved horseman, Seagram had a beard and moustache and looked very much like King Edward VII. His friends recognized his behaviour as a mask for his true camaraderie, generosity and loyalty. Sometimes embarrassed by a display of gratitude for one of his numerous philanthropies, he would put a gruff check to the eulogy and quickly change the conversation. Norman Seagram, another grandson, once described him as "a very warm person behind the stern exterior. As a boy I was very scared

of him. He always wore a tail coat and would pick a dandelion from the infield and wear it in his lapel. He thought it was lucky. A strange thing about him was that he seldom watched a race. He would turn his back and would say that a certain horse should be the leader by one or two lengths, or who was at the quarter pole as he visualized the race." Frowde recalled that when he died, he still had his own carriage horses stabled behind the house on Willow Street. "He never did own a car and in his later years I used to drive him to the office."

Seagram was a visionary. He once put away fourteen acres of land to be used for hospital purposes. Later the Kitchener–Waterloo Hospital was built on the site. He believed in free enterprise and liked competition. At one time the only railroad in Waterloo was the Grand Trunk Railway, and he wanted another line in Waterloo. They had trouble getting the line through as they did not have enough land, so he cut off the corner of the warehouse to make it possible. As his business grew, new buildings were painted differently so that he could easily see how it was expanding. Another Seagram tradition was the raising of the Union Jack whenever one of his horses won the Plate. It was a day for Waterloo and his employees to celebrate because it often meant that an addition would be built onto the distillery.

His string of successes, finishing one-two for an unrivaled six years in a row, never seemed to dull his enthusiasm as each Plate race approached. Although he was the first to congratulate William Hendrie, his chief rival in that period and a fellow merchant and president of the Ontario Jockey Club, he was upset when *Butter Scotch* beat *Dalmoor* in 1899. He described the filly as a "common mare," believing that *Dalmoor* was one of the best horses foaled at Waterloo. He condemned *Dalmoor* to perdition with a vivid and comprehensive stream of invective and castigation. The following year, at six, *Dalmoor* won.

Hendrie was the only owner to challenge Seagram until the early 1900s when Nathaniel Dyment, a wealthy lumberman from Barrie, split up the monopoly that the men from Hamilton and Waterloo held on the Plate. Hendrie, who developed the cartage business by the force of his own acumen, was a tall, broad-shouldered gentleman with a handsome face full of character and

one that responded with a sunny smile to any remark that pleased his fancy. He never bet on his horses, a trait of Seagram's too. To Hendrie, the pleasure of winning was satisfaction enough. Once, a young owner whose horse had just been beaten by Hendrie's, declared that he was prepared to run the race again and wager $1,000 he would defeat the Hendrie horse. "I hope I am a sportsman, not a gambler," he replied. Hendrie's racing successes could be traced to *Martimas*, a colt that had won the rich Futurity Stakes in New York, **Derwentwater*, an English sire that had stood in North West Canada (Alberta), and *Spark*, a mare that Seagram had disposed of when she was unable to produce in his breeding shed. **Derwentwater* sired *Butter Scotch*, and later when mated with *Spark*, produced *Lyddite*, first winner of the King's Plate in 1902. **Derwentwater* was also the sire of *Springwells*, dam of George M. Hendrie's 1918 Plate winner *Springside*. Meanwhile, *Martimas* sired 1909 Plate winner *Shimonese* (out of *Lyddite)* owned by Hendrie's sons, Colonel John S. Hendrie and George M. Hendrie, and *Kelvin*, a colt that Toronto's Ambrose Woods won the Plate with in 1907 after acquiring it as a yearling for ninety dollars at a dispersal sale of the Valley Farm Stable estate of the late William Hendrie.

Johnny Dyment was a charismatic figure, who developed three Plate winners in the 1903–1912 period. Nathaniel Dyment's grand-nephew, Johnny was an energetic, ruddy-faced sportsman who had once ridden in the Plate for his father. *Thessalon* and *Sapper* won in 1903–1904 for Nathaniel's Brookdale Stable; when he died, his sons, Albert and Simon, along with Johnny Dyment, took over. The year of *Heresy*'s triumph in 1912 was a tragic one for the Dyments: Johnny died after striking his head on the ice while skating on a pond behind the barns in Barrie. *Herendesy*, a son of *Heresy*, won for Brookdale in 1921.

Two other families took up the challenge of the Seagrams after the Dyments and Hendries faded as serious contenders—Harry Giddings Senior of Oakville and the Thorncliffe Stable of the Toronto suburb of Todmorden in the Don Valley. Trained by his son Harry Junior, three offspring of **Bassetlaw—St. Bass, Hearts of Oak* and *Beehive*—won before World War I and in 1920, *Panthea*, a daughter of **Bassetlaw*, produced a Plate winner in *St. Paul*. Robert Davies, one of Canada's most knowledgeable horsemen and founder of Thorncliffe Stud and Stock Farm in the hills of the Don Valley, possessed an unique role in Plate history. At age sixteen he rode in the controversial Plate of 1865 in London, finishing second on *Nora Criena* against *Lady Norfolk* in a run-off after the two earlier heat winners had been disqualified. He both owned and trained Plate winners in the 1870s and was rumoured to have ridden one of them in the actual Plate race. He had also been a director and vice-president of the OJC before resigning in 1904, following a dispute with fellow members over several matters, one being the relaxing of the rules of Plate eligibility. He wanted the race opened to horses foaled outside the province. After his death in 1916 his sons took over his stable and won the Plate in 1922 with *South Shore*, a sore-ankled mare who later foaled Plate winners *Shorelint* in 1929 and *Sally Fuller* in 1935. *Sally Fuller* was the sole property of Edward F. Seagram, Joe's oldest son, who had controlled the Seagram Stable operations after his dad's death. Before going out on his own, Edward and his brothers, Norman and Thomas, kept the yellow and gold silks flying with victories by *Flowerful, Haplite, Young Kitty* and *King O'Connor* (the last four-year-old to win the Plate). *Sally Fuller*'s win in

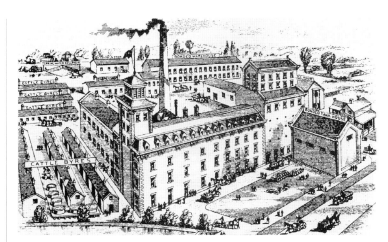

1935 was the twentieth and last for the men of Waterloo. The Depression was a fatal blow to the stable that for three years in the Roaring Twenties had led all stable earnings in North America. It was gradually reduced in numbers from the days when a hundred mares filled the barns in Waterloo. By the 1970s the famed Seagram silks had disappeared from the entries for the Plate.

The 1891–1935 period has always been acknowledged as the reign of the greatest dynasty of the Canadian turf. It also saw one of the most sweeping changes in laws affecting the operations of racing in Canada. The colourful strolling bookmakers with their chalkboards—the Knights of the Pencil—disappeared along with their betting booths from the tracks in 1911 and were replaced by betting machines; the pari-mutuel system of gambling was introduced with the arrival of the "iron machines." The system was hailed as "speculation without bookmakers." While the system was generally welcomed by fans, who had had to endure muscling matches to get close to the machines and then wait twenty or thirty minutes to cash a ticket, attendance at racetracks steadily increased as crowds soared above thirty thousand on holidays and on Plate day at Woodbine. Big profits meant one thing—governments wanted their share—and a never-ending tussle with provincial and federal authorities developed during the latter years of the war and the 1920s. It was government pressure that had chased away the legal bookies. It began levying a daily racing tax as well as taking a percentage of each dollar wagered. The big loser was the fan, who was getting less and less for his two-dollar bet whenever a new tax was introduced.

A side issue, but the most important as far as the continuity of the Plate was concerned, developed in the final years of World War I in Europe. Ottawa insisted that tracks should close to aid the war effort, and finally introduced legislation doing so in 1917. The ban was not lifted until the summer of 1919, six months after hostilities ceased. North America's oldest continuously run stakes race were "non-betting" events in 1918–1919 as the OJC defied the government and staged the Plate in conjunction with the Toronto Hunt Club's open air horse show, proceeds going to the Red Cross. These were the only sanctioned races for thoroughbreds in a two-year period. The reigning riders of this era were Harry Lewis, Frankie Mann, Johnny Wilson, James Butwell and Frank Robinson. Leading trainers were Seagrams' John R. Walker, Charles Boyle, Harry Blair, Barry Littlefield and William Bringloe; Ed Whyte, John Nixon, Fred Schelke, Johnny Dyment and Harry Giddings Junior. (All but Blair were later inducted into Canada's Hall of Fame.)

VICTORIOUS, THE "TERROR COLT," AND TRAINER JOHN R. WALKER.

oseph Emm Seagram's odyssey, which would lead him to an incredible total of sixteen Plate triumphs, was launched long before the appearance of the *"Terror Colt,"* his horse that returned to the barn on Plate day with the fifty guineas and a name. *Victorious*, a title graciously bestowed upon him by Lord Stanley, the Governor General.

Seagram was still in his teens and a recent graduate of Dr. Tassie's Boarding School for Boys in Galt when he first became the owner of a racehorse. However, because he was still a minor and his affairs were in the hands of a guardian, a Church of England clergyman, he was not anxious for it to be known that he had gone into partnership with Francis Lowell, the noted Galt horseman, who had been deprived of the Plate in 1876, the year the Plate was first run at Woodbine Park, when judges disqualified his mare, *Mary L.* So Seagram's name did not appear on the transaction and all entries for horse races were made in Lowell's name. Ironically, the first horse owned by Seagram was believed to have been a trotter, not a thoroughbred, a breed whose bloodlines and physical characteris-

tics he would later relentlessly pursue.

A small, ruled ledger book, synonymous of an era when inkwells and quill pens were the tools of a clerk, is the first tangible evidence of exactly when the distiller's unquenchable desire to influence horse racing began to take root at his two hundred–acre stud farm on Bridgeport Road in Waterloo. Detailed breeding reports, with corrections or results penciled in later, record many of the mares that Seagram owned, including the initial purchase of two mares in 1884 from John Forbes, the Woodstock bookmaker and breeder. One was *Maumee,* dam of the 1888 Plate winner *Harry Cooper.* Two of her three foals died, but the one that lived, *Helen Leigh,* captured the first running of the important Breeders' Stakes for Seagram in 1889.

The other mare was *Bonnie Vic,* who aged like good whisky and produced repeated dividends during the Seagram reign. One of them was *Victorious,* who contrary to newspaper headlines ("The *Terror Colt's* Plate," and "He Is *Victorious* Now, The *Terror Colt* Wins the Queen's Plate and a Name") was actually a gelding on Plate day. Huge crowds packed Woodbine. *The World* in its account, wrote:

FAMILY BOOK THAT CHRONICLED JOSEPH E. SEAGRAM'S STORIED CAREER.

VICTORIOUS | 3-year-old bay gelding

Owner: Joseph E. Seagram, Waterloo; *Trainer:* John Walker
Jockey: Michael Gorman; *Breeder:* J.E. Seagram

"Such a galaxy of handsome women in handsome costumes were never before seen on a Canadian racetrack and the sporting men from all over the country were on hand with plenty of money to back their favourites." *The Globe* applauded the win of the fifty-year-old Seagram, saying: "It was a very popular one indeed, for all followers of the Canadian turf like him and his pluck." *The World* went on: "After the race the popular distiller from Waterloo was presented to His Excellency, who handed him the certificate and cheque and asked him to name the winner 'Victorious.' Joseph was more than pleased to agree with Lord Stanley."

In running the fastest Plate in history (2:14 1/2 for a mile-and-a-quarter), *Victorious* was described as a big, long-striding, bay-brown gelding with a great turn of speed. "He's rather high on the leg, and has a shambling gait about him in his slow paces that would hardly recommend him to the connoisseur at the first glance. He has, however, the one needful quality—endurance—as have all the members of his family." *Victorious,* who afterwards met and defeated some of the best handicap horses on New York tracks, was endowed with tremendous stamina; he won the Plate, the Breeders' Stakes at a mile-and-an-eighth and the Dominion Day Handicap at a mile-and-a-quarter in the space of seven days for trainer John Walker and jockey Mike Gorman.

Although Seagram later enjoyed considerable success with mares he had imported in foal to English stallions, *Victorious* was of old Canadian lineage; his dam, *Bonnie Vic,* was a full-sister to two Plate winners, and his sire was John White's famous stallion *Terror.*

Besides its report on the race, *The Globe* carried a fanciful description of the various tiers of society to be seen at the track:

Above the viceregal apartment, with its elaborate carpeting and upholstered seats, was the second section, whose occupants were less inclined to indulge in betting than were visitors in other parts of the stand. Here there was little room for prom-

enading. In the third section was to be found the element which invariably produces sensation. Directly under this part of the stand was the saloon in connection with the track, which was recently granted a license. It is only just to observe that this new departure did not in the least lessen the carrying out of the OJC meeting with tranquility. Just east of here were stationed fourteen bookmakers, who were hemmed in by a crowd of men eager to expropriate their money. Although the bookmakers were more numerous than on previous years, it was learned that the majority of them had been successful. The dust in this portion of the grounds was very unpleasant and before the day was over those who visited the betting stands were in no condition to appear before His Excellency and the gay throng of beautiful women surrounding him.

Police in plain clothes expelled about twenty men who entered through a broken gate but were spotted as having no badges. In another gate incident, a ten-dollar U.S. bill was presented for a fifty-cent ticket. A keen-eyed ticket seller saw that instead of being signed by the president of the bank, it was signed "Who is he?" There was no police officer at hand or the man with the bill might have been asked the same question at the station.

1891 QUEEN'S PLATE STAKES

SECOND RACE
Woodbine Park
MAY 23, 1891

THE QUEEN'S PLATE. 50 Guineas. For all ages; for horses owned, bred, raised and trained in the Province of Ontario, that have never won public money. Added to a conditional sweep stake, payable $5 at the time of entry, February 1, and an additional $5 unless declared out on or before May 1. Entries can be made between February 1 and May 1, on which day the stake finally closes, by payment of $20 p.p. The club will give $75 to the second horse and $25 to the third. Plate, 50 guineas and stakes to the winner. Horses that have ever left Canada, or horses that have been more than one month out of this Province are ineligible. Twenty-five entries. Distance 1¼ miles. Value to winner $407.

Horse	A	Wt.	Fin	Jockey	Owner	Betting
VICTORIOUS	3	106	1²	M Gorman	J E Seagram	2-1
LA BLANCHE	5	121	2¹	A Gates	A E Gates	3-1
MYANNA	3	101	3	Myers	A E Gates	2-1
COUNTESS	4	117	4	Shauer	T D Hodgens	2-1
ELLA B.	3	105	5	Doane	E Burgess	3-1
PAPPOOSE	4	121	6	Lewis	G Pepper	6-1
GLADSTONE	3	106	7	J Dyment	Orkney Stable	12-1
VOLGA	3	101	8	Hueston	Orkney Stable	10-1
JIM BERRY	4	122	9	H Douglas	D Roche	5-1
DAISY DEANE	aged	121	10	Snider	Dr J A Watson	12-1
LADY BLAIR	4	117	11	Bowman	Oakville Stable	10-1
NELLIE	5	121	12	Hickson	J Pratt	12-1

Start good. Track fast. Time: 2:14½ (Plate record).
Winner: Three-year-old bay gelding by Terror—Bonnie Vic, by Vicksburg. Bred by J. E. Seagram. Trained by John R. Walker.
As expected JIM BERRY sprinted to the lead as the field passed the stand but as speedy as the leader was it was obvious the Terror horse could outsprint him as he took the lead early in the game in the lower turn. PAPPOOSE was also close with the leaders. JIM BERRY faded badly in the backstretch and the Terror horse, running under a pull, had the race won. MYANNA and LA BLANCHE took up the pursuit as well as COUNTESS but all they could do was to keep the Terror horse hustling. He won by a couple of lengths.

Joseph Seagram's formula for success was simple—purchase and import the best stock available. After a studious research of the thoroughbred, he acquired a deep respect for the founders of the breed, the English, and began the importation of true blue-bloods, particularly broodmares, to form the foundation of his stud in Waterloo. Good colts come only from good stock, and without good stock, the racing structure of a new country was bound to be weak. The venture was costly but rewarding, and it made Seagram a giant of the turf—a symbol of success throughout North America.

John F. Ryan, writing about the "Canadian Invader of the American Turf" in New York's *Morning Telegraph* in 1903, explained Seagram's theory, which had been put into effect before his first Queen's Plate triumph with *Victorious*:

> Seagram was ambitious to continue his success, and he went about doing so in a manner which was expensive and novel, and which gave him such a big start on the other owners that they never succeeded in defeating him for the coveted prize until eight years later. Securing a first-class buyer, he sent him to England with instructions to purchase mares in foal. The buyer was given a free hand, and he brought back the right kind of stock. Seagram's Platers arrived in utero. As they were foaled in the province they were eligible for the race, and as many of them would also have been eligible for the great classics of England, it can readily be seen that the out-and-out province breds had little chance against them.

In an article entitled *"The Seagram Reign,"* Robert McCarthy said the late J.E. Frowde Seagram recalled that his grandfather "was a firm believer that a good broodmare was seventy to seventy-five per cent of a good breeding establishment and that a good stallion was much easier to find."

The man Seagram chose to dispatch on a

JOSEPH EMM SEAGRAM, THE LAIRD OF WATERLOO.

shopping trip to England was Edmund H. Haines of Owen Sound. Haines obviously was an acute judge of horseflesh because he purchased *Milley*, who would foal three Plate winners (*O'Donohue, Joe Miller* and *Millbrook*) before dying tragically after giving birth to the third one; *Counterscarp*, dam of another Plate winner (*Martello*); *Clarionet* and *Objection*. He paid only $2,000 for the four horses, an incredible bargain when you consider that Seagram later sold *Objection* for $5,000 after winning several purses with him. But it was *Milley* who was the coup in Haines' acquisition.

Years later (in 1904), in a letter to T.C. Patteson, Seagram discussed his theory of breeding imported English mares to English stallions or to native stallions, saying that "*Milley* was the best mare I think I ever owned. I believe, had she been sent to a good imported English stallion, or any first class American stallion, would have thrown a stake horse." *Crom-a-boo*, the stallion Seagram chose to mate with *Milley* to produce *O'Donohue*, sired 1893 Plate

1892 QUEEN'S PLATE STAKES

SECOND RACE
Woodbine Park
MAY 24, 1892

THE QUEEN'S PLATE. 50 Guineas. The gift of Her Majesty; for all ages. Open to horses owned, bred, raised and trained in the Province of Ontario, that have never left Canada, and have never been for a period of more than one month out of the province; added to a sweepstakes of $5 each payable at time of entry, March 1, and $5 additional, unless declared out by May 1, between which days entries can be made on payment of $20 p.p.; the first horse to receive the guineas and stakes, and $100 added by the club; the second horse $100 and the third $50. Distance 1¼ miles. Value to winner $422.

Horse	A	Wt.	Fin	Jockey	Owner	Betting
O'DONOHUE	3	106	1²	F Horton	J E Seagram	2-1
QUEEN MARY	3	101	2¼	Hueston	Orkney Stable	3-1
HEATHER BLOOM	3	101	3	F Doane	William Hendrie	5-1
BARONET	5	126	4	Pope	Doane Brothers	20-1
GLADSTONE	4	122	5	O'Leary	M Gorman	6-1
DOM PEDRO	5	126	6	Steeds	J Harkley	15-1
MARTELLO	3	106	7	Sharrard	J E Seagram	10-1
BAY COURT	4	122	8	Regan	T D Hodgens	10-1
JAPONICA	3	101	9	Cook	A Finkle	8-1
THUNDER MAID	5	121	10	C Wise	J Harkley	10-1
BOB KING	3	101	11	Flint	M Gorman	20-1
FLY	5	121	12	Graham	E Phillips	30-1
HINDOO	3	106	13	Allison	C M Lang	50-1
ALBERT VICTOR	3	106	14	Bernard	T Brady	4-1
AIDE-DE-CAMP	7	126	15	Goff	Col Milligan	50-1
KING JOHN	3	106	16	Sinclair	Orkney Stable	6-1

Start good. Time: 2:22. Track slow.

Winner: Three-year-old black colt by Crom-a-boo—*Milley, by Struan. Bred by J. E. Seagram. Trained by John R. Walker.

After a short delay at the post, the field broke cleanly and the winner, O'DONOHUE, quickly went to the lead by two lengths over HEATHER BLOOM and QUEEN MARY. O'DONOHUE led throughout and was only challenged in the stretch by QUEEN MARY and HEATHER BLOOM. When jockey Horton went to the whip O'DONOHUE swerved in towards QUEEN MARY. But he straightened his colt out and won by two lengths with QUEEN MARY finishing a half-length in front of HEATHER BLOOM.

Scratched—Roseland, Longbend, Harry A., Flemish Beauty, Terrebonne, Charley D., Phlox, Lalita and Lightwood.

winner *Martello* out of *Counterscarp*.

In foal to *Crom-a-boo*, *Milley* dropped a big, rakish-looking black colt, who by the time he was a three-year-old stood over sixteen hands high. Seagram called him *O'Donohue*, naming him after his chief distiller, James O'Donohue, who was paraded about Woodbine on the shoulders of a troop of fans from Waterloo after the colt's electrifying triumph over fifteen Plate opponents. *O'Donohue*, who was rumoured to be painfully lame in the days before the race, allowed his pedigree to overcome the infirmities before an excited throng celebrating Queen Victoria's seventy-second birthday.

JOHN F. RYAN CHRONICLED SEAGRAM'S "FORMULA FOR SUCCESS."

"He is such a good racehorse," *The Globe* maintained, "that it seemed only a question of his ability to stand up to get the money. Some time ago one of his knees developed considerable soreness and fever, and trainer [John] Walker began to have fears of getting him to the post. Then two days ago the other knee was found to be affected, and it was thought then that for a certainty *O'Donohue* would not be a starter, but care and skill have done much. He had only two good legs yesterday, but he won at that, and Walker can take no little credit to himself for his work."

Bookmakers and their slates were in great evidence for the thirty-third running of the Plate. The Ontario Jockey Club enlarged the betting paddock, pushing the track further south towards Lake Ontario, and built a stand for the bookies, allowing twenty-two pencillers to establish the odds. However, *The Mail*'s correspondent was both praiseworthy and critical of one of the changes to the track, stating, "The officials of the OJC showed a great deal of wisdom in enlarging the betting paddock," but added, "The building, or shed, is so constructed that those in the boxes cannot see the track itself, not to speak of the races. The roof should be raised four or five feet, and there should also be a redistribution of the bookmakers' boxes, so that each may have an equal chance of handling the public money."

The Evening News was critical too: "The architect for the bookmakers' stand, if there was one, made a mistake. The roof is so low that a man as tall as King Coal Smith could not enter the place without smashing his high hat. The bookmakers from their stalls cannot even get a glimpse at the track, not to speak of seeing how the money goes."

The following day, before the second day of the meeting, *The Evening News* reported, "Prior to the opening, the bookmakers met and appointed a deputation to ask management to change the ring by placing the boxes opposite each other. The change was made immediately and is a great improvement. It is more convenient for the public as well as for the bookies."

O'DONOHUE | 3-year-old black colt

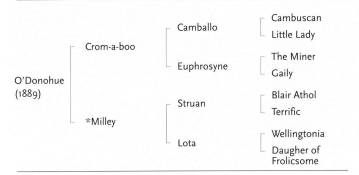

			Cambuscan
		Camballo	Little Lady
	Crom-a-boo		
			The Miner
		Euphrosyne	Gaily
O'Donohue (1889)			
			Blair Athol
		Struan	Terrific
	*Milley		
			Wellingtonia
		Lota	Daugher of Frolicsome

Owner: Joseph E. Seagram, Waterloo; *Trainer:* John Walker
Jockey: Mr. F. Horton; *Breeder:* J.E. Seagram

The same newspaper, in a gimmick to boost circulation, attempted to cash in on the public's growing interest in the Plate, offering twenty-five dollars to any reader who could select the first three finishers. "Each competitor can guess as often as he pleases so long as his choices are written on the blank printed below."

At its annual meeting that fall, the OJC requested vice-president T.C. Patteson to "enter into negotiations respecting the purchase of a pari-mutuels machine." Shareholders also approved the spending of "not more than $12,000" to erect a new iron grandstand.

MARTELLO LEADS STABLEMATE *ATHALO* ACROSS THE FINISH LINE AT WOODBINE.

Martello was Edward Frowde Seagram's "Plate horse" as far as his father was concerned, when he proudly stepped forward to accept the historic scrip for the fifty guineas from Sir George Kirkpatrick, Ontario's Lieutenant Governor. It was a significant occasion, the stands at Woodbine Park creaking and bending while a 24 May holiday crowd estimated at nineteen thousand loudly roared its approval of Joseph Seagram's feat of becoming the first owner to win the Queen's Plate three years in a row. The triumph meant that a little game, a family tradition, had also been maintained. A few years earlier, when his Waterloo stable was just beginning to monopolize racing, Seagram began the charming custom of giving each of his sons a Plate horse. In 1891 and the following year, *Victorious* and *O'Donohue* launched the Seagram reign by winning the Plate for Edward's younger teenage brothers, Joseph and Norman; Thomas, who was five, was "too young at the time."

Martello's win was considered remarkable by previously suspicious turf writers: he not only ran the fastest Plate ever (2:14), lowering *Victorious'* record by a half second, but he did it despite the fact that he was practically lame and had been a questionable starter on the morning of the race. Afterwards *The Empire* said: "That Lame Leg of *Martello*'s Was Game." However, his career was not nearly as bright as that of his nineteen-year-old owner, who eventually would take control of the Seagram stable after the death of his father in 1919. In observing Seagram's family custom, *The Empire* said: "All of his three sons have now won the Plate with

horses he had previously given them. Curiously enough his eldest son was the last to win the Plate, but his patience was rewarded. *Martello*'s future, however, is not rosy, as his habit of striking himself will mar his usefulness as a racer."

Before the race, stories persisted that *Martello* was lame and was "all but hors de combat." Although trainer John Walker had worked diligently to get rid of the lameness, placing a leather shield on the foreleg in workouts to prevent him from striking himself, horsemen suggested that the field was one of the weakest assembled for some years and if *Martello* started, "a cripple" could again win the Plate. After his record win, *The Empire* said: "The public may be inclined

1893 QUEEN'S PLATE STAKES

FOURTH RACE
Woodbine Park
MAY 24, 1893

THE QUEEN'S PLATE. 50 Guineas, the gift of Her Majesty. For all ages. Open to horses owned, bred, raised and trained in the Province of Ontario, that have never won public money, have never left Canada, and have never been for a period of more than one month out of this Province; added to a sweepstakes of $5 each, payable at time of entry, March 1, and $5 additional, unless declared out by May 1, between which days entries can be made on payment of $20 p.p. The first horse to receive the guineas and stakes, and $300 added by the club. The second horse $150 and the third $50. Distance 1¼ miles. Value to winner $830.

Horse	A	Wt.	Fin	Jockey	Owner	Odds $1
MARTELLO	4	119	1²	H Blaylock	J E Seagram	3-1
ATHALO	3	103	2³½	A Brooker	J E Seagram	2-1
HEATHER BLOOM	4	117	3¹	Doane	William Hendrie	5-2
LOU DALY	3	101	4	Boyle	T D Hodgens	7-1
ASPINELL	3	103	5	Mason	N Smillie	10-1
MEDIATOR	3	104	6	Sharrard	J Pascoe	30-1
KING JOE	3	106	7	Shields	J Dyment	4-1
SALTPETRE JR.	5	123	8	Smith	F Godson	60-1
MERCURY	4	119	9	Harrison	O M Arnoldi	20-1

Time: 2:14 (Plate record). Mutuels paid $8.25 (Seagram's Stable). Track good.

Winner: Four-year-old bay gelding by Crom-a-boo—*Counterscarp, by Rattle. Bred by J. E. Seagram. Trained by J. R. Walker.

The start was delayed as MERCURY ran nearly a mile before he was pulled up and returned to the gate. MERCURY broke away again, travelling a quarter-mile, and cooked his chances. The flag fell to a straggling start with ATHALO on the lead followed by MARTELLO and KING JOE. At the quarter KING JOE fell back and HEATHER BLOOM moved up to challenge the Seagram twosome. LOU DALY was a length back of HEATHER BLOOM. ATHALO continued to set the pace down the backstretch with MARTELLO a length back. Doane on HEATHER BLOOM made a futile attempt to overtake the leaders at this point while the rest of the field was stretched out an eighth of a mile. At the mile it was still ATHALO on top in 1:48 but entering the stretch MARTELLO came on and in a strong gallop finished two lengths in front of his stablemate.

Scratched—Gypsy, King Harry, Strathclip, Woodbine, Bonnie Buff, Coriander and Stattern gelding.

Joseph Seagram's oldest son, Edward, and his family in 1910, from left: Campbell, Elenor and Frowde.

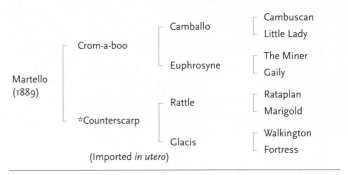

MARTELLO | 4-year-old bay gelding

			Camballo	Cambuscan
Martello (1889)	Crom-a-boo			Little Lady
			Euphrosyne	The Miner
				Gaily
	*Counterscarp		Rattle	Rataplan
				Marigold
			Glacis	Walkington
	(Imported *in utero*)			Fortress

Owner: Joseph E. Seagram, Waterloo; *Trainer:* John Walker
Jockey: Harry Blaylock; *Breeder:* J.E. Seagram

The winner, imported *in utero* from England, was described in *The Mail* as "the alleged counterfeit." *The World* whined: "*Athalo* was by all odds a better horse than *Martello*. But because he ran second nobody noticed him. He only ran second to let *Martello* win. He could beat *Martello* by two seconds. Probably Joseph of Waterloo will keep him on ice until next year."

Trailing the Seagram entry was William Hendrie's *Heather Bloom*. The Ontario Jockey Club president would encounter many more frustrating defeats before finally upsetting the Waterloo stable in 1899. A prophetic note in *The World* added: "The Gods have given everything to William Hendrie but a Queen's Plate. But they'll give it to him yet."

Another matter, however, was distressing Hendrie. A stairway leading from the closed stand to the open stand collapsed shortly before the running of the Plate, when partially rotted planks gave way under the weight of the immense crowd. *The World* said that dozens of fans sank ten feet into an opening. Women fainted, a man suffered a broken leg and dozens luckily escaped with only bruises. *The Mail* dismissed the incident, saying: "It should be mentioned that there was a slight accident to one of the stands, but happily it was not of a serious nature as to mar the general effect of a deservedly popular holiday occasion." *The World*, the only paper to give any details of the accident, did manage to extract some humour: "When the eastern stand gave way a man had his wooden leg broken. He exclaimed, as he was extricated from the debris: 'Be jabers, I'll make the Jockey Club buy me a cork leg now.'"

The OJC, which had leased Woodbine in 1881 from Joseph Duggan and had been continually embroiled in disputes with The Deacon over "the terms of the contract," was immediately assailed by fans, and reluctantly paid $4,415.50 in out-of-court settlements and legal injury claims as well as the costs for repairs of the damage to the aging grandstand, built in 1875. However, the matter was not resolved until three years later when litigation against Duggan was dropped as he agreed to deduct $1,750 from the OJC's annual rent of the track.

to think that Mr. Seagram was playing possum, but such was not the case. For a week his leg has rested in the soak barrel, soaking until most of the lameness had been taken out of it."

Wagering was especially lively, as *The Mail* reported: "A system new to the majority at Woodbine was the 'Paris mutuels' [*sic*], operated by two local speculators, who were liberally patronized. So far as they are concerned, it matters not which horse wins; they simply take in all the money offered, and after the race divide it among those holding tickets on the winning horse, of course retaining a small commission for themselves. In this way the public makes its own odds." Most of the betting, however, was with the fifteen bookmakers, who refused to couple the Waterloo horses in the betting. They feared *Martello* might not start, leaving *Athalo* to carry the Seagram colours. But there was a wild plunge on *Athalo,* and betting, which had gone on for some time before Seagram declared he would "win with *Martello,*" was so strong that *Athalo* went to the post a 6-to-5 favourite; 2-to-1 could be obtained on *Martello.*

T.C. PATTESON (LEFT) AND WILLIAM HENDRIE FEUDED WHILE JOSEPH SEAGRAM (RIGHT) WON THE PLATE.

The major contest of 1894 did not occur on Woodbine's muddy oval, where another of Joseph Seagram's horses, *Joe Miller*, a spirited gelding with the stamina of a team of Clydesdales, slogged his way to win the Queen's Plate. Instead, it took place in the boardrooms of the Ontario Jockey Club, in court and in the newspapers. It was fought with such ferocity that it took months for peace to be restored. Indeed, no single dispute in the history of the Ontario Jockey Club has ever been as acrimonious as this quarrel.

It was largely a power struggle between Thomas C. Patteson, the autocratic, scholarly Englishman who helped found the Ontario Jockey Club in 1881 and so restored the integrity of horse racing in the province, and Scotsman William Hendrie, the railway and cartage magnate from Hamilton, who was one of the founding fathers of the Club and its long-time president. Both men were warm-tempered and had often clashed in the past. However, a series of incidents that spring prompted vice-president Patteson, along with executive committee chairman George Torrance and director J.H. Mead, to demand Hendrie's resignation. The coup failed because when "all the dirty linen had been washed," the trio were no longer on the board of directors; meanwhile Hendrie, who despite *The World*'s prediction that he would lose his office, was still firmly entrenched in the presidency.

On the surface, the event that triggered the ruckus was the reaction of the president and his sons (James W., manager of the stable, and William Junior) to the executive committee's decision to postpone the Plate for two days until 24 May. Hendrie protested vigorously about the delay, while James sent a telegram to OJC secretary Lyndhurst Ogden, threatening to send the stable's entry, *Lochinvar*, around the track on the originally scheduled date, and thus claim the Plate and stakes.

A majority of the executive decided that the track, which was partially submerged under water because of heavy rainstorms, was "too dangerous" for both horses and riders. There had been flooding throughout the city and racing had also been cancelled at other tracks. Matters worsened a day later when the Hendries travelled from Hamilton to inspect the course. A scuffle erupted in front of the judges' stand when young William, taking exception to remarks in *The Empire* concerning his father's position, attacked the newspaper's sports editor Stewart Houston. Later Hendrie senior and Patteson became embroiled in a heated discussion, which almost led to blows.

The World summarized the incident as follows: "Patteson, according to a witness, expressed the opinion that young Hendrie's assault on Mr. Houston was unprovoked and disgraceful. This was resented by Mr. Hendrie in words that led Mr. Patteson to threaten bodily harm to the president. Better counsels prevailed, and there the matter ended." In a letter to the Club's shareholders, Hendrie said he "was insulted in a most gross and uncalled for manner by Mr. Patteson, and it was only the intervention of Mr. Seagram, Mr. Torrance and Professor Smith that peace was restored." Hendrie was at least consistent in criticizing the postponement. The same committee, led by Patteson, delayed the opening of the 1890 season by a day despite Hendrie's opposition. On that occasion the Toronto press praised him.

At the heart of the dissension, besides the Patteson/Hendrie

1894 QUEEN'S PLATE STAKES

FOURTH RACE
Woodbine Park
MAY 24, 1894

THE QUEEN'S PLATE. 50 Guineas. The Gift of Her Majesty. For all ages. Open to horses owned, bred, raised and trained in the Province of Ontario that have never won public money, have never left Canada, and have never been for a period of more than one month out of this Province; added to a Sweepstakes of $5 each, payable at time of entry, 1st March, and $5 additional, unless declared out by 1st May, between which days entries can be made on payment of $20 p.p. The first horse to receive the guineas and stakes, and $500 added by the Club. The second horse $200, and the third $100. Distance 1¼ miles. Value to winner $785.

Horse	A	Wt.	St	¼	½	¾	Str	Fin	Jockey	Owner	Odds $1
JOE MILLER	3	103	2	2	1	1	1	1½	F Regan	J E Seagram	6-5
VICAR OF WAKEFIELD	3	106	1	1	2	2	2	2⁶	A Brooker	J E Seagram	6-5
LOU DALY	4	117	5	5	4	3	3	3	Doane	T D Hodgens	2-1
THORNCLIFFE	3	106	6	7	6	5	4	4	H Blaylock	R Davies	5-1
BEN HUR	4	122	7	8	7	6	7	5	Barnes	A G Alexander	10-1
LOCHINVAR	3	103	3	6	3	7	6	6	Flint	Wm Hendrie	5-1
DICTATOR	3	106	4	4	5	4	5	7	S White	Dr Lang	8-1
HARRY A.	5	126	11	11	11	8	8	8	H Douglas	H B Alley	30-1
ANNIE D.	6	121	9	10	10	11	9	9	Stewart	Brookdale Stable	30-1
MAY BLOSSOM	3	101	8	9	9	10	11	10	Smith	J Dyment	30-1
MERRYTHOUGHT	3	101	10	8	8	9	10	11	Harrison	J Duggan	20-1

Start good. Time: 2:28½. Seagram entry paid $7.10; straight, place $8.05. Track muddy.
Winner: Three-year-old brown gelding by Springfield—*Milley, by Struan. Bred by J. E. Seagram. Trained by John R. Walker.

BEN HUR caused a lot of trouble at the post but the flag fell to a perfect start. Brooker on VICAR OF WAKEFIELD set the pace. Going by the stand he was clear of JOE MILLER, on whom LOU DALY was lapped. LOCHINVAR was fourth with the others bunched. Around the turn JOE MILLER and LOU DALY moved up. At the half JOE MILLER went to the front as LOU DALY was unable to stand the pace and had to settle for third. JOE MILLER coasted home a half-length in front of his stablemate with LOU DALY third, six lengths back.

JOE MILLER WAS ONE OF SEAGRAM'S BEST PLATE WINNERS.

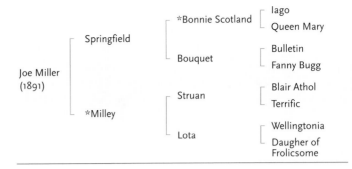

Owner: Joseph E. Seagram, Waterloo; *Trainer:* John Walker
Jockey: Frank Regan; *Breeder:* J.E. Seagram

rivalry, was a festering feud between Toronto and Hamilton interests—professional people versus merchants such as Hendrie and Seagram, non-horse-owning directors opposing officers who operated racing stables or other tracks, and the violation of a Club bylaw, which forbade shareholders from transferring stock and voting privileges to friends.

Patteson, Torrance and Mead wrote to Hendrie, requesting his resignation and denouncing his presidency. They declared that because he kept a racing stable "he should remain on the outside as does Mr. Seagram, another large owner of horses non-resident in Toronto," and that his sympathies lay on the side of Hamilton interests, which had to postpone the opening of its meet because the OJC's was delayed. "When the Club was the only one in Canada, the design of its early promoters was to make it Provincial in its character. Now there are several Jockey Clubs in the country, including one in Hamilton, and it is generally felt by Toronto people that *in future Toronto races will best be controlled by Toronto men.*" Patteson, who later claimed that Hendrie had very little to do with making the OJC the success it was, emphasized that he was responsible for "conferring the presidency upon him when I was urged to accept it myself, but I thought him a better figurehead." Patteson also prevented Hendrie from taking the chair at the OJC's annual meeting in June because Hendrie had been served with a court injunction, which forbade the transaction of any business until the validity of certain transfers of stock had been adjudicated upon. He disputed Hendrie's assertion that he had put some of his stock in the names of immediate family connections to "keep the Club out of the control of the trotting faction."

Hendrie informed shareholders that "persistent efforts were being made to mislead them and create a prejudice against him in the public's mind by charging him with intentions that exist only in the prolific imaginations of his detractors." He also denied that his residence made him "unfit to be president of the Club," and said he had done everything in his power to uphold its provincial charter. In October Hendrie was elected president after "eulogistic comments" by the Honourable Sir Frank Smith, an influential Cabinet minister and member of the Canadian senate who helped found the Canadian Pacific Railway, and Toronto lawyer William Mulock, who later was knighted and appointed Chief Justice of Ontario.

The annual meeting, a harmonious gathering that was "almost as colourless as a Sunday School teachers meeting," was not attended by "Patteson and his adherents." However, Hendrie's election did not calm the hostilities between the two men. In a statement to the press, Hendrie said: "The Patteson party are defeated, and they knew it a week ago, and I am perfectly sure had the victory been the other way they would have scorned any proposal for compromise. All through this unfortunate controversy they have shown me scant courtesy, and a taste of their own medicine may teach them a useful lesson for the future." Patteson, whose diligence was rewarded in 1883 when Buckingham Palace gave its approval of the Plate, thus elevating the race's importance and prestige, would never again enter the gates of Woodbine. Hendrie's thirteen-year presidency would temporarily end in 1896 when he was replaced by Sir Frank Smith, but he would regain the seat in 1901.

Patteson would retire to his Eastwood Stock Farm, the former home of Rear Admiral Henry Vansittart of the Royal Navy, who in 1834 helped found the village of Woodstock. Patteson raised Shropshire sheep, shorthorn cattle, saddle and carriage horses on his farm four miles east of Woodstock. However, his often caustic criticism of the sport of horse racing would continue in letters to the editor of the Toronto newspapers until his death in 1907. Patteson's immense contributions to racing, however, were recognized in 1976 when he was among the first group of builders inducted into the Canadian Horse Racing Hall of Fame. Also inducted that year were William Hendrie and Joseph Seagram.

As for *Joe Miller,* a three-year-old son of Seagram's imported mare **Milley* and a half-brother to *O'Donohue,* he went on to perform Herculean feats. The following day, 25 May, he finished second in the Breeders' Stakes, conceding seven pounds to Nancy Lee. Joe Miller then sped home the winner in the Stanley Produce Stakes on 26 May and won the Dominion Handicap three days later at Woodbine. Shipping to Hamilton, the gelding won the Prince of Wales Plate on 31 May and the Canadian Handicap the following day. In a space of nine days he won five races and was second in another. *Joe Miller* also set two track records on the turf at Sheepshead Bay, New York, for a mile-and-a-half and a mile-and-three-quarters that stood for several years. In 1900 the aging gelding was still successful. He won the Hunters Flat Race Handicap while carrying 170 pounds. Joe's son, E.F. Seagram, was in the saddle.

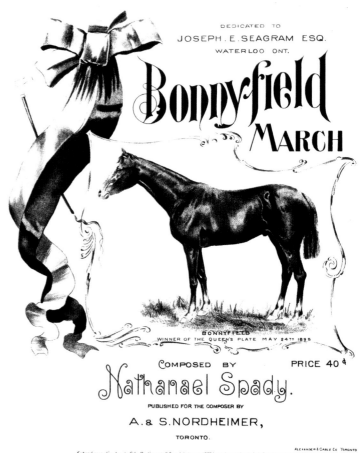

Legends persist that the Laird of Waterloo, Joseph E. Seagram, didn't mind sampling the fine whiskies he distilled, but he wasn't a betting man and rarely wagered on the horses carrying his black and yellow silks. Neither did William Hendrie, the ebullient president of the Ontario Jockey Club.

Although these two friendly rivals spent millions in building sumptuous studs and training centres, and importing high quality breeding stock so that they could compete against the top stables south of the border, they apparently abstained when the bookmakers began pencilling odds on their horses. An anecdote, however, surfaced following *Bonniefield*'s Queen's Plate victory, which suggests that the two sportsmen were not adverse to loosening their purse strings in a bankroll-to-bankroll contest. The yarn was told when the Waterloo stable continued its blitzkrieg by running a four-horse entry and finishing first and second for the third year in a row. *Bonniefield*'s win was especially rewarding for Seagram: it not only gave him the Plate for an unprecedented fifth consecutive year, but enabled him to collect a sizeable wager, almost ten times the value of the Plate purse and fifty guineas.

"IT TOOK FIVE YEARS"—but "Joe" Seagram in the end won his bet, reported Toronto's *Evening News*. The story, which the newspaper said "may or may not be true," recounted a bet "Joe" Seagram and President Hendrie had made in 1890, a year neither had a horse in the Plate:

> The two met and got arguing about the respective merits of their stables. 'Pshaw!' said Seagram, 'I'm going to carry off the Plate for the next five years.' 'Bet you ten thousand dollars to five thousand you don't,' retorted Hendrie. 'I'll go you,' said the man from Waterloo and the bet was made. By yesterday's victory Seagram gets the $10,000.

Seagram's hand was so strong in this Plate against the six horses that opposed him, including Hendrie's gallant *Lochinvar*, who finished third, that he reluctantly refused to declare who he would win with among his four starters. It was suspected that Seagram would have preferred a win by *Vicar of Wakefield*, a four-year-old maiden and second to *Joe Miller* the previous year. *The Globe* commented: "The way they've been training for [John] Walker he [Seagram] could not very well have separated them. He's said, in effect: 'There's the four. There is no difference among them that justifies me making a choice.'"

A jubilant crowd of ten thousand was almost as perplexed as the twenty-five bookmakers in the betting ring, about which of the Seagram horses would win. The majority fortunately plumped for *Bonniefield*, who went off as the even money favourite; two of the other three Waterloo horses, runner-up *Millbrook* and *Vicar of Wakefield*, a disappointing fourth, were second and third choices in the wagering. The throng, many of which sported badges and scarfs in the Seagram colours, followed those silks so loyally, and the favourites won with such regularity, that several books had a

DEDICATED TO
JOSEPH. E. SEAGRAM ESQ.
WATERLOO ONT.

Bonnyfield
MARCH

BONNIEFIELD
WINNER OF THE QUEEN'S PLATE MAY 24TH 1895

COMPOSED BY   PRICE 40¢

Nathanael Spady.

PUBLISHED FOR THE COMPOSER BY

A. & S. NORDHEIMER,

TORONTO.

Entered according to act of the Parliament of Canada in the year 1895 by Nathanael Spady in the Department of Agriculture.

SEAGRAM'S HORSES WERE SO POPULAR THAT MUSICAL SCORES WERE WRITTEN OF *BONNYFIELD*. PRINTER MISSPELLED *BONNIEFIELD*'S NAME.

severe "crimp" put in their bank rolls; the ring on the whole sustained tremendous losses, as Waterloo-owned horses won all five races in which the stable was entered. The only other race on the card, the Red Coat Steeplechase, went to a jumper owned by William Hendrie Jr.

The five-day meet was a remarkable success for Seagram: the Walker-trained stable won fifteen races. Praise was also heaped on Alfie Brooker, a local jockey replacing Seagram's imported rider, Harry Lewis, whose suspension in the United States was observed by the OJC. Brooker, who won the Plate and the Breeders' Stakes (a day later) on *Bonniefield*, had four of Seagram's five opening day victories.

Seagram also scored important wins with *Saragossa* when the five-year-old won the Walker Cup and the Toronto Cup, beating 1893 Kentucky Derby winner *Lookout* in the latter. Appropriately, Hiram Walker presented the Walker Cup to a fellow distiller, who was entitled to permanent possession of the trophy since it was the fourth year in a row he had won the Cup. The popular Waterloo horseman was lionized throughout the meet and whenever one of his

A CLOSE FINISH.

favourites would win, a long line of lucky bettors would file into the cavernous depths of the grandstand and chorus "Seagram, Seagram" in thirsty and appreciative tones.

As for the OJC, an attitude that horse racing could be a profitable business as well as an elegant sport, was beginning to take shape. The Club ordered that an office be built for secretary Lyndhurst Ogden and arranged for Alexander Graham Bell's latest invention,

BONNIEFIELD | 3-year-old brown gelding

Owner: Joseph E. Seagram, Waterloo; *Trainer:* John Walker
Jockey: Alf Brooker; *Breeder:* J.E. Seagram

a telephone, to be installed. Quarters for gentlemen riders were also built and the numbers of winning horses were painted on a board for the convenience of patrons. To insure high-class racing, the Club imported New York's leading officials: Alfred Post, Francis Trevelyan and famed handicapper William Vosburgh. Innovations were costly but were paid for as the Club sold program rights to Mr. Bryan for $550 and charged Mr. Meek $50 to peddle a "tip" sheet. The sale of liquor privileges went to George Briggs, who also was allowed to hold a pigeon shooting meet. The Hunt Club was allowed to lease the track for two days in September for $400, but the Club turned down a request from Hamilton horsemen George M. Hendrie and his brother William Junior, to rent Woodbine for a ten-day fall meeting, because "a matter of so great importance" could not be decided upon since the president, their father, and a full board of directors, were not at the meeting.

1895 QUEEN'S PLATE STAKES

FIFTH RACE
Woodbine Park
MAY 21, 1895

THE QUEEN'S PLATE; 50 Guineas, the Gift of Her Majesty. For all ages. Open to horses, owned, bred, raised and trained in the Province of Ontario that have never won public money, have never left Canada, and have never been for a period of more than one month out of this Province; added to a Sweepstakes of $5 each, payable at time of entry, March 1, and an additional $5 unless declared out by May 1, between which dates entries can be made on payment of $20 at post. The first horse to receive the guineas and stakes, and $500 added by the Club. The second horse $200 and the third $100. Net value to winner $995. Distance, one mile and a quarter.

Horse	A	Wt.	St	¼	½	Str	Fin	Jockey	Owner	Odds $1
BONNIEFIELD	3	104½	1	1	1	1	1nk	BrookerA	SeagramJE	Even
MILLBROOK	3	110	6	4	3	4	2³	Knapp	SeagramJE	4-1
LOCHINVAR	4	119	9	7	6	6	3	Flint	HendrieWm	8-1
VICAR OF WAKEFIELD	4	119	5	6	5	3	4	Connolly	SeagramJE	5-2
CHICKIE	3	104½	3	3	2	5	5	Snedker	DugganJos.	6-1
CONFECTIONER	3	103	4	5	4	2	6	McManus	SeagramJE	8-1
LADY SINCLAIR	5	121	7	8	8	7	7	Stewart	DickensonJob	15-1
KILTIE	3	103	9	9	7	8	8	Lendrum	HendrieWm	50-1
SUSQUEHANNA	3	107	10	10	9	9	9	BlaylockH	OrkneyStable	20-1
ANNIE MILLER	5	121	2	2	10	10	10	Welch	WrightAE	50-1

Time, 2:17½. Track good. Start fair.

Winner: Three-year-old brown gelding by Springfield—Bonnie Ino, by *Strachino. Bred by Mr. J. E. Seagram. Trained by John R. Walker.

BONNIEFIELD and CHICKIE were the leaders along with ANNIE MILLER until the head of the backstretch was reached, where MILLBROOK moved up. CHICKIE died away and MILLBROOK got to BONNIEFIELD's saddle girth a sixteenth of a mile from home. BONNIEFIELD beat his stable companion by a half-length while LOCHINVAR was three lengths back. The others were very much strung out.

Scratched—Dictator, Little Chief, Mediator, Wild Mark and Alice Barnes.
Overweight—Bonniefield, 1½ lbs.; Millbrook, 4 lbs.; Chickie, 3½ lbs.; Susquehanna, 4 lbs.

OPENING DAY AT THE WOODBINE.

The voice of horse racing in 1896 and the Ontario Jockey Club's most outspoken critic was the "exiled" Thomas C. Patteson, the former vice-president and founding father who had lost a bitter power struggle with president William Hendrie two years before. Although he no longer ruled Woodbine Park in his strident manner, barking out orders and admonishing minor officials if they were lax in fulfilling their duties, Patteson's presence was still palpable. A turf historian and former editor of *The Mail*, he continued to vent his views through letters to the editor and his freelance columns.

Never one to mince words, Patteson, in an unsigned article in *The Sunday World,* made it clear that he felt the Queen's Plate was diminishing in importance:

Everybody appears to be of the opinion that the field, outside the Seagram representatives, will be the poorest in quality seen for many a year. I must confess I am inclined to be of that way of thinking, but the indications are that the field in the other events will much more than compensate for any short-comings in a race that, after all, is considerably over-rated in importance. Before the days of Messrs Hendrie, Seagram and Dawes, that is before they went in for breeding and racing on the scale that they follow now, the struggle for Her Majesty's Guineas was undoubtedly of prime importance, but now it has receded in interest into an affair that is given prominence only

on account of the tradition attached to it and because it is for maiden horses nominated some months ahead. To the stranger the Queen's Plate is probably one of the least interesting events of the meeting, but for loyal Canadians, no matter how poor the field and how certain the issue, the event will always command respect and attention.

But Patteson had not finished: "A trainer of repute and a Canadian of experience too, said that outside the Seagram quartette [*sic*]—*Millbrook, Springal, Moorland* and *Dandelion*—he would not give a hundred dollars for a single horse." Earlier the Club's erstwhile vice-president displeased stockholders when he advised them to petition Sir John Thompson, the Minister of Justice, to have the clause permitting betting at racetracks withdrawn; he argued that such a step would prevent continuous racing at any one track, and that the Club could afford to relinquish the amount they derived from betting privileges. In 1896 the OJC offered six races daily during a six-day spring meeting and sold betting privileges to bookmaker Max Franks for $1,500 per day for fifteen books, giving him one free book for managing the betting-ring.

The supervising and regulating of betting was really developing into a distressing problem for the OJC, and in more ways than one. *The Globe* was delighted that the gaudily dressed bookmaker found at an English race meeting, offering odds against the field in stentorian tones, was nowhere to be seen at Woodbine. "The bookies here

T.C. PATTESON, HORSERACING'S OUTSPOKEN CRITIC.

MILLBROOK | 4-year-old brown colt

Millbrook (1892)	Springfield	*Bonnie Scotland	Iago
			Queen Mary
		Bouquet	Bulletin
			Fanny Bugg
	*Milley	Struan	Blair Athol
			Terrific
		Lota	Wellingtonia
			Daughter of Frolicsome

Owner: Joseph E. Seagram, Waterloo; *Trainer:* John Walker
Jockey: Harry Lewis; *Breeder:* J.E. Seagram

conduct their business under strict principles in little railed off spaces, and they mark up the odds—and uncommonly short odds they are, too, compared with those offered under similar circumstances by their British brothers—on specially prepared cards, issued by the management of the Club." *The Mail and Empire* grumbled that there was always a commotion in the vicinity of the betting-ring:

> The same old scene was enacted and it was almost impossible to make one's way through the surging crowd. The Club should either enlarge the stand or devise a scheme which would ensure the comfort of backers and pencillers alike. It would be a good plan to place some of the books out in the open air, as a trip to the bookies' stamping grounds is far from pleasant.

The Club also had to address another issue: Seagram's remarkable string of Plate victories. Would he win his sixth successive Plate with *Millbrook* and finish one-two for the fourth year in a row? The bookies, recognizing the "fealty of the public" to the black and yellow jackets, made the Waterloo stable favourite in the four races it entered on Plate day, "and in some cases at an absurdly short price." In almost every instance, Seagram horses were not coupled in the betting, a fact that had been objected to in 1895 when the stable ran four horses in the Plate. Trainer John Walker had also planned to run four more again in 1896, but ran three when he scratched Dandelion. Some punters complained that they were forced to select which candidate would win and had lost money when *Bonniefield* had won a year earlier. The argument against combining the Waterloo horses was that quotations against the stable would be absurdly short. For their part, the bookies said they were willing to quote odds-only on the stable, but their customers invariably demanded that the horses be priced individually. After a lengthy discussion, the Club's

executive committee deferred a decision about allowing an owner to run more than two horses in a race; but they dismissed a proposal to rid the Plate of also-rans by making horses who were entered more than once carry extra weight.

Millbrook, runner-up the year before, went off as the 2-to-5 favourite, even though the crowd knew he was unsound. He managed to stagger home ahead of *Springal,* but pulled up lame. Another Seagram horse, *Moorland,* was fourth; *Dictator* prevented a Waterloo clean sweep. Somebody quipped that Walker had now won the Plate with three cripples.

A starting gate was introduced for the first time at Woodbine in two races, but received faint praise from *The Mail and Empire.* "It hardly is the kind of thing to soothe the nerves of a fractious horse." The gate should no doubt have been used for the Plate race: there were seven false breaks before the flag fell.

PRESIDENT WILLIAM HENDRIE WATCHES *LOCHINVAR.*

1896 QUEEN'S PLATE STAKES

FOURTH RACE
Woodbine Park
MAY 23, 1896

THE QUEEN'S PLATE; 50 Guineas, the Gift of Her Majesty. For horses of all ages, owned, bred, raised and trained in the Province of Ontario that have never won public money, have never left Canada, and have never been for a period of more than one month out of this Province. A Sweepstakes of $5 each at time of entry, March 2, and $5 additional, unless declared out by May 1, between which days entries can be made on payment of $20 at post position. First horse to receive the Guineas and stakes and $500 added by the Club. Second horse $200 and third $100. Value to winner $975. Distance one mile and one-quarter.

Horse	A	Wt.	St	¼	½	¾	Str	Fin	Jockey	Owner	Op.	Cl.
MILLBROOK	4	122	5	7	6	1hd	1nk	1½	LewisH	SeagramJE	1-3	2-5
SPRINGAL	3	102	4nk	6	5	3¹	2½	2³	McManusT	SeagramJE	4-1	6-1
DICTATOR	5	126	2nk	3nk	2½	2½	3²	3⁵	Murray	Gladstone&Everleigh	6-1	8-1
MOORLAND	3	103	6	1⁴	1¹	4²	5	4²	Johnston	SeagramJE	6-1	8-1
BROTHER BOB	5	123	1½	2¹	3nk	6	6	5	BrookerA	BrookdaleStable	10-1	8-1
LOCHINVAR	5	123	3½	4²	4¹	5	4²	6	FlintJ	HendrieW	6-1	8-1
BRADLAUGH	3	103	7	5	7	7	7	7	Ballard	HoarA	12-1	20-1
MARCELLA	5	121	8	8	9	8	8	8	Paget	GlenoakStable	10-1	8-1
CLIPMOUNT	3	103	9	9	8	9	9	9	Condon	DoaneJH	15-1	10-1

Time, 2:19. Track slow. Good start; at post 10 minutes. Won handily; place under a pull.
Winner: Four-year-old brown colt by Springfield—*Milley, by Struan. Trained by John R. Walker. Bred by Joseph E. Seagram.

Seven breaks occurred before the flagfall. MARCELLA was the chief culprit. MOORLAND sprinted to the lead ahead of BROTHER BOB, who dropped back after a half-mile. DICTATOR then moved to contend but failed to threaten the Seagram pair. After a game struggle MILLBROOK and SPRINGAL moved confidently to the lead and took control in the stretch. LOCHINVAR showed early speed but faltered. MILLBROOK pulled up lame.
Scratched—Dandelion, Garter King, Armada, Boston, Dan Gordon and Alice Barnes.

In 1897 a great number of Torontonians doubted whether the introduction of Sunday streetcar service and Joseph Seagram's indomitable grasp of the Queen's Plate could be halted, as they braced themselves for the 24 May weekend festivities honouring the Queen's Diamond Jubilee. The answer was no on both counts. Despite vigorous protests from the city's mayor, who threatened legal action, and physical attempts to block the streetcars from running by citizens who had narrowly lost a referendum vote, the trams did begin to rattle around the city every sabbath. They were termed a blessing by churchgoers when it began to rain on that first Sunday morning.

A day earlier at Woodbine Park a patriotic throng was in a capricious mood. It had come to cheer Miss Elsie

PLATE WINNER *FERDINAND* WORE A GARLAND OF ROSES AND A PHOTO OF QUEEN VICTORIA.

Jones, "the popular and courageous lady from Brockville who had boldly entered the race and thrown down the gauntlet to such veterans as Seagram and Hendrie in the contest for the blue ribbon of the Canadian turf." The crowd was rooting for an upset by *Wicker,* her chestnut colt, but instead it graciously applauded another Plate triumph by the Waterloo stable.

A colourful paddock scene unfolded when veteran trainer Charley Boyle, who thirty-five years earlier in 1862 saddled his first Plate winner, *Palermo,* but had not trained a Plate horse in fourteen years, led *Ferdinand* into the winner's circle. Boyle was justifiably proud because he had just taken over the stable from John Walker (who later accepted an offer from Lord Derby to train in England) and had extended its Plate streak to seven. The custom of draping a garland of roses around the shoulders of the winning horse occurred for the first time in Plate history when the wife of Lieutenant Governor Sir George Kirkpatrick bestowed the floral wreath on *Ferdinand.* Sir George then elicited three rousing cheers from the crowd before it joined the Royal Grenadiers' band in singing "God Save the Queen."

Although the bettors' hearts were with Miss Jones, they judiciously made Seagram's three-horse entry the 1-to-2 choice. For the first time entries were coupled in the betting. Miss Jones, who saw her colt narrowly defeated for second place by *Bon Ino,* a future Seagram winner, was the first to congratulate the distiller. Years later Seagram recalled *Wicker's* gallant third-place finish and his conversation with Miss Jones before the running of the race. "I did not think I would ever like to lose the Queen's Plate,

but if I am beaten today I will be glad to know that it was by a horse owned by such an estimable lady as you."

The Mail and Empire also captured the mood of the crowd: "Many men backed *Wicker* from a spirit of gallantry that was worthy of mediaeval times. Their gallantry was exceedingly costly, and is all the more admirable on that account. Very many people would have liked to have seen Miss Jones' *Wicker* win, simply because the horse is owned by a woman. But *Wicker* never had a chance."

But some did not welcome *Ferdinand's* victory, accomplished in a record 2:13 by veteran jockey Harry Lewis. The win by the classically bred colt, who like *O'Donohue* and *Martello* was imported *in utero* from England on the advice of Seagram's astute agent Edmund Haines, received something of a bad press. While horsemen marvelled at Seagram's prosperity in winning so often and finishing in the top two places for the last five years, others were disgruntled, arguing that it was his wealth that was responsible and that he was taking advantage of the "loosely written" province-bred stipulation in the Plate rules. *The Evening News* said testily that the primary object of the Plate was to provide an incentive for provincial horsemen to breed thoroughbreds, and contended that the wealthy horse owner had a tremendous advantage over his poorer associates since he could afford to buy a mare in foal in England and bring her across to Canada.

MIXED REVIEWS BY CITIZENS GREETED THE INTRODUCTION OF SUNDAY STREETCAR SERVICE.

Moreover, the newspapers maintained that each breeder should have only one entry in the race. Seagram, who weeks earlier had been appointed to the executive committee of the Ontario Jockey Club to replace Senator J.H. Ferguson, was the butt of additional sardonic comment, when *The Evening News* added: "If Mr. Seagram was put on the same footing as others a great deal more interest would be added to the race." The newspaper also lampooned *Ferdinand*'s "English heritage" by printing a mock interview with the colt: "'Why, blawst it, old fellow, donchernow,' he said good naturedly, 'I 'ad to win—me hon'r depended on it. H'll, a true British gentleman couldn't h'afford to let any bloomin' Colonial nag win'er Majesty's "Guineas" in Jubilee Year—not I. We English are the stuff, donchernow.'"

Secretary Lyndhurst Odgen of the OJC was accused of "injudicious conduct" by *The Evening News* when he yelled and gesticulated in front of *Wicker* during the parade before the race. The colt faced the starter in a "peevish and fretful state," thus delaying the start for nearly twenty-five minutes. A Plate first was recorded as the start was made from "Gus Hamilton's rubber-band machine," an elastic barrier that sprung up at the starter's signal. Only once did the Plate field break through the barrier. As for *Ferdinand,* who was on the small side but had the "nice long style of galloping that bespeaks speed," Lewis told *The Mail and Empire*'s representative: "I knew what the horse I had under me could do and I played a waiting game. The race was mine as soon as we struck the stretch."

Bookmakers reported a sluggish day's business: Seagram horses dominated the seven races at short odds. One of the bookies that day was the Woodstock Wonder, Edward (Tip) O'Neill, the Canadian-born outfielder of manager Charles Comiskey's champion St. Louis Browns of 1888. When the Browns went on a barnstorming tour in 1887, O'Neill was billed as "baseball's greatest hitter" after batting .492. He had a career batting average of .326 over ten seasons. He was also the American Association's leading hitter in 1888. The son of a Woodstock, Ontario, innkeeper, O'Neill in 1883 became the first Canadian to pitch in the major leagues. But it was his hitting that prompted writers to proclaim him as Canada's first baseball hero. He was so adored by his public that hundreds of children were named after him, including Thomas (Tip) O'Neill, who would one day gain fame as the U.S. Speaker of the House of Representatives. It was said that every time the tall, handsome James (Tip) O'Neill came to bat for the St. Louis Browns, a dozen women wearing flowing robes would rise from the crowd and sound a fanfare on silver trumpets. When his playing days were over, he became a bookmaker and also ran a saloon in Montreal before he died in 1915.

FERDINAND | 3-year-old chestnut colt

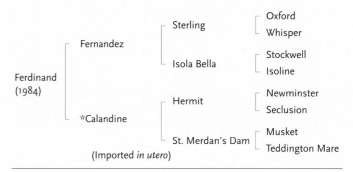

Ferdinand (1984)
- Fernandez
  - Sterling
    - Oxford
    - Whisper
  - Isola Bella
    - Stockwell
    - Isoline
- *Calandine (Imported *in utero*)
  - Hermit
    - Newminster
    - Seclusion
  - St. Merdan's Dam
    - Musket
    - Teddington Mare

Owner: Joseph E. Seagram, Waterloo; *Trainer:* Charles Boyle
Jockey: Harry Lewis; *Breeder:* J.E. Seagram

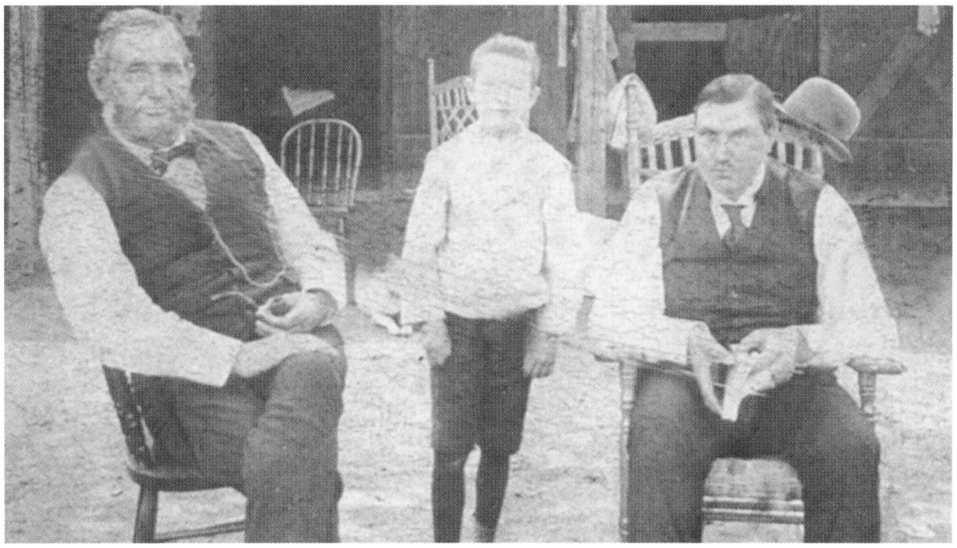

Trainer Charles Boyle (left), his grandson, Joe Boyle Junior, and son David relax at "The Firs" in Woodstock.

1897 QUEEN'S PLATE STAKES

FOURTH RACE
Woodbine Park
MAY 22, 1897

THE QUEEN'S PLATE; 50 Guineas, the Gift of Her Majesty Queen Victoria. For 3-year-olds and upward. Open to horses owned, bred, foaled, raised and trained in the Province of Ontario that have never won a race, either on the flat or across country; have never left Canada, and have never been for a period of more than one month out of this Province. A Sweepstakes of $5, payable at time of entry, March 1, and $5 additional unless declared out by May 1, between which days entries can be made on payment of $20 p.p. The first horse to receive the Guineas and stakes and $500 added by the Club. Net value to winner $1,016. Second horse $200 and third horse $100. Distance, one and one-quarter miles.

Horse	A	Wt.	St	¼	½	¾	Str	Fin	Jockey	Owner	Odds $1
FERDINAND	3	106	2^{nk}	3^{nk}	3^{2}	2½	1^{hd}	1^{2}	LewisH	SeagramJE	a-1-2
BON INO	3	101	6	8	1½	1^{1}	2½	2½	FlintJ	SeagramJE	a-1-2
WICKER	3	106	3½	1^{hd}	2^{hd}	3^{4}	3^{5}	3^{15}	SongerA	JonesMissElsie	2-1
DALMOOR	3	106	5	6	4^{hd}	4^{1}	4^{4}	4^{5}	McGloneJ	SeagramJE	a-1-2
FIDDLE	3	101	7	4^{2}	6	5	5	5	WhyteE	HendrieWm	b-8-1
LEADING LADY	3	101	4½	7	7	6	6	6	Walker	HendrieWm	b-8-1
SPRINGBOK	4	119	1^{nk}	2^{1}	5	7	7	7	LendrumR	SwartzJE	40-1
BOSTON	4	119	8	5	8	8	8	8	Davis	BateTC	100-1
BILLY DINMOUNT	4	119	10	9	9	9	9	9	Wyatt	WyattS	100-1
KING KEN	7	123	9	10	10	10	10	10	Stewart	McIntyreJ	100-1

a-Coupled, Ferdinand, Bon Ino and Dalmoor; b-Fiddle and Leading Lady.

Time, :26½, :52, 1:18½, 1:45½, 2:13 (Plate record). Track fast.

Winner: Three-year-old chestnut colt by Fernandez—*Celandine, by Hermit. Trained by Charles Boyle. Bred by Mr. J. E. Seagram.

Start good; won galloping. Place driving. There was a 20 minute delay before the flag fell, due chiefly to WICKER's misbehaviour. FERDINAND was also fretful. But on the fourth breakaway the flag dropped to a splendid start. SPRINGBOK went to the front early but gave away the lead to BON INO, the real work horse of the race. It was her burst of speed up the backstretch that cooked WICKER, yet she was able to go and beat him for place. FERDINAND was never far off the leaders and took control with a burst in the far turn and won handily under jockey Harry Lewis. LEADING LADY was a tremendous disappointment and went all to pieces when asked to race. DALMOOR was with the bunch up the backstretch and easily outclassed the remainder of the field.

Scratched—Dandelion.

Disenchanted with Joseph Seagram's effective monopoly of the Queen's Plate, which was sapping much of the race's excitement and popularity, Toronto newspapers began to focus on other aspects of the event besides the result. Their rationale was that there was little sense discussing the outcome since it was apparent that *Bon Ino* would stroll home as she pleased under jockey Robert (Tiny) Williams, who during his career had six mounts in the Kentucky Derby. She had been second in 1897 while acting as *Ferdinand*'s workhorse, and bookmakers were predicting prohibitive odds of 1-to-5 on Seagram's black jackets and yellow sashes. Hardly a betting affair, moaned the public and the pencillers.

The Daily Star boldly said:

> The Woodbine is unique in many ways. It is, as it were, a great rock in a weary land for Yankee horsemen. Nowhere in America is the sport of Kings conducted so cleanly and honestly. Nowhere is it held so much as a social function, simulating in this respect the English tracks. In Toronto, society has made the Woodbine its own, and turfmen, after dealing with the trash and rabble at Yankee tracks, are mightily refreshed to run their horses before good people. The Ontario Jockey Club, what with the regular purses and extra money, gives away about $4,000 a day, or $28,000 during the whole meeting. This in itself is worth coming after, even if there were no other attractions. . . .
>
> It makes no difference that there are thirty races during the meet which are better from a speculative standpoint, that the people are so anxious to bet on the Queen's Plate that the 'bookies' can offer almost any odds, or that there are other races made in better time. To make even a small wager on the event is to express your patriotism to your province, your loyalty to the Queen, and your respect for the aristocracy. Among the people, it is a pleasure even to lose on the Queen's Plate.

Very few of the ten thousand at Woodbine who wagered on the thirty-ninth running of the Plate lost their money: the Waterloo stable experienced its sixth one-two finish and its eighth consecutive win. The victory was worth $1,010 plus the fifty guineas for Seagram—a paltry sum when you consider the outlay in employing the large number of people to operate his mushrooming racing and breeding operations.

For the second year, a starting machine was used in the Plate. But this one was an improvement over the earlier model. It had been invented by starter C.H. Pettingill, who in 1919 would be blamed, along with jockey Johnny Loftus, for mighty *Man o' War*'s only loss because of a poor, straggling start in the Sanford Memorial at Saratoga Springs. Pettingill's machine was very simple, an elastic band stretched across the track from a cross pole. An electric button released the spring, sending the band up and away. It was considered much more effective than the old barrier machine. Trainers of two-year-olds were requested to take advantage of the opportunity to

A DAPPER ELMER JAMES HANDED OUT JACKETS TO THE GROOMS TAKING HORSES TO THE PADDOCK WHEN WOODBINE OPENED IN 1956. JAMES, WHO RODE IN THE 1898 AND 1899 PLATE RACES, WAS THE NEPHEW AND SON OF THE LEGENDARY TRAIN AND BANK ROBBERS, JESSE AND FRANK JAMES.

teach their horses to break from the machine, which would be used during the meeting.

It posed no problems for *Bon Ino* as she defeated eight foes, four of whom had previously run in the Plate: "She did not have to extend herself. She led all the way, under double wraps, and won by as much as she pleased," said *The World*. Only Nathaniel Dyment's *Maritana II*, who was nosed out for second place, challenged *Bon Ino* and runner-up *Dalmoor*, who would win the Plate for Seagram two years later. *Bon Ino*'s win prompted *The Mail and Empire* to observe facetiously: "The betting public will still continue to drink Seagram's. If by chance *Maritana II* had won, popular sentiment would have forced Mr. Dyment to start a distillery." Dyment was a Barrie lumberman.

The only disturbing aspect was that it seemed as if Seagram's Plate appetite was insatiable. The Waterloo stable appeared to be invincible, and for any horseman looking down the road, hoping the well would soon dry up so he might capture Her Majesty's guineas, the prospects were abysmal. There was a better chance that Seagram's vast stills of spirits would be emptied before the liquor merchant's stable would be beaten. His supply of fresh, talented stock seemed to be endless and if his trainers did not have an impertinent youngster from an imported mare ready to run against you, Seagram would challenge with one of his experienced maidens who had been saved for another Plate canter. Besides employing the top trainers, grooms and exercise boys, Seagram also imported the leading jockeys.

Little notice in Toronto newspapers was directed toward the appearance of jockey Elmer James, riding Nathaniel Dyment's third-place finisher *Maritana II*. His uncle was the legendary criminal figure of the lawless Wild West, Jesse James, who was gunned down in his living room in St. Joseph's, Missouri, by fellow gang member Robert Ford in 1882. Elmer's father, Frank, who fought on the Confederate side during the Civil War, was a member of the vicious Quantrill Raiders during and after the war, and with his younger brother, Jesse, later formed the rampaging James brothers and Cole Younger brothers' gang that terrorized the public with its cold-blooded crimes while carrying out a daring string of bank, stagecoach and train robberies throughout the U.S. Midwest in the 1860s, 1870s and 1880s.

Elmer James, who also rode in the 1899 Plate, finishing third on William Hendrie's *Toddy Ladle,* was born in Waco, Texas, and as a youth went to England to ride, winning the Duke of York Stakes before going to France in the employ of Baron de Rothschild. Elmer was eminently successful riding in the United States and Canada. He later worked at racetracks throughout Ontario in numerous capacities and was employed by the Ontario Jockey Club when Woodbine opened in 1956. *The Toronto Star,* in an article on his life, said, "Shedrow at New Woodbine has a dapper little man with a spirit and good humor that make him popular with jockeys and trainers alike. He is 79 and he couldn't be happier with his daily task of handing out white jackets to the grooms who take horses to the paddock." In his obituary in *The Globe and Mail* in 1959, the newspaper reprinted a 1949 interview with James, in which he recalled the details of the slaying of his uncle from his aunt's account of the event. Jesse was shot in the back of his head by Ford as he stood on a chair dusting a picture on the wall. "My aunt ran into the room and held Uncle Jesse's head in her arms as he died. But he lived long enough to tell her what happened and I've heard every one of the details," said Elmer James. A resident of Toronto for almost fifty years, James was buried in St. John's Norway Cemetery.

In August 1898 the OJC's directors mourned the death of Sir Casimir Stanislaus Gzowski, the man who was largely instrumental in the ultimate success of horse racing in Ontario in the 1860s and the founding of the Club. He presided over its first meeting in the fall of 1881. Born in Russia in 1813, Gzowski immigrated to the U.S. and studied law before embarking on an engineering and railroad construction career. He came to Ontario in 1841

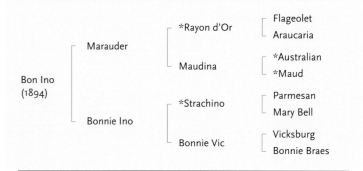

BON INO | 4-year-old bay filly

			Flageolet
		*Rayon d'Or	Araucaria
	Marauder		
		Maudina	*Australian
Bon Ino			*Maud
(1894)			
			Parmesan
		*Strachino	Mary Bell
	Bonnie Ino		
		Bonnie Vic	Vicksburg
			Bonnie Braes

Owner: Joseph E. Seagram, Waterloo; *Trainer:* Charles Boyle
Jockey: R. (Tiny) Williams; *Breeder:* J.E. Seagram

to work on the Welland Canal and from 1852 to 1860 constructed the Grand Trunk Railway between Toronto and Sarnia. He built the International Bridge between Fort Erie and Buffalo in 1871.

FOR THE SECOND YEAR C.H. PETTINGILL'S STARTING MACHINE WAS USED.

1898 QUEEN'S PLATE STAKES

FOURTH RACE
Woodbine Park
MAY 21, 1898

THE QUEEN'S PLATE; 50 Guineas, the gift of Her Majesty. For 3-year-olds and upward. Open to horses owned, bred, raised and trained in the Province of Ontario that have never won a race, either on the flat or across country; have never left Canada, and have never been for a period of more than one month out of this Province. Added to a Sweepstakes of $5 each, payable at time of entry March 8, and $5 additional unless declared out by May 2, between which days entries can be made on payment of $20 p.p. The net value to winner $1,010 and Guineas. Second horse to receive $200 and third $100. 30 entries, 6 declared. Distance one mile and a quarter.

Horse	A	Wt.	St	½	Str	Fin	Jockey	Owner	Odds $1
BON INO	4	117	1	1no	1no	11½	WilliamsR	SeagramJE	a-1-6
DALMOOR	4	122	2	3²	3⁴	2no	McGlone	SeagramJE	a-1-6
MARITANA II.	3	101	4	2¹⁵	2⁶	3¹⁵	JamesE	DymentN	b-8-1
THE TAR	4	119	7	6¹	4⁸	4⁸	Sullivan	SeagramJE	a-1-6
JESSAMINE PORTER II.	3	101	6	5²	6¹⁵	5no	Shields	DymentN	b-8-1
LEADING LADY	4	117	3	4²	5½	6²⁰	Walker	HendrieW	8-1
BRISTLES	4	119	5	7	8	7	Brooker	DaviesR	15-1
SPRINGBOK	5	123	9	8	9	8	Flint	SwartzJohnE	15-1
LADY SINCLAIR	8	121	8	9	7	9	Randall	DickensonJ	30-1

a–Coupled, Bon Ino, Dalmoor and The Tar; **b**–Maritana II. and Jessamine Porter II.
Time, 2:15½. Track good.
Winner: Four-year-old br. f, by Marauder—Bonnie Ino, by *Strachino. Trained by Charles Boyle. Bred by J. E. Seagram.
Start good. After a considerable delay at the start because of the bad behaviour of MARITANA II. and SPRINGBOK the field broke cleanly with BON INO taking a short lead with DALMOOR and LEADING LADY close behind. LEADING LADY pressed BON INO the first time past the stand. MARITANA II. took up the chase of the leader down the backstretch and was only a neck out but she tired badly in the stretch and surrendered second place by a neck to DALMOOR at the wire.
Scratched—Disorder.

I n *The Hamilton Spectator*'s opinion, the general sentiment of the great majority of the racing public was: "After eight years of wearing the 'black and yellow,' it is time for a change." Wearing a tie or scarf in the colours of the Plate winner was a custom the haberdashers encouraged in this period. Fans did not wish any misfortune against Joseph Seagram's stable, whose reign seemed almost as long as Queen Victoria's; it was simply that it was about time that another owner won Her Majesty's "Guineas."

The inevitable occurred on a warm 20 May afternoon at Woodbine Park and it unquestionably was the biggest and most welcome boost ever given to the Queen's Plate in its forty-year history. *Butter Scotch,* a combative three-year-old bay filly who was making her first start, accomplished a feat few horsemen or the betting public thought possible. She courageously skipped away from "another Seagram herd" to win the "guineas" for Hamilton's William Hendrie, the man who had striven so diligently to dismantle turf's longest winning streak. The sight of a jockey wearing a brown jacket with yellow sleeves barging past the older and more experienced *Dalmoor*—the odds-on choice of the four-horse Waterloo stable entry—caused pandemonium at the lakeshore track and warmth in the heart of every haberdasher. Even though the favourite had been beaten, the people rose up and cheered. From all sides could be heard: "Well, Hendrie has beaten Seagram at last. I'm glad of it." The crowd was exuberant as Hendrie received a loving cup from the Earl of Minto, Canada's Governor General. *The World,* in its description of the presentation, said, "The piece of plate which, it may be mentioned, will be given annually by the Ontario Jockey Club, in addition to the added money (and the record Plate purse of $1,331) is a handsome loving cup. In it was placed the certificate for the fifty guineas," which comes from Her Majesty's privy purse. It read: "This is to certify that Mr. William Hendrie's bay filly, *Butter Scotch*, is entitled to the fifty guineas generously donated by her most gracious majesty, Queen Victoria." The trophy, which cost the OJC $116, was the first ever presented to a Plate winner. The scene, as Seagram walked over to congratulate Hendrie, was vividly recorded by *The Mail and Empire:*

ORNATELY CRAFTED QUEEN'S PLATE TROPHY WAS AWARDED FOR THE FIRST TIME IN PLATE HISTORY.

> Then there was a rush to the paddock to see the jockeys weighed in, and to find out if no bitter chance was to rob *Butter Scotch* of her victory. Mr. Seagram was standing at the secretary's office door. He looked philosophic. Perhaps he had felt that his luck could not last forever. Mr. Hendrie stepped into the paddock with his horse and his jockey beside him. A mighty cheer arose from the mass of spectators; the ladies in the members' stand clapped their hands and waved their 'kerchiefs. The two famous rivals of Canadian horsedom advanced with outstretched hands, and as they gripped another cheer went up. To the excited spectators it was as important as a meeting between the Czar and Kaiser. The little jockey from Nashville, Tennessee, R.J. Mason, riding in his first and only Plate race, was cheered also.

Mr. Hendrie's victory will have a far-reaching effect, by which the Canadian turf will be greatly benefitted. The Queen's Plate is a prize all breeders strive to win, and now that Mr. Seagram's luck has turned, other breeders will be encouraged to continue their efforts to land the prize, and it will be well for the turf if other than the Hendrie and Seagram horses are the contending ones in the race for the 'guineas' in future years [seven of the fourteen horses in the race were owned either by Seagram or Hendrie]. . . . The Plate has been restored to the position of a game of chance. It will no longer be a walkover.

While *The Hamilton Spectator* expressed the view that "Toronto people seemed to take as much pleasure out of the victory as the Hamilton folks, even though they regard the Seagram stable as their own," it is said that Seagram felt that *Dalmoor*'s illness a few days earlier had a great deal to do with his loss of the race. The fact that he carried twenty-five pounds more than *Butter Scotch* was also a major factor. *The Globe* said that Seagram harboured no bitterness.

'They've beaten me', he said, 'but it was a good horse and a

BUTTER SCOTCH RETURNING TO SCALE.

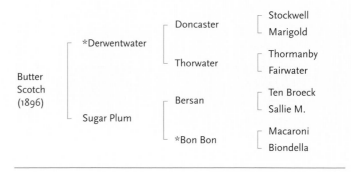

			Stockwell
		Doncaster	Marigold
	*Derwentwater		Thormanby
		Thorwater	Fairwater
Butter Scotch (1896)			Ten Broeck
		Bersan	Sallie M.
	Sugar Plum		Macaroni
		*Bon Bon	Biondella

Owner: William Hendrie, Hamilton; *Trainer:* Eddie Whyte
Jockey: R.J. Mason; *Breeder:* Valley Farm Stud (William Hendrie)

good owner that won.' For two score years Mr. Hendrie has been a worthy open-handed supporter of the turf, calculating the cost of racing and paying it willingly. With him a good year was only one that was less expensive than a bad one, but he never stopped, and whether the years were lean or fat, you never missed the horses from the Valley Farm the following season. Such a man likes winning just as much as the poorest professional, but he races on whether winning or losing.

Butter Scotch's win was apparently a bonanza for the book-makers, who "won barrels on the turnover. Men bet $500 to win $100, neglecting the tempting $5 to $1 against Hendrie's three-horse entry." Unraced as a two-year-old, the Hendrie-bred filly won a prize in the thoroughbred class at the September Exhibition in Toronto. "This is the winner of next year's Queen's Plate," Archie Whyte predicted as he led her out of the ring. Trained by his son, Eddie, *Butter Scotch* showed speed in her trials as a two-year-old, but she was not very big and it was doubted if she could go the distance. She helped popularize *Derwentwater,* an English stud purchased by Hendrie from a breeder who had imported him into Alberta.

A canny Scotsman and former clerk with the Great Western Railway, Hendrie's initial brush with horses was through the draught horses that later helped him develop Canada's largest cartage business. He was a founding father of the OJC and its president for thirteen years until he stepped down in 1896 to serve as vice-president. His ambition to win the Plate had possessed him as early as 1866 when he acted as starter for *Beacon*'s Plate triumph in Hamilton. After winning one of North America's richest races, the Futurity, at New York's Sheepshead Bay racetrack in 1898 with his two-year-old colt *Martimas,* Hendrie admitted that his real goal was still the Plate.

This was the ultimate prize in his eyes, even though the Futurity's value was thirty times greater than the Plate purse. Hendrie was extremely popular in Hamilton. He frequently donated large amounts of money to charitable causes and after winning the Futurity bestowed part of the $36,610 purse for the construction of a new wing at Hamilton General Hospital. It was named the *Martimas* Wing.

Hamiltonians, who had eagerly read bulletins in the windows of local newspapers describing *Butter Scotch*'s triumph, crowded the streets and platforms around the Hunter Street railway station to welcome Hendrie home that evening. *The Spectator* reported that as the train drew up to the platform, the Thirteenth Battalion band struck up "See the Conquering Hero Comes," while the crowds cheered themselves hoarse.

One pertinent item ignored by the press was a sentence that had been inserted into the Club's advertisement regarding Queen's Plate conditions, which advised horsemen and the racing public that the race was "The oldest fixture run continuously on this Continent."

1899 QUEEN'S PLATE STAKES

FOURTH RACE
Woodbine Park
MAY 20, 1899

Fortieth Running of THE QUEEN'S PLATE. (The oldest fixture run continuously on this continent.) 50 Guineas, the gift of Her Majesty Queen Victoria, with $1,000 added by the Club. First horse to receive the Guineas and stakes (net value $1,331), with second horse to receive $200 and third $100. A sweepstakes of $5 payable at time of entry and $5 additional unless declared by May 10. For maiden 3-year-olds and upward (non-winners on flat or cross country), foaled, raised and trained and owned in the Province of Ontario, have never left Canada, and never been for a period of more than one month out of this province. A piece of plate will be presented by the Club to the winner. One mile and a quarter.

Horse	A	Wt.	St	¼	½	Str	Fin	Jockey	Owner	Odds $1
BUTTER SCOTCH	3	101	2	9	6²	3½	1²	MasonRJ	HendrieWm	a-5-1
DALMOOR	5	126	1	7	4nk	1¹	2nk	WilliamsR	SeagramJE	b-1-6
TODDY LADLE	3	103	6	3¹	2½	4¹	3⁵	JamesE	HendrieWm	a-5-1
CURFEW BELL	3	105	9	11	5¹	2nk	4⁸	Sullivan	SeagramJE	b-1-6
TERRALTA	3	101	3	5¹	7	7	5³	Blair	SeagramJE	b-1-6
DALLIANCE	5	123	4	6½	8	6²	6¹⁵	Valentine	CaptForester	100-1
BELLCOURT	3	101	14	14	14	10	7¹	Kitley	DymentN	100-1
SARDONYX	4	119	8	2nk	1hd	5²	8	McGlone	SeagramJE	b-1-6
COCOANUT	3	107	11	12	12	11	9	Hewitt	ArnottDJ	c-100-1
PLAY FUN	3	104	5	4½	3nk	8	10	McDermott	HendrieWm	a-5-1
SPRING BLOSSOM	3	104	10	8	9	9	11	Bastien	ArnottDJ	c-100-1
NICK WHITE	3	106	7	1hd	10	12	12	Flint	ClanceyEB	100-1
TARTAN	3	108	12	13	13	13	13	Hamilton	McCollMr	100-1
DR. JACK	3	103	13	10	11	14	14	Tanner	TymonMr	100-1

a–Coupled as William Hendrie entry; b–Joseph E. Seagram entry; c–D. J. Arnott entry.
Time: 2:15½. Track slow.
Winner: B. f (3), by *Derwentwater—Sugar Plum, by Bersan. Trained by Ed Whyte. Bred by William Hendrie.
Start good. After a seven-minute wait at the post the field broke evenly. NICK WHITE went to the front the first time past the grandstand, followed by SARDONYX and TODDY LADLE. CURFEW BELL and DALMOOR moved up in the backstretch as BUTTER SCOTCH worked her way nobly along the inside. The Seagram pair held the lead approaching the stretch followed by Hendrie's duo of BUTTER SCOTCH and TODDY LADLE. Mason on BUTTER SCOTCH slipped through along the rail and was almost cruel with his whip as he outduelled Tiny Williams on DALMOOR, pulling away to win by two lengths. DALMOOR hung on for the place, a neck in front of TODDY LADLE.
Overweight—Toddy Ladle, 2 lbs.; Curfew Bell, 4 lbs.; Cocoanut, 4 lbs.; Play Fun, 2 lbs.; Spring Blossom, 3 lbs.

It was claimed by *The Daily Star*, perhaps with tongue in cheek, that over *Dalmoor's* stable door a placard hung upon which was inscribed the motto: "If at first you don't succeed, try, try, try again." Even if it was facetious, there is no arguing that the adage was appropriately Victorian and in keeping with the archaic rules still regulating the running of the Queen's Plate as it and the Ontario Jockey Club cautiously drifted into the twentieth century. The race was still an incredibly restricted contest for maidens foaled, raised, trained and owned in the province who had never left Canada or who had never spent more than a month outside Ontario.

A stalwart six-year-old campaigner, *Dalmoor* was owned by the omnipotent Joseph Seagram stable. However, his reputation was somewhat tarnished after setbacks in the Plate races of 1897, 1898 and 1899. The Waterloo stable could overlook the first two losses since they were to stablemates. However, the son of *Louis XIII* was culpably negligent in allowing the Hamilton filly *Butter Scotch* to shatter Seagram's unrivaled stream of eight successive Plate wins.

Give *Dalmoor* another chance was new trainer Harry Blair's view. He reminded everyone that the horse was ill; his teeth were bothering him and he was carrying twenty-five pounds more than William Hendrie's filly a year earlier. *Dalmoor* did try again, but it was not easy as he hooked up with another Hendrie youngster, *The Provost*, who was in receipt of a twenty-pound edge in weights. A grim head-to-head struggle in the stretch, calling for all jockey Harry Lewis' skill and encouragement, spurred *Dalmoor* into winning the race that had eluded him the year before.

The belated triumph was welcomed with a sigh of relief by the majority of an estimated Victoria Day crowd of eighteen thousand. The punters had made Seagram's two-horse entry the 11-to-10 favourites, and they sweated out *Dalmoor's* nerve-wracking neck decision. Their bankrolls were in his hands because the other half of the Seagram entry in the fifteen-horse field, *Ottoman*, lolloped home in eleventh place.

Dalmoor's triumph, it was unanimously agreed, was due solely to Lewis' superior jockeyship: he outrode Tommy Powers on *The Provost* in winning his third Plate race.

"At the weights *The Provost* was the best horse in the race, but Powers made too much use of him early, displaying poor judgment," *The Spectator* observed.

DALMOOR WON THE PLATE ON HIS FOURTH ATTEMPT.

Powers chased after the pacesetter, *Bonnie Maid,* and then *Bellcourt,* but was unable to hold off *Dalmoor's* furious charge in the final furlong. Harry Lewis afterwards said that he had "hugged the rail as closely as possible for fear someone might interfere with me." At one point he thought his horse might buckle, but when he drew his whip, "*Dalmoor* proved game to the core or else he would not have won."

Like three previous Seagram Plate winners—*O'Donohue, Martello* and *Ferdinand*—*Dalmoor* was imported *in utero* after being conceived in England. An Englishman, witnessing his first Queen's Plate, offered a curious critique of the proceedings in *The Evening News:*

The crowd was large and listless, but good natured and well-behaved. One portion of the crowd, and one only, was moved to real activity during the races. The bookmakers were early to work and did a splendid business. These gentlemen had the prosperous air of their colleagues on the English turf, but, strange to say, their clients seemed equally well-fed. The lean and haggard plumper, so familiar in the Old Country, was not to be seen, nor decayed nobleman, the bankrupt squire, the

Jack-at-all-crimes, who can be found in plenty of fairer places. The costers of Epsom, the miners of Doncaster, have not their counterpart in Toronto, where for the Ontario Jockey Club should be deeply grateful. . . . By and by the ground was strewn with tiny pieces of paper, tokens of distress, and after each race men might be seen tearing up with spiteful pains the valueless tickets they had bought from the bookies. In time the ground became more white than green.

The men in the mob were wonderfully well dressed. Some might have just stepped from Piccadilly or Belgravia.

Even the meanest had creased his trousers to a knife edge with a flat iron. And the ladies—who shall find words to describe them? It was a splendid day for waiting. . . . even a bugler who appeared in the scoring box was not noticed. There was hardly bustle to alarm a sparrow at her nest in the eaves of the stand, and, save after the screeching din of the Queen's Plate, the roll of the trams in the rear would have easily drowned the applause. . . . The scene in the paddock was striking; Mr. Seagram patting his gallant horse, and Mr. Hendrie generously congratulating his victorious friend.

Although Seagram had won yet again, his defeat the year before had revived interest in the oldest uninterrupted racing fixture on the continent: forty-one horses were nominated for the Plate—a record. Unquestionably the race's rules were too restrictive. However, *The Daily Star* took a positive view of things: "Not only does it command respect on account of its long standing, but because the "guineas" is a gift from Her Majesty's privy purse, and there is not today, even in England, a race for which funds are contributed by the Head of State."

One of Seagram's stable riders at the turn of the century was

DALMOOR | 6-year-old bay horse

Owner: Joseph E. Seagram, Waterloo; *Trainer:* Harry Blair
Jockey: Harry Lewis; *Breeder:* J.E. Seagram

Otto Wonderly, a Canadian boy who started as a "candy butcher" on the Canadian Pacific Railway. He twice rode in the Plate on mounts owned by Sir Adam Beck. Wonderly was one of the top riders in the U.S., and won the Suburban Handicap at Belmont, N.Y., in 1902 on Diamond Jim Brady's *Gold Heels*. J.B. Holmes, a New York resident and frequent contributor to thoroughbred magazines, had galloped horses for several leading stables, including the Seagram string, and wrote of Wonderly in *The Canadian Horse:* "What a rider he was! A clean-cut, handsome youth—a regular Beau Brummel—he attended church on Sundays in a top hat and cutaways and was lionized by the ladies." Holmes was of the opinion that Wonderly was the best jockey ever developed in Canada. "He was on par or better than Ron Turcotte, who is very good today. Wonderly had a way with horses and was strong, as well as being a clever boy." Wonderly, who had just led the jockey's list at Hot Springs, Arkansas, was killed in Memphis, Tennessee, on 5 April 1905, while schooling his own horse at the barrier.

Not a May snow fall—Just a citizen casting away his un-cashed tickets.

WINNERS AND LOSER.

1900 QUEEN'S PLATE STAKES

FOURTH RACE
Woodbine Park
MAY 24, 1900

The Forty-First Running of the QUEEN'S PLATE. $1,250 added. (The oldest fixture run continuously on this continent.) Value to winner $1,395. 50 Guineas, the gift of Her Majesty Queen Victoria, with $1,000 added by the Club. The second horse to receive $200 and the third $100. A sweepstakes of $5 payable at time of entry and $5 additional unless declared out by May 10. For maiden 3-year-olds and upward, owned, foaled, raised and trained in the Province of Ontario, that have never won a race on the flat or across country, have never left Canada, and have never been out of this province. A piece of plate will be presented by the Club. 41 entries. One mile and a quarter.

Horse	A	Wt.	St	¼	½	¾	Str	Fin	Jockey	Owner	Op.	Cl.	Pl.
DALMOOR	6	126	9	7^2	4^{nk}	$3\frac{1}{2}$	3^2	1^{nk}	LewisH	SeagramJE	a-6-5	11-10	3-5
THE PROVOST	3	106	2	2^1	$2\frac{1}{2}$	$2\frac{1}{2}$	1^1	2^2	Powers	HendrieW	b-7-2	7-2	8-5
BELLCOURT	4	117	6	$4\frac{1}{2}$	$11\frac{1}{2}$	1^3	2^1	3^5	Howell	DymentN	c-5-1	6-1	2-1
MAGOG	3	101	12	$11\frac{1}{2}$	10^6	8^1	$4\frac{1}{2}$	4^{nk}	Thompson	DymentN	c-5-1	6-1	2-1
BARLEY SUGAR	3	101	8	6^{hd}	7^{hd}	7^{hd}	7^{nk}	5^{nk}	McQuade	HendrieW	b-7-2	7-2	8-5
EUCLAIRE	3	101	7	5^2	3^{nk}	4^{nk}	5^2	$6\frac{1}{2}$	Boyle	ClanceyEB	40-1	100-1	40-1
WHITE CLOVER	3	101	13	10^{hd}	13^{10}	13^2	$8\frac{1}{2}$	7^{hd}	Southard	HendrieW	b-7-2	7-2	8-5
BONNIE MAID	3	101	14	$1\frac{1}{2}$	$6\frac{1}{2}$	6^{nk}	$6\frac{1}{2}$	8^3	Landry	ChappellH	40-1	100-1	40-1
MISS DART	3	101	11	$8\frac{1}{2}$	9^3	9^4	9^5	9^5	WonderlyO	BeckA	5-1	6-1	2-1
OPUNTIA	3	103	1	3^1	$5\frac{1}{2}$	10^3	10^4	10^{30}	Irvin	DaviesR	40-1	100-1	40-1
OTTOMAN	4	119	10	$9\frac{1}{2}$	12^1	11^1	11^1	11^{nk}	BlairC	SeagramJE	a-6-5	11-10	3-5
CURFEW BELL	4	117	15	13^{10}	11^{nk}	$5\frac{1}{2}$	12^1	12^{10}	Sullivan	PepperM	50-1	30-1	10-1
TARTAN	4	119	3	12^5	$8\frac{1}{2}$	12^2	13^6	13^8	Warshire	GalvinJF	40-1	100-1	40-1
BRINGLOE	3	106	14	15	14^{10}	13^{10}	14^{15}	14^{20}	WeberA	BoyleDA	40-1	100-1	40-1
ROSA D.	4	117	5	14^1	15	15	15	15	Castro	NolanJ	40-1	60-1	20-1

Coupled in betting: a—J. E. Seagram entry; b—William Hendrie entry; c—Nathaniel Dyment entry.

Time, :25, :51, 1:04, 1:33, 1:47, 2:14. Track good.

Winner: B.h. (6), by Louis XIII.—*Lady Dalmeny, by Town Moor. Trained by Harry Blair. Bred by Mr. Joseph E. Seagram.

Went to post at 4:25. At post nine minutes. Start good. Won all out; second easily. Away at a leisurely pace, DALMOOR moved swiftly in the backstretch and only got up in the final sixteenth and it took a hard ride by his jockey to barely outgame THE PROVOST at the finish. THE PROVOST prompted the early pace and appeared to have won the race but was nailed in the final strides. DALMOOR bore in badly in the last sixty yards. BELLCOURT, after fighting for the lead with THE PROVOST, tired in the stretch run. MAGOG, slow to get going, closed a big gap. WHITE CLOVER ran impressively.

Scratched—Play Fun, Sir Wilfrid.

1901 | JOHN RUSKIN

. . . Her gracious memory evermore must lend
A pathos to this springtime holiday;
To us its splendid hues of joy must blend
With sorrows tender grey.
Yet but to bless it with a nobler air
And loftier purpose. With true hearts we sing
Our empire's anthem, and send up the prayer—
God save our noble King!

    J.W. BENGOUGH (*THE GLOBE*, 24 MAY 1901)

Queen Victoria was dead and *John Ruskin*, named after the eminent Victorian author, critic and social reformer, became the last horse to capture the Queen's Plate until the ascension of Elizabeth II in 1952. The horse romped leisurely through the mud at Woodbine to earn the "guineas." On this occasion, however, the royal gift came from the privy purse of the new monarch, King Edward VII, who belatedly advised the Earl of Minto that he "would continue the grant of Fifty 'Guineas' towards the Queen's Plate for the improvement of thorough-bred horses in Ontario," a tradition his mother had inaugurated in 1860. For a time that spring, directors of the Ontario Jockey Club had feared it might have to put up the money for the "guineas" since it had not received official confirmation from Buckingham Palace. In July the Club unanimously agreed to the Governor General's suggestion that "the name of the race to which 'His Majesty The King donates the sum of Fifty "Guineas"' should in future be known as the King's Plate."

The "guineas" from Edward VII were understandably delayed as the monarch was involved in a dramatic sailing incident on 22 May, the day before the Plate, while participating in a trial match aboard *Shamrock II*, Sir Thomas Lipton's challenger for the America's Cup. The monarch escaped injury after a sudden squall blew up off Southampton, which left the Cup challenger badly damaged.

At Woodbine, under gloomy and threatening skies, a non-holiday crowd of less than six thousand presented itself for "the greatest outdoor social and sporting event of the year." It witnessed yet another victory for the black and yellow silks of Joseph Seagram, his tenth out of the last eleven Plates. "Was it a race?" *The World* asked rhetorically after the odds-on favourite had romped to a six-length win. *The Mail and Empire* headed its report: "SEAGRAM WINS QUEEN'S PLATE IN THE HOLLOWEST FASHION."

A three-year-old chestnut gelding, *John Ruskin* warmed up for his win by galloping more than a quarter-of-a-mile after a false break. Since no bugle had sounded to signal an official start, *John Ruskin* and five others were recalled to the barrier. He was another of bloodstock agent Edmund Haines' English imports, conceived in England but shipped across the Atlantic before his dam foaled. The son of *Juggler* triumphed in the easiest imaginable fashion over Nathaniel Dyment's

JOHN RUSKIN WON HANDILY UNDER JOCKEY HARRY VITITOE.

Bellcourt. The second place finish by the Barrie industrialist's horse marked the first time since 1892 that either a Seagram or a William Hendrie horse had failed to gain the runner-up spot. Hendrie, who had again taken over as the OJC's president, did nail down third and fourth places as horses owned by Seagram, Dyment, Hendrie and Robert Davies, another Club director, dominated the race, taking nine of the first eleven places in the fifteen-horse field.

John Ruskin's jockey was Harry Vititoe, an American who allegedly was brought in by Seagram because he said he could ride at one hundred pounds if necessary. Vititoe, who rode in the Kentucky Derby in 1900, was two-and-a-half pounds overweight and rode the winner at 105 1/2 pounds instead of the 103 pounds allowed under Plate conditions for three-year-olds. After the race he was "all out," and had to abandon the remainder of his mounts that day because he was so weakened from his loss of weight. Veteran Harry Lewis, seeking his fourth Plate victory for the Seagram stable, was similarly fatigued and later fainted; the effort of getting down to 108 pounds had overtaxed his strength. Jockeys were allowed to ride five pounds overweight, which Lewis barely managed on Seagram's other main challenger, *Oneiros;* he finished a tardy eleventh.

Vititoe was said to be a member of a family of thirty-five, which may explain why newspapers and racing journals frequently misspelled his name, spelling it Vittatoe. Nevertheless, he would gain far more notice in later years for another accomplishment. He was the rider whom trainer Louis Feustel chose to break *Man o' War* at Saratoga Springs after owner Sam Riddle had purchased the gangling yearling for $5,000 from August Belmont II. Dorothy Ours, in her highly acclaimed book *Man o' War: A Legend Like Lightning,* wrote: "The person trainer [Louis] Feustel trusted with this delicate task was a slim young man named Harry Vititoe, a

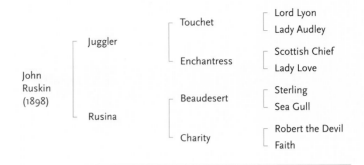

JOHN RUSKIN | 3-year-old chestnut gelding

			Lord Lyon
		Touchet	Lady Audley
	Juggler		
		Enchantress	Scottish Chief
John			Lady Love
Ruskin			
(1898)			Sterling
		Beaudesert	Sea Gull
	Rusina		
		Charity	Robert the Devil
			Faith

Owner: Joseph E. Seagram, Waterloo; *Trainer:* Harry Blair
Jockey: Harry Vititoe; *Breeder:* J.E. Seagram

former jockey with a kinship for wild creatures. Vititoe had ridden many a bucking horse. . . . But Vititoe's patience didn't make this colt trust a squeeze around his middle, a breathing weight behind his shoulders, and a human voice three feet behind his ears. When Vititoe settled into the saddle, *Man o' War* exploded. . . . To his human handlers, the red colt's explosive energy would remain a constant threat. . . . Vititoe balanced on Red's back for fifteen or twenty minutes almost every day, educating Red with each tug on a rein, shift of weight, and verbal command." It was Vititoe who was also credited with *Man o' War's* incredible ability to take command of a race at the break from the barrier. In training sessions, Vititoe would steady Red behind the bouncing net, teaching him to vault underneath and spring down the track. In workouts with other juveniles, *Man o' War* would always get away first.

WILLIAMS' MUSICAL LIBRARY NO. 8

QUEEN'S PLATE

MARCH AND TWO-STEP

The R. S. Williams & Sons Co., Limited

Head Office: 143 Yonge Street, Toronto.

DURING VICTORIA'S REIGN, ONE OF THE POPULAR DANCES WAS THE QUEEN'S PLATE MARCH AND TWO-STEP.

1901 QUEEN'S PLATE STAKES

FOURTH RACE
Woodbine Park
MAY 23, 1901

The Forty-Second Running of the QUEEN'S PLATE, the oldest fixture run continuously on this continent. 50 Guineas, formerly the Gift of Queen Victoria, with $1,250 added by the Club. Winner to receive Guineas plus $1,570; second horse $300 and third horse $150. A sweepstakes of $5 payable at time of entry; an additional $5 unless declared out by May 9. For maiden 3-year-olds and upward, owned, foaled, raised and trained in the Province of Ontario, that have never won a race, either on the flat or across country, have never left Canada, and have never been for a period of more than one month out of this province. A piece of Plate will be presented by the club. 27 entries. Distance, one and one-quarter miles.

Horse	A	Wt.	St	1/4	1/2	3/4	Str	Fin	Jockey	Owner	Op.	Cl.	Pl.
JOHN RUSKIN	3	103	9	8hd	8nk	2^1	1^5	1^6	VititoeH	SeagramJE	a-3-5	4-5	—
BELLCOURT	5	121	15	9nk	9$\frac{1}{2}$	8hd	4^2	2^8	Dugan	DymentN	b-6-1	7-1	2-1
FERNEY TICKLE	3	101	6	5$\frac{1}{2}$	5hd	6^3	6^1	3^1	Pemberton	HendrieWm	c-4-1	5-1	2-1
MAPLE SUGAR	3	105	12	7nk	7^2	9	8	4nk	Aker	HendrieWm	c-4-1	5-1	2-1
EUCLAIRE	4	117	7	6nk	6^1	7^1	5$\frac{1}{2}$	5^3	Murray	ClanceyEB	8-1	30-1	10-1
PARISIAN LADY	3	101	5	2^5	2hd	1hd	3^3	6^4	O'ConnorJ	DaviesRobert	d-6-1	12-1	4-1
KASLO	4	119	4	4^1	4nk	5$\frac{1}{2}$	7	7	Neel	SimonAD	15-1	15-1	6-1
PANDO	3	101	11	13	12	11	11	8	Forehand	HendrieWm	c-4-1	5-1	2-1
LADY BERKELEY	3	101	3	12	1^2	8^1	9	9	ThompsonL	DymentN	b-6-1	7-1	2-1
OPUNTIA	4	119	14	11	10	10	10	10	Crowhurst	DaviesRobert	d-6-1	12-1	4-1
ONEIROS	3	108	3	3$\frac{1}{2}$	3hd	3^1	2^2	11	LewisH	SeagramJE	a-3-5	4-5	—
PAARDEBURG	3	106	8	10	11	12	12	12	Lendrum	CookGW	10-1	20-1	8-1
SILVER LOCKS	4	117	13	14	14	13	13	13	Powers	DymentN	b-6-1	7-1	2-1
DADDY	3	103	1	12	13	14	14	14	MartinJ	BoyleDA	30-1	30-1	10-1
JUVENCUS	3	103	10	15	15	15	15	15	Blair	SeagramJE	a-3-5	4-5	—

Coupled in betting, a–J. E. Seagram entry; b–N. Dyment entry; c–Wm. Hendrie entry; d–Robert Davies entry.
WENT TO POST AT 4:45. OFF AT 5:00. Time, :25, :51, 1:19, 1:44, 2:18¾. Track muddy.
Winner: Ch. g (3), by Juggler—*Rusina, by Beaudesert. Trainer, Harry Blair. Bred by J. E. Seagram.
Start fair. Won easily; second the same. JOHN RUSKIN went to the front at his leisure and won as he pleased. He was by far the best. BELLCOURT ran a fine race from a bad beginning. She finished strongly. So did FERNEY TICKLE. ONEIROS and LADY BERKELEY stopped to a walk after setting the early pace along with PARISIAN LADY. PARISIAN LADY galloped three furlongs in a false break with JOHN RUSKIN, and then she tried to run away going back to the start and had little left after a mile. MAPLE SUGAR did well despite poor start. A claim of foul by Lorne Thompson, the rider of LADY BERKELEY, against the winner for bumping and inferfering around the top bend was disallowed by the stewards.
Overweight—Oneiros, 5 pounds.

RACE OFFICIALS LOOK ON AS WILLIAM HENDRIE AND TRAINER EDWARD WHYTE POSE WITH *LYDDITE*, FIRST WINNER OF THE KING'S PLATE

William Hendrie practically stole the historic first running of the King's Plate from his friendly adversary, Joseph Seagram, when *Lyddite*, an explosive chestnut daughter of a broodmare that the Laird of Waterloo had deemed a failure and had sold for $120 at an auction sale, easily outdistanced the greatest number of starters in the forty-three-year history of the race.

It marked the second time in four years that the brown and yellow silks of the Hamilton cartage tycoon's Valley Road Stable had earned the fifty "guineas" with a three-year-old filly, and on both occasions it had been accomplished at the expense of an odds-on favourite from Seagram's prepotent stable. Except for *Butter Scotch* and *Lyddite*, who had interrupted Seagram's annual spring ritual, the stable had captured each running of the Plate since 1891. Newspapers mentioned this fact while detailing the irony of Seagram's upset in an event which the owners of eighteen horses had so eagerly sought the prestige of claiming the first King's Plate and "guineas" donated by the new monarch, Edward VII. "Cast-off beats Seagram," was the tone of race accounts as the sports writers told the story of *Spark*, the unwanted dam of the Plate-winning filly. The columnists claimed that Seagram had sold the mare to Hendrie for the "paltry sum of $70" after his dismal performances in the breeding shed in Waterloo. A classy daughter by *Spendthrift*, out of *Torchlight*, and a full-sister to *Lamplighter*, "one of the crack racehorses of the day," *Spark* had been purchased in New York for $1,500, a price one prominent trainer thought was such a steal, he immediately offered Seagram $2,000 for the filly. The bid was declined.

Joseph Seagram had bright hopes that *Spark* would be the star matron of his Waterloo stud. Her first foal, however, was clubfooted and had to be destroyed. The second foal was also deformed and shared the same fate. Her third was "no account," and E. King Dodds, an author and turf historian, was asked to catalogue *Spark* for Grand's annual auction sale at The Repository on Toronto's Queen Street. Dodds said that the mare had been knocked down for $120 to veterinarian Dr. Andrew Smith. He in turn passed *Spark* on to Hendrie, who immediately bred her to his own stallion, *Derwentwater*, sire of 1899 Plate winner *Butter Scotch*. The deal accumulated a future dividend when *Lyddite* foaled *Shimonese*, Plate winner in 1909 for Hendrie's sons John and George.

Fate clearly was in Hendrie's hands on a bright, sunny day at Woodbine. Not only did he finish two lengths in front of *Fly-in-Amber*, one of Seagram's three-horse entry, but he did it with *Lyddite*, who was expected to set the pace for her more experienced stable-mate, *Maple Sugar*, and *Scotland Yet*. Trainer Ed Whyte—who had been attached to the stable on Plains Road in Burlington since his youth, and was lauded for his untiring efforts in preparing the four-horse entry—had difficulty finding a competent lightweight jockey at Woodbine who "could do" 101 pounds and he was forced to import an American rider for *Lyddite*. *The Daily Star*, which like most newspapers rarely printed a jockey's first name, reported: "Failing to get jockey Gormley at St. Louis, jockey Lindsey was engaged, but he could not leave Louisville in time to get here for the race. Wainwright was thereupon engaged at the last minute."

Sam Wainwright, from Nashville, was under contract to Sam Parmer's Tennessee stable. He rode a faultless race, avoiding the early crowding that the favoured *Fly-in-Amber* encountered, and won as he pleased. "Well, y'see, from the start I just got her into a nice spot and stayed there until the three-eighth pole, when I made my move. I was in fifth position all the time, and she was pricking her ears at the finish." *The Mail and Empire* added: "And away he went, as if the winning of a King's Plate was an everyday event with him."

The newspaper said that the "victory might have been more popular, perhaps, had a Toronto man been the owner of the winner, but even this is doubtful, for Mr. Hendrie has a warm place in the hearts of sportsmen, and the cheers which greeted the posting of the numbers were cheers for the President of the Ontario Jockey Club rather than for *Lyddite*." While the winner was being "Kodaked" in the paddock, Seagram was among the first to congratulate her owner, saying: "Well, I'm glad you won the first King's Plate." Hendrie jocularly replied: "Didn't I tell you I was going to do it?"

THE KING'S PLATE TROPHY WAS PRESENTED FOR THE FIRST TIME.

Two days later Hendrie received a cablegram from England and Sir Dighton Probyn, His Majesty's Equerry, with a one-word message: "Congratulations." The prompt testimony of King Edward's interest in the race delighted Hendrie. But turf patrons found it hard to break themselves of an ingrained habit—and nine out of ten of them still spoke of the race as the Queen's Plate. They did lavish praise, though, upon the Club's opening day program, which was enclosed inside a royal purple cover and bore the monogram of King Edward VII.

Considerable interest was focussed on the new Maxwell starting machine and its sturdy rubber barrier, which the OJC engaged along with starter Marshall "Mars" Cassidy and two assistants at a cost of fifty-five dollars a day during the nine-day meeting. Cassidy, America's most respected starter, was complimented on his skill in keeping the record Plate field at the post for just seven minutes. The Club introduced the machine when it adopted the "no recall rule." It was an unqualified success.

The OJC's joint lease of Woodbine Park with Joseph Duggan, a sensitive subject ever since 1881 when it had agreed to an initial five-year deal of $10,000 with the former publican, was still a matter of contention as it sought an extension of the lease. The OJC threatened to move racing to Exhibition Park in the city's west-end while it was in the process of adding stabling facilities at Woodbine. It was also pondering the acquisition of property on Don Mills Road, on which to build a track.

Early in 1902 Duggan informed the OJC that he would sell Woodbine Park for $175,000, a price almost triple the Club's evaluation figure of $53,750. He later lowered the sale price but the Club instead took out a twenty-one-year lease on the property, with an option to buy for $150,000. In 1907, three years after Duggan's death, the OJC exercised its option to purchase the racetrack and the Woodbine Park Hotel. The protracted deal finally settled the estate, but for some years afterwards Duggan's lone surviving daughter, Mrs. John J. (Annie) Dixon, held a $100,000 mortgage on the racecourse.

LYDDITE | 3-year-old chestnut filly

Lyddite (1899)	*Derwentwater	Doncaster	Stockwell
			Marigold
		Thorwater	Thormanby
			Fairwater
	Spark	Spendthrift	*Australian
			Aerolite
		*Torchlight	Speculum
			Midnight

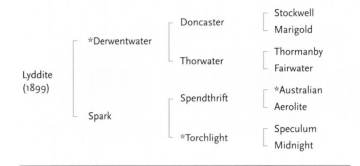

Owner: William Hendrie, Hamilton; *Trainer:* Eddie Whyte
Jockey: Sam Wainwright; *Breeder:* William Hendrie

KING EDWARD VII WAS FEATURED ON A POST-RACE DINNER MENU.

1902 KING'S PLATE STAKES

FIFTH RACE
Woodbine Park
MAY 22, 1902

The Forty-Third Running of the KING'S PLATE. $1,750 added. 50 Guineas, the gift of His Majesty King Edward VII, with $1,500 added by the Club. The first horse to receive the Guineas and stakes. The second horse $350 and the third $150. A sweepstakes of $5 payable at time of entry, and $5 additional, unless declared out by 8th May. For 3-year-olds and upward, owned, foaled, raised and trained in the Province of Ontario, that have never won a race, either on the flat or across country, have never left Canada, and have never been for a period of more than one month out of this Province. One mile and a quarter. Value to winner $1,725.

Horse	Eqt	A	Wt.	St	¼	½	¾	Str	Fin	Jockey	Owner	Odds to $1
LYDDITE		3	101	3½	3½	4^{1}	3^{4}	1½	1^{2}	WainwrightS	HendrieWm	a-5-2
FLY-IN-AMBER		4	117	6^{hd}	4^{hd}	2½	5^{hd}	3^{8}	2^{hd}	Lendrum	SeagramJE	b-3-5
OPUNTIA		5	123	5^{4}	7^{3}	3½	1^{2}	2^{2}	3^{1}	BolandJ	DaviesR	c-10-1
PICKTIME	s	3	106	17	10^{2}	5^{2}	7½	6^{1}	4^{4}	Hayden	ClanceyEB	d-15-1
MAPLE SUGAR	s	4	117	9^{2}	6^{hd}	6½	6^{4}	4^{2}	5^{4}	WalkerT	HendrieWm	a-5-2
SCOTLAND YET	s	3	106	8	8	8	8	8	6^{3}	Blake	HendrieWm	a-5-2
PARISIAN LADY		4	117	1^{1}	1^{1}	1^{2}	2^{1}	5^{1}	7^{1}	McQuade	DaviesR	c-10-1
EASTERN PRINCE	s	3	103	11	13	11	10	10	8^{2}	ThorpeJ	SeagramJE	b-3-5
DOONSIDE		3	101	2^{2}	2^{nk}	7	9	9	9^{1}	Kingston	HendrieWm	a-5-2
ONEIROS	s	4	119	10	12	10	4½	7	10^{2}	Dangman	SeagramJE	b-3-5
REVELSTOKE		3	103	7	5^{hd}	9	11	11	11^{1}	Thompson	DymentN	15-1
ST. ROSANNA		3	101	13	17	15	14	14	12^{2}	Hodgson	ClanceyEB	d-15-1
LADY ESSEX	s	3	101	4^{hd}	9	12	12	12	13^{4}	McKeand	ChappellH	20-1
GOLDEN WAY		4	119	12	11	13	13	13	14^{3}	Ellis	Doley&O'Neill	20-1
FERNEY TICKLE	s	4	117	14	14	14	15	15	15^{2}	Flint	BurgessJ	50-1
LADY BEVYS	s	3	101	15	15	16	16	16	16	MurphyR	MackenzieAW	50-1
LADY M.	s	5	121	18	18	18	17	17	17	McFadden	DavisP	40-1
*SAUCY SALLY		4	117	16	16	17	18	18	18	Pemberton	MeagherT	50-1

*Added starter.
a-Coupled as William Hendrie entry; b-J. E. Seagram entry; c-Robert Davies entry; d-E. B. Clancey entry.
WENT TO POST AT 5:29. OFF AT 5:34. Time, :12¾, :24¾, :51, 1:18, 1:47, 2:15. Track fast.
Winner: Ch. f (3), by *Derwentwater—Spark, by Spendthrift. Trained by Edward Whyte. Bred by Mr. William Hendrie.
Start perfect. Won easily; second driving. LYDITTE crowded the early pace, escaping the interference which FLY-IN-AMBER and PICKTIME encountered, and came fast in the stretch, running away from the others and finished with something in reserve. FLY-IN-AMBER and OPUNTIA were driving to the limit. PARISIAN LADY tired after going a mile. A mile is her limit.
Scratched—Cardigan and Court K.

During the 1890s, a period when Joseph Seagram and, to a lesser extent, William Hendrie, were controlling the Queen's Plate, Nathaniel Dyment made an inconspicuous debut in the contest for the fifty "guineas." Predictably, it was a Seagram horse, *Joe Miller*, that galloped to a decisive victory in 1894, while the Brookdale Stable's unheralded *Annie D.*, a six-year-old mare trained by Nathaniel's eighteen-year-old grand-nephew, Johnny Dyment, ran an unthreatening ninth. It was hardly an omen of what might lay ahead for the wealthy Barrie lumberman, his trainer and the mare, a maiden daughter "of the famed provincial sire *Terror*."

The Dyment name, through the efforts of John Dyment, a nephew of Nathaniel's and Johnny's father, had long been associated with the racing and the breeding of thoroughbred stock in Ontario. By 1883, the year the Plate became a fixture at Woodbine Park, horses racing in Dyment's silks were entered in the race each year, running either under his name or that of the Orkney Stable, his stock farm in the Orkney hills near the communities of Copetown and Lynden, just west of Hamilton. Three times Dyment's horses placed among the top three, but he was a "small owner and breeder" and was not in the same league as Seagram or Hendrie.

KING'S PLATE WINNER *THESSALON* (LEFT) AND STABLEMATE *NESTO* (9).

However, his Uncle Nathaniel began to build a racing and breeding establishment in Barrie, spending thousands of dollars to import the finest mares and stallions, such as **Courtown*, for his Brookdale Stable. This had been the site of the 1873 Plate race in Barrie and provided Nathaniel with an excellent training track. Soon the lumber baron began to compete with his fellow merchants and horsemen—Seagram, the Waterloo distiller; Hendrie, the Hamilton cartage magnate; and Robert Davies, the Toronto brewer and owner of Thorncliffe Stock Farm.

In his biography of the Dyment family, *The Dyments*, John Nathaniel Dyment, the great-grandson of Nathaniel, quotes a sketch that had appeared in *Lovers of the Horse*: "The thoroughbred never had a warmer friend nor more ardent admirer than Nathaniel Dyment. . . . He neither spared time nor money in the encouragement of breeding and racing thoroughbreds. In later years he maintained that this hobby had added years to his life (1832–1906) and only regretted that he had not taken to it when he was a much younger man. . . . Mr. Dyment had all the qualities of a sportsman, the betting ring had no attraction to him, as he seldom wagered on a horse, but spent thousands of dollars on foreign breds for the purpose of bettering his string; this being done for the pure love of the sport and not for the financial benefit to be derived therefore." The article Dyment quoted said that Nathaniel grew up in Beverley

1903 KING'S PLATE STAKES

FIFTH RACE
Woodbine Park
MAY 23, 1903

The Forty–Fourth Running of the KING'S PLATE. $2,000 added. 50 Guineas (the gift of His Majesty) with $1,750 added by the Club. The first horse to receive the Guineas and stakes and $1,250 added by the club; the second horse $350 and the third $150. A sweepstakes of $5 payable at time of entry, and $5 additional unless declared out by May 7. Allowances. For 3-year-olds and upward, owned, foaled, raised and trained in the Province of Ontario, that have never won a race, either on the flat or across country, have never left Canada, and have never been for a period of more than one month out of this Province. A piece of plate will be presented by the Club to the winner. Closed March 2, 1903, with 50 entries. Distance, mile and one quarter. Value to winner $1,960.

Horse	Eqt	A	Wt.	St	¼	½	¾	Str	Fin	Jockey	Owner	Odds to $1
THESSALON		3	103	7	1¹	2²	2¹	1ⁿᵏ	1³	CastroQ	DymentN	a-5-2
NESTO		3	103	5	2ʰᵈ	1ʰᵈ	1ʰᵈ	2³	2¹	DalyJ	DymentN	a-5-2
GOLDEN CREST	s	4	117	6	3¹	6¹	6⁵	3¹	3¹¹	Flint	OsborneHC	20-1
HAWKINS	sb	3	106	10	9	8	8	4¹	4ⁿᵏ	Pickering	BeckAdam	150-1
PICKTIME	sb	4	122	3	5ⁿᵏ	5³	4¹	5¹	5²	Hodgson	ClanceyEB	100-1
WAR MEDAL		3	101	8	7	7	7	7	6²	ThorpeJ	SeagramJE	b-7-5
CARDIGAN		4	119	4	4¹	3¹	3³	6ⁿᵏ	7	Jenkins	HigginsD	7-2
MAPLE SUGAR		5	121	14	6¹²	4¹	5¹	8	8	Munro	HendrieW	c-6-1
JACK CANUCK		4	119	1	13	9	9	9	9	Lendrum	SimpsonCB	100-1
PERFECT DREAM		3	101	13	10	10	10	10	10	WalshJ	SeagramJE	b-7-5
FARMER'S FOE		4	119	9	11	11	11	11	11	Rutter	DaviesRobert	30-1
DESERONTO	s	3	103	11	12	12	12	12	12	Kingston	HendrieW	c-6-1
MARSTON MOOR		4	119	12	8	10	13	13	13	Blake	CookGW	60-1
WHITEWARD		5	126	15	15	14	14	14	14	JonesA	McCulloughMrsJA	60-1
FLY-IN-AMBER		5	121	2	10	Broke down				SimmsW	SeagramJE	b-7-5

Coupled in betting: a–N. Dyment entry; b–J. E. Seagram entry; c–W. Hendrie entry.
WENT TO POST AT 5:01. OFF AT 5:08. Time, :24½, :51½, 1:19½, 1:47½, 2:15½. Track fast.
Winner: Blk. c (3), by *Cannie Boy—Annie D., by Terror. Trained by John Dyment. Bred by Brookdale Stable, Barrie.
Start good. Won easily; second driving. THESSALON was well handled and free from all interference, was waited with until the stretch was reached and came away with ease when Castro called on him. NESTO showed much speed, but was tiring in the last furlong and had all he could do to stall off GOLDEN CREST. The latter ran well throughout. HAWKINS ran a good race and finished fast. CARDIGAN tired after going a mile. FLY-IN-AMBER, the favorite, broke quickly on top but stopped badly after a quarter-mile. Simms scrambled off the mare when he noted she had broken her ankle. The mare was later destroyed.
Scratched—Elcho, Sheridan and Lady Essex.

BARRIE LUMBER MERCHANT
NATHANIEL DYMENT.

Township, Wentworth County, and at age sixteen began business for himself by purchasing a big pine tree, which he felled and had taken to a mill; as he made more money he purchased more pine, and from lumber amassed a large fortune and remained in this business until the time of his death.

The green jacket and orange sleeves of Nathaniel Dyment were prominent in 1898 when *Maritana II*, a daughter of *Annie D.*, was nosed out for second place by future Plate winner *Dalmoor.* Three years later, Dyment again was a threat in the race when *Bellcourt*, another filly out of *Annie D.*, was runner-up to *John Ruskin.* But there was no denying them in the forty-fourth running of the King's Plate in 1903 as *Thessalon* and *Nesto*, a pair of three-year-olds bred by the seventy-one-year-old Nathaniel and trained by Johnny Dyment, pranced away from the field for a one-two finish. *Thessalon,* a black gelded son of *Annie D.*, and named after the community where Dyment built his first major lumber mill, was ridden by Quintin Castro, who had shipped in from Nashville, Tennessee, to ride the gelding: "It was pretty easy. When *Nesto* [the Dyment horse most expected to win] came at me in the stretch, I shook the black fellow up and he came on like a good horse." Remarkably, no Seagram or Hendrie horse finished in the first five, an event that prompted *The Globe* to inform its readers:

> Mr. Dyment's victory was decided and complete, for the two horses that carried his green and orange jacket were first and second at the beginning, the middle and the end. The crowd saw the Seagram, Hendrie dynasty that had controlled the fortunes of the Plate for twelve years set aside for the House of Dyment, and without wishing any ill-luck to the gentlemen who have so long and so generously supported Canadian racing, a vast throng demonstrated genuine satisfaction that another good sportsman had reached his long delayed turn at the most coveted honour of the Canadian turf.

With his family at his side, Nathaniel Dyment accepted the cup and certificate from Lord Minto; his son, Albert E. Dyment, Member of Parliament for Algoma and future president of the Ontario Jockey Club, was there as well as his twenty-seven-year-old trainer and grandnephew.

The Governor General, Lord Minto, was a King's representative highly regarded in horse racing circles in England. T.C. Patteson recalled that Lord Minto once rode five winners in one day at a race course near Cambridge. "He was then Lord Melgund, and rode under the name of 'Mr. Roily.' It is not generally known that Lord Minto was one of the greatest jockeys the world had ever seen, the best in fact to my mind. . . . He rode three times in the Grand National."

The good luck of racing, which had been with Seagram's stable for years, shunned him in a dramatic and pathetic turn of events in this Plate race. Handicappers and the betting public believed that

THESSALON | 3-year-old black gelding

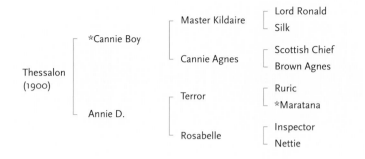

Owner: Nathaniel Dyment, Barrie; *Trainer:* John Dyment
Jockey: Quintin Castro; *Breeder:* Orkney Stud (John Dyment), Barrie

Fly-in-Amber was a cinch to win for the Waterloo stable, but she stumbled, falling in front of the packed stands. Her ankle was shattered. Later, moments after *Thessalon* and *Nesto* had crossed the finish line, the sound of a pistol stunned everyone. *Fly-in-Amber* had been destroyed. She had been runner-up in the previous Plate, and trainer Barry T. Littlefield, who had recently taken over the Canadian division of Seagram's vast racing stable, was anxious to see her win. As a precaution he brought in Willie Simms, considered the last of the great black-skinned riders. Simms, the only one at the time to win the Kentucky Derby, Preakness and Belmont Stakes, who had twice won the Kentucky Derby, once on the legendary *Ben Brush,* and later on *Plaudit,* quickly dismounted when he realized that *Fly-in-Amber* was in trouble.

Although he was sorely disappointed, Seagram took the misfortune in "his usual good spirit," as *The Globe* put it. Greeting Simms when he returned to the scales, the owner said: "Well, Simms, hard luck; broke her leg, eh? Can't be helped. That's horse racing."

In delving into the Plate winner's background, newspapers disclosed that *Thessalon* in 1902 had come within a nose of losing his maiden status and therefore his race eligibility when he was narrowly beaten in the first running of the Coronation Stakes (now the Futurity), which today is Canada's richest race for juveniles. They also wrote that the fate of his dam was a mystery. Two years earlier *Annie D.* had been sold at auction to a "Stratford man named Kelly for $45," and was apparently in foal to **Cannie Boy,* the sire of *Thessalon.*

OWNER NATHANIEL DYMENT, TRAINER JOHN DYMENT AND *THESSALON*.

On the morning after *Sapper*'s consummate triumph in the fastest running of the Plate, Jimmy Walsh, a Toronto boy from Breadalbane Street, was "togged in faultless tailor-mades, with a dapper felt hat and silk umbrella." He rode for Ryan and Dunn's stable in Chicago, where he now made his home. Walsh was described as a precocious, cool-headed jockey, with an "almost girlishly demure" face.

Since riding his first winner in New York at the age of thirteen, Walsh had taken four hundred races, but "unlike the average downy-lipped youth of nineteen, he already has a past—a luridly chequered dream of horses and big stakes, of money, ups and shouts from 'the gods,' of tawny tracks and fair women." This spicy sentence was part of an article in *The News* entitled "The Glamor of a Jockey's Life—Jockeys Have a Swift Time While They Are At It. But They All Get Consumption."

While recounting his experiences to the reporter, Walsh kept flipping a gold coin, as aimlessly as most boys toss coppers. "A sovereign," he said laconically. "An English gentleman threw it at me after the race f'r the Plate. You bet he won it on *Sapper*!"

Always rode the fast races f'r the big stakes. Always liked horses. Yes, *Sapper*'s a good horse, handy and quiet, and a fine breaker. No fuss at the net. Gits away clean an' easy. That's half the game. I told everybody *Sapper* would win the Plate after he worked a mile and a quarter in 2:14. Yes, he led all the way. Had everybody dizzy behind him.

Sapper's time of 2:12 clipped a full second off the record that had been set by *Ferdinand* in 1897; indeed, many thought that if Walsh had been pressed, Nathaniel Dyment's black gelding could have been another second faster.

Weighed 'undred and three in the Plate, but get up to an 'undred and eight 'n in the winter. Oh, we train down on toast an' tea, an' Turkish baths, and hitt'n the road. Do a five-mile clip out an' back, come in' take medsun on an empty stomach. Pshaw! The main thing is redoocin' an' hitt'n the road. Flesh that comes off that way stays off, you bet! Can't depend on the baths. They're flabby.

"Pretty gay life you jockeys lead?" the reporter supposed.

Yes—[with a meditative swing of his umbrella]—jockeys er a pretty bunch all right, but the money's the swiftest. Most 'v 'em spend it as fast as it comes—wine, cards an' women. The average jockey is played out by the time he's old enough to

JIMMY WALSH, A TORONTO BOY, RODE *SAPPER* TO A CONVINCING VICTORY.

vote. They all have consumption. It's the redoocin' an' hitt'n the road on a slack stomach is what fetches it on.

"So you have to make hay while the sun shines, eh?"

Bet we do. A jockey's only got a few years t' live anyhow—same as a horse. As long as he wins he's a favourite with the crowd. Yes, the crowd's a queer thing too, 'specially when they yell, and all yeh c'n see is a strech a hats a-wavin' an' yeh know it's your horse that's got the resta the bunch dizzy. If you're wuna the dizzy bunch, you feels queer too.

Sapper would be Walsh's lone hurrah in the Plate. He rode in the race only once more—the following year, when he finished third on *Half Seas Over*, the pacesetter for the mighty *Inferno*. However, the kid with the riding savvy of a veteran would provide only a fragment of the year's events.

It was a good year for the Ontario Jockey Club, whose profits were described as "highly satisfactory." Bookmakers' betting privileges for the thirteen-day spring meeting alone had netted $28,000. The Club was considering adding more stalls to the 343 they already had on the property. However, 1904 was a tragic year for many Torontonians: it was the year of the Great Fire. On 19 April flames destroyed almost every downtown building in the area of the commercial warehouses along both Front and Wellington Streets. Property losses were estimated at fifteen million dollars, and some of the 139 structures that survived were still smouldering a month later. The present Union Station owes its location to the fire. From the rubble and ashes of the leveled buildings, land for a new station that was required by the Canada's two

VICE-PRESIDENT ROBERT DAVIES WANTED THE PLATE RULES RELAXED.

national railways—the CPR and CNR—became available. Construction of Union Station started in 1916 and was completed in 1924 after delays caused by squabbling over the location of the tracks, located south of the Queen's Hotel (later to become the Royal York).

Dyment's *Sapper* was also "sizzling" when he galloped to a six-length win over William Hendrie's *Nimble Dick* and Alex Mackenzie's favoured *War Whoop,* who had cost the Kirkfield horseman $4,000—a record for a provincially bred horse.

Dyment, who had bought *Sapper* for about one hundred dollars from Richard Wells of Aurora, was politely chided by Joseph Seagram when he acknowledged the Barrie lumberman's second Plate victory. "Well, you had to do it with a mare of mine." *Kate Hardcastle, Sapper*'s dam, was formerly owned by Seagram, who sold her to Wells for a small sum at an auction. Wells in turn bred the mare to Dyment's stallion **Courtown* and sold the offspring to Dyment.

SAPPER | 3-year-old black gelding

Sapper (1901)	*Courtown	Haberstown	Belladrum
			Nora
		Lady Alice	Master Bagot
			Boomerang
	Kate Hardcastle	Clarendon	*St. Blaise
			Clara
		Miss Harding	Great Tom
			Melita

Owner: Nathaniel Dyment, Barrie; *Trainer:* John Dyment
Jockey: Jimmy Walsh; *Breeder:* Richard Wells, Aurora

The first film of the Plate was shot in 1904 when the OJC reluctantly allowed Shea's Theatre "to take a photo [moving picture]; so long as the race and racing was not in any way interfered with." However, it denied a request by a promoter to stage automobile races at The Woodbine.

Someone not in attendance for the running of the 1904 Plate was Woodbine's proprietor, Joseph Duggan, whose Kingston Road property was the site on which Messrs. Pardee and Howell had built the racetrack in 1875. "The Deacon," a former innkeeper and one of the city's best-known personalities, died two weeks before the Plate, a race he had won in 1889. It was Duggan who had influenced postmaster T.C. Patteson to "take a hold of horse racing and remedy its corruption" by organizing the Ontario Jockey Club. Another horseman, Henry (Grandpa) Chappell of Sandwich, Ontario, who had been racing horses since 1838 and was implicated in the great fiasco of 1865 in London with a foreign-bred ringer, the so-called *Stone Plover,* ran his last Plate horse, *Chappell Boy.* He finished twelfth.

In 1904 the OJC was startled to lose the services of one of its most knowledgeable directors, Robert Davies, the Club's first vice-president. Davies had been just sixteen when he rode *Nora Criena* to a second-place finish behind Chappell's ringer in the first heat of the Plate's most controversial race. In later years he would go on to own, train or breed two Plate winners, to establish the Thorncliffe Stock Farm, a prominent stud and racing stable, and to build one of Canada's leading breweries. The minutes of the Club's board meetings do not reveal why Davies resigned. But the board's failure to act on his suggestion of relaxing the rules of eligibility for the King's Plate, thus allowing into the racehorses who had been foaled outside Ontario, may have been a contributing factor.

THE GREAT FIRE OF 1904 DESTROYED MOST BUILDINGS ALONG TORONTO'S FRONT AND WELLINGTON STREETS.

1904 KING'S PLATE STAKES

FIFTH RACE
Woodbine Park
MAY 21, 1904

The Forty-Fifth Running of the KING'S PLATE. 50 Guineas (the Gift of His Majesty King Edward VII) with $2,000 added by the Club. Net value to winner $1,975 plus 50 Guineas; the second horse $450 and the third $250. A sweepstakes of $5, payable at time of entry; $5 additional unless declared out by May 10, and $15 additional for starters. For maiden three-year-olds and upward, owned foaled, rasied and trained in the Province of Ontario, have never left Canada and have never been for a period of more than one month out of this province. A piece of Plate will be presented by the Club to the winner. 39 entries. One mile and a quarter.

Horse	Eqt	A	Wt.	PP	St	¼	½	¾	Str	Fin	Jockey	Owner	Op.	Cl.	Pl.
SAPPER		3	103	5	8	$1\frac{1}{2}$	$1^{1\frac{1}{2}}$	1^{5}	1^{3}	1^{6}	WalshJ	Dyment N	a-2-1	5-2	4-5
NIMBLE DICK	b	3	106	4	9	$2^{1\frac{1}{2}}$	2^{8}	2^{4}	2^{2}	$2\frac{1}{2}$	Kingston	Hendrie W	b-3-1	3-1	1-1
WAR WHOOP		3	106	6	12	8^{nk}	8^{1}	8^{1}	3^{1}	3^{8}	Romanelli	KirkfieldStable	8-5	5-2	1-1
HAWKINS	sb	4	119	7	13	7	4^{hd}	$3\frac{1}{2}$	4^{2}	4^{3}	WonderlyO	BeckAdam	d-12-1	15-1	6-1
HEATHER JOCK		3	106	9	6	9	9	$6\frac{1}{2}$	5^{2}	5^{1}	MichaelsH	HendrieW	b-3-1	3-1	1-1
CON AMORE	b	3	101	3	3	10	10	5^{nk}	6^{2}	6^{8}	Olandt	SeagramJE	c-11-1	10-1	4-1
GOLDEN CREST		5	121	2	2	4^{1}	5^{hd}	4^{1}	7^{8}	$7\frac{1}{2}$	DalyJ	OsborneHC	e-8-1	10-1	4-1
BUTTER LADLE		3	101	12	14	11	11	7	8	8^{3}	DalyW	OsborneHC	e-8-1	10-1	4-1
GRAND LODGE	sb	4	119	14	10	$6\frac{1}{2}$	12	9	9	9^{1}	Songer	BeckAdam	d-12-1	15-1	6-1
NESTO	b	4	119	13	7	5^{1}	$3\frac{1}{2}$	10	10	10^{2}	Troxler	DymentN	a-2-1	5-2	4-5
NAROD		4	119	11	11	12	6^{nk}	11	11	11^{1}	Murray	AlexanderH	20-1	40-1	15-1
CHAPPELL BOY		3	106	10	5	3^{1}	7	12	12	12^{2}	JohnsonM	ChappellH	15-1	20-1	8-1
VIRTUOSO	b	3	103	1	1	13	13	13	13	13^{5}	ThorpeJ	SeagramJE	c-11-1	10-1	4-1
PERFECT DREAM		4	117	8	4	14	14	14	14	14	Castro	Kidd Brothers	15-1	20-1	8-1

a-Coupled as N. Dyment entry; b-Wm. Hendrie entry; c-J. E. Seagram entry; d-Adam Beck entry; e-H. C. Osborne entry.

WENT TO POST AT 4:45. OFF AT 4:55. Time, :23½, :49½, 1:15¼, 1:44, 2:12 (Plate record). Track fast.

Winner: Blk. g (3), by *Courtown—Kate Hardcastle, by Clarendon. Trained by J. Dyment. Bred by Richard Wells, Aurora.

Start good. Won easily; second driving. SAPPER was best at all stages and went to the front shortly after the start, raced NIMBLE DICK into submission and came away as his rider pleased. NIMBLE DICK ran well and was the only one able to keep the winner company. WAR WHOOP began slowly, but closed up a lot of ground and put NIMBLE DICK to a hard drive at the end. HAWKINS ran a good race but tired at the end. GOLDEN CREST kept up well for seven furlongs. The race was run with no mishaps.

Scratched—Hawkeye, Eastern Prince and War Medal.

nferno was Canada's first great racehorse, and for years no discussion of past Plate winners, or of who was the fleetest Canadian-bred horse, could proceed until someone had said, "I mean next to *Inferno*, who was the most memorable?"

More than fifty years after the 20 May afternoon the awesome bay colt almost rope-towed the field home while capturing the forty-sixth running of the King's Plate, Jack Thorpe would not hesitate a moment in stating that *Inferno* was "the greatest." He had galloped the rugged colt and had worked for three generations of the Seagram family as stable boy, exercise rider, jockey, assistant trainer and head trainer. "There was never in my time a Plate winner quite the equal of *Inferno,* and if it is any information, the old-timers of my younger days told me that there was nothing before who was in the same class.

He was the greatest." To emphasize his opinion, Thorpe told of *Inferno*'s performance at Saratoga Springs. "In those days there were no graded handicaps and when you ran at Saratoga you met the best in America. He won two handicaps there and he had to beat good horses."

In 1905, an excited public sensed that Joseph Seagram's colt was a cut above any other they had seen race at Woodbine, but few were aware that the swift son of *Havoc* would shortly become a legend and the subject of numerous articles up to and after his death in 1919. The horse's herculean deeds were legion, and it mattered not that when he died in obscurity, *Inferno* was an ill-tempered

"rogue," dangerous to the unwary and a hopeless failure at stud. He kicked down so many wooden stall gates at Seagram's Waterloo farm that an iron door had to be placed on his stall, and the only man able to manage the fiery bay was "Stricker," a ninety-five-pound groom.

A year before he died, *Inferno* had been sold to a man by the name of "Fish"; but the infamous colt, once affectionately known as "The Fastest Provincial yet Uncovered" fetched a bid of only one hundred dollars at auction. It was written that when the bay died, Seagram had him opened up. "His heart was the most massive I've ever seen," he said, a trifle awed.

1905 KING'S PLATE STAKES

FIFTH RACE
Woodbine Park
MAY 20, 1905

The Forty-Sixth Running of the KING'S PLATE. 50 Guineas (the gift of His Majesty), with $2,250 added by the Club. The first horse to receive the guineas, stakes and $1,300; the second horse $450, and the third $250. A sweepstakes of $5 payable at time of entry, $5 additional, unless declared out by May 10, and $25 additional for starters. For maiden 3-year-olds and upward, owned, foaled, raised and trained in the Province of Ontario, have never left Canada, and have never been for a period of more than one month out of this Province. A piece of Plate will be presented by the Club to the winner. Declarations Wednesday, May 10. Closed March 1, 1905, with 37 entries; 22 paid, $5 additional. One mile and a quarter. Weight for age. Value to winner $2,210.

Horse	Eqt	A	Wt.	PP	St	¼	½	¾	Str	Fin	Jockey	Owner	Odds to $1
INFERNO		3	106	1	1	2³	2³	2½	3²	1²	PhillipsH	SeagramJE	a-3-5
WILL KING	s	3	106	3	2	4⁴	4³	3²	2²	2³	BurnsT	DymentN	b-6-5
HALF SEAS OVER		3	106	2	4	1¹½	1¹½	1⁴	1³	3⁴	WalshJ	SeagramJE	a-3-5
MAID OF BARRIE		3	101	4	5	3³	3²	4³	4⁵	4⁴	WalshE	DymentN	b-6-5
GOLDEN CREST	s	6	121	6	6	5³	5³	5³	5¹⁰	5²⁰	FlintGeo	OsborneHC	40-1
CROSS OF GOLD	s	4	122	5	3	6	6	6	6	6	CrawfordA	PounderRH	30-1

a–Coupled, Inferno and Half Seas Over; b–Will King and Maid of Barrie. Coupled in straight betting only.
WENT TO POST AT 4:45. OFF AT 4:47. Time, :25¾, :49¾, 1:16¼, 1:43, 2:12. Track fast.
Winner: B. c (3), by Havoc—Bon Ino, by Marauder. Trained by B. T. Littlefield. Bred by Mr. J. E. Seagram, Waterloo.
Start good. Won easily; second the same. INFERNO allowed his stable companion to make the pace and when Phillips called on him in the last quarter came away with ease. WILL KING ran a good race, finished gamely and disposed of HALF SEAS OVER. The latter, away well, but tired from setting the pace. MAID OF BARRIE showed early speed. The others cut no figure.
Scratched—Heather Jock, Tony Hat, Chappell Boy, Stock Exchange, Dileas.

JACK THORPE WORKED FOR SEAGRAM'S FOR MORE THAN FIFTY YEARS.

Foaled at 10:30 pm on 9 March 1902, *Inferno* had a star on his forehead and one white rear foot. His feet would plague him throughout his prodigious career; they were so bad at times that a clocker, asked where *Inferno* could be found, replied, "Just follow the blood marks." From his very conception *Inferno* was destined to be a "good one"; his parents represented the Waterloo breeder's finest male and female stirps. His sire, *Havoc,* had been bred in Illinois and had performed with great distinction against the best handicap horses in the United States. He himself was a son of the formidable speed sire, *Himyar,* who achieved undying fame as the sire of the "Black Whirlwind," *Domino,* a pillar of the American Stud Book. As Seagram's stud, *Havoc* would sire three more Plate winners besides *Inferno*—*Slaughter, Seismic* and *Mandarin.*

The maternal side of *Inferno*'s pedigree was amply endowed with stamina and more than complemented *Havoc*'s fast blood. His dam, *Bon Ino,* won the Plate for Seagram in 1898 and was out of *Bonnie Ino,* the dam of another Plate victor. Several other winners of the race were also sprinkled throughout *Bon Ino*'s family, a fact that did not go overlooked by the more than sixteen thousand who were lucky to gain entrance to the overcrowded course (hundreds were turned away). His incredibly quick workouts that spring had tipped off railbirds, who made him the overwhelming 3-to-5 choice. So great was *Inferno*'s superiority that only three other owners were willing to pay the rider's fee plus the twenty-five dollars to start in the Plate, worth a record $2,210 for the winner.

Kelly Phillips, *Inferno*'s rider, allowed his stable-mate, *Half Seas Over,* to set the early pace before he surged into a ten-length lead and loped home effortlessly, tying the race record of 2:12. As he accepted the "guineas" from Governor General Earl Grey, Seagram found it difficult to express his delight at his first Plate win since 1901. "He's a nice horse, and it was a good race. . . . Oh, he just walked in!" Phillips admitted that the handsome colt could have "walked home three seconds faster if I'd asked him. It's a shame to take the money; he simply outclassed this field. I just had to sit still and let him run." A Texan, Phillips made his debut in 1903 and was one of America's great jockeys after the turn of the century.

Inferno lost his only race as a two-year-old and was intentionally put away by trainer Barry Littlefield so that he would not lose his maiden status for the Plate. A son of Charles Littlefield, the man who rode the first Plate winner in 1860, Littlefield showed extreme patience and skill in keeping *Inferno* competitive throughout his career, despite the horse's sore feet.

Active until he was six, *Inferno* often "spotted" his foes up to thirty pounds while setting track records and winning thirteen of his thirty-one races. He won the King Edward Gold Cup three times, the Durham Cup twice, the Toronto Cup, Queen's Hotel Cup and Stanley Produce Stakes, as well as two handicap races at Saratoga Springs. At five, his popularity blossomed to new heights. The public's faith in the big son of *Havoc* was "as boundless as the ocean." The bookmakers, on the other hand, despised the Seagram colt, who

INFERNO | 3-year-old bay colt

			Alarm
		Himyar	
	Havoc		Hira
			Elkhorn
		Elletta	
Inferno			Billetta Jr.
(1902)			*Rayon d'Or
		Marauder	
			Maudina
	Bon Ino		
			*Strachino
		Bonnie Ino	
			Bonnie Vic

Owner: Joseph E. Seagram, Waterloo; *Trainer:* Barry T. Littlefield
Jockey: H. (Kelly) Phillips; *Breeder:* J.E. Seagram

STRICKER THE GROOM WAS THE ONLY MAN ABLE TO MANAGE *INFERNO.*

in an eight-day span in May, won his only three starts that season.

Fittingly, *Inferno* departed racing in spectacular fashion, winning the mile and three-quarter Durham Cup in 1908. The Woodbine crowd, showing its respect and admiration for the venerable champion, cheered loud and long as he returned to the weigh scales. Accolades poured in for the gallant bay. *The Hamilton Spectator* said: "*Inferno* is now six years old and has been a most creditable representative of Canadian breeding. Season after season he has come out in the spring to run long distance races, with substantial weight on his back and turn away everything that could be brought here to win big prizes."

Historian and pedigree authority Michael Palethorpe had one explanation for *Inferno*'s inability to reproduce his own brilliance: "Perhaps Seagram's bloodstock was already saturated with the strains *of Havoc* and *Bon Ino.*" He was certainly the best colt Seagram ever bred but perhaps he burned himself out on the track. A red-brick building erected in 1905, Fire Station 227, would become an imposing landmark for residents of the Beach well into the twenty-first century. It is located at the corner of Queen St. E. and Herbert Avenue.

TRAINER BARRY T. LITTLEFIELD SADDLED FIVE PLATE WINNERS FOR JOSEPH E. SEAGRAM.

THE TALL STRAIGHT, IMPOSING FIGURE OF WILLIAM HENDRIE WAS ABSENT FROM WOODBINE ON PLATE DAY.

The tall, straight figure of William Hendrie was notably absent from Woodbine when a crowd of twenty thousand jammed the grounds on 22 May to view the King's Plate and applaud a record win by *Slaughter*. The president of the Ontario Jockey Club was critically ill in his Hamilton home, unable to view the annual contest for the "guineas" or congratulate his long-time rival, Joseph Seagram, who again was victorious with a son of *Havoc*. *Slaughter* sliced two-fifths of a second off the old record and provided the distiller with his twelfth Plate win.

It was the second year in a row that Hendrie's familiar brown and yellow silks were not represented in the race. In two months the seventy-four-year-old self-made tycoon, who had just become the first Canadian to be named an honourary member of Britain's Jockey Club, would be dead. His position as Club president would be assumed by Joseph Seagram, now the Member of Parliament for Waterloo North.

Later, praising his former rival, Seagram said: "He always looked forward to seeing his colours in first; but could take defeat equally well. His career was a model for sportsmen."

The Daily Star, in a 1902 story depicting the personalities and characteristics of the two men after Hendrie's *Lyddite* had upset Seagram's favoured entry, observed:

> The races are all right, but the centre and cynosure of opening day at the Woodbine is the King's Plate. It is not only a horse race, but custom and circumstance has made it a man's race—a contest between Hendrie and Seagram [Nathaniel Dyment and Harry Giddings Senior had yet to make it a four-way fight]. Just as the personal equation lends excitement to an election, so it enhances a horse race. Mr. Seagram has won many of the royal guineas; Mr. Hendrie not quite so many. Mr. Seagram runs horses because he likes 'em, and because a Seagram victory is good advertising for the Fourteen Year Old (whisky); Mr. Hendrie runs horses for the love of the sport and because horses—not racehorses, by the way—made his fortune. Mr. Seagram is bluff and democratic, and he smokes his cigar at an upward angle; Mr. Hendrie is a gentleman of the old school, dressed like an English squire, and smokes a cigar very grandly and deliberately, like a statesman pondering over a new tariff policy. Both have an enthusiastic following, and both are keen to win; but both are friendly rivals, and have nothing but good words for each other.

Hendrie's illness did not dampen the general spirit of the day as Seagram's three-year-old colt, *Slaughter*, cruised to a three-length victory over Nathaniel Dyment's odds-on choice, *Court Martial,* and Kirkfield Stable's *Kirkfield* at 3-to-1 odds. The small field was made up of two others horses, both rather inferior. Woodbine's gracious surroundings, and its annual King's Plate festivities, were beginning to attract visitors from across Canada and abroad. A special train travelled up from Louisville, Kentucky. Another excursion came in from Buffalo, and the city's hotels were filled to capacity for days before the race.

In Woodstock, where interest in the Plate was always keen because of local horsemen Charlie Boyle and Ras Burgess, *The Daily Sentinel* said: "A cosmopolitan crowd surged about The Woodbine, which is certainly a horseman's paradise. This year the improvement to the grandstand, track and betting ring have added to what was already the Belmont Park of Canada."

The public seemed to be faced with three major headaches: getting to the track, making a bet and fending off pickpockets. *The Mail and Empire* set the scene for its readers:

> Thousands hurried to the grounds, jostling, nervous and expectant. Rich and poor, cultured and uncultured, refined and in the rough, rubbed elbows and made obeisance at the shrine of the

equine. The procession of autos, carriages, tally-hos and electric cars was strung along the road from the corner of King and Yonge Streets clear down to the track. All streetcars heading east were jammed to the limit. Everybody seemed to be actuated by a desire to board the first one. Climbing on a crowded, moving car is one way of inviting a visit to the hospital, or a trip to the cemetery, but stylishly dressed women, men as well, were eager and willing to take the chance.

The old ramshackle shed that does duty as a betting ring fairly groaned under the strain. The 'talent' were wedged in like sardines, and men literally fought with each other to place their money in the capacious maws of the perspiring bookmakers, the thirty-six books doing a roaring trade. Only one favourite landed in front, and that one at a short price. The lambs were pretty well shorn, as in almost every race it was the unexpected that happened. The usual quota of bank clerks and store clerks, and others unable to lose, went broke.

There was quite a collection of light-fingered gentry plying their profession in the jam, relieving the fortunate ones of the increment obtained from the 'bookies.' Two of the gang were caught red-handed by the Pinkerton detectives engaged for this purpose, and the ranks in the cells will likely be further augmented today. Race frequenters will give a fervent 'Amen' to this, as they are of the opinion that there is more excitement in losing money in the regular way, by putting it on the 'also rans,' than being relieved of it in any such surreptitious manner.

For its part, *The Toronto Sunday World* described the start of the Plate in a quite charming way:

Down the track in a cloud of dust six black spots are moving—not so fast as an automobile, but with a speed that is alluring and with a stride and swing that forces the lump into the throat of the most phlegmatic beholder. As the dust cloud lifts the colours of the jockeys can be seen. . . . Anybody's race. . . . The stand takes fire. With a roar, *Slaughter*'s name is cut loose from 15,000 throats. *Court Martial* is after the leader, and Louis Smith is beginning to apply the whip. 'Come on *Slaughter*' To have heard the roar of the voices, to have seen the frenzied enthusiasm of the crowd is never to forget it. Hats are in the air, dainty women are splitting gloves, men are shouting. Perfect pandemonium breaks loose, for the race is won and the wise money has made good.

SLAUGHTER | 3-year-old bay colt

Owner: Joseph E. Seagram, Waterloo; *Trainer:* Barry T. Littlefield
Jockey: J.K. Treubel; *Breeder:* J.E. Seagram

THE PLATE RACE ANNUALLY ATTRACTED TORONTO'S GRAND SOCIETY IN LARGE NUMBERS.

1906 KING'S PLATE STAKES

FIFTH RACE
Woodbine Park
MAY 22, 1906

1 1–4 MILES (2:05). The Forty-Seventh Running of the KING'S PLATE. 50 Guineas, the gift of His Majesty King Edward VII, with $4,000 added by the Club. Value to winner $3,395 plus the Guineas. Second horse $700 and third horse $300. Breeder of the winner to receive $250. A sweepstakes of $5 payable at time of entry, $5 additional unless declared out by May 10, and $25 additional for starters. For maidens, three–year–olds and upward, owned, foaled, raised and trained in Ontario that have never left Canada, and have never been for a period of more than one month out of this Province. A piece of Plate will be presented by the Club. Closed with 37 entries, March 1, 1906.

Horse	A	Wt.	St	½	¾	Str	Fin	Jockey	Owner	Odds $1
SLAUGHTER	3	106	2	4	2	1	1³	TreubelJK	SeagramJE	a-5-2
COURT MARTIAL	3	106	1	1	1	2	2⁴	SmithL	DymentN	9-10
HARUKO	3	101	3	2	3	3	3¹½	Olandt	SeagramJE	a-5-2
WICKLIGHT	3	106	4	3	4	4	4⁸	Doyle	KirkfieldStable	3-1
STOCK EXCHANGE	4	117	5	5	5	5	5⁴⁰	Moreland	PowerBros	100-1
FIRST ROBBER	4	119	6	6	6	6	6	Renecamp	CanfieldGS	100-1

a–Coupled as J. E. Seagram entry.

Time, :12⅕, :25, :38, 1:06, 1:18, 1:43, 2:11⅗ (Plate record). Track fast.

B. c (3), by Havoc—Martyrdom, by *St. Blaise. Trainer, Barry T. Littlefield. Bred by J. E. Seagram, Waterloo.

Start good. Won easily. Second same. SLAUGHTER was splendidly ridden as Treubel waited on the leaders until the last turn was reached, and then came away, and won with plenty in reserve. COURT MARTIAL jumped into the lead at the start, set out a torrid clip to head of the stretch, where he tired. HARUKO finished strong, outgaming WICKLIGHT, who swerved to the inside when the barrier was released and bumped HARUKO, causing him to lose much ground. The others were outclassed.

Scratched—Bilberry, Forty Winks and Sword Dance.

1907 | KELVIN

Kelvin's unexpected triumph in the 1907 King's Plate was one of the more fascinating happenings in an event which was gaining a certain amount of curious recognition in the United States because of the fact that it was the continent's oldest continuously run horse race.

The Plate was fifteen years old before the Kentucky Derby was run for the first time, but unlike the extravaganza in Louisville, the conditions governing the contest for His Majesty's guineas favoured the owners of large stables. These men could afford to reserve their good horses until they were three years olds, just for the purpose of racing them in the Plate. Consequently, longshots rarely romped home for bettors looking to get rich with an unknown outsider.

Kelvin changed all this on a sultry May afternoon at Woodbine. The three-year-old brown colt, a "$90 cast-off," portrayed as "the despised outsider who demonstrated beyond doubt the dictum that nothing is so uncertain as a horse race," won the forty-eighth

HORSE SALES WERE LIVELY EVENTS AT THE REPOSITORY.

running of the Plate. Bookmakers, harassed by police throughout the afternoon and later summoned and charged with frequenting a common betting house, paid off *Kelvin*'s few supporters at odds up to 50-to-1. Most fans, meanwhile, were consulting their programs and asking, "Who's the number eleven horse?" "Who's *Kelvin*?" and "Who's T. Ambrose Woods?"

Ambrose J. Small, the theatrical entrepreneur and owner of Toronto's Grand Opera House who had mysteriously disappeared six months earlier, they knew about. A $5,000 reward had been posted for information about his whereabouts. But this Ambrose, who six weeks previously had married the daughter of bookmaker and horseman A.M. (Abe) Orpen, they knew nothing of, since it was his first attempt to win the Plate.

Ironically, *Kelvin* was bred by the late president of the Ontario Jockey Club, William Hendrie, and was out of *Nancy Lee,* whose dam *Bonnie Bird,* won the Plate in 1880, and was a half-sister to several Plate winners owned by Joseph Seagram, the incumbent head of the OJC. But on Plate day *Kelvin* was the property of "Pud" Woods, a wholesale liquor merchant and a member of the Toronto Hunt Club. He had spotted the cast-off at one of Hendrie's weeding-out sales at The Repository, and had bid on it mainly because of its well-proportioned build and the fact it was the lone offering of *Martimas,* still the only Canadian-owned horse to have won the Futurity in New York. In spite of these credentials, Woods was able to buy the youngster for just $90. *Kelvin* was immediately groomed for the show ring because of his perfect confirmation. He twice won blue ribbons in the stallion competition at the Canadian National Exhibition. However, as a three-year-old he was put into training for the Plate, although it was thought that at best he had a chance of "placing."

At the Plate presentation, the elated Woods said: "It's the first

King's Plate I have ever seen. Too bad it can't be used as a loving cup." Both Woods and trainer Charley Phair had put small bets on *Kelvin;* but Orpen "made thousands" by betting his money outside the track. While most players lost money supporting Seagram's 3-to-5 favourite, *Half a Crown,* who was second by a neck, and Adam Beck's *Photographer,* they cheered wildly when they realized that "Pud" Woods had become the first Toronto owner in eighteen years to win the Plate. The race was worth a record $3,895, just $3,805 more than Woods had paid for the horse as a yearling.

Aboard Seagram's odds-on favourite was Dave Nichol, a jockey from Chicago who was North America's leading rider in 1905. One of the finest natural riders ever seen in the saddle, Nichol enjoyed huge success in Canada, winning the Maple Leaf Stakes, Ontario Jockey Club Handicap twice, Toronto Cup and Hamilton Derby. Nichol was the rider of the immortal *Sysonby,* a horse who won fourteen of his fifteen starts and one that veteran U.S. horsemen at one time ranked only with *Man o' War, Colin* and *Citation* as America's greatest horses.

Kelvin's strong surge in the stretch provided an all-Toronto victory: he was ridden by twenty-three-year-old Jimmy Foley, and trained by Charley Phair, an ex-jockey who had won the Plate in 1880 on *Bonnie Bird,* the colt's grand-dam. Wood's wife, Elsie Belle Orper, whose father would later own Dufferin, Long Branch and Hillcrest racetracks in Toronto, and one in London as well as Windsor's Kenilworth Park (where he staged the historic match race between *Man o' War* and *Sir Barton* in 1920) was given some credit for *Kelvin*'s win. She had made the rider's royal blue silks, which were emblazoned with a black diamond, and apparently had prevailed upon her husband to enter the colt in the sixteen-horse field, which included *Halfcaste,* a horse owned by her father, and the eccentric lawyer Charles Millar. Trainer Phair expected *Halfcaste* to

Martimas, winner of the rich Futurity in New York for William Hendrie, sired Plate winners *Kelvin* and *Shimonese*. Trainer Ed Whyte tends the colt.

KELVIN | 3-year-old brown colt

Kelvin (1904)	Martimas	*Candlemas	Hermit
			Fusee
		Biggonet	Bramble
			Bobinet
	Nancy Lee	Strathspey	*Glenelg
			La Polka
		Bonnie Bird	Judge Curtis
			Bonnie Braes

Owner: T. Ambrose Woods, Toronto; *Trainer:* Charles Phair
Jockey: James Foley; *Breeder:* Valley Farm Stable, Hamilton

outrun *Kelvin,* but the colt was severely injured after being kicked at the start.

Kelvin did all that had been asked of him in training, but his work was far from impressive. Phair admitted that no efforts had been made to attract public attention by pulling off fast workouts. Foley's trip on the winner was lauded by *The Hamilton Spectator:* "He is entitled to share in the credit, for he rode a great race. His rush on *Kelvin* was well-timed and his finish stamped him as a rider of ability. Under a poorer rider it is doubtful if *Kelvin* could have withstood *Half a Crown*'s rush." *Bilberry,* whom bookmakers offered at odds of 100-to-1, was an even greater surprise after his game third-place finish. The gelding was a not very successful jumper, and his appearance in the Plate was regarded as a joke.

What was not a joke, as far as fans were concerned, was Woodbine's new admission charge of $1.50. Some blamed the fifty-cent increase on the OJC's expected loss of revenue caused by the federal Government's attempt to put racetrack bookmakers out of business. The Club had reluctantly introduced a new betting system following amendments to the Criminal Code by the Supreme Court and the Morality Department's zealous interpretation of the law. A year before, most of the bookies had been summoned and fined $250 apiece "for frequenting a common gaming house." The OJC said that bookmakers were living up to a literal interpretation of that judgment. The new law stated that the bookies could not occupy a "fixed place" to conduct business but must "keep moving." Previously, they had been housed in the betting shed to the east of the grandstand. Now they were spread all across the lawn. Newspapers agreed that the new system was a poor substitute. *The Hamilton Spectator* summed it up this way:

> Instead of using booths, the bookmakers, satchels in hand, occupied places on the lawns and exhibited odds on small slates. They were supposed to keep moving, just like peanut vendors with their push carts, but, like the latter, the majority of them remained in the same place practically all afternoon. Consensus was that the new system was a farce and the public was going to suffer by the change. About the only thing accomplished by the change was putting the public to a lot of unnecessary inconvenience. The quotations were no more liberal than in the past, the pencillers being afraid to loosen up, as they could not tell just what their neighbours were doing. The bettors had to fight their way through a struggling mass of humanity in order to get close enough to see what the quotations were or to place their wagers. That did not deter them any, and if there were any Moral Reformers present they must have realized that little had been accomplished by the change. The worst feature of the new system was the method of paying off. The cashiers paid off on the lawn, and in the big crowd it was often difficult for a speculator to locate the man with whom he had placed a bet. Many bets were unpaid and bookies did not handle as much money as in former years.

1907 KING'S PLATE STAKES

FIFTH RACE
Woodbine Park
MAY 18, 1907

1 1–4 MILES (2:05–4–117). The Forty-Eighth Running of the KING'S PLATE. 50 Guineas, the gift of His Majesty. $4,250 added. Three-years-olds and upward. Maidens. Weight-for-age. Winner to receive $3,895 plus 50 Guineas.

Horse	Eqt	A	Wt	PP	St	¼	½	¾	Str	Fin	Jockey	Owner	O.	C.	P.	S.
KELVIN		3	106	9	9	9^1	3^1	4^1	$1^{1\frac{1}{2}}$	1^{nk}	FoleyJ	WoodsTA	15	20	8	4
HALF A CROWN		3	110½	2	5	2^1	4½	3^2	5½	2^2	Nicol	SeagramJE	a-3-5	4-5	1-3	1-10
BILBERRY		5	123	7	6	2½	2^{hd}	2^1	2^2	3^{nk}	AustinJ	DeloreyM	30	50	20	10
WICKLIGHT		4	119	1	1	7^1	7^1	5^1	6^2	4^{hd}	Bullman	KirkfieldStable	b-6	8	3	8-5
KIRKFIELD		3	106	8	8	8^2	9^1	8^1	8^2	5^2	Kunz	KirkfieldStable	b-6	8	3	8-5
PHOTOGRAPHER	s	3	106	3	2	5^1	1½	1½	4½	6^{nk}	KellyJ	BeckA	2	2	4-5	2-5
KELPIE	s	3	101	4	3	4^{hd}	6½	7^1	7^{nk}	7^2	McCarthy	HendrieJS	20	40	15	6
UP-TO-DATE	s	3	101	12	10	11½	10^3	10^2	9^1	8^1	GoldsteinP	GiddingsJrH	40	30	10	4
GAY DORA		3	101	13	12	12^1	11½	11^1	10½	$9^{1\frac{1}{2}}$	AlexH	DaviesR	c-40	30	10	4
CAPSTAN	s	3	103	16	11	13^1	12^1	12½	14½	10^2	SmithL	DaviesR	c-40	30	10	4
EXCUSE		4	117	11	16	15½	14½	14^1	11^1	11^2	Diggins	BarryG	100	50	20	8
*BILLENEER	s	4	122	6	13	10^2	13^2	15^2	13^1	12^1	DennisonJ	BarbourJW	40	50	20	10
SEA WALL		3	101	14	7	6½	5^1	6½	3^{nk}	13^3	McDanielR	SeagramJE	a-3-5	4-5	1-3	1-10
HALFCASTE		3	103	5	14	14^1	15^1	13^1	12½	14^2	Lloyd	Orpen&Millar	10	15	6	3
SUPPER DANCE		3	101	15	4	1^1	8½	$9^{1\frac{1}{2}}$	15^1	15^2	Olandt	SeagramJE	a-3-5	4-5	1-3	1-10
WILD FLOWER II.	s	5	121	10	15	16	16	16	16	16	McBrideJ	BabcockR	10	15	6	3

*Added starter.

a–Coupled as J. E. Seagram entry; b–Kirkfield Stable entry; c–Robert Davies entry.

WENT TO POST AT 4:39. OFF AT 4:45. Time, :23⅗, :48⅘, 1:14⅘, 1:44, 2:12⅗. Track fast.

Br. c (3), by Martimas—Nancy Lee, by Strathspey. Trained by Charles Phair. Bred by Valley Farm Stable, Hamilton.

Start good. Won driving. KELVIN closed an early gap into a good position, then ran in behind the leader until rounding the far turn, where he moved up with a rush on the outside and was under a drive all of the last furlong to stall off HALF A CROWN. The latter came when straightened out for the final run, but tired at the sixteenth post and Nicol had to stop riding to straighten him out. BILBERRY ran a good race, but was tiring at the end. WICKLIGHT closed a big gap. PHOTOGRAPHER showed speed, but was tiring fast at the end.

Overweight—Half A Crown, 4½ pounds.

By 1908 it was clear that the King's Plate, on the verge of its fiftieth birthday, was no longer a race for older horses. Three-year-olds were starting to assume control, and this was an inevitability if North America's oldest uninterrupted horse race was going to flourish. Conditions governing the Plate badly needed to be brought into the twentieth century.

Critics had begun to question the feasibility of shelving Plate "also rans" for a year, thus ensuring their maiden status and eligibility. Unsuccessful aged geldings and infertile mares had often packed the fields during Queen Victoria's reign, but since 1898 the Plate had become the domain of youngsters. The only exception was Joseph Seagram's 1900 winner *Dalmoor,* a six-year-old. He was runner-up twice before graduating in his fourth try, which remarkably was not a record as "ol' *Fred Henry*" was a five-time loser in the 1880s before he gave up in disgust.

THE LITTLEFIELDS, CHARLES (SEATED) AND HIS SON, BARRY, WHO TRAINED *SEISMIC* FOR J.E. SEAGRAM.

The decisive defeat of *Half a Crown* by two three-year-olds is interesting in view of the belief earlier advanced. An exceptional animal might justify such a course, but the difficulty about recognizing an exceptional horse before he runs is that every owner thinks his horse is something above the common. The competition from younger horses is growing keener annually, and there may be something, too, in the contention a three-year-old has an advantage in May under the scale of weight [colts received a thirteen-pound advantage and fillies eighteen], though that is presumed to equalize matters.

The horse that *The Globe* writer predicted would win, Valley Farm Stable's three-year-old filly *Shimonese,* received a poor ride from her jockey, Willie Mulcahey, and lost by a neck to Seagram's fleet-footed colt, *Seismic.* Ironically, she would return and win the Plate the next year, but it would be ten years

The Globe, assessing the chances of the possible starters, reminded readers that if the Seagram stable was pinning its hopes on *Half a Crown,* who had been beaten by a neck the year before, and if Woodstock Stable's best bet was *Supper Dance,* another four-year-old, it may be of interest to recall that *Dalmoor* was the only horse over the age of three who has won the Plate in nine years.

This year the best looking chances in the Seagram and Woodstock Stables, and the only starter from Thorncliffe, are all four-year-olds, and if the winner is found in a horse younger than these, it will be a further demonstration of the futility of keeping over a horse especially for this race after he is three years old.

In his account of the race, *The Globe*'s reporter kept up his rhetoric:

before another older horse triumphed. Three decades (1939) would also elapse after *Seismic*'s thunderous and record-breaking win before the Ontario Jockey Club would finally revise the race's archaic regulations and allow only three-year-olds to participate.

Seismic, a bay colt by *Havoc* out of the imported dam *Semley,* followed in the footsteps of his sire's other Plate winners, *Inferno* and *Slaughter,* in either tying or breaking the race's record; his 2:11 clocking clipped three-fifths of a second off *Slaughter*'s 1906 time. In 1907 Woodbine became a much quicker course when C.W. Leavitt Junior, who was responsible for building the Belmont and Saratoga tracks, was put in charge of making it the fastest new course in North America.

Seismic's effort would probably have been wasted if it had not been for Mulcahey's ineffectual riding in the stretch and for the skilful ride of Charley Fairbrother, a nineteen-year-old jockey from Brooklyn, New York, who at the far turn drove through a gap on the

SEISMIC AND TRAINER *BARRY* T. *LITTLEFIELD*.

SEISMIC | 3-year-old bay colt

			Himyar	Alarm
		Havoc		Hira
			Elletta	Elkhorn
Seismic (1905)				Billetta Jr.
			St. Serf	St. Simon
	*Semley			Feronia
			Anne Page	Tibthorpe
				Windsor

Owner: Joseph E. Seagram, Waterloo; *Trainer:* Barry T. Littlefield
Jockey: Charles Fairbrother; *Breeder:* J.E. Seagram

inside to gain the lead. *Shimonese* (fractious at the barrier as she twice broke through the webbing) overhauled *Seismic* at the top of the stretch, but at the critical moment Mulcahey became rattled and let go of *Shimonese*'s head when the filly tired and swerved to the inside. Her rider then had to fuss with his lines in an effort to straighten the filly out again, but despite rallying her with the whip, she lost by a neck.

Seagram took his thirteenth Plate win in his stride, bowing as he accepted the congratulations and cup from Earl Grey. "Thank you, your Excellency," he said simply. Then, with a flash of humour, he added, "I hope you'll come back next year and do the same thing."

"It would be a great pleasure to me to do so," the Governor General replied, as he joined in the laughter.

Seagram was characteristically reticent to talk about his win. He told *The Mail and Empire*'s reporter: "It was a good race and I'm satisfied. You know as much about the race as I do, so what more need I say?" Trainer Barry Littlefield was almost as terse as his employer. "I always thought *Seismic* was the one to beat. Of course, it's easy enough to say it now after the race, but that has really been my conviction all along." Fairbrother was also to the point: "I felt from the first that he had it in him to win. All I had to do was wait for the proper time. When it came, I brought him along and won. That's all there was to my part of the race."

GOVERNOR GENERAL EARL GREY AND LADY GREY (LEFT) OFTEN OFFICIATED AT KING'S PLATE CEREMONIES.

1908 KING'S PLATE STAKES

FIFTH RACE
Woodbine Park
MAY 23, 1908

1 1-4 MILES (2:05). The Forty-Ninth Running of the KING'S PLATE. 50 Guineas, the Gift of His Majesty; with $4,000 added by the Club. The first horse to receive The Guineas, Stakes and $2,750; the second horse $700 and third horse $300. The breeder of the winner to receive $250. A sweepstakes of $5 payable at time of entry, $5 additional unless declared out by May 8, and $25 additional for starters. For three-year-olds and upward, owned, foaled, raised and trained in the Province of Ontario that have never won a race, either on the flat or across country, have never left Canada, and have never been for a period of more than one month out of this Province. Closed March 2, 1908, with 27 entries.

Horse	A	Wt.	St	¼	½	¾	Str	Fin	Jockey	Owner	Odds $1
SEISMIC	3	106	8	5¹	5hd	3½	1¹	1nk	FairbrotherC	SeagramJE	a-1.00
SHIMONESE	3	101	9	7¹	6¹	4½	2nk	2⁵	MulcaheyW	ValleyFarmStable	b-3.00
HALF A CROWN	4	122	7	6¹	7¹½	5²	3⁴	3¹⁰	SchillingCH	SeagramJE	a-1.00
TABLE BAY	3	101	4	3²	4¹	1nk	4³	4³	GoldsteinP	WoodstockStable	c-4.50
SUPPER DANCE	4	117	1	1¹½	1¹½	2²	5⁴	5²	WalshE	WoodstockStable	c-4.50
NEWGUILE	3	109	5	4½	2½	7½	8²	6¹½	PowersV	PowersBrothers	18.00
DOG OF WAR	3	106	6	8²	9²	9²	9³	7²	OlandtG	SeagramJE	a-1.00
ARCHIE WHYTE	3	106	3	9¹	8²	8¹	7¹	8¹½	RiceT	ValleyFarmStable	b-3.00
CAPSTAN	4	119	2	2hd	3½	6²	6½	9¹½	BurnsT	ThorncliffeStable	12.00
WICKLIGHT	5	123	13	10⁴	10⁴	10⁸	10¹⁰	10¹⁵	FoleyJ	AmbroseWoodsT	60.00
SAUCE O' GOLD	3	105	12	11³	11⁶	11⁶	11¹⁰	11¹⁵	LeibertE	MacLeanHJ	100.00
GOOD LIKENESS	4	117	11	13	13	13	13	12²	MartinC	CampbellWC	50.00
TWO LIPS II	3	106	10	12⁴	12⁴	12³	12²	13	PerryG	McKeeJames	150.00

a–Coupled as J. E. Seagram entry; b–Valley Farm Stable entry; c–Woodstock Stable entry.
Time, :24, :49⅘, 1:15⅘, 1:46, 2:11 (Plate record). Track fast.
B. c (3), by Havoc—*Semley, by St. Serf. Trained by Barry T. Littlefield. Bred by Joseph E. Seagram, Waterloo.
At post six minutes. Start good. Won driving. Place easily. SEISMIC broke slow and was outrun in the first half and was carried wide at first turn and forced to work his way up on outside. Came through on inside entering stretch with Fairbrother outriding Mulcahey when it came to a finish. SHIMONESE messed about in the early stages, moved up strong entering stretch and closed stoutly. Would have won had her rider kept her straight. But Mulcahey let go of her head and she swerved. HALF A CROWN, in the pack, closed with a rush. TABLE BAY was close to the pacesetters but tired in the stretch. SUPPER DANCE tired badly in last half after setting pace. NEWGUILE and CAPSTAN also faltered in stretch. WICKLIGHT acted up at the gate and did his best to cripple, with his heels, every horse near him, and did land severely on HALF A CROWN, clearly third best while running on the outside.
Scratched—The Lintie.

The tale of *Shimonese* and her resplendent victory in the Silver Jubilee King's Plate was quite dissimilar to the romantic "Cinderella" or "rags to riches" anecdotes usually associated with racetrack lore. Rather, she was a "riches, to riches, to riches" horse that simply ran the fastest mile-and-a-quarter in the Plate's history.

A four-year-old chestnut filly, *Shimonese* was the "retrieved property" of Colonel John S. Hendrie and George M. Hendrie of Hamilton, sons of William Hendrie, the late president of the Ontario Jockey Club and the filly's breeder. How and why she was able to run under the brown and yellow silks of Valley Farm Stable affords another example of the bizarre conditions that regulated the running of the Plate before World War II.

Shimonese, a daughter of 1902 Plate winner *Lyddite*, was among the consignment of yearlings from Hendrie's estate being offered for sale at a special auction in 1906 at Toronto's Repository on Simcoe Street. She was bought by Alexander Mackenzie's affluent Kirkfield Stable. A young but highly respected horseman and railway executive, Mackenzie had grown up in the village of Kirkfield, east of Lake Simcoe in Victoria County. Later he moved to Toronto and built one of the most beautiful homes in the fashionable Rosedale district. Mackenzie was the son of Sir William Mackenzie, who along with his partner Sir Donald Mann, built the Canadian Northern Railway in 1895, a company which became one of Canada's three transcontinental links. The senior Mackenzie helped develop Ontario's first major hydro-electric power system, ensuring his electric streetcar system in Toronto would have a supply of relatively inexpensive power generated from the falling waters at Niagara. He also constructed transit systems in Winnipeg, Great Britain, China, Mexico, Argentina, Brazil and developed mines. Brascan began its existence as one of Mackenzie's many entrepreneurial creations. In 2000 a plaque was unveiled at the Sir

THE "EXPLOSIVE" *SHIMONESE* WON THE SILVER JUBILEE RUNNING OF THE PLATE.

William Mackenzie Inn, his former summer residence in Kirkfield, a small community not far from Beaverton, Ontario. Mackenzie was born in a log cabin in Kirkfield in 1849. From 1897 until his death in 1923 Mackenzie owned Benvenuto, an ornate Norman castle of stone with turrets, located where today's Edmund Street runs into Avenue Road in Toronto. It was demolished in 1927, but Benvenuto Place exists today.

Less than a year after buying *Shimonese*, the thirty-one-year-old Mackenzie "met an untimely and lamentable death," which left the ownership of Kirkfield Stable in the hands of his older brother, Roderick Mackenzie. However, the surviving member of the stable was ineligible to run a horse in the Plate because of the race's antiquated conditions, which stipulated that a horse had to be "owned by a resident of Ontario." Mackenzie, who lived in Winnipeg, reluctantly returned *Shimonese* to the Hendries for "a sum considerably in advance of the purchase price," according to *The Globe*.

Newspapers paid little attention to the fact that both Rod Mackenzie and George Hendrie became the first Canadian owners to run a horse in the Kentucky Derby that year. Mackenzie's *Direct* finished sixth, three lengths ahead of Hendrie's *Michael Angelo*.

The fortuitous circumstances involving Mackenzie's ineligibility to participate in the Plate were naturally welcomed by the Hendries, although some horsemen felt they should have won the Plate a year earlier with *Shimonese*. Her defeat by a neck to *Seismic* occurred when she suddenly swerved in the stretch, displaying some of the bad habits of her sire, *Martimas*,

1909 KING'S PLATE STAKES

FIFTH RACE
Woodbine Park
MAY 22, 1909

1 1-4 MILES (2:05). The Fiftieth Running of the KING'S PLATE. 50 Guineas, the gift of His Majesty King Edward VII. 3-year-olds and upward, owned, foaled, raised and trained in the Province of Ontario, that have never won a race on the flat or across country. Estimated value $5,000. Net value to winner $3,250; second horse, $700; third horse, $300. Club will present a piece of plate to owner of winner. Breeding award $250. Closed March 1 with 34 entries at $5. To start $25.

Horse	Eqt	A	Wt.	PP	St	¼	½	¾	Str	Fin	Jockey	Owner	Op.	Cl.
SHIMONESE		4	119	7	5	6hd	4¹	11½	1⁵	1⁵	GilbertC	ValleyFarmStable	1	4-5
TOLLENDAL	sb	3	108	1	3	2³	2⁶	2²	2¹⁰	2¹⁵	Goldstein	SeagramJE	a-3	4-1
FORT GARRY	b	3	108	3	2	1²	1¹½	3¹⁰	3⁸	3⁸	Mentry	DymentJ	3	16-5
DESERT STAR		3	108	4	6	8	7hd	5½	4½	4³	McCarthyD	CookGW	30	40-1
COURTIER	sb	3	108	6	4	4hd	3¹	4⁶	5¹⁰	5⁶	MusgraveP	SeagramJE	a-3	4-1
DOG OF WAR		4	124	5	1	5²	5²	6⁴	6⁴	6⁶	Quarrington	SeagramJE	a-3	4-1
SAUCE O'GOLD		4	119	8	8	7¹½	8	7³	7³	7⁴	FoleyJ	MacLeanHJ	30	60-1
GENEROUS MOOR		3	110	2	7	3½	6¹	8	8	8	WalshE	BeckA	30	20-1

a–Coupled as J. E. Seagram entry.
WENT TO POST AT 4:55. OFF AT 5:00. Time, :23³/₅, :48⁴/₅, 1:15, 1:43, 2:10²/₅ (Plate record). Track fast.
(NO SEPARATE PLACE OR SHOW WAGERING)
Ch. f (4), by Martimas—Lyddite, by *Derwentwater. Trainer, John Nixon. Bred by Valley Farm Stable, Hamilton.
Start good. Won cantering; second and third easily. SHIMONESE ran under stout restraint for the first half mile, then moved up with a rush on the turn out of the backstretch, caught and passed the leaders easily and drew away under restraint in the last quarter. TOLLENDAL followed the fast early pacemaker closely, but had nothing left when the winner challenged. FORT GARRY, made entirely too much use of in the first half, showed the most early speed, but tired badly in the last mile. The others were beaten off and are very ordinary.
Scratched—Mendip and Capetown.
Overweight—Generous Moor, 2 pounds.

SHIMONESE WAS SOLD AT THE REPOSITORY ON TORONTO'S SIMCOE STREET.

SHIMONESE | 4-year-old chestnut filly

Shimonese (1905)	Martimas	*Candlemas	Hermit
			Fusee
		Biggoner	Bramble
			Bobinet
	Lyddite	*Derwentwater	Doncaster
			Thorwater
		Spark	Spendthrift
			*Torchlight

Owner: Valley Farm Stable (Colonel John S. Hendrie and George M. Hendrie), Hamilton; *Trainer:* John Nixon; *Jockey:* Clifford Gilbert
Breeder: Valley Farm Stable

who more than once was responsible for the same costly sidestep.

There was no swerving or sidesteps in the 1909 Plate; *Shimonese* ran as straight as an arrow, rushing into the lead despite the "stout restraint" of the jockey, Clifford Gilbert.

In the weeks leading up to this Plate, most newspaper articles conceded the race to the filly. But certain critics still queried her courage and performance as a three-year-old. She was second in all six of her starts, including being runner-up to the great *Inferno* in the gruelling mile and three-quarter Durham Cup in 1908. The tendency to remain a bridesmaid did enable *Shimonese* to build up a $1,780 dowry while retaining her eligibility for the Plate. At post-time, she was the 4-to-5 favourite.

As he presented the cup to the Honourable Colonel Hendrie, MPP for Wentworth County, Governor General Earl Grey said cheerfully: "It gives me the greatest possible pleasure to give you this Plate. I feel it is your turn, as I have already given it to Mr. Seagram several times." The Governor General then turned and smiled at Seagram, who was standing at his elbow. The Laird of Waterloo, always gracious in defeat, must have experienced some discomfiture.

It was Joseph Seagram who had gone to New York in 1891 and purchased a much-touted yearling out of *Torchlight*, which he named *Spark*. He expected her to become the star matron in his broodmare band. But after her repeated failures, Seagram sold her for just $120 to William Hendrie, who reaped a bountiful harvest out of the mare as he bred her to his stallions. *Spark* was the dam of Plate winner *Lyddite*, who in turn was the dam of *Shimonese*.

An article in *The Globe*, entitled "Nomenclature of the Turf," acknowledged the appropriateness of the filly's name:

> *Shimonese* is a Japanese high explosive, and the name is eminently suitable for a daughter of *Lyddite*, another preparation of dynamite, and the mare thus named a daughter of *Spark*.

It was hoped that the Plate victory of the Japanese-named horse would be an omen for the upcoming running of the English Derby, where King Edward VII's colours would be carried by *Minoru*, the Japanese word for "success." As it turned out, *Minoru* did win. A racetrack in Vancouver was later named in honour of the monarch's horse.

GEORGE M. HENDRIE.

ALEXANDER MACKENZIE.

COLONEL JOHN S. HENDRIE.

A mong the many forgotten anecdotes of Plate history is one about a small provincial breeder who upstaged the wealthy studs of Seagram, the Hendries, Brookdale, Thorncliffe, and the Giddings, the formidable newcomers from Oakville's Cedar Grove. It was a feat most horsemen believed impossible, or at best a fluke. Unfortunately, few people knew anything about the man who had bred the first two finishers in the fifty-first running of the King's Plate, the first under the patronage of the race's third monarch, King George V.

His identity was played down largely because he no longer owned *Parmer*, a three-year-old bay gelding who jogged home an awesome ten lengths in front of his stablemate *Commola*, an unraced filly. The untried three-year-olds had run under the silks of Colonel John S. Hendrie and George M. Hendrie, owners of Hamilton's Valley Farm Stable, easily outclassing Seagram's odds-on entry of *Jane Shore* and *Tollendal*. Only one newspaper, *The Mail and Empire*, gave any details about the breeder, Joseph James, who owned a handful of broodmares on his small farm in Windsor.

James had sold *Parmer* and *Commola* as yearlings to George Hendrie after he had spotted them romping in a field opposite the Windsor racecourse in 1908. He was much impressed by their looks, the newspaper said, and bought the yearlings as well as the mares:

> Joe James was an enthusiastic horseman, anxious to win a King's Plate. With this end in view he picked out a few of his best bred mares and shipped them to Walter O. Parmer's Edenwold Stud near Nashville, Tennessee, to be bred to the *Hanover* stallion, *The Commoner*. The mares were *Losiola* and *Placena*, and the produce proved to be *Commola* and *Parmer*.

The amount Hendrie paid for the four horses was never disclosed, but the newspaper said that James would share in the one-two finish of the horses he bred and would receive "something like $850," which included a $250 award to the breeder.

Johnny Wilson, a young Kentuckian, was riding *Parmer*, who was named after the owner of the Nashville stud where he was conceived:

> It was the easiest kind of win. When we got to the stretch, I shouted to Stanley Davis, 'Stan, I'm going after the money.' Stanley [on *Commola*] shouted back, 'Go ahead, kid, and win.' Then I hit my horse a couple of times with the whip because I wasn't going to take any chances, but I won easy.

Davis, a Toronto boy, went on: "I shouted to Wilson to go and win because my horse was getting dead. It was all I could do to save the place. There were no orders given us to let one another get ahead. We were just told to do our best to win.

THE COLOURFUL BOOKMAKERS, THE "KNIGHTS OF THE PENCIL," MADE THEIR LAST APPEARANCE AT WOODBINE IN 1910.

Parmer's one-sided triumph over a slow surface at Woodbine was the Hendrie's second Plate in a row; they had taken over Valley Farm Stable in 1906 after the death of their father, William Hendrie. The win also gave the Hendrie family the distinction of winning the first (1902) and the last (1909) runnings of the King's Plate during the reign of King Edward VII and the first under the patronage of the new monarch, George V. The Prince of Wales assumed the crown on 8 May 1910. Out of respect for the bereaved King, who had owned a large racing stable, the Ontario Jockey Club delayed the opening of the season until 24 May, four days after the "peace-maker of Europe's" elaborate state funeral. The postponement was applauded by *The World*, who praised the Club's directors for displaying "true loyalty" while facing "a serious curtailment of receipts in giving up the lucrative holiday weekend dates."

The Globe noted that the absence of Earl Grey, who had returned to England to attend the funeral, "undoubtedly dimmed the social lustre of the occasion." However, Club president Joseph Seagram added a witty touch in the presentation ceremonies: "It gives me great pleasure to present to you this well won trophy. As I have been unable to win it myself, I am glad that such good sportsmen have captured it."

When Seagram was informed by Colonel Hendrie that his share of the purse, $3,323, would go to George Hendrie, "who was primarily responsible for the success of our good horse, *Parmer*; and besides, we are partners in Valley Farm and always divide the honours," the Waterloo horseman jocularly inquired: "Do you and your brother propose to keep on dividing the Plate year by year?" "That is a matter for the future to decide," Colonel Hendrie rejoindered with a smile.

The future of horseracing at racetracks was in jeopardy in 1910 as politicians debated a contentious bill in the House of Commons. The agitation against racetracks and gambling was spearheaded by the Moral and Social Association, under the secretaryship of Rev. Dr. Shearer of Toronto. On 16 November 1909, H.H. Miller, MP (South Grey), introduced a bill which was designed to prohibit "the business of betting" on racetracks in any place in Canada. Known as the Miller Bill, an act to amend the Criminal Code (as it affected racetracks) which, if passed, would have changed the whole racing

JOHNNY WILSON, A KENTUCKIAN, RODE *PARMER*.

picture. The bill was designed to "curtail the evils of racetrack gambling." The Hon. Alan Bristol Aylesworth, Minister of Justice, was credited as the chief person responsible for the defeat of the bill and the deciding factor in saving racing for Canadians. It was accomplished by passing an amendment. Prime Minister Sir Wilfrid Laurier supported the amendment. Until the amended Miller Bill was passed the only method of betting on Canadian racetracks was by the English method of bookmaking.

While the bill was being dealt with in the House, Aylesworth, who was severely critical of the promoters of this bill, said: "Where is this thing going to end? We have made it a crime for a man to go fishing on Sunday. We have branded as a criminal a boy, nearly grown, who smokes a cigarette. I believe the day is not far distant when the influences behind the Miller bill will demand criminal statute against card-playing, dancing and any other form of amusement which certain people may regard as sinful."

After numerous stormy debates the amendment was saved by a single vote. On 15 April 1910 the compromise legislation was given third reading and passed by the House of Commons. It allowed seven-day meetings and prohibited betting as a business. Permission was granted for bookmaking to take place during those periods.

As it turned out, the 1910 Plate marked the last year of legalized bookmaking at Woodbine. Diluted amendments to the Criminal Code allowed the introduction of the French pari-mutuel betting system and machines were ordered. "Speculation without bookmakers," was the message relayed from Churchill Downs when betting machines had been introduced for the Kentucky Derby two years before. The roaming "Knights of the Pencil" with their slates were to be replaced by the "colourless iron monsters."

Evicted from their old-fashioned booths in 1906, bookmakers had been forced to circulate in front of the stands or face prosecution. This law was often ignored, and on Plate day 1910, fans found it difficult to place a wager. *The Mail and Empire* set down the bettors' predicament: "At times it would require a hardened athlete, or an organized football team in the form of a

wedge, to break in to make a bet. It was, in fact, a great sight to see how the people perspired and strove, submitted to have toes trampled upon and their clothing disarranged, in the great feat of placing money upon their respective choices."

The impending demise of the pencillers was forecast in an editorial by *The World* the day before the Plate: "Probably the time is coming when the bookmaker is to disappear from the race meeting, and if betting is to be allowed, then it will be limited to betting machines. Bookmakers are not so bad as they are painted, but they are an unnecessary part of racing, or ought soon to be."

Also in 1920, Fred (Busher) Herbert became the first Canadian-born jockey to win the Kentucky Derby, guiding *Donau* to victory. Born in Ontario in 1887, Herbert was one of the first contract riders for E.R. Bradley's Idle Hour stable that dominated racing in North America during the 1920s and '30s. He won the first race in 1903 at Churchill Downs, weighing in at 89 pounds, equipment and all, for that race, and was never troubled afterward in having to diet. Two years after his Derby victory he moved to England. From that base he explored the world, riding in Russia, England, France, Hungary, India, Australia and Argentina. Though the exact totals were never assembled, Herbert reckoned that he had ridden 25,000 horses and 3,000 winners. Wherever he went he was known for his skill in getting mounts away quickly from the start. He retired in 1974 at age 61, and died on June 8, 1955, at his residence in Maidenhead, near London.

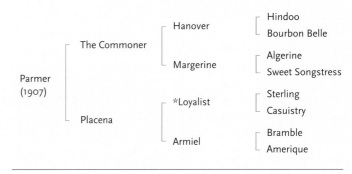

PARMER | 3-year-old bay gelding

Parmer (1907)
- The Commoner
  - Hanover
    - Hindoo
    - Bourbon Belle
  - Margerine
    - Algerine
    - Sweet Songstress
- Placena
  - *Loyalist
    - Sterling
    - Casuistry
  - Armiel
    - Bramble
    - Amerique

Owner: Valley Farm Stable (Colonel John S. Hendrie and George M. Hendrie), Hamilton; *Trainer:* John Nixon; *Jockey:* Johnny Wilson; *Breeder:* Joseph James, Windsor

1910 KING'S PLATE STAKES

FIFTH RACE
Woodbine Park
MAY 24, 1910

1 1–4 MILES (2:05). The Fifty–First Running of THE KING'S PLATE. 50 Guineas, the Gift of His Majesty King George V, with $4,000 added by the Club. The first horse to receive The Guineas, stakes and $2,750 (net value $3,322.50), second horse $700 and third horse $330. The breeder of the winner to receive $250. A sweepstakes of $5 payable at time of entry, and $25 additional for starters. For maiden 3–year–olds and upward, owned

foaled, raised and trained in the Province of Ontario.

Horse	Eqt A	Wt.	PP	St	¼	½	¾	Str	Fin	Jockey	Owner	Op.	Cl.	Pl.
PARMER	3	105	2	2	4½	4¹½	2¹	1¹	1¹⁰	WilsonJ	ValleyFarmStable	a-3	5-2	7-10
COMMOLA	3	104½	4	5	3²	2²	3⁵	3⁴	2ⁿᵏ	DavisS	ValleyFarmStable	a-3	5-2	7-10
JANE SHORE	3	103	3	3	1²	1⁵	1⁶	2⁶	3ʰᵈ	TaplinE	SeagramJE	b-7-10	7-10	1-4
WHAUP	3	108	1	1	10	10	9	8	4¹	BurnsG	ValleyFarmStable	a-3	5-2	7-10
VALYDON	s 4	124	9	8	6ʰᵈ	5ʰᵈ	7²	6²	5⁴	HenryJ	MacLeanHJ	30	60	20
FROLIC	3	103	7	10	9	7	4½	4¹	6¹	McCarthyD	DaviesR	5	6	2
TOLLENDAL	sb 4	121	5	9	7ʰᵈ	6ⁿᵏ	5ⁿᵏ	5¹	7⁵	MusgraveP	SeagramJE	b-7-10	7-10	1-4
ONAPING	7	124	6	4	2¹½	3½	6¹	7ʰᵈ	8²	TroxlerR	NewellR	25	50	15
*PARADE	s 5	124	8	7	8	9	10	9	9	KellyA	MeagherM	40	80	30
SANDY KIRKWOOD	3	105	10	6	5ʰᵈ	8	8	10	10	PhairCJr	SmillieAN	6	6	2

*Added starter.
a–Coupled as Valley Farm Stable entry; b–J. E. Seagram entry.
WENT TO POST AT 4:30. OFF AT 4:32. Time, :24¹/₅, :49²/₅, 1:15³/₅, 1:44, 2:12²/₅. Track slow.
B. g (3), by The Commoner—Placena, by *Loyalist. Trainer, John Nixon. Bred by Joseph James, Windsor.
Start good. Won cantering; second and third driving. PARMER, under slight restraint, followed the leaders until rounding the far turn, from where he closed up rapidly and, catching JANE SHORE tiring, drew away into a long lead.

1911 | ST. BASS

From a historic viewpoint, the fifty-second running of the King's Plate was notable for several reasons, not the least of which was the overwhelming performance of *St. Bass*, whose record time would never be bettered at Woodbine. Perhaps of more lasting significance were the formal inductions into Plate history of Harry C. Giddings Senior, the owner and breeder of the three-year-old Plate winner, and the pari-mutuel betting system, with its "iron men" that had replaced the colourful bookmakers.

Giddings' fame as a breeder (initially in Europe with the trotters) and horse dealer was well-documented, while the pari-mutuel system had been successful for years in France, the Argentine, Australia (where it was known as the Totalisator) and the

PARI-MUTUEL BETTING WAS INTRODUCED AS THE "IRON MEN" REPLACED THE BOOKMAKERS. THE MUTUELS CREATED A NEW RACETRACK EXPRESSION, "THE HANDLE." THE CROWD OF 12,000 BET $74,403.

United States. "The pari-mutuel sounds French, but really means English 'fair play,'" *The Mail and Empire* explained.

Giddings, wearing a silk top hat and "looking like a Methodist parson with his white tie and grey beard," accepted the cup and scrip for the fifty "guineas" from Governor General Earl Grey. He owned the Cedar Grove Stud in Oakville and was an American by birth; his family had moved from Cleveland, Ohio, when he was a boy.

Giddings would win three more Plates in the next ten years under the guidance of his son, Harry Junior, whose success as a trainer of Plate winners would remain unrivalled.

As early as 1893 there were newspaper reports of Giddings' sales of breeding stock to German and French harnessmen. But it was not until the early 1900s that he became seriously interested in thoroughbreds when he fortuitously purchased a filly from a neighbour who was in financial difficulties. The unraced mare would later foal a Plate winner, *Hearts of Oak*, but by this time Giddings and his son were deeply involved "with the runners."

Giddings startled fellow breeders in 1903 when he sold two horses to Alexander Mackenzie's Kirkfield Stable for $7,000, a record price for provincially bred horses. A few years later, when *St. Bass* was a two-year-old, Giddings turned down an even higher offer, which would have been a record for a provincially bred horse. On Plate day, Giddings explained why he had rejected the bid. "I was confident from the first that *St. Bass* had the race at his mercy, and that is why I refused to sell him for $7,500 when I had the offer. I do not know positively who wanted to buy him, but I think the offer was made on behalf of Sir

1911 KING'S PLATE STAKES

FIFTH RACE
Woodbine Park
MAY 20, 1911

1 1–4 MILES (2:05). The Fifty-Second Running of THE KING'S PLATE. Value $4,000 added. Three-year-olds and upward. Maidens. Weight-for-age. Ontario-bred, owned and trained. Net value to winner $3,395, including 50 Guineas presented by His Majesty King George V and Plate presented by the Ontario Jockey Club; second $700; third $300.

Horse	Eqt	A	Wt.	PP	St	¼	½	¾	Str	Fin	Jockey	Owner	Equiv. Odds Str't
ST. BASS	b	3	108	5	4	1¹	1³	1¹	1¹	1⁶	DuganE	GiddingsH	190-100
POWDERMAN		3	105	1	1	7	4¹	2½	2²	2⁵	KoernerT	ValleyFarmStable	a-11-10
JANE SHORE		4	119	4	3	5¹	5½	4⁸	4¹⁰	3¹	Goldstein	SeagramJE	b-43-10
HAVROCK	b	3	108	8	6	4ⁿᵏ	2ʰᵈ	3¹	3¹½	4¹²	Musgrave	SeagramJE	b-43-10
PLACERLAND		3	105	2	2	3ʰᵈ	7	6²	6²	5½	Fain	WoodsTA	82.1
SANDERLING		3	108	7	5	2¹	3¹	5²	5¹	6¹	BurnsG	DaviesR	102-1
LEGISLATOR		3	105	6	7	6ʰᵈ	6²	7	7	7³	FodenN	ValleyFarmStable	a-11-10
MISS MARTIMAS		3	103	8	8	8	8	8	8	8	Taplin	MackenzieJM	35-1

a–Coupled as Valley Farm Stable entry; b–J. E. Seagram entry.
WENT TO POST AT 4:31. OFF AT 4:33. Time, :23¹/s, :48³/s, 1:15, 1:42, 2:08⁴/s (Plate record). Track fast.

$2 Mutuel Prices:

ST. BASS	5.80	2.80	2.40
POWDERMAN (a-Entry)		2.40	2.20
JANE SHORE (b-Entry)			2.30

B. c, by *Bassetlaw—Lady Betz, by Hanover. Trained by Giddings H. Jr. Bred by Giddings H. Sr., Cedar Grove Stud, Oakville.

Start good. Won easily; second and third driving. ST. BASS outbroke his opponents and, setting the pace under slight restraint to the stretch turn, drew away again and won in a canter. POWDERMAN had a very rough trip, was repeatedly cut off in the first half and forced to go to the outside, then came on fast. JANE SHORE ran well and outstayed HAVROCK for third place. SANDERLING ran well for a mile and tired. The others were always outpaced.

ST. BASS, RIDDEN BY EDDIE DUGAN, WAS THE FIRST OF FOUR PLATE WINNERS OWNED BY OAKVILLE'S HARRY GIDDINGS AND TRAINED BY HARRY JUNIOR.

Owner: Harry Giddings Sr., Oakville; *Trainer:* Harry Giddings Jr.
Jockey: Eddie Dugan; *Breeder:* Harry Giddings Sr.

Donald Mann. I knew that he was the fastest two-year-old I ever raised, not excepting *Wire In* and *War Whoop* [the pair he sold in the $7,000 deal]. I have had other good offers for *St. Bass,* but I never set any price upon him, simply because I knew his value, and was not prepared to sell him at any price." (Sir Donald Mann and Sir William Mackenzie were the founders of the Canadian Northern Railway as well as other key transcontinental links. It was Mackenzie's youngest son, Alexander, who bought *War Whoop* and *Wire In* from Giddings in 1903.)

The three-year-old bay colt was impeccably bred: he was by the Kentucky-based stallion, **Bassetlaw,* an imported son of *St. Simon,* and out of *Lady Betz,* a member of one of America's most important equine families, *Hanover.* Giddings' fondness for **Bassetlaw* was royally rewarded since all four of his Plate winners descended from the English sire. *St. Bass'* breeding was also noted by the Governor General when he told Giddings, "With such a frame and the blood of that fine horse *St. Simon* in his veins, *St. Bass* ought to have a great turf career."

The colt, who won the Breeders' Stakes three days later and went on to capture two other major stakes, was ridden by Eddie Dugan, a nineteen-year-old Californian. Dugan easily kept *St. Bass* in the lead throughout the one-sided contest and pulled away to win by six lengths over his closest foe, *Powderman,* from the Valley Farm Stable. Afterwards, *The Mail and Empire*'s reporter asked Dugan about his excessive use of the whip. "My orders were to break the record for the race, and I had the whole length of the stretch to do it in. When *Powderman* showed up [turning into the stretch] I let the colt have the whip and he walked away."

The mile-and-one-quarter clocking of 2:08 4/5 was an incredible one and three-fifths seconds faster than *Shimonese*'s Plate record—an eight-length difference between the two winners. The record would later be equalled by *Belle Mahone* and *Springside,* but it would remain the Plate standard at "Old" Woodbine (later Greenwood) because in 1924 the distance for the race was shortened to a mile and an eighth until 1957, a year after the Plate was shifted to the "New" Woodbine in the Toronto suburb of Rexdale.

The fans had a mixed reaction to the newly installed "aluminum and steel-built pari-mutuel betting machines," which were set up in a special building to the east of the grandstand; they gave the officials "numerous headaches." Earlier that year, the Ontario Jockey Club had bought twenty-one machines, at $430 apiece, from a Kentucky firm, and boasted that they could handle either straight, place or show betting and would be "operated by electricity and manipulated by experts." However, only eight of the machines were set up to handle two-dollar wagering (the others handled five- and ten-dollar bets), and the crowd congested about the unfamiliar machines. Cashiers also did not have enough small bills to pay the winners, and this caused further delays.

In its criticism of the new system, which did away with the "pencillers," *The Mail and Empire* wrote:

> . . . expressions of dissatisfaction were heard at the inability of many to place their bets. It was a severe test of the system, as the jam in the betting ring was something terrific at times. A laudable attempt was made by attendants to keep the crowds in line, and, as might be expected, the chief crush was around the two-dollar machines.
>
> With the exception of the five per cent taken by the club for operating expenses and privileges, all the money wagered is returned to the public on an equitable basis of division, the public by their choices establishing the odds. The system is absolutely honest, and it is quite evident that on the general average, it will give greater odds to the public than yielded by the observant bookmaker, who gave the 'talent' just what he thought the traffic would stand. It must be admitted that the bookmaker with his slate and markers was a picturesque figure, but it is safe to say that in an official capacity the Woodbine will know him no more.

The pari-mutuels did create a new racetrack expression, "the handle," when *The World* was able to announce that the crowd of twelve thousand had bet $74,403 on straight [win] betting alone. The place and show pools were not disclosed, but for the first time race charts revealed how much had been bet to win on each horse and the win, place and show payoffs. In spite of predictions that *St. Bass* was the logical betting favourite, he was sent off as second choice behind the Valley Farm entry and returned $5.80 for each two-dollar straight wager.

Among the twenty thousand people who witnessed *Heresy*'s regal triumph in the King's Plate were their Royal Highnesses, the Duke and Duchess of Connaught and Princess Patricia, and an elderly gentleman who had become an exalted figure in his own commonwealth—the racetrack.

The occasion was a memorable one because it was the first time that members of the royal family had attended the contest for the monarch's fifty "guineas." Almost as noteworthy was the patronage of Charles Littlefield, a slender, spritely gentleman who sported a short grey beard; in his black garb, he could easily have been mistaken for a member of the clergy. The description would have amused horsemen who had seen the crafty jockey in his prime more than fifty years earlier. Littlefield was the man who rode *Don Juan,* the first winner of the Queen's Plate in 1860 at the village of Carleton (now known as The Junction in west Toronto). The American-born jockey also rode two other Plate winners, but one was disqualified a few weeks later.

Littlefield's presence elicited considerable comment, especially after he was photographed in the paddock congratulating Robert Small, the jockey who had ridden *Heresy* to his three-length victory. Understatement was the order of the day as *The Globe* captioned the photo: "The Most Remarkable Racing Picture Ever Taken." Its report stated, "The occurrence is unique, and as the veteran said to the lad when they shook hands, 'I doubt, my boy, if you will ever see what I have seen this day—the fifty-third race of which I rode the first winner. I hope you may.'"

Littlefield was at Woodbine as a guest of one of the track's racing officials, Charles Boyle, his former partner from the days when the two ran a successful stable on the New York and New Jersey racing circuits. The two men had been involved in many Plate escapades before 1900. Littlefield not only was one of the best riders of his era, but he trained several champions for some of the biggest stables in North America. His visit to Toronto enabled him to spend some time with his son, Barry, who was in the midst of a brilliant career that would see him train five Plate winners for Joseph Seagram's Waterloo stable.

The man who, tragically, was not at the Plate was the trainer and part-owner of Brookdale Stable, John Dyment, a ruddy-faced sportsman with a cheerful personality. He had died earlier that year at the age of thirty-five. As a teenager, Dyment had ridden one of his father's horses (*Gladstone,* 1891) in the Plate, and when his grand-uncle, lumber millionaire Nathaniel Dyment, went into the racing game on a large scale in 1894, it was "young Johnny" (he was just eighteen) who took over the management of the Barrie stable. His ability to hone a runner for a big race was soon recognized when *Thessalon* and *Sapper* won the Plate in successive years. Dyment was also an astute judge of horseflesh, as can be attested by a string of victories in major stakes races at other tracks with the great handi-cappers *Fort Hunter* and *Tongorder.*

Following his grand-uncle's death in 1907, John Dyment assumed control of the large racing and breeding establishment

CHARLES LITTLEFIELD, THE MAN WHO RODE THE FIRST QUEEN'S PLATE WINNER IN 1860, VISITED WOODBINE PARK. HERE HE CHATS WITH *HERESY*'S WINNING RIDER, ROBERT SMALL.

near Lake Simcoe, along with Nathaniel's two sons—Simon and Albert, who later would serve as president of the Ontario Jockey Club for eighteen years. John Dyment's sudden death on 12 January was reported to have been caused "by a blood clot on the brain." He had been unconscious for a week after suffering an apoplectic stroke and partial paralysis. His son, Jack Dyment, who became an engi-neer and aviation consultant, was seven years old when his father died. "I remember him being carried into the bran mash hut and being laid on the bench after falling on the pond at Brookdale. He had hit his head on the ice. But I remember being told by an uncle that he had also hurt himself a week earlier when he fell in Toronto."

(In 2000 and 2001 the Canadian Horse Racing Hall of Fame acknowledged the skill and talents of these accomplished horsemen when it inducted the two Littlefields, Barry and Charles, the Dyment family—Nathaniel, Albert and John—and Charles Boyle.)

Dyment's death at the height of his career was mourned not only by horsemen, but by hockey people too; he had been an enthu-siastic president of the Barrie Hockey Club for several years and was an executive with the Ontario Hockey Association.

Heresy's triumph was a poignant remembrance for racing fans, for it was John Dyment who had gone to Missouri, purchased *Hera,* a valued daughter of *Hamburg,* and brought her to Brookdale while she was in foal to the imported sire, **Sain.* Dyment was not forgotten. Presenting the silverware and certificate for the "guineas" (the winner's share exceeded $4,000 for the first time), the Duke of Connaught, who had watched the race from the judges' stand, said: "Well, Mr. Dyment, the horse ran a great race, just as you said he would." Albert Dyment's response was an emotional tribute. "This has been the greatest day in my racing career, but I want to give credit for owning this horse to the late Mr. John Dyment, who selected the mother [dam] and trained the colt as a two-year-old. Even a year ago he confidently looked forward to the time when the cup would be his."

TRAINER JOHN DYMENT.

HERESY | 3-year-old brown colt

Heresy (1909)
- *Sain
  - St. Serf
    - St. Simon
    - Feronia
  - *The Task
    - Barcaldine
    - Satchel
- Hera
  - Hamburg
    - Hanover
    - Lady Reeta
  - Tara Blackburn
    - Luke Blackburn
    - Tarantula

Owner: Brookdale Stable (Albert E. Dyment and Simon Dyment), Barrie
Trainer: John Nixon; *Jockey:* Robert Small; *Breeder:* John Dyment, Barrie

The race proved to be a rough trip for *Heresy:* he almost went to his knees when *Havrock* barged into the tightly bunched field in the rush for the rail. Small was able to hold the black colt up and guide him back into the race, but *Jane Shore* had to be pulled up. Phil Musgrave, *Havrock*'s rider, was immediately handed a two-day suspension by the stewards for "rough riding."

Heresy's victory was welcomed by the fans, who had made him the solid choice at 6-to-5, betting $10,670 on him in the straight (win) pool of $25,001. Although wagering was up on the day, bettors found it hard going to place a two-dollar bet. There simply were not enough machines to handle the holiday crowd. "It required the strength of a trained rugby player to purchase or cash tickets." Many fans were shut out at the windows while winners were still waiting to be paid off after the next race had begun. "Lines were clean down to the fence after the last race, and were not cleaned up until 7:30 o'clock," *The Daily Star* reported.

While the profits of $48,432 for the meeting were "highly satis-

factory," officials harboured some reservations about the new pari-mutuel betting system. Shortages had developed in the cash room, possibly the fault of calculators, and cashier John Spencer was short $1,500 from his "box." His quick exit from the city was noted and a warrant for his arrest was issued. A claim for a lost two-dollar ticket was also allowed, although one director said it was a "dangerous precedent."

Estimates of the huge crowd at Woodbine ranged up to twenty thousand, a figure that *Hoofprints of the Century* claimed was the largest to appear at any racetrack in North America in 1912, the second year of the "blackout" at New York tracks. Anti-gambling legislation, enacted by the New York State Assembly in September 1910, was not lifted until May 1913. The "blackout" forced the Metropolitan stables to ship their horses to European tracks or to Canada, which welcomed the Belmonts, the Whitneys, John Schorr, Phil Chinn, Guy Bedwell, Sam Hildreth and the champions *King James* and *Fitz Herbert*.

HER ROYAL HIGHNESS PRINCESS PATRICIA (CENTRE) ATTENDED ALONG WITH HER HUSBAND, THE DUKE OF CONNAUGHT (LEFT).

1912 KING'S PLATE STAKES

FIFTH RACE
Woodbine Park
MAY 18, 1912

1 1–4 MILES (2:04⅕–3–113, May 27, 1911). The Fifty–Third Running of THE KING'S PLATE. (The oldest fixture run continuously on this continent). 50 Guineas, the gift of His Majesty King George V, with $5,000 added by the Club. First horse to receive $4,285 and Plate, presented by the OJC; second horse $700 and third horse $300. The breeder of the winner to receive $500. A Sweepstakes of $5 payable at time of entry, $5 additional unless declared out by May 1, and $25 additional for starters. For 3–year–olds and upward, owned, foaled, raised and trained in the Province of Ontario that have never won a race, either on the flat or across country, have never left Canada, and have never been for a period of more than one month out of this Province. Closed with 35 nominations.

Horse	Eqt	A	Wt.	PP	St	¼	½	¾	Str	Fin	Jockey	Owner	Equiv. Odds Str't
HERESY	b	3	108	6	4	3¹½	3¹	1²	1³	1³	SmallR	BrookdaleStable	a-120-100
AMBERITE		3	103	10	3	1½	1¹	2⁴	2⁴	2³	Hopkins	CrewCA	27-5
RUSTLING		3	103	4	6	4nk	4¹	3½	3²	3½	Schuttinger	SeagramJE	b-16-5
CALUMNY		3	107½	2	1	9⁶	7¹	6¹½	6⁸	4½	McTaggartJ	GormanJG	c-50.00
TROPAEOLUM		3	105	5	7	2¹	2nd	4¹	5¹½	5¹	TurnerC	BrookdaleStable	a-120-100
GOLD BUD		3	103	7	8	5³	5⁴	5¹½	4½	6¹⁰	MartinE	DaviesR	27-5
HAVROCK	b	4	124	9	5	6¹½	6²	7⁶	7⁶	7⁶	Musgrave	SeagramJE	b-16-5
MARYBUD		3	103	3	2	7³	8¹⁵	8²⁵	8²⁵	8²⁵	GouldG	GormanJG	c-50.00
JOE GAIETY	b	3	105	8	10	8½	9⁶	9⁶	9⁶	9⁶	Lounsberry	GlasscoE	125.00
*JANE SHORE		5	122	1	9	10	10	10	10	10	BurnsG	WoodsTA	38.00

*Added starter.
a–Coupled, Brookdale Stable entry; b–J. E. Seagram entry; c–J. G. Gorman entry.

WENT TO POST AT 5:10. OFF AT 5:15. Time, :24⁵, :49, 1:15²⁄₅, 1:42, 2:11. Track good.

$2 Mutuel Prices:

HERESY (a–Entry)	4.40	2.90	2.40
AMBERITE		4.00	2.70
RUSTLING (b–Entry)			2.90

Br. c (3), by *Sain—Hera, by Hamburg. Trained by John Nixon. Bred by John Dyment, Brookdale Stable, Barrie.

Start good and slow. Won easily; second and third driving. HERESY was a forward contender from the start and, after being saved for seven furlongs, moved up rapidly while rounding the far turn and drew away into an easy lead in the last quarter. AMBERITE took the lead at once and set a fast pace, but tired when challenged by the winner. RUSTLING ran well, but was tiring at the end and just lasted long enough to outstay CALUMNY for third place. HAVROCK swerved across to the inside at the start and caused a jam in which JANE SHORE was forced to pull up. CALUMNY was also interfered with and, closing a big gap, ran a good race. TROPAEOLUM showed speed, but failed to stay the route.

Scratched—Le d'Or and Porcupine.
Overweight—Calumny, 4½ pounds.

1913 | HEARTS OF OAK

The rules governing the King's Plate were still hopelessly antiquated before World War I, a fact that upset horsemen who were seeking major changes to eradicate its provincialism and modernize the regulations. But the public seemed unconcerned, and the crowds grew larger with each running at Woodbine. They were lured by the pageantry and royal tradition; a chance to mingle with the upper crust in sport's largest outdoor social event—the Plate.

For years now people throughout the province had made a habit of attending the race for the King's "guineas." It was suggested that the six other races on the card "are but feeders to the race for Province-bred maidens. All of these races have better class horses; more experienced than those that run for the Plate, but all the same they are but fillers for this event."

In 1913, however, the most significant modification of the original rules (drafted in 1860) would occur—winners of races for two-year-olds were now eligible. It would take thirty years before this rule was eased to allow three-year-old winners into the Plate. The revision came at a time when the country was on the move. Cars were now rolling off the Ford assembly line and electric light bulbs, rather than gaslights, were glowing brightly in many homes. Toronto's 400,000 people, however, were still allowed to see only certain stage plays. A committee of forty men (but no women) known as "theatre purifiers" had brought charges against the cast of *Deborah* for staging "an immoral production." The Reverend Mr. Coburn, secretary of the censorious group and the Crown's first witness, gave a vivid description of the downfall of dear *Deborah* and how she had ruined two lives. Three church ministers said that the play "taught a great moral lesson." However, *Deborah* was banned and each member of the cast was fined five dollars by Magistrate Denison.

On Sunday afternoons the verandah of Cedar Grove Farm in Oakville was crowded with members of the Giddings family. Harry Sr. (in white suit) is seated next to his dog.

In Calgary, Alberta, on the same day as the fifty-fourth running of the King's Plate, seven thousand boxing fans packed a barn-like structure to witness a "mismatch" between Luther McCarthy of Lincoln, Nebraska, the "white" heavyweight champion of the world (Jack Johnson, a black man, was the recognized world champion at this time) and Arthur Pelkey of Quebec. Minutes after "a minister of the Gospel climbed between the ropes and in a five-minute address extolled boxing as a pastime and an exercise" McCarthy was dead from a first-round blow "delivered somewhere in the solar plexus region." Pelkey, who was a pupil of former Canadian world heavyweight champion Tommy Burns, was arrested by the North West Mounted Police and charged with manslaughter. The sports world was shocked to learn of the death of the white hope at the hands of a cotton-mill worker who had been fighting for less than two years and was considered a third rater.

At Woodbine a mismatch of another sort occurred when Harry C. Giddings' *Hearts of Oak* ran precisely the way everyone had expected him to in winning the Plate by ten lengths over Joseph Seagram's *Maid of Frome*. *Hearts of Oak* and the Oakville owner-breeder were the first beneficiaries of the new Plate

1913 KING'S PLATE STAKES

FIFTH RACE
Woodbine Park
MAY 24, 1913

1 1-4 MILES (2:04 1/5). The Fifty-Fourth Running of THE KING'S PLATE. $5,000 added by the OJC. 50 Guineas presented by His Majesty King George V and plate presented by the Club. 3-year-olds and upward, the property of a British subject resident in Ontario, foaled, raised and trained in Ontario, that have never won a race either on the flat or across country, OTHER THAN A RACE EXCLUSIVELY FOR 2-YEAR-OLDS, have never left Canada, and have never been for a period of more than one month out of the Province. Winner to carry 5 pounds extra. Net value to winner $4,085 and 50 Guineas; second, $700; third, $300.

Horse	Eqt	A	Wt.	PP	St	¼	½	¾	Str	Fin	Jockey	Owner	Equiv. Odds Str't
HEARTS OF OAK		3	113	4	2	1^1	1^1	1^1	1^4	1^{10}	Wilson J	Giddings H	a-.35
MAID OF FROME		3	108	5	5	2^1	2^2	2^3	2^5	2^2	ButwellJ	SeagramJE	b-10.50
GOLD BUD		4	119	10	8	$4^{\frac{1}{2}}$	5^1	3^1	3^5	3^{hd}	KnappW	DaviesR	8.00
VOIVODE		3	105	2	3	$8^{\frac{1}{2}}$	6^2	5^2	4^2	4^8	Montour	SeagramJE	b-10.50
MAUSOLUS	b	3	108	6	10	5^{hd}	3^{nk}	$4^{1\frac{1}{2}}$	5^2	5^2	AdamsF	Roberts HH	15.00
ONDRAMIDA	b	3	108	1	1	3^1	4^{hd}	6^6	6^6	$6^{1\frac{1}{2}}$	GrayH	GiddingsH	a-.35
ELFAIN	b	3	103	3	4	10	9^5	9^{15}	9^{20}	7^6	Wolfe	BrookdaleStable	c-20.00
CRYSTIAWOGA	b	3	110	7	9	7^{hd}	7^3	7^1	$7^{1\frac{1}{2}}$	8^2	BurnsG	BrookdaleStable	c-20.00
ROCKSPRING	b	4	121	9	7	9^6	8^4	8^2	$8^{1\frac{1}{2}}$	9^{20}	SmallR	HendrieJS	56.00
PORCUPINE	b	4	121	8	6	$6^{\frac{1}{2}}$	10	10	10	10	WarringtonW	HamiltonJL	187.00

a-Coupled as Harry Giddings entry; b-J. E. Seagram entry; c-Brookdale Stable entry.

WENT TO POST AT 5:24. OFF AT 5:26. Time, :23 3/5, :49 2/5, 1:15 3/5, 1:42 3/5, 2:09 1/5. Track fast.

$2 Mutuel Prices:			
HEARTS OF OAK (a-Entry)	2.70	2.50	2.30
MAID OF FROME (b-Entry)		4.20	2.90
GOLD BUD			2.70

B. c (3), by *Bassetlaw—Lady Lightfoot II, by *Greenback. Trainer, Harry Giddings Jr. Bred by Harry Giddings Sr, Cedar Grove Stud, Oakville.

Start good and slow. Won cantering; second and third driving. HEARTS OF OAK drew clear of interference in the first eighth and, after being rated along in front under restraint to the stretch turn, drew away into along lead and won pulling up. MAID OF FROME ran in closest and game pursuit all the way, but tired badly in the last quarter. GOLD BUD ran well, but also tired in the stretch racing. VIOVODE dropped back while rounding the first turn, but finished resolutely and would have been third in another stride. MAUSOLUS showed a flash of speed on the backstretch, but tailed off at the end.

Overweights—Ondramida, 3 pounds; Crystiawoga, 5.

rule; the colt had won four of his seven starts as a juvenile and was said to be pounds the best two-year-old in the country.

The Sunday World summed up the race neatly: "The story may be told in a very few words, as it was a case of *Hearts of Oak* being first and the others nowhere. Once the big three-year-old got into his stride he made the others look very ordinary, and jockey [Johnny] Wilson had but to rate him out in front, and this he did to perfection. When [Jimmy] Butwell was about to make his challenge on *Maid of Frome,* he let out a wrap and 'clucked.' *Hearts of Oak* bounded away like a scared rabbit and showed his class by making his own pace— a pace that was killing to the nine other contestants. He demonstrated he was a stayer as well." Wilson, a Kentucky-born rider, had won the Plate in 1910 on *Parmer.*

The winner paid just $2.70 for a $2.00 straight wager and was officially clocked at 2:09 1/5. However, it was claimed that "a number of expert clockers at the track caught the full time in 2:08 3/5, and some got it a fraction faster." The unofficial clockings would have broken the mark established by Giddings' first Plate winner, *St. Bass* in 1911, the colt that the breeder had reportedly refused to sell for $7,500, a record offer for a provincially bred horse. At the time Giddings stated that he had rejected the offer because the horse was the "fastest two-year-old he had ever raised."

Giddings' credibility, however, became suspect that spring when he was asked to compare *St. Bass* with Plate hopeful *Hearts of Oak.* It was only then that *Sunday World* readers learned that *St. Bass* "was unfortunate as a youngster," almost dying of distemper as a weanling and being blind for several days. His owner often expected to find him dead in his stable. As a yearling, *St. Bass* suffered "a couple of broken bones in his foot," and it was a long time before he could "even walk, to say nothing of galloping." It was not until his final workout that trainer Harry Giddings Junior was confident he had himself a Plate starter. So much for horsemen's tales.

It was obvious in 1913 that a new double-decked grandstand was needed desperately to replace the cramped quarters of the old public stand to the east of the members' enclosed stand. The two-tiered stand, which would seat 8,050 and would be built that fall at a cost of $160,000 (additional horse-stalls were also erected on property formerly occupied by the Woodbine Park Hotel on Queen Street), had become a priority of the Ontario Jockey Club. For the second time in its history, fans were turned away, and estimates of the Plate day crowd ranged from seventeen to twenty five thousand. *The Mail and Empire* summed it up:

Long before the horses were called to the post for the opening race, standing room in the grandstand was at a premium. Still the crowd poured through the gates, and when the big spacious lawns became so crowded that it became uncomfortable to get about, the gates were closed and no more were admitted to the course. Possibly a couple of thousand were shut out.

HEARTS OF OAK | 3-year-old brown colt

Hearts of Oak (1910)	*Bassetlaw	St. Simon	Galopin
			St. Angela
		Marquesa	Blair Athol
			Murcia
	Lady Lightfoot II	*Greenback	Dollar
			Music
		Prosperine	Daniel Boone
			Anna H.

Owner: Harry Giddings Sr., Oakville; *Trainer:* Harry Giddings Jr.
Jockey: Johnny Wilson; *Breeder:* Cedar Grove Stud (H. Giddings Sr.)

PLATE DAY WAS ALWAYS AN OCCASION FOR THE LADIES TO DISPLAY THE LATEST FASHIONS.

THE STEELWORKERS AND MEN WHO CONSTRUCTED THE NEW GRANDSTAND AT WOODBINE PARK IN MAY 1914.

THE WOODBINE HOTEL ON KING ST. W. WAS AN ATTRACTIVE PLACE IN 1914 WHERE HORSES AND CARS SHARED PARKING SPACE. BY THE 1930S IT WAS RENAMED THE PICADILLY AND LATER WINSTON'S. IN THE 1930S *THE GLOBE AND MAIL*'S OFFICES WERE BUILT NEXT DOOR BY WILLIAM H. WRIGHT, THE MINING PROSPECTOR AND STOCK PROMOTER FROM BARRIE WHO BRED 1939 KING'S PLATE WINNER *ARCHWORTH*.

N o horse in the history of the Plate had ever strutted up to the starting post with the gaudy credentials that *Beehive* possessed on 23 May 1914. The three-year-old bay colt had been unbeaten as a juvenile, winning all six of his starts (including the Coronation Futurity in record time) and was clearly the "winterbook" betting favourite for the King's Plate.

A large holiday crowd of more than fifteen thousand had been lured to Woodbine, not only by *Beehive*'s anticipated victory but also by the presence of the Duke and Duchess of Connaught and Princess Patricia, and the track's new concrete and steel grandstand, a towering double-decked structure that glistened with its freshly painted coat of green and white. "What more picturesque scene could one imagine than was presented when the flower of the Dominion paraded the lawns awaiting the mounted troops and the royal carriage?" one passionate author asked. "Why, the echoes of the cheers, rebounding from the stands and floating over the infield and shores of Lake Ontario, made one feel as though life was really worth living."

The day's main attraction was the question of *Beehive*'s invincibility, and the undefeated streak of the mighty son of *Bassetlaw* and *My Honey,* who would be carrying the red, white and blue silks of owner and breeder Harry C. Giddings Senior of Oakville. The 1913 season had been only two days old when *Beehive* "broke his maiden" in handy fashion, and before it was over he would earn $3,995, winning five more starts without ever being seriously extended. However, the new rule that allowed winners of two-year-old races to run in the Plate, penalized these horses, since they had to carry five pounds extra.

To add further lustre to *Beehive*'s crown, an article in *The Globe* the day before the race stated that Giddings had turned down an offer of $10,000 for the colt. "The offer was made the other morning to trainer Harry Giddings Junior by Mr. J.E. Laxton, a horse owner who also trains for Mr. Edward Trotter. It is believed to be the biggest offer ever made for a Plater."

By this time, horsemen had already conceded the Plate to Cedar Grove Stud, which was aiming for its third victory in four years in an event that newspapers were describing as "the famous classic of the Canadian turf." Only seven opponents contested the issue with *Beehive,* including a trio from the Joseph Seagram stable. Observers felt that *Beehive*'s running style, which was similar to that of Giddings' other Plate winners, *St. Bass* and *Hearts of Oak,* would intimidate his foes; he liked to take a commanding position early and then await the gasping challengers at the top of the stretch. There was no deviation from the script in this Plate as fans, who received just thirty cents for every two dollars they had wagered on the colt to win, saw *Beehive* "make all his own pace and stall off determined opposition from the Seagram entry. The

UNDEFEATED *BEEHIVE* AND JOCKEY GUY BURNS.

BEEHIVE | 3-year-old bay colt

Owner: Harry Giddings Sr., Oakville; *Trainer:* Harry Giddings Jr.
Jockey: Guy Burns; *Breeder:* Cedar Grove Stud (H. Giddings Sr.)

race was truly run; the winner was ridden by Guy Burns, a Canadian. *Beehive* merely acted like it was a workout. Burns sat still and steered the shortest route, but a lick or two were necessary when [Jimmy] Butwell urged on *Dark Rosaleen*. Then the unbeaten colt drew away, and it was only a matter of how far he could win."

Although the track was rated "fast" on Plate day, the spring of 1914 was recalled as the worst ever for horsemen. "It rained for twenty-two days in a row that spring," said Tom Bird, the veteran handicapper and clocker at both the old and new Woodbines. He first worked at the Queen Street East track in 1894. "It wasn't all during the meeting itself, but horseman had a terrible time trying to condition their racers." The location of Woodbine on the shores of Lake Ontario would be a financial burden for the OJC until it closed the track in 1993. It's increased maninntenance costs were aggravated by the low-lying property, plus the high-water levl of the lake.

Beehive followed up his Plate success by winning the Breeders' Stakes and the William Hendrie Memorial Handicap under top weight in a space of seven days. His streak of victories ended at nine in Hamilton a month later when he finished third in the Dominion Plate against older horses, again under high weight. Throughout the season, which saw him travel to Fort Erie, Windsor and Hamilton before returning to Woodbine, *Beehive* toted the heaviest imposts in all but one race, and often against more seasoned runners. He gave away from nine to twenty-eight pounds in the one-mile Canadian Handicap at Windsor and was still much the best horse.

Only once in twelve starts that year did *Beehive* finish as low as fourth, and his eight wins also included successes in the important Stanley Produce Stakes and the Dominion Handicap. When Giddings finally stopped

racing the colt that fall, his career record showed eighteen starts, fourteen wins, one second and two thirds for total earnings of $16,105, a lofty bankroll for a provincial-bred in a period when some winning purses were as low as $450.

However, the heyday *of Beehive*'s sparkling career quickly soured and it would be all downhill until the combative, free-running horse discovered a new career. Injuries had sidelined him for most of 1915 and he beat only one horse in two races. He was then gelded and sold by Giddings to fellow Oakville horseman, Willie Wilson, who years later would spring the greatest upset in Plate history with *Maternal Pride*. At five the Plate champion was "washed up," losing all eleven starts and ending his racing career in lowly claiming (selling) races. *Beehive* resurfaced in 1918 as a champion lightweight hunter class jumper for Major Joseph Kilgour's Sunnybrook Farms. Under Wilson's tutelage and riding, old *Beehive* strutted to jumping laurels and dozens of blue ribbons festooned his stable. His jumping career lasted well into the 1920s.

1914 KING'S PLATE STAKES

FOURTH RACE
Woodbine Park
MAY 23, 1914

1 1–4 MILES (2:04⅕). The Fifty–Fifth Running of THE KING'S PLATE. (The oldest fixture run continuously on this continent). 50 Guineas, the gift of His Majesty King George V with $5,000 added by the Club. The first horse to receive $4,735, including Guineas; second horse $700 and third horse $300. The breeder of the winner to receive $500. A Sweepstakes of $5 payable at time of entry, $5 additional unless declared out by May 1st, and $25 additional for starters. For three–year–olds and upward, the property of a British subject resident in Ontario, foaled, raised and trained in Ontario that have never won a race, either on the flat or across country, other than a race exclusively for two–year–olds, and have never left Canada, and have never been for a period of more than one month out of this Province. Winners to carry 5 lbs. extra. A piece of plate will be presented by the Club to the winner. Closed with 32 nominations of which 6 declared at $5 each.

Horse	Eqt	A	Wt.	PP	St	¼	½	¾	Str	Fin	Jockey	Owner	Equiv. Odds Str't
BEEHIVE	b	3	113	3	3	1²	1²	11½	1²	1³	BurnsG	GiddingsH	.15
DARK ROSALEEN		3	108	1	1	2¹	21½	2³	2³	2⁴	ButwellJ	SeagramJE	a-5.00
SEA LORD		3	105	5	7	5½	5ʰᵈ	4²	3²	3⁸	TaplinE	SeagramJE	a-5.00
OLD RELIABLE		3	113	6	5	3½	3²	3⁴	4³	4¹	TeahanF	MintzSol	21.90
GOLD BUD		5	122	8	4	6ʰᵈ	7²	5½	5⁶	5⁶	ClaverA	DaviesRobt	30.00
EXMER	b	4	121	7	6	4²	41½	6⁵	6²	6⁵	PeakC	StewartAT	12.40
FROISSART		3	110	4	8	8	6½	7⁵	7⁶	7¹⁰	GouldG	SeagramJE	a-5.00
*PORCUPINE		5	124	2	2	7ʰᵈ	8	8	8	8	HanoverJ	HamiltonJL	30.90

*Added starter.
a-Coupled as J. E. Seagram entry.
WENT TO POST AT 4:45. OFF AT 4:51. Time, :23⁴/₅, :49⁴/₅, 1:16¹/₅, 1:43²/₅, 2:10³/₅. Track fast.

$2 Mutuel Prices:

BEEHIVE	2.30	2.10	2.20
DARK ROSALEEN (a-Entry)		2.10	2.60
SEA LORD (a-Entry)		2.10	2.60

B. c (3), by *Bassetlaw—My Honey, by Yo El Rey. Trainer, Harry Giddings Jr. Bred by Harry Giddings Sr, Oakville.
Start good and slow. Won easily, second and third driving. BEEHIVE, outrunning the others from the start, moved into an easy lead in the first quarter and was rated along until rounding the far turn, where he seemed to tire and his rider went to a drive, but withstood DARK ROSALEEN's challenge and was going away at the end. DARK ROSALEEN made a threatening effort on the stretch turn, but tired in the last eighth. SEA LORD easily disposed of OLD RELIABLE in the last quarter. The latter ran well for a mile. EXMER showed early speed.
Scratched—Vastatio.

Aroused by the daily despatches of heavy Allied casualties suffered at Ypres and Gallipoli, anti-German feeling in Toronto was at its height in the spring of 1915 when Charles Vance Millar, a wealthy but eccentric lawyer, chose to ignore the ceremonies honouring the upset triumph of his King's Plate winner, *Tartarean*.

The consternation provoked by Millar's absence was tranquil compared to the outrage fomented in 1926 by his "uncommon and capricious" will. It bequeathed the bulk of his estate to the woman (or women) who gave birth to the most children in Toronto over the next ten years. The father of the maligned "Great Stork Derby" during the Depression years apparently perceived that much poverty stemmed from "uncontrolled child-bearing" and it was Millar's way of embarrassing the city into relaxing its strictures against birth control. In his obituary, *The Toronto Star* said that Millar's strange legacy was "written five years before his death" (31 October 1926) and that he'd told a friend about it and confided: "I am going to make [love making] the most popular sport in Canada in the next ten years." The satirical will of the avowed bachelor left shares of his estate in breweries to temperance militants, racetrack stock to clergymen and other known opponents of alcohol and gambling, as well as $500 to the Roman Catholic church to say regular Masses for a Protestant acquaintance (it was declined). The remainder of the estate would be invested and paid in cash to the winner of the "maternity marathon." It produced a flurry of lawsuits and an attempt of government intervention. *The Star* identified five mothers who appeared ahead of the field. Certainly the Dionne quintuplets, born during the ten-year "race-time," would have Elzire Dionne well ahead. But her children were born outside Toronto and didn't qualify. Eventually, four mothers were declared the winners with nine children each. They each received $100,000 immediately, followed by a further $25,000. When the City of Toronto's welfare department called on the winners demanding repayment of the welfare benefits they'd received, one mother abandoned her children and headed for Detroit, never to be heard of again.

Millar was described as a man devoted to his mother, partially deaf with an unpleasant voice and who dressed indifferently. His clients included the pugilist Jack Johnson, hotelmen, racing men, merchants, widows, orphans, publishers and corporations. However, Millar's assumed absence from Woodbine on 22 May 1915

CHARLES MILLAR, ECCENTRIC LAWYER AND FATHER OF THE "GREAT STORK DERBY."

was pardonable, as Harcourt Ferguson, a partner in Millar's law firm, explained when he accepted the "guineas." "His [*Tartarean*] win came as a surprise, and had Mr. Millar anticipated it, he would have been present." But Millar *was* at the track, and witnessed the stirring one-two finish of his two horses, *Tartarean* and *Fair Montague*. His vantage point was not *Tartarean*'s stable, as some colleagues said, but rather the running board of his car in the automobile enclosure. "Many of his friends were ready to give Charlie a cheer, but the modest lawyer suddenly vanished," *The World* said.

Millar's ostensible shyness was possibly his way of protesting about the hardening resentment being shown to Canadians of German descent. He was of German parentage, the son of Simon Millar, a farmer from the southwestern Ontario community of Aylmer. Here the man who later became an award-winning scholar and "a shrewd lawyer with a keen sense of humour" was born in 1853. Although it revealed that Millar was "of German parentage," *The World* assured readers that he was "Canadian all over . . . and has been so devoted to his old mother, that he has never married." But public xenophobia was high that spring following grim reports that eighty-three Canadians were among the many victims who had drowned when the liner *Lusitania* was sunk by a German submarine, and the mounting number of Canadian casualties in Belgium from mustard gas.

Repercussions of the war in Europe had prompted directors of the Ontario Jockey Club to advise John W. Schorr, who trained many of the finest horses in North America, and previously was a most welcome visitor at Woodbine, that "on account of strong anti-German feeling, it would be advisable to withdraw your entries to stakes and not come to Toronto." Equally disturbing in Millar's mind was the fact that William Krausmann, who owned one of the favourites for the Plate, *Hampton Dame*, was told to "haul down his colours," and sell his highly regarded daughter of *Inferno*.

He reluctantly complied, "selling" the three-year-old filly to E.J. Davies of the Copland Brewery Company, who was a cousin of Robert Davies, head of the brewery, Thorncliffe Stable and a former OJC vice-president. *The Mail and Empire* declared that the sale of *Hampton Dame* would "clear a situation arising out of the objection to her running in the plate in Mr. Krausmann's name. Naturally, he regrets parting with *Hampton Dame*, as any owner of a good horse would do. 'Yes, I am going to sell the filly. But I am a better Britisher than ever.'"

In a race that included jockeys named Obert, Shilling and

Groth, *Hampton Dame* finished fifth for her new "owner." However, the following year she was again running for the man who owned the Hotel Krausmann at Toronto's King and Church Streets. Ironically, soldiers returning from the war in 1918 were billeted at Krausmann's hotel, which had been converted into a hostel by the Salvation Army.

While Millar railed against injustices throughout his career, his acquisition of *Tartarean* for the Plate was solely possible because of a restriction that discriminated against horse owners who were not British subjects. Not only did a horse have to be the property of a resident of Ontario, but the owner had to be a British subject. This rule became a contentious issue in 1912 when Mrs. Lily A. Livingston, an American, established the Pontiac Stud in Cobourg. She had imported some of the leading studs and broodmares from her renowned Rancocas Stud in New Jersey (which she inherited in 1901 on the death of its founder, tobacco millionaire Pierre Lorillard), and had ambitions of one day winning the Plate. Mrs. Livington (who was Miss Eileen Barnes when she was Lorillard's hostess at Rancocas) operated the four-hundred-acre stud until 1920, when she sold the farm to oil magnate Harry F. Sinclair, whose companies reached around the world.

Club directors were not in agreement when faced with the problem of allowing a non-British subject to enter a horse that otherwise would qualify. But a "British majority" ruled the boardroom and Mrs. Lily Livingston was forced to sell her Plate eligibles, two of which (*Tartarean* and *Fair Montague*) were acquired by Millar. *The World* noted in its Woodbine Gossip column that the breeder of the first two horses across the finish line "was an absentee." (But Mrs. Livingston received five hundred dollars from the OJC as the breeder of the winner.) Both horses were maidens but they easily outclassed the ten other Plate starters as *Tartarean* hit the wire a short neck in front of his stablemate, who was thought to be the

TARTAREAN | 3-year-old bay colt

Tartarean (1912)
- *Stanhope II
  - Florizell II
    - St. Simon
    - Perdita II
  - King's Daughter
    - Kingfisher
    - *Voila
- Tarletan
  - *Uhlan
    - The Ranger
    - La Mechante
  - War Dress
    - War Dance
    - Brocade

Owner: Charles Millar, Toronto; *Trainer:* John Nixon
Jockey: Harry Watts; *Breeder:* Pontiac Stud (Mrs. Lily A. Livingston), Cobourg

superior one in trainer John Nixon's barn.

Although the Governor General, the Duke of Connaught, could not attend the Plate, he declared: "It would be inadvisable to stop racing in Canada, as it is most important that nothing should be done to discourage breeders of horses at this time." And so it was business as usual at Woodbine in its first wartime meeting. "A feeling of dignified reserve seemed to pervade the greetings of those who promenaded in front of the members' stand," *The Toronto Sunday World* reported. Flags were plentiful and patriotic selections from the military band frequently evoked applause, but the attendance was lower than that on previous Plate days, which was partially attributed to the absence of the royal party from Ottawa. "The prevailing note of black and white in feminine fashion lent an appropriate, if not altogether premeditated aspect to the picturesque spectacle on the lawn, and with the profusion of khaki uniforms, constituted the only features significant of war," one fashion critic noted.

TRAINER JOHN NIXON WON FIVE PLATES.

1915 KING'S PLATE STAKES

FIFTH RACE
Woodbine Park
MAY 22, 1915

1 1–4 MILES (2:04 1/5). The KING'S PLATE. Fifty–Sixth Running of the oldest fixture run continuously on this continent. 50 Guineas, the Gift of His Majesty King George V. Net value to winner $4,310, second, $700; third, $300. The breeder of the winner to receive $500. A sweepstakes of $5 payable at time of entry, $5 additional, unless declared out by May 1st, and $25 additional for starters. For three–year–olds and upward, the property of a British subject resident in Ontario, foaled, raised and trained in Ontario that have never won a race, either on the flat or across country, other than a race exclusively for two–year–olds, have never left Canada, and have never been for a period of more than one month out of this Province. Winners to carry 5 lbs. extra. A piece of plate will be presented by the Club to the winner. Declarations Saturday, May 1st. Closed March 1st with 29 nominations.

Horse	Eqt	A	Wt.	PP	St	1/4	1/2	3/4	Str	Fin	Jockey	Owner	Equiv. Odds Str't
TARTAREAN		3	108	3	4	6nk	61	52	21	1nk	WattsH	MillarChas.	a-3.80
FAIR MONTAGUE		3	108	2	2	42	1½	12	12	24	RiceT	MillarChas.	a-3.80
PEPPER SAUCE	b	3	113	5	8	91	71	3nk	43	35	TaplinE	CrewCA	8.00
LADY CURZON		3	108	9	9	8nk	5nk	21	3hd	42	ShillingR	BrookdaleStable	1.50
HAMPTON DAME		3	108	6	3	101	111½	91	61	53	ObertW	DaviesEJ	5.05
LAST SPARK		3	110	7	5	2hd	2hd	4nk	52	66	AmbroseE	HendrieJS	b-20.00
SPLUTTER		3	110	11	6	11	31½	61	71	71	MetcalfJ	HendrieJS	b-20.00
CHARON		3	108	4	12	12	10nk	101	91	82	GrothJ	SeagramJE	c-10.70
HARRY BASSETT II.	b	3	105	12	10	5hd	81	81	81	91½	StevensonW	GiddingsH	47.00
VASTATIO	b	4	121	1	1	111	12	12	111	101	BurnsG	SeagramJE	c-10.70
OKEMUS	b	3	113	10	7	3½	4hd	71	101	113	ClaverA	DolanJF	47.00
SMITHFIELD	b	3	113	8	11	71	91	11	12	12	GoldsteinP	SeagramJE	c-10.70

a–Coupled as Chas. Millar entry; b–J. S. Hendrie entry; c–J. E. Seagram entry.
WENT TO POST AT 5:11. OFF AT 5:19. Time, :24 4/5, :49 3/5, 1:14 3/5, 1:42 3/5, 2:09 1/5. Track good.

$2 Mutuel Prices:

TARTAREAN (a–Entry)	9.60	11.60	6.90
FAIR MONTAGUE (a–Entry)	9.60	11.60	6.90
PEPPER SAUCE			4.50

B. c (3), by *Stanhope II.—Tarletan, by *Uhlan. Trained by John Nixon. Bred by Mrs Lily A. Livingston, Pontiac Stud, Cobourg.

Start good and slow. Won driving; second and third the same. TARTAREAN followed the leaders until the far turn, then moved up steadily and, finishing fast, outstayed FAIR MONTAGUE in a close finish. The latter easily raced into the lead after going the first half-mile, but tired when the winner challenged. PEPPER SAUCE was shuffled back in the first eighth when there was much crowding and jostling, but closed a gap and finished fast. LADY CURZON and HAMPTON DAME suffered from being crowded back and the former moved up with a rush on the far turn, but tired in the homestretch. HAMPTON DAME closed a big gap. LAST SPARK and OKEMUS showed speed, but tired.

1916 | MANDARIN

The black jackets with the yellow sashes had been noticeably absent from the King's Plate winner's circle since 1908, an event that was remedied with a flourish in the fifty-seventh running of the historic race. The familiar silks of Joseph Seagram were all that could be seen as the six-horse field galloped into the long stretch at Woodbine on 20 May.

It was an occasion without precedent in the annals of Canada's most important horse race: Seagram's trio finished first, second and third. The seven-year drought for the Waterloo stable had ended in historic fashion with *Mandarin*'s one-sided victory. But more important, the unlucky thirteen jinx had been shattered by the three-year-old chestnut colt as he gave Seagram his much anticipated fourteenth Plate win. In sweeping the Plate clean, Seagram also collected every available prize, which included a $500

EDWARD FROWDE SEAGRAM REPLACED HIS ILL FATHER IN THE WINNER'S CIRCLE WITH ARTHUR PICKENS ON *MANDARIN*.

award for the breeder of the victor. In all, the sweep totalled $5,515 for the once dominant stable, which in recent years had been forced to share the spoils more equitably at Ontario tracks with the stables of Harry Giddings, Brookdale, Thorncliffe and Valley Farm.

The result was not unexpected. In fact, some newspapers had boldly predicted that the race could wind up in a "clean sweep" for trainer Barry Littlefield's stable. The wartime crowd was so confident that this may occur, it made the Seagram entry the prohibitive 1-to-5 favourites. (There was no show betting because of the small field; the $2.50 payoff that place bettors received was better than the win price of $2.40, a common occurrence when an entry finishes one-two.)

From the drop of the flag, the Seagram horses were in command, and there was little likelihood that they would be challenged. *Mandarin*, who was under restraint, led every step of the way, and jockey Arthur Pickens was almost an incidental passenger. In winning the King's Plate. Pickens became the first jockey to win both the Kentucky Derby and the Plate. Born in Norwood, Ohio, in 1888, Pickens began his riding career in New Orleans in 1906. In 1916 he was under contract to Seagram and in a space of six days won the Plate, Breeders' Stakes (on *Mandarin*), the Coronation Futurity and Maple Leaf Stakes. At age nineteen Pickens won the 1908 Kentucky Derby on long-shot *Stone Street*.

Described as "a pretty shifty sort who should prove a frequent winner in races for Canadian breds," *Mandarin* glided home four lengths in front of stablemates *Gala Water* and *Gala Day*. *Johnnie Austin*, who

MANDARIN LEADS THE FIELD THE FIRST TIME PAST THE GRANDSTAND DURING AN UNPRECEDENTED *SEAGRAM* SWEEP.

finished more than seventy lengths behind the winner, was so far back that "he got in when the others were weighing in." One newspaper noted that the odds on the long shot had been driven down because "too many fans hoped to get the price of an automobile by investing a 'deuce' spot on *Johnnie Austin,* who arrived home about a quarter to seven. Proof positive that there is 'one born every minute,' even in Toronto."

While Joseph Seagram's colours were back on top, the man leading *Mandarin* into the winners' enclosure, and receiving the certificate for the King's guineas from Lieutenant Governor Sir John S. Hendrie, was not the Laird of Waterloo. Seagram was seriously sick and was unable to attend. Accepting on his behalf was his oldest son, Edward Frowde Seagram, who would take control of the stable following his father's death in 1919. "Send him a telegram at once; it will be joyful news of a well-earned victory," Sir John advised while presenting the Plate. In response, Seagram said: "I am sure when he hears that his three entries carried off the entire honours he will undoubtedly urge his physician to permit him to come from Waterloo to see *Mandarin* race before the close of the meet."

Mandarin, who won the important Breeders' Stakes a few days later, was sired by Seagram's own stud, *Havoc,* and was indeed royally bred. He was out of **Royal China,* a mare that was imported as a weanling in 1904 from England along with her dam, **Chinka,* who was born in the Royal Mews of King Edward VII at Sandringham. The man who had a hand in this win, Edmund Haines, the bloodstock agent from Owen Sound who had been responsible for so many of Seagram's earlier Plate victories with English mares he had selected for him, afterwards recalled how he was able to purchase Edward VII's bloodstock.

The King was looking over his horses along with a party chaperoned by Mr. Richard Marsh, his trainer, and Mrs. Marsh, who greatly fancied the mare. The King, on hearing her express of admiration, asked her: 'Do you really fancy **Chinkal,*' and, of course, was doubly assured she did. 'Well,' replied His Majesty, 'she is your property.' The mare was duly transferred, and the next year in Mr. Marsh's own stables, she foaled **Royal China.*

Haines, who was in England on a shopping trip for Seagram that season, visited the renowned trainer's stud and selected the broodmare and her weanling, **Royal China.*

The Dyments of the prominent Brookdale Stable were also doing some shopping that year as they joined the flurry of small companies making "horseless carriages." One such car was the Barrie Bell, made by Dyment's Barrie Carriage Company from 1916 to 1918. The Barrie Bell was apparently "not a fun car to drive," said Brian Jackson, mayor of Innisfil Township and an antique-car

MANDARIN | 3-year-old chestnut colt

			Alarm
		Himyar	Hira
	Havoc		
		Elletta	Elkhorn
Mandarin			Billetta Jr.
(1913)			
			Saraband
		Worcester	Elegance
	*Royal China		
		*Chinka	Florizell II
			*Chinkara

Owner: Joseph E. Seagram, Waterloo; *Trainer:* Barry T. Littlefield
Jockey: Arthur Pickens; *Breeder:* J.E. Seagram

JOSEPH SEAGRAM HORSES FINISHED ONE-TWO-THREE: *MANDARIN, GALA WATER* (LEFT) AND *GALA DAY* (RIGHT).

1916 KING'S PLATE STAKES

FOURTH RACE
Woodbine Park
MAY 20, 1916

1 1-4 MILES (2:04⅕). Fifty-Seventh Running of THE KING'S PLATE. $5,000 added. 3-year-olds and upward. Allowances. Foaled, raised, owned and trained in Ontario. Net value to winner $4,015, including 50 Guineas, the Gift of His Majesty King George V; second, $700; third, $300. Breeder of winner to receive $500.

Horse	Eqt A	Wt.	PP	St	¼	½	¾	Str	Fin	Jockey	Owner	Equiv. Odds Str't
MANDARIN	b 3	113	3	2	1²	1²	1³	1³	1⁴	PickensA	SeagramJE	a-.20
GALA WATER	3	108	2	3	3¹	3²	3⁴	3⁵	2½	SmythJ	SeagramJE	a-.20
GALA DAY	b 3	113	1	1	2⁴	2⁵	2⁶	2⁴	3⁸	WarringtonW	SeagramJE	a-.20
OLD POP	b 3	113	4	4	5²	4⁵	4⁶	4⁶	4⁸	BurnsG	CrewCA	6.45
LAST SPARK	b 4	126	5	5	4²	5¹⁵	5²⁵	5⁴⁰	5⁵⁰	MottA	HendrieJS	13.75
JOHNNIE AUSTIN	s 4	124	6	6	6	6	6	6	6	AustinJ	BarbourJG	42.85

a-Coupled as J. E. Seagram entry.

WENT TO POST AT 4:15. OFF AT 4:17. Time, :23⅗, :49, 1:14⅗, 1:43⅕, 2:12. Track good.

$2 Mutuel Prices:

MANDARIN (a-Entry)	2.40	2.50	—
GALA WATER (a-Entry)	2.40	2.50	—
GALA DAY (a-Entry)	2.40	2.50	—

(NO SHOW WAGERING)

Ch. c (3), by Havoc—*Royal China, by Worcester. Trained by Barry T. Littlefield. Bred by J. E. Seagram, Waterloo.

Start good and slow. Won easily; second and third driving. MANDARIN led, under restraint, all the way, and was eased up at the finish. GALA WATER wore the tiring GALA DAY down in the last few strides. The latter raced in closed pursuit to the stretch and finished gamely. The others were outpaced and beaten off at the end.

enthusiast. He bought a 1917 model in 1990 and finished restoration in 2004. The car is now displayed at the Simcoe County Museum in nearby Midhurst. Fewer than forty were built and when the Royal Bank called its loan of $750,000 for start-up costs, the Dyment family was reportedly almost bankrupt. However, its stable continued to flourish until the mid 1920s, winning the King's Plate in 1921 with *Herendesy.*

1917 | BELLE MAHONE

HORSES PARADE IN THE SADDLING PADDOCK BEFORE THE RACE.

Fellow riders, valets and assorted well-wishers squeezed into the crowded jockey's quarters at Woodbine, eagerly thrusting their hands forward to pat or shake hands with Frankie Robinson after his return from the winner's enclosure and the presentation of the King's Plate to Edward Frowde Seagram.

"Aye, Frankie. When did you think you had the race won?"

Minutes earlier Robinson had guided *Belle Mahone* through heavy congestion in the early running before taking command in the stretch to win the guineas in a time that equalled the Plate record.

"You might say when I got to the track," he replied with an impish grin. "I wasn't sure they would even allow me to ride. Heck, the horses were goin' to the post for the third race and ours [the Plate] was up next. Then when I get to the jock's room to weigh in, I learnt that the people had made arrangements for another boy to ride the filly."

As it turned out, Robinson's major obstacle on 19 May was the hectic journey from Buffalo to Woodbine, not the mile-and-one-quarter trip on *Belle Mahone,* who not only became the fastest filly in Plate history, but also the first three-year-old filly to win the race since 1902. A "heady" jockey who possessed exceptional ability and twice would win more races than any other rider in North America (he was also the leading money winner the year he won the Plate), Robinson's tardiness was the result of a missed train connection in Buffalo.

I was on the overnighter from Baltimore [he had been riding at Pimlico], but when we arrived in Buffalo Saturday mornin' they told us, 'sorry, you're late, the Toronto train has just pulled out.' I wasn't going to miss riding Mr. Seagram's filly, not if I could help it. You see, I gave him my word last fall I'd be up here to ride her in the Plate.

Robinson immediately hired a fast automobile to Hamilton, where another machine had also been ordered and was waiting. Unlike harried racegoers, who years later would travel bumper-to-bumper in arduous trips along the two-lane highway through the Niagara peninsula to Fort Erie and Buffalo, Robinson fortunately had no mishaps en route to Woodbine.

Two years later he suffered serious injuries

1917 KING'S PLATE STAKES

FOURTH RACE
Woodbine Park
MAY 19, 1917

1 1–4 MILES (2:04⅕). North America's Longest–Established Stake Race. The Fifty–Eighth Running of THE KING'S PLATE. 50 Guineas, the Gift of His Majesty King George V, with $7,500 added by the club and a piece of plate for the winner. Net value to winner $6,125; second $1,000, third $500 and the breeder of the winner to receive $500. A sweep-stakes of $5 payable at time of entry, and $25 additional to start. For three–year–olds and upward, the property of a British subject resident in Ontario, foaled, raised and trained in Ontario that have never won a race, either on the flat or across country, other than a race exclusively for two–year–olds, have never left Canada, and have never been for a period of more than one month out of this province. Winners to carry 5 lbs. extra.

Horse	Eqt	A	Wt.	PP	St	¼	½	¾	Str	Fin	Jockey	Owner	Odds $1
BELLE MAHONE	b	3	108	5	5	6nk	5³	3¹	1nk	1¹	RobinsonF	SeagramJE	a-.40
TARAHERA		3	108	8	4	2½	2¹	1¹	2⁸	2⁶	MinkL	BrookdaleStable	9.10
GALA DRESS		3	108	2	2	7½	4½	5nk	4½	3½	ParringtonT	SeagramJE	a-.40
CAPTAIN B.	b	3	110	1	1	1¹	1nk	2½	3²	4²	CrumpW	GooderhamMRoss	10.00
GALLEY HEAD		3	115	9	8	5⁸	6¹	6⁵	5⁸	5⁵	CooperF	SeagramJE	a-.40
LADDER OF LIGHT	b	3	103	7	7	3½	3²	4¹	6¹⁰	6¹⁰	CollinsW	BeardmoreGW	b-12.65
RINGDOVE		3	108	4	6	4nk	7³	7²	7²	7¹½	HaynesE	BeardmoreGW	b-12.65
WOODRUFF	s	3	105	6	9	8¹	9	8⁵	8¹⁰	8¹⁵	WardW	GormanJG	108.30
BRITANNIA		3	108	3	3	9	8½	9	9	9	RiceT	ThorncliffeStable	11.90

a–Coupled as J. E. Seagram entry; b–George W. Beardmore entry.
WENT TO POST AT 4:12. OFF AT 4:14. Time, :22⅘, :48⅖, 1:14⅕, 1:41⅘, 2:08⅘. Track fast.

Mutuel Prices:

	$2 Mutuels Paid			Odds to $1		
BELLE MAHONE (a–Entry)	2.80	2.10	2.20	.40	.05	.10
TARAHERA		3.50	3.30		.75	.65
GALA DRESS (a–Entry)	2.80	2.10	2.20	.40	.05	.10

B. f (3), by Ypsilanti II.—*Irish Lass, by Donovan. Trained by Barry T. Littlefield. Bred by J. E. Seagram, Waterloo.
Start good and slow. Won easily; second and third driving. BELLE MAHONE met with repeated interference in the early running and was crowded back, but responded with a rush when called on and was going away at the end. TARAHERA was much used in forcing the terrific early pace and tired in the last quarter after having raced into the lead. GALA DRESS ran a good race and outstayed CAPTAIN B. for third place. The latter set a fast early pace and tired badly. LADDER OF LIGHT showed speed and ran well to the stretch.

FRANK ROBINSON WAS TWICE NORTH AMERICA'S LEADING RIDER. HE WON THE PLATE ON *BELLE MAHONE*. TWO YEARS LATER HE DIED IN A FALL AT BOWIE, MD.

BELLE MAHONE | 3-year-old bay filly

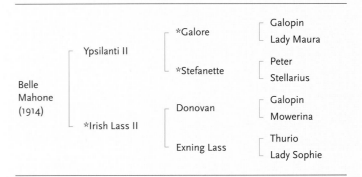

			Galopin
	*Galore	
Ypsilanti II			Lady Maura
			Peter
	*Stefanette	
Belle			Stellarius
Mahone			Galopin
(1914)		Donovan	
			Mowerina
*Irish Lass II		
			Thurio
	Exning Lass	
			Lady Sophie

Owner: Joseph E. Seagram, Waterloo; *Trainer:* Barry T. Littlefield
Jockey: Frank Robinson; *Breeder:* J.E. Seagram

in a fall at the Bowie track in Maryland. The *American Turf Monthly* said in 1978 that Robinson's "death was due in part to the delay of an ambulance stalled in heavy traffic."

Belle Mahone had been touted heavily that spring as a "sure thing" because of the way she had performed for trainer Barry T. Littlefield, who would win his fifth Plate for the Waterloo stable of the seriously ailing Joseph Seagram. One critic, who predicted another clean sweep for Seagram, suggested that she might lower *St. Bass'* Plate record of 2:08 4/5. The bay filly tied the mark, paying just forty cents for every dollar wagered, while the black and yellow silks finished one-three-five in the nine-horse field. (Because a three-year-old filly had not won the Plate in fifteen years, many horsemen were amazed when fillies captured the top three positions.) Although the Ontario Jockey Club president was again absent for opening day and his Plate victory, his vigilant emissary to the thoroughbred breeding grounds of England, Edmund Haines, was at Woodbine and was delighted with the result, for it was he who had imported both the sire and dam of the winner, *Ypsilanti II* and *Irish Lass II.*

Meanwhile, the war in Europe was still in progress as another racing season opened in Toronto. Horsemen were concerned that a possible ban on racing might soon materialize; indeed, the government had already suggested to officials that this could be the final Plate race until the war was over. Although racing continued during the Great War in England, France, Germany, Italy and Austria, the fall meet at Woodbine was cancelled and was replaced by a two-day Red Cross Horse Show. That summer, owners were advised that they would be allowed, "without prejudice," to take their Plate eligibles out of the country for training purposes "until a period of six months after the war had ended."

Reminders of the battles being fought in Europe were inescapable as newspapers printed daily casualty lists and photos of well-known athletes who had been killed in action. Even the Toronto Maple Leaf baseball team, on its way to another International League pennant behind the .380 hitting of manager Napoleon (Nap) Lajoie, was doing its bit to boost morale. They drilled each day with their bats. Mayor Tommy Church was so impressed that he offered

twenty-five rifles to replace the bats. On Plate day, a spirit of patriotism was in the air because of the presence of several thousand khaki-clad soldiers, who were the guests of the Club. "On the lawn to the east of the track were parked autos, filled with returned heroes unable to get out by themselves, while all of the front boxes in the grandstand were set apart for the soldiers. An added attraction was an aviator from the Long Branch training school, who performed some thrilling stunts, including a neatly executed loop-the-loop over the steeplechase course."

The racetrack was an ideal site to stir up emotions with the inherent pageantry and pomp of the Plate, one writer observed:

> The Queen's Own Band, to the great delight of the vast throng, played as its first number a military air entitled 'Conscription,' which the directors of the Ontario Jockey Club had selected several days prior to the announcement by Premier Borden that selective conscription would be put into effect in Canada. When the band struck up the air, the returned soldiers arose as one man and cheered lustily. The scene was most impressive.

One man who thought otherwise was the Reverend Mr. Stauffer, who wrote a letter to *The Globe* suggesting that Woodbine should be "ploughed up for the purpose of planting potatoes." He possibly came up with the idea after learning that the infield at Churchill Downs, home of the Kentucky Derby, was being used to grow potatoes for the needy. The clergyman stated that the racetrack should be closed until after the war and criticized horsemen for being unwilling "to give up their private profit in this national emergency."

Harry Giddings quickly responded to this charge: "His proposition is about what might be expected from such a source. If he had more knowledge of land, he would know the Woodbine racecourse is unsuitable for grain or root growing." Giddings then offered the Reverend Stauffer and his congregation the free use of a hundred acres "of as good land as can be found between Toronto and Hamilton, situated two and one-half miles east of Oakville, and ready for the ploughs. On it there is an eight-room house and a good barn, the use of which is included."

The minister accepted the offer, saying: "A West Toronto church, desirous of placing some eighty boys for the summer, will call on Mr. Giddings' solicitors before the day is over."

GEORGE M. HENDRIE, *SPRINGSIDE* AND JOCKEY LEE MINK.

Eight of the most indispensable minutes in King's Plate history occurred on 24 May 1918 at Woodbine racetrack. At 3:21 that afternoon the Canadian racing season opened with a field of thirteen horses parading to the post for the fifty-ninth renewal of North America's oldest continuously run stakes race. The perfunctory season was over at approximately 3:29, moments after George M. Hendrie's three-year-old chestnut colt *Springside* flashed past the finish line.

The race result was anticipated, but it was anti-climactic. What was at stake, the continuity of the Plate race, was the really crucial issue. It had been preserved when the Ontario Jockey Club brazenly staged the only thoroughbred race in Canada in 1918 during the opening day of the Toronto Hunt Club's open-air horse show. All proceeds of the two-day event went to the Red Cross, including a $1,000 donation from Hendrie, owner of Valley Farm Stable of Hamilton and the breeder of *Springside*. The OJC was prompted to take arbitrary steps following an Order-in-Council by the Federal government in the summer of 1917 banning all organized racing meetings for the duration of the war in Europe. Aware that the Plate's continuity was in jeopardy and seeking a suitable alternative, the Club first agreed to put its grounds at Woodbine at the disposal of the Toronto Hunt Club, at no charge, on 24–25 May. It then appealed directly to Sir Robert Borden, the prime minister, boldly informing him that "directors have decided to permit the running of the King's Plate, according to the old custom." They reminded Sir Robert that the race would not only act as a "slight encouragement for the breeders of thoroughbred horses in Ontario," but its continuity should be maintained. They promised that no other races would be allowed at the horse show, nor would betting be, in any way, sanctioned or permitted upon the premises.

In attempting to soften their contemplated step, which they felt "is not of course in any way in conflict with the Order-in-Council of last year," the Club's directors said they "wished to explain fully what was proposed as they would greatly regret it if their position in the matter were misapprehended or if the Government should in any way gain the impression that the Ontario Jockey Club was not loyally following its decision."

The "Red Cross" Plate attracted a crowd of five thousand, including the Governor General, the Duke of Devonshire, who told Hendrie he was extremely pleased with the decision to run the race

and prevent a lapse in the long record of consecutive contests for His Majesty's "guineas." It was obvious, however, that the spectators were not there to watch the heavyweight hunters and the ladies' saddle horse competition, or even the officers' chargers. "That the crowd came for the race was amply demonstrated by the rapidity with which the attendance decreased as soon as the race was run."

While the noise of the "iron men" was missing and newspapers headlined stories "Betless King's Plate for Hendrie Colt," betting in one form or another occurred as the *Daily Racing Form*'s race chart revealed opening and closing win odds as well as place and show, noting that

PROGRAMME

Open Air Horse Show

Under the Auspices of

✚ **Toronto Hunt Club** ✚

Woodbine Park, Toronto

MAY 24TH □ 1918 □ MAY 25TH

Proceeds in Aid of the
**Red Cross Society
of Canada**

The King's Plate will be run Victoria Day.

Price 15 Cents

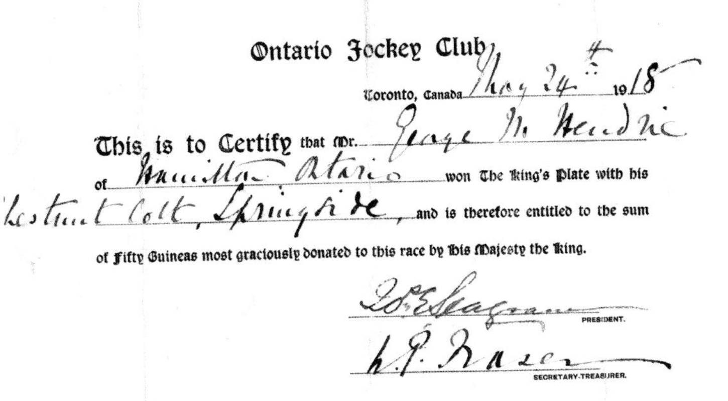

Ontario Jockey Club

Toronto, Canada May 24th 1918

This is to Certify that Mr. George M. Hendrie of Hamilton Ontario won The King's Plate with his Chestnut Colt, Springside, and is therefore entitled to the sum of Fifty Guineas most graciously donated to this race by His Majesty the King.

W. E. Seagram PRESIDENT.

W. P. Fraser SECRETARY-TREASURER.

Ontario Jockey Club certificate made it official.

SPRINGSIDE | 3-year-old chestnut colt

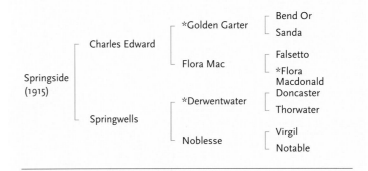

Springside (1915)	Charles Edward	*Golden Garter	Bend Or
			Sanda
		Flora Mac	Falsetto
			*Flora Macdonald
	Springwells	*Derwentwater	Doncaster
			Thorwater
		Noblesse	Virgil
			Notable

Owner: George M. Hendrie, Hamilton; *Trainer:* Ed Whyte
Jockey: Lee Mink; *Breeder:* George M. Hendrie

show bets were not accepted on *Springside,* the heavily favoured colt that everyone predicted would win the Plate.

The previous summer owners were notified that they would be allowed to train Plate eligibles outside the country. Hendrie was the only owner to take advantage of the "wartime rule" as he shipped *Springside* to trainer John Walters in Kentucky, where he broke his maiden that November in a claiming race at the Latonia track. The following spring the colt's coat was sparkling after the sojourn in the Blue Grass State. He had prepared for the Plate with a judicious defeat at Churchill Downs in Louisville, losing by only two lengths (a victory would have disqualified *Springside* from Plate competition as the only winners allowed were those of two-year-old races). Two weeks before the Plate, *Springside* was shipped to Hendrie's local trainer, Ed Whyte, who merely had to "breeze" the colt a couple of times at Woodbine, then slip a saddle on his back and toss up jockey Lee Mink. One of seven American riders imported from Kentucky for the Plate, Mink received five hundred dollars for his day's work.

A delightful aside to *Springside*'s dash for the "guineas" was the heroic battlefield tale of his half-brother, *Rockspring,* who had been credited with leading a Canadian calvary charge at the Somme. The gelding had finished ninth in the 1913 Plate and had gone off to France early in the War as the charger of Major Ian Hendrie, the son of Lieutenant Governor Sir John S. Hendrie and George Hendrie's nephew. "Brother to King's Plate Winner Leads Charge Which Saves Allies," reported one newspaper as it related the feats of *Rockspring,* "who dashed into the hordes of advancing Germans and cut them to ribbons at the moment when it appeared as if the tide of battle was turning against the brave defenders of democracy. Correspondents at the front substantiate reports of the memorable charge of the Canadian calvary. "The admirable warhorse thrives on the work and dangers he goes through."

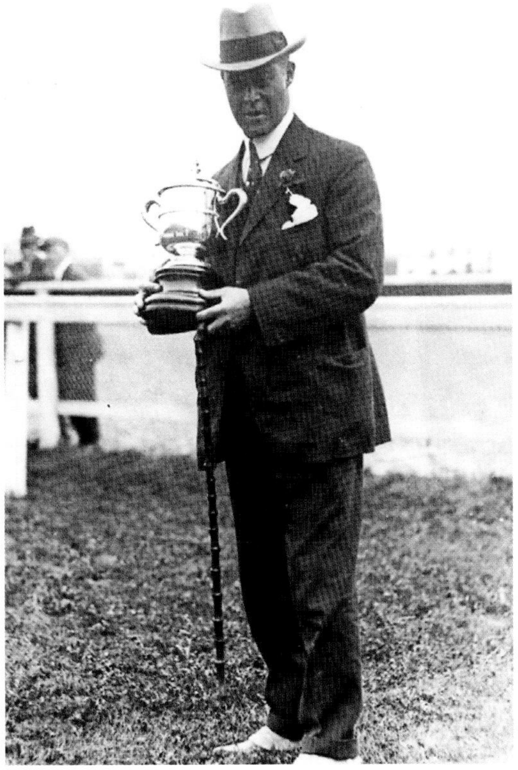

The proud owner holds the coveted King's Plate, his "loving cup."

1918 KING'S PLATE STAKES

Woodbine Park
MAY 24, 1918

1 1-4 MILES (2:04⅕). Fifty-Ninth Running of THE KING'S PLATE. $3,250 added and 50 Guineas, the Gift of His Majesty, King George V of England. Feature event of The Toronto Hunt Open Air Horse Show (proceeds in aid of Red Cross Society of Canada). For 3-year-olds and upward, the property of a British subject resident in Ontario, foaled, raised and trained in Ontario, that have never won a race, either on the flat or across country, other than a race exclusively for 2-year-olds, have never left Canada. (Note—Because of War-time conditions horses are allowed to train outside of province). Winners to carry five pounds extra. A piece of plate will be presented to winner. Net value to winner, $2,540 and 50 Guineas; second, $600 and third, $250. Breeder of winner to receive $150. A sweepstake of $5 at entry and $10 to start.

Horse	Eqt	A	Wt.	PP	St	¼	½	¾	Str	Fin	Jockey	Owner	Odds $1
SPRINGSIDE		3	113	11	5	6^{2}	$3\frac{1}{2}$	2^{3}	1^{1}	1^{3}	MinkL	HendrieGM	1.00
LADDER OF LIGHT		4	119	5	6	3^{1}	$1\frac{1}{2}$	1^{hd}	2^{3}	2^{4}	EnsorL	BeardmoreGW	a-6.00
MAY BLOOM		3	108	10	8	$5\frac{1}{2}$	5^{1}	3^{hd}	3^{2}	3^{3}	RodriguezJ	BrookdaleStable	b-2.50
BLACKBURN		3	110	3	1	1^{1}	$2^{1\frac{1}{2}}$	4^{1}	4^{1}	4^{hd}	ScherrerG	BrookdaleStable	b-2.50
GOLD GALORE		4	124	8	7	$8\frac{1}{2}$	$9\frac{1}{2}$	7^{hd}	$7\frac{1}{2}$	5^{hd}	CrumpW	SeagramJE	c-4.00
PLEASURE BENT		3	110	12	4	4^{hd}	6^{1}	5^{1}	5^{hd}	6^{hd}	MolesworthG	ThorncliffeStable	7.00
SADDUCEE		3	110	7	9	10^{hd}	10^{2}	10^{2}	8^{1}	7^{3}	SutherlandG	BrookdaleStable	b-2.50
SEA FROTH		3	108	2	2	2^{hd}	$4^{1\frac{1}{2}}$	$6\frac{1}{2}$	6^{hd}	8^{2}	EnnisR	SeagramJE	c-4.00
TWELVE BELLS		3	112	6	10	9^{1}	$7\frac{1}{2}$	8^{1}	10^{1}	9^{2}	CollinsW	SeagramJE	c-4.00
BENCHER	b	3	110	4	12	11^{6}	8^{1}	9^{1}	$9\frac{1}{2}$	10^{3}	FodenN	GiddingsH	3.00
RED ADMIRAL		3	114	1	3	7^{nk}	11^{3}	11^{2}	11^{4}	11^{1}	CheyneR	BeardmoreGW	a-6.00
SCARBORO BEACH		3	105	9	13	12^{5}	12^{8}	12^{6}	12^{5}	12^{5}	GibsonH	LeRoyM	40.00
McCORBURN		4	121	13	11	13	13	13	13	13	WattsR	MillarC	40.00

a-Coupled as George W. Beardmore entry; b-Brookdale Stable entry; c-J. E. Seagram entry.

WENT TO POST AT 3:21. OFF AT 3:26. Time, :23⅘, :48⅘, 1:15⅖, 1:42⅖, 2:08⅘. Track fast.

$2 Mutuel Prices: **SPRINGSIDE** .... 4.00 — —

(NO SEPARATE PLACE OR SHOW WAGERING)

Ch. c (3), by Charles Edward—Springwells, by *Derwentwater. Trained by Edward Whyte. Bred by George M. Hendrie, Hamilton.

Start good and slow. Won easily; second and third driving. SPRINGSIDE, much the best, move up to the leaders on the far turn and easily drew away in the homestretch. LADDER OF LIGHT took the lead when entering the backstretch, held on well in the last eighth and was easily best of the others. MAY BLOOM made a game effort when rounding the last turn but tired in the final drive. BLACKBURN tired after setting initial pace. GOLD GALORE suffered from early interference and finished last. BENCHER wheeled at the start.

Overweights—Twelve Bells, 2 pounds; Red Admiral, 4.

By the spring of 1919 the war in Europe had been over for six months, the soldiers were home, and only the formal signing of the peace treaty was necessary for the official proclamation. Naturally, horse racing was quick to resume its activities, everywhere except Canada, where a stubborn government dragged its feet on lifting the Order-in-Council that had banned wagering at racetracks for the "duration of the war and six months thereafter."

Optimistic horsemen, anticipating the resumption of racing under normal conditions, had eagerly organized programs throughout the country, as well as the Diamond Jubilee of the continent's oldest continuously run stakes race, the King's Plate. To their dismay, the government instead introduced a bill in April prohibiting betting at tracks until the summer; it extended the Order-in-Council under the War Measures Act to the close of that session in Parliament.

Undaunted, harness horse-men immediately announced that they would go ahead with meets, betting or no betting, at Picton, Galt, Belleville and the Toronto Exhibition track. The Ontario Jockey Club, faced with the alternatives of postponing the opening of its 24–31 May meeting until later in the summer, or staging a non-betting Plate race for the second year in a row, reluctantly cancelled the $7,500-added Plate. It then reopened the event for original subscribers, but offered a meagre purse of $3,000. Thus, the sixtieth running of the Plate on 24 May was a "betless affair." The press was sympathetic towards the Ontario Jockey Club's plight:

LADDER OF LIGHT's OWNER GEORGE BEARDMORE (LEFT) WITH LADY EATON AND HER SON, TIMOTHY CRAIG EATON, AT A SHOW.

> The historic event was run under the auspices of the Toronto Hunt Open Air Horse Show, and while the Ontario Jockey Club looked after the details, it was a case of everything going out and nothing coming in for them. They supplied the King's Plate purse, while the Horse Show people received the receipts for the day. Everything was conducted in keeping with Woodbine tradition, but nevertheless, Plate day without additional races was like a duck out of water to the majority of the

spectators present, and it was noticed immediately after the Plate race there was a scurry to get home by a large number.

However, judging by the *Daily Racing Form*'s detailed race chart in the Toronto newspapers, wagering on the twelve-horse field was evident. Money exchanged hands at the mutuel windows as the winner paid seven dollars for a two-dollar bet. The Seagram entry was heavily favoured at even money while the Thorncliffe Stable entry was bet down to odds of 6-to-1. *Hemisphere* was the long shot at 40-to-1.

The rather subdued crowd, which numbered about five thousand, was mainly a society one, according to the *Evening Telegram*. What was missing was the feeling of pent-up enthusiasm; the murmur of admiration as the horses paraded to the post; the death-like stillness of expectancy as the runners stood in the chute awaiting the start; the expectation of something worth remembering.

The result provided a double triumph for the horse show crowd as the winner, *Ladder of Light,* was owned by OJC director George

Uniformed women of the Red Cross Society mingle with racing fans while collecting for charity.

LADDER OF LIGHT | 5-year-old brown mare

Ladder of Light (1914)	*Stanhope II	Florizel II	St. Simon
			Perdita II
		King's Daughter	Kingfisher
			*Viola
	Missing Link	*Isidor	Amphion
			*Isis
		Miss Laudeman	Hanover
			Elizabeth L.

Owner: George W. Beardmore, Toronto; *Trainer:* J.H. (Joe) Doane
Jockey: Lawrence (Larry) Lyke
Breeder: Pontiac Stud (Mrs. A. Lily Livingston), Cobourg

Wathen Beardmore, a founder of the Toronto Hunt Club and for years the Master of the Fox Hounds. Beardmore, whose stately residence on Toronto's Beverley Street was named "Chudleigh," was rewarded in his third Plate attempt with the five-year-old mare. He had bought her as a yearling from Mrs. Lily Livingston, the Cobourg breeder who was not allowed to run her Ontario-bred horses in the Plate because she was an American. (A motion by director Major Joseph Kilgour in 1919 to have "the property of a British subject" deleted from the Plate conditions was dismissed by the executive committee.) However, Mrs. Livingston received the breeder's award ($150) for the second time—1915 Plate winner *Tartarean* was bred at her Pontiac Stud.

Following the half-length win over Joseph Seagram's favoured *Doleful,* Beardmore announced that he shared the opinion of his trainer, Joseph Doane, that the mare could win money in New York; but he declared that he was opposed to sending his horses away when they should have the opportunity to race in Canada. *Ladder of Light,* runnerup in the 1918 Plate, was still a maiden despite being given four starts that fall in Maryland. (She was one of the seven in the field of twelve whose owner had taken advantage of the wartime rule allowing horses to train or race outside the country.) However, in this King's Plate, according to *The Mail and Empire,* Lawrence Lyke, whose riding fee was five hundred dollars, "gave the winner a million-dollar ride."

> Without a less capable boy up, *Doleful*, would have secured the honours, although no fault could be found with the ride [George] Walls gave the second horse. Lyke, in difficulty at times, had to ease his mount to escape the jam, but was content to lay off the pace. But when *Uncle John* faltered going around the last turn, Lyke brought the mare in on the rail to pass *Hong Kong.* To horsemen at the top of the stretch, including starter James Milton, *Ladder of Light* looked like a beaten horse.

The fact that Lyke was in the irons on *Ladder of Light* was a surprise to him since he had come up from New York's Belmont racetrack under the impression that he would ride one of Seagram's three-horse entry. But when he was unable to make the weight, Lyke accepted a ride on Beardmore's mare. Lyke was a veteran U.S. rider who later lost the Kentucky Derby by a head in 1921 aboard *Black Servant.*

The war was over, but the reminders of it were evident in the Plate field—*Salvo, Ammunition* and *Bugle March.*

1919 KING'S PLATE STAKES

Woodbine Park
MAY 24, 1919

1 1–4 MILES (2:04 1/5). Sixtieth Running of THE KING'S PLATE. 50 Guineas, the gift of His Majesty King George V, with $3,000 added by the Ontario Jockey Club. The principal feature of the Toronto Hunt Club's one-day horse meeting. For 3-year-olds and upward, the property of a British subject resident in Ontario; foaled and raised in Ontario. Due to war-time conditions, rules regarding horses leaving province are waived. Horses which have won a race exclusively for 2-year-olds are eligible. Winners to carry five pounds extra. Nominations closed March 4 (23 nominations). Sweepstake of $5 to enter and $10 to start. A piece of plate will be presented by the club to the winner. Net value to winner, $2,470 and 50 Guineas; second, $600 and third, $250. Breeder of winner to receive $150.

Horse	Eqt	A	Wt.	PP	St	¼	½	¾	Str	Fin	Jockey	Owner	Odds $1
LADDER OF LIGHT		5	122	1	3	6^{1}	6^{1}	3^{3}	2^{3}	$1\frac{1}{2}$	LykeL	BeardmoreGW	2.50
DOLEFUL		3	108	6	5	$4\frac{1}{2}$	4^{hd}	$1\frac{1}{2}$	1^{hd}	2^{6}	WallsG	SeagramJE	a-1.00
HONG KONG	sb	3	113	11	2	2^{hd}	2^{1}	2^{1}	3^{2}	3^{1}	KummerC	SeagramJE	a-1.00
UNCLE JOHN		3	108	2	6	3^{hd}	3^{1}	4^{1}	4^{2}	4^{2}	FodenN	SunnysideStable	8.00
SALVO		3	110	4	4	$5\frac{1}{2}$	5^{1}	5^{5}	5^{5}	5^{5}	WilliamsJ	HendrieGM	b-3.50
CORA W.		3	103	9	10	10^{2}	10^{4}	8^{1}	$6\frac{1}{2}$	6^{2}	ScottJ	WalkerW	30.00
AMMUNITION		4	121	7	8	$7\frac{1}{2}$	$8\frac{1}{2}$	6^{hd}	7^{1}	7^{3}	DishmonC	HendrieGM	b-3.50
GALWAY	b	3	108	12	1	$1\frac{1}{2}$	1^{hd}	$7\frac{1}{2}$	$8\frac{1}{2}$	8^{2}	EricksonH	SeagramJE	a-1.00
PLEASURE BENT		4	126	8	9	8^{1}	7^{1}	9^{1}	9^{2}	9^{4}	CaseyA	ThorncliffeStable	c-6.00
BUGLE MARCH		3	105	5	7	9^{1}	9^{1}	11^{1}	10^{2}	10^{2}	FoleyJ	ThorncliffeStable	c-6.00
HEMISPHERE		3	105	3	11	12	12	12	11^{1}	11^{5}	GibsonW	LeRoyM	40.00
FAIR AND WARMER		3	103	10	12	11^{1}	11^{5}	$10\frac{1}{2}$	12	12	FallenM	ThorncliffeStable	c-6.00

a–Coupled as J. E. Seagram entry; b–G. M. Hendrie entry; c–Thorncliffe Stable entry.

WENT TO POST AT 3:26. OFF AT 3:28. Time, :23 1/5, :48 3/5, 1:15 2/5, 1:41 4/5, 2:09 2/5. Track slow.

Mutuel Prices:

	$2 Mutuels Paid			Odds to $1		
LADDER OF LIGHT	7.00	—	—	2.50	—	—
DOLEFUL (a-Entry)		—	—		—	—
HONG KONG (a-Entry)		—	—		—	—

(NO SEPARATE PLACE OR SHOW WAGERING)

Br. m (5), by *Stanhope II.—Missing Link, by *Isidor. Trained by Joseph H. Doane. Bred by Mrs. Lily A. Livingston, Pontiac Stud, Cobourg.

Start good and slow. Won driving; second and third the same. LADDER OF LIGHT moved up rapidly after rounding the stretch turn, caught DOLEFUL tiring in the last eighth and outstayed him in the final drive. DOLEFUL took the lead on the far turn and held on in the final drive. HONG KONG showed speed, but tired badly in the last quarter. UNCLE JOHN was on the outside of the leaders most of the race and failed to respond when called on. SALVO met with interference in the early running. CORA W. finished with a belated rush. GALWAY ran well for three-quarters, then retired.

Scratched—Jim Petrie and Master Fox.

Windsor, Ont. (Kenilworth Park)—
Striding with rhythm that rivaled friction-less mechanism, *Man o' War*, the "horse of the century," made farcical pretensions of his much-heralded rival, *Sir Barton*, and beat him to the finish in the most hollow style, in their mile-and-a-quarter test, entailing a cash prize of $75,000 in American currency and a supplementary prize of a $5,000 gold cup.

JOCKEY ROXY ROMANELLI.

WILY ENTREPRENEUR A.M. (ABE) ORPEN.

The greatest day in Canadian horse racing? Positively. It was the Roaring Twenties and this match race would be one of the most memorable turf spectacles of the Golden Era of Sports. Two champions clashed that afternoon: Sam Riddle's immortal *Man o' War*, holder of more records than any other horse and the leading three-year-old of 1920, and *Sir Barton*, the Canadian-owned champion of the older-horse division and America's first Triple Crown winner in 1919; he was owned by Commander J.K.L. Ross of Montreal.

The supremacy of the American turf was settled conclusively before an estimated thirty thousand spectators, who made Big Red a prohibitive 1-to-20 favourite, the shortest odds that can prevail in the mutuel system of betting. The big, strapping racing machine came striding down the stretch, knocking almost seven seconds off the track record. His speed made the critics forget the one-sideness of the race, but it was *Man o' War*'s last before going to stud, and, like the wins of "Old Bones," *Exterminator,* and a later "Big Red," *Secretariat,* it came on Canadian soil. *Sir Barton*'s rider that day, Frank Keosh, was a last-minute substitution for Earl Sande and rode in the King's Plate the following year, finishing second on *Royal Visitor.*

The daring gamble of putting up such an enormous purse was a huge personal triumph for A.M. (Abe) Orpen, Toronto's wily entre-preneur who operated Kenilworth and Toronto's Dufferin Park, and later Hillcrest, Long Branch and London racetracks. Orpen's race coup was a badly needed boost for Canadian horse racing, which

MAN O' WAR OUTCLASSED *SIR BARTON* AT WINDSOR'S KENILWORTH PARK.

had suffered needlessly because of the government's wartime ban on betting in 1918 and 1919. Its glorious and welcome return was never more evident than on that eventful day in Windsor, or at Woodbine earlier in the season when *St. Paul*, a three-year-old gelding owned by Harry Giddings Senior of Oakville and trained by his son, Harry, won the King's Plate before a crowd that Toronto newspapers declared was the largest in the track's history. Estimates ranged from nineteen to twenty thousand.

The Mail and Empire claimed: "Over 20,000 paid homage to King Horse at the Ontario Jockey Club opening. At least this is the estimation of secretary W.P. Fraser. This is open to argument from the throng that invaded the mutuels, as in their opinion, 'there must have been a million,' so hemmed in were they." The struggle to place a wager was so difficult, said *The Evening Telegram,* that "men were simply carried off their feet in the rush, and it was hope-less to even dream of seeing the racing and get a little down at the same time. At least half the money that went down there to be put up, never left the pockets."

Because of the congestion, fans travelling on streetcars were forced to alight a mile or so from the track and walk the balance of the way, while late-arriving automobiles were parked blocks from their destination. Several thousand people were still trying to gain admit-tance long after the races had begun, and it was suggested that the centre field should be opened to the public on special occasions, a

Tuesday, October 12, 1920
KENILWORTH PARK WINDSOR

GLEN RIDDLE FARM'S
MAN O' WAR
(3) By Fair Play—Mahubah

and J. K. L. ROSS'
SIR BARTON
(4) By Star Shoot—Lady Sterling

Match Race
$75,000 PURSE AND GOLD CUP
17506

GENERAL ADMISSION $5.00

THIS TICKET STUB IS NOW A COLLECTOR'S ITEM.

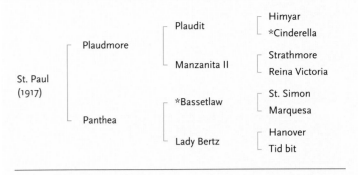

ST. PAUL | 3-year-old brown gelding

			Himyar
		Plaudit	*Cinderella
	Plaudmore		Strathmore
St. Paul		Manzanita II	Reina Victoria
(1917)			St. Simon
		*Bassetlaw	Marquesa
	Panthea		Hanover
		Lady Bertz	Tid bit

Owner: Harry Giddings Sr., Oakville; *Trainer:* Harry Giddings Jr.
Jockey: R.C. (Roxy) Romanelli; *Breeder:* Cedar Grove Stud (Harry Giddings Sr.)

custom at Maryland tracks. "If there is one class that should be catered to where racing is concerned, that class is made up of those who go to the mutuels often to back their honest opinions. Keep them away and members' badges will not pay the $80,000 in purses very long."

For Giddings Senior, who received the piece of plate and the scrip for the guineas from the Duke of Devonshire, it was his fourth Plate win with a horse he had bred, and like *St. Bass, Hearts of Oak* and *Beehive,* it would go on to win the Breeders' Stakes. However, Giddings Senior would be severely censured by Ontario Jockey Club officials later in the year when he "sold the scrip drawn by the Governor General upon the Keeper of the King's Privy Purse for the sum of Fifty 'Guineas' to Mr. Charles Millar." (Millar, who had won the Plate in 1915, was the brilliant but eccentric Toronto lawyer. One of his clients and a previous partner in his racing stable was Abe Orpen.)

Although Giddings' three-horse entry was second choice in the wagering behind the favoured Seagram Stable entry, *St. Paul*'s impressive win was cheered loudly, partly because of his veteran jockey, Roxy Romanelli, "who not so far back was rated as one of the cleverest riders on the Canadian circuit." Romanelli was back at Woodbine after

a long stint in the Argentine and Peru.

Horse racing had also returned and the promise of an exciting era could be measured by the renewed interest of the large American outfits applying for stall space for their top stakes horses. They came from the stables of the Whitneys, Willis Kilmer, Walter Salmon and Commander J.K.L. Ross. *Exterminator, Boniface, Display, Tattling, Billy Kelly, My Dear, Spot Cash, Hallucination,* along with Seagram's good ones—*Gaffsman, Sir Harry, Edisto* and *Golden Sphere*—would win the big races for the top riders, Earle Sande, Frank Keogh, Johnny Maiben, Pete Walls, Mack Garner and Al Claver in the 1920s. But there was a tempering note. The Ontario government wanted in on the action and had levied a daily licence fee of $7,500 per day, plus the amusement tax. The fans were the losers. To counter the taxes, the OJC increased the "bite" taken out of every bet from five to ten per cent.

ROMANELLI ON CEDAR GROVE STABLE'S *ST. PAUL.*

1920 KING'S PLATE STAKES

FOURTH RACE
Woodbine Park
MAY 22, 1920

1 1–4 MILES (2:04⅕). Sixty–First Running of THE KING'S PLATE. (The oldest continuously run fixture on this Continent.) 50 Guineas, the Gift of His Majesty King George V, with $7,500 added by the Ontario Jockey Club. (Note—The conditions of this race were extended to meet war conditions until Dec. 31, 1919.) Net value to winner $5,755 and 50 Guineas; second, $1,000; third, $500. The breeder of the winner to receive $500. A sweepstakes of $5 payable at time of entry, and $10 additional to start. For 3-year-olds and upward, foaled in Ontario that have never won a race, either on the flat or across country, other than a race exclusively for 2-year-olds. Winners to carry 5 lbs. extra. A piece of Plate will be presented to winning owner by club.

Horse	Eqt A	Wt.	PP	St	¼	½	¾	Str	Fin	Jockey	Owner	Odds $1
ST. PAUL	b 3	105	5	4	3hd	2²	2²	1³	1⁴	RomanelliR	GiddingsH	a–1.70
BUGLE MARCH	4	121	13	8	1¹	1¹	1nk	2⁴	2⁶	WilliamsJ	RiddellT	12.65
PRIMO	b 3	108	12	10	2hd	3¹	3¹½	3⁵	3³	MorrisL	GiddingsH	a–1.70
ANMUT	3	103	14	12	8¹	6³	5½	4½	4²	DugganC	BrookdaleStable	50.30
GALLANT KITTY	4	124	11	9	9¹½	7¹½	7¹⁵	5¹½	5¹½	RichcreekA	SeagramStable	b–.95
AZRAEL	b 4	124	8	7	4¹½	4hd	6nk	6hd	6³	WillisO	MurphyT	29.45
CROWN OF GOLD	b 3	109	9	11	5¹	5³	4⁴	7³	7⁵	RodriguezJ	SeagramStable	b–.95
BENCHER	b 5	129	4	13	6¹	8³	8²	8¹⁰	8¹⁰	PrimroseW	GiddingsH	a–1.70
ANTIPHON	b 4	119	7	6	11⁸	9¹⁰	9¹⁵	9¹⁵	9⁶	JohnstonWJ	WarnerAW	61.25
LIVELY SLEEPER	4	119	3	2	7¹	10³	10¹½	10¹	10¹	GarnerH	BeardmoreGW	120.90
FAIR AND WARMER sb	4	119	6	5	14	14	11¹	11¹	11¹	DishmonC	ThorncliffeStable	63.10
WASKA	5	122	1	1	13¹⁰	13¹⁰	12³	13¹⁰	12¹⁵	WhitewoodR	BrodieWA	f–141.80
PLEASURE BENT	b 5	129	10	14	10½	11½	13¹	13⁸	13⁸	MetcalfJ	CornellG	15.60
KELTIE	b 4	121	2	3	12¹½	12²	14	14	14	BlackA	FoxheadMews	f–141.80

a–Coupled as H. Giddings Sr. entry; b–Seagram Stable entry. f–Mutuel field.
WENT TO POST AT 4:33. OFF AT 4:36. Time, :23⅘, :48⅘, 1:14⅘, 1:41⅗, 2:09. Track fast.

Mutuel Prices:

	$2 Mutuels Paid			Odds to $1		
ST. PAUL (a–Entry)	5.40	3.30	4.80	1.70	.65	1.40
BUGLE MARCH		8.30	5.10		3.15	1.55
PRIMO (a–Entry)	5.40	3.30	4.80	1.70	.65	1.40

Br. g (3), by Plaudmore—Panthea, by *Bassetlaw. Trainer, Harry Giddings Jr. Bred by Harry Giddings Sr. of Cedar Grove Stud, Oakville.

Start good and slow. Won easily; second and third driving. ST. PAUL was saved under sight restraint for the first mile, then took an easy lead when his rider was ready and won in a canter. BUGLE MARCH showed the most early speed, but tired when challenged. PRIMO stopped after twice failing to get past the leaders in the turn into the eastern run and later in the turn into the backstretch. CROWN OF GOLD tired badly in the backstretch after lying fifth and finished in the ruck.

Scratched—Sweet Bouquet.

1921 | HERENDESY

The noise and movement of the throngs who had been herded into the infield had an unnerving effect on the nine Plate starters as they anxiously stomped about behind the barrier, waiting for it to spring upwards. Most fractious of all was *Herendesy*, the little "black colt" of Brookdale Stable. He was the betting favourite, but he wheeled and bucked repeatedly under jockey Jimmy Butwell, a Toronto boy, who had been the continent's leading rider in 1920 and had won almost every major race in North America, except the Kenucky Derby and the King's Plate.

The colt's roguishness was out of character; as a two-year-old he had been quite mild. Suddenly *Herendesy* made a menacing lunge towards the barrier, which startled the masses milling about near the starting chute. They had been anticipating the "off" for almost eight minutes. Those who had bet on the colt from Barrie were stunned when the starter ordered him to be removed from the number five post position and taken to the outside fence after he had lashed out and kicked *Moll Cutpurse*.

BROOKDALE STABLE'S *HERENDESY* AND JOCKEY JIMMY BUTWELL.

Finally the field was away, and cleanly, but in the dash out of the chute towards the inside rail, some bumping occurred. *Royal Visitor* jostled *Fuse*, then Butwell allowed *Herendesy* to swerve from the outside fence down to the inside, rocking *Royal Visitor* with a bodycheck. Rough riding tactics? The stewards thought there might have been and after the race had a talk with Butwell and Frank Keogh, who finished second on *Royal Visitor*. But they did not alter the result or fine the jockeys. Some reporters, however, were unimpressed with the collision, saying: "The bumping had no effect on the final result." They lauded the colt's six-length victory under a choking pull: "*Herendesy* First and Rest Nowhere in Plate," and "It was strictly a two-horse race for a mile, and a one-horse race the final quarter."

Herendesy's win was a Canadian breeding milestone as he became the first Plate victor to be sired by a previous winner. He was by 1912 Plate winner *Heresy*. That was the year Albert and Simon Dyment took control of Brookdale following the tragic death of Johnny Dyment, their second cousin, who had built the stable into one of Canada's leading racing and breeding establishments.

1921 KING'S PLATE STAKES

FOURTH RACE
Woodbine Park
MAY 21, 1921

1 1–4 MILES (2:04$\frac{1}{5}$). Sixty-Second Running of THE KING'S PLATE. $7,500 added and 50 Guineas the Gift of King George V. 3-year-olds and upward. Foaled in Ontario. Net value to winner $5,070; second, $1,500; third, $1,000; fourth, $500.

Horse	Eqt	A	Wt.	PP	St	¼	½	¾	Str	Fin	Jockey	Owner	Odds $1
HERENDESY	b	3	113	5	4	$1^{1\frac{1}{2}}$	1^{3}	1^{3}	1^{3}	1^{6}	ButwellJ	BrookdaleStable	a-.87½
ROYAL VISITOR	b	3	113	9	3	2^{hd}	2^{2}	2^{10}	2^{15}	2^{15}	KeoughF	BrennerM	b-2.35
MOLL CUTPURSE		3	103	7	8	9	8^{nk}	5^{1}	5^{4}	3½	WeinerF	LivingstonMrsLA	c-13.45
HEATH BELL		3	108	3	7	8^{2}	9	9	6^{2}	4^{2}	ParringtonK	BrennerM	b-2.35
CROWN OF GOLD	b	4	124	8	9	$7^{1\frac{1}{2}}$	5^{nk}	4^{4}	3^{2}	5^{10}	LancasterR	SeagramStable	11.05
GAY KAP	b	3	108	6	6	6^{hd}	7^{1}	7^{nk}	8^{3}	$6^{1\frac{1}{2}}$	RomanelliR	MapleLeafStable	44.90
RESARF	b	3	113	4	5	4^{1}	$3^{1\frac{1}{2}}$	3½	4^{3}	$7^{1\frac{1}{2}}$	RichcreekA	BrookdaleStable	a-.87½
FUSE		3	105½	1	1	5½	6^{2}	6^{3}	7^{6}	8^{6}	McTaggartJ	ThorncliffeStable	30.40
FLEA		3	103	2	2	3^{1}	4^{hd}	8^{1}	9	9	GregoryH	LivingstonMrs LA	c-13.45

a-Coupled as Brookdale Stable entry; b-M. Brenner entry; c-Mrs. L. A. Livingston entry.

WENT TO POST AT 4:15. OFF AT 4:23. Time, :24$\frac{1}{5}$, :49$\frac{3}{5}$, 1:15$\frac{4}{5}$, 1:42$\frac{3}{5}$, 2:10. Track fast.

Mutuel Prices:

	$2 Mutuels Paid			Odds to $1		
HERENDESY (a-Entry)	3.75	2.45	2.20	.87½	.22½	.10
ROYAL VISITOR (b-Entry)		2.80	2.30		.40	.15
MOLL CUTPURSE (c-Entry)			2.70			.35

Br. c (3), by Heresy—Depends, by *The Friar. Trainer, George Walker. Bred by Albert & Simon Dyment, Barrie.

Start good and slow. Won easily; second and third driving. HERENDESY began from the extreme outside and, rushing across to the inner rail, bumped ROYAL VISITOR slightly and was under restraint until rounding the first turn, when he raced to the front and easily held the race safe to win in a canter. ROYAL VISITOR raced in closest pursuit and made a game challenge at the end of the stretch after being unable to get to the front. MOLL CUTPURSE was kicked on the side by the winner while at the post and was badly outrun, finished gamely and outstayed the others for third place. HEATH BELL closed a gap and finished resolutely.

Overweight—Fuse, 2½ pounds.

The win by *Herendesy* also kept a racetrack superstition alive: "When horse is 'black,' bet Brookdale." Its three previous winners, *Thessalon*, *Sapper* and *Heresy*, had black- or brown-coloured hides. In this era horses were usually identified as bays or browns instead of blacks if there were some brown-coloured hairs among the black hairs of their coats.

The Plate again attracted a huge crowd, and about two thousand were allowed into the infield to ease congestion in the stands. Women fainted in the crush at the gates, and most fans "arrived more or less dishevelled in clothing, or a bit out of temper." However, the crowd of more than twenty-five thousand was delighted at the sight of veteran trainer George Walker winning his first Plate. Two weeks before the race, it appeared that he would not have a starter because *Herendesy* was ailing. But Walker's careful nursing and a couple of tight

THE DUKE AND DUCHESS OF DEVONSHIRE STROLL ACROSS WOODBINE'S LAWN.

Herendesy (1918)

- Heresy
  - *Sain
    - St. Serf
    - *The Task
  - Hera
    - Hamburg
    - Tara Blackburn
- Depends
  - *The Friar
    - Friar's Balsam
    - Lizzie Baker
  - *Device
    - Sir Bevys
    - Lady Plotwell

Owner: Brookdale Stable (Albert Dyment and Simon Dyment), Barrie
Trainer: George Walker; *Jockey:* James (Jimmy) Butwell
Breeder: Albert Dyment and Simon Dyment

drills a week before the race enabled him to send a "fit horse post-ward." A horseman from Memphis, Tennessee, Walker joined Brookdale shortly before World War I, bringing with him a world-wide reputation. He had been one of America's top trainers before moving to Europe in 1905, where his horses earned more than 3.3 million marks in six seasons and twice won the German Derby and Grand Prix of Baden; he took almost every turf classic in Germany and Austria.

While the sixty-second Plate was hardly a classic, it provided a notable tableau. Mrs. Lily Livingston, who owned the sprawling Rancocas Stud in New Jersey and the Pontiac Stock Farm in Cobourg, was eligible to race a horse in the Plate for the first time. Conditions had been revised to allow any person (even non-residents of Canada) to enter, providing the horse had been "foaled, raised and trained in the province of Ontario." Mrs. Livingston, who had earlier bred Plate winners *Tartarean* and *Ladder of Light,* but was unable to race them in her own silks, entered two fillies—*Moll Cutpurse,* which finished third after being kicked at the starting barrier by the rowdy *Herendesy,* and *Flea,* which finished last. The grand dowager of the turf had become only the third woman to ever run a horse in the Plate.

A sign of the times in 1921 was the presence of the Royal Canadian Mounted Police, who had been put in charge of supervising the federal government's new betting regulations. Late betting was immediately eliminated as "the iron men" were

closed during the post parade. However, payoff prices were now quickly posted. In a move to gain control of racetrack revenues, Ottawa introduced legislation that limited the mutuel percentage allowed to tracks on a scale of from seven to three per cent, according to the amount of money wagered. Woodbine was taking ten per cent. The move came a year after the Ontario government had levied a daily licence fee of $7,500 on the larger tracks along with a twenty-five-cents per ticket amusement tax. The Ontario Jockey Club, complaining of diminishing revenues and the financial threats faced by owners and breeders, angrily denounced both governments for their attempts to "bleed the racing industry." General admission tickets were increased from $1.50 to $2.00 to offset increased costs. The club also claimed a rebate from the province "for races given for horses bred and owned in Canada."

A less serious problem was Prohibition. Police nabbed several "flask-carrying Members," who were convicted. The Club was then prosecuted for a breach of the new Temperance Act and fined $1,000. Later, the courts quashed the sentence, following an appeal.

HATS, HATS, HATS! LADIES' DAY AT WOODBINE PARK.

outh Shore stood alone in the historic records of the oldest racing fixture in North America, for she not only won the King's Plate on 20 May, after standing for more than a day in an ice pack to soothe a bad leg, but she later gave birth to two foals who would also capture the Plate. *South Shore's* feat would be matched almost eighty years later by another Hall of Fame filly, *Dance Smartly*, winner of the Queen's Plate in 1991, and the dam of Plate winners *Scatter The Gold* in 2000 and *Dancethruthedawn* in 2001.

In 1929, her son *Shorelint* won the classic, and six years later a daughter, *Sally Fuller*, made off with the Plate. The odds against a modern-day mare matching this feat were truly astronomical. The only other Plate-winning mares to produce a victor of the fifty "guineas" were *Nettie* in 1882 (with *Fanny Wiser*), *Lyddite*, the dam of *Shimonese*, in 1908, and *Dance Smartly*.

South Shore, who was by the imported English sire **Orme Shore*, was blessed with speed throughout her pedigree. She was the first offspring of *Southern Maid*, a daughter of Kentucky Derby winner *Plaudit*, and was acquired by the Thorncliffe Stable for just $400 as a yearling. The Kentucky-bred filly was an instant local heroine in 1913 when she broke a long-standing spring record at Woodbine in her first race, and later that year narrowly missed winning the Futurity in New York, the richest event for juveniles in North America, losing to the indomitable *Pennant*.

While *Southern Maid* was carrying *South Shore*, veteran trainer Charles Patterson, who saddled Kentucky Derby winner **Omar Khayyam*, predicted that if the foal was a filly, the Thorncliffe people would have one of the best bred mares in America. The foal was a filly and she did go on to win the Plate. However, *South Shore* was not the soundest of horses. She was hampered by an ailing leg throughout her limited racing career, and at the age of four was entered in the Plate with only one start. Racetrackers who remembered her dam's blazing speed, and who had witnessed some of *South Shore's* workouts, knew she was capable of winning the race. But there was also speculation that making it as far as the post parade on Saturday might require the talents of Houdini.

Trainer Fred Schelke, who boasted before the race that "If she's sound I'd be willing to wager the City Hall on her," remained at the stable till Friday midnight in order that the ice would be properly applied to the bad leg. *The Mail and Empire* also reported: "The icing

PRESIDING STEWARD DAVID BOYLE (LEFT) AND *SOUTH SHORE'S* TRAINER FRED SCHELKE.

was renewed immediately after the filly had been out in the morning until race time. The way she ran, however, left no doubt that she was not only a game mare, but had been sent to the post a very fit horse."

South Shore's gimpy leg was dismissed by a good proportion of the large crowd, which turned out on a "cool, rainy, disagreeable day" as she and stablemate *Fuse* went off as the 5-to-2 second choice behind Brookdale Stable's three-year-old *Paddle*. It was an interesting contest as *South Shore*, ridden by Toronto's Kenny Parrington, saved ground on the inside while stalking the early pacesetters, *Paddle* and *King's Court*. After rushing her to the lead in the backstretch, Parrington eased up when he knew the race was won and appeared satisfied to allow a close finish, winning by a length over *Paddle*, who had come on again with a belated rush.

The Plate victory for the familiar canary- and black-coloured silks of Thorncliffe Stable was dearly cherished; it ended a drought that had lasted for more than fifty years, back to 1871 when Robert Davies, the man who built the racing and breeding establishment in Todmorden Mills (now part of the Toronto borough of East York), won with *Floss* at Kingston. After the death of one of Canada's most respected horsemen in 1916, Davies' oldest son, George, assumed control of the stable. Three of Davies' other six sons, Wilfred, Robert and Norman, also played prominent roles in the powerful stable. Another son, Melville, ran horses under his own name. While the colourful Thorncliffe jackets were frequently victorious on the Ontario circuit and at American tracks, the Plate had eluded the Davies boys until the victory of *South Shore*, the filly whose dam (*Southern Maid*) was purchased by their father from the famed Kentucky breeder, John E. Madden. The Plate was presented to George Taylor Davies by Canada's newly appointed Governor General, Lord Byng of Vimy.

Byng was in command of the Canadian Corps in 1916 and 1917. It was as "Byng's Boys" that the corps came to be known, and Byng was in command when the Canadians took Vimy Ridge during Easter 1917, the first great British victory of the war. Byng said after Vimy, "what a mouthful to swallow [the Prussian Guard] being beaten to hell by what they called 'untrained colonial levies.'" Loved by his troops for his many appearances in the front lines, it was only natural that Byng should come to Canada as Governor General. The appearance of Byng was almost deferred because of the OJC's

One of Canada's greatest mares, *South Shore*; King's Plate champion and dam of two Plate winners.

SOUTH SHORE | 4-year-old black filly

South Shore (1918)	*Orme Shore	Orme	*Ormonde
			Angelica
		Virginia Shore	John Davis
			Distant Shore
	Southern Maid	Plaudit	Himyar
			*Cinderella
		Sally K.	*Mirthful
			Unsightly

Owner: Thorncliffe Stable, (Robert, George, Wilfred and Melville Davies), Todmorden; *Trainer:* Fred Schelke; *Jockey:* Kenny Parrington
Breeder: Thorncliffe Stable

vigorous, but losing taxation battle with the Hon. Peter Smith and the provincial government.

The "Smith Bill," which was rushed through the legislature while its chief opponents were absent from the House, allowed the government to collect five per cent on all money wagered through the mutuel machines. The act was passed just three days before the Plate, and it prompted legal wrangling, protests and threats to postpone the opening of the racing season. On the morning of the race Mr. Justice Middleton declared in favour of an application by the Ontario Jockey Club for an injunction restraining the provincial treasurer from instructing the Provincial Police to stop all racing at Woodbine.

W.A. Hewitt, writing in *The Toronto Star,* noted that it was the fans who would be "contributing to the provincial coffers," and "the new tax is not going to break anybody nor to cause any great hardship."

Four years later, Byng was involved in the "King-Byng" affair, the euphonious name given the convoluted constitutional and political squabble surrounding the struggle in 1926 between an embattled Prime Minister Mackenzie King, the slightly naive Governor General and the Leader of the Opposition, Arthur Meighen. King lost office to Meighen briefly when Byng refused to accept his advance to dissolve Parliament. Author J.L. Granatstein, in his review of Jeffrey Williams' book, *Byng of Vimy,* said, "In the subsequent election King was returned triumphantly to power. Meighen's career came to a close and Byng, badly bruised by his encounter with the sharp elbows on the Rideau, returned to England a broken man." Mackenzie King was not one to allow any Governor General to stand in his way, and the Prime Minister was quite ruthless in riding roughshod over Byng.

George Davies of Thorncliffe Stable with the Plate trophy.

1922 KING'S PLATE STAKES

FOURTH RACE
Woodbine Park
MAY 20, 1922

1 1-4 MILES (2:04 1/5). Sixty-Third Running of THE KING'S PLATE. The oldest fixture run continuously on this Continent. 50 Guineas the Gift of His Majesty King George V, and $10,000 added by the OJC. The first horse to receive The Guineas, Stakes, and $7,000: the second horse $1,500, and the third horse $1,000. The breeder of the winner to receive $500. A Sweepstakes of $5 payable at time of entry, and $10 additional to start. For three-year-olds and upward, foaled, raised and trained in the Province of Ontario, that have never won a race, either on the flat or across country, other than a race exclusively for two-year-olds, have never left Canada, and have never been more than one month out of Province. Winners to carry 5 lbs. extra. Net value to winner $7,315 and 50 Guineas.

Horse	Eqt	A	Wt.	PP	St	¼	½	¾	Str	Fin	Jockey	Owner	Odds $1
SOUTH SHORE		4	122	11	6	3^{1}	2^{hd}	$1^{½}$	1^{nk}	1^{1}	ParringtonK	ThorncliffeStable	a-2.37½
PADDLE		3	113	8	4	1^{1}	$1^{½}$	2^{2}	2^{1}	2no	BuxtonM	BrookdaleStable	1.85
EL JESMAR	b	3	113	5	2	4^{1}	3^{4}	3^{8}	3^{8}	3^{6}	LangC	FletcherJC	b-4.50
ROYAL GIFT	b	3	111	3	9	7^{1}	$5^{½}$	4^{3}	4^{10}	4^{15}	TaylorE	BrennerMrsDora	26.00
FUSE		4	122	4	1	5^{2}	6^{2}	5^{4}	$5^{½}$	$5^{1½}$	McDermottL	ThorncliffeStable	a-2.37½
MOLL CUTPURSE		4	122	1	10	11	$9^{1½}$	8^{6}	6^{2}	6^{2}	ClaverA	LivingstonMrsLA	23.20
CHEECHAKO	sb	3	105	7	11	8^{2}	7^{6}	7^{2}	7^{10}	7^{15}	RowanJ	FletcherJC	b-4.50
GREYBOURNE		4	127	6	8	9^{1}	10^{15}	9^{5}	$8^{½}$	8^{4}	RomanelliR	NewellR	11.75
KING'S COURT		3	102	2	3	2^{1}	4^{2}	$6^{½}$	9^{8}	9^{3}	TurnerC	SeagramStable	c-9.40
IMPERSONATOR		3	108	9	5	6^{hd}	$8^{½}$	10^{30}	10^{30}	10^{30}	ThompsonC	SeagramStable	c-9.40
ISLANDER		5	124	10	7	10^{3}	11	11	11	11	BlackA	BellDJ	85.70

a-Coupled as Thorncliffe Stable entry; b-J. C. Fletcher entry; c-Seagram Stable entry.

WENT TO POST AT 4:29. OFF AT 4:33. Time, :24, :49 2/5, 1:15 4/5, 1:44, 2:12. Track slow.

Mutuel Prices:

	$2 Mutuels Paid			Odds to $1		
SOUTH SHORE (a-Entry)	6.75	3.20	2.55	2.37½	.60	.27½
PADDLE		3.15	2.40		.57½	.20
EL JESMAR (b-Entry)			2.70			.35

Blk. f (4), by Orme Shore—Southern Maid, by Plaudit. Trainer, Fred Schelke. Bred by Thorncliffe Stable, Todmorden.

Start good and slow. Won easily; second and third driving. SOUTH SHORE was saved close up for the first three-quarters, then raced into the lead and was under restraint at the end. PADDLE set the pace to the last turn and tired, but finished gamely. EL JESMAR saved ground on the far turn and when entering the homestretch and was game at the finish, almost getting up for second place. ROYAL GIFT closed a gap and finished gamely. The others were beaten off at the end. KING'S COURT showed early speed but tired.

Scratched—Resarf, Tipsy Dance and Shoulder Arms.

Overweights—Impersonator, 3 pounds; King's Court, 2; Royal Gift, 1.

1923 | FLOWERFUL

Lord and Lady Byng arrive at Woodbine Park in an open laudau.

Joseph Seagram had been at rest in Waterloo's Mount Hope Cemetery for nearly four years, but to the crowd of almost thirty thousand at Woodbine on 19 May 1923, his presence and influence were conspicuously visible. It was as if the Laird of Waterloo had willed his heirs the sixty-fourth running of the King's Plate when a brash young colt, *Flowerful*, cruised home a three-length winner after setting all the pace.

Edward Frowde Seagram, who had taken control of the Seagram racing empire following the death of his father, proudly accepted the silver cup from Lady Byng, who two years later would present a trophy named in her honour to Frank Boucher of the New York Rangers, the National Hockey League's "most gentlemanly player."

1923 KING'S PLATE STAKES

FOURTH RACE
Woodbine Park
MAY 19, 1923

1 1-4 MILES (2:04⅕). Sixty-Fourth Running KING'S PLATE. 50 Guineas, the gift of His Majesty King George V, and $10,000 added by the Ontario Jockey Club. The first horse to receive The Guineas, Stakes, and $7,000, the second horse $1,500, and the third horse $1,000. The breeder of the winner to receive $500. A Sweepstakes of $5 payable at time of entry, and $25 additional to start. For three-year-olds and upward, foaled, raised and trained in the Province of Ontario, that have never won a race, either on the flat or across country, other than a race exclusively for two-year-olds, have never left Canada, and have never been for a period of more than one month out of this Province. Winners to carry 5 lbs. extra. Death of nominator does not render entry void. A piece of plate will be presented by the Club to the owner of the winner. Net value to winner $7,495 and 50 Guineas.

Horse	A	Wt.	PP	St	¼	½	¾	Str	Fin	Jockey	Owner	Odds $1
FLOWERFUL	3	113	8	1	1^{1}	$1^{1\frac{1}{2}}$	1^{1}	1^{3}	1^{3}	WilsonT	SeagramStable	a-9.50
CHEECHAKO	4	124	11	12	7^{nk}	6^{hd}	4^{hd}	4^{2}	$2\frac{1}{2}$	AbelA	FletcherJC	11.65
TRAIL BLAZER	3	105	4	4	2^{nk}	2^{hd}	3^{2}	$2\frac{1}{2}$	3^{2}	SmallwoodE	ThorncliffeStable	b-1.20
RALLIM	3	108	9	5	5^{1}	3^{1}	2^{hd}	3^{hd}	4^{4}	ScobieE	MillarC	3.30
MAYPOLE	3	108	10	6	3^{hd}	5^{2}	5^{1}	5^{2}	5^{1}	ParringtonT	BrookdaleStable	c-11.15
VESPRA	3	108	5	9	$10^{1\frac{1}{2}}$	7^{3}	6^{6}	6^{3}	$6^{1\frac{1}{2}}$	ChalmersJ	BrookdaleStable	c-11.15
PELF	3	103	6	11	13	13	11^{1}	8^{6}	7^{3}	ClaverA	SeagramStable	a-9.50
OCEAN CREST	3	110	12	7	6^{hd}	10^{4}	7^{2}	7^{3}	8^{8}	StirlingD	ThorncliffeStable	b-1.20
HEARTS OF ROCK	4	122	7	13	11^{1}	$11\frac{1}{2}$	$10\frac{1}{2}$	9^{2}	9^{3}	MaibenJ	ElliottEJ	70.60
HONEY'S JEWEL	3	110	13	3	$4^{1\frac{1}{2}}$	4^{hd}	$9\frac{1}{2}$	11^{2}	10^{2}	RomanelliR	GiddingsH	8.25
GAME SCRAPPER	3	110	3	2	9^{hd}	9^{nk}	12^{3}	12^{3}	11^{1}	RowanJ	SmallmanJE	71.40
FLORALIA	3	103	1	8	8^{2}	8^{nk}	$8^{1\frac{1}{2}}$	10^{hd}	12^{8}	WallsP	SeagramStable	a-9.50
MY SOLACE	3	103	2	10	$12\frac{1}{2}$	12^{1}	13	13	13	StevensF	LivingstonMrsLA	46.45

a-Coupled as Seagram Stable entry; b-Thorncliffe Stable entry; c-Brookdale Stable entry.

WENT TO POST AT 4:30. OFF AT 4:31. Time, :23⅘, :49, 1:15⅖, 1:43⅗, 2:11. Track good.

Mutuel Prices:

	$2 Mutuels Paid			Odds to $1		
FLOWERFUL (a-Entry)	21.00	9.75	4.85	9.50	3.87½	1.42½
CHEECHAKO		11.80	4.15		4.90	2.07½
TRAIL BLAZER(b-Entry)			2.55			.27½

Br. c (3), by Ypsilanti II.—Bouquet, by Kinley Mack. Trainer, William H. Bringloe. Bred by Seagram Stable, Waterloo.

Start good and slow for all but HEARTS OF ROCK. Won easily; second and third driving. FLOWERFUL began well and, setting a fast pace from the start, kept his lead under slight restraint to the stretch turn, where he drew away to win easing up. CHEECHAKO gained steadily from a slow beginning and, finishing fast, outgamed TRAIL BLAZER in the final drive. The latter raced well and finished gamely. RALLIM also raced forwardly, but tired in the last quarter. HONEY'S JEWEL was in a jam at the half-mile pole, where he was pulled up. MAYPOLE was in contention early and maintained his position but never threatened.

It was a propitious day—in England the Duke of York was married to Lady Elizabeth Bowes-Lyon, whose appearance at Woodbine in 1939 as King George VI and Queen Elizabeth stirred the nation; the resolute *Zev* captured the Kentucky Derby, and a long shot who enjoyed an "off" track, *Flowerful*, paid twenty-one dollars, an unheard of price for a stable noted for sending out horses that the public routinely made the favourite.

The great throng that packed the stands and lawns, and overflowed two thousand strong to the infield to watch the event, heartily roared its approval when *Flowerful* and jockey Terry Wilson, wearing the famed black silks with the yellow sash, were led into the unsaddling ring by the oldest son of "old Joe." It was the Seagram's sixteenth Plate victory, but the first for Joe's sons—Edward, Norman and Thomas. The following day they received a telegram from Aldershot, England: a congratulatory cable from His Majesty, King George V. To the knowledgeable, this Plate really belonged to the former president of the Ontario Jockey Club. During

THE GOVERNOR GENERAL'S WIFE, LADY BYNG, PRESENTS TROPHY TO EDWARD F. SEAGRAM.

Flowerful (1920)	Ypsilanti II	*Galore	Galopin
			Lady Maura
		*Stefanete	Peter
			Stellarius
	Bouquet	Kinley Mack	*Islington
			Songstress
		Briar Sweet	*Sir Modred
			Sweetbriar

Owner: Seagram Stable (Edward F., Norman and Thomas W. Seagram), Waterloo; *Trainer:* Wiliam H. (Bill) Bringloe
Jockey: Terrence (Terry) Wilson; *Breeder:* J.E. Seagram

World War I and into 1919, Seagram methodically disposed of almost every broodmare he owned at the Waterloo farm. One exception was *Bouquet*, an especially combative mare that twice beat the males in the Autumn Cup. She was a great favourite of Seagram, and one of his final acts before his death on 18 August 1919, was to breed her to *Ypsilanti II*, a Maryland-bred stallion Seagram had imported from England after it had won several classic races on the British turf. He was an immediate success—sire of Seagram's 1917 Plate winner *Belle Mahone*. But Seagram was not alive when *Bouquet* dropped her *Ypsilanti II* foal, *Flowerful*, who was the only colt raised at the Waterloo stud in 1920, a fact that was recalled when toasts were drunk in honouring the man and his last Plate winner.

Although he was part of a three-horse entry, *Flowerful* was given only a slight chance of capturing the Plate. As a two-year-old, he had won only once in nine starts. "If track conditions are bad, he is a contender on his one good race in the mud last year at the Hamilton track," prophesized *The Star*'s W.A. Hewitt. It had been a wet spring and the rain had been falling off-and-on for almost a week before the season was to open with the traditional Plate race. However, officials were predicting a fast track if they had one dry day before the opener: "The Woodbine course, being of a light soil, dries out rapidly and in twenty-four hours changes from mud to a lightning fast track."

On Plate day the sun shone brightly for the vice-regal party, which included the Governor General, Lord Byng of Vimy and Harry Cockshutt, Ontario's Lieutenant Governor, and the handsomely dressed ladies, whose "dazzling footgear rivaled hats in vividness; old-time 'Ascot' finery replaced by tailor-mades and sports attire." In spite of the drenching it had taken, the track was rated as "good," and *Flowerful*, breaking from the middle of the field, went immedi-ately to the lead, which he never surrendered. Trainer William Bringloe, who would later add five more Plates to his portfolio, was complimented by *The Mail and Empire*: "He not only had the horse in grand condition, but fooled the clockers completely, and it's a smart trainer that can fool them."

Wilson's ride on the colt, whose career went downhill afterwards, was also praised by Francis Nelson, a racetrack steward who moon-lighted as a columnist for *The Star*. "Seagram's new rider gave a fine exhibition of skill in race riding when he made the pace in the Plate, and rated his horse out in front—a much more difficult task than judging the pace when following it."

TRAINER BILL BRINGLOE AND JOCKEY TERRY WILSON.

Flowerful's time for the mile-and-one-quarter was 2:11, respectable over an "off track." It would be the last time the Plate was contested at that distance until 1957 at the new Woodbine in suburban Etobicoke. After consider-able debate, the Ontario Jockey Club, which was now under the direction of the sons of former presi-dents—Colonel William Hendrie, who had been president since replacing Joseph Seagram, and directors Sir John Hendrie and Edward F. Seagram, along with A.E. Dyment, G.W. Beardmore, R.J. Christie, Major Joseph Kilgour and D. King-Smith, bowed to requests by horsemen and shortened the Plate to a mile-and-one-eighth. They complained that a longer race was a severe test for any horse, first crack out of the box. Rules at this time did not allow horses to be trained outside Ontario. Because it had been a long, drawn-out winter, abetted by an unusually wet spring, a majority of the Platers in 1923 were not as fit as in previous years.

There was hardly a racetrack in the 1910s that had not been worked over by either *Mother* or *Useeit*, two of the "toughest, hard knockin' mares" ever to feel the urgent jabs of a jockey's spurs. They rattled about like gypsies, often at the same track, wherever their itinerant trainers fancied they might swipe a meagre purse.

Mother was a Kentucky-bred who toiled at the small Ontario and Quebec tracks until she was raced out and was sold to Jack Bater, a farmer in Trafalgar Township. A.W. Hoots, an illiterate Oklahoma Indian, who periodically would trek his small string of nags from Juarez, Mexico, to the Montreal courses, often bedded down in Toronto to run *Useeit* at Dufferin Park's homey "bullring." However, Hoots was later ruled off the turf for refusing to part with the old mare when she was claimed out of a cheap race at one of the "leaky-roof half-milers of the West." He told the judges that his wife would run him off the reserve if he went back without *Useeit*, and that he would rather be ruled off by them than by his wife.

A number of years later and many miles apart, *Mother* and *Useeit* were bred. According to Mrs. Rosa M. Hoots, it was a deathbed wish of her husband's that the mare be bred to *Black Toney*, the greatest stallion in Kentucky, because he had a vision that *Useeit* would "throw" a black colt that would win the Kentucky Derby. Jack Bater had no such premonition in 1921 when *Mother* foaled a chestnut colt at his small breeding farm near Oakville. The foal was by *Plaudmore*, sire of the 1920 King's Plate winner *St. Paul*. His arrival was no occasion for celebration; just another horse into the world.

Mother's first foal was a spindly legged little fellow who kept pretty much to himself when he was turned loose to roam the paddock. He never liked to mix with the other horses. Later, when Bater was paid a visit by the neighbouring Wilson brothers of Oakville, Hugh and Willie, he had himself prospective clients.

"Years later I remember my dad [Hugh] telling me how he and Willie first laid their eyes on this young weanling. He had caught his leg in this old wire fence and they went over to untangle him. Willie held him while Dad pulled the leg out. He had a nasty cut in the leg and it left a pretty good scar. But it didn't seem to bother the little guy as he scampered over to his mare [*Mother*]," William H. Wilson recalled in 1984.

"You like him?" Bater asked when the Wilsons showed interest.

"Well, I don't know," replied Hugh.

"Tell you what I'll do. I'll sell him to you for $500."

"Can he run?" the Wilson brothers wanted to know.

"Well, why don't you take him back to your place and see if he can run," Bater suggested.

"Buy him then," advised Willie, who would later train the horse.

On 17 May 1924, the lore of horse racing would be further enriched when *Useeit*'s son, named *Black Gold* after the oil of Oklahoma, won the Golden Jubilee running of the Kentucky Derby at Churchill Downs, while at Woodbine Park, *Maternal Pride*, the gelded son *of Mother*, won the sixty-fifth running of the King's Plate and earned immortality by returning the greatest price in the race's

WAS IT REALLY *MATERNAL PRIDE*? OR A "RINGER" WHO PAID $193.25 FOR $2.00? JOCKEY GEORGE WALLS LOOSENS SADDLE.

history. A two-dollar wager to win on the unheralded gelding was worth $193.35. The similarities between these two horses ends here as *Black Gold*, who was the best three-year-old in America, paid $5.50.

He was trained by an Indian, Hedley (Three-Fingered) Webb, who would not talk to the press, and was ridden by a man who five years later would win the Plate, J.D. Mooney (his son, John Mooney, would hold the presidency of the Ontario Jockey Club from 1971 to 1974). Legend has it that when Mrs. Hoots was ceremoniously presented with a cheque for $52,775, she refused to accept it. She graciously received the silver trophy, but did not trust cheques. Mrs. Hoots wanted it all in cash. She was finally persuaded that it was dangerous to carry that much cash all the way to Oklahoma and took the cheque, but she made the Club certify it. The saga of *Black Gold* ended on the proper melodramatic note at the Fair Grounds in New Orleans in 1928 when he attempted a comeback after three years at stud. He gamely finished the race, but on three legs, and had to be destroyed. A stone marks the spot where he was buried at the track.

Unlike the Derby hero, *Maternal Pride* was "King Horse—but only for a day," and then because he was ignored by the bettors who had overlooked his workouts. His only race before the Plate was as a two-year-old; it was in one of the cheaper races in the fall and he finished last. Wilson took *Maternal Pride* back to his Oakville farm for the winter, but in April, when the Ontario Jockey Club announced the names of the forty-six horses nominated for the Plate, the list included *Mother*'s chestnut gelding. The Wilsons were the butt of many a joke, especially Hugh, who knew he would be the laughing stock of the racing fraternity if his horse made a miserable showing. Just before the race Wilson was standing in the members' enclosure speaking with owner Jim Fletcher. Behind them were Harry Giddings Senior, Tom Phelan and Allie Loudon, president of the Hamilton Jockey Club. Wilson heard either Phelan

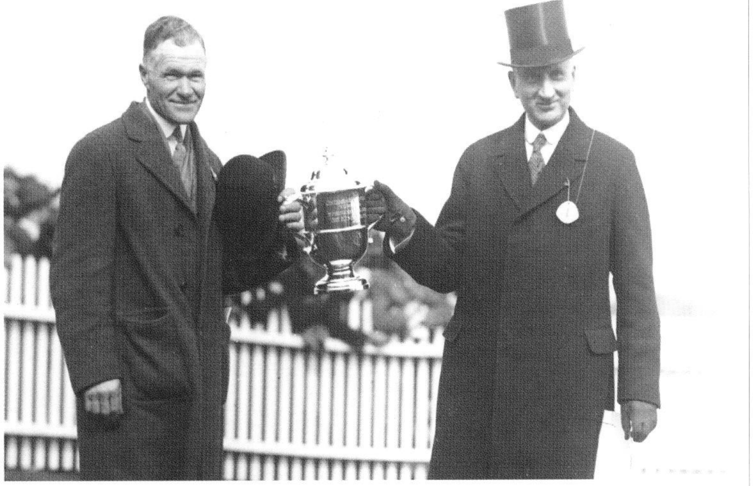

Lt. Governor Henry Cockshutt awards Plate trophy to owner Hugh Wilson.

MATERNAL PRIDE | 3-year-old chestnut gelding

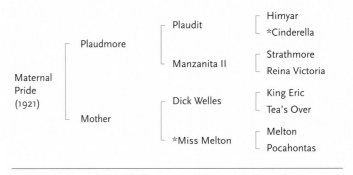

Maternal Pride (1921)	Plaudmore	Plaudit	Himyar
			*Cinderella
		Manzanita II	Strathmore
			Reina Victoria
	Mother	Dick Welles	King Eric
			Tea's Over
		*Miss Melton	Melton
			Pocahontas

Owner: Hugh S. Wilson, Oakville; *Trainer:* William G. (Willie) Wilson
Jockey: George Walls; *Breeder:* Jack Bater, Oakville

or Giddings say: "That colt [*sic*] of Wilson's is nothing but a plug. He'll break a leg at the quarter pole. Don't waste dough on him." Mother's pride and instinct caused a few women to frivolously put up two-dollars on the underdog. He was the first to show and quickly opened up a two-length lead. The sudden departure had enabled him to avoid the jostling at the first turn as *Catamaran* fell. Although the challenges would come, the race seemed to be no contest as *Maternal Pride* opened up eight lengths. But, predictably, his margin began to shrink as *Thorndyke* made his move, stride by stride whittling away at the lead. *Maternal Pride* was faltering, his lead two lengths as the fox and hound chase continued around the turn into the stretch. Georgie Walls went to his "bat," touching up the tiring upstart. No response. The crowd of twenty-five thousand was on its feet, roaring, anticipating his collapse. It never came. A two-dollar wager for win, place or show returned $193.35, $95.45 and $43.65. Afterwards rumours circulated that *Maternal Pride* was a "ringer." Frank Armstrong, writing in *The Telegram* in 1961, disagreed:

> He was considered 'nuthin' before the Plate and was 'nuthin' after it. So suspicion was voiced and printed that another horse had been substituted in the name of *Maternal Pride*. . . . I don't subscribe to that theory, and never believed that Hugh Wilson, who was essentially a show-ring rider as well as a trainer of hunters and jumpers, would ever resort to such trickery. . . . I visited Wilson's farm after *Maternal Pride* had won the Plate and asked him pointblank if the horse was a ringer. . . . He told me he adhered to the theory that the Plate run was survival of the fittest. In that era, a horse made his first start of the year at one mile and a furlong without benefit of racing as a three-year-old. Wilson related how he had trained *Maternal Pride* throughout the winter on his five-eighths mile track near the Trafalgar Road and about the permanent scar on his leg, the one he picked up when he stepped through wire fence at Jack Bater's place as a weanling. Wilson showed me pictures taken in the winner's ring. The identical scar showed up on both shots. In my book that identification was as good as the lip tattoo of today.

William Wilson remembers his father's version of the incident: "He was no ringer. After the race my father called over the Bater brothers, who had bred him and knew all about the scar, to confirm that the horse was *Maternal Pride*. But it was no secret that the ICRA didn't like Dad."

Although *Maternal Pride* could only beat mediocre fields afterwards, he still retained a touch of class, for he won the final race of his career, on 7 November 1925, at Beulah Park in Ohio.

1924 KING'S PLATE STAKES

FOURTH RACE
Woodbine Park
MAY 17, 1924

1 1-8 MILES (May 24, 1922, 1:51²/₅-4-109). Sixty-Fifth Running KING'S PLATE. 50 Guineas, gift of His Majesty King George V, and $10,000 added by the OJC. The first horse to receive the Guineas, Stakes and $7,000; the second horse $1,500, and the third horse $1,000. The breeder of the winner to receive $500. A Sweepstakes of $5 payable at time of entry, and $25 additional to start. For three-year-olds and upward, foaled, raised and trained in the Province of Ontario, that have never won a race, either on the flat or across country, other than a race exclusively for two-year-olds, have never left Canada, and have never been for a period of more than one month out of this Province. Winners to carry 5 lbs. extra. A piece of plate will be presented by the Club to the owner of the winner. The Club reserves the right to cancel this race upon the repayment of all entrance fees paid in advance. Net value to winner $7,575 and 50 Guineas.

Horse	Eqt	A	Wt.	PP	St	¼	½	¾	Str	Fin	Jockey	Owner	Equiv. Odds Str't
MATERNAL PRIDE	b	3	110	6	5	1^{hd}	1^{4}	1^{6}	1^{3}	1^{2}	WallsG	WilsonHS	95.67½
THORNDYKE		3	109	3	2	3^{1}	3^{2}	2^{3}	2^{5}	2^{6}	BurkeHJ	ThorncliffeStable	5.95
MAYPOLE		4	127	5	4	$7^{1\frac{1}{2}}$	$7\frac{1}{2}$	$3^{1\frac{1}{2}}$	$3^{1\frac{1}{2}}$	$3^{1\frac{1}{2}}$	SharpF	BrookdaleStable	a-15.95
ISOLETTA		3	112	2	1	$6^{1\frac{1}{2}}$	4^{hd}	5^{2}	4^{2}	4^{3}	ScobieE	SeagramStable	b-1.45
SEVEN OAKS		3	112	4	8	$9\frac{1}{2}$	6^{1}	6^{6}	$5\frac{1}{2}$	5^{4}	RomanelliR	RobsonC	c-3.85
TIGER TIM		3	109	15	10	11^{hd}	$8^{1\frac{1}{2}}$	7^{2}	7^{2}	$6^{1\frac{1}{2}}$	StevensF	CiceriPL	f-7.00
MEXICAN PETE	b	3	112	13	9	$2^{1\frac{1}{2}}$	$2^{1\frac{1}{2}}$	4^{hd}	6^{3}	$7\frac{1}{2}$	AbelA	FletcherJC	f-7.00
PELF		4	122	11	7	$12^{1\frac{1}{2}}$	11^{3}	9^{4}	8^{2}	8^{3}	GariepyF	ElliottStable	43.25
HONEY DEAR		3	112	8	6	4^{6}	9^{1}	8^{hd}	9^{6}	9^{8}	ChalmersJ	GiddingsH	c-3.85
REBUS		3	107	7	14	14	12^{2}	12^{1}	10^{3}	$10\frac{1}{2}$	StirlingD	FairJG	104.60
BEAU OF THE WEST	b	3	109	12	10	13^{3}	13^{3}	13^{1}	12^{4}	11^{1}	WilsonT	SeagramStable	b-1.45
OCEAN CREST		4	129	1	3	$10^{1\frac{1}{2}}$	14	14	$11\frac{1}{2}$	12^{15}	McTaggartJ	DaviesMR	23.30
*ANN K.		5	123	10	12	$5\frac{1}{2}$	$10^{1\frac{1}{2}}$	$11\frac{1}{2}$	13^{1}	$13\frac{1}{2}$	SchwartzM	BakerSH	f-7.00
THORNTON		3	109	14	11	8^{nk}	5^{3}	10^{1}	14	14	WallsP	BrookdaleStable	a-15.95
CATAMARAN		3	112	9	13	Fell.					MilnerW	SmallmanJE	12.70

a–Coupled as Brookdale Stable; b–Seagram Stable entry; c–C. Robson and H. Giddings entry.
f–Mutuel field. *Added starter.

OFF AT 4:34. Time, :24¹/₅, :49, 1:15¹/₅, 1:43³/₅, 1:57³/₅. Track slow.

Mutuel Prices:

	$2 Mutuels Paid			Odds to $1		
MATERNAL PRIDE	193.35	95.45	43.65	95.67½	46.72½	20.82½
THORNDYKE		7.95	6.70		2.97½	2.35
MAYPOLE (a–Entry)			11.15			4.57½

Ch. g, by Plaudmore—Mother, by Dick Welles. Trainer, William G. Wilson. Bred by Bater Brothers, Oakville.

Start good and slow. Won easily; second and third driving. MATERNAL PRIDE began quickly and, setting a good pace, raced into a long lead and tired somewhat in the stretch, but easily withstood THORNDYKE's challenge. The latter finished resolutely and was gradually gaining on the winner at the finish. MAYPOLE made up ground and outraced ISOLETTA through the homestretch. ISOLETTA finished gamely. There was much jostling and crowding while going into the first turn and the rider on CATAMARAN was unseated when his mount stumbled. SEVEN OAKS had a rough race in the early running.

By 1925, twelve years after it had happened in England, people still remembered the shocking event, but not the name of the militant suffragette who had dashed out of the crowd of spectators at Tattenham Corner, one of the critical turns on the Epsom racecourse. Miss Emily Wilding Davison had been trampled to death after tackling King George V's colt, *Anmer, sending him to the turf during the running of the 1913 Derby. The suicidal lunge into the tightly bunched field, and her desperate clutching on *Anmer's bridle rein, were not entirely unexpected as the Rights of Women movement was at its height in England that spring. To attract attention to their cause, Miss Davison had threatened to prevent the Derby from being run.

However, the tragic event and the name of the suffragette was vividly recalled on 23 May 1925, for that ironically, was the Day of the Filly and the triumph

FOSTER HEWITT (BACK TO CAMERA) HOLDS A MICROPHONE, WHILE J.C. FLETCHER (RIGHT) RECEIVES THE PLATE FROM GOVERNOR GENERAL LORD BYNG. OJC SECRETARY W.P. FRASER IS IN THE CENTRE.

of *Anmer's three-year-old chestnut daughter, *Fairbank,* in the sixty-sixth running of the King's Plate. It had never happened before, but the first five to finish were fillies. Only *Goldlands,* a gelding, prevented a six-horse sweep by the opposite gender on the cold, murky afternoon at Woodbine Park. At the wire, in one of the race's most exacting finishes, it was *Fairbank* by the width of a fluttering eyelash over *Duchess.*

Fairbank was owned and bred by James C. Fletcher, a man with both a remarkable and colourful career, and her victory was immediately hailed by the monarch. The following day a cablegram was received by the secretary of the Ontario Jockey Club:

> The King asks if you will kindly convey His Majesty's congratulations to Mr. J.C. Fletcher on his winning the King's Plate. The King is much pleased that the winner was bred by *Anmer, formerly the property of His Majesty.—Equerry.

A royally bred stallion, *Anmer had been donated by George V to the federal Department of Agriculture in 1916 for the purpose of military remounts and "light horse breeding" and to improve the

calibre of local draught animals whose quality and numbers had been decimated in World War I. He was the first of many studs the monarch would present to the National Bureau of Breeding and later to the Canadian Racing Association, which placed stallions at various tracks and localities in Ontario. The fee to breed was a mere ten dollars.

*Anmer was by *Florizel II* (a full-brother to *Persimmon* and *Diamond Jubilee,* both of which won the Derby and St. Leger for Edward VII) and stood for several years at Fletcher's farm in Downsview (now part of Toronto) before being sent to Major Palmer Wright's stud at Chaffey's Locks, near the Rideau Canal and Ottawa.

Curiously, there was some question following *Fairbank*'s win of the identity of her sire—*Anmer or *Sobieski. *Rock On,* her dam who had several Derby winners in her pedigree, had been bred to both stallions. *The Mail and Empire* reported: "She acts like an *Anmer and Mr. Fletcher has always maintained that she is by *Anmer." *The Globe,* however, wrote: "Mr. Fletcher is of the opinion that *Anmer sired the Plate winner, although she would have been equally well bred had she been by *Sobieski. The *Anmer cross will undoubtedly guide him in his breeding operations in the future."

FAIRBANK AND FUTURE HALL OF FAME JOCKEY CHIC LANG. HE LATER WON THE KENTUCKY DERBY.

FAIRBANK | 3-year-old chestnut filly

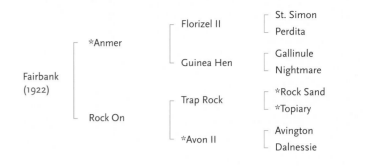

Owner: J.C. Fletcher, Downsview; *Trainer:* Jack Givens
Jockey: Charles (Chick) Lang; *Breeder:* J.C. Fletcher

Fletcher, who lived at one time near the village of Fairbank, had enjoyed a prolific racing career abroad before returning to Canada just before World War I. He had lived in Japan for years and also raced horses with the famed Kentucky breeders, Jack and Ham Keene, in Japan, India and Russia. In those days he used to ride his own horses and his skill as a jockey brought him as much fame as his horses. When he decided to go into the breeding game, Fletcher went to Kentucky and purchased several mares from his old friends, the Keene brothers, and also picked up some useful matrons around Ontario, including *Rock On*.

In Fletcher's first two cracks at the Plate, his runners twice were among the first three finishers. But in 1925 he and trainer Jack Givens knew they had a big shot to win with *Fairbank* in spite of the presence of Seagram Stable's favoured three-horse entry, headed by *Duchess*. As a two-year-old *Fairbank* had won the important Coronation Stakes, defeating *Duchess*. Astride the filly, who overtook *Duchess* in the final strides when she dropped her nose on the finish line, was Charles (Chic) Lang, a young jockey from Hamilton, Ontario. His meteoric rise was such that he progressed from an exercise boy to a top flight race rider almost overnight.

Lang realized his "life's ambition" in 1928 when he won the Kentucky Derby on *Reigh Count*, the champion three-year-old that season, winning six stakes rces. Lang joined another Hamilton-born jockey, Robert Frederick (Brusher) Herbert, as the first two Canadian-born jockeys to win America's most famous race. Herbert won the 1910 Derby on *Donau* before heading to Germany to ride for Kaiser Wilhelm. The exclusive club includes Smokey Saunders (*Omaha*), who was born in Montana, but raised in Alberta, Ron Turcotte (*Riva Ridge* and *Secretariat*) and Stewart Elliott (*Smarty Jones*).

Plagued with weight problems, Lang retired following his big year of 1928. He

shipped to England, where he rode in several races. Besides the Kentucky Derby win, Lang won numerous stakes races, including the Jockey Club Gold Cup (1923 and 1928), Saratoga Cup, Gazelle, Dwyer, Belmont Futurity and Lawrence Realization. He made a brief comeback in 1932 and retired with 601 wins. He turned to training at east coast tracks in the 1930s and 1940s and died in 1947 at age 42 in Wilmington, Delaware.

An historic first in 1925 was the broadcasting of the Plate race by Toronto station CFCA, which was owned by *The Star*. W.A. Hewitt, the newspaper's sports editor, described each step of the race. He wrote: "Thousands of fans all over Canada and in various parts of the United States 'went to the races' by radio." Stationed in the judges' enclosure, Hewitt and his son Foster, who would later earn world-wide fame as a hockey announcer, were able to give listeners the result of the close Plate finish before the numbers were posted on the race result board.

1925 KING'S PLATE STAKES

FOURTH RACE
Woodbine Park
MAY 23, 1925

1 1–8 MILES (1:51²/₅). Sixty–Sixth Running of the KING'S PLATE. 50 Guineas, the Gift of His Majesty King George V, with $10,000 added by the Club. The first horse to receive $7,585 and 50 Guineas; second $1,500, third $1,000. Breeder of the winner to receive $500. A Sweepstakes of $5 payable at time of entry and an additional $25 to start. 3–year–olds and upward, the property of a British subject resident in Ontario, foaled, raised and trained in Ontario, that have never won a race, either on the flat or across country, other than a race exclusively for 2–year–olds, have never left Canada, and have never been for a period of more than one month out of this Province. Winner to carry 5 lbs. extra. A piece of plate will be presented to owner of winner. Closed with 48 nominations.

Horse	Eqt	A	Wt.	PP	St	¼	½	¾	Str	Fin	Jockey	Owner	Odds $1 Str't
FAIRBANK		3	112	8	5	4²	3ʰᵈ	4¹	3²	1ⁿᵒ	LangC	FletcherJC	a-4.87½
DUCHESS		3	112	10	9	3ʰᵈ	4¹	3½	1½	2⁴	KennedyB	SeagramStable	b-1.05
JEAN CREST		3	112	3	2	1ⁿᵏ	1ʰᵈ	1ʰᵈ	2²	3⁴	SchaeferL	WhiteJP	16.15
FORECAST II.		3	112	5	4	2¹½	2¹	2½	4⁴	4⁵	MooneyJD	RiverdaleStable	7.80
CATAMARAN		4	127	13	12	7¹	5¹	6¹½	5¹	5¹½	StevensF	SmallmanJE	6.50
GOLDLANDS		3	112	9	11	10⁴	8⁴	5ʰᵈ	6¹½	6³	WallsP	SeagramStable	b-1.05
HOI POLLOI		3	112	4	7	8¹	7ⁿᵏ	7¹	7¹	7²	McTagueJ	FletcherJC	a-4.87½
OCEAN CREST		5	130	2	3	6ʰᵈ	9²	9⁴	8¹	8½	LeylandJ	MorrisonGW	77.85
CLOTH HALL	sb	3	112	14	15	13¹	11⁴	11⁶	11⁴	9³	MooreR	RiddellT	f-26.90
TRICKY TAKE OFF		3	107	7	14	15	15	12ʰᵈ	12²	10²	LiebgoldM	HannaWC	f-26.90
TAMARIND		3	112	12	10	5¹	6ʰᵈ	8ʰᵈ	9¹	11⁴	FisherR	SeagramStable	b-1.05
SHADOW DANCE		3	112	11	6	9ʰᵈ	10⁵	10½	10²	12³	ClaverA	ThorncliffeStable	33.80
PANKETA	b	3	112	6	8	11³	12¹	13²	13⁶	13⁶	TauletteP	PopularFarmStable	29.25
REBUS		4	122	15	13	14¹⁰	14⁶	15	15	14²	EricksonH	FairJG	f-26.90
BYNG BOY	b	4	127	1	1	12⁵	13²	14⁴	14¹	15	BakerFJ	HogarthT	28.40

a-Coupled as J. C. Fletcher entry.   f-Mutuel field.

WENT TO POST 4:28. AT POST 9 MINUTES. Time, :24²/₅, :49, 1:16²/₅, 1:43²/₅, 1:56²/₅. (Plate record.) Track good.

	——$2 Mutuels Paid——			——Official Booking Odds——		
FAIRBANK (a-Entry)	$11.75	$ 4.00	$ 3.40	487½—100	100—100	70—100
DUCHESS (b-Entry)		2.75	2.35		37½—100	17½—100
JEAN CREST			5.80			190—100

Ch. f (3), by *Anmer—Rock On, by Trap Rock. Trainer, Jack Givens. Bred by Mr. J. C. Fletcher, Downsview.

Start good and slow. Won driving; second and third the same. FAIRBANK, away well, was forwardly placed in the early running and, coming on the outside in the stretch, caught DUCHESS tiring in the last sixteenth and outgamed her in a hard drive. The latter, close from the start, raced into the lead after entering the stretch, but tired with victory seemingly soon. JEAN CREST set a good pace to the head of the stretch, then came again after being passed by DUCHESS and FAIRBANK and was gaining at the end. FORECAST II. followed close up to JEAN CREST in the early running, but failed to respond when called on.

1926 | HAPLITE

Tattling was lengths the best three-year-old in Canada in 1926, but her handsome, millionaire owner, Commander J.K.L. Ross of Montreal, was confronted with an anachronistic rule that prohibited him from entering the filly in the sixty-seventh running of the King's Plate. In one respect, the rule was similar to baseball's "colour-barrier," which had barred blacks from playing in the major leagues until it was lifted in 1947, opening the door for Jackie Robinson's ebullient debut with the old Brooklyn Dodgers.

Like baseball, which was run by segregationist owners, and influenced by a powerful clique of players who were fearful of losing their jobs if the sport was opened to black athletes, there were many horse owners and breeders in Ontario who enjoyed the monopoly they had on His Majesty's fifty "guineas" and were not anxious to open up the race to outsiders.

In *Tattling*'s case, she was ineligible because she had been foaled in Quebec, at Commander Ross' stock farm in Vercheres. Thus, instead of going to the post in the historic Plate on 22 May, a race that she surely would have won, *Tattling* reposed in her stall at Woodbine while Seagram Stable's *Haplite* "stole" the honours in her absence. It mattered not in 1926 that *Tattling* was far superior to any other Plate horse, including *Haplite*. At two she had beat him easily in the Lansdowne Nursery Handicap at Woodbine, and her record at three was simply incredible. A daughter of *Marathon*, *Tattling* regularly challenged the males and older horses, capturing the most important race for fillies and the mares, the Maple Leaf Stakes, in 1926 (and again in 1927), Stanley Produce and Breeders' Stakes at Woodbine, the Quebec Derby at Dorval, the Canadian Handicap at Windsor and the Dominion Plate at Hamilton. She faced *Haplite* only once in 1926, in the important Breeders' Stakes, which she won handily when he was unplaced and was retired for the year. During her career *Tattling* started twenty-one times, winning thirteen races and finishing second on four occasions. When Woodbine was opened in 1956, a stakes race—the *Tattling* Stakes, for fillies and mares foaled in Canada, naturally—was named in her honour. The race was discontinued in 1995.

The injustice of barring horses that had not been foaled in Ontario from the Plate had increasingly become a sensitive point among horsemen, especially those from outside the province. Some went as far as recommending that the issue should be brought to the attention of the man who donated the "guineas," King George V. A story which appeared in *The Canadian Sports and Daily Racing Form* stated:

> There has been born a general suggestion that the King's Plate conditions should be brought to the attention of King George V; that it would be advisable to make the classic open

OJC PRESIDENT A.E. DYMENT WITH KING'S PLATE AND OWNER E.F. SEAGRAM. AT RIGHT, JOCKEY HENRY ERICKSON WEIGHS OUT.

to all Canadian foals instead of restricting it to those born in the Province of Ontario. If adopted this suggestion would permit the participation by Commander Ross who breeds in Quebec and to prominent western producers, including the Prince of Wales, who has a big ranch and breeding establishment in Alberta.

An outstanding amateur rider who had broken a track record in Brisbane, Australia, the young Prince in 1919 purchased a four-thousand-acre spread near Calgary, which he named the EP (for Edward Prince) Ranch. He soon became involved in breeding racing stock, cattle and sheep, saying: "It would be a good thing for the farmers and ranchers around here." His Majesty also encouraged the growth of hunting and amateur riding in the East, donating a silver cup for steeplechasing to the Toronto Hunt Club. The Prince of Wales Stakes (first run in 1929) is also still one of the major races for Canadian-bred three-year-olds.

Almost as popular as His Majesty was Ross, who had gained national recognition in 1919 when his colt, *Sir Barton*, won the Kentucky Derby, the Preakness and the Belmont Stakes to become the first winner of America's Triple Crown. Ross, a naval commander in World War I, was the son of James R. Ross, one of the builders of the Canadian Pacific Railway. His farms in Kentucky and Maryland were showplaces, as well as the stable in Vercheres, a farm often visited by Ontario breeders. They would breed to one of Ross' studs, then ship their mares home to foal, thus remaining eligible for the Plate.

In the 1920s, one of the arguments against opening Ontario's Plate race was that Quebec had a King's Plate of its own—restricted to foals of that province. The dilemma would not be resolved until 1944 when the OJC opened the King's Plate to all Canadian-bred foals.

Ironically, while *Tattling* stood idle on Plate day in 1926, the honours would instead go to a three-year-old gelding which had been imported *in utero* from England—*Haplite*. He won a rousing duel with Riverdale Stable's filly *Attack*, gaining a slim neck decision before twenty thousand chilled racegoers who endured driving rains and sodden lawns. The track was so muddy that riders wore "mud silks" instead of the usual brilliant new silks seen on Plate day. A member of Waterloo stable's favoured three-horse entry, *Haplite* was fully expected to win for trainer Bill Bringloe and jockey Henry Erickson, and give Edward Seagram and his brothers Norman and Thomas their second Plate and the family's seventeenth. The chief diversion of the crowd that day seemed to be finding something to beat *Haplite*. *Attack* came within a neck of an upset, due mainly to the forceful ride of J.D. (Jaydee) Mooney, who had won the Kentucky Derby two years earlier, and was riding the filly for his father-in-law, James Heffering.

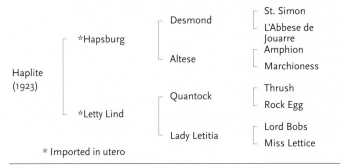

HAPLITE | 3-year-old gelding

Haplite (1923)	*Hapsburg	Desmond	St. Simon
			L'Abbese de Jouarre
		Altese	Amphion
			Marchioness
	*Letty Lind	Quantock	Thrush
			Rock Egg
		Lady Letitia	Lord Bobs
			Miss Lettice

* Imported in utero

Owner: Seagram Stable, Waterloo; *Trainer:* William H. (Bill) Bringloe
Jockey: Henry Erickson; *Breeder:* Seagram Stable

HAPLITE GETS UP BY A NECK TO DEFEAT RIVERDALE STABLE'S *ATTACK*, RIDDEN BY J.D. MOONEY.

COMMANDER J.K.L. ROSS WAS ONE OF NORTH AMERICA'S LEADING OWNERS AND BREEDERS BUT WASN'T ALLOWED TO RUN *TATTLING* IN THE KING'S PLATE BECAUSE SHE HAD BEEN FOALED IN QUEBEC. ROSS ALSO WAS NOT A RESIDENT OF ONTARIO. AT LEFT IS TRAINER H.G. (GUY) BEDWELL.

1926 KING'S PLATE STAKES

FOURTH RACE
Woodbine Park
MAY 22, 1926

1 1-8 MILES (1:51 2/5). Sixty-Seventh Running of the KING'S PLATE. $10,000 added and 50 Guineas, the gift of King George V. 3-year-olds and upward. Allowances. Horses foaled and raised in the Province of Ontario. Net value to winner $7,550; second, $1,500; third, $1,000; fourth, $500.

Horse	Eqt	A	Wt.	PP	St	¼	½	¾	Str	Fin	Jockey	Owner	Odds $1
HAPLITE		3	117	7	5	2^{nk}	2^{nk}	2½	2^{3}	1^{nk}	EricksonH	SeagramStable	a-.65
ATTACK		3	113	6	6	1^{1}½	1^{1}	1^{1}	1½	2^{10}	MooneyJD	RiverdaleStable	14.15
TAURUS		3	112	10	9	4^{hd}	4^{4}	3^{5}	3^{4}	3^{3}	StrettonJ	MillarChas.	b-6.50
DAVENPORT		3	117	1	1	6½	10^{1}	8½	5^{4}	4^{2}½	LangC	FletcherJC	c-6.15
HERETRIX		3	112	13	13	11^{1}½	9^{3}	4^{1}	4^{2}	5½	HastingsF	MillarChas.	b-6.50
PHANARIOT		3	117	11	11	10^{hd}	8½	10^{4}	7^{2}	6^{1}	SchaeferL	SeagramStable	a-.65
CLOTH HALL	b	4	127	5	4	7½	7^{1}	7^{3}	8^{hd}	7^{1}	FairbrotherC	RiddellT	22.70
JUST IN FUN		3	112	8	7	9^{hd}	11^{2}	11^{4}	10^{3}	8^{1}½	LoganJ	FletcherJC	c-6.15
SOUTHERN GLOW		4	122	14	8	5^{2}	5^{1}	6½	9^{2}	9^{3}	ClaverA	ThorncliffeStable	15.90
QUARTZ-SINTER	b	3	117	4	2	3^{nk}	3^{hd}	5^{hd}	6^{hd}	10½	ThompsonB	SeagramStable	a-.65
IFS AND ANDS		3	112	9	12	13^{6}	12^{2}	12^{1}	11^{1}	11^{1}	MooreR	SmallmanJE	43.70
SIBERIAN		4	127	2	3	8½	6^{hd}	9^{nk}	12^{1}	12^{1}½	AbelA	FletcherJC	c-6.15
REBUS		5	122	12	14	14	13^{5}	13^{20}	13^{20}	13^{25}	RenzettiE	FairAE	137.60
HUCKLEBERRY		3	112	3	10	12^{2}	14	14	14	14	RomanelliR	HammallW	29.25

a-Coupled as Seagram Stable entry; b-Charles Miller entry; c-J. C. Fletcher entry.

WENT TO POST AT 4:16. AT POST 6 MINUTES. Time, :24 4/5, :50 3/5, 1:17 2/5, 1:46, 1:59 3/5. Track heavy.

$2 Mutuel Prices:			
HAPLITE (a-Entry)	**3.30**	**2.35**	**2.10**
ATTACK		**6.85**	**3.60**
TAURUS (b-Entry)			**2.95**

B. g (3), by Hapsburg—*Letty Lind, by Quantock. Trainer, W. H. Bringloe. Bred by Seagram Stable, Waterloo.

Start good and slow. Won driving; second and third the same. HAPLITE was waited with after dropping in behind ATTACK on the turn into the backstretch and, responding gamely when called on, gradually wore the leader down in the last fifty yards and outfinished her. ATTACK was rushed into the lead quickly and set a good pace until in the last eighth, where she began to tire. TAURUS moved up rapidly after rounding the far turn, but also tired. DAVENPORT closed a big gap after being shuffled back on the first turn. HERETRIX and PHANARIOT closed big gaps.

Scratched—Atwood, Ben Hur, Night Off and Oh See.

1927 | TROUTLET

Fifty-six years of Plate races had passed, but for the impeccably dressed gentleman who seemed to gain a renewed fortitude each spring when another crop of Plate hopefuls warmed to the task ahead, his reminiscences in 1970 were as fresh as the carnation in his lapel. Ryland H. New was eighty-two, but he vividly recalled attending his first Plate race in 1914, travelling from Oakville to the "old" Woodbine in a horse-drawn carriage with his wife Isabel. Their neighbour, Harry Giddings, won it with *Beehive*.

That was the year after I got married. My wife had horses in those days. In fact she won the lady phaeton class at the Exhibition against American-owned harness horses. But we gave up horses when we could not enjoy them on the highway. Bunny [his wife] had a close call on her dog-cart.

There was also the year his close friend, Hugh Wilson, "stole" the Plate with the unheralded longshot, *Maternal Pride*, which paid a record $193.35 for a two-dollar wager.

Hugh and I went over to England in 1924 to look at some hunters and I remember when we came back he ran this horse called *Maternal Pride* in the Plate. I had a little friendly bet on him—twenty dollars—that day. I'm really not the gambler in my family. Mrs. New is the big bettor. I don't think Hugh bet a dime.

New's wager earned him almost $2,000, and two years later he told his wife he was going to buy the winner of the 1927 Plate.

Do you remember Charles Millar, the lawyer who left all that money to the woman who had the most babies in Toronto? He died in 1926, but he had this filly called *Troutlet* which had won the Clarendon Stakes for two-year-olds that year. Two months after he died I tried to buy *Troutlet* from John Nixon, Millar's trainer. But to get the filly I had to buy her full brother, *Taurus*, who was four. He had been third in the 1926 Plate. The two cost me $15,000 and I ran them as an entry in the Plate, which was quite unique at the time to run a brother and sister. (It hasn't since 1927.) I put down $5,000, paid $5,000 a little later and the rest at a later date. I still have the cancelled cheques.

A fractious sort of filly who would dawdle at the start but possessed a powerful finishing kick, *Troutlet* was a light bay and was an offspring of imported English stock, by *Sobieski* and out of *Troutling*. She had been bred at Raymond Dale and Bill Dalziel's farm in King Township, north of Toronto, and later sold to Millar, who shortly before he died predicted: "That's the filly who is going to win the Plate next year."

RYLAND H. NEW CLASPS THE TROPHY AND HIS "CHRISTY" WHILE RECEIVING CONGRATULATIONS FROM LORD AND LADY WILLINGDON.

Crisp in New's memory, as well, were the accompanying events of a chilly, but memorable, 21 May Saturday afternoon in 1927 when his scarlet and white silks appeared for the first time in the historic race. It was an auspicious debut as *Troutlet* captured the sixty-eighth running of the King's Plate, winning it by a nose in her final stride, and earning the major portion of the record purse of $15,000. She had saved the day for New, as most of the experts preferred her older brother, *Taurus*, who finished out of the money. An account of the race said that the Plate appeared to belong to *Mr. Gaiety*, but jockey Frankie Horn gave New's feared filly a "hiding," and she responded with courage. Her clocking of 1:55 4/5 was a Plate record for the mile-and-one-eighth race at Toronto's east end track. For Nixon it was his fifth Plate winner, a record that would be bettered by only four other trainers in the race's history.

I can still see them handing the lead strap to the other trainer to lead his horse [*Mr. Gaiety*] into the circle as we waited for the judge's decision. But then they announced that Troutlet had won and the strap was handed to [John] Nixon. It was quite a day. Earlier, when Mrs. New and I arrived at the track, everybody was excited over the news of [Charles] Lindbergh flying the Atlantic. 'Did you hear about Lindbergh? He's just landed in France—in Paris!' our friends kept saying.

It was a memorable occasion in another respect, as never before had the Plate attracted such an assembly of official and political dignitaries. It was a social carnival, a day of pageantry and displays of loyalty to the monarchy; a day for Canadians to acknowledge the diamond jubilee of Confederation by singing the national hymn, "*O Canada*." To oblige those unfamiliar with the words, the Ontario Jockey Club printed the anthem in its program.

Canada's Prime Minister, the Right Honourable W.L. Mackenzie King, was in attendance, along with Lieutenant Governor W.D. Ross of Ontario and provincial premier Howard Ferguson. However, it was the state arrival of the newly appointed Governor General that brought the great crowd on the lawns and in the stands to its feet. "A spreading salvo of handclapping" greeted Lord and Lady Willingdon as they made their way up a strip of red carpet to the royal box, the socially elect within the sacred precincts of the members' enclosure forming a human lane for the reception of their excellencies. Former governor of Bombay and Madras, he was made Governor General of Canada in 1926 against the wishes of the British parliament (he was a friend and tennis partner of King George V). Well liked by Canadians, he introduced arts competitions for excellence in music, literature, painting, sculpture and the Willingdon Cup, an inter-provincial team competition for amateur golfers.

When the fifty "guineas" were presented to *Troutlet*'s owner, it was not difficult to locate Ryland Herbert New amidst the throng of grey and black silk top hats. The Oakville horseman, who made his fortune in the sewer pipe business and would later help organize the formation of the Canadian Thoroughbred Horse Society, disdained wearing a top hat on Plate day like the rest of his fellow owners and Club officials. Instead he wore a "Christy" (bowler). "I was a rebel in those days, but a constructive rebel. I was always advocating changes. I remember the years when there wasn't even outhouse facilities for the men."

TROUTLET | 3-year-old bay filly

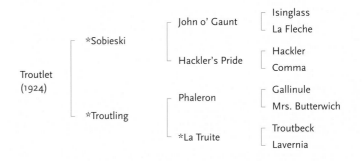

Troutlet (1924)	*Sobieski	John o' Gaunt	Isinglass
			La Fleche
		Hackler's Pride	Hackler
			Comma
	*Troutling	Phaleron	Gallinule
			Mrs. Butterwich
		*La Truite	Troutbeck
			Lavernia

Owner: Ryland H. New, Oakville; *Trainer:* John Nixon; *Jockey:* Francis Horn
Breeder: Raymond M. Dale and William Dalziel, King, Ont.

TROUTLET WAS A NOSE WINNER OVER *MR. GAIETY* FOR TRAINER JOHN NIXON.

JOCKEY FRANKIE HORN.

1927 KING'S PLATE STAKES

FOURTH RACE
Woodbine Park
MAY 21, 1927

1 1-8 MILES (1:51 2/5). Sixty-Eighth Running KING'S PLATE. $15,000 added and 50 Guineas, the gift of His Majesty King George V of England. 3-year-olds and upward; foaled, raised and trained in Ontario. Net value to winner $10,570 and 50 Guineas; second, $2,500; third, $1,000; fourth, $500.

Horse	Eqt	A	Wt.	PP	St	¼	½	¾	Str	Fin	Jockey	Owner	Odds $1 Str't
TROUTLET		3	112	3	1	8^{3}	5^{nk}	$3^{1\frac{1}{2}}$	3^{6}	1no	HornF	NewRH	a-2.80
MR. GAIETY		3	112	8	6	3^{nk}	2^{4}	1^{hd}	$1^{\frac{1}{2}}$	2^{3}	FisherR	GlasscoMrsE	b-3.35
GEMS TO LET	b	3	117	5	5	1^{1}	1^{1}	2^{4}	$2^{1\frac{1}{2}}$	3^{4}	EricksonH	SeagramStable	c-5.00
PERLAPIDES	b	3	112	14	15	$11^{\frac{1}{2}}$	$10^{\frac{1}{2}}$	10^{1}	6^{hd}	4^{hd}	SchaeferL	FletcherJC	5.85
TAURUS		4	127	2	2	10^{3}	8^{hd}	8^{1}	$5^{1\frac{1}{2}}$	5^{4}	ButwellJ	NewRH	a-2.80
CAPITOL		3	117	15	9	5^{hd}	4^{hd}	4^{hd}	4^{1}	$6^{1\frac{1}{2}}$	MooreR	GlasscoMrsE	b-3.35
TIPPANCE		3	112	4	3	$6^{\frac{1}{2}}$	9^{hd}	$9^{\frac{1}{2}}$	7^{2}	7^{hd}	BarrW	DonValleyStable	52.00
GAY PARISIAN		3	117	6	11	15^{1}	11^{3}	$11^{1\frac{1}{2}}$	8^{1}	$8^{1\frac{1}{2}}$	BourassaO	SeagramStable	c-5.00
ELIZA JANE		3	112	7	4	2^{1}	3^{1}	7^{1}	$9^{1\frac{1}{2}}$	9^{2}	WilsonT	CowieRWR	11.95
BLOOMTIP		3	117	1	10	9^{hd}	$12^{1\frac{1}{2}}$	12^{1}	$11^{\frac{1}{2}}$	10^{1}	KennedyE	WrightWH	d-26.15
MEERAN		3	112	16	13	13^{3}	14^{1}	13^{2}	10^{hd}	11^{1}	PetreccaJ	SmallmanJE	130.45
MISS CONTENT		3	107	10	12	12^{hd}	13^{1}	14^{2}	12^{1}	$12^{1\frac{1}{2}}$	MacIverJ	WrightWH	d-26.15
LADY McNEILL	b	3	112	12	8	$7^{\frac{1}{2}}$	6^{4}	6^{2}	13^{2}	13^{12}	MooneyJD	RiverdaleStable	53.70
SOUTHERN DAWN		3	108	13	16	16	16	15^{6}	15^{2}	14^{8}	HartE	ThorncliffeStable	61.60
LISTERINE	b	3	112	11	7	4^{1}	$7^{\frac{1}{2}}$	5^{hd}	14^{4}	15^{2}	McCannG	WhiteJP	7.05
QUARTZITE	b	4	132	9	14	14^{1}	15^{2}	16	16	16	McCoyJ	SeagramStable	c-5.00

a-Coupled as R. H. New entry; b-Mrs. E. Glassco entry; c-Seagram Stable entry; d-W. H. Wright entry.

WENT TO POST AT 4:31. OFF AT 4:35. Time, :24 2/5, :49, 1:15 2/5, 1:42 3/5, 1:55 4/5. (Plate record.) Track fast.

Mutuel Prices:

	$2 Mutuels Paid			Odds to $1		
TROUTLET (a-Entry)	7.60	3.90	2.85	2.80	.95	.42½
MR. GAIETY (b-Entry)		4.25	3.00		1.12½	.50
GEMS TO LET (c-Entry)			2.90			.45

B. f (3), by *Sobieski—*Troutling, by Phaleron. Trainer, Nixon J. Bred by Dale R M & Dalziel Wm., King.

Start good and slow. Won driving; second and third the same. TROUTLET closed an early gap, came through a narrow opening when rounding the far turn, then came to the outside of the leaders and, finishing fast and gamely, wore MR. GAIETY down to win in the last stride. MR. GAIETY was always a prominent contender and passed GEMS TO LET when entering the home stretch, then finished gamely when put to a drive. GEMS TO LET took the lead and set a good pace, but tired in the final drive. PERLAPIDES raced well. TAURUS began slowly, was forced very wide on the first turn, then continued to race wide to secure racing room and closed a gap. CAPITOL also raced well throughout. LISTERINE quit.

Scratched—Rex Muscarum and Lazibones.

Overweight—Southern Dawn, 1 Pound.

Running came easy to *Young Kitty*, the impertinent three-year-old filly who effortlessly spread-eagled her thirteen opponents in the sixty-ninth running of the King's Plate. Throughout her career it so often appeared that she instinctively was in motion the moment the barrier would lift, a flurry of legs and hooves quickly propelling her into an impulsive lead. Her attitude towards running was quite brazen; daring the impatient ones to chase her, and maybe even torment her if she started to tire when the contest approached the stretch and the run to the wire.

Young Kitty had been the exciting sensation in the 1927 crop of two-year-olds, delighting racegoers as she wildly sprinted to the front, winning all but one of her seven starts. After taking the Coronation Futurity at Woodbine, she closed out the season on a sloppy track at Thorncliffe Park, capturing the Clarendon Stakes, a race that has usually provided the following year's top Plate contender. Her only setback had come in her first start, losing to J.C. Fletcher's *Dushka,* who was expected to be her chief foe in the battle for the "guineas."

The battle, however, was over as soon as the field left the barrier as, in a flash, the silks of the Seagram Stable were alone in front. Staged in a drizzling, misty rain over a slippery track, the Plate could hardly be described as a contest as it was *Young Kitty* every inch of the journey, coasting home twelve lengths ahead of R.W.R. Cowie's filly *Bonnington.* Incredibly, the next four finishers were also three-year-old fillies. Horsemen were unable to explain the fillies' domination. However, they were unanimous that *Young Kitty*'s margin of victory would have been greater if jockey Leslie Pichon had ever asked the dark bay filly to run, noting that she was "under stout restraint as she flashed by the judges' stand."

Critics immediately compared her to one of the greatest Canadian breds of the 1900s—*Inferno,* another Seagram horse—predicting that if she met no mishaps, and continued to train on, she could equal his wonderful record. In future years she would earn the reputation as "a great racemare, one of the finest ever bred in Canada." However, *Young Kitty* was a product of an era when motherhood was important, and her maternal instincts, or lack of them, would eventually lead to her demise—a disappointment for those who had hoped she might produce an offspring that was bolder, and faster, than she. What ability she had was reserved for the racetrack, not the broodmare barn.

A man who knew her well was Jack Thorpe, who had been exercising horses for the Seagrams ever since 1898. *Young Kitty* was one of his favourites. "She was a great racemare. But we were all sorely disappointed when she failed to prove herself after retiring to the broodmare farm. She

WOODBINE PARK'S STANDS BULGED WITH HUGE CROWDS SHORTLY BEFORE THE STOCK MARKET CRASH OF 1929.

JACK THORPE HAD EXERCISED SEAGRAM HORSES SINCE 1898 AND *YOUNG KITTY* WAS ONE OF HIS FAVOURITES.

refused to mother her foals, and though we took two away from her and developed them for racing, they were of little account."

Initially, *Young Kitty* fascinated people who studied pedigrees. She was by *Old Koenig,* who had been only a "fair sort of runner," and until *Young Kitty* came along was considered "not a horse of any great quality." The same could be said of the Plate winner's dam, *Gallant Kitty,* a mare of uncertain parentage who developed into one of Seagram's most productive broodmares during the late 1920s and 1930s, and in 1977 was inducted into Canada's Hall of Fame. A daughter *of Kate Kittleberry, Gallant Kitty*'s sire was debatable. It might have been the imported stallion **Galatine,* but likely was Seagram's great stallion *Havoc,* who sired a record four King's Plate winners. Despite the confusion of her parentage, *Gallant Kitty*'s reputation would forever be enhanced by her first offspring of any significance. At the time, though, horsemen believed that *Young Kitty* was "a fluke." A fluke or not, she was tough and swift despite her "tender underpinning." In her only other start in 1928, *Young Kitty* returned nine days after her Plate triumph to win the Breeders' Stakes. At four she again was undefeated, extending her record to ten wins in eleven starts, winning the Connaught Cup and the William Hendrie Memorial Handicap.

Her first trip to the breeding shed in 1930 ended in failure. A few months later trainer Bill Bringloe had *Young Kitty* facing quality American breds at Havre de Grace in Maryland. A second-place finish was the best she could manage in three

EDWARD F. SEAGRAM, JOCKEY LESLIE PICHON AND THE FILLY WHO WON BY TWELVE LENGTHS, *YOUNG KITTY*.

YOUNG KITTY | 3-year-old brown filly

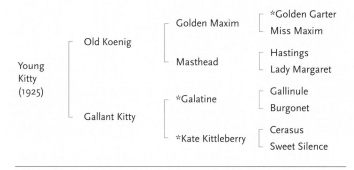

```
                                              ┌ Golden Maxim ┌ *Golden Garter
                          ┌ Old Koenig ──────┤              └ Miss Maxim
                          │                   └ Masthead     ┌ Hastings
Young                     │                                  └ Lady Margaret
Kitty    ─────────────────┤
(1925)                    │                   ┌ *Galatine    ┌ Gallinule
                          └ Gallant Kitty ───┤              └ Burgonet
                                              └ *Kate Kittleberry ┌ Cerasus
                                                                  └ Sweet Silence
```

Owner: Seagram Stable, Waterloo; *Trainer:* William H. (Bill) Bringloe
Jockey: Lester Pichon; *Breeder:* Seagram Stable

races, and it was back to the breeding shed for two years. Again the results were negative. Four years later her fertility record read: barren; barren; foal dead; not covered. Eventually she managed to drop two foals, *Young Man* and *Kitty Jean*, but they were hardly worth the time and energy expended by her handlers.

In between her unobliging visits to the boudoir, *Young Kitty* would be allowed to engage in her favourite pastime—running. Unsound at times and aging, she never abandoned her familiar style of quickly barging to the front, hoping that her early speed was enough. She was at her best one afternoon in 1932 at the Hamilton track when she upset Plate winners *Aymond* and *Queensway*. However, she did not win a race in 1933. The following year the nine-year-old mare was her old self, winning five times and finishing out of the money only once in ten races. On 23 May 1935, *Young Kitty* made her final start in a $2,200 claiming event at Woodbine. She was the betting choice, but the flare was absent as she finished fifth. "Never in contention," was her final review in the racecharts.

During her lengthy career, *Young Kitty* won eighteen of thirty-eight starts with her major victories coming in the Clarendon Plate, Coronation Futurity, King's Plate, Breeders' Stakes, Connaught Cup and William Hendrie Memorial Handicap.

In 1928 the Plate, and racing in general, were undergoing vital modifications. Only one older horse was entered that year, four-year-old Little Margie B, which finished last. A request by two Oshawa breeders, Charles Robson and Sam McLaughlin, apparently helped bring about a change in Plate rules concerning the length of time a mare could spend visiting a stallion outside the province. The revision allowed three months instead of one. Another change was the glistening appearance of Woodbine Park. The Ontario Jockey Club, which in 1927 had given serious consideration as to the feasibility of moving the racecourse to

another property, completed construction of a new double-decked members' stand and directors' room. A covered paddock was also built while the jockeys' quarters were moved from behind the directors' wooden building, to the westerly members' entrance on Queen Street. Cost of the renovations was $300,000, an expenditure which likely prompted the resignation of director Colonel D. King Smith.

Besides the physical changes at the track, an almost complete transition of the men directing the OJC's development had taken place during a four-year period. The vacancies caused by the deaths of president Colonel William Hendrie, directors Sir John S. Hendrie, Major Joseph Kilgour, Sir Edmund Osler and Colin Campbell had been filled by Albert E. Dyment, the new president, along with an executive which included George M. Hendrie, Colonel K.R. Marshall, Allen Case, Edward Seagram and W.G. Gooderham.

1928 KING'S PLATE STAKES

FOURTH RACE
Woodbine Park
MAY 19, 1928

1 1-8 MILES (1:51²/5). Sixty-Ninth Running of THE KING'S PLATE. $15,000 added. 3-year-olds and upward, the property of a British subject resident in Ontario, foaled, raised and trained in Ontario, that have never won a race, either on the flat or across country, other than a race exclusively for 2-year-olds, have never left Canada, and have never been for a period of more than one month out of this Province. A silver cup will be presented by the Club to the owner of the winner. Breeder of winner to receive $1,000. A sweepstakes of $5 at entry; $25 to start. Allowances. Net value to winner $10,525 and 50 Guineas, the Gift of His Majesty King George V.; second, $2,500; third, $1,000; fourth, $500.

Horse	Eqt	A	Wt.	PP	St	¼	½	¾	Str	Fin	Jockey	Owner	Odds $1
YOUNG KITTY		3	112	6	4	1¹	1¹	1⁴	1⁶	1¹²	PichonL	SeagramStable	a-.50
BONNINGTON		3	112	11	7	2¹	2ʰᵈ	2¹	2³	2²½	TownrowR	CowieRWR	b-7.60
HANNA DEEBE		3	107	12	8	5½	5½	5¹	3ⁿᵏ	3ʰᵈ	MannF	FletcherJC	c-3.60
BEST BONNET		3	109	1	3	3ʰᵈ	4¹½	4½	4¹½	4¹½	SchaeferL	SeagramStable	a-.50
WHITE DOVE	b	3	107	7	10	8ʰᵈ	6¹	6ʰᵈ	5ⁿᵏ	5¹	StevensJ	McKayMrsW	90.50
DUSHKA		3	113	14	11	9³	8ⁿᵏ	7ʰᵈ	6³	6⁴	PeternellR	FletcherJC	c-3.60
ICHITARO		3	117	10	9	11⁵	11³	8ⁿᵏ	7⁴	7⁸	GwynneJ	FletcherJC	c-3.60
GRUBSTAKE		3	112	4	2	10ʰᵈ	10½	9½	8⁶	8ⁿᵏ	StarkeyA	WrightWH	d-54.40
CEDAR CREST	b	3	112	5	5	7ⁿᵏ	9ⁿᵏ	10½	9²	9⁴	ThomasJ	WhiteJP	60.20
GOLD ERA		3	107	9	13	13⁸	13²⁰	11²	10⁶	10⁸	FlemingE	WrightWH	d-54.40
BIKOS		3	117	3	1	12¹	12½	12ⁿᵏ	12¹½	11½	HarveyW	RobsonC	b-7.60
HEAD LAD	sb	3	112	8	6	4²	3ⁿᵏ	3ʰᵈ	11½	12¹½	TryonA	ThorncliffeStable	e-23.10
MYSTIC STAR		3	117	13	12	6ⁿᵏ	7ʰᵈ	13³⁰	13⁴⁰	13⁴⁰	MerglerD	ThorncliffeStable	e-23.10
LITTLE MARGIE B.		4	122	2	14	2	14	14	14	14	MarrJ	GlasscoTM	40.10

a–Coupled as Seagram Stable entry; b–R. W. R. Cowie & C. Robson entry; c–J. C. Fletcher entry; d–W. H. Wright entry; e–Thorncliffe Stable entry.

WENT TO POST AT 4:38. OFF AT 4:47. Time, :24³/5, :50, 1:16⁴/5, 1:44³/5, 1:57. Track fast.

Mutuel Prices:

			—$2 Mutuels Paid—			—Odds to $1—		
YOUNG KITTY (a–Entry)			3.00	2.60	2.05	.50	.30	.02½
BONNINGTON (b–Entry)				4.55	2.25		1.27½	.12½
HANNA DEEBE (c–Entry)					2.10			.05

Br. f (3), by Old Koenig–Gallant Kitty, by *Galatine or Havoc. Trainer, Bringloe W H. Bred by Seagram Stable, Waterloo.

Start good and slow. Won easily; second and third the same. YOUNG KITTY took the lead while going to the first turn and led under restraint until reaching the far turn, then drew far away and won in a canter. BONNINGTON raced closest up and made a game rush when called on, but tired in the final drive. HANNA DEEBE was close up in the early racing and raced gamely through the final drive. BEST BONNET was hard ridden throughout. WHITE DOVE began slowly, but worked his way up on the outside and finished gamely. DUSHKA reared up into the air at the start. HEAD LAD raced well for three-quarters.

Scratched—Flying Column.
Overweights—Best Bonnet, 1 pound; Dushka 1.
Corrected weight—Best Bonnet, 108 pounds.

In 1929, the year of the stock market crash on Wall Street, trainer Fred Schelke gloomily concluded that a series of ill-timed events had practically eliminated any chance of him winning another King's Plate for the Thorncliffe Stable.

That winter an epidemic of coughing had swept through his Leaside stabling quarters. It afflicted *Pin Wheel*, the winterbook favourite and the barn's best bet for the Plate, and caused the death of two promising two-year-olds. This left Schelke with *Shorelint*, the first foal of a mare who had won the 1922 Plate for the Davies' family. Although the brown colt had shown little in 1928 as a two-year-old, his trials at the Thorncliffe track were encouraging for owners George and Wilfred Davies. His workers were said to be faster than those of any candidate at Woodbine. However, with the Plate only days away, *Shorelint* pulled up lame following a workout. He had stepped on a stone and had suffered a quarter crack—a small split in the wall of his hoof.

Shorelint's condition was not the only reason for the benign trainer's permanent frown; there was some doubt whether jockey John (Jaydee) Mooney, who was attempting a comeback, would be able to make the weight of 117 pounds on the day of the race. His weight, which had plagued him throughout his career, had a habit of "ballooning." It finally forced Mooney to quit riding in 1928 and

FRED H. SCHELKE WAS A "HANDS ON" TRAINER FOR THORNCLIFFE STABLE.

turn to training a string of horses for Senator Frank O'Connor, the man who had founded the Laura Secord candy company. But poor racing luck, illness and accidents haunted his horses, and the following spring Mooney wearily announced: "I've resigned and I'm applyin' fo' a riding license. I hope I get lucky." The twenty-eight-year-old from New Orleans had been offered a ride on *Shorelint* if he could shed forty pounds and regain his riding weight.

"I can remember as a boy driving my father's car slowly in first gear. He would run behind it for three or four miles every morning," recalled John J. Mooney, former president of the Ontario Jockey Club. "He had a terrible problem. At the track in the morning he would weigh in, and in a matter of hours he'd pick up ten pounds. I think he rode two pounds over on *Shorelint*."

Schelke's hopes of a Plate, thus, were in the hands of a jockey who had not been in the saddle for more than a year, and might be weak after his tortuous reducing program, and an ailing horse with a crack in its hoof. The raw talent was there for a possible upset, but only if Mooney still retained the "touch" that had earned him the Kentucky Derby in 1924—and if *Shorelint* had the courage of his dam, *South Shore*, who also had physical problems and was nursed all night before her 1922 Plate win by Schelke as he "iced" her sore legs.

The seventieth running of the Plate was one that played strange pranks on the emotions of the immense throng that stood shoulder-to-shoulder across the spacious lawns and jammed every seat and aisleway of the double-decked stands. It was a race spectators fully expected would go to the Seagram Stable and its imposing entry. Partially out of respect for the riding ability of Johnny Maiben, the

THORNCLIFFE STABLE'S WILFRED DAVIES, *SHORELINT* AND JOCKEY J.D. MOONEY.

Trainer Fred Schelke leads *Shorelint* to the track.

SHORELINT | 3-year-old brown colt

Shorelint (1926)	Oil Man	*North Star III	Sunstar
			Angelic
		Bandello	Kingston
			*Maid of Erin
	South Shore	*Orme Shore	Orme
			Virginia Shore
		Southern Maid	Plaudit
			Sally K

Owner: Thorncliffe Stable, Todmorden; *Trainer:* F.H. Fred Schelke
Jockey: J.D. (Jaydee) Mooney; *Breeder:* Thorncliffe Stable

"black-browed booter" brought in from New York, the punters had bet his mount, *Circulet*, the promising half-brother to 1926 Plate winner *Haplite*, and his stablemates *Dance Circle* and *Irish Sphere*, down to odds of 1-to-4.

The crowd watched as the large field of eighteen starters surged off the mark and lengthened out into a ragged, multicoloured stream that whirled past the grandstand. However, the tension-relieving shout "They're Off" held a note of dismay as the heavily favoured *Circulet* broke flatfooted and in a tangle with *Meteor Sparks*. Hope rose again, though, as another Seagram candidate, *Dance Circle*, flashed into an early lead; then suspense and uncertainty and disbelief replaced it as J.C. Fletcher's *Ichitaro* made his gallant bid under the crushing impost of 132 pounds.

The line of vision from the stands could not reveal which of the front phalanx was the threat as it swung into the stretch, but halfway down the straightaway, like a high violin note over the deep rumble of the stands, came the cry, "Thorncliffe! Thorncliffe! Thorncliffe!" With "Sit-Still" Mooney riding in perfect rhythm, *Shorelint* swung over the line with a handful of daylight behind him. It marked the second time that the sons of Robert Davies, who had won the 1871 Plate, had led his canary and black striped silks into the winner's circle. The victory had also restored a jockey's confidence:

> He was in remarkable condition. Mistah Schelke was right worried after the colt hurt himself and I nevah did see a man work so hard to get him back in shape. He had to be much the best to get up to win after the bad luck at the break. [*Shorelint* got kicked in the flank before the start and Mooney had to take the colt back of the field to see if he was hurt.] When the barrier went up he sort of dwelt; we were off bad, only three or four horses behind us. I took him on the rail to save all the ground I could. When I saw I couldn't get through on the rail I took him out. At the three-eighths pole, like the man said, I let the colt out and at the last corner we cut back on the rail and went after the hoss out in front, one of Fletcher's. That ole colt shore did turn it on and I was sittin' still at the wire. Mistah Schelke deserves all the credit—and say, did you notice that since he's done another good job trainin' that smile o' his is back into shape again?

1929 KING'S PLATE STAKES

FOURTH RACE
Woodbine Park
MAY 18, 1929

1 1-8 MILES (1:51$\frac{2}{5}$). Seventieth Running KING'S PLATE. $15,000 added. 3-year-olds and upward. Horses foaled, raised and trained in the Province of Ontario. Allowances. Net value to winner $10,710 and 50 Guineas, the Gift of His Majesty, King George V, and silver cup; second, $2,500; third, $1,000; fourth, $500.

Horse	Eqt	A	Wt.	PP	St	¼	½	¾	Str	Fin	Jockey	Owner	Odds $1 Str't
SHORELINT	b	3	117	15	15	9^{3}	5^{hd}	4^{hd}	2^{5}	$1^{1\frac{1}{2}}$	MooneyJD	ThorncliffeStable	13.15
ICHITARO		4	132	1	1	4^{hd}	$2^{1\frac{1}{2}}$	1^{3}	1^{2}	2^{3}	GwynneJ	FletcherJC	a-16.10
LINDSAY	b	3	107	6	6	8^{hd}	8^{hd}	$7^{1\frac{1}{2}}$	3^{3}	3^{5}	MannF	FletcherJC	a-16.10
VESTIP		3	112	5	11	15^{8}	13^{3}	$11^{2\frac{1}{2}}$	7^{1}	4^{1}	LittleH	NewRH	97.55
CUDDLE DOON		3	112	8	4	2^{nk}	$4^{1\frac{1}{2}}$	5^{hd}	4^{1}	$5^{1\frac{1}{2}}$	SchaeferL	HastingsStable	b-6.20
ASSAIL		3	112	10	7	3^{hd}	3^{2}	3^{1}	$6^{1\frac{1}{2}}$	6^{hd}	MannJ	RussellMrsW	20.30
DUSHKA		4	127	9	16	13^{2}	$12^{1\frac{1}{2}}$	10^{3}	10^{5}	$7^{1\frac{1}{2}}$	ConveyJ	FletcherJC	a-16.10
METEOR SPARKS		3	112	11	13	10^{hd}	10^{2}	$6^{\frac{1}{2}}$	5^{hd}	$8^{1\frac{1}{2}}$	LeonardR	HastingsStable	b-6.20
MASTER BOBBIE		3	117	13	9	11^{2}	14^{4}	$9^{1\frac{1}{2}}$	9^{hd}	$9^{\frac{1}{2}}$	TownrowR	CowieRWR	63.65
DAISY FAIR	b	3	112	7	12	12^{nk}	11^{1}	8^{hd}	$8^{1\frac{1}{2}}$	10^{8}	PhillipsC	GlasscoMrsE	16.65
DANCE CIRCLE		3	107	4	2	$1^{1\frac{1}{2}}$	1^{hd}	2^{nk}	$1^{1\frac{1}{2}}$	11^{1}	GoodwinP	SeagramStable	c-.25
SON OF HARMONY	b	3	112	18	5	6^{hd}	6^{8}	15^{5}	$12^{1\frac{1}{2}}$	12^{2}	CarlisleC	HastingsStable	b-6.20
AIRDROME		3	117	16	8	5^{hd}	7^{nk}	12^{2}	13^{6}	13^{8}	StrettonS	NewellR	63.15
CIRCULET		3	117	17	14	$14^{1\frac{1}{2}}$	$15^{\frac{1}{2}}$	14^{1}	14^{1}	14^{2}	MaibenJ	SeagramStable	c-.25
IRISH SPHERE	b	3	117	2	3	7^{1}	$9^{\frac{1}{2}}$	13^{1}	15^{1}	$15^{1\frac{1}{2}}$	McGinnisP	SeagramStable	c-.25
PANDER		4	127	14	17	17^{2}	17^{10}	17^{10}	16^{5}	16^{2}	JonesJ	McKayWm	352.80
BRILLIANT DIAMOND		3	112	3	10	16^{8}	16^{8}	16^{5}	17	17	HornG	MacKayRR	196.45
CAREY	b	4	127	12	18	18	18	18	P'l'dup		FishmanM	DayJN	103.10

a-Coupled as J. C. Fletcher entry; b-Hastings Stable entry; c-Seagram Stable entry.

WENT TO POST AT 4:36. OFF AT 4:42. Time, :24$\frac{3}{5}$, :50, 1:17$\frac{2}{5}$, 1:43$\frac{3}{5}$, 1:57$\frac{3}{5}$. Track fast.

Mutuel Prices:

	$2 Mutuels Paid			Odds to $1		
SHORELINT	28.30	10.50	8.10	13.15	4.25	3.05
ICHITARO (a-Entry)		11.20	12.40		4.60	5.20
LINDSAY (a-Entry)		11.20	12.40		4.60	5.20

Br. c (3), by Oil Man—South Shore, by *Orme Shore. Trainer, Schelke F H. Bred by Thorncliffe Stable, Todmorden.

Start good and slow. Won driving; second and third easily. SHORELINT, away slowly and forced to race on the outside to reach a forward position, secured a clear course after entering the home stretch, and passing ICHITARO, won going away. ICHITARO raced into a clear lead, but tired right at the end under his impost. LINDSAY, on the outside all the way, finished gamely. VESTIP finished gamely also. CUDDLE DOON was hard ridden and had no mishaps. ASSAIL tired in the last quarter. DANCE CIRCLE set the early pace and quit. CIRCULET was bumped and knocked off his stride by METEOR SPARKS on the first turn and was never dangerous afterwards. CAREY was pulled up after going five-eighths.

Scratched—Canadian Flag.

Woodbine had never looked more attractive than it did on 17 May, the afternoon the 1930 horse racing season opened in Canada. The infield, with its velvet carpet of green, looked fresh and soothing to the eye; the steeplechase course was a picture and the immense throng in the public enclosure, the clubhouse lawn and stand, made a moving picture that was "thrilling." Gathered in the club members' enclosure were many prominent in Canada's official and social life. Governor General and Viscountess Willingdon attended in state. The King's Plate was the attraction—eighteen horses foaled in Ontario running for a record purse of almost $16,000—but in a way the day was a tribute to W.P. Fraser, who had died that winter. For more than thirty years he had been secretary-treasurer of the Ontario Jockey Club, and it was through his efforts that the continuity of the Plate had been maintained through the difficult years of World War I.

Meanwhile, occupying a two-dollar seat in the top row of the public grandstand instead of one in the more comfortable members' stand, was Ryland H. New, who had won the race in 1927 with *Troutlet*. Even though he owned a luxurious estate along the lakeshore in Oakville, a clay sewer pipe company and had extensive interests in other building firms, New was a renegade at times, ignoring the social ritual that surrounded the Plate. He loved horses and the honest running of a race, and was often depicted as a "true sportsman." New had framed the "fifty-guinea" note he had won in 1927 and hung it on the wall of his home, but donated the entire prize money to The Star Fresh Air Fund for needy children.

In the seventy-first running of the Plate, New had an entry— *Aymond*, ridden by Henry Little, and *Vestip*, whose jockey was Pete McCann, a Toronto boy who would later train so many of E.P. Taylor's Plate winners. But it was *Aymond*, the three-year-old bay

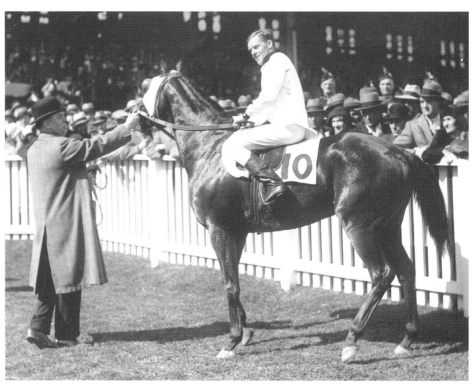

RYLAND H. NEW HOLDS BRIDLE OF *AYMOND*. JOCKEY HENRY LITTLE UP.

gelding, that New and trainer Jack Hutton figured was the strength in the entry even though the crowd had largely ignored the twosome, letting it go off at 14-to-1 as it fancied Thorncliffe Stable's *Whale Oil*. Mike Rodden, sports editor of *The Globe*, was moved by the contest:

What an epic of the turf! Not like last year's thrilling win by *Shorelint*, not like other races that have gone before, but nevertheless a victory that shows the uncertainty that exists, and will continue to exist, in the sport of kings. That's just how it happened at Woodbine when *Aymond*, carrying the scarlet and white colours of R.H. New, made every post a winning one. He wasn't a pre-race favourite by any means, but what did it matter to this gallant son of *Roselyon and Ablaze*. It was his day, his opportunity, and he did not fail.

Breaking quickly after a tedious thirteen-minute delay at the post, Little hustled *Aymond* over to the rail and said: "Catch us if you can." It was a race that was won at the start, not in the final eighth of a mile, as the bay showed speed, courage and staying power. Had he failed to get the rail it

AYMOND, WITH JOCKEY HENRY LITTLE, LED FROM WIRE-TO-WIRE.

Trainer Jack Hutton and Oakville owner Ryland H. New.

AYMOND | 3-year-old bay gelding

Aymond (1927)	*Roselyon	Sunstar	Sundridge
			Doris
		Desmond's Rose	Desmond
			Electric Rose
	Ablaze	Tony Bonero	*Sain
			America
		Abrasion	Smile
			Attrition

Owner: Ryland H. New, Oakville; *Trainer:* Jack Hutton
Jockey: Henry Little; *Breeder:* James Heffering, Whitby, Ont.

might have been another story. *Whale Oil*, who was on the outside, repeatedly attempted to overhaul New's gelding. He drew up to level terms on the run into the backstretch and the two raced like a team until midway down the lane before *Aymond* gradually pulled away to win by a length. The five-year-old *Ichitaro*, who finished a "game" third, lugged 133 pounds, sixteen more than the three-year-olds as officials had increased the Plate weight allowances to dissuade owners from entering older horses. He was ridden by Norman (Dude) Foden, the "Demon of Dufferin" who was a master of the quarter-mile "bull rings" but never got a Plate mount home first during his career.

Meanwhile, New, who had intently watched the duel between *Aymond* and *Whale Oil* with binoculars from his distant vantage point, must have grown excited for, during the race, someone in the row ahead of him said: "For the love of Mike, shut up." "Shut up, nothing," New yelled back. "That's my horse coming in first."

Afterwards, in the stables where *Aymond* was being cooled off, trainers and backstretchers dropped by to congratulate Jack Hutton, the Cobourg horseman; Henry Little, the shy, fair-haired eighteen-year-old jockey from North Toronto who had been sidelined for a year because of the injuries he had suffered in a fall; and New, who chuckled as he recalled how he had "paid $25 too much" for the horse which had just earned him almost $11,000. New told of the day he dispatched Hutton and his friend Hughie Wilson to the Frank O'Connor dispersal sale in 1929 to look over a rangy, unraced two-year-old that had been bred at Jim Heffering's farm out on the Kingston Road near Pickering. Their instructions were not to pay more than $1,000 for him. "Somehow Jack and Hughie got their signs crossed as they started bidding against each other, and before they realized it, the price was twenty-five dollars more than I had wanted to pay."

An irony of the race was that Heffering's Riverdale Stable was represented by *Love's Arrow*, one of Mrs. Lily Livingston's breeding. It finished thirteenth. However, Heffering earned $1,000 that day because he was the breeder of *Aymond*. He had also come close in 1926 with *Attack*, losing by a short neck to *Haplite*—but over a twenty-year span Heffering's determined efforts to parade his white and black silks into the Plate winner's circle would be denied.

1930 KING'S PLATE STAKES

FOURTH RACE
Woodbine Park
MAY 17, 1930

1 1-8 MILES. (Spot Cash, May 23, 1923, 1:51²/₅, 3, 103.) Seventy-First running KING'S PLATE. 50 Guineas the Gift of His Majesty King George V, with $15,000 added by the Ontario Jockey Club. The first horse to receive the Guineas, Stakes and $10,000, the second horse $2,500, the third horse $1,000 and the fourth horse $500. The breeder of the winner to receive $1,000. A Sweepstakes of $5 payable at time of entry, and $25 additional to start. For three-year-olds and upward, the property of a British subject resident in Ontario, foaled, raised and trained in Ontario, that have never won a race, either on the flat or across country, other than a race exclusively for two-year-olds, have never left Canada, and have never been for a period of more than three months out of this Province. Winners to carry 5 lbs. extra. Death of nominator does not render entry void. No gelding allowance. A Silver Cup will be presented by the Club to the owner of the winner. Entries closed Friday, March 14, with 62 nominations. The Club reserves the right to cancel this race upon the repayment of all entrance fees paid in advance. Net value to winner, $10,730 and 50 Guineas.

Horse	Eqt	A	Wt.	PP	St.	¼	½	¾	Str	Fin	Jockey	Owner	Odds $1
AYMOND	b	3	117	3	1	1^{1}	1^{hd}	1^{hd}	1^{nk}	1^{1}	LittleH	NewRH	a-14.10
WHALE OIL		3	117	5	5	3½	2^{1}	2^{4}	2^{2}	2^{2}	BurkeJH	ThorncliffeStable	b-2.35
ICHITARO	b	5	133	1	3	2^{hd}	3½	3^{3}	3^{5}	$3^{1\frac{1}{2}}$	FodenN	FletcherJC	c-4.75
VESTIP	b	4	127	10	8	6^{hd}	9^{1}	7^{nk}	5½	$4^{1\frac{1}{2}}$	McCannG	NewRH	a-14.10
QUATRA BRAS		3	117	4	2	7½	7^{1}	6½	$6^{1\frac{1}{2}}$	5^{nk}	SlateF	CochenourTS	7.65
PAT GAIETY		3	112	11	14	15^{1}	15^{1}	14^{2}	7½	6^{1}	NoelW	GlasscoTM	82.35
LINDSAY	b	4	122	7	6	12^{3}	10½	10½	8^{1}	7½	McTagueJ	FletcherJC	c-4.75
STAR CREST	b	3	117	9	10	8½	$6^{1\frac{1}{2}}$	4½	4^{hd}	8½	QuattlebaumC	HastingsStable	20.20
PANDORUS	b	3	117	14	17	14^{hd}	13^{3}	13^{2}	9^{1}	9½	MaibenJ	SeagramStable	d-2.70
BRAVE ALONZO	b	3	112	2	4	9½	8½	8½	10^{2}	10^{3}	SniderA	McIntyreJR	25.50
VARSITY		3	117	17	15	13½	12^{1}	11^{1}	11^{1}	11½	AimersT	ThorncliffeStable	b-2.35
SPHERE OF BEAUTY		3	112	8	7	5^{2}	5^{hd}	5½	12^{2}	12^{2}	MannF	SeagramStable	d-2.70
LOVE'S ARROW		3	112	15	9	4^{1}	4½	9^{1}	13^{1}	13^{1}	CarlisleC	RiverdaleStable	46.70
GRANITE ROCK		3	117	12	16	10½	11^{hd}	12^{1}	14^{2}	14^{3}	KurtsingerC	LamantiaP	52.40
ZARF		3	112	16	18	18	16^{1}	16^{1}	15^{1}	15^{2}	DaintyF	HalliwellA	49.65
FAIR FORTUNE	b	3	117	13	13	11½	14^{2}	15^{1}	16^{1}	16^{4}	TownrowR	SmallmanJE	111.70
PERTNESS	b	3	110	6	12	16½	18	17½	17^{1}	17^{12}	StrettonS	ElliottGB	60.40
GILDED CASINO		3	107	18	11	17^{1}	17^{1}	18	18	18	McGinnisP	SeagramStable	d-2.70

a-Coupled as R. H. New entry; b-Thorncliffe Stable entry; c-J. C. Fletcher entry; d-Seagram Stable entry.
Time, :24, :49²/₅, 1:15, 1:42⁴/₅, 1:57¹/₅. Track fast.

	$2 Mutuels Paid			Official Booking Odds		
AYMOND (a-Entry)	$30.20	$11.25	$ 6.15	1410—100	462½—100	207½—100
WHALEOIL (b-Entry)		4.15	3.35		107½—100	67½—100
ICHITARO (c-Entry)			3.95			97½—100

B. g (3), by *Roselyon—Ablaze, by Tony Bonero. Trained by J. Hutton. Bred by Mr. J. Heffering, Whitby.
WENT TO POST—4:23. AT POST—13 minutes.

Start good and slow. Won driving, second and third the same.

AYMOND, beginning fast and hurried to get clear of interference, was steadied along in front, shook off repeated challenges from WHALE OIL and, holding on tenaciously, was slowly moving clear in the last eighth. WHALE OIL offered keen contention, made several efforts, but tired slowly in the final drive. ICHITARO, in close quarters early, saved ground and continued gamely under his heavy impost. VESTIP, outrun early, worked his way up on the outside to close with good energy. QUATRA BRAS ran a good race. PAT GAIETY gained much ground. PANDORUS lacked speed and could not get into contention under severe punishment. LOVE'S ARROW had early speed. The others were outrun.

Scratched—Refiner and Nature's Eye.

Overweight—Pertness, 3 pounds.

By 1931 the first alarming effects of the Depression had finally caught up with horse racing across Canada. Statistics released by the federal Department of Agriculture showed that betting and attendance figures had plunged for the second year in a row, resulting in smaller purses and fewer racing days. Wagering at Kenilworth Park in Windsor and at Woodbine were both down more than $800,000 that year. In its annual report to shareholders, the Ontario Jockey Club noted that the size of its purses and stakes were fast getting back to what they were twenty-five years ago. Although the Ontario Government reduced its daily racing tax from $5,000 to $4,000, the OJC was still unhappy: "Racing in Ontario is being taxed out of existence." Ottawa also contributed to the fears of horsemen in regard to the future of the sport when the Honourable Ernest Lapointe proposed an amendment to the Criminal Code that would prohibit newspapers and racing tabloids from printing information that aided the public in its handicapping of, and betting on, horses.

The economical woes of the troubled thirties would wipe out, or curtail, several of the biggest stables. Brookdale Stable folded when Albert Dyment, president of the Ontario Jockey Club, and his brother Simon "took a beating" in the stock market crash. Also feeling the pinch was Riverdale Stable, which had won the Plate in 1929 and bred the winner the following year, but did not send out another Plate candidate until 1938. Dispersal sales were commonplace as G.M. Hendrie and E.F. Seagram pruned the size of their stables.

The most vivid sign of horse racing's distressful state was exhibited on 23 May at Woodbine when the smallest crowd since the "betless" Plates of 1918 and 1919 watched R.W.R. Cowie's *Froth Blower* splash through a deep muddy track to win the Plate, which had been devalued by $5,000 from a year earlier and was a $10,000-added event. Some critics blamed the cold, rainy weather for the unenthusiastic turnout, which "was not more than 12,000." There was not the usual clamouring at the gates when they opened at noon. Also, the accustomed parade of fashions was replaced by heavy coats, slickers and bobbing umbrellas. Another suggestion for the "thinnest crowd in years" was the fact that the Thorncliffe track in neighbouring Leaside had hosted the opening of the season a week earlier. Lou Marsh of *The Daily Star* gave his views:

> The reason? Anybody is entitled to his guess, but the outstanding reasons for lack of a reach cinch are undoubtedly tight money and the cool, chilly weather. Some folks say that when the Ontario Jockey Club accepted second place on the list of Toronto openings that they cost themselves plenty in

BOB COWIE (LEFT) AWAITS THE TROPHY PRESENTATION FROM GOVERNOR GENERAL LORD BESSBOROUGH. HOLDING TROPHY IS OJC SECRETARY PALMER WRIGHT.

attendance. There is no doubt that Thorncliffe took the gilt off the gingerbread. A lot of the regulars finished the northend meet with the old wallet somewhat anemic to say the least. And then again, the track conditions hurt the crowd. There are plenty who like to go gunning for the puddle jumpers and the beetles with the web feet, but there are still some who hate to lay in the hot cross buns when track conditions are not perfect or nearly perfect. They insist that picking horses on a muddy racing strip is just a guessing contest.

The usual glitter and splendour of Plate day was also absent. For the first time in years the state arrival of the vice-regal carriage was cancelled because of the cold winds, rain and the muddy track. Instead, Canada's new Governor General, Lord Bessborough, made an unostentatious appearance, arriving by auto in the parking lot. The crowd was not aware of his presence in the royal box until after the band struck up the National Anthem and his blue and gold standard was hoisted up the infield flagpole. "There wasn't even a mild cheer. What a contrast to the usual showy parade down the long stretch and the roaring acclaim of thousands of racegoers," noted *The Daily Star*. An official said the open coach arrival was dispensed with because Lord Bessborough had sciatica. One of his aides disagreed. "It looks like the deuce on an afternoon like this."

The small crowd obviously surprised track officials, who for the first time since 1927 had opened extra wickets to handle advance betting on the Plate. Wagering was down by a sizeable total. The adverse conditions had little effect on trainer Harry Giddings, English-born jockey Frank Mann and R.W.R. (Bob) Cowie, a Scotsman from Edinburgh who was able to operate a stable with the profits he made from importing novelties from all over the world. The favoured *Froth Blower* was his fourth Plate horse. After the presentation of the cup from Lord Bessborough, Cowie confided: "I'm still walking on air. I did a lot of stall walking while the horses were at the post."

For Giddings the win signalled a rejuvenation of his career. He had won four Plates for his father, Harry Senior, but had not won the race since 1920. Mann, who would go on to win two more Plates, was lauded for his patience and cool manner while stalking R.S. (Sam) McLaughlin's pacesetting *Skygazer* before taking command in the stretch. The brown colt was almost three lengths better than the runner-up, *Bronze*, of the Thorncliffe Stable. Although the day was generally disagreeable to many, *The Mail and Empire*'s Ed Allan wrote about an amusing incident that took place in the judges' enclosure:

> Following the running of the King's Plate, the boy who looks after *Froth Blower*, brushed by everybody and ran over and doffed his hat and stood beside his horse, ready to be snapped by the camera man. The individual goes by the nickname of 'Goat Eye,' and has a habit of bobbing up at inopportune times. He bobbed out quickly on Saturday, but he surely wanted to get his photograph taken with the Plate winner. Somehow or other 'Goat Eye' generally manages to get with a winner. Last fall he was looking after Connie Smythe's *Rare Jewel* [who paid $214.40 in upsetting *Froth Blower*] when the latter won the Coronation Stakes.

"Goat Eye" had himself a winner in hockey's Smythe, who bought defenseman Francis (King) Clancy from the Ottawa Senators with the $15,000 he collected on *Rare Jewel*'s surprise win. Six months after the 1931 Plate, Smythe opened one of the best-known sports arenas in North America—Maple Leaf Gardens.

A glimpse of what beckoned in the annals of Canadian horseracing was significant in the race chart of the Kentucky Derby of 1931. *Boys Howdy*, who finished fifth, was owned by Harry Clifford Hatch, the self-made millionaire Canadian industrialist and head of one of the world's largest distilleries. He would be Hatch's only starter in the Derby. However, Hatch would later by described as "the E.P. Taylor of his time" as his stable thoroughly dominated Canadian racing, capturing the King's Plate five times between 1936 and 1945. Also in that Derby in 1931 was *Ladder*. He would go on to sire Plate winner and Canada's Horse-of-the-Half-Century *Bunty Lawless*. *Bunty Lawless* later sired *Windfields*, the cornerstone of Taylor's breeding empire, as well as Taylor's first Plate winner, *Epic*. Also, the rider of *Prince d'Amour* in the 1931 Derby was Elmer James, nephew of the infamous U.S. Midwest bank robber and murderer Jesse James. The jockey would later ride in Canada and was employed for years by the Ontario Jockey Club.

FROTH BLOWER | 3-year-old brown colt

Froth Blower (1928)	Cudgel	Broomstick	Ben Brush
			*Elf
		Eugenia Burch	*Ben Strome
			*The Humber
	*Chrysoberil	Verdun	Rabelais
			Vellana
		New Moon	Flying Fox
			New Mown Hay

Owner: R.W.R. Cowie, Toronto; *Trainer:* H. Giddings Jr.
Jockey: Frankie Mann; *Breeder:* R.W.R. Cowie

Jockey Frankie Mann won his first of three Plates on *Froth Blower*.

1931 KING'S PLATE STAKES

FOURTH RACE
Woodbine Park
MAY 23, 1931

1 1–8 MILES. (Spot Cash, May 23, 1923, 1:51 2/5, 3, 103.) Seventy-Second Running KING'S PLATE. $10,000 added and 50 Guineas. 3-year-olds and upward. Foaled in Ontario. Net value to winner, $7,850 and 50 Guineas; second, $1,500; third, $1,000.

Horse	Eqt	A	Wt.	PP	St.	¼	½	¾	Str	Fin	Jockey	Owner	Odds $1
FROTH BLOWER		3	117	5	1	$4^{1\frac{1}{2}}$	$2\frac{1}{2}$	2^{hd}	2^{2}	$1^{2\frac{1}{2}}$	MannF	CowieRWR	1.62½
BRONZE	b	3	112	11	7	$6^{1\frac{1}{2}}$	4^{nk}	3^{1}	3^{3}	2no	CanfieldL	ThorncliffeStable	a-3.65
SKYGAZER		3	112	8	2	$1\frac{1}{2}$	1^{1}	$1\frac{1}{2}$	1^{nk}	3^{3}	PhillipsC	McLaughlinRS	13.10
PAR EXCELLENCE	b	4	127	3	3	5^{1}	6^{1}	5^{hd}	$4^{1\frac{1}{2}}$	$4^{1\frac{1}{2}}$	LoumanH	NewRH	13.10
OIL RITE		3	112	7	8	$7\frac{1}{2}$	5^{nk}	$4\frac{1}{2}$	5^{1}	5^{1}	SimpsonR	ThorncliffeStable	a-3.65
FESS		3	112	2	11	$10\frac{1}{2}$	7^{nk}	6^{2}	6^{5}	6^{10}	AimersT	ThorncliffeStable	a-3.65
VESTIP		5	128	12	9	$8\frac{1}{2}$	9^{2}	$8^{1\frac{1}{2}}$	7^{2}	7^{5}	GwynneJ	UplandFarmStable	20.55
FREETHINKER		4	132	10	5	3^{hd}	3^{3}	7^{3}	8^{4}	$8^{1\frac{1}{2}}$	RobertsonA	SeagramStable	b-2.65
GOLADER		3	117	6	10	11^{4}	10^{hd}	9^{nk}	10^{10}	9^{6}	MooneyJD	SeagramStable	b-2.65
MYTHICAL LORE		3	112	1	4	9^{nk}	11^{12}	10^{5}	9^{nk}	10^{1}	McGinnisP	SeagramStable	b-2.65
KIRKLAND POST		3	107	9	6	2^{hd}	8^{hd}	11^{10}	11^{1}	$11^{1\frac{1}{2}}$	CleverleyW	WrightWH	27.50
SEDGEROSE		3	107	4	12	12	12	12	12	12	DaintyF	HarberStable	48.05

a-Coupled as Thorncliffe Stable entry; b-Seagram Stable entry.
Time, :25, :50, 1:16 3/5, 1:42 2/5, 1:59 1/5. Track muddy.

	$2 Mutuels Paid			Official Booking Odds		
FROTH BLOWER	$ 5.25	$ 3.70	$ 3.35	162½—100	85—100	67½—100
BRONZE (Thorncliffe Stable entry)		3.45	3.10		72½—100	55—100
SKYGAZER			5.15			157½—100

Br. c (3), by Cudgel—*Chrysoberil, by Verdun. Trained by Harry Giddings Jr. Bred by Mr. R. W. R. Cowie, Toronto.
WENT TO POST—4:26½. AT POST—3½ minutes.

Start good and slow. Won ridden out; second and third driving.

FROTH BLOWER, hustled into a forward position, was rated along until leaving the backstretch and, wearing down SKYGAZER, was kept under pressure thereafter. BRONZE, slow to get going, worked his way up, saved ground on the stretch turn and got up in the final drive. SKYGAZER showed good speed and held on gamely. PAR EXCELLENCE was unable to get up. OIL RITE raced evenly. FESS closed a big gap. VESTIP had no mishaps. FREETHINKER, in hand for three-quarters, tired. The others were never a factor.

Flying low in her red and gold monoplane, the daring aviatrix, Amelia Earhart, made history on 21 May 1932. Not only did she become the first woman to achieve a solo flight across the Atlantic ocean, but she made the journey from Newfoundland to Northern Ireland in record time. In Toronto another "lady" also established a record that day when *Queensway*, a three-year-old chestnut filly, became the fastest winner of the King's Plate as she waltzed across the finish line three lengths in front of *King O'Connor*.

Earhart's magnificent achievement, and *Queensway*'s stirring victory for owner R.W.R. (Bob) Cowie of Weston, who had now seen his gold and Alice blue silks paraded into the winner's circle for the second year in a row, were earned with a minimum of discomfort. After landing in a field near Londonderry, the wife of New York publisher George Palmer Putnam explained that the fifteen-hour flight from Harbor Grace, Newfoundland, had slightly affected her hearing: "I am afraid I am a bit deaf after that terrible roar of the engine in my ears all the time, but at any rate I have done it. Now, perhaps, I think I would like to go to London, but the only clothes I have with me are the flying suit I'm wearing and I didn't bring any money."

Queensway suffered a few minor cuts about the legs during a nearly ten-minute skirmish at the new "Wake" starting gate—a stationary barrier that was used for the first (and last) time in a Plate race. It resembled a set of low racetrack stalls, minus the overhead bridge. However, she was hardly puffing after her mile and one furlong dash around the Woodbine oval, and the cuts were accepted as normal under the circumstances. Visitors to trainer Harry

AVIATRIX AMELIA EARHART, THE FIRST WOMAN TO FLY SOLO ACROSS THE ATLANTIC.

Giddings' barn thought that she had returned looking about the same as she did twenty minutes before lining up at the post.

Even though she had been full of run at the finish as jockey Frank Mann had her "under wraps," *Queensway* did not win as she pleased. The Cowie-bred filly had received a stubborn challenge from Harry Hatch's *Easter Hatter* for three-quarters of her journey which had been expected as the gelding had been established as a slight favourite ahead of Seagram Stable's strong entry of *Shady Well* and *King O'Connor*. However, once Mann wheeled the filly to the outside, finally conquering the persistent *Easter Hatter*, *Queensway* had little to worry about, nor did her pilot, owner or her backers. Her 1:55 1/5 clocking bettered *Troutlet*'s 1927 record by three-fifths of a second.

"Mann rode the winner of this race last year for the same outfit and I think that if she had been pressed, we mean urged, there is no doubt that she would have clipped more than a full second off the record," wrote Ed Allan in *The Mail and Empire*. Writers agreed that *Queensway* was the superior horse in this Plate race, but they expressed mixed feelings over the showing of the Seagram entry—*King O'Connor*, because he ran such a smashing race, and *Shady Well*, because she ran so much below the "dope." Her race was too bad to be true. *King O'Connor*, who would win the Plate the following year, had been shuffled back at the start but was running over the top of the field to

1932 KING'S PLATE STAKES

FOURTH RACE

Woodbine Park

MAY 21, 1932

1 1–8 MILES. (Spot Cash, May 23, 1923, 1:51²/₅, 3, 103.) Seventy-Third Running of the KING'S PLATE. $7,500 added. 3-year-olds and upward. Foaled in Ontario. Allowances. Net value to winner, $5,620 and 50 Guineas; second, $1,200; third, $800.

Horse	Eqt	A	Wt.	PP	St.	¼	½	¾	Str	Fin	Jockey	Owner	Odds $1
QUEENSWAY		3	112	8	4	1½	2³	11½	12½	1³	MannF	CowieRWR	3.00
KING O'CONNOR		3	112	1	11	11	8³	41½	2⁴	2⁴	BurkeJH	SeagramStable	a-2.85
SPEY CREST	b	3	112	5	3	4¹½	4⁵	3⁴	3⁴	3⁵	SchaeferL	WrightWH	b-6.50
SHADY WELL		3	112	9	9	7⁴	5ⁿᵏ	5³	5³	4½	LegereE	SeagramStable	a-2.85
EASTER HATTER	b	3	117	11	5	2ⁿᵏ	1¹	2½	4⁴	5³	RileyG	HatchHC	2.40
EASTER DANDY		3	112	4	10	8³	7½	7¹½	6½	6⁴	O'MalleyJ	RidgewoodFarm	c-22.30
BRONZE	b	4	127	7	7	10½	11	9³	9³	7ⁿᵏ	RallsC	ThorncliffeStable	d-10.45
SERFMAN		3	112	10	8	6ʰᵈ	6¹	8²	8²	8⁴	AimersT	ThorncliffeStable	d-10.45
MISS GORMLEY		3	107	3	2	3³	3ⁿᵏ	6⁴	7¹	9³	FodenN	SchelkeFH	20.00
FRAGRANT GIFT		3	112	6	6	9¹½	9½	10²	10²	10¹	MalleyT	WrightWH	b-6.50
ROYAL GUEST	b	4	122	2	1	5ⁿᵏ	10½	11	11	11	McCabeW	NewRH	c-22.30

a-Coupled as Seagram Stable entry; b-W.H. Wright entry; c-Ridgewood Farm and R. H. New entry; d-Thorncliffe Stable entry.

Time, :24, :48³/₅, 1:13⁴/₅, 1:41, 1:55¹/₅.(Plate record.) Track fast.

	——$2 Mutuels Paid——			——Official Booking Odds——	
QUEENSWAY	$ 8.00	$ 4.10	$ 3.00	300—100	104—100	50—100
KING O'CONNOR (Seagram entry)		3.75	2.75		87½—100	37½—100
SPEY CREST (W. H. Wright entry)			3.30			65—100

Ch. f (3), by Old Koenig—*Chrysoberil, by Verdun. Trained by H. Giddings Jr. Bred by Mr. R. W. R. Cowie, Toronto.
WENT TO POST—4:18. AT POST—9½ minutes.
Start good out of machine. Won easily, second and third driving.
QUEENSWAY, away well, was taken under restraint for three quarters and, wearing down EASTER HATTER, increased his advantage and was never menaced. KING O'CONNOR, slow to get going, moved up gamely in the last half mile but could not overtake the winner. SPEY CREST, in hand early, moved up when called upon and finished gamely. SHADY WELL closed a gap. EASTER HATTER set the pace, then tired. BRONZE, an early trailer, closed resolutely. MISS GORMLEY showed speed.
Scratched—Skygazer.

get up for second money. Many considered that the first-time starter was in the race just to help *Shady Well*. But she was in no mood to run. "She will not be so bumble-footed later on in the season." It was suggested by stablehands that she was "horsin'." It was "that time" of the month. History would later record that the stories were true as *Shady Well* would dominate racing and a stakes race would later be named in her honour.

R.W.R. COWIE, FRANK MANN AND GOVERNOR GENERAL LORD BESSBOROUGH.

Cowie, who had been so overjoyed with *Froth Blower*'s victory in 1931 that he immediately went out and got married, came in for some needling from Giddings during the post-race stable party. "What do you think of a man who deliberately dresses up with top hat and everything, ready to receive the King's Plate?" asked Giddings, who had just become only the second man to train six Plate winners (John Walker had done it in the 1890s for Joseph Seagram). "He didn't do that for *Froth Blower*—go ahead and tell him Bob."

"I wasn't so sure of *Froth Blower* last year."

"You mean you didn't wear your glad rags to the meet—not being sure of the hoss?" added Giddings. "That's it," Cowie replied.

"And today you were so sure *Queensway* would do her stuff that you turned up in a tony get-up all set for the headline attraction?"

"Yes—I knew if the track was fast nothing could touch her. You noticed that she burst the speed mark, too."

Horsemen noted that Cowie, whose introduction into racing in 1916 was with a horse called *Starter*, had pulled off an unusual feat of breeding back-to-back Plate winners with horses out of the same mare, the imported *Chrysoberil*. (Liberty in 1862 and 1863 and *Dance Smartly* in 2000 and 2001 are the only mares to do it.) Seventy-one years later, in 2003, Queensway gained induction into the Hall of Fame when she was celebrated as the first unofficial winner of Canada's Triple Crown. In a two-week period she won the Plate, Breeders' Stakes and the Prince of Wales Stakes, the three races that comprise the event that was inaugurated in 1959.

A gloomy note of 1932 was the diminished value of the Plate race. In two years its worth had been cut in half—down to a $7,500-added event. Retrenchment was an expression often used by the Ontario Jockey Club as horse racing, and the country in general, suffered through another year of the Depression. The handle on opening day (handle is racing slang for a day's betting) was down twenty per cent from 1931, which had been a dismal year as well. But the most distressing statistic supplied by the federal Government revealed that betting at Woodbine had dropped from $5.1 million in 1929 to $1.4 million for the seven-day spring meeting. Only Thorncliffe in nearby Leaside showed a seasonal increase in 1932.

Deeply concerned that the overall calibre of racing would dete-

QUEENSWAY | 3-year-old chestnut filly

			*Golden Gerter
		Golden Maxim	Miss Maxim
	Old Koenig		
			Hastings
Queensway		Masthead	Lady Margaret
(1929)			
			Rabelais
		Verdun	Vellana
	Chrysoberil		
			Flying Fox
		New Moon	New Mown Hay

Owner: R.W.R. Cowie, Toronto; *Trainer:* H. Giddings Jr.
Jockey: Frankie Mann; *Breeder:* R.W.R. Cowie

riorate when it was forced to lower the value of its stakes race program and cut its minimum purse value from $1,200 to $800, the OJC retrenched as best as it could. There would be no dividend for stockholders, and secretary Palmer Wright was instructed to defer any painting or renovations to the track that could reasonably be put off to another season, and to keep expenditures down to a minimum. Instead of featuring military bands every day, they would be used only on opening and closing day, and their fees would be cut by one to five dollars. The number of bandsmen was also reduced.

To attract fans, general admission was lowered to one dollar (plus tax), daily double wagering was introduced (on the second and fifth races) and the one-two-three bet (across the board) was lowered from six to three dollars. The OJC also made a blatant attempt to increase its membership when it advised members that their sons, should they be approved by the board, would be admitted without paying the usual initiation fee of one hundred dollars. It also decided that ladies (not women), upon approval, may become members upon the same basis as ordinary members. A backward step was the banning of race broadcasts during the fall meet.

A FILLY, *QUEENSWAY*, WON THE PLATE ON THE DAY OF MRS. EARHART'S HISTORIC ACHIEVEMENT. JOCKEY FRANK MANN IN THE SADDLE.

Plate history has always acknowledged that King *O'Connor*'s triumph in 1933 for the once powerful Seagram Stable was notable on two accounts: it marked the last time a four-year-old would win the fifty guineas, and the race attracted its largest field in history when twenty-two horses paraded to the post at Woodbine.

Overlooked, regrettably, were the circumstances which allowed the rangy, brown gelding to join the "rodeo" which, for

PRESENTATION CEREMONIES: (FROM LEFT) LADY BESSBOROUGH, TRAINER BILL BRINGLOE, JOCKEY ED LEGERE, OWNER EDWARD SEAGRAM, LORD BESSBOROUGH AND CLUB PRESIDENT A.E. DYMENT.

twenty-three minutes, thrashed about behind the starting barrier—his early background and, more important, the impending demise of Canada's most famous racing establishment which, for the first time, would win the Plate with a horse it did not breed. The black silks with the yellow sash of the Seagram Stable, whose tradition of winning had fallen into the secure hands of Edward, Norman and Thomas, the sons of founder Joseph Emm Seagram, no longer dominated racing in Canada. It had been in a slump since 1930, but it had managed to win its nineteenth Plate almost as an afterthought.

Some thought the Plate win was the farewell gesture of a national institution in horse racing. The dispersal sales later that year would further decimate the dwindling ranks of the Waterloo racing empire which, in its heyday, owned the largest and classiest band of broodmares, and had entries running simultaneously at four or five tracks in the United States and Canada. However, before Edward Frowde Seagram would go out on his own when he dissolved the partnership with his brothers and terminated the contract of the stable's longtime trainer, Billy Bringloe, there

would be a Plate victory with a horse that logically had no right to be among the field that reared and pawed the dirt behind the webbing for twenty-three minutes while the impatient crowd shouted "Let 'em go."

He was eligible that day, but for all the wrong reasons. It wasn't a case of a trainer putting a horse on the shelf and "saving" him for another Plate race after a strong showing, which had often been Seagram's practice during his amazing streak of eight successive Plates in the 1890s. Unraced as a juvenile because he was awkward and undeveloped, *King O'Connor* stunned everyone connected with the stable in his 1932 Plate debut as a three-year-old when he finished ahead of his more publicized stablemate, *Shady Well*, and was second to *Queensway*.

Trainer Bringloe obviously had no thought of a future Plate win for the gelding. If he had, he would have sent him back to the farm and not risked endangering his maiden status and Plate eligibility. Instead, *King O'Connor* ran four days later in the Breeders' Stakes, but finished fourth. At Thorncliffe in Leaside the long-striding gelding was second, beaten by a length in the Prince of Wales Stakes. In the three races which now comprise Canada's Triple Crown, *King O'Connor* had been a factor in each one.

Later that summer he ran three times in four days at Fort Erie. A win in any one of these races would have prevented him from joining the bulky 1933 field that left the barrier like the charge of the Light Brigade and straggled home like Napoleon's retreat from Moscow.

Bringloe's fourth winner for Seagrams was "lengths" the best conditioned horse in the race. "He's so fit he could have run to the Rocky Mountains," said one horseman. He

KING O'CONNOR CHALLENGED *EASTER HATTER* IN THE STRETCH AND WON HANDILY.

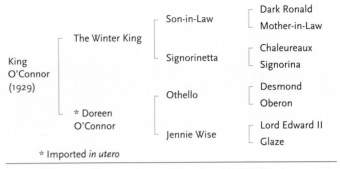

KING O'CONNOR | 4-year-old brown gelding

			Son-in-Law	Dark Ronald
		The Winter King		Mother-in-Law
King			Signorinetta	Chaleureaux
O'Connor				Signorina
(1929)			Othello	Desmond
		* Doreen		Oberon
		O'Connor	Jennie Wise	Lord Edward II
				Glaze

* Imported *in utero*

Owner: Seagram Stable, Waterloo; *Trainer:* William H. (Bill) Bringloe
Jockey: Eddie Legere; *Breeder:* Frederick Harris, Oakville, Ont.

EDDIE LEGERE WAS LAUDED FOR HIS SKILLFUL RIDE ON *KING O'CONNOR*.

had to be, considering the obstacles he encountered on Plate day. Because he was four, *King O'Connor* had to carry 127 pounds. Thus, not only did he bear this burden during the long delay (at one point the riders dismounted for five minutes while a new bridle was placed on *Que Toi*), he was forced to concede from five to twenty pounds to all but three of his foes.

Starter Mars Cassidy, who had no stall-gates to assist him because the field was too big, was forced to line them up in the old-fashioned open manner. He was lauded for his expertise and patience in ensuring that everyone received a fair start before he "pulled the trigger." Also noted was jockey Eddie Legere's ride, the way he skilfully threaded the traffic and avoided the bumping and interference before taking *King O'Connor* to the outside in the backstretch and making his spirited charge away from the field.

The final curious chapter in *King O'Connor's* win was the manner in which he was acquired. At the turn of the century, Joseph Seagram had often been criticized because several of his Plate winners were imported *in utero* after being conceived in England. His adversaries claimed that his wealth gave him an advantage over the smaller and less affluent owners and breeders. Ironically, *King O'Connor* was also imported *in utero*, but by Frederick Harris, a Hamilton newspaper editor who lived in Oakville. Later Harris sold the mare, **Doreen O'Connor*, and her foal to a neighbour, Ryland H. New, who had twice won the Plate with horses he had not bred. But this time New consigned the yearling to a public auction at the Woodbine Park Paddock in 1930, a sale at which

Seagrams were active as consignors.

At that sale Harris watched with eager interest as the auctioneer presided over the sale of a large, rangy gelding by *The Winter King*. He looked almost out of place among the other youngsters offered for sale. When the hammer came down after a final bid of $500 by Bringloe, acting for the Seagram Stable, Harris went over to the trainer and said: "You have just bought a King's Plate winner." He could have added, "and perhaps the last winner to be imported *in utero*." There has not been another "import" in more than seventy-five years.

1933 KING'S PLATE STAKES

FOURTH RACE
Woodbine Park
MAY 20, 1933

1 1–8 MILES. (Spot Cash, May 23, 1923, 1:51²/₅, 3, 103.) Seventy-Fourth Running KING'S PLATE. $7,500 Added. 3-year-olds and upward, the property of a British subject resident in Ontario, foaled, raised and trained in Ontario, that have never won a race, either on the flat or across country, other than a race exclusively for 2-year-olds, have never left Canada, and have never been for a period of more than three months out of this Province. Winners to carry 5 lbs. extra. No gelding allowance. A Silver Cup will be presented by the Club to the owner of the winner. Entries closed March 21st with 55 nominations. Net value to winner, $6,100 and 50 Guineas; second, $1,200; third, $800.

Horse	Eqt	A	Wt.	PP	St.	1/4	1/2	3/4	Str	Fin	Jockey	Owner	Odds $1
KING O'CONNOR		4	127	12	6	9nk	81	61	21	13	LegereE	SeagramStable	2.75
EASTER HATTER	b	4	132	4	1	2½	22	1½	1½	2½	MozierR	HatchHC	a-4.75
SYNGO		3	117	8	2	6½	6½1	71	41	34	McCoyJ	WebsterMrsRE	b-6.35
COURT BUTTERFLY	b	3	117	16	20	101	101	101	81	4½	FodenN	SmytheC	c-15.60
ROYAL VINTAGE	b	3	112	1	9	82	91	4hd	32	5½	RemillardP	WrightWH	d-20.60
FRIGID FROSTY		4	127	15	21	161	161	14hd	131	6¹½	WellsL	CoxC	f-8.45
HEAP GOOD	b	3	112	7	4	121	11hd	111	61	72	MadeleyF	NewmarchWI	f-8.45
SYNDIC	b	3	117	11	16	171	14hd	9hd	91	8½	CraverL	WebsterMrsRE	b-6.35
BETHANKFUL	b	3	112	9	11	141	151	151	151	9nk	TownrowR	MountainRoseStable	f-8.45
KHAKI JOHN	b	3	117	3	14	31	3hd	31	101	101½	MattioliJ	ThorncliffeStable	e-5.00
PENSWEEP	b	3	117	22	8	5nk	5½	5hd	7½	114	RileyG	HatchHC	a-4.75
JUNIAM		3	117	5	19	15½	17²	131	12¹½	121	HornF	NewRH	g-16.60
CANNY AGE		3	117	2	3	1½	1hd	2hd	5²	133	DoughertyF	SmytheC	c-15.60
CARTWHEEL		3	107	18	13	19½	181	171	171	143	ThomasJ	McLaughlinRS	h-16.80
QUE TOI	b	4	122	13	22	22	22	22	201	15²	GwynneJ	MarkhamStable	f-8.45
OUR SONNY	b	3	117	6	7	11hd	121	12hd	11hd	161	PollardJ	FletcherJC	f-8.45
BRONZE	b	5	128	19	18	73	7²	8½	161	173	AimersT	McElroyJ	f-8.45
PERTOXICAL		3	117	17	12	18hd	15²	18½	18²	181	HallsworthS	NewRH	g-16.60
PEPPER PRINCE		3	112	10	15	13½	13²	16hd	141	19²	MannF	McLaughlinRS	h-16.80
BY THE SEA		3	112	20	17	21⁵	191	191	201	201	DugganR	ThorncliffeStable	e-5.00
PAPALICO		3	117	14	8	4hd	6hd	8hd	21³	21⁵	MannJ	CochenourTS	17.30
LADY WORTHMORE		3	112	21	10	201	21³	21hd	22	22	OsborneH	WrightWH	d-20.60

a-Coupled as H. C. Hatch entry; b-Mrs. R. E. Webster entry; c-Conn Smythe entry; d-W. H. Wright entry; e-Thorncliffe Stable entry; g-R. H. New entry; h-R. S. McLaughlin entry. f-Mutuel field.

Time, :24²/s. :49²/s, 1:15, 1:42³/s, 1:56²/s. Track fast.

Official Program Numbers

Mutuel Prices:

	—$2 Mutuels Paid—			—Odds to $1—		
12-KING O'CONNOR	7.50	4.80	3.70	2.75	1.40	.85
4-EASTER HATTER (a-Entry)		5.80	4.30		1.90	1.15
8-SYNGO (b-Entry)			4.35			1.17½

Br. g (4), by The Winter King—*Doreen O'Connor, by Othello. Trained by Wm. H. Bringloe. Bred by Frederick Harris, Oakville.

IN GATE—4:29. AT POST—23 minutes.

Start good and slow. Won easily. KING O'CONNOR moved up leaving the backstretch and, wearing down EASTER HATTER in the stretch, won in hand. The latter took command when CANNY AGE tired but was no match for the winner. SYNGO moved up near the end. COURT BUTTERFLY saved ground and finished gamely. CANNY AGE set the pace but tired. HEAP GOOD was close up. PENSWEEP was unable to improve his position. KHAKI JOHN raced well for seven-eighths. PAPALICO was not a factor. QUE TOI broke a bridle at the post which was one of the causes for the long delay.

Scratched—Corsinax and Trickys Son.

Atwo-dollar bet on *Horometer*, the horse critics believed might become the greatest King's Plate winner of them all, was a chance to earn a sure dime, which was not easy during the years of rampant unemployment and breadlines. It was 1934, and Mitch Hepburn and the Liberals had just swept the Tories out of Queen's Park. Toronto celebrated its Centennial and welcomed actress Mary Pickford, "America's Sweetheart," who had been born on the street where the Hospital for Sick Children now stands. And skipper Angus Walters sailed his fishing schooner *Bluenose* so close to the shores of Lake Ontario that the crowd at Woodbine could hear the canvas snapping as she tacked up into the wind.

It was also the year of the seventy-fifth running of the Plate, which attracted twenty-three thousand people. The only reason for the largest mob since 1930 was *Horometer*.

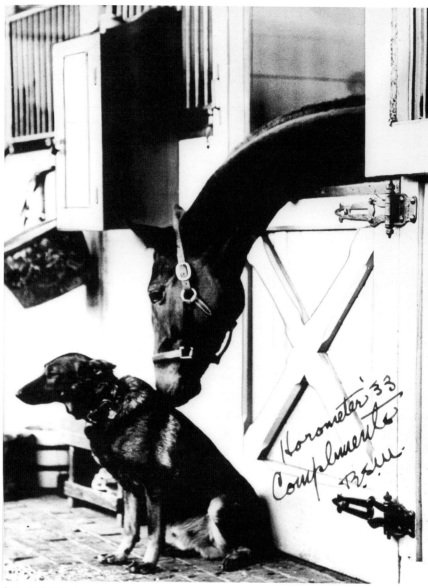

ONE OF CANADA'S GREATEST HORSES, *HOROMETER*, NUZZLES STABLE PET. HE LOST ONLY ONCE IN NINE CAREER STARTS AND PAID JUST FIVE CENTS ON A DOLLAR WHEN HE WON THE PLATE.

"Every mother's son had made up his mind that *Horometer* was the only possible winner, and everyone wanted to be on hand to see his judgment vindicated. When the big horse came from behind and took a commanding lead coming into the stretch, thousands of heads were literally nodding their 'I told you so's,'" wrote *The Mail and Empire*.

For a brief period it was *Horometer*'s year. But his meteoric ascent would suddenly crumble less than six weeks after he had romped to a record time in the Plate, paying a minimal $2.10. He faced token opposition that day as just five other horses were entered in a race that some felt should have been either a "non-betting affair" or a "walk-over." However, before his greatness could be tested against top notch runners in the United States, he suffered a broken bone in his foot, an injury which would prevent him from racing again.

Years later, when the merits of the greatest winners in the Plate's first one hundred years were assessed, books, essays in magazines and newspapers claimed that "one of the all-time great Canadian-bred horses, the ill-fated *Horometer*," died shortly after his major triumph from a "mysterious cerebral ailment." There was no mention of a crippling foot injury. Thus the charisma and legend of the horse was forever enhanced.

An insider who debunks the mysterious illness and suggests it was more likely a bullet to the head that did in *Horometer*, is Frank Mann, the jockey who often said: "He was the greatest Canadian-bred I'd ever ridden." The sleek brown gelding provided Mann with his third Plate victory.

I'm not sure when he hurt the foot. In fact, I don't recall his last race at Long Branch. But I do remember galloping him the following spring [18 May 1935]. He pulled up lame. In those days they weren't able to repair a horse's foot like they can today, so he'd had it. He was a gelding and had no stud value, so they 'put him down' at the farm in Oshawa. You couldn't blame them [owner R.S. McLaughlin and trainer Harry Giddings], I guess. But I kinda felt bad when I heard, because I'd tried to buy him for a pet and give him a home. He was a real nice horse, kinda quiet, but smart.

Andy Lytle, writing in *The Star Weekly* on Plate day a year later, confirmed part of Mann's account: "There was a touch of the tragic around the Parkwood stables, for *Horometer*, Plate winner last year and being groomed for another season of racing, broke down this morning going three-quarters of a mile. Frankie Mann was obliged to pull up sharply and dismount. *Horometer*, his gleaming eyes sobbing with pain and limping badly, hobbled to the stables and experts anxiously went to work on his hoof, the one broken last season and severely reopened in today's gallop."

Mann also disputed the date of the death notice in the *American Racing Manual*, that stated *Horometer* died in 1936 at the age of five. "Don't believe it or that he died of some ailment. I know when it happened."

From the day *Horometer* went to the post for the first time as a two-year-old, his reputation of superiority would gain in momentum. Following his win in the Goodwood Plate, a reference to his noble bloodlines was made and it was suggested that off this start it would take a horse that "was above the ordinary to take the measure of the Oshawa owned youngster." None did as the son of **Hourless* won the Clarendon, Coronation and Grey Stakes Handicap. He was five-for-five.

The following spring his workouts were enough to scare off most owners and it was predicted that he would smash *Queenway*'s 1932 Plate record of 1:55 1/5, which he did by a full second. The clocking would stand for eleven years. On 23 May, four days after his Plate win, he captured the Breeders' Stakes. But three races in the space of eight days would be too taxing for the gelding, for on 26 May he lost the Hendrie Memorial Handicap by inches to an older horse carrying nine pounds less. It would be the only blot on *Horometer*'s record.

On 9 June, at the Long Branch track west of Toronto, the horse who went about his business in an almost haughty, aloof manner, and whose eyes flamed when he caught a glimpse of a rival, would make his final start, winning the Canadian Breeders' Handicap. His eight wins and a second in nine starts came at a time when purses were declining, and were worth but $14,605 (fifty years later the fourth place finisher in the Plate would earn $16,435).

The injury, which eventually cost him his life, was a cruel blow to the men who had closely witnessed his majestic development: owner Robert Samuel McLaughlin, trainer Harry Giddings and Mann. *Horometer* was the first of three Plate wins for the sixty-three-year-old McLaughlin, who would make Parkwood Stable, his breeding and racing establishment north of Oshawa, one of the finest on the continent before selling out to another industrialist, E.P. Taylor.

The day he won the guineas, McLaughlin had reason to be jubilant; his runners had set two track records and tied another. It was an afternoon that would live long in the memory of the man who had turned his father's carriage business into a successful motor car company before selling out to General Motors. McLaughlin proudly admitted: "I am as happy as the day I was married."

For Giddings it was perhaps his greatest afternoon as he not only saddled winners in four of the seven races, but gained the distinction of earning a record seventh King's Plate. But for Mann, who had emigrated from Nottingham, England, in 1920, and had long been judged as one of the smartest riders in Canada, it would be his final Plate win. Three years later he would be banned from riding in Ontario "for suspicious behaviour" along with seven other riders by the Incorporated Canadian Racing Association. "I accepted some money, you see, but I got six years while the other guys got off with two or three," said Mann, who would be inducted as a Legend to the Hall of Fame in 2000.

It was at this spring meeting that the ICRA, aided by the Royal Canadian Mounted Police and the Department of Agriculture, seriously began to exert its authority in an effort to deal with horses that were suspected of being "doped." The saliva box was introduced, two winners each day were tested and registration papers for first-time starters were required.

HOROMETER | 3-year-old brown gelding

Horometer (1931)	*Hourglass	*Hegofol	Childwick
			Nebrouze
		Hour Glass II	*Rock Sand
			*Hautesse II
	Star Pal	*North Star III	Sunstar
			Angelic
		*Palestra	*Prince Palatine
			Adana

Owner: R.S. (Sam) McLaughlin, Oshawa; *Trainer:* Harry Giddings Jr.
Jockey: Frank Mann; *Breeder:* R.S. McLaughlin

1934 KING'S PLATE STAKES

FOURTH RACE
Woodbine Park
MAY 19, 1934

1 1–8 MILES. (Spot Cash, May 23, 1923—1:51 2/5—3—103.) Seventy-Fifth Running of the KING'S PLATE. 50 Guineas, the gift of His Majesty the King, with $7,500 added by the Ontario Jockey Club. The first horse to receive the Guineas, Stakes and $5,000; the second horse $1,200 and the third horse $800. The breeder of the winner to receive $500. A Sweepstakes of $5 payable at time of entry, and $40 additional to start. For three-year-olds and upward, the property of a British subject resident in Ontario, foaled, raised and trained in Ontario, that have never won a race, either on the flat or across country, other than a race exclusively for two-year-olds, have never left Canada, and have never been for a period of more than three months out of this Province. Winners to carry 5 lbs. extra. No gelding allowance. Acceptances to be named through the entry box the day before the race, at usual time of closing. Death of nominator does not render entry void. A Silver Cup will be presented by the Club to the owner of the winner. The Club reserves the right to cancel this race upon the repayment of all entrance fees paid in advance. Closed with 41 nominations. Net value to winner, $5,400 and 50 Guineas.

Horse	Eqt	Wt.	PP	St	¼	½	¾	Str	Fin	Jockey	Owner	Equiv. Odds Str't
HOROMETER	3	117	2	1	3½	1^{1}	$1^{2\frac{1}{2}}$	$1^{2\frac{1}{2}}$	1^{4}	MannF	McLaughlinRS	a-.05
SPEYGOLD	b 3	117	4	6	$5^{1\frac{1}{2}}$	5^{6}	4^{4}	$3^{2\frac{1}{2}}$	$2^{1\frac{1}{2}}$	MorrisonR	WrightWH	b-12.50
PAPALICO	4	132	6	4	2^{nk}	4^{5}	2^{1}	2^{nk}	3^{4}	FodenN	CochenourTS	24.50
PITCHBLENDE	3	117	5	5	6	6	5^{2}	5^{8}	4^{nk}	TownrowR	CowieRWR	a-.05
CANDY FEAST	3	112	3	3	3^{1}	2^{hd}	3^{2}	4^{3}	5^{12}	WallN	SeagramEF	12.70
SAM WORTHY	b 3	117	1	2	$4^{2\frac{1}{2}}$	$3^{1\frac{1}{2}}$	6	6	6	VercherT	WrightWH	b-12.50

a–Coupled as R. S. McLaughlin and R. W. R. Cowie entry; b–W. H. Wright entry.
Time, :24 1/5, :49 2/5, 1:15, 1:41, 1:54 1/5. (Plate record.) Track fast.

	—$2 Mutuels Paid—		
HOROMETER (McLaughlin and Cowie entry)	$ 2.10	$ 2.05	$ 2.05
SPEYGOLD (W. H. Wright entry)		2.05	2.15
PAPALICO			2.30

Br. g (3), by *Hourless—Star Pal, by *North Wales II. Trained by H. Giddings Jr. Bred by R. S. McLaughlin, Oshawa.
WENT TO POST—4:31. AT POST—3 minutes.

Start good and slow from gate. Won easily; second and third driving.

HOROMETER, much the best and under stout restraint, went into the lead approaching the five-furlong pole, drew clear, was roused once midway of the far turn and held his field safe while still under reserve. SPEYGOLD, taken back of the pace, began to improve his position nearing the turn out of the backstretch and closed gamely though no match for the winner. PAPALICO, well placed from the start, moved up briefly at the five-sixteenth ground but was unable to improve his position in the stretch drive. PITCHBLENDE dropped far out of it in the opening six furlongs and passed tired horses in the last quarter-mile. CANDY FEAST went well for the first six furlongs. SAM WORTHY had early speed.

1935 | SALLY FULLER

Decisions that Edward Frowde Seagram made shortly after the Seagram Stable of Waterloo was unceremoniously dismantled in 1933 would figure prominently two years later in yet another Plate victory for the famed racing colours—the black jackets with a yellow sash and black cap—which had been around since the 1880s.

One of the first moves Eddie Seagram made after buying out the interests of his brothers, Norman and Thomas, was superficial, but it distinguished his silks from those of Joseph E. Seagram and the estate's stable. He subtly altered his father's colours, adding a yellow cuff to the jacket and a yellow band to the cap. Next step was to put Johnny Thorpe in full charge of the handful of horses he had retained after the dispersal sales.

Thorpe had been with the stable ever since he had timidly asked for a job one morning in 1898 while the Seagram string was training at the old Newmarket track on The Danforth in Toronto. Performing as a groom, exercise rider, jockey and assistant trainer, he would later boast that he had galloped more Plate winners than any other rider—twelve. Thorpe had also been a keen student of the men he had formerly served—Billy Bringloe, Barry Littlefield, Harry Blair and Charlie Boyle—for it was only a matter of weeks before he and Eddie were in the winner's circle with *Shady Well*, one of the great racemares of the 1930s.

Another of Seagram's decisions that year was to spend five hundred dollars for a brown filly, a yearling that had been bred by Thorncliffe Stable. Even in this depressed period it looked like a piece of grand larceny, for she was a sister to Plate winner *Shorelint* and was out of *South Shore*, who had also captured the fifty guineas for the sons of Robert Davies. Her name was *Sally Fuller* and initially she made Seagram think that he had made a colossal blunder. In four starts as a two-year-old

SEAGRAM STABLE IN WATERLOO. NOTE THE TRAINING TRACK (TOP) AND THE COVERED TRACK (BOTTOM LEFT).

JOCKEY HERB LINDBERG CAME UP WITH "ACES" ON *SALLY FULLER*.

her earnings were fifty dollars, a sum she had collected for a third-place finish in a $1,500 claiming race. It was hardly the type of company that a future Plate winner should be associated with.

The final piece of the triumvirate fell into place during the 1934–1935 winter racing season in Florida when Seagram bought the contract of twenty-six-year-old apprentice jockey named Herb Lindberg. "Lindy," who had spent five years exercising horses for the powerful Brookmeade Stable of Virginia, rode more like a seasoned veteran than an apprentice. He welcomed the opportunity to join Seagram, for it allowed him to escape a contract which paid him just twenty-five dollars a week. Forty years later, Lindberg recalled: "I wrote up my own contract, but I didn't care about it at the time, just as long as [George] Henze gave me a chance to ride. He had given me my start in 1934, letting me ride for him at Hawthorne Park in Chicago. A year later I win [*sic*] four races in one day, including the Plate."

Thorpe entered two fillies in 1935—*Gay Sympathy* and *Sally Fuller*—and instructed Lindberg to either go the front early, or to force the pace to set it up for the other half of the entry, who would save ground and make a bid late in the race. *Gay Sympathy*'s rider was Bobby Watson who, a few years later, would win three Plates in a space of five years. Thorpe afterwards admitted: "She [*Sally Fuller*] hadn't shown me too much in training until about a week before the Plate. Then she moved up with a corking good trial, and from then on she continued to improve."

The crowd made Seagram's fillies third choice in the betting behind the undefeated *Listaro* of Parkwood Stable and Harry Hatch's good entry of *Chickpen* and *Donstick*. The race, however, did not go exactly the way Thorpe had figured. After running *Worthing* into the

Sally Fuller was the last Plate winner to carry the familiar black and yellow diagonal sash racing silks of Joseph E. Seagram and family.

SALLY FULLER | 3-year-old brown filly

Sally Fuller (1932)	*Judge Fuller	Great Sport	Gallinule
			Gondolette
		Maglona	Fugleman
			Rayon
	South Shore	*Orme Shore	Orme
			Virginia Shore
		Southern Maid	Plaudit
			Sally K.

Owner: Edward F. Seagram, Waterloo; *Trainer:* Johnny Thorpe
Jockey: Herb Lindberg; *Breeder:* Thorncliffe Stable, Todmorden, Ont.

ground, *Sally Fuller* took command, but instead of faltering in the stretch, she pulled away and won by three lengths "with her ears pricking." A distant eleventh in the race was the five-year-old *Papalico*, who carried twenty-six pounds more than the winner (133 to 107).

The first three finishers were "feathery-weighted" fillies. *Chickpen*, who lost several lengths while taking the overland route around both turns, was second ahead of *Gay Sympathy*, who made a late challenge, as expected. (Four days later *Gay Sympathy* would win the Breeders' Stakes as she took advantage of an extra thirteen pounds assigned to *Sally Fuller* because of her Plate victory.)

"The Men of Waterloo" had just won their twentieth Plate, which had been devalued to a $5,000-added event that year, its lowest gross since 1919. However, its value would slowly climb. One observer that day optimistically asked: "Who says the Depression isn't over? It was an old-time Seagram field day, as not only did he win the Plate, but two other races as well. The stable is back in its stride."

It would flourish, racing and winning big races with horses like *Stand Pat* in Chicago and New York, and at racetracks in Florida, California, Texas, Canada and even England. But Edward Frowde Seagram would be dead in two years time and, despite the efforts of his son, J.E. Frowde Seagram, who took over the reins of the stable until his death in 1979, the black and yellow silks had won its last Plate.

For Thorpe, who exercised and trained horses for three generations of Seagrams, *Sally Fuller* would represent his lone Plate victory as a trainer. Lindberg would finish second with *Mona Bell* in 1938 and third on the favoured *King Maple* in 1954, but he also would have to live off the memory of *Sally Fuller*'s unexpected win. Both Lindberg and Thorpe would later be inducted into Canada's Hall of Fame.

Trainer John Thorpe, Herb Lindberg and Edward Frowde Seagram.

1935 KING'S PLATE STAKES

FOURTH RACE
Woodbine Park
MAY 18, 1935

1 1-8 MILES. (Spot Cash, May 23, 1923—1:51²/₅—3—103.) Seventy-Sixth Running of the KING'S PLATE. 50 Guineas, the gift of His Majesty the King, with $5,000 added by the Club, the first horse to receive the Guineas, Stakes and $3,400; the second horse $800 and the third horse $500. The breeder of the winner to receive $300. A Sweepstakes of $5 payable at time of entry, and $40 additional to start. For three-year-olds and upward, the property of a British subject resident in Ontario, foaled, raised and trained in Ontario, that have never won a race, either on the flat or across country, other than a race exclusively for two-year-olds, have never left Canada, and have never been for a period of more than three months out of this Province. Winners to carry 5 lbs. extra. No gelding allowance. Acceptances to be named through the entry box the day before the race, at usual time of closing. Death of nominator does not render entry void. A Silver Cup will be presented by the Club to the owner of the winner. The Club reserves the right to cancel this race upon the repayment of all entrance fees paid in advance. Net value to winner, $4,404 and 50 Guineas.

Horse	Eqt	Wt.	PP	St	¼	½	¾	Str	Fin	Jockey	Owner	Odds $1
SALLY FULLER	3	107	4	4	$2^{1\frac{1}{2}}$	2^{2}	1^{2}	$1^{2\frac{1}{2}}$	1^{3}	LindbergH	SeagramEF	a-4.07½
CHICKPEN	3	112	11	3	4^{hd}	$4^{\frac{1}{2}}$	$3^{1\frac{1}{2}}$	$2^{1\frac{1}{2}}$	2^{2}	YoungS	HatchHC	b-3.15
GAY SYMPATHY	3	109	5	10	9^{1}	8^{1}	7^{1}	4^{2}	3^{4}	WatsonR	SeagramEF	a-4.07½
EPICURUS	b 3	117	6	12	10^{1}	6^{1}	6^{hd}	6^{6}	4^{6}	McDonaldC	ParkwoodStable	c-1.00
DONSTICK	b 3	112	2	6	5^{hd}	$5^{\frac{1}{2}}$	5^{1}	5^{2}	5^{2}	MadeleyF	HatchHC	b-3.15
EILEEN D.	3	112	9	5	6^{1}	$3^{1\frac{1}{2}}$	$2^{\frac{1}{2}}$	$3^{1\frac{1}{2}}$	$6^{3\frac{1}{2}}$	FodenN	ParkwoodStable	c-1.00
WORTHING	b 3	117	3	2	$1^{\frac{1}{2}}$	$1^{1\frac{1}{2}}$	$4^{\frac{1}{2}}$	7^{1}	7^{hd}	DoughertyF	WrightWH	d-13.20
TAX FREE	3	112	1	7	8^{hd}	$11^{1\frac{1}{2}}$	11^{4}	10^{1}	8^{4}	CourtneyG	WrightWH	d-13.20
BEECHVIEW	3	112	8	8	11^{1}	$10^{1\frac{1}{2}}$	9^{1}	9^{1}	$9^{3\frac{1}{2}}$	BurrillJ	GrahamR	86.00
LISTARO	3	117	12	9	7^{1}	7^{hd}	8^{1}	8^{1}	$10^{\frac{1}{2}}$	MannF	ParkwoodStable	c-1.00
PAPALICO	b 5	133	7	1	9^{2}	9^{1}	10^{1}	11^{6}	11^{4}	ParkerW	CochenourTS	19.70
GOGGLES	b 3	117	10	11	12	12	12	12	12	BarnesE	CrawfordSB	14.60

a–Coupled as the E. F. Seagram entry; b–H. C. Hatch entry; c–Parkwood Stable entry; d–W. H. Wright entry.
Time, :24, :48³/₅, 1:14²/₅, 1:42, 1:55²/₅. Track fast.

	$2 Mutuels Paid			Official Booking Odds		
SALLY FULLER (Seagram entry)	$10.15	$ 4.85	$ 7.30	407½—100	142½—100	265—100
CHICKPEN (Hatch entry)		4.30	4.60		115—100	130—100
GAY SYMPATHY (Seagram entry)	10.15	4.85	7.30	407½—100	142½—100	265—100

Br. f (3), by *Judge Fuller—South Shore, by *Orme Shore. Trained by John Thorpe. Bred by Thorncliffe Stable, Todmorden.

WENT TO POST—4:44½. AT POST—3 minutes.

Start good and slow. Won easily, second and third driving.

SALLY FULLER, away in the first flight, forced the early pace of WORTHING, moved to the front easily after reaching the half-mile post, was rated in front for the balance of the journey and held CHICKPEN safe. The latter, in the first flight from the outset, moved up with a rush in the stretch, closed well, but could not menace the winner. GAY SYMPATHY saved ground while racing on the inside in the early stages, but lacked early speed, then closed stoutly when finding her best speed. EPICURUS, away slowly and suffering some interference in the early stages, gradually worked his way up and closed with good speed. DONSTICK raced evenly, but could not better his position. EILEEN D. had some early speed but quit at the end. WORTHING had good early speed but quit after three-quarters. LISTARO was never prominent, showing a dull performance.

Scratched—Easteroam, Vingt Cinq.

Overweight—Gay Sympathy, 2 lbs.

The Plate Grows Up: Race Opens for All Canadian Horsemen—*Bunty, Horometer* the Dominant Winners

Nothing, in my opinion, has done more good for horse breeding in Canada than the King's Plate run at Toronto.

THE EARL OF MINTO

Canada's eighth Governor General spoke these words on his return to England in 1904, and few could argue with them. The race, under the control of the Ontario Jockey Club, had amply fulfilled its original purpose of encouraging the breeding of thoroughbreds in the province of Ontario. But like horse-drawn carriages and high button shoes, the original rules set down for the Plate soon became obsolete when horsemen throughout Canada began to develop horses that could run as fast or as far as any province-bred. They wanted an opportunity to win the fifty guineas and the prestige that went with Canada's historic racing event; although it was a lengthy journey from British Columbia or Alberta, the railroads had made it possible for a westerner to ship east for the race.

The Plate had been an exclusive neighbourhood clambake for Ontario's dogmatic horsemen and many refused to budge and move with the times, despite the protestations of breeders from the prairies in the 1920s. Quebeckers such as Commander J.K.L. Ross (whose horses finished one-two in the Kentucky Derby in 1919 and was owner of *Sir Barton*, America's first Triple Crown winner that year) and fellow Montreal horseman Wilfrid Viau (who raced former Kentucky Derby winner **Omar Khayyam*) would be reminded that La Belle Province had its own Plate, one that was restricted to horses bred in their province. The OJC encouraged the stables of Ross, Viau and Manitoba's R. James Speers to campaign in the major stakes races in Ontario, except of course the Plate. While Plate candidates could not train outside Ontario, the OJC did put in a rule that allowed breeders to take their mares to Quebec (or the United States) for a three-month period and breed them to Ross' good stallions at his stud in Vercheres, Quebec.

Rules for the race, which originally was open only to maidens—horses bred, foaled and raised in Upper Canada that had never won public money—had undergone modifications periodically as the OJC gradually lifted restrictions because of the persistent demands of horsemen. For a brief period during the latter years of World War I, owners were allowed to train their horses in the United States; some of the more wealthy sportsmen took advantage of this. The winner in 1918, George M. Hendrie's Springside, broke his maiden at Latonia, Kentucky, in the fall and had a "tightener" the following spring, finishing second by two lengths at Churchill Downs, Louisville, before returning to Toronto and galloping home an easy winner.

In 1913 the OJC had opened the race for horses that had won a race exclusively for two-year-olds. It also increased the difference in weight a four- or five-year-old had to carry against a three-year-old, which weeded out many of the older maidens from the list of Plate starters. In 1938 the Plate was restricted to three- and four-year-olds only, and in 1939, when King George VI and Queen Elizabeth visited Woodbine Park, the first ruling monarch to attend the Plate since the original donation of fifty guineas from Queen Victoria, it was for three-year-olds.

However, in November 1943, one of the bleakest moments during World War II, the Plate grew up as the gates of Woodbine were thrown open, an event that delighted Jim Coleman, columnist for *The Globe and Mail* and the severest critic of the OJC's policy of "Ontario only." This was how he

CANADA'S HORSE OF THE HALF-CENTURY AND PROLIFIC SIRE, *BUNTY LAWLESS*.

THE GIANT ELM TREE (LEFT) AND GRASSY INFIELD STEEPLECHASE COURSE WERE FAMILIAR SIGHTS AT THE WOODBINE IN ITS EARLY YEARS.

the New Woodbine in 1956.

One of the classic examples of the unfairness of this archaic condition involved Mrs. Lily A. Livingston, once described as "one of the most gracious ladies that ever graced the turf in any country." She had inherited the great Rancocas Stud of Jobstown, New Jersey, following the death of tobacco magnate, Pierre Lorillard, but later sold it to oilman Harry Sinclair when she established Pontiac Stud in Cobourg, Ontario. Her stock farm near the shores of Lake Ontario rivaled that of the Seagrams, Thorncliffe and Brookdale; she spent almost a million dollars bringing to Canada some of the choice blooded stock of Kentucky, Virginia and Maryland. Mrs. Livingston was regarded as a menace to the existing sportsmen in control, and despite support

greeted Colonel Kenric R. Marshall's announcement that all Canadian owners in 1944 would be allowed to compete: "Nothing, in my opinion, has done more good for horse breeding in Canada than opening the race to all the unfortunates who live in benighted sections of the wastelands, beyond the borders of our beloved Province. . . . The Plate finally has grown up, but eighty-four years is a rather prolonged period of adolescence." King George VI, who approved of the restructuring of the Plate's conditions, advised the OJC that he "considered the idea one of encouragement to the expanding breeding industry in Canada."

Another important change was a new rule that permitted horsemen to give their hopefuls a race before the Plate. The OJC introduced the Plate Trial Stakes, which was scheduled to be run a week before the Plate. Instead of the big race opening the spring meeting, it became the closing-day attraction. However, the OJC could not make up its mind whether a man had the right to train wherever he pleased before the Plate; some preferred warmer climes—Florida, South Carolina or California—because it rescinded the rule in the early 1950s after initially agreeing that Ontario's long, cold winters and wet springs hindered the training of expensive horses. Another contentious rule—a flagrant act of discrimination—was one stipulating that owners had to be "British subjects resident in Canada." It had evoked considerable ridicule and embarrassment from time to time for the pious board of the OJC, but would not be deleted until the opening of

from some of the OJC directors, she was not allowed to nominate for the Plate the horses she had bred and foaled in Ontario. Their fears were justified. After selling her stock, two runners from her first crop, *Tartarean* and *Fair Montague*, finished one-two in the 1915 Plate. That was the year Club officials told Toronto hotel owner William Krausmann that it would be advisable for him to sell his Plate filly, *Hampton Dame*, because of anti-German sentiment. Four years later, *Ladder of Light*, a mare that the Cobourg horsewoman had sold to OJC director George W. Beardmore, also won the Plate.

In 1921 the OJC relaxed the "British subject" clause and allowed Lily Livingston to run her horses in the Plate under her blue and silver braid coloured silks with a black cap. She was a major supporter of the Cobourg Horse Show, spoken of as the finest in the province. But the rule was inserted again in 1925 and Lily returned to Virginia in the 1930s. When she died, *The Blood-Horse* magazine of Kentucky said her passing "removed from the Thoroughbred scene one of the last links with the fabulous racing days of the Gay Nineties." Another victim of the discrimination

MRS. LILY LIVINGSTON, OWNER OF THE FAMED PONTIAC STUD FARM IN COBOURG, ONT., BRED TWO PLATE WINNERS THAT RAN UNDER THE COLOURS OF OTHER OWNERS. FOR SEVERAL YEARS SHE WAS NOT ELIGIBLE TO ENTER A HORSE AS SHE WAS A U.S. CITIZEN.

King's Plate Day 1939

Ontario Jockey Club Limited Toronto Canada Official Programme

Palmer Wright
Secretary-Treasurer

COMMEMORATIVE 1939 KING'S PLATE PROGRAM.

was Henry Deimler, an American citizen who had run a refrigeration company in Toronto for nineteen years. In 1931 he owned *Hayloft*, a three-year-old maiden bred by the Seagram Stable in Waterloo. Familiar with the Plate conditions, Deimler transferred ownership to his wife, a Canadian and an Ontario resident, born in Walkerton. But *Hayloft*'s nomination was refused because Mrs. Deimler was married to an American. *Hayloft* never recovered from the embarrassing slight; his record for his first two seasons was zero for forty. In eighty-seven career starts, he earned just $2,475.

The brightest moment in Plate history during the 1936–1948 period came when Willie Morrissey, the feisty Irishman, won the 1938 Plate with the "little guy's horse," *Bunty Lawless*. Two years later, Miss Mildred Kane, a close friend of Morrissey's, won the race with an untried maiden, *Willie the Kid*. The huge throngs of two-dollar bettors at Woodbine were enthralled when someone with whom they could identify won the Plate. Charlie Hemstead, another hotel owner, won it in 1943 with *Paolita*, but the greatest triumph for the underdog came in 1948 when Jim Fair, the dirt farmer from Cainsville, almost lost his overcoat and suit as he pushed through the adoring crowd on his way to the winner's circle following *Last Mark's* victory.

The triumphs by Morrissey, Fair and Miss Kane, the first woman to win the race, opened up the Plate to the little guy after an endless parade of victories by owners with seemingly unlim-

COLONEL R.S. (SAM) MCLAUGHLIN, THE AUTO TYCOON WHO OWNED PARKWOOD STABLE.

PARKWOOD STABLE IN OSHAWA, LATER NAMED THE NATIONAL STUD, THEN WINDFIELDS FARM.

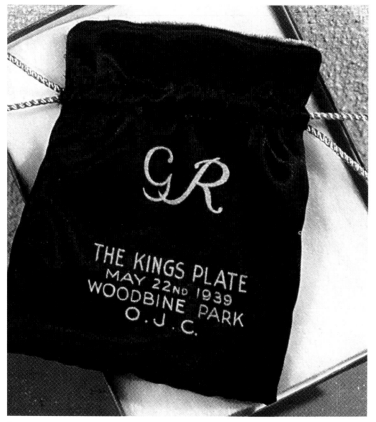

PURPLE VELVET BAG WITH THE TRADITIONAL "50 GUINEAS." (OFFICIALLY SOVEREIGNS.)

COLONEL McLAUGHLIN AND FUTURE HALL OF FAME INDUCTEES *HOROMETER* AND JOCKEY FRANK MANN.

PLATE WINNER *ARCHWORTH* AND TRAINER MARK COWELL.

ited resources. Millionaires dominated the Plate, and when the Seagram, Hendrie, Dyment, Davies, Giddings, New and Cowie stables were no longer contenders, they were replaced by Harry Hatch, a liquor merchant and industrialist, who won five Plates in a space of ten years, and automobile pioneer Robert Samuel McLaughlin of Oshawa, winner of three Plates, including one by the great *Horometer*.

Until *Bunty Lawless*, a rugged individual who could sprint and carry weight a distance of ground, the finest Canadian-breds had been *Inferno* (1905) and *Horometer* (1934). While they were both outstanding racehorses, *Bunty* added a second dimension—he was the first great Canadian-foaled sire since *Terror* in the 1870s. He dominated the sires' lists of most winners and highest earnings for years, with offspring that included *Windfields*, who in turn was a great sire, Plate winners *Epic* and *McGill*, *Senator Jim*, *Heptad*, *Dorenes Lad* and *Major Flight*. Before he died, *Bunty Lawless* was named Canada's "Horse of the Half-Century."

A RADIANT QUEEN ELIZABETH AND KING GEORGE VI ENTER WOODBINE'S ROYAL BOX. PRIME MINISTER MACKENZIE KING, RIGHT, AND FAR RIGHT ONTARIO PREMIER MITCHELL HEPBURN.

During a period when Canada was recovering from the Depression and surviving another world war, horse racing thrived, despite betting scandals, strikes and wartime shortages of gasoline and manpower. On the eve of the 1937 Plate, and the week afterwards, the Incorporated Canadian Racing Association, which governed racing at Woodbine, Hamilton and Fort Erie, broke up a jockey's betting ring and suspended eight jockeys, several of whom were considered the finest in Canada—Frankie Mann, Bobby Watson, Colin McDonald, Johnny Passero and Frankie Dougherty. All were later reinstated. Also policing the sport were the Department of Agriculture and its representatives, the Royal Canadian Mounted Police, who supervised the betting machines and the taking of winners' blood tests. To protect themselves, the Horsemen's Benevolent and Protective Association was formed for owners, trainers and backstretch employees. The arrival of electrically controlled starting gates was introduced during this period, along with cameras, to decide photo-finishes and film every step of a race to detect possible infractions.

Harry Giddings in 1942 became the "winningest" trainer in Plate history when his *Ten to Ace* won handily. It was Giddings' eighth Plate victory, but his first as an owner. Other leading trainers during this period were Cecil Howard, Arthur Brent and Billy Bringloe. *Sweepster* and *Teddy Wrack* each sired two Plate champions in the 1930s and 1940s.

HARRY HATCH DOMINATED CANADIAN RACING IN THE 1930S AND 1940S.

Seldom in the seventy-seven-year history of the Plate had there been a more glorious day for the races than that sunny Saturday, 23 May 1936. Does that sound familiar? It was an introduction that journalists repeatedly adopted in the 1920s and 1930s, but here it was applied by *The Daily Star*'s globe-trotting Gordon Sinclair. "Never before had Woodbine looked better. A south wind day, warm and misty and lazy. . . ." Torontonians heeded the welcoming call and thronged to the racecourse. By half-past one the stands were full, including the newly built seats at the east end of the track. By two o'clock, about the same time as Norman "Red" Ryan, the notorious criminal, was robbing a Sarnia liquor store in the last grisly episode of a life of crime, the park was bulging with a crowd of more than twenty-two thousand.

Because of the death of George V, His Majesty's donation of fifty guineas that year was granted by his son, the new and handsome young monarch, Edward VII. "Today," Alexandrine Gibb confided to *the Daily Star*'s readers, "owners are all more than usually anxious to win; it is the first allotment of the new King's money." Even the press, though, had no prescience of just how unique that gift would be; before the running of the next Plate, Edward would abdicate his throne and the historic race would have a new patron.

Some of the usual colour of the occasion was lost because no vice-regal representative was present: mourning for the late King was still being observed. The absence was regretted by some, but others saw it as imparting a distinct and attractive character to the event. As Sinclair put it: "In many ways staged luxury gave way to natural magnificence. For the first time in twenty years no Governor sat, top-hatted, in a flag-draped box. No prancing greys kicked up dust pulling a royal carriage down the straight. Instead of the open victoria, or whatever they call that museum piece they haul down the track twice a year, Pete Mahony sat astride a sprinkling cart and watered a fast dry track." OJC President A.E. Dyment subbed for the Governor General.

It turned out to be a particularly memorable day for Harry C. Hatch, millionaire industrialist and horse-owner. Harry Hatch's stable had led winning owners in the previous autumn meeting of the Ontario Jockey Club, but his hopes for a Plate in 1935 with *Chickpen*, who had been second, were snuffed out by *Sally Fuller*'s powerful effort; as one observer noted, "nobody, living or dead, was more anxious to win the Plate than Harry Hatch."

Hatch would claim much more than a normal portion of the day's glory. Not only would his two-year-old *Goldlure* win the Goodwood Stakes in record-breaking time, but *Monsweep*, Hatch's three-year-old brown gelding, would weave his way through the field to earn a purse of more than $5,000 plus the guineas. By the end of the program, the Hatch stable would score three wins, thrusting the owner to a dominant position in Canadian racing.

Harry Hatch, born in the small hamlet of Robin's Landing in Ontario's Prince Edward County in 1884, began his apprenticeship and eventual rise from a saloon keeper to the very pinnacle of the liquor business with his brother Herb, rather inauspiciously. For

HARRY C. HATCH, MILLIONAIRE INDUSTRIALIST, LIQUOR TYCOON AND BREEDER OF DISTINCTION, WON THE PLATE FIVE TIMES.

several years he worked in the often violent atmosphere of dingy, smoked-filled rooms of hotels and saloons in Eastern Ontario's Deseronto, the Tyedinaga Indian Territory and for a time at Indian Head, Saskatchewan, before returning east in 1908 with his father, Bill Hatch, to work at the family's hotel in Oshawa. In 1911 he opened a package liquor store in Whitby, and two years later he and Herb went into partnership in a liquor store on Yonge Street in Toronto. When the provincial government passed the Ontario Temperance Act in 1916, closing down the liquor stores and saloons, the Hatch boys relocated to Montreal, opening a mail-order business. Harry shrewdly anticipated the enormous profit to be made by selling booze through the mail to residents of Ontario. After World War I he went into business with another liquor merchant, T.A. (Pud) Woods, winner of the King's Plate in 1907 with *Kelvin*, and son-in-law of Abe Orpen, the celebrated bookie and racetrack owner.

Hatch soon prospered to the point where he was able to purchase the controlling interest of Gooderham & Worts Ltd. in 1923, and four years later pulled off a major business coup when he acquired Hiram Walker & Sons Ltd. based in Walkerville, Ontario. In 1927 he merged the two companies, to make it one of the largest distilling companies in the world. During the U.S. Prohibition and the rum-running war (exporting liquor was not illegal) of the 1920s, Harry and Herb's knowledge of boats, their friendship with the seamen and smugglers who cruised the Great Lakes in their swift

Camera-shy Hatch always delegated his sons to accept the Plate. Here Cliff poses with *Monsweep* and jockey Danny Brammer.

craft (one of the fastest was a boat from Hamilton, *Martimas,* named after William Hendrie's great horse and sire), and their prowess in moving large shipments of liquor across Lake Ontario and Lake Erie to American ports, was a factor in the success of the man who was personally insured for the then unheard amount of $1.5 million. Hatch was also a director of several companies, including Canada Malting and Canadian Steamship Lines. In 1933 he bought one of the largest wineries in Canada, T.G. Bright and Company Ltd., and helped promote an intensive program of grape research.

The year 1927 saw Hatch enter horseracing when he bought Agincourt Farms (northeast of Toronto), the stable of Commander J.K.L. Ross, which had gone under the auctioneers hammer, along with some of his horses, including the celebrated racemare, *Tattling,* who dominated racing in Canada in 1926. A year later he purchased *Sweepster,* which became one of the most successful studs in Canada, siring Plate winners *Monsweep* and *Goldlure,* and *Luress,* the dam of Plate winners *Budpath* and *Acara.*

A combination of shrewd purchases and his knowledge of bloodlines would establish Hatch as the most successful Canadian breeder and owner during the late 1930s and 1940s. But until 1936, the King's Plate had eluded him. That year *Monsweep,* coupled in the betting with *Sweepouch,* was second choice behind Edward Seagram's entry of *Samoan* and *Judge Pool.* The preceding year had been a lacklustre one for the Billy Bringloe–trained gelding, with only a single win in four starts. There was, however, no doubt at the end of the race which horse was the best that day. While Seagram's *Samoan* took the lead early, it was *Monsweep,* with the skilful Danny Brammer aboard, who was moving the fastest going down the backstretch. He overtook the frontrunner

MONSWEEP | 3-year-old brown gelding

Monsweep (1933)	Sweepster	Sweep	Ben Brush
			Pink Domino
		Oktibbena	*Rock Sand
			Octoroon
	*Mona Maris	Twelve Pointer	Royal Realm
			Fin Glen
		Madelon	*Teddy
			Miss Glover

Owner: H.C. (Harry) Hatch, Toronto; *Trainer:* William H. (Bill) Bringloe; *Jockey:* Danny Brammer; *Breeder:* H.C. Hatch

and pulled away to win by almost three lengths. George M. Hendrie's *Stormblown* had to settle for second money.

By Monday, Norman "Red" Ryan would nudge *Monsweep* from the front pages of the Toronto press. Ryan, a well-known criminal turned reformed model prisoner, had been paroled just ten months earlier in an unprecedented move by the Bennett government. An idol of prison reformists, he was shot dead by a Sarnia police officer while robbing a liquor store.

But Harry Hatch, whose own business career began in a small liquor store, had built his breeding farm and stable into a prominent position that would last for more than a decade. *Monsweep* was the first of his five Plate winners to carry the light and dark blue hooped silks in the next ten years, and during that time Hatch would earn more newspaper column space than Red Ryan ever dreamed of.

1936 KING'S PLATE STAKES

FOURTH RACE
Woodbine Park
MAY 23, 1936

1 1–8 MILES. (Spot Cash, May 23, 1923—1:51 2/5—3—103.) Seventy-Seventh Running of the KING'S PLATE. $6,000 Added and 50 Guineas, the gift of His Majesty, King Edward VIII. 3-year-olds and upward. Foaled in Ontario. Allowances. Net value to winner, $5,110 and 50 Guineas; second, $1,000; third, $600.

Horse	Eqt	A	Wt.	PP	St.	¼	½	¾	Str	Fin	Jockey	Owner	Equiv. Odds Str't
MONSWEEP		3	117	4	2	7½	$3^{1\frac{1}{2}}$	2½	1^{1}	$1^{2\frac{1}{2}}$	BrammerD	HatchHC	a-3.07½
STORMBLOWN		3	112	5	11	9^{8}	7½	3½	2^{4}	2^{4}	BarnesF	HendrieGM	b-3.10
EPICURUS		4	132	6	5	8^{1}	9½	4^{1}	$3^{1\frac{1}{2}}$	$3^{1\frac{1}{2}}$	TownrowR	ParkwoodStable	c-5.00
LADYMUCH		3	112	11	9	10^{3}	10^{3}	7^{5}	6½	4^{5}	WatsonR	SmallmanJE	16.45
SAMOAN	b	3	117	13	7	1^{hd}	1^{4}	1^{1}	5^{4}	5^{5}	HunterJ	SeagramEF	d-1.90
CHALGO	b	3	112	10	4	$4^{1\frac{1}{2}}$	4^{1}	5^{4}	4^{3}	6^{2}	FeeneyR	WebsterMrsRE	33.20
SPEARMAN	b	3	117	8	8	$5^{1\frac{1}{2}}$	6^{1}	6^{2}	7^{hd}	7^{15}	McDonaldC	ParkwoodStable	c-5.00
SANDALMAN		3	112	7	10	12^{5}	12^{5}	10^{3}	9^{1}	8^{1}	PasseroJ	ErindaleStable	128.10
ODD CATCH		3	117	1	13	13	13	13	12^{1}	9^{5}	RemillardP	LucasGW	81.80
ROCK SURE	b	3	117	3	6	2^{nk}	2^{hd}	9^{4}	10^{4}	10^{hd}	FodenN	HendrieGM	b-3.10
DESERT PLACE	b	5	123	2	12	11^{3}	11½	12^{3}	11^{1}	11^{4}	AimersT	HarrisMrsL	111.10
SWEEPOUCH	b	3	117	12	1	6^{hd}	8^{hd}	8^{3}	8^{hd}	12^{10}	YoungS	HatchHC	a-3.07½
JUDGE POOL	b	3	113	9	3	3^{2}	5^{5}	11½	13	13	MannF	SeagramEF	d-1.90

a-Coupled as H. C. Hatch entry; b-G. M. Hendrie entry; c-Parkwood Stable entry; d-E. F. Seagram entry.
Time, :24, :48 3/5, 1:13 3/5, 1:40 2/5, 1:55. Track fast.

	$2 Mutuels Paid			Official Booking Odds		
MONSWEEP (H. C. Hatch entry)	$ 8.15	$ 3.95	$ 3.10	307½—100	97½—100	55—100
STORMBLOWN (G. M. Hendrie entry)		4.00	3.40		100—100	70—100
EPICURUS (Parkwood Stable entry)			3.60			80—100

Br. g (3), by Sweepster—*Mona Maris, by Twelve Pointer. Trained by Wm. H. Bringloe. Bred by H. C. Hatch, Toronto.
WENT TO POST—4:10. AT POST—10½ minutes.

Start good and slow. Won driving, second and third the same.

MONSWEEP weaved his way between the leaders when reaching the backstretch, engaged the pacemakers when reaching the final turn, then continued stoutly after moving to the front and came out gradually nearing the end. STORMBLOWN, shuffled back going to the first turn, raced into contention swiftly when in full stride, obtained racing room on the inside at the final turn, but had too much taken out of him and he tired in the last eighth. EPICURUS bettered his position steadily and finished gamely. LADYMUCH, slow to get into full stride, circled her field and came willingly at the close. SAMOAN was made too much use of setting the pace and tired badly after seven eighths. CHALGO raced forwardly, but was not good enough. SPEARMAN was never a factor. ROCK SURE was placed on the outside and quit early. JUDGE POOL showed a flash of early speed.

Scratched—Tough Timber, Hurry Fox.

Overweight—Judge Pool, 1 lb.

GOVERNOR GENERAL LORD TWEEDSMUIR AND LADY TWEEDSMUIR (PATTERNED DRESS) TO THE LEFT OF OJC PRESIDENT A.E. DYMENT, POSE ON THE LAWN WITH OJC DIRECTORS PRIOR TO THE PLATE RACE.

In the spring of 1937, as Plate day approached, three events took place that would affect the Plate—each in their own time and way. The effect of the first was symbolic and immediate. George VI had been crowned king to fill the throne left vacant by his brother, Edward VIII, who had abdicated to marry the beautiful divorcee, Mrs. Wallis Simpson. Thus, for the second year in a row, the "guineas" would be donated by a new monarch. In both cases the Plate would be captured by a horse owned by Harry C. Hatch, and as had been the case the year before, it would be Harry's son Clifford who would accept because of his father's reluctance to enter the winner's circle, a trait he maintained while winning five Plate races. Presenting the trophy and script was Governor General Lord Tweedsmuir. The first commoner to become royalty's official representative was John Buchan, the famed novelist and biographer. He was the author of the best-selling novel *The Thirty-Nine Steps*—later turned into three separate feature films—and in 1937 inspired the creation of the Governor General's Literary Awards. Canadian publishers and booksellers welcomed the author, who quickly became their champion.

Handicappers and touts had forecast that *Silver Jubilee,* a colt out of *Silver Wedding,* would earn the Plate in Coronation Year. The crowd of almost twenty-four thousand went along with their advice and made the Parkwood Stable entry the heavy favourite. But it was *Goldlure,* another son of *Sweepster,* who would win by a length over *Cease Fire.* The second event, the replacement of Stanley Baldwin by Neville Chamberlain as British prime minister, had a more far-reaching impact, for it signalled the adoption by the Conservative government of a policy of appeasement with German chancellor Adolf Hitler, and the beginning of the descent into a war which would have an important effect on every Canadian institution.

But the storm signals from Europe went largely unnoticed in Toronto; horsemen were more concerned with a third event, an impending scandal implicating many of Canada's leading jockeys. A tremor, which was felt on the eve of the seventy-eighth running of the Plate, erupted into a full-scale earthquake a week later when the Incorporated Canadian Racing Association announced that it had revoked the licences of eight riders—Frankie Mann, Johnny Passero, Bobby Watson, Henry Palaez, Frank Dougherty, Colin McDonald, Frank Madeley and Gordon Atkins. Years later, Mann, Passero and Watson would be inducted into Canada's Horse Racing Hall of Fame at Woodbine.

It was the biggest bombshell involving a jockey's betting ring to ever hit racing in Toronto and owners and trainers were left in consternation as they desperately sought replacements and what evidence the ICRA had in expelling the riders. Horsemen knew problems were brewing after several lengthy meetings had been held between five of the riders and the ICRA, which controlled the sport at Woodbine, Hamilton and Fort Erie. The ICRA's board, which included Ontario Jockey Club president A.E. Dyment, George M. Hendrie, James Heffering, R.S. McLaughlin, George Hardy, Robert Simpson and John Madigan, had initially withdrawn the temporary licences of Mann, who was seeking a record fourth Plate victory, Passero, Palaez, Dougherty and Atkins. It gave no explanation for its action.

Mann had been scheduled to ride stockbroker Rupert Bain's *Isleworth,* while Passero, who nineteen years later would saddle the winner of the first Plate race held at "new" Woodbine, was in the employ of Erindale Stable and was to have ridden *Sandalman.* Three of the jockeys who were suspended a week later, however, had been allowed to ride, and two of them were on the favoured Parkwood Stable entry of *Silver Jubilee* and *Red Pirate.* Bobby Watson, who would be reinstated in 1939 and would later win three Plates, was on fifth-place finisher *Red Pirate.* Another jockey who rode that day,

Edward VIII abdicated his throne before the seventy-eighth running of the Plate to marry Mrs. Wallis Simpson.

GOLDLURE | 3-year-old chestnut colt

Goldlure (1934)	Sweeptster	Sweep	Ben Brush
			Pink Domino
		Oktibbena	*Rock Sand
			Octoroon
	*Golden Lure	*Golden Boss	The Boss
			Golden Hen
		Perfidious	Bachelor's Double
			Obsequious

Owner: H.C. (Harry) Hatch, Toronto; *Trainer:* William H. (Bill) Bringoe; *Jockey:* Sterling Young; *Breeder:* H.C. Hatch

Colin McDonald—he was on *Silver Jubilee* and finished third—would also serve his sentence and return to capture the 1947 Plate on *Moldy*. Madeley, who replaced Passero on *Sandalman*, finished a distant twelfth.

"Suspicious behaviour" was the reason later given for the suspensions; all eight jockeys were unable to show cause why they should not be barred from ICRA tracks. The talented and handsome Frankie Mann, who had won with the great *Horometer*, *Queensway* and *Froth Blower*, was considered the "ring-leader" of the group and was not reinstated until 1943. However, he continued his successful career in Quebec. The other seven riders were denied licences for two to three years before they were allowed to drift back to full-time racing.

Jim Coleman, writing in *The Globe and Mail* in 1943, welcomed the return of "Ferocious Francis Mann, the iron-armed hard-boot. . . . He has been reinstated by the racing dukes after serving a six-year suspension for professional shenanigans. While Francis was under official displeasure, he kept in shape by riding around the uninhibited Quebec circuit, where boat races occur with great frequency, and veteran habitues of the tracks always go armed with a pair of high rubber boots."

Clifford Hatch, Sterling Young and trainer W.H. (Bill) Bringloe.

1937 KING'S PLATE STAKES

FOURTH RACE
Woodbine Park
MAY 22, 1937

1 1-8 MILES. (Tempestuous, Oct. 3, 1936—1:51 1/5—4—109.) The Seventy-Eighth Running of the King's Plate. 50 Guineas, the Gift of His Majesty King George VI, with $7,000 added by the Ontario Jockey Club. The first horse to receive the Guineas, stakes and $4,700; the second horse $1,150 and the third horse $700. The breeder of the winner to receive $450. A Sweepstakes of $10 payable at time of entry and $50 additional to start. For 3-year-olds and upward, the property of a British subject resident in Ontario, foaled, raised and trained in Ontario, that have never won a race, either on the flat or across country, other than a race exclusively for 2-year-olds, have never left Canada, and have never been for a period of more than three months out of this Province. Winners to carry 5 lbs. extra. No gelding allowance. Acceptances to be named through the entry box the day before the race, at usual time of closing. Death of nominator does not render entry void. A Silver Cup will be presented by the Club to the owner of the winner. The Club reserves the right to cancel this race upon the repayment of all entrance fees paid in advance. Net value to winner, $5,930 and 50 Guineas.

Horse	Eqt	A	Wt.	PP	St	¼	½	¾	Str	Fin	Jockey	Owner	Equiv. Odds Str't
GOLDLURE		3	117	5	3	$2^{1\frac{1}{2}}$	2^{hd}	$1\frac{1}{2}$	1^{hd}	1^{1}	YoungS	HatchHC	a-$4.27\frac{1}{2}$
CEASE FIRE		3	117	3	5	$3\frac{1}{2}$	$3\frac{1}{2}$	$3^{1\frac{1}{2}}$	3^{3}	$2^{1\frac{1}{2}}$	CritchfieldC	BainHR	b-13.35
SILVER JUBILEE		3	117	10	2	4^{hd}	$4\frac{1}{2}$	2^{2}	2^{hd}	3^{1}	McDonaldC	ParkwoodStable	c-1.10
BUDRON		3	117	4	12	5^{1}	5^{1}	5^{2}	5^{4}	$4\frac{1}{2}$	LindbergH	HatchHC	a-$4.27\frac{1}{2}$
RED PIRATE		3	117	11	11	9^{1}	9^{hd}	$6^{1\frac{1}{2}}$	6^{1}	5^{3}	WatsonR	ParkwoodStable	c-1.10
ALDWYCH		3	112	15	4	1^{4}	$1\frac{1}{2}$	4^{2}	4^{hd}	$6^{1\frac{1}{2}}$	ValleeF	CowieRWR	5.65
ISLEWORTH	b	3	112	7	14	$13^{1\frac{1}{2}}$	13^{2}	$9^{1\frac{1}{2}}$	7^{5}	7^{1}	BrysonJ	BainHR	b-13.35
GOLDEN SILENCE		3	117	16	6	$7\frac{1}{2}$	$8\frac{1}{2}$	10^{2}	10^{1}	$8^{1\frac{1}{2}}$	AimersT	ErindaleStable	d-9.75
SLYCAT		3	112	13	8	8^{1}	7^{hd}	$7^{1\frac{1}{2}}$	8^{hd}	9^{hd}	RemillardP	MedwayStable	8.10
POVERTY STRUCK	b	3	112	9	10	11^{1}	$11\frac{1}{2}$	11^{hd}	11^{2}	10^{hd}	BurnsE	EFSeagramEstate	e-43.15
GOLD GUARD	b	3	107	2	13	14^{4}	14^{3}	13^{2}	13^{2}	11^{1}	FodenN	EFSeagramEstate	e-43.15
SANDALMAN	b	4	127	6	15	12^{1}	12^{hd}	12^{2}	$12^{1\frac{1}{2}}$	12^{2}	MadeleyF	ErindaleStable	d-9.75
NOTROUBLE	b	3	112	12	9	$15\frac{1}{2}$	$15^{1\frac{1}{2}}$	15^{1}	14^{1}	13^{1}	FairR	FairJG	140.20
PAGAN KING	b	3	117	8	1	$6\frac{1}{2}$	6^{2}	$8^{1\frac{1}{2}}$	$9\frac{1}{2}$	14^{1}	BlackH	ParkwoodStable	c-1.10
FORE ISUS	b	3	112	1	16	16	16	16	16	15^{1}	McTagueC	ErindaleStable	d-9.75
TIGNABRUICH	b	4	127	14	7	$10\frac{1}{2}$	10^{hd}	14^{1}	15^{1}	16	JohnstoneR	CampbellDA	192.70

a-Coupled as H. C. Hatch entry; b-H. R. Bain entry; c-Parkwood Stable entry; d-Erindale Stable entry; e-E. F. Seagram Estate entry.

Time, :23 2/5, :47 3/5, 1:14 2/5, 1:41 2/5, 1:55 2/5. Track fast.

	$2 Mutuels Paid			Official Booking Odds		
GOLDLURE (H. C. Hatch entry)	$10.55	$ 6.00	$ 3.30	$427\frac{1}{2}$—100	200—100	65—100
CEASE FIRE (H. R. Bain entry)		12.70	5.50		535—100	$152\frac{1}{2}$—100
SILVER JUBILEE (Parkwood Stable entry)			2.35			$17\frac{1}{2}$—100

Ch. c (3), by Sweepster—*Golden Lure, by *Golden Boss. Trained by Wm. H. Bringloe. Bred by H. C. Hatch, Toronto.
WENT TO POST—4:17. AT POST—13 minutes.

Start fair and slow. Won driving, second and third the same.

GOLDLURE, having clear racing room going to the first turn, followed in nearest attendance of ALDWYCH in the first three-quarters, took a slight lead midway of the final turn, then withstood a long, hard drive gamely in the last quarter mile. CEASE FIRE, in the first flight from the beginning, rallied gamely for the final drive after saving much ground and held on determinedly to the finish. SILVER JUBILEE, well placed in the early running, challenged strongly nearing the stretch, but tired in the final eighth. BUDRON broke out and bothered horses at the break, then raced well placed and finished with good energy in the final drive. RED PIRATE could not enter contention. ALDWYCH flattened out badly. ISLEWORTH was unable to reach contention. GOLDEN SILENCE was done early. SLYCAT had a rough trip. FORE ISUS held up the start and was placed on the outside.

Scratched—Dalamac and Goster.

Bunty Lawless was "the little guy's horse" when he won the King's Plate before an adoring throng at the old racetrack on Queen Street. The chunky, durable colt was owned by a feisty Irishman—a boxing promoter, hotel owner and ex-newsboy from Toronto's east-end gas-house district; was trained by a former teamster who knew little about thoroughbreds; was ridden by a jockey who was greeted in the winner's circle by his sobbing, grey-haired mother; was named after the owner's boyhood hero, James (Bunty) Lawless, a sort of big brother to countless youngsters in Toronto's tough Cabbagetown district; and was sired by a stallion who was killed in a stable fire before his only runner was foaled.

When *Bunty Lawless* died in 1956, just three days before the opening of the new Woodbine racetrack on land close to the farm where he used to roam, he belonged to everyone, from the kind who wore silk hats to those with holes in their boots. He had been acclaimed as Canada's "Horse of the Half-Century," an honour bestowed upon him in a poll conducted by the Canadian Press in 1951. The voters selected *Bunty Lawless* over *Inferno* and *Horometer*, for he had not only earned an ever-lasting reputation as a gifted racehorse, but his legacy as a sire left an indelible mark on the history of the Plate; his bloodlines would be traced through a succession of Plate winners for years afterwards.

But *Bunty*'s story is not only one of statistics, victorious progeny and sire lists, or triumphs on New York and Canadian tracks. It exudes melodrama played out in an era of scant purses and impoverished facilities, when the two-dollar bettor craved a hero to soar or despair over. It is a story that began largely because of the vindictive attitude of one man who was rebuffed by another owner.

The man who owned, bred and championed *Bunty Lawless* was W.F. (Willie) Morrissey, an eccentric character

ONE OF RACING'S MOST CONTROVERSIAL FIGURES, THE FEISTY IRISHMAN WILLIE MORRISSEY.

with a fiery temper but a sentimental disposition. Most people loved him; he was "one of the gang" who sat in the cheap seats. Racetrack officials usually disliked him since he was not a conformist, but Morrissey was the man who opened the race to everyone, confounding the tradition that the Plate was the property of the privileged. He proved small owners could send a winner into the race.

A former carnival barker who managed a string of prize fighters and a three-horse stable, Morrissey grew up as a street scrapper and hustler from the Eastern Avenue and Trinity Street district in Toronto. On many a Plate day the penniless "newsie" would stand outside the fence, looking through a knothole, wondering if he would ever have enough money to get inside to see a horse race, never dreaming of owning a horse, much less a King's Plate winner.

When it happened, Willie politely doffed the pearl-grey fedora that friends coaxed him to wear, shook hands with Lord Tweedsmuir, then disappeared with the cup into the milling crowds of the twenty-five-cent section in the grandstand. There he shook hands and exchanged greetings with the lifelong friends and "oldtimers" from his boyhood neighbourhood. In the moment of his greatest sports triumph, the ex-newsie did not forget the companions of his deprived days, any more than he forgot *Bunty Lawless* when he named the first horse he ever bred in the memory of the man who taught boys how to box, play hockey and baseball, and had acted as their lifeguard when they took prohibited swims in Lake Ontario.

On the Sunday morning, while thumbing over a sheaf of congratulatory telegrams in his suite at the Morrissey House on Yonge Street, he sounded like the golfer, who, after making a hole-in-one with his first shot of his first game, threw the clubs away. "I'm satisfied for the rest of my life; I never expected to live to see a day like yesterday. It was the best day of my life and I never expect to experience another thrill like the one it gave me to see *Bunty* win."

The triumph provided an extra stipend besides the almost $7,000 in purse money, for Morrissey had won a side-bet of $4,000

TRAINER JACK ANDERSON LEADS *BUNTY LAWLESS* INTO ENCLOSURE.

BUNTY LAWLESS | 3-year-old bay colt

Bunty Lawless (1935)	Ladder	Ladkin	Fair Play
			*Lading
		Panoply	Peter Pan
			Inaugural
	Mintwina	Mint Briar	*Assagai
			*Sweet Briar II
		Edwina	Celt
			Lady Godiva

Owner: W.F. (Willie) Morrissey, Toronto; *Trainer:* Jack Anderson; *Jockey:* J.W. (John) Bailey; *Breeder:* W.F. Morrissey

from a group of sportsmen known as the Stock Exchange Syndicate. It was a horse-to-horse wager, pitting *Bunty Lawless* against Harry Hatch's *Suffern*, who quit badly after forcing the pace for a mile. Morrissey was on a roll.

It began when he sent an agent to buy a horse for eight-hundred dollars. When the owner, Jack Whyte, realized who the buyer was, he upped the price to $1,000. The deal collapsed, but Morrissey, still simmering, retaliated a few days later when he claimed Whyte's well-bred filly, *Mintwina*, for $2,000 at Fort Erie. In her first start, however, she broke a bone in her foot. Morrissey wanted to put her down, but "Doc" Hodgson convinced him that he could save the filly by placing a cast on her leg. Later, an offer to breed to *Ladder*, a young stud owned by Frank Selke (a future hockey genius in Montreal and breeder of Hall of Fame inductee *Wonder Where*), was accepted—a mating that produced *Bunty Lawless*.

He was impressive at two, winning or placing second in all but one of his ten starts. Curiously, his only real setback came as the result of an equipment failure and it later prompted his owner to bet a bundle that his horse would win the Plate. It seemed that Morrissey was able to turn every misfortune to his advantage.

> Everything that happened to me was all for the best. If *Mintwina* hadn't been injured, *Bunty* wouldn't have been bred. And that defeat in Mrs. Orpen's Cup and Saucer race, when his bridle broke, was a bit of luck, too, though it didn't look like it at the time. If he had won the race I'd never have had the $4,000 horse-for-horse bet that *Bunty* would beat *Suffern* in the Plate.

Horsemen generally conceded that *Bunty Lawless* was the class of the fourteen starters in the Plate which, for the first time, was restricted to three- and four-year-olds. But many wondered whether his lengthy training schedule might have been too strenuous. He had been in training since 13 January at Dufferin Park, racing's "Little Saratoga," toiling all winter in the snow and over the frozen half-mile oval.

On Plate day his rider was J.W. (Jackie) Bailey, a Toronto boy who got a one-day release from his New York contract so he could ride the horse whose name would appear in the pedigrees of two future greats—*Victoria Park* and the magnificent *Windfields*, the stud who later proved to be an early cornerstone in E.P. Taylor's breeding empire. Ironically, the runnerup to *Bunty Lawless* was *Mona Bell*, a filly owned by James Cosgrave and a new OJC shareholder, E.P. Taylor.

With *Bunty*'s victory, Morrissey's ambitions had been realized and he declared that his silks would never be carried in the race again. He promised that if he ever developed another Plate candidate he would turn it over to a friend, Miss Mildred Kane. (He fulfilled half that promise when *Willie the Kid* won the 1940 Plate in her name. But he would run *Arbor Vita* under his burnt orange silks in 1943.)

1938 KING'S PLATE STAKES

FOURTH RACE
Woodbine Park
MAY 21, 1938

1 1-8 MILES. (Tempestuous, Oct. 3, 1936—1:51 1/5—4—109.) Seventy-Ninth Running KING'S PLATE. 50 Guineas, the gift of His Majesty King George VI, with $7,500 added by the Ontario Jockey Club. FOR 3- AND 4-YEAR-OLDS, the property of a British subject, residents of Ontario. Foaled, raised and trained in Ontario which have never won a race, either on the flat or across country, other than a race exclusively for 2-year-olds, and have never left Canada and have never been for a period of more than three months out of this province.

Horse	Eqt	A	Wt.	PP	St	¼	½	¾	Str	Fin	Jockey	Owner	Equiv. Odds Str't
BUNTY LAWLESS		3	117	5	1	3^{1}	3^{1}	3^{1}	1^{hd}	$1^{1\frac{1}{2}}$	BaileyJW	MorrisseyWmF	2.97½
MONA BELL		3	112	6	2	$1^{2\frac{1}{2}}$	$1^{2\frac{1}{2}}$	1^{1}	$2^{2\frac{1}{2}}$	2^{4}	LindbergH	CosgraveStable	25.20
CABIN GAL		3	112	11	8	7^{1}	$7^{\frac{1}{2}}$	$7^{1\frac{1}{2}}$	4^{1}	$3^{2\frac{1}{2}}$	PascumaA	GiddingsH	10.05
GRAND DAME		3	113	9	4	$5^{2\frac{1}{2}}$	4^{nk}	4^{nk}	$3^{\frac{1}{2}}$	$4^{1\frac{1}{2}}$	RemillardP	HendrieGM	3.75
CARACOLE		3	117	14	9	11^{4}	$10^{\frac{1}{2}}$	$8^{\frac{1}{2}}$	$8^{\frac{1}{2}}$	$5^{2\frac{1}{2}}$	McTagueC	HatchHC	a-4.20
SLYCAT	b	4	127	1	10	$9^{\frac{1}{2}}$	$6^{1\frac{1}{2}}$	6^{2}	6^{2}	$6^{\frac{1}{2}}$	SchiehF	MedwayStable	7.60
TABMARK		3	112	10	13	$6^{1\frac{1}{2}}$	5^{nk}	$11^{\frac{1}{2}}$	11^{1}	$7^{\frac{1}{2}}$	AimersT	FairJG	b-37.05
ALDWYCH		4	127	12	11	10^{nk}	11^{2}	10^{1}	9^{3}	8^{nk}	ValleeF	CowieRWR	25.45
SUFFERN	b	3	117	2	6	$2^{1\frac{1}{2}}$	2^{1}	$2^{\frac{1}{2}}$	5^{hd}	$9^{2\frac{1}{2}}$	BrammerD	HatchHC	a-4.20
RED PIRATE		4	132	8	3	$8^{\frac{1}{2}}$	$9^{\frac{1}{2}}$	5^{1}	10^{1}	10^{1}	DabsonH	ParkwoodStable	c-11.25
TABHIM		4	127	7	12	$12^{1\frac{1}{2}}$	$12^{1\frac{1}{2}}$	$13^{\frac{1}{2}}$	$13^{\frac{1}{2}}$	$11^{\frac{1}{2}}$	CourtneyG	SeagramP	b-37.05
TROUBLEMARK		3	117	4	7	$13^{2\frac{1}{2}}$	13^{2}	$12^{\frac{1}{2}}$	$7^{\frac{1}{2}}$	12^{1}	FairR	FairJG	b-37.05
BUCHAREST	b	3	112	13	14	14	14	14	14	$13^{\frac{1}{2}}$	SchmidlA	ParkwoodStable	c-11.25
WICKLOW	b	3	117	3	5	4^{nk}	8^{nk}	9^{nk}	12^{nk}	14	RallsC	RiverdaleStable	13.70

a-Coupled as H. C. Hatch entry; b-J. G. Fair and Phillip Seagram entry; c-Parkwood Stable entry.

Time, :24, :49, 1:14 2/5, 1:41 2/5, 1:54 2/5. Track fast.

Official Program Numbers↘	$2 Mutuels Paid			Official Booking Odds		
5-BUNTY LAWLESS..	$ 7.95	$ 5.95	$ 4.20	297½—100	197½—100	110—100
6-MONA BELL		19.30	10.65		865—100	432½—100
11-CABIN GAL			7.15			257½—100

B. c (3), by Ladder—Mintwina, by Mint Briar or *Traumer. Trained by Jack Anderson. Bred by W. F. Morrissey, Toronto.

WENT TO POST—3:59. AT POST—10½ minutes.

Start good and slow. Won handily, second and third driving.

BUNTY LAWLESS, well handled, was rated in close attendance of the pace the first mile, came to the outside of the pacemaker MONA BELL, wore her down and drew clear nearing the end. MONA BELL had speed from the start, was hustled into the lead at once, drew clear through the backstretch and held on gamely, but was unable to contend with the closing rush of the winner. CABIN GAL, rated off the pace the first seven-eighths, moved up threateningly entering the stretch, but was unable to threaten the leaders. GRAND DAME made a move after going a mile, then tired. CARACOLE came with a rush through the final half mile. TABMARK raced evenly. SLYCAT was in close quarters at the start, then made up ground. ALDWYCH could never threaten. SUFFERN forced the pace, then quit badly after going a mile.

On a chilly, cloudy Monday afternoon in May at the aging but majestic Woodbine Park, newspaper publisher George McCullagh captured the most coveted honour in Canada with Archworth, a mercury-footed colt he had bought for a mere $500 at a public auction of yearlings in 1937.

It was the most memorable moment in the eighty-year history of the Plate as King George VI became the first reigning monarch to witness the race that sprang into existence through the original gift of fifty "guineas" from his royal ancestor, Queen Victoria. He would bestow fifty sovereigns and a gold-plated trophy to the horseman whose orange and black silks had prevailed—an owner who had gained his love for horses in his boyhood while driving a butcher's delivery wagon.

"Royalty saluted royalty with the timeless love of a good man for a good horse," wrote Ralph Allen of *The Globe and Mail*, the newspaper that McCullagh published in a building named after William H. Wright, the mining prospector and stock promoter from Barrie who had bred the chestnut colt.

THE ROYAL LANDAU ARRIVES AT WOODBINE PARK WITH QUEEN ELIZABETH AND KING GEORGE VI, THE FIRST RULING MONARCH TO ATTEND THE KING'S PLATE.

The slender, brown-haired man who is Canada's King looked across the high maroon dais and held out his hand. 'I congratulate you. You have a great thoroughbred there.' The beautiful lady in blue smiled her soft lambent smile and voiced gracious agreement. 'Your horse is a real champion. He was never extended.' In this high moment, while 50,000 [the crowd was not more than 25,000] acclaiming subjects of Their Majesties pressed close for a first-hand look at history, a proud three-year-old colt called Archworth—royalty himself in the bravest equine tradition—danced lightly back to his stall and the niche of immortality turfdom reserves for its King's Plate winners.

Archworth's victory obviously delighted the royal party as His Majesty, an owner-breeder himself, had detected the supple chestnut colt in the post parade and asked Premier Mitchell Hepburn for the horse's name. The King's binoculars were rarely off the colt, who would streak away from the barrier when the webbing went up and maintain his searing pace, lengthening out with each stride over his straggling pursuers, to win by ten lengths. "Never have I seen a horse go out and take such a long lead and hold it," observed Queen Elizabeth. The Queen, interested and versed in racing's every detail, asked during the presentation ceremony if Mr. McCullagh had bred his champion himself. "No, ma'am," Mr. McCullagh replied. "He was bred by a soldier of the Queen, my old sidekick, Bill Wright. The credit for winning was not due to me, but to Bill."

Later McCullagh said that he had pleaded with the diffident Wright to go to the royal dais and take the honour in his place. "It's a great day for me, but I am only the stuffed shirt who bought him for $500. My thrill is nothing at all compared to the joy in Bill Wright's heart. It's been a lifelong dream. When he came to this country from England in 1907 he used to watch the races at Woodbine from a knothole in the fence. Standing there he vowed that if he ever struck it rich, he would try to breed the winner of the Plate. That dream came true today. All the credit goes to Bill, to trainer Mark Cowell, and to jockey [Denny] Birley."

Wright, a financier and miner, served in the Boer War and immigrated to Canada in 1907. In 1911 he and his brother-in-law, Ed Hargreaves, went prospecting near Porcupine, Ontario, and on a rabbit-shooting expedition discovered a vein of silver that would become the world's richest silver deposit. Wright served in World War I in France as a "millionaire private" and during the 1920s and 1930s invested in insurance and banking. In 1936 he bought Toronto's *Globe* newspaper and later *The Mail and Empire*. He then merged the two newspapers, putting McCullagh in charge as publisher.

Archworth's owner almost missed the Plate as he did not arrive at the track until the last minute. He had been visiting his seriously ill mother in London, and had motored to Toronto at the insistence of his parent. When he ascended the carpeted stairs to the royal plat-

TRAINER MARK COWELL, *ARCHWORTH* AND SYDNEY BIRLEY.

ARCHWORTH | 3-year-old chestnut colt

```
                          ┌─ Thunderer ──┬─ Broomstick
              Worthmore ──┤              └─ Jersy Lightning
              │           └─ Lady Moon'et ┬─ Dick Welles
Archworth ────┤                           └─ Moon'et
(1936)        │           ┌─ *Archiac ────┬─ Polymelus
              Archipelago ┤               └─ Keystone II
                          └─ *Samoa ──────┬─ Cylglad
                                          └─ Theresa II
```

Owner: C. George McCullagh, Toronto; *Trainer:* M.R. (Mark) Cowell; *Jockey:* Sydney D. Birley; *Breeder:* William H. Wright, Barrie, Ont.

---

form, he was minus a hat and wore a grey business suit.

In the weeks leading up to the much-anticipated royal visit, *Archworth* was put through an unorthodox training schedule by Cowell, one that was criticized by the media and some horsemen as being too punishing. They felt his horse might be "over-trained," and that either *Sea General* or *Jelwell*, who had beaten *Archworth* the year before, could upset the horse that had earned juvenile honours after winning the important Cup and Saucer and Clarendon Stakes. But *Archworth* toyed with his twelve foes in a race that signalled an important change in rules: it was now open only to three-year-olds.

The colt would later capture the Breeders' and Prince of Wales Stakes, but was never recognized as the winner of Canada's Triple Crown. The trio of races became an official event in 1959, the year of the next royal visit. When he was retired to stud at Wright's farm in Barrie, *Archworth* had won fifteen times and was second or third in sixteen other races, but

ROYALTY MEETS OWNER, *THE GLOBE AND MAIL* PUBLISHER GEORGE MCCULLAGH.

his gross purse earnings were just $31,234.

The only disappointing aspect of the Plate was the unexpected low turnout. Ontario Jockey Club officials predicted it might exceed one hundred thousand, and they printed seventy-thousand programs, most of which were later burned. Gallons of coffee and thousands of hot dogs were also dumped. Mutuel machines, which had been installed in the centrefield, as well as extra lavatory facilities, were hardly patronized. The armies of police and soldiers, employed to handle the hordes, could have stayed at home.

President A.E. Dyment blamed the press and police for scaring people away from the track because of the feared traffic congestion and overcrowding. He also said: "The lack of experience by those in charge of the Royal Tour was a prime cause of what can only be termed a fiasco."

1939 KING'S PLATE STAKES

THIRD RACE
Woodbine Park
MAY 22, 1939

1 1-8 MILES. (Tempestuous, Oct. 3, 1936—1:51⅕—4—109.) Eightieth Running KING'S PLATE. $50 Guineas, the gift of His Majesty, the King, with $10,000 added by the Club, the first horse to receive the Guineas, Stakes and $7,000; the second horse $1,500; the third horse $800, and the fourth horse $200. The breeder of the winner to receive $500. A Sweepstakes of $10 payable at time of entry, and $100 additional to start. FOR THREE-YEAR-OLDS, weight 112 lbs., the property of a British subject resident in Ontario, foaled, raised and trained in Ontario, that have never won a race, either on the flat or across country, other than a race exclusively for two-year-olds, have never left Canada, and have never been for a period of more than three months out of this Province. Winners to carry 5 lbs extra. No gelding allowances. Acceptances to be named through the entry box the day before the race, at usual time of closing. A Cup will be presented by the Club to the owner of the winner. Net value to winner, $8,720 and 50 Guineas.

Horse	Eqt	Wt.	PP	St	¼	½	¾	Str	Fin	Jockey	Owner	Equiv. Odds Str't
ARCHWORTH		117	12	1	1⁵	1⁵	1⁴	1⁶	1¹⁰	BirleySD	McCullaghCG	1.70
SEA GENERAL	b	117	8	7	8¹½	5½	4²	3⁴	2ʰᵈ	PascumaA	GiddingsH	2.25
SKYRUNNER	b	117	6	3	2½	2ⁿᵏ	2¹½	2ⁿᵏ	3³	WatsonR	ParkwoodStable	f-12.55
SYNGO BAY		112	7	11	4ʰᵈ	6¹	5²	4²	4⁵	LongdenJ	WebsterMrsRE	a-f-12.55
JELWELL		112	4	4	5ʰᵈ	4ⁿᵏ	3ⁿᵏ	5²	5¹	DeeringJ	CosgraveStable	6.85
BUDSIS	b	112	11	5	3¹	3ʰᵈ	6ⁿᵏ	6ⁿᵏ	6ʰᵈ	NashR	HatchHC	10.35
MILIUS	b	117	13	9	10½	10½	8½	8ʰᵈ	7¹½	RemillardP	MedwayStable	24.50
ENSIGN MARY		112	5	10	9²	7²½	7½	7ʰᵈ	8ⁿᵏ	BurnsE	H&RStable	22.80
THE CALF		117	9	12	12²	11²	10¹	9²	9³	McTagueC	WebsterMrsRE	a-f-12.55
RYE GRASS	b	112	10	8	7½	9¹	9ⁿᵏ	10²	10²	YoungS	BainHR	23.30
SEA CADET		117	3	2	11⁴	8²	11⁴	11⁵	11⁵	ThomasJ	RainesWT	63.95
McMARK		117	1	13	13	12	12	12	12	FodenN	FairJG	60.40
GOLD FAWN	b	112	2	6	6ⁿᵏ	Pulled up.				LindbergH	SeagramJEF	f-12.55

f–Mutuel field. a–Coupled as Mrs. R. E. Webster entry.

Time, :23³/₅, :48³/₅, 1:13³/₅, 1:40³/₅, 1:54²/₅. Track good.

	—$2 Mutuels Paid—			—Official Booking Odds—		
ARCHWORTH	$ 5.40	$ 3.60	$ 3.50	170—100	80—100	75—100
SEA GENERAL		3.60	2.90		80—100	45—100
SKYRUNNER (f-Field)			3.55			77½—100

Ch. c, by Worthmore—Archipelago, by *Archiac. Trained by Mark R. Cowell. Bred by Mr. William H. Wright, Barrie.
WENT TO POST—3:57½. AT POST—6 minutes.

Start good and slow. Won easily, second and third driving.
ARCHWORTH, much the best, sprinted into a clear lead at once, was steadied along under steady restraint the first three-quarters, then drew away to win as rider pleased. SEA GENERAL, shuffled back at the start and carried out at the first turn, worked way forward steadily thereafter and, closing gamely, outfinished SKYRUNNER. The latter raced in nearest pursuit of the pacemaker and held on well to the end. SYNGO BAY bumped at the first turn, saved ground thereafter and raced evenly. JELWELL, away slowly, made up ground. BUDSIS faltered after three-quarters. MILIUS could never threaten. RYE GRASS tired. GOLD FAWN pulled up after five-eighths and appeared to break down.

Scratched—Lightful and Saragossa.

If Willie Morrissey was the swash-buckling and wayward Rhett Butler, then surely Miss Mildred Kane was his glamorous temptress, Scarlett O'Hara, as they strolled into the winner's circle with her capricious bay colt, *Willie the Kid*. No woman had ever owned a Plate winner before, but it was her cerise silks that jockey Ronnie Nash wore while guiding the green and untried colt to a circuitous victory, and it was her "Rhett," the man who had bred the horse, who was wearing a big white sombrero, as he gallantly escorted Miss Kane.

Approval was immediate. The throng in Woodbine's densely packed grandstands roared and applauded loudly, welcoming the captivating spectacle, which looked more like a scene from Hollywood's greatest romantic film, *Gone With the Wind,* than a pious presentation of the King's Plate trophy by one of His Majesty's representatives.

In Ralph Allen's account in *The Globe and Mail,* where he said that the race was won by "a Dizzy Dean of a horse," he likened *Willie the Kid* to his unofficial guardian and godfather, Willie Morrissey:

PLATE CHAMPION *WILLIE THE KID* WAS UNRACED AT TWO AND A MAIDEN BEFORE PLATE WIN FOR JOCKEY RON NASH.

Better combinations of horse and man, and also worse, have won the King's Plate, but you may be sure that no more irresponsible twosome ever put the snatch on a monarch's gold. In practically every phase of this arresting project, from the start of the training season in early April until the race was over in the middle of a fine Saturday afternoon, the two Willies persisted in breaking all the rules, assaulting the conventions and waylaying the traditions of the oldest horse race in North America. Not that they did so in anything but the most gentlemanly way. Even the silk hat owners were warmed to the cockles of their aristocratic hearts by the sight of the dapper little man from Cabbagetown standing there in the enclosure with one of those atrocious Rhett Butler sombreros in his hand and his eyes resting fondly on the chucky colt that had won in spite of himself.

This Plate renewal was pure romance, the story of the ex-newsie, speculator and manager of prizefighters who had got lucky with a colt named *Bunty Lawless* and had vowed that his next good horse would run in his girlfriend's name. The Ontario Jockey Club frowned on Plate candidates being the ornament of an owner's female companion, and had also sighed with relief when the hotelman's coarsely named *Gas House* was unable to go to the post the year before when King George VI and Queen Elizabeth were at Woodbine.

Morrissey was a caustic individual who had an alarming habit of disrupting the establishment. He was a crusader for the lowly paid workers in the backstretch and eventually helped found an association in their behalf. He was also a prophet, who had put up a huge sum to back his claim that *Bunty Lawless* would win the 1938 Plate, and it was said that he had practically conducted a house-to-house canvass to tell everybody that *Bunty*'s half-brother, *Willie the Kid,* would "get you the money."

If he had been selling magazine subscriptions or vacuum cleaners, he could not have worked any harder in starting the slogan, "Listen, *Willie*'s in," and in so doing, knocking his odds down to almost 3-to-1. The son of *Mintwina* was unraced at two because his

WILLIE MORRISSEY'S ENTOURAGE (FROM LEFT) MILDRED KANE WITH SILVERWARE, MISS OLIVE ARMSTRONG ON HIS ARM AND JOCKEY RON NASH.

WILLIE THE KID | 3-year-old bay colt

Willie the Kid (1937)	*Roselyon	Sunstar	Sundridge
			Doris
		Desmond's Rose	Desmond
			Electric Rose
	Mintwina	Mint Briar	*Assagai
			*Sweet Briar II
		Edwina	Celt
			Lady Godiva

Owner: Miss Mildred A. Kane, Toronto; *Trainer:* Gordon (Pete) McCann; *Jockey:* Ronnie Nash; *Breeder:* William F. (Willie) Morrissey, Toronto

front legs were unsound. But he had trained smartly for Morrissey's close friend, Dr. Robert Hodgson, and the young man officially listed as his trainer, Gordon (Pete) McCann, a former jockey who had taken out his training licence only that year. Years later, Morrissey, McCann and Hodgson would all be inducted into Canada's Hall of Fame.

McCann had exercised him at Dufferin Park that winter, as well as *Hood,* which finished third behind the favoured *Curwen.* "I used to gallop *Hood* 'on the sly' for his trainer, Charlie Mitchell, while I trained *Willie the Kid* for Morrissey," said McCann years later. "I'd get a few dollars to gallop him. Morrissey didn't pay you much, but I at least knew what the other horse could do."

McCann did not have fond memories of the colt, who later lost the Prince of Wales Stakes to *Hood* by a length and did not race again that year. He made only ten starts in an injury-plagued career. "He had everything wrong with him. He was a cripple; a mixed-up thing." Jockey Nash, a Toronto boy whom Morrissey had hastily recruited from New York the day before the race when he found out that his regular rider. Tommy Aimers, who had broken his collar bone, might have agreed with McCann. Nash had to fight the inexperienced colt throughout the race as he went wide in both turns, drifting towards the outside fence before Nash was able to straighten him out. "You could have docked the Queen Mary in the room he took swinging into the homestretch," one horseman noted.

Another "bad actor" in the Plate was the new Clay Puett starting gate, being used for the first time in eastern Canada. Puett, an ex-jockey as well as starter from Arizona, was the inventor of the enclosed electric starting gate. It made its Canadian debut on 1 July 1939 at Vancouver's Exhibition Park, and was an immediate success. It was set on wheels so that it could be pulled off the racecourse quickly. By the end of 1940 Puett's gate was a fixture at all major North American tracks. In 1994, the Clay Puett Award was inaugurated by the University of Arizona to honour a person or persons for their outstanding contributions to the racing industry.

For starter Thomas (Nipper) Rowe, his first Plate experience with the "bomb" release electric activated gate was "a disaster" and resulted in one horse being left at the Puett gate. Unfortunately, Rowe and his staff allowed the eleven-horse field to start while *Ring Wise,* a 13-to-1 shot, was wheeling in reverse and out of the gate. One of the assistants had failed to secure the bar at the rear of the stall, which allowed *Ring Wise* to retreat. Rowe, who had done a head count, did not notice that he was minus a starter and pressed the button too soon. The OJC was sharply criticized for its failure to refund those who had wagered on Harry Giddings' gelding. The veteran trainer was philosophical: "Forget it Nipper. That's horse racing."

1940 KING'S PLATE STAKES

FOURTH RACE
Woodbine Park
MAY 18, 1940

1 1-8 MILES (1:51 1/5). Eighty-First Running KING'S PLATE. 50 Guineas, the gift of His Majesty, the King, with $7,500 added by the Ontario Jockey Club. 3-year-olds. Weight, 112 lbs. Winners to carry 5 lbs. extra. Owned by a British subject resident in Ontario. Foaled, raised and trained in Ontario which have never won a race, either on the flat or across country, other than a race exclusively for two-year-olds, have never left Canada and have never been for a period of more than three months out of this province. Breeder of winner to receive $500. Net value to winner $6,720; second, $1,200; third, $700; fourth, $100.

Horse	Eqt	Wt.	PP	St	¼	½	¾	Str	Fin	Jockey	Owner	Equiv. Odds Str't
WILLIE THE KID	b	112	10	4	$3^{1\frac{1}{2}}$	3^{1}	2^{2}	$2^{2\frac{1}{2}}$	1^{3}	NashR	KaneMissMA	3.35
CURWEN	b	117	11	5	2½	2½	1^{1}	1^{1}	2^{1}	WatsonR	HatchHC	3.20
HOOD		117	6	8	6^{hd}	6^{2}	$6^{1\frac{1}{2}}$	3½	$3^{3\frac{1}{2}}$	RemillardP	McIntyreJR	5.25
FROBISHER		117	7	6	4½	4^{hd}	$5^{1\frac{1}{2}}$	6^{3}	4^{2}	YoungS	ParkwoodStable	a-4.90
ROSE MOUNTAIN	b	117	2	9	$8^{1\frac{1}{2}}$	$8^{1\frac{1}{2}}$	4^{2}	4½	$5^{1\frac{1}{2}}$	McTagueC	RoseMountainStable	14.30
SILVOS	b	112	1	2	7^{1}	7^{2}	$8^{1\frac{1}{2}}$	7^{8}	6^{2}	LindbergH	SeagramJEF	12.05
KATIE BUD		112	8	7	5^{1}	5^{1}	3½	5^{1}	7^{4}	FodenN	GarrityD	12.60
STORM LIGHT		107	5	10	10	10	10	8^{2}	8^{4}	SpineN	HendrieGM	59.50
STAR GAIETY		112	4	3	9^{2}	$9^{3\frac{1}{2}}$	9^{2}	9^{hd}	9^{1}	CourtneyG	ErindaleStable	60.10
ABYDOS	b	117	3	1	$1^{2\frac{1}{2}}$	1½	7½	10	10	SchmidlA	ParkwoodStable	a-4.90
RING WISE		117	9	Wheeled						SmithCW	GiddingsH	13.10

a-Coupled as Parkwood Stable entry.

WENT TO POST 3:57. Time, :23 3/5, :48, 1:14 1/5, 1:42 2/5, 1:55 4/5. Track fast.

Mutuel Prices:

	$2 Mutuels Paid			Odds $1		
WILLIE THE KID	8.70	4.45	3.70	3.35	1.22½	.85
CURWEN		4.20	3.15		1.10	.57½
HOOD			4.30			1.15

B. c, by *Roselyon—Mintwina, by Mint Briar or *Traumer. Trainer, McCann Gordon (Pete). Bred by Morrissey W F, Toronto.

Start good and slow. Won easily; second and third driving. WILLIE THE KID, steadied in close attendance of the pace for three-quarters, moved up with a rush entering the stretch, bore out sharply, then closed with good courage and was going away at the end. CURWEN forced the pace of ABYDOS, took the lead when the latter faltered, saved ground and closed willingly to the finish. HOOD, away slowly, was steadied along and closed ground in the stretch run. FROBISHER came gamely through the final quarter mile after being blocked at the half-mile post. ROSE MOUNTAIN moved into contention after going a half mile, but was unable to threaten the leaders. SILVOS went evenly. KATIE BUD tired. ABYDOS quit. RING WISE wheeled at the start. STORM LIGHT was shuffled back sharply.

Scratched—Ffafryn.

BUDPATH OUTDISTANCED *UNDISTURBED* WHEN IT COUNTED—ON PLATE DAY.

BUDPATH AND BOBBY WATSON.

By 1941 the war in Europe was having an effect on every institution in Canada, and the King's Plate was no exception. The trophy, wrought by a silversmith in England and imported each spring for thirty years, was resting at the bottom of the Atlantic ocean. It had been lost at sea with a convoy sunk by German submarines. Hastily, a replica of the ornate cup with its carved handles and lid had to be fashioned by a Toronto artisan.

More significant, neither the Governor General nor Ontario's Lieutenant Governor Albert Matthews would be in attendance in 1941. Representatives of the throne were following King George VI's policy that no public appearance should be made other than those directly related to the furtherance of the war effort. This policy did not extend to His Majesty's horses, which continued to race with great success that year, in spite of objections by a vociferous anti-racing fraternity. The group, believing that the sport drained resources at a time when a total war effort was needed to ensure Britain's victory, was chagrined and frustrated by the King's patronage of the sport. To withdraw his support that year, however, would have been particularly painful since by November his filly *Sun Chariot* and his colt *Big Game* were at the top of the list of leading two-year-olds.

The Ontario Jockey Club was itself concerned about the future of its operations for what people now referred to as "The Duration." It was feeling the growing pressure that the King's Plate should be opened up to all Canadians, and that Jim Speers in Winnipeg and Fred Orpen at Toronto's Dufferin Park were offering larger purses for their major races than for the race that still outdrew any other in Canada. A costly horsemen's strike also occurred during the spring meeting as trainers were charged with inciting grooms to refuse to take horses over to the paddock. Although racing went on with small

fields, OJC officials ordered trainers to remove their horses and equipment from the grounds. At Thorncliffe Park in Leaside, officials denied track privileges to horsemen who had taken part in the Woodbine strike. It was also clear that the continuance of racing was putting some strain on resources needed elsewhere, including labour and transportation, and it had its opponents at home. Any indication that King George VI supported its continuance in Britain, then, would have influenced the government in Ottawa.

By taxing betting, however, the government had created an important source of revenue for itself that year; it took five per cent out of all monies wagered and put a twenty per cent tax on all paid admissions. So in early 1941 at least, no interdict on racing seemed near at hand and the OJC began preparations for the opening of the spring meeting, including the Plate race and a Charity Day five days later, the proceeds of which were to go to the Lord Mayor's Fund for War Sufferers in Britain.

On 17 May, a crowd of more than twenty eight thousand assembled at Woodbine. It soon looked to them as if the day would belong to the round and rubicund Squire of Oakville, Harry Giddings. In the first race, his speedster, *Ten to Ace*, a highly regarded son of *Stand Pat*, easily sped away from the field. *Ten to Ace*'s win further heightened interest in the Plate because *Undisturbed*, a towering bay gelding who was also sired by *Stand Pat*, had won the opening day feature the year before and was the horse that handicappers figured would give Giddings a record eighth Plate victory. All he had to do to beat his eight foes was to run on his 1940 form. Parkwood Stable's entry of *Skyliner* and *Warrigan* was given a chance, as well as Harry Hatch's *Budpath*, who had raced well as a two-year-old but could never catch *Undisturbed* in the important races. However, the *Budpath* that *Undisturbed* faced in their first meeting as three-year-

BUDPATH | 3-year-old chestnut colt

```
                                    ┌─ Sunstar
                     ┌─ *North Star III ─┤
                     │              └─ Angelic
          ┌─ *Buddy Bauer ─┤
          │          │              ┌─ Cunard
          │          └─ Bed of Roses ─┤
Budpath ──┤                          └─ *Melton Mowbray
(1938)    │
          │                         ┌─ Sweep
          │          ┌─ Sweepster ──┤
          │          │              └─ Oktibbena
          └─ Luress ─┤
                     │              ┌─ *Golden Boss
                     └─ *Golden Lure ─┤
                                    └─ Perfidious
```

Owner: H.C. (Henry) Hatch, Toronto; *Trainer:* Lloyd Gentry
Jockey: Robert (Bobby) Watson; *Breeder:* H.C. Hatch

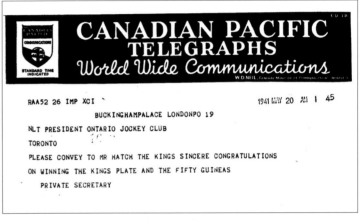

CONGRATULATIONS FROM KING GEORGE VI'S PRIVATE SECRETARY.

SUB-LIEUTENANT CLIFF HATCH JR. ACCEPTED THE TROPHY WITH TRAINER LLOYD GENTRY, JOCKEY WATSON AND OJC PRESIDENT A.E. DYMENT.

olds had been thoroughly prepared and was "dead fit." Lloyd Gentry had trained *Budpath* that spring at Dufferin, when the track was still under snow and ice, with a view of running the horse out in front from the break and staying there. "Have him give his Sunday best for five furlongs or so and break his rivals' hearts," was the way *The Daily Star*'s Joe Perlove described Gentry's conditioning program. When the gates opened it was *Budpath* jack-rabbiting into the lead, opening up a length or two against *Passa Grille* and *Undisturbed* at various stages of the contest. This was where he won the race, in the first six furlongs, for when the run down the stretch arrived, *Budpath* was still cruising under the hand-riding of jockey Bobby Watson.

Harry Hatch's son, Sub-Lieutenant Clifford Hatch, again accepted the Plate for his father, who watched the presentation from his box. The victory was his third and confirmed Hatch as one of Canada's most astute breeders. His successes, which surfaced with the Plate wins of two sons by *Sweepster*, *Monsweep* and *Goldlure* in 1936 and 1937, had continued through *Budpath*'s dam, *Luress*, a daughter of *Sweepster* and a full-sister to *Goldlure*. *Luress* would later foal the 1944 Plate winner *Acara*. While *Budpath* was universally acknowledged as a strong and durable horse, he would collapse and die of a heart attack in 1942. He won five of his twelve starts, including the Canadian Derby at Polo Park in Winnipeg, and was out of the money only twice.

Two interested spectators at the opening day of the race meeting were Canadian industrialists E.P. Taylor, who became OJC shareholder that year, and Harry Carmichael, the "dollar-a-year men" Canada had loaned to Washington and London. They resumed their racing stables in 1944.

1941 KING'S PLATE STAKES

FOURTH RACE
Woodbine Park
MAY 17, 1941

1 1–8 MILES (1:51⅕). Eighty-Second Running KING'S PLATE. $8,000 Added and Fifty Guineas, the gift of His Majesty, King George VI. 3-year-olds. Net value to winner $6,670 and fifty guineas; second, $1,200; third, $700; fourth, $100.

Horse	Eqt	Wt.	PP	St	¼	½	¾	Str	Fin	Jockey	Owner	Odds $1
BUDPATH	b	117	9	1	1²	1¹	1¹	1¹	1²½	WatsonR	HatchHC	3.25
UNDISTURBED	b	117	5	2	3ⁿᵏ	3²	2¹½	2²½	2³½	SmithCW	GiddingsH	1.05
ATTRISIUS	b	112	4	7	7²½	6²½	6²½	4½	3½	PraterD	RiverdaleStable	61.80
TAFFRAIL		112	3	4	4¹½	4¹½	4²	3½	4¹½	BirleySD	SeagramJEF	9.95
SKYLINER		117	8	9	8²	8⁵	8⁵	7⁵	5½	ConveyJ	ParkwoodStable	a-2.70
WARRIGAN		117	7	8	5¹	5¹½	5¹½	6¹	6²	McTagueC	ParkwoodStable	a-2.70
PASSA GRILLE	b	112	1	3	2¹½	2ⁿᵏ	3¹½	5¹½	7⁵	McDougallE	HendrieGM	b-35.90
DEPOSITOR	b	112	6	5	9	9	9	8²½	8⁵	RemillardP	MedwayStable	17.45
LADY WALES	b	112	2	6	6¹½	7¹½	7²	9	9	MeynellH	HendrieGM	b-35.90

a–Coupled as Parkwood Stable entry; b–G. M. Hendrie entry.
WENT TO POST—4:07. AT POST—½ minute. Time, :23³/5, :47⁴/5, 1:14, 1:41²/5, 1:56⁴/5. Track fast.

Mutuel Prices:

		—$2 Mutuels Paid——			——Odds $1——		
BUDPATH		8.50	3.40	3.25	3.25	.70	.62½
UNDISTURBED			2.90	2.75		.45	.37½
ATTRISIUS				9.05			3.52½

Ch. c, by Buddy Bauer—Luress, by Sweepster. Trainer, Gentry Lloyd. Bred by Hatch H C, Toronto.

Start good and slow. Won handily; second and third driving. BUDPATH took command going to the first turn, was steadied along the backstretch, shook off UNDISTURBED and won under strong hand riding. UNDISTURBED moved up to force the pace after three-quarters, but was not good enough. ATTRISIUS moved up in the closing five-eighths and finished willingly. TAFFRAIL raced close up throughout. SKYLINER closed well. PASSA GRILLE tired after three-quarters. WARRIGAN did not menace the leaders. The others were outrun.

Scratched—Andsan and Top Boots.

1942 | TEN TO ACE

Harry Giddings became a horseman early in his teens because of a claustrophobic fear of schoolrooms and the fact that his father, Harry Senior, had some of the finest thoroughbred racing stock in Canada on his Cedar Grove farm and needed somebody to take care of them. "He eventually gave up trying to force me to get an education and bought me a few mares for $25 or $30 apiece, and then put me to work," recalled the ruddy-faced Squire of Oakville in 1942 after saddling his eighth Plate winner, one more than any trainer has achieved in the race's 150-year history. It was the first race to be run under his distinctive red, white and blue silks of the man who bred, owned and trained the horses in his stable. A robust horseman who had been a sturdy shot-putter in his schooldays and later owned "the best stable of fighting cocks in these parts," Giddings won four Plates for his father, the first in 1911 with *St. Bass*, two for R.W.R. (Bob) Cowie, and had saddled the future Hall of Famer, *Horometer*, for Oshawa automobile industrialist Sam McLaughlin.

Ten to Ace OPENED UP A FIFTEEN-LENGTH LEAD AND COASTED HOME ALONE.

Ten to Ace was Gidding's first Plate winner, and his last, and it would inject more drama and pathos into his life than he or any blasé observer could possibly have imagined. A striking chestnut colt with a white face, *Ten to Ace* was Giddings' royal flush, a horse that he described as being, "Maybe the fastest horse I've ever trained. After the way he ran today I can't tell you how good he is going to be." The comment was made after *Ten to Ace* opened up a fifteen-length lead on a sloppy racetrack at Woodbine and then coasted home ten lengths in front of his closest opponent in the Plate.

When the colt was still nursing from his mother, Giddings pointed to him with the pride of a connoisseur: "That one will write turf history. Don't say anything about him. Anything can happen to a growing colt. If he goes to the races, as he should in due course, mark what I tell you—he'll show his heels to the fastest of them. He's the best foal ever dropped on this farm."

What happened on 23 May, when *Ten to Ace*

1942 KING'S PLATE STAKES

FOURTH RACE
Woodbine Park
MAY 23, 1942

1 1-8 MILES (1:51$\frac{1}{5}$). Eighty-Third Running KING'S PLATE. $8,000 Added and Fifty Guineas, the gift of His Majesty, King George VI. 3-year-olds. Foaled in Ontario. Allowances. Net value to winner $6,430 and 50 Guineas; second, $1,200; third, $700; fourth, $100.

Horse	Eqt	Wt.	PP	St	¼	½	¾	Str	Fin	Jockey	Owner	Odds $1
TEN TO ACE		117	1	1	1^{10}	1^{15}	1^{15}	1^{12}	1^{10}	SmithCW	GiddingsH	.27½
COSSACK POST	b	117	3	3	$3^{2\frac{1}{2}}$	3^{3}	$2^{2\frac{1}{2}}$	2^{5}	$2^{2\frac{1}{2}}$	WatsonR	HatchHC	5.15
DEPRESSOR		117	4	6	$4^{1\frac{1}{2}}$	$4^{2\frac{1}{2}}$	$3^{\frac{1}{2}}$	3^{6}	3^{8}	HorvathK	MedwayStable	7.60
NORTH SWEPT		112	2	2	$2^{2\frac{1}{2}}$	2^{2}	4^{10}	5^{1}	4no	AimersT	MacDonaldStable	38.50
VALKYRIAN		112	5	4	5^{1}	5^{1}	5^{1}	4^{1}	$5^{3\frac{1}{2}}$	NashR	ParkwoodStable	31.40
MUCKLE		117	6	5	6^{3}	6^{3}	7	$6^{\frac{1}{2}}$	$6^{3\frac{1}{2}}$	LeavittR	CowieRWR	13.10
JAYEFFDEE		112	7	7	7	7	$6^{\frac{1}{2}}$	7	7	WoodhouseH	PickeringStable	64.25

OFF AT 4:47 (Eastern War Time). Time, :23$\frac{1}{5}$, :48, 1:14$\frac{2}{5}$, 1:42$\frac{4}{5}$, 1:57$\frac{4}{5}$. Track muddy.

Mutuel Prices:

	$2 Mutuels Paid			Odds $1		
TEN TO ACE	2.55	2.50	2.40	.27½	.25	.20
COSSACK POST		3.00	2.50		.50	.25
DEPRESSOR			2.70			.35

Ch. c, by Stand Pat—Royalite, by Lucullite. Trainer, Giddings Harry. Bred by Giddings Harry, Oakville, Ont.

Start good from stall gate. Won easily; second and third driving. TEN TO ACE, easily best, sprinted into command at the start, was taken under strong restraint going to the first turn, opened up a long lead after straightening away in the backstretch, saved ground entering the stretch and finished with speed in reserve. COSSACK POST, never far back from the leaders while under stout reserve, was placed under urging midway of the final turn and closed with good courage, but was no match for the winner. DEPRESSOR, also under early reserve, was placed to punishment in the final three-eighths, came extremely wide entering the stretch and finished willingly. NORTH SWEPT forced the pace for three-quarters, but tired steadily when urged. VALKYRIAN was unable to reach the leaders at any stage. MUCKLE never threatened at any stage. JAYEFFDEE was outrun throughout.

Scratched—Bill's Gift, Single Claim, Rhadagus and Clocklike.

TRAINER HARRY GIDDINGS' RECORD COLLECTION OF PLATE TROPHIES REACHED EIGHT AS HE ACCEPTS PLATE FROM LIEUTENANT GOVERNOR ALBERT MATTHEWS. C.W. (CHARLIE) SMITH RODE THE WINNER.

TEN TO ACE | 3-year-old chestnut colt

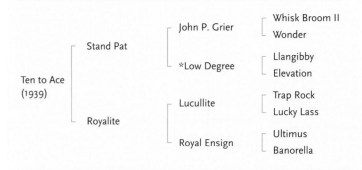

Owner: Harry Giddings Jr., Oakville; *Trainer:* Harry Giddings Jr.
Jockey: C.W. (Charlie) Smith; *Breeder:* Harry Giddings Jr.

won "by as far as a small country boy can throw a big red apple," was best described by *The Globe and Mail*'s Jim Coleman:

> The 1942 racing season hasn't opened yet as far as *Ten to Ace* is concerned. It's quite true that *Ten to Ace* was under racing silks on Saturday afternoon, but it was only a workout. . . . It would be nothing short of puckish humour to refer to the eighty-third running of the King's Plate as a 'race.' Of course, it had all the essential earmarks of a race for approximately the first fifteen yards but, after that, the *Ace* bounded ahead in a manner which suggested that a bee must have taken a bite out of his buttocks. . . . He was five lengths on top going around the clubhouse turn and jockey Charlie Smith was employing a combination half-nelson and stranglehold in an attempt to slow him down. But, after that, the horse's superior strength asserted itself so Smith just pursed his lips, blew his wad of bubble gum into the infield and hung on for his very life. . . . Two extremely important questions are before the house. They are: (a) Is *Ten to Ace* really as good as his ridiculously easy victory would indicate? (b) Are the other domestic three-year-olds, who sloshed through the mud behind *Ten to Ace*, merely a bunch of blue-blooded equine bums?

Coleman reported that the colt's next race was in Winnipeg and suggested that R. James Speers, the breeder and turf tycoon who promoted the Canadian Derby, would save everybody a lot of trouble if he sat down and mailed Giddings a cheque for $5,000, thus obviating the necessity of the *Ace* taking a lengthy and cramped railway journey to Manitoba. "*Ten to Ace* won't lose at Winnipeg unless some exasperated Western gambler shoots the colt before he crosses the finishing line."

What happened out West would fall under the category of "That's horse racing." *Ten to Ace* came out of the starting gate at Polo Park "like a runaway locomotive" and opened up a twenty-length lead. But suddenly his long, long stride began to shorten. *Maginot Line* overtook him, as did the rest of the field. The eastern invader finished last. His trainer's excuse was that the horse had contracted "car fever" en route to Winnipeg and it had ruined his constitution. But perhaps he was, as many horsemen suspected, just a sprinter.

Ten to Ace's highs and lows had come at a time when Canadians needed both entertainment and relief from the grim war news, the daily reports of death and destruction. Earlier in 1942 there had been reports that racing would continue undisturbed, at least for the foreseeable future, in spite of the war. OJC president A.E. Dyment summed up that confidence in his report to the board: "When it is realized that racing is still being carried on in the Old Country even through the worst phases of the war up to date, and that horse racing has continued in both occupied and unoccupied France, it is difficult to see why we should look forward to any serious interruption of the sport in this country."

While racing would survive the food and fuel rationing and the lack of stable help, one notable casualty in 1942 was the black and yellow silks of the Seagrams. For the first time since 1890, the family colours were absent. Philip Seagram, who had kept the family streak alive in 1938, was killed in action in 1941.

TEN TO ACE BROKE LIKE A ROCKET FROM THE FIRST STALL OF THE STARTING GATE.

n May 1943 stories in certain newspapers predicted that a "Seadrome Route to Europe" would be built: a series of floating islands, with deep draughts for stability, that would allow planes to transport cargo and passengers across the Atlantic in 800-mile hops, "with hotels for those who wish to await the next plane." Such futuristic proposals were often part of the Allied propaganda effort to keep spirits up on the home front during the war that seemed destined to continue for another two years. The Seadrome, of course, never became a reality, but deep-draughted sea platforms were later developed to mine the ocean beds for fuel.

Another rumour, which had circulated during the weeks leading up to the eighty-fourth running of the King's Plate, did become a reality later that year when the Ontario Jockey Club announced on 25 November that any three-year-old thoroughbred foaled in Canada would be eligible for future runnings of the historic race. The OJC had departed from its long-standing policy of restricting the Plate to horses foaled in Ontario; from now on, it was opened up to owners in any part of the Dominion. The change, announced by Club president Colonel K.R. Marshall, was greeted by *The Globe and Mail*'s Jim Coleman in his usual candid, biting style:

> Yes, gents, from now on the King's Plate is going to be a horse race instead of an exclusive neighbourhood clambake. The Woodbine gates have been flung open to admit those unfortunates who live in benighted sections of the wastelands, beyond the borders of our own glorious Province! The Plate finally has grown up, but 84 years is a rather prolonged period of adolescence. . . . Colonel Marshall and his fellow directors should be congratulated. It demonstrates that they are progressive and open-minded. As an illustration of the wide scope of their interests, it is necessary only to point out that they have opened up the Plate and also have decided to build lavatories

for the stable help. . . . Seriously, though, the OJC decision will be good for racing.

The OJC also removed a restriction that prevented horsemen from training their Plate candidates outside Canada, and (of more importance) announced the introduction of the Plate Trial Stakes, which would allow trainers to give their horses a "tightener" instead of having to run them a mile-and-a-furlong on the first day of the spring meeting. A champion for western rights and a horseowner himself, Coleman noted:

> Horsemen will be delighted that the OJC has finally abandoned that ridiculous scheme of running the King's Plate on the very first day of the season. A lot of good racing stock was ruined before the OJC agreed with those critics who protested plaintively that three-year-olds aren't ready to run nine furlongs on their first trip to the post. Under ordinary circumstances most of the horses which ran in the Plate weren't worth the price of hamburger by the end of the season. Look at this year's field. Only one of those horses—*Tulachmore*—still was in training by the end of the season. The rest of them—*Paolita*, *Grandpal*, *Sweepgold*, *Arbor Vita*—were washed up, perhaps for all time.

The restructuring of the Plate's conditions had to be approved by King George VI, who advised the Club that he "considered the idea one of encouragement to the expanding breeding industry in Canada." It is noteworthy that the OJC's attitude towards horsemen, breeders and the changing times had occurred after the influx of new faces on the board—the new president Colonel Marshall, Allen Case, J.E. Smallman, J.E. Frowde Seagram, George C. Hendrie and Sam McLaughlin, who all owned horses themselves.

However, the deplorable weather conditions through the spring

OWNER CHARLES H. HEMSTEAD AND JOCKEY PAT REMILLARD.

PAOLITA | 3-year-old black filly

Paolita (1940)
- *North Wales II
  - Blandford
    - Swyndford
    - Blanche
  - *Chaucrita
    - Chaucer
    - Cry Help
- Boca Grande
  - *Hourless
    - *Negofol
    - Hour Glass II
  - Captiva
    - *Brown Prince II
    - Thirty-third

Owner: Charles H. Hemstead, Toronto; *Trainer:* William (Willie) Thurner
Jockey: Pat Remillard; *Breeder:* George M. Hendrie, Hamilton, Ont.

training period, along with a coughing epidemic that eliminated all four Parkwood Stable entries, had a profound effect on the board's decision to permit a "tightener" before the Plate. Few horses in the field of eight survivors were barely fit on 22 May when Charles Hemstead's lightly raced filly *Paolita* paid a bundle as she stumbled through the mud to score the biggest upset since *Maternal Pride* in 1924. Trained by Willie Thurner and ridden by Pat Remillard, the filly paid $76.50 for a victory that was achieved in 2:02 3/5, the slowest time ever recorded while the Plate was still a nine-furlong event.

Described as a "ploughing match," the race produced a bizarre finish for a crowd estimated at more than thirty-five thousand. Remillard, who bounced off the inside rail as he shot through a small opening in the far turn, hit the top of the stretch with a filly that first of all drifted out, then lugged in, narrowly avoiding the three horses on her heels—*Arbor Vita, Tulachmore* and *Grandpal*. Seconds after *Paolita* staggered across the finish line, the objection sign flashed on the infield board. The riders of the first four finishers, Remillard, Tommy Aimers, Alf Shelhammer and Frankie Mann, whose six-year suspension had been lifted by the Incorporated Canadian Racing Associations that season, were subsequently interviewed by the

stewards and told that *Paolita* had not caused interference. Mann was the last of the eight riders involved in the 1937 probe into a gambling scandal to be restored to good standing. He was allowed to ride in Quebec and the U.S. during his ICRA suspension in Ontario, and during his career won six King's Plates—three at Woodbine and three at Blue Bonnets in Montreal. Mann was inducted into the Hall of Fame in 2000 in the Legends category.

Hemstead paid $1,175 for the black filly at a yearling auction sale. Its breeder was George M. Hendrie, who won the King's Plate in 1918 with *Springside* and was president of the OJC for just two months before he died in 1942. Owner of the St. Regis and Carson Hotels and a restaurant at the Canadian National Exhibition, Hemstead at one time held a trainer's licence and was a breeder of some reputation. He was one of the first directors of the Canadian Thoroughbred Horse Society and later a director of the Horsemen's Benevolent and Protective Association. On the afternoon of *Paolita*'s huge upset a guest in his box at Woodbine was Toronto-born Hollywood idol, Mary Pickford. Hemstead died in 1961, shortly after fires destroyed the Carson Hotel and his restaurant at the CNE. He also lost the St. Regis in legal action with its former owner. It was said by his family doctor "that he died of a broken heart."

TRAINER WILLIE THURNER.

1943 KING'S PLATE STAKES

FOURTH RACE
Woodbine Park
MAY 22, 1943

1 1-8 MILES (1:51⅕). Eighty–Fourth Running KING'S PLATE. $8,000 Added and 50 Guineas, the gift of His Majesty, King George VI. 3-year-olds. Foaled in Ontario. Weight 112 lbs. Winners, 5 lbs. extra. Net value to winner $6,640; second, $1,200; third, $700; fourth, $100; breeder, $500.

Horse	Eqt	Wt.	PP	St	¼	½	¾	Str	Fin	Jockey	Owner	Odds $1
PAOLITA		112	6	3	6½	5nk	3nk	1hd	12½	RemillardP	HemsteadCH	37.25
ARBOR VITA		117	7	5	5²	7⁵	7⁴	4⁴	2²	AimersT	MorrisseyWF	1.10
TULACHMORE	b	117	2	7	7²	6nk	6¹	3½	3²	MannF	MacDonaldStable	3.10
GRANDPAL	b	117	1	6	4¹½	4³	4½	2¹	4⁶	ShelhammerA	HatchHC	a-4.95
GRAY SYNGO		112	5	8	8	8	8	7nk	5²½	SmithCW	WebsterMrsRE	32.25
PACIFIC ISLE		107	4	1	3²	3nk	2nk	8	6⁶	BirleySD	NorthgraveWTJr	35.90
SWEEPGOLD	b	117	3	4	1½	1²	1²	5½	7¹½	HorvathK	HatchHC	a-4.95
GALLANT FOE	b	112	8	2	2²	2²	5½	6nk	8	PalaezH	RiverdaleStable	2.40

a-Coupled as H. C. Hatch entry.

WENT TO POST—4:58½. OFF AT 4:59 (Eastern War Time). Time, :24³/₅, :50, 1:17³/₅, 1:48, 2:02³/₅. Track heavy.

Mutuel Prices:

	—$2 Mutuels Paid—			—Odds $1—		
PAOLITA	76.50	19.30	6.05	37.25	8.65	2.02½
ARBOR VITA		3.75	2.90		.87½	.45
TULACHMORE			3.20			.60

Blk. f, by *North Wales II.—Boca Grande, by *Hourless. Trainer, Thurner Willie. Bred by Hendrie George M., Hamilton, Ont.

Start good from stall gate. Won driving; second and third the same. PAOLITA, away well and taken in hand when outrun. moved into a short lead entering the stretch, was taken out into the better footing midway of the stretch and, responding to vigorous urging, held ARBOR VITA safe at the close. The latter was allowed to settle into his best stride before being called upon, began moving up leaving the backstretch, responded willingly to strong urging and fought it out stubbornly at the close. TULACHMORE, rated behind the leaders and sent up on the outside on the lower turn, finished stubbornly. GRANDPAL, never far back, moved up menacingly entering the stretch, but could not keep up. GRAY SYNGO closed a gap. PACIFIC ISLE raced well for three-quarters, then tired. SWEEPGOLD set the pace for seven-eighths, then faltered. GALLANT FOE showed speed for three-quarters and tired badly.

Pronounced by his critics as "purely a sprinter" and by other critics as "fast horse, but no heart," *Acara* disproved both theories as he easily won the eighty-fifth running of the King's Plate before a throng in excess of thirty-six thousand at Woodbine Park. While proving he was more than a weak-hearted sprinter who "ran out of gas" (a hardship motorists could identify with during the wartime rationing of fuel) after six furlongs, *Acara* became the first grey-coloured horse to ever win the show-piece of Canadian racing.

Owned and bred by distiller Harry C. Hatch, who again shied away from the winner's circle while his son Sub-Lieutenant Douglas Hatch, accepted the Plate, *Acara* was a grey colt by the imported French stallion, **Belfonds*, who stood in Virginia. Hatch had sent his stable's great producing mare, *Luress*, a half-sister to 1937 Plate winner *Goldlure* and dam of 1941 Plate victor, *Budpath*, to the United States and the court of the aging grey sire, but returned her to foal the colt at his Agincourt farm northeast of Toronto.

JOCKEY BOBBY WATSON DISPLAYS KING'S PLATE TROPHY WITH HARRY HATCH'S SON, SUB-LIEUTENANT DOUGLAS HATCH.

The 27 May Plate was another "Hurry home with Hatch" day, a popular slogan at Woodbine in the 1930s and 1940s, as the runners of the former liquor store owner finished second and fourth. *Ompalo,* ridden by a future steward and starter for the Ontario Jockey Club, Sam Hall, and *Sayonara,* grabbed off second and fourth place. Only Medway Stable's *Korafloyd* prevented a complete sweep by Hatch, who was winning his fourth Plate in nine years. It was also noted that half the field was either bred by Hatch, or was by his stallion, *Sweepster,* who, unfortunately, had been allowed to "escape" to California. Another salient point was that the first four finishers had all taken advantage of the new Plate rule which allowed owners to winter their candidates in the southern climes of the United States.

While jockey Bobby Watson was accepting the acclaim of the huge crowd, telling reporters that *Acara* had almost pulled his arms from the sockets when he tried to keep him off the early pace before taking command in the far turn, his fellow jockeys were not quite as hospitable when he returned to the riders' quarters. They blamed him for the traffic jam at the first turn, claiming that he came over sharply on three horses and almost caused Riverdale Stable's *Attester* to fall. He would have fallen, except he was jammed between two horses. *Attester*'s jockey, Henry Palaez, who came close to sliding out of his saddle, was shoved back into it by Herb Lindberg, the rider aboard the favoured *Heulwen*. Lindberg momentarily checked his horse while rescuing Palaez, who later

had to be restrained from going after Watson. *Heulwen, Nimblefoot,* who had both defeated *Acara* in the major races the year before, along with *Gypster* and *Attester* all suffered cuts and injuries in the melee of flying hooves.

Before the Plate, stewards had warned the riders that they "wanted a clean race," and obviously felt there was no need for an inquiry; they did not call any of the riders to the stand. The jocks similarly avoided a confrontation and lodged no claims of foul. Ironically, Watson got the ride on *Acara* three days before the Plate when the colt's regular rider, Bobby Summers, suffered a knee injury.

One horse that escaped the bumping, Dr. L.H. Appleby's *Cum Laude,* who

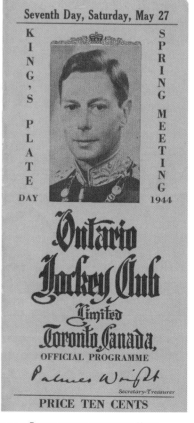

Seventh Day, Saturday, May 27

KING'S PLATE DAY

SPRING MEETING

1944

Ontario Jockey Club Limited Toronto, Canada.

OFFICIAL PROGRAMME

Palmer Wright
Secretary-Treasurer

PRICE TEN CENTS

1944 PLATE COVER FEATURED KING GEORGE VI.

Acara MADE HISTORY WHEN HE BECAME THE FIRST GREY STARTER TO EVER WIN THE PLATE.

ACARA | 3-year-old grey colt

Acara (1941)	*Belfonds	Isard II	Le Samaritain
			Irish Idyll
		La Buire	Perth
			Lark
	Luress	Sweepster	Sweep
			Oktibbena
		*Golden Lure	*Golden Boss
			Perfidious

Owner: Harry C. Hatch, Toronto; *Trainer:* Cecil Howard
Jockey: Robert (Bobby) Watson; *Breeder:* H.C. Hatch

finished fifth, had the "longest trip" that day as he had made the arduous journey by rail from Vancouver to become the first non-Ontario horse to ever run in the Plate.

This was the first Plate open to westerners, or Quebeckers, and it was an honour that Jim Speers of Winnipeg, who had done so much to improve the quality of racing in the West, had longed to achieve. His hopes that year would have been carried by *Gower Mon*, a horse that Lester (Whittlin' Knifey) Knifong, was wintering in California. However, when *Gower Mon* stumbled off a boxcar in Toronto after an ordeal that "Knifey" swore took twenty-nine days, the horse was so thin that he resembled a coat rack. In the course of the trip, which had stopovers in Kansas City, Chicago, New Orleans, Chicago (again) and Detroit, *Gower Mon* had developed a distressing phobia. Whenever a locomotive whistled, he would throw himself on his back in the straw, his eyeballs would tumble into his skull and they would rattle like castanets. Turf historian James Coleman swears that *Gower Mon* spent most of the trip on his back, and when the horses went to the post for the Plate at Woodbine, he was cowering fearfully in his barn.

Knifey would later gain revenge, for he knew that *Acara* was going to Winnipeg for the Canadian Derby, and immediately sent *Gower Mon* home, but this time in style—in the express car on a passenger train which required thirty-six hours to reach Winnipeg. The locomotive engineer was under instructions to blow his whistle only in the direst emergency; Speer's close friend was the president of the Canadian Pacific Railway. It rained for a week before the race at Polo Park, a track whose "gumbo" was infamous throughout the racing world. "The bottom fell out of the track," said Coleman, "and it was sticky enough to stop a hungry elephant going for a bale of hay."

As expected, *Acara* was leading turning for home but *Gower Mon* was abruptly steered across the track to the outside rail. He lost ten lengths by this manoeuvre but, suddenly, he was travelling twice as swiftly as his rivals. Knifey had outwitted his mud-boggled foes. When *Gower Mon* went to the outside fence, he was running along a solid clay path, over which the jockeys and valets had been walking on their two-hundred-yard journey from the finish line to the paddock after each race for a week. *Acara* had to settle for third behind *Cum Laude*.

1944 KING'S PLATE STAKES

FOURTH RACE
Woodbine Park
MAY 27, 1944

1 1-8 MILES (1:51⅕).The Eighty-Fifth Running KING'S PLATE. 50 Guineas, the gift of His Majesty King George VI. Estimated value $13,085 ($10,000 added by OJC). Winner to receive $9,100 and 50 Guineas; the second horse $1,500; the third horse $1,000, and the fourth horse $300. The breeder of the winner to receive $700. By subscription of $10 each at time of entry; $25 by May 1, 1944, to continue eligibility and $100 additional to start. For CANADIAN-BRED 3-YEAR-OLDS, the property of a British subject resident in Canada, which have never won a race either on the flat or across country other than a race exclusively for two-year-olds or the Plate Trial as offered by the Ontario Jockey Club for three-year-olds; which have never started in a race outside of Canada, and which have never been outside of Canada except as a foal and then for a period not exceeding three months, nor again until after the 31st of October of their two-year-old year. Weight 112 lbs. Winners in 1943 to carry 5 lbs. extra. Winner of Plate Trial, 5 lbs. additional. No gelding allowance. Death of nominator does not render entry void. A Cup will be presented by the Club to the owner of the winner. Closed March 20, 1944, with 56 nominations.

Horse	Eqt	Wt.	PP	St	¼	½	¾	Str	Fin	Jockey	Owner	Odds $1
ACARA	b	117	10	3	3nk	2½	2¹	1¹½	1³½	WatsonR	HatchHC	b-2.42½
OMPALO	b	117	8	10	10½	7½	3¹½	2²	2¹½	HallS	HatchHC	b-2.42½
KORAFLOYD		117	9	11	11½	9³	5⁴	3²½	3²	CourtneyG	MedwayStable	a-4.00
SAYONARA		112	3	7	8¹	11½	11½	5½	4²½	DewhurstJ	HatchHC	b-2.42½
CUM LAUDE		112	11	9	9¹	10nk	7nk	6²	5nk	HolydayF	ApplebyLH	28.45
HEYSIRIS	b	112	12	12	12	12	10½	8½	6nk	RogersC	ParkwoodStable	c-1.75
HEMFOX	b	117	2	2	1hd	1½	1hd	4¹	7nk	RemillardP	HemsteadCH	4.30
HEULWEN	b	117	4	4	5¹	4nk	8nk	7²½	8¹½	LindberghH	ParkwoodStable	c-1.75
NIMBLEFOOT	b	117	7	5	7³	6¹	9nk	9¹	9⁵	PariseS	RiverdaleStable	d-8.75
ATTESTER	b	117	5	8	6²	5¹	4½	10¹½	10²	PalaezH	RiverdaleStable	d-8.75
HAGGERTY	b	112	1	1	4¹½	8nk	12	11nk	11nk	LeavittR	TheDukeStable	14.75
GYPSTER	b	117	6	6	2½	3¹	6nk	12	12	BirleySD	CosgraveStable	a-4.00

a-Coupled, Korafloyd and Gypster; b-Acara, Ompalo and Sayonara; c-Heulwen and Heysiris; d-Nimblefoot and Attester.

OFF AT 4:54. Time, :23³/₅, :48³/₅, 1:13⁴/₅, 1:41, 1:54⁴/₅. Track fast.

Mutuel Prices:

	—$2 Mutuels Paid—			—Odds $1—		
ACARA (b-Entry)	6.85	5.90	4.40	2.42½	1.95	1.20
OMPALO (b-Entry)	6.85	5.90	4.40	2.42½	1.95	1.20
KORAFLOYD (a-Entry)			3.70			.85

Gr. c, by *Belfonds—Luress, by Sweepster. Trained by Cecil Howard. Bred by Harry C. Hatch, Toronto.

Start good from stall gate. Won easily; second and third driving. ACARA was rated close to the leaders from the start, moved into the lead before entering the stretch and drew out smartly. OMPALO moved up gradually, was sent to the outside for the drive and closed resolutely. KORAFLOYD, outrun early, moved up leaving the backstretch, but failed to menace the first two. SAYONARA moved up slowly, and closed well. CUM LAUDE made up ground from a slow start. HEYSIRIS was outrun. HEMFOX made the pace to the final quarter. HEULWEN showed speed and tired. NIMBLEFOOT was in trouble on the first turn. ATTESTER was crowded going into the first turn and tired after seven furlongs. GYPSTER quit badly.

Scratched—Patafryn.

1945 | UTTERMOST

Eighteen days after the war ended in Europe a joyful milling throng of nearly forty thousand fought a second Battle of the Bulge while cramming its way into Woodbine Park to watch the eighty-sixth running of the King's Plate, and more importantly, a record-shattering effort by a small bay colt whose owner had once remarked—facetiously, perhaps—that, "He's the sorriest looking two-year-old we have in our barn."

The assessment of Harry C. Hatch, the prominent but reclusive Canadian breeder, whose light and dark blue silks had already captured the Plate four times during the reign of three monarchs, was made several hours before the "peanut-sized" colt stepped out on the Polo Park racetrack in Winnipeg to duplicate the feat of his half-brother, *Sayonara*, who had won the Futurity in 1943. Before the 1944 racing season was concluded, *Uttermost* was judged Canada's outstanding two-year-old, winning practically every trophy in the country. He was the first to win the juvenile "triple crown," Mrs. Orpen's Cup and Saucer, the Claredon and Coronation Futurity Stakes.

Uttermost quickly proved he was no one-year wonder, a fluke, as he opened his 1945 campaign with a convincing win in the Plate Trial Stakes, winning his division a "tick" (fifth of a second) faster than *The Sheriff*, who had won the other division under jockey Chris Rogers. To further reinforce his chances of winning the Plate, Hatch and his California-born trainer, Cecil Howard, had imported veteran American rider Wayne Wright, who had won the 1942 Kentucky Derby on *Shut Out*, upsetting the great *Alsab*, to ride the other half of his entry, *Fair Jester*, a horse that critics were touting "would be better" than *Uttermost*. Thus, there were few punters in the packed grandstands who figured that the odds-on entry from the Hatch stable could possibly be extended by the fourteen other starters.

Uttermost was small, and not too chunky either. In fact, looking at him in the paddock one would have to guess he would need the help of a tractor to get him to go the nine-furlong Plate

CARR HATCH, ANOTHER OF HARRY HATCH'S SONS DELEGATED TO ACCEPT THE KING'S PLATE, AND LIEUTENANT GOVERNOR ALBERT MATTHEWS.

distance, a race which appeared to favour the long-striding gait of *Fair Jester*. However, as jockey Bobby Watson would later put it in summing up his colt's ability, *Uttermost* had "oomph," and was as game as horses come. "Call on him, and he always gives."

Watson had to call on his colt only one or two times despite having to start from the Number 13 post position. The winner was one of four starters who had to start from outside the twelve-stall starting gate, but *Uttermost* broke well. He escaped the crowding in the clubhouse turn, began moving at the *Optionor* and *Fair Patsy*

UTTERMOST DRAWS AWAY FROM FIFTEEN CHALLENGERS.

leaving the backstretch and easily held off *Tarian*, the 41-to-1 longshot, in the stretch run. Fourth was *Fair Jester*, who never really got rolling until the final turn, moving from a distant thirteenth to within five lengths of his stablemate at the wire. *Uttermost* added lustre to his crowning achievement when the clockers announced that his time of 1:53 4/5 had broken *Horometer*'s 1934 record by two-fifths of a second. Later that season *Uttermost* swept the major races for his age, the Prince of Wales and Breeders' Stakes, to affirm his position as a worthy champion. Thus he had won the "triple crown" for both juvenile and three-year-olds, a feat that has never been equalled.

In the Plate, Watson had his colt under a restraining hold for much of the way. "I touched him only once, at the eighth pole, and the way he took the lead satisfied me I was riding my third Plate winner. Oh yes, number thirteen is a lucky number and don't try to tell me any different. I drew Number 13 post position and when *Uttermost* won, it was the 1,013th win of my career."

Lieutenant Governor Albert Matthews, who made the Plate presentation in the unsaddling paddock, handed the trophy to another of Harry's three sons, Lieutenant Carr Hatch of the Royal Canadian Navy. He had recently returned to Canada after serving in the invasion of France. It was a Hatch tradition, his sons accepting the Plate, one that had begun with *Monsweep* and *Goldlure* in 1936 and 1937. Clifford and Douglas, also naval officers, had accepted the Plates after the wins of *Budpath* (1941) and *Acara* (1944).

Jim Coleman, writing in *The Globe and Mail*, singled out "two unobtrusive little fellows" who were almost forgotten during the presentations—trainer Cecil Howard and John Annesley, the Irishman who looked after the horses on Hatch's farm at Agincourt. "Howard, who took over the training of the Hatch horses with very little fuss, has given his patron two remarkably successful years. And, for that matter, if Mr. Hatch lost little John he'd lose one of the 'best horses' in his barn."

Radio broadcasting personality Gordon Sinclair interviews jockey Bobby Watson.

UTTERMOST | 3-year-old bay colt

Uttermost (1942)	*Soleil du Midi	*Teddy	Ajax
			Rondeau
		Midnight Folly	Black Jester
			Only Girl
	Uppermost	*Cohort	Grand Parade
			Tetrabbazia
		Summit	Ultimus
			*Torpenhow

Owner: H.C. (Harry) Hatch, Toronto; *Trainer:* Cecil Howard
Jockey: Robert (Bobby) Watson; *Breeder:* H.C. Hatch

An item that was overlooked were the names of the prominent owners whose horses were coupled in the four-horse mutuel betting field—industrialists Sam McLaughlin and Harry Carmichael, and distiller J.E. Frowde Seagram.

Uttermost would be the fifth, but final Plate triumph, for Harry C. Hatch, the quiet, gentle, self-made millionaire who had dominated Canadian racing since the mid-1930s. He was seriously ill, and the energy and direction which he gave the stable that bore his name gradually weakened with his own fading health. With his death, just weeks before the 1946 Plate, an important chapter in the history of the Plate closed. The track lost one of its most discerning and enterprising breeders. He would be inducted as Legend in Canada's Horse Racing Hall of Fame in 2000.

1945 KING'S PLATE STAKES

FOURTH RACE
Woodbine Park
MAY 26, 1945

1 1-8 MILES (Bon Jour, Sept. 16, 1944—1:50 3/5—6—126). The Eighty-Sixth Running KING'S PLATE. $10,000 Added and 50 Guineas, the gift of His Majesty King George VI. 3-year-olds. Foaled and owned in Canada. Weight, 119 lbs. Fillies allowed 5 lbs. No gelding allowance. (Non-winners of a race other than one exclusively for 2-year-olds or the Plate Trial as offered by the Ontario Jockey Club for 3-year-olds, who have never started as a 3-year-old except in the Plate Trial.) A cup will be presented by the Club to the owner of the winner, and mementos to the trainer and rider of the winner. Closed November 14, 1944, with 68 nominations; 42 remained eligible May 1, 1945. Net value to winner, $9,695 and 50 guineas; second, $1,500; third, $1,000; fourth, $300; breeder award, $700.

Horse	Eqt	Wt.	PP	St	¼	½	¾	Str	Fin	Jockey	Owner	Odds $1
UTTERMOST	b	119	13	10	6^{nk}	3^{nk}	3½	$2^{1½}$	1^{2}	WatsonR	HatchHC	a-.55
TARIAN	b	119	11	12	$8^{2½}$	5^{1}	4^{1}	3^{1}	2^{nk}	ParisoN	GilpinF	40.55
FERRY PILOT		119	7	13	9^{nk}	10½	8^{1}	$4^{1½}$	$3^{2½}$	HarrisH	HaltonBrookStable	b-13.10
FAIR JESTER		119	6	1	13½	13½	9^{1}	5½	4no	WrightWD	HatchHC	a-.55
OPTIONOR	b	119	9	3	3^{nk}	2^{1}	2^{1}	1½	5^{2}	SummersR	TaylorHW	6.75
HEYDUNETTE		114	16	16	11^{1}	8½	7^{nk}	6^{2}	6^{2}	HallerA	ParkwoodStable	f-17.90
HUSTLING DOM	b	119	2	7	10^{3}	11^{1}	11½	11^{1}	7^{1}	BarberE	HalliwellAJ	f-17.90
CORVITA		114	10	2	5½	6½	6½	7½	$8^{2½}$	DewhurstJ	McCarthyL	30.15
HEMJOHN	b	119	3	8	4^{1}	7½	10½	$9^{1½}$	9^{2}	WilliamsH	Bur-FitStable	35.60
THE SHERIFF	b	119	1	5	2^{nk}	4^{1}	5^{nk}	10½	10½	RogersC	StuartJ	3.45
FAIR PATSY		114	8	6	$1^{1½}$	1^{2}	1½	8½	$11^{2½}$	LeavittR	HaltonBrookStable	b-13.10
FLORAL GIFT		114	15	4	12^{1}	12^{1}	13^{1}	12^{2}	12^{4}	BlackH	MedwayStable	51.50
VICTORY MARK		119	5	15	16	16	16	14½	13½	AtkinsG	FairJG	f-17.90
PATTOY	b	119	12	11	7^{1}	9^{1}	12^{nk}	13^{nk}	14^{1}	CowleyJ	SeagramJEF	f-17.90
SMOKEY JOE	b	119	4	14	14^{nk}	14^{nk}	14^{nk}	15½	15^{1}	LindbergH	GardenCityStable	f-17.90
HEMSEVEN		119	14	9	15^{3}	15^{1}	15^{1}	16	16	RemillardP	HemsteadCH	4.65

a-Coupled, Uttermost and Fair Jester; b-Ferry Pilot and Fair Patsy. f-Mutuel field.

WENT TO POST—4:27½. OFF AT 4:29. Time, :23 3/5, :48 2/5, 1:13 3/5, 1:40 2/5, 1:53 4/5. Track fast.

Mutuel Prices:

	$2 Mutuels Paid			Odds to $1		
UTTERMOST (a-Entry)	3.10	2.60	2.40	.55	.30	.20
TARIAN		22.00	10.90		10.00	4.45
FERRY PILOT (b-Entry)			4.85			1.42½

B. c, by *Soleil du Midi—Uppermost, by *Cohort. Trainer, Cecil Howard. Bred by Hatch H C, Toronto.

Start good from stall gate. Won handily; second and third driving. UTTERMOST escaped the crowding on the first turn, began moving up to the leaders leaving the backstretch and wore down OPTIONOR and held TARIAN safe. The latter was hard urged reaching the stretch and closed well, but did not menace the winner. FERRY PILOT moved up gradually and closed well. FAIR JESTER broke fast, was taken back going to the first turn and closed gamely. OPTIONOR showed speed and took command entering the stretch, but tired suddenly in the final furlong. HEYDUNETTE closed a big gap. HUSTLING DOM could not reach the leaders. CORVITA could not threaten under pressure. HEMJOHN had early speed. THE SHERIFF, tired after six furlongs. FLORAL GIFT was never a threat. FAIR PATSY took the lead going to the first turn, but quit badly.

By all the rules of superstition, 25 May 1946 should have been a fine day. The war was over and young men had returned from the fronts and munitions plants to resume their racing careers. The King's Plate had been run each year since 1860, despite the many difficulties, and thereby maintained its reputation as the oldest continuously run stakes race on the continent. In fact, despite the rationing of food and fuel, the blackouts and the drain on manpower, racing had prospered during World War II, since it provided relaxation and distraction from worry during those desperate years. At long last, after six years of vice-regal absence, the new Governor General would attend the Plate and present the gift of "guineas." King George VI's choice of Lord Alexander, the Viscount of Tunis, who was accompanied by his wife, Lady Margaret, could not have been more appropriate or more enthusiastically received by Canadians. Not only was Viscount Alexander a venerated war hero, but he was associated with the Italian campaign in which Canadians played such a significant role. The youngest major-general in the British army during World War I, Viscount Alexander supervised the army's retreat from Dunkirk in 1940 and was the last Briton to be Governor General of Canada.

PHOTOGRAPHERS CAPTURE KING'S PLATE PRESENTATION—COL. R.S. MCLAUGHLIN (LEFT) AND GOVERNOR GENERAL VISCOUNT ALEXANDER.

But the Gods were not cooperative. The day was colder than usual, and it had rained continuously for several days, which had left the lawns a morass, the paddock muddy, the track looking like a Mississippi swamp and the stands and betting sheds jammed with wet, steaming humanity. It was impossible for all in the throng of more than thirty-six thousand to find shelter from the steady downpour. Many thousands just stood in the rain, or sat it out in the upperstands, nailed to their posts. They could not get to the wickets in any case because of the crush in the betting enclosures.

But none left, at least not until *Kingarvie*, a stringy chestnut gelding with a long, skinny neck and a heart as large as a cannon ball, had won the eighty-seventh running of the Plate, winning it with such facility that not one of his sleek red hairs was ruffled when he tiptoed back to the winner's enclosure. The public had supported Colonel Sam McLaughlin's gelding at odds of 1-to-2, and he won like a horse that should have been backed down to 1-to-100. At the finish the chart-callers gave him a margin of six lengths but, in reality, it was not even a contest after he turned for home. *David T.*, struggled past the wire in second place, but it was obvious that he could not have raised *Kingarvie*'s blood pressure if they had given him a headstart of ten lengths.

An implacable individual who certainly would not win an equine beauty contest, *Kingarvie* had shambled along behind the lead pony in the post parade as if the race was a forgone conclusion—after all, he had beaten everything else in the field previously, and convincingly, and it was an old story to him. There were better looking horses than *Kingarvie*, and there were horses faster than he, like E.P. Taylor's *Windfields*, who had bypassed the classic to go after the major American races, but there was not a horse which could look *Kingarvie* in the eye and make him quit.

It was a splendid triumph for jockey Johnny Dewhurst, trainer Arthur Brent and especially for Sam McLaughlin, a man who had done more than any other person to improve the class of horses bred in Canada. He had been in inferior health for many months, but when *Kingarvie* bounded past the winning post he tossed his pearl-grey topper into the air. It was only the second Plate ever won by the automobile pioneer and, although the genial gentleman's laugh was as hearty as usual, there was a hint of moisture around his eyes when he walked—not without a hint of a swagger—into the enclosure to accept His Majesty's gift from the Governor General. McLaughlin had lavished a fortune on the racing game, but he had been waiting for his second Plate since 1934, the year *Horometer* outclassed his field. It was no novelty for *Kingarvie* to be led into the winner's circle, for the Plate victory marked his tenth consecutive victory after losing his first two starts to *Windfields* as a two-year-old. Then his rampage began, winning the Coronation Futurity, the Clarendon and Mrs. Orpen's Cup and Saucer Stakes, and finally prepping for the Plate

KINGARVIE WAS "AN IRON HORSE" STARTING 169 TIMES AND EARNING $97,700.

KINGARVIE | 3-year-old chestnut gelding

		*Bull Dog	*Teddy
	Teddy Wrack		Plucky Liege
		Decree	*Wrack
Kingarvie			Royal Message
(1943)		Bachelor's	Tredennis
		Double	Lady Bawn
	*Forsworn		The Tetrarch
		Forequarter	Lamb Mint

Owner: Parkwood Stable (Colonel R.S. McLaughlin), Oshawa;
Trainer: Arthur Brent; *Jockey:* Johnny Dewhurst;
Breeder: Woodlands Investments, Ltd., Oshawa

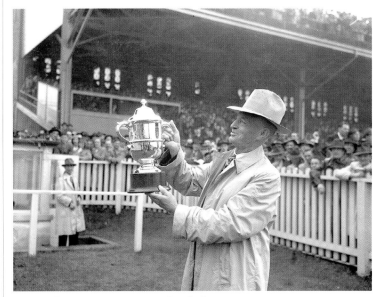

TRAINER ARTHUR BRENT AND THE KING'S PLATE.

with an opening day win in the Plate Trial Stakes.

Later that season history would be made when *Windfields* became the first horse ever flown into Toronto to compete in a stakes race. He met *Kingarvie* in the Breeders' Stakes and managed to outlast the Plate winner, who had atrocious racing luck, falling to his knees at the start of the mile and one-sixteenth race.

While *Windfields* would go on to become one of Canada's great sires, *Kingarvie* would carve out a career as "an iron horse," running at any distance, on any type of track, and against some of the best handicap horses in both the United States and Canada. The son of *Teddy Wrack* won the Canadian Championship at Long Branch later in 1946 and the following winter in Florida won the Hallandale Handicap at Gulfstream, was second in the Tropical Park Handicap and third in the Bougainvillea Handicap at Hialeah.

He would also finish first, second and third in successive runnings of the King Edward Gold Cup at Woodbine. His final stakes victory came in 1950 at Montreal when he equalled the track record in capturing the Cattarinich Memorial Handicap at Blue Bonnets. In 1953, at the age of ten, *Kingarvie* ended his career in a $2,000 claiming race at Detroit's Hazel Park. Later he would be inducted into Canada's Hall of Fame: his remarkable career showed 169 starts—thirty wins, twenty-one seconds and twenty-seven thirds—for earnings of $97,700, a record for a Canadian-bred horse.

JOHNNY DEWHURST AND KINGARVIE.

1946 KING'S PLATE STAKES

FOURTH RACE
Woodbine Park
MAY 25, 1946

1 1-8 MILES (1:50³⁄₅). The Eighty–Seventh Running KING'S PLATE. $10,000 Added and 50 Guineas, the gift of His Majesty King George VI. For Canadian–bred 3–year–olds. Weight, 119 lbs. Fillies allowed 5 lbs. No gelding allowance. Net value to winner, $9,850 and 50 guineas; second, $1,500; third, $1,000; fourth, $300. Breeder award, $700.

Horse	Eqt	Wt.	PP	St	¼	½	¾	Str	Fin	Jockey	Owner	Odds $1
KINGARVIE		119	4	3	3²	2¹	1²	1³	1⁶	DewhurstJ	ParkwoodStable	.50
DAVID T.	b	119	5	6	6²	6²	3¹¹⁄₂	2¹¹⁄₂	2⁴	CourtneyG	TurnerD	7.55
BLUESWEEP	b	119	1	10	9¹	9¹¹⁄₂	8³	2¹¹⁄₂	3¹	WatsonR	HCHatchEstate	4.85
KHABULA		114	9	7	8¹⁄₂	7²	5¹	5¹	4²	KeaneR	MedwayStable	30.20
DOUBLE BRIAR	b	119	10	5	5ⁿᵏ	5ⁿᵏ	2ⁿᵏ	3¹⁄₂	5⁴	RemillardP	WebsterMrsRE	a-5.45
WILLEGIVIT	b	114	6	4	4¹⁄₂	4ⁿᵏ	7²	7³	6⁴	BarberE	HeiseNL	15.25
KANSHORE	b	114	7	2	2¹	3²	4¹⁄₂	4¹⁄₂	7¹	LeavittR	SeagramJEF	75.15
BAREFOOT JOE	b	119	8	8	7¹¹⁄₂	8¹⁄₂	6ⁿᵏ	8²	8³	ParisoN	GrovesG	a-5.45
NODDY'S NUMBER		119	3	9	10	10	10	9¹	9¹¹⁄₂	BirleySD	HaltonBrookStable	52.45
ROYAL WORTH	b	119	2	1	1¹¹⁄₂	1¹⁄₂	9¹	10	10	FisherR	SimonL	82.60

a–Coupled, Double Briar and Barefoot Joe.
WENT TO POST—4:35. OFF AT 4:36¹⁄₂. Time, :23³⁄₅, :47³⁄₅, 1:13²⁄₅, 1:41²⁄₅, 1:55³⁄₅. Track sloppy.

Mutuel Prices:

	—$2 Mutuels Paid—			—Odds $1—		
KINGARVIE	3.00	2.50	2.40	.50	.25	.20
DAVID T.		4.25	2.90		1.12¹⁄₂	.45
BLUESWEEP			2.85			.42¹⁄₂

Ch. g, by Teddy Wrack–*Forsworn, by Bachelor's Double. Trainer, Arthur Brent. Bred by Woodlands Investments Ltd., Oshawa, Ont.

Start good from stall gate. Won easily; second and third driving. KINGARVIE, much the best and at home in the footing, raced close to the pace while strongly reserved for a half mile and, going to the front when ready, drew out with ease through the stretch run. DAVID T., rated back of the leaders, was placed to punishment midway of the stretch and closed with determination, but was no match for the winner. BLUESWEEP, sluggish in the early stages, began to improve his position leaving the backstretch and closed willingly, but was no threat at the finish. KHABULA, permitted to settle into stride before being called on, closed with good courage on the outside. DOUBLE BRIAR, never far from the pace, moved up threateningly after going five-eighths, but faltered when the real racing began. WILLEGIVIT did not threaten. KANSHORE showed speed for seven-eighths, then began to falter. BAREFOOT JOE was never dangerous. NODDY'S NUMBER raced far back throughout. ROYAL WORTH had speed for a half mile, then quit badly.

Scratched—Palermo, Karakas.

The unlikely winner of the eighty-eighth running of the King's Plate was *Moldy*, a bay gelding with a "fishy" name; he had survived more misadventures than Pearl White or any of those other movie serial queens of the silent screen. *Moldy* startled the form players in a crowd of 48,015 at Woodbine Park, the largest ever to witness a sporting event in Canada, when he hurtled across the finishing line barely ahead of a three-horse posse. Aboard the winner, who held off the desperate charge of *Burboy*, *Watch Wrack* and *Kanlee* in the stretch, was Colin McDonald, a jockey who had recently been released from his job in an Oshawa war factory.

Owned and bred by Colonel Sam McLaughlin's Parkwood Stable of Oshawa, which had captured the Plate the year before with *Kingarvie* (another son of *Teddy Wrack*), the unheralded *Moldy* was allowed to go off as the long shot in a field of sixteen, despite a rousing second-place finish to *Tularch* the week before in the Plate Trial Stakes. He returned $36.50 for the two-dollar bettors, who had dismissed his dismal efforts as a two-year-old (a lone win in nine starts, one that came against maidens late in the season at Long Branch) and the reports of his hair-raising exploits while wintering in Florida.

COLIN McDONALD AMUSES FELLOW JOCKEYS ON HOW HE WON THE KING'S PLATE.

Moldy had reluctantly been selected by trainer Arthur Brent for a winter of sunshine and a chance to prove himself because the stable's other hopefuls had either shown a distaste to travel the nine-furlong distance, or were broken down. But *Moldy* was hardly a fit specimen. He ran as if he would like to tuck his legs up underneath his arms, and was, as horsemen would say, "a sore-goin' horse." Racetrackers shrugged their shoulders and thought "Brent was daft" when he put *Moldy* on a van headed south.

Circumstances, however, would prevent Brent from ever really training the gelding. After remedial work had been carried out on the shins of *Moldy*'s forelegs, Brent one morning found out that his star boarder had escaped, making a dash through and over several fences before he was corralled. Fortunately, he sustained no injuries. The next time Brent's crew had *Moldy* ready for a workout, he again took off, crashing into a hydrant and tearing shoulder muscles before his handlers could catch him. So much for training. Brent was lucky to have his Plate horse in one piece when he shipped him back to Woodbine for workouts in a less dangerous atmosphere.

"He wasn't the best horse to ever win the Plate. But he was a courageous fellow, and in view of the accidents which had befallen him, it was a wonder that he even managed to stagger out onto the track for the Plate," wrote Jim Coleman of *The Globe and Mail* after *Moldy*'s unexpected triumph. "Obviously he had refused to read his own past performance charts, as he ran as if he was in a hurry to make

1947 KING'S PLATE STAKES

FOURTH RACE

Woodbine Park

MAY 24, 1947

1 1-8 MILES (1:50⅗). The Eighty-Eighth Running KING'S PLATE. $10,000 Added plus 50 Guineas, the gift of His Majesty King George VI. Weight, 119 lbs. For Canadian-bred 3-year-olds. Fillies allowed 5 lbs. No gelding allowance. Net value to winner, $10,335; second, $1,500; third, $1,000; fourth, $300. Breeder award, $700.

Horse	Eqt	Wt.	PP	St	¼	½	¾	Str	Fin	Jockey	Owner	Odds $1
MOLDY	b	119	6	6	6¹	4¹½	2²½	1³	1½	McDonaldC	ParkwoodStable	17.25
BURBOY	b	119	10	12	14½	9½	4¹½	2nk	2nk	FisherR	Bur-FitStable	a-9.75
WATCH WRACK		119	11	8	10nk	11nk	11nk	6¹	3nk	BavingtonA	DonEarlStable	5.30
KANLEE	b	119	16	15	15¹½	12¹	6²	4¹	4²	WatsonR	LahmanH	2.95
YELLOWKNIFE		114	5	4	4½	3½	1½	3nk	5²	BirleySD	CowieRWR	b-10.75
VICTORY CHIMES	b	119	12	10	13²	10½	7½	5½	6nk	YoungS	LawsonCW	a-9.75
MULLIGAN		119	14	16	16	16	14½	7½	7²	DewhurstJ	TheDukeStable	f-8.90
SWEEP COMET	b	119	3	9	7nk	14¹	10¹	8¹½	8¹½	RogersC	ZakoorD	15.20
TREGARON	b	119	8	7	8¹	6½	12½	12½	9nk	LeavittR	SeagramJEF	13.55
FLORIST		119	1	2	2¹	1nk	9¹	9¹	10½	BarberE	MedwayStable	f-8.90
WELSH MAN	b	119	9	11	9½	7nk	5½	10½	11nk	RemillardP	StonedeneStable	b-10.75
LEONFORTE		119	2	5	5nk	5nk	8nk	11nk	12½	CourtneyG	BraesideStable	18.05
DIRIGO	b	119	7	13	11nk	8nk	13½	14½	13½	ConveyJ	HardyG	f-8.90
CURLY J.		119	13	14	12½	15¹	15¹½	15⁴	14¹	KeeneH	HerdmanL	f-8.90
TULARCH		119	15	1	1¹½	2¹	3nk	13¹	15⁶	VinaJ	McCullaghCG	2.25
SIR ACHTOI		119	4	3	3²	13½	16	16	16	SivewrightJ	DrumhellerJV	f-8.90

a-Coupled, Burboy and Victory Chimes; b-Yellowknife and Welsh Man. f-Mutuel field.

WENT TO POST—4:49. OFF AT 4:51. Time, :23⅗, :48⅗, 1:14⅖, 1:41, 1:54⅕. Track fast.

Mutuel Prices:

		—$2 Mutuels Paid—			—Odds $1—		
MOLDY		36.50	13.35	7.60	17.25	5.67½	2.80
BURBOY (a-Entry)			8.95	5.65		3.47½	1.82½
WATCH WRACK				4.80			1.40

B. g, by Teddy Wrack—*Obituary, by Obliterate. Trainer, Arthur Brent. Bred by Woodlands Investments Ltd, Oshawa, Ont.

Start good from stall gate. Won driving; second and third the same. MOLDY, away well, moved into the lead at the last turn, drew clear and held BURBOY safe. The latter, outrun in the early stages, closed well and fought it out at the end. WATCH WRACK closed with a rush. KANLEE closed well. YELLOWKNIFE had early speed. VICTORY CHIMES closed strongly. MULLIGAN was away slowly. SWEEP COMET could not keep up. TREGARON failed to respond to punishment. FLORIST faltered. WELSH MAN tired. LEONFORTE had speed. TULARCH faltered. SIR ACHTOI had brief speed.

GOVERNOR GENERAL VISCOUNT ALEXANDER HAS THE ATTENTION OF TRAINER ARTHUR BRENT, COLIN MCDONALD AND COL. R.S. (SAM) MCLAUGHLIN.

MOLDY | 3-year-old bay gelding

			*Teddy
		*Bull Dog	Plucky Liege
	Teddy Wrack		*Wrack
		Decree	Royal Message
Moldy (1944)			Tracery
		Obliterate	Damage
	*Obituary		Sunder
		Au Revoir	Howdyedo

Owner: Parkwood Stable (Colonel R.S. McLaughlin), Oshawa;
Trainer: Arthur Brent; *Jockey:* Colin McDonald;
Breeder: Woodlands Investments, Ltd., Oshawa

the acquaintance of Viscount Alexander, the Governor General." Coleman advised Sam McLaughlin that he should retire the gelding immediately before he was kidnapped and held for ransom by the Sioux, or before he was found dangling from some precipice, clinging by his teeth to the yielding branch of a small tree.

This facetious suggestion amused McLaughlin, who then recalled an amusing incident which had provoked him into giving *Moldy* his inapt name. "I had sent a salmon from my salmon stream [in Nova Scotia] to Bertie and Molly Cassels, friends in Toronto. So they'd know it was coming, I sent them a wire and told them I hoped the salmon would save them some meat coupons [war-time rationing was still in effect]. In a few days, back came a wire saying the fish had arrived, but what did I mean by 'moldy'? That had me puzzled, so I sent my chauffeur to the telegraph office. He discovered the wire had been sent to Bertie and Moldy Cassels. The telegrapher had hit a 'd' instead of an 'l' for Molly."

At about the same time, McLaughlin was having a problem with The Jockey Club in New York, which had just rejected all six names he had suggested for the yearling by *Teddy Wrack*, out of the imported mare, *Obituary*. In frustration, McLaughlin sent them one more name—*Moldy*, which was accepted. The gelding turned out to be a little better horse than many at first had predicted; he raced until he was five, winning the Durham Cup at Woodbine in his final season. He retired with earnings of $37,260 from sixty-five starts, eleven of which were wins, and was in the money for more than half his starts.

Nineteen forty-seven was a significant year in several respects. Earlier in the season the Ontario Jockey Club

INAPTLY NAMED *MOLDY* ENJOYED A WINTER OF FLORIDA SUNSHINE.

was forced to postpone its scheduled nine-day Greenwood Racing Club meeting, which was to have preceded the Club's own spring card, because of a dispute with the Horsemen's Protective and Benevolent Association over minimum purses. The HBPA, headed by Willie Morrissey and Charles Hemstead, two hotel owners who had previously won the Plate, was demanding a minimum purse of $1,500; the OJC said it could not afford to pay more than $1,200. At the annual meeting that fall, OJC president Colonel K.R. Marshall reported an operating loss, citing the increased purses paid out as a result of negotiations with the HBPA, inclement weather and a substantial reduction in betting revenues. A new director was elected at that meeting—horseman and industrialist, E.P. Taylor.

Meanwhile, the OJC was in a period of transition and was obviously optimistic about the sport's future. It had purchased the Greenwood charter from racing interests in Petrolia, a town in southwestern Ontario that had prospered in the nineteenth century as the centre of Canada's pioneer oil industry, and had installed the "eye-in-the-sky" photo-finish camera and new totalisator machines.

Little attention was paid by Toronto newspapers that May when *Jet Pilot,* a horse owned by Florence Nightingale Graham, won the Kentucky Derby. She was born in Woodbridge, Ontario, and lived there until she was twenty-four years of age. At one time she travelled to the St. Lawrence Market to sell the produce from her father's farm. However, by 1947 her name was now Elizabeth Arden Graham, the most renowned name in the world of glamour and the cosmetics industry. She owned Maine Chance Farm in Lexington, Kentucky, one of the leading racing and breeding stables in North America. In 1954 Elizabeth Arden officiated in the opening of Black Creek Pioneer Village in the tree-planting ceremony, and in 2003 was inducted into the Legends category of the Canadian Horse Racing Hall of Fame.

Years later horsemen would coyly suggest that James G. (Jim) Fair, the Squire of Cainsville, had "slipped one by the stewards" when he captured the King's Plate with *Last Mark*, a robust brown colt that many suspected was not a three-year-old, but a year older, and thus ineligible.

"Uncle Jim," who owned, bred and trained the colt, had never won the Plate, not even close, in more than twenty years of challenges with a string of cheap horses. He would put up the one-hundred dollar starting fee and get nothing back. Yet he kept smiling: "My year will come." When *Last Mark* came along, the Squire confidently predicted that he would "gallop" on Plate day. He not only "galloped," winning by almost five lengths over Jim Speers' *Lord Fairmond*, the first good western horse to come east for the Plate, but he ran faster than all but one Plate winner during the thirty-two years it was a mile-and-one-eighth test at Woodbine. (Collisteo would equal the time in 1954.) Astonished clockers had to check their stopwatches, *Last Mark*'s time of 1:52 was one and four-fifths seconds faster than *Uttermost*'s Plate record, and quicker than those of the great *Bunty Lawless* and *Horometer*.

Talking with Bobby Hewitson, sports editor of *The Evening Telegram*, a month before the race, Fair said: "Robert, I want to show you the winner of the King's Plate. Come fast track or slow track; come large field or small, this horse has class, plenty of it. He'll beat his rivals doing anything, anytime. He'll win the Plate as far as you can throw an apple."

Big Jim was a rubber boots and overalls guy, not inclined to fuss with the finery worn by the fashionable in the Turf Club. But he startled officials one morning, arriving at their office to answer charges of a minor illegality, wearing a top hat, silk tie and tails. Creaseless trousers, a collarless shirt and suspenders comprised the cigar-smoking Squire's normal ensemble. But he had an acute sense of sartorial timing. He would dress up whenever it seemed certain one of his horses would win and he would be required to pose in the winner's circle. On those days the two-buck bettors would notice Fair's Sunday raiment and plunge the money on his livestock. "Oh, oh," they would say, "Jim's shined up like he's got a winner." One day, wearing his finest off-the-track suit, Fair seemed a trifle annoyed when he learned everybody was betting on his entry. Unloosening the tie that was choking him, he said, a trifle mournful, "I'm gussied up like this because I just come from a funeral."

Oldtimers recall that Fair used to tramp barefooted across the damp infield grass at Woodbine in the mornings, explaining, "The dew is good for corns." A customary scene around Fair's tack room at breakfast: "What's to eat?" he once said to his three stablehands. "Two eggs," replied one. "Okay," Fair said. "Fry one egg for me, and scramble the other one for yourselves." He was a shoestring operator, from the old line of independent storekeepers—tough and proud, witty and irreverent, close-fisted, desperately durable, always working close to the line of financial extinction. In two years he had run the gamut, one day lucky to be eating chicken feathers, the next day fussing about how the chicken would be fried. In 1946 the

JOCKEY HOWARD BAILEY, JIM FAIR AND LIEUTENANT GOVERNOR RAY LAWSON.

bailiff had seized his racing stock and sold it at auction at Thorncliffe. But friends bought most of it, turning it back to Fair, to be paid for as he went along.

Legend, or not, if he did commit an act of chicanery that day at Woodbine, nobody could prove that *Last Mark* was a four-year-old. "Who could tell?" said Joseph (Yonnie) Starr, who was around the track in that era and would later win four Plate races. "Everybody took a close look at him. But Jim did breed big horses and sometimes his horses were bigger than others their age." Another veteran, the late Jim Bentley, often related colourful tales of "Fair," and would insist the colt was a four-year-old. "You can bet your last dollar on it. He was no three-year-old, and you have my word on it." However Bentley, or other veterans who admired Fair's carefree, Huckleberry Finn style, never spoke malevolently about the big dirt farmer and horseman. "Everybody on the track knew that Jim's horse wasn't a three-year-old. His teeth were too big. Ask anybody who was around in those days. Fair had a farm up near Brantford, and he possibly got him mixed up with another horse, or maybe he wandered off into the bush for a year. Who knows if he [*Last Mark*] was even out of the mare that he was supposed to be? . . . they didn't bother to check in those days as closely as they do now. Also, Fair owned both the stallion [*Koenigsmark*] and the mare [*McTab*]."

Racegoers in 1948 certainly were not about to object, for they had made *Last Mark* the 5-to-2 favourite, and never was there a more popular victory in the Canadian classic. The only comparison was when Willie Morrissey won with *Bunty Lawless*. That was a case of a

Howard Bailey's only Plate mount—*Last Mark*. Trainer Jim Fair adjusts bridle.

LAST MARK | 3-year-old brown colt

Last Mark (1945)	*Koenigsmark II	Ellangowan	Lemberg
			Lammermuir
		Lady Kroon	Kroonstad
			Needle Rock
	McTab	Lovetie	Ildrim
			Luray
		Mutchkin	*Giganteum
			Miss Lois

Owner: James G. (Jim) Fair, Cainsville, Ont.; *Trainer:* James G. Fair
Jockey: Howard Bailey; *Breeder:* James G. Fair

"boy from the other side of the tracks" stepping into the winner's circle. On 24 May it was the same with Jim Fair. As he shambled out of the grandstand, "Uncle Jim" almost lost his overcoat as he was mobbed by hundreds of fans in a crowd of forty-two thousand.

It was strictly a Canadian victory, wrote Hewitson. "A victory for Canadian training and Canadian weather. *Kingarvie* and *Moldy*, previous winners, had been conditioned in Florida. They were fitter than those trained in Canada. But Fair prepared his horse at Cainsville this winter and finished up his work this spring at Woodbine." Fair's cherubic-faced jockey, Howard "Hard-Riding" Bailey, who had never ridden in the Plate before, was lauded for his "clever ride" as he sat off the pace before making his move. It would be his only Plate ride; the man he beat, Johnny Longden, would go on to win more than six thousand races in a forty-year career, but fail in his four attempts to win the Plate. Another Hall of Fame jockey imported from New York for the race, Toronto-born Ted Atkinson, finished thirteenth on *All British*, the horse many thought might upset *Last Mark*.

Before he concluded his racing career, *Last Mark* would gain a distinction unequalled in the annals of Canadian horse racing—he would win two King's Plate races. In 1949, the last year that Quebec's version of the Plate was open to older horses, Fair shipped his colt to Blue Bonnets and won the fifty "guineas" again.

When Fair died in 1957, *Globe and Mail* sports editor Jim Vipond wrote: "He was a symbol of the little man." Bill Risewick, a veteran steward representing the Ontario Racing Commission, added: "The common man felt part of Fair."

1948 KING'S PLATE STAKES

FOURTH RACE
Woodbine Park
MAY 24, 1948

1 1–8 MILES (1:50$\frac{3}{5}$). The Eighty–Ninth Running KING'S PLATE. 50 Guineas, the gift of His Majesty King George VI, with $10,000 added by Ontario Jockey Club. 3–year–olds. Foaled in Canada. Property of British subjects resident in Canada who have not started in a race in 1948 (Plate Trial as offered by Ontario Jockey Club excepted). Weight, 119 lbs. Fillies allowed 5 lbs. (No gelding allowance.) Gross value, $14,660. Net value to winner, $11,010 plus 50 guineas; second, $1,500; third, $1,000; fourth, $300. Breeder of winner, $700.

Horse	Eqt	Wt.	PP	St	¼	½	¾	Str	Fin	Jockey	Owner	Odds $1
LAST MARK		119	3	10	$7^{2\frac{1}{2}}$	6^{2}	4^{2}	$1^{\frac{1}{2}}$	$1^{4\frac{3}{4}}$	BaileyHR	FairJG	a-2.52½
LORD FAIRMOND		110	12	3	4^{2}	4^{1}	2^{2}	3^{3}	$2^{\frac{3}{4}}$	LongdenJ	WhittierParkStockFarm	4.60
JOEY BOMBER	b	119	5	1	2^{nk}	$1^{\frac{1}{2}}$	$1^{2\frac{1}{2}}$	$2^{\frac{1}{2}}$	3^{3}	FisherR	FewsterWJ	38.35
SWEEPBLU		119	10	12	$13^{1\frac{1}{2}}$	8^{1}	6^{3}	$4^{1\frac{1}{2}}$	4^{5}	WatsonR	HatchC	4.05
POLIPAT		119	7	15	16	16	12^{hd}	7^{nk}	5^{1}	BovineV	MittenRC	f-5.75
MEAL TIME		119	1	2	1^{1}	$2^{1\frac{1}{2}}$	3^{nk}	$5^{1\frac{1}{2}}$	$6^{\frac{3}{4}}$	DreweryJ	BlackJH	7.45
RED BOTTLE	b	120	11	13	12^{nk}	$9^{\frac{1}{2}}$	10^{1}	$8^{\frac{1}{2}}$	$7^{\frac{1}{2}}$	MannF	deL'OrrEV	f-5.75
KID RUMBLE		119	4	8	9^{1}	7^{nk}	5^{nk}	$6^{2\frac{1}{2}}$	$8^{1\frac{3}{4}}$	ShufeltR	HeiseNL	38.05
MISTY WATERS	b	114	9	6	8^{nk}	10^{nk}	11^{1}	$9^{3\frac{1}{2}}$	9^{4}	WagnerJ	KennedyDJ	f-5.75
FACE OFF	b	119	2	14	11^{1}	11^{1}	$9^{\frac{1}{2}}$	10^{4}	$10^{5\frac{1}{2}}$	DewhurstJ	SeagramJEF	25.20
CHANCE TOSS	b	119	8	11	$15^{\frac{1}{2}}$	$15^{\frac{1}{2}}$	13^{1}	$11^{2\frac{1}{2}}$	11^{3}	RemillardP	KinraraStable	f-5.75
WAR WRACK	b	119	13	9	14^{1}	14^{1}	14^{2}	13^{4}	12^{1}	RoyE	ParkwoodStable	b-39.05
ALL BRITISH	b	119	6	5	3^{1}	3^{2}	7^{2}	12^{1}	13^{6}	AtkinsonT	TurnerS	3.30
FAIR MARK	b	119	15	7	6^{1}	$5^{1\frac{1}{2}}$	8^{nk}	14^{1}	14^{nk}	DoughertyF	FairJG	a-2.52½
COLERAINE	b	119	14	4	$5^{\frac{1}{2}}$	$12^{\frac{1}{2}}$	$15^{1\frac{1}{2}}$	15^{1}	15^{1}	RogersC	ShortE	f-5.75
ANUDONA	b	114	16	16	10^{nk}	$13^{\frac{1}{2}}$	16	16	16	StantonJ	ParkwoodStable	b-39.05

a–Coupled, Last Mark and Fair Mark; b–War Wrack and Anudona. f–Mutuel field.

WENT TO POST—4:37½. OFF AT 4:39. Time, :23$\frac{2}{5}$, :47$\frac{2}{5}$, 1:12$\frac{3}{5}$, 1:38$\frac{4}{5}$, 1:52. (Plate record.) Track fast.

Mutuel Prices:

	$2 Mutuels Paid			Odds $1		
LAST MARK (a–Entry)	7.05	4.40	3.50	2.52½	1.20	.75
LORD FAIRMOND		5.45	4.05		1.72½	1.02½
JOEY BOMBER			11.40			4.70

Br. c, by *Koenigsmark II—McTab, by Lovetie. Trainer, James G. Fair. Bred by Fair J G, Cainsville, Ont.

Start good from stall gate. Won easily; second and third driving. LAST MARK, easily best, was rated close to the pace under strong restraint, moved to the leaders leaving the backstretch, then drew out steadily. LORD FAIRMOND, forwardly placed from the start, was hard urged through the last quarter, but was no match for the winner. JOEY BOMBER broke fast, took command from MEAL TIME, drew clear, but began to falter when the real racing began. ALL BRITISH ran close to the lead but faltered badly in the backstretch when the pace quickened.

Scratched—Graydon Trace, Waycross.

Overweight—Red Bottle, 1 lb.

The Squire of Cainsville in familiar track attire.

The Taylor Years: An *Epic* to the *Dancer*— Hello Woodbine, Farewell "Leaky-Roof Circuit"

I n the 1948 Christmas edition of *The Blood-Horse*, a magazine published in Kentucky for the thoroughbred racing and breeding industry, a feature article was devoted to Edward Plunket Taylor and his "plans for the future."

> E.P. Taylor lends truth to the saying that everyone should have a hobby and a worry. . . . Canadian breeders during the past few years have taken a more progressive attitude towards the improvement of their bloodstock. E.P. Taylor will undoubtedly be an important factor in helping Canada take a prominent place in the breeding world.

These were the opening and closing statements of a story that would unfold like a prepared script during the next four decades, of "likeable Eddie, who at forty-seven controls and operates as much industry as anybody else in Canada . . . a big vigorous man with a sparkling personality and a rare ability to organize and direct." At the time, Taylor owned one outstanding racehorse, *Windfields*, a handful of promising mares in *Nandi*, *Iribelle* and *Fairy Imp*, a 600-acre farm in Willowdale, north of Toronto, and a reputation of being a good horseman from the days he and fellow brewer Jimmy Cosgrave ran an enterprising stable to advertise their beer before World War II. It was one that trainer Bert Alexandra had built up out of Taylor's initial $6,000 investment, featuring *Jack Patches*, *Madfest*, *Annimessic*, *Jelwell* and the ill-fated *Mona Bell*, a full sister to *Iribelle* and one of Taylor's favourite horses up to that time, a filly that ran second to *Bunty Lawless* in the King's Plate in 1938 and then beat him in the Breeders' Stakes. A year later, at Stamford Park in Niagara Falls, *Mona Bell* suffered a broken leg and had to be destroyed. Taylor was shocked by the mishap. It was also a severe blow to plans already being made to assemble a small group of

WINNIFRED AND E.P. TAYLOR.

mares to raise young stock for racing, plans that would be shelved because of the war.

Ten years later, the revolution would formally erupt as the future of Canadian horse racing slowly began to soar under the deft leadership of the powerful industrialist and visionary. Elected as a director of the Ontario Jockey Club in 1947, Eddie Taylor had also successfully pursued quality breeding stock in Kentucky shortly after the war. With the purchase in 1950 of R.S. McLaughlin's famed Parkwood Stables north of Oshawa, a 640-acre spread he would name The National Stud Farm, Taylor was now firmly committed to his "future plans," with the purchases of *Bull Page*, *Navy Chief* and *Flaring Top*, the grand-dam of *Nijinsky II*.

He bred five successive Plate winners from 1949 to 1953; two of them ran for other owners because Taylor sold *McGill* and lost *Epigram* in a cheap claiming race. By 1954 he and Gil Darlington, the man Taylor initially put in charge of his farm, introduced an innovative method of both selling his young stock and giving more owners a chance to own quality racehorses—a sale of pre-priced yearlings. Darlington was an astute horseman—he brought *Chop Chop*, a horse he had initially stood at his own Trafalgar Farm, and who would later sired four Plate winners, with him to join the National's stallion roster. At first, Taylor offered only half of his crop, keeping what was left over for his own racing stable. By 1968 he would integrate his sale with the annual Canadian Thoroughbred Horse Society yearling auction and make it one of the major markets, attracting buyers from Europe and the United States. In the first ten years of his sale at Windfields, Taylor disposed of Plate winners *Canadian Champ*, *Blue Light* and *Titled Hero*. Rejected by the buyers were *Nearctic*, *Lyford Cay*, *New Providence*, *Victoria Park*, *Flaming Page*, *Canebora* and *Northern Dancer*. By 1970, these horses would either win Taylor the Plate or help establish him as the world's leading breeder, an honour he would retain for an unparalleled length of time.

The chairman of Argus Corporation, Taylor was the personifi-

BILL REEVES CHECKS THE CHALKBOARD TO SEE WHICH OF WINDFIELDS' PRE-PRICED YEARLINGS HAD NOT BEEN BOUGHT.

cation of riches gained and power wielded before he severed his boardroom connections in 1966. An associate once said: "Eddie can read a balance sheet like a poem, and tell you where it doesn't scan." As a director of the OJC, Taylor became actively involved in the conduct of racing in Ontario, and soon began to fall back on the techniques that had become the hallmark of his business life: consolidation and merger. Working closely with George C. Hendrie and J.E. Frowde Seagram, grandsons of the dominant racing families at the turn of the century, Taylor was the driving force behind a concerted program of purchasing racetracks (Hamilton, Thorncliffe, Long Branch, Dufferin and Stamford) and closing them, much to the consternation and outrage of fans in these areas. Those that were kept were refurbished—Woodbine Park (later Greenwood), which had been built in 1875, and Fort Erie, a track that had been operating since 1900. Taylor's aim was to create an economically workable Ontario circuit, one that he achieved by buying up dozens of inactive racing charters, which enabled him to create a nine-month racing season.

But before he put such a scheme into operation, Taylor first had to acquire a substantial block of company shares, which at the time were trading on the stock market at six hundred dollars. He negotiated a deal with the Seagram family, which held the largest number of shares, although not control. Taylor knew that if he was to acquire the largest single holding, he would have to pay a premium and negotiate a deal with

RIBBON-CUTTING CEREMONY TO OPEN THE "NEW" WOODBINE. MANAGING DIRECTOR GEORGE C. HENDRIE, PRESIDENT E.P. TAYLOR AND ONTARIO PREMIER LESLIE FROST.

Frowde Seagram to purchase his family's shares at $1,500 each. Once he had become the largest shareholder in the OJC, he could proceed with his future plans from a position of strength. The key to his plan was a modern racing plant, equal to any in North America, that would be located south of the village of Malton, in the Toronto suburb of Etobicoke and close to the city's major airport. With the assistance of a retired farmer, Taylor's sub-committee began buying up parcels of land in the winter of 1952, acquiring four hundred acres at $1,550 per acre near Rexdale Boulevard and Highway 27. Over the next twelve months, another 280 acres were acquired and the site of Taylor's posh new $13 million "supertrack" was announced. Originally it was to open in 1955 but racing did not begin there until the following year, in June, when *Landscape*, running under Taylor's own turquoise and gold polka dots, won the first race.

While the "new" Woodbine offered unlimited potential with its turf and dirt tracks, spacious training facilities and modern barns, sprawling parking lots and comfortable accommodation, Greenwood and Fort Erie were not overlooked. The OJC improved facilities, built a half-mile harness track inside the main dirt course and installed lights for night trotting races at the venerable old track on Queen Street. Millions were also spent making Fort Erie an attractive summer retreat for both Canadian and American horsemen. Yet on occasion, Taylor would err. The OJC built tracks for standardbreds at St. Catharines (Garden City) and Campbellville (Mohawk) to give harnessmen top tracks to race at when the thoroughbreds occupied Greenwood. St. Catharines turned out to be a costly venture and was later sold.

Charles Taylor, who with John J. Mooney, Jack Kenney,

THE PLATE CELEBRATES ITS 100TH BIRTHDAY WITH GEORGE C. HENDRIE DOING THE HONOURS.

GIL DARLINGTON MANAGED NATIONAL STUD, LATER NAMED WINDFIELDS FARM.

GEORGE BLACKWELL, BRITISH BLOODSTOCK AGENT WHO BOUGHT *NEARCTIC*'S DAM, *LADY ANGELA*.

Charles Baker, Joe Thomas and Peter Poole, would assume many of the portfolios or duties held by Eddie after he gradually phased himself out of racetrack administration, as well as Windfields' comprehensive breeding and marketing programs and racing stable, once commented that his father's success as a breeder was remarkable, but "people tend not to pay much attention to his success in racetrack management. He was a pioneer in this field and was instrumental in establishing Sunday racing, turf races, emphasizing the importance of stakes races for fillies and mares and a comprehensive stakes schedule patterned on the English program of classic racing."

The most profound decision Eddie Taylor ever made in regard to his hobby—horses—was in 1952. Although he was gratified with the success of the horses he had bred in Canada, he sought wider recognition. And so he asked George Blackwell of the British Bloodstock Agency to buy him the best mare in the Newmarket December sales. Blackwell chose *Lady Angela*, a daughter of *Hyperion*, the leading English sire at the time and an outstanding sire of broodmares. The British considered *Hyperion*, winner of the Epsom Derby and the St. Leger, to be the "best little horse that ever lived." She was in foal to the great Italian sire, *Nearco*, and one of the conditions of the purchase was that she be bred back to *Nearco* in 1953. Taylor paid $35,000 for the eight-year-old mare, the top price of the sale, and for a mare that had only one win in eleven starts. After foaling *Empire Day* in England, she was bred back to the Italian stud and when pronounced in foal was shipped to Taylor's National Stud in Oshawa, where she dropped a nearly black colt, later named *Nearctic*. He was to prove the

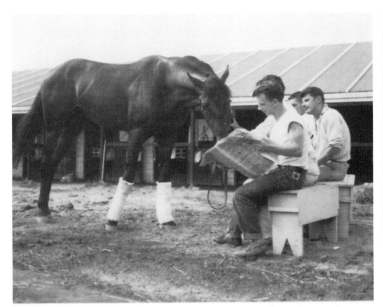

1959 PLATE WINNER *NEW PROVIDENCE* CHECKS OUT THE *DAILY RACING FORM*.

cornerstone on which Windfields' international reputation was built. Rejected by buyers at Taylor's sale in 1955 as "too expensive" at $35,000, *Nearctic* was a fast, high-class horse, but was sometimes erratic while winning twenty-one races, some of them against the top handicap horses in the United States. At stud, he stood for a record $2,500, and exceeded all expectations. Few breeders, if any, anticipated that he would create a new branch of the *Nearco* sire line, which would influence the future development of the thoroughbred world-wide. Kentucky Derby winner *Northern Dancer* was out of his first crop. Breeding history would be made in the ensuing twenty years as offspring and grandsons of *Nearctic* hit the racing headlines. The average cost of yearlings in 1968, the year Taylor consigned his first crop to the CTHS sales, was $5,923. In 1983 the average price soared to $61,922. Taylor had put Canadian racing on the map, and *Nearctic* and his son *Northern Dancer* led the way. *Nijinsky II* and *The Minstrel*, both sons of *Northern Dancer*, made an impact in Europe, winning the classics before other sons of *Northern Dancer* followed in their footsteps—*Shareef Dancer*, *El Gran Senor* and *Storm Bird*. The best decision Taylor did not make was to geld *Northern Dancer*, a move contemplated in 1963 but rejected because of the failure of an expensive *Ribot* colt that had been gelded.

While Taylor was influential during the 1949–1970 era, jockeys Avelino Gomez, Ron Turcotte, Hugo Ditfach, Jim Fitzsimmons and Chris Rogers stamped themselves as candidates for racing's Hall of Fame. The excitable Cuban arrived in Canada in the mid-1950s and won four Plates. Rogers, who like Turcotte, also went south seeking greater fame, won three Plates in a space of six years. The dominant trainers were Pete McCann of Windfields with five Plates in ten years, and Yonnie Starr and Horatio Luro with three apiece. Roy Johnson would saddle the first two Plate victories for the West in *Whistling Sea* and *Merger* during the 1960s.

The pomp, pageantry and tradition of the historic race would never be greater than in 1959 when Queen Elizabeth II became the second ruling monarch to attend the race for the "guineas."

NOTE THE PROXIMITY OF THE PHOTOGRAPHER AT THE CLUBHOUSE TURN AND THE CEMENT BLOCKS SUPPORTING THE RAILS BEFORE A PACKED GRANDSTAND FOR WOODBINE'S FIRST PLATE RACE.

1949 | EPIC

THE FILLY *FILSIS* STARTED OUTSIDE THE TWELVE-STALL STARTING GATE. SHE FINISHED THIRD AT ODDS OF 76-TO-1. *EPIC*, THE WINNER, BROKE FROM NO. 12 STALL.

Of *Epic*, after his convincing triumph over twelve rivals in the ninetieth running of the King's Plate, it would be said: "He came, he saw, he conquered." The same would later be said of the colt's owner, Edward Plunket Taylor, the man who would build Windfields Farm of Ontario and Maryland into one of the world's greatest racing and breeding empires.

Taylor said there was no particular significance in the colt's name; it was one that he had found while thumbing through a dictionary in the library of his Bayview Avenue home in Willowdale. "It appealed to me. It was short. It was easily remembered. An epic is a poem, or is an event of importance."

Epic was E.P. Taylor's first Plate winner, and also the first horse to ever carry the turquoise silks with the gold-coloured polka dots on the sleeves in Canada's most important race, one that in the future Taylor would thoroughly dominate in the manner which Joseph E. Seagram had at the turn of the twentieth century. Unlike Seagram, whose stable controlled the future of the historic race almost from the day he ventured into racing, Taylor bided his time before he made the Plate a goal

He had already established himself as a knowledgable horseman in the 1930s, a time in which he was devoted to winning races, not classics. When Taylor bought or claimed his first racehorses (*Madfast, Annimessic, Jack Patches, Nandi* and *Mona Bell*) in 1936 with an initial investment of $6,000, it was to further indulge his hobby of attending races and wagering, and also to promote his chief commercial enterprise at the time—beer. The advertising of beer was forbidden by the Canadian government in those days, and with the acquisition of Cosgrave's Brewery in Toronto, Taylor saw a way to popularize his brand among beer-drinking racegoers by racing in the name of his newly acquired brewery. As a result Cosgrave Stable, with its light blue silks and gold-coloured cap, was formed. In five years it became one of America's leaders in races won, accounting for 308 victories, but no Plates. *Mona Bell* was second to *Bunty Lawless* in 1938 while *Jelwell* and *Gypster* were out of the money in the war years while Taylor curtailed his racing activities.

Windfields, a son of *Nandi,* one of Taylor's $1,500 claims in Maryland in 1936, looked almost invincible for the Plate in 1946, but trainer A.E. (Bert) Alexandra and Taylor decided he "was too good" for homebrews and sent him up to Florida and New York against horses like Triple Crown winner *Assault.* Sired by *Bunty Lawless,* Taylor would name his farm Windfields after his first stakes winner and great progenitor of future champions. However, when another of *Bunty*'s offsprings was foaled that

1949 KING'S PLATE STAKES

FOURTH RACE
Woodbine Park
MAY 28, 1949

1 1–8 MILES (1:50$\frac{3}{5}$). Ninetieth Running KING'S PLATE. $10,000 added. 3–year–olds. Foaled in Canada. Allowances. Gross value, $14,310. Net value to winner $10,810, plus 50 guineas; second, $1,500; third, $1,000; fourth,$300.

Horse	Eqt	Wt.	PP	St	¼	½	¾	Str	Fin	Jockey	Owner	Odds $1
EPIC		119	12	3	2^{2}	2^{3}	$1\frac{1}{2}$	$1^{2\frac{1}{2}}$	$1^{2\frac{1}{4}}$	RogersC	TaylorEP	1.40
SPEEDY IRISH	b	119	9	13	13	11^{1}	7^{3}	$3^{1\frac{1}{2}}$	2^{6}	DewhurstJ	McCullaghCG	1.20
*FILSIS	b	114	13	4	3^{2}	3^{3}	3^{1}	2^{1}	$3\frac{1}{2}$	RobillardG	ElliottGB	76.20
BUNTY LINE	b	119	5	5	6^{hd}	6^{nk}	4^{3}	4^{3}	$4^{6\frac{1}{4}}$	CourtneyG	JStuartStable	6.65
BUNTY JEWEL		114	6	9	$9\frac{1}{2}$	$8^{1\frac{1}{2}}$	9^{1}	9^{1}	5^{4}	KeenanJ	HemsteadCH	a-f-19.80
BAY COMPANION		114	2	12	10^{1}	10^{1}	$5^{1\frac{1}{2}}$	6^{1}	$6^{1\frac{3}{4}}$	McKlemurryA	GrantRW	f-19.80
REGAN LAD	b	119	4	10	$12\frac{1}{2}$	$12\frac{1}{2}$	12^{1}	12^{2}	7^{3}	O'SullivanE	FairJG	f-19.80
BOLARIS	b	114	10	1	$1^{1\frac{1}{2}}$	1^{hd}	$2^{1\frac{1}{2}}$	5^{1}	8^{2}	StroudL	ChrisS	13.60
ROYAL BOMBER	b	119	1	11	$4^{3\frac{1}{2}}$	4^{1}	6^{nk}	$7\frac{1}{2}$	9^{2}	FisherR	DellerMrsG	a-f-19.80
RAMILLION		119	3	2	5^{hd}	$9\frac{1}{2}$	11^{1}	10^{1}	$10^{1\frac{3}{4}}$	RoyE	HaltonBrookStable	161.10
GRAYDON TINA		114	11	6	7^{2}	5^{1}	8^{1}	8^{1}	$11^{2\frac{1}{2}}$	DodgeF	BainHR	26.45
FOXY RYTHM	b	114	7	7	8^{1}	7^{nk}	$10\frac{1}{2}$	11^{2}	12^{4}	StrettonS	SheridanVJ	56.75
KAN DIS	b	119	8	8	11^{4}	13	13	13	13	HolbornW	TaylorHW	132.00

a–Coupled, Bunty Jewel and Royal Bomber. f–Mutuel field. *Started from outside gate.

WENT TO POST—4:21. OFF AT 4:22. Time, :23, :46$\frac{3}{5}$, 1:12$\frac{2}{5}$, 1:38, 1:52$\frac{1}{5}$. Track fast.

Mutuel Prices:

	$2 Mutuels Paid			Odds $1		
EPIC	4.80	2.75	3.15	1.40	.37½	.57½
SPEEDY IRISH		2.45	2.55		.22½	.27½
FILSIS			9.50			3.75

Br. c, by Bunty Lawless—Fairy Imp, by *Gino. Trainer, A. E. (Bert) Alexandra. Bred by Taylor E P.

Start good from stall gate. Won handily; second and third driving. EPIC, away fast, was under mild reserve while forcing the pace established by BOLARIS, moved into the lead approaching the half-mile pole, drew clear, then continued smartly at the close to hold SPEEDY IRISH safe. The latter, very sluggish in the early stages as usual, gradually bettered his position, closed with good energy when placed under punishment, but failed to threaten the winner at the end. FILSIS raced in close attendance of the pace from the outset, moved up gamely entering the stretch and continued gamely to the close, although tiring slightly at the end.

THE FIRST OF MANY PLATES FOR E.P. TAYLOR. GOVERNOR GENERAL VISCOUNT ALEXANDER (LEFT) AND TRAINER BERT ALEXANDRA AND JOCKEY CHRIS ROGERS.

EPIC | 3-year-old brown colt

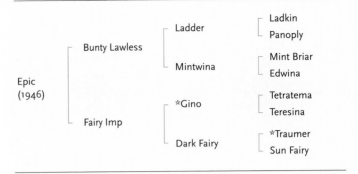

Epic (1946)
- Bunty Lawless
  - Ladder
    - Ladkin
    - Panoply
  - Mintwina
    - Mint Briar
    - Edwina
- Fairy Imp
  - *Gino
    - Tetratema
    - Teresina
  - Dark Fairy
    - *Traumer
    - Sun Fairy

Owner: E.P. Taylor, Willowdale; *Trainer:* A.E. (Bert) Alexandra
Jockey: Chris Rogers; *Breeder:* E.P. Taylor

year at the nursery in Oshawa, a "growthy" dark brown-coloured colt, his goal would always be the 1949 Plate.

Ridden by Hamilton-born jockey Chris Rogers, who like Alexandra and Taylor were experiencing their first Plate victories, *Epic* would toy with his field on 28 May, and support a statement Taylor had made three months before the race, a time when *Epic* was more or less an unknown and had never started in any kind of race. The colt was too big as a two-year-old to support his weak ankles and trainer Alexandra decided to take him to California and "go slow with him" before finishing off his conditioning program in New York that spring.

"Without any hemming, hawing or perhapses, he told me that *Epic* would win the Plate if he made it to the starting gate," recalled *The Daily Star*'s Joe Perlove. Taylor greeted the writer after the race, saying "We sure put ourselves away out on a limb that day, didn't we?" However, few people, if any, were aware that a last-minute decision by Alexandra almost cost *Epic* the opportunity to run. Seventeen horses were expected to run, so the Ontario Jockey Club decided to start the remainder of the field (five horses) outside the barrier. When Alexandra found out that *Epic* had drawn a post position outside the twelve-stall starting gate, he complained loudly that all horses should have an equal chance and should start from the old open barrier. The stewards refused, whereupon Alexandra announced that *Epic* would be scratched from the race. Taylor, however, was not in agreement with the scratch and while they were arguing the point, four other owners removed their horses from the race, with the result that *Epic* went into the last stall of the starting gate. *Filsis*, a filly, started outside the gate, and finished third at 76-to-1 odds.

Despite *Epic*'s impressive Plate Trial win in his first start, he was second choice in the betting to George McCullagh's *Speedy Irish*, who chased the winner home after a slow start. "Give Johnny [Collins], my assistant, credit for this win," said

YOUTHFUL CHRIS ROGERS AFTER HIS FIRST PLATE VICTORY.

Alexandra. "He stuck with him, saying he was a great horse after I just about gave up on him. He had bad ankles, a front hoof that wasn't too good and we had to fire one leg three times for a bad splint. Before the third firing, I gave up on him. Said he wouldn't do. Collins disagreed and stuck with him practically day and night. Do you realize the hours of drilling we gave this horse? It went on for months and months. No racing. Just conditioning. It was awful. Now I think he deserves a rest, maybe two months, before we try the New York horses."

While the late 1940s was a time when attendance soared, and purse money slowly increased, the OJC was faced with two threats—the City of Toronto and horsemen, who were demanding a greater say in the operation of racing. Toronto was attempting to raise taxes by increasing the assessment of Woodbine by $500,000 and was threatening to expropriate the property. Because of the City's threats to take action in the next few years, and the looming expediency to change the site of the track, the OJC said "it was advisable that we should be extremely careful in seeking another property." In the next couple of years agents for the OJC would quietly begin acquiring land in Rexdale, the vicinity northwest of Toronto. Meanwhile, the Horsemen's Benevolent and Protective Association was formed, and resolved to put an end to the "dictatorial" Incorporated Canadian Racing Association, the governing body of the sport in Ontario. The HBPA would win this "show of strength and unanimity" as the ICRA collapsed. The action, however, led to the birth of the Ontario Racing Commission, which would become a far more autocratic and restrictive body than the ICRA.

The OJC announced that steeplechasing, which had been a feature at Woodbine Park since its opening in 1876, would be cancelled on Saturdays and holidays the following year. Steeplechasing was getting little support at the betting windows, and fields were small. The once popular sport for the "timber toppers" and major event on the two-and-one-half-mile course in the infield, the Woodbine Autumn Steeplechase Handicap, was discontinued after the 1952 season.

Little Frankie Dougherty, an ex-jockey who was among the eight riders nailed in the 1937 race-fixing scandal, had a future King's Plate winner in his barn in the spring of 1950, a bay colt that had been bred by E.P. Taylor. It was named after McGill, the Montreal university the industrialist had attended. A horse who preferred going a distance of ground, such as a mile-and-one-eighth, *McGill* was the winterbook favourite for the ninety-first running of the Plate, but unfortunately, if he won the race, it would have to be in the silks of another owner, and not Dougherty's wife, whose name and colours the horse ran under.

Under prevailing conditions, Dougherty was not eligible to enter the colt in the Plate because he was not "a British subject resident in Canada." Although he had lived and worked sporadically in Canada since the early 1930s, Dougherty and his wife were American citizens from New York. Naturally, Dougherty had a multitude of offers for the colt, especially after *McGill* had won the richest running of the Cup and Saucer Stakes in the fall of 1949, establishing himself as the horse to whip for

MCGILL (INSIDE) EKES OUT A NECK VICTORY OVER *SIR STROME*.

the Plate the following spring. But Dougherty, a shrewd bargainer, was not about to be shoved into any deal. He told reporters: "I expect to sell the horse so he can run in the Plate. But if I don't get my price, I'll sell him cheap to Willie Russell, just to try and get Willie a Plate winner." Russell was an owner-trainer with a couple of cheap horses.

"Fast Frankie" had ridden in the Plate as recently as 1948, when he was on the losing half of Jim Fair's winning entry of *Last Mark* and *Fair Mark*. He knew of the prestige and glamour attached to having your name on the scroll along with the Seagrams, Hendries, McLaughlins and Hatches. Nobody had to remind him that, among

VINCE SHERIDAN, TRAINER PETE KEISER AND *MCGILL* WITH CHRIS ROGERS UP.

Canadian owners, the Plate was the most keenly sought prize of all racing diadems and that men had paid huge sums for two-year-olds with shiny records for the express purpose of winning the historic race. R. James Speers, the dedicated Winnipeg horseman, had once stood near the finish line in front of Santa Anita's grandstands in California on the day of the $100,000 Santa Anita Handicap. "This is pretty nice," he observed, his eye scanning the fifty-seven thousand people in attendance, "but I'll tell you the truth: I'd rather win the King's Plate than this one here today."

Dougherty must have been a slick dealer to acquire the horse for "about" $7,000 from E.P. Taylor, the man who had bred *McGill*. The colt had looked rather ordinary after his first couple of starts, and Taylor sold the offspring of *Bunty Lawless*, the celebrated Plate champion and sire of *Epic*, his first Plate winner, that same year. His stable's hopes were riding on *Bonvivant*, which had cost him $11,000, and *Bennington*. However, before the season was over, owners were lining up at Dougherty's barn, while Taylor's hopes for a second successive Plate were scuttled as *Bonvivant* was unable to train; the horse was later sold for $5,000, while *Bennington* was claimed for $7,500 by a Mrs. Lottie Wolf.

Meanwhile, *McGill* went to the post twenty times, winning three races; but, more importantly, he beat the best two-year-olds in Canada when winning the Cup and Saucer, and had banked $17,000. A newcomer to racing, Bill Beasley, offered Dougherty $17,000 several days before the stakes race, but Dougherty refused. He wanted the $10,000 purse before he would sell. Another person interested in *McGill* was Vince J. Sheridan, owner of a successful heavy machinery business and president of the Ontario division of the Horsemen's Benevolent and Protective Association. That winter he offered $15,000, a sizeable sum in 1950, and one that many

Vince Sheridan, Chris Rogers and trainer Pete Keiser are congratulated by Governor General Viscount Alexander.

McGILL | 3-year-old bay colt

McGill (1947)	Bunty Lawless	Ladder	Ladkin
			Panoply
		Mintwina	Mint Briar
			Edwina
	Tinted Chick	Tintagel	*Sir Gallahad III
			Heloise
		Brown Chick	Brown Bud
			Chickadee

Owner: Vincent J. Sheridan, Toronto; *Trainer:* Pete Keiser
Jockey: Chris Rogers; *Breeder:* E.P. Taylor, Willowdale, Ont.

horsemen thought was "friendly." No deal. Dougherty had to have $17,500, he explained, because he wanted to put $15,000 in the bank and bet the remaining $2,500 on *McGill* to win the Plate.

Eventually "Fast Frankie" got what he wanted, but that made Sheridan a target for all the second-guessers. They noticed that the colt looked thin, and questioned the methods of Sheridan's trainer, Pete Keiser. Other horses, such as *Nephisto,* were working quicker that spring, and when *McGill* finished fourth in the Plate Trial Stakes, the critics harped on the fact that Sheridan "got took." His reply to all the needlers was that he did not pretend to know that much about a horse himself, but that his trainer assured him that *McGill* was a good colt, and that the horse was doing everything that was being asked of him. Sheridan said repeatedly that he had confidence in Keiser and that was why he was keeping the horse.

On Plate day a crowd of thirty-five thousand backed Sheridan's judgment: it made the colt the 2-to-1 favourite over Carr Hatch's *Unionville,* which finished third. Perhaps the hero of the day was jockey Chris Rogers, the Hamilton youth who was winning his second Plate in a row. He gave *McGill* a "million-dollar ride" in gaining a neck decision over Joe Holbeck's *Sir Strome.* Rogers outrode American rider Ted Johnson in the stretch when the two colts ran head-to-head. "We got beat by a superior rider," Holbeck said afterwards. "I think we had the best horse, but the other horse had the best rider." Ironically, *Sir Strome* was bred by R. James Speers, who never again came that close to winning the race he cherished above all others; several weeks later, however, the colt would win the Quebec edition of the King's Plate in Montreal. Among the also-rans at Woodbine was *Brazen Buz,* owned and trained by Mrs. Estelle Giddings, wife of the late Harry Giddings, who had trained eight Plate winners.

Feminists should have been proud that day, but no fuss was made over the face that she had become the first woman to ever saddle a horse in the Plate.

Taylor was philosophical when he was questioned about selling a Plate winner, which later in his breeding career would become a routine practice of Windfields Farm. "A person can't race them all. It's a great thrill to breed two successive Plate winners." Frank Selke, who gave up the breeding business and a job with Conn Smythe and the Toronto Maple Leafs for a chance to build a hockey dynasty with the Canadiens in Montreal, best summed up Taylor's predicament: "After a while I got tired of never being right. If I sold a horse that didn't win, I was called a crook for peddling poor stock. If I sold a horse that won, I was ridiculed for not realizing I had a good thing, which I should have kept for my own stable."

1950 KING'S PLATE STAKES

FOURTH RACE
Woodbine Park
MAY 27, 1950

1 1-8 MILES (1:50⅗). Ninety-First Running of the KING'S PLATE. Fifty guineas, the gift of His Majesty the King, with $15,000 added by the Ontario Jockey Club. (Estimated value, $21,000). 3-year-olds. Bred in Canada. Property of a British subject resident in Canada, which have not started in 1950, the Plate Trial excepted. Weight, 119 lbs. Fillies allowed 5 lbs. No gelding allowance. Gross value, $19,440. Net to winner $14,040; second, $2,250; third, $1,500; fourth, $450. Breeder award, $1,050.

Horse	Eqt	Wt.	PP	St	¼	½	¾	Str	Fin	Jockey	Owner	Odds $1
McGILL	b	119	6	13	10^{nk}	6^{hd}	$3\frac{1}{2}$	$2\frac{1}{2}$	1^{nk}	RogersC	SheridanV	2.10
SIR STROME	b	119	7	8	$9^{1\frac{1}{2}}$	7^{nk}	$5\frac{1}{2}$	3^{hd}	2^{2}	JohnsonT	DoubleBlueStable	a-5.25
UNIONVILLE	b	119	9	12	11^{3}	10^{nk}	$6^{1\frac{1}{2}}$	$4^{2\frac{1}{2}}$	$3^{1\frac{1}{2}}$	NicholsJ	HatchC	4.40
*MEDALOFREEDOM		119	13	4	12^{1}	12^{1}	$11\frac{1}{2}$	$5^{1\frac{1}{2}}$	4no	BavingtonA	DoubleBlueStable	a-5.25
NEPHISTO	b	119	12	5	$2\frac{1}{2}$	2^{2}	$1^{1\frac{1}{2}}$	$1^{1\frac{1}{2}}$	$5^{1\frac{3}{4}}$	StewartJ	ParkwoodStable	b-4.90
MAPLE WOOD	b	119	8	7	8^{hd}	11^{4}	9^{3}	6^{2}	$6^{5\frac{1}{2}}$	StantonJ	MaplewoodFarm	33.35
TINDERILL	b	119	10	10	$7^{1\frac{1}{2}}$	8^{hd}	$8\frac{1}{2}$	7^{nk}	$7^{4\frac{3}{4}}$	MorrealeL	JStuartStable	f-25.20
LADY'S LOVER	b	119	3	2	3^{2}	$3^{2\frac{1}{2}}$	$4^{1\frac{1}{2}}$	8^{1}	$8^{1\frac{1}{4}}$	ZakoorW	MerrillFW	f-25.20
BARD OF AVON		119	2	6	$4^{1\frac{1}{2}}$	4^{3}	7^{nk}	$9\frac{1}{2}$	9^{hd}	LicataA	McCullaghCG	59.65
*PINE RIVER	b	119	14	11	14	14	13^{1}	$12\frac{1}{2}$	$10\frac{1}{2}$	DewhurstJ	ParkwoodStable	b-4.90
BRAZEN BUZ	b	119	5	9	6^{2}	5^{hd}	$10\frac{1}{2}$	11^{1}	11^{3}	RemillardP	GiddingsMrsE	9.80
BLUE DANCE		119	11	1	$1^{1\frac{1}{2}}$	$1\frac{1}{2}$	2^{3}	$10\frac{1}{2}$	$12^{1\frac{1}{2}}$	PicouC	McIntyreJR	5.60
ROANITE	b	119	1	3	5^{hd}	9^{nk}	$12\frac{1}{2}$	13^{1}	13^{2}	HolbornW	SeagramJEF	14.00
JIM'S ICRA		119	4	14	13^{2}	13^{1}	14	14	14	RobillardG	HardyG	f-25.20

a-Coupled, Sir Strome and Medalofreedom; b-Nephisto and Pine River. *Started from outside gate. f-Mutuel field.

WENT TO POST—3:55. OFF AT 3:55½. Time, :23, :47⅖, 1:12, 1:38⅗, 1:52⅖. Track fast.

Mutuel Prices:

	$2 Mutuels Paid			Odds $1		
McGILL	6.20	3.85	3.05	2.10	.92½	.52½
SIR STROME (a-Entry)		4.95	3.50		1.47½	.75
UNIONVILLE			3.50			.75

B. c, by Bunty Lawless—Tinted Chick, by Tintagel. Trainer, Pete Keiser. Bred by Taylor E P.

Start good from stall gate. Won driving; second and third the same. McGILL, allowed to settle in stride before being called upon, began to better his position leaving the backstretch run, came between horses on reaching the homestretch, took command inside the final seventy yards, then continued gamely under punishment to outlast SIR STROME. The latter, sluggish in the early stages, was placed under pressure entering the last three furlongs, came to the outside for the drive, closed with determination under pressure and fought it out stubbornly at the finish. UNIONVILLE, steadied in back of the pace, responded when roused entering the final half, came stoutly through the homestretch and finished with good energy. MEDALOFREEDOM closed willingly after failing to keep up in the early stages. NEPHISTO set the pace for the opening five furlongs, raced BLUE DANCE into defeat to draw clear, but faltered inside the final furlong. MAPLE WOOD made up ground in the last three furlongs. TINDERILL could not engage the leaders. LADY'S LOVER showed speed for the opening seven furlongs then began to falter. BLUE DANCE took command in the run to the first turn but began to weaken after going seven furlongs.

Scratched—Day's Eye.

The bandsmen of the Queen's Own Rifles broke into "Rule Britannia" as a big field of twenty-one horses started its long parade out of the paddock and towards the two starting gates for the ninety-second running of the King's Plate. An appropriate selection, many in the crowd of thirty-five thousand thought—E.P. Taylor's entry, the fleet, multiple stakes-winning filly, *Britannia*, and her plodding stablemate, *Major Factor*, were at $3.15-to-$1 in the betting odds behind the favourite, Medway Stable's gelding, *Libertine*, who was at $2.65-to-$1 odds.

Horsemen and stable connections figured that *Britannia*, the handsomely bred daughter of *Bunty Lawless* and *Iribelle* (a foundation mare in Windfields Farm's breeding empire), had only to beat Colonel J.E. Smallman's *Libertine* to earn the guineas for Taylor. *Major Factor*, a lightly regarded gelding that horsemen had ignored the year before

LIEUTENANT COLONEL CHARLES BAKER (LEFT), HONOURARY AIDE TO GOVERNOR GENERAL VISCOUNT ALEXANDER, JOCKEY ALF BAVINGTON AND E.P. TAYLOR.

when he ran repeatedly in $2,500 claiming races, was a contender only if the track was muddy. On 26 May 1951 the track at Woodbine was dry and fast.

Major Factor, ridden by a jockey whose scheduled Plate mount had been withdrawn, would, however, win that day, beating *Libertine* by a length, an event that prompted *The Daily Star*'s Milt Dunnell to write: "Which just goes to prove a musician is no smarter than anyone else. When the man who trained the E.P. Taylor pair was fooled, and the jockey who had his choice of mounts made the wrong pick, there's some excuse for the man who came to the track to swing a baton."

Thirty-three years later, three of these men recalled the major roles they played in what was to be the last running of the King's Plate, as such, in the first 125 years of the historic Canadian classic. King George VI passed away in February 1952, and the race once again became the Queen's Plate when he was succeeded by his daughter, Elizabeth II.

In 1984, Pete McCann, *Major Factor*'s trainer, was still training and galloping his own horses at the age of seventy-five. Alf Bavington, who won his only Plate in 1951, was on daily parade at the racetrack, leading the horses to the post as an outrider, while Gil Robillard, who chose the wrong horse but made up for it the following year when he won with a long shot, was trying to win his first Plate as a trainer. Gordon (Pete) McCann, an ex-fighter and jockey who once rode four winners on a program in Havana and was the leading rider in Cuba in 1926, was too shy to enter the winner's circle when his boss accepted the coveted "guineas" in 1951. He refused to be lured out of the shaded paddock, where well-wishers found him standing beside the jockey's quarters. Finally he retreated to the stables.

Yet he did talk later about the race: "[*Major Factor*] was just a horse who happened to be better than anything else around on that day. I remember watching the race from the centrefield. The filly [*Britannia*] was in front and Alfie [Bavington] was eighteenth when the horses disappeared behind the mutuels board. I lost sight of [Alfie]. But at the top of the lane, I saw our silks." McCann actually saw two sets. Robillard and the filly were beginning to falter after setting the pace, while Bavington and *Major Factor* were flying on the outside of the pack, taking a run at the leader, *Libertine*.

Bavington, a nephew of Mildred Kane, the first woman to win the Plate (the McCann-trained *Willie the Kid* in 1940), knew more about the horse he had to catch than his own mount. The year before, he had ridden *Libertine* to victory in the rich Cup and Saucer Stakes, but had lost the mount the following spring to Johnny Dewhurst. At the time, Bavington was under contract to Bill Beasley's stable, which ran a candidate in each division of the Plate Trial Stakes.

> I was on both of them, but they did nothing. Our trainer, [Johnny] Passero, talked Beasley out of entering them in the Plate, which wasn't a bad idea as there was talk of maybe twenty-five or so horses going into the Plate and the likelihood of splitting the race. As it was they had to borrow a couple of gates from Dufferin, and then we had to still start one horse outside the gates. [Two days later the OJC acquired the new fourteen-stall Puett starting gate from New Jersey. It had fool-proof magnetic locks to prevent horses from breaking through the barrier. Also, a green light signaled when all the horses had been loaded.] Really all I wanted that day was a mount. He would have been a longshot if he'd not been part of Mr. Taylor's entry.

Bavington's timing was impeccable in 1951: he also won the Prince of Wales Stakes on *Major Factor,* again beating *Libertine.* Later that year he was replaced on *Major Factor* for the Breeders' Stakes by Jose Vina. But Alfie was asked to ride *Libertine* and won the race! Gilbert H. Robillard, whose career ended in 1956 when he suffered a broken leg in a morning workout accident, well remembered his reasons for choosing the filly, but disagreed with a version of the story which claimed that McCann believed *Britannia* would win the Plate.

> I had first call for Mr. Taylor's horses that year, and had won the Coronation and Princess Elizabeth Stakes with the filly when she was a two-year-old. We also beat the colts in the Plate Trial. I knew both horses well, as I had ridden and won on *Major Factor.* Pete [McCann] said he thought I was making a mistake. The gelding had started out as a claimer and had improved, but I never thought he was as good as the filly. I figured she was fit and ready. But she went a mile and collapsed. Mr. Taylor gave me my choice. In fact he was going to bring up Hedley Woodhouse from New York to ride the filly. It was up to me. I still received my ten per cent of the Plate purse. But it wasn't the money—it's the prestige.

MAJOR FACTOR | 3-year-old brown gelding

Major Factor (1948)	*Boswell	Bosworth	Son-in-Law
			Serenisima
		Flying Gal	*Sir Gallahad III
			*Filante
	Aldwych	Marine	Man o' War
			*Damaris II
		*Chrysoberil	Verdun
			New Moon

Owner: E.P. Taylor, Willowdale, Ont.; *Trainer:* Gordon (Pete) McCann
Jockey: Alf Bavington; *Breeder:* E.P. Taylor

An apprentice rider employed by Jim Speers' Whittier Stock Farm of Winnipeg, which ran a two-horse entry in the Plate, was Gerald Lavigne, who later trained Plate winners *Almoner* (1970) and *Son of Briartic* (1982). Another horseman emerging on the scene, and who would make Plate history, winning three Queen's Plates in the 1970s, was Jack Stafford. He won his first two races ever at Woodbine Park that spring.

Major Factor's owner E.P. Taylor with King's Plate.

Trainer Gordon (Pete) McCann.

1951 KING'S PLATE STAKES

FOURTH RACE
Woodbine Park
MAY 26, 1951

1 1-8 MILES (Beau Dandy, Sept. 23, 1950—1:50—5—121). Ninety-Second Running of the KING'S PLATE. Fifty guineas, the gift of His Majesty the King, with $15,000 added by The Ontario Jockey Club. (Estimated value, $21,000). The first horse to receive the guineas, stakes and 65 per cent of the added money; the second horse, 15 per cent; the third horse, 10 per cent, and the fourth horse, 3 per cent. The breeder of the winner to receive 7 per cent. For Canadian-bred 3-year-olds, the property of a British subject resident in Canada, who have not started in a race in 1951, the Plate Trial as offered by the Ontario Jockey Club excepted, and which have not been outside Canada at any time during 1951. Weight, 119 lbs. Fillies allowed 5 lbs. No gelding allowance. Gross value, $21,405. Net to winner $16,005; second, $2,250; third, $1,500; fourth, $450. Breeder award, $1,050.

Horse	Eqt	Wt.	PP	St	¼	½	¾	Str	Fin	Jockey	Owner	Odds $1
MAJOR FACTOR		119	2	18	$17^{2\frac{1}{2}}$	$10\frac{1}{2}$	9^{nk}	6^{4}	1^{1}	BavingtonA	TaylorEP	a-3.15
LIBERTINE	b	119	1	10	$9\frac{1}{2}$	$5^{1\frac{1}{2}}$	$2^{1\frac{1}{2}}$	1^{nk}	$2^{3\frac{1}{4}}$	DewhurstJ	MedwayStable	2.65
BEAR FIELD		119	14	12	12^{hd}	8^{1}	4^{1}	$4\frac{1}{2}$	3^{1}	BrightC	FairJG	f-4.95
BRITANNIA		114	4	1	$1^{2\frac{1}{2}}$	1^{5}	$1^{1\frac{1}{2}}$	2^{3}	$4^{1\frac{1}{4}}$	RobillardG	TaylorEP	a-3.15
MR. HOOD	b	119	5	17	$10\frac{1}{2}$	$7\frac{1}{2}$	$6^{1\frac{1}{2}}$	5^{2}	$5\frac{3}{4}$	JohnsonT	McIntyreJR	b-9.25
MOUNT BRANCA	b	119	20	9	$7^{1\frac{1}{2}}$	3^{hd}	3^{4}	$3\frac{1}{2}$	$6^{2\frac{1}{4}}$	NicholsJ	DoubleBlueStable	c-5.95
CYMRO		119	13	13	15^{nk}	15^{1}	11^{1}	10^{hd}	7no	McTagueC	WhittierParkStockFarm	d-7.55
CARALITA		114	16	8	8^{1}	$9^{1\frac{1}{2}}$	8^{3}	7^{1}	8^{nk}	PalaezH	MinnekahdaStable	f-4.95
PANDAMOND	b	119	19	19	20	20	$14\frac{1}{2}$	$12^{1\frac{1}{2}}$	$9\frac{1}{2}$	PolkV	HolbeckMrsJE	c-5.95
*PREY SEVEN		119	21	20	19^{2}	19^{2}	$13^{2\frac{1}{2}}$	11^{2}	10^{5}	BuissonR	McMackenMrsG	f-4.95
BILL ARMSTRONG		119	10	4	5^{nk}	6^{1}	5^{nk}	$8^{1\frac{1}{2}}$	11^{nk}	PermaneR	MorrisseyWF	e-34.30
SCAPA BLOW		114	17	16	18^{5}	16^{1}	17^{nk}	$13^{1\frac{1}{2}}$	12^{3}	HartleyD	WhittierParkStockFarm	d-7.55
FAIRLOW		119	6	3	$3\frac{1}{2}$	2^{nk}	7^{2}	$9\frac{1}{2}$	$13^{1\frac{1}{4}}$	RemillardP	NorthDownsFarm	28.45
DONSTAN	b	119	11	6	$6\frac{1}{2}$	$11\frac{1}{2}$	12^{1}	14^{2}	$14^{1\frac{1}{2}}$	ChurchK	CheslerL	8.45
SIR ALGAHAD		119	12	11	$13\frac{1}{2}$	13^{1}	15^{1}	15^{1}	15^{1}	CampbellH	KinraraStable	f-4.95
TEDDY'S SISTER		114	18	7	11^{2}	14^{1}	$16\frac{1}{2}$	$16^{1\frac{1}{2}}$	16^{3}	BernardoN	FlemingJJ	b-9.25
IMPONE		119	15	15	$16\frac{1}{2}$	17^{nk}	19^{2}	17^{8}	17^{15}	StantonJ	FaulknerAE	f-4.95
CORWYNT	b	119	8	2	$2^{1\frac{1}{2}}$	$4\frac{1}{2}$	$10^{1\frac{1}{2}}$	18^{6}	18^{7}	FisherR	HemsteadCH	42.50
LUSCOE'S PRIDE	b	119	3	5	4^{hd}	12^{nk}	18^{4}	19^{6}	19^{2}	NashA	LuscoeStable	f-4.95
WILLIE GEORGE		119	9	14	$14^{1\frac{1}{2}}$	$19\frac{1}{2}$	20	20	20	WankmuellerR	HardyG	e-34.30
ERINDALE KID	b	119	7	Lost rdr.						ZakoorW	ErindaleStable	f-4.95

a-Coupled, Major Factor and Britannia; b-Mr. Hood and Teddy's Sister; c-Mount Branca and Pandamond; d-Cymro and Scapa Blow; e-Bill Armstrong and Willie George. f-Mutuel field. *Started from outside the gate.

WENT TO POST—3:45. OFF AT 3:45½. Time, :23 2/5, :47 2/5, 1:12 3/5, 1:39 3/5, 1:53. Track fast.

Mutuel Prices:

	$2 Mutuels Paid			Odds $1		
MAJOR FACTOR (a-Entry)	8.30	3.90	2.75	3.15	.95	.37½
LIBERTINE		4.05	2.70		1.02½	.35
BEAR FIELD (f-Field)			2.70			.35

Br. g, by *Boswell—Aldwych, by Marine. Trainer, McCann Gordon (Pete). Bred by Taylor E P.

Start good from Orpen-Clark gate. Won driving; second and third the same. MAJOR FACTOR was slow getting under way, worked his way into contention slowly, came with a rush through the stretch and was up at the end to best LIBERTINE. The latter suffered some interference at the start, was roused midway of the last turn, forged into a slight lead midway of the stretch, was unable to stall off the top one, but hung on determinedly to easily best the others. BEAR FIELD was unable to keep up early, moved to the leaders slowly, closed stoutly under hard urging, but could not reach the top pair. BRITANNIA sprinted into the lead in the run to the turn, drew clear after settling on the backstretch, then faltered after straightening out in the stretch. MR. HOOD showed a game effort. MOUNT BRANCA raced evenly within striking distance of the pace, then faltered inside the final furlong when put to urging. CYMRO could not reach contention. CARALITA was never formidable. BILL ARMSTRONG had early foot. DONSTAN tired. FAIRLOW was though early. CORWYNT stopped. ERINDALE KID lost his rider at the start.

Scratched—Sis Bunty.

The impact of E.P. Taylor's influence on horse racing in Canada had already begun to take a firm hold the year the race became the Queen's Plate again. For the fourth successive year a horse bred by Taylor would win the Plate as *Epigram*, a maiden with career earnings of just seventy-five dollars, splashed home in front of twenty mud-coated rivals to earn a purse of $16,875, plus Her Majesty's fifty "guineas." But, as was the case in 1950, the winner would run under the silks of another stable. The Three Vs Stable of Frank, Lawrence and Gordon Veal, three Toronto men who ran a Studebaker auto dealership, had claimed the well-bred colt for $2,500 from Taylor the year before.

A trainer now, jockey Gil Robillard had mud trickling out of his ears and off his nose the day he won with the "Cinderella" horse for the Veals and trainer Stanley (Rip) Bowden:

> The Veal boys wanted to get another rider, but Rip [Bowden] stuck by me and said they'd better get another trainer if I didn't ride the horse. Later he wasn't much; just a big bullish horse that was fit and ready on Plate day. I told everybody that the big sulky bastard would win the race after the Plate Trial Stakes. In those days it was a sprint and Mr. Taylor's horse, *Acadian*, won. *Epigram* was fifth, but we were flying at the end. . . . When the track came up a sea of mud I knew we'd win because *Acadian* couldn't handle it. Then he [*Acadian*] gets stuck under the gate. . . . I'd never seen anything like it before, or since. Doug [Haig], who was the starter, had every problem imaginable. First one of the gates got stuck in the mud in the infield, then they can't get the two gates together and it's like a half-hour and we're still standing around. When *Acadian* flipped on his back, he managed to tear off his blinkers and bridle, which means more delay. Oh yes, the vets also had to check him out. Then Haig finds out he can't operate the electrical system because of the dampness, and we had to start from open stalls. With a half-mile to go we had maybe two horses beat. I hit him twice and he took off in the slop. I hit him again turning into the stretch, but I think if I'd hit one more time he would have quit. He was scared.

Taylor was disappointed on that foggy 24 May afternoon when the skies seemed to drip rain interminably; he was concerned over the health of *Acadian,* who limped home ninth, and the seventh-place finish of *Dance Circle,* the filly owned by his wife, Winifred. Their entry was the 3-to-2 favourite because each had won a division of the Plate Trial Stakes, and another horse bred by Taylor, *Epigram,* had won the Plate. Breeding stakes winners, after all, was Taylor's business. He had sold the 1950 Plate winner *McGill* to Vince Sheridan and had wished the Veals luck with *Epigram,* a horse that he had little regard for in the first place. He later told author Richard Rohmer that he considered the colt to be one of the worst horses ever to win the Queen's Plate. However, the powerful business magnate, who owned Windfields Farm in suburban York Mills and

FAMED AUTHOR AND RACING REPORTER JIM COLEMAN INTERVIEWS GIL ROBILLARD FOR TORONTO RADIO STARTION CFRB.

the National Stud in Oshawa, was suitably pleased that another horse he had bred had won Canada's most distinguished race. "There's almost as much thrill in breeding a Plate winner as there is in owning one. But it seems that I'm the only interested person who didn't have a hedge bet on the colt." *Epigram* paid $25.05.

In 1952 Taylor's long-range plans for his breeding and racing operations were just beginning to fall into place, as were his designs for the future steps that the Ontario Jockey Club and racing in Canada would take. Taylor was an expansionist, both in the hardknocking world of corporate finance and development and in horse racing. His blueprints for it had the same ingredients he had used to put together Canadian Breweries: acquisitions, shutdowns, mergers, all leading to fewer, but much more attractive, facilities.

Tracks at Hamilton and Fort Erie would be acquired, along with several disused racing charters, which allowed the OJC to race a greater length of time at Woodbine. In a few years, racing at tracks in and around Toronto—Thorncliffe, Dufferin and Long Branch—would cease. But before Taylor's master plan could take effect, he needed a reduction of taxes from Premier Leslie Frost's Conservative government at Queen's Park, which was taking twelve cents out of every dollar wagered. Taylor gave a hint of his expansionist proposals at the *Daily Racing Form*'s first Horse of the Year awards dinner in 1952, at which he was the guest of honour. *Bull Page,* a colt that he had purchased for $38,000 in Kentucky in 1948, and one that would

Premier Leslie Frost presents the Queen's Plate to the Veal brothers (from left) Frank, Lawrence and Gordon, while Gil Robillard extends a hand towards well-wishers.

EPIGRAM | 3-year-old bay colt

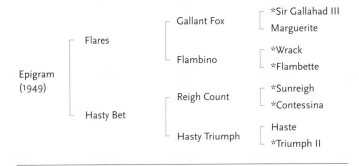

Epigram (1949)	Flares	Gallant Fox	*Sir Gallahad III
			Marguerite
		Flambino	*Wrack
			*Flambette
	Hasty Bet	Reigh Count	*Sunreigh
			*Contessina
		Hasty Triumph	Haste
			*Triumph II

Owner: Three Vs Stable (Frank, Lawrence and Gordon Veal), Toronto
Trainer: Stanley V. (Rip) Bowden; *Jockey:* Gil Robillard
Breeder: E.P. Taylor, Willowdale, Ont.

join *Chop Chop* and *Windfields* in projecting his breeding aspirations to great heights, had been the unanimous choice in the 1951 poll. Taylor told the horsemen and politicians:

> All our tracks are outmoded and inadequate for present-day racing. We need improvement in racing itself, better conditions for horsemen, and more facilities for the public. This can only be accomplished with modern racing plants. There has been some progress made to reduce taxation, but the present structure is still excessive. It should be lowered so that racetracks will have a higher per centage in order to provide higher purse distribution. The establishment [by Frost] of the Ontario Racing Commission is the best thing that could have happened to our racing.

Headed by Magistrate Tupper Bigelow, George C. Hendrie, D.A. Mcintosh, Bert McLean and supervisor Bill Risewick, the ORC took over the job of legislating the sport in Ontario. One of its first moves was the introduction of the "film patrol." The motion picture camera, which was used to film races from several vantage points, enabled the ORC to build up its case in a betting-ring scandal in 1951 at Fort Erie, one that saw ten jockeys and a trainer ruled off North American tracks for life.

During the jockey scandal of 1951 Risewick received threats to his life and frequently changed hotels in Niagara Falls, checking into the Foxhead Hotel and sleeping in another. One day his car was crowded off the road on the way back to Toronto from Fort Erie and on another occasion his car was gouged with an ice pick. Risewick was the ideal man for the role as he grew up around horses; his grandfather owned standardbreds. Risewick's career had been mainly centred around the motion picture business before coming to Canada in 1929 to edit and process newsreel films. In a *Globe and Mail* interview, he said, "When I came to Toronto I immediately got into the thoroughbred business along with motion pictures."

At the same awards dinner, Taylor leaked the news to Nelson Dunstan, a *Daily Racing Form* columnist from New York, that in 1953, or possibly the year after, the Queen's Plate would be transferred to a course that would be one of the most modern on the North American continent. Taylor, who had a habit of tipping off American writers of major happenings during his days in the spotlight, said that he and several of the leading businessmen and sportsmen of Ontario had joined together for the purpose of constructing a new track in or near Toronto. They had already acquired control at Woodbine. The new plant would cost $5 million, or more. The "new" Woodbine was on the horizon.

1952 QUEEN'S PLATE STAKES

SIXTH RACE
Woodbine Park
MAY 24, 1952

1 1-8 MILES (1:50). Ninety-Third Running of the QUEEN'S PLATE. Fifty guineas, the gift of Her Majesty, Queen Elizabeth II, with $15,000 added by the Ontario Jockey Club. (Estimated value, $21,000). Gross value, $22,125.

Net to winner $16,875, plus 50 guineas; second, $2,250; third, $1,500; fourth, $450. Breeder award, $1,050.

Horse	Eqt	Wt.	PP	St	¼	½	¾	Str	Fin	Jockey	Owner	Odds $1
EPIGRAM	b	119	2	13	15^{1}	14^{1}	10^{1}	8½	1^{1}	RobillardG	ThreeV'sStable	11.52½
GENTHORN	b	114	3	9	9^{1}	8^{1}½	8^{2}	4^{1}½	2^{5}¾	FlutieE	FourL'sStable	79.80
LATIN LAD		119	21	6	5½	5½	2^{1}½	1^{nk}	3¾	VinaJ	GardenCityStable	23.95
BLUE WRACK	b	119	15	1	1½	2^{1}½	3^{1}½	2^{nk}	4^{1}¼	LicataA	AvestaStable	3.35
ERIC'S GIRL		114	20	16	18^{1}	18^{1}	19^{1}½	9^{nk}	5no	BreckonsJ	NorthDownsFarm	a-11.95
HIELAN LADDIE		119	17	14	14½	15½	16^{1}	12^{1}	6^{1}	McTagueC	SeagramJEF	b-7.35
DRESS CIRCLE	b	114	1	7	7^{1}	7½	7½	5½	7^{1}½	OtisR	TaylorMrsEP	c-1.55
LORD STROME	b	119	10	15	17^{1}	16½	15^{1}½	15½	8^{1}¼	BavingtonA	WhittierParkStkFm	d-11.95
ACADIAN	b	119	7	17	12^{1}	11½	11½	10^{2}	9^{2}¼	NashR	TaylorEP	c-1.55
ALLISON PASS	b	119	6	8	8^{nk}	9^{2}	9^{1}½	11½	10½	DewhurstJ	ElmarStable	d-11.95
TOUR DE FORCE		119	19	4	3^{hd}	3^{hd}	1^{hd}	3^{nk}	11^{nk}	RoyE	HaltonBrookStable	f-22.95
SOD FIELD	b	119	8	11	11^{nk}	12½	13½	17½	12^{1}¼	BarberE	FairJG	f-22.95
WAIT ON ME	b	119	18	20	20^{1}½	20^{1}	19^{1}½	13^{1}	13¾	CorollaC	Jo-AnnStable	11.60
KOOFLA	b	119	14	12	13^{nk}	13^{nk}	14^{2}½	16^{1}	14^{7}½	PongL	HalliwellAJ	f-22.95
OUR OMAR	b	119	2	13	2½	1½	4^{1}	7^{1}	15^{2}	RemillardP	KennedyAG	a-11.95
LUCKY PASS	b	119	16	10	10½	10^{hd}	12½	14^{nk}	16^{4}	MafaleM	BelliJ	79.75
MINNEDOSA	b	114	11	11	4^{2}	4^{2}	5^{1}	6^{nk}	17^{1}¾	ClemesK	BayParkStable	f-22.95
TRING FAIR		119	4	18	16^{nk}	17^{1}	17^{1}	18^{nk}	18^{nk}	JohnsonT	HRBainEstate	a-11.95
FLAREDAY	b	114	9	19	19½	19½	20^{1}	19^{1}	19^{15}	BuissonR	SeagramJEF	b-7.35
FIREY GAL	b	114	12	21	21	21	21	21	20^{1}	EllisM	StormFarm	f-22.95
SUNNYCREST	b	119	5	5	6½	6½	6^{nk}	20^{1}	21	RogersC	SheridanVJ	18.95

a-Coupled, Eric's Girl, Our Omar and Tring Fair; b-Hielan Laddie and Flareday; c-Dress Circle and Acadian; d-Lord Strome and Allison Pass. f-Mutuel field.

OFF AT 5:48. Time, :24, :49²/s, 1:16²/s, 1:45, 1:58³/s. Track sloppy.

Mutuel Prices:

	$2 Mutuels Paid			Odds $1		
EPIGRAM	25.05	14.30	10.80	11.52½	6.15	4.40
GENTHORN		64.35	30.70		31.17½	14.35
LATIN LAD			10.95			4.47½

B. c, by Flares—Hasty Bet, by Reigh Count. Trainer, Stanley V. Bowden. Bred by Taylor E P.

Start good from open stalls. Won driving; second and third the same. EPIGRAM, steadied in back of the pace, improved his position gradually, closed boldly through the homestretch run to wear down the leaders and drew clear at the end. GENTHORN, also outpaced in the early stages, came between horses for the drive and finished stoutly. LATIN LAD raced forwardly placed from the beginning, but weakened in the closing drive.

On 2 June, the day of Elizabeth II's coronation, "Ol' Banana Nose," Eddie Arcaro, was tossed up on the back of *Canadiana*, replacing regular jockey Jose Vina for the ninety-fourth running of the Queen's Plate. The expertise of the world's leading jockey, winner of the Kentucky Derby a record five times, was scarcely required as the slender, long-striding bay filly, whom horsemen had already dubbed the "Queen of the Track," broke smartly out of the Number 17 post position and cruised home more than five lengths ahead of her closest rival. Eased up in the stretch, *Canadiana*'s unrushed clocking was just one-fifth of a second off the Plate record.

The delighted owner of the first Canadian-bred to win more than $100,000 in its career was E.P. Taylor, who had become only the third man to win both the King's Plate and the Queen's Plate. (At the turn of the century, two of horse racing's great pioneers, Joseph Seagram and William Hendrie, had registered Plate victories during the reigns of Queen Victoria and Edward VII.)

"OL' BANANA NOSE" EDDIE ARCARO WAS ABOARD *CANADIANA* IN HER WIRE-TO-WIRE VICTORY FOR E.P. TAYLOR. SHE WAS THE FIRST CANADIAN-BRED TO EARN MORE THAN $100,000.

How good was *Canadiana* that day? "She would've won that one with Kate Smith ridin' her. That's a good filly, a real good one," was veteran jockey Sammy Boulmetis' observation of the filly who would earn more tributes than any other horse in Canada before she was retired at the age of five with a record bankroll of $177,116. "Another mile and *Canadiana* would have lapped 'em," another rider claimed.

Canadiana had shocked the racing community in the Plate Trial Stakes a week earlier, finishing fourth, a result that prompted her owner to send out the distress signal for Arcaro. Taylor was criticized for "bumping off" the Cuban, who had guided her to the Horse-of-the-Year title as a two-year-old, an honour usually reserved for older horses; Vina had been her only rider in twelve earlier races. Taylor defended his action: "This is no reflection on Vina. Arcaro has ridden my horses in New York on many occasions. My idea mainly was to add some extra colour to the race." Taylor had also entered another filly, *Lively Action*, in the Plate. She had won her division of the Plate Trial Stakes, and Taylor facetiously suggested: "Let them choose which mount they ride." Jose Vina chose *Lively*

A BUBBLE GUM CARD FEATURED *CANADIANA*'S WIN.

Action and finished third, four lengths behind the runner-up, *Blue Scooter,* but he was invited into the winner's circle by Taylor. The Cuban also received the winning jockey's share of the purse, about $2,100, the amount he would have earned if he had finished first.

Arcaro, known as the "jock with the clock in his conk," sparkled in the attention he received on his arrival in Toronto. He had never ridden before at Woodbine, and recalled that the last time he rode in Canada, in 1932 when he was "a punk kid," he had been suspended while riding at either Kenilworth or Devonshire Park in Windsor. When reminded by W.A. Hewitt, formerly the presiding steward on Ontario tracks, that "I gave you the first suspension you ever had," Arcaro's dark eyes twinkled before he replied: "That's right, sir. The horse was *Bag Smasher.*"

Years later, while assessing the Plate winners he had saddled for Windfields, trainer Pete McCann remarked: "A helluva filly, a nice filly. Vina was a good rider, too. He would have won that day on her. I knew she would do it that day, even though I was kidded about leading her [on a pony] to the starting gate in my business suit. She had a little trick step she did when she left her stall before a race; it told

WOODBINE'S PACKED STANDS AND ITS FAMOUS ELM PROVIDE A BACKDROP FOR *CANADIANA*'S DOMINANT WIN.

CANADIANA | 3-year-old bay filly

Canadiana (1950)	Chop Chop	Flares	Gallant Fox
			Flambino
		*Sceptical	Buchan
			Clodagh
	Iribelle	*Osiris	Papyrus
			Most Beautiful
		Belmona	King James
			Belmon

Owner: E.P. Taylor, Willowdale, Ont.; *Trainer:* Gordon (Pete) McCann
Jockey: Eddie Arcaro; *Breeder:* E.P. Taylor

me whether she was ready. She didn't want to do her jig step before the Trial, and she just didn't run her race that day."

Canadiana was a daughter of *Chop Chop*, a stakes winner in the U.S. who would go on to sire three more Plate winners, including Taylor's first Kentucky Derby starter *Victoria Park* in 1960. The filly was his first good horse and was the tip of the iceberg as far as his stud career was concerned. *Chop Chop* was by Ascot Gold Cup winner *Flares* (whose full brother was 1935 American Triple Crown winner *Omaha*). His offspring were usually anything but show horses to the eye; nevertheless, they almost invariably outran their looks as *Chop Chop* was credited with twenty-nine stakes winners. If *Canadiana* inherited her class from *Chop Chop*, no doubt she got her toughness from the bottom half of her pedigree, *Iribelle*, one of the cornerstone mares of Taylor's breeding operations. *Canadiana* was also his first major stakes winner in the United States, winning the Test Stakes at Saratoga Springs in 1952, and the Vagrancy Handicap later at Aqueduct. Her conquests on both sides of the border had breeders eagerly anticipating her progeny when she finally retired to the broodmare shed. After witnessing her Plate victory, A.G. Vanderbilt, owner of the great *Native Dancer*, said that he hoped the two horses would one day meet each other, "but preferably after they have both concluded their careers."

Unlike many of his promising fillies, who were bred shortly after winning a stakes race, Taylor allowed *Canadiana* to do what she did best—run. She made sixty-two starts in four seasons, winning a lot of races and a great deal of money (more than all her offspring did collectively), but there is little doubt that the strenuous racing compromised her career as a producer. When she finally "caught," it was to a cover by *Windfields*, a mating that produced *All Canadian*, her lone stakes winner in fifteen frantic years. Ironically, *All Canadian* won the race that she had failed in, the Plate Trial Stakes. Subsequent years, however, proved to be discouraging for her handlers at Oshawa. Despite their efforts with *Nearctic, Northern Dancer, *Menetrier, New Providence* and *Right Combination*, the results were fruitless. She was pronounced in foal on many occasions, but would abort or lose them in every conceivable manner.

Peter Poole, general manager of Windfields Farm's breeding operations, said he was a firm believer that you "get it either one way or another, but rarely both. *Canadiana* was one horse who was what she was—a runner. At the time Mr. Taylor was breeding many of his young fillies, and he wanted to have one good racehorse in his barn. She also wasn't a good mother with her first few foals, and wouldn't feed them properly."

1953 QUEEN'S PLATE STAKES

SEVENTH RACE
Woodbine Park
JUNE 2, 1953

1 1-8 MILES (1:50). Ninety-Fourth Running of QUEEN'S PLATE (50 Guineas, the gift of Her Majesty the Queen), with additional guaranteed value of $20,000. The owner of the first horse to receive the Guineas, stakes and 65 per cent of the added money; of the second horse, 15 per cent; of the third horse, 10 per cent, and the fourth horse, 3 per cent. The breeder of the winner to receive 7 per cent. Special weights. 3-year-olds. Bred in Canada. The bona fide property of a British resident in Canada who have not started in a race in 1953. Weight, 119 lbs. Fillies allowed 5 lbs. No gelding allowance. Gross value, $26,070. Net to winner $20,445; second, $2,250; third, $1,500; fourth, $450. Breeder award, $1,050.

Horse	Eqt	Wt.	PP	St	¼	½	¾	Str	Fin	Jockey	Owner	Odds $1
CANADIANA	b	114	17	3	1^{2}	1^{5}	1^{6}	1^{8}	$1^{5\frac{1}{2}}$	ArcaroE	TaylorEP	a-.60
BLUE SCOOTER		119	13	6	6^{2}	4^{nk}	$2^{\frac{1}{2}}$	$2^{1\frac{1}{2}}$	2^{4}	JohnsonT	McIntyreJR	7.75
LIVELY ACTION	b	114	12	16	13^{1}	9^{2}	6^{nk}	$4^{\frac{1}{2}}$	3no	VinaJ	TaylorEP	a-.60
BELFLARES		114	9	17	$15^{\frac{1}{2}}$	$14^{\frac{1}{2}}$	$10^{\frac{1}{2}}$	$7^{\frac{1}{2}}$	$4^{\frac{3}{4}}$	PedersonG	ArmstrongBrothers	91.05
VIRGINIA FAIR		114	18	2	3^{1}	$3^{\frac{1}{2}}$	$3^{\frac{1}{2}}$	$3^{\frac{1}{2}}$	5^{3}	RichardsD	CharlesworthJA	11.70
BIG HEAP	b	119	3	7	$8^{1\frac{1}{2}}$	$6^{1\frac{1}{2}}$	5^{2}	6^{nk}	6^{hd}	RoyE	StaffordFarm	f-15.50
CHAIN REACTION		119	11	1	2^{1}	2^{hd}	$4^{\frac{1}{2}}$	5^{hd}	7^{nk}	McTagueC	TomlinsonMrsJ	f-15.50
LOWMOND		114	10	10	12^{nk}	12^{1}	9^{1}	$8^{1\frac{1}{2}}$	$8^{\frac{3}{4}}$	RemillardP	NorthDownsFarm	13.40
FOOD FOR THOT		119	19	8	$9^{\frac{1}{2}}$	11^{1}	11^{1}	11^{nk}	$9^{\frac{1}{2}}$	DyeG	ApplebyLH	43.40
BONSAND		119	7	9	$14^{\frac{1}{2}}$	15^{1}	13^{hd}	$9^{\frac{1}{2}}$	10^{2}	LicataA	KruppC	16.05
BALLYRAY	b	119	6	14	16^{3}	16^{2}	$15^{1\frac{1}{2}}$	13^{1}	$11^{\frac{1}{2}}$	OtisR	SeagramJEF	f-15.50
SUNITA	b	119	16	15	17^{2}	17^{1}	$16^{\frac{1}{2}}$	$15^{\frac{1}{2}}$	$12^{\frac{3}{4}}$	BuissonR	SheridanVJ	b-34.10
BRIARCREST	b	119	4	13	7^{nk}	$8^{\frac{1}{2}}$	7^{nk}	$10^{\frac{1}{2}}$	13^{6}	BirleySD	SheridanVJ	b-34.10
MILLBROOK		119	2	12	$10^{1\frac{1}{2}}$	$10^{\frac{1}{2}}$	$12^{\frac{1}{2}}$	14^{1}	$14^{\frac{3}{4}}$	AllgaierH	RusanaStable	f-15.50
TEDDYBROOK	b	119	15	4	5^{1}	7^{nk}	8^{nk}	$12^{\frac{1}{2}}$	15^{hd}	CombestN	CowanJG	f-15.50
WINTER LADY		114	8	19	19	18^{2}	18^{5}	16^{1}	$16^{2\frac{3}{4}}$	LindbergH	ArmstrongMissOR	34.15
BETTERGO		119	5	18	18^{2}	19	19	19	$17^{1\frac{1}{4}}$	FonteC	HemsteadCH	f-15.50
AVELLA	b	114	14	11	11^{nk}	13^{hd}	17^{1}	17^{2}	18^{6}	BoulmetisS	AddisonStable	11.60
NORTH OF SEVEN	b	119	1	5	$4^{1\frac{1}{2}}$	5^{nk}	$14^{\frac{1}{2}}$	18^{1}	19	FiskB	CheslerL	22.75

a-Coupled, Canadiana and Lively Action; b-Sunita and Briarcrest. f-Mutuel field.
OFF AT 5:01. Time, :23^{2}/s, :47^{2}/s, 1:12, 1:38^{2}/s, 1:52^{1}/s. Track fast.

Mutuel Prices:

	$2 Mutuels Paid			Odds $1		
CANADIANA (a-Entry)	3.20	2.70	4.20	.60	.35	1.10
BLUE SCOOTER		5.10	5.30		1.55	1.65
LIVELY ACTION (a-Entry)	3.20	2.70	4.20	.60	.35	1.10

B. f, by Chop Chop—Iribelle, by *Osiris II. Trainer, McCann Gordon (Pete). Bred by Taylor E P.

Start good from stall gate. Won easily; second and third driving. CANADIANA, much the best and having the speed to reach the first turn on top, took a clear lead before entering the backstretch, widened on her field at will and, in the last furlong, was being taken in hand the final yards. BLUE SCOOTER, away with the leaders, moved up to force the pace after the opening half mile, closed with determination when set down for his best, could not menace the top one, but was best of the others. LIVELY ACTION, unable to keep pace in the early stages, saved some ground entering the home stretch and finished with fine energy. BELFLARES, outpaced early, closed some ground in the last three furlongs. VIRGINIA FAIR raced in close attendance of the pace but weakened inside the last furlong. BIG HEAP could not reach the leaders. BONSAND was outrun. CHAIN REACTION tired. BRIARCREST was outrun. TEDDYBROOK had brief speed. AVELLA was never a factor. NORTH OF SEVEN went well for a half-mile then faltered.

When Gordon McMacken bought Maplewood Farm in Todmorden, a sleepy suburb north of Toronto, he told his good friends from Hamilton, Peter Burton and Walter Fitzgerald, that he expected many a Queen's Plate winner to pass through its gates. Undoubtedly, the owner of *King Maple*, who in 1953 had been selected as Canada's Horse of the Year in the *Daily Racing Form*'s annual poll, was looking ahead to 12 June 1954 and the sight of the bay-coloured son of *Fairaris* and *Noon Maid* carrying his red and white silks into the winner's enclosure.

McMacken's prophecy proved to be partially accurate; the Plate winner did pass through his farm gates that winter, but he belonged instead to Burton and Fitzgerald, who had wintered *Collisteo* and seven other members of their Bur-Fit Stable at Maplewood. Ridden with incredible skill by Hamilton-born Chris Rogers, who that afternoon equalled the record of three Plate wins held by Bobby Watson, Frankie Mann, Harry Lewis and Richard O'Leary, *Collisteo*

A HALO FOR CHRIS ROGERS? *COLLISTEO*'S OWNERS, WALTER FITZGERALD (LEFT) AND PETER BURTON HOIST TROPHY.

stole the race by a head from E.P. Taylor's *Queen's Own* (later named the outstanding horse of 1954) and McMacken's 1-to-4 favourite, *King Maple*. The silks Rogers wore were yellow and black; Peter Burton had been a former football quarterback for the old Hamilton Tigers in the late 1920s.

"I stole the Plate," Rogers said to reporters afterwards. "I stole it like I did on *McGill* in 1950. I set a false pace in the stretch and relaxed my horse a bit. You could say I was playing possum, eh? I let the boy on Mr. Taylor's horse [Bert Albert on *Queen's Own*] move up with me. Then I moved again when he thought he had us beaten. When I moved with my colt, the other boy didn't have time to realize it, and we were at the finish—and in front. As I always told the boys, you can win more races in the final twenty yards than at the eighth pole."

A head separated the two horses in a race that, at 1:52, equalled *Last Mark*'s 1948 record. Pete McCann, trainer of Taylor's entry of *Queen's Own* and *Staff Reporter*, second choice in the betting after registering wins in their divisions of the Trial Stakes, credited Rogers for his ride. "He made a bum of Albert an American rider they brought in from Montreal. It was one of Rogers' big rides of his life, and that's all there was to it."

The colt's win, plus the fourth place finish of *Collisteo*'s stable-mate, *Pancho*, was worth more than $23,000. However, both owners failed to cash in at the mutuels: "Fitz" only had twenty dollars and "Petey" forty on their entry, which paid $24.20. They were so sure that it would be the McMackens who would be meeting Canada's first native-born Governor General, the Honourable Vincent Massey, that they did not bring formal dinner jackets in the event they might be the guests of honour at the Jockey Club's posh post-race dinner at the Toronto Club.

It was a crushing blow for Mrs. Gordon McMacken to see her colt lose the race that she and her husband most coveted. Still, it was not completely *King Maple*'s fault, considering the knocking about he and jockey Herb Lindberg received at least twice. Before the Plate, there had been much talk of how *King Maple* would trounce his eight challengers. If horses could have read, the rest of the field would never have left their stalls. Congratulatory wires had poured into the McMacken home days before the race, and North Downs Farm had sent a flowered horseshoe as a premature prize. The general optimism about *King Maple* was not unfounded. Trainer Johnny Hornsby had him fit and on his toes following an impressive win in the Plate Trial Stakes, and had kidded *Collisteo*'s trainer, Dick Townrow, who was saddling his first Plate horse, "to make sure and show up" at his place for the party Saturday night. Townrow, an ex-jockey, replied: "Maybe the party will be at my house." Mrs. McMacken was generous in defeat: "If it couldn't have been *King*

Collisteo holds off *Queen's Own* charge to win by a head.

COLLISTEO | 3-year-old brown colt

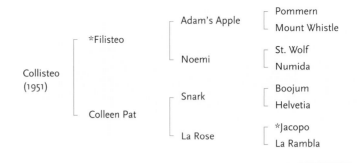

Collisteo (1951)	*Filisteo	Adam's Apple	Pommern
			Mount Whistle
		Noemi	St. Wolf
			Numida
	Colleen Pat	Snark	Boojum
			Helvetia
		La Rose	*Jacopo
			La Rambla

Owner: Bur-Fit Stable, Hamilton, Ont. (Walter Fitzgerald, Peter Burton)
Trainer: Richard (Dick) Townrow; *Jockey:* Chris Rogers
Breeder: Malcolm D. Richardson, Aurora, Ont.

Maple, I'm very happy it was *Collisteo* that won it."

Collisteo, who had set a track record in winning the Victoria Stakes as a two-year-old, served as a tribute to his breeder, Malcolm Richardson. He had had a long career as an amateur steeplechase and hunt rider, and at the annual yearlings auction had sold the colt for $3,600 to Bur-Fit Stable. Richardson was as proud of the win as the owners, for the Plate had been a Richardson family tradition. He had seen his first Plate in 1911 when his father, bank manager Harry A. Richardson, brought him to the track at a time when children were not allowed into the member's enclosure. He watched the race from the back seat of a roadster parked on the fringe of the track. In 1928 Richardson bought Foxley Green, a farm in the rolling hills of Aurora, thirty miles north of Toronto. He would later call it "the biggest little breeding farm in Canada" after he got into the breeding game in an earnest, but modest fashion in 1945.

Two years later, Richardson went to Kentucky with E.P. Taylor for the Keeneland fall sales. "I knew little about breeding in those days. It was at this sale that I bought *Colleen Pat.* She was by *Snark,* a very fast sprinter, and I bred her to **Filisteo,* who was a real 'killer' if you weren't careful around him. He was a noted distance runner. I figured this breeding might produce a good horse."

The foal was *Collisteo.* "The really unusual fact about the sale was that two of the mares that were sold in it, later produced Plate winners. They were led in one after the other. *Colleen Pat* was first. She was in foal, carrying a filly [*Gaiety*] that I later sold to Taylor. She cost me $2,900. I was glad that he [Taylor] didn't bid on her. He was interested in the next mare, *Hasty Bet,* the dam of *Epigram,* who won the Plate in 1952. Something, eh?"

Trainer Richard Townrow.

1954 QUEEN'S PLATE STAKES

SEVENTH RACE
Woodbine Park
JUNE 12, 1954

1 1-8 MILES (1:50). Ninety-Fifth Running QUEEN'S PLATE. Fifty guineas, the gift of Her Majesty the Queen, with additional guaranteed value of $20,000. The owner of the first horse to receive the guineas, stakes and 65 per cent of the added money; of the second horse, 15 per cent; the third horse, 10 per cent, and the fourth horse, 3 per cent. The breeder of the winner to receive 7 per cent. 3-year-olds. Bred in Canada. Special weights. The bona fide property of a British subject resident in Canada which have not started in a race in 1954, excluding the Plate Trial and excluding such other race or races as may be determined by the Ontario Jockey Club Limited, and who have not been outside of Canada at any time during 1954. Weight, 119 lbs. Fillies allowed 5 lbs. Gross value, $29,680. Net to winner $22,305, second, $3,000; third, $2,000; fourth, $600. Mutuel Pool, $103,552. Breeder award to winner $1,400.

Horse	Eqt	Wt.	PP	St	¼	½	¾	Str	Fin	Jockey	Owner	Odds $1
COLLISTEO	b	119	7	2	3^2	$2^{1\frac{1}{2}}$	1^1	1^2	1^{hd}	RogersC	Bur-FitStable	b-11.10
QUEEN'S OWN		119	6	8	9	7^{hd}	4^{hd}	$2^{2\frac{1}{2}}$	$2^{3\frac{3}{4}}$	AlbertB	TaylorEP	a-3.00
KING MAPLE		119	3	9	$6\frac{1}{2}$	4^{hd}	3^{hd}	3^1	$3^{2\frac{1}{2}}$	LindbergH	McMackenStable	.25
PANCHO	b	119	9	5	$5\frac{1}{2}$	8^{hd}	6^3	$4\frac{1}{2}$	4^3	BavingtonA	Bur-FitStable	b-11.10
HI LAUDE	b	119	8	4	8^{hd}	9	5^{hd}	5^3	5^2	RoyE	ApplebyLH	22.80
STAFF REPORTER	b	119	4	1	1^1	1^1	$2^{1\frac{1}{2}}$	6^2	6^1	BrownC	TaylorEP	a-3.00
HEPTAD		119	2	7	7^{hd}	5^{hd}	$7\frac{1}{2}$	7^1	$7^{2\frac{1}{4}}$	ClemesK	ArmstrongBrothers	41.75
THREE STRIPER		119	5	6	4^{hd}	8^{hd}	8^{10}	8^{12}	8^{15}	OtisR	SeagramJEF	65.05
WELCOME HOME		119	1	3	$2\frac{1}{2}$	3^{hd}	9	9	9	StevensonD	ArmstrongMissOR	76.55

a–Coupled, Queen's Own and Staff Reporter; b–Collisteo and Pancho.

OFF AT 5:25. Time, :23²/₅, :47²/₅, 1:11³/₅, 1:38²/₅, 1:52. Track fast.

Mutuel Prices:

	$2 Mutuels Paid			Odds $1		
COLLISTEO (b–Entry)	24.20	5.40	2.20	11.10	1.70	.10
QUEEN'S OWN (a–Entry)		3.70	2.10		.85	.05
KING MAPLE			2.10			.05

Br. c, by *Filisteo—Colleen Pat, by Snark. Trainer, Richard Townrow. Bred by Malcolm Richardson, Aurora, Ont.

Start good. Won driving; second and third the same. COLLISTEO, well handled, raced in the thick of contention from the beginning while saving ground, forged to the front midway of the last turn, drew good and clear after straightening out in the homestretch and hung on tenaciously at the close to outlast QUEEN'S OWN. The latter, taken in hand in the run to the first turn, was set down for his best after straightening out in the homestretch and fought it out with determination at the close. KING MAPLE lacked racing room after the first turn, worked his way between horses after reaching the backstretch and came with good energy when clear in the last furlong. PANCHO, steadied early, could not better his position in the final drive. HI LAUDE could not engage the leaders. STAFF REPORTER, sent to the front at once, began to shorten strides after going five furlongs. HEPTAD was never troublesome. THREE STRIPER had brief speed. WELCOME HOME tired badly.

Scratched—Miss Luscoe.

L arkin Maloney, a dour man with an irascible temperament, went out one evening to buy a paper, or perhaps it was an excuse to seek shelter because his wife was having the girls in for bridge. He strayed farther than the newsstand that night, after reading that an auction of year-lings was taking place at Woodbine. A man who had made a fortune in the building materials business, Maloney took refuge at the sales in 1953, and with the assistance of Dave Garrity, who did the bidding, came home poorer by $8,500, but the owner of *Ace Marine*. He was a chestnut colt that would capture the final running of the Plate at Woodbine Park, the aging, but still beautiful track that had hosted its first Queen's Plate in 1876, and where the race had been run since 1883.

From the days of Victoria, the track had mellowed to the pounding hooves of thousands of horses, and its stands had heard the whoops and moans of millions of winners and losers. Like many Torontonians who had trekked out to the suburbs during the post-war baby boom in search of cheaper housing and more living space, the Ontario Jockey Club was on the move too. It fashioned a racetrack out of the mudflats northwest of Metro Toronto, in Rexdale, near Highway 27 and Malton Airport. The mid-fifties were clearly an era in which tradi-tions were destroyed: both the Brooklyn Dodgers and the New York Giants moved their franchises to California.

For years Toronto had been expropriating little pieces of the property that was once owned by horseman and publican Joseph Duggan. Woodbine was now an island, surrounded by streetcar tracks, houses, newly built roads, cut off from Lake Ontario and the sandy beaches over which the horses once galloped. The track would soon become known as Greenwood—a name taken from a disused racing charter the OJC had acquired from horsemen in the old Ontario oil town of Petrolia. The final running of the Plate was a nostalgic one for fans, horsemen and officials, whose lives or fami-lies had spanned the days of the race's earliest years until the ninety-sixth renewal, which would become the first ever televised by the CBC. Clocker Tom Bird was one of the oldtimers who remembered the great races over the years; he had seen *Joe Miller* win the Plate in 1894. M.C. Smith, the first mayor of Burlington in 1912, had not missed a Plate since 1891, the year *Victorious* started an avalanche of wins for Joseph Seagram. Frowde Seagram, Joe's grandson, was there, along with George C. Hendrie, grandson of William Hendrie, the Laird of Waterloo's friendly adversary, and the new track manager, the energetic J.J. Mooney, whose father, J.D. Mooney, had ridden both a Kentucky Derby and a King's Plate winner in the 1920s.

It was fitting that the last Plate winner at old Woodbine should

FANS PACKED WOODBINE PARK (LATER RENAMED OLD WOODBINE, THEN GREENWOOD) FOR THE FINAL RUNNING OF THE PLATE AT THE EIGHTY-YEAR-OLD TRACK. *ACE MARINE* LED EVERY STEP OF THE WAY.

be bred by Carr Hatch, son of Harry Hatch, the man who had bred five Plate winners between 1936 and 1945, and that it should be trained by Joseph (Yonnie) Starr. A former newspaper boy who had been around Toronto racetracks since 1922, Starr's beginnings were "walking hots" (cooling out horses that had had a workout), jockey's agent, assistant trainer and owner of a one-horse stable. His first horse was *Exhibition,* one that Conn Smythe had sold him "on the cuff" (payments were made whenever the horse earned the share of a purse). It was Smythe, too, who had recommended Starr to Maloney shortly after he had strayed into the night and become enamoured of a yearling that reminded him of "Ol' *Eucalyptus,*" a horse that he had owned years ago.

A small, compact colt, *Ace Marine* was not regarded as being among the elite of the 1954 crop of two-year-olds. He had two wins in modest company that year; his best effort was finishing third in a stakes race at Narragansett to *Boston Doge,* the world's fastest sprinter at the time. The OJC announced that instead of one Plate Trial Stakes race before the Queen's Plate, it would stage two—one at six furlongs and the other at one mile and seventy yards. To further confuse handicappers, the two stakes races attracted so many entries that seven divisions were needed to facilitate eager trainers. The only horse to win at each distance was *Ace Marine,* who was ridden by George Walker, a Syrian-born jockey from Pawtucket, Rhode Island.

Walker had been Stafford Farm's regular jockey in 1954. But Jack

Stafford hired a new rider that winter—Avelino Gomez. The Cuban would climb aboard *Senator Jim,* while Conn McCreary, hero of two Kentucky Derbies, would ride the other half of his entry, *Bernford.* A week before the first session of the Plate tuneups, Walker got the break he needed: Chris Rogers, a three-time winner of the Plate, cancelled his riding obligation with Starr. Walker fitted neatly aboard *Ace Marine,* winning the Plate in commanding fashion.

A colt with a classic pedigree, stamina mixed with speed, *Ace Marine* sped to the lead coming out of the gate and was never seriously threatened. His sire, *Ace Admiral,* once set a mile-and-five-furlong track record, while his dam, *Sweepster's* daughter *Mazarine,* was a filly noted for her blazing speed. Despite his Trial wins, *Ace Marine* was third choice in the betting and paid $13.20; the Stafford Farm entry was the choice at 13-to-10. *Baffin Bay* finished second, ahead of *Senator Jim.*

"I think I just about drove my exercise boys dizzy getting the horse ready for the race," Starr remembered years later. "It was like training on a merry-go-round that winter. We were stabled in one of the old six-stall barns—four this way and two the other way. That didn't give us much room, but Murray Clarke, Larry Thompson and young Donnie Noyes, jogged him a mile-and-a-half each morning, round and round under the shed on those cold mornings. You know that he's the only horse to ever win the Plate Trial *twice?*"

Starr also recalled that if it had not been for a box of sanitary napkins, *Ace Marine* might never have won the Plate. "A few weeks before the race, he developed a terrible rash, some kind of infection. Small boils. The vet prescribed penicillin, but that sometimes knocks a horse off for a month. We got rid of the rash with hot towels. It was a real assembly line, four of us passing them one to another for three hours, but it worked. On the day of the race I went across the road to the drugstore and bought a box of pads. People thought I was crazy, but I put them on to protect his girth when I tightened up the saddle strap. Funny, eh?"

A rugged competitor, *Ace Marine* developed into a versatile performer after his Plate victory, winning the Prince of Wales, the Breeders', the Seagram Cup Stakes, the Durham Cup Handicap and Horse-of-the-Year honours. At four, running at the "new" Woodbine, he captured the Dominion Day Handicap in record time, and won the Canadian Maturity against his old rivals, *Senator Jim* and *Baffin Bay.* Despite fourteen lifetime wins, including nine in stakes races, *Ace Marine* failed by $999 to achieve the coveted "$100,000 Club." In 2003 Ace Marine was inducted into the Legends category of the Hall of Fame at Woodbine.

Nearly three weeks before the final running of the Plate at Woodbine Park, K.R. (Rud) Marshall, the OJC's chairman, reported to the board that he had been approached verbally by the Governor-General's secretary, who said Queen Elizabeth II had suggested that the name of the Queen's Plate be changed to the Queen's Cup and that the Fifty Guineas she awarded each year be replaced with a challenge cup. The chairman said that he had requested the complete details in writing and it was decided to defer the decision pending receipt of these details.

ACE MARINE | 3-year-old chestnut colt

Ace Marine (1952)	Ace Admiral	*Heliopolis	Hyperion
			Drift
		War Flower	Man o' War
			Crotala
	Mazarine	Sweepster	Sweep
			Oktibbena
		*Mandataria	Lombardo
			Manda

Owner: Larkin Maloney, Toronto; *Trainer:* Joseph (Yonnie) Starr
Jockey: George Walker; *Breeder:* Carr Hatch, Agincourt, Ont.

Ace Marine's owner Larkin Maloney shoulders the Queen's Plate trophy.

1955 QUEEN'S PLATE STAKES

SEVENTH RACE
Woodbine Park
JUNE 11, 1955

1 1-8 MILES (1:50). Ninety-Sixth Running QUEEN'S PLATE. $20,000 added and Fifty Guineas, the gift of Her Majesty the Queen. 3-year-olds. Foaled in Canada. Special weights. Bona fide property of a British subject resident in Canada, which have not started in a race in 1955, excluding the Plate Trials, and excluding such other races as may be determined by the Ontario Jockey Club Limited, which have not been outside of Canada at any time during 1955. Fillies allowed 5 lbs. No gelding allowance. Gross value, $32,645. Net value to winner $25,270 plus 50 guineas; second, $3,000; third, $2,000; fourth, $1,000. Mutuel Pool, $177,413.

Horse	Eqt	Wt.	PP	St	¼	½	¾	Str	Fin	Jockey	Owner	Odds $1
ACE MARINE	b	119	11	1	$1^{1\frac12}$	1^{1}	1^{2}	$1^{\frac12}$	1^{3}	WalkerG	MaloneyL	5.60
BAFFIN BAY	b	114	10	4	$5^{1\frac12}$	$5^{1\frac12}$	2^{hd}	$2^{2\frac12}$	2^{1}	BuissonR	GraulMrsRYJr	9.50
SENATOR JIM		119	2	15	14^{3}	14^{1}	$9^{\frac12}$	$3^{2\frac12}$	3^{4}	GomezA	StaffordFarm	a-1.30
LOYALIST	b	115	17	14	13^{1}	12^{1}	8^{hd}	$4^{1\frac12}$	$4^{2\frac12}$	StevensonD	MoffattWA	3.45
SPRINGHURST	b	119	8	17	$15^{\frac12}$	15^{1}	$12^{\frac12}$	$6^{1\frac12}$	5^{3}	RichardsL	SheridanVJ	f-30.85
SCARBORO LASS	b	114	16	5	4^{1}	$4^{\frac12}$	5^{1}	5^{1}	$6^{1\frac14}$	RemillardP	SteenBR	b-14.20
WINDERMERE	b	119	12	11	10^{1}	$8^{\frac12}$	7^{1}	7^{2}	$7^{2\frac12}$	JohnsonT	TaylorEP	b-14.20
BERNFORD		119	7	6	6^{1}	$7^{\frac12}$	6^{hd}	$8^{\frac12}$	$8^{\frac12}$	McCrearyC	StaffordFarm	a-1.30
SILVER SPAT		119	14	9	9^{1}	13^{1}	13^{1}	12^{1}	9^{3}	DewhurstJ	AdamsA	32.60
MERRY LIFE		114	13	2	2^{1}	$2^{\frac12}$	$3^{1\frac12}$	9^{1}	10^{hd}	WilliamsR	TaylorMrsEP	b-14.20
BIRCH HILLS	b	119	9	3	3^{hd}	$3^{\frac12}$	$4^{\frac12}$	$10^{\frac12}$	11no	HawksworthW	NorthDownsFarm	f-30.85
DORENES LAD	b	119	4	10	$7^{\frac12}$	$6^{\frac12}$	$11^{\frac12}$	11^{hd}	12^{hd}	BovineV	BennettC	49.10
FLEET BRENDA		114	1	8	$11^{\frac12}$	$10^{\frac12}$	10^{nk}	13^{2}	$13^{1\frac14}$	JamesB	BegenJ	49.35
FLEET COUNTESS		114	5	16	16	16	16	14^{nk}	14^{2}	PicouC	CookMrsRE	69.00
FAIR SHORE		119	15	7	$8^{\frac12}$	9^{hd}	15^{2}	$15^{\frac12}$	$15^{\frac34}$	DupreG	SeagramJEF	136.50
FAIRATOR	b	119	3	13	12^{3}	11^{2}	14^{1}	16	16	VinaJ	FairJG	9.45
GREAT WEST	b	119	6	12	Lost rdr.					WickA	KennedyMrsDJ	30.85

a-Coupled, Senator Jim and Bernford; b-Scarboro Lass, Windermere and Merry Life. f-Mutuel field.
OFF AT 5:23. Time, :23 2/5, :47 2/5, 1:12 2/5, 1:39, 1:52 2/5. Track fast.

Mutuel Prices:	$2 Mutuels Paid			Odds to $1		
8-ACE MARINE	13.20	6.80	3.50	5.60	2.40	.75
7-BAFFIN BAY		10.10	4.50		4.05	1.25
1-SENATOR JIM (a-Entry)			2.30			.15

Ch. c, by Ace Admiral—Mazarine, by Sweepster. Trainer, Starr J. (Yonnie). Bred by Carr Hatch, Agincourt Ont.

Start good. Won handily; second and third driving. ACE MARINE sprinted to the front in the run to the first turn, was cleverly rated in front, shook off a bold challenge from BAFFIN BAY after straightening out in the home stretch and came away smartly inside the final sixteenth. BAFFIN BAY raced in the first flight from the beginning, responded when punished entering the stretch, made a determined effort to overhaul the winner but was held safe, then continued gamely to the end. SENATOR JIM lacked speed, moved to the leaders on the last turn and finished with determination.

Horsemen were not too sure whether the "New" Woodbine, the imposing, neoteric racetrack located in the jet stream area of Malton Airport, was too far out in the sticks. On 12 June, the afternoon the track opened, Jim Fair, the rumpled Squire of Cainsville, got dressed up for the occasion, but complained that the barns were so far away from the paddock that it had taken him twenty-five minutes to bring his horse over for a race. It was no place to be on a scorching day either. The two-dollar bettors could not even buy a beer. Malton was "dry" and the only people quaffing were Turf Club members, who had obtained a liquor licence for the day.

"To be honest, at first I thought E.P. [Taylor] was crazy putting it way out there," trainer Frank Merrill said in 1979, as he reminisced about the day that Bill Beasley's colt, *Canadian Champ*, overwhelmed the opposition to win the Queen's Plate at the Ontario Jockey Club's $13-million

THE FIRST QUEEN'S PLATE AT THE "NEW" WOODBINE WAS WON BY *CANADIAN CHAMP*. OWNER BILL BEASLEY SHAKES THE HAND OF GOVERNOR GENERAL VINCENT MASSEY. TO THE LEFT ARE TRAINER JOHN PASSERO AND JOCKEY DAVE STEVENSON.

showplace. "We'd been accustomed to tracks you could walk to, or take a bus or streetcar. You know, handy to get at . . . like Dufferin, Thorncliffe or 'old' Woodbine. The new one was way out by itself, surrounded by empty fields in those days. Not like today, with shopping plazas, hotels and housing developments everywhere. But it didn't take long to figure out that maybe E.P. might know what he was doing. So I buy up some property close by the track, about five hundred acres at $800 an acre. A week or so ago I had an offer of $50,000 an acre for a chunk of it."

It was befitting that the man who was responsible for Woodbine, Edward Plunket Taylor, should win the Hopeful Purse, the first race on the program, with *Landscape*. Ridden by Numero Uno, the indefatigable Avelino Gomez, the three-year-old maiden wore Number 1, broke from the Number 1 post and was the first horse to step on the track following the opening ceremonies, when Premier Leslie Frost snipped a ribbon that extended across the track at the finish line. Jim Proudfoot, who covered opening day for *The Toronto Star,* wrote: ". . . for with the lakes and waterfalls, sunken pools and statues, shrubs and lawns. New Woodbine is Taylor's Landscape for sure."

Three days later, all six fillies in the first running of the rich Canadian Oaks were Taylor-breds, a fact that punters the following day acknowledged when they made the colt bred by Taylor the 3-to-10 favourite to capture the fifty "guineas." Sired by *Windfields, Canadian Champ* was a grandson of the illustrious *Bunty Lawless,* who had died at a nearby farm in Etobicoke three days before the new track opened. *Bunty* was the colt who had beaten the first horse Taylor ever ran in the Plate—*Mona Bell.*

While horsemen may have had their doubts about the industrialist's long-range plans to make Woodbine the "Giant of the North," there was soon no question in the minds of the sceptics that Taylor's sale of yearlings at his National Stud in Oshawa was the route an owner should follow if he wanted an equal chance at competing with him for the Plate. He had bred six of the last eight Plate winners. Seeking a method to encourage a broader ownership of good horses, Taylor and farm manager Gil Darlington had devised a sale format that would allow Mr. and Mrs. Taylor to continue being owners on the circuit. The desire was to sell only part of the crop, yet avoid the stigma of "culling"—buyers thinking those offered were the less desirable. To achieve this, all Taylor's yearlings were catalogued and offered at individual fixed prices. The number sold was to be limited to half the fillies, and half the colts. Should more than one customer seek the same animal, the buyer would be determined by lot.

In Windfields' first sale, September 1954, thirty-six yearlings were offered, with buyers taking eight of them at a total cost of $51,500. The following year, fifteen of the thirty-five offered sold for $102,000. Meanwhile, those purchased at the first sale had started running, and by the time of the third sale in the fall of 1956, five of the eight had

Canadian
Champ
(1953)

- Windfields
  - Bunty Lawless
    - Ladder
    - Mintwina
  - Nandi
    - Stimulus
    - *Golden Feast
- Bolesteo
  - *Filisteo
    - Adam's Apple
    - Noemi
  - Bold Fay
    - *Bull Dog
    - Busy Fairy

Owner: Bill Beasley Stable, Toronto; *Trainer:* John Passero
Jockey: Dave Stevenson; *Breeder:* E.P. Taylor, Willowdale, Ont.

CANADIAN CHAMP RECEIVES A KISS FROM JOCKEY DAVE STEVENSON.

become stakes winners. They included Queen's Plate winner *Canadian Champ,* which Beasley had bought for $7,500. Taylor was pleased to have sold a Plate winner in that first lot, but equally satisfying in 1955 was the fact that among those ignored were *Nearctic* ($35,000 was too steep), who would later sire the world's greatest stallion of the twentieth century, *Northern Dancer,* and the 1957 Plate winner *Lyford Cay.*

Beasley, who had made a fortune in bingo games and children's rides at carnivals and amusement parks, had high hopes for the bay colt the moment he looked him over. "The first thought that came to my mind was that I had bought a champ." He was a horse that groom Bruce Naylor and Beasley's other stablehands called "George," and later "King George" when he conquered every two-year-old in Canada. Throughout his career he was practically unbeatable on home ground, winning fifteen stakes races in Canada, but he was a step or two behind the good American colts whenever he went south. Beasley's $7,500 investment grossed $152,000 in purses before he sold "George" back to Taylor for "about $150,000." At stud he would sire *Canebora,* Plate and Triple Crown winner of 1963, and *Titled Hero,* who won the Plate in 1966.

On Plate day, the Johnny Passero–trained colt gave Beasley and a crowd of 19,120 something to worry about for a fraction of a second as he broke sideways coming out of the outside Number 10 post position. Nineteen-year-old Dave Stevenson, who years later would take over Woodbine's racing operations, had to stand in his stirrups to prevent his mount from bothering horses on the inside. "When Stevenson nearly came out of the saddle, my heart went down to my stomach," Beasley admitted. Moments later the colt was in front, and continued to open up ground right to the wire. *Argent,* who refused to leave the gate with the field, finished gamely to earn second money.

Although the first Plate race at New Woodbine (the "New" would be dropped in 1963) was a triumph for *Canadian Champ,* it was also a notable year in Plate history because an owner no longer had to be a British subject resident in Canada. Anybody could now enter a Canadian-foaled three-year-old, "even Bulganin [the Russian premier] if he had a Canadian-one," quipped James Coleman, the OJC's publicity director.

1956 QUEEN'S PLATE STAKES

SEVENTH RACE
(New) Woodbine
JUNE 16, 1956

1 1-8 MILES. Ninety–Seventh Running QUEEN'S PLATE. $25,000 added and Fifty Guineas, the gift of Her Majesty the Queen. 3–year–olds. Canadian–Foaled. Special weights. The owner of the first horse to receive the Guineas, stakes and 60% of the added money; the second horse, 20%; the third, 10% and the fourth horse, 5%. The breeder of the winner to receive 5%. For non–starters in a race in 1956, excluding the Plate Trial, and such other race or races as may be determined by the Ontario Jockey Club Limited, and which have not been outside of Canada at any time during 1956. Weight, 119 lbs. Fillies allowed 5 lbs. Gross value, $35,660. Net to winner $25,285 and 50 guineas; second, $5,000; third, $2,500; fourth, $1,250. Breeder of winner, $1,250. Mutuel Pool, $128,652.

Horse	Eqt	Wt.	PP	St	¼	½	¾	Str	Fin	Jockey	Owner	Odds $1
CANADIAN CHAMP		119	10	1	1^{hd}	1^1	1^2	1^4	$1^{4\frac{3}{4}}$	StevensonD	BillBeasleyStable	.30
ARGENT		119	9	10	8^{hd}	$6\frac{1}{2}$	6^2	2^1	2^1	BovineV	SteenBR	10.20
LONDON CALLING	b	119	3	7	$6^1\frac{1}{2}$	7^2	$7^3\frac{1}{2}$	3^3	$3^6\frac{1}{2}$	RobillardG	TaylorEP	a-10.35
CENSOR	b	119	4	3	3^2	2^{hd}	3^2	4^{hd}	$4\frac{3}{4}$	GomezA	TaylorMrsEP	a-10.35
BIG BERNE	b	119	8	5	$5^1\frac{1}{2}$	$5^3\frac{1}{2}$	$4\frac{1}{2}$	7^2	5^{nk}	RemillardP	StaffordFarm	60.55
BUNTY'S FLIGHT		119	7	4	4^1	$4^1\frac{1}{2}$	$4^2\frac{1}{2}$	$6\frac{1}{2}$	6^2	WalkerG	Maloney&Smythe	4.20
LAWDAY	b	119	1	9	10	9^{nk}	9^4	9^7	7^{nk}	WilsonHB	SeagramJEF	77.85
O'MORRISSEY		119	2	2	$2^1\frac{1}{2}$	$3^3\frac{1}{2}$	2^1	5^{nk}	$8\frac{3}{4}$	PlesaE	ArmstrongMissOR	37.20
WINCHESTER	b	119	5	6	$9^1\frac{1}{2}$	10	$8^2\frac{1}{2}$	8^{hd}	9^{10}	BuissonR	LuxianaStable	105.10
BERNMAR	b	119	6	8	7^2	$8^1\frac{1}{2}$	10	10	10	GubbinsG	McGarryPJ	165.00

a-Coupled, London Calling and Censor.

OFF AT 4:45. Time, :23 1/5, :47 2/5, 1:13 2/5, 1:41, 1:55. Track slow.

Mutuel Prices:

		—$2 Mutuels Paid—			—Odds to $1—		
9–CANADIAN CHAMP		2.60	2.50	2.20	.30	.25	.10
8–ARGENT			3.80	2.70		.90	.35
1–LONDON CALLING (a–Entry)				2.90			.45

B. c, by Windfields—Bolesteo, by *Filisteo. Trainer, John Passero. Bred by Taylor E P.

Start good for all but ARGENT. Won easily; second and third driving. CANADIAN CHAMP, away alertly, was sent to the front in the run to the first turn, was snugged along in front while saving ground, rapidly drew out into a commanding advantage early in the stretch and won with something left. ARGENT, unprepared at the start, steadily worked his way forward to attain the runner-up position early in the stretch, closed gamely and though unable to threaten the top one, held on well to outfinish LONDON CALLING. The latter, unable to keep up early, closed with good energy through the stretch to easily best the others. CENSOR displayed speed to the stretch and tired. BUNTY'S FLIGHT could not engage the leaders. O'MORRISSEY attended the pace closely for six furlongs, then weakened.

1957 | LYFORD CAY

One of the fascinations of horse racing is that no man can point to a yearling and say, with any ring of certitude, "that one will be a stakes winner." If they could, it might have altered the racing career of the world's most successful breeder, E.P. Taylor.

In September 1955, the second year of Taylor's innovative pre-priced sale of yearlings at his Windfields Farm in Oshawa, the stud stations he had purchased from car pioneer Sam McLaughlin, he offered *Nearctic,* later the sire of *Northern Dancer* and grandsire of *Nijinsky II* and *The Minstrel,* for $35,000. Nobody in Canada had ever paid that much for a Canadian-bred colt, and it was not surprising that the price was considered to be too expensive. Catalogued at $10,000 were two sons of *Chop Chop,* a stallion that had already established himself as a top sire through the first of his four Plate winners, *Canadiana.* She was the first horse to earn more than $100,000 in Canada. One of the yearlings was out of *Famous Maid,* which stockbroker M.J. Boylen bought. When Boylen later complained that his horse had an unsound knee, Taylor graciously offered him either his money back or another yearling by the same sire (this one was out of *Bernadette S.*). Boylen took the cash refund, and later bought a colt bred by late Jim Fair—*Lad Ator,* winner of the Cup and Saucer Handicap in 1956.

Lyford Cay WENT TO THE FRONT OUT OF THE GATE AND WAS NEVER THREATENED.

Named after Taylor's home and the luxurious private club that he had developed on the north coast of New Providence Island in the Bahamas, *Lyford Cay* came back to haunt Boylen and other horsemen who had rejected *Famous Maid*'s bay son—"the cripple with the gimpy knee." He led every stride of the way to win the ninety-eighth running of the Queen's Plate by almost twelve lengths over Mrs. E.P. Taylor's *Chopadette,* the colt Boylen had rejected as a substitute for *Lyford Cay.* A distant ninth in the twelve-horse field was *Lad Ator,* who ran under the colours of Mrs. M.J. Boylen.

Ridden by the colourful Cuban, Avelino Gomez, who merrily waved his whip at a crowd of 26,705 as he coasted to his first of four Plate victories, *Lyford Cay*'s time of 2:02 3/5ths was a record at the new track. It would be broken by another of *Chop Chop*'s sons in 1960, *Victoria Park,* and later by *Northern Dancer, Regal Embrace,* and *Izvestia,* but it was a tribute to the gelding's courage, and trainer Pete McCann's tender care, that in the next twenty-seven runnings of the Plate, only these three horses (all bred by Taylor but turned down by buyers) and *Izvestia* would better his time.

Nineteen fifty-seven marked the first time that the Plate had been contested at a mile-and-a-quarter since the Ontario Jockey Club had shortened the distance to a mile-and-an-eighth in 1924 at the "old" Woodbine. The Club had decided wisely that it was asking too much of a

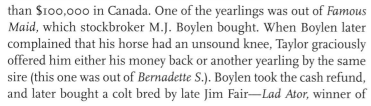

1957 QUEEN'S PLATE STAKES

SEVENTH RACE
Woodbine
JUNE 8, 1957

1 1-4 MILES (Ballydonnell, Oct. 13, 1956—2:03 2/5—4—122). Ninety-Eighth Running QUEEN'S PLATE. $25,000 added and Fifty Guineas, the gift of Her Majesty the Queen. 3-year-olds. Canadian-Foaled. Scale weight. The owner of the first horse to receive the Guineas, stakes and 65% of the added money; the second horse, 20%; the third horse, 10% and the fourth horse, 5% By subscription of $10 each, to accompany the nomination by December 15, 1955; second subscription of $15 by December 15, 1956; third subscription of $100 by May 1, 1957, and an additional $250 when entering. For those not starting in a race in 1957, excluding the Plate Trial, and excluding such other races as determined by the Ontario Jockey Club Limited, and have not been outside of Canada at any time during 1957. Weight, 126 lbs. Fillies allowed 5 lbs. Nominations closed December 15, 1955. Gross value, $35,195. Net to winner, $26,070, plus 50 Guineas; second, $5,000; third, $2,500; fourth, $1,250. Mutuel Pool, $209,371.

Horse	Eqt	Wt.	PP	¼	½	¾	1	Str	Fin	Jockey	Owner	Odds $1
LYFORD CAY	b	126	12	1	1^{2}	$1^{2\frac{1}{2}}$	1^{3}	1^{5}	$1^{11\frac{1}{2}}$	GomezA	TaylorEP	a-.55
CHOPADETTE		126	7	2	$3^{2\frac{1}{2}}$	3^{5}	2^{3}	2^{6}	2^{4}	RogersC	TaylorMrsEP	a-.55
FLYING ATOM	b	126	6	6	5^{2}	$5^{1\frac{1}{2}}$	5^{nk}	3^{nk}	$3^{\frac{3}{4}}$	RodriguezEA	BayfieldFarm	15.85
HENRY B. GOOD		126	11	7	8^{hd}	8^{hd}	7^{hd}	4^{nk}	$4^{1\frac{1}{2}}$	UyeyamaH	PasqualeEC	34.75
ALI'S PRIDE		126	9	8	7^{2}	6^{nk}	$8^{1\frac{1}{2}}$	8^{1}	$5^{\frac{1}{2}}$	BovineV	Farr&Ellins	3.95
OUR SIRDAR	b	126	10	5	$4^{\frac{1}{2}}$	$4^{\frac{1}{2}}$	$6^{1\frac{1}{2}}$	6^{1}	6^{nk}	DunnW	ShermanorFarm	36.15
HOLIDAY TED	b	126	4	3	2^{2}	2^{hd}	3^{1}	$7^{\frac{1}{2}}$	$7^{\frac{1}{2}}$	ClemesK	CullinghamMrsJD	67.40
THE SCHREIBER		126	1	9	12	11^{5}	$9^{2\frac{1}{2}}$	9^{4}	8^{hd}	CoyA	ArmstrongMissCB	27.00
LAD ATOR	b	126	3	10	$10^{1\frac{1}{2}}$	$7^{\frac{1}{2}}$	4^{nk}	5^{hd}	9^{9}	PlesaE	BoylenMrsMJ	6.95
SENOR TEDDY	b	126	5	12	11^{hd}	10^{1}	$10^{2\frac{1}{2}}$	10^{5}	$10^{6\frac{1}{4}}$	PongL	MarshallKR	22.85
COUNT TEDDY	b	126	8	11	9^{hd}	$9^{1\frac{1}{2}}$	11^{8}	11^{8}	11^{9}	WalkerG	DewValleyFarm	97.55
MIDI BLUE		126	2	4	6^{hd}	12	12	12	12	CizikN	AssiniboineStable	61.50

a-Coupled, Lyford Cay and Chopadette.

OFF AT 5:29. Time, :23, :46 1/5, 1:11, 1:36 4/5, 2:02 3/5 (Track Record). Track fast.

Mutuel Prices:		$2 Mutuels Paid			Odds to $1		
	1-LYFORD CAY (a-Entry)	3.10	2.50	2.40	.55	.25	.20
	1-CHOPADETTE (a-Entry)	3.10	2.50	2.40	.55	.25	.20
	7-FLYING ATOM			4.50			1.25

B. g, by Chop Chop—Famous Maid, by *Fairaris. Trained by McCann Gordon (Pete). Bred by Taylor E P.

Start good. Won easily. LYFORD CAY stepped to the front immediately following the start, was well rated while showing the way, drew out into a long lead entering the stretch and won as though much the best. CHOPADETTE, a sharp factor from the beginning, raced in closest pursuit of the leader after going a half-mile, closed with good energy when roused during the stretch run and though no match for the top one, was easily best of the others. FLYING ATOM, away in the first flight, responded readily when shaken for the drive, finished with good courage but was no threat to the top pair. HENRY B. GOOD finished fairly well on end. ALI'S PRIDE was never troublesome. OUR SIRDAR failed to stay.

horse to run that far in his first race of the year. Comparisons of times were futile as everyone realized that Canadian breeding, and the condition of racetracks, had improved immeasurably from the afternoon in 1911 that *St. Bass* had established the previous Plate record of 2:08 4/5ths.

The Taylors' entry, bet down to fifty-five cents to the dollar by the first crowd in Canada to wager more than $1 million, had earlier established themselves as the clear favourites after they had each captured their divisions of the Plate Trial Stakes. The only horse afforded a chance of catching Gomez and Chris Rogers, who was brought in to ride *Chopadette*, was *Ali's Pride*, owned by Frank Ellins and Wilf Farr. But he did not fancy the track's hard surface and finished an unthreatening fifth. "If it hadn't of been the Plate, we wouldn't have raced," trainer Willie Thurner confessed. "The track stung his feet all the way." It was the condition of the track that had convinced Gomez to ride *Lyford Cay* instead of *Chopadette*. He had spent weeks drilling both horses in morning trials and had ridden them a week earlier in the stakes' races. El Senor knew that *Chopadette*'s only chance of beating his stablemate was on a muddy track. The track was like cement that day. Besides, he and Rogers had agreed to split the winner's ten per cent share of the $26,070 purse. They each wound up with about $1,500 as *Chopadette*'s second place finish added $5,000 more to the pot. "I win the Plate my first step out of the gate," the press was informed. "I knew he would win before we take thirty steps. I no let him go until we're at the three-sixteenths' pole."

Mud or no mud, few figured *Lyford Cay* would win with such authority. However, Rogers' prediction that *Chopadette,* who beat his rival in the rich Coronation Futurity the year before, was the better horse was later confirmed; he retired with more stakes victories and purse money than *Lyford Cay*. Because of his numerous problems, every race looked as if it would be the gelding's last. When he bowed a tendon the following year, he was retired to stud at Windfields Farm, but as a "teaser," whose job it was to discern, sometimes painfully, which mares were anxious to be bred, and which ones were unfriendly.

E.P. Taylor, who had now bred seven Plate winners in nine years, accepted his triumph with his usual sang-froid. "I would rather that my wife win this Queen's Plate. On the other hand, I'm quite happy that I did." But then Taylor was not given to extravagance in his public utterances; the purse would help at home, but was not a lot of money to a man of his financial girth. In six years his main residence would be his retreat at Lyford Cay, his home where he and Winnie had entertained United States president John F. Kennedy in 1962 for his summit meeting with British prime minister Harold Macmillan.

LYFORD CAY | 3-year-old bay gelding

Owner: E.P. Taylor, Toronto; *Trainer:* Gordon (Pete) McCann
Jockey: Avelino Gomez; *Breeder:* E.P. Taylor

Lyford Cay and jockey Avelino Gomez delighted a crowd of 26,705, who wagered over a $1 million for the first time in Plate history.

1958 | CALEDON BEAU

Fellow owners, trainers and even "hot walkers," had concluded that Conn Smythe, the feisty owner of the Toronto Maple Leafs, who seldom used a velvet glove if he had a hammer handy when training his hockey troops, and Yonnie Starr, the unassuming little guy who trained Smythe's horses, were simply asking too much of *Caledon Beau* to expect him to run a creditable race in the ninety-ninth running of the Plate.

"What," the critics asked, "does that Smythe think he's doing, running a three-year-old in back-to-back races like that? And then run him back in the Plate four days later. Is he nuts? What does he think he's got? Another *Exterminator*?" An old gelding who was worshipped by legions of racing fans in the 1920s, "Ol' Bones' handlers thought nothing of running him two or three times a week against the best horses on the continent, and winning to boot. But this was the late 1950s, the modern era, not like the old days at Dufferin's bullring when there were seven-day meets and horsemen used to break their necks to get horses into three races—Saturday, Tuesday or Wednesday, and then Saturday again.

In *Caledon Beau*'s case, Smythe and Starr had thrown away the trainers' almanac on a horse that would earn the title "The Major's Iron Horse," training and racing him for the Plate at a relentless pace, a grind that began only days after his temperature had come down. He was one of the fortunate ones that had survived the coughing epidemic, which spread through the stabling area that spring at the "new" Woodbine. Thoroughbreds were the pampered darlings of the horse world to most owners, but not to The Major, who had never been one to pamper man or beast.

Conn Smythe, hat in one hand and Plate in other, with his wife Irene and Al Coy.

Smythe's dark brown colt, who had been foaled at his farm near the gravel pits in the Caledon Hills, was a stakes winner at two, but like other horses his age, his efforts had been

1958 QUEEN'S PLATE STAKES

SEVENTH RACE
Woodbine
JUNE 7, 1958

1 1–4 MILES. (Flying Trapeze, November 2, 1957. 2:01⁴/₅, 4, 118.) Ninety–Ninth Running QUEEN'S PLATE. Fifty Guineas, the gift of Her Majesty the Queen, with $25,000 added. 3–year–olds. Canadian–foaled. Scale Weight. By subscription of $10 each, to accompany the nomination by December 15, 1956; second subscription of $25 by December 15, 1957; third subscription of $100 by May 1, 1958, and an additional $250 when making entry the day before the race. The owner of the first horse to receive the Guineas, stakes and 50% of the added money, the second horse 25%, the third horse 15%, and the fourth horse 10%. Weight, 126 lbs. Fillies allowed 5 lbs. Nominations closed December 15, 1956. Gross value, $38,895. Net to winner, $26,010 and 50 Guineas; second, $6,250; third, $3,750; fourth, $2,500. Mutuel Pool $188,439.

Horse	Eqt	Wt.	PP	¼	½	¾	1	Str	Fin	Jockey	Owner	Odds $1
CALEDON BEAU		126	9	8^{nk}	7^{1}	3^{1}	$1^{\frac{1}{2}}$	1^{6}	$1^{9\frac{1}{2}}$	CoyA	SmytheC	d-2.90
WHITE APACHE	b	126	13	9^{2}	$11^{2\frac{1}{2}}$	7^{hd}	$5^{2\frac{1}{2}}$	3^{3}	$2^{5\frac{1}{4}}$	HaleD	FourL'sStable	23.55
STOLE THE RING		121	1	1^{1}	$1^{1\frac{1}{2}}$	$1^{1\frac{1}{2}}$	2^{5}	$2^{2\frac{1}{2}}$	$3^{3\frac{1}{2}}$	LongdenJ	ArmstrongMissCB	1.25
DR. EM JAY	b	126	3	5^{hd}	5^{1}	$4^{1\frac{1}{2}}$	$4^{1\frac{1}{2}}$	$4^{2\frac{1}{2}}$	$4^{2\frac{1}{4}}$	GubbinsG	LansonFarms	a-3.15
HAPPY HARRY	b	126	11	$2^{\frac{1}{2}}$	2^{2}	2^{2}	3^{hd}	5^{2}	$5^{2\frac{1}{4}}$	RodriguezE	BillBeasleyStable	c-14.95
FOXY PHIL	b	126	7	10^{2}	10^{hd}	10^{1}	6^{1}	6^{4}	6^{1}	McLaughlinR	LansonFarms	a-3.15
TAMARIND		126	10	14	14	14	14	$7^{\frac{1}{2}}$	7^{4}	GoodwinA	WindfieldsFarm	b-17.65
CHOMIRU	b	121	2	$11^{\frac{1}{2}}$	9^{nk}	9^{1}	$7^{1\frac{1}{2}}$	8^{2}	$8^{\frac{1}{2}}$	DunnW	ShermanorFarm	29.60
EPIC LAD	b	126	4	12^{8}	12^{4}	11^{4}	$9^{2\frac{1}{2}}$	$9^{2\frac{1}{2}}$	$9^{2\frac{1}{4}}$	SorensenB	WindfieldsFarm	b-17.65
ESKIMO FLYER		126	8	4^{1}	$6^{\frac{1}{2}}$	6^{nk}	$8^{\frac{1}{2}}$	10^{3}	$10^{2\frac{1}{4}}$	O'BrienC	Maloney&Smythe	d-2.90
JOKERS HILL	b	126	14	$7^{\frac{1}{2}}$	8^{nk}	8^{nk}	10^{1}	11^{1}	$11^{\frac{1}{2}}$	NashA	ViewHulloaFarm	109.10
STROKE O'TWELVE		126	12	13^{1}	13^{10}	$12^{2\frac{1}{2}}$	$12^{1\frac{1}{2}}$	$12^{\frac{1}{2}}$	12^{1}	LeidN	GardenCityStable	79.95
CANADIAN FLYER	b	126	6	3^{hd}	4^{hd}	5^{hd}	$11^{\frac{1}{2}}$	13^{5}	13^{12}	VanHookE	BillBeasleyStable	c-14.95
JEANSEN	b	126	5	$6^{\frac{1}{2}}$	3^{hd}	13^{6}	13^{4}	14	14	ContradaG	DesnoyersS	26.70

a–Coupled, Dr. Em Jay and Foxy Phil; b–Tamarind and Epic Lad; c–Happy Harry and Canadian Flyer; d–Caledon Beau and Eskimo Flyer.

IN GATE—5:44. OFF AT 5:44. Time, :23³/₅, :47³/₅, 1:12⁴/₅, 1:38¹/₅, 2:04¹/₅. Track fast.

Mutuel Prices:

	$2 Mutuels Paid			Odds to $1		
4–CALEDON BEAU (d–Entry)	7.80	4.00	2.90	2.90	1.00	.45
9–WHITE APACHE		12.40	5.30		5.20	1.65
5–STOLE THE RING			3.30			.65

Br. c, by County Delight—Seemly, by *Beau Pere. Trained by J. (Yonnie) Starr. Bred by Conn Smythe, Caledon, Ont.

Start good. Won easily. CALEDON BEAU steadily improved his position while saving ground, moved to the front along the inside leaving the backstretch, then came away from his opposition thereafter, winning as if much the best. WHITE APACHE gradually worked his way forward to the stretch, closed with good energy and, while no match for the winner, was easily best of the others. STOLE THE RING stepped to the front immediately, made the pace to the far turn and weakened when placed to a drive. DR. EM JAY finished willingly but was unable to improve his position in the late stages. HAPPY HARRY pressed the pace for six furlongs and tired. FOXY PHIL was never prominent. EPIC LAD never menaced. CANADIAN FLYER could not keep up.

Trainer Yonnie Starr.

eclipsed by *Stole the Ring*, the undefeated filly bred by another maverick, Willie Morrissey, and leased to Miss Blanche Armstrong, an associate of Willie's, who generally managed the Morrissey House on Yonge Street in Toronto along with her sister, Olive.

Smythe had been in and out of horse racing for almost thirty years but had never won the Plate, while Starr had trained 1955 winner *Ace Marine* for Larkin Maloney, Smythe's business and horse racing partner. The Plate tuneup for *Caledon Beau* originally called for a start in the Marine Stakes on Saturday 31 May, the final day of the Old Woodbine meeting before the action moved north to the "new" Woodbine for the Plate the following Saturday. The colt had also been entered in the Plate Trial Stakes on 2 June, the opening day feature at Woodbine, but nobody expected that he would run in both races. Wrong. Ridden by Alfonso Coy, *Caledon Beau* made a rush at the leaders before he tired and finished fourth in the Marine. But Smythe noted that his colt showed signs of "toughness" and decided to run him back forty-eight hours later, a move that confounded horsemen. "Something popped inside of Smythe's skull," wrote *The Telegram*'s George Dulmage. "It was like Smythe had watched his Leafs take a licking on any Saturday night, a good Leaf team being beaten by an inferior one. So he ordered the horse entered in the Plate Trials Monday, and tightened him with a two-mile slow work on Sunday. *Caledon Beau* whipped his Trial field like a champion, and in the big test for the Queen's Plate he killed the field. He murdered 'em." Three races and a two-mile workout in eight days. *Caledon Beau* had proved once again the old adage that practice makes perfect.

The cocky, bantam-sized Smythe, exultant as he waved the Plate over his head, told everybody he wished it was the Stanley Cup. He needled onlookers: "Here's a horse that has been overtrained and overworked." Then he pulled a slip of paper out of his pocket: "Take a look at these figures. *Caledon Beau* knocked off the final quarter in 24 and 3/5th seconds. That's when you got to beat them, and that's when you find out what your opposition is like, whether the other horses have it or not." They did not, because *Caledon Beau* came into the last quarter like an express train, winning by almost ten lengths over Domenic Lamantia and Tony LoPresti's longshot, *White Apache*. The favourite, *Stole the Ring*, who had not raced that spring because of the croup she had caught during the coughing epidemic, was a retreating third. Her rider, the world's leading jockey, Johnny Longden, said: "She suddenly weakened; she's a tired filly. It's difficult for a filly which hasn't had a race to compete against colts at a mile-and-a-quarter."

Nobody had to tell Coy, or Starr, that *Caledon Beau* was a "tough little horse." Coy had thrashed the colt twice with his whip, the first time when a hole opened for him in the backstretch. "Boy, did I cut him up then. He likes it, you know. When we went through that hole, I gave him his head. His ears just flattened and I hit him with everything. By the time we hit the head of the stretch, I stopped and just let him run." The winner paid $7.80.

"He's a tough horse, an iron horse, but I've been trying to tell you guys this all along," Starr politely reminded writers. He

CALEDON BEAU | 3-year-old brown colt

			Reigh Count
		Count Fleet	Quickly
	County Delight		
		Matriarch	*Sir Gallahad III
Caledon			Sunstroke
Beau			
(1955)			Son-in-Law
		*Beau Pere	Cinna
	Seemly		
			Jamestown
		Pertinent	Kings Choice

Owner: Conn Smythe, Toronto; *Trainer:* Joseph (Yonnie) Starr
Jockey: Al Coy; *Breeder:* Conn Smythe

CALEDON BEAU AND AL COY.

mentioned the anecdote about the morning Smythe had excitedly called him over to the foaling barn at Caledon to take a look at a colt out of *Seemly*. Smythe had bought the mare in foal to *County Delight* in Kentucky, and the foal was the first to be born at his farm since his return to racing. "I was amazed. Eight hours after he was foaled, he was frisking around after his mother as if he'd been in the world for weeks. Mr. Smythe and I agreed there and then that 'this is a powerful colt.'" A record New Woodbine crowd of 28,386 certainly had to agree.

In 1958 "The Woodbine" gate, designed and constructed by OJC engineers Ralph Pick and J.K. McMillan, was used for the first time. It weighed nine tons, five tons lighter than the conventional fourteen-stall gate used on U.S. tracks, and the first here with its own motorized mobile unit.

It was a pale grey Tuesday afternoon, 30 June, when Queen Elizabeth made her first visit to the "new" Woodbine, walking through the mud in open-toed white shoes to inspect a field of twenty starters for the centennial running of the Plate, a race that had been given royal assent and the donation of a sum representing fifty "guineas" by Her Majesty's great-great-grandmother in 1860. The day was similar to the one that Elizabeth's parents had encountered during their memorable royal visit to Woodbine Park in 1939—overcast, with a few showers and a crowd far below expectations. Less than twenty-five thousand showed up that day, a third of the total that had been estimated by Ontario Jockey Club officials.

Twenty years later, the threat of colossal traffic jams and a shortage of seats again deterred racegoers, and only 19,846 (less than half the expected total) made the trip to the resplendent, but isolated, racecourse in Etobicoke to witness the glamorous arrival of the royal couple in the same elegant landau that had

FANS JAMMED THE RAMPS AND BALCONIES TO VIEW E.P. TAYLOR ESCORT HER MAJESTY QUEEN ELIZABETH IN THE SADDLING PADDOCK.

been used in 1939. People stayed home to watch the spectacle on television, in spite of the OJC's advertisements in the newspapers that thousands of free seats were available, that general admission was only one dollar (entrance to the Club House was five dollars), and that there was parking for twenty-five thousand cars.

The fact that the richest running of the Plate, which carried a gross purse of $77,300, plus the fifty gold sovereigns, was held on a working day, the day before the 1 July holiday, instead of Saturday, was a major factor in the smallest Plate turnout in thirty years. Moreover, fans had been forewarned by jockey Avelino Gomez, the talented but noisy Cuban rider, that John Evans' swift colt, *Winning Shot*, was a cinch to beat Conn Smythe's *Major Flight*, E.P. Taylor's *New Providence* and *Sunday Sail*, owned by James Boylen, the only horses he figured had a reasonable chance of finishing in the money. "All I know is Gomez has the winner. The only way that horse can lose is for Avelino to fall off. If I don't win, never again will I sit in a saddle." Gomez would later ride more than four thousand winners and win a record four Plates. But the horse that had been bet down to fifty-five cents on the dollar, a colt bred by one of Conn Smythe's former employees, Frank Selke, who had won a fifth successive Stanley Cup for the Montreal Canadiens that spring, had to settle for the show money, a sagging nose behind the charging *Major Flight* and *New Providence*,

who cruised home the winner in Taylor's turquoise and gold polka-dot silks, paying $15.10.

"As everyone said at the time," wrote *The Toronto Star*'s Milt Dunnell, "there couldn't have been a more appropriate winner than E.P. Taylor. The Queen sat in a $13-million plant for her first look at Canadian racing. The first Queen Elizabeth, in 1585, had a special stand erected at Croydon from which she could watch the races. Cost of the stand was thirty-four shillings. That's approximately the kind of accommodation the second Elizabeth would have found here if she had paid her visit before Taylor took Ontario out of the leaky roof circuit." These sentiments had earlier been made by one of the Queen's most loyal subjects, Smythe, when he spoke of his chances of winning with *Major Flight*. "If I lose, I hope the winner is owned by some person who has been good for racing. Who would be a more appropriate winner than E.P. Taylor? If it hadn't of been for Taylor, would we have the wonderful new racetrack? No person ever did so much for the racing game in Canada."

Smythe's sagacity proved to be wiser than the boasts of Gomez, for when the bulky field hit the head of the stretch, the small crowd was in a frenzy as two game thoroughbreds battled for the lead. One was *New Providence*, a bay colt that Taylor could not find a buyer for when he offered him for $10,000 at his annual yearling sale. On his heels was Smythe's colt, *Major Flight*. The favourite had been shuffled back in the early running, prompting El Senor to moan: "I'll tell you it wasn't a truly run race. It was very rough and there was a lot of interference. But I didn't have the horse this time either. When I try to turn him loose . . . I have a hand full of nothing." Both Gomez and Hugo Dittfach, who was on fourth-place finisher *Sunday Sail*, complained of the way jockey Bob Ussery had navigated the winner, saying that they had been fouled by the hot-shot rider from New York. Later the track's film patrol cameras revealed that the ride by the twenty-three-year-old Oklahoman was as "clean as a whistle."

Taylor's knowledge of the racing game and the wisdom of his racing manager, Joe Thomas, may have provided them with the winning margin when they decided that Ussery should ride *New Providence*, who had been a mild disappointment that spring after his promising two-year-old season. Eddie Arcaro was their original choice, but he got hurt in the Belmont Stakes. Johnny Longden was also not available; he was sitting out a ten-day suspension. Ussery

Obviously intrigued on her first visit to Woodbine, Queen Elizabeth is joined in the Royal Box by E.P. Taylor (left) and Lieutenant Governor J. Keillor Mackay.

gave Taylor's colt a flawless ride, even though he was unable to follow the pre-race instructions given him by Thomas. The son of *Bull Page* went to the front sooner than expected, but this time he did not loaf when he got the lead. After his Plate win, the colt would go on to become the first winner of Canada's new Triple Crown trophy and the Horse-of-the-Year; he retired with earnings of $130,000.

Hosted by Mr. and Mrs. Taylor in the royal box, the Queen was well acquainted with the winner's pedigree. She had been given the bloodlines of several of the contenders on the advice of her staff, who a few years earlier had sent a message to officials in Australia: "For heaven's sake, put someone in the royal box who really can talk about the horses. Her Majesty knows the *Stud Book* and the pedigrees all the way back to *Eclipse*."

"How nice of you to win it today," the Queen said to Eddie and Winifred Taylor in the winner's circle. Four years earlier the Taylors had been in England while the ground was being broken on the site of "new" Woodbine, and had attended the Royal Ascot meeting, where they were the Queen's guests in the royal box. At the time she acknowledged great interest in the project, and

Trainer Gordon (Pete) McCann, jockey Robert Ussery and Her Majesty.

NEW PROVIDENCE | 3-year-old bay colt

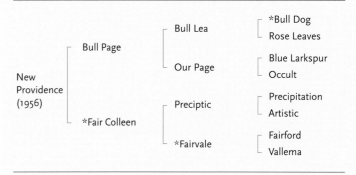

New Providence (1956)	Bull Page	Bull Lea	*Bull Dog
			Rose Leaves
		Our Page	Blue Larkspur
			Occult
	*Fair Colleen	Preciptic	Precipitation
			Artistic
		*Fairvale	Fairford
			Vallema

Owner: Windfields Farm, Oshawa, Ont.; *Trainer:* Gordon (Pete) McCann
Jockey: Robert Ussery; *Breeder:* E.P. Taylor, Toronto

said that she hoped one day to visit the track. For Taylor the day could not have been a greater success, despite the small turnout. Since January 1958, he and his top men at the OJC had been in constant contact with the co-ordinator of the Royal tour, in order to time the Queen's tour to coincide with the one-hundredth running of the Plate. They failed to arrange the visit in early June, but was able to persuade tour organizers that he wanted Elizabeth at the track longer than the seventy minutes that originally had been scheduled. He got two hours and ten minutes instead.

Among the myriad of problems of protocol that were eventually ironed out was informing Lieutenant Governor J. Keiller Mackay that he could not be the first person to greet the royal party. He would have to wait his turn in the royal box. Taylor, who later sent a cheque for $150 to reimburse the OJC for the cost of the fifty gold sovereigns he had accepted, was on hand to welcome the monarch. It was his show.

QUEEN'S PLATE STAKES CENTENNIAL

SIXTH RACE
Woodbine
JUNE 30, 1959

1 1–4 MILES. (2:01 4/5). One Hundredth Running THE QUEEN'S PLATE. $50,000 Added and Fifty Guineas, the Gift of Her Majesty the Queen. 3–year–olds. Canadian–foaled. By subscription of $25 each to accompany the nomination by Dec. 15, 1957; second subscription of $50 by Dec. 15, 1958; third subscription of $100 by May 1, 1959; and an additional $500 when making entry two days before the race.

Horse	Eqt	Wt.	PP	¼	½	¾	1	Str	Fin	Jockey	Owner	Odds $1
NEW PROVIDENCE	b	126	18	8^{hd}	8^{hd}	3^{hd}	1½	1^{4}	$1^{1\frac{1}{4}}$	UsseryR	WindfieldsFarm	b-6.55
MAJOR FLIGHT	b	126	10	17^{3}	15½	11^{1}	5^{hd}	$3^{1\frac{1}{2}}$	2no	CoyA	SmytheC	a-4.25
WINNING SHOT		126	2	10^{nk}	11^{1}	9^{nk}	4^{1}	2^{hd}	3¾	GomezA	EvansJS	.55
SUNDAY SAIL		126	5	15^{nk}	9^{nk}	8^{hd}	7½	4^{4}	$4^{9\frac{1}{2}}$	DittfachH	BoylenJA	10.70
MR. ROOSTER		126	15	9^{1}	$7^{1\frac{1}{2}}$	7^{1}	2½	$5^{3\frac{1}{2}}$	5^{2}	ContradaG	LatimerWD	139.35
CHOPAVANE	b	126	11	4^{hd}	10^{2}	10^{1}	8^{2}	7^{2}	6^{nk}	LeidN	ViscountHardinge	330.80
FLYING GREY		121	14	6^{nk}	3^{hd}	2^{1}	$3^{1\frac{1}{2}}$	6^{hd}	7^{1}	DodsonD	RossDG	f-15.75
FARSHORE		126	20	20	20	20	20	9^{hd}	$8^{4\frac{1}{2}}$	HawksworthW	McGarryPJ	f-15.75
BROWN PANTHER	b	126	8	3^{1}	2^{3}	1^{2}	6^{hd}	8^{1}	9^{hd}	PottsC	StaffordFarm	f-15.75
SIR CHOP	b	126	1	13^{1}	12^{hd}	12^{1}	11½	11^{1}	10¾	WickA	CarterGJ	f-15.75
THEO GEO	b	126	12	7½	$4^{1\frac{1}{2}}$	4^{nk}	9½	10½	11^{1}	RogersC	ChrisMrsBS	37.35
SOLARWAY		126	9	11^{hd}	13^{1}	13^{nk}	12½	12^{1}	$12^{1\frac{1}{4}}$	RoyE	NewMissSB	f-15.75
LE GRAND ROUGE		126	4	18^{2}	19½	18½	14^{nk}	14^{hd}	13^{hd}	BaileyPJ	Maloney&Smythe	a-4.25
CASTLEBERRY	b	126	17	19¾	$19^{1\frac{1}{2}}$	19^{2}	19^{1}	15^{1}	14^{3}	GuitierrezR	SeagramJEF	303.15
THE MOHAWK	b	126	19	5^{nk}	5^{hd}	5^{nk}	10^{1}	13^{nk}	$15^{1\frac{1}{2}}$	WarmeE	Kennedy&Lannoo	f-15.75
SEA PAGE	b	126	6	2^{hd}	6^{1}	6½	13^{1}	16^{1}	16½	SorensenB	WindfieldsFarm	b-6.55
CHADA	b	126	16	12^{1}	14½	17^{1}	17½	17½	17^{nk}	BairdRL	AddisonH	42.65
GEORGE HARDY		126	3	14½	16^{2}	16^{1}	15½	18^{2}	$18^{1\frac{1}{2}}$	ClarkCM	ArmstrongMissOR	66.40
MISS WHISKIT	b	121	13	16^{2}	17^{4}	18^{3}	18^{1}	19^{5}	19^{8}	RemillardP	ViewHulloaFarm	f-15.75
PAGE SERVICE	b	126	7	1^{nk}	1½	14½	16^{hd}	20	20	SorrentinoM	GardenCityStable	115.15

a–Coupled, Major Flight and Le Grand Rouge; b–New Providence and Sea Page. f–Mutuel field.
IN GATE—5:29. OFF AT 5:29. Start good. Won handily. Time, :23 1/5, :46 3/5, 1:12 3/5, 1:39, 2:04 4/5. Track fast.

Mutuel Prices:

	$2 Mutuels Paid			Odds to $1		
2–NEW PROVIDENCE (b–Entry)	15.10	5.70	3.00	6.55	1.85	.50
1–MAJOR FLIGHT (a–Entry)		4.30	2.60		1.15	.30
3–WINNING SHOT			2.20			.10

B. c, by Bull Page—*Fair Colleen, by Preciptic, trained by Gordon (Pete) McCann; bred by E. P. Taylor.

NEW PROVIDENCE, never far off the pace, moved to the front on leaving the backstretch, opened up a commanding lead and was kept under steady pressure to the finish. MAJOR FLIGHT, badly outpaced in the early stages, improved his position gradually, finished with fine courage through the homestretch run, but could not overtake the winner. WINNING SHOT, taken in hand in the run to the first turn, raced on the outside early and closed gamely when placed to a drive.

On the day that *Victoria Park* might have won the famed Belmont Stakes in New York, he was at home, at Woodbine, acting like a big kid with the children, running the fastest Queen's Plate—2:02—in its 101-year history. It would be thirty years before Izvestia in 1990 would clip a fifth of a second (2:01 4/5) off the old plate record that "Ol' Pigeon Toes" established that day.

If he ever regretted the decision to go after the Plate instead of the Belmont Stakes, the "classic test of stamina and courage" and a race that was contested on the same day, and was won by *Celtic Ash*, a horse that *Victoria Park* had repeatedly manhandled that spring, owner E.P. Taylor never publicly admitted remorse. Taylor was president of the Ontario Jockey Club and had never wavered from his commitment that the Canadian public was entitled to see the colt in the country's most important race. In the first six months of 1960, he

"OL' PIGEON TOES," *VICTORIA PARK*, CRUISED DOWN THE STRETCH, RUNNING THE FASTEST PLATE IN HISTORY (2:02) AND RETURNING JUST $2.10 FOR A $2 WAGER.

had done more for Canadian breeding than any previous home-bred had done in a lifetime: multiple stakes winner in two countries, first horse to earn more than $100,000 in a season and a record career bankroll of $250,000.

It was a distinction he held until another colt from Windfields Farm, *Northern Dancer*, came along a few years later to win the Kentucky Derby and the Preakness Stakes, races in which *Victoria Park* had made history for a Canuck, finishing third at Louisville and a fast-closing second to *Bally Ache* at Pimlico in Maryland. When *Bally Ache* was scratched from the Belmont, horsemen were quick to claim that Taylor had erred in going after another Plate victory instead of the big dollars in New York and a chance to emphasize the point that Canada's breeding industry, which he monopolized, was as good as any in the world. Taylor agreed that his horse would likely have won the third jewel in America's Triple Crown, but insisted that even the scratching of *Bally Ache* would not have influenced his decision.

Taylor was in a "no-win" situation in any case. If *Victoria Park* and trainer Horatio Luro had remained in New York, he was in effect telling the world that the Queen's Plate, the continent's oldest continuously run horse race, was one for Canadian-breds that were not good enough to run somewhere else; that, as president of the OJC, he proclaimed the glamour of the country's top sports spectacle—then hopped off to Belmont Park on the day of the Plate.

To the delight of more than twenty-five thousand spectators, *Victoria Park* and jockey Avelino Gomez put on an unforgettable display as they waltzed to a one-sided triumph, one that would cost the OJC $3,515 in mutuel payoffs. He returned the minimum, $2.10, to win, but because so much money was bet on him in the show pool, the track had to make up the difference. As a side attraction, the crowd witnessed the clowning of El Senor, who stood high in his irons while cruising down the stretch, peering behind him to see if there was any opposition, and daring a crank, who had telephoned the police and track officials with a threat that he intended to shoot Gomez out of the saddle at the clubhouse turn. To hit the Cuban caballero would have taken the steady eye and aim of a Bisley

THE THREAT OF A SNIPER SHOOTING HIM OUT OF THE SADDLE DIDN'T DAUNT THE CUBAN CABALLERO.

VICTORIA PARK | 3-year-old bay colt

Victoria Park (1957)	Chop Chop	Flares	Gallant Fox
			Flambino
		*Sceptical	Buchan
			Clodagh
	Victoriana	Windfields	Bunty Lawless
			Nandi
		Iribelle	*Osiris II
			Belmona

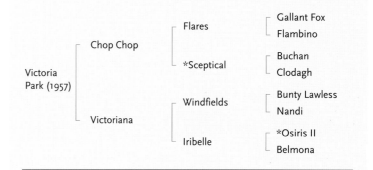

Owner: Windfields Farm, Oshawa, Ont.; *Trainer:* Horatio A. Luro
Jockey: Avelino Gomez; *Breeder:* E.P. Taylor, Toronto

marksman because *Victoria Park* was neatly boxed in by a phalanx of fellow travellers.

Later, Gomez laughed off the incident that a sniper had been sent up from Cuba. "Shoot! We go too fast. Why do you theenk I'm in a pocket goan' to the first bend? We get away a bit slow, but that's okay. They want me to stay off the pace a while and this way I doan have to snatch heem. Den I get in a little pocket of horses so dat man can't shoot me. But I never let him run one leetle bit. He was crying to get loose all the time, just looking for more horses to whip, but the trainer tell me win it easy as I can because the horse runs next week." Prepared for his early two-year-old successes by Taylor's Canadian-based trainer, Pete McCann, the colt had been moved that fall to Luro's barn for his major races in the United States.

The Plate, unfortunately, would be *Victoria Park*'s last race in Canada. The colt who had the ability to carry his blazing speed over impressive distances, to glide past opponents with contemptuous ease in the stretch, won the Leonard Richards Handicap at Delaware Park on 18 June, beating *Tompion* in track record time, then was shipped by air to California for the rich Hollywood Derby. Apparently fit when he boarded the plane, *Victoria Park* arrived on the west coast after a rough, eleven-hour trip with a bowed tendon in his foreleg. His racing career was over.

"No question at all in my mind, he was the greatest Canadian horse I ever ride," said Gomez years later. "*Nearctic* was very fast, and I never get a chance to ride *Northern Dancer.*" Shortly after the Plate victory, Avelino's wife, Patricia, gave birth to a daughter that they christened "Vicky."

Victoria Park, the colt yearling buyers had spurned at a price of $12,500 because he was pigeon-toed and "had a pair of front knees which were reminiscent of those of a housemaid who had spent her life scrubbing kitchen floors" was equally good at stud as his sire, *Chop Chop*. He produced a flurry of stakes winners, including Plate champions *Almoner, Kennedy Road* and *Victoria Song* in successive years. As good a racehorse as he was, and later the leading sire in Canada, *Victoria Park* would forever live in the shadow of *Northern Dancer*. The *Dancer* would gain everlasting international fame with his progeny while standing at Windfields' farm in Maryland, the fancy of every breeder in the world, while "Ol' Pigeon Toes" romanced mainly domestic mares at home, in Oshawa.

1960 QUEEN'S PLATE STAKES

SEVENTH RACE
Woodbine
JUNE 11, 1960

1 1–4 MILES. (2:01⅘). One Hundred and First Running THE QUEEN'S PLATE (The oldest fixture run continuously on this continent). Fifty Guineas, the gift of Her Majesty the Queen. $50,000 Added. 3–year–olds. Canadian–foaled. Fillies for whom the final payments have been made for the Woodbine Oaks Stakes may be made eligible for the Queen's Plate not later than May 1, 1960, upon payment of $100 each. The owner of the first horse to receive the Guineas, stakes and 50% of the added money; the second horse, 25%; the third horse, 15%; the fourth horse 10%. Scale weight, 126 lbs. Fillies allowed 5 lbs. A gold cup will be presented by the Club to the owner of the winner, and mementos to the trainer and rider of the winner. Nominations closed December 15, 1958. Nomination fees—189 remained eligible upon a payment of $25 on December 15, 1958, $4,725; 98 remained eligible upon a payment of $50 on December 15, 1959, $4,900; 48 remained eligible upon a payment of $100 on May 1, 1960, $4,800. Gross value, $68,425. Net to winner, $42,750 and 50 Guineas; second, $12,500; third, $7,500; fourth, $5,000. Mutuel Pool, $99,504. Quinella Pool, $53,556.

Horse	Eqt	Wt.	PP	¼	½	¾	1	Str	Fin	Jockey	Owner	Odds $1
VICTORIA PARK	b	126	3	4^{hd}	$3^{1\frac{1}{2}}$	1^{1}	1^{4}	1^{7}	$1^{7\frac{3}{4}}$	GomezA	WindfieldsFarm	b-.05
QUINTAIN	b	126	4	$5^{1\frac{1}{2}}$	$5^{1\frac{1}{2}}$	$4\frac{1}{2}$	$3\frac{1}{2}$	2^{4}	$2^{3\frac{1}{4}}$	PottsC	KingfieldFarm	36.60
CHAMPAGNE VELVET	b	126	7	1^{hd}	1^{1}	3^{2}	4^{4}	4^{1}	3^{nk}	RemillardP	BillBeasleyStable	a-7.85
MEN AT PLAY		126	6	6^{hd}	7^{5}	7^{5}	6^{4}	5^{3}	4^{1}	SmithFA	Maloney&Smythe	25.50
HIDDEN TREASURE	b	126	1	3^{nk}	$4\frac{1}{2}$	2^{nk}	$2^{2\frac{1}{2}}$	$3^{1\frac{1}{2}}$	$5^{1\frac{1}{4}}$	CoyA	BillBeasleyStable	a-7.85
TORONTO BOY	b	126	8	8	8	8	8	6^{3}	$6^{4\frac{1}{4}}$	DittfachH	TaylorCharles	b-.05
BULPAMIRU	b	121	2	$7^{1\frac{1}{2}}$	$6^{2\frac{1}{2}}$	6^{2}	5^{hd}	7^{6}	$7^{9\frac{1}{4}}$	SmithGL	ShermanorFarm	15.50
GARDEN GREEK	b	126	5	2^{1}	2^{hd}	5^{1}	7^{1}	8	8	VelezH	GardenCityStable	49.00

a–Coupled, Champagne Velvet and Hidden Treasure; b–Victoria Park and Toronto Boy.

IN GATE—5:43. OFF AT 5:43. Start good. Won easily. Time, :23⅘, :47⅘, 1:12⅕, 1:36⅘, 2:02 (Plate record). Track fast.

Mutuel Prices:

	$2 Mutuels Paid			Odds to $1		
2–VICTORIA PARK (b–entry)	2.10	2.20	2.10	.05	.10	.05
4–QUINTAIN		5.70	2.10		1.85	.05
1–CHAMPAGNE VELVET (a–entry)			2.10			.05

$2 QUINELLA 2–4 PAID $26.80

B. c. by Chop Chop—Victoriana, by Windfields. Trained by Horatio A. Luro; bred by E. P. Taylor.

VICTORIA PARK was bumped and shuffled back at the start, quickly moved up when clear to attain a striking position in the run to the first turn, assumed command from the outside midway of the backstretch, then came away from his opposition at will to win as his rider pleased. QUINTAIN, never far from the pace, closed with good energy to easily best the others. CHAMPAGNE VELVET took an early lead, dropped back leaving the backstretch, then came again when roused during the drive but could not threaten the top pair. MEN AT PLAY failed to menace. HIDDEN TREASURE tired after a mile. TORONTO BOY was never a factor. BULPAMIRU never threatened. GARDEN GREEK forced the pace for a half-mile, then gave way.

HUGO DITTFACH SIPS VICTORY OUT OF QUEEN'S PLATE TROPHY.

A man's lifetime had slipped away between the day his parents had taken him in an open carriage to watch his first Queen's Plate race in 1892, until an afternoon seventy years later when he finally won the guineas by the "width of a hockey puck," the closest finish in the 102-year history of the race in which he had played such an instrumental role when its antiquated rules were restructured.

At the age of eighty-one, Colonel Kenric Rudolphus ("Rud") Marshall was one of horse racing's "grand old gentlemen." On this June afternoon his 18-to-1 longshot, *Blue Light*, hit the finish line inches ahead of Conn Smythe's *Just Don't Shove*, a colt that most handicappers had figured would not be beaten under Johnny Longden. The world's most victorious jockey was gunning for one of the few major races in North America that had eluded him during his thirty-four-year career. Born in Wakefield, England, but raised near the mining community of Taber, Alberta, Longden had led for all but one step of the mile-and-a-quarter distance, the final one, when Hugo Dittfach, the Displaced Person who had escaped from East Germany as a penniless refugee, shoved his colt's nose ahead.

The standing ovation from the crowd of 28,302 that day was deafening for the unheralded colt, *Hustlin' Hugo*, Patrick MacMurchy, the shy Scottish-born trainer, and "Rud," the ex-polo player and steeplechase rider, chairman of the board and former president of the Ontario Jockey Club, a decorated war hero at the Battle of the Somme and at Amiens in World War I and later commanding officer of the 48th Highlanders. Marshall was a business tycoon in the fuel, dock and shipping industry, who served on the boards of various charitable foundations, Marshall was a quiet, gentle-spoken, self-effacing sportsman. The boisterous applause startled him as he walked across the track to the winner's circle. It should not have, for it was in recognition of the part he had played in bringing the Plate into the modern era, opening it to all Canadians in 1944, and introducing a stakes race that allowed trainers to give their horses a race before the Plate. The overdue changes took place while the race retained a touch of glamour and class possessed by no other in North America. Ted Reeve in *The Telegram* paid Marshall a fitting tribute the day before the Plate: ". . . we will be rooting for *Blue Light*. Col. Marshall, when he was head of the proceedings at Old Woodbine, was a good neighbour. Many a football practice was had in the infield there, with the use of tack room or so also. And our kid lacrosse teams always had a stretch of grass there for their games when requested. A gentleman who has done much for racing and other matters Canadian or Torontonian, it would be a goodly sight to see the Colonel in the winner's circle on this special occasion."

His father, N.G.L. Marshall, ran the aged gelding *Fred Henry* in the 1889 Plate, and "Rud" recalled going to Woodbine a few years later to see *O'Donohue* win for the Seagrams. "My parents took me in an open carriage. I remember that we joined the grand parade to the course along Queen Street and Eastern Avenue. There was no age-limit for children in those days. To me, it appeared to be a tremendous crowd, although I suppose that there were 10,000 to 12,000 persons in the grounds. It was a very gay crowd, with the ladies and gentlemen dressed in the height of fashion. In retrospect, it was reminiscent of a race meeting at a fashionable racecourse."

Although his silks—cerise and white blocks with a white cap—were first registered in 1901, Marshall had owned few good horses in that sixty-year span. His main interest was always with the jumpers. That changed in 1952 when he paid $3,300 for a colt bred by Jim Speers of Winnipeg at the annual sale of yearlings. Named *Hartney*, the colt went on to earn Horse-of-the-Year honours in 1957. His next acquisitions were at E.P. Taylor's pre-priced sale of yearlings: *Gai Gai* and *Blue Light*, a son of *Chop Chop*, that cost him $7,500. A disappointment as a two-year-old, *Blue Light* earned some praise with a second-plate finish to *Just Don't Shove* in one of the divisions of the Plate Trial Stakes. He looked like he was fit and

The thickness of a nose separated long shot *Blue Light* (blinkers) from favourite *Just Don't Shove* and its Hall of Fame jockey Johnny Longden.

BLUE LIGHT | 3-year-old bay colt

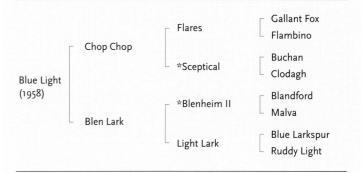

Blue Light (1958)	Chop Chop	Flares	Gallant Fox
			Flambino
		*Sceptical	Buchan
			Clodagh
	Blen Lark	*Blenheim II	Blandford
			Malva
		Light Lark	Blue Larkspur
			Ruddy Light

Owner: K.R. Marshall, Toronto, Ont.; *Trainer:* Patrick MacMurchy
Jockey: Hugo Dittfach; *Breeder:* E.P. Taylor, Toronto

would improve in a longer race. An offer to "ride" the more experienced Eddie Arcaro was vetoed by Marshall and MacMurchy. Their rider would be the ex-Calgary restaurant busboy, the Hustlin' Hessian—Dittfach, who became available when his Plate mount, *Axeman*, suffered bucked shins. "Hugo fitted the colt very well. He was a horse that had to be hustled hard, and Hugo could do that. He was such a lazy horse that he laid down to eat. But Hugo made him go that day," MacMurchy later said. *Blue Light* would be Dittfach's lone Plate winner in a career of more than 3,800 victories. "He [*Blue Light*] never got to be the champion he could have been. He had quarter cracks in his feet, and after the Plate he bled in both legs. It was the only stakes race he ever won. But that day we won through his kindness." Dittfach explained:

> Well, Longden's horse [*Just Don't Shove*] went to the lead coming out of the gate. But he is batting him to keep him going and the horse is trying to stop, and pull out, and he's laying his ears back, fightin Johnny . . . and my colt just runs. He's kind. He broke good and we save ground and he gave me no trouble anytime, and when I started to drive, hit him to get him going, he went.

Smythe, talking to author Scott Young years later, recalled the race differently. "I asked him [Longden] why he didn't give that horse one crack? He said, 'Mr. Smythe, your trainer asked me not to hit him because he might bolt.' Well, if he had bolted he would have bolted more than three inches and would have won the Plate! Even when it cost me that Plate, I really marvelled at a man like him, winner of more than 5,000 races, still obeying instructions!"

Trainer Pat MacMurchy, Hugo Dittfach and *Blue Light*'s owner, Col. K.R. (Rud) Marshall.

1961 QUEEN'S PLATE STAKES

SEVENTH RACE
Woodbine
JUNE 17, 1961

1 1-4 MILES (2:01⅘). One Hundred and Second Running QUEEN'S PLATE STAKES. $50,145 Added of which 50 Guineas was the gift of Her Majesty the Queen. 3-year-olds. Canadian foaled. Colts and geldings, 126 lbs.; fillies, 121 lbs. By subscription of $25 each, which shall accompany the nomination by December 15, 1959; second subscription of $50 by December 15, 1960; third subscription of $100 by May 1, 1961, and an additional $500 when making entry two days before the race. Fillies for whom the final payments for the Canadian Oak Stakes have been made, may be made eligible for the Queen's Plate not later than May 1, 1961, upon payment of $100 each. Closed Dec. 15, 1959, with 181 nominations at $25 each; 83 remained eligible on Dec. 15, 1960, by payment of $50 each; 63 remained eligible on May 1, 1961, by payment of $100 each. Value of race, $71,620. Value to winner, $47,620; second, $12,500; third, $7,500; fourth, $5,000. Mutuel Pool, $214,220.

Horse	Eqt	Wt.	PP	¼	½	¾	1	Str	Fin	Jockey	Owner	Odds $1
BLUE LIGHT	b	126	9	$6^{1½}$	6^{1}	6^{1}	5½	2^{2}	1no	DittfachH	MarshallKR	18.75
JUST DON'T SHOVE		126	5	$1^{1½}$	$1^{1½}$	$1^{1½}$	1^{1}	$1^{1½}$	2^{2}	LongdenJ	SmytheC	b-1.45
RAMBLIN WRECK	b	126	10	3^{nk}	3½	$4^{1½}$	4^{1}	3½	$3^{2¼}$	GomezA	BeasleyB	2.85
VICTORIA REGINA	b	121	8	11^{nk}	11^{nk}	11^{nk}	$8^{1½}$	6^{3}	4^{hd}	ParnellJ	WindfieldsFarm	a-3.90
GRAMP'S PRIDE		126	13	5½	5½	5^{hd}	6^{1}	5^{nk}	5¾	BorgemenkeR	MorrisseyWF	7.55
QUEEN'S PARK	b	126	4	4½	4½	3^{hd}	2^{1}	4^{hd}	$6^{3¼}$	CosentinoS	WindfieldsFarm	a-3.90
MILTON MAN		126	1	9½	$10^{2½}$	10^{3}	7^{nk}	7½	7½	GibbG	MaloneyL	107.55
JAMMED LUCKY	b	126	11	10^{hd}	9^{nk}	9^{hd}	9^{1}	8^{2}	$8^{3¾}$	CoyA	SmytheC	b-1.45
FLASHING TOP	b	121	3	8½	1^{1}	8½	10^{2}	9^{2}	$9^{4¼}$	FitzsimmonsJ	WindfieldsFarm	a-3.90
PRINCE TOUR	b	126	7	13	13	12½	12½	10^{2}	10^{3}	BrownC	LuxianaFarm	26.65
MAID O' NORTH		121	2	7½	7½	7^{nk}	11^{1}	11^{1}	11^{nk}	PottsC	ShermanorFarm	11.00
EDGOR'S LANE		126	12	$12^{2½}$	12^{2}	13	13	12½	$12^{4½}$	ZehrF	EdgorRidgeStable	213.60
TEHRAN'S DAN	b	126	6	2^{1}	2^{1}	2½	3^{hd}	13	13	RoyE	GormleyStudFarm	81.50

a-Coupled, Victoria Regina and Flashing Top; b-Just Don't Shove and Jammed Lucky.

OFF AT 5:46. Start good. Won driving. Time, :23⅖, :47⅕, 1:12⅕, 1:37⅘, 2:05. Track fast.

$2 Mutuel Prices:			
7-BLUE LIGHT	39.50	10.60	4.80
2-JUST DON'T SHOVE (b-Entry)		3.30	2.50
8-RAMBLIN WRECK			3.00

B. c, by Chop Chop—Blen Lark, by *Blenheim II. Trainer, MacMurchy Pat. Bred by Taylor E. P.

BLUE LIGHT, outrun in the early stages, gradually bettered his position, was set down for his best after straightening out in the homestretch and, responding gallantly, was along in the final strides to wear down JUST DON'T SHOVE. The latter moved to the front at once, opened up a clear lead, was smoothly rated in advance, responded when vigorously roused in the final yards and just failed to last long enough. RAMBLIN WRECK raced in the thick of contention from the beginning, saved ground entering the homestretch run and finished stoutly under pressure. VICTORIA REGINA stumbled at the start, raced far back in the early stages, was forced to come to the outside entering the homestretch and finished with fine courage. GRAMP'S PRIDE raced forwardly placed in the early racing but failed to better his position when roused. QUEEN'S PARK raced forwardly placed, moved up threateningly after going six furlongs, then began to falter. MILTON MAN could not gain a contending position. JAMMED LUCKY failed to threaten. FLASHING TOP failed to menace. PRINCE TOUR was squeezed back at the start. MAID O' NORTH could not reach the leaders. EDGOR'S LANE showed nothing. TEHRAN'S DAN forced the early pace and stopped badly.

1962 | FLAMING PAGE

Flaming Page, a stout-hearted daughter of *Bull Page,* was different from any other Canadian-bred filly. She was not only a superior runner—a distinction she earned when she became the first filly to win the two most important races for three-year-olds in Canada, the Queen's Plate and the Canadian Oaks, in a space of seven days—but her eminence as a broodmare when she retired would be a success story that knew no bounds. The classic test of a thoroughbred's quality is if it can outproduce itself—sire or foal a horse better than he or she was. In a relatively short period, *Flaming Page* achieved the accolades: dam of *Nijinsky II,* the first winner of Britain's Triple Crown since *Bahram* in 1935; and grand-dam of *The Minstrel,* also the champion horse of Europe.

THE CELEBRATED BROODMARE *FLAMING PAGE* (RIGHT), DAM OF *NIJINSKY II*, AND HER FIRST FOAL, *FLEUR*, AT WINDFIELDS FARM.

Retired after only sixteen races, *Flaming Page*'s first foal was *Fleur,* a stakes-placed daughter by *Victoria Park.* She later became a valued property for breeder E.P. Taylor when she foaled *The Minstrel,* a colt that English sportsman Robert Sangster had paid $200,000 for at the Keeneland sales in Kentucky. A son of *Northern Dancer,* the colt captured the Epsom and the Irish Derbys and the King George VI and Queen Elizabeth Stakes at Ascot before Taylor bought back a half-share in him and teamed up with the betting-pools' millionaire to syndicate the colt for a record $9 million in 1977. *The Minstrel*—along with his three-quarters brother, *Nijinsky II*—was regarded in Europe as one of the finest horses to race there during the last decade. In winning the Derby, *Nijinsky II* gave his breeder the distinction of being the first in history to breed winners of both the Kentucky Derby and the Epsom Derby. His Canadian-breds could no longer be considered second-class citizens in the world of the thoroughbred; they were dominant on both sides of the Atlantic.

1962 QUEEN'S PLATE STAKES

SEVENTH RACE
Woodbine
JUNE 16, 1962

1 1–4 MILES (2:01$\frac{4}{5}$). One Hundred and Third Running QUEEN'S PLATE STAKES. $50,000 Added, with 50 Guineas, the gift of Her Majesty the Queen. 3–year–olds. Canadian–foaled. Scale weights: colts and geldings, 126 lbs.; fillies, 121 lbs. By subscription of $25 each, which shall accompany the nomination by December 15, 1960; second subscription of $50 by December 15, 1961; third subscription of $100 by May 1, 1962; an additional $500 to make entry two days before the race. Winner to receive the Guineas, all nomination, subscription and entry fees and 50% of the added money; second, 25%; third, 15% and fourth, 10%. Closed Dec. 15, 1960, with 301 nominations. On December 15, 1961, 120 remained eligible. On May 1, 1962, 57 remained eligible. Value of race, $76,225. Value to winner, $51,225; second, $12,500; third, $7,500; fourth, $5,000. Mutuel Pool, $252,290.

Horse	Eqt	Wt.	PP	¼	½	¾	1	Str	Fin	Jockey	Owner	Odds $1
FLAMING PAGE	b	121	5	12^{2}	$11^{1\frac{1}{2}}$	6^{nk}	1^{nk}	$1^{2\frac{1}{2}}$	$1^{1\frac{3}{4}}$	FitzsimmonsJ	WindfieldsFarm	b-1.10
CHOPERION		126	1	7^{nk}	9^{1}	$11^{\frac{1}{2}}$	$5^{\frac{1}{2}}$	3^{2}	$2^{1\frac{1}{4}}$	HartackW	WindfieldsFarm	b-1.10
PETER'S CHOP		126	9	$8^{\frac{1}{2}}$	$6^{\frac{1}{2}}$	3^{hd}	$2^{\frac{1}{2}}$	$2^{\frac{1}{2}}$	$3^{1\frac{1}{4}}$	McCombS	DelGrecoP	3.25
KING GORM		126	6	10^{2}	10^{1}	8^{nk}	6^{1}	$4^{1\frac{1}{2}}$	$4^{4\frac{1}{2}}$	DittfachH	LansonFarm	c-4.55
SUN DAN		126	13	3^{nk}	3^{nk}	1^{hd}	$3^{1\frac{1}{2}}$	5^{4}	$5^{4\frac{3}{4}}$	PottsC	FarrWJ	10.70
TRES SUAVE		126	4	1^{nk}	$2^{1\frac{1}{2}}$	2^{nk}	$4^{1\frac{1}{2}}$	$6^{2\frac{1}{2}}$	$6^{1\frac{1}{4}}$	RasmussenG	LansonFarm	c-4.55
HAMMER'N TONGS		126	7	$5^{1\frac{1}{2}}$	7^{1}	$10^{\frac{1}{2}}$	9^{2}	8^{2}	7^{nk}	RobinsonK	Bo-TeekFarm	82.35
LAVELLA	b	121	2	6^{hd}	5^{1}	4^{1}	$7^{2\frac{1}{2}}$	$7^{\frac{1}{2}}$	$8^{2\frac{1}{2}}$	HaleD	MarshallKR	83.30
MONARCH PARK	b	126	10	4^{1}	4^{hd}	$7^{2\frac{1}{2}}$	8^{1}	9^{2}	$9^{1\frac{1}{4}}$	DaltonH	AddisonHallStable	28.55
ARGUE AROUND	b	126	11	11^{1}	13	13	13	12^{4}	10^{hd}	RemillardP	TripleRStable	30.40
WELCOME EFFORT	b	126	8	13	$12^{\frac{1}{2}}$	$12^{3\frac{1}{2}}$	12^{2}	$11^{\frac{1}{2}}$	$11^{\frac{1}{2}}$	RogersC	GoldenWestFarm	24.15
RECKLESS RICK	b	126	12	$9^{\frac{1}{2}}$	$8^{\frac{1}{2}}$	9^{nk}	10^{1}	$10^{\frac{1}{2}}$	$12^{6\frac{1}{4}}$	AnyonE	DoubleKFarm	13.55
NAVY JAY		126	3	2^{hd}	$1^{\frac{1}{2}}$	5^{hd}	11^{1}	13	13	RoserG	BurtonHC	87.40

b–Coupled, Flaming Page and Choperion; c–King Gorm and Tres Suave.

OFF AT 6:10. Start good. Won ridden out. Time, :23$\frac{4}{5}$, :47$\frac{4}{5}$, 1:12$\frac{3}{5}$, 1:38$\frac{2}{5}$, 2:04$\frac{3}{5}$. Track fast.

$2 Mutuel Prices:

2–FLAMING PAGE (b–Entry)	4.20	3.80	2.60
2–CHOPERION (b–Entry)	4.20	3.80	2.60
7–PETER'S CHOP			3.10

B. f, by Bull Page—Flaring Top, by Menow. Trainer, Luro Horatio A. Bred by Taylor E. P.

FLAMING PAGE, allowed to settle into best stride, moved up fast on the outside when advancing along the backstretch and around the far turn, took command approaching the stretch, briskly drew clear and was intermittently urged to maintain a safe advantage over CHOPERION. The latter, slow to respond while racing along the inside early, was taken to the outside when commencing his rally on the final turn and continued on strongly through the stretch but could not reach the winner. PETER'S CHOP, never too far back, joined the leaders along the backstretch and lacked the needed late response. KING GORM, unhurried through the first half mile, steadily worked his way up to reach a striking position entering the stretch and closed determinedly.

Scratched—New Perspective.

In the fall of 1968, Taylor sold his yearlings not at Windfields, as he had since 1954, but through the annual Canadian Thoroughbred Horse Society (CTHS) sales. At his pre-priced sale two years earlier, only ten of his sixty-two yearlings had been purchased; it became clear then to Taylor and general manager Joe Thomas that the sales pattern had to change. To accommodate the auction, the pre-prices became reserves, and selling quotas were abandoned. Buyers could take them all, as long as they paid the minimum reserve bids.

Many of the breeders expressed concern that the entry of Taylor's own horses would swamp the market. George Frostad, president of the CTHS, a shrewd businessman, a land developer and a successful breeder, thought that the Taylor horses would elevate a parochial event to one of international stature. It did offer offspring of the *Dancer,* and Frostad was right; sales for the first time grossed more than $1 million, and Windfields' immediate objective was achieved when fifty-two of the eighty-one consigned horses sold for $576,000.

Charles Englehard, the ultra-rich mining

EL SENOR FROM THE ARGENTINE, HORATIO LURO.

Owner: Windfields Farm, Oshawa, Ont.; *Trainer:* Horatio A. Luro
Jockey: Jim Fitzsimmons; *Breeder:* E.P. Taylor, Toronto

industrialist from New Jersey and South Africa, sent Vincent O'Brien, his Irish-born trainer, to the CTHS sale to inspect a colt by the famed Italian sire, *Ribot*. O'Brien rejected the yearling, but was impressed by a big, superbly built colt out of *Flaming Page*. O'Brien's advice to Englehard was to buy the colt by *Northern Dancer,* not the one by *Ribot*. Unable to attend the sales, the platinum magnate sent one of his Canadian executives, George Scott, who bid $84,000, a record for a domestic yearling. In an era of $100,000 yearlings, the initial significance of the purchase was mostly local. But when the colt turned out to be *Nijinsky II,* the CTHS had secured itself a place in thoroughbred sales history. Undefeated at two, *Nijinsky II* concluded his career with only two losses, one a photo-finish in the Prix de l'Arc de Triomphe at Longchamp to **Sassafras;* he had record winnings of $677,117 for a horse raced in Europe, and international Horse of the Year honours in every racing community except Canada (he was not eligible because he had never raced beneath the Maple Leaf). Englehard's syndication of *Nijinsky II* was for $5.4 million, making him the most expensive stud in the history of horse racing. Eddie Taylor bought two shares, which cost him $340,000, or four times the amount he received when he sold the horse in 1968. Like his sire and dam, *Nijinsky II* out-produced himself; he was the progenitor of more than seventy stakes winners and horses, which earned in excess of $13 million.

In 1960, the year after Taylor's *New Providence* had won the Plate for his sire, a filly by the same stallion, called *Bull Page,* was offered at Windfields Farm in Willowdale for $20,000. She was out of *Flaring Top,* a multiple stakes-producing mare. Buyers ignored the bay filly (later named *Flaming Page*) that Taylor had assigned to his American-based trainer, the charming and nattily attired Argentinian, Horatio Luro. At two, she finished out of the money only once in seven races, winning the Shady Well

MRS. WINNIE TAYLOR LEADS PLATE WINNER *FLAMING PAGE* AND JIM FITZSIMMONS ACROSS WOODBINE'S TURF COURSE.

Stakes, coming second in the Princess Elizabeth and third against the colts in the Coronation Futurity.

Wintered in Florida, *Flaming Page* ran against the best fillies in North America at Hialeah, and later at Churchill Downs, Kentucky, where she finished second to *Cicada* on a sloppy track in the Kentucky Oaks. Champion for three successive years, *Cicada* earned almost $800,000, a record for a mare at the time. Luro that year became the first trainer to win both the Kentucky Derby, with *Decidedly* in record time, and the Plate in the same year. After *Flaming Page*'s effort against *Cicada,* Luro was convinced that she might have the stamina to win the two demanding Canadian races in a one-week span. She won the Oaks easily, and then on 16 June, before a record crowd of 32,169, which included Her Majesty Queen Elizabeth, the Queen Mother, jockey Jim Fitzsimmons bided his time in the thirteen-horse field before launching a determined drive coming out of the backstretch. Her powerful kick sent the filly into command at the top of the homestretch and she pulled away to win by almost two lengths over her stablemate, *Choperion,* ridden by Bill Hartack. Before the race, the two jockeys had agreed to split the ten per cent share of the winning purse, on condition that the loser would also be presented to the Queen Mother. The first four finishers were all bred by Taylor. "You don't have to have a Windfields-bred thoroughbred to win the Queen's Plate—but it sure helps," *The Daily Star*'s Joe Perlove observed afterwards.

How good was Taylor's filly that afternoon? Hugo Dittfach, who was on fourth-place finisher *King Gorm,* expressed his admiration: "Get this. Fitzie [Fitzsimmons] had her under a pull when they flew by me. She went by me like I was standin' still. Before the race I thought I had one helluva shot. Now, I have no excuses. There wasn't any way we were gonna beat her." A week later, competing in her third distance race in twenty-one days, the Coaching Club of America Oaks at Belmont, New York, *Flaming Page* held the lead for a mile before tiring in the stretch to finish fourth by three lengths to *Bramalea, Cicada* and *Firm Policy.* It was her final race.

Nothing in Canadian racing had stirred as much furore as the announcement on 22 May 1963 that *Jet Traffic* had been barred from the Queen's Plate by directors of the Jockey Club Limited (Ontario). He was ineligible because of a minor and flimsy technicality. The decision seriously exacerbated the sense of frustration many horsemen and the public felt over the continued monopoly of the Plate by Windfields Farm, since it eliminated the one horse that would likely have beaten *Canebora*, E.P. Taylor's big horse that year.

Owned by Russell A. Firestone Junior, the American rubber tire tycoon from Dallas, the Canadian-foaled colt had been established as the winterbook favourite because of his impressive record as a two-year-old in the United States. To further enhance his flashy credentials, the bay colt that had been bred by Frank Conklin at his Midway Farms near Brantford, Ontario, sped to an easy victory in the Bay Shore Stakes at Aqueduct, New York, on 27 March. In knocking off two good colts, *Bonjour* and *Top Gallant,* the Plate hopeful was timed in 1:34 1/5, the fastest mile ever by a three-year old so early in the spring. "By coincidence," wrote Milt Dunnell in *The Toronto Daily Star,* after a conversation with Firestone, "that's when the first doubts of the colt's eligibility for the Plate cropped up." No American-owned horse had ever won the Plate.

Acting on an "anonymous" claim that *Jet Traffic* had been nominated incorrectly, Jockey Club directors investigated the allegation and, after discussing the matter with the principals, voted unanimously to bar Firestone's colt on two counts: that Frank Conklin, the breeder, was not acting as a deputy for Firestone when he paid his original twenty-five dollar nomination fee on 15 December 1961, and that the nomination was paid by Conklin in the name of Warren L. Jones Junior of Hermitage Farm, Goshen, Kentucky. Four months earlier Jones had consigned and sold the yearling to Firestone for $10,000 at the Keeneland summer sales in Kentucky. Firestone made the second subscription on 15 December 1962. Shortly afterwards, the Jockey Club Limited became aware that the Ontario Racing Commission's rules of racing had been violated; they notified Firestone that there appeared to be doubt about *Jet Traffic's* eligibility, and that the payment of any subscription (the next one was due on 1 May) and the receipt thereof was not an assurance of eligibility and that he should be prepared to establish eligibility.

In essence, *Jet Traffic* was grounded because Conklin nominated the colt under Jones' name—the man he had sold him to in 1960 (along with his dam, *Valis Regina*)—instead of Firestone, who had bought him in July 1961. This contravened the Ontario rules, which stipulated that only an authorized agent or a person deputized by the owner could make the nomination payment. E.P. Taylor, chairman of the meeting, together with J.E. Armstrong, Wolfgang von Richthofen, Harry Carmichael and J.E. Frowde Seagram, declared a conflict of interest and refrained from voting. The vote of the other directors was 8-0 and so the subscription payments were returned.

"At first the Jockey Club told me how happy they were to have my horse in the list of nominees," Firestone told Dunnell. "We pulled

FANS BOOED OWNER E.P. TAYLOR AND *CANEBORA* FOLLOWING ITS CONTROVERSIAL VICTORY. WITH TAYLOR ARE PANAMANIAN JOCKEY MANNY YCAZA AND LIEUTENANT GOVERNOR EARL ROWE.

Jet Traffic out of the [Kentucky] Derby because we intended to run in the Queen's Plate. His last half dozen races were planned with an eye for your race in Canada. Then I was informed by telegram that my horse couldn't run. It's a shame that people would take advantage of a loophole, if one exists, to bar a horse. It's all politics, of course. I'm glad the Jockey Club doesn't operate that way down here."

George C. Hendrie, president of the Jockey Club Limited, and general manager John J. Mooney, were in charge of the investigation. Mooney revealed that several ways were tried to see if the horse could be found eligible. "We called Mr. Firestone, asking if he had made Mr. Conklin a deputy for the payments. Mr. Firestone said he really didn't know Mr. Conklin." This killed it, in the eyes of directors. Ironically, the man who trained *Jet Traffic,* Del Carroll, later was one of Taylor's top trainers when he moved part of his breeding and racing operations to Maryland.

Fans were further alienated when a local favourite, Hugo Dittfach, who had won the Plate Trial Stakes on *Canebora,* was replaced on the horse two days before the race by the controversial Manny Ycaza, the talented but fiery Panamanian who was noted (like Dittfach) as "a slashin' type of rider." Dittfach could not believe his ears when trainer Pete McCann told him that Ycaza had been brought in from New York to ride the Plate favourite. He would have to ride the filly, *Breezy Answer,* which finished fifth. "I thought McCann was kiddin'. Mr. Taylor thanked me after we won the Trial and said 'You're going to ride and I guess you're going to win.' Why break up a winning combo? Even McCann didn't know why they brought in Ycaza. Nobody ever told me." In cases such as this, riders in an entry often split the ten per cent of the winning purse, which was a record $55,000, but an irate Dittfach knew this would not happen: "He [Ycaza] wouldn't split a nickel."

Ycaza, who arrived in Toronto with his new wife, a Miss Universe, vigorously tattooed the colt, especially when he broke the race open at the top of the stretch, pulling away from *Son Blue* and the tiring *Warriors Day* and *Royal Maple,* second choice in the betting behind Taylor's favoured 3-to-1 entry. A colt that would go on to become Canada's second winner of the Triple Crown with subsequent wins in the Prince of Wales and the Breeders' Stakes, and earn $141,414, *Canebora* was another of the yearlings that buyers had rejected at Taylor's pre-priced sale that would go on to win the Plate. He was available for $7,500 in 1961, "but," wrote Mike Armstrong of *The Toronto Telegram,* "buyers in the past have ignored such bargains as *Victoria Park, Flaming Page, New Providence, Lyford Cay* and *Blue Light.* It seems that buyers at his sale wouldn't know a bargain if they got into a stall with one."

Taylor's monopoly of the Plate—he had now bred twelve of the last fifteen winners, eight of them running under his turquoise and gold polka-dot silks—was roundly booed by the patrons as he walked across to the winner's circle. He stood for a while, smiling, and holding *Canebora*'s white rein, but the booing did not stop. Taylor was a victim of the rules. *The Globe and Mail* had earlier demanded that Taylor reinstate *Jet Traffic,* saying that if he did not, "sportsmanship will have a sadder meaning in the lexicon of the game." Taylor pointed out that if *Jet Traffic* were reinstated and he won, the Jockey Club would be faced with a lawsuit from the other owners. There was nothing he could do. "It's a fiasco. Now the poor person who wins the Plate is going to get the raspberry."

While Taylor was feeling the resentment of the public, *Jet Traffic* was performing at Chicago's Washington Park, finishing seventh in the $113,333 Chicagoan Stakes to *B. Major* and *Candy Spots.* Russell Firestone has since competed in such races as the Rothman's International at Woodbine, but he has never run a horse in the Plate.

Canebora, nevertheless, provided marvelous copy for the media. Along with the *Jet Traffic* controversy, many columns were written regarding *Canebora*'s intense dislike of bugle music as well as just who his father was. Dick Beddoes in *The Globe and Mail* said: "*Canebora* cannot identify his sire for the incontestable reason that his mother was the equine equivalent of a bigamist. Her name was *Menebora* and in 1959 she had barnyard romances with gentlemen called *Navy Page* and *Canadian Champ. Canebora* was foaled eleven months later. *Canebora*'s old man, whoever he is, could whinny with pride after Saturday's romp."

Out of deference to *Canebora* no bugle was blown in the paddock area before the race. No traditional *Saddle Up* or *Post Call.* Jim Proudfoot in *The Daily Star* wrote, "Most of all he dislikes bugle music, which of course is a vital part of the racetrack show. . . . These sounds, sweet to most ears, strike *Canebora* like a fingernail scraped down a blackboard." Also enjoying the situation was Scott Young in *The Globe and Mail,* who wrote, "As a two-year-old he once chased an entire Salvation Army band of Christmas carollers all the way from Windfields Farm to the Eglinton Avenue subway station at a speed that qualified three cornet players for our next Olympic team."

CANEBORA | 3-year-old brown colt

Canebora (1960)	Canadian Champ	Windfields	Bunty Lawless
			Nandi
		Bolesteo	*Filisteo
			Bold Fay
	Menebora	*Menetrier	Fair Copy
			La Melodie
		*La Bora	Mistral
			La Divine

Owner: Windfields Farm, Oshawa, Ont.; *Trainer:* Gordon (Pete) McCann
Jockey: Manuel Ycaza; *Breeder:* E.P. Taylor, Toronto

1963 QUEEN'S PLATE STAKES

SEVENTH RACE
Woodbine
JUNE 15, 1963

1 1–4 MILES (2:01 4/5). One Hundred and Fourth Running QUEEN'S PLATE STAKES. $50,000 Added, with 50 Guineas, the gift of Her Majesty the Queen. 3-year-olds. Canadian-Foaled. Scale weights: colts and geldings, 126 lbs.; fillies, 121 lbs. By subscription of $25 each, which shall accompany the nomination by December 15, 1961; second subscription of $50 by December 15, 1962; third subscription of $100 by May 1, 1963; an additional $500 to make entry two days before the race. Winner to receive the Guineas, all nomination, subscription and entry fees and 50 per cent of the added money; second, 25 per cent; third, 15 per cent, and fourth, 10 per cent. Closed Dec. 15, 1961, with 282 nominations at $25 each. 132 remained eligible Dec. 15, 1962, on payment of $50 each. 67 remained eligible May 1, 1963, on payment of $100 each. Value of race, $79,850. Value to winner, $54,850; second, $12,500; third, $7,500; fourth, $5,000. Mutuel Pool, $257,109.

Horse	Eqt	Wt.	PP	¼	½	¾	1	Str	Fin	Jockey	Owner	Odds $1
CANEBORA	b	126	10	$7^{1½}$	7^{nk}	4^{nk}	1^{hd}	1^{hd}	1^{1}	YcazaM	WindfieldsFarm	a-3.20
SON BLUE	b	126	8	9^{1}	8^{1}	8^{nk}	$3^{1½}$	3^{3}	2½	FitzsimmonsJ	FarrWJ	4.65
WARRIORS DAY		126	19	4^{nk}	3^{nk}	$2^{2½}$	2^{1}	2^{1}	$3^{3¾}$	RobinsonK	SmytheC	6.10
ROYAL MAPLE	b	126	5	18^{nk}	12½	11^{1}	9½	4^{hd}	4^{nk}	TurcotteR	LevesqueJL	3.50
BREEZY ANSWER		121	1	12^{hd}	13^{2}	13^{2}	$8^{1½}$	6^{2}	$5^{1¾}$	DittfachH	WindfieldsFarm	a-3.20
PRINCE BUBI	b	126	4	6½	6^{1}	3½	$5^{2½}$	5½	6^{1}	McCombS	DellioM	69.95
MENEDICT		121	9	3^{hd}	4^{2}	5^{1}	6^{hd}	7½	7no	BohenkoP	GrantHA	c-7.15
RICH		126	3	5½	5^{hd}	6^{hd}	7½	9½	8no	LanowayG	LansonFarm	35.25
MAJOR'S CHOICE		126	11	10½	9½	9½	10^{1}	10^{1}	9^{hd}	GordonG	ArmstrongBros	f-21.35
HOP HOP	b	126	16	16^{1}	16^{1}	16½	11^{2}	11^{2}	$10^{3¾}$	DaltonH	MaloneyL	c-7.15
WELCOME PARDNER		126	12	17^{nk}	17½	17½	15^{1}	15^{3}	11^{hd}	ShieldsS	GoldenWestFarm	b-9.05
BLACK N' RED		126	14	19	19	19	16½	12^{nk}	12½	ChambersW	RossDG	f-21.35
COMMON MARKET		126	2	15^{1}	15^{1}	15^{1}	13½	13^{nk}	13^{nk}	BurtonJ	Gardiner-GoldenWestFm	b-9.05
PRINCE MAPLE		126	18	14^{hd}	14^{1}	14^{1}	14^{1}	14½	$14^{1¼}$	HarrisonJ	R-RStable	33.65
MORNINS' MORNIN	b	126	15	11^{hd}	11½	12^{1}	12^{1}	16^{3}	15^{3}	SellersJ	Mann-Knox	17.05
ASKUM	b	126	13	1^{nk}	$1^{2½}$	1^{5}	4^{hd}	8^{nk}	$16^{7½}$	HaleD	NaturalFarmStable	59.35
LADY B. FAST	b	121	6	8^{1}	10^{1}	10^{nk}	17^{1}	17^{15}	$17^{18½}$	UyeyamaH	OlivierRanches	f-21.35
MEDALIA S.	b	126	17	13^{hd}	18^{4}	18^{2}	18^{2}	18^{6}	$18^{8½}$	GubbinsG	JacobsJM	f-21.35
GUIDING WAVE		126	7	$2^{1½}$	2^{2}	7½	19	19	19	PottsC	TripiMrsJT	f-21.35

a-Coupled, Canebora and Breezy Answer; b-Welcome Pardner and Common Market; c-Menedict and Hop Hop. f-Mutuel field.

OFF AT 5:21. Start good. Won driving. Time, :22 4/5, :46, 1:10 4/5, 1:37 1/5, 2:04. Track fast.

$2 Mutuel Prices:

1-CANEBORA (a-Entry)	8.40	4.40	3.10
7-SON BLUE		5.50	4.00
11-WARRIORS DAY			4.40

Br. c, by Navy Page or Canadian Champ—Menebora, by *Menetrier. Trainer, McCann Gordon (Pete). Bred by Taylor E. P.

CANEBORA, unhurried through the first half mile, moved steadily from the outside to wrest command shortly before reaching the stretch and was kept under pressure during the drive to dispose of WARRIORS DAY and held SON BLUE safe. The latter, never a great distance back, moved to the leaders on the second turn, launched his bid from the outside when shaken for the stretch run, outfinished WARRIORS DAY but could not overtake the winner. WARRIORS DAY, well placed early, moved nearest the leader along the backstretch, attained a slight advantage from the inside between calls on the final turn and held on determinedly.

1964 | NORTHERN DANCER

Northern Dancer SAUNTERS HOME ALONE IN A ONE-SIDED Queen's Plate VICTORY.

He had a stride that looked two sizes too big for him, but it was perfectly controlled, like something they did at the Bolshoi Ballet . . . his dimensions were that of a vest-pocket Hercules who was fashioned more along the lines of a speedball than a stayer.

CHARLES HATTON, *DAILY RACING FORM*

Leon Rasmussen, like other students of thoroughbred pedigrees and the confirmation of great racehorses, enjoyed writing about *Northern Dancer* as much as any turf authority, quoting Hatton's favourite description of the Canadian-bred colt during an eight-part series in 1983 that examined the "most remarkable racing and breeding story of our time." Hatton's words about the muscular, chunky bay colt were written immediately after *Northern Dancer*

became the first Canadian-bred to win the Kentucky Derby. He knew how special the blocky, feisty little bay colt was. But he couldn't possibly have known that a Canadian from the backwaters of racing would become the most influential sire in the world, not only in the most hallowed halls of the sport in North America, Europe and Asia, but in countries like Peru, Denmark, Greece, India, Korea, Thailand and Zimbabwe.

Northern Dancer spilled his pearls everywhere. People all over the world recognize his name.

Of the five Kentucky Derbies that Hall of Fame jockey Bill Hartack won, his stirring, upset victory with *Northern Dancer* over the splendid, racy looking *Hill Rise*, holds a special place in his heart. Perhaps it was because *Northern Dancer* was always the underdog.

THE CITY OF TORONTO WELCOMED ITS KENTUCKY DERBY HERO WITH A BILLBOARD.

NORTHERN DANCER | 3-year-old bay colt

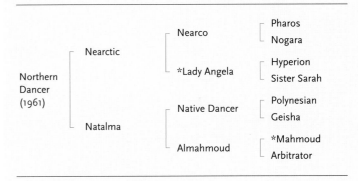

Owner: Windfields Farm, Oshawa, Ont.; *Trainer:* Horatio Luro
Jockey: William Hartack; *Breeder:* E.P. Taylor, Toronto

Or that another jockey had turned down the opportunity to ride him in the Derby. Although he'd won the Flamingo Stakes (the first Canadian-bred to win a $100,000 race) and the Florida Derby with the colt, Bill Shoemaker ditched him in favor of *Hill Rise*, winner of

eight consecutive races before the 1964 Derby. "I don't know if it was because he was Canadian-bred or if it was because he was on the small side," Hartack said. "Every time he ran, he showed he could run further than anybody thought he could. It was a great challenge for me to ride him."

As a yearling, nobody was willing to pay the pre-set price of $25,000 that owner E.P. Taylor put on *Northern Dancer*'s head. Andre

A CLASSIC DUEL UNDER THE TWIN SPIRES OF LOUISVILLE'S CHURCHILL DOWNS—*NORTHERN DANCER* (BLINKERS) BY A MUSCULAR NECK WINNER OVER CALIFORNIA FAVOURITE *HILL RISE*.

Blaettler, who had been with Taylor since 1951, recalled how Larkin Maloney, a regular buyer at the sales, vacillated when he and his trainer, Carl Chapman, attended the annual inspection of yearlings the day before the sale at the Willowdale farm on Bayview Avenue. "We would bring them out in pairs, and *Northern Dancer* was led out with *Brockton Boy*. He was a bigger animal and Maloney didn't like small horses. I knew about his preference and told him the horse he was learning toward [*Brockton Boy*] was by a proven sire [*Menetrier*] and the mare had produced a stakes winner." *Northern Dancer* was by two "maidens" to the breeding business.

It was Peter Richards, son of the famed English rider and trainer, Sir Gordon Richards, who broke the colt to saddle at Oshawa before he was shipped to trainer Horatio Luro. Several times, Luro recommended that he be gelded, so ornery was the son of *Nearctic* in his fledgling days. "Napoleonic," they called him. The colt's temperament was described as feisty, willful and anything but cuddly.

E.P. TAYLOR, TRAINER HORATIO LURO, BILL HARTACK AND PREAKNESS STAKES CHAMPION *NORTHERN DANCER* DRAPED WITH THE TRADITIONAL "BLACK-EYED SUSAN" BLANKET.

Northern Dancer was born at Taylor's Windfields Farm in Oshawa (then called the National Stud), on 27 May 1961, three weeks early, but a late foal at that. He was fortunate to be born. His dam, *Natalma*, who Taylor purchased for $35,000 as a yearling, had chipped a bone in her knee, and rather than try to continue racing her at age three, Taylor decided to breed her to his first-year sire *Nearctic*. *Natalma* had enormous ability, but also a sour disposition. As a two-year-old she lost the Spinaway Stakes on a disqualification. The breeding took place so late in the season that Windfields decided she would be bred only once, and if she didn't catch, they wouldn't try again that season. She conceived.

Of all the weanlings foaled at Windfields that year, *Northern Dancer* was the smallest, standing only 15.2 hands when fully grown. What he lacked in size, he had in muscle and strength and attitude. His seventy-three-inch girth was equal to that of *Kelso*, five times Horse of the Year, who stood sixteen hands high. He was willful and difficult as a youngster, and known as a bad ride among the exercise boys, said Windfields racing manager Joe Thomas. "The low lad on the totem pole had to ride him and if he didn't use all his expertise, he would put him on his butt," he said. "Even at the track he would do tricks, bolting, buckjumping, all sorts of things. He was a handful. Gradually, as he became more successful, he seemed to realize he should conduct himself more to his station in life and he became more tractable. He was never really mean. He was just full of himself. He was full of character. In my mind I believe *Northern Dancer* realized who he was and what he was and was demanding

NORTHERN DANCER.

the attention he thought he deserved."

In his two-year-old season *Northern Dancer* won seven of nine starts, including four in stakes races, the Summer Stakes, Coronation Futurity, Carleton and Remsen Stakes at Aqueduct. It was his win at the New York track that established the *Dancer* as a horse to watch in the Triple Crown races of 1964.

After *Northern Dancer* won the Kentucky Derby, *The Globe and Mail* devoted a two-page spread to him. The mayor of Toronto awarded him the key to the city, although it took the form of a specially carved carrot. In 1965, he became the first non-human to be voted into Canada's Sports Hall of Fame. Thirty-five years after his Derby victory and nine years after his death, Canada Post in 1999 placed his image on a stamp. He's just not a horse that can be forgotten easily. He demands no less.

NORTHERN DANCER WINNING THE CORONATION STAKES AS A TWO-YEAR OLD.

But his win in the Derby still didn't get him the stamp of approval from the Kentucky hardboots. The betting public still made *Hill Rise* the favourite to win the Preakness two weeks later. *Northern Dancer* won it by two and a half lengths. Hartack expressed reservations about the colt's ability to handle the mile and a half distance of the Belmont Stakes, and Luro announced to the media that the colt would not run in the race. Both were overruled by Taylor, who wanted to see his colt become the ninth Triple Crown winner. After *Northern Dancer* finished third, some—including a furious Luro—said that Hartack lost the Belmont because the colt fought the tight hold Hartack had on him during a sluggish early pace. Hartack said forty-three years later: "I nursed him as long as I could and just couldn't make him go a mile and a half."

According to Avalyn Hunter's book *The Kingmaker: How Northern Dancer Founded a Racing Dynasty*, Hartack confided to Ron Turcotte—the first jockey to ride *Northern Dancer*—that race strategy didn't defeat the Canadian-bred in the Belmont, but soundness did. Sound or not, *Northern Dancer* went home to race in the Queen's Plate two weeks later, with Hartack still aboard. He was regarded like a rock star coming home. *The Toronto Telegram* alone sent ten reporters and photographers to cover the event, and their work was spread out over several pages. Jack Price, the owner of 1961 Kentucky Derby and Preakness winner *Carry Back*, who like *Northern Dancer* failed to win the Belmont and the Triple Crown,

1964 QUEEN'S PLATE STAKES

SEVENTH RACE
Woodbine
JUNE 20, 1964

1 1–4 MILES (2:01⅘s). One Hundred and Fifth Running QUEEN'S PLATE STAKES. $50,000 added, with 50 Guineas, the gift of Her Majesty the Queen. 3–year–olds. Canadian–foaled. Scale weights: colts and geldings, 126 lbs.; fillies, 121 lbs. By subscription of $25 each, which shall accompany the nomination by December 15, 1962; second subscription of $50 by December 15, 1963; third subscription of $100 by May 1, 1964; an additional $500 when making entry two days before the race. Winner to receive the Guineas, the stakes and 50% of the added money; second, 25%; third, 15%, and fourth, 10%. Closed Dec. 15, 1962, with 333 nominations at $25 each. On Dec. 15, 1963, 123 remained eligible at $50 each. On May 1, 1964, 56 remained eligible at $100 each. Gross value of race, $74,075 (plus 50 Guineas). Value to winner, $49,075; second, $12,500; third, $7,500; fourth, $5,000. Mutuel Pool, $171,949. Quinella Pool, $68,706.

Horse	Eqt	Wt.	PP	¼	½	¾	1	Str	Fin	Jockey	Owner	Odds $1
NORTHERN DANCER	b	126	1	7^{hd}	8	6^{3}	$1^{\frac{1}{2}}$	1^{4}	$1^{7\frac{1}{2}}$	HartackW	WindfieldsFarm	.15
LANGCREST		126	8	$2^{\frac{1}{2}}$	2^{1}	1^{hd}	2^{hd}	$2^{1\frac{1}{2}}$	$2^{4\frac{1}{2}}$	McCombS	LangillSJ	57.00
GRAND GARCON		126	6	$4^{\frac{1}{2}}$	3^{nk}	$3^{2\frac{1}{2}}$	3^{5}	3^{4}	$3^{1\frac{1}{4}}$	FitzsimmonsJ	Sherman FA	a-10.70
RETURN TRIP		126	7	6^{1}	6^{1}	5^{hd}	4^{2}	4^{2}	$4^{2\frac{1}{4}}$	MorenoH	GoldenWestFarm	21.50
PIERLOU	b	126	4	5^{1}	5^{1}	4^{hd}	5^{2}	5^{3}	$5^{3\frac{1}{2}}$	GomezA	LevesqueJL	7.00
LATER MEL		121	3	8	$7^{\frac{1}{2}}$	7^{1}	6^{4}	6^{7}	$6^{10\frac{3}{4}}$	ShukN	FarrWJ	20.05
TOP RULER		126	5	1^{nk}	1^{1}	2^{nk}	7^{2}	7^{6}	$7^{12\frac{1}{4}}$	DittfachH	CarmichaelJBW	a-10.70
ALL SEASONS	b	126	2	3^{1}	4^{hd}	8	8	8	8	HarrisonJ	McGuinnessLJ	90.00

a–Coupled, Grand Garcon and Top Ruler.

OFF AT 5:22. Start good. Won easily. Time, :23⅗s, :47⅘s, 1:12⅗s, 1:36⅘s, 2:02⅕s. Track fast.

$2 Mutuel Prices:				
	2–NORTHERN DANCER	2.30	2.40	2.10
	7–LANGCREST		18.40	3.90
	1–GRAND GARCON (a–Entry)			2.40

$2 QUINELLA 2–7 PAID $48.80

B. c, by Nearctic—Natalma, by Native Dancer. Trainer, Horatio A. Luro. Bred by Taylor E. P.

NORTHERN DANCER, taken in hand and allowed to settle in stride while saving ground early, was steadied momentarily when blocked entering the backstretch, moved through between horses when clear, rapidly worked his way up on the outside to wrest command midway of the far turn and came away from his opposition at will thereafter, winning as his rider pleased. LANGCREST, under light restraint while pressing the issue, attained a narrow advantage midway of the backstretch and continued gamely when displaced to be easily best of the others. GRAND GARCON was with the pace to the stretch turn and weakened. RETURN TRIP was never dangerous. PIERLOU, within easy striking distance of the leaders early, faltered after six furlongs. LATER MEL was never a factor. TOP RULER displayed speed for six furlongs, then gave way.

E.P. Taylor and wife Winnie join Bill Hartack and the *Dancer* in Woodbine's winner's circle.

Horatio Luro relaxes while the *Dancer* munches on Kentucky Bluegrass.

showed up at the Queen's Plate for the first time to have a look. Price was one of 31,228 people that thronged Woodbine, and they seemed ever noisier than the number.

In a tribute rare to a thoroughbred, the spectators cheered and applauded *Northern Dancer* in the paddock before the race. When he made his move during the race, the noisy vocal support from the crowd drowned out the public address system. And he was loudly cheered again as he was led back to the winner's circle ceremonies. In the race *Northern Dancer* and Hartack created a dramatic show after lagging behind the field in the early running. He was last with only a half mile to the wire. The crowd wasn't anticipating this type of run for a champion who went off at odds of fifteen cents to the dollar. They expected the race to be a one-sided affair. Boxed in early behind his seven opponents, the *Dancer* found a hole down the backside and bulled his way to the front, winning by almost eight lengths in a hand ride by Hartack down the stretch. Track announcer Daryl Wells probably said it best as the *Dancer* sprinted away from the field, saying, ". . . coming to the wire here's the great little horse, *Northern Dancer.*"

But Hartack knew something was amiss. When he warmed up for the race, "he wasn't the *Northern Dancer* that I knew. He didn't give me that brilliant speed he usually has." It was his last race. Sure enough, *Northern Dancer* pulled up with heat in the main tendon of his left foreleg after a workout at Woodbine several weeks later. He had suffered a strained rather than a truly bowed tendon and when it didn't improve, he was retired from racing. One of Blaettler's memories was the *Dancer*'s habit of never "putting out" in the morning. He saved himself for the afternoons, winning fourteen of his eighteen starts. He was never worse than third during his career.

The racing game's loss was the breeding game's gain. *Northern Dancer*, standing initially for a stud fee of $10,000 at Windfields, produced ten stakes winners in his first crop, an astonishing 47.6 per cent success rate. But it was only the beginning. In his second crop, *Northern Dancer* begat *Nijinsky II*, which became the first English Triple Crown winner since 1935 and spawned his own line of classic winners and sires. His incredible sire statistics were

unheard of and in 1968 he was shipped to Taylor's farm in Maryland. *Northern Dancer*'s 1974 crop was one of the best of his career. From it came *The Minstrel*, a flashy, small and stocky chestnut that was a three-quarter brother to *Nijinsky II*. He was a bargain yearling purchase at $200,000 and was best known for his lion-hearted efforts, including a spirited drive to win the Epsom Derby. *The Minstrel* was instrumental in setting off international bidding wars for *Northern Dancer* offspring.

Afterwards the sky was the limit. Soccer pools magnate Robert Sangster had become enamored with *Northern Dancer*, as had Sheikh Mohammed bin Rashid al Maktoum of oil-rich Dubai. In 1983 at Keeneland, the two powerful bidders went toe to toe, and the sheikh came out the winner of a $10.2-million son of *Northern Dancer* our of *My Bupers*. Named *Snaafi Dancer*, he was a complete bust. He never raced and failed at stud. By 1985, *Northern Dancer* commanded a reported $1-million stud fee with no guarantee of a live foal—if you could get a breeding. Few of them were offered on the open market. And it appeared that *Northern Dancer* was worth more than gold. In the fall of 1981, when he was twenty years old, a group of Europeans, led by a French veterinarian, offered to buy *Northern Dancer* outright for $40 million—at a time when his best breeding days might be behind him. Some of the original twenty-three shareholders were interested. Others, like Windfields, were not. The group withdrew its bid. They wanted all of *Northern Dancer* or nothing. In 2004 all eighteen starters in Europe's most famous race, the Prix de l'Arc de Triomphe in Paris, had *Northern Dancer's* blood in their pedigrees.

As for *Northern Dancer*, he sired 147 stakes winners, at his time a record, and an astonishing twenty-three per cent of his 645 foals. And the pint-sized Canadian upstart usually bred only about thirty-five mares a year, maybe as many as forty-four. He was from an era that preceded shuttling stallions back and forth between hemispheres and large books of mares. And he indeed became a kingmaker. His sons, *Nijinsky II* and *Sadler's Wells* (thirteen times English leading sire), *Lyphard* (who most closely resembled *Northern Dancer* in conformation and personality), *Nureyev, Danzig, Storm Bird* also became sires of sires. Not all of *Northern Dancer's* sons had to succeed at the racetrack to make it big in the breeding shed. Lightly raced *Vice Regent* became one of the *Dancer's* best sons at stud, siring 105 stakes winners, and producing *Deputy Minister*, which in turn begat *Touch Gold, Awesome Again* (sire of the brilliant *Ghostzapper*) and *Silver Deputy* (sire of *Silverbulletday*). *Sadler's Wells* sired 265 stakes winners. On and on it went.

In a February issue of *The Blood-Horse*, author Terry Conway remembered the great stallion with great warmth and insight, quoting the men who were in charge during his Maryland stud duties. "Back in the day, when a truck stacked with hay rumbled onto the farm, *Northern Dancer* never paid it a lick of attention from his stall across the lane from the breeding shed. But if he laid eyes on an approaching van with a mare onboard, all hell broke loose. He would rear up, rest his forelegs on the sill of the bottom half of the door, and whinny and squawk as the loading ramp dropped," recalled Benny Miller, who would become Windfields Maryland farm manager. "He acted like every mare on the farm would be his conquest. To calm things down, we moved him to the backside of the stallion barn."

At the height of his glory, *People* magazine described *Northern Dancer* as the only celebrity that could earn a million dollars before breakfast. His stud fees soared from $10,000 to $500,000. However, private deals saw $1 million changes hands for the services of the world's top sire. Conway, quoting Windfields Maryland general manager Joe Hickey, wrote, "He knew he was the star. We had a lot of significant people come by to look at *The Minstrel. Northern Dancer* would get very impatient and start stomping his hoof. He didn't want any horse taking his place."

E.P. Taylor died on 14 May 1989, the leading breeder in the world with 349 stakes wins. On the evening of 15 November 1990, the grand old stallion was suffering from another bout of colic. It was the same ailment that took the life of his dam, *Natalma*, who also died at age twenty-nine. By early the next morning the condition worsened. Charles Taylor, E.P.'s son, and veterinarian Alan McCarthy vetoed the idea of taking him to the New Bolton Equine Center for medical intervention. Junior Clevenger, the *Dancer's* caretaker for the last decade of his life, snapped a lead shank to the stallion, then steered him to an area off to the side of the training barn. "The horse hadn't been in a van for years, and the vets weren't sure he would even survive the trip up there," said Clevenger. "His companion horse, *T.V. Commercial*, was brought out to be with him. His systems were shutting down and he was visibly suffering. It was the humane thing to do."

Five years earlier, Hickey had secretly commissioned an oak casket. The gallant champion was placed in the box draped in a turquoise cooler offset by gold piping (the colours of Windfields silks) with the name "*Northern Dancer*" scripted on it. A Windfields refrigerated van transported his body across the Canadian border at Fort Erie to Windfields in Oshawa. A national hero was welcomed home by staff late at night. *Northern Dancer* was buried midway between the barn where he was born and the barn where he created his first classic winner. He rests under a simple granite headstone. For years after his death he received birthday cards. And three or four times a year deliveries of flowers, sometimes roses, would arrive from his fans.

"He was the horse of a lifetime," said Bernard McCormack, director of sales and marketing for Windfields. "He might very well be a horse of three lifetimes." Hickey added, "He was the greatest commercial sire ever. They'll be selling horses for a lot of years to come, but they'll never experience the worldwide influence *Northern Dancer* delivered.

I like to think my horse has done something for Canadian racing—just as Northern Dancer *did when he won those big stakes in the United States last year.*

WHISTLING SEA'S OWNER, PAUL OLIVIER

Whistling Sea definitely did something for Canadian racing when he became the first Plate winner to have been foaled outside Ontario. In proving that a Windfields Farm address was not essential to take the Plate—although the record certainly indicated that it helped, since all but three of the previous sixteen winners had been bred by E.P. Taylor—Paul Olivier's triumph with an unfashionably bred colt from Okotoks, Alberta, might have set Canadian breeding back a step or two. Breed the best to the best, pay large sums, wine and dine the horses in Florida during the winter and import a hotshot rider from New York for the coup de grace: this was the modus operandi for success.

Olivier dispelled all this on a sunny June afternoon as a Woodbine crowd of almost thirty two thousand, including the Queen Mother, saw his rags-to-riches Cinderella colt, *Whistling Sea*, lead all the way to the wire. The horse was by *Alibastro*, a stallion that he had bought for $1,600—about the amount he earned while losing thirty-three successive races. The dam was by 1938 Plate winner *Bunty Lawless*, but breeder Les Saunders was able to buy *B Fast* for a mere three hundred dollars. Go back a generation in the *Whistler*'s pedigree and the bloodlines were quality. The class had skipped a generation, but the colt reestablished it that afternoon, whipping half-brothers to *Northern Dancer* and *Flaming Page*; Canada's champion two-year-old in 1964, *Good Old Mort;* and *Flyalong*, a multiple stakes-winning colt that had been running in fashionable company in Florida all winter.

Whistling Sea had glared back at the challenges of the best horses from Ontario and Quebec, had withstood a frivolous claim of foul by Ron Turcotte on a horse that finished eighth, but still collected the fifty gold coins from the Queen Mother, as well as a cheque for $47,694. The tall, handsome American from Woonsocket, Rhode Island, had grown up in Ventura, California, before making a fortune as a "mud merchant" in Calgary, importing a special type of soil from Oklahoma for packing oil drills and, incidentally, for cooling thoroughbreds' feet.

His rider was Tak Inouye of Vancouver Island and Vernon, British Columbia. The son of a Japanese logger, Inouye was raised in the interior of the province where his parents were shipped during World War II, lest they provide aid to an enemy that might invade the West Coast. Inouye, the least experienced rider in the Plate, had got his start with Les Lear, the former football coach of the Calgary Stampeders, who had a string of ponies out west. "Lear taught me all I know about horses, which is to get up before six in the morning and work till after five in the afternoon," Inouye quipped. Unlike New York riders Turcotte, *Des Erables'* pilot, and Heliodoro Gustines, who was hired to ride the favoured *Native Victor* of Windfields Farm, Inouye was an import from the "B" circuit bull-

MR. AND MRS. PAUL OLIVIER ACCEPT PLATE TROPHY FROM QUEEN ELIZABETH, THE QUEEN MOTHER.

rings of Vancouver, Ohio, Michigan and northern Kentucky. He shipped to Woodbine that spring with a sour outlook on life, but a determination to do well. A long scar on his shoulder was a relic of a critical operation: a silver clip had been inserted to keep the joint from constant dislocation. Several months earlier, Inouye had suffered a broken shoulder, then later tore all the muscles in the same shoulder in a training accident.

Tak Inouye's break came the morning he went to Roy Johnson's barn looking for some horses to exercise. Johnson, an ex-jock himself, from Airdrie, Alberta, was seeking a replacement for Hugo Dittfach to ride *Whistling Sea* in the Woodstock Stakes. Dittfach had been given the chance to ride one of the favourites, and so abandoned the long-shot colt, who seemed to have little future in the distance events. Besides, he was a free spirit. Jockeys did not ride him, they more or less accompanied him on the trip because he preferred to ignore the instructions tapped on his hide. Johnson agreed, admitting that he doubted whether the colt could stagger a mile. He came to this conclusion when *Whistling Sea* refused to "rate" and was beaten by twelve lengths. "That's when we thought he was a sprinter."

Western Canada's first Plate winner, *Whistling Sea*, Tak Inouye and Paul Olivier, a transplanted American from Rhode Island and California living in Calgary.

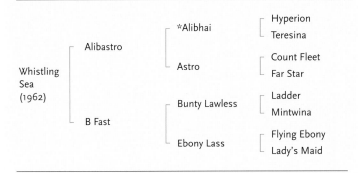

WHISTLING SEA | 3-year-old dark bay or brown colt

Whistling Sea (1962)	Alibastro	*Alibhai	Hyperion
			Teresina
		Astro	Count Fleet
			Far Star
	B Fast	Bunty Lawless	Ladder
			Mintwina
		Ebony Lass	Flying Ebony
			Lady's Maid

Owner: Olivier Ranches (Paul Olivier), Calgary, Alberta; *Trainer:* Roy Johnson
Jockey: Tak Inouye; *Breeder:* L.R. Saunders, Calgary

Whistling Sea outsprinted American-bred horses in the Woodstock, then led all the way in his division of the Plate Trial Stakes, upsetting the winterbook favourite, *Flyalong*, owned by Tom Hays of Oakville and Doug Weldon of London, Ontario. A fluke, horsemen concluded. Even Johnson had to be pressed by Olivier to enter him in the Trial. "I really only ran him in the Trial to prove to his owner that he was a sprinter. I thought he'd get hit in the head with the quarter-pole. After that race I thought, well maybe we had a runner that could carry his speed over a distance of ground." Olivier, who had seen his colt win at odds of 143-to-1 the year before, needed little convincing. When *Whistling Sea* turned two, Olivier invited two hundred people to his spread near Calgary for a party to view the "future Queen's Plate winner." Olivier had purchased him from Saunders for $5,000. "I had given Les three free stud services and he agreed to let me have first shot at buying the foals. All three out of *B Fast* were stakes winners." One of them was *Lady B. Fast*, which finished seventeenth for Olivier in the 1963 Plate.

Olivier ignored the earlier failures and was not listening when people told him the colt would be whistling *"Show Me the Way to Go Home"* if anybody asked him to go more than seven furlongs faster than a brisk walk. Slammed by *Butterscotch* at the break, *Whistling Sea* ricocheted off Turcotte's colt, *Des Erables*, before accelerating clear of any further trouble. Inouye sat there, his hands low on his mount's neck, letting him go about things his own way. He shook off *Butterscotch*, but halfway down the back stretch encountered *Des Erables* again. Inouye hoisted his hands a trifle to see how his mount felt. He had lots of horse, so he lowered his hands. In the turn *Good Old Mort*, with Avelino Gomez aboard, charged up to breathe on the "Whistler." Inouye lifted his hands again. Still lots of horse. Turning for home, up stormed *Flyalong*, ridden by Cliff Potts, a westerner. At the sixteenth pole, *Flyalong* was lapped on the leader. Inouye merely waved his whip alongside his mount's nose.

The only time the race was ever in doubt was when the stewards viewed the films. The last time a Plate winner had been disqualified was in 1876, ninety years before. Cliff Potts lamented: "The West finally wins the race, and he [*Whistling Sea*] has to win at my expense." In congratulating him on his ride, Gomez needled Inouye. "You win that one for Japan, eh?" "No," Inouye said solemnly. "For Western Canada."

Jim Coleman, a transplanted westerner and a veteran Toronto columnist, had been rooting for horses from western Canada ever since 1944, when *Cum Laude* shipped east, and especially for the entries of Winnipeg's R. James Speers. Coleman wrote: "Thoroughbred racing came of age in Canada on Saturday afternoon. The shackles have been removed . . . the Plate is now an event of genuine national interest." It was a *great* day for the West. Earlier, in Ireland, *Meadow Court*, owned by Max Bell of Calgary, Frank McMahon of Vancouver and singer Bing Crosby of Hollywood, won the Irish Sweeps Derby at The Curragh.

1965 QUEEN'S PLATE STAKES

SEVENTH RACE
Woodbine
JUNE 26, 1965

1 1–4 MILES (2:01$\frac{4}{5}$). One Hundred and Sixth Running QUEEN'S PLATE STAKES. $50,000 added, with 50 Guineas, the gift of Her Majesty the Queen. 3–year–olds. Canadian–foaled. Scale weights: colts and geldings, 126 lbs.; fillies, 121 lbs. By subscription of $25 each, which shall accompany the nomination by December 15, 1963; second subscription of $50 by December 15, 1964; third subscription of $100 by May 1, 1965; and an additional $500 when making entry two days before the race. The added money and all fees to be divided 65% to the winner, 20% to second, 10% to third and 5% to fourth. Closed Dec. 15, 1963, with 303 nominations at $25 each. On Dec. 15, 1964, 90 remained eligible upon payment of $50 each. On May 1, 1965, 53 remained eligible upon payment of $100 each. Gross value of race, $73,375. Value to winner, $47,693.75, plus 50 Guineas; second, $14,675; third, $7,337.50; fourth, $3,668.75. Mutuel Pool, $292,734.

Horse	Eqt	Wt.	PP	¼	½	¾	1	Str	Fin	Jockey	Owner	Odds $1
WHISTLING SEA		126	4	1^{1}	$1^{2\frac{1}{2}}$	1^{2}	$1^{2\frac{1}{2}}$	$1^{1\frac{1}{2}}$	$1^{1\frac{3}{4}}$	InouyeT	OlivierRanches	a-7.20
FLYALONG	b	126	12	11^{2}	10^{5}	$7^{\frac{1}{2}}$	4^{3}	2^{4}	$2^{2\frac{1}{4}}$	PottsC	Hays&Weldon	b-2.45
BLUE MEL		126	11	12	11^{4}	11^{8}	8^{1}	5^{2}	$3^{\frac{3}{4}}$	DittfachH	BoylenPE	29.50
NATIVE VICTOR	b	126	7	6^{hd}	6^{nk}	$6^{1\frac{1}{2}}$	$5^{\frac{1}{2}}$	4^{1}	$4^{2\frac{1}{4}}$	GustinesH	WindfieldsFarm	c-1.40
GOOD OLD MORT	b	126	1	5^{hd}	5^{hd}	$4^{\frac{1}{2}}$	2^{hd}	3^{nk}	$5^{2\frac{3}{4}}$	GomezA	DaneHillAcres	3.45
LUCKY MARINE		126	2	2^{hd}	7^{2}	$8^{1\frac{1}{2}}$	$7^{2\frac{1}{2}}$	8^{2}	6^{hd}	MaxwellP	MaloneyL	35.95
SUPER FLOW	b	126	9	4^{1}	3^{nk}	5^{1}	6^{1}	7^{hd}	$7^{1\frac{1}{4}}$	RobinsonK	BeasleyB	66.55
DES ERABLES		126	5	8^{2}	4^{3}	$3^{\frac{1}{2}}$	3^{1}	$6^{\frac{1}{2}}$	$8^{\frac{1}{2}}$	TurcotteR	ThomasMrsS	b-2.45
TOP VICTORY	b	126	10	$7^{1\frac{1}{2}}$	$9^{\frac{1}{2}}$	9^{1}	$9^{1\frac{1}{2}}$	9^{5}	$9^{4\frac{3}{4}}$	LeBlancJ	WindfieldsFarm	c-1.40
CHIEF BRANT		126	8	9^{hd}	12	12	12	11^{2}	$10^{1\frac{3}{4}}$	RemillardP	MartinMrsVJr	16.65
SPOTTED FLYER	b	126	6	10^{nk}	8^{hd}	$10^{2\frac{1}{2}}$	11^{6}	$10^{1\frac{1}{2}}$	$11^{6\frac{1}{2}}$	GordonG	GoldenWestFarm	a-7.20
BUTTERSCOTCH	b	126	3	$3^{\frac{1}{2}}$	$2^{2\frac{1}{2}}$	2^{1}	10^{hd}	12	12	HaleD	ViscountHardinge	101.90

a–Coupled, Whistling Sea and Spotted Flyer; b–Flyalong and Des Erables; c–Native Victor and Top Victory.
OFF AT 5:31. Start good. Won driving. Time, :23$\frac{1}{5}$, :46$\frac{2}{5}$, 1:11$\frac{3}{5}$, 1:37$\frac{3}{5}$, 2:03$\frac{4}{5}$. Track fast.

$2 Mutuel Prices:

1–WHISTLING SEA (a–Entry)	16.40	5.90	4.60
2–FLYALONG (b–Entry)		3.70	3.00
9–BLUE MEL			7.00

Dk. b. or br. c, by Alibastro—B Fast, by Bunty Lawless. Trainer, Roy Johnson. Bred by Saunders Lloyd R., Calgary, Alta.
WHISTLING SEA assumed command soon after the start, set the pace to the stretch under good rating and responding readily to pressure, turned back a challenge from FLYALONG and won going away. FLYALONG, allowed to settle in stride, gradually worked his way up on the outside to reach closer contention on the final turn and continuing strongly, joined the leader inside the last eighth but was not good enough. BLUE MEL, unhurried when outrun early, steadily improved his position from the outside and finished strongly when set down.

In 1964 a big, black yearling colt, who later would be named *Titled Hero*, persuaded Patrick MacMurchy that perhaps he should postpone his retirement for another couple of years. MacMurchy, a trifle shy and retiring in his demeanour, was a patient and laconic trainer. A Scotsman from Port Patrick, who had been around racetracks since the early 1920s, MacMurchy had faced the capricious luck of racing, tending to the cheap plugs as well as the great ones, like *Zev* and *Grey Lag*, while apprenticing for Samuel Clay Hildreth at Rancocas Farm in New Jersey, and later as foreman for the famed Greentree Stud of Harry Payne Whitney in Lexington, Kentucky.

Pat saddled a couple of good runners after returning to Canada—*Yellowknife, Senor Teddy* and *Blue Wrack*—and then took over the stable of Colonel Kenric R. Marshall, president of the Jockey Club Limited. In the 1950s he proceeded to give "Rud" Marshall the most exciting afternoons of his life with *Hartney,* judged Canada's best horse in 1957, and *Blue Light,* who won the 1961 Queen's Plate by a throbbing nose, upsetting the favourite, *Just Don't Shove*. MacMurchy was now sixty-seven, but the racetrack was the only place he felt at home. And so his decision to hang around for one more good horse was done partially to give him a place to go to in the mornings.

A year after his 1961 Plate win, Colonel Marshall died, leaving his stable in the hands of his son, Peter, who had played a little polo, and MacMurchy. A pseudo-photographer in New York City, Peter Marshall had grown up in a family whose enthusiasm for horses was limitless. His grandfather ran a Plate horse in 1889, and his father had registered his own silks twelve years later. Marion Marshall, his mother, would tell Peter of her first Plate races when she was married to Alexander Mackenzie, who had died in his early thirties. His father, Sir William Mackenzie, whose home was the fashionable One Benvenuto Place on Toronto's Avenue Road, was head of the streetcar railway and had his own private coach. On racing days it would be brought through the gates and into the grounds of Woodbine Park. "It was a fine old car complete with ball-fringed curtains on the windows," Peter's mother would say. "What fun it was to watch the races from it." Marshall, who inherited his father's cerise and white silks, left the training

AVELINO'S PATENTED LEAP FROM *TITLED HERO*'S SADDLE EXCITED RACING FANS AND OWNER PETER MARSHALL.

VETERAN TRAINER PAT MACMURCHY.

and buying of yearlings to MacMurchy, staying well away from the barns and workouts.

In the fall of 1964 Marshall and MacMurchy looked at a colt by *Canadian Champ* out of *Countess Angela* at E.P. Taylor's annual sale of pre-priced yearlings. He was on sale for $15,000. "We both thought he was the best looking colt for sale, regardless of price. But we really didn't have a priority to buy him because we hadn't bought since 1962. However, Joe Thomas, Windfields' racing manager, helped us get him. Later Conn Smythe offered me $35,000 for him. But I turned him down because I wanted to see *my* horse in the Plate," said MacMurchy. Fate, which had favoured his father in 1961 when *Blue Light* upset Smythe's *Just Don't Shove,* was with Peter Marshall five years later. It was Smythe's *Bye and Near* who chased *Titled Hero* across the finish line in the 1966 Plate.

Bye and Near was the only one to challenge the 1-to-4 favourite on a day when Marshall's colt was lacking his usual enthusiasm. *Titled Hero* practically staggered home, running the final quarter in twenty-

Titled Hero staggered home ahead of *Bye and Near*.

seven seconds for jockey Avelino Gomez. "He didn't run with his old fire. It wasn't a good race for him," MacMurchy admitted later. The two colts had clashed for several strides in the turn approaching the top of the stretch, and it looked to many observers as if Gomez had "squeezed" *Bye and Near* and jockey Sam McComb at the crucial moment.

In 1980, when Gomez died from injuries he suffered in a spill at Woodbine, Smythe recalled the race and the feuds the two jockeys had had over the years. "In those days I didn't claim foul, and that was the year he stole the Plate from me. *Bye and Near* would have won if he [Gomez] hadn't shut him off." Actually, what the Cuban did was to reach out and grab the saddle cloth of Smythe's horse. McComb was infuriated that he could not claim foul. But Smythe admired him: "He was always beating our stable. But that's what I loved about the man. He would do anything to win. Gomez was a soldier. He never asked for an inch, and he never backed off from anybody or anything."

When MacMurchy's last "good horse" retired, *Titled Hero* was the fourth leading Canadian-bred, surpassed in earnings by only *Northern Dancer, George Royal* and *Victoria Park*. But he was never an easy task for MacMurchy and his aides, Jimmy and Billy Lynn, Alex Anderson and Frank Austin. *Titled Hero* was Canada's leading juvenile in 1965, winning eight of his twelve starts, including the Coronation Futurity, Grey Handicap, Summer and Colin Stakes and placing second in the Cup and Saucer and Vandal Stakes and winning $101,076.

TITLED HERO | 3-year-old black colt

Titled Hero (1963)	Canadian Champ	Windfields	Bunty Lawless
			Nandi
		Bolesteo	*Filisteo
			Bold Fay
	Countess Angela	Bull Page	Bull Lea
			Our Page
		*Lady Angela	Hyperion
			Sister Sarah

Owner: Peter K. Marshall, Toronto, Ont.; *Trainer:* Pat MacMurchy; *Jockey:* Avelino Gomez; *Breeder:* E.P. Taylor, Toronto

That spring MacMurchy considered entering the colt in the Kentucky Derby and a date with *Graustark* and *Moccasin*. None of them made it; injuries sidelined the two American horses, while *Titled Hero* was hit by a virus that shot his temperature up to 104 degrees Ferenheit. Later, when the colt got to the races, he bruised a heel and missed three weeks of training. Meanwhile, *Stevie B. Good* beat him in two of their three clashes before the Plate, a race for which *Stevie B. Good* was ineligible because his owner had failed to make an eligibility payment in 1965.

After his Plate win, *Titled Hero* looked more like a loser. His right eye was swollen, two teeth were missing and he finished the race on a cracked hoof. The left fore quarter, bruised by a stone earlier in the season, split and later became infected. It prevented him from running in the Prince of Wales Stakes, but he did return to win the Breeders' Stakes. But before he was to go to stud in 1968 at Windfields, he had to be put down because of an incapacitating injury.

1966 QUEEN'S PLATE STAKES

SEVENTH RACE
Woodbine
JUNE 25, 1966

1 1-4 MILES (2:01⅘). One Hundred and Seventh Running QUEEN'S PLATE STAKES. $50,000 added, with 50 Guineas, the gift of Her Majesty the Queen. 3-year-olds. Canadian-foaled. Scale weights: colts and geldings, 126 lbs.; fillies, 121 lbs. By subscription of $25 each, which shall accompany the nomination by December 15, 1964 (closed with 259 nominations). To continue eligibility, the following additional payments must be made: second subscription of $50 by December 15, 1965 (116 remained eligible); third subscription of $100 by May 1, 1966 (69 remained eligible); and an additional $1,000 when making entry. Winner to receive the Guineas. The added money and all fees to be divided 65% to the winner, 20% to second, 10% to third and 5% to fourth. Gross value of race, $80,175. Value to winner, $52,113.75 plus 50 Guineas; second, $16,035; third, $8,017.50; fourth, $4,008.75. Mutuel Pool, $236,646.

Horse	Eqt	Wt.	PP	¼	½	¾	1	Str	Fin	Jockey	Owner	Odds $1
TITLED HERO		126	5	4^{nk}	2^{1}	2^{6}	$1\frac{1}{2}$	1^{1}	1^{3}	GomezA	MarshallPK	.25
BYE AND NEAR		126	8	2^{2}	1^{4}	$1^{1\frac{1}{2}}$	2^{7}	2^{7}	$2^{6\frac{1}{4}}$	McCombS	SmytheC	13.30
BRIGHT MONARCH	b	126	3	$5^{1\frac{1}{2}}$	5^{1}	4^{3}	3^{4}	3^{3}	$3^{4\frac{3}{4}}$	BazeJ	McMahonMrsFM	7.45
HOLARCTIC	b	126	9	9^{hd}	$9^{1\frac{1}{2}}$	7^{1}	6^{1}	$4^{2\frac{1}{2}}$	$4\frac{1}{2}$	FitzsimmonsJ	ShermanFA&FH	a-9.35
ECHO LAD		126	1	11	10^{1}	8^{1}	8^{7}	7^{4}	$5\frac{1}{2}$	BarrobyF	ShortE	59.65
THE HANGMAN	b	126	2	8^{1}	$7^{2\frac{1}{2}}$	5^{nk}	4^{hd}	$5\frac{1}{2}$	6^{hd}	TurcotteN	HillcrestStable	98.20
SOLAR PARK	b	121	11	$6\frac{1}{2}$	6^{1}	6^{2}	$5\frac{1}{2}$	$6\frac{1}{2}$	$7^{5\frac{1}{4}}$	HarrisW	Hays&Weldon	71.55
ARCTIC TROOPS	b	126	4	$3^{1\frac{1}{2}}$	3^{2}	3^{nk}	7^{2}	8^{10}	8^{13}	DittfachH	WindfieldsFarm	12.80
BIG JIVE	b	126	10	7^{nk}	8^{nk}	$9^{1\frac{1}{2}}$	9^{4}	9^{10}	$9^{13\frac{1}{2}}$	PottsC	LiebermanE	134.05
RADIANT COLORS	b	126	7	$10\frac{1}{2}$	11	10^{8}	10^{15}	10	10	RobinsonK	JosephPF	121.60
FAMOUS MONARCH		126	6	$1\frac{1}{2}$	$4^{2\frac{1}{4}}$	11	11		Outdist.	ZivkovicV	ShermanFA	a-9.35

a-Coupled, Holarctic and Famous Monarch.

OFF AT 5:13. Start good. Won driving. Time, :23⅕, :46⅘, 1:11⅕, 1:36⅗, 2:03⅗. Track fast.

$2 Mutuel Prices:

6-TITLED HERO	**2.50**	**2.30**	**2.10**
8-BYE AND NEAR		**4.70**	**3.00**
4-BRIGHT MONARCH			**2.70**

Blk. c, by Canadian Champ—Countess Angela, by Bull Page. Trainer, Pat MacMurchy. Bred by Taylor E. P.

TITLED HERO, forwardly placed from the beginning, moved closest to the leader before going a half-mile, assumed command from the outside on the second turn and was roused to increase his advantage through the stretch. BYE AND NEAR raced FAMOUS MONARCH into defeat early to establish a commanding advantage on the initial turn, continued gamely when challenged and, while unable to stay with the winner in the late stages, was easily best of the others. BRIGHT MONARCH, unhurried through the first half-mile, finished willingly when put to pressure but could not improve his position in the late stages. HOLARCTIC gradually improved his position to the stretch and lacked further response. ECHO LAD, void of early speed, never entered contention. ARCTIC TROOPS raced forwardly for six furlongs and faltered.

Trainer Yonnie Starr and jockey Jim Fitzsimmons always did have a way with fillies. Conn Smythe's *Jammed Lovely* would be no exception for these two veterans when she startled the bettors with her upset win over Saul Wagman's *Pine Point*, ridden by North America's leading 1966 jockey, Avelino Gomez. During a career that would earn him an induction into horse racing's Hall of Fame, Starr conditioned some of the finest fillies and mares on the continent: champions *La Prevoyante, Wonder Where, Fanfreluche*, the combative *Kitty Girl* and the great producer *Ciboulette*. Fitzsimmons, with his blond crewcut and swaggering strut, was equally proficient with the distaff members. The Calgary rider rode two Plate winners, both fillies— *Flaming Page* (1962) and *Jammed Lovely*. The only other fillies to win the Plate since Woodbine opened in 1956, besides these two, were *La Lorgnette* (1985), *Dance Smartly*

It's the filly, *Jammed Lovely*, by a neck over *Pine Point*.

(1991) and *Dancethruthedawn* (2001). Fitzsimmons and his two Plate-winning fillies would later earn induction to the Hall of Fame. Jammed Lovely was also successful as a broodmare, producing the marvelous multiple stakes winning champion *Lovely Sunrise* and stakes-placed *Jammed Bear*. As a lasting tribute to the filly, every November there's a race at Woodbine for Canada's top three-year-old fillies—the *Jammed Lovely* Stakes.

Jammed Lovely was the lone filly in a fourteen-horse field. She defied the handicappers, winning by a neck and posting a mutuel payoff of $24.90 for the two-dollar punters. It was a costly and emotional victory for that grand old curmudgeon, Smythe. He was so confident that his filly would beat the colts, that he offered every owner in the race a bet—his horse against theirs. The winner would send $5,000 to the Ontario Crippled Children's Society. His optimism cost him $10,000.

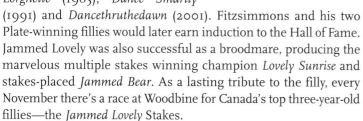

I couldn't get anybody to bet, even though my horse was at 11- or 12-to-1. Finally just before the race, Jean-Louis Lévesque of Montreal, owner of *Courant d'Air*, said he wouldn't take my bet but would donate $10,000 to the Crippled Children if he won. In a moment of exuberance I said I'd do the same if I won. It was some horse race. Fitzie kept *Jammed Lovely* in striking distance all the way but coming into the stretch he was running fourth on the rail and was boxed in. . . . Just as I was thinking I

didn't know how he was going to get out, he showed me. He came out from the rail to go around *Ette Rule*, then cut back to the rail where there was enough room for him to pound into the lead. As they came down the stretch his big challenge came from Gomez on *Pine Point*, but when they got up to his boot Fitzie let *Jammed Lovely* out another notch and won by a neck. Later he sounded very brave. 'If we'd gone another time around the track, we still would have won,' he said.

Smythe admired Fitzsimmons for his "loyalty" in turning down a chance to ride the favoured *Betemight*, owned by Noel Hickey and trained by another Irishman, Jim Bentley. Smythe had told him he was free to choose his mount. Fitzsimmons, who had guided the filly to two-year-old honours in 1966 and had finished second in the slop in the Canadian Oaks, did not hesitate. She was far more impressive on a fast track. "I got to stay with you. I'm going to stick together with the whole outfit."

Fitzsimmons' decision, however, was not predicated on loyalty to Smythe and to Yonnie Starr. He firmly believed *Jammed Lovely* had a better chance to win the Plate than the gelding, and had said so all week. "I knew this horse. I knew what she could do. She's a really tough filly, a sweetheart." He rejected *Betemight*, who had been running with the best horses in the United States that year, because he had always come up empty for him. Canadian Ron Turcotte, who

Jim Fitzsimmons tells Conn Smythe how he outduelled Avelino Gomez and *Pine Point*.

JAMMED LOVELY | 3-year-old bay filly

Jammed Lovely (1964)	Jamie K.	Crowfoot	Blue Larkspur
			*Ann Earn
		Sea Elf	Halcyon
			Royal Duchess
	*Eolia	Brick	Congreve
			Gavia
		Eos	Strip the Willow
			Endecha

Owner: Conn Smythe, Caledon, Ont.; *Trainer:* Joseph (Yonnie) Starr
Jockey: Jim Fitzsimmons; *Breeder:* Conn Smythe

flew up from Aqueduct racetrack in New York, finished sixth on *Betemight* and agreed with Fitz's assessment. "No excuses. I didn't ask anything out of him for the first mile and when I did at the quarter-pole I got nothing out of him. There was nothing there."

Escorting his three granddaughters across the maroon carpet to the stakes enclosure, Smythe could not help but remember how he had come up with the name for the *Jamie K.–Eolia* filly. He named her while accompanying his wife, Irene, who would die of cancer in 1965, on a stroll through the paddocks of his Caledon farm. "This little filly was lying down and then jumped up and nestled against her mother the way foals do, and Irene said, "Isn't she lovely? I looked at Irene and thought it could be applied either to my wife or to the filly, and thought, wouldn't that be a good name—*Jammed Lovely*."

Later an exultant Smythe proclaimed, "The Red Ensign. They've got to fly my colours for a year now, and this is what I want flown! The Canadian ensign, the one that I and so many soldiers fought under during two wars!" It was a tradition that the winner's silks be flown from the tall flagpole in Woodbine's infield gardens. Conn's racing colours featured a blue maple leaf on a white background but, instead of that bright bunting, he preferred the ensign with the Union Jack in the corner. Three years earlier, during the great flag debate, Smythe had protested vehemently when Prime Minister Lester Pearson replaced the Red Ensign with a distinctive red maple flag.

"What a great combination," he proudly said as a flag was draped over the rail in front of *Jammed Lovely*'s stall. "Yonnie's a Jew, Fitz is a Catholic and I'm a Protestant. And we've got the Canadian ensign. How can you beat that combination?"

In 1967 Canada celebrated its Centennial in a year when *Cool Reception* would have been the 1-to-10 favourite for the Plate. He never got a chance; he was destroyed after breaking his leg in losing a gallant struggle in the final furlong to *Damascus* in the Belmont Stakes at New York. Smythe's horse thus became the thirtieth filly to win the Plate, which was perhaps fitting as *Wild Rose*, an aged mare, had won in 1867, the year of Confederation.

1967 QUEEN'S PLATE STAKES

SEVENTH RACE
Woodbine
JUNE 24, 1967

1 1–4 MILES (2:01⅘s). One Hundred and Eighth Running QUEEN'S PLATE STAKES. $50,000 added, with 50 Guineas, the gift of Her Majesty the Queen. 3–year–olds. Canadian–foaled. Scale weights: colts and geldings, 126 lbs.; fillies, 121 lbs. By subscription of $25 each, which shall accompany the nomination by December 15, 1965 (closed with 257 nominations). To continue eligibility, the following additional payments must be made: second subscription of $50 by December 15, 1966 (100 remained eligible); third subscription of $100 by May 1, 1967 (43 remained eligible); and an additional $1,000 when making entry. Owner of winner to receive the Guineas. The added money and all fees to be divided 65 per cent to the winner, 20 per cent to second, 10 per cent to third, and 5 per cent to fourth. Value of race $79,882.50. Value to winner $51,978.75; second $15,945; third $7,972.50; fourth $3,986.25. Mutuel Pool $273,380.

Horse	Eqt	Wt.	PP	¼	½	¾	1	Str	Fin	Jockey	Owner	Odds $1
JAMMED LOVELY	b	121	13	2½	3^{1}	4^{4}	$3^{1\frac{1}{2}}$	1^{1}	1^{nk}	FitzsimmonsJ	SmytheC	11.45
PINE POINT	b	126	3	5½	5^{4}	5^{5}	4½	2½	$2^{3\frac{1}{4}}$	GomezA	WillowDownsFarm	2.80
COME BY CHANCE		126	7	10½	8½	6^{1}	7^{hd}	4^{hd}	3^{hd}	BarrobyF	LansonFarm	d-4.30
MORE OF MORT	b	126	8	9½	9^{hd}	8^{1}	6½	5^{hd}	4^{nk}	TurcotteN	HaysTE	b-13.00
BLENHEIM PARK		126	11	$4^{2\frac{1}{2}}$	4^{5}	3^{1}	2^{1}	3^{1}	5^{nk}	GordonG	WindfieldsFarm	a-8.25
BETEMIGHT	b	126	6	14	12^{1}	7^{nk}	8^{4}	6^{4}	$6^{3\frac{3}{4}}$	TurcotteR	HickeyPN	2.70
MR. SWEET DREAMS		126	9	13^{2}	13^{2}	11^{2}	9^{4}	7^{4}	$7^{4\frac{1}{2}}$	FerraroR	CoulterMrsDH	d-4.30
GILMORE	b	126	5	12½	14	13^{5}	10^{4}	9^{5}	$8^{3\frac{1}{4}}$	WalshE	GoldenWestFarm	c-34.10
BATTLING	b	126	1	$3^{2\frac{1}{2}}$	2½	1^{hd}	1^{1}	8^{hd}	$9^{3\frac{1}{2}}$	DittfachH	WindfieldsFarm	a-8.25
DAUPHIN BLEU		126	4	8^{1}	11^{1}	12^{1}	$12^{3\frac{1}{2}}$	$10^{3\frac{1}{2}}$	$10^{4\frac{1}{2}}$	KellyJ	GoldenWestFarm	c-34.10
FILS DU NORD	b	126	2	7^{1}	6½	9^{hd}	13^{8}	$12^{1\frac{1}{2}}$	11¾	HaleD	EstateofShermanFA	b-13.00
ETTE RULE		126	14	1^{2}	2½	2^{1}	5^{1}	$11^{1\frac{1}{2}}$	12^{2}	InouyeT	ThePheasantStable	55.60
COURANT D'AIR	b	126	12	11^{1}	10½	10½	11^{1}	13	13	HinojosaH	LevesqueJL	5.70
IN THE RING		126	10	6^{1}	$7^{1\frac{1}{2}}$	14	14	14	Out.	KeegansH	LarchTreeFarm	109.25

a–Coupled, Blenheim Park and Battling; b–More of Mort and Fils du Nord; c–Gilmore and Dauphin Bleu; d–Come by Chance and Mr. Sweet Dreams.

OFF AT 5:13. Start good. Won driving. Time, :22⅖s, :45⅘s, 1:10⅗s, 1:36⅗s, 2:03. Track fast.

$2 Mutuel Prices:

9–JAMMED LOVELY	**24.90**	**8.50**	**5.10**
5–PINE POINT		**4.80**	**3.20**
4–COME BY CHANCE (d–Entry)			**3.60**

B. f, by Jamie K.—*Eolia, by Brick. Trainer, J. (Yonnie) Starr. Bred by Conn Smythe, Caledon, Ont.

JAMMED LOVELY prompted the issue in the opening quarter, was taken in hand and reserved back of the leaders until leaving the backstretch, slipped through along the inside to take command from BATTLING after entering the stretch and responded well during the drive to hold PINE POINT safe. The latter, away in the first flight and unhurried for six furlongs, circled his field while rallying on the final turn, closed determinedly but could not overtake the winner. COME BY CHANCE steadily improved his position to the stretch and finished willingly without menacing the top ones. MORE OF MORT raced evenly for six furlongs and closed with good energy when set down for his best. BLENHEIM PARK, forwardly placed from the beginning, moved up menacingly on the second turn and weakened in the stretch. BETEMIGHT, sluggish early, gradually worked his way forward to reach a striking position in the early stretch and lacked further response.

1968 | MERGER

During a morning workout at Woodbine in the spring of 1968, trainer Roy Johnson learned that Merger was a colt that responded to a whip, but he abhorred the sight of a jockey tattooing his bay's hide with it.

One morning I've got Georgie Gordon, who had ridden him as a two-year-old and again in April, working him five-eighths of a mile. With about two furlongs to go he went to hit him. But Georgie never did hit him as the next thing he knew, he was on the ground. He [Merger] ran out from under him, and Georgie wound up on his butt. He had got a look at Georgie with the whip in his hand. That's about the time I decided to change from the cup blinkers to the French type of blinkers. They are cut away and permit the horse to see the other horses but not the jockey. That incident, along with a race in May when he pulled himself up and was beaten a head after losing sight of the other horses, convinced me. He was getting beaten by noses and heads. The only bad race he had wasn't his fault, he was in the process of rebucking his shins and I shouldn't have run in the Coronation Futurity, which was an important race. But he wasn't anywhere near his best form and it was the only time in his life he wasn't one-two.

The Queen's Plate was won for the prairies for the second time in four years when Golden West Farm's *Merger,* the blocky bay colt from the Calgary suburb of Okotoks, bulled his way through the deep, clinging mud to win the Plate in the final seventy yards from Lanson Farm's *Big Blunder.*

WAYNE HARRIS, THE TWENTY-YEAR-OLD FROM VANCOUVER, ACKNOWLEDGES THE CHEERS FROM THE PACKED WOODBINE STANDS AFTER HIS WIN ON *MERGER* FOR ALBERTA-BORN TRAINER ROY JOHNSON.

A WESTERN CANADIAN TRIUMPH—FRANK MCMAHON, ROY JOHNSON, MAX BELL, *MERGER,* THE COLT FROM OKOTOKS, ALBERTA, AND WAYNE HARRIS.

A short neck separated the two colts in a contest that had see-sawed back and forth down Heartbreak Lane. Moving from the rear of the thirteen-horse field, Jim Fitzsimmons had gunned *Big Blunder* to the lead at the top of the stretch, plodding his way through the porridge past *Merger.* In the ensuing neck-to-neck duel, *Merger* responded to jockey Wayne Harris' punishing stick and again took over the lead. It was Alberta, Ontario and Quebec, since *Rouletabille,* owned by Jean-Louis Lévesque of Montreal, was third, although he had been checked when he ran into a "blind switch" at the top of the stretch.

The field was perhaps the best balanced in Plate history; only two had failed to win a stakes race in their careers. The crowd bet the first four finishers (Frowde Seagram's *Phelodie* was fourth) down to odds of less than 4-to-1. This Plate was

Tycoons from the west, Golden West Farm's Frank McMahon of Vancouver and Calgary's Max Bell.

MERGER | 3-year-old bay colt

Merger (1965)	*Prince d'Amour	Tantieme	Deux pur Cent
			Terka
		Princesse d'Amour	Prince Bio
			Vers l'Amour
	*Anglirish	Ballyogan	Fair Trial
			Serial
		Irish Brume	Brumeux
			Snakeless

Owner: Golden West Farm (Max Bell, Frank McMahon), Calgary, Alberta
Trainer: Roy Johnson; *Jockey:* Wayne Harris; *Breeder:* Golden West Farm Ltd

in every way an all-Western triumph, even though the colt's breeding was of Irish and French bloodlines. **Prince d'Amour,* who stood in Alberta, was the sire of the winner. He was a son of *Tantieme,* one of the few horses to win the Prix de l'Arc de Triomphe twice, and was imported after being kicked and injured during the 1962 Epsom Derby. The dam, **Anglirish,* a daughter of *Ballyogan,* was a proven stakes producer before *Merger* came along, through her high calibre winners in Ontario, *Naughty Flirt* and *Gilmore.*

Merger was greeted in the winner's circle by Max Bell of Calgary, the wealthy industrialist and publisher, and Vancouver's Frank McMahon, an oil and gas pipeline tycoon, who at the time was putting a National Hockey League franchise into the west coast city. The win was Bell's second major triumph; his colt *Meadow Court,* ridden by Lester Piggott, had won the Irish Sweeps Derby at The Curragh in 1965. Leading *Merger* was Johnson, the tall, lean prairie weed-bender, who also saddled *Whistling Sea* for the West's 1965 Plate win. Jockey Harris was an angelic-looking twenty-year-old from Vancouver with a quick tongue and a fiery temperament. He had learned his skills in Ontario in 1965, but had discovered that riding in California was a more lucrative way to earn a living.

In his golden moment of triumph, Wayne Harris could not resist socking it to his old rival, Jim Fitzsimmons, who was seeking his third Plate victory. As the pair crossed the finish line within inches of each other, Harris yelled over: "You made me ride like hell." A frustrated Fitzsimmons ignored the crack, but later said, "It's kind of hard to get beat in a race like that. But he's a loudmouth . . . Just a kid. My horse ran his guts out and he was trying right to the end. You win some and you lose some, but this is the toughest kind to lose. It was a shame to run a race like this on a muddy track." He recalled an earlier altercation the pair had had in 1966 when stewards suspended Harris for twenty days for attacking and almost unseating the veteran while pulling up after a race. Harris also had been disciplined and fined after two incidents at the starting gate.

One jockey notable for his absence was El Perfecto, who had declared that he wasn't interested in riding that year; indeed, he had "retired" to become an owner-trainer. "Eef I want, I could have ride in the Plate. I turn down three horses that were offered me this week." In Plate week, Avelino Gomez fell prey to the wiles of Walter (The Halter) Woods who claimed *Pink Passion,* the first horse he had saddled in his new vocation. Gomez threatened to punch Woods in the mouth the next time he came by his barn. An unrepentant Woods recalled that Gomez had once claimed foul against one of his horses and he had lost the purse. It was an inauspicious beginning to Gomez's short-lived career as a trainer, but he was never a stranger to controversy and his fans loved him none the less for it.

1968 QUEEN'S PLATE STAKES

SEVENTH RACE
Woodbine
JUNE 22, 1968

1 1-4 MILES (2:01 4/5). One Hundred and Ninth Running QUEEN'S PLATE STAKES. $50,000 added, with 50 Guineas ($134), the gift of Her Majesty the Queen. 3-year-olds. Canadian-foaled. Scale Weight. By subscription of $25 each to accompany the nomination by December 15, 1966 (273 nominated); second subscription of $50 by December 15, 1967 (118 remained eligible); third subscription of $100 by May 1, 1968 (68 remained eligible); and an additional $1,000 when making entry. The added money and all fees to be divided 65 per cent to the winner, 20 per cent to second, 10 per cent to third, and 5 per cent to fourth. Colts and geldings, 126 lbs.; fillies, 121 lbs. Value of race $82,659. Value to winner $53,775.25; second $16,505; third $8,252.50; fourth $4,126.25. Mutuel Pool $354,049.

Horse	Eqt	Wt.	PP	¼	½	¾	1	Str	Fin	Jockey	Owner	Odds $1
MERGER	b	126	4	$3\frac{1}{2}$	2^{nk}	3^1	$1\frac{1}{2}$	2^5	1^{nk}	HarrisW	GoldenWestFarm	3.20
BIG BLUNDER		126	8	11^1	11^{hd}	10^3	3^{hd}	1^{hd}	$2^{2\frac{3}{4}}$	FitzsimmonsJ	LansonFarm	a-3.70
ROULETABILLE	b	126	6	$8\frac{1}{2}$	9^{nk}	$8\frac{1}{2}$	7^3	3^2	$3^{2\frac{1}{4}}$	GrubbRL	LevesqueJL	3.05
PHELODIE		126	2	13	13	12^1	$8^{1\frac{1}{2}}$	5^6	$4^{1\frac{1}{4}}$	DittfachH	SeagramJEF	3.95
NORTHERN OIL		126	3	10^2	7^1	$4\frac{1}{2}$	$5^{1\frac{1}{2}}$	4^1	$5^{7\frac{1}{2}}$	RobinsonK	SmytheC	33.00
DAINTY DAVIE		126	10	6^{hd}	$8\frac{1}{2}$	9^{hd}	6^{hd}	6^{hd}	6^1	PlattsR	GardinerFarm	14.05
SOLOMETEOR	b	121	9	7^1	$6\frac{1}{2}$	6^1	$4^{2\frac{1}{2}}$	7^{nk}	$7\frac{3}{4}$	BolandW	WindfieldsFarm	9.00
SON COSTUME	b	126	13	$9\frac{1}{2}$	$10\frac{1}{2}$	$7\frac{1}{2}$	2^{hd}	$8^{1\frac{1}{2}}$	$8^{1\frac{1}{4}}$	GrimmP	AgroJ&J-Pol'atoL-Ip'litoJ	30.90
NO PARANDO	b	126	5	$5^{2\frac{1}{2}}$	5^1	$5\frac{1}{2}$	$9^{3\frac{1}{2}}$	9^8	9^{10}	LeBlancJ	ShermanFH	66.95
POLAR ZONE		126	7	2^{hd}	$3^{3\frac{1}{2}}$	$3^{1\frac{1}{2}}$	10^2	10^2	10^2	TurcotteN	LansonFarm	a-3.70
WINNING ISLE		121	1	12^2	12^5	$11^{2\frac{1}{2}}$	11^{nk}	11^{10}	11^{14}	GibsonM	PrimeRacingStable	80.05
McSAM	b	126	11	4^{nk}	4^1	13	13	13	$12^{3\frac{3}{4}}$	AlterF	Eaton-AssafStable	100.90
MINK STOLE		121	12	1^1	$1^{1\frac{1}{2}}$	1^1	12^7	$12^{1\frac{1}{2}}$	13	ChambersW	AngrosaStable	22.60

a-Coupled, Big Blunder and Polar Zone.

OFF AT 4:40. Start good. Won driving. Time, :23 1/5, :46 4/5, 1:12 1/5, 1:39, 2:05 2/5. Track muddy.

$2 Mutuel Prices:

5–MERGER	8.40	5.00	3.70
1–BIG BLUNDER (a-Entry)		4.80	3.30
7–ROULETABILLE			3.30

B. c, by *Prince d'Amour—*Anglirish, by Ballyogan. Trainer, Roy Johnson. Bred by Golden West Farm Ltd., Calgary.

MERGER prominently placed early while saving ground, took command from MINK STOLE when ready on the far turn, remained close to the pace when headed and came again under strong handling during the drive to outfinish BIG BLUNDER. The latter, permitted to settle in stride, moved up fast on the outside when commencing his rally on the backstretch and after reaching the front entering the stretch, g his bid entering the stretch, and sent to the inside for the drive and closed determinedly but could not seriously threaten the top pair. PHELODIE outrun early, closed stoutly in the final quarter mile. NORTHERN OIL moved through along the inside to reach closer contention on the backstretch and lacked the needed late response. DAINTY DAVIE was never dangerous. SOLOMETEOR raced evenly for six furlongs, moved up menacingly between horses on the far turn and faltered. SON COSTUME, unhurried for a half mile, loomed a threat on the final turn and weakened. NO PARANDO raced forwardly for six furlongs and retired. POLAR ZONE in the thick of contention from the beginning, was taken up when in close quarters on the far turn and failed to recover. WINNING ISLE was never a contender. McSAM was finished early. MINK STOLE displayed speed for seven furlongs and quit.

When Avelino Gomez tried his hand as an owner and trainer of a modest-sized stable in 1968, one of the first horses he sought to buy was a two-year-old colt by *Pago Pago, owned by Warren Beasley. Beasley told Gomez that the price for Jumpin Joseph, who had been bred by his late father, Bill Beasley, was $50,000, and that's where the conversation stopped. "You can't replace a good colt for $50,000," was the advice of Beasley's trainer, Bobby Bateman. *Pago Pago was the best horse to come out of Australia since the immortal, but ill-fated *Phar Lap, the New Zealand-bred gelding who died of colic in 1932 after becoming the world's second leading money winner. When Beasley talked with A.B. (Bull) Hancock of Claiborne Farms in Kentucky about breeding a mare to the stallion, he had little problem as *Pago Pago's ability as a sire was unknown. The mare he wanted serviced was Skinny Minny, a daughter of Kentucky Derby winner Ponder. She was a proven producer, a multiple stakes winner herself and the dam of Canadian Oaks winner All We Have. The mating produced a big, but passive, chestnut-coloured foal that was named Jumpin Joseph.

AVELINO GOMEZ'S RECORD FOURTH PLATE VICTORY.

The following winter Gomez decided to return to the saddle. Like so many of his earlier retirements, it failed to work, partially because El Senor could not get anybody as good as himself to ride his stock. Slimmed down to his former riding weight of 116 pounds, the forty-year-old Gomez talked to Beasley again. He wanted to ride Jumpin Joseph in the Queen's Plate. The excitable but ingenious Cuban would be an ideal partner because the colt had matured as a three-year-old. At age two he showed considerable ability, winning the Grey Stakes Handicap, the Display Stakes, the Fleur de Lys Stakes (in Montreal) and finished third in the Summer and Carleton Stakes. He was at the top of his class, overshadowed in the annual handicappers' polls only by Windfields Farms' undefeated, but injury-prone Viceregal, Canada's Horse of the Year, and to a lesser degree by H.W Hatch's Grey Whiz. However, Jumpin Joseph's chances for the Plate took a mighty leap forward the following spring. The overwhelming winterbook favourite for the 110th running of the plate after his eight-for-eight season, Viceregal, suffered a broken coffin bone in his left forefoot in a stakes races at Keeneland in April, ending his career and eliminating him from the starting field of the Kentucky Derby. Taylor was bitterly disappointed. Years later he expressed the opinion that Viceregal might have been the best colt he ever bred. At stud Viceregal was a disappointment in Canada, although several of his Canadian daughters were good producers, and had fair success in France, siring French and German stakes winners before being sold to Japan, where he was the sire of Gold City, the Japanese juvenile champion of 1986). Chronic injuries and ailments prompted handicappers to dismiss Grey Whiz's chances of being a threat until the major turf races later that summer.

Suddenly Jumpin Joseph and Gomez were the bosses. Beasley's colt won the Queenston, the Toronto Cup and the Marine Stakes. Trainer Bateman wanted him fresh for the big race, so they passed up the Plate Trial. He also hoped to overcome the jinx that had plagued winners of the Toronto Cup and the Marine—he wanted Jumpin Joseph to become the first horse to win these stakes and then capture the Plate. Fourteen went to the post that day, but only five were given a chance of upsetting the even-money favourite: Fire n Desire, the Cinderella horse that had miraculously risen out of the ranks of claiming races to establish himself as a genuine Plate candidate, Conn Smythe's Sailor Conn, Jean-Louis Lévesque's Fanfaron and Windfields' Northern Native, a full-brother to Northern Dancer.

Fire n Desire, a son of Nearctic, was owned by Sam Lima, who operated a billiards lounge in Etobicoke, and Morris Rose, an ex-jockey who once rode five winners on a program at Churchill Downs, Kentucky. He was the sentimental favourite of the record crowd of 32,806, which would bet a new mutuels high of $1,742,675. Claimed by trainer Larry Moorhead from owner Saul Wagman for $12,000 at Fort Erie in April, the colt was second choice in the wagering following three successive wins, one at odds of 53-to-1 over Fanfaron, a well-bred son of Victoria Park, and another in the Plate Trial Stakes over Northern Native, who was trained by Peter Richards, son of England's famed jockey and trainer Sir Gordon Richards.

The day on which the Plate was run, wrote The Globe and Mail's Jim Vipond, could have been retitled "Avelino Gomez Day." Gomez had carefully picked his spots that spring, riding largely top-calibre horses. In the days before the Plate, he refused to ride

Governor General Roland Michener congratulates trainer Robert Bateman (left) and Warren and Noreen Beasley, owners of *Jumpin Joseph*.

JUMPIN JOSEPH | 3-year-old chestnut colt

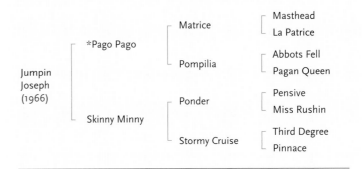

Jumpin Joseph (1966)	*Pago Pago	Matrice	Masthead
			La Patrice
		Pompilia	Abbots Fell
			Pagan Queen
	Skinny Minny	Ponder	Pensive
			Miss Rushin
		Stormy Cruise	Third Degree
			Pinnace

Owner: Warren Beasley, Myrtle, Ont.; *Trainer:* Robert S. (Bobby) Bateman
Jockey: Avelino Gomez; *Breeder:* William (Bill) Beasley, Myrtle, Ont.

for fear of a possible riding violation and a subsequent five-day suspension, which would cost him the chance to ride a record fourth Plate winner. El Perfecto rode five horses on Plate day and won them all, three of them while wearing the flamingo and black silks of the Beasley stable. He could have ridden seven horses, but cancelled two mounts: "Five's plenty. I'm 40 not 20." In gaining his record fourth Plate, Gomez had the throng roaring its appreciation of his performance. He had dispelled the doubters, who presumed *Jumpin Joseph* could be had in a mile-and-a-quarter race, and the colt outclassed the opposition, winning by two lengths over *Fanfaron*. Unhurried in the early going, Gomez went to work on the back stretch and in one big move darted between *Sailor Conn* and *Blithe Victor* before taking aim at *Fire n Desire* in the far turn leading to the top of the stretch.

Hugo Dittfach, aboard *Sailor Conn,* felt he had Gomez boxed in going down the backside. "But when you're riding for $50,000, you don't start handing out favours. I could hear Gomez yelling for room, but nobody was giving any ground. Suddenly he was through the hole. He had too much horse." Afterwards Gomez agreed: "Good to be on the favourite. Not many more chances for me. Perhaps two or three years." The colt paid $4.10, the largest payoff on any of El Senor's four Plate winners.

The jockey who eventually would replace Gomez as Canada's King of the Saddle was already winning two or three races a day on a regular basis, nineteen-year-old Sanford (Sandy) Hawley, an apprentice who did not have a mount in the 1969 Plate. He would never be neglected again. Before this season was over, he had notched up 230 wins, more than double the number of the runner-up, Gomez.

Warren Beasley, wearing the same nubby beige jacket his father did when *Canadian Champ* won the Plate in 1956, had an idea for the blanket of yellow daisies they flung on *Jumpin Joseph*'s shoulders. "We're going to take it up to Mount Pleasant Cemetery and put it on dad's grave." Asked if there would be a champagne party at his barn after the races, Beasley laughed. "No, we're serving watermelons. We're abstainers." It was a day when the losers served the bubbly.

1969 QUEEN'S PLATE STAKES

SEVENTH RACE
Woodbine
JUNE 21, 1969

1 1-4 MILES (2:01⅘). One Hundred and Tenth Running QUEEN'S PLATE STAKES. $50,000 Added. 3-year-olds. Canadian-Foaled. Scale weights: Colts and Geldings, 126 lbs.; Fillies, 121 lbs. By subscription of $25 each which shall accompany the nomination by December 15, 1967 (300 nominated); second subscription of $50 by December 15, 1968 (133 remained eligible); third subscription of $100 by May 1, 1969 (65 remained eligible); and an additional $1,000 when making final entry. The owner of the first horse receives the guineas. The added money and all fees to be divided 65% to the winner, 20% to second, 10% to third, and 5% to fourth. Gross value of race, $84,650, plus 50 Guineas. Value to winner, $55,022.50, plus 50 Guineas; second, $16,930; third, $8,465; fourth, $4,232.50. Mutuel Pool, $421,408.

Horse	Eqt	Wt.	PP	¼	½	¾	1	Str	Fin	Jockey	Owner	Odds $1
JUMPIN JOSEPH	b	126	2	$8^{1\frac{1}{2}}$	$8^{2\frac{1}{2}}$	$4^{1\frac{1}{2}}$	2^{4}	1^{2}	1^{2}	GomezA	BeasleyWarren	1.05
FANFARON	b	126	13	9^{hd}	10^{1}	8^{2}	4^{nk}	2^{3}	$2^{4\frac{3}{4}}$	CruguetJ	LevesqueJL	9.20
FIRE N DESIRE		126	11	1^{hd}	1^{hd}	1^{4}	1^{1}	3^{nk}	3^{hd}	DuffyL	LimaSV&RoseM	2.90
JAMMED RED		126	3	5^{hd}	3^{2}	2^{1}	3½	4½	4^{hd}	PionR	HempelLJ	69.70
NORTHERN NATIVE	b	126	14	4½	6^{nk}	7½	5^{nk}	5^{1}	$5^{1\frac{1}{2}}$	GrubbR	WindfieldsFarm	10.60
GREY WHIZ	b	126	5	12^{2}	$12^{2\frac{1}{2}}$	12^{1}	9^{1}	7^{6}	6^{1}	LeBlancJ	HatchHW	18.85
SAILOR CONN		126	9	7^{1}	7½	$5^{1\frac{1}{2}}$	6^{7}	6^{4}	$7^{6\frac{1}{2}}$	DittfachH	SmytheC	8.00
LUCKY RED PATCH		126	6	$13^{1\frac{1}{2}}$	$13^{2\frac{1}{2}}$	13^{4}	$11^{2\frac{1}{2}}$	8^{2}	$8^{1\frac{1}{4}}$	KellyJ	MacGregorMrsDG	f-47.65
NORTHERN MYTH	b	126	10	14	14	14	$13^{2\frac{1}{2}}$	9^{4}	$9^{5\frac{1}{4}}$	GibbG	GardenCityStable	f-47.65
BLITHE VICTOR	b	126	8	$6^{1\frac{1}{2}}$	5^{1}	$6^{1\frac{1}{2}}$	$7^{2\frac{1}{2}}$	10^{4}	$10^{2\frac{3}{4}}$	SorrentinoM	MarchLD	40.50
WYN D'AMOUR		126	7	11^{nk}	9^{hd}	9^{1}	$10^{1\frac{1}{2}}$	11^{hd}	11¾	RogersC	FMRStable	24.80
WICKED WYNNIE	b	126	4	2^{hd}	2^{2}	3^{hd}	12½	12^{nk}	12^{hd}	FitzsimmonsJ	McLawsD	115.10
NEWS TO ME	b	126	1	$10^{2\frac{1}{2}}$	$11^{1\frac{1}{2}}$	11^{hd}	8^{nk}	13^{5}	$13^{5\frac{1}{2}}$	BehrensR	SeedhouseE	83.80
DAY WILL COME	b	126	12	$3^{1\frac{1}{2}}$	4^{1}	10^{hd}	14	14	14	GordonG	MoffattWA	f-47.65

f-Mutuel field.

OFF AT 4:52. Start good. Won handily. Time, :23⅕, :46⅖, 1:11⅕, 1:37⅖, 2:04⅕. Track fast.

$2 Mutuel Prices:

2-JUMPIN JOSEPH	4.10	3.20	2.50
10-FANFARON		6.50	3.90
9-FIRE N DESIRE			3.00

Ch. c, by *Pago Pago—Skinny Minny, by Ponder. Trainer, Bateman R S (Bob). Bred by Beasley Bill, Myrtle, Ont.

JUMPIN JOSEPH, unhurried early while saving ground, was sent between horses while advancing along the backstretch, moved strongly from the outside to take command from FIRE N DESIRE approaching the stretch and drew good and clear and needed only mild urging to retain a comfortable margin. FANFARON, permitted to settle in stride, gradually improved his position to reach closer contention nearing the stretch and close gamely along the inside when set down for the drive but could not seriously threaten the winner while easily second best. FIRE N DESIRE, hustled to the front soon after the start, shook off his early opposition to establish a long lead along the backstretch and held on willingly when displaced. JAMMED RED, away in the first flight, moved nearest to the leader on the backstretch and lacked the necessary closing response. NORTHERN NATIVE, unable to keep up early, finished willingly without menacing. GREY WHIZ, void of early speed, never entered serious contention. SAILOR CONN failed to threaten. LUCKY RED PATCH was never a factor. WICKED WYNNIE gave way after vieing for the early lead. NEWS TO ME showed little. DAY WILL COME was finished early.

World-Wide Recognition: New Owners, Breeders and Jockeys Take Over from E.P. and Avelino

I can remember years ago people asking what would ever happen when the Seagrams, Hendries, Dyments, Davies and Giddings left the game. But along came the Hatches and the McLaughlins to fill the gap. . . . then came Taylor. There's always somebody.

GEORGE C. HENDRIE, PRESIDENT OF
THE JOCKEY CLUB LIMITED, 1971

The announcement from Windfields Farm a week before the 112th running of the Queen's Plate was quite straightforward. For the second successive year, Canada's dominant racing stable would not have a starter in the race, stated Joe Thomas, the man who supervised the thoroughbred operations of E.P. Taylor. Few were surprised, especially those in the breeding industry who had witnessed Windfields shift its emphasis from racing to breeding; it was now committed to selling yearlings and developing its commercial breeding facilities and stallion rosters in Oshawa and Maryland. This move was inevitable if Taylor was going to remain the world's leading breeder of thoroughbreds, a goal he achieved in 1970 when his stock earned more than $1.7 million. That was the year *Northern Dancer*, the colt buyers had spurned in 1962 when Taylor put a $25,000 tag on him at his novel pre-priced sale of yearlings, was the world's leading sire, ahead of *Hail to Reason* and *Bold Ruler*, while *Nijinsky II*, a colt the industrialist had

bred, led all runners in total earnings.

Something had to suffer, and in this case it was Taylor's racing operations at Woodbine, the "supertrack" he had built in the then distant suburbs of Toronto in 1956, and at Greenwood and Fort Erie, the tracks he culled out of the old "leaky roof circuit" and restored under innovative management. The turquoise and gold polka dot silks of Windfields had not been ushered into the winner's circle for the traditional shawl of flowers and fifty guineas since *Northern Dancer*'s year, 1964, a pivotal one in that he became the first Canadian-bred to win the Kentucky Derby. It would be fourteen years before *Regal Embrace*, a grandson of the world's greatest sire, would stroll before the dais for owners Eddie and Winnie Taylor. In the interim, Windfields had sold four Plate winners at public auction. Like his grandsire, who had also been rejected by the buyers, *Regal Embrace* would be the eighteenth and final Plate winner for the Taylors: the former Winifred Duguid died at the family home in the Bahamas in January 1982, two years after her husband had suffered a debilitating stroke. This had placed their son Charles in the demanding role of maintaining Windfields' position as the predominant breeder of stakes horses in the world, as well as serving on the executive committee of the board of trustees of the Ontario Jockey Club.

Charles Taylor's enthusiasm and interest in the family's racing

THE MEN DIRECTING THE ONTARIO JOCKEY CLUB—ALLAN G. ISBISTER, J.H. (JACK) KENNEY, JOHN J. MOONEY, GEORGE C. HENDRIE AND E.P. TAYLOR.

tradition was deep-rooted. In the 1960s and 1970s he was *The Globe and Mail*'s correspondent in London, Africa and Peking. When he moved back to Canada in 1972, his love of racing was aroused. In a conversation with *The Globe and Mail*'s Neil A. Campbell, Taylor said: ". . . I get a tremendous amount of enjoyment out of Windfields Farm. When it comes to direct involvement in the running of the farm, I started in sort of a sideline capacity in 1972. I would sit in whenever possible at meetings between my father and Joe Thomas and go to the farms, horse sales, and so on. As the decade went on, my father's health declined and his ability to concentrate on aspects of the horse business correspondingly declined. With his active encouragement, I became more and more involved. When he had his stroke he was

WINDFIELDS FARM IN OSHAWA PRODUCED CANADA'S GREATEST THOROUGHBREDS.

completely out of the Windfield's operation; that was in the autumn of 1980. I think it has been a very smooth transition."

A measure of what Taylor had accomplished in the thirty years he had been selling yearlings might be partly reflected in the prices buyers were willing to pay in 1984, compared to his first sale in Oshawa in 1954 when eight were sold for $51,500. In 1984 Windfields sold seventy-three colts and fillies for $25.7 million at sales in Kentucky and at the Canadian Thoroughbred Horse Society auction at Woodbine. These figures may not have surprised even Taylor, whose investment of $6,000 in the mid-1930s for a handful of claimers eventually led him to every conceivable honour in horse racing. When ill health forced him to cut back from his role at Windfields, Taylor said: "Each decade has seen significant changes in our operations. Right now, I think we are well equipped for our present modus operandi, which is selling yearlings and standing stallions."

CHARLES TAYLOR TOOK OVER THE REINS OF WINDFIELDS AFTER THE DEATH OF HIS FATHER.

While Windfields really only had three top contenders in the Plate during the 1970–1984 period—*Police Car*, fourth in 1974; 1978 Plate winner *Regal Embrace* and *Bold Agent*, runner-up in 1979—it nevertheless had a direct influence on most of the renewals of the coveted event. Home-based *Victoria Park* sired three successive Plate winners in the 1970s. He also bred *Victoria Song, Norcliffe, Sound Reason* and *Son of Briartic*, while studs he had bred, *Briartic* and *Nice Dancer*, sired Plate winners *Steady Growth* and *Fiddle Dancer Boy*. Even *L'Enjoleur* and *Key to the Moon*, bred by their owners, had the Windfields' touch: one was out of a *Northern Dancer* mare, *Fanfreluche*, while the other was a grandson of *Square Angel*, a Canadian Oaks–winning filly bred by Taylor.

The stables that replaced Taylor for racing honours in the 1970s were owned by Jean-Louis Lévesque, George Gardiner, D.G. (Bud) Willmot and Jack Stafford. In the 1980s the men that were spending millions for yearlings to develop elite racing stables or breeding establishments were Ernie Samuel of Sam-Son Farm, Bahnam K. Yousif, John Sikura, Richard Kennedy, R.M. Anderson and Frank Stronach. While Lévesque, Gardiner, Willmot and Stronach took turns at winning many of the stakes races in the 1970s, it was Stafford who enjoyed the greatest success, winning major races in the United States with *Tudor Queen* and *Overskate* (perhaps the best horse to finish second in the Plate) and the fifty guineas three times, twice with horses bred by *Amber Morn*. Jack and Florence Stafford had the opportunity to shake hands with Queen Elizabeth II and Prince Philip in 1973 when *Royal Chocolate* romped home at long odds in the mud, and the following year they met the Queen Mother, when *Amber Herod* was victorious. A Taylor-bred, *Sound Reason*, gave the Staffords and trainer Gil Rowntree their third win of the decade in 1977. After Jack died, Rowntree moved to the Yousif stables and won a fourth Plate with *Key to the Moon*. The only men besides Rowntree to win more than one Plate during this era were Jim Bentley (*Kennedy Road* and *Fiddle Dancer Boy*) and Jerry Lavigne (*Almoner* and *Son of Briartic*).

During the 1970s three jockeys emerged who were talented enough to ride against any in the world—Sandy Hawley, Robin Platts and Jeff Fell. In a fifteen-year span they would capture nine Plates; Hawley, the first man to ride more than five hundred winners (515 in 1973), and Platts, each won the race four times, tying them with Avelino Gomez for most victories in Plate history. Fell, the slender, quiet kid from Hamilton, Ontario, won only one Plate, largely because he had been lured to the United States early in his career—following Hawley—but annually he was placed among the top riders in New York and Florida in money earnings.

In 1970 Sandy Hawley was the rider who took over from the aging Gomez, who died in a spill in 1980. He averaged more than four hundred winners a year while capturing the North American title four times, and was also the leading apprentice rider on the continent in his first full season. Hawley was a protege of trainer Duke Campbell and once rode seven winners on a single card. He also won the Oaks, the major race for fillies in Canada, a record five years in a row. His secret? "The kid rides all eight or nine races on the card and rides them all the same way; he tries as hard for fourth place as he does for first," said Alfie Bavington, a former rider who won the Plate for Taylor on *Major Factor*. "The kid's got it upstairs too. Even when he gets into trouble, he doesn't panic; he waits until he gets his opening and then makes his move. Like Gomez, he's a great drawing card too."

Horse racing underwent major changes in the 1970s. In 1971 the OJC became a non-profit organization, a move prompted by Taylor, who was following a trend of major racing jurisdictions throughout the world. Sunday racing was introduced and illegal off-track gambling was tried for a short period. In the 1980s inter-track wagering helped balance the track's sagging economy since it enabled fans in Fort Erie, or even Montreal, to bet on daily racecards at Woodbine and on the Queen's Plate.

1970 | ALMONER

There are a number of elements which have set the 111th running of the Plate into a category all of its own. It was the Plate that *Two Violins* "should" have won for one of North America's leading trainers, Louis Cavalaris; the race that showcased a young apprentice jockey, Sanford Desmond (Sandy) Hawley, and one that informed breeders that Windfields Farm might have the best stallion this side of *Northern Dancer* in Canada, the former Plate winner, *Victoria Park*. It was also the Plate that a daughter of the great *Dancer*, *Fanfreluche*, a mare that would be involved in an intriguing tale of abduction and would later be sold for $2 million, finished second to *Almoner*, a compact brown gelding who richly deserved his victory with a gritty stretch run.

No trainer had ever won the Kentucky Derby and then have the stewards deny him one of racing's biggest prizes. But it happened to Cavalaris in 1968 when it was discovered that someone had put an illegal drug in the feedbucket of *Dancer's Image*. It also seemed that the man who so diligently trained the horses for several of America's most important owners was truly possessed of some hex or hoodoo when it came to the Queen's Plate. Year after year he somehow would get shuffled out of contention in Canada's major horse race.

In 1965 he had the best colt in the country in his barn, *Victorian Era*. But Allen Case, its owner, neglected to make one of the eligibility payments for the Plate. Two years later "Large Lou" went to the United States seeking richer prizes with an exceptional colt, *Cool Reception*. He was a cinch to win the Plate that year, but first he would tackle the great *Damascus* in the Belmont Stakes. The colt got beat in the final strides, but breaking his leg and had to be destroyed. *Arctic Blizzard* was pounds the best in 1968 when handicappers assessed the Plate, but again Cavalaris' hopes went

TEENAGE APPRENTICE SENSATION SANDY HAWLEY TOASTS HIS FIRST PLATE VICTORY.

"poof" when the colt was forced into an early retirement because of a smashed foot. Then in 1970 the Plate "kiss of death" that had haunted Cavalaris would afflict another favourite, owner George Gardiner's undefeated *Two Violins*. The bay gelding who walked "like an arthritic person," had sprawled to his knees in a workout four days before the race and on the morning he was to be entered, a grim Cavalaris declared that "Ol' Ugly" was lame in the left foreleg, the victim of a fractured splint bone.

The Plate was suddenly a wide-open event. However, jockey Avelino Gomez, who was involved in one of his "retirements," took a more jaundiced view of the fifteen-horse field: "The worse bunch I see in my last fifteen years in the country." Nonetheless, when asked what horse he would like to be aboard, Gomez opted for *Almoner*, a gelding that had been bred by Phil Sherwood and

bought by owner Malcolm Smith of Parkview Stable. Smith had been persuaded to spent $25,000 for the son of *Victoria Park* by Joseph (Jerry) Lavigne, his "wiley" trainer and the man better known as "The Weasel" because of his ability "to ferret out" the best in an animal or find a way of confusing his contemporaries. Hawley and his agent, Colin Wick, had closely inspected the serious contenders during both runnings of the Plate Trial Stakes, and wisely chose *Almoner*, whose odds suddenly dipped when it was announced that "the hottest young rider" in Canada would be on his back. The horse they might have preferred, *Fanfreluche*, was already spoken for; Ron Turcotte would be her rider. Undistinguished as a two-year-old while winning just two of twelve starts, *Almoner* had shown vital signs that he was coming up to a peak before the Plate. John LeBlanc rode him in one of the Plate

Trainer Jerry Lavigne (left), *Almoner*, Hawley and owner Malcolm Smith.

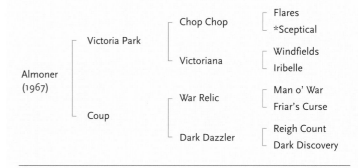

ALMONER | 3-year-old dark bay or brown gelding

Almoner (1967)	Victoria Park	Chop Chop	Flares
			*Sceptical
		Victoriana	Windfields
			Iribelle
	Coup	War Relic	Man o' War
			Friar's Curse
		Dark Dazzler	Reigh Count
			Dark Discovery

Owner: Parkview Stable (Malcolm Smith), King, Ont.; *Trainer:* J.H. (Jerry) Lavigne; *Jockey:* Sandy Hawley; *Breeder:* P.A. (Phil) Sherwood, King, Ont.

Trials, finishing second despite having his saddle slip on him and losing considerable ground. But onlookers liked the way he was running in the final eighth of a mile—it looked like he might prefer the longer Plate distance. Also, his sire had set a Plate record of 2:02 when he won it in 1960.

Responding to Hawley's energetic handling in the stretch-run, *Almoner* went ahead of the exhausted *Dance to Market,* and beat the fading *Fanfreluche* in the final fifty yards, winning by less than a length. A jubilant Hawley afterwards said: "All I was concerned with before I made my move was not to get boxed in. When I looked over my shoulder and didn't see anything coming, I just followed the field around the turn and moved to the outside. I had a lot of horse underneath me at the finish."

One man who agreed was E.P. Taylor, who said he had bet on *Almoner* "because I bred his pappy." For the record, it should be noted that Taylor's stallions sired seven of the fifteen starters, including the Cavalaris-trained *Mary of Scotland,* who later that year would prevent *Almoner* from sweeping Canada's Triple Crown by upsetting him on a deep, soggy turf in the Breeders' Stakes.

Years later, the dour man who led *Almoner* into the winner's circle confessed: "Maybe I'm an oddball—and I guess I hate to say this—but at the time I was in shock over the win, mixed up because I'd told myself it was to be just another race. I know now how lucky I was to have a winner. As the years go by, I realize it more and more. Since then we've had a few horses that I thought were better than *Almoner,* but they never came close to winning the Plate." When *Almoner* was retired to become a show jumper for Smith's daughter, Karen, the gelding had career earnings of $171,130. "He was sound as a bell. But we refused to run him into the ground. After all he had done it wouldn't have been fair. These days, kids at the shows still come up to him and stroke his neck."

1970 QUEEN'S PLATE STAKES

SEVENTH RACE
Woodbine
JUNE 20, 1970

1 1-4 MILES (2:01⅘). One Hundred and Eleventh Running QUEEN'S PLATE STAKES. $50,000 Added. 3-year-olds. Canadian-Foaled. Scale weights: Colts and Geldings, 126 lbs.; Fillies, 121 lbs. By subscription of $25 each which shall accompany the nomination by December 15, 1968 (332 nominated); second subscription of $50 by December 15, 1969 (146 remained eligible); third subscription of $100 by May 1, 1970 (77 remained eligible); and an additional $1,000 when making final entry, with $50,000 added. The owner of the winner receives 50 guineas, the gift of Her Majesty Queen Elizabeth II. The added money and all fees to be divided 65% to the winner, 20% to second, 10% to third, and 5% to fourth. Value of race $88,450. Value to winner $57,525; second, $17,660; third, $8,830; fourth, $4,415. Mutuel Pool, $355,388.

Horse	Eqt	Wt.	PP	¼	½	¾	1	Str	Fin	Jockey	Owner	Odds $1
ALMONER	b	126	5	9½	$9^{3\frac{1}{2}}$	7^{4}	5^{1}	3^{nk}	1¾	HawleyS	ParkviewStable	2.85
FANFRELUCHE		121	10	3^{hd}	3^{1}	2^{1}	2^{2}	1^{1}	2½	TurcotteR	LevesqueJL	b-3.45
TOP CALL	b	126	15	8½	7^{1}	5½	$4^{1\frac{1}{2}}$	4^{6}	3^{5}	DuffyL	TenneyI	4.10
DANCE TO MARKET	b	126	8	$2^{1\frac{1}{2}}$	1½	$1^{2\frac{1}{2}}$	$1^{1\frac{1}{2}}$	2^{3}	4¾	RogersC	MartinVJr	5.20
MARY OF SCOTLAND		121	4	13^{1}	13^{hd}	15	11½	6^{3}	$5^{3\frac{1}{4}}$	PlattsR	GardinerFarm	c-8.85
BIG BLUE BOMBER		126	14	4^{1}	4^{3}	3^{nk}	3½	5^{1}	$6^{1\frac{1}{4}}$	SwatukB	SmytheC	9.35
TEDDIKUS		126	1	12^{hd}	10^{hd}	10¼	7^{1}	$7^{1\frac{1}{2}}$	$7^{1\frac{1}{2}}$	TurcotteN	SeagramJEF	a-34.40
YORK RANGER		126	6	15	15	14^{1}	13^{2}	9½	8^{2}	HinojosaH	ArdwoldStable	58.80
DEAN OF YORK		126	11	11½	12^{hd}	11½	10^{1}	8½	$9^{1\frac{1}{4}}$	GreenW	GardinerFarm	c-8.85
CROQUEMITAINE	b	126	3	$10^{2\frac{1}{2}}$	$11^{2\frac{1}{2}}$	12^{1}	12^{1}	$11^{1\frac{1}{2}}$	10no	GrubbR	LevesqueJL	b-3.45
REGAL ADMIRAL		126	12	6^{4}	$6^{2\frac{1}{2}}$	6½	6^{5}	10^{1}	$11^{2\frac{1}{4}}$	DittfachH	HatchHW	26.65
TRUE WILLIE	b	126	13	14¼	14^{hd}	13^{hd}	8^{nk}	12^{4}	$12^{5\frac{1}{4}}$	KellyJ	GarciaP&AyarraF	49.00
KING'S CHAMPION	b	126	2	7½	5^{hd}	9^{hd}	9^{3}	13^{nk}	13no	BellJ	SeagramJEF	a-34.40
MILDENHALL		126	7	5^{1}	8^{1}	8^{hd}	14^{7}	14^{15}	14	LeBlancJ	StolleryMrsAW	59.40
BEES WAX		126	9	16	$2^{1\frac{1}{2}}$	4½	15	15	Out'd	ArmstrongR	StaffordFarm	18.75

b-Coupled, Fanfreluche and Croquemitaine; c-Mary of Scotland and Dean of York; a-Teddikus and King's Champion.

IN GATE 4:48. OFF AT 4:48. Start good. Won driving. Time, :23, :46⅕, 1:11⅕, 1:37⅖, 2:04⅘. Track fast.

$2 Mutuel Prices:			
4-ALMONER	7.70	3.80	3.10
2-FANFRELUCHE (b-Entry)		3.90	3.10
12-TOP CALL			3.80

Dk. b. or br. g, by Victoria Park—Coup, by War Relic. Trainer, Lavigne J. G. (Jerry). Bred by Sherwood Phil A., King, Ont.

ALMONER, unhurried through the first half-mile, moved steadily from the outside to reach a striking position entering the stretch and, responding to energetic handling, wore down FANFRELUCHE in the closing yards. FANFRELUCHE, close to the leaders while saving ground, moved up on the outside to take command from DANCE TO MARKET soon after straightening out in the stretch, drew clear but could not resist the bid of the winner. TOP CALL gradually improved his position from the outside to become a more serious factor on the final turn and finished determinedly in a good effort. DANCE TO MARKET raced BEES WAX into defeat early to establish a good lead on the backstretch, made the pace to inside the stretch and weakened when challenged. MARY OF SCOTLAND, slow to gain her best stride, made up considerable ground in the late stages. BIG BLUE BOMBER was a factor to the stretch and faltered. TEDDIKUS was never prominent. YORK RANGER was without early speed and never entered contention. DEAN OF YORK failed to attain prominence. CROQUEMITAINE never menaced. REGAL ADMIRAL, within striking distance of the leaders, failed to respond when called upon. BEES WAX gave way after setting and pressing the early pace and was not persevered with in the late stages.

The mahogany-coloured *Kennedy Road* was quite unlike any previous winner of the Queen's Plate. He was a tall, lean colt with bulging muscles and he looked invincible on the June afternoon he sprinted away from the field in eighty-five-degree weather at Woodbine.

Owned and bred by Arthur and Helen Stollery's Angus Glen Farm of Unionville, Ontario, *Kennedy Road* had a temperamental streak that severely tested the patience of the men who trained him—Jim Bentley, Charles Whittingham and Clarke Whitaker. One day he would streak into the lead against the best horses in North America, and often win, then, there would be afternoons when he sulked and refused to respond to his rider's desperate urging.

However, it was not his behaviour that distinguished him from any number of Plate winners. Instead of fading into oblivion after his day in the sun, *Kennedy Road* developed into a great racehorse, maturing from a wild-eyed sprinter with an uncontrollable habit of attempting to flee from his opponents, into a swift older horse

WOODBINE'S PACKED STANDS APPLAUDED *KENNEDY ROAD*, TRAINER JIM BENTLEY AND SANDY HAWLEY.

who occasionally could be "rated" and could perform in a more relaxed style.

The second successive Plate winner to be sired by *Victoria Park*, the colt was Canada's champion of his age and sex at two, three and four before finally being honoured as the country's outstanding horse in 1973. That year he was syndicated for $1.5 million and retired to stud after his brilliant performances in California against *Autobiography*, *Quack*, *Cougar II*, *Big Spruce*, *Kentuckian* and *Tri Jet*, while winning the Hollywood Gold Cup and three stakes races. He was also invited to New York for the Marlboro Cup, facing *Secretariat* and *Riva Ridge*. He was sixth ahead of *Key to the Mint*. Although he was older and more cagey at five, he was still the old *Kennedy Road* in his final week at the track.

He had been nominated to run in Woodbine's rich Canadian International Championship Stakes, a demanding mile-and-five-eighths endurance test against many of the world's top grass specialists. Also in the lineup was the incomparable *Secretariat*, the colt many horsemen insisted was as good or better than *Man o' War*. To prep him for this contest, which was at a distance at which the horse did not excel, trainer Whitaker ran *Kennedy* in a six-furlong sprint just four days before the turf championship. With Avelino Gomez up, *Kennedy Road* was never quicker, running the distance in a record 1:08 3/5, a timing which stood for twenty-six years.

However, the race ruined whatever chance *Kennedy* had of springing an upset against the classic field. He came out of it with a bowed tendon. On Championship day *Kennedy* was as exciting as ever before a crowd of more than 35,000, barging into the lead and then duelling with *Secretariat* for more than a mile before he slowly backed up, perhaps in pain. "He came out of [the gate] running like the wild man from Borneo," Whitaker recalled.

Kennedy Road would forever be remembered by Sandy Hawley. He was the twenty-two-year-old jockey's second successive Plate winner. More than a decade later, while assessing his Plate mounts, Hawley would say: "*Kennedy* was the greatest. He was the type of horse who would fight you. But on that day he simply waited for horses to come to him after we took the lead. I had a good hold on him, but I didn't want to strangle him, so I let him run easily. When I clucked he took off."

Stollery, a fifty-six-year-old mining engineer and cattle breeder, was the man who bred *Kennedy Road*, along with the champion filly *Lauries Dancer* and stakes winning *Gallant Glen* in 1968. They were foaled a year after he had gone out and bought three broodmares. "It was a miracle to be blessed with the winner of the Oaks and Plate in my first try." Stollery loved the action he received from the studdish, raw-boned colt, and was never too bashful to admit: "I loved *Kennedy*." The day he and his wife walked across the track to receive the Plate, he whispered to a bystander: "Just think, anybody could have had *Kennedy*, *Laurie* and the other horse [*Gallant Glen*] for $90,000 last spring. I priced them at $30,000 apiece before they got to the races, but I didn't have any buyers."

OWNERS ART AND HELEN STOLLERY WITH JOCKEY HAWLEY.

KENNEDY ROAD | 3-year-old bay colt

			Chop Chop	Flares
				*Sceptical
	Victoria Park			
			Victoriana	Windfields
Kennedy				Iribelle
Road				
(1968)			Nearctic	Nearco
				*Lady Angela
	Nearis			
			Bolaris	*Fairaris
				Bold Fay

Owner: Mrs Arthur W. Stollery, Toronto, Ont.
Trainer: James C. Bentley; *Jockey:* Sandy Hawley
Breeder: Angus Glen Farm (Arthur Stollery), Unionville, Ont.

Another "miracle" was performed by the Irish-born Bentley, who had been around racetracks in Canada since 1927, the year he was given a chance to gallop Plate winner *Troutlet*. Bentley was the man who developed *Kennedy Road* as he won most of Canada's important two-year-old races. But on New Year's Day 1971, the colt's chances of even starting in the Plate, let alone winning it as the overwhelming favourite, were in considerable doubt. The son of *Nearis* had been injured in the Remsen Stakes in New York, and had just undergone an operation to remove a piece of bone from a hind ankle. Underweight and confined to a stall near Miami, Florida, he was a long time convalescing before Bentley was able to put him

"under tack" in the middle of March, and into light training in April.

Briartic beat him in the Marine Stakes a month before the Plate, and there were those who feared that Bentley would not have the colt fit enough to run by Plate day. More doubt was raised when *Kennedy*'s ankle swelled because of an infection. But Bentley persevered, and would compare the colt to *Arise*, which had won the Travers Stakes at Saratoga Springs. They were the best horses he had ever trained. Later he was more categorical: "He was a great horse . . . the best horse I ever had. He had the confirmation and power, and was very sound. He was also masculine, with a great idea of his own strength—rough, tough and hard, which is as it should be. If he had been gelded, he would have been one helluva horse. But Art [Stollery] wouldn't hear of it. There were times you had to put the fear of God into him, or he wouldn't put out."

Years later Bentley, *Arise*, *Lauries Dancer* and *Kennedy Road* were inducted into the Canadian Horse Racing Hall of Fame.

A SPONGE BATH FOR *KENNEDY ROAD*.

1971 QUEEN'S PLATE STAKES

SEVENTH RACE
Woodbine
JUNE 19, 1971

1 1–4 MILES (2:01⅘). One Hundred and Twelfth Running QUEEN'S PLATE STAKES. $50,000 Added. 3-year-olds. Canadian–Foaled. Scale weights: Colts and Geldings, 126 lbs.; Fillies, 121 lbs. By subscription of $25 each which shall accompany the nomination by December 15, 1969 (321 nominated); second subscription of $50 by December 15, 1970 (169 remained eligible); third subscription of $100 by May 1, 1971 (82 remained eligible); and an additional $1,000 when making final entry, with $50,000 added. The owner of the winner receives 50 guineas, the gift of Her Majesty Queen Elizabeth II. The added money and all fees to be divided 65 per cent to the winner, 20 per cent to second, 10 per cent to third, and 5 per cent to fourth. Value of race $83,675, plus 50 Guineas. Value to winner $54,388.75; second, $16,735; third, $8,367.50; fourth, $4,183.75. Mutuel Pool, $358,422.

Horse	Eqt	Wt.	PP	¼	½	¾	1	Str	Fin	Jockey	Owner	Odds $1
KENNEDY ROAD		126	4	6¹½	5ⁿᵏ	2ʰᵈ	1¹	1³	1³½	HawleyS	StolleryMrsAW	.45
FABE COUNT		126	9	8ʰᵈ	7²½	5²½	3¹½	2½	2³½	KellyJ	ParkviewStable	32.60
GREAT GABE		126	2	7ⁿᵏ	8ʰᵈ	7½	7⁴	6²	3ⁿᵒ	BaboolalJ	WillowDownsFarm	51.35
COOL MOON		126	3	9	9	6³	6¹	4ʰᵈ	4ⁿᵒ	DuffyL	GilbrideWP	14.20
CHATTY CAVALIER	b	126	1	5ʰᵈ	3½	4²½	5¹	5ʰᵈ	5ʰᵈ	UsseryR	GardinerFarm	5.50
BRIARTIC		126	7	3²	4¹½	1ʰᵈ	2³½	3⁴	6¹¾	GrubbR	BennettFarm	41.80
LORD VANCOUVER	b	126	6	4²	6¹½	8¹½	8³	7⁵	7⁵	DittfachH	SmytheC	29.70
SPEEDY ZEPHYR	b	126	5	2¹½	1³	3¹	4³	8¹½	8ⁿᵏ	TurcotteR	RathgebC	4.90
WINTER HOLIDAY		126	8	1²½	2ⁿᵏ	9	9	9	9	StahlbaumG	ViscountHardinge	89.95

OFF AT 4:46. Start good. Won handily. Time, :22⅘, :46⅖, 1:11⅕, 1:37, 2:03. Track fast.

$2 Mutuel Prices:

4–KENNEDY ROAD	2.90	2.70	2.70
9–FABE COUNT		9.90	5.60
2–GREAT GABE			9.00

B. c, by Victoria Park—Nearis, by Nearctic. Trainer, Bentley James C. Bred by Angus Glen Farm, Unionville, Ont.

KENNEDY ROAD, unhurried early, steadily improved his position from the outside to take command from BRIARTIC on the far turn and establishing a good lead in the stretch, was not seriously threatened while being mildly encouraged. FABE COUNT gradually worked his way forward from the outside to be nearest to the winner soon after straightening out in the stretch and closed determinedly to be easily second best. GREAT GABE, slow to gain his best stride, came between horses while rallying through the stretch and closed gamely without threatening the top ones. COOL MOON, without early speed, was sent to the outside for the stretch run and finished willingly. CHATTY CAVALIER tired after three-quarters. BRIARTIC, well placed early, moved between horses to wrest command at the half-mile pole and weakened upon reaching the stretch. LORD VANCOUVER could not keep pace. SPEEDY ZEPHYR prompted the issue, moved through on the inside to gain the lead on the first turn, drew clear and gave way after six furlongs. WINTER HOLIDAY tired abruptly.

1972 | VICTORIA SONG

Trainer Larry Grant was not about to change his mind about the bay gelding, even though he was in the presence of the horse's ecstatic owner, Mrs. Margaret Seitz, and even though the purple and yellow mums had been draped over the shoulders of *Victoria Song*, the surprise winner of the 113th running of the Plate.

"He's still ugly as sin," maintained the former computer programmer from Montreal, "but what a beautiful runner today. Like I said before this race, the Plate is not a beauty contest. It's a contest of speed and endurance, and I thought that the extra distance would definitely benefit this guy. There was lots of speed in the race, which were plus factors for us. When the speed started to back up, I knew ol' ugly would just be shifting into high gear, which is what happened today. Robin [Platts] was still sitting on our horse, and hadn't really got into him yet, but he was picking them off without trying. Ol' ugly's a plodder and doesn't get serious until the last three-eighths [of a mile]."

ROBIN PLATTS VAULTS OUT OF THE SADDLE AFTER *VICTORIA SONG*'S WIN.

The daughter of Larkin Maloney, Marg Seitz had been around horses since she was three, and before her father died she promised him she would try to win the Queen's Plate. Maloney had won the Plate with *Ace Marine* in 1955, the last year the race was run at the "old" Woodbine, now Greenwood. Gazing at the flop-eared and cantankerous horse that had cost her $16,500 at the yearlings sale (she and Grant were both impressed with its pedigree—a son of *Victoria Park* and out of a *Nearctic* mare), Mrs. Seitz reacted to Grant's needle: "He's beautiful; simply beautiful. I've never said he was ugly. That's Larry's opinion. As far as I'm concerned, he's never looked better."

It was Grant's carefully detailed training schedule, which looked as if it had been programmed on one of the complex computers he used to operate, that had the son of *Victoria Park* (his third winner in as many years) at the absolute peak of his physical ability. Another major factor in the gelding's two-length victory over *Barachois*—who courageously held on for second place after suffering a broken coffin bone in his left forefoot during the stretch run, and the favoured *Gentleman Conn*—was jockey Robin Platts, whose judgment and execution were faultless. Platts patiently trailed the fourteen other starters before sending *Victoria Song* on one of his patented come-from-behind rallies. They were crowd pleasers because the fans never knew whether "Ol' ugly" would arrive at the finish line in time.

Platts, a muscular twenty-two-year-old from Leicester, England, who was gaining his first Plate victory, was aware of the gelding's idiosyncrasies. He often dropped his exercise riders in morning trials, and in the afternoon races had a habit of ducking in and bothering other horses, which not only cost him a chance to break his maiden as a two-year-old, but led to a five-day

1972 QUEEN'S PLATE STAKES

SEVENTH RACE
Woodbine
JUNE 17, 1972

1 1–4 MILES (2:01$\frac{4}{5}$). One Hundred and Thirteenth Running QUEEN'S PLATE STAKES. $50,000 Added. 3–year–olds. Canadian–Foaled. Scale Weights: Colts and Geldings, 126 lbs.; Fillies, 121 lbs. By subscription of $25 each to accompany the nomination by December 15, 1970 (293 nominated); second subscription of $50 by December 15, 1971 (125 remained eligible); third subscription of $100 by May 1, 1972 (78 remained eligible); and an additional $1,000 when making final entry. The owner of the first horse receives the Guineas. The added money and all fees to be divided 65% to the winner, 20% to second, 10% to third, and 5% to fourth. Gross value of race $86,375. Value to winner $56,143.75; second, $17,275; third, $8,637.50; fourth, $4,318.75. Mutuel Pool, $471,870.

Horse	Eqt	Wt.	PP	¼	½	¾	1	Str	Fin	Jockey	Owner	Odds $1
VICTORIA SONG		126	3	15	15	$11^{1\frac{1}{2}}$	6^{2}	2^{1}	1^{2}	PlattsR	GreenHillsFarm	6.30
BARACHOIS	b	126	13	$4^{1\frac{1}{2}}$	3^{hd}	$4^{1\frac{1}{2}}$	$3^{1\frac{1}{2}}$	1^{hd}	$2^{\frac{1}{2}}$	StahlbaumG	LevesqueJL	12.15
GENTLEMAN CONN		126	9	$10^{1\frac{1}{2}}$	$9^{\frac{1}{2}}$	5^{1}	$4^{\frac{1}{2}}$	$3^{\frac{1}{2}}$	$3^{\frac{1}{2}}$	BaboolalJ	WillowDownsFarm	1.45
SUFFIX		126	2	13^{5}	12^{1}	$7^{2\frac{1}{2}}$	7^{hd}	6^{3}	$4^{3\frac{1}{2}}$	KellyJ	MinshallAW	9.45
HENRY TUDOR		126	6	$8^{\frac{1}{2}}$	$7^{\frac{1}{2}}$	3^{hd}	2^{1}	4^{1}	$5^{1\frac{3}{4}}$	GomezA	GardinerFarm	7.60
GEORGE OF CANADA	b	126	4	12^{hd}	10^{1}	$8^{\frac{1}{2}}$	8^{2}	7^{2}	6^{hd}	GrubbR	ThreeStarStable	f-25.20
NICE DANCER	b	126	5	$1^{1\frac{1}{2}}$	$1^{2\frac{1}{2}}$	$1^{2\frac{1}{2}}$	1^{hd}	5^{hd}	7^{1}	McCarronG	MortonTA&Harlequin	11.35
PRESIDIAL		126	8	14^{3}	14^{3}	12^{1}	9^{4}	9^{7}	$8^{3\frac{1}{2}}$	LeBlancJ	WindfieldsFarm	9.00
PARKRANGLE		126	11	$3^{\frac{1}{2}}$	$2^{1\frac{1}{2}}$	2^{hd}	5^{1}	8^{2}	$9^{3\frac{1}{2}}$	DuffyL	ParkviewStable	7.55
FIFTY GUINEAS	b	126	1	9^{hd}	$11^{1\frac{1}{2}}$	15	$12^{\frac{1}{2}}$	$10^{3\frac{1}{2}}$	10^{3}	RyanM	SmytheC	88.80
BARLEY SUGAR	b	126	7	5^{1}	8^{1}	13^{2}	11^{2}	12^{5}	$11^{1\frac{1}{2}}$	DittfachH	BanksD	65.45
TOMMY JACK	b	126	15	$2^{\frac{1}{2}}$	4^{1}	6^{hd}	10^{7}	$11^{\frac{1}{2}}$	12^{3}	CoombsW	BragagnoloN	f-25.20
MADLY MAGIC	b	126	10	6^{hd}	5^{1}	$9^{\frac{1}{2}}$	14^{3}	13^{4}	$13^{4\frac{1}{2}}$	BellJ	BennettRJ	f-25.20
BURNT GRASS	b	126	12	$11^{1\frac{1}{2}}$	$13^{\frac{1}{2}}$	$14^{2\frac{1}{2}}$	13^{1}	14^{5}	$14^{4\frac{1}{2}}$	PinedaR	ViscountHardinge	53.00
FORT MYERS	b	126	14	7^{1}	$6^{1\frac{1}{2}}$	10^{hd}	15	15	15	MiceliM	MarkoW	f-25.20

f–Mutuel field.

IN GATE—4:46. OFF AT 4:46. Start good. Won ridden out. Time, :23, :46, 1:11, 1:37$\frac{2}{5}$, 2:03$\frac{1}{5}$. Track fast.

$2 Mutuel Prices:

3–VICTORIA SONG	14.60	6.70	4.20
11–BARACHOIS		11.40	5.60
8–GENTLEMAN CONN			3.20

B. g, by Victoria Park—Arctic Song, by Nearctic. Trainer, Grant Larry G. Bred by Taylor E. P.

VICTORIA SONG, unhurried early, moved up gradually outside, came widest into the stretch to take aim on the leaders and drew off under intermittent pressure. BARACHOIS, within striking distance, came outside around the final turn, took command in midstretch but could not hold the winner and pulled up lame. GENTLEMAN CONN, off the inner rail around the final turn while in contention, came outside into the stretch but lacked a closing bid.

TRAINER LARRY GRANT, PLATTS AND *VICTORIA SONG*.

			Chop Chop	Flares
Victoria Song (1969)	Victoria Park			*Sceptical
		Victoriana	Windfields
				Iribelle
	Arctic Song	Nearctic	Nearco
				*Lady Angela
		*Evensong	The Phoenix
			Angelus

Owner: Green Hills Farm (Mrs. William Seitz), Milton, Ont.
Trainer: Larry Grant; *Jockey:* Robin Platts; *Breeder:* E.P. Taylor, Toronto

MRS. MARGARET SEITZ WAS DELIGHTED AFTER DUPLICATING THE FEAT OF HER FATHER, LARKIN MALONEY, WHO WON THE PLATE IN 1955.

suspension for Platts. "He usually did things his way, and when you rode him it was always a case of hoping he would fire at the right time. He fired when he wanted to, not when I wanted him to. That was an old trick of his as well as his lackadaisical way of walking out of the gate. In the Plate Trial a week before the Plate I cussed and swore at him. I couldn't get him pulled up until well after the race was over. He was really moving past the finish line, but we were fourth."

Platts knew his horse had the ability; the trick was to be around on the day it surfaced. The year before, *Victoria Song* had started thirteen times, earning $25,044, which largely came from six second-place finishes and included frustrating losses in the rich Coronation Futurity and the Cup and Saucer Stakes. "No horse in Canada has ever won as much money without winning a race," Grant lamented as he prepped the strong-willed maiden, a horse that went through more pairs of shoes than Fred Astaire. "He's awfully tough on shoes. It's the way he moves." Positive things, however, began to happen to the horse which had been winless in thirteen races in 1971. On 13 April he broke his maiden with Platts up. The jockey had reason to celebrate because on the same day his wife Debbie gave birth to their first child. Platts, who had a chance to ride Gardiner Farms' *Henry Tudor*, said it would be tough to decide which mount to ride.

The morning before the race, Larry Grant wondered whether thirteen might prove to be a lucky omen. "I just hope 13 is our lucky number. Robin had a dream about 13 the other night. This is the 113th running of the Plate and the car sticker the Ontario Jockey Club gave me was 113. This horse also broke his maiden on 13 April. We'd hoped to get Number 13 post, but got Number 3 instead, which is part of the number." He was unaware that *Victoria Song* was also the thirteenth horse sold at the Canadian Thoroughbred Horse Society yearling sales in 1970.

For all but Platts, it would be their luckiest Plate day. It helped them when Canada's leading jockey, Sandy Hawley, was unavailable to ride the pre-race favourite, *Gentleman Conn*, because of a ten-day suspension the stewards had meted out when his unruly mount was guilty of intimidation in the Plate Trial Stakes. The crippling injury suffered in the final yards by *Barachois*, a son of *Northern Dancer*, was another factor. Jockey Gary Stahlbaum felt he would have won had this not happened. *Victoria Song* beat the odds that day. In future races he reverted to form, a charging second or third in a succession of stakes races. Mrs. Seitz and Larry Grant would soon fade out of further Plate competition, while Platts' career was just beginning. The day was also notable because 34,367 racegoers, the largest turnout in Plate history at Woodbine, wagered more than $2 million, a record.

Jack Stafford had waited a long time for this day, almost twenty-five years, and had gone through almost as many horses as trainers in order to achieve his goal. When it happened, when he finally won his first Queen's Plate, the man who at one time made a living selling jams, jellies and syrups from store-to-store across Canada, was as amiable, but as delightfully bombastic, as ever before a crowd of 40,137, the largest ever to view the historic race at Woodbine in Rexdale.

Big Jack Stafford rarely did anything in a small way, and he held form on this occasion as well, winning the 114th running of the race in the presence of Queen Elizabeth II and Prince Philip. "How's that for timing?" he wisecracked as he led his wife

JOCKEY TED COLANGELO IS GREETED BY QUEEN ELIZABETH II WHILE JACK AND FLORENCE STAFFORD AND PRINCE PHILIP LOOK ON.

Florence, their sons Gordon and Howard, and trainer Gil Rowntree across the racetrack to the winner's circle. "No Lieutenant Governors for this poor boy from the country trying to make good in the city."

It was a regal performance by a 23-to-1 longshot, appropriately named *Royal Chocolate*, that earned Stafford a cheque for $80,698 and a purple pouch containing fifty gold sovereigns—the royal gift that winners normally receive in the form of a cheque, but one that is presented in the form of gold coins whenever a reigning monarch is in attendance. Stafford's command performance was equally entertaining. When the Queen was presented to the man who was known as the "King of Jams" or the "Monarch of Marmalades," she was quoted as saying: "Congratulations. I was surprised to see a horse win by so much in such an important race." Stafford chortled: "Your Majesty, we just slewed 'em, that's all."

Later, chatting with Dick Beddoes of *The Globe and Mail*, Stafford was chastised for using such language to royalty. "Oh, I thought I'd give the Queen some Kentucky talk. Down there, when they slay something big in racing, they say slewed. We slewed 'em."

The Queen handed Jack a gold cup and passed the gold and purple leather pouch from her "pantry purse" to Mrs. Stafford, who told Prince Philip, "I'm going to look in the bag if you don't mind."

Clutching a handful of bright coins adorned with engravings of Elizabeth II, Mrs. Stafford murmured: "What a prize for the trophy case." Prince Philip was just as curious: "Let *me* look, too. I don't get to see a lot of those."

A tall, chestnut colt, known as "*Chuckle*" to Stafford's stablehands, *Royal Chocolate* won the Plate by almost six lengths. His move was timed perfectly by an inexperienced and unheralded jockey who was making his one and only appearance in the race. Ted Colangelo, a twenty-four-year-old, had emigrated from Italy to Canada in 1966, and was on the winner only because he had lost a discussion with trainer Rowntree, who was also winning his first Plate after two resounding last-place defeats. "Ted was our main contract rider and he wanted to ride the other half of the entry, *Good Port*. But I told him 'You'll ride *Royal Chocolate* or nothing.' I remember that I fired him the first time he came to work for me. I ran him off shedrow because he kept falling off my horses in the morning. Later I had a couple of nutty horses, kooks that other jocks refused to ride, and he came by one morning and asked if he could have a chance on them. He was okay, so I started using him and we clicked together. His Plate ride was perfect. I couldn't have asked for a better ride, even if I was sitting alongside him, telling

Royal Chocolate was a "royal surprise" for bettors as he won handily.

him what to do."

Rowntree, who had been with Stafford for seven years, longer than any trainer had ever survived with the Port Elgin horseman, had a feeling that "*Chuckle*" was coming up to the race in "perfect condition." Sired by one of Stafford's stallions, *Amber Morn,* the colt was considered inferior as a two-year-old to Big Jack's other Plate horses—*Tara Road* and *Good Port.* Indeed, he had been relegated to a stall at the far end of the barn at Woodbine. But as spring progressed and the colt put on a hundred pounds in weight, Rowntree started to have second thoughts about his son of *Rocket Shot,* a mare that was a particular favourite of Stafford's. She had a fiery temperament similar to her owner's, but she never did get to the races: she tried to kick down a cement wall at the track and broke bones in both feet. As a broodmare she had foaled a good stakes winner in *Amber Orbit,* and later would mate with the same sire (*Amber Morn*) to produce *Royal Chocolate.*

Tara Road and *Good Port* would both go on to become stakes winners. But on Plate day, *Tara Road* was in his barn, the victim of a freak accident—he had put his foot through some floorboards on shedrow—while *Good Port* had yet to get "untracked" in four starts that season. "What I liked about *Royal Chocolate* was the way he handled his training. He put on weight and became robust off the training. Also, I think he put out the message he was ready when he won his division of the Plate Trial by almost two seconds quicker than the other winner [*Queen's Splendour*]."

The colt won the Plate when he fled past the exhausted 7-to-5 favourite, the filly *La Prevoyante,* and *Queen's Splendour,* at the top of the stretch and then outdistanced *Sinister Purpose,* who reinjured a bowed tendon, and the improbable *My Archie Bald.* Rowntree's reaction to the victory did not surprise those who knew him: "I can't think of any person I'd rather see win the Plate than myself."

ROYAL CHOCOLATE | 3-year-old chestnut colt

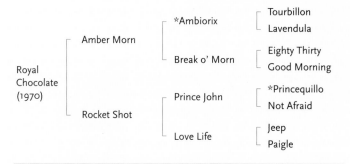

Royal Chocolate (1970)	Amber Morn	*Ambiorix	Tourbillon
			Lavendula
		Break o' Morn	Eighty Thirty
			Good Morning
	Rocket Shot	Prince John	*Princequillo
			Not Afraid
		Love Life	Jeep
			Paigle

Owner: Stafford Farm (Jack Stafford), King City, Ont.
Trainer: G.H. (Gil) Rowntree; *Jockey:* Ted Colangelo; *Breeder:* Stafford Farm

Trainer Gil Rowntree, *Royal Chocolate* and Ted Colangelo.

1973 QUEEN'S PLATE STAKES

SIXTH RACE
Woodbine
JUNE 30, 1973

1 1-4 MILES ($2:01\frac{1}{5}$—Monte Christo II—5—116—Sept. 23, 1972). One Hundred and Fourteenth Running QUEEN'S PLATE STAKES. $75,000 Added. 3-year-olds. Canadian-Foaled. Scale Weight: Colts and Geldings, 126 lbs; Fillies, 121 lbs. By subscription of $25 each to accompany the nomination by December 15, 1971 (328 nominated); second subscription of $50 by December 15, 1972 (138 remained eligible); third subscription of $150 by May 1, 1973 (57 remained eligible); and an additional $1,500 when making final entry. The added money and all fees to be divided 65% to the winner, 20% to second, 10% to third, and 5% to fourth. Gross value of race $124,150. Value to winner $80,697.50, plus 50 Guineas ($136.50); second $24,830; third $12,415; fourth $6,207.50. Mutuel Pool, $521,336.

Horse	Eqt	Wt.	PP	¼	½	¾	1	Str	Fin	Jockey	Owner	Odds $1
ROYAL CHOCOLATE	b	126	3	10^{1}	7^{1}	7^{hd}	5^{3}	1^{3}	$1^{5\frac{1}{2}}$	ColangeloT	StaffordFarm	a-23.05
SINISTER PURPOSE		126	13	6^{hd}	5^{hd}	5^{1}	6^{2}	4^{hd}	2^{nk}	StahlbaumG	RiverRoadStable	3.35
MY ARCHIE BALD	b	126	12	1^{hd}	3^{hd}	4^{3}	3^{hd}	5^{1}	3^{1}	RichieS	SevenSStable	f-26.05
ALBERT THE CONSORT		126	11	16^{2}	16^{hd}	15^{3}	12^{1}	8^{1}	$4^{\frac{1}{2}}$	PlattsR	GardinerFarm	10.00
SINGING SPIRIT		126	14	15^{1}	14^{1}	11^{hd}	10^{hd}	$6^{\frac{1}{2}}$	$5^{\frac{1}{2}}$	HoleM	BoswellW&McLawsDP	67.80
FABIUSAND	b	126	4	14^{3}	15^{3}	10^{1}	9^{1}	7^{1}	6^{2}	KellyJ	ParkviewStable	111.95
INGENIOUS DEVICE	b	126	5	17	17	14^{1}	13^{4}	10^{2}	$7^{\frac{1}{2}}$	GreenW	SeedhouseEB	f-26.05
LA PREVOYANTE	b	121	15	2^{hd}	2^{hd}	2^{2}	2^{3}	2^{1}	8^{1}	LeBlancJB	LevesqueJ	1.40
LUCKY MASTER	b	126	7	9^{2}	$7^{1\frac{1}{2}}$	7^{hd}	8^{1}	11^{1}	$9^{\frac{1}{2}}$	BellJ	DeToro&BridlePathFm	f-26.05
COMBAT DAY		126	2	8^{2}	$9^{\frac{1}{2}}$	9^{hd}	7^{hd}	9^{hd}	$10^{\frac{1}{2}}$	TurcotteN	MayAJR	34.35
QUEEN'S SPLENDOUR		126	9	7^{1}	1^{2}	1^{hd}	1^{hd}	3^{1}	$11^{\frac{3}{4}}$	DuffyL	ViscountHardinge	58.45
ZACA SPIRIT	b	126	8	5^{2}	4^{2}	$3^{\frac{1}{2}}$	$4^{\frac{1}{2}}$	12^{3}	12^{1}	GomezA	Bo-TeekFarm	16.00
GOOD PORT	b	126	16	4^{2}	12^{2}	12^{1}	$14^{\frac{1}{2}}$	14^{7}	13^{1}	GrubbR	StaffordFarm	a-23.05
VICTORIAN PRINCE	b	126	1	13^{hd}	$13^{\frac{1}{2}}$	13^{2}	11^{1}	13^{hd}	14^{8}	HawleyS	Grovetree&BCStable	4.10
IMPRESSIVE LADY		121	7	3^{hd}	$6^{1\frac{1}{2}}$	6^{hd}	15^{10}	15^{20}	15^{24}	DittfachH	BruntonJM	12.50
TIME OF PLENTY		126	10	12^{1}	$8^{\frac{1}{2}}$	16^{2}	17	17	$16^{\frac{1}{2}}$	WalfordJ	Sam-SonFarm	f-26.05
RUSTY SCISSORS		126	6	11^{1}	11^{2}	17	16^{2}	16^{hd}	17	GordonG	SlomaH	f-26.05

a-Coupled, Royal Chocolate and Good Port. f-Mutuel field.

OFF AT 4:16. Start good. Won handily. Time, $:23\frac{2}{5}$, $:47\frac{1}{5}$, $1:13\frac{1}{5}$, 1:41, 2:08. Track slow.

$2 Mutuel Prices:

1-ROYAL CHOCOLATE (a-Entry)	48.10	14.50	9.00
8-SINISTER PURPOSE		5.40	4.70
16-MY ARCHIE BALD (f-Field)			5.50

Ch. c, by Amber Morn—Rocket Shot, by Prince John. Trainer, Rowntree Gil H. Bred by Stafford Farm, King City.

ROYAL CHOCOLATE, reserved early, and saving ground, came outside the leaders around the final turn to challenge for the lead, took command into the home lane and pulled away with authority. SINISTER PURPOSE, never far back, circled foes around the final turn behind the winner and finished willingly while outside. MY ARCHIE BALD, hustled quickly to press the opening pace, stalked the leaders in the backstretch while outside and closed off the rail.

When Gil Rowntree was told that *Amber Herod* had eagerly taken a flop in the mud while he was being led from his barn to the walking ring, where he would be saddled for a Plate race worth a record $148,525, the forty-year-old trainer rationalized that the colt was trying to tell him something. "At first I didn't know what to think when Kenny [Zweig] walked into the paddock. I guess my eyes bugged out, and my stomach went into a knot. The colt has mud splattered all over the white blanket that his exercise rider [Gail Powell] had sewn for him. Then my groom tells me the horse had taken a roll in the slop just as they came out of the tunnel and onto the track, but he's okay. So I figured he must like it. That was his sign of approval."

Earlier in the day, Rowntree had attempted to get a line on how *Amber Herod* might perform before a crowd that would include Queen Elizabeth, the Queen Mother, by taking him out for a stroll in the barn area. "He walked like a big fat cow. I thought if I took him beside the track he might perk up and show some interest. He didn't. It wasn't until I saddled him, when the people in the crowd began clapping and he got buckin' and actin' up, that I knew he was feeling as good as you could get him. Never before had he shown such signs of life before a race."

AMBER HEROD HAD LITTLE TROUBLE HANDLING A SLOPPY TRACK.

Although the track was deep and muddy, and the rains that fell that morning had added a further layer of "black puree" to the slippery surface, Rowntree welcomed an "off track." He reasoned that a sloppy surface was the equalizer he needed to beat his major rivals, George Hendrie's *Native Aid*, the roan colt that champion jockey Sandy Hawley had chosen to ride, and Windfields Farm's undefeated *Police Car*. Jack Stafford's trainer could excuse the colt's only previous race on a sloppy racetrack, an eighteen-length loss the previous fall while he was still a maiden. He had not yet learned how to run without "lugging" in on other horses. Rowntree was still experimenting with various types of equipment such as blinkers, special bits and a burr. About a month before the Plate, it was discovered that *Amber Herod* had a sharp wolf tooth in his lower left jaw, which irritated him when he ran, so it was extracted.

Jockey Robin Platts, who would make all the correct moves that enabled Stafford Farms to win its second successive Plate in front of a member of the royal family, recalled that his seven sets of goggles had aided him in gaining his second triumph in the race. Scooting along the rail, Platts had flipped each set of goggles onto his forehead as they became coated with the flying mud. "Sometimes you get lucky. That day everybody stayed outside. He was a distance horse and on a track like that one, it was a case of who could out-plod the others. I won two Plates because of the off track, where if it had been fast, I might have got beaten. *Amber Herod* was a big clown who was inclined to loaf when he got the lead, and I had to get to know him. When my agent [Alan Dunn] went to Mr. Stafford that spring to see if I could ride for him, he said I sure could, as long as I was prepared to get to the track in the mornings and work with the horses. Well, that's what I preferred to do anyway."

Platts did not think that the burr, which had been attached on the rail side of the colt's bit, and had stung the left side of his mouth whenever Platts tugged on the reins, was really a factor. Whether it was the burr, or Platts' vigorous right-handed hitting, *Amber Herod* returned to running dead ahead, and to an unexpected length-and-a-half win over *Native Aid*. "He would have preferred a fast track,"

The Queen Mother presents Plate to Jack and Florence Stafford while their sons, Gordon and Howard look on. Jockey Robin Platts ignores presentation while talking with trainer Gil Rowntree and Chairman of the Board Charles Baker.

Hawley said. Fourth-place finisher *Police Car* also had to struggle in the slop.

Astonishingly, the crowd of 32,674 had allowed the winner of the Plate Trial and the Queenston Stakes to go off at odds of 10-to-1. "Our plan was to get to the inside rail and stay there. On a lot of sloppy tracks, you don't get as much mud in your face down there, and neither does the horse. Mind you, on many sloppy tracks the footing's bad down on the inside. But it was fine that day. We just sat in there and saved ground and let the others take the long way around." When *Muddy York*, a sprinter, tired and drifted wide, Platts slipped through and easily splashed home in 2:09 1/5, the slowest time since the race was moved to Woodbine in 1956. "But it was still too fast for the second horse," said Rowntree, who praised Platts for making the proper adjustments. "[Robin] made one big move, but that's why you ride good jocks."

The effusive Stafford, a youthful seventy-nine-year-old who had just bred two successive Plate winners by his Kentucky-based sire *Amber Morn*, could not resist reminding the Queen Mother that her daughter had presented him with the gold sovereigns the previous year. "Your daughter was here last year, y' know. Real nice girl you have there." The Queen Mother said "Thank you," and the crusty Stafford replied, "Thanks for coming." Full of himself, and as ebullient as ever as the cameras clicked, Stafford advised the Queen Mother: "Would you mind just turning around there a little so the boys can get everybody in?" Earlier, in the paddock when he first met the Queen Mother, he reminded her: "You're from Scotland, and that's good. They breed good folks there. My wife [Florence] is from Edinburgh."

AMBER HEROD | 3-year-old bay colt

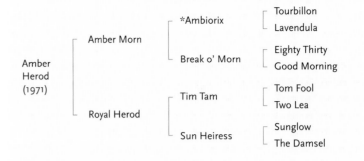

Amber Herod (1971)	Amber Morn	*Ambiorix	Tourbillon
			Lavendula
		Break o' Morn	Eighty Thirty
			Good Morning
	Royal Herod	Tim Tam	Tom Fool
			Two Lea
		Sun Heiress	Sunglow
			The Damsel

Owner: Stafford Farm (Jack Stafford), King City, Ont.
Trainer: G.H. (Gil) Rowntree; *Jockey:* Robin Platts; *Breeder:* Stafford Farm

Guardsman Andrew Ritchie remained at attention even though he was dumped during the parade of the Governor General's Horse Guard.

1974 QUEEN'S PLATE STAKES

SEVENTH RACE
Woodbine
JUNE 29, 1974

1 1-4 MILES (2:01 1/5). One Hundred and Fifteenth Running QUEEN'S PLATE STAKES. $75,000 Added. 3-year-olds. Canadian-Foaled. Scale Weight: Colts and Geldings, 126 lbs.; Fillies, 121 lbs. By subscription of $35 each to accompany the nomination by December 15, 1972 (355 nominated); second subscription of $100 by December 15, 1973 (157 remained eligible); third subscription of $200 by May 1, 1974 (77 remained eligible); and an additional $2,000 when making final entry. The owner of the first horse receives the Guineas. The added money and all fees to be divided 65% to the winner, 20% to second, 10% to third, and 5% to fourth. Gross value of race $148,525. Value to winner $96,541.25, plus 50 Guineas ($129.50); second $29,705; third $14,852; fourth $7,426.25. Mutuel Pool, $537,108.

Horse	Eqt	Wt.	PP	¼	½	¾	1	Str	Fin	Jockey	Owner	Odds $1
AMBER HEROD		126	3	11½	7½	4^{1}	1^{hd}	$1^{1\frac{1}{2}}$	$1^{1\frac{1}{2}}$	PlattsR	StaffordFarm	9.75
NATIVE AID	b	126	4	7^{2}	5^{hd}	3^{hd}	3^{3}	$3^{2\frac{1}{2}}$	2^{hd}	HawleyS	HendrieGC	3.95
RUSHTON'S CORSAIR		126	1	3^{hd}	$3^{2\frac{1}{2}}$	$2^{1\frac{1}{2}}$	$2^{1\frac{1}{2}}$	2^{2}	3^{3}	GreenW	MinshallAW	8.00
POLICE CAR		126	6	6½	$9^{1\frac{1}{2}}$	6½	$4^{1\frac{1}{2}}$	4^{3}	4½	DuffyL	WindfieldsFarm	1.40
BUTTERBUMP	b	126	7	14	$13^{1\frac{1}{2}}$	11^{4}	11^{2}	12^{3}	$5^{7\frac{1}{2}}$	ArellanoJ	ViscountHardinge	a-7.20
LINCOLN FIELDS	b	126	2	$13^{1\frac{1}{2}}$	12^{2}	8½	9^{5}	7^{5}	6^{nk}	BaboolalJ	ShefryFarm	f-33.40
LOVELY SUNRISE	b	121	8	5½	6^{hd}	10^{hd}	8^{hd}	6^{hd}	$7^{11\frac{1}{2}}$	GrubbR	SmytheC	14.15
MUDDY YORK	b	126	14	1^{hd}	1^{4}	12½	6^{1}	9^{5}	8½	DittfachH	StolleryMrsAW	22.55
RASH MOVE	b	126	10	12½	$8^{2\frac{1}{2}}$	5^{2}	7^{3}	10½	$9^{5\frac{1}{2}}$	RogersC	KinghavenFarm	b-12.55
CHANGEABOUT	b	126	9	2^{2}	2^{hd}	$7^{1\frac{1}{2}}$	10^{1}	8½	10^{1}	HinojosaH	GardenCityStable	f-33.40
NAIGO		126	13	10½	14	12^{3}	12^{6}	11^{3}	$11^{2\frac{1}{2}}$	KellyJ	KinghavenFarm	b-12.55
NOBLE ANSWER	b	126	11	8^{hd}	$11^{1\frac{1}{2}}$	9^{hd}	5^{2}	5^{7}	$12^{2\frac{1}{2}}$	WoodhouseR	ViscountHardinge	a-7.20
CONVERSATION		126	12	$9^{2\frac{1}{2}}$	10^{1}	13^{2}	13^{3}	13^{12}	13	CastanedaM	GardinerFarm	31.90
DOCTOR McKAY	b	126	5	4½	4^{hd}	14	14	14	Out'd.	GustinesH	E&F RacingStable	34.65

a–Coupled, Butterbump and Noble Answer; b–Rash Move and Naigo. f–Mutuel field.

OFF AT 4:46. Start good. Won ridden out. Time, :22 4/5, :47 2/5, 1:14 1/5, 1:41 2/5, 2:09 1/5. Track sloppy.

$2 Mutuel Prices:				
	4–AMBER HEROD	21.50	8.20	5.60
	5–NATIVE AID		5.30	4.10
	3–RUSHTON'S CORSAIR			5.20

B. c, by Amber Morn—Royal Herod, by Tim Tam. Trainer, Rowntree Gil H. Bred by Stafford Farm, King City, Ont.

AMBER HEROD advanced into the backstretch turn along the rail, stayed that way into the far turn to duel from there to the final turn, was roused into the stretch to open up and retained his margin under intermittent pressure. NATIVE AID, well placed early outside, had aim on the leaders around the far turn outside, stayed outside in the stretch and edged RUSHTON'S CORSAIR. The latter saved ground early stalking the pace, came off the rail midway of the backstretch, dueled with AMBER HEROD around the far turn just outside but failed to stay in the early stretch. POLICE CAR, between foes early, saved ground around the far turn, stayed inside to the home lane then closed willingly off the rail. BUTTERBUMP made a strong belated bid outside. MUDDY YORK moved quickly to the fore, set the early pace and tired. RASH MOVE, a contender early, could not keep up. NOBLE ANSWER lacked a closing response.

Scratched—Bill Fields.

Jean-Louis Lévesque, born on the Gaspé coast of Quebec and brought up around horses that were used like taxis for salesmen visiting his village, later surrounded himself with some of the finest thoroughbreds that money could buy after fulfilling a promise to himself as a young businessman that the day he could afford to buy a horse, it would be a racehorse.

It did not happen overnight, and as it turned out, it was a pair of stakes-winning standardbreds that he would own first. But two years later, in 1958, the man who was trying to revive the flagging interest in "the runners" at Blue Bonnets racetrack in Montreal, would begin his quest to own a Queen's Plate winner. Writing in *The Blood-Horse* shortly after Lévesque's colt *L'Enjoleur* had overpowered his opposition on 28 June, Edward Bowen recalled that Lévesque did what most Canadians do when they take up thoroughbred racing: "Two things are likely to happen: He will set as his goal winning the Queen's Plate, and he will go shopping for some Windfields Farm blood."

THE CLASSICALLY BRED *L'ENJOLEUR*, BY *BUCKPASSER* AND OUT OF *NORTHERN DANCER*'S DAUGHTER *FANFRELUCHE*, WENT TO STUD AT GATEWAY FARMS IN FLORIDA.

Lévesque, who often admitted "I don't know that much about racehorses," became a regular visitor and buyer in 1962 at E.P. Taylor's breeding establishment in Oshawa, and would spend millions for horses that would carry his silks to important victories at almost every track in North America and earn him numerous horse-of-the-year titles. There would be *La Prevoyante*, undefeated champion at two years old in Canada and the U.S.; the great "Fanny," *Northern Dancer*'s sturdy daughter, *Fanfreluche;* along with *Rouletabille, Fanfaron, Barachois* and the broodmares who got his stable started, *Ciboulette* and *Arctic Dancer.* (*Fanfreluche, Fanfaron* and *Barachois* all finished as runners-up in their bid for Plate glory while *Rouletabille* was third.)

However, this quiet, proud man who had worked forward in the business world from a $500-a-year clerical position to build a major financial empire in Quebec, soon learned, and accepted philosophically, that it took more than dollars to put an owner into the winner's circle on Plate day. He was also aware that since 1944, the year the restrictions were taken off the historic race, opening it to all Canadian horsemen, no Quebec owner had won the Plate.

On the day that *Fanfreluche*'s glamorous son *L'Enjoleur* vindicated his breeding (he was sired by millionaire *Buckpasser*) and erased the claims that he was "a disappointment, an enigma, over-rated and perhaps lame," with a five-and-one-half length victory that was a mere three-fifths of a second off the Plate record, Lévesque would allow his son Pierre, and his trainer, Joseph (Yonnie) Starr, to speak for him. He had been "stung" by the media after *La Prevoyante*'s ill-timed death in an inconsequential stakes race in Florida that winter, and might have heard the boos in the post parade as jockey Sandy Hawley guided his erratic colt to the starting gate along with twelve other hopefuls.

Lévesque did not deserve the jeers any more than E.P. Taylor did when he dominated the Plate in the 1950s and early 1960s. "This win was very important for my father," his son Pierre said. "It meant more to him than winning the Kentucky Derby." The betting favourite at $1.15 to $1, even though he had won only one (the Quebec Derby) of seven previous starts as a three-year-old, *L'Enjoleur*

JEAN-LOUIS LEVESQUE, SANDY HAWLEY AND *L'ENJOLEUR*.

L'ENJOLEUR | 3-year-old bay colt

L'Enjoleur (1972)	Buckpasser	Tom Fool	Menow
			Gaga
		Busanda	War Admiral
			Businesslike
	Fanfreluche	Northern Dancer	Nearctic
			Natalma
		Ciboulette	Chop Chop
			Windy Answer

Owner: Jean-Louis Lévesque, Montreal, Que.; *Trainer:* Joseph (Yonnie) Starr
Jockey: Sandy Hawley; *Breeder:* J.-L. Lévesque

CALL TO THE POST BY TRUMPETER ED PILAR IN WOODBINE'S SADDLING PADDOCK.

accomplished what nine other horses had failed to do for Lévesque's trainers Duke Campbell, Lucien Laurin and Starr, and jockeys Ron Turcotte, Jean Cruget, Avelino Gomez and Herb Hinojosa.

In winning his third Plate, Hawley had travelled from his full-time home in California, to ride the colt at Lévesque's request. He had been warned that Preston Gilbride's *Greek Answer* would attempt to steal the race and that trainer Frank Merrill Jr. was attempting to "stretch out" the speedster. The *Daily Racing Form* wrote that *Greek Answer* trained at times with his nose in a bag full of cotton soaked in oil of eucalyptus. Merrill's strategy was to force the colt to take deeper breaths and expand his lungs. "No excuses," Merrill said after his colt had sped briefly to the lead and was responsible for six furlongs in 1:10 2/5 ths before quitting. "He just can't go that distance." Although he drifted wide in the stretch, *L'Enjoleur* was never in any danger from *Greek Answer* as he opened up a seven-length lead entering the stretch. "All I tried to do that day was to get him to relax, which he did," Sandy Hawley said. After a brief duel in the backstretch, *L'Enjoleur* moved away with authority, opening up a huge lead that was enough to withstand the late charges of *Near the High Sea* and *Mystery Time*.

1975 QUEEN'S PLATE STAKES

SEVENTH RACE
Woodbine
JUNE 28, 1975

1 1–4 MILES (2:01⅕). One Hundred and Sixteenth Running QUEEN'S PLATE STAKES. Scale weights. $75,000 Added (plus 50 Guineas). 3-year-olds. Canadian–Foaled. Colts and Geldings, 126 lbs.; Fillies, 121 lbs. By subscription of $35 each to accompany the nominations by Dec. 15, 1973 (417 nominated); second subscription of $100 by December 15, 1974 (157 remained eligible); third subscription of $200 by May 1, 1975 (77 remained eligible); and an additional $2,000 when making final entry. The owner of the first horse receives the Guineas. The added money and all fees to be divided 65% to the winner, 20% to second, 10% to third, and 5% to fourth. Value of race $146,695. Value to winner $95,351.75 (plus 50 Guineas—$113.50); second $29,339; third $14,669.50; fourth $7,334.75. Mutuel Pool, $533,804.

Horse	Eqt	Wt.	PP	¼	½	¾	1	Str	Fin	Jockey	Owner	Odds $1
L'ENJOLEUR	b	126	6	3½	3²½	1ʰᵈ	1⁴	1⁷	15½	HawleyS	LevesqueJL	1.15
NEAR THE HIGH SEA		126	1	8²½	8¹½	8¹	7⁴	3¹½	2²½	GrubbR	LaistJ & FrymanEI	53.55
MYSTERY TIME		126	5	5²	4½	4⁴	3¹½	4⁴	3ʰᵈ	ParsonsW	DouglasSM	11.00
NEW ORIENT	b	126	4	12³	10½	10¹	9ʰᵈ	7½	4ʰᵈ	SwatukB	RossMrsGretchen	32.50
BRILLIANT SANDY		126	2	9¹	9²½	9²	8²	6ʰᵈ	5²½	KellyJ	SmithT-WillowDowns	31.15
REX FAVOR		126	11	10ʰᵈ	11²½	11²½	11³	9³	6¹½	DittfachH	FarrellGE	18.25
UPPER SHELF	b	126	10	4ʰᵈ	5²	6²	5¹	8²½	7ⁿᵏ	StahlbaumG	KinghavenFarm	a-7.65
COUNTRYMAN	b	126	9	2ʰᵈ	2²½	3³	4³	5½	8¹½	DuffyL	KinghavenFarm	a-7.65
GREEK ANSWER		126	13	1½	1ʰᵈ	2²	2⁵	2²	9¹½	SolomoneM	GilbrideWP	2.15
TRUSTED FRIEND		126	7	7ʰᵈ	7¹	7½	10²	10¹½	102½	FellJ	WindfieldsFarm	13.70
ESKIMO BAY		126	8	6ʰᵈ	6³½	5¹	6ʰᵈ	11⁶	11³½	McMahonW	VaseyMr & MrsG	84.35
JOHNNY ONE STEP		126	12	11²	12³½	12⁵	12⁸	12⁵	12²	GreenW	SlomaH	113.20
COUP DE SOLEIL		126	3	13	13	13	13	13	13	PlattsR	ViscountHardinge	65.65

a–Coupled, Upper Shelf and Countryman.

OFF AT 4:44. Start good. Won handily. Time, :23, :45³/₅, 1:10²/₅, 1:35³/₅, 2:02³/₅. Track fast.

$2 Mutuel Prices:

7-L'ENJOLEUR	4.30	4.10	3.70
2-NEAR THE HIGH SEA		25.80	11.40
6-MYSTERY TIME			5.30

B. c, by Buckpasser—Fanfreluche, by Northern Dancer. Trainer, Starr J. (Yonnie). Bred by Levesque J. L., Montreal.

L'ENJOLEUR, away with the first flight, saved ground around the first turn, moved outside midway of the backstretch to duel with GREEK ANSWER, edged away around the far turn to widen thereafter and won with authority while drifting out in the stretch. NEAR THE HIGH SEA moved between foes around the final turn and closed determinedly without threatening. MYSTERY TIME, alert at the start, was taken back slightly and saving ground came off the rail in the backstretch just outside of COUNTRYMAN into the far turn, saved ground into the homestretch and held NEW ORIENT safe. The latter made a belated bid while wide. BRILLIANT SANDY, outfinished the balance. UPPER SHELF, well placed early, saved ground around the final turn and faded. COUNTRYMAN duelled for the early lead along the rail, was even with the winner to midway of the backstretch and was fading around the far turn. GREEK ANSWER duelled early outside, edged away in the backstretch, was even with L'ENJOLEUR approaching the far turn, could not stay and weakened a furlong out between foes.

The 117th running of the Queen's Plate will forever be remembered as the one that produced a classic duel between the Old Man and The Kid; the race that the forty-eight-year-old Avelino Gomez grudgingly lost, not the one that young Jeffrey Fell deservedly won. It was one of horse racing's most appealing spectacles: the climactic struggle of an underdog being nursed through the stretch by a resourceful veteran attempting a comeback, grimly clinging to a lead that he knows is shrinking, while the powerful favourite and his vigorous twenty-year-old rider maintain their relentless chase, refusing to bow to tradition.

A Woodbine throng of 34,877 would noisily applaud both winner and loser. They had bet their money on the best horse in the race, the determined bay colt *Norcliffe*, who jogged towards the winner's circle with Fell on his back and owner Colonel Charles Baker and trainer Roger Attfield alongside. But they took time to acknowledge Jim Corcoran's *Military Bearing*, the weary challenger, and El Perfecto, the Cuban-born jockey who had turned this Plate into such a thriller. The cheers should have been reserved for *Norcliffe* and Fell, but instead the crowd was on its feet, clapping and hooting as Gomez brought his horse back to the finish line. He stood in the irons and waved his whip towards the stewards' stand and the legion of followers who had witnessed his triumphant rides in four other Plate races

"I almost steal it, eh?" Gomez said afterwards, his craggy face drained, but his Latin eyes expressing satisfaction. "I did every thin' possible. But no excuse. The best horse beat me today." Gomez insisted that he was not guilty of allowing his horse to drift at the top of the stretch so that *Norcliffe* would have just that much farther to travel to get past his horse. "I kept my course. If I drift out and brush him, I get disqualified anyway. I had 99 1/2 tricks, but I run out of tricks, that's all, and I run out of horse." Avelino's tricks had worked until his colt was about ten strides from the wire. That's when *Norcliffe* got his head in front and would edge away to win by a half-length.

Trained by Jim Bentley, *Military Bearing* had jumped into an early lead and at the end proved to be a better horse than *Ambassador B.*, the roan colt of Stafford Farms that had been expected to challenge *Norcliffe*, and Jean-Louis Lévesque's *Laissez-Passer*, a son of *Northern Dancer*, ridden by Sandy Hawley. However, it was the class horse that prevailed, a Windfields Farm–bred yearling that Colonel Baker had paid $80,000 for at the sales in Saratoga Springs, New York. "When you have a horse two or three lengths in front of you with only three furlongs to go, you've got to be worried. But we knew this horse [*Norcliffe*] had to have something to run at, and I did say that if somebody carried us to the quarter pole we would be in pretty good shape. Gomez couldn't have ridden a better race for us," Colonel Baker explained afterwards.

THOUSANDS WATCH AS BOARD CHAIRMAN CHARLES BAKER AND MRS. SUE BAKER LEAD *NORCLIFFE* AND JEFFREY FELL INTO THE WINNER'S CIRCLE.

The Plate victory was the first for the fifty-six-year-old owner. Chairman of the board of the Ontario Jockey Club, a medal winning member of Canada's Olympic Team and International Equestrian Teams (1948–1960) and a former Commanding Officer of the Governor General's Horse Guard, Colonel Baker was twice wounded and three times mentioned in dispatches while serving in Europe during World War II. It was also a first for Attfield, an Englishman from Berkshire, and was certainly Fell's biggest moment in the Plate. The rider from Hamilton, Ontario, had gained the chance to ride *Norcliffe* largely because he was the best jockey riding on a regular basis in Canada. Hawley was at meets in California that spring, and although he had won the rich Coronation Futurity on the colt as a two-year-old and said he would be available on Plate day, Colonel Baker and Attfield decided to "ride" the boy who had been aboard on all four of his previous races that year. Fell was also in the irons the day that *Norcliffe* broke his maiden at Fort Erie by sixteen lengths.

A QUITE PROPER ROGER ATTFIELD IS MUSCLED BY *NORCLIFFE*.

Jeffrey Fell predicted he would win the Plate

MILITARY BEARING BATTLED *NORCLIFFE* TO THE WIRE.

and kept telling friends to ignore *Norcliffe*'s fourth-place finish to *Military Bearing* on the grass in the Toronto Cup: "You're crazy if you don't go with me." Afterwards he admitted that *Military Bearing* had surprised him. "I didn't think he'd open up three or four lengths down the backstretch, and then hold the lead that long. I pretty well knew that he was going to tire and what would happen. But Gomez kept getting more and more out of his horse. Boy, did he make me ride!"

Attfield's main concern before the race was that the colt's training schedule had been changed in May because of a bruised foot. "It put me off key a little bit on how to bring him to the race. I had to run him three weeks in a row at a mile-and-a-sixteenth, which usually wouldn't be my ideal way of bringing a horse up to the Plate. But he needed that. This is a funny game. If I get beaten, I'm wrong. Now I won, so I did the right thing. But I had always thought he was the best horse. He could be an even better horse than he showed today."

Roger Attfield's assessment was correct. The son of *Buckpasser* and *Drama School*, a daughter of *Northern Dancer*, would go on to become Canada's Horse-of-the-Year in 1976 and would be selected as the champion male handicap horse of 1977.

During his racing career *Norcliffe* accomplished a feat no other horse has ever managed by completing a unique triple—winning the richest races in Canada for two-, three- and four-year-olds—the Coronation Futurity, a race he won in record time (1:49.1, for a mile and an eighth, a record for the juvenile race that has never been bettered more than thirty years later), the Queen's Plate and the Canadian Maturity, a race that is no longer contested. *Norcliffe* also won the Prince of Wales and captured the Carling O'Keefe Invitational Handicap twice, setting a track record for a mile and a half in his 1977 Carling O'Keefe victory.

NORCLIFFE | 3-year-old bay colt

Norcliffe (1973)	Buckpasser	Tom Fool	Menow
			Gaga
		Busanda	War Admiral
			Businesslike
	Drama School	Northern Dancer	Nearctic
			Natalma
		*Stalina	Stalino
			Boscabell

Owner: Norcliffe Stable (Charles "Bud" Baker), King, Ont.
Trainer: Roger Attfield; *Jockey:* Jeffrey Fell; *Breeder:* E.P. Taylor, Toronto

That year he finished second by less than a length to the legendary *Forego* in the Nassau County Stakes Handicap at Belmont, New York. Nine of his fourteen wins came in stakes races and he was first, second or third in twenty-five of his thirty-three starts. He retired with a bankroll of $434,066.

After his four-year-old season he was purchased and syndicated by Roy Kennedy to stand at stud at his Gateway Farms in Ocala, Florida, and later at Patricia Kennedy's Hyllview Stallion Station in that state. His progeny allowed him to surpass *Nodouble* as Florida's leading stallion. *Norcliffe* later stood at Crescent Farm in Kentucky before his untimely death at age eleven in 1984 at Shadowland Farm in Midway, Kentucky. During his abbreviated career as stud, he sired thirty-three stakes winners from only seven crops of foals. He was North America's leading juvenile sire by number of wins and second in earnings in 1981. His most notable sons were the Eclipse Award sprint champion *Groovy*, who earned more than $1 million, and *At the Threshold*, winner of the Arlington Classic and American Derby, and sire of Kentucky Derby winner *Lil E. Tee*.

1976 QUEEN'S PLATE STAKES

SEVENTH RACE
Woodbine
JUNE 26, 1976

1 1–4 MILES (2:01 1/5). One Hundred and Seventeenth Running QUEEN'S PLATE STAKES. $75,000 Added. 3-year-olds. Canadian-Foaled. Scale Weight: Colts and Geldings, 126 lbs.; Fillies, 121 lbs. By subscription of $35 each to accompany the nomination by December 15, 1974 (375 nominated); second subscription of $100 by December 31, 1975 (139 remained eligible); third subscription of $200 by May 1, 1976 (70 remained eligible); and an additional $2,000 when making final entry. The owner of the first horse receives the Guineas. The added money and all fees to be divided 65% to the winner, 20% to second, 10% to third, and 5% to fourth. Gross value of race $138,025. Value to winner $89,716.25 (plus 50 guineas); second $27,805; third $12,802.50; fourth $6,901.25. Mutuel Pool, $669,547.

Horse	Eqt	Wt.	PP	¼	½	¾	1	Str	Fin	Jockey	Owner	Odds $1
NORCLIFFE	b	126	7	5^{2}	3½	2^{2}	2^{5}	$2^{3\frac{1}{2}}$	1½	FellJ	NorcliffeStable	1.60
MILITARY BEARING		126	1	$1^{1\frac{1}{2}}$	1^{1}	$1^{1\frac{1}{2}}$	1^{2}	$1^{1\frac{1}{2}}$	$2^{2\frac{1}{4}}$	GomezA	CorcoranJD	11.55
CONFEDERATION	b	126	9	$7^{2\frac{1}{2}}$	7^{2}	6^{3}	3^{3}	3^{5}	3^{6}	McCarronC	WindfieldsFarm	9.80
LAISSEZ-PASSER	b	126	4	9^{5}	8^{1}	7^{2}	5^{2}	4^{3}	4^{hd}	HawleyS	LevesqueJL	a-2.60
HOOK AND DRAW	b	126	2	10^{5}	10^{3}	10^{2}	9^{5}	5^{2}	5^{3}	ParsonsW	HillcrestStable	23.25
LAKE HURON	b	126	11	11	11	11	10^{12}	$8^{2\frac{1}{2}}$	6^{2}	GrubbR	StaffordFarm	b-3.40
NATIVE ICE		126	6	$8^{1\frac{1}{2}}$	9^{7}	8^{2}	6½	6^{2}	$7^{2\frac{1}{2}}$	StahlbaumG	d'AndreaF&P	37.55
LE GASPESIEN	b	126	10	$6^{2\frac{1}{2}}$	6^{2}	5^{hd}	7^{hd}	9^{6}	8^{nk}	DuffyL	LevesqueJL	a-2.60
AMBASSADOR B.	b	126	8	2^{hd}	4^{1}	3½	4^{1}	7^{1}	$9^{8\frac{1}{2}}$	PlattsR	StaffordFarm	b-3.40
BYE BYE PARIS		121	5	4^{hd}	5^{2}	$4^{2\frac{1}{2}}$	8^{2}	10	10	RogersC	SmytheC	12.25
INTREPID SPIRIT		126	3	3^{hd}	2^{1}	9^{6}	11	Outdist.		LeBlancJB	Bo-Teek Farm	98.55

a-Coupled, Laissez-Passer and Le Gaspesien; b-Ambassador B. and Lake Huron.

OFF AT 4:44. Start good. Won ridden out. Time, :23, :47, 1:12, 1:37 4/5, 2:05. Track fast.

$2 Mutuel Prices:				
	8-NORCLIFFE	**5.20**	**4.00**	**3.10**
	3-MILITARY BEARING		**8.80**	**4.90**
	9-CONFEDERATION			**4.70**

B. c, by Buckpasser—Drama School, by Northern Dancer. Trainer, Attfield Roger. Bred by Taylor E. P.

NORCLIFFE stalked the early pace outside, made a mild challenge into the far turn, was in behind MILITARY BEARING around the final turn and into the stretch, stayed outside thereafter wearing his rival down and took command in the final stages. MILITARY BEARING broke alertly to take command under rating, edged away around the far turn to increase the margin on NORCLIFFE round the final turn, came slightly wide into the stretch, set the pace to deep in the stretch and just failed in a very game effort. CONFEDERATION saved ground advancing around the far turn, stayed inside thereafter and finished willingly. LAISSEZ-PASSER was never dangerous. HOOK AND DRAW closed belatedly. LAKE HURON showed nothing. LE GASPESIEN could not keep up. AMBASSADOR B. stayed contentious to the far turn then dropped back. BYE BYE PARIS was through around the far turn. INTREPID SPIRIT stopped badly.

Races at Woodbine are often not decided until the horses have passed the sixteenth pole, a black-and-white-striped stake placed just inside the inner rail 120 yards from the finish line. It was at this point in the 1977 running of the Plate that *Northernette*, a good filly that had been stretched to the limit and was running her third race in twenty-one days, encountered *Sound Reason*, a colt running with one eye covered in mud.

At the wire the distance separating the two animals who had dominated their categories as two-year-olds was barely a half-length as the pursuing colt of Stafford Farms had simply worn down the filly despite her gritty display. But was that not the way it was expected to happen? Fillies are not supposed to beat the colts. Syl Asadoorian, a land developer from Cambridge,

SOUND REASON HANDLED THE SLOPPY GOING, CATCHING *NORTHERNETTE* IN THE FINAL SEVENTY YARDS.

Ontario, who owned the daughter of *Northern Dancer* in partnership with Toronto's Sam Cosentino, smiled and grudgingly agreed: "I guess that's why they have filly races. But, you know, our filly never got a breather and I'm proud of her. After her big win in the Canadian Oaks [the richest Canadian race for fillies], I think second place is a big accomplishment. It's the first time anyone ever caught *Northernette* in the stretch. What a helluva time for a first, eh?"

Trainer Jerry Meyer would not completely accept the filly versus colt theory, reminding visitors to his barn that he had lost the Plate ten years earlier when a colt that he saddled, the favoured *Pine Point*, was beaten a neck by *Jammed Lovely*, the last filly to win the Plate. "Everything went our way except winning the race. She ran big—*Sound Reason* ran bigger. Robin [Platts] gave that colt a tremendous ride. But I can't help reminding myself of the role that *Plus de Rien* played in the outcome. I have to feel he cost us the race. He stayed out front much longer than I thought he would. If that colt wasn't in it, our filly would have been out front by herself. As it was, [Avelino] Gomez had to use our filly three times in the heavy going."

Both Asadoorian and Meyer, who had never won the Plate despite developing numerous outstanding horses in Canada and the United States, could only reflect after the race on what might have happened if they had been willing to spend more than $45,000 for a dark bay colt that had been consigned by Windfields Farm to the annual auction of Canadian-foaled yearlings in September 1975. "Take a look at this page," Meyer said as he thumbed through an old yearling sales catalogue. The page listing the pedigree of a colt by *Bold Reason*, which Windfields pre-priced at $20,000, had the word "Syl" written in heavy letters. Asadoorian did not get the yearling, and instead went to Saratoga Springs and paid $50,000 for a bay filly out of Canadian Oaks champion *South Ocean*, also bred by E.P. Taylor (for the second year in a row, Taylor had bred the first four Plate finishers). "I guess if I had been a little more persistent that night, I might have had an entry racing today."

Jack Stafford, an octogenarian with horse farms in Port Elgin and King, Ontario, also remembered the sales at Woodbine. "I bought yearlings that year for $116,000 and $165,000 but the $45,000 one turned out to be the good one." It gave him, trainer

Mud-splattered Robin Platts and *Sound Reason* accompany Jack Stafford's son Howard to the winner's enclosure.

SOUND REASON | 3-year-old dark bay or brown colt

Sound Reason (1974)	Bold Reason	Hail to Reason	*Turn-to
			Nothirdchance
		Lalun	*Djeddah
			Be Faithful
	New Tune	New Providence	Bull Page
			*Fair Colleen
		Song of Victory	Victoria Park
			*Evensong

Owner: Stafford Farm, King City, Ont.; *Trainer:* Gil Rowntree
Jockey: Robin Platts; *Breeder:* E.P. Taylor, Toronto

Gil Rowntree and Platts their third Plate victory of the 1970s. "We actually trained for the Plate this time," Rowntree boasted in the post-race celebrations. "The other times [1973 and 1974] we were going into the Plate and got lucky with what were mediocre horses at the time. This time we knew what our horse could do, and I probably spent more time with him than any other horse. The big thing was getting him to relax and settle down so that he could be rated, although there was one time in the race that I thought he was a little too relaxed. That was the only time I was worried; when Robin reached back and gunned him at the five-eighths pole, I thought it was kind of early to be doing that."

Platts, who had used up his six sets of goggles and was being stung by the mud as it hit an eye that had required stitches to close following an accident in the jockeys' quarters a week earlier, said his horse was reacting to the slop. "He tried to pull up on me. It was the first time he'd ever had slop in his face. He'd won in the slop before, but he was in the lead that time."

A trainer who at times treated major wins as if they were his just reward, Rowntree would later say: "What did three Plate victories mean then? It meant that I had a job for at least another couple of weeks, and I had more money in the bank. Working for Stafford, though, was not as difficult as a lot of people thought. He wasn't difficult. He gave me the material and left me alone."

Jack Stafford often said that his work ethic was simple: "My system was always to work harder than anyone else. If you bum for an hour, you lose money. Time is money." Rowntree, who had been a groom, hot walker, jockey, valet and an assistant trainer with Lou Cavalaris before jumping at the chance to train for Stafford, kept his job because he was able to satisfy his owner's major aim in life—to win the Plate, not once but three times. The favourite of the three? "*Royal Chocolate* will always be my favourite. That's because he's the one that won the year the Queen was here. It's just a great honour to be able to meet and talk with your Queen. It's once in a lifetime."

1977 QUEEN'S PLATE STAKES

SEVENTH RACE
Woodbine
JUNE 25, 1977

1 1-4 MILES (2:01 1/5). One Hundred and Eighteenth Running QUEEN'S PLATE STAKES. $75,000 Added. 3-year-olds. Canadian-Foaled. Scale Weight: Colts and Geldings, 126 lbs.; Fillies, 121 lbs. By subscription of $35 each to accompany the nomination by December 15, 1975 (381 nominated); second subscription of $100 by December 15, 1976 (134 remained eligible); third subscription of $200 by May 1, 1977 (67 remained eligible); and an additional $2,000 when making final entry. The owner of the first horse receives the Guineas. The added money and all fees to be divided 65% to the winner, 20% to second, 10% to third, and 5% to fourth. Value of race $133,135. Value to winner $86,537.75; second $26,527; third $13,313.50; fourth $6,656.75. Mutuel Pool, $608,154.

Horse	Eqt	Wt.	PP	¼	½	¾	1	Str	Fin	Jockey	Owner	Odds $1
SOUND REASON		126	2	7^{3}	5^{hd}	$4^{2\frac{1}{2}}$	3^{1}	2^{3}	$1\frac{1}{2}$	PlattsR	StaffordFarm	1.55
NORTHERNETTE	b	121	3	$3^{1\frac{1}{2}}$	2^{2}	2^{2}	2^{2}	$1\frac{1}{2}$	$2^{3\frac{1}{2}}$	GomezA	AsadoorianS-CosentinoS	1.45
GIBOULEE	b	126	1	8	8	7^{1}	5^{4}	5^{8}	3^{5}	CruguetJ	LevesqueJL	a-2.45
PRO CONSUL	b	126	6	$4\frac{1}{2}$	$3\frac{1}{2}$	3^{4}	4^{3}	$4\frac{1}{2}$	4^{7}	DuffyL	McCulloughMrsG	20.55
PLUS DE RIEN		126	7	1^{2}	$1^{1\frac{1}{2}}$	$1^{1\frac{1}{2}}$	1^{1}	$3\frac{1}{2}$	5^{2}	StahlbaumG	BurnettT&J	26.80
SOCIAL PLEASURE	b	126	4	$5^{2\frac{1}{2}}$	$6^{2\frac{1}{2}}$	$6^{1\frac{1}{2}}$	6^{5}	6^{10}	6^{10}	GrubbR	HKStable	33.60
GRAND LUXE		121	5	6^{hd}	7^{3}	8	$7^{2\frac{1}{2}}$	7^{5}	7^{13}	FellJJ	LevesqueJL	a-2.45
REGENT BIRD	b	126	8	2^{hd}	$4^{2\frac{1}{2}}$	$5\frac{1}{2}$	8	8	8	DittfachH	RequestFarm	47.65

a-Coupled, Giboulee and Grand Luxe.

OFF AT 4:43. Start good. Won ridden out. Time, :23 2/5, :47 2/5, 1:13, 1:40, 2:06 3/5. Track sloppy.

$2 Mutuel Prices:			
2-SOUND REASON	5.10	2.60	2.30
4-NORTHERNETTE		2.60	2.30
1-GIBOULEE (a-Entry)			2.50

Dk. b. or br. c, by Bold Reason—New Tune, by New Providence. Trainer, Rowntree Gil H. Bred by Taylor E. P.

SOUND REASON, unhurried for the first half-mile, advanced around the far turn, was moving well on the outside around the final turn, stayed outside pressing NORTHERNETTE at the furlong pole, then responding to intermittent handling, got the measure of that one in the latter stages. NORTHERNETTE stalked the early pace, moved up on the leader around the final turn on the outside, had command in early stretch, but failed to hold the winner in the final seventy yards. GIBOULEE, trailing early advanced around the final turn, and proved best of the balance. PRO CONSUL saved ground and was contentious to midway of the far turn, but lacked a closing response. PLUS DE RIEN moved quickly to the fore, set the pace to the home lane, then weakened. GRAND LUXE was never dangerous.

Scratched—Crossword Puzzle.

For once, the hero of the Queen's Plate was not a four-legged beast which ran long and hard, or a rider who knew how to make the right moves, or a trainer who brought a fine thoroughbred to a peak at the right time—but a seventy-seven-year-old man with his binoculars dangling from his left hand as he walked slowly and carefully away from the winner's circle at Woodbine. Edward Plunket Taylor: the man the crowds once loved best to boo.

The red carpet on which he and his wife, Winnie, had crossed the main track to the winner's circle, had been rolled up before they returned, and they picked their way through the dirt to the sound of warm applause. Along the path under the stands where the horses come from the walking ring Taylor walked, secluded. A few moments later he sank onto a settee, facing a forest of men who in years gone by had made him a target for everything from cheap shots to faint praise. The piquancy was lost on no one. Here was a man who had done it yet again, with feeling. Done it in his special way, offering for sale every yearling he had bred, then racing in his own colours what others would not buy. This had been the case with *Regal Embrace*, a colt that could have purchased by any buyer at the 1976 yearling sales for $15,000. There were no takers. And he had won the Plate, beating the heavily favoured *Overskate*, Stafford Farms' muscular chestnut colt that twice would be named Canada's Horse of the Year.

For these reasons, plus the fact that it had been fourteen years since his previous Plate win with the great *Northern Dancer*, Taylor mused a bit on where this victory rated in his ten Plate wins since *Epic*, his first, in 1949. "After a long interval, it's a great pleasure. It's hard to win when you offer everything for sale, as we do. But of course I get pleasure, too, when a horse we've bred wins the Plate, and that's happened pretty often, you know." Eighteen times to be precise.

Regal Embrace had something in common with his sire, *Vice Regent*, and his grandsire, *Northern Dancer*: each one had failed to meet the reserve price Windfields Farm had placed on them when they were offered for sale as yearlings. However, in 1976, horsemen were aware that an occasional lemon would occur in the Windfields' consignment, and they backed away from the bay colt with the suspect ankles. Their judgment was supported when he was unraced as a two-year-old because of his size—he was too big and gangly—and his ailing ankles. *Regal Embrace* was listed in the Plate winterbook at odds of 150-to-1.

There were still many who doubted *Regal Embrace*'s quality on Plate day, despite his breeding (a half-brother to champion *Viceregal*) and his record of four wins in five starts. He had matured nicely under trainer Macdonald (Mac) Benson's care, but had never met the challenge of a colt of *Overskate*'s stature, and had no previous experience in a stakes race. But he did have jockey

A FITTING AND REGAL FAREWELL FOR EDWARD PLUNKET TAYLOR AND WINNIE.

Sandy Hawley on his back, and in the end this would be the determining factor in a race that he would tie *Victoria Park*'s 1960 Plate track record of 2:02. Sandy Hawley would win his fourth Plate, tying Avelino Gomez's record, and would, on this occasion, outride Robin Platts.

Hawley, who had hustled his mount to the front of the field at the clubhouse turn, kept the lead throughout the race, and held off *Overskate*'s desperate, but poorly timed charge. A neck separated the two horses at the wire. Platts may have been guilty of underestimating *Regal Embrace*'s ability to run as fast, and as far, as he managed that afternoon. "Early, when I saw them rolling, I tried to keep my horse off the pace. I thought I was being set up perfectly. Then I saw that Sandy's horse was running so easily, so I thought I'd better get moving," Platts said to explain the loss. He could not understand why his colt had failed to catch the winner.

The forty-eight-year-old Benson, a native of Wilmington, Delaware, who had just taken over the job as Windfields' exclusive

Sandy Hawley has *Regal Embrace* in a neck decision over the heavily favoured *Overskate*.

REGAL EMBRACE | 3-year-old bay colt

Regal Embrace (1975)	Vice Regent	Northern Dancer	Nearctic
			Natalma
		Victoria Regina	*Menetrier
			Victoriana
	Close Embrace	*Nentego	Never Say Die
			Tideless
		Hold Me Close	Native Dancer
			*Sticky Case

Owner: Windfields Farm, Oshawa, Ont.; *Trainer:* Macdonald (Mac) Benson
Jockey: Sandy Hawley; *Breeder:* E.P. Taylor, Toronto

Ontario trainer, was delighted with the unexpected triumph. "What can you say? Your first year here and you win the Plate."

"It was a combination of things that beat us," trainer Gil Rowntree observed several years later. "*Overskate* was the best horse I ever trained, a genuine racehorse; sound, and like a machine. He won something like $800,000. But on that day it was a great ride by Hawley; a mistake, or whatever you want to call it, by Platts; and racing luck. The best horse doesn't always have to win. That was the only time that horse [*Regal Embrace*] ever beat him. The Plate is one race, one day. It's like the Kentucky Derby. *Native Dancer* lost one race, the Derby."

While *Regal Embrace*'s ailing ankles would force him into an early retirement and stud, *Overskate* would roll to eighteen stakes victories in New York, Chicago, Ontario and Manitoba and a record nine Sovereign titles in the annual polls of Canada's leading horses and induction into the Canadian Horse Racing Hall of Fame. Ironically, when he was finally retired to stud at the age of six, *Overskate* was shipped to Tivoli Farms in New York, which was just around the corner from Blue Sky Farms and one of its studs, *Regal Embrace*.

Trainer Mac Benson.

1978 QUEEN'S PLATE STAKES

SEVENTH RACE
Woodbine
JUNE 24, 1978

1 1–4 MILES (2:01¹/₅). One Hundred and Nineteenth Running QUEEN'S PLATE STAKES. $100,000 Added. 3-year-olds. Foaled in Canada in 1975. By subscription of $35 each to accompany the nomination by December 15, 1976; second subscription of $100 by December 15, 1977; third subscription of $200 by May 1, 1978 and an additional $2,000 when making final entry. The owner of the first horse receives the guineas. The added money and all fees to be divided 65% to the winner, 20% to second, 10% to third, and 5% to fourth. Weight, 126 lbs.; fillies allowed 5 lbs. Final entries to be made through the entry box on a date and time to be determined by the racing secretary. A gold cup will be presented by the Club to the owner of the winner and mementos to the trainer and the rider of the winner. Nominations closed Wednesday, December 15, 1976, with 373 eligible. Value of race $164,755, value to winner $107,091; second, $32,951; third, $16,475; fourth, $8,238. Mutuel Pool, $481,029. Exactor Pool, $270,873.

Horse	Eqt	Wt.	PP	¼	½	¾	1	Str	Fin	Jockey	Owner	Odds $1
REGAL EMBRACE		126	8	2^{1}½	1^{hd}	1^{2}	1^{2}	1^{2}½	1^{nk}	HawleyS	WindfieldsFarm	2.55
OVERSKATE		126	3	5^{hd}	5^{2}	4^{2}	2^{1}	2^{3}	2^{7}½	PlattsR	StaffordFarm	1.45
L'ALEZANE		121	4	6½	7^{2}	6^{2}	5^{3}	3^{2}	3¾	SouterJP	LevesqueJL	12.75
COLOURFUL CONN		126	1	8½	6^{hd}	5^{hd}	6^{2}½	7^{2}½	4^{hd}	DittfachH	WillowDownsFarm	123.45
PREACHER JOE	b	126	5	11	11	9^{3}	7^{2}	6½	5^{hd}	DuffyL	PattersonMrsB	64.00
LUCKY COLONEL S.	b	126	11	1^{hd}	2^{2}	2^{hd}	4½	4^{2}	6^{3}¼	GrubbR	SmytheC	a-6.25
HIGH ROLLER		126	7	4^{2}	4^{2}½	3½	3½	5^{2}	7½	GomezA	IndigJ&KennedyRA	7.30
PLEASURE BENT	b	126	9	10½	8^{1}½	8^{hd}	8½	8^{4}	8^{1}¼	ToroF	Harl'q'n-V'nWiel'g'n-B'h'n	5.75
MAPLE GROVE	b	126	10	7^{2}	9^{2}	11	11	9^{1}½	9^{5}	WalfordJ	E&FRacingStable	72.80
PORTAGE BAY		126	6	9^{hd}	10½	10½	10^{3}	10^{1}	10^{1}½	KellyJ	HollandJV	132.55
FORTY BYE TWO		126	2	3^{hd}	3^{hd}	7^{2}	9^{2}½	11	11	BeckonD	SmytheC	a-6.25

a–Coupled, Lucky Colonel S. and Forty Bye Two.

OFF AT 4:45. Start good for all but PLEASURE BENT. Won ridden out. Time, :23, :46, 1:10⁴/₅, 1:37, 2:02. Track fast.

$2 Mutuel Prices:

8–REGAL EMBRACE	7.10	3.30	2.80
3–OVERSKATE		2.90	2.50
4–L'ALEZANE			4.20

$2 EXACTOR 8–3 PAID $17.80,

B. c, by Vice Regent—Close Embrace, by *Nentego. Trainer, Benson MacDonald (Mac). Bred by Taylor E. P.

REGAL EMBRACE moved quickly from the outset to duel into the first turn on the inside, had command into the backstretch when pressed, edged away with a clear lead into the far turn, retained a good margin into the home lane, was under intermittent urging thereafter and bested OVERSKATE. The latter advanced midway of the backstretch between foes, saved ground around the turn, was in behind REGAL EMBRACE into the home lane and closed gamely thereafter to just fail on the outside. L'ALEZANE advanced around the final turn when widest and finished willingly to best the balance. COLOURFUL CONN finished widest to edge PREACHER JOE, who was never dangerous. LUCKY COLONEL S. engaged the winner on the outside, stayed within striking distance to the final turn then weakened along the rail. HIGH ROLLER was well placed early on the outside but lacked a closing response. PLEASURE BENT lunged at the start and showed nothing thereafter. FORTY BYE TWO saved ground early in contention then dropped back.

I f John Tammaro had been the owner of *Steady Growth* he would have scratched the colt out of the 120th running of the Queen's Plate. But Tammaro was only the trainer of the prodigious chestnut colt who splashed effortlessly through the mud at Woodbine to win the fifty guineas and a major share of the $163,910 purse. Furious and disgusted at the condition of a racetrack that was deep, sloppy and covered with a layer of water, Tammaro earlier that day had suggested to D.G. (Bud) Willmot, owner of Kinghaven Farms, that the colt should not run.

Willmot listened to Tammaro's deep concern of the situation, but quickly vetoed the suggestion. "He [Willmot] said the Queen Mother is here and we run under any circumstances. I really didn't have a choice. He wouldn't let me put in a scratch. But if he'd been my horse . . ." said the portly ex-jockey from Baltimore, Maryland.

Tammaro accepted his employer's decision. However, even after the colt's two-and-one-half length victory over the odds-on favourite, *Bold Agent*, he was still decidedly critical of Woodbine's ground crew for allowing the

BRIAN SWATUK SALUTES FANS ABOARD D.G. (BUD) WILLMOT'S *STEADY GROWTH*.

surface to become so muddy after the heavy rains the day before and on the morning of the race. He had complained at length to racing secretary Lou Cavalaris, threatening to scratch the horse, and stating that in his opinion the crew "didn't do the best they could do." He said that the surface would have been far better if they had squeezed the water from it.

"It wasn't that he didn't have respect for the Plate or how much it meant to the Willmots after all the years they had waited to have a good horse in the race. Dad was thinking about the horse, that's all," recalled Cathy Tammaro, the daughter and an assistant to the trainer. "A lot of people forget that when he came back after the race his feet were really stinging, and we had to take all four shoes off and let him walk on the grass for a couple of days. We wanted to rest his feet longer, but he was so wound up and eager to run, that we had to put his shoes back on and get him back to the track." Tammaro had boldly predicted that the angry colt with the manners of a bully would beat *Bold Agent*, the heavily touted colt of Windfields Farm. "This [*Steady Growth*] is the best three-year-old colt in Canada," he would proclaim. Afterwards, he would quietly remind people of these statements: "Like I said before the race, the other horse isn't in the same league as our horse. I wasn't concerned with him [*Steady Growth*], or how well he'd run in the mud. I knew he could handle it. It was the chance of an injury on a bad track which concerned me. Look back and see how many times a horse gets injured on a bad track. The odds are 15-to-1 that it happened on a muddy instead of a fast track. Why gamble for a $100,000 purse

THE QUEEN MOTHER GREETS JOCKEY BRIAN SWATUK.

TRAINER JOHN TAMMARO AND HIS DAUGHTER, CATHY, EMBRACE AFTERWARDS.

STEADY GROWTH | 3-year-old chestnut colt

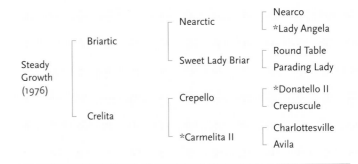

Steady Growth (1976)	Briartic	Nearctic	Nearco
			*Lady Angela
		Sweet Lady Briar	Round Table
			Parading Lady
	Crelita	Crepello	*Donatello II
			Crepuscule
		*Carmelita II	Charlottesville
			Avila

Owner: Kinghaven Farm (D.G. "Bud" Wilmot), King, Ont.
Trainer: John Tammaro; *Jockey:* Brian Swatuk; *Breeder:* Kinghaven Farm

with a million dollar animal? But the man said that we would run, and we did."

A towering colt who it seemed was all legs and no body when he first came to the racetrack, *Steady Growth* gave the sixty-two-year-old industrialist, his trainer and jockey Brian Swatuk their first taste of a Plate victory. It was an emotional but ecstatic Willmot family that gathered in the winner's circle to receive a gold cup and a $4,500 bank draft drawn against the royal household account of Her Majesty, the Queen Mother, and later a cheque for $106,510.

For Willmot, a member of the Ontario Jockey Club's board of trustees, the chairman of Molson Companies Limited and a man of power mentioned no fewer than twelve times in volume one alone of Peter Newman's *The Canadian Establishment*, the victory crowned twelve years of concentrated effort and finances to establish himself in the thoroughbred racing industry. No man had spent as many millions during this period as he did and receive so little in return. "Twelve years we've waited for this day," said his son David, who was deeply involved in the operations of the farm's racing and breeding operations in the fashionable horse country of King, north of Toronto. "I remember the day three years ago when I was on the way to the track one morning about six o'clock and Ian [Black], our farm manager, called me into the foaling barn. He said 'come on in here, I've just foaled the biggest horse I've ever seen.' It was. There was this big gangly colt."

He would grow to almost 1,200 pounds. "He was so tall that he had to duck his head when he walked under the overhang of our barn here [at the track]," remembers Cathy Tammaro. He also developed a habit of crowding his groom against the wall in his stall. On Plate week he was in a particularly incorrigible mood, biting two of his handlers, one on the shoulder and the other on the stomach.

Steady Growth's Plate trip went just about the way Tammaro and the twenty-nine-year-old Swatuk had figured it would. They had diagrammed a "game plan" a few days earlier—drop in around the first turn and go back out on the backside. They figured that the speed horses, *Bold Agent, Bridle Path* and *Coup de Chance*, would cut out the early fractions, before they made their move. Everything worked to perfection largely because Sandy Hawley, who was on *Bold Agent*, could not escape the rail. He got pinned in early, and Swatuk kept him there. Afterwards Hawley praised the horse that had beaten him out of a possible fifth Plate victory. "He ran a big race in the mud and we didn't. I think the track conditions hurt us. If we'd had a fast track I think it might have been different. But we both had to run over a bad track."

Before retiring later that year with a hind leg injury, *Steady Growth* would travel to Chicago and win the $100,000-added Arlington Classic.

1979 QUEEN'S PLATE STAKES

SEVENTH RACE
Woodbine
JUNE 30, 1979

1 1-4 MILES (2:01 1/5). One Hundred and Twentieth Running QUEEN'S PLATE STAKES. $100,000 Added For 3-year-olds, foaled in Canada in 1976. By subscription of $35 each to accompany the nomination by December 15, 1977 (366 nominated); second subscription of $100 by December 15, 1978 (161 remained eligible); third subscription of $200 by May 1, 1979 (85 remained eligible), and an additional $2,000 when making final entry. The owner of the first horse receives the Guineas. The added money and all fees to be divided 65% to the winner, 20% to second, 10% to third and 5% to fourth. Weight, 126 lbs. Fillies allowed 5 lbs. Final entries to be made through the entry box on a date and time to be determined by the racing secretary. A gold cup will be presented by the Club to the owner of the winner, and mementos to the trainer and the rider of the winner. Value of race $163,910, value to winner $106,542; second $32,782; third $16,391, fourth $8,195. Mutuel Pool $444,096. Exactor Pool $303,091.

Horse	Eqt	Wt.	PP	¼	½	¾	1	Str	Fin	Jockey	Owner	Odds $1
STEADY GROWTH		126	7	5^{4}	5^{3}	4^{3}	1^{1}	1^{2}	$1^{2\frac{1}{2}}$	SwatukB	KinghavenFarm	1.65
BOLD REGENT	b	126	3	4^{2}	$4^{4\frac{1}{2}}$	2^{hd}	$2^{2\frac{1}{2}}$	$2^{3\frac{1}{2}}$	2^{2}	HawleyS	WindfieldsFarm	a-.70
RAM GOOD	b	126	2	9	9	9	8^{10}	4^{5}	$3^{\frac{1}{2}}$	QuongMD	SmytheC	58.80
NONPARRELL	b	126	1	8^{6}	8^{9}	8^{12}	$4^{4\frac{1}{2}}$	3^{4}	4^{10}	BeckonD	AsadoorianS	42.35
LINDA'S LAUGHIN		126	4	6^{hd}	7^{5}	$6^{2\frac{1}{2}}$	5^{2}	5^{2}	$5^{5\frac{1}{2}}$	ToroF	RMCStable&ShefreyFm	18.85
BRIDLE PATH	b	126	9	$2^{4\frac{1}{2}}$	$2^{3\frac{1}{2}}$	$1^{1\frac{1}{2}}$	3^{1}	6^{6}	$6^{1\frac{1}{2}}$	PlattsR	WindfieldsFarm	a-70
GREAT STATE	b	126	5	7^{7}	6^{hd}	7^{hd}	7^{2}	7^{4}	$7^{7\frac{1}{2}}$	BelowusJ	StaffordFarm	21.80
COUP DE CHANCE		126	6	3^{hd}	3^{hd}	$3^{2\frac{1}{2}}$	6^{2}	8^{15}	8	SouterJP	LevesqueJL	15.45
BULL REGENT	b	126	8	1^{hd}	1^{hd}	5^{hd}	9	9	Eased	GomezA	PentlandCK	16.25

a-Coupled, Bold Agent and Bridle Path.

OFF AT 4:45. Start good. Won ridden out. Time, :22 2/5, :45 2/5, 1:11 3/5, 1:38 3/5, 2:06 3/5. Track sloppy.

$2 Mutuel Prices:				
	7-STEADY GROWTH	**5.30**	**2.30**	**2.70**
	1-BOLD REGENT (a-Entry)		**2.10**	**2.20**
	3-RAM GOOD			**4.90**

$2 EXACTOR 7-1 PAID $8.70,

Ch. c, by Briartic—Crelita, by Crepello. Trainer, Tammaro John. Bred by Kinghaven Farm, King, Ont.

STEADY GROWTH stalked the early pace into the clubhouse turn when saving ground, eased off the rail in the backstretch advancing, moved with a very quick rush on the outside around the far turn to take command when pressed, retained command into the home lane, opened up a clear lead at the furlong marker under intermittent urging and retained the advantage in the run for the wire. BOLD AGENT was well placed early, advanced along the rail into the far turn to challenge for the lead, pressed the winner around the final turn but failed to threaten in the stretch run.

The 121st running of the Queen's Plate produced a finish that would have inspired the wizardry in the late Avelino Gomez to reach into his bag of tricks and seize yet one more victory with some miraculous gesture. Ten of the eighteen starters approached the wire at Woodbine in a swirling mass of horseflesh, racing silks and flailing whips, but it was the little-known jockey from Placentia Bay, Newfoundland, Bill Parsons, who would act like Moses parting the sea of horses as he "stole" the Plate on long shot *Driving Home*. He would have made El Perfecto proud.

The race had been dedicated to the memory of Gomez, one of the world's most colourful and accomplished riders, dead from injuries suffered a week earlier in a three-horse spill on the track where four times he had won the historic Plate, and so many of his 4,200 victories. Parsons, jubilant in his moment of triumph, momentarily paid tribute to "Gomey" as he plucked two yellow blooms out of *Driving Home*'s floral wreath and tossed them high into the air. "Those are for Gomey," he whispered to Marg Magnusson, wife of the gelding's trainer, Glenn Magnusson, as they walked into the grassy winner's circle. Many in the crowd of 26,598 had observed the gesture and warmly applauded.

"We decided in the jocks' room that whoever won the race would do it. We'd like it to become a tradition," said the thirty-seven-year-old who had earned most of his paycheques on the smaller tracks of the "B" circuit. Riding with the confidence of Sandy Hawley or Ron Turcotte or the late Gomez, men that he admired while he struggled to ride "live mounts" during a mediocre career, Parsons had spotted his seventeen rivals a sizable lead on the muddy track before unleashing his winning charge in the final turn on the $2.95-to-$1 long shot.

A superbly bred son by *Roberto*, and out of a *Native Charger* mare, *Pagan Pagan, Driving Home* was hardly graceful as he bulled his way through and around the snarled traffic to arrive at the finish line at the precise moment, winning by more than a length over *Someolio Man* and *Allan Blue*, and seven other opponents, who suddenly seemed more interested in admiring the winner's dramatic dash up the stretch. *Driving Home* would never win an equine beauty contest, but he had again proved he was a determined runner over a distance of ground, and it was a surprise that the crowd had favoured five other horses and chose to ignore the dark bay gelding's impressive come-from-behind win two weeks earlier in the Plate Trial Stakes, a race that had provided Parsons with his first stakes victory in five years.

This Plate race would provide more than its normal quota of moments of elation and despair. The race was a triumph for the West. The gelding was trained by Magnusson, a former exercise rider from Wynward, Saskatchewan, who had been attempting to win the Plate since 1955, the year he won the Plate Trial with *Silver Spat* at the "old" Woodbine. The owner was Hal Yerxa, who operated a country-western radio station in Camrose, Alberta, and at one time was known as "Uncle Hal" on a children's program, earning six dollars a week. That was long before he scraped up enough money to establish a modest

DRIVING HOME (LEFT) BULLED HIS WAY THROUGH TRAFFIC FROM SEVENTEENTH PLACE TO WIN AT THE WIRE OVER *SOMELIO MAN* AND *ALLAN BLUE*, FAR RIGHT.

Owner Hal Yerxa receives Plate from Lieutenant Governor Pauline McGibbon. Mrs. Yerxa and trainer Glenn Magnusson look on.

DRIVING HOME | 3-year-old dark bay or brown gelding

Driving Home (1977)	Roberto	Hail to Reason	*Turn-to Nothirdchance
		Bramalea	Nashua Rarelea
	Pagan Pagan	Native Charger	Native Dancer Greek Blond
		Pagan Princess	*Toulouse Lautrec Polly

Owner: CFCW Racing Stable (Hal Yerxa), Camrose, Alberta
Trainer: Glenn Magnusson; *Jockey:* Bill Parsons
Breeder: Hill 'n' Dale Farm (John Sikura Sr.), Gormley, Ont.

stable, then later spend $60,000 in U.S. funds for a horse he had never seen. "I had hired a bloodstock agent, Patrick Lawley-Wakelin, to buy some horses for me in Kentucky in the summer of 1978. I didn't know too much about this business, and Patrick had been recommended to me. But I can remember getting a call from Patrick and him telling me, 'Hal, I've just bought you a *Roberto* colt and it's going to cost you about $70,000 in Canadian dough.' 'My God Patrick, what are we doing now?' I asked. Patrick told me this was a big strong animal and a Canadian to boot. He later had to be gelded, he was so big and he had a nasty temperament."

Yerxa had never attended a Plate race before, and was delighted to find out that the eastern folks at Woodbine were quite hospitable, presenting him a cheque for $119,554 (and fifty cents), the winner's share of a record Plate purse of $183,930, and a gold cup. "I was down here last year when my filly [*Country Romance*] finished third in the Oaks, but it always seemed I had something else to do when the Plate came up, so I would watch it on TV." Attired in the quite proper morning suit, which he had rented in Edmonton, Yerxa related the circumstances he had encountered while leasing duds quite unlike the blue jeans, western boots and Stetson he normally wears. "They weren't going to rent me the suit unless I

Bill Parsons plucked a bloom, tossing it into the air, dedicating his Plate win to Avelino Gomez, who died a week earlier in the Canadian Oaks.

consented to bet the horse for them. Right now I would say there are about thirty tailors counting their money. They gave me an envelope with $250 in it. Thank goodness I remembered to put up the bet."

Mister Country, the other half of Yerxa's entry, finished seventh. He was among the tightly bunched ruck that included the heavy favourite, Norcliffe Stable's *Duns Scotus,* who would never race again. Purchased for $300,000 as a yearling by Charles Baker, the colt was a son of *Buckpasser* and was out of *Alma North,* a daughter of *Northern Dancer.* The sleek, dark bay colt suddenly faltered with a furlong to go. Jockey Robin Platts had the colt in a perfect position to make a winning move, fourth and three lengths off the lead, when he "took a couple of funny steps, and I thought 'Oh, oh.'" Running with a fractured knee, *Duns Scotus* gamely finished tenth on three legs.

1980 QUEEN'S PLATE STAKES

EIGHTH RACE
Woodbine
JUNE 28, 1980

1¼ MILES. (2.01⅕) One Hundred and Twenty-First Running QUEEN'S PLATE STAKES. $100,000 added 3-year-olds, foaled in Canada in 1977. By subscription of $35 each to accompany the nomination by December 15, 1978 (378 nominated); second subscription of $100 by December 15, 1979 (177 remained eligible); third subscription of $200 by May 1, 1980 (85 remained eligible), and an additional $2,000 when making final entry. The added money and all fees to be divided 65% to the winner, 20% to second, 10% to third and 5% to fourth. Weights, 126 lbs. Fillies allowed 5 lbs. Value of race $183,930, value to winner $119,555, second $36,786, third $18,393, fourth $9,196. Mutuel Pool $719,388.

Horse	Eqt	Wt.	PP	¼	½	¾	1	Str	Fin	Jockey	Owner	Odds $1
DRIVING HOME	b	126	16	17hd	172	173	122	7½	11½	ParsonsW	CFCWRacingStable	b-20.95
SOMEOLIO MAN		126	5	13hd	121	12hd	11½	82	2no	DifffachH	TerdikJ	24.30
ALLAN BLUE		126	2	102	10½	8hd	6¹½	3½	3½	BelowusJ	StaffordFarm	3.20
DUSTY OLD FARMER	b	126	6	163	155	6hd	7hd	51	4½	BeckonD	PaddockhurstStable	a-57.10
BEJILLA		126	9	3hd	32	32	1½	11	52	LeBlancJB	PaddockhurstStable	a-57.10
DECENT DAVEY	b	126	13	8hd	91	92	51	6½	6nk	SwatukB	FosterDJ	10.20
MISTER COUNTRY	b	126	11	144	13½	7hd	82	92	7nk	HansenR	CFCWRacing Stable	b-20.95
HASTY RICK		126	3	1½	11½	11½	23½	21	8nk	SouterJP	RMCSta&ShefryFm	f-55.50
ARCTIC MORNING		126	8	154	164	16hd	132	108	9hd	HoSangG	Sam-SonFarm	81.20
DUNS SCOTUS	b	126	12	5½	4½	4hd	3½	4½	105½	PlattsR	NorcliffeStable	1.30
BYE BYE TONY		126	10	92	6hd	112	103	114	112	DuffyL	SmytheC	27.50
HAWAIIAN FIGHTER		126	17	7hd	7½	52	41	12hd	122	VasquezJ	BKYStable	21.70
LORD COSTUME	b	126	15	62	8½	131	143	134	13½	McMahonWG	IppolitoJ	f-55.50
PAR EXCELLANCE		121	1	12hd	142	153	151½	14hd	143	StahlbaumG	BigBoy-KnightsbridgeSta	6.20
CORVETTE CHRIS		126	14	11hd	11hd	10½	163	163	151½	ClarkD	SeedhouseEB	14.60
PONTILLION		126	7	22½	21½	21	91	17	16no	VanKeurenM	RodeV	65.70
THORNY QUESTION		126	4	18	18	18	172	15hd	17	StandringJS	SutherlandMrsM	f-55.50
KINSMANS GLORY		126	18	42	51	14hd	18	Eased		CruguetJ	SoboIJ&S	56.40

a–Coupled, Dusty Old Farmer and Bejilla; b–Driving Home and Mister Country. f–Mutuel field.

OFF AT 4:53. Start good. Won driving. Time, :23, :46⅗, 1:12, 1:38, 2:04⅕. Track muddy.

$2 Mutuel Prices:

2–DRIVING HOME (b-Entry)	43.90	17.30	11.20
5–SOMEOLIO MAN		20.60	10.40
4–ALLAN BLUE			4.40

Dk. b. or br. g, by Roberto—Pagan Pagan, by Native Charger. Trainer Glenn Magnusson. Bred by Hill 'n' Dale Farm, Gormley, Ont.

DRIVING HOME was far back around the clubhouse turn, was still well back into the far turn, moved between foes midway of the turn, stayed outrun into the home lane, came widest gaining strongly in midstretch, then, responding to very brisk urging, drew clear in the latter stages. SOMEOLIO MAN was outrun early, advanced between foes midway of the far turn, moved strongly approaching the furlong marker in the middle, then, when roused for the drive, edged ALLAN BLUE. ALLAN BLUE lodged his bid midway of the far turn on the outside, came between horses a strong contender a furlong out, duelled in midstretch, had command between calls in deep stretch but failed to hold the top pair.

James Charles Bentley was in his eightieth year, still active and doing what he enjoyed most in life, fibbing a little while supervising the training of *Fiddle Dancer Boy*. This was the colt that had just captured the most hotly contested Queen's Plate in its 122-year history. It was so humid that July afternoon that twenty-five people were treated for heat prostration at Woodbine's medical centre. The finish was tight, six horses straining to get their noses on the wire first, and it was left to the photo-finish camera to decide the names of which owner and horse would be painted on the imposing oak scroll of Plate winners.

The distance between Bentley's colt with the aching foot, and *Le Grand Seigneur*, who finished sixth, was less than that at a supermarket checkout counter on a Friday night. In between was *Frost King*, the best horse in the race, champion every year he raced until he finally broke down. He finished third behind *Wayover*, who was accused of interfering him in the far turn. Racing history, however, abounds with good horses who have failed on a particular day because of injuries or racing luck: *Man o' War*, *Native Dancer*, *Nashua*, *Forego*, *Kelso* and Canadian-breds *Northern Dancer*, *Sunny's Halo*, *Overskate* and *Cool Reception*.

Tall and slimmer than a leprechaun, Bentley had a charming way of paraphrasing a situation, whether he was the beneficiary or the victim. "I remember something Joe Estes wrote years ago in *The Blood-Horse*. He really knew pedigrees, but he also understood harseracing [*sic*]. 'It doesn't matter if you win by an inch, or by three inches, a length, or by five lengths. The margin of victory isn't important. Only victory is important.'" Get home in front, that's what counted. Win by a wide edge, or a wide lip. A week, a month, a year later, it would not matter how Jim Bentley's horse had won. It only mattered that on the day when the whole country and Queen Elizabeth, the Queen Mother, were watching, Bentley's colt, the one for which owner Jack Carmichael paid the training bills, was first by the width of a cigar butt.

Bentley's eyes twinkled when he told a story, especially if the listener was gullible. "Why that Bentley can't tell when he's tellin' you the truth, or pullin' your leg, I swear," Carl Chapman, another trainer of Irish descent said after listening to the Irishman's blarney. "Jus' listen to him! He should be ashamed telling some of those Black-Irish fibs of his." Bentley, who rarely ever appeared for work in anything but a white shirt, tie, tweed jacket and grey flannels, would wear an overcoat on rainy days as he rode his pony to the training track. He was the son of a County

THE QUEEN MOTHER EXTENDS A GRACIOUS HAND TO OUTRIDER GORDON MOSES IN WALKING RING. AT LEFT, OJC CHAIRMAN CHARLES BAKER.

A SIX-HORSE PHOTO FINISH WON BY *FIDDLE DANCER BOY*'S NOSE.

Limerick farmer who used to run a string of steeplechasers. "He had about twenty-seven, and they didn't run very well. Like a lot of owners I've met since, he used to blame the riders, so I became his jockey."

In the early 1920s Bentley ventured to America and eventually wound up working for Colonel E.R. Bradley's Idle Hour Farm in Kentucky. "One summer we're at Saratoga [Springs] and I met John Nixon, a big, old gruff trainer from Canada. He talked me into coming to Toronto with a trainload of horses. He said the sidewalks were paved with gold and I've been digging for it ever since." In subsequent years Bentley had trained a barnful of stakes winners: *Arise*, winner of the Travers Stakes at Saratoga Springs; champion filly *Lauries Dancer*; and 1971 Plate winner *Kennedy Road*. In 1981 there was considerable doubt whether the cagey veteran had any tricks left in preparing one more horse for the Plate. He managed, but only because of the skill of blacksmith Frank Huarte.

A grandson of *Northern Dancer*, and out of a mare who

was a half-sister to *Skinny Minny*, dam of Plate winner *Jumpin Joseph*, *Fiddle Dancer Boy* had always showed a willingness to perform, even when he was ailing. Having to continually face future Hall of Fame inductee *Frost King*, champion at the ages of two, three and four, did not help either. The colt's gravest crisis came after his second-place finish in the Marine Stakes, when it was noticed that his right forefoot had been pierced by a sharp object, possibly a nail, and had become infected under the wall of the hoof. Bentley despaired of being able to get him ready for the Plate after a part of the hoof was cut away and patched by Huarte. "He didn't miss any training as I didn't take pity on him. I had him galloped two miles every day, and when he'd come back he was lame on it and there'd be a pool of blood. But he ran well in the Plate Trial."

On 4 July *Fiddle Dancer Boy* ran with a bar shoe on the foot and a patch secured by nine nails and taped with what is known as "vet rap." David Clark, who was up, made his winning move when he circled the dense traffic in the far turn, hitting the wire an inch in front of *Wayover*, the horse that had been disqualified for interfering with his colt in the Plate Trial. In this race it was *Frost King* who received the bump. *Frost King*'s rider, Lloyd Duffy, told the stewards that *Wayover*'s nudge had knocked his horse off stride. "He spit out bit . . . it knocked the legs out from under him. I would say it cost us the race." When the stewards looked at the film, they did not detect any signs of wrongdoing by *Wayover* and his jockey, Larry Attard, and the order of finish stood. "In a race like this, I guess you almost have to knock a horse down to get a foul called. It's nice to ride the 3-to-5 favourite and everything, but if you don't win, you can't sit in the corner and cry," Duffy lamented afterwards.

The affable Bentley was charming as he chatted with the Queen Mother in the winner's enclosure. He told her that he thought *Fiddle Dancer Boy* was her type of horse—a steeplechase type. "She told me after the race that she had been admiring the horse in the paddock, and agreed with me." Bentley was not too sure why he rated this Plate win as a greater thrill than that of *Kennedy Road*. "Not too sure I've got many more in me," he said with a twinkle in his eyes.

Lyin' Jim, who was inducted into Canada's horse racing Hall of Fame in 1982 and named Man of the Year by his peers, died in 1984. *Fiddle Dancer Boy*, the $20,000 yearling that Jack Carmichael had purchased from the estate of his father, Harry Carmichael, a long-time director of the Ontario Jockey Club and an owner who had been unsuccessful in his attempts to capture the Plate, would forever be hampered by the damaged foot, despite compiling career earnings of $364,773.

FIDDLE DANCER BOY | 3-year-old bay colt

Fiddle Dancer Boy (1978)	Nice Dancer	Northern Dancer	Nearctic
			Natalma
		Nice Princess	*Le Beau Prince
			*Happy Night II
	Fiddly Dee	Hidden Treasure	Dark Star
			Ratine
		Stormy Cruise	Third Degree
			Pinnace

Owner: J.B.W. (Jack) Carmichael, Toronto; *Trainer:* James C. Bentley
Jockey: David Clark; *Breeder:* William Beasley Enterprises Ltd., Toronto

Jack Carmichael accompanies *Fiddle Dancer Boy* and David Clark.

1981 QUEEN'S PLATE STAKES

EIGHTH RACE
Woodbine
JULY 4, 1981

1 1-4 MILES (2:01 1/5). One Hundred and Twenty-Second Running QUEEN'S PLATE STAKES (Gr.IC). $100,000 Added. 3-year-olds. Foaled in Canada in 1978. Scale weights: Colts and Geldings, 126 lbs.; Fillies, 121 lbs. By subscription of $35 each which shall accompany the nomination by December 15, 1979 (375 nominated); second subscription of $100 by December 31, 1980 (177 remained eligible); third subscription of $200 by May 1, 1981 (106 remained eligible); and an additional $2,000 when making final entry two days prior to the race. The owner of the first horse receives the Guineas. The added money and all fees to be divided 65% to the winner, 20% to second, 10% to third, and 5% to fourth. Final entries to be made through the entry box on a date and a time to be determined by the racing secretary. Value of race $184,025, value to winner $119,616; second, $36,805; third, $18,403; fourth, $9,201. Mutuel Pool, $695,956.

Horse	Eqt	Wt.	PP	¼	½	¾	1	Str	Fin	Jockey	Owner	Odds $1
FIDDLE DANCER BOY		126	11	7^{hd}	$8^{1\frac{1}{2}}$	6^{hd}	5^{1}	3^{hd}	1no	ClarkD	CarmichaelJBW	8.45
WAYOVER	b	126	5	6½	5^{2}	5^{2}	$1^{1\frac{1}{2}}$	$1^{1\frac{1}{2}}$	2½	AttardL	CarnwithJ&H	14.35
FROST KING		126	6	4^{1}	4^{1}	4^{1}	2½	2½	3½	DuffyL	MarkoW&SmithT	a-.70
AL SARAB	b	126	1	11^{2}	7^{2}	8^{2}	4^{1}	4^{1}	$4^{1\frac{1}{4}}$	PlattsR	BKYStable	23.05
REGAL STAFFORD	b	126	4	10^{hd}	10½	11^{2}	9½	6^{2}	5no	DittfachH	EatonHallFarm	30.65
LE GRAND SEIGNEUR	b	126	9	9^{hd}	9^{1}	9^{2}	6^{1}	5^{2}	$6^{2\frac{1}{2}}$	BeckonD	LevesqueJL	b-7.65
SOLAR COMMAND		121	12	5½	6½	7^{hd}	8^{hd}	7½	7½	LeBlancJB	SherwoodP	37.95
MORE SPIRIT		126	3	14^{2}	14^{1}	12^{1}	12^{2}	$9^{1\frac{1}{2}}$	8^{nk}	GrubbR	McCollJB	4.40
LE BOTANISTE	b	126	13	8^{2}	11^{3}	$10^{1\frac{1}{2}}$	$10^{1\frac{1}{2}}$	8^{hd}	9^{1}	PennaD	LevesqueJL	b-7.65
REGIMEN		126	10	3^{hd}	2½	$1^{1\frac{1}{2}}$	3½	10½	10^{nk}	HoSangG	RauschBarbara	63.20
MR. ACHIEVER	b	126	7	$15^{1\frac{1}{2}}$	$15^{1\frac{1}{2}}$	15^{7}	11^{2}	$11^{1\frac{1}{2}}$	$11^{1\frac{1}{4}}$	BellJJ	SmithT	a-.70
MISTY MOGUL		126	15	12	13^{2}	13½	13^{1}	12^{2}	$12^{1\frac{1}{2}}$	BelowusJ	JimDandyStable	78.25
YOURS TO COMMAND	b	126	2	13^{2}	12½	14^{1}	15^{5}	13^{4}	$13^{2\frac{1}{2}}$	McMahonWG	GardinerFarmLtd	107.95
REGENT CAT		126	16	2½	3^{3}	3½	7^{1}	14½	14½	QuongMD	StieglanL	143.00
REGAL KAPERS		126	8	16	16	16	16	15½	15½	SwatukB	WillowDownsFarm	56.85
LE PROMENEUR	b	126	14	1^{hd}	1^{hd}	2^{1}	14^{hd}	16	16	SouterJP	LevesqueJL	b-7.65

a-Coupled, Frost King and Mr. Achiever; b-Le Grand Seigneur, Le Botaniste and Le Promeneur.

OFF AT 4:47. Start good for all but REGAL KAPERS. Won ridden out. Time, :24 2/5, :47, 1:11 2/5, 1:37 2/5, 2:04 4/5. Track fast.

$2 Mutuel Prices:			
10-FIDDLE DANCER BOY	18.90	7.50	4.10
7-WAYOVER		10.30	4.90
1-FROST KING (a-Entry)			2.70

B. c, by Nice Dancer—Fiddly Dee, by Hidden Treasure. Trainer, Bentley Jim. Bred by Beasley Wm Enterprises Ltd, Toronto.

FIDDLE DANCER BOY was in contention in the opening quarter, was outrun midway of the backstretch, advanced when widest into the far turn, circled foes around the final turn, stayed slightly wide in midstretch gaining, then responding to intermittent handling, got up in time. WAYOVER stalked the early pace in contention, lodged a bid on the outside to challenge strongly around the far turn, had command midway of the turn, opened up a clear lead in early stretch and just failed to last. FROST KING was well placed early, moved to challenge into the far turn, pressed the issue along the rail in the stretch and finished gamely. The rider on FROST KING claimed foul against WAYOVER for interference around the far turn which was disallowed.

Attrition would decide the 123rd running of the Queen's Plate, the first to be held on a Sunday. The favourite was a big, virile colt named *Le Danseur*. Bred by E.P. Taylor and owned by Jean-Louis Lévesque, *Le Danseur* was a bay, with a body of rich brown, and a mane, tail and stockings of black, as if his first coat had been touched up with a tar brush. He was the 1-to-4 favourite because of his past performances, earning $260,000—more than any of the other seventeen starters, and because he was a *survivor*.

By 15 December 1980, a total of 364 horses had been nominated at a cost of thirty-five dollars, but one by one they had fallen by the wayside, either victims of untoward injury, or simply because they could not live up to their promise. The swiftest of the crop had been *Deputy Minister*, a colt of great potential. He had swept two-year-old honours for the continent and, had he stayed sound, would have been the overwhelming favourite for the Plate. *Deputy Minister* went on to become one of the leading sires in North America in the 1990s. *Le Danseur* rolled on. Through most of the spring, he waged practically a two-horse campaign against *Brave Regent*, a dark brown colt of mighty Windfields Farm. The two colts had divided Canada's richest races for two-year-olds, *Le Danseur* winning the Coronation Futurity, and *Brave Regent* the Cup and Saucer Stakes. They had met twice in stakes races in May, and each time *Brave Regent* had withstood determined stretch drives by *Le Danseur*. Then, in mid-June, just two weeks before the Plate, *Le Danseur* demolished his rival in the Plate Trial Stakes, sweeping by him at the turn into the stretch and leaving *Brave Regent* to limp off to the stud farm.

The only contenders still healthy were *Briar Wind*, *Exclusive Canadian*, and *Son of Briartic*, good colts, but not the calibre of *Lord Durham*'s son out of *Dancing Angela*. There was also a colt in the field to which handicappers paid too little attention—*Runaway Groom*, a grey by the French sire, **Blushing Groom;* he had been bred by Gardiner Farms of Caledon, Ontario, but had then been sold as a yearling in Kentucky for $39,000 to Albert C. Coppola of McLean, Virginia. *Runaway Groom* was bred to run a distance, but was hardly a threat; he had never raced further than seven furlongs in his four previous starts, all in Kentucky. Besides, only one grey had ever won the Plate—*Acara* in 1944.

However, inconsistency is the only consistent factor a horseman should swear by, and it was common knowledge that *Le Danseur* had his problems: a bowed tendon had made him vulnerable. All winter, trainer Jacques Dumas had watched in dismay as the foreleg assumed the arclike shape that gave the injury its name. A knot had appeared on the flexor tendon of the colt's right foreleg and it was a constant threat to his racing future. Tendons are both a weight-bearing and a shock-absorbing part of the galloping mechanism, and in both those functions they bear enormous strain. The rupture in the tendon had almost healed, but inflammation in the sheath around it was still generating fluid. By spring, the bow had distended the pastern until even the untrained eye could detect its awkwardness. To veteran horsemen, *Le Danseur* seemed to be running on the thin edge of luck—a frail machine awaiting the one extra moment of

PAUL SOUTER AND OWNER DAVE KAPCHINSKY ARE ALL SMILES WITH PLATE WINNER *SON OF BRIARTIC*.

force that would explode one of its most delicate parts.

David Kapchinsky, a burly forty-nine-year-old from Edmonton, whose wealth had come from Kap Transport during the opening of oil exploration in Alberta, and later real estate development, had his own problems at the time. In 1979 one of the major investments in thoroughbreds had been a colt out of *Dancing Angela*, and he had done so well with him that at the sales the following year he wanted to buy his half-brother by *Lord Durham*. But his trainer, Jerry Lavigne, had said it was bad policy to buy offspring of the same mare two years in a row. Now Kapchinsky wished he had stuck by his guns. *Son of Briartic*, for which Lavigne advised him to pay $105,000, turned out to be a sound investment, winning six races and $170,620 as a two-year-old. But he kept running into the *Lord Durham* colt "Kap" had wanted to buy, losing twice to *Le Danseur* that year and again in stakes races the following spring.

On 29 May *Son of Briartic* won his first race of the year, on Woodbine's turf course, beating good horses in the Toronto Cup, a race for which his nemesis had not been entered. Two weeks later, Lavigne procrastinated about entering him for the Plate Trial, walking around all morning with the entry form in his pocket. He was not anxious to enter unless the race was split into two divisions, and it was not certain that it would be. When the entries closed and the race was split, Lavigne was left holding the entry. The next two weeks would prove nerve-wracking for Kapchinsky, who had learned never to question Lavigne's confusing moves. The trainer had once told him, "If you've got the money, I've got the experience." Now Kapchinsky liked to say, "Lavigne has the money, and I've got the experience."

A remote man who thrived on subterfuge, Lavigne had not earned the title, "*The Weasel,*" for nothing. He had another race in mind for the colt—a mile-and-a-furlong allowance event a week before the Plate. Murphy's Law—"if something can go wrong, it will"—was invoked when the colt popped a splint in his foreleg; he was scratched after failing to pass the veterinarian's test that day. (A splint is a bony growth that develops between the cannon bone, which is like the shin bone, and the pencil-like splint bones that go down the sides of the leg.) A nitrogen freeze treatment enabled Lavigne to "gallop" the colt into the Plate—he put two swift workouts into him over muddy tracks on Tuesday and Wednesday. Critics thought *Son of Briartic* was a "short horse," lacking the stamina to travel the Plate distance. Because he had been on the vet's list of disabled horses, Lavigne could not enter him in a race for five days—Friday at the earliest. When the Plate is run on a Saturday, entries are traditionally made on a Thursday. But the 1982 race had been scheduled for a Sunday, and entries were filed on the previous Friday, the day *Son of Briartic* became eligible. "I used the same entry form for the Plate that I'd filled out for the Plate Trial," Lavigne said with a sly grin. "I used it for luck."

Lavigne, who had won the Plate with *Almoner* in 1970, and jockey John-Paul Souter got the only break they needed when *Arctic Regent*, a speed horse, was scratched. The strategy changed: "Go to the front and improve your position," were Lavigne's instructions. "He exploded, like a good horse," Souter said. "I couldn't believe it; he'd been off for a month. I was just sittin' on him, goin' down the backstretch movin' easy while everybody else was riding." *Runaway Groom*, the 38-to-1 longshot, made one menacing move and finished second. "That's when I started whalin' away." While *Son of Briartic* motored, the others struggled. Third was *Le Danseur*; his bowed tendon had doubled in size and he was retired to stud.

Dave Kapchinsky shows off newly created Aynsley English fine bone china Queen's Plate trophy.

SON OF BRIARTIC | 3-year-old chestnut colt

Son of Briartic (1979)	Briartic	Nearctic	Nearco
			*Lady Angela
		Sweet Lady Briar	Round Table
			Parading Lady
	Tabola	Round Table	*Princequillo
			*Knight's Daughter
		Bambola	Botticelli
			*Mamounia

Owner: Paddockhurst Stable (Dave Kapchinsky), Edmonton, Alberta
Trainer: J.C. Lavigne; *Jockey:* John-Paul Souter; *Breeder:* E.P. Taylor, Toronto

This Plate was marred by a three-horse spill; as a result of which one of the eighteen starters failed to survive. *Transcendent*, who along with *Cliff House* and *Sea Chestnut*, fell in the far turn, died from an apparent heart attack. The culprit in the three-horse spill was *Icy Circle*, who finished fourth but was disqualified by the stewards.

Deemed a weak field, it did produce several top runners. *Runaway Groom* went on to win the Prince of Wales, the Breeders' Stakes and the illustrious Travers Stakes at Saratoga, defeating the winners of the three U.S. Triple Crown races—Kentucky Derby winner *Gato Del Sol*, Preakness champion *Aloma's Ruler* and *Conquistador Cielo*, winner of the Belmont Stakes. *Runaway Groom* was Canada's champion three-year-old and was inducted into the Canadian Horse Racing Hall of Fame in 2001.

1982 QUEEN'S PLATE STAKES

SEVENTH RACE
Woodbine
JUNE 27, 1982

1 1-4 MILES (2:01 1/5). One Hundred and Twenty-Third Running QUEEN'S PLATE STAKES (Gr.IC). $150,000 Added and Fifty Guineas. 3-year-olds, foaled in Canada. Weights, 126 lbs. Fillies allowed 5 lbs. By subscription of $35 each which shall accompany the nomination by Dec. 15, 1980 (364 nominated); second subscription of $100 by Dec. 15, 1981 (165 remained eligible); third subscription of $200 by May 1, 1982 (93 remained eligible) and an additional $2,000 when making final entry. Owner of first horse receives the Guineas. The added money and all fees to be divided: 60% to the winner, 20% to second, 11% to third, 6% to fourth and 3% to fifth. Value of race $235,840, value to winner $141,504, second $47,168, third $25,943, fourth $14,150, fifth $7,075. Mutuel pool $715,302.

Horse	Eqt	Wt.	PP	¼	½	¾	1	Str	Fin	Jockey	Owner	Odds $1
SON OF BRIARTIC	b	126	5	$1^{1/2}$	$1^{1\,1/2}$	1^{1}	1^{2}	$1^{4\,1/2}$	$1^{2\,1/2}$	SouterJP	PaddockhurstStable	8.75
RUNAWAY GROOM		126	14	18	$17^{1/2}$	$8^{1/2}$	2^{3}	2^{4}	$2^{3\,1/4}$	ClarkD	CoppolaA	38.20
LE DANSEUR		126	11	17^{4}	16^{1}	$15^{1/2}$	$6^{1/2}$	4^{3}	3^{hd}	VasquezJ	JLouisLevesqueStaInc	a-.50
[D]ICY CIRCLE	b	126	3	$9^{1/2}$	$11^{1\,1/2}$	$10^{1/2}$	10^{1}	7^{3}	4no	HoSangG	McCulloughMrsG	20.25
LE GRAND ARGENTIER		126	4	$2^{1/2}$	$5^{1/2}$	4^{hd}	$3^{1\,1/2}$	$3^{2\,1/2}$	5^{4}	GrubbR	JLouisLevesqueStaInc	a-.50
EXCLUSIVE CANADIAN	b	126	12	14^{hd}	$15^{1\,1/2}$	16^{2}	11^{4}	8^{2}	$6^{2\,1/2}$	BeckonD	BKYStable	8.80
GIFTED PRINCE		126	1	$11^{1\,1/2}$	9^{hd}	$5^{1/2}$	7^{2}	5^{hd}	$7^{1\,1/4}$	BellJJ	BCSta&RobillardMrsG	96.50
NO NO'S BOY		126	15	$12^{1/2}$	12^{1}	12^{2}	9^{1}	9^{4}	8^{nk}	DennieD	SpraggStable	43.50
VALIANT PRINCE	b	126	9	$7^{1/2}$	$8^{1/2}$	7^{1}	4^{2}	6^{hd}	$9^{4\,1/2}$	ParsonsW	PickeringCE&Partners	f-34.95
GREAT STAKE	b	126	7	3^{1}	2^{1}	11^{hd}	8^{hd}	11^{1}	$10^{1/2}$	AttardL	CarmichaelJBW	f-34.95
AKHTIAR	b	126	2	13^{hd}	13^{1}	13^{hd}	13^{hd}	$12^{1/2}$	11^{hd}	DuffyL	NorcliffeStable	10.80
BRIAR WIND	b	126	18	10^{1}	7^{hd}	$3^{1/2}$	5^{2}	10^{hd}	12^{nk}	StahlbaumG	HatchHW	8.30
REGENCY GOLD		121	13	$8^{1/2}$	10^{2}	$9^{1/2}$	14^{4}	$13^{1\,1/2}$	13^{2}	BelowusJ	Sam-SonFarm	114.20
FRIGID LADY		121	10	4^{hd}	3^{hd}	6^{1}	12^{2}	14^{8}	14^{10}	McMahonWG	LivergantMrsL	128.50
BACKWOODSMAN	b	126	8	$5^{1\,1/2}$	6^{hd}	18	15	15	15	PennaD	AkumaStable	f-34.85
SEA CHESTNUT		126	6	$16^{2\,1/2}$	18	$17^{1/2}$	Fell			DePassR	Schaf'n-Manos-Stewart	269.60
TRANSCENDENT		126	16	$15^{3\,1/2}$	14^{hd}	$14^{1/2}$	Fell			SwatukB	Bo-Teek Farm	103.40
CLIFF HOUSE	b	126	17	$6^{1/2}$	$4^{1/2}$	$2^{1/2}$	Fell			FazioJJ	WindfieldsFarm	f-34.85

[D]-Icy Circle disqualified and placed eighteenth.
a-Coupled, Le Danseur and Le Grand Argentier. f-Mutuel field.
OFF AT 4:45. Start good. Won ridden out. Time, :23 3/5, :47 3/5, 1:13, 1:37 4/5, 2:04 3/5. Track fast.

$2 Mutuel Prices:				
	5-SON OF BRIARTIC	19.50	8.60	5.00
	10-RUNAWAY GROOM		27.80	9.70
	1-LE DANSEUR (a-Entry)			2.70

Ch. c, by Briartic—Tabola, by Round Table. Trainer, Lavigne J. G. (Jerry). Bred by Taylor E. P. (Ont-C).
SON OF BRIARTIC rushed up quickly to take the early lead when pressed, had a clear lead around the clubhouse turn, retained the advantage in the backstretch was roused around the far turn when challenged, opened into the homelane, widened in midstretch then was under intermittent urging to retain the advantage. RUNAWAY GROOM trailed into the clubhouse turn, stalked that one thereafter but failed to menace. LE DANSEUR was outrun early, advanced around the final turn but was never dangerous in the stretch run.

Horse racing moved from the sports pages to the front pages in the spring of 1983, the topic of conversation of people who would not know a pastern from a pitchfork, as they read, or watched on television, the colourful exploits of the second coming of *Northern Dancer*—a tall, virile, glamorous chestnut colt called *Sunny's Halo*, who was Canada's champion two-year-old. It was the type of Cinderella story the public revelled in. David (Pud) Foster, the ex-newsie who used to hustle the late editions of Toronto's newspapers outside Dufferin Park, and trainer David C. Cross Jr., a tough-nosed kid from B.C. and a racetracker whose Christmas meal one year was a dish of carrots he had scrounged from a friendly feedwoman—walking into "hardboot" and mint julep territory and winning the Kentucky Derby before a boisterous throng of 135,000 and a television audience of many millions.

LARRY ATTARD CELEBRATES AS TRAINER JOHNNY CARDELLA LEADS *BOMPAGO* THROUGH CROWD.

Nineteen years earlier, E.P. Taylor had stood on the same dais with the governor of Kentucky; *Northern Dancer*'s victory gave Canadians the same euphoric feeling as on an afternoon in 1972 when Paul Henderson scored the winning goal with seconds to play in Moscow.

This time the feeling was different: in 1964 the *Dancer* proved that a Canadian-foaled steed could beat the world's best bred horses, a fact that had hit home every time one of his offspring would win a major event in Europe or North America. Canadians expected *Sunny's Halo* to win the Derby, after his winter recuperating in California and easy victories in the Rebel Handicap and the Arkansas Derby at Hot Springs. Some of the early Derby favourites—*Copelan* for one—had retired because of injuries, and the astute handicappers liked the colt out of a $3,900 mare, one of which was Derby commentator Bill Hartack, *Northern Dancer*'s jockey.

Braving a sudden rain shower, "Pud" nervously accepted the accolades along with his wife Shirley, Dave and Patti Cross, and jockey Eddie Delahoussaye. David Fineberg (later, when he got into the securities business on Bay Street, he changed his name to Foster) emotionally dedicated *Sunny*'s victory to the people of Toronto and Canada. He had run *Decent Davey*, a 10-to-1 outsider in the 1980 Queen's Plate, and now in 1983, he was bringing home a colt worth an estimated $12 million—he had turned down $6 million before the Derby—that would pay five cents on the dollar in the Plate. Some Torontonians were so excited that they were naming cocktails, and even model homes, after *Sunny's Halo*. But first there would be the Preakness Stakes and Chicago's Arlington Classic.

The Plate was *Sunny's*, as long as he remained healthy. A stumbling start on a sloppy track spoiled his chances in the Preakness. He wrenched an ankle in the Arlington Classic and a mysterious skin virus that vets were unable to diagnose knocked him out of the Plate.

Meanwhile, in Toronto, The Cold Water Kid, trainer Johnny Cardella, awaited a chance to run his gelding *Bompago* against *Sunny's Halo*. He told the media that he "would not be ashamed to come second to a horse that had won the Derby." Cardella had been knocking around racetracks as long as Cross; he had been a hot-walker, a janitor of stalls and a groom for his older brother, Danny, and was later assistant to Frank Merrill Jr., who loved the quick turnover of discounted claiming horses, an equine game of Russian roulette. In every basket of fruit, said his old boss, occasionally there was a lemon. "When you reach into the basket, you might get an apple or an orange, or even a . . ." Cardella was acquainted with the day-to-day problems that can beset the best laid plans of gaining access to the treasury. He had reached "into the basket of fruit" at Fort Erie in August and had plucked "a peach of a runner," claiming *Bompago*, a roguish, unpredictable gelding, for $40,000 from trainer Gord Huntley and owners Sam Young and Lionel and Carol Schipper of Toronto.

Bred by Eaton Hall Farm, owned by Thor and John Craig Eaton, an old Toronto family that had built the famous department stores, *Bompago* had been raised by Tom Webb. He consigned him to the annual yearling sales at Woodbine, and when the bidding stalled, Huntley bought him for $25,000. "The first time he was out, July at Woodbine, I had a horse running in the same race—*Caustic Ruler. Bompago* beat him, which got me to thinking that he may be a better horse than mine," Cardella recalled. "Two races later he was in for $40,000 at Fort Erie, that's when I took him. That's a lot of money, but that winter my brothers Gerry and Carl, and Danny's son, Paul, went in with me as partners."

A couple of weeks later, *Bompago* finished third in the Achievement Stakes, an encouraging sign. What was not was his behaviour. He was a problem horse, highly strung and difficult to ride. *Bompago* regularly dumped exercise riders, and few jockeys wanted to ride him because the races were more like wrestling matches. He failed to win his next four races, but Cardella, still

Kentucky Derby winner *Sunny's Halo* had to skip the Plate because of a skin infection.

BOMPAGO | 3-year-old bay gelding

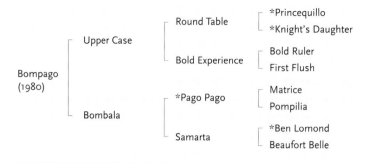

Bompago (1980)	Upper Case	Round Table	*Princequillo
			*Knight's Daughter
		Bold Experience	Bold Ruler
			First Flush
	Bombala	*Pago Pago	Matrice
			Pompilia
		Samarta	*Ben Lomond
			Beaufort Belle

Owner: Carl, Gerry, John and Paul Cardella, Toronto; *Trainer:* John Cardella
Jockey: Larry Attard; *Breeder:* Eaton Hall Farm, King City, Ont.

hopeful, ran him in the rich Cup and Saucer Stakes, an October test of stamina for juveniles. *Bompago* had the race won, but in the stretch, where the outside Marshall turf course crosses the main track to the inner grass course, he made a right-hand turn to the outer rail, a move that ended up earning him only second-place money.

Rated at odds of 30-to-1 in the winterbook (*Sunny's Halo* was 3-to-5), *Bompago* was inconsistent as a three-year-old, winning a stakes race, and then failing to finish in the money in two of his next three starts. In the space of three weeks, two important events would occur. The first was prompted by jockey Larry Attard, who suggested an equipment change: discard the ring bit. Cardella replaced the bit, a loop that tightens around the horse's jaws, clamping the mouth and locking the head in place, with a leather-covered slide bit that was softer on the horse's mouth. It worked as *Bompago*, a 25-to-1 long shot, won the Plate Trial Stakes by five lengths. That same weekend that *Bompago* won the Plate Trial, *Sunny's Halo* injured his ankle in the Arlington Classic at Chicago He also developed a severe skin infection that veterinarians were unable to diagnose, preventing *Sunny* from running in the Plate. Foster, Cross and *Sunny's Halo* were spectators at Woodbine when *Bompago* and *Sir Khaled*, trained by Bill Marko, left the gate quickly and staged a two-horse duel until the top of the stretch when it became a one-horse contest—*Bompago* pulled away to win by almost five lengths. A race later, *Bompago* bowed a tendon and was retired. In his first start in 1984 he bowed a tendon in his other leg. *Sunny's Halo* came back in 1983 to win the Super Derby in Louisiana, before retiring to stud—syndicated for $7 million—with record earnings of $1,247,791.

Sunny's trainer, David C. Cross Jr.

1983 QUEEN'S PLATE STAKES

EIGHTH RACE
Woodbine
JUNE 26, 1983

1 1–4 MILES (2:01$\frac{1}{5}$). One Hundred and Twenty-Fourth Running QUEEN'S PLATE STAKES. (Gr. IC). $175,000 Added and Fifty Guineas. 3–year–olds, foaled in Canada. Scale weight: Colts and Geldings, 126 lbs.; Fillies, 121 lbs. By subscription of $35 each which shall accompany the nomination by Dec. 30, 1981 (406 remained eligible); second subscription of $100 each by Dec. 30, 1982 (191 remained eligible); third subscription of $200 by May 1, 1983 (80 remained eligible) and an additional $2,000 when making final entry. The added money and all fees to be divided: 60% to the winner, 20% to second, 11% to third, 6% to fourth and 3% to fifth. Value of race $252,310, value to winner $151,386, second $50,462, third $27,755, fourth $15,138, fifth $7,569. Mutuel Pool $467,612. Exactor Pool $183,843. FE Pool $33,709. FE Exactor Pool $21,382.

Horse	Eqt	Wt.	PP	¼	½	¾	1	Str	Fin	Jockey	Owner	Odds $1
BOMPAGO		126	5	2^{2}	$2^{1\frac{1}{2}}$	2^{3}	$1^{1\frac{1}{2}}$	$1^{2\frac{1}{2}}$	$1^{4\frac{1}{2}}$	AttardL	Cardella&Partner	2.45
SIR KHALED	b	126	1	$1\frac{1}{2}$	1^{1}	1^{hd}	2^{5}	$2^{2\frac{1}{2}}$	$2^{1\frac{1}{2}}$	DosRamosRA	MarkoB&ReliableStable	a-8.60
ROCKCLIFFE		126	2	$7^{1\frac{1}{2}}$	$3\frac{1}{2}$	$3\frac{1}{2}$	3^{2}	3^{4}	3^{1}	PlattsR	NorcliffeStable	4.15
GONE TO ROYALTY		126	8	$10\frac{1}{2}$	10^{1}	$8\frac{1}{2}$	5^{3}	4^{3}	$4^{5\frac{1}{4}}$	TurcotteYA	LevesquePL	6.85
RISING YOUNG STAR		126	12	$6\frac{1}{2}$	$6\frac{1}{2}$	$6\frac{1}{2}$	7^{1}	$5^{1\frac{1}{2}}$	$5^{1\frac{1}{4}}$	DuffyL	Marko&Romeo&Marcello	a-8.60
DIAPASON	b	126	9	$11\frac{1}{2}$	14	9^{2}	6^{1}	$8^{3\frac{1}{2}}$	$6^{1\frac{1}{4}}$	LeBlancJB	LaPointeJ	5.70
FEU D'ENFER		126	6	$12\frac{1}{2}$	13^{hd}	11^{1}	10^{4}	7^{hd}	7^{nk}	StahlbaumG	JLLevesqueStable	21.45
WISE STRATEGY	b	126	13	3^{1}	4^{hd}	$4\frac{1}{2}$	$4^{1\frac{1}{2}}$	6^{2}	8^{5}	GrubbR	Meadowview&Ventura	41.05
CRUSHED ICE	b	126	7	5^{1}	5^{2}	5^{5}	$9^{1\frac{1}{2}}$	9^{1}	$9^{1\frac{1}{2}}$	BraccialeVJr	KinghavenFarm	23.25
NAC ELLES' PAL		126	3	12^{1}	11^{hd}	$12^{1\frac{1}{2}}$	12^{3}	11^{hd}	10^{hd}	LindbergG	HatchWD	144.35
HIGH CHICAGO		126	11	8^{hd}	7^{2}	8^{hd}	$8\frac{1}{2}$	$10^{2\frac{1}{2}}$	$11^{1\frac{1}{4}}$	DittfachH	McDougaldMrsJA	34.20
SECOND CANDY		126	4	4^{hd}	$9^{1\frac{1}{2}}$	14	11^{1}	$12^{2\frac{1}{2}}$	$12^{2\frac{1}{2}}$	BelowusJ	BCStable	93.95
AUTUMN ALLEY		126	14	14	12^{hd}	$12^{1\frac{1}{2}}$	$13^{1\frac{1}{2}}$	$13^{4\frac{1}{2}}$	$13^{4\frac{1}{2}}$	BeckonD	Alexander&Stielgan	10.30
REGAL DECISION		126	10	9^{1}	$8\frac{1}{2}$	10^{hd}	14	14	14	ClarkD	WindfieldsFarm	13.35

a–Coupled, Sir Khaled and Rising Young Star.

OFF AT 5:15. Start good. Won handily. Time, :23$\frac{4}{5}$, :48, 1:12, 1:36$\frac{4}{5}$, 2:04$\frac{1}{5}$. Track fast.

$2 Mutuel Prices:			
5–BOMPAGO	6.90	4.80	3.40
1–SIR KHALED (a–Entry)		8.80	5.00
2–ROCKCLIFFE			3.60

$2 EXACTOR 5–1 PAID $54.00.

B. g, by Upper Case—Bombala, by *Pago Pago. Trainer, Cardella John. Bred by Eaton Hall Farm (Ont–C).

BOMPAGO broke alertly and was away with the first flight, was outside pressing the leader around the clubhouse turn, stayed pressing in the backstretch under restraint, took command around the far turn with a clear lead, increased the margin in early stretch along the rail then widened in deep stretch to win under a hand ride. SIR KHALED moved quickly to take command under rating, stayed inside and even with the winner approaching the far turn, was outrun around the final turn then closed gamely. ROCKCLIFFE saved ground around the clubhouse turn, stayed along the rail around the final turn, failed to menace the top pair.

It had never happened before in the piquant history of the Queen's Plate: a winning jockey lodging a protest against one of the losing horses. Jockeys know better: let the horses, not the stewards, decide. But this was the 125th running for Her Majesty's fifty "guineas," the year the riders aboard the first two finishers, *Key to the Moon* and *Let's Go Blue*, claimed foul against each other. It had been almost twenty years since an interference call had been laid against the winner, so it is understandable that this renewal of the continent's oldest fixture will one day be judged as one of the most engrossing ever.

There had been many rollicking races during the Plate's adolescence: at the Carleton course in the Toronto Junction in 1863, when *Willie Wonder* was disqualified two weeks after the race; at the Newmarket course in London two years later, when the judges sent two possible winners packing because of blatant infractions; and in 1876, the first year the race was held at The Woodbine, when *Mary L.* was placed last for interfering with her opponents in the stretch. But this was 1984, and not even Orwell could have forecast such a fanciful outcome.

Although pomp and pageantry suffered because Queen Elizabeth II was asked to postpone her tour of Canada and a visit to Woodbine, in view of the pending federal election, a crowd of 32,019 did witness a race oozing with excitement, a spectacle that would continue long after the fierce competitive contest had reached its climax. Bahnam K. Yousif's *Key to the Moon* had muscled his way across the finish line, a half-length in front of the favoured *Let's Go Blue,* while another of Yousif's horses, *Ten Gold Pots*, the catalyst in BKY Stable's victory, was third after fulfilling his role as the stable's "rabbit."

Roars of approval for the dramatic struggle were still cascading from the stands when suddenly (at least for those who had failed to notice an incident in the final fifty yards) the inquiry sign on the infield tote board began to flash. In quick succession three announcements came over the public address system. The stewards wanted to take a look at video tapes of the stretch run to determine if the winner had fouled the rallying loser. Larry Attard had claimed foul against Robin Platts and *Key to the Moon*, stating that the winner had bothered *Let's Go Blue* twice inside the seventy-yard pole. Platts, who had just won his fourth Plate, tying him with Avelino Gomez and Sandy Hawley for most wins, added to the confusion by making a counter-claim that Attard's horse had bumped him as the fourteen-horse field swung out of the turn into the long run down the backstretch.

After lengthy deliberation, viewing the head-on and pan shots

CONTROVERSY! BOTH JOCKEYS CLAIMED FOUL. PLATE WINNER *KEY TO THE MOON* (LEFT) AND *LET'S GO BLUE*.

of the contentious point in the race where *Key to the Moon* was alleged to have fouled *Let's Go Blue*, stewards Eddie Hall, Ted Kennedy and Ivan McHutchion ruled that there was "insufficient reason" to alter the finish. Hall claimed that the films revealed that *Key to the Moon* had veered in toward the rail, crowding the loser as he attempted to regain the lead, but he and his fellow stewards were uncertain whether it had happened "a jump or two before the wire or past it. We were handicapped because the films do not clearly pinpoint the location. The fact that the race was the Queen's Plate had no bearing on the decision." The man who owned and bred *Let's Go Blue*, Mel Lawson, a Burlington lumber merchant, trainer Janet Bedford and Attard, angrily disputed the decision, claiming that the bumping had cost them the race. Many racegoers felt the decision would have been different if the Plate had not been at stake. Hall said: "It is only human nature. We are never going to be able to convince people who thought otherwise." He admitted that if the stewards had been able to determine that the bumping had occurred before the finish line, *Key to the Moon* would have been disqualified. Films did show that *Let's Go Blue* did swing outwards as the field swung into the backstretch, possibly pushing Platts' mount wide. But it was not enough to merit his counter-claim of foul, one that Platts said he made "just for protection." The one point in the race where most fans and television viewers thought *Let's Go Blue* was erratic was at the top of the stretch. After taking the lead from the pace-setting *Ten Gold Pots*, Attard's horse now had to contend with

Key to the Moon is all grins for owner Bahnam Yousif and wife Fetoun.

KEY TO THE MOON | 3-year-old dark bay or brown colt

Key to the Moon (1981)	Wajima	Bold Ruler	*Nasrullah
			Miss Disco
		*Iskra	Le Haar
			Fasciola
	Kamar	King to the Mint	Graustark
			Key Bridge
		Square Angel	Quadrangle
			Nangela

Owner: BKY Stable, Woodbridge, Ont.; *Trainer:* Gil H. Rowntree
Jockey: Robin Platts; *Breeder:* Bahnam K. Yousif

the other half of the entry, the horse that was expected to prefer the Plate distance. *Key to the Moon,* strong and full of run, attempted to sweep by on the outside but was taken out into the middle of the track by *Let's Go Blue.* The tactic only delayed his surge for the lead. "I was on my way down to call the stewards and claim foul myself," trainer Gil Rowntree remarked after the hullabaloo was over. I almost got sick when I heard that Robin was claiming foul. You don't claim foul when you're on the winner."

It was a three-horse race—Team Yousif against Lawson's colt. Yousif, forty-eight, an Arabian multi-millionaire business consultant from Saudi Arabia, had raced horses in Europe before opening up a Canadian division in 1977. He had built an indoor training track near Woodbridge and had bred the Plate winner out of a mare (*Kamar*) he had purchased for $65,000. She had won the Canadian Oaks, and when it came time to breed her, Yousif sent her to *Wajima,* the last champion to be sired by *Bold Ruler.* Before the result became official, Yousif was perhaps the calmest individual in his exuberant party.

Until 1984 only two other women had saddled a horse for the Plate—Estelle Giddings in 1950 and Olive Armstrong in 1953. Estelle was the widow of Harry Giddings, who had saddled a record eight Plate winners before his death. For a short period afterwards she handled his stable. Following the race the thirty-eight-year-old English-born Ms. Bedford, who became the first woman to ever condition the favourite for the Plate, admitted that she felt like flinging her purse to the ground in bitter frustration:

> I did stamp my feet, but just for a moment and I might have cursed quietly. But that's horse racing. I was more disappointed for Mr. Lawson. In all the years I have trained for him I had never seen him that upset before. He's an extremely fair man, not the type to complain. 'I know I wuz robbed.' We got beat by one of the best, Robin Platts.

Platts admitted that it perturbed him to claim foul: "But a lot of money was at stake today." Attard later agreed that the BKY team effort had been effective. "I wasn't surprised my claim of foul was disallowed. I did my job and they [the stewards] did their job."

While fans anticipated a future clash between these two rivals, which never happened, there was no arguing the fact that the Plate, enlivened by their fierce duel, did, in fact, realize its potential as Canada's greatest one-day annual sporting and social festival once again, and was an immense success despite the absence of royalty.

1984 QUEEN'S PLATE STAKES

SEVENTH RACE
Woodbine
JULY 22, 1984

1 1–4 MILES (2:01$\frac{1}{5}$). One Hundred and Twenty-Fifth Running QUEEN'S PLATE STAKES. (Gr. IC). Purse $175,000 Added. 3-year-olds, foaled in Canada. Scale weight: Colts and geldings, 126 lbs.; fillies, 121 lbs. By subscription of $35 each which shall accompany the nomination by Dec. 30, 1982 (472 nominated); second subscription of $100 each by December 15, 1983 (217 remained eligible); third subscription of $200 by May 1, 1984 (116 remained eligible), and an additional $2,500 when making final entry. In order to remain eligible each subscription or payment must be paid on or before due date. The owner of the first horse receives the Guineas. The added money and all fees to be divided: 60% to the winner, 20% to second, 11% to third, 6% to fourth and 3% to fifth. Final entries to be made through the entry box on a date and time to be determined by the Racing Secretary. Value of race $273,920, value to winner $164,352, second $54,784, third $30,131, fourth $16,435, fifth $8,218. Mutuel Pools (including Fort Erie) $662,165. Exactor Pool $324,479.

Horse	Eqt	Wt.	PP	¼	½	¾	1	Str	Fin	Jockey	Owner	Odds $1
KEY TO THE MOON	b	126	8	6^{1}	$4\frac{1}{2}$	4^{3}	$3^{4\frac{1}{2}}$	$1^{1\frac{1}{2}}$	$1\frac{1}{2}$	PlattsR	BKYStable	b-2.90
LET'S GO BLUE		126	5	3^{1}	$3\frac{1}{2}$	2^{2}	2^{1}	2^{2}	$2^{3\frac{1}{4}}$	AttardL	JimDandyStable	.85
TEN GOLD POTS	b	126	7	$2\frac{1}{2}$	2^{2}	$1\frac{1}{2}$	1^{hd}	3^{5}	$3^{3\frac{1}{2}}$	StahlbaumG	BKYStable	b-2.90
VAL DANSANT		126	4	13^{2}	13^{2}	8^{2}	6^{3}	4^{2}	4^{nk}	LeBlancJB	Norman& Sanderson	6.75
COOL NORTHERNER		126	10	12^{3}	11^{1}	$9\frac{1}{2}$	8^{2}	6^{3}	$5^{2\frac{1}{2}}$	DriedgerI	D'AndreaF&P	13.20
PARK REGENT	b	126	11	$10\frac{1}{2}$	6^{2}	$6\frac{1}{2}$	$4^{1\frac{1}{2}}$	5^{hd}	$6^{1\frac{1}{2}}$	ClarkD	ParkviewStable	10.55
DANCING HARE		126	14	14	14	11^{4}	7^{1}	8^{9}	7^{nk}	DosRamosRA	FranksJ	a-25.05
MISTER LORENZO		126	3	11^{2}	8^{1}	$5\frac{1}{2}$	5^{2}	$7\frac{1}{2}$	$8^{9\frac{1}{2}}$	DuffyL	DeToro, Longo&Fidani	60.45
DAYSPRING	b	126	9	8^{hd}	10^{hd}	10^{2}	10^{5}	$9^{1\frac{1}{2}}$	$9^{1\frac{1}{4}}$	KingRJr	KingfieldFarm	47.50
AXE T.V.	b	126	6	1^{1}	1^{hd}	3^{hd}	9^{2}	10^{5}	$10^{4\frac{1}{2}}$	FellJ	FranksJ	a-25.05
NICO DEMUS	b	126	2	4^{hd}	9^{1}	12^{8}	12^{12}	11^{2}	$11^{1\frac{1}{2}}$	FenechSC	BrnjasJ	212.05
MALE EGO	b	126	1	$5\frac{1}{2}$	$5^{3\frac{1}{2}}$	7^{2}	11^{hd}	12^{15}	12^{26}	LauzonJM	AnakaMrs H	90.40
TROPARE	b	126	12	$9\frac{1}{2}$	$12\frac{1}{2}$	14	13^{2}	13^{2}	13^{2}	SouterJP	AndersonFm&HarlequinR	125.80
REPATRIATE	b	126	13	7^{2}	7^{hd}	13^{2}	14	14	14	BeckonD	FosterDJ	131.80

a–Coupled: Dancing Hare and Axe T.V.; b–Key to the Moon and Ten Gold Pots.

OFF AT 4:41. Start good. Won ridden out. Time, :23$\frac{4}{5}$, :47$\frac{1}{5}$, 1:12, 1:37$\frac{2}{5}$, 2:03$\frac{4}{5}$. Track fast.

$2 Mutuel Prices:			
2–KEY TO THE MOON (b–Entry)	**7.80**	**2.90**	**3.50**
7–LET'S GO BLUE		**2.70**	**2.60**
2–TEN GOLD POTS (b–Entry)	**7.80**	**2.90**	**3.50**

$2 EXACTOR 2–7 PAID $15.70.

Dk. b. or br. c, by Wajima—Kamar, by Key to the Mint. Trainer, Rowntree Gil H. Bred by Yousif B K (Ont–C).

KEY TO THE MOON was well placed early on the outside and, under rating, moved up approaching the far turn, lodged a bid around the final turn and was carried wide into the home lane, had a clear advantage at the furlong marker then was under intermittent handling to prevail. LET'S GO BLUE was contentious early, pressed the issue around the far turn, had a slight advantage around the final turn then drifted out, was outrun a furlong out then closed gamely inside the winner. The rider on LET'S GO BLUE claimed foul against KEY TO THE MOON for interference at the wire, and the rider on KEY TO THE MOON claimed foul against LET'S GO BLUE for interference into the backstretch, and both claims were disallowed. TEN GOLD POTS pressed the early pace, had command in the backstretch, stayed inside and contentious into the stretch and weakened thereafter.

Scratched—Mascot.

End of an Era: A New Golden Age of Racing Launched by Samuel, Willmot, Stronach, Stavro

Edward Plunket Taylor was seventy-seven years old when *Regal Embrace* won Canada's most famous horse race, the Queen's Plate, in 1978. As E.P.—Eddie, the name his close friends often called him—crossed the track, grey topper and all, to a warm ovation, many thought they were seeing the end of an era. Perhaps they were. Perhaps they thought they'd never see the like of him again, a man who transformed a leaky roof circuit into a world-class racing destination that brewed international respect. All of the members of his era, Viscount Hardinge, Preston Gilbride, Jean-Louis Lévesque, Jack Stafford, Frowde Seagram and Conn Smythe, were also in their seventies and eighties. Many wondered who would step up to the plate to replace them when they moved on.

Two years later, after Taylor had witnessed Windfields' tenth Plate winner, he suffered a debilitating stroke and the effects lingered until he died in 1989, a year before *Northern Dancer* drew his last breath. Taylor's son,

DANCE SMARTLY, CANADA'S FIRST BREEDERS' CUP CHAMPION, TRIUMPHS UNDER THE TWIN SPIRES OF CHURCHILL DOWNS.

Not at all. During the 1980s a new wave of committed, horse-loving owners and breeders took the helm, with Ernie Samuel and his Sam-Son Farm and the Willmot family's Kinghaven Farm battling each other for supremacy, and a handful of others, including Toronto lawyer Rick Kennedy, market breeder Bob Anderson, Bahnam Yousif and Steve Stavro, with his Knob Hill Farm colouring up the racing landscape with some well-bred, classy horses. And there was this young auto parts maker, too, called Frank Stronach, who began to make noises in 1980 with Eclipse award-winning mare *Glorious Song*.

This new, young enthusiastic guard launched a new golden age of racing in Canada, buying and breeding horses with goosebump power which were competitive south of the border as well. But it didn't happen overnight. Both Sam-Son and Kinghaven built their empires, one filly at a time over decades.

Charles, inherited the presidency of the farm, and was ringside during the dizzying boom times, when *Northern Dancer*'s cachet drove yearling prices to new heights. But even as *Northern Dancer* yearlings were setting world records, Taylor could see that problems were looming. The market couldn't climb forever. It hurt when Joe Thomas, Windfields' astute racing manager, died prematurely at age fifty-nine after a battle with cancer in 1984, the same year the farm sold a colt for $8.25 million. Peter Poole, the farm manger, retired a couple of years later. And in 1988 Windfields closed its farm in Chesapeake City, Maryland, laying off fifty people and moving its band of one hundred broodmares to Oshawa. Costs had spiraled out of control and Windfields had suffered significant losses. Charles battled melanoma for a decade, until he died in 1997. Windfields lived on, and it will always be the most important name in Canadian racing, but some wondered if the Canadian scene would have the life sucked out of it as the magic makers began to disappear.

"Our plan was very similar to Sam-Son's," said David Willmot, who built Kinghaven along with his father D.G. (Bud) Willmot. They bought quality fillies, raced them, retired the best ones to their broodmare band and then bred them to the best U.S. stallions that money could buy.

David Willmot's life was forever changed when he saw *Northern Dancer* win the Kentucky Derby in 1964, the first thoroughbred race he ever laid eyes on. When he and his father attended their first sale, the Keeneland summer yearling sale of 1967 in Kentucky, they bought four yearlings. One of them was *Cool Mood*, a daughter of *Northern Dancer* from his unproven first crop, a wonderful buy at US$31,000. *Cool Mood* not only won the Canadian Oaks for Kinghaven but was the granddam of both of its Triple Crown winners, *With Approval* and *Izvestia*, more than two decades later.

Samuel went on to become one of the most influential builders

SAM-SON FARM'S ERNIE SAMUEL AND *REGAL CLASSIC*.

in Canadian racing. He was born in London, England, the son of Dr. Bernard Willinsky, the former chief surgeon at Mount Sinai Hospital in Toronto. The young Ernie eventually assumed his grandfather's surname of Samuel, and carried on with the family business in Toronto: Samuel, Son & Co. Ltd., a steel manufacturing firm that he turned into a multi-billion dollar conglomerate with operations in three countries.

Samuel's first love was show jumping. He owned *Canadian*

Club, the talented jumper that carried Jim Day to an Olympic team gold medal in Mexico in 1968. He quickly switched to thoroughbred racing, founded Sam-Son Farm in 1972 and began with two foundation mares. Samuel was a winner off the bat with trainer Art Warner. His first racehorse, *Bronze Sand*, won the first race he contested at Fort Erie during the early 1970s. "You might say we were hooked coming out of the first gate," he once said. Samuel ran his first Plate horse in 1973, but had no illusions of winning. The horse, *Time of Plenty*, was a hopeless long shot and staggered in sixteenth. But the best was yet to come. Day joined Samuel as trainer in 1977 and the farm's fortunes began to ascend. In 1980 Samuel was owner of the year in Canada for the first time, helped by stakes wins from his star, *Stutz Bearcat*. Kinghaven was close on his heels, and getting excited about homebreds *Bayford* and *Passing Mood*, all in the same year that thoroughbreds ran under the lights for the first time at Greenwood.

Kinghaven got its first taste of the major-league spotlight when the farm bought a half-interest in 1981 Horse of the Year, *Deputy Minister*, winner of an Eclipse Award after winning the Laurel Futurity and Young America Stakes. By the next year, Sam-Son and Kinghaven were officially locked in a battle for supremacy. During the mid-1980s, Sam-Son horses were flooding Queen's Plate fields three at a time, earning roles as favorites. In 1984 Sam-Son was reaching its might, becoming the first owner to win more than $1 million in purses in a single season. Samuel horses won 12 stakes, with such classy steeds as *Classy 'n Smart* (later dam of *Dance Smartly*), *In My Cap* and *Dauphin Fabuleux*. For an encore the following year Samuel was leading owner with $1.5 million, won a remarkable 17 stakes races, a dozen more than BKY Stable in second place, while Kinghaven had two.

The battle of the titans was even more hard-fought in 1986, with Kinghaven turning the tables, leading Woodbine owners with winnings of $1,962,335 and eighteen stakes wins, with Sam-Son narrowly back in second place with $1,920,496 and eighteen stakes wins. Kinghaven dominated the scene with its incredible group of

PLAY THE KING, JOCKEY DON SEYMOUR, MICHAEL WILLMOT AND ROGER ATTFIELD.

KINGHAVEN'S *WITH APPROVAL* TEAM—JOCKEY DON SEYMOUR, DAVID WILLMOT, TRAINER ROGER ATTFIELD AND D.G. (BUD) WILLMOT.

fillies all destined to swell the broodmare band with black type hype: *Triple Wow, Playlist* and the grass-loving *Carotene*, a world beater and Breeders' Stakes winner against the colts. With North American earnings taken into account, Kinghaven became the first Canadian stable to earn more than $2 million in a season, ending at about $2.5 million.

In 1987 Kinghaven earned $3.6 million in North America, second only to Nelson Bunker Hunt as North America's leading breeder. During the 1980s, the Willmots' fortunes were swelled by the addition of natty British-born trainer Roger Attfield; in 1987 he won 101 races for them, third to D. Wayne Lukas and Jack Van Berg. In 1989 Kinghaven horses earned more than $5 million, second in North America again but this time to Ogden Phipps. One of Attfield's greatest triumphs was to turn ugly duckling *Play The King* into one of the best sprinters in North America, even though he hadn't been fashion-

WINDFIELDS FARM, MARYLAND DIVISION.

ably bred and was so clumsy Kinghaven once tried to sell him as a saddle horse with no takers. Horse of the Year in 1988 in Canada, *Play The King* turned into one of the most beloved horses Kinghaven owned before he suffered a critical ankle injury in the Maryland Breeders' Cup at Pimlico in 1989. In 1990, Kinghaven stood first among all stables in North America with $5,041,280, ahead of Frances Genter, whose Kentucky Derby winner *Unbridled* made up most of her sum.

Ironically, just as Kinghaven was at its height, the Willmots planned to scale down the operations, which at one point had 250 horses, and farms in Toronto, Ocala, Florida, and Lexington, Kentucky. Like Windfields, they discovered that such a huge operation was costly. At first Kinghaven sought to raise cash by selling up to $54 million shares to the public but the plans were torpedoed by the stock market collapse in 1988. In November that year Kinghaven liquidated its breeding stock, selling off sixty-nine of its best broodmares for $10.7 million. Both Willmots wept; it was hardest to let *Carotene* go. The four-time Canadian champion mare and future Hall of Fame inductee sold for $1.3 million to Sheikh Mohammed

bin Rashid al Maktoum of Dubai. Bud Willmot figured he had too much capital invested in the business at his stage of life.

Kinghaven kept all its racing stock, and gradually built up a smaller, more modest broodmare band. Ironically, within the next three years, it celebrated its best two seasons with back-to-back Triple Crown wins. "We had 80 mares before the dispersal, and we never got back to that size," said David Willmot. "Nor did we want to." Even with Kinghaven's lofty winnings column at the racetrack, the liquidation sale allowed it to break even, he said. "We had been big. We had more than one hundred employees and we were operating three farms. The key to this game is a bad horse costs as much as a good horse, so you focus on the good horses that can make enough, and they can carry themselves and make a profit. And that profit doesn't have to be used to carry a whole bunch of bad ones." Eventually, Kinghaven bred as few as a dozen mares, but still to top U.S. stallions. Attfield began to take on other clients.

With Kinghaven retrenching, Sam-Son rose to the fore, almost alone, although even Samuel admitted that he was downsizing a bit too. He took over with a vengeance. In 1991 he became the first Canadian to win the Eclipse Award in the U.S. as owner of the year. He lost by only one vote to John Mabee as breeder of the year, while his Breeders' Cup champion *Dance Smartly* was the top three-year-old filly and Jim Day was runner-up in voting as trainer of the year. Day had twenty-five stakes wins for Sam-Son in Ontario, another record that season. By this tme, Sam-Son had won thirty-one Sovereign Awards.

In 1992 another face emerged on the Canadian scene. Steve Stavro, owner of the grocery chain, Knob Hill Farms, and who had just

WHERE SPORT AND BUSINESS ARE KING—KINGHAVEN FARMS, KING, ONTARIO.

become chairman of Maple Leaf Gardens Ltd. upstaged Samuel and Kinghaven by winning honours as Canada's top owner and breeder. His Knob Hill Farm won nine stakes, and from just ninety-four starters, won $1,894,248, second to Sam-Son, who had far more starters: 235. The star of the Knob Hill stable that year was *Benburb*, which had to pull off major upsets to get attention. And he did, more than once, upsetting Queen's Plate winner *Alydeed* in the Prince of Wales and odds-on favorite *A.P. Indy* in the Molson Export Million.

In 1967 Stavro, who was born in Macedonia, acquired his first horses—*Boy Bandit* and *Danforth Dan*. He had first visited the old Woodbine Park on a bicycle, delivering groceries from his father's store on Queen Street East, and often selling produce to passengers on the streetcars. He's a guy who came down from the greys, someone once said. He doesn't crave attention. By 1988 Stavros had a horse, *Granacus*, in the Kentucky Derby. It had won the

Grade I Blue Grass Stakes at Keeneland and had a shot. However, *Granacus* finished eleventh in the Derby after nearly falling down at the three-eighths pole. He ended third in the Queen's Plate, foiled by a slow early pace. *Granacus* had been named for the first battle Alexander the Great won in Asia Minor, near the banks of the Granacus River. The blue and gold colours of Knob Hill Farm are also the official hues of the fabled warrior king who is a key figure in Macedonian culture.

GLORIOUS SONG, WITH JOHN LEBLANC AND FRANK STRONACH, WAS CANADA'S FIRST MILLIONAIRE.

Also emerging was another Canadian immigrant, Frank Stronach, who left school in Austria at age fourteen to work as a tool and die apprentice. He arrived in Canada with a forty dollars in his pocket and eventually became Canada's highest paid executive.

He bought *Glorious Song* as a yearling for $36,000 and she became a millionaire by the time he sold an interest in her to Nelson Bunker Hunt. During the 1980s, Stronach tried to buy success by snapping up proven older horses, but it wasn't that easy. The $1.5 million he spent on *Alwuhush* produced a fourth place finish in the 1990 Breeders' Cup Turf. Stronach finally made a major breakthrough during the late 1990s by buying a seventy-five per cent interest in *Touch Gold* as a yearling for $375,000. *Touch Gold* won the Belmont Stakes. While Samuel and Kinghaven were firmly rooted in Canada, Stronach always looked far beyond. "He wants to be No. 1," said breeder Bob Anderson, who sold a few million-dollar yearlings in his day. "Frank is going for the jugular. He wants it. He understands and has the love of the game to do it. And he's got money. He's probably, without question, the most important owner in North America today."

One of the most important riders in North America, Sandy Hawley, returned to ride at Woodbine during the 1980s, a likeable natural lightweight who had been so successful in Canada, that fans at California's Hollywood Park called the track at which he rode, Hawleywood Park. Hawley immediately took over as leading rider when he returned, but the jockey colony was also boosted by budding stars Todd Kabel, apprentice Jim McAleney and Don Seymour.

The 1980s and early 1990s were a heady time. Thoroughbred wagering showed sharp increases during the late 1980s before the wheels came off. The popularity of inter-track wagering made the difference, and Toronto's booming economy didn't hurt either. For example, nearly 14 percent more fans showed up at Woodbine in 1987, and they bet 8.3 percent more on track. And for the first time in 1988, Woodbine offered two $1 million purses, one of them for the new Challenge race, meant to attract top three-year-olds from south of the border. Woodbine also inherited the Arlington Million for a year, after the Chicago grandstand burned down.

La Lorgnette was a gift. A big gift. It's just that Charles Taylor, squire of Windfields Farm, didn't know it at first. She was a tall, lanky daughter of French Derby winner *Val de l'Orne* that, by the time she won the 126th running of the $290,840 Queen's Plate, stood 17.1 hands high in her stocking feet. "You wouldn't have called her a swan by any means," said Bernard McCormack, marketing and sales manager for Windfields Farm, referring to her as a yearling. "Legs going everywhere. Tall and narrow. I don't think we would have had a very high reserve on her had she gone through the sales ring." As trainer Mac Benson put it, she wasn't exactly a knockout.

La Lorgnette found a way to escape the sales ring. About three days before the annual Woodbine yearling sales, she developed an impaction in her colon, with colic-like symptoms. Medication didn't help her settle down, so off to the University of Guelph's veterinary clinic she went. The vets shaved her belly for surgery, but she didn't need it after all. La Lorgnette responded to other medical treatment. "Well, she can go back to the sale, if you want," the vets told Windfields. With a shaved belly? It would have been like attending the prom without a gown. La Lorgnette was withdrawn from the sales and remained the property of Windfields.

CHARLES TAYLOR LEADS *LA LORGNETTE* AND DAVID CLARK INTO THE WINNER'S CIRCLE.

"Hrmmph," Taylor said of the giraffe-like filly with the unusual sense of timing. "Of all the ones that I'm left with, do I have to be stuck with her?" Taylor ate those words many times after that. He changed his tune, so much so, that when Windfields dispersed its blue-blooded broodmare band in 1996, Taylor found it hardest of all to part with *La Lorgnette*. After all, *La Lorgnette*, named after a set of long-handled opera glasses worn by the fashionable women of the early 1800s, was an endearing sort. She gave the farm a boost in a bleak year, and became its last of eleven Plate winners (and twentieth Windfields-bred winner). Her Queen's Plate win gave Windfields only its second triumph of the year in any race. The first was *La Lorgnette*'s Canadian Oaks victory. *La Lorgnette* became only the second filly in history (after *Flaming Page* in 1962) to sweep both the Canadian Oaks and the Plate, putting her in a special elite group of fillies. And she was the first filly to win the Plate in eighteen years. The four-legged accident had become the farm flagbearer.

American-born Benson, winning his second Queen's Plate, wiped away tears in the winner's circle. "She's always been a favourite with me," he said. "Lots of people like the runt of the litter. She's like the giant of the litter, but I love her." And the big plain-looking filly with a regal aura had done it in the presence of the Queen Mother, who seemed to have a good effect on jockey David Clark. Both of his Queen's Plate wins had come in the presence of the Queen Mum. "It was just coincidence," said Clark, who had won four years before with *Fiddle Dancer Boy*. He told the Queen Mother

that he'd met her before and said afterward: "Maybe she should come here every day." The Queen Mother told Clark that she had really admired the filly. But she hadn't placed a wager on *La Lorgnette*. She, like most others, gave the nod to the powerful three-horse Sam-Son Farm entry that included the flashy *Dauphin Fabuleux*, which had been Horse of the Year the previous year; *Imperial Choice*, a sore-kneed colt nicknamed *Lumpy*; and *In My Cap*, second to *La Lorgnette* in the Oaks. They went off at 3-to-5, *La Lorgnette* second choice at 7-to-2.

The 126th Queen's Plate had all the elements of a potboiler, whoever bet on it. Torrential rains fell five hours before the race, and the Woodbine dirt track was a sea of slop, a condition that favoured pace setters. However, the rain stopped by the first race, the sun came out when the Queen Mother arrived, and the track was rated good by the time the Plate was run. Benson changed *La Lorgnette*'s shoes, putting inserts in them. Sam-Son star *Dauphin Fabuleux*, sound as a dollar going into the race, broke down at the five-eighths pole with a condylar fracture of his right front leg. *La Lorgnette*, as massive as she was, wasn't quick from the gate, and had only two horses beaten in the first half of the race. But by the three-quarter mile mark, *La Lorgnette* started her roll, almost pulling Clark out of the saddle. "When I hit the backside, I had so much horse, it was unbelievable," he said. "She's just too big to fight. I just had to hang on." At first she picked up horses along the rail, then Clark swung his filly four-wide to the outside and began to run down the field with fluid, ground-eating strides. Like a freight train

THE QUEEN MOTHER PRESENTS SILVERWARE—TRAINER MAC BENSON, JOCKEY DAVID CLARK, JUDY MAPPIN AND HER BROTHER CHARLES TAYLOR. AT RIGHT OJC CHAIRMAN OF THE BOARD CHARLES BAKER.

LA LORGNETTE | 3-year-old bay filly

Owner: Windfields Farm; *Trainer:* Mac Benson;
Jockey: David Clark; *Breeder:* E.P. Taylor (Ont-C)

under full steam, she won easily by two-and-three-quarters lengths, loafing at the end. A crowd of 31,195 viewed as *La Lorgnette* overhauled *Imperial Choice* in 2:04 3/5.

The Plate hadn't been in Windfields' plans until *La Lorgnette* had won the Oaks so impressively. And besides, the Queen Mother was a patron of Woodbine and the Taylor family had good personal rapport with her. The Oaks had always been her main goal, especially after breaking her maiden in the Natalma Stakes as a two-year-old. She showed hints of a happy future in that event, although she raced like an ungainly goose. "If you look at her head-on, all you could see was just legs going in all directions," Benson said. She wintered in Maryland, but got colic again although the second attack proved inconsequential. As usual, *La Lorgnette* would handle everything in a unique way. "Whenever she got colic, she would lie on her back with her four legs straight up in the air," Benson marvelled.

Taylor had intended in giving *La Lorgnette* six weeks off after the Plate to prepare her for a fall campaign. But under pressure to run her in the mile-and-a-half Prince of Wales, Taylor gave in, after checking with Benson that the race wouldn't hurt the filly. However, Benson admits he made a mistake by working *La Lorgnette* by herself at Fort Erie before the race, because she didn't get enough out of the work. *La Lorgnette* finished second to *Imperial Choice*. Benson was never able to get her back into winning shape again. They aimed for the Breeders' Cup at Aqueduct in New York, but a dull effort in a prep race at home made them decide to leave her at home. *La Lorgnette* retired with $488,610, with five wins in nineteen starts.

When she went to the broodmare shed, Windfields sought stallions with a more compact build because after all, big gangly yearlings that looked like *La Lorgnette* aren't terribly saleable. After she was sold at the farm dispersal for US$95,000 to John Sikura, she was matched up with *Woodman*, a very tidy, compact kind of sire. The result was the offspring that made *La Lorgnette's* name in the breeding world: *Hawk Wing*, winner of $1.6 million and the Eclipse Stakes in England. *La Lorgnette's* first foal was *Alexandrina*, dam of *Thornfield*, winner of the Canadian International Championship. Because *Thornfield* was a gelding, *La Lorgnette's* name will live on mostly in the offspring of *Hawk Wing*, which stands at stud at Coolmore in Ireland.

SEVENTH RACE
Woodbine
JULY 14, 1985

1 1-4 MILES (2:01⅕). One Hundred and Twenty-Sixth Running QUEEN'S PLATE STAKES. (Gr. IC). Purse $200,000 Added. 3-year-olds. Foaled in Canada. Scale weight: Colts and geldings, 126 lbs.; fillies, 121 lbs. By subscription of $35 each which shall accompany the nomination by Dec. 15, 1983 (444 nominated); second subscription of $100 each by December 15, 1984 (193 remained eligible); third subscription of $200 by May 1, 1985 (105 remained eligible), and an additional $2,500 when making final entry. In order to remain eligible each subscription or payment must be paid on or before due date. The owner of the first horse receives the Guineas. The added money and all fees to be divided: 60% to the winner, 20% to second, 11% to third, 6% to fourth and 3% to fifth.
Value of race $290,840, value to winner $174,504; second $58,168; third $31,992; fourth $13,088 each. Mutuel Pool $600,788.
Exactor Pool $286,238.

Horse	Eqt.	Wt.	PP	¼	½	¾	1	Str	Fin	Jockey	Owner	Odds $1
LA LORGNETTE		121	12	12³½	10½	6½	1½	11½	12¾	Clark D	Windfields Farm	3.80
IMPERIAL CHOICE		126	6	7²	4ʰᵈ	5½	3¹	3⁵	2ʰᵈ	Driedgerl	Sam-Son Farm	b-.70
PRE EMPTIVE STRIKE	b	126	14	6ʰᵈ	6²½	4½	2¹	2ʰᵈ	3⁵	PlattsR	Cullen & Kennedy	a-8.30
DH -CROWNING HONORS		126	5	13ʰᵈ	14	12²½	8³	6²	4	SwatukB	Cullen & Kennedy	a-8.30
DH -IN MY CAP		121	13	14	13ʰᵈ	11ʰᵈ	7³	5½	4¹	StahlbaumG	Sam-Son Farm	b-.70
ROMAN EMPORER	b	126	8	3ʰᵈ	3¹	3½	4³	4²½	6³	KingRJr	DeToro & Longo	41.70
NORTHERN SISTER		121	4	11¹½	11¹	9½	5ʰᵈ	7⁴	7⁴½	BeckonD	BKY Stable	79.40
STOLE THE PRINCE	b	126	11	9³½	8ʰᵈ	8ʰᵈ	6²	8²½	8²½	LindbergG	Jonassen & Ross	97.00
FIGHTING CHAMP	b	126	9	5½	7³	10²½	9²	9⁶	9⁶½	AttardL	Marcello & Romeo	62.25
WILD STYLE	b	126	2	8ʰᵈ	9ʰᵈ	13	11⁵	11⁹	10ⁿᵏ	LauzonJM	Kinghaven Farms	50.20
S. S. ENTERPRISE		126	10	4¹	5ʰᵈ	7¹	10⁵	10½	11¹⁴	DuffyL	Dixon & Riso	13.30
OLD GUN POWDER	b	126	3	2³	2²½	2ʰᵈ	12⁶	12¹⁰	12²⁰	HosangG	Paddockhurst Stable	39.75
FUSTUKIAN	b	126	1	1ʰᵈ	1½	1ʰᵈ	13	13	13	SeymourD	Derby Farm & SmithRK	8.80
DAUPHIN FABULEUX	b	126	7	10¹	12⁴	---	--	--	--	FellJ	Sam-Son Farm	b-.7C

Dauphin Fabuleux pulled up.
DH -Dead-heat.
a-Coupled: Pre Emptive Strike and Crowning Honors; b-Imperial Choice, In My Cap and Dauphin Fabuleux.
OFF AT 4:39. Start good. Won handily. Time, :23³/₅, :47²/₅, 1:12⁴/₅, 1:38²/₅, 2:04³/₅. Track good.

$2 Mutuel Prices:			
11-LA LORGNETTE	9.60	3.10	2.70
2-IMPERIAL CHOICE (b-Entry)		2.30	2.10
1-PRE EMPTIVE STRIKE (a-Entry)			3.20

$2 EXACTOR 11-2 PAID $16.20
B. f, by Val de l'Orne-The Temptress, by Nijinsky II. Trainer, Benson M. Bred by Taylor E P (Ont-C).
LA LORGNETTE was unhurried for a half-mile and allowed to settle in stride, advanced on the leaders into the far turn in the middle but lacked room, got clear around the turn, moved strongly to take a slight advantage around the final turn, stayed well in early stretch to open up a furlong out, then with a clear margin in deep stretch prevailed in hand. IMPERIAL CHOICE staked the early pace in contention, saved ground around the final turn, dueling, stayed along the rail in the stretch and edged PRE EMPTIVE STRIKE, who was contentious on the outside into the far turn, was inside LA LORGNETTE around the final turn and closed gamely just off the rail. CROWNING HONORS was well back early then closed belatedly off the rail to dead-heat with IN MY CAP, who was well back early, lodged a bid around the final turn and finished on even terms with CROWNING HONORS. ROMAN EMPORER lacked a closing response, as did NORTHERN SISTER. OLD GUN POWDER tired. DAUPHIN FABULEUX was never dangerous,pulled up lame in the backstretch and was vanned off.
Trainers-1, Benson M; 2, Day James E; 3, Warner Arthur H; 4, Warner Arthur H; 5, Day James E; 6, Detoro N; 7, Rowntree Gil H; 8, Carter George M; 9, Marko Bill; 10, Attfield Roger; 11, Dixon Samuel G; 12, Lavigne Jerry G; 13, Smith R K; 14, Day James E.

1986 | GOLDEN CHOICE

Golden Choice just did what he was bred to do, run forever, mud or shine. But when the ebullient colt won the 127th running of the Queen's Plate, the first maiden to score in thirty-four years, the sparks began to fly.

It wasn't a boring year in the annals of Queen's Plate history. Mud flew everywhere, and it wasn't just because the angry heavens poured rain on the Woodbine track for a day before the race. A feud between owner Richard Sanderson, a food broker from Mississauga, Ontario, and Gerry Belanger, his former trainer and the man who had selected *Golden Choice* at the yearling sales, simmered in the year before the Plate, but boiled over afterward into the public domain. Both men were lively raconteurs, outspoken, controversial and with strong personalities. Sanderson wasn't part of the racing establishment. Morning suits weren't for him. Belanger, a veteran horseman, was an astute judge of thoroughbreds.

Things began to go horribly wrong in 1985 after Sanderson moved from Montreal to Mississauga. He was tired of his horses losing and fired Belanger in September, a year before the Plate and chose thirty-one-year-old Mike Tammaro, who had never started a horse in the race. But Sanderson couldn't get rid of Belanger so easily. At the yearling sales in 1984, Sanderson urged Belanger to pick him out a yearling that could run in the Plate. Belanger agreed to forgo his commission for finding the colt, which was to be his top pick of the sale. But when the colt earned out his purchase price, Belanger had the option to buy twenty per cent of him for one dollar. When *Golden Choice* won the Plate, more than winning out his purchase price of $60,000, Sanderson welcomed Belanger to exercise his option. He did. Trouble ensued.

Belanger had enjoyed a successful association with Sanderson. A couple of years earlier he picked out *Val Dansant*, a son of *Val de l'Orne*, for $55,000 at the Woodbine Select Yearling Sales. *Val Dansant* finished fourth in the 1984 Queen's Plate and then won the Prince of Wales Stakes. Belanger had bought a twenty per cent share of him, too, for one dollar, but Sanderson grew weary of paying the training bills when *Val Dansant* went winless in fourteen starts and sold him for stud purposes in New Zealand. Belanger collected twenty per cent of the sale.

Belanger was flying high in the early 1980s. He was considered an astute judge of yearlings after having picked out Eclipse Award winner *Glorious Song* for Frank Stronach and then Canadian champion *Rainbow Connection*. Add to that stakes winner and champion *Corvette Chris*, which earned Belanger a Sovereign Award. Although Sanderson knew he wasn't in Frank Stronach's league, he contacted Belanger out of the blue and learned that he was no longer working for Stronach.

Golden Choice was the sixth horse Belanger had bought for Sanderson, a fifty-five-year-old from Leeds, England, who moved to Canada in 1957. Sanderson wanted a colt that could that could run one-and-a-half miles, the way they do in England. Belanger told him *Golden Choice*, who was also by *Val de l'Orne*, was the only yearling in the sale that could fill the bill. Windfields Farm, which bred

RICHARD SANDERSON HOISTS PLATE TROPHY. AT LEFT, TRAINER MICHAEL TAMMARO AND MRS. SANDERSON.

Golden Choice, trotted him out for inspection by Belanger at the sales, but "he didn't take six steps and I told them to take him back to the barn. I knew he was the one."

Golden Choice was the fourth last horse to sell that night. By the time his hip number came up, Belanger and Sanderson were about the only people left in the sales arena—except for Ernie Samuel, sitting nearby. Belanger despaired. Samuel owned *Golden Choice*'s older half-brother, *Imperial Choice*, who later earned honours as Canada's top three-year-old colt. Said Belanger to

OFT-CONTROVERSIAL GERRY BELANGER.

Sanderson: "We haven't got a prayer. Ernie Samuel will buy him."

Sanderson gave the impression he was leaving the sale, but quietly held up six fingers at the back of the arena. Samuel quit at $55,000. As a two-year-old, *Golden Choice* started only three times, winning $2,897. Belanger was preparing him for the Coronation

Futurity, at a distance he would have favoured, when *Golden Choice* developed a problem with his ankle. Belanger said that things fell apart between two men when he had to face the job he hated the most: telling an owner bad news. It didn't go well, he said.

Sanderson wrote in his book, published in 1988, *The Choice Was Golden*, he just didn't trust Belanger any more. "When we lost and lost and lost, I wanted to ask a lot of questions and have them answered. I was tired with bombast and bravado."

More troubles ensued just before the Plate. Belanger, as president of the Ontario Association of Horse Trainers (which was against foreign horsemen taking jobs from locals), wrote a letter to the federal government to try to have Sanderson's new trainer, Tammaro, a U.S. citizen, deported. (Tammaro, whose father, John, had won the Queen's Plate in 1979 with *Steady Growth*, had spent ten years in Canada.) The move failed. The volatile situation didn't subside when Tammaro brought in Maryland-based jockey Vince Bracciale to ride *Golden Choice* after Brian Swatuk had given up the mount to ride favored *Grey Classic*, the two-year-old champion. Tammaro thought Vince's patient ways would be perfect for *Golden Choice*.

Tammaro warned Sanderson that the jockey was "no oil painting," but not to worry. When Bracciale finally showed up for the Plate, Sanderson saw a scrubby, dark, unshaven man with a huge wad of chewing tobacco in his cheek. "He looked like he'd been on the red eye from somewhere for a week," Sanderson wrote. But Sanderson loved him. And he loved Bracciale's "hillbilly" accent. Without him, Sanderson believes he would not have won the Plate.

Winless in seven starts before the Plate, the big colt went off at odds of more than 11-to-1, had only one horse beaten early, then swung around horses to win easily by four and a half lengths in 2:07 1/5 on the slow track. The last horse to win the Queen's Plate as a maiden was *Epigram* in 1952.

"Winning the Queen's Plate is the biggest surprise of my life," said Sanderson who served in the British army for eight years. "I thought we'd finish in the money, but I'm just a little guy. I'm not big in this business."

GOLDEN CHOICE | 3-year-old bay colt

Owner: Richard Sanderson; *Trainer:* Michael Tammaro
Jockey: Vince Bracciale Jr.; *Breeder:* E.P. Taylor (Ont-C)

Golden Choice won the Prince of Wales, and had a chance to become Canada's third Triple Crown winner but he finished a close third to *Carotene* in the Breeders' Stakes. Later that summer he captured the Niagara Stakes against older horses at Woodbine.

The battles between owner and former trainer continued, with Belanger filing an injunction with the Supreme Court of Ontario to prohibit surgery to correct a fractured splint bone on the horse. As it was, the legal wrangles prevented *Golden Choice* from having a splint bone removed. Eventually, Belanger sold his twenty per cent share back to Sanderson.

Almost two decades later, Belanger encountered Sanderson at a breeders' award ceremony. The two had dinner together and had a few laughs about their misadventures. "We kind of got along with each other. It was a beautiful thing when we left," recalled Belanger.

Golden Choice, Vince Bracciale and groom Cathy Tammaro.

SEVENTH RACE
Woodbine
JULY 13, 1986

1 ¼ MILES (2.01 ⅘). 127th Running THE QUEEN'S PLATE STAKES (Gr IC). Purse $200,000 Added. 3-year-olds, foaled in Canada. Scale Weight: Colts and Geldings 126 lbs.; Fillies 121 lbs. By subscription of $35.00 each to accompany the nomination by December 15, 1984 (465 nominated); second subscription of $100.00 each by December 15, 1985 (204 remained eligible); third subscription of $200.00 by May 1, 1986 (108 remained eligible); and an additional $2,500.00 when making final entry two days prior to the race. In order to remain eligible each subscription or payment must be paid on or before due date. The owner of the first horse receives the Guineas. The added money and all fees to be divided: 60% to the winner, 20% to second, 11% to third, 6% to fourth and 3% to fifth. Final entries to be made through the entry box on a date and time to be determined by the Racing Secretary.
Value of race $290,775; value to winner $174,465; second $58,155; third $31,985; fourth $17,447; fifth $8,723. Mutuel pool $599,473. Exactor Pool $320,030.

Horse	Eqt.	A.	Wt.	PP	¼	½	¾	1	Str	Fin	Jockey	Odds $1
Golden Choice		3	126	6	12²½	11⁶	9¹½	4¹	1¹½	1⁴½	Bracciale V Jr	11.60
Cool Halo		3	126	3	9½	10ʰᵈ	11⁷	7¹½	5⁴	2½	Penna D	12.20
Steady Effort	b	3	126	5	1½	1⁴	1²	2³	3⁴	3ⁿᵒ	Platts R	19.70
No Louder		3	126	2	2½	2²	2¹½	1ʰᵈ	2ʰᵈ	4³¾	Fell J	a-.95
Royal Treasurer		3	126	13	11²	9¹	10¹	6²½	4½	5ⁿᵏ	Clark D	a-.95
Cap Trinite	b	3	126	9	5ʰᵈ	7²	4½	5²	6¹	6⁴½	Attard L	10.90
In The East		3	126	1	8⁷	5½	3²	3½	7⁷	7³½	Beckon D	81.15
Grey Classic	b	3	126	12	10¹	13	12⁷	10³	8²	8⁴	Swatuk B	a-.95
Wolark		3	126	10	6½	6¹	5½	8⁴	9⁶	9²¾	Duffy L	5.10
Bold Costume		3	126	11	13	12ʰᵈ	13	13	11⁸	10²½	Leblanc J B	123.05
Essa Lad	b	3	126	8	7ʰᵈ	8⁶	6½	9¹	10ʰᵈ	11¹⁰	Lauzon J M	42.60
Trooper John	b	3	126	7	4½	3ʰᵈ	7ʰᵈ	12¹	13	12²	Hosang G	18.50
Storm On The Loose		3	126	4	3½	4½	8¹	11³	12²	13	Day P	6.75

a-Coupled: No Louder, Royal Treasurer and Grey Classic
OFF AT 4:41 Start good, Won ridden out. Time, :24¹/₅, :48, 1:13³/₅, 1:40³/₅, 2:07¹/₅ Track slow.

$2 Mutuel Prices:

6-GOLDEN CHOICE	25.20	10.30	7.10
3--COOL HALO		11.20	7.30
5--STEADY EFFORT			11.90
$2 EXACTOR 6-3 PAID $158.40.			

B. c, by Val de l'Orne-Your My Choice, by Barachois. Trainer Tammaro Michael. Bred by Taylor E P (Ont-C).
GOLDEN CHOICE was unhurried when well back early, stayed that way in the backstretch, advanced around the far turn, was outside the dueling leaders into the home lane, stayed outside to take command a furlong out then increased his margin under strong handling. COOL HALO was outrun in the backstretch, was well back around the final turn, came outside in full flight in midstretch and closed willingly. STEADY EFFORT was away with the first flight to take command when pressed, opened up around the clubhouse turn, vied for command around the final turn, stayed dueling in the stretch and outnodded NO LOUDER.

Market Control was the odd one. The one that prepared for the 128th Queen's Plate by hurdling a fallen horse in Detroit. The one that a *Daily Racing Form* handicapper completely discounted, shrugging him off with a terse "Not with these" comment in his Plate predictions. The one that Kinghaven Farms entered only on the urging of a jockey they did not usually hire. But win *Market Control* did, in dramatic fashion with a last-to-first swoop, dashing off all the hot favourites to score by three-and-one-quarter lengths, and earning the best part of a record $340,365 purse. *Market Control* won in 2:03 3/5, the fastest Plate in a decade, since *Regal Embrace* equaled *Victoria Park*'s stakes record of 2:02. And he did it in front of royalty: Prince Andrew, the Duke of York and his gregarious bride, Sarah Ferguson.

Afleet was the glamour boy that was supposed to dazzle the field, and he was supported by his precocious female sidekick *One From Heaven*, winner of the Canadian

THE WILLMOTS—MICHAEL, BUD, DAVID AND IVY—RECEIVE THE AYNSLEY BONE CHINA QUEEN'S PLATE FROM LADY SARAH AND PRINCE ANDREW.

Oaks, and seven of nine starts. Together they were 3-to-5 favourites from Toronto lawyer Rick Kennedy's barn. In a ten-week span, *Afleet*, a son of the top U.S. stallion *Mr. Prospector*, had swashbuckled his way into everybody's hearts, winning four of five starts in impressive fashion. He seemed unbeatable.

While *Afleet* was winning the Plate Trial, *Market Control* was off in the Motor City, running in the humble Piston Stakes—the first stakes race of his career—when a horse broke his leg in front of him and fell. "*Market Control* jumped him, did the Ali shuffle around the jockey and still finished up in third," trainer Roger Attfield said. Jockey Ken Skinner was so impressed by *Market Control*'s response to adversity and his furious stretch kick, that he urged Attfield to run him in the Queen's Plate. In the words of Kinghaven owner David Willmot, Skinner said they'd be crazy not to. Then Skinner had to pray that he'd get the mount. After all, Don Seymour had first call on all the Kinghaven horses, and top U.S. jockey Jose Santos had already approached Attfield to ride *Market Control*. Attfield stuck with Skinner and his enthusiasm. At twenty-nine, Skinner was already a seasoned veteran of twelve years. Born in Edinburgh, Scotland, Skinner moved to Vancouver when he was eighteen months old and launched his career at Exhibition Park. He had moved to the New York circuit in 1979. "The Plate has been on my mind all my life," Skinner said. "When we moved here from New York [where he had been riding until the 1987 season], it was on my mind, but I didn't think we'd be able to do it so quickly."

Market Control, which had made a career of running in allowance races, had never met *Afleet*. Gary Stahlbaum, riding *Afleet*, wanted badly to win his first Plate after eleven unsuccessful tries.

Kennedy had enlisted the world's winningest jockey, Bill Shoemaker, to ride *One From Heaven*. By all accounts, Attfield knew he shouldn't have run *Market Control* in the Plate, if the experts had their way. "According to the dosage index, *Market Control* had no chance," he mused. Because he didn't pretend to understand the index, Attfield said he ran the son of Kentucky Derby winner *Foolish Pleasure* because he thought he deserved a chance. He thought all three Kinghaven horses deserved to be in the race.

Once *Market Control* was finished with him, *Afleet* became the seventh consecutive odds-on favourite to be defeated in the Plate and it looked like the jinx would end when *Afleet* had a length lead turning into the stretch, and *One From Heaven* was making her move on the outside. However, in the early stages of the race, *Market Control* was making his backers relieved there were two other Kinghaven horses in the entry. He trailed the field, three or four lengths behind the next-to-last horse. *Market Control* didn't start moving until the five-eighths pole, but then he began picking up horses relentlessly.

Willmot had been watching his other two starters, noticing that *Steady Power* was making no headway, and neither was *Bodmin Moor*. He switched to look at *Market Control*, just as Skinner dropped his hands, and the big colt began a furious drive. Willmot leaned over and told his wife, Susan, that they were going to win. Harry Addison Jr., sitting in the next box, expressed disbelief. Nobody had been watching *Market Control*. Suddenly, *Market Control* loomed up alongside *Afleet*, undaunted by the fact that *One From Heaven* had carried him wide around the turn. "Where the hell did he come from?" Stahlbaum recalled later. "On the turn when Shoe came up beside me, he said: 'It looks like it's going to be me and you' and he

Alone at the wire, Ken Skinner and *Market Control*.

MARKET CONTROL | 3-year-old bay colt

Market Control (1984)	Foolish Pleasure	What a Pleasure	Bold Ruler
			Grey Flight
		Fool-Me-Not	Tom Fool
			*Cuadrilla
	Amerigirl	Drone	Sir Gaylord
			Caps and Bells
		Lady Amigo	*Amerigo
			Jolly Princess

Owner: Kinghaven Farms; *Trainer:* Roger Attfield
Jockey: Ken Skinner; *Breeder:* Kinghaven Farms Ltd. (Ont-C)

said just to sit chilly because we've got the thing won. I said, 'Yeah, *Afleet*'s gonna be the man now.' I moved off and Shoe was following me and wherever *Market Control* came from, I don't know." *Afleet* finished second, with *One From Heaven* third.

Kennedy, who had rented a large tent for his friends east of the grandstand, thought he had the race won at the head of the stretch and finally had to admit that *Afleet*'s pedigree stopped him. "If he could have gone a mile and a quarter, he would have won," he said. "But he couldn't. His limit is definitely 1 1/8 miles. *Market Control* ran a hell of a race." Kennedy quickly changed plans to run *Afleet* in the one-and-a-quarter-mile Travers, and instead sent him to New York to win the one-mile Jerome Stakes, where he demolished a top-class field and earned enough admiring glances to eventually be sold to Taylor-Made Farm in Kentucky, where he enjoyed an exceptional stud career. *Afleet* was chosen as Canada's Horse of the Year in 1987. He was a multiple stakes winner in the U.S.

Afleet and *Market Control* never met again. *Market Control* failed to hit the board in two starts after the Queen's Plate. He finished fifth in a rain-soaked Prince of Wales and fourth in the Breeders' Stakes. He won the Horometer Stakes. Attfield had been so impressed with the way that *Market Control* worked in the fall, that he nominated him to the Widener Stakes at Hialeah, but almost immediately afterward, the colt suffered a slab fracture of his right knee. He stood at stud for a short time at Kinghaven, but was later sold to Oklahoma interests.

Skinner bounced from track to track afterward, eventually riding at Singapore for a couple of years, then returning home to Vancouver for a few mounts, always scoring with longshots. He was last seen doing race analysis on in-house track broadcasts in New York.

It was the second Queen's Plate win for Kinghaven, the first with *Steady Growth* in 1979. "*Market Control* was one of the most exciting Queen's Plate winners we ever had," Willmot said. "*Steady Growth* was satisfying, because we had been trying to win for a few years and he was our first. But *Market Control* was the most fun. It was totally unexpected." Willmot said of the three horses that Kinghaven entered, *Market Control* was thought the least likely to win. "I fully expected *Afleet* to win this race," he said at the time. "He's still the best three-year-old in Canada. This was just one race on one day, but I'm sure glad this was the one day. My dad [Bud Willmot] told the Duke in the winner's circle that the last time we won the race, he met his grandmother."

SEVENTH RACE
Woodbine
JULY 19, 1987

1 ¼ MILES. (2.01 /5) 128th Running THE QUEEN'S PLATE STAKES (Gr 1C). Purse $225,000 added. (Plus Fifty Guineas). 3-year-olds, foaled in Canada. Scale weight: Colts and Geldings, 126 lbs. Fillies, 121 lbs. By subscription of $35.00 each to accompany the nomination by December 15, 1985 (519 nominated); second subscription of $100.00 by December 15, 1986 (270 remained eligible); third subscription $200 by May 1, 1987 (141 remained eligible) and an additional $3,000 when making final entry two days prior to the race. In order to remain eligible each subscription or payment must be paid on or before due date. The owner of the first horse receives the Guineas. The added money and all fees to be divided 60% to the winner, 20% to second, 11% to third, 6% to fourth and 3% to fifth. Final entries to be made through the entry box on a date and time to be determined by the Racing Secretary.
Value of race $340,365; value to winner $204,219; second $68,073; third $37,440; fourth $20,422; fifth $10,211. Mutuel pool $674,056. Exactor Pool $344,659.

Horse	Eqt.	A.	Wt.	PP	¼	½	¾	1	Str	Fin	Jockey	Odds $1
Market Control	b	3	126	5	14	14	11^{2}	6^{3}	2^{3}	$1^{3¾}$	Skinner K	b-9.30
Afleet	b	3	126	14	6^{1}	7^{1}	6^{hd}	$1^{½}$	$1^{½}$	2^{2}	Stahlbaum G	c-.60
One From Heaven	b	3	121	12	9^{1}	$9^{1½}$	$7^{2½}$	4^{2}	3^{3}	$3^{2½}$	Shoemaker W	c-.60
Duckpower	b	3	126	1	11^{hd}	$10^{1½}$	9^{hd}	7^{2}	$4^{1½}$	$4^{2½}$	Penna D	a-5.30
Steady Power	b	3	126	9	$13^{1½}$	12^{hd}	12^{2}	10^{1}	$8^{4½}$	$5^{¾}$	Dos Ramos R A	b-9.30
Steady Zephyr	b	3	126	11	7^{hd}	6^{hd}	4^{hd}	5^{hd}	7^{hd}	$6^{¾}$	Platts R	16.85
Bold Revenue	b	3	126	6	5^{hd}	3^{hd}	3^{hd}	2^{hd}	$5^{1½}$	$7^{3½}$	Attard L	26.95
Bold Executive		3	126	2	2^{1}	2^{1}	2^{hd}	3^{1}	6^{1}	8^{1}	Hawley S	4.45
Chance For Green		3	126	7	12^{2}	$11^{2½}$	$10^{2½}$	$8^{1½}$	9^{5}	$9^{3½}$	Clark D	31.8
Skate the World		3	126	13	10^{hd}	$13^{1½}$	14	13^{9}	10^{1}	$10^{½}$	Lindberg G	100.05
Bodmin Moor	b	3	126	3	3^{hd}	$4^{½}$	$5^{½}$	11^{5}	$11^{3½}$	$11^{3½}$	Seymour D J	b-9.30
Soggy Sixpense	b	3	126	4	1^{1}	1^{2}	$1^{1½}$	$9^{1½}$	12^{3}	$12^{2½}$	Lauzon J M	a-5.30
Hangin On a Star	b	3	121	10	$8^{1½}$	8^{1}	8^{1}	12^{1}	13^{15}	13	Duffy L	a-5.30
That's A Blunder	b	3	126	8	$4^{1½}$	$5^{1½}$	13^{hd}	14	14	--	Espinoza J C	98.25

That's A Blunder, Distanced.
a-Coupled: Duckpower, Soggy Sixpense and Hangin On a Star; b-Market Control, Steady Power and Bodmin Moor; c-Afleet and One From Heaven.
OFF AT 5:13, Start good, Won handily. Time, :22 /5, :45 /5, 1:11 /5, 1:37 /5, 2:03 /5 Track fast.

$2 Mutuel Prices:			
2-MARKET CONTROL (b-entry)	20.60	5.50	4.00
3-AFLEET (c-entry)		2.60	2.30
3-ONE FROM HEAVEN (c-entry)		2.60	2.30

$2 EXACTOR 2-3 PAID $44.90.

B. c, by Foolish Pleasure-Amerigirl, By Drone. Trainer Attfield Roger. Bred by Kinghaven Farms Ltd (Ont-C).
MARKET CONTROL was well back early when saving ground, was well back after a half mile, advanced around the far turn on the outside, stayed outside into the home late, challenged AFLEET strongly a furlong out then drew away and won under a hand ride. AFLEET was contentious early but well outside, lodged a bid around the far turn, had command around the final turn, opened up in early stretch but could not match the winner. ONE FROM HEAVEN was contentious around the far turn, was inside and even with MARKET CONTROL into the home lane but could not match.

Sam-Son Farm owner Ernie Samuel never would have dreamed he would have won his first Queen's Plate with his second-stringer, *Regal Intention*. Jockey Jack Lauzon did. After several years of presenting favoured three-horse entries that all came a cropper on Plate day, Samuel figured his best chance ever was with *Regal Classic*, a lovely red push-button kind of colt with such an impressive turn of foot, Samuel had sent him on the U.S. Triple Crown trail. At one point, *Regal Classic*, who was co-owned by Windfields Farm, was no more than 10-to-1 to sweep the U.S. Triple Crown in some Nevada betting books.

The big dark colt he called "the other *Regal*" stayed at home and cleaned up at Greenwood and Woodbine, winning four stakes and an allowance race in six starts. However, these accomplishments still didn't suggest a Plate win, particularly with the classy field he had to face. But on a sizzling hot day (thirty-three degrees Celsius), not only did *Regal Intention* put the boots to *Regal Classic* in the $332,495 Queen's Plate, but also to Steve Stavro's star, *Granacus*, winner of the Blue Grass Stakes at Keeneland, a Kentucky Derby starter, and a fifth-place finisher in the Belmont Stakes.

So what if *Regal Classic* had finished second in the Breeders' Cup Juvenile as a two-year-old and finished fifth in the 1988 Kentucky Derby, less than four lengths behind *Winning Colours*? Lauzon had a dream that he would win the Queen's Plate with *Regal Intention*, even with the odds stacked against him. And just to put a further stamp on the matter, his wife's soothsayer, known only as Jessie, predicted the win, too. Lauzon had all the clues. It made him nervous. He never got nervous. But then, he had never won a Plate before either. "Spooky as hell," said Lauzon, who maintained he didn't believe in fortune tellers.

A week before the draw, the seer had told Lauzon's wife, Geraldine, that Lauzon would win the Plate, and she could see the number six on her radar screen. Days later, *Regal Intention* drew post six. "I got up and told myself I'm going to win this race," Lauzon said. But a rash of nerves hit him the night before the race. "I was kind of tossing and turning. Is this true? Is this going to really happen? I slept maybe four hours. I was nervous because I felt like I almost knew I was going to win the race. I never get nervous. I never get butterflies, but this is the worst I ever had them."

What helped him was that he knew he was the underdog, and all the pressure was on *Regal Classic* and Sandy Hawley, who had just rejoined the Woodbine rider colony, after undergoing treatment for cancer in California. Obviously trainer Jim Day, who trained both "*Regals*," didn't see it coming at all. He was almost speechless after the race, happy that his 0-for-11 record in the Plate had finally been broken, but stunned at who had done it for him. Finally, he said: "I don't think *Regal Classic* ran his best race. The other horse outdid himself. *Regal Intention* has never beaten *Regal Classic* doing anything, running against him in the afternoon or working with him in the morning."

On the surface, *Regal Intention*'s job in the Plate was to ensure an honest pace for *Regal Classic*, who was such a hot equine prospect

REGAL INTENTION ENJOYS THE ATTENTION OF OWNER ERNIE SAMUEL AND JOCKEY JACK LAUZON.

that Windfields Farm had purchased a twenty-five per cent share the previous autumn. But neither Samuel nor Day gave Lauzon such instructions. Samuel told Lauzon to go for the win. Day had told Lauzon to take a stiff hold on *Regal Intention* early, because he figured *Baldski's Prize* would take the lead.

Usually *Regal Intention* would pull Lauzon right to the lead. But something blessed happened; *Baldski* knocked dirt in *Regal Intention*'s face, causing the Sam-Son speedster to spit the bit for a while and relax. *Baldski's Prize* set rocking-horse fractions of forty-eight for the half, 1:13 2/5 for the six furlongs, with *Regal Intention* five lengths behind him. They crawled the mile in a ridiculous 1:39, deadly fractions for a stretch runner. With three furlongs to go, *Regal Intention* took the lead, and won in 2:06 1/5, and only had to kick home a final quarter in a leisurely 27 1/5 seconds to keep the rest of the field at bay. "I looked behind and the rest of them weren't getting close," Lauzon said. "I started nudging him and he really went on. I said, 'This is it. I'm going for it all.'"

Regal Classic was second. *Granacus*, ridden by U.S. star Jacinto Vasquez, was third. Trainer Pat Collins said he (*Granacus*) ran out of energy, and he didn't like the hard track. Perhaps both were also spent from their tough U.S. campaign. *Granacus* and *Regal Classic*

SAMUEL'S "SECOND-STRINGER" *REGAL INTENTION* UPSET FAVOURED STABLEMATE.

REGAL INTENTION | 3-year-old dark bay or brown colt

Regal Intention (1985)	Vice Regent	Northern Dancer	Nearctic
			Natalma
		Victoria Regina	*Menetrier
			Victoriana
	Tiffany Tam	Tentam	Intentionally
			Tamerett
		Loudrangle	Quadrangle
			Lady Known as Lou

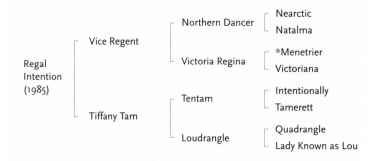

Owner: Sam-Son Farms; *Trainer:* James E. Day
Jockey: Jack M. Lauzon; *Breeder:* Sam-Son Farms (Ont-C)

were only the fourth and fifth horses to run in both the Kentucky Derby and the Plate, the first three being *Victoria Park, Northern Dancer* and *Giboulee*, seventh in the Derby in 1977. *Regal Intention*, like *Regal Classic*, a son of *Vice Regent*, was a fresh horse. Julie Krone became the first woman to ride in the Queen's Plate and finished fifth with *No Malice*, saying it was "the most exciting race I've been a part of."

Samuel was ecstatic, even though he'd strained his back in the morning while lifting a crate of liquor at his home in Milton, Ontario. "There was too much excitement to think about which horse was leading," he said. "You just want to get there first. When a horse is running that strong, you just knew nobody could get to him." In spite of his loss, *Regal Classic* hit a milestone. With his Plate effort, he increased his earnings to $1,030,517, making him the fourth richest Canadian thoroughbred in history. As for *Regal Intention*, he was lucky to be alive. His dam, the stakes winning *Tiffany Tam*, was originally carrying twins, which are a curse in thoroughbred racing. One of them was pinched a month into the pregnancy, leaving *Regal Intention* to survive and become a Queen's Plate winner.

The race was simulcast to ten tracks, including six in the U.S., and broadcast for an hour on CBC. A crowd of 28,812 showed up, the smallest since 1980, and only the second time in twenty years that fewer than thirty thousand witnessed the Plate. Even Princess Margaret's presence couldn't make people leave the comfort of their air-conditioned homes that day. Sam-Son was the first owner in twenty-six years to send out both the first- and second-place finishers, echoing the achievement of Windfields Farm in 1962.

The best was yet to come. The two *Regals* hooked up again in the Prince of Wales at Fort Erie, and created one of the most memorable stretch duels in Canadian racing history. The race was switched to one-and-three-sixteenth mile on the dirt, to spice up the Canadian Triple Crown and make it more attractive for Plate horses, and the result was electrifying. This time *Regal Classic* won by the bob of a nose. The final quarter mile was grand theatre. *Regal Intention* set the pace, but *Regal Classic* loomed up at the top of the stretch. To the eighth pole *Regal Intention* stayed on top by a few inches. For the next sixteenth of a mile the two were dead even. *Regal Classic* inched ahead, and seemed the victor, but *Regal Intention* fought back in the last ten yards and caught up. Neither jockey knew which had won. The two "*Regals*" never met again.

SEVENTH RACE
Woodbine
JULY 10, 1988

1 ¼ MILES. (2.01 /5) 129th Running QUEENS PLATE STAKES (Grade I-C). Purse $225,000 Added. 3-year-olds foaled in Canada. (Closed) Scale Weight: Colts and geldings, 126 lbs. Fillies, 121 lbs. By subscription of $35 each to accompany the nomination by December 15, 1986 (597 nominated); second subscription of $100 each by December 15, 1987 (284 remained eligible); third subscription of $200 by May 1, 1988 (126 remained eligible); and an additional $3,000 when making final entry two days prior to the race. In order to remain eligible each subscription or payment must be paid on or before due date. The owner of the first horse receives the Guineas. The added money and all fees to be divided: 60% to the winner, 20% to second, 11% to third, 6% to fourth and 3% to fifth. Final entries to be made through the entry box on a date and time to be determined by the Racing Secretary.
Value of race $332,495; value to winner $199,497; second $66,499; third $36,574; fourth $19,950; fifth $9,975. Mutuel pool $665,948. Exactor Pool $348,071.

Horse	Eqt.	A.	Wt.	PP	¼	½	¾	1	Str	Fin	Jockey	Odds $1
Regal Intention		3	126	6	2^{1}	2^{3}	2^{1}	$1^{2½}$	$1^{3½}$	$1^{3¼}$	Lauzon J M	a-.55
Regal Classic		3	126	3	4^{1}	3^{hd}	4^{hd}	$3^{1½}$	2^{2}	$2^{2½}$	Hawley S	a-.55
Granacus		3	126	8	$8^{½}$	8^{hd}	7^{2}	$4^{1½}$	3^{4}	$3^{1¼}$	Vasquez J	2.40
Grey Skelly		3	121	1	$10^{1½}$	$10^{½}$	$10^{½}$	$8^{2½}$	$5^{1½}$	4^{nk}	Swatuk B	38.00
No Malice		3	126	10	$3^{1½}$	$4^{½}$	$6^{1½}$	$5^{½}$	4^{hd}	5^{nk}	Krone J A	36.10
Tejabob		3	126	9	9^{3}	9^{7}	$8^{1½}$	9^{3}	$7^{4½}$	$6^{3½}$	Clark D	b-11.95
Sweeping Change	b	3	126	2	6^{hd}	5^{hd}	$5^{½}$	$6^{1½}$	6^{3}	7^{4}	Seymour D J	34.30
Rather Theatrical	b	3	126	5	11	11	11	11	9^{3}	8^{4}	Penna D	b-11.95
Lucky J. W.		3	126	4	$7^{½}$	7^{hd}	$9^{4½}$	$10^{½}$	11	$9^{½}$	Ravera P P	108.80
Plate Dancer	b	3	126	11	$5^{½}$	$6^{3½}$	$3^{½}$	7^{hd}	10^{hd}	10^{nk}	Ward W	97.05
Baldski's Prize		3	126	7	$1^{2½}$	1^{5}	$1^{1½}$	2^{hd}	$8^{½}$	11	Platts R	9.85

a-Coupled: Regal Intention and Regal Classic; b-Tejabo and Rather Theatrical.
OFF AT 5:13 Start good, Won handily. Time, :24, :48, 1:13 2/5, 1:39, 2:06 1/3 Track fast.

$2 Mutuel Prices:

1-REGAL INTENTION (a-entry)	3.10	3.00	2.10
1-REGAL CLASSIC (a-entry)	3.10	3.00	2.10
7-GRANACUS			2.50

$2 EXACTOR 1-1 PAID $12.80.

Dk. b. or br. c, by Vice Regent-Tiffany Tam, by Tentam. Trainer Day James E. Bred by Sam-Son Farms (Ont-C).
REGAL INTENTION was well placed early in the early leader, was outrun around the clubhouse turn, moved up on the leader approaching the far turn, took command around the turn to open up, had a clear advantage in midstretch and retained it with authority. REGAL CLASSIC was unhurried early when between rivals, advanced around the far turn, was just outside into the home lane then closed evenly off the rail. GRANACUS was well back early, lodged his bid around the final turn but never threatening in the run for the wire. GREY SKELLY was far back early then finished with determination.

Those who knew *With Approval* very well called him "Snoopy," because he was so laid-back. But those who watched him in action called him the "Cardiac Kid," because his racing style kept them on the edge of their seats. This was no more so than in the Queen's Plate, when *With Approval* overcame the worst of trips to win by the bob of his pert roan nose, and set up the first Triple Crown sweep in twenty-six years. It was the first Plate win for twenty-eight-year-old jockey Don Seymour, and the third in ten years for Kinghaven Farms.

With Approval was only the second grey or roan to win the Queen's Plate in its 130 runnings, the first being *Acara* in 1944. The plan was to have *With Approval* five or six lengths off the lead, but before anybody could say Queen Mum, he was bumped around badly, shuffled back by fifteen lengths by the first turn, bogged down on the rail, in danger of clipping heels, ahead of only three horses and off the bit. "I said at the five-eighths pole, forget it," said Kinghaven Farm president David Willmot. Trainer Roger Attfield had all but given up on *With Approval* after the first quarter mile. "I must say, I wasn't very confident after the first turn," said Attfield, after winning his third Plate. Seymour was worried, too. *With Approval* was getting too much dirt in his face, so Seymour wheeled him to the outside. With a half-mile left to run *With Approval* was fifth, and suddenly by the top of the stretch, was in striking position. Just then, Sam-Son Farm's irritable, unpredictable *Most Valiant* (after he bit a groom, he was dubbed "Most Violent") launched a blistering stretch drive for a screaming Jack Lauzon, who thought he was going to win two Plates in a row.

The battle in front of 32,485 fans and Queen Elizabeth, the Queen Mother was epic. The two colts fought stride for stride, noses apart the length of the stretch. "I did everything I could come up with once I realized *Most Valiant* had a shot," Lauzon told writer Jim Proudfoot after the race. "I hit him with the whip. I jumped up and down and I yelled my fool head off. . . . I don't think he had anything left to give. He ran his eyeballs out." Seymour said he didn't know where the finish line was. "I just had my head down and I was riding as hard as I could. . . . I was glad the wire came when it did." Neither Lauzon nor Seymour knew who had won until the mutuels numbers flashed onto the infield board. The wait took longer than the race did: 2:03. *Domasca Dan*, the lunch-bucket colt with a big

MRS. IVY WILLMOT CHIRPS TO *WITH APPROVAL* AFTER HIS NOSE VICTORY. OWNER BUD WILLMOT, TRAINER ROGER ATTFIELD AND DON SEYMOUR.

heart, finished third, one-and-one-quarter lengths behind the leaders. The purse was a record $429,434 and the race was shown to thirty outlets through simulcast in Canada and the United States.

With Approval had been the 11-to-10 betting favourite and was regarded so highly by Kinghaven after winning his only two starts as a two-year-old that they put him on the U.S. Triple Crown trail earlier in the season. He finished second in the Tampa Bay Stakes, but then misbehaved in the post parade and acted up in the starting gate in the Flamingo Stakes. He didn't run a lick and finished sixth. Attfield gave him a break, brought him home and schooled him, reasoning afterward that the Florida disaster was a blessing in disguise. If he had done well in Florida at the Flamingo, they would have been tempted to go after the big U.S. races, although not the Kentucky Derby; Attfield had seen *Easy Goer* train in Florida and wanted no part of him.

The Bank of Montreal was paying a $1 million bonus for the first time to the Canadian Triple Crown winner. They were able to get away with paying reasonable insurance fees—$100,000, plus a $50,000 deductible if the money had to be paid out—because the likelihood of anybody accomplishing the feat seemed remote. It hadn't been accomplished since 1963 when *Canebora* won it. Kinghaven made the Canadian Triple Crown its main objective and *With Approval* picked a fine time to prove the insurance agents wrong.

A NOSE SEPARATED *WITH APPROVAL* (LEFT) AND *MOST VALIANT*.

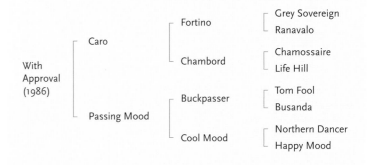

WITH APPROVAL | 3-year-old roan colt

With Approval (1986)	Caro	Fortino	Grey Sovereign
			Ranavalo
		Chambord	Chamossaire
			Life Hill
	Passing Mood	Buckpasser	Tom Fool
			Busanda
		Cool Mood	Northern Dancer
			Happy Mood

Owner: Kinghaven Farms; *Trainer:* Roger Attfield
Jockey: Donald J. Seymour; *Breeder:* Kinghaven Farms Ltd. (Ont-C)

In the Queen's Plate *With Approval* encountered problems at the starting gate, having to stand while *Domasca Dan* refused to be loaded, then remaining calm when British Columbia entry *Rear Admiral* acted up in the next stall, almost jumping over the barrier. *Rear Admiral,* owned in part by Edmonton businessman Nelson Skalbania, had been undefeated before he came east, but finished last in the Plate Trial.

The Prince of Wales wasn't any easier for *With Approval,* winning it by only a head after staying close to the pace of *Domasca Dan.* "In the last seventy yards, that's when you've got to keep busy on him to make sure he's paying attention," Seymour said. "If you ask him a little too early . . . he'll relax on you and think it's all over when he gets his head in front." *With Approval* won in 1:56 4/5, just four-fifths off the track record. This time everything went according to plan, but it kept Attfield on his toes. "It's pretty hair-raising," he said. "You'd like to have him pull aways a little more so you don't get palpitations. I'll tell you one thing about horses like this—they're very hard on the trainer and they're a lot easier on themselves." *With Approval*'s grandsire, *Buckpasser,* ran the same way.

With Approval never won by much on dirt, but on grass he excelled. Attfield expected more in the Breeders' Stakes and he got it. *With Approval* thrashed *Most Valiant* to win by seven and a half lengths on the turf. "We would have needed wings to catch *With Approval,*" Lauzon said. The Triple Crown win made *With Approval* Canada's richest racehorse with earnings of $1,819,700. *With Approval* didn't get a chance to test the best three-year-old colts in the United States after minor back and leg ailments forced him to the sidelines, but his efforts were good enough to make him Canada's Horse of the Year.

Kept on the grass at age four, *With Approval* proved to be one of the top turf runners in North America, setting a world record of 2:10.46 for eleven furlongs in winning the Bowling Green Handicap at Belmont, thereby breaking a mark set by the mighty *Cougar II*; defeating *Alwuhush* in the Tidal Handicap at Belmont in stakes record time, finishing second to Wayne Gretzky's *Golden Pheasant* in the $1 million Arlington Million in Chicago—and better yet, earning a valiant second by a half-length in the Breeders' Cup Turf at Belmont. Although he was supposed to race as a five-year-old, *With Approval* was retired late in his four-year-old career after he suffered a slight tear to a suspensory ligament. Plans to race in the $2 million Japan Cup were cancelled. At stud, he excelled with numerous stakes winners.

SEVENTH RACE
Woodbine
JULY 9, 1989

1 ¼ MILES. (2.01 1/5) 130th Running QUEEN'S PLATE STAKES (Grade Ic). Canada's Triple Crown Series. Purse $250,000 added. (Plus Fifty Guineas) 3-year-olds, foaled in Canada. (Closed). Weights: colts and geldings, 126 lbs.; fillies, 121 lbs. By subscription of $100 each to accompany the nomination by December 15, 1987 (558 nominated); second subscription of $500 by December 15, 1988 (235 remained eligible); the first two payments due December 15, 1987 and December 15, 1988 are split equally among the Queen's Plate, Prince of Wales and Breeders' Stakes; third subscription of $1,000 by May 15, 1989 (80 remained eligible) and an additional $5,000 when making final entry two days prior to the race applies to Queen's Plate only. In order to remain eligible each subscription and payment must be paid on or before due date. The added money and all applicable fees to be divided 60% to the winner, 20% to second, 11% to third, 6% to fourth and 3% to fifth. Final entries to be made through the entry box on a date and time to be determined by the racing secretary. $1,000,000 bonus offered by the Bank of Montreal to the winner of all three races: The Queen's Plate, Prince of Wales and Breeders' Stakes, or $250,000 to the horse that accumulates the most points competing in all three races. Points accredited: 5 for win, 3 for second, and 1 for third.
Value of race $429,434; value to winner $257,660; second $85,887; third $47,238; fourth $25,766; fifth $12,883. Mutuel pool $809,234. Exactor Pool $396,037.

Horse	Eqt.	A.	Wt.	PP	¼	½	¾	1	Str	Fin	Jockey	Odds $1
With Approval		3	126	8	12^{1}	11^{2}	$10^{1/2}$	5^{hd}	$3^{1/2}$	1no	Seymour D J	1.10
Most Valiant		3	126	1	2^{hd}	$3^{1/2}$	5^{1}	$4^{1/2}$	$2^{1\frac{1}{2}}$	$2^{1\frac{1}{4}}$	Lauzon J M	a-8.95
Domasca Dan	b	3	126	10	$4^{1/2}$	1^{hd}	1^{hd}	1^{hd}	1^{hd}	$3^{1\frac{1}{4}}$	Sabourin R B	4.95
Blondeinamotel		3	121	2	$8^{1/2}$	5^{hd}	6^{1}	7^{3}	$5^{1\frac{1}{2}}$	4^{hd}	Day P	4.65
Splasing Success	b	3	126	3	$3^{1/2}$	$4^{1\frac{1}{2}}$	3^{hd}	$2^{1/2}$	$4^{1\frac{1}{2}}$	$5^{1/2}$	Attard L	99.65
Stellar Night		3	126	5	$6^{1/2}$	$7^{1/2}$	7^{1}	6^{1}	6^{4}	$6^{4\frac{1}{2}}$	Penna D	5.20
Lone Pine		3	126	6	$10^{1/2}$	$14^{1/2}$	15	10^{4}	8^{3}	7^{1}	David D J	101.90
Creed	b	3	126	4	7^{1}	6^{2}	$4^{1/2}$	$3^{2\frac{1}{2}}$	7^{hd}	$8^{2\frac{1}{2}}$	Lindberg G	25.65
Forum Fighter		3	126	13	11^{1}	$9^{1/2}$	$9^{1/2}$	9^{1}	9^{4}	$9^{2\frac{3}{4}}$	Stahlbaum G	123.70
Harry Laric		3	126	14	15	15	12^{hd}	11^{3}	$10^{1/2}$	10^{1}	Clark D	116.70
Ivory Dance		3	121	12	5^{hd}	8^{2}	8^{2}	8^{hd}	11^{10}	11^{11}	Landry R C	a-8.95
Rear Admiral		3	126	7	$13^{1/2}$	13^{1}	$13^{1\frac{1}{2}}$	13^{4}	12^{3}	12^{2}	Walker M	32.75
Antigonos	b	3	126	11	$14^{2\frac{1}{2}}$	12^{hd}	14^{hd}	$14^{1/2}$	13^{3}	$13^{2\frac{1}{2}}$	McAleney J	b-80.20
Wave Wise	b	3	126	9	$1^{1/2}$	$2^{1\frac{1}{2}}$	$2^{1\frac{1}{2}}$	12^{3}	14^{1}	$14^{3/4}$	Hawley S	a-8.95
Askar		3	126	15	9^{hd}	$10^{2\frac{1}{2}}$	11^{4}	15	15	15	Dos Ramos R A	b-80.20

a-Coupled: Most Valiant, Ivory Dance and Wave Wise; b-Antigonos and Askar.
OFF AT 5:13 Start good, Won driving. Time, :24, :47 3/5, 1:12 2/5, 1:37 3/5, 2:03 Track fast.

$2 Mutuel Prices:			
9--WITH APPROVAL	4.20	3.10	2.50
1--MOST VALIANT (a-entry)		6.20	3.60
10- DOMASCA DAN			3.00

$2 EXACTOR 9-1 PAID $29.40.

Ro. c, by Caro-Passing Mood, By Buckpasser. Trainer Attfield Roger. Bred by Kinghaven Farms Ltd (Ont-C).
WITH APPROVAL was well back coming by the grandstand for the first time along the rail, eased just outside in the backstretch and still unhurried, lodged a bid around the far turn, stayed outside into the home lane, dueled with a rival in midstretch then responding to a strong drive, outnodded his foes. MOST VALIANT was away smartly to vie for the early lead when saving ground, stalked the issue around the far turn came between foes into the home lane inside the winner, dueled for command in the stretch run and just missed. DOMASCA DAN vied for the early lead, had command in the backstretch, retained command in midstretch along the rail but failed to match the top pair. BLONDEINAMOTEL was well placed early, was inside into the home lane but failed to menace between foes thereafter. SPLASHING SUCCESS vied for command around the final turn but weakened in the stretch run.

The odds were against Kinghaven Farms—or anybody—having two superstars in back-to-back seasons. Kinghaven proprietor David Willmot didn't foresee a sparkling future for *Izvestia* when he first laid eyes on the rakish little grey as a foal. *Izvestia* wasn't exactly a showstopper. He more closely resembled a Russian-built Lada.

"*Izzy* [as Willmot still fondly calls him today] was one of the smallest, worst-looking, pathetic foals we ever had born on the farm," he said. "He was never a big, strapping horse." But wait, *Izzy* must have said. He managed to become not only the easiest of Queen's Plate winners in 131 years and only the fourth Triple Crown winner in history, but he marched through his three-year-old season draped in superlatives.

The crown was supposed to have fallen to Sam-Son's marvellous looker *Sky Classic*, a royally bred son of *Nijinsky II* that had been marked for the Kentucky Derby trail until he cracked a hind cannon bone early in his three-year-old season. While *Sky Classic* had been chosen Canada's top two-year-old colt, *Izvestia* was flying under the radar, racing only twice, finishing sixth in the Coronation Futurity on a sloppy track that he didn't seem to relish. His first race was more impressive. In the paddock before the

LIEUTENANT GOVERNOR LINCOLN ALEXANDER, BETWEEN D.G. WILLMOT (LEFT) AND OJC BOARD CHAIRMAN CHARLES BAKER, RIGHT, CONGRATULATE JOCKEY DON SEYMOUR.

race, a horse nearby kicked a wall, prompting *Izzy* to jump over backwards and fall. The colt seemed so dazed afterward that trainer Roger Attfield told rider Don Seymour to have him scratched if he didn't wake up. But he went out and won the race by six lengths.

In 1990 *Izvestia* blossomed. Even before he faced the starting gate of the $392,000 Queen's Plate, most deemed him unbeatable. It was "*Izvestia* and the rest o' ya," the backstretch colony hummed. With five wins in seven starts under his belt, *Izvestia* didn't disappoint at odds of 3-to-5. From post 12 he absolutely destroyed his twelve opponents, winning by thirteen lengths, the greatest winning margin in the race's history. Even though jockey Don Seymour never cocked his whip, *Izvestia* sped the distance in an astonishing 2:01 4/5, shaving one-fifth of a second off the thirty-year-old stakes record set by *Victoria Park* and equalled in 1978 by *Regal Embrace*. The time was two-fifths faster than *Northern Dancer*'s clocking in 1964 and a fifth faster than *With Approval*'s time the previous year. His time was as fast or faster than all but eleven Kentucky Derby winners, including *Unbridled*, the Derby winner of 1990. Izvestia ran the final two furlongs in 24 1/5 seconds, unpushed and unthreatened. *With Approval* did it in 25 3/5 seconds the year before. There are few that have run faster final quarters in any of the Kentucky Derbies or Queen's Plates to date. Only *Secretariat*'s final quarter clocking of twenty-three seconds in 1973 was faster than Izvestia's final sprint to the wire. As for lopsided victories, Izvestia's effort was the ultimate. *Young Kitty* won the Plate in 1928 by twelve

lengths. *Lyford Cay* won the 1957 Plate by eleven and a half lengths.

"He wasn't even tired," Willmot said in a whisper, having lost his voice yelling for the colt down the homestretch. "He wasn't even blowing hard in the winner's circle. I was breathing harder than he was. I was absolutely awestruck. If he belonged to somebody else I would have been excited. I would have said it was the most impressive Plate I've ever seen." He wasn't the only one. Richard Migliore, who came from New York to ride Steve Stavro's *Iskandar Elakbar* to a third-place finish, was most vocal, saying it was "the strongest race I've seen any three-year-old run this year, including [Preakness winner] *Summer Squall* and [Kentucky Derby winner] *Unbridled*. And [Belmont Stakes winner] *Go and Go* ran a powerful race at a mile and a half, but I can't think he wants to see this horse."

Migliore was one of four U.S. jockeys to ship in for the race—an unusually high number of invaders—but none could crack Seymour's grasp on the Plate. Pat Day, Jorge Velasquez and Ron Hansen all watched *Izvestia*'s rump disappear into the Woodbine distance. The crowd of 28,494 applauded enthusiastically in tribute to the little grey for his cool fireworks. It was Kinghaven's fourth Plate win, and its third in four years. Willmot admitted afterward he was a nervous wreck, unable to sleep and eight times more nervous than he'd been before *With Approval*'s Plate score. "I just found it so hard to believe we had a shot at two consecutive Queen's Plates."

Izvestia, a son of *Icecapade*, was named after a Russian hockey tournament. Attfield dubbed him *Izzy Goer*. Whatever his moniker,

IZVESTIA AND NOBODY. THE GREY COLT WON BY THIRTEEN LENGTHS.

IZVESTIA | 3-year-old grey colt

Owner: Kinghaven Farms; *Trainer:* Roger Attfield
Jockey: Donald J. Seymour; *Breeder:* Kinghaven Farms Ltd. (Ont-C)

Izvestia was hot, very hot, all season en route to Horse of the Year honours. He won the $191,500 Prince of Wales Stakes by six-and-a-quarter lengths over *Very Formal*. He ran the one-and-three-sixteenths mile in 1:56 2/5, only two-fifths of a second slower than the track record." He has gears left he hasn't used yet," said Seymour. "I get numb when he comes down the stretch," Willmot said.

Every detail of his life soon became public knowledge: *Izvestia* is allergic to hay dust, so he eats a special diet; *Izvestia* loves oranges and grapes, eating them one at a time. Just before the Prince of Wales, Gainesway Farm in Kentucky bought a half-interest in *Izvestia* to stand him at stud at the end of his four-year-old career. The farm had been looking for a replacement for *Icecapade*, which had died two years before. *Izzy* was supposed to live in his sire's old stall, eventually.

Imagine the Kinghaven nerves when the turf came up soft for the Breeders' Stakes. *Izvestia* answered the doubt by winning the one-and-a-half mile race by six lengths. Along with it came the $1 million Bank of Montreal bonus for sweeping all three legs. Seymour was in tears. Willmot, of course, had feared the worst. "This is the most emotional race I've ever been involved with in my entire life," he said. A few weeks later *Izvestia* won the Molson Million by three lengths. Attield said, "*Izvestia* could end up being a better horse than *With Approval* and that's saying a lot, isn't it? He's the real thing. There's no doubt about it."

Unfortunately, *Izvestia* will always be remembered for the race he didn't finish as much as for the races he did. "We mismanaged him as a four-year-old," Willmot recalled years later. "I feel very badly about it. We took him to some weird races we shouldn't have done, and we never got him on the right path. Roger felt he was finally coming right, just before the [Rothman's International] that year." As the field moved in front of the grand-

stand for the first time in the one-and-a-half mile race, *Izvestia* broke a hind leg, suffering a compound fracture of his left hind cannon bone and demolishing his pastern into fifteen pieces, like a bag of ice. He could not be saved. "That was our worst day in the business, ever," said Willmot, who had also lived through the euthanasia of their former Horse of the Year, *Play The King*, a short time before.

"Dad and I were driving home after that, and it was just awful and everybody was weeping," he said. "Both of us looked at each other and said: 'We can't handle this. We've got to get out of the business.' But you go back to the farm, and you see the young horses out in the fields, and you just say it's a terrible part of the business but you have to understand this is part of the business and go on. It was hard. When you have two Horses of the Year go down on the racetrack, it really was hard."

SEVENTH RACE
Woodbine
JULY 8, 1990

1 ¼ MILES. (2.01 /5) 131st Running THE QUEEN'S PLATE STAKES (Grade IC). Purse $250,000 Added (Plus Fifty Guineas, The Gift Of Her Majesty The Queen-Canada's Triple Crown Series). 3-year-olds. Foaled in Canada. Weight: Colts and Geldings, 126 lbs. Fillies,121 lbs. By subscription of $100.00 each to accompany the nomination by December 15, 1989 (188 remained eligible) the first two payments due December 15, 1988 and December 15, 1989 are split equally among the Queen's Plate, Prince of Wales and the Breeders' Stakes; third subscription of $1,000 by May 15, 1990 (61 remained eligible) and an additional $5,000.00 when making final entry two days prior to the race applies to Queen's Plate only. In order to remain eligible each subscription and payment must be paid on or before due date. The added money and all applicable fees to be divided: 60% to the winner, 20% to second, 11% to third, 6% to fourth and 3% to fifth. The owner of the winner receives the Guineas. Final entries to be made through the entry box on a date and time to be determined by the Racing Secretary. $1,000,000 bonus offered by the Bank of Montreal to the winner of all three races: The Queen's Plate, Prince of Wales and Breeders' Stakes or $250,000 to the horse that accumulates the most points competing in all three races. Points accredited 5 for win, 3 for second and 1 for third.
Value of race $392,000; value to winner $235,200; second $78,400; third $43,120; fourth $23,520; fifth $11,760. Mutuel pool $606,580. Exactor Pool $391,463

Horse	Eqt.	A.	Wt.	PP	¼	½	¾	1	Str	Fin	Jockey	Odds $1
Izvestia	b	3	126	12	5½	6¹	3½	1hd	1⁹	1¹³	Seymour D J	b-.60
Very Formal	b	3	126	9	10³	10²	10²	5¹	3³	2¹¼	Hawley S	a-4.95
Iskandar Elakbar		3	126	5	3hd	3½	1hd	2½	2⁴½	3nk	Migliore R	7.20
Secret 'n Classy	b	3	126	11	11²½	11²½	12¹⁵	10hd	6hd	4¹¼	Swatuk B	a-4.95
Key Timing		3	126	7	12³	12⁸	11¹	9²½	7⁸	5⁴½	Hansen R	44.65
Bundle Bits		3	121	10	6¹½	5¹	5hd	3¹½	4¹	6½	McAleney J S	b-.60
Roll the Dice		3	126	8	4¹½	4¹	2hd	4³½	5½	7²½	Day P	9.35
Cozzene's Prince		3	126	2	1hd	2½	6¹	12²⁰	9¹½	8²½	Fenech S C	78.00
Ordinary Superstar	b	3	126	6	8hd	8¹½	8²	8hd	8hd	9½	Penna D	70.60
Halo's Honey		3	126	4	7hd	7hd	7hd	7hd	10¹½	10½	Dos Ramos R A	27.55
Truth Squad	b	3	126	13	9¹½	9¹	9³	11²	11²	11³½	Attard L	93.85
French King	b	3	126	3	2½	1hd	4²	6½	12²⁵	12	Velasquez J	12.60
King Riviera		3	126	1	13	13	13	13	13	--	Platts R	93.30

King Riviera, Distanced.
a-Coupled: Very Formal and Secret 'n Classy; b-Izvestia and Bundle Bits.
OFF AT 5:10 Start good. Won handily. Time, :23 ²/₅, :47 ⁴/₅, 1:13, 1:37 ³/₅, 2:01 ⁴/₅ Track fast.

$2 Mutuel Prices:				
2-IZVESTIA (b-entry)		3.20	2.50	2.20
1-- VERY FORMAL (a-entry)			3.50	2.90
7-- ISKANDAR ELAKBAR				3.10

$2 EXACTOR 2-1 PAID $9.40.
Gr. c, (May), by Icecapade-Shy Spirit, by Personality. Trainer Attfield Roger. Bred by Kinghaven Farms Ltd. (Ont-C).

IZVESTIA was unhurried coming by the grandstand for the first time on the outside, lost some ground around the clubhouse turn, moved up on the leader in the backstretch, dueled around the far turn, had command around the final turn to open up in early stretch, then increased his margin with every stride. VERY FORMAL was well back early, advanced around the final turn and closed with determination well off the rail. ISKANDAR ELAKBAR pressed the early pace, vied for command inside the winner around the far turn but lacked a closing response.

Dance Smartly always knew she was something special. She had a cocky way about her, an attitude that breathed: "Peel me a grape." It's just that in the spring of 1991, not everybody knew yet how very, very good she was.

Trainer Jim Day, who had an intimate knowledge of all his Sam-Son Farm charges, said early in the season that the colt, *Rainbows for Life*, was a more likely winner of the Queen's Plate than *Dance Smartly*. At two, Ernie Samuel thought *Radiant Ring* was better. A reporter wrote that the Bank of Montreal's $1-million bonus for sweeping the Triple Crown was safe this year, because there just wasn't another *With Approval* or *Izvestia* on the prowl. They didn't reckon with *Dance Smartly*, who scared the fillies—and the colts—out of their bridles and bits in 1991. By the end of the year, *Rainbows for Life* was staying out of *Dance Smartly*'s way in her quest for the Triple Crown. Although the filly, *Queensway*, won all three races in 1932, *Dance Smartly* is credited as being the first and only filly Triple Crown winner in Canada. The trio of races—the Queen's Plate, Prince of Wales and the Breeders' Stakes—hadn't been strung together officially as a series until 1959.

Dance Smartly was a happy accident. Her mother, *Classy 'n Smart*, a future Hall of Fame inductee, was headed for the court of English Triple Crown winner *Nijinsky II*, but he was ailing, so she was sent to another son of *Northern Dancer*, *Danzig*, to be bred. The result was a dark bay filly that grew larger than her mother, and, with more of an attitude. "*Classy 'n Smart* was the nicest horse you could ever be around," said Irwin Driedger, her regular rider. "And she had a lot of ability. She was just a class act. She was a push-button horse. She was a real sweetheart. A little kid could lead her around."

Driedger was on the verge of retirement and no longer riding regularly for them, but when *Dance Smartly* made her first start, the Sam-Son establishment gave him the ride, just for old times sake. He remembers that *Dance Smartly* was stubborn loading into the gate. "She was not as easy-going [as *Classy 'n Smart*]," he said. "*Dance Smartly* was pretty good from the word go." Under Driedger, she won, going off at 1-to-2 and winning with authority by three and a half lengths. Driedger retired shortly afterward, with a bright memory.

Winning the Queen's Plate by eight lengths with authoritative ease was just her first coronation. *Dance Smartly* won all eight starts as a three-year-old, including her thrashing of some good U.S. colts in the Molson Export Million at Woodbine. She then made history in the Breeders' Cup, the showcase event for the best thoroughbreds in the world. Eighteen previous Canadian-based horses, including *Dance Smartly* (third the year before in the Juvenile Fillies) had run in the Breeders' Cup and had been beaten. But at Kentucky's Churchill Downs she became the first Canadian-bred to win, capturing the rich Distaff in convincing fashion against America's best fillies and mares. When she did, she surpassed *Lady Secret*'s world record earnings for a female, garnering a total of $3,263,836 when she retired at four. Her exploits also earned her a Sovereign and Horse of the Year honours in Canada and an Eclipse Award in the United States as the champion three-year-old filly. Like *Northern*

DANCE SMARTLY'S WINNING TEAM—TRAINER JIM DAY, JOCKEY PAT DAY AND OWNER ERNIE SAMUEL.

Dancer before her, she helped put Canada on the horse-racing map.

Samuel figured *Dance Smartly* deserved a shot at the boys after winning the Canadian Oaks over her stablemate *Wilderness Song*, which eventually became Sam-Son's first Grade 1 winner, with a victory in the Spinster Stakes in Kentucky. *Dance Smartly* won the Oaks without breaking a gallop, according to her rider Pat Day. She created minus betting pools, and the filly they called *Daisy* because of the marking on her forehead, was just beginning. Ditto for the Queen's Plate, even though she ran against Plate Trial winners *Bolulight* and the big, lumbering *Megas Vukefalos*, the royally bred *Rainbows for Life*, who had been the champion two-year-old in Canada the previous year, U.S. import British Banker from the mighty Dogwood Stable, and *Shudanz*, who had won the Victoria Park Stakes by eight and a half lengths.

So what? *Dance Smartly* seemed to say. "She only ran today for maybe three or four jumps," Pat Day said after the victory. *Wilderness Song* set the pace and hung on gamely as Pat Day lowered his hands for only a few moments and *Dance Smartly* plunged by her. The filly one-two was the first such finish since *Sally Fuller* won in 1935 ahead of *Chickpen*. "I guess if they're even-steven, a tough colt will beat a tough filly," Samuel said afterward. "But this is a great filly." A crowd of 26,932 witnessed the spectacle, and had bet the three-horse Sam-

Son entry down to odds-on favourites. The Prince of Wales drew only six entries, and *Dance Smartly* was the only horse anybody wanted to talk about, although she had two talented stablemates in the race, and 8,350 fans bet them down to 1-to-9.

"Before the Queen's Plate, I thought *Rainbows for Life* could beat *Dance Smartly* and I hoped he would," Jim Day said. "Now I don't think he can and I hope he won't." He didn't. *Dance Smartly* won by two lengths over 23-to-1 shot *Professor Rabbit*, with *Rainbows for Life* fourth and *Wilderness Song* fifth after setting a pace that was more torrid than the Queen's Plate. The Ontario Jockey Club allowed only win and exactor betting on the race. *Dance Smartly* won in 1:56 3/5, only three-fifths of a second off the track record. Day tapped her on the shoulder only twice in the stretch. She had to work a little harder for this one, and was puffing a bit in the winner's circle, something she did not do in the Queen's Plate.

Even so, eleven horses lined up for the Breeders' Stakes, and this time she was on her own. *Rainbows for Life* was scratched the morning of the race when it became clear that *Dance Smartly* had no injuries or problems. She won the big Bank of Montreal $1-million boodle when she cruised to an eight-length victory in the Breeders' over *Shiny Key*. Day took her to the lead with a half-mile left and she never was seriously threatened. "We haven't been to the bottom of the well yet," Pat Day said.

Jim Day would like to have skipped the Molson Million to give *Dance Smartly* a rest before the Breeders' Cup, but with a $1 million purse, a healthy horse in the barn, and pressure to show up against U.S. imports at the home track, there was no option. She also worked for the race too fast: five furlongs in 58 2/5 seconds, although well within herself. Day's concern? *Dance Smartly* had wear and tear on her ankles as a two-year-old. Before the Million, they brought in U.S. veterinarian Steve Selway to double-check her ankles. Her ankles were remarkably intact, despite the tough campaign she had experienced. *Dance Smartly* was second choice in the Molson Million behind U.S. 1990 juvenile champion *Fly So Free*, who was hampered with a gimpy leg. The filly broke in a tangle, sat off a crawling pace, and cruised to a win under a hand ride. *Fly So Free* was fourth. "There ain't no filly in America that can beat

her," said Leon Blusiewicz, trainer of another horse in the race that saw only her heels. "She doesn't have to prove nothing to me. She could have carried 136 [pounds] and whipped this field."

Sam-Son considered running her in the Breeders' Cup Classic, but decided the Distaff was the best spot for her. But the Americans weren't convinced of her ability. Steve Crist, editor of *The Racing Times*, wrote: "Every Canadian wonder horse—*With Approval* and *Izvestia* and *Afleet*—has gotten its head handed to it at a short price. *Dance Smartly* is one of the most vulnerable favourites on the card." But *Dance Smartly* launched herself into legendary status at Churchill Downs when she won the Breeders' Cup Distaff, taking charge with a furlong to go, and winning by a half-length over *Versailles Treaty*, the best three-year-old filly in the United States. *Daisy* had been clipped on her right hind heel by another filly, and returned to the barn bleeding, but a patch she had on the inside quarter saved her from career-ending injury. "The incredible thing is that she wins stakes sprinting on the dirt and going a mile and a half on the turf," marvelled Samuel. "And she does it easy. Just magic." A U.S. writer proclaimed: "She's a woman. The rest are little girls."

She later became a top broodmare, foaling Queen's Plate winners *Scatter the Gold* and *Dancethruthedawn*. All of her foals came with attitude, just like her.

DANCE SMARTLY | 3-year-old dark bay or brown filly

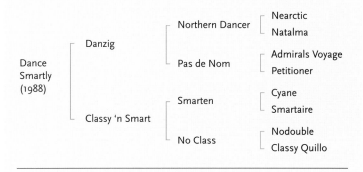

```
                                    ┌ Northern Dancer ┌ Nearctic
                      ┌ Danzig ─────┤                 └ Natalma
                      │             │
Dance                 │             └ Pas de Nom ──────┌ Admirals Voyage
Smartly ──────────────┤                                └ Petitioner
(1988)                │
                      │             ┌ Smarten ─────────┌ Cyane
                      └ Classy 'n Smart                 └ Smartaire
                                    │
                                    └ No Class ────────┌ Nodouble
                                                       └ Classy Quillo
```

Owner: Sam-Son Farms; *Trainer:* James E. Day
Jockey: Pat Day; *Breeder:* Sam-Son Farms (Ont-C)

NORTH AMERICA'S DOMINANT FILLY AND PLATE CHAMPION PRODUCING BROODMARE *DANCE SMARTLY*.

EIGHTH RACE   1¼ MILES. QUEEN'S PLATE S. Purse $250,000

Woodbine

JULY 7, 1991

Value of Race: $391,400 Winner $234,840; second $78,280; third $43,054; fourth $23,484; fifth $11,742. Mutuel Pool $.00

Last Raced	Horse	M/Eqt.	A.	Wt.	PP	¼	½	¾	1	Str	Fin	Jockey	Odds $1
16Jun91 8WO1	Dance Smartly		3	121	3	4½	42	3hd	3½	12	18	Day P	x–0.55
16Jun91 8WO2	Wilderness Song		3	121	1	11	1½	11½	11	23	23½	Villeneuve F A	x–0.55
30Jun91 9WO1	Shudanz		3	126	6	3½	3hd	42	42	41	3½	Platts R	x–2.50
23Jun91 9WO3	Rainbows for Life	b	3	126	7	72	6½	61½	83	5nk	4½	Swatuk B	x–0.55
23Jun91 9WO1	Megas Vukefalos		3	126	8	61½	72	82	6hd	61½	5½	Walls M K	8.20
23Jun91 9WO1	Bolulight		3	126	5	21	21½	21½	2½	3hd	62½	Seymour D J	x–2.50
9Jun91 9WO2	Professor Rabbit		3	126	2	8hd	8hd	71	5hd	72	7no	McAleney J S	21.05
8Jun91 8WO3	San Cielo	bf	3	126	4	9	9	9	9	9	83½	Penna D	27.20
20Jun91 5AP1	British Banker		3	126	9	5hd	5½	5hd	7½	81	9	Hawley S	10.65

x–Coupled: Dance Smartly and Wilderness Song and Shudanz and Rainbows for Life and Bolulight.

OFF AT Start Good For All But. Won . Track fast.

TIME :23³, :47², 1:11⁴, 1:37¹, 2:03² (:23.70, :47.50, 1:11.90, 1:37.30, 2:03.50)

1A– DANCE SMARTLY (x–entry)	—	—
1 – WILDERNESS SONG (x–entry)	—	—
2B– SHUDANZ (x–entry)	—	—

$2 Mutuel Prices:

Dk. b or br. f, (Apr), by Danzig – Classy 'n Smart , by Smarten . Trainer Day James E. Bred by Sam–Son Farms (Ont–C).

Owners– 1, Sam-son Farms; 2, Sam-son Farms; 3, Kinghaven Farms Richardson & T C Racing; 4, Sam-son Farms; 5, Knob Hill Stable; 6, Kinghaven Farms; 7, King Caledon Farm; 8, Firestone D M; 9, Dogwood Stable

Trainers– 1, Day James E; 2, Day James E; 3, Attfield Roger L; 4, Day James E; 5, Meyer Jerome C; 6, Attfield Roger L; 7, Pearce Grant; 8, Quanbeck Alton H; 9, Vestal Peter M

N ever had a horse been draped in so many superlatives early in his career as *Alydeed*. But never had a horse sent his trainer, owner, jockey and betting backers into such apoplexy as *Alydeed*. So much talent. So little predictability of seeing it. Fortunately, for the one-hundred-and-thirty-third running of the Queen's Plate, *Alydeed* was at full throttle and in full bloom. He won the race by eleven-and-a-half lengths with such laughable ease that some said he could have arrived late and still beat the rest of the field. The best seemed yet to come.

Even before he set foot on a racetrack, *Alydeed* sent the pulse of trainer Roger Attfield racing. That shouldn't have been easy to do: Attfield had already trained a string of world-beaters and Triple Crown winners. Still, Attfield said *Alydeed* may have been the best of them all. "He was very precocious," Attfield said. "He was a great specimen physically. He just had so much ability. He just stood head and shoulders above any two-year-old we had in the barn. He probably had as much ability as any horse I'd ever seen." So confident was Attfield that he picked a stakes race for *Alydeed*'s first start: the flashy son of *Shadeed* won the Victoria Stakes easily, by three-and-one-quarter lengths as a heavy 2-to-5 favourite at Woodbine. Problems occurred after the race as X-rays showed a minor bone chip in his left ankle, three in his right, as tiny as grains of sand. That sent *Alydeed* off for arthroscopic surgery and Attfield gave him the rest of his two-year-old season off. Still, he was made the Queen's Plate winterbook favourite.

Alydeed, a $100,000 yearling purchase by Kinghaven Farms, was sent on the 1992 Kentucky Derby trail. He won his first start at age three at Gulfstream by nine-and-a-half lengths, barely raising a sweat. His impressive stretch move prompted trainer Allen Jerkens to say that *Alydeed* was the best three-year-old he'd seen in Florida in five years. A cough and a lung infection aborted his Derby march, but still, *Alydeed* created a buzz by winning the Derby Trial in stunning fashion, with a speed rating of 110. Attfield knew he just wasn't ready for the Derby. But he stamped himself as one of the top three-year-olds on the continent when he finished a close second to *Pine Bluff* in the Preakness Stakes at Pimlico, Maryland, in only the fifth start of his career.

By the time *Alydeed* got to the Plate, he'd won five of seven lifetime starts and New York–based jockey Craig Perret had already given up the mount on *Pine Bluff* after the Kentucky Derby to ride the Canadian colt. It cost him money; *Pine Bluff* won $1 million for being the top point earner in the U.S. Triple Crown series, but Perret thought *Alydeed* could do more. By this time, *Alydeed* was practically a legend, said to be the best Canadian thoroughbred to come along since 1964 when *Northern Dancer* won the Kentucky Derby. Around the barn, he was known as *Alydude*. At 1-to-5, the shortest-priced morning line Plate favourite since the *Dancer* (1-to-9), the headlines were already blaring: "This one is already over." Eleven others bravely entered the Plate to run against *Alydeed* but "there has not been a

THE WILLMOTS, IVY AND HUSBAND BUD, ENJOY THE COMMENTS OF LIEUTENANT GOVERNOR HAROLD (HAL) JACKMAN AND JOCKEY CRAIG PERRET.

mismatch of such sporting proportions since Mike Tyson decided to fight Miss Piggy," wrote *Toronto Sun* columnist Steve Simmons.

Indeed. *Alydeed* settled into fourth place early. On the backside, he crept up with ease and greeted surprise pacesetter *Grand Hooley* at the three-eighths pole. Perret said he let the colt run "a little bit" at the head of the stretch, but "there was an awful lot left in the tank." *Alydeed* finished in a pedestrian 2:04 3/5, the slowest Plate in four years but there was a stiff wind blowing in the horses' faces in the homestretch and Perret shut the colt down in the final furlong. *Alydeed* displayed his prowess in front of only 24,101 bettors, the smallest Woodbine crowd since 1967. *Alydeed* was such a heavy favourite, he cost the Ontario Jockey Club $33,938.40 in minus pools. A day later, Kinghaven sold *Alydeed*'s mother, *Bialy*, for US$1 million.

Perret didn't raise his whip during the race. He called *Alydeed* scary. "This horse is just incredible," said Perret, winning his first Queen's Plate in his first try. "I never moved on him. This is a different horse than the *Alydeed* I rode in the Preakness. I just wish that I'd had a race under him before we went to the Preakness because I'm convinced that if he'd had that extra seasoning, he'd have won that race. This is the kind of colt horsemen can only dream about having once in their lifetime."

Alydeed had the last laugh, winning the Plate by almost twelve lengths.

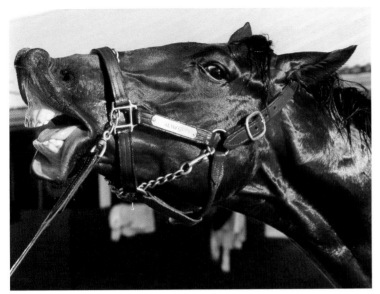

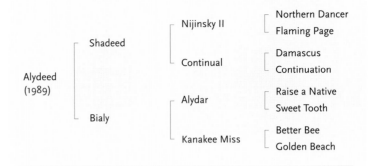

ALYDEED | 3-year-old dark bay or brown colt

Alydeed (1989)	Shadeed	Nijinsky II	Northern Dancer
			Flaming Page
		Continual	Damascus
			Continuation
	Bialy	Alydar	Raise a Native
			Sweet Tooth
		Kanakee Miss	Better Bee
			Golden Beach

Owner: Kinghaven Farms; *Trainer:* Roger Attfield
Jockey: Craig Perret; *Breeder:* Anderson Farms (Ont-C)

What was it about *Alydeed* that was so special? He had more gears than a Jaguar. And he could shift them all quickly, with the litheness of a cat. When *Alydeed* won the Marine Stakes several weeks before the Queen's Plate, Perret had a brief conversation with jockey Dave Penna, who was running head and head with him at the head of the stretch. Perret yelled over: "Watch what happens when I push the button." *Alydeed* took off so fast that Perret didn't hear Penna's reply. It seemed impossible for *Alydeed* to lose the Prince of Wales Stakes. Fort Erie oddsmaker Jerry Davis made *Alydeed* the 1-to-9 morning line favourite, for the first time in his life. Place and show betting were banned. Only five others showed up to run against him. "Nobody will beat this horse unless he falls down," said the owner of a 15-to-1 shot.

When it rained the night before the race, Attfield considered scratching *Alydeed* because he was uncertain how he would handle the footing, but soldiered on. Kinghaven president David Willmot said he counted every raindrop. "I didn't feel good all day," he said. When upstart *Benburb* defeated *Alydeed* by a half length in the strength-sapping mud, it was one of Fort Erie's biggest upsets in the track's ninety-five years and one of the most unexpected defeats in thoroughbred racing history. One bettor had wagered $40,000 on *Alydeed* to win. Owned by Steve Stavro's Knob Hill Farm, *Benburb* paid fifty-one dollars to win. As a two-year-old, he hadn't won a race.

Alydeed showed no signs of bleeding or lameness after the race. But dreams were broken. Still, he had an excuse: he couldn't handle mud. With no shot at winning a Triple Crown $1 million bonus, *Alydeed* headed for the Travers, but finished a tired eighth, twenty-four-and-a-quarter lengths behind the winner. "A huge disappointment," Attfield said afterwards.

"He was a very hard horse to train mentally," Attfield said, years later. "The older he got, the more difficult he got to train. He could self-destruct really, really quickly. Before a race, sometimes he'd get very hot and sweaty, and anxious to a degree. Sometimes he'd get nasty. He'd get very, very hot and hard to saddle. He's got a lot of *Nijinksy* in him. He'll get hot some mornings for no reason at all. At other times, he's as mellow as you like." He knew that as *Alydeed* got older, the problems would become even worse and he wouldn't be able to overcome *Alydeed*'s moods. He was right. Although *Alydeed* won his first three races as a four-year-old, equalling a thirty-six-year-old track record in one of them, breaking another, all at sprint distances, he inexplicably faltered half way into the season. When he finished sixth in a field of seven in the King Edward Gold Cup Stakes at Woodbine, beaten by *Beau Fasa*, an old former claimer. *Alydeed's* jockey Craig Perret was loudly booed by fans. Attfield discovered the horse had an elevated temperature the next day.

EIGHTH RACE **$1\frac{1}{4}$ MILES. QUEEN'S PLATE S. Purse $265,000**

Woodbine

JULY 5, 1992

Value of Race: $381,500 Winner $228,900; second $76,300; third $41,965; fourth $22,890; fifth $11,445. Mutuel Pool $51,876,200.00 Exacta Pool $344,280.00

Last Raced	Horse	M/Eqt.	A.	Wt	PP	¼	½	¾	1	Str	Fin	Jockey	Odds $1
21Jun92 ^{10}WO^{1}	Alydeed	L	3	126	7	4^{hd}	$4\frac{1}{2}$	$4^{1\frac{1}{2}}$	1^{2}	1^{7}	$1^{11\frac{1}{2}}$	Perret C	0.10
21Jun92 ^{10}WO^{2}	Grand Hooley	b	3	126	2	1^{1}	$1^{1\frac{1}{2}}$	1^{hd}	$2^{1\frac{1}{2}}$	2^{2}	$2\frac{3}{4}$	David D J	20.85
6Jun92 ^{8}WO^{1}	Benburb	L	3	126	9	$7\frac{1}{2}$	6^{hd}	6^{hd}	$6^{1\frac{1}{2}}$	5^{hd}	$3\frac{3}{4}$	Attard L	13.90
14Jun92 ^{10}WO^{2}	Rodin	L b	3	126	3	12	12	12	$8^{1\frac{1}{2}}$	$4\frac{1}{2}$	$4\frac{1}{2}$	McAleney J S	x-24.40
28Jun92 ^{10}WO^{2}	Judge Carson	L	3	126	8	$11^{2\frac{1}{2}}$	10^{hd}	$10\frac{1}{2}$	11^{4}	7^{2}	5^{1}	Clark D	72.75
21Jun92 ^{10}WO^{3}	Tannenberg	L	3	126	1	2^{1}	3^{3}	3^{hd}	3^{hd}	$3\frac{1}{2}$	6^{2}	Kabel T K	54.90
21Jun92 ^{10}WO^{4}	Blitzer	f	3	126	5	$5\frac{1}{2}$	$5^{1\frac{1}{2}}$	5^{hd}	4^{hd}	6^{hd}	7^{nk}	Seymour D J	x-24.40
14Jun92 ^{9}WO^{2}	Bright Feather	b	3	121	11	$6\frac{1}{2}$	$7\frac{1}{2}$	7^{2}	5^{hd}	9^{hd}	$8\frac{3}{4}$	Swatuk B	35.95
27Jun92 ^{8}WO^{6}	Change of Fortune		3	126	4	$3^{1\frac{1}{2}}$	2^{hd}	$2\frac{1}{2}$	$7\frac{1}{2}$	$10\frac{1}{2}$	9^{nk}	Landry R C	108.45
21Jun92 ^{10}WO^{7}	Keen Falcon		3	126	6	$8\frac{1}{2}$	8^{3}	8^{2}	12	$8\frac{1}{2}$	$10\frac{1}{2}$	Hawley S	30.80
21Jun92 ^{10}WO^{5}	Cambridge Champ	b	3	126	12	9^{2}	9^{2}	$9^{1\frac{1}{2}}$	$9\frac{1}{2}$	11^{5}	11^{6}	King R Jr	104.60
28Jun92 ^{3}WO^{1}	Ragnarok	L	3	126	10	$10\frac{1}{2}$	11^{4}	11^{hd}	$10\frac{1}{2}$	12	12	Villeneuve F A	49.25

x-Coupled: Rodin and Blitzer.

OFF AT 5:12 Start Good For All But. Won . Track fast.

TIME :24, :48, 1:13^{2}, 1:38^{3}, 2:04^{3} (:24.00, :48.00, 1:13.40, 1:38.60, 2:04.60)

$2 Mutuel Prices:				
	6 – ALYDEED	2.20	2.20	2.10
	3 – GRAND HOOLEY		3.80	2.10
	8 – BENBURB			2.10

$2 EXACTA 6–3 PAID $8.70

Dk. b or br. c, (Mar), by Shadeed – Bialy , by Alydar . Trainer Attfield Roger L. Bred by Anderson Farms (Ont–C).

Owners– 1, Kinghaven Farms; 2, P E L Racing Stable; 3, Knob Hill Stable; 4, Stronach Frank; 5, Meyers Gerald J; 6, Schickedanz Gustav; 7, Stronach Frank; 8, Sam Son Farm; 9, Dominion Bloodstock RBuchanan and Partner; 10, Syndicate Keen; 11, Pedigree Farm; 12, Haines Colin

Trainers– 1, Attfield Roger L; 2, Attard Sid C; 3, England Phillip; 4, Vella Daniel J; 5, Marko Bill; 6, Bankuti George N; 7, Vella Daniel J; 8, Day James E; 9, Lane Robert W; 10, Allain Emile M; 11, Sheehan Kevin; 12, Reid Jim

Peteski used to be the horse that nobody wanted. He wasn't even the favourite to win the 134th running of the Queen's Plate, but he did, en route to becoming Canada's sixth Triple Crown winner. Within a few short months, *Peteski* became a mesmerizing Canadian star, even a candidate for U.S. year-end honours. He'd fooled just about everybody.

He was the first horse ever bred by Montreal real estate dealer Barry Schwartz. But with the real estate world reeling from a recession, Schwartz eventually sold the resulting foal, *Peteski*, early in his three-year-old season to New York real estate developer Earle I. Mack, who became the first American resident to own a Queen's Plate winner. (Californian Paul Olivier owned 1965 winner *Whistling Sea*, but he had long been a resident of Calgary.) Mack bought *Peteski* for a reported US$150,000 in a package deal with an unraced two-year-old after *Peteski* had won the third start of his career by ten lengths.

Schwartz regarded *Peteski* most fondly, even considered him a member of the family. He named him after his teenage son, Pete. But nobody made a reasonable offer when *Peteski* went on the auction block as a yearling, and Schwartz also bought him back for $37,000 from a two-year-old sale. The copper-coloured colt earned the barn name of *Chowderhead* at the time he was broken in Florida by a man who figured he wasn't much. Schwartz went looking for buyers in Toronto, but nobody took him. Jockey Don Seymour thought *Peteski* wouldn't go much past five furlongs, so speed crazy was he. Later, when he had the choice of choosing trainer Roger Attfield's *Cheery Knight* or Mack's *Peteski* to ride in the Queen's Plate, Seymour picked *Cheery Knight*, figuring that *Peteski* wouldn't relax enough to go one-and-one-quarter miles and that *Cheery Knight* was a more seasoned competitor.

Peteski started only once as a two-year-old, finishing fifth to *Cheery Knight* in a four-and-a-half-furlong sprint. Attfield had warned the seventeen syndicate owners of *Cheery Knight* they wouldn't win that race because "they say there's a horse in there who's just a rocket." That was *Peteski*, but not at his best. A few weeks later, *Peteski* was in Attfield's barn. Attfield spent the winter in Florida trying to quell *Peteski*'s aggressiveness. "He was a hard horse to get settled in his work," Attfield said. "He always wanted to do everything too fast. I spent the whole winter, just trying to get him to settle." But by the time he got to the Queen's Plate, *Peteski* had won three races by open lengths. He was favoured to win the Plate Trial under Mack's burgundy and yellow rising-sun silks, but finished second amid a storm of controversy. Craig Perret, who also rode *Alydeed* for Attfield, took over the ride on *Peteski* for the Plate Trial and told reporters after the Plate that *Peteski* could have won the Plate Trial if he'd pushed him harder, that he was just trying to experiment with the colt when challenged in the stretch. This statement didn't go over well with the betting public and with the Ontario Racing Commission.

Perret testified that he made the unfortunate remarks out of confusion. The ORC eventually exonerated Perret, who had struck *Peteski* eight times with the whip down the stretch; Perret had made every effort to win, they concluded. However, because of his loose

U.S. OWNER EARLE MACK DONNED A BALL CAP TO LEAD *PETESKI* AND CRAIG PERRET INTO THE WINNER'S CIRCLE.

lips, the ORC fined the Cajun jockey $4,000, suspended him for fifteen days, and ordered him to make a public apology. The suspension caused Perret to miss the ride on *Peteski* in the Prince of Wales.

Before that storm broke, *Peteski* ran away with the Queen's Plate. *Cheery Knight* had been made the 8-to-5 favourite while *Peteski* was 4-to-1. *Peteski* hardly got a mention in pre-race predictions from horsemen and handicappers. Even though there was supposedly a surfeit of speed horses in the race, *Peteski* rolled out of the starting gate to the lead and no horse seriously challenged him. He won easily by six lengths over *Cheery Knight*.

"Nobody pushed him because nobody thought he could go a mile and a quarter," Seymour said. *Peteski* needed only a final quarter of twenty-seven seconds to win. The win was the sixth Plate victory for Attfield, and his fifth in seven years. Because of Kinghaven Farm cutbacks, Attfield had just opened up a public stable. Mack, who had owned a handful of Canadian horses since 1964, said he was "flattered" to win. "Of all the races I wanted to win, the Queen's Plate and the Kentucky Derby are the two I wanted to win the most," he said, as he doffed his topper to wear a baseball cap with "Canada" written on it into the winner's circle. "It's my good luck cap," he said. Mack's love of Canada got a test in the Prince of Wales, the victim of a major cut in stakes purses on ORC tracks because of wagering declines. Both the Prince of Wales and the Breeders' Stakes were cut by $50,000, leaving only a total purse of $120,333 for the Fort Erie event. But under heavy pressure to run *Peteski* in the Jim Dandy Stakes at Saratoga, Mack decided to support Canadian racing, even though this year there remained only a $100,000 bonus based on the best points accumulated through the three races. The $1 million Bank of Montreal bonus was gone.

In the Prince of Wales, *Peteski* didn't get away with the easy lead he had in the Plate and the pace was much faster. *Peteski* finally stuck his head in front just before the three-eighths pole and pulled away from seven rivals in the stretch to win by four lengths. By winning in 1:54 2/5 for the one-and-three-sixteenths mile, *Peteski* obliterated a twenty-three-year-old track record of 1:56. Jockey Dave Penna said the media never gave *Peteski* credit for what he did in the Plate. "I read that the fractions were very mediocre and slow and he stole the race with an easy and uncontested lead. The way I saw it, they were driving to stay within two lengths of him." Perret got the mount back for the Breeders' Stakes and once again, Mack overcame the temptation to run *Peteski* in the $1 million Travers at Saratogo in favor of the $250,000 Breeders' Stakes at Woodbine.

Attfield began to rub his hands with glee. "If you think *Peteski* is good on dirt, wait'll you see him on turf," he said. Before the Breeders' Stakes, he astonished Woodbine clockers by breezing seven furlongs on the lawn in 1:22 4/5. Only four horses started in the third leg of the Triple Crown, the shortest field in the 103-year history of the race. *Peteski* went wire-to-wire, winning by six lengths, but in dramatic fashion: his saddle slipped up to his neck several strides out of the starting gate. Perret sat still throughout, and won. The payoff of $2.20 for a two-dollar wager was the lowest since the Breeders' Stakes became part of the Triple Crown in 1959.

However, *Peteski* truly made his mark in his next start, the $1 million Molson Export Million at Woodbine, for which Mack had to pay a $15,000 supplemental fee to start. *Peteski* ran up against Kentucky Derby and Travers winner *Sea Hero*, Belmont Stakes winner *Colonial Affair*, and Haskell Invitational winner *Kissin Kris*, and

PETESKI | 3-year-old chestnut colt

```
                                          ┌─ Raise a Native
                      ┌─ Exclusive Native ┤
           ┌─ Affirmed┤                   └─ Exclusive
           │          │                   ┌─ Crafty Admiral
           │          └─ Wont Tell You    ┤
Peteski    │             Again            └─ Scarlet Ribbon
(1990)     │                              ┌─ Northern Dancer
           │          ┌─ Nureyev          ┤
           └─ Vive    ┤                   └─ Special
                      │                   ┌─ His Majesty
                      └─ Viva Regina      ┤
                                          └─ Second the Motion
```

Owner: Earle I. Mack; *Trainer:* Roger Attfield
Jockey: Craig Perret; *Breeder:* Barry Schwartz (Ont-C)

defeated them all. "He thinks he's King Kong and he showed today he is one of the best," Perret said. "I didn't think in our wildest dream that he could do what he did today." *Peteski* hadn't won his first race until six days after *Sea Hero* won the Kentucky Derby. At this point, a win in the $750,000 Super Derby in Louisiana could have catapulted *Peteski* to the three-year-old championship in North America.

Heavily favored in the Super Derby, he finished third in a five-horse blanket finish, after chasing the pacesetters during the fastest pace in the history of the race. The US$3-million Breeders' Cup Classic was only five weeks later, but *Peteski* was scratched the morning of the race with a wrenched ankle. The ankle healed and Attfield was eagerly drawing up a schedule to keep *Peteski* in turf races as a four-year-old when Mack suddenly decided to retire *Peteski* and prevent further injury. The 1993 Canadian Horse of the Year was retired to stud duty at Darby Dan Farm in Pennsylvania (he got one vote in horse of the year voting in the United States) for a fee of $7,500. *Peteski* died prematurely at age eleven in 2001, the same year that his sire, *Affirmed*, also died.

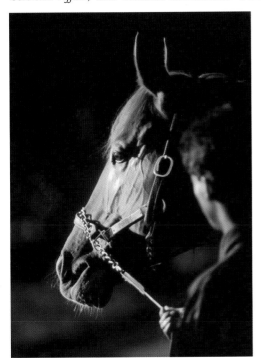

TRIPLE CROWN CHAMPION *PETESKI*.

NINTH RACE 1¼ MILES. QUEEN'S PLATE S. Purse $250,000
Woodbine
JULY 11, 1993
Value of Race: $364,332 Winner $218,600; second $72,866; third $40,076; fourth $21,860; fifth $10,930. Mutuel Pool $55,012,900.00 Exacta Pool $315,158.00

Last Raced	Horse	M/Eqt. A. Wt	PP	¼	½	¾	1	Str	Fin	Jockey	Odds $1
27Jun93 9WO2	Peteski	L 3 126	5	1½	1¹	1¹½	1³	1⁴	1⁶	Perret C	4.15
13Jun93 10WO1	Cheery Knight	L 3 126	9	4ʰᵈ	6ʰᵈ	6¹½	4¹	2¹½	2¹¼	Seymour D J	1.65
27Jun93 9WO3	Janraffole	b 3 126	1	10³½	8ʰᵈ	5ʰᵈ	5³	3ʰᵈ	3ⁿᵒ	Walls M K	7.55
1Jly93 8WO3	Flashy Regent	L 3 126	7	1¹	1¹	1¹	7²	5¹	4²	Hawley S	33.35
16Jun93 9WO1	Explosive Red	3 126	2	9²½	7¹½	3²	3ʰᵈ	4²	5⁸	Larsen M G	8.35
27Jun93 9WO1	Circulating	L 3 126	6	2ʰᵈ	2²	2¹	2½	6⁶	6²½	Dos Ramos R A	7.85
27Jun93 9WO4	Regent Runner	f 3 126	11	7ʰᵈ	10⁴	10²	8¹½	8³	7³½	Clark D	4.95
26Jun93 7WO3	Corporate Revenue	L bf 3 126	8	3¹½	4ʰᵈ	4½	6½	7½	8²	David D J	91.05
26Jun93 7WO1	Briartic Star	3 126	4	6½	5¹	8ʰᵈ	1¹	10¹½	9²¾	Platts R	24.30
27Jun93 9WO5	Fleetward	b 3 126	3	5¹	3½	7¹½	9½	1¹	10ⁿᵒ	Kabel T K	40.35
13Jun93 9WO3	Imperial Bandit	L 3 126	10	8½	9¹	9ʰᵈ	10²	9ʰᵈ	11	Landry R C	77.95

OFF AT 5:41 Start Good For All But . Won . Track fast.
TIME :23⁴, :47⁴, 1:12², 1:37¹, 2:04¹ (:23.80, :47.80, 1:12.40, 1:37.20, 2:04.20)

$2 Mutuel Prices:	5 – PETESKI	10.30	4.40	3.40
	9 – CHEERY KNIGHT		3.40	2.70
	1 – JANRAFFOLE			4.60

$2 EXACTA 5–9 PAID $25.90

Ch. c, (Apr), by Affirmed – Vive , by Nureyev . Trainer Attfield Roger L. Bred by Barry Schwartz (Ont–C).

Owners– 1, Earle I Mack; 2, Kinghaven Farms RFerguson & TCRacing Stable; 3, J Louis Levesque Stable; 4, Kaydann Farms; 5, Frank Stronach; 6, PASherwood and Sheehan Farms; 7, Knob Hill Stable; 8, Meadow Val Stable; 9, FZupet; 10, Huntington Stud Farm Inc; 11, Maple Croft Farms

Trainers– 1, Attfield Roger L; 2, Attfield Roger L; 3, Dumas Jacques; 4, Campbell Donald J; 5, Vella Daniel J; 6, Wright Roderick W; 7, England Phillip; 8, Kocsis Eugene; 9, Ross Bob; 10, Ross John A; 11, Lockhurst Debi

Thirty-two years after Frank Stronach bought his first racehorse, he finally won the Queen's Plate. Ironically, the sixty-two-year-old Austrian-born citizen of Canada, who was in the early stages of building a breeding and racing empire, did it with a gelding, *Basqueian*, a horse he and trainer Danny Vella initially didn't even consider the best in their barn.

The 135th Queen's Plate was the year of the gelding as the Canadian Triple Crown proved to be a tight contest between two big tough rangy geldings, the other being *Bruce's Mill*, so big his chestnut body would fill the starting gate and his head would poke out over the screen. Undefeated in four starts in 1994, *Bruce's Mill* was also the first Queen's Plate horse trained by Mark Frostad, who had his trainer's licence for only five years and would later prove to be a major force on the Canadian scene.

Owned by Earle I. Mack, *Bruce's Mill*'s only match was *Basqueian*, one of three horses that carried Stronach's blue and black diamond silks in the Plate. Before the 1994 Plate, Stronach had entered only four horses in Canada's most prestigious race, with the stable's best effort coming from *Sinister Purpose's* second place finish in 1973. It seemed as if 1994 was the year that Stronach would snatch the torch as the dominant owner at Woodbine. For the first time in ten years, neither Kinghaven Farm nor trainer Roger Attfield had a Plate entry. And Sam-Son Farm had only a long shot, *Comet Shine*, which hadn't lived up to his billing after earning honours as Canada's top two-year-old the previous season.

Neither *Basqueian* nor *Bruce's Mill* were stars as two-year-olds. Stronach and Vella thought their pint-sized colt *Road Rush*, who had won the Grey Stakes and was third in both the Coronation Futurity and Cup and Saucer, was better than *Basqueian*, who had only one win in eight starts as a juvenile. At three in Florida, *Road Rush* defeated horses that later won the Illinois Derby and Flamingo Stakes, then was out of action for two months after bleeding badly in the Jim Beam Stakes. He was a rush job for the Queen's Plate and had only one start in three months. The winterbook favourite for the Plate was *Parental Pressure*. He had won the Coronation Futurity and Kingarvie Stakes at age two and won twice that winter in Florida with jockey Jack Lauzon in the irons. *Parental Pressure* also had defeated *Basqueian* in their first meeting at age three in the Queenston Stakes.

Parental Pressure provided high drama in the Plate in ways nobody would have expected. He had been ridden in all of his starts by Jack Lauzon, who finished third with him in the Tampa Bay Derby in late March. However, after that loss, breeder, part-owner and trainer Fred Loschke fired Lauzon, who showed up at Danny Vella's Florida digs over the winter and eventually became *Basqueian*'s regular rider. Even though *Basqueian* suffered a nose defeat in the Plate Trial to *Bruce's Mill*, Lauzon was so confident of the big gelding's ability, he declared him the Plate winner. *Basqueian* in the Trial had been caught in traffic, and wasn't the type of horse that could quickly accelerate out of trouble. To top it off, Lauzon's wife, Geraldine consulted her fortune teller, who predicted her energetic husband

FRANK STRONACH AND JOCKEY JACK LAUZON ACCOMPANY *BASQUEIAN*.

would win with a horse whose name started with the letter B.

In spite of his defeat in the Plate Trial, *Basqueian* was the Plate favourite over his nemesis *Bruce's Mill* and *Parental Pressure*. *Basqueian* dropped back to tenth of eleven starters early in the race after being bumped mildly a couple of times. Racing wide throughout the early going, the big gelding made an explosive move on the final turn, jumping the shadow of one of Woodbine's new light standards as he hurtled forward. "I thought, oh geez," Lauzon said afterward. "My feet came out of the stirrups but I was lucky to jump back into them. It didn't really stop him, didn't really lose any stride whatsoever." *Parental Pressure*, ridden by Dave Penna, had pressed the quick pace and had taken the lead at the mile mark, and as *Basqueian* fired past, Lauzon yelled to Penna: "See you later, Dave." He won by seven lengths ahead of *Bruce's Mill*, while *Parental Pressure* drifted out badly in the stretch and held onto third place ahead of *Road Rush*.

JACK LAUZON ACKNOWLEDGES ACCOLADES FROM THE PLATE AUDIENCE.

BASQUEIAN | 3-year-old bay gelding

Bassqueian (1991)
- Bounding Basque
  - Grey Dawn
    - Herbager
    - Polamia
  - La Basque
    - Jean-Pierre
    - Lady Dulcinea
- Valse Musette
  - Halo
    - Hail to Reason
    - Cosmah
  - Miss Dancer
    - Legend Dancer
    - Mrs. Brummer

Owner: Frank Stronach; *Trainer:* Daniel J. Vella
Jockey: Jack M. Lauzon; *Breeder:* Frank Stronach (Ont-C)

"They say winning your first [Queen's Plate] is the best," said Lauzon, who won the Plate in 1988 with *Regal Intention*. "But for me, this is more special. Being fired from *Parental Pressure*, there was a personal motivation, a vendetta maybe. All I can do is thank Mr. Loschke for firing me and Mr. Stronach for hiring me." Lauzon said that Loschke had fired him because he had been hitting the horse (*Parental Pressure*) too aggressively. But he added that he was hired in the first place because Loschke wanted a strong, aggressive rider to handle the horse. *Basqueian*'s win was the first by a gelding in the Plate since 1983 when *Bompago* won. Only 18,202 witnessed the race at Woodbine, the smallest Plate crowd in forty years. However, this was the first season that the Ontario Jockey Club had set up a series of off-track betting operations in the Toronto area.

Basqueian and *Bruce's Mill* hooked up for another exciting match in the Prince of Wales at Fort Erie, but while eleven contested the Queen's Plate, only four ran in the Prince of Wales, and only seven in the Breeders' Stakes. The reason? Perhaps losing any vestige of a Triple Crown bonus had something to do with it. This was the first season that there was no bonus at all, not even $100,000 for top point earners. *Basqueian* ended up being the only horse to compete in all three legs. The Prince of Wales belonged to *Bruce's Mill*. Frostad, realizing that the big chestnut had a bad habit of gawking around, put a set of orange blinkers on him. It worked. *Bruce's Mill* won in 1:53 4/5 for the one-and-three-sixteenth miles, eclipsing the track and stakes record set by *Peteski* the year before.

Basqueian came back to win the Breeders' Stakes on a turf that was so soggy that trainer Roger Attfield lost a shoe while walking it in the morning and promptly scratched the tough filly *Alywow*. *Basqueian* overcame tardy fractions and outlasted tired horses, winning the one-and-a-half mile race. The race was run at Fort Erie because Woodbine's new turf course had not yet been completely refurbished. In October *Basqueian* won the Durham Cup against older horses, a victory that enhanced his chances for year-end honours as he defeated *Bruce's Mill* as the top three-year-old and finished third in Horse of the Year balloting to Alywow.

Stronach ended the season with twenty-two stakes wins in Canada, three short of Sam-Son's record set in 1991. In 1995, *Basqueian* was Canada's top older horse. That season he was second by a nose in the $250,000 Hawthorne Gold Cup in Chicago. In 1996, he won his third consecutive Durham Cup with a dramatic last-to-first sweep. The following year, at age six, *Basqueian* was a useful stakes horse at sprint distances in the United States.

NINTH RACE 1¼ MILES. QUEEN'S PLATE S. Purse $250,000
Woodbine
JULY 10, 1994
Value of Race: $460,700 Winner $276,420; second $92,140; third $50,677; fourth $27,642; fifth $13,821. Mutuel Pool $54,848,700.00 Exactor Pool $329,635.00

Last Raced	Horse	M/Eqt. A. Wt	PP	¼	½	¾	1	Str	Fin	Jockey	Odds $1
26Jun94 9WO2	Basqueian	L b 3 126	3	10³	9hd	7½	2½	1⁴	1⁷	Lauzon J M	a- 1.75
26Jun94 9WO1	Bruce's Mill	L 3 126	5	7²½	5½	5³½	4²½	3²	2½	Perret C	1.90
18Jun94 11Tdn6	Parental Pressure	L 3 126	9	2hd	2hd	2½	1½	2¹	3¹½	Penna D	2.90
1Jly94 7WO2	Road Rush	L b 3 126	6	9½	10⁴	10½	6¹	4³½	4⁴½	Landry R C	a- 1.75
18Jun94 8FE4	Comet Shine	L b 3 126	2	11	11	11	8²½	5²½	5⁵	Clark D	17.30
11Jun94 7WO1	Von Fleet	L b 3 126	1	8²½	8²½	6hd	7½	6½	6⁴½	Seymour D J	a- 1.75
26Jun94 9WO3	Tall in the Saddle	b 3 126	4	6hd	4hd	4½	5½	7⁶	7²½	Hawley S	12.00
26Jun94 9WO5	Prix de Crouton	L 3 126	11	3½	3¹	3½	9⁴	9¹⁰	8⁸	McAleney J S	14.85
12Jun94 10WO2	Tuxedo Landing	L f 3 126	8	1hd	1²	11½	3½	8hd	9⁵½	Attard L	28.10
25Jun94 8WO2	Dynamite Stuff	L 3 126	10	4¹½	6hd	8³	10²	10³	10⁵½	Sabourin R B	71.65
18Jun94 8WO2	Barron Road	L 3 126	7	5hd	7²½	9hd	11	11	11	Bahen S R	41.50

a–Coupled: Basqueian and Road Rush and Von Fleet.

OFF AT 5:42 Start Good For All But. Won . Track fast.
TIME :23¹, :46⁴, 1:11, 1:37², 2:03² (:23.20, :46.80, 1:11.00, 1:37.40, 2:03.40)

$2 Mutuel Prices:				
1A–BASQUEIAN(a–entry)	5.50	2.60	2.30
4 – BRUCE'S MILL		2.90	2.50
7 – PARENTAL PRESSURE			3.00

$2 EXACTOR 1A–4 PAID $15.40

B. g, (Feb), by Bounding Basque – Valse Musette , by Halo . Trainer Vella Daniel J. Bred by Frank Stronach (Ont–C).
Owners– 1, Frank Stronach; 2, Eimack and Partners; 3, Hammer Kopf Farm jcorrente and Partners; 4, Frank Stronach; 5, Sam Son Farm; 6, Frank Stronach; 7, J M B Stables; 8, Berg Racing Stable; 9, C E C Farms; 10, Pedigree Farm; 11, Reade Baker and Janis Maine
Trainers– 1, Vella Daniel J; 2, Frostad Mark; 3, Loschke Fred H; 4, Vella Daniel J; 5, Day James E; 6, Tiller Robert P; 7, Cox Greg D; 8, Berg Lorne E; 9, Cardella John; 10, Ross Brian; 11, Baker Reade

The Shaddock family was lucky the day they lit upon a yearling called *Regal Discovery* at a Kentucky sale in 1993. He was their first yearling purchase. Not only did he win the Queen's Plate for them, the powerful bay colt brought more to their lives than they ever dreamed. Together they won the 136th running of the Queen's Plate in a sensational upset, surprising everybody but themselves and giving the top-hatted trainer Roger Attfield his seventh Queen's Plate victory and the spurned Canadian jockey Todd Kabel his first.

Attfield was supposed to have won the Queen's Plate with a talented colt called *Talkin Man*, who was owned by David Willmot and Mrs. Helen Stollery. Kabel was supposed to have won the race aboard one of Frank Stronach's powerful three-horse entry because he'd been riding them all spring. And the Shaddocks, with their two-and-a-half-horse racing stable, weren't supposed to defeat the Stronachs, Willmots and Samuels and the bigger barns of the sport. Winterbook favourite *Talkin Man* had been sent on the U.S. Triple Crown trail, but suffered an injury before the Plate. Samuel also had the impressive *Smart Strike*, a horse he considered the equal of Horse of the Year champions *Dance Smartly* and *Sky Classic*. But *Smart Strike* pulled a ligament in his foot just before the Plate and was out for the year. That left the Stronach entry of the brilliant little *Honky Tonk Tune*, the top two-year-old filly in Canada the previous year, *All Firmed Up*, a $125,000 yearling purchase and *Freedom Fleet*, a royally bred son of two Canadian champions, *Afleet* and *Avowal*, to capture all the pre-race hype. The entry went off as the heavy favourites.

Kabel had ridden *All Firmed Up* and *Freedom Fleet* with excellent success, but come Plate time Stronach's management team ditched Kabel and brought in two top U.S. jockeys: Mike Smith for *Freedom Fleet* and Shane Sellers for *All Firmed Up*. Attfield hadn't seen too many agents knocking at his door to ride *Regal Discovery* until Kabel showed up. Dave Penna was supposed to have ridden him, but the Monday before the Plate he broke his collarbone in a spill during the Colin Stakes. The next morning Kabel worked *Regal Discovery* and loved what he saw. The strong colt pattered over five furlongs of a muddy track in 1:00 4/5, with a final three-eighths in 35 2/5 and "galloped out like a Trojan," Attfield said. Kabel was confident, even though *Regal Discovery* had won only one race in seven career starts—although he'd been fourth in the Plate Trial. His other good start was as a two-year-old when he finished third to *Talkin Man* in the Coronation Futurity.

Both Attfield and Kabel knew they had a horse for the course, though. "He was an out-and-out stayer. He was a horse that was just coming to the Plate in fantastic shape. Two weeks before the Plate I said to the owners that I felt a number of horses in the race wouldn't be true mile-and-a-quarter horses and once they headed into the stretch, he would be flying at them," said Attfield. He was right. *Regal Discovery* settled in eighth place early while Langfuhr and Kiridashi waged war on the front end. *Freedom Fleet* flew to the

TODD KABEL REVELS IN HIS FIRST PLATE VICTORY ON UPSETTER *REGAL DISCOVERY*.

front around the final turn from twelfth place. *Regal Discovery* slipped up along the rail and darted through a hole along inside with only 150 yards to go. Kabel had one ace: from having ridden *Freedom Fleet* he knew he would pull himself up while on the lead. Smith said later he didn't know that. As *Freedom Fleet* was loafing, *Regal Discovery* swept past him to win.

For the co-owners, Ron and Anne Shaddock of Whitby, and their daughter, Lesley, it was the ultimate dream. Everywhere, people were thrusting thumbs up in the air, perhaps a tribute to their stable name: the No. 1 Stable, named after the jersey worn by NHL Vancouver Canucks goalie Kirk McLean, who had been married to Lesley at the time. "I think it was one of the most memorable events in all of our lives," Lesley said. "We were all very nervous. It all became a bit of a blur." *Regal Discovery* won $261,660, from the record purse of $436,100, a marvelous achievement for a little stable that had never before run a horse in the Queen's Plate.

The Shaddocks had made a habit of attending the Kentucky yearling sales every year and decided to buy a Canadian-bred colt or filly. In 1993 they couldn't find anything in their price range until *Regal Discovery*, from the second crop of *Regal Classic*, came into the ring. They got him for US$22,000. "*Regal Classic* hadn't thrown a ton of black type horses at the time and we were actually scoffed at by a few people who said they thought we paid more than the market value," Lesley said. "We weren't fazed by that."

Reggie needed surgery at the end of his two-year-old season to remove some bone chips, and then wintered at Payson Park in Florida, where his groom, Jennifer Smith, doted on him. While there, *Reggie*, as he was called by his friends, became quite fond of fresh fruit. He loved grapefruit, oranges and bananas, but he was a particularly soft touch for peaches, his favourite. "We'll still go and visit him with a tin

Anne Shaddock and daughter Lesley happily parade *Regal Discovery* and Todd Kabel across Woodbine's track. At right are trainer Roger Attfield and owner Ron Shaddock.

of peaches, and put them in a bowl," Lesley said. "He'll slurp them right down." The morning after the Plate, *Reggie* lay exhausted in his stall as Kabel came by with his sons to bring him a big Tupperware container of fruit cocktail. "He ate the whole thing lying down," Lesley said. "He was so tired, he didn't even bother to get up."

Reggie was always a special horse to the Shaddocks. He loved people and he loved attention. He had a kind manner. And he gave them unique life experiences: the Shaddocks got to attend the Sovereign Awards, as *Regal Discovery* was nominated as top three-year-old colt after finishing second in the Prince of Wales and in the Woodbine Million; they met Queen Elizabeth II when she came to Canada on a jubilee tour and asked to see a Queen's Plate winner. They were also invited by Sheikh Mohammed to be his guests in Dubai when *Regal Discovery* ran in the $500,000 Duty Free Handicap.

Reggie retired after his four-year-old season and stood at stud at Goshen, N.Y., then at Gardiner Farm in Caledon. But interest in him waned. Also the Shaddocks didn't have a large broodmare band to support him. In 2005 a farm in Vancouver expressed an interest in standing him at stud, but the Shaddocks were loathe to see him go. They wanted him nearby, so that they could visit him and ensure that he was well cared for. But they did not own a farm. In stepped Eric Coatrieux, who was Attfield's assistant trainer at the time. He had also served as *Regal Discovery*'s exercise rider. Reggie had found a spot in his heart, too, particularly since he had accompanied him to Dubai.

In the winter of 2005–06, Coatrieux offered to give *Reggie* a home for life his farm in King City. The Shaddocks had *Reggie* gelded, to make him more tractable around people. "He's out in the field with a little donkey," Coatrieux said. "They are good friends. They just love each other."

REGAL DISCOVERY | 3-year-old bay colt

Regal Discovery (1992)	Regal Classic	Vice Regent	Northern Dancer
			Victoria Regina
		No Class	Nodouble
			Classy Quillo
	Royal Discovery	Tom Tulle	Tom Rolfe
			Tulle
		Great Discovery	Pan Dancer
			Sadie Hawkins

Owner: No. 1 Stable; *Trainer:* Roger Attfield
Jockey: Todd K. Kabel; *Breeder:* C.G. Scott (Ont-C)

"*Reggie*" in retirement with his paddock pals.

NINTH RACE **$1\frac{1}{4}$ MILES. QUEEN'S PLATE S. Purse $265,000**

Woodbine

JULY 9, 1995

Value of Race: $436,100 Winner $261,660; second $87,220; third $47,971; fourth $26,166; fifth $13,083. Mutuel Pool $60,573,100.00 Exactor Pool $355,292.00

Last Raced	Horse	M/Eqt.	A.	Wt	PP	¼	½	¾	1	Str	Fin	Jockey	Odds $1
25Jun95 ^{8}WO^{4}	Regal Discovery	L	3	126	2	8^{hd}	$7\frac{1}{2}$	$5\frac{1}{2}$	$5^{1\frac{1}{2}}$	2^{3}	$1^{1\frac{1}{4}}$	Kabel T K	9.05
11Jun95 ^{8}WO^{2}	Freedom Fleet	b	3	126	12	$12\frac{1}{2}$	11^{hd}	10^{2}	4^{hd}	$1^{1\frac{1}{2}}$	$2^{4\frac{1}{2}}$	Smith M E	x- 1.30
25Jun95 ^{8}WO^{3}	Mt. Sassafras	L	3	126	9	7^{1}	8^{hd}	$7\frac{1}{2}$	$7^{1\frac{1}{2}}$	6^{4}	$3\frac{3}{4}$	Bahen S R	x- 3.90
2Jly95 ^{4}WO^{3}	Kiridashi	L	3	126	5	$2\frac{1}{2}$	$2^{2\frac{1}{2}}$	1^{hd}	1^{hd}	$4\frac{1}{2}$	$4\frac{1}{2}$	Attard L	x- 3.90
25Jun95 ^{8}WO^{1}	All Firmed Up	L b	3	126	6	$3\frac{1}{2}$	$3\frac{1}{2}$	3^{1}	3^{1}	3^{hd}	$5\frac{1}{2}$	Sellers S J	x- 1.30
25Jun95 ^{8}WO^{2}	Langfuhr		3	126	8	1^{hd}	1^{hd}	$2\frac{1}{2}$	2^{hd}	5^{1}	$6^{4\frac{1}{2}}$	Stevens G L	2.15
22Jun95 ^{6}WO^{1}	For Pete's Sake		3	126	1	5^{hd}	4^{2}	4^{3}	$6^{1\frac{1}{2}}$	7^{1}	$7^{1\frac{1}{4}}$	Dos Ramos R A	47.35
25Jun95 ^{7}WO^{7}	Disciple		3	126	7	13^{4}	12^{4}	$8\frac{1}{2}$	$8^{2\frac{1}{2}}$	8^{3}	8^{2}	Baird J	63.95
2Jly95 ^{4}WO^{4}	Your Majestic	L	3	126	11	14	14	12^{2}	12^{4}	9^{6}	9^{6}	McAleney J S	48.90
3Jly95 ^{5}WO^{3}	Prince of North	L b	3	126	14	11^{hd}	13^{hd}	$13^{1\frac{1}{2}}$	$11^{2\frac{1}{2}}$	10^{1}	$10^{3\frac{1}{2}}$	Husbands P	72.90
18Jun95 ^{9}WO^{3}	Honky Tonk Tune	L	3	121	13	10^{1}	10^{hd}	6^{hd}	9^{2}	11^{3}	$11^{1\frac{1}{4}}$	Hawley S	x- 1.30
10Jun95 ^{6}WO^{3}	Stanley Silver	L b	3	126	10	$9\frac{1}{2}$	9^{hd}	11^{4}	10^{hd}	12^{15}	12	McKnight J	44.50
21Jun95 ^{8}WO^{2}	Ice Agent	L b	3	126	4	$6\frac{1}{2}$	6^{hd}	9^{hd}	13^{10}	13^{12}	—	Landry R C	12.90
8Jun95 ^{8}WO^{3}	Desert Falcon	b	3	126	3	4^{hd}	$5^{2\frac{1}{2}}$	14	14	14	—	Platts R	51.80

x–Coupled: Freedom Fleet and Mt. Sassafras and Kiridashi and All Firmed Up and Honky Tonk Tune.

OFF AT 5:42 Start Good For All But DISCIPLE. Won . Track fast.

TIME :23, :45^{4}, 1:10^{3}, 1:37, 2:03^{4} (:23.00, :45.80, 1:10.60, 1:37.00, 2:03.80)

$2 Mutuel Prices:				
	4 – REGAL DISCOVERY	20.10	5.20	3.30
	2b– FREEDOM FLEET(x–entry)		2.70	2.20
	1a– MT. SASSAFRAS(x–entry)			3.10

$2 EXACTOR 4–2B PAID $59.20

B. c, (May), by Regal Classic – Royal Discovery , by Tom Tulle . Trainer Attfield Roger L. Bred by C G Scott (Ont–C).

Owners– 1, No 1 Stable; 2, Frank Stronach; 3, Minshall Farms; 4, Minshall Farms; 5, Frank Stronach; 6, Gustav Schickedanz; 7, Mickey and Phyllis Canino; 8, Hope Stock Farm and Bpowell; 9, William Sorokolit; 10, Schickedanz Bruno; 11, Frank Stronach; 12, Double B Racing Stable & The Estate of Jbearss; 13, Gsl Don Meehan & Friends Stables & Sleslie; 14, Tp Paras Stable

Trainers– 1, Attfield Roger L; 2, Vella Daniel J; 3, Minshall Barbara J; 4, Minshall Barbara J; 5, Vella Daniel J; 6, Keogh Michael; 7, Attfield Roger L; 8, Ranford Kathryn; 9, Erwin Dennis M; 10, Cheadle James W; 11, Vella Daniel J; 12, Luider Michael John; 13, Lorimer Suzanne; 14, DePaulo Michael P

Best and Worst of Times: Breeders' Cup Triumph— Greenwood Gone, Financial Woes, Slots a Saviour

As the twentieth century drew to a close, Woodbine experienced the best of times and the worst of times. The largest track in Canada rode more ups and downs than the roller coasters at Canada's Wonderland. One of the big upswings was Woodbine's staging of the thirteenth Breeders' Cup in 1996, the only time the international extravaganza had been held outside of the United States. A record crowd of 42,243 filed into Woodbine, blessed with unseasonably warm October weather, to watch the $11 million spectacle, headlined by racing's richest thoroughbred, *Cigar*.

Cigar didn't win (he was third), but Woodbine did. The total worldwide betting handle on the race was about $69.5 million, way ahead of the previous year's total, although about $10 million below the record Breeders' Cup handle. The consensus was that Woodbine was an excellent Breeders' Cup host. "They won me over," said Wayne Lukas, who trained *Boston Harbor* to win the $1 million Juvenile.

AWESOME AGAIN STUNNED THE RACING WORLD WITH HIS UPSET VICTORY AGAINST THE GREATEST HORSES IN THE WORLD IN THE $5 MILLION BREEDERS' CUP CLASSIC AT LOUISVILLE.

"And I was one of the most critical ones about having it up here. It was an outstanding Breeders' Cup, maybe the best yet. I don't know what they could have done to be a better host."

But sour notes lurked behind the Breeders' Cup glamour. Woodbine officials had to stave off a work stoppage by mutuel clerks, which almost resulted in Woodbine losing the Breeders' Cup at a late hour. Worst of all, Woodbine, like many tracks in North America, was in a precarious financial position, the victim of the proliferation of gaming opportunities from the 649 lottery to scratch-and-wins, to three casinos that began operating in Ontario. In 1999, craps made its debut at the casinos, although they had been banned in Canada since Confederation. Woodbine officials struggled to adapt to change. One way to reduce expenses was to sell properties, and it sold its old stalwart, Greenwood. For the standardbred business, Greenwood had been a little Fort Knox, taking advantage of its stop on a Toronto Transit Commission streetcar line.

But with Greenwood being turned into flashy, expensive lakeside condos, it meant the harness folk had to find another home. Woodbine officials created a supertrack, moved harness racing to Woodbine and constructed three ovals, none of which crossed each other. The transition from downtown Greenwood to the Rexdale track in the suburbs was accomplished practically overnight. New Year's Eve 1993 witnessed the last race at the track that welcomed

harness racing in 1875 and the following day, 1 January 1994, the trotters and pacers had invaded Woodbine for the first time, racing on a seven-eighths mile oval, chalking up faster clockings than ever. It was the only place in the world that could stage a thoroughbred race in the afternoon and a harness race in the evening. Initially, fans weren't thrilled. Average daily attendance and wagering plummeted in the first fifty days of the standardbred meet, dipping by almost twenty per cent, even counting revenue from intertrack. Gradually, Woodbine opened up standardbred opportunities at its Mohawk Raceway near Campbellville, created a summer meet and, by 2007, had moved all three of its $1 million harness races (The North America Cup, the Metro Pace and the Canadian Trotting Classic). Woodbine hosted few Breeders' Crown races, leaving Mohawk to take that glory. The Canadian Pacing Derby also left Woodbine in 2005.

Still, the best pacers and trotters and drivers in the business frequented Woodbine. *Moni Maker*, the richest trotting mare in history, set world records at Woodbine. *Rocknroll Hanover* became the first two-year-old in harness history to go faster than 1:50 when he won the Metro Pace at Woodbine, then returned next year to win Canada's richest harness race, the $1.5 million North America Cup at Woodbine. *Real Desire* was another superstar. Although he was never fond of the footing at Woodbine, he won the Canadian Pacing

Derby there in 2002 as the 2-to-5 favourite. Other champions to grace Woodbine's harness track were *Eternal Camnation*, *Rainbow Blue*, Hambletonian winner *Yankee Paco* and the best the Breeders' Crown could offer.

In 1996, Woodbine suffered an $8 million operating loss—a regular occurrence during the 1990s—and was burdened with an estimated $77 million in debt. Daily average attendance bottomed out in 1995 at 8,000 people a day on the weekends and barely 4,000 on weekdays. So serious was the OJC's predicament that it began selling the equine art off the walls of the trustees' private room. "There's no question, racing was on a downward spiral in the late '80s and '90s," said David Willmot, who faced a tough task turning around the Ontario Jockey Club tracks after he took leadership in 1995. "We just weren't competing with other entertainment venues." Willmot got the job as president and chief executive officer in 1995, beating out more than 150 applicants. But when he took over the reins, the horizon was bleak. "There wasn't one part of the organization that I'm aware of that was operating on eight cylinders," said director Bob Anderson.

The first task before the OJC was to get tax relief from the province, a must if tracks were to compete against lotteries and casinos. The seven per cent levy that Ontario took from every betting dollar (nine per cent for triactors) was the highest takeout at any track in North America. Finally, the province agreed to take only half of one

WOODBINE'S GREATEST DAY! THE PERFECT HOSTS FOR BREEDERS' CUP '96, WHICH ATTRACTED THE GLOBE'S BEST HORSES, JOCKEYS, TRAINERS, A HUGE CROWD AND A WORLD-WIDE TV AUDIENCE.

per cent, turning 2.5 per cent back to the bettor, one per cent to the tracks and the rest to horsemen, to help increase purses. The tax relief was expected to return $50 million back into the industry. It proved to be racing's saving grace. But a delay in getting it in 1996 caused a purse cut of about ten per cent the month before the Breeders' Cup. On top of that, Woodbine had to drop six racing dates at the end of the season to prevent further purse cuts. When the tax relief did come, it gave racing in Ontario new life. Woodbine began to use the money to spiff up the old cinderblock and cement grandstand, something that hadn't been done since the track was built in 1956.

Beginning in 1994, another trend—teletheatres—also took patrons away from the racetrack. In 1993, only simulcasting from the OJC's other tracks existed. In 1994, Woodbine established nine teletheatres. In the second year there were twenty-four of them and in the third year, twenty-seven. The intent? To make it more convenient for patrons to skip the traffic jams and wager from a neighborhood outlet. But teletheatres also took about half of the crowd away from Woodbine and created empty, yawning grandstands. The buzz died. To combat this development—Woodbine lost an estimated eight dollar per patron in food and beverage charges—the track allowed customers to park for free in February of 1996—costing the OJC $1.3 million in lost revenue. And on 1 January 1997, to lure yet more people back to the track, the OJC dropped the four dollars general admissions charge. Attendance for

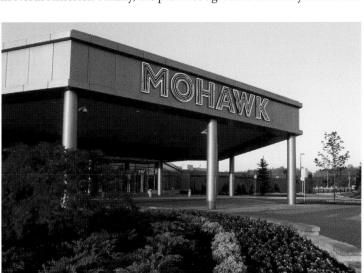

MOHAWK IN CAMPBELLVILLE BECAME THE "HOME" FOR WEG'S MAJOR HARNESS RACING EVENTS IN 2007.

THE INTRODUCTION OF SLOTS AT WOODBINE AND MOHAWK WAS AN ENORMOUS FINANCIAL BOON FOR HORSEMEN AND WEG.

NHL OWNER AND PHARMACEUTICAL ENTREPRENEUR EUGENE MELNYK.

TWO OF HORSE RACING'S MAJOR PLAYERS IN NORTH AMERICA—FRANK STRONACH AND STEVE STAVRO.

thoroughbred racing on-track had dropped from 2.3 million in 1995 to 1.24 million in 1996. However, factor in the teletheatres and attendance actually wasn't dropping. It remained constant.

But constant wasn't good enough. Willmot realized OJC tracks needed a major overhaul to survive and compete against other forms of entertainment. With various initiatives were undertaken, including telephone account betting and a Horseplayer Interactive betting service—allowing fans to watch and wager on races from the comfort of their homes—and $45 million in upgrades to the front entrance, the jockey room and the paddock. Woodbine's boat began to turn around about 1997. Telephone account betting had been legal in Canada since 1982, but had never been tried before by the OJC. "It's no secret that we have been labeled a dying industry but from this day forward, that is about to change," Willmot said, in announcing the initiatives in 1997.

And then along came slots, the one-armed bandits that would make Woodbine the envy of North American tracks. In May of 1996, the Ontario government allowed slots at racetracks, but they weren't installed at Mohawk Raceway until August of 1999 (750 of them) and at Woodbine until March of 2000, when 1,700 machines began humming in a newly renovated 60,000 square-foot setting. The refurbishment to create an area for the slots and also to modernize the wagering area for races, hit $150 million. Slots had already been allowed in Quebec, Manitoba and Alberta. "The greatest thing slots bring is the resurgence in morale and the renewal of confidence we have in ourselves," Willmot said. "No longer are people in the industry sitting around hanging their heads, wondering what we're going to do with our lives when we go out of business." Now Woodbine seats nearly 700 diners with a view of the track, another 1,000 with close access to television in another five restaurants, 400 pari-mutuels windows, 150 automated betting machines, a food court, a race book, walls decorated with enormous posters of horses, drivers and jockeys, and the cabinets and displays of Canada's legends in the Canadian Horse Racing Hall of Fame.

The advent of slots hit racing in Ontario like a windstorm. Slots were an enormous boon, more than anybody expected, including the Ontario Lottery and Gaming Corporation, which manages them. Purses shot up anywhere from 60 to 400 per cent at Ontario tracks because of them. They pumped at least $20 million into the thoroughbred purses in the first season. And they brought back the buzz

to Woodbine. Within the first twenty-five minutes of the introduction of the slots on 29 March 2000, 1,300 people were at the machines. After the first week, 100,000 people had found their way to the track slots. It took only ninety-two days for the OJC to attract one million visitors to its slot-machine operation. Overall in 2000, more than seven million people visited Woodbine and Mohawk, mostly because of the slots, which are open longer hours than the racetrack program. At the peak of its popularity, Woodbine would attract 50,000 bettors a week. In the years after the slots were installed, both Mohawk and Woodbine averaged between 140,000 to 150,000 customers a week. The slots would eventually be open twenty-four hours a day, seven days a week.

Slots weren't the only success. The foal crop in Canada grew 7.8 per cent from 1999 to 2001, nearly four times the growth of the overall North America foal crop during the same period. More owners, including an increasingly powerful Canadian entrepreneur, Eugene Melnyk, began sending mares to Canada to drop their foals and become eligible for breeding bonuses—and the Queen's Plate, whose purse had risen by $500,000 to $1 million in 2000. Willmot's Kinghaven Farms had reduced its broodmare band to fifteen from eighty in its heyday, but with the advent of slots, Kinghaven bred twenty-seven mares in 2000.

According to a story in the *Lexington Herald-Leader*, track executives began to talk about Woodbine "the way teenage girls talk about Britney Spears. It's everybody they want to be," (at least in that era). An executive from the Kentucky Thoroughbred Association, said if he were to pick a model for Kentucky to compete with the riverboat gambling, it would be Woodbine. A string of U.S. racing executives came to Toronto for a look. But Woodbine was particularly interesting, because it seemed to be bucking trends of slots cannibalizing patrons from the racing side. "It would appear that we bucked that trend because of the extensive distribution system we have in play with telephone accounts, teletheatres and simulcasts," the OJC's Hugh Mitchell said.

But although slots were the sexy part of racing in Ontario in the early 2000s, the OJC also proved that horse racing was very much alive. In the twenty-six months before the opening of slots, there had been seven purse increases. The OJC handled a record $1.2 billion in wagering at both thoroughbred and harness operations in 2000, an increase of 11.6 per cent over 1999. And those numbers had nothing to do with slot revenue. Within two years there had been an increase of $100 million in wagering on horse racing in the Toronto area. In 1998 wagering on and off track had risen 7.7 per cent from the previous year. And U.S. patrons wagered 17 per cent more on OJC races. Willmot estimated the racing attendance rose between 20 and 25 per cent. In 1998 Woodbine had an operating profit of $4.5 million. In 1999 the daily average purse distribution for thoroughbreds shot up to $470,000 a day from $304,000. Slots provided only about 40 per cent of the increase.

Slots have been a gold mine, but telephone account wagering proved to be the largest growing segment of the local racing industry, tying in perfectly with simulcasting and Woodbine's push for a channel on satellite TV. Telephone account wagering on OJC throughbred races soared to $9.7 million in 2000 from $5.9 million in 1999.

Woodbine spent $7 million to upgrade its on-site TV studio, after signing a three-year deal with CTV Sportsnet to provide live coverage of racing during the winter of 1998–99. Woodbine also launched a new horse racing satellite TV channel in May 1999, in conjunction with Philadelphia Park.

TORONTO'S SPECTACULAR SKYLINE PROVIDED A TOWERING BACKDROP AS A THOROUGHBRED GALLOPS FOR THE FINAL TIME IN 1993 AT GREENWOOD, FORMERLY WOODBINE PARK OR OLD WOODBINE.

In 2001 the Ontario Jockey Club changed its name to Woodbine Entertainment Group to reflect its new direction and in 1999 it had already put out a request for proposals to develop 300 acres to the west of the track, complete with hotel and an arena. Still, the new WEG was quickly to find new challenges.

In the racetrack arena, the Queen's Plate was also subject to change. By the year 2000, homebreds from the big-name stables such as Windfields, Kinghaven and Sam-Son were largely disappearing, replaced by horses bought at auctions. About half of the horses in the 2000 Plate were purchased at auction. The reason? Canadians had begun to sell their yearlings in the United States. When the Canadian economy recovered in the late 1990s, Canadians weren't buying south of the border. The major stables raced with small stables, and even Kinghaven took to becoming a seller. The exception to the rule was Eugene Melnyk, a Toronto-born resident of Barbados and owner of the Ottawa Senators of the National Hockey League. He made his fortune with pharmaceuticals. His Queen's Plate victory with *Archers Bay* in 1998, the first horse he'd ever entered in the race, marked the end of one era, but the start of another one.

Archers Bay became the twentieth Windfields alumnus to win the Plate, but the first one since *La Lorgnette* in 1985. Eleven of them were owned by E.P. Taylor himself, who died nine

years before *Archers Bay* won. Melnyk seemed bent on taking up the Windfields' torch and becoming an international power in the sport. The thought wasn't far from his mind when he purchased *Archers Bay* at a Kentucky auction for US$120,000. The blood that ran through *Archers Bay*'s veins meant so much to the Windfields folk that they had retained *Archers Bay*'s full sister, *Acadia*, as a broodmare even after a rash of cutbacks. Eventually, *Archers Bay* stood stud at Windfields before he died.

"It's something I was keenly aware of when I bought this horse," Melnyk said. "I knew he was just about the perfect Windfields-bred, sort of a throwback to the past—and eligible to the Plate of course." *Archers Bay* was the start of Melnyk's yearling buying spree, as he set aside his practice of claiming older horses. That season in 1996, when he bought *Archers Bay*, he spent $1.5 million to buy eight to ten yearlings in the United States. The next year, he spent $3.5 million on fifteen yearlings, making him the second-leading buyer of select yearlings south of the border in 1997. In 2000, he spent about US$16 million on yearlings. Melnyk owned *Archers Bay* in partnership with Iris and Bill Bristow, a stockbroker with Nesbitt Burns, who predicted back then that Melnyk would become a major force in the thoroughbred racing game, on the same level as Canadian industrialist Frank Stronach. The Austrian-born auto and racetrack magnate had set a benchmark during the late 1990s and early 2000s when his horses won five Breeders' Cup races—Classic winners *Awesome Again* and *Ghostzapper*, *Macho Uno* in the Juvenile, Distaff champion *Ginger Punch* and *Perfect Sting* in the Filly and Mare Turf.

By the year 2000, when slots came to Woodbine, Melnyk was about to race his first horse, U.S.-bred Graeme Hall, in the Kentucky Derby. But his first regret was that there wasn't a Canadian-bred horse in the race. "Canada needs another *Northern Dancer*, another *Sunny's Halo*," he said. He's poised to put Canada on the map. And he's sending at least ten of his mares home to foal in Canada, so their offspring will be eligible for races such as the Queen's Plate.

JIM AND FLORENCE BEGG ACCOMPANY *VICTOR COOLEY* AND EMILE RAMSAMMY.

A little star in his own heaven, that's what he was. The horse with the sooty coat, *Victor Cooley*, was bound for big things from the day he was born—which was Oscar awards night in Hollywood. It's no surprise that he won the very first start of his career on another Oscar night. And it's no surprise that his handlers dubbed him *Oscar*. He was just as temperamental as any Oscar winner, too. That's why he became a gelding.

With more than three months to go before the 137th Queen's Plate, well-respected journalist Jim Proudfoot was lamenting the poor quality of the field headed for the race. "It's all so damnably depressing," he wrote. But by the time the Plate rolled around, many trainers were saying that it was a very tough, competitive Plate, with a field that included horses that could be competitive south of the border. And *Victor Cooley* was at the head of this class. He had to be. He was saddled with post no. 1 in the Plate, and no horse since *Northern Dancer*, in 1964, had won from that post. When trainer Mark Frostad heard this news, he admitted he got a lump in his throat. *Victor Cooley* had to be on his toes to claim that $255,480 winner's pot. *Victor Cooley* toyed with the field, winning by one-and-a-half lengths. He outclassed the lot of them for Emile Ramsammy, a Trinidad-born jockey who had never ridden in the Queen's Plate before and owners Windways Farms, which included Jim and Florence Begg and their son, Jeff and his wife, Annabel. He also delivered the first of many Plate wins for trainer Mark Frostad.

The Beggs were shopping-centre developers, but Jeff in particular had first been lured to the show-jumping arena, where he made the long list for the national team during the 1970s. He turned to training thoroughbreds when one of his jumpers, *Cicero Creek*, showed a reluctance to leap over fences. *Cicero Creek* went back to racing. Jeff trained for five years but traded in his backstretch boots in 1986. Windways is primarily a breeding organization and races only those horses it cannot sell. *Victor Cooley*'s dam, *Willow Flight*, had been a $15,000 private purchase that had been a step behind crack fillies like *Avowal*, *Eternal Search* and *Sintrillium*, finishing second eighteen times. In the only stakes race she won, the 1983 Tattling Stakes, she had finished in a dead heat for first.

Victor Cooley, a son of *Cool Victor*, had an attitude that overshadowed any kind of humble beginning. The Beggs couldn't get rid of him and his silly displays of unrestrained energy as a youngster. One of those performances caused him to be scratched from a Woodbine horse sale. "He was always a handful," said Annabel, who operated Windways Farm and broke *Victor Cooley* to saddle. "He was pretty cocky. When the sales inspectors came to look at him, I don't think he ever had one foot on the ground all the time they were there. He was leaping and

"OSCAR STAR" *VICTOR COOLEY*.

TRAINER MARK FROSTAD.

jumping and running." He was accepted for the sale, but wrenched a hock in a playful caper and was scratched. The Beggs figured he would have brought $30,000 with all four corners intact.

The Beggs also had links to polo and thank goodness. They turned to polo pony riders, accustomed to riding horses that turned on a dime, to start riding *Victor Cooley*. But even they couldn't always stay aboard him. Frostad used to call him "mentally challenged."

Frostad said, "It took a long time for him to get things straight about what he was supposed to do. In fact, in his first few races [over the winter] in New Orleans, he wandered all over the track. He did the same thing at two." At two *Victor Cooley* won the princely sum of $1,870, which may have contributed to Proudfoot's pre-Plate angst. *Dance Smartly*, he wasn't. But his winter campaign was another story. He broke his maiden at Fair Grounds in New Orleans in February, added a couple more U.S. wins, then ran fifth in the Lexington Stakes in Kentucky behind some good colts

OWNER/BREEDER JIM BEGG (RIGHT) AND HIS FATHER, JAMES T. BEGG.

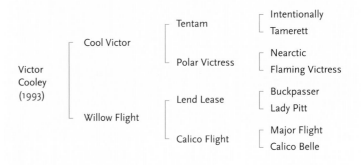

VICTOR COOLEY | 3-year-old dark bay or brown gelding

Victor Cooley (1993)
- Cool Victor
  - Tentam
    - Intentionally
    - Tamerett
  - Polar Victress
    - Nearctic
    - Flaming Victress
- Willow Flight
  - Lend Lease
    - Buckpasser
    - Lady Pitt
  - Calico Flight
    - Major Flight
    - Calico Belle

Owner: Windways Farm; *Trainer:* Mark Frostad
Jockey: Emile Ramsammy; *Breeder:* Jeff Begg (Ont-C)

such as *Prince of Thieves* and *Roar*. The Beggs rejected an offer of $200,000 for a half-interest in the colt.

When *Victor Cooley* thundered back to Canada, he won the Queenston and the Marine Stakes, equaling the track record, making him the morning line favourite. By post time, however, he was a close second choice to another promising Frostad colt, *Chief Bearhart*, who went on later to win the Breeders' Stakes and Canadian International at Woodbine, and eventually the Breeders' Cup Turf at Hollywood against the best in the world. But the question was—and Frostad was needled about this the week before the Plate—while many offspring of *Cool Victor* had won at one-and-one-eighth miles, none had got one-and-one-quarter miles. *Victor Cooley* proved them wrong. He worried Ramsammy when he broke flatfooted, but the thirty-three-year-old jockey settled him in behind horses. During a period of bumping on the backstretch, he had to muscle his way off the rail because the other jockeys were doing their best to hem him in. Around the final turn, *Victor Cooley* traded the lead with pacesetter *Stephanotis*, but then the gelding "exploded," according to Ramsammy. As *Victor Cooley* swept to the lead, Ramsammy thought: "So much for the people doubting this horse."

Ramsammy was mobbed by his enthusiastic fan club, a group of Caribbeans, after the race. However, the race was watched by only 16,025 people, the smallest since 1955. Princess Margaret was supposed to have presented the gold trophy to the winner, but cancelled her trip when the race was moved back a week after officials decided it conflicted with the Toronto Indy auto race. It was a healthy win for Frostad, who had a standing bet with Ontario Jockey Club president David

Willmot that if either were to win the Queen's Plate, they'd stop smoking. "I thought I'd never have to worry about it," Frostad said.

The Beggs turned down an invitation to race *Victor Cooley* in the Haskell Invitational at Monmouth Park in favour of running him in the Prince of Wales, where he was expected to smoke the competition. He finished fifth to *Stephanotis*.

At four, *Victor Cooley* became a world beater, winning the Commonwealth Breeders' Cup at Keeneland, and the $250,000 Vosburgh Handicap at Belmont when he showed his Canadian heels to *Tale of the Cat*. By this time he was described as "a hard knocking horse that had earned $1 million, primarily in minor stakes." *Victor Cooley* continued to race until he was seven He's now living out his days on Windways Farm. Age hasn't mellowed him much. He still is a cut-up, keeping the Beggs on their toes. "We don't have yearlings that are as tough as he is," he said. "And he's kind of spoiled."

EIGHTH RACE
Woodbine
JULY 7, 1996

1¼ MILES. QUEEN'S PLATE S. Purse $265,000 FOR THREE-YEAR-OLDS, FOALED IN CANADA. Colts and Geldings 126 lbs. Fillies 121 lbs.

Value of Race: $425,800 Winner $255,480; second $85,160; third $46,838; fourth $25,548; fifth $12,774. Mutuel Pool $693,762.00 Exactor Pool $483,119.00

Last Raced	Horse	M/Eqt. A. Wt	PP	¼	½	¾	1	Str	Fin	Jockey	Odds $1
9Jun96 10WO1	Victor Cooley	L b 3 126	1	5hd	4 1½	3hd	33	23	11½	Ramsammy E	2.55
23Jun96 6WO4	Stephanotis	L b 3 126	10	11	1½	1hd	1hd	1hd	2¾	Walls M K	a- 11.50
19May96 9WO4	Kristy Krunch	L b 3 126	4	3hd	2 1½	2 1½	2hd	34	31½	Platts R	21.95
23Jun96 6WO3	Chief Bearhart	L b 3 126	2	13	13	123	108	5½	4hd	Hawley S	*2.55
23Jun96 6WO2	Firm Dancer	L 3 126	13	92	9½	72	41	42½	52½	Penna D	3.45
12Jun96 8WO4	Northernprospector	L bf 3 126	5	81½	7hd	5½	5hd	7hd	61¼	Montpellier C	33.35
27Jun96 2WO3	Crown Attorney	L 3 126	12	11hd	112	91	71	82	72½	Clark D	10.50
16Jun96 8WO4	Intended Passage	L 3 126	3	123	10½	102	6½	6½	82¼	McAleney J S	89.55
23Jun96 6WO1	Northface	L bf 3 126	9	41	31	43	8½	93	93½	Kabel T K	b- 5.20
29Jun96 9WO1	Spider Wire	L b 3 126	8	71	5hd	61	91	102	101¼	Landry R C	a- 11.50
9Jun96 7WO5	Lorries Mane Man	L 3 126	6	10½	122	13	117	1110	1119	Attard L	53.25
23Jun96 2WO2	Handsome Hansel	L f 3 126	11	6hd	6½	8½	125	128	128½	Dos Ramos R A	b- 5.20
27Jun96 7WO3	Domasca Dave	L b 3 126	7	2hd	84	11½	13	13	13	Poznansky N E5	91.05

*-Actual Betting Favorite.
a-Coupled: Stephanotis and Spider Wire.
b-Coupled: Northface and Handsome Hansel.

OFF AT 4:42 Start Good For All But . Won . Track fast.
TIME :224, :46, 1:111, 1:37, 2:034 (:22.80, :46.00, 1:11.20, 1:37.00, 2:03.80)

$2 Mutuel Prices:				
3 – VICTOR COOLEY		7.10	4.90	4.00
1a– STEPHANOTIS (a–entry)			9.50	6.30
6 – KRISTY KRUNCH				8.10

$2 EXACTOR 3–1A PAID $53.90

Dk. b or br. g, (Mar), by Cool Victor – Willow Flight , by Lend Lease . Trainer Frostad Mark. Bred by J Begg (Ont-C).

Owners– 1, Windways Farm; 2, Minshall Farms; 3, Molincroft Farms; 4, Sam-Son Farms; 5, Schickedanz Gustav; 6, K 5 Stables; 7, Lamb A and M; 8, Abbott Charles S; 9, Stronach Frank H; 10, Minshall Farms; 11, Pitoscia C and Adamo M; 12, Stronach Frank H; 13, Grace-Lyn Farms and Norseman Racing Stable

Trainers– 1, Frostad Mark; 2, Minshall Barbara J; 3, Schnitzler Rita A; 4, Frostad Mark; 5, Keogh Michael; 6, Johnson Joseph H; 7, MacKenzie John P; 8, Pearce Grant; 9, Vella Daniel J; 10, Minshall Barbara J; 11, DePaulo Michael P; 12, Vella Daniel J; 13, Mattine Tony

Awesome Again always lived up to his name. It's just that hardly anybody knew it when he surfaced in Toronto the week before the 138th running of the Queen's Plate, with only $25,680 of winnings in his pocket. A couple of months before the Plate, he didn't even have a name. Finally, owner Frank Stronach of Newmarket, Ontario, went with the thought that struck him first when he saw the big colt as a youngster: awesome. He was a son of Canadian champion *Deputy Minister*, one of the leading sires in North America.

Awesome Again was a rookie at the racing game, having made only two previous starts in his life, all in the five weeks before the Plate. How could a horse win a tough one-and-one-quarter-mile race with a record like that? None of the four *Daily Racing Form* handicappers picked him to win. Nobody had won a Plate in their third career start. He did. And he did it in front of Queen Elizabeth II, her first visit to Woodbine in twenty-four years. *Awesome Again* was one of twenty-one horses that Stronach originally nominated to the Plate, although he was one of only three that actually started. *Awesome Again* left clues. In his second start, a one-and-one-sixteenth mile allowance race at Hollywood Park, he had been headed twice early, then pounced and won easily by six lengths. That got people talking. They also should have been listening to trainer David Hofmans when he said that *Awesome Again* reminded him of his stablemate, *Touch Gold*, which had just won the Belmont Stakes and foiled the Triple Crown bid of Silver Charm. "They have the same sire [*Deputy Minister*], and some of the same mannerisms," Hofmans said. "He's a very intelligent horse. And he acts like he wants to run on." Hofmans admitted that a mile-and-one-quarter race was an ambitious plan: "But the way he's acting right now, it's worth taking a shot." Hofmans had had him only a few weeks. He'd been developed by Toronto trainer Danny Vella, who had won the Plate for Stronach in 1994 with *Basquerian*.

In the Plate, *Awesome Again* was up against favored *Cryptocloser*, who had raced ten times, rubbed shoulders with some good American horses, and won the Plate Trial in a five-and-three-quarter-length jog. But *Awesome Again* was like a tank mowing down a corn-field, and *Cryptocloser* had poor racing luck.

A heavy-bodied colt, low to the ground, *Awesome Again* ran in the middle of a tightly bunched field and made his move before the quarter pole. He wrestled the lead from *Air Cool* and won by three and a half lengths ahead of *Cryptocloser*. He won, laughing, even though he gawked and lugged in toward the inner rail when he heard the noise of the crowd of 20,098 in the stretch. Top U.S. jockey Mike Smith—who hadn't even seen the colt until the morning of the race—was left speechless in the Queen's presence, but gushed afterward. "Awesome," he said. "It's amazing to do what he just did. He kind of ran in hand, really. I was more busy than he was."

The racetrack stewards were almost as busy following the race. They launched an inquiry concerning *Cryptocloser*, who was forced to check sharply in the stretch when a tiring *Cowboy Cop*, who was

FRANK STRONACH AND TRAINER DAVID HOFMANS CONGRATULATE *AWESOME AGAIN*.

running as part of the Stronach entry, appeared to come in on him. *Cryptocloser* in turn bumped *Sky and Sea* to the inside. Emile Ramsammy, riding *Sky and Sea*, also lodged a claim against *Cowboy Cop*. After a lengthy review, the stewards threw out both claims. That should have ended any controversy. It didn't.

The Plate of 1997 wasn't really over for almost two months. Part-owner Bill Sorokolit Jr. (New Jersey real estate tycoon, Earle I. Mack, had purchased a half-interest in the horse before the Plate for US$100,000) appealed the decision, saying because *Awesome Again*'s entrymate (*Cowboy Cop*) fouled him, that *Awesome Again*'s number should have come down—even though *Awesome Again* had nothing to do with the bumping. "*Cryptocloser* did an amazing thing just to come back and only get beaten by three lengths," Sorokolit said."I think it cost him seven lengths." In the end, a tribunal of the Ontario Racing Commission turned down the appeal, saying the crowding incident resulted from a combination of events, and that there was nothing to suggest collusion between riders of entrymates.

Awesome Again got to keep his Queen's Plate win, but there would be no sniffing of Triple Crown glory. Immediately after the race, Stronach scuttled any plans to send him on the Canadian Triple Crown trail. "I'm saying this right now before I get tempted," he said. "We rushed him a bit to get here, and we know he is a really good horse. You can't squeeze him too much." *Awesome Again* never raced in Canada again.

Meanwhile, *Cryptocloser* won the Prince of Wales, prompting Sorokolit to propose a rematch with *Awesome Again*. He'd put up the $117,660 winner's purse from the Fort Erie race, if Stronach would match it. But Stronach was after bigger things. On the day that Stronach's *Touch Gold* won the $1 million Haskell Invitational at Monmouth Park, *Awesome Again*—in only his fourth start—won the $250,000 Jim Dandy at Saratoga by three lengths on a sloppy track, running erratically, but still defeating Behrens. *Awesome Again* ended up playing pinch hitter in the $750,000 Travers Stakes, after *Touch Gold* withdrew with a troublesome left front foot. And he had his rematch with *Cryptocloser*. Still, he seemed to be the underdog of the stable. *Touch Gold* was the more aggressive of the two, the street fighter of the barn, while *Awesome Again* was so amiable, he was known as "*Tony the Pony*." *Awesome Again* went off as the favourite in the Travers, but finished third after tiring badly behind Deputy Commander. *Cryptocloser* finished fifth.

It was a different story the next year. This time, Stronach had "consolidated" his stable and put his racing string in the hands of Patrick Byrne, who campaigned *Awesome Again* as if—in the words of one scribe—he was "the cross-eyed stepchild," inferior to *Touch Gold*. "He didn't impress me when I first saw him," Byrne said of the unassuming colt. In 1998, *Awesome Again* prepared for the $5.12 million Breeders' Cup Classic in anonymity, even though he had been undefeated in five previous starts. Although he had defeated 1997 Kentucky Derby winner *Silver Charm* early in the season in the Stephen Foster Handicap at Churchill Downs, he spent the rest of his time ducking mighty *Skip Away*, winner of the 1997 Breeders' Cup Classic, but winning the Whitney, the Saratoga Breeders' Cup Handicap, and the Hawthorne Gold Cup. Interestingly enough, Pat Day had his pick of Stronach mounts in the richest thoroughbred horse race ever run, with the classiest field of millionaires (eight of them) ever assembled. He picked *Awesome Again* over *Touch Gold*.

Awesome Again created shock waves when he blasted through a hole that opened up in the stretch and won by three-quarters of a length over *Silver Charm*, English champion *Swain* and Belmont Stakes winner *Victory Gallop*, with *Skip Away* sixth and *Touch Gold* eighth. Byrne admitted he probably made a mistake in underestimating *Awesome Again*, which became the richest Canadian-bred horse in history, with winnings of $4,374,589 and nine victories in twelve starts. He was retired to stud after the Classic. He stood at stud at Stronach's Kentucky farm, beginning at $50,000. *Touch Gold* stood for $30,000. But when *Deputy Minister*'s son became the first Breeders' Cup winner to sire another Breeders' Cup winner (*Ghostzapper*, a brilliant U.S. Horse of the Year) and also to sire multiple Breeders' Cup winners on the same day (*Ghostzapper* and *Wilko*), *Awesome Again*'s fee soared to $125,000 for 2005. He is no longer second banana. He was and is awesome, in every way.

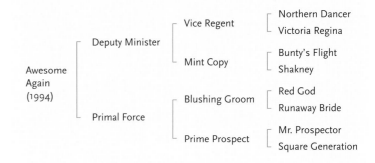

AWESOME AGAIN | 3-year-old bay colt

Awesome Again (1994)	Deputy Minister	Vice Regent	Northern Dancer
			Victoria Regina
		Mint Copy	Bunty's Flight
			Shakney
	Primal Force	Blushing Groom	Red God
			Runaway Bride
		Prime Prospect	Mr. Prospector
			Square Generation

Owner: Frank Stronach; *Trainer:* David Hofmans
Jockey: Michael E. Smith; *Breeder:* Frank Stronach (Ont-C)

Mike Smith doffs his helmet in an "awesome" win.

EIGHTH RACE Woodbine JUNE 29, 1997

1¼ MILES. QUEEN'S PLATE S. Purse $285,000 FOR THREE-YEAR-OLDS, FOALED IN CANADA. Weights: Colts and Geldings, 126 lbs. Fillies, 121 lbs.

Value of Race: $425,700 Winner $255,420; second $85,140; third $46,827; fourth $25,542; fifth $12,771. Mutuel Pool $632,263.00 Exactor Pool $187,323.00 Trifecta Pool $257,209.00

Last Raced	Horse	M/Eqt.		A.	Wt	PP	1/4	1/2	3/4	1	Str	Fin	Jockey	Odds $1
5Jun97 ^{5}Hol^{1}	Awesome Again	L		3	126	3	9^{2}	7^{2}	7½	2^{hd}	12½	13½	Smith M E	a-3.00
8Jun97 ^{8}WO^{1}	Cryptocloser	L		3	126	4	11^{hd}	9^{1}	9^{4}	6½	4^{hd}	2^{hd}	Martinez W	1.25
7Jun97 ^{6}Pim^{1}	Sovereign Storm	L	b	3	126	14	14	13½	11½	81½	52½	3^{1}	Hamilton S D	50.95
8Jun97 ^{8}WO^{2}	Air Cool	L	f	3	126	2	5^{1}	4^{hd}	4^{hd}	1½	2^{4}	4^{5}	Platts R	20.30
8Jun97 ^{8}WO^{3}	Love View	L	b	3	126	11	13^{hd}	14	12½	11^{2}	8^{3}	53½	Walls M K	5.30
1Jun97 ^{9}WO^{1}	Cowboy Cop		b	3	126	5	8^{hd}	8½	8^{hd}	41½	3^{hd}	62½	Landry R C	a-3.00
31May97 ^{7}WO^{1}	Sky and Sea	L		3	126	1	4^{hd}	5^{2}	51½	5^{hd}	6½	71½	Ramsammy E	29.70
15Jun97 ^{1}WO^{1}	Annihilate	L	f	3	126	12	10^{hd}	12^{2}	10½	9^{2}	7^{hd}	8^{1}	Hawley S	15.35
15Jun97 ^{3}WO^{2}	Rabbit in a Hat	L		3	126	9	7^{hd}	6^{hd}	6^{1}	10^{2}	10^{2}	91¼	Bahen S R	11.95
8Jun97 ^{8}WO^{4}	John the Magician	L		3	126	7	2½	2^{hd}	2½	7^{1}	9^{hd}	10^{3}	Sabourin R B	14.95
7Jun97 ^{3}WO^{4}	Tempolake	L		3	126	13	12^{1}	11^{1}	13^{hd}	12^{hd}	12^{4}	11^{2}	Poznansky N E	134.65
15Jun97 ^{1}WO^{3}	Sloane Ranger	L	b	3	126	10	3^{1}	1^{hd}	1^{1}	3^{hd}	11^{2}	123¼	Gryder A T	101.65
7Jun97 ^{3}WO^{1}	C. C. On Ice	L		3	126	8	1^{hd}	31½	3^{hd}	13^{3}	13^{6}	13^{11}	Kabel T K	a-3.00
15Jun97 ^{1}WO^{5}	Bowmore	L	b	3	126	6	6^{1}	10½	14	14	14	14	Somsanith N	57.90

a-Coupled: Awesome Again and Cowboy Cop and C. C. On Ice.

OFF AT 4:40 Start Good For All But. Won . Track fast.

TIME :22^{4}, :46^{1}, 1:11^{4}, 1:38, 2:04^{1} (:22.80, :46.20, 1:11.80, 1:38.00, 2:04.20)

$2 Mutuel Prices:			
1 – AWESOME AGAIN(a-entry)..........	8.00	3.90	3.00
4 – CRYPTOCLOSER....................		3.30	2.90
12 – SOVEREIGN STORM.................			11.70

$2 EXACTOR 1–4 PAID $16.20 $2 TRIFECTA 1–4–12 PAID $344.60

B. c, (Mar), by Deputy Minister – Primal Force , by Blushing Groom–Fr . Trainer Hofmans David. Bred by Frank Stronach (Ont–C).

Owners– 1, Stronach Frank H; 2, Sorokolit Jr William A and Mack Earle I; 3, H and D Stable; 4, Colebrook Farms; 5, Shaw Richard F and Jo Ellen; 6, Stronach Frank H; 7, Pin Oak Stable and Sam-Son Farm; 8, Maine J and Baker R; 9, Minshall Farms; 10, RMC Stable; 11, Molincroft Farms; 12, Sugar Stable Park Stud and Partners; 13, Stronach Frank H; 14, McArthur Angus

Trainers– 1, Hofmans David; 2, Frostad Mark; 3, Campitelli Francis P; 4, Bowden Thomas R; 5, Bell David R; 6, Vella Daniel J; 7, Frostad Mark; 8, Baker Reade; 9, Minshall Barbara J; 10, Ross John A; 11, Schnitzler Rita A; 12, Carroll Josie; 13, Vella Daniel J; 14, Couse Maggie P

At first glance, even a few weeks out, the 139th Queen's Plate was confusing and apparently devoid of heroes. *Archers Bay*, making only the sixth start of his career, cleared things up very nicely, winning by almost five lengths. Furthermore, he won in 2:02 1/5, just two-fifths of a second off *Izvestia*'s 1990 stakes record of 2:01 4/5. *Archers Bay*'s time was also identical to *Real Quiet*'s clocking in winning the Kentucky Derby a month earlier. With so few starts the crowd of almost 20,000 made him second choice behind Plate Trial winner, the giant-sized *Brite Adam*.

Before *Archers Bay* breezed into the picture, all the talk was of Canadian-bred *Victory Gallop*, which had finished second in the Kentucky Derby and Preakness and was therefore made the 8-to-5 favourite to win the Plate. However, he didn't make the trip to Canada, as he continued on to stymie *Real Quiet*'s Triple Crown bid by winning the Belmont Stakes. Then there was winterbook favourite *Classic Result*, the top two-year-old that injured himself a couple of weeks before the Plate and did not contest the event. American-based hopeful *Nite Dreamer*, tabbed early as a Kentucky Derby contender after a second-place finish in the Louisiana Derby, hadn't raced since 15 March and had a troubled trip in the Plate.

At the last minute, Kinghaven Farm, fired up by how wide-open the race was, supplemented the filly *Primaly* for $15,000, feeling that she was back to her form of the previous season, when she finished third in the Breeders' Cup Juvenile Fillies at Hollywood Park. This created lively controversy when jockey Todd Kabel ditched his regular mount, *Zap Happy*, to ride David Willmot's *Primaly*, thinking the filly was stronger than the colt. *Zap Happy*'s trainer, Bob Tiller, said he was "extremely hurt and insulted," and had to scramble to find another rider at the last minute. He charged that Kabel was getting even for him for taking him off a couple of horses that subsequently won with David Clark. Ironically, *Zap Happy* was owned by a syndicate that included Willmot's wife, Susan. In the end, *Zap Happy* finished a length ahead of *Primaly*, but alas, without a cheque in ninth place in the thirteen-horse field.

It should have been an indication that *Archers Bay* was a horse on the move when jockey Kent Desormeaux gave up a day of riding at Hollywood Park to come to Canada, even though *Archers Bay* had been almost nine lengths behind *Brite Adam* in his first Canadian start, the Plate Trial. At the time, Desormeaux was one of the hottest riders in the sport, the regular rider of Kentucky Derby champion *Real Quiet*. Desormeaux met *Archers Bay* only in the saddling ring before the Plate, and admitted he didn't even know the big bay colt's name. Both trainer Todd Pletcher and owner Eugene Melnyk were at the very beginnings of their top-flight careers. In fact, Melnyk was one of Pletcher's first supporters when the young trainer left the employ of D. Wayne Lukas. When Pletcher came to Toronto, he was a fresh face that was among the sports top-twenty money makers in 1998.

"It's everyone's dream. You can't imagine what it's like to come here and win the Queen's Plate," Melnyk said of winning the Plate with his first entry. "I've owned claiming horses and I've run stan-

KENT DESORMEAUX PUMPS FIST TO SIGNAL *ARCHERS BAY*'S PLATE WIN.

dardbreds at small tracks. But to come here and win a race like this is incredible. To have a horse run in the Queen's Plate is wondeful, to have one that can win the Queen's Plate is something one can only dream of. This [Woodbine] is my old stomping ground. I used to come here every weekend. It's home."

The head of the large pharmaceutical company Biovail in Mississauga, Ontario, Melnyk purchased the Windfields Farm–bred son of *Silver Deputy* for $125,000 as a yearling at Kentucky in partnership with Bill Bristow, a stockbroker at Nesbitt Burns, and his wife Iris of Campbellville, Ont. Melnyk named the colt, as is his custom, after an area in his adopted home of Barbados. Archers Bay is an area in northwest Barbados, one of the prettiest spots on the island and famous for its sunsets.

In the beginning, *Archers Bay* was a Kentucky Derby hopeful, but missed too much time because of sore shins. No other horse in the Plate had fewer starts in 1998 than *Archers Bay* (two). Aboard *Archers Bay*, Desormeaux became the second jockey to win the most important stakes race in Canada and the United States the same year. Bill Hartack, aboard *Northern Dancer* had been the first in 1964 to win both the Kentucky Derby and Queen's Plate. To Louisiana-born Desormeaux, it seemed like a big deal to win the Plate. Desormeaux pumped his arms as he crossed the wire, screamed and hopped up and down on the awards stand, holding aloft a large silver plate. "Look what I got," he said. "The Queen's Plate." His only anxious moment was on the far turn, when he was trapped

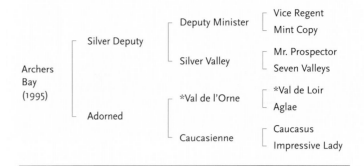

Owner: Eugene N. Melnyk and R. Bristow Farm; *Trainer:* Todd Fletcher
Jockey: Kent J. Desmoreaux; *Breeder:* Windfields Farm (Ont-C)

AN EXULTANT EUGENE MELNYK AND CO-OWNER MRS. IRIS BRISTOW ARE APPLAUDED BY LIEUTENANT GOVERNOR HILARY WESTON AND OJC'S CHAIRMAN OF THE BOARD GEORGE M. HENDRIE.

behind a wall of *Brite Adam, Kinkennie* and *One Way Love.* After steadying his mount, Desormeaux swung *Archers Bay* outside of the leading threesome and wrested the lead from *Brite Adam.* "I had no place to go and I was all dressed up," Desormeaux said. "I had very much difficulty finding a spot. There were horses everywhere." Desormeaux said they hadn't seen the best of *Archers Bay* yet. "Turning for home, he really put on a gear that not many horses have, only true champions can find."

Melnyk, ever the patriotic Canadian, vowed to take *Archers Bay* to the Prince of Wales—partly because the colt needed one more start in Canada to be eligible for a Sovereign Award at year's end. In the Prince of Wales, *Archers Bay* bumbled around early, not getting hold of the track, giving Melnyk a dose of butterflies, but then charged home to win impressively, turning back a stiff challenge from *Nite Dreamer.* *Archers Bay* put himself in line to become the seventh Triple Crown winner, but the colt was too good to stay in Canada: he had a date in the $750,000 Travers Stakes at Saratoga. If only the Breeders' Stakes were a week earlier, Melnyk might have taken a shot. A $1 million bonus wouldn't have changed the plans, he said. The bonus had been dropped a few years earlier. Melnyk turned down an invitation to run in the $1 million Haskell Invitational at Monmouth, New Jersey, to run in the Jim Dandy at Saratoga and to get a race over the track before the Travers, but finished sixth. Jockey Pat Day said the colt didn't handle the track that day.

That effort almost led Pletcher to pull *Archers Bay* from the Travers, but ran him and finished fourth behind *Coronado's Quest, Victory Gallop* and *Raffie's Majesty,* beaten five lengths. The colt was sideswiped at the start from a chain-reaction bumping incident caused by *Victory Gallop.* He dropped far behind the dawdling pace. Still, he won a Sovereign Award as Canada's champion three-year-old colt. *Archers Bay* returned at four and hooked up with *Behrens,* finishing second to him in the $350,000 Gulfstream Park Handicap in February.

He retired with earnings of $666,200 and it was only fitting that he stood at stud at Windfields Farm. After all, he had been the final Queen's Plate winner bred by Windfields and represented eight generations of Windfields breeding. Melnyk was determined to make him a success at stud and bought nearly twenty broodmares that would link up perfectly to his bloodlines. It was a great blow to Melnyk, when *Archers Bay* was euthanized on 3 October 2002 because of complications from colic surgery after siring only three crops. He was buried across from the grave of his great-great-grandsire, *Northern Dancer.*

EIGHTH RACE
Woodbine
JUNE 21, 1998

1¼ MILES. QUEEN'S PLATE S. Purse $500,000 FOR THREE–YEAR–OLDS, FOALED IN CANADA. 126 lbs.

Value of Race: $500,000 Winner $300,000; second $100,000; third $55,000; fourth $30,000; fifth $15,000. Mutuel Pool $583,653.00 Exactor Pool $190,727.00 Triactor Pool $303,954.00

Last Raced	Horse	M/Eqt.	A.	Wt	PP	¼	½	¾	1	Str	Fin	Jockey	Odds $1
3Jun98 3WO2	Archers Bay		3	126	7	6¹½	5¹½	5½	4½	1hd	1⁴¾	Desormeaux K J	3.95
3Jun98 3WO1	Brite Adam	L	3	126	3	4¹	42½	4¹	1hd	22½	24¼	McKnight J	2.30
6Jun98 3WO5	Kinkennie	b	3	126	11	3²	32½	3²	2hd	32½	3no	Platts R	7.40
29Mar98 11TP6	Nite Dreamer	L	3	126	1	9hd	10¹	6¹	5¹	4¹	4¾	Perret C	6.05
6Jun98 8WO3	Pinafore Park	L	3	121	13	11²	12hd9½		7½	6²	5¹	Landry R C	45.20
30May98 7WO1	The Fed		3	126	12	10³	6hd	7hd	8hd	74½	6³	Walls M K	9.00
6Jun98 7WO1	One Way Love	L b	3	126	4	2hd	2³	22½	31½	5½	7²	Clark D	41.10
6Jun98 3WO6	Bronze Shoal	L f	3	126	9	8hd	9¹	11¹	10hd8hd	8¹		Husbands P	108.20
3Jun98 3WO3	Zap Happy	L b	3	126	5	5hd	7hd	10¹½113	9hd	9¹		McCauley W H	12.05
6Jun98 8WO2	Primaly	L	3	121	6	12¹	11hd8hd	9²	10⁸	10⁸		Kabel T K	6.80
6Jun98 5Del3	Platino	L b	3	126	10	13	13	13	13	12hd111		Montpellier C	a-12.95
7Jun98 4Del3	Star On Fire	L bf	3	126	8	7hd	8hd	12¹	12¹	13	12¹½	Bahen S R	a-12.95
10Jun98 5Del1	Yodelman	L b	3	126	2	12½	11	1hd	6hd	11hd13		Ramsammy E	a-12.95

a–Coupled: Platino and Star On Fire and Yodelman.

OFF AT 5:14 Start Good For All But. Won . Track fast.

TIME :22², :45³, 1:10², 1:36⁴, 2:02¹ (:22.40, :45.60, 1:10.40, 1:36.80, 2:02.20)

$2 Mutuel Prices:			
7 – ARCHERS BAY	9.90	4.70	3.90
3 – BRITE ADAM		4.00	3.10
9 – KINKENNIE			5.20

$2 EXACTOR 7–3 PAID $28.20 $2 TRIACTOR 7–3–9 PAID $195.70

B. c, (Mar), by Silver Deputy – Adorned , by Val de l'Orne-Fr . Trainer Pletcher Todd A. Bred by Windfields Farm (Ont–C).

Owners– 1, Melnyk Eugene and Laura and Bristow Iris; 2, RMC Stable; 3, Schickedanz Gustav; 4, Pabst Henry E; 5, Anderson Farms and Ferguson Roderick; 6, Shaw Richard F and Jo Ellen; 7, Schickedanz Bruno and Hillier John; 8, Boissonneault Patrick Nancy and Paul; 9, Laser Quest Racing and Partners; 10, Kinghaven Farms; 11, Stronach Stables; 12, Stronach Stables; 13, Stronach Stables

Trainers– 1, Pletcher Todd A; 2, Schnitzler Rita A; 3, Keogh Michael; 4, O'Callaghan Niall M; 5, Attfield Roger L; 6, Bell David R; 7, Wright Michael Jr; 8, DiMarco John; 9, Tiller Robert P; 10, Attfield Roger L; 11, Vella Daniel J; 12, Vella Daniel J; 13, Vella Daniel J

1999 | WOODCARVER

Woodcarver was a splendid animal. A fetching big grey, with dark dapples scattered over his rump, he had to win the 140th Queen's Plate. Just had to. His owner, the venerable Toronto real estate developer, Gustav Schickedanz, had been in the racing business for twenty years without a Plate winner. Jockey Mickey Walls, already an Eclipse Award winner by the time he was seventeen, was battling burnout by age twenty-five and needed a Plate win to put a nice bow on his career. Trainer Mike Keogh's parents were coming from England, and his mother was to celebrate her birthday that day. "My mom is the strongest person I've ever known, having battled and beaten cancer twice," said Keogh, former assistant to Roger Attfield.

The gods smiled on *Woodcarver* that wet, mucky day at Woodbine in suffocating humidity. He ran the race of his life, charging down the lane with such power that he prompted race announcer Dan Loiselle to call him a "one-horse wrecking crew." He was the best of an interesting, but undistinguished crew, with so few standouts that a field of nineteen lined up to pay the starting fee. The only trouble was Woodbine could offer only seventeen starting spots, after a redesign of the dirt course in 1994 that narrowed the track. It was the largest field in seventeen years. Among this crew, *Zaha* was the early winterbook favourite off the only win of his career, the Coronation Futurity the previous fall. He, *Woodcarver* and *Euchre* had all been originally nominated to the U.S. Triple Crown. Frank Stronach withdrew his talented filly *Bag Lady Jane*, which allowed *Euchre* to get into the field with only two starts and earnings of $25,920. Also scratched was *Maple Syrup*, who had insufficient earnings to gain a starting spot ahead of *Euchre*. It was a smart move for *Eurchre*'s trainer Robert Frankel: *Euchre* finished third behind *Gandria*, a 67-to-1 shot and one of three fillies in the race.

There was no shortage of storylines for this Plate. Rags to riches stories abounded. You had to love the chances of *Sir Lloyd*, a $6,000 purchase that was co-owned by postal employee Lloyd Simpson, who named the colt after himself (and knighted him, too, anticipating a bow to royalty at the Plate). Then there was *Lenny the Lender*, Canada's answer to *Charismatic*, the horse that went from claimer to Kentucky Derby winner that year. Toronto philanthropist and auto and computer parts expediter Victor Deschenes, plucked him out of a $40,000 maiden claimer on 18 April. Among other things, the colourful Deschenes was famous for having rescued seven Ukrainian dwarfs who were unable to speak English and were stranded in Canada without work promised to them. He paid their flights home. Deschenes claimed the horse from Walls' father, Joe, who said that if *Lenny the Lender* won the Plate, he'd turn in his trainer's licence. Lenny fnished with a late rally to finish fourth.

As for *Woodcarver*, he was the best-bred horse in the race (what else would you call a horse by *Woodman* and out of *Sharpening Up?*) and rattled the sabres early in the season when he won the

WOODCARVER'S TEAM—TRAINER MICHAEL KEOGH, JOCKEY MICKEY WALLS AND OWNER-BREEDER GUSTAV SCHICKEDANZ.

Queenston Stakes by seven lengths in his first start of the season. His connections had thought so highly of him as a two-year-old that they had considered running him in the Breeders' Cup Juvenile at Churchill Downs. A minor injury sidelined him. After he had broken his maiden as a two-year-old, a hopeful buyer offered $1 million for him. Schickedanz filed it away. "I like horses like him and we want to race him," Schickedanz said. "He makes us feel good." He considered the horse a member of his family. He also didn't sell his champion sprinter *Langfuhr*, when he stood at stud in Kentucky.

Woodcarver became the Plate favourite after that Queenston effort, but finished only fifth in the Marine Stakes. However, Keogh said the horse came back "dead lame," suffering a stone bruise in a front foot during the race. In the Plate Trial he wore orthopedic pads on both front feet when he finished second, beaten only a head, but Keogh was pleased, considering that rains had bungled his training plans leading up to the race. After his early misfortunes, *Woodcarver* trained like a champ before the Plate. Schickedanz prayed for post Number 1 and got it, although he had the ninth selection of posts. There had been precious few Plate winners from the pole position. "This year he has only one win and he was Number 1 that day," Schickedanz reasoned. "I said, 'Lord, give us one, please.' It's the shortest way around." Keogh kept the orthopedic pads on *Woodcarver* until the day before the Plate, just in case he stepped on something else.

Woodcarver had one more hurdle to overcome: it rained buckets during the morning and the afternoon. No matter. The colt bounced out of the gate with a rush, stayed close to the leaders, and took the lead on the backstretch. It was easy. Walls swatted him only once, just to keep his mind on his business. Keogh's nifty black brogues were coated with mud after the race. "It's the best dirt in the world,"

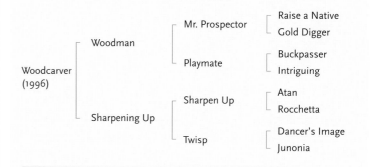

		Mr. Prospector	Raise a Native
	Woodman		Gold Digger
Woodcarver		Playmate	Buckpasser
(1996)			Intriguing
		Sharpen Up	Atan
	Sharpening Up		Rocchetta
		Twisp	Dancer's Image
			Junonia

Owner: Gustav Schickedanz; *Trainer:* Michael Keogh
Jockey: Mickey Walls; *Breeder:* Gustav Schickedanz (Ont-C)

IT'S *WOODCARVER* IN A GALLOP, WINNING BY FIVE LENGTHS.

he said, smiling. Walls oozed confidence about the colt all week, and gave Keogh confidence too. Walls was on a roll after a difficult winter. He had won the Canadian Oaks with *Touch Dial* as well, the first jockey since Pat Day in 1991 to record an Oaks-Plate double. All this after he had taken the winter off, and in his words, "got fat, enjoyed myself, went skiing, played golf and basically laid around all winter." He figured he gained twenty pounds, and didn't dare look at the weight scales. But he felt rejuvenated after having his first winter off in many years. "The stretch run was a blur," Walls said. "I was tired, thirsty and excited to finally win this race. I don't know what to think." It was a happy time for the *Woodcarver* family.

Woodcarver worked better before the Prince of Wales Stakes than he had before the Plate. But at Fort Erie, *Gandria* got the better of *Woodcarver*, after wearing him down in the stretch. He had taken the lead just past the three-furlong pole and seemed to be on his way to victory. He dug in again, but *Gandria* had another gear. "She's got five of them," said her rider Constant Montpellier. *Woodcarver* returned two weeks later to finish last in the Haskell Invitational at Monmouth, New Jersey, after pressing the early pace. To do this, he skipped the Breeders' Stakes, won by another filly, *Free Vacation*.

Two months after his Plate win, tragedy struck. Nearing the end of a six-furlong work at Woodbine in September, *Woodcarver* took a bad step, somersaulted twice, tossing Walls to the ground, and was eventually euthanized on the track, after having shattered his left foreleg. He suffered a condylar fracture to the left cannon bone, totally ruptured one branch of the suspensory ligament and dislocated his

ankle. Walls was unhurt in the fall, but was smarting in other ways. He had also lost his sister, Nicola, in a car accident the previous month.

"It was a total shock," said Keogh of *Woodcarver*'s accident. The Schickedanzes accepted a Sovereign Award for *Woodcarver* later that year as the top three-year-old colt in Canada with a tearful speech. He had won $455,126 in his brief career of nine starts.

NINTH RACE
Woodbine
JUNE 27, 1999

1¼ MILES. QUEEN'S PLATE S. Purse $500,000 For Three-Year-Olds, Foaled in Canada. Weight: 126lbs.

Value of Race: $500,000 Winner $300,000; second $100,000; third $55,000; fourth $30,000; fifth $15,000. Mutuel Pool $609,212.00 Exactor Pool $190,006.00 Triactor Pool $332,193.00

Last Raced	Horse	M/Eqt. A. Wt	PP	¼	½	¾	1	Str	Fin	Jockey	Odds $1
6Jun99 8WO2	Woodcarver	L 3 126	1	41	21½	1½	1½	12	15	Walls M K	3.65
12Jun99 8WO4	Gandria	L 3 121	14	11hd	132½	13hd	7hd	33½	2nk	Montpellier C	67.40
3Jun99 1Hol1	Euchre	L 3 126	7	8½	4hd	3hd	24	23	34½	Ramsammy E	b- 2.35
23May99 8WO2	Lenny the Lender	L 3 126	17	151	152	11½	8hd	4hd	42¾	Kabel T K	10.30
12Jun99 3WO5	Festive Knight	L f 3 126	3	135	6hd	6hd	4hd	51½	5nk	Bahen S R	41.25
5Jun99 11Bel7	Zaha	L 3 126	16	17	17	157	131½	85	61	Davis R G	7.40
6Jun99 8WO1	Catahoula Parish	L b 3 126	12	61	8hd	8hd	6hd	6hd	71¾	Landry R C	5.05
6Jun99 8WO4	Dave the Comet	L b 3 126	11	5hd	10hd	102	92	7hd	83	Baze R A	a- 29.55
12Jun99 8WO2	Roaring Twenties	L b 3 121	10	141	14hd	7½	11hd	9hd	92	Antley C W	b- 2.35
6Jun99 8WO8	The Feeber	L b 3 126	5	3hd	3hd	51½	5hd	10½	101	McAleney J S	a- 29.55
6Jun99 8WO3	Sir Lloyd	L 3 126	9	2hd	51	4hd	3½	112	111	Husbands P	11.90
23May99 3Hol2	Touching	L b 3 121	6	12½	91	9hd	12hd	127	1210	Clark D	b- 2.35
6Jun99 8WO5	Time for Judith	L 3 126	2	16hd	16hd	16hd	1612	149	131	Lauzon J M	69.25
12Jun99 7WO1	Fadder Ted	L f 3 126	15	91	121	12hd	143	13½	1413½	Poznansky N E	56.90
12Jun99 3WO2	Geraint	L b 3 126	13	7½	7hd	141½	154	16	151	McKnight J	26.85
22May99 9WO1	Great Defender	L b 3 126	8	11	11	22	101½	15hd	16	Callaghan S	11.55
12Jun99 7WO3	Beauty's Boy	L 3 126	4	10hd	111½	17	17	—	—	Somsanith N	70.40

a-Coupled: Dave the Comet and The Feeber.
b-Coupled: Euchre and Roaring Twenties and Touching.

OFF AT 5:05 Start Good For All But. Won . Track muddy.
TIME :222, :46, 1:111, 1:371, 2:03 (:22.46, :46.05, 1:11.21, 1:37.24, 2:03.13)

	3 – WOODCARVER	9.30	6.40	4.50
$2 Mutuel Prices:	11 – GANDRIA		44.60	17.20
	2b– EUCHRE(b–entry)			2.90

$2 EXACTOR 3–11 PAID $561.60 $2 TRIACTOR 3–11–2 PAID $2,094.40

Gr/ro. c, (Apr), by Woodman – Sharpening Up , by Sharpen Up–GB . Trainer Keogh Michael. Bred by Gustav Schickedanz (Ont-C).

WOODCARVER was in hand pressing the early pace set by GREAT DEFENDER from the rail, assumed command along the rail on the backstretch, turned away EUCHRE around the turn and drew clear in the drive under constant handling. GANDRIA was unhurried early while off the rail, circled the field while five wide on the turn turn and closed willingly from outside in the drive. EUCHRE stalked the early pace along the rail, drew even with the winner on the 2nd turn but failed to sustain the bid and weakened in the drive.

Owners– 1, Schickedanz Gustav; 2, Arosa Farms; 3, Stronach Stables; 4, Deschenes Victor and Rosanne and Alcamo Tom; 5, Overheath Stable; 6, Shadwell Stable; 7, Jam Jar Racing Stable; 8, RMC Stable; 9, Stronach Stables; 10, RMC Stable; 11, Simpson L Barkin A and Partner; 12, Stronach Stables; 13, Tenenbaum Racing Stables; 14, Shelter Valley Farms and Walls C; 15, Kingfield Racing Stable Ltd; 16, Wilson Robert and Shirley; 17, Rainbow End Racing Stable House Ronald K and Alexander A

Trainers– 1, Keogh Michael; 2, Cheadle James W; 3, Frankel Robert; 4, Schnitzler Rita A; 5, DePaulo Michael P; 6, McLaughlin Kiaran P; 7, Ross John A; 8, Baker Reade; 9, Orseno Joseph; 10, Baker Reade; 11, Baker Reade; 12, Attard Tino; 13, Seymour Gerald E; 14, Walls Joe F; 15, Day Catherine M; 16, Armata Ross; 17, Glennon Darren C

The racing career of *Scatter the Gold* was brief but luminous, and strikingly special for a leading Canadian racing family, the Samuels. Bred in the purple, *Scatter the Gold* raced only seven times in his life but he was at his best at the right time, winning the 141st Queen's Plate, with its flashy record purse of $1 million, and throwing light into a year with some dark corners. The darkest was that Ernie Samuel, winner of thirty-nine Sovereign Awards, breeder of international champions, died a few months before the Plate on 25 March at age sixty-nine after a long illness. His voice, always the loudest when his horses came charging down the stretch, was silenced. But his family could take cheer that Samuel left with a stable full of horses that bore his legacy of excellence. And that his prize, *Dance Smartly*, had foaled her first Queen's Plate winner: *Scatter the Gold*.

The Samuels were already on top of the world with Plate winterbook favourite, *Dixieland Diamond*, but the colt suffered a fracture of a cannon bone in February. *Strike Smartly*, a half brother to *Dance Smartly*, looked to be the next to take up the torch but finished a lacklustre fifth in

TAMMY SAMUEL-BALAZ AND HER MOTHER, LIZA, HOIST QUEEN'S PLATE TROPHY.

the Plate Trial, beaten almost twenty lengths by 22-to-1 long shot *Pete's Sake*. *Pete's Sake* was a son of *Peteski* that was owned by Jerry Frankel, a Texan who produced the 1973 movie *Slapshot*, starring Paul Newman. Frankel specifically bought a Canadian-bred to run in the Queen's Plate, and suddenly, he was in the picture with the colt's runaway six-length victory.

But in the year 2000 nobody was producing Canadian-breds with as much spit and fire as Ernie Samuel. The fifth foal of *Dance Smartly*, *Scatter the Gold* was goofy and silly, and not at all precocious. He hadn't won a race before the Plate, so jockey Todd Kabel raised a few eyebrows three days before the Plate when he switched from *Strike Smartly* to the maiden *Scatter the Gold*, who hadn't raced as a two-year-old. No maiden had won the Queen's Plate since *Golden Choice* in 1986. Also, no maiden had won the Plate without a start at two since the race was moved to Woodbine in 1956. Still, Kabel got excited after a six-furlong work when *Scatter the Gold* handily edged out *Strike Smartly*, which had suffered an infected hock before the Plate and hadn't been quite the same as he was earlier in the year.

Pete's Sake went off as a narrow favourite over the two-horse Sam-Son entry, both sons of the world-class stallion *Mr. Prospector*. With no standouts, a large field of sixteen went to the post. Five of them were maidens. *Pete's Sake* ended up last and was vanned off the track after Patrick Husbands pulled him up, saying that he was not injured, but just had nothing left after the first turn. It's too bad Ernie Samuel couldn't have seen what happened. *Scatter the*

Gold was only tenth up the backstretch, but rushed up on the outside to be third at the head of the stretch. He mowed down pacesetters *Wake at Noon* and *For Our Sake* to win easily by four and a half lengths.

Everywhere tears of joy rained down cheeks, mixed with memories of how proud Samuel would have been. "The sad thing is that he is not here to share it," said Tammy Samuel-Balaz, Samuel's daughter and the manager of the Sam-Son operation. "But we feel that he was here with us. And he will continue to be a part [of the Sam-Son outfit], certainly in spirit." Samuel's widow, Liza, said: "I know that Ernie is right here with me today, and he couldn't be more excited or happy and thrilled as I am."

It was an emotional day for Kabel, whose last-minute choice was vindicated. After he crossed the wire, he pumped and pumped and pumped his fists and looked like the smartest guy alive. "I was thinking a lot of [Samuel] today," Kabel said in winning his second Plate. "I'm still thinking about him. I get pretty emotional about it. I said to [trainer] Mark [Frostad] before I got up on the horse, 'This one's for Mr. Samuel.'" It was the third Plate win for the Samuels, and the first for Mark Frostad in the six years he had trained for the stable. He had earlier trained *Victor Cooley* for another farm.

Scatter the Gold, bred like Kentucky Derby winner *Fusaichi Pegasus*, was still a little coltish and green, although big and tough and powerful by the time he got to the Plate. Everybody called him a big playboy. His mind was never on the game. "He's a big clown," Frostad said. "He's always doing things that annoy you. As he gets older and gets more experience, he'll stop doing that stuff." He didn't know that

TODD KABEL'S FIST PUMP EMPHASIZES HIS VICTORY ON *SCATTER THE GOLD*.

SCATTER THE GOLD | 3-year-old dark bay or brown colt

Scatter the Gold (1997)	Mr. Prospector	Raise a Native	Native Dancer
			Raise You
		Gold Digger	Nashua
			Sequence
	Dance Smartly	Danzig	Northern Dancer
			Pas de Nom
		Classy 'n Smart	Smarten
			No Class

Owner: Sam-Son Farms; *Trainer:* Mark Frostad
Jockey: Todd Kabel; *Breeder:* Sam-Son Farm (Ont-C)

Scatter the Gold had only two more starts left in his career. Frostad knew that the Prince of Wales was not the ideal race for the colt that loved distance, and the bigger, sweeping turns of Woodbine. Still, he was made the heavy 6-to-5 favourite in the morning line to defeat six others. Frostad said his works coming up to the Prince of Wales were a lot better than they were going into the Plate. But his greenness showed in the POW. He won it by a neck, but not easily. Dropping back to last place after a poor start he was ten lengths out of it, unwilling to pick up the bridle, until he made a bold move on the second turn. He weaved his way among horses, bullied his way between rivals, and tried to pull up short of the finish line. Kabel earned every cent of his pay cheque that day. "He stumbled leaving the gate real bad," Kabel said. "I was a bit concerned because he struggled getting a hold of the track. He did need a lot of encouraging today, but from the quarter pole home, he dug in game and hard."

Frostad said he was more confident going into the Breeders' Stakes. Samuel-Balaz was nervous. "It feels like a little more pressure, only because he's [*Dance Smartly*'s] son and you would absolutely love it if that all could come together," she said, recalling *Dance Smartly*'s Triple Crown win. It wasn't to be. *Scatter the Gold* just didn't show his turn of foot when Kabel asked him to run. He finished third behind *Lodge Hill* and *Master Stuart*. It was his final race. Afterward, he underwent surgery to remove a bone chip, and although Sam-Son intended to race him at four, they got an offer they couldn't refuse from the Shizunai Stallion Station in Japan. He was exported to Japan before the Sovereign Awards, where he lost three-year-old colt honours to *Kiss A Native*, winner of four stakes at Woodbine and the Pegasus at The Meadowlands. *Scatter the Gold* retired with two wins in seven starts for $845,854 in earnings. "I don't think there will ever be another *Dance Smartly*, because she was magic," said Samuel-Balaz. "But *Scatter the Gold* was exciting. He allows you to dream."

TENTH RACE
Woodbine
JUNE 25, 2000

$1\frac{1}{4}$ MILES. QUEEN'S PLATE S. Purse $1,000,000 For Three-Year-Olds, Foaled in Canada. Weight: 126 lbs

Value of Race: $1,000,000 Winner $600,000; second $200,000; third $110,000; fourth $60,000; fifth $30,000. Mutuel Pool $705,124.00 Exactor Pool $235,204.00 Triactor Pool $399,252.00 Superfecta Pool $84,132.00

Last Raced	Horse	M/Eqt.	A.	Wt	PP	¼	½	¾	1	Str	Fin	Jockey	Odds $1
3Jun00 ^{10}WO^{2}	Scatter the Gold	L b	3	126	13	$9\frac{1}{2}$	$10^{2\frac{1}{2}}$	7^{1}	$3^{1\frac{1}{2}}$	1^{2}	$1^{4\frac{1}{4}}$	Kabel T K	a- 3.65
4Jun00 ^{6}WO^{2}	I and I		3	126	2	$11\frac{1}{2}$	$11^{2\frac{1}{2}}$	10^{5}	4^{hd}	3^{1}	2^{4}	McAleney J S	10.35
4Jun00 ^{6}WO^{4}	For Our Sake	L b	3	126	16	$4\frac{1}{2}$	$2\frac{1}{2}$	$2^{1\frac{1}{2}}$	$2^{2\frac{1}{2}}$	2^{1}	$3^{4\frac{1}{4}}$	Landry R C	13.25
2Jun00 ^{5}WO^{1}	Allende	L bf	3	126	8	10^{3}	9^{1}	8^{hd}	$9^{1\frac{1}{2}}$	$5^{1\frac{1}{2}}$	$4^{2\frac{3}{4}}$	Somsanith N	37.15
21May00 ^{8}WO^{3}	Wake At Noon	L b	3	126	3	1^{1}	1^{1}	1^{1}	1^{hd}	4^{7}	$5^{1\frac{1}{4}}$	Clark D	5.95
9Jun00 ^{4}Bel^{2}	Lodge Hill	L	3	126	15	16	16	16	$14\frac{1}{2}$	$8\frac{1}{2}$	$6^{1\frac{1}{4}}$	Velazquez J R	8.60
4Jun00 ^{6}WO^{3}	Bold n' Fancy	L b	3	126	10	6^{1}	6^{1}	6^{1}	$6^{1\frac{1}{2}}$	6^{4}	7^{1}	Walls M K	31.85
4Jun00 ^{6}WO^{7}	Touch of Power	L bf	3	126	6	7^{2}	5^{hd}	$4\frac{1}{2}$	$7\frac{1}{2}$	7^{hd}	8^{nk}	Dos Ramos R A	66.45
1Jun00 ^{8}WO^{5}	Ace of Suedes	L	3	126	14	15^{2}	15^{3}	$13\frac{1}{2}$	$12\frac{1}{2}$	$10\frac{1}{2}$	$9\frac{1}{2}$	Olguin G L	f- 35.15
4Jun00 ^{6}WO^{5}	Strike Smartly	L f	3	126	9	14^{5}	13^{hd}	15^{2}	15^{12}	$12\frac{1}{2}$	$10^{1\frac{3}{4}}$	Boulanger G	a- 3.65
4Jun00 ^{10}WO^{2}	Attawapiskat	L bf	3	126	12	$12\frac{1}{2}$	14^{2}	14^{hd}	13^{1}	$13\frac{1}{2}$	$11\frac{3}{4}$	McKnight J	f- 35.15
10Jun00 ^{3}WO^{2}	Twistingbythepool	L b	3	126	7	8^{1}	8^{1}	9^{1}	10^{3}	11^{hd}	$12^{1\frac{1}{4}}$	Montpellier C	32.15
21May00 ^{6}WO^{2}	Fartherthanuthink	L b	3	126	1	13^{hd}	12^{2}	12^{hd}	11^{hd}	14^{6}	$13\frac{1}{2}$	Ramsammy E	13.50
10Jun00 ^{3}WO^{1}	Runaway Love	L bf	3	126	4	3^{hd}	4^{2}	$5\frac{1}{2}$	8^{hd}	9^{hd}	$14^{13\frac{1}{4}}$	Day P	6.20
4Jun00 ^{6}WO^{8}	Tricky Hearts	L b	3	126	5	2^{hd}	$3^{1\frac{1}{2}}$	3^{3}	5^{1}	15	15	Bahen S R	64.60
4Jun00 ^{6}WO^{1}	Pete's Sake	L	3	126	11	$5\frac{1}{2}$	7^{2}	11^{hd}	16	—	—	Husbands P	3.25

a-Coupled: Scatter the Gold and Strike Smartly.
f-Mutuel field: Ace of Suedes and Attawapiskat.

OFF AT 5:45 Start Good For All But LODGE HILL. Won driving. Track fast.
TIME :23^{1}, :46^{2}, 1:11^{2}, 1:38, 2:05^{2} (:23.21, :46.52, 1:11.48, 1:38.08, 2:05.53)

$2 Mutuel Prices:				
	1A- SCATTER THE GOLD(a-entry)	**9.30**	**4.70**	**3.10**
	3 - I AND I		**9.10**	**6.70**
	13 - FOR OUR SAKE			**7.40**

$2 EXACTOR 1-3 PAID $91.30 $2 TRIACTOR 1-3-13 PAID $838.20
$1 SUPERFECTA 1-3-13-9 PAID $5,176.50

Dk. b or br. c, (Feb), by Mr. Prospector - Dance Smartly , by Danzig . Trainer Frostad Mark. Bred by Sam-Son Farm (Ont-C).

SCATTER THE GOLD was unhurried early while racing off the rail, continued outside of rivals along the backstretch, made a quick move four wide on the second turn, assumed command in upper stretch and drew clear under steady urging. I AND I saved ground through the first turn, angled out on the backstretch, rallied four wide on the second turn then closed willingly in the drive, but was no match for the winner. FOR OUR SAKE was in hand pressing the early pace, drew even with the pacesetter on the second turn, battled heads apart in upper stretch then weakened in the late stages.

Owners- 1, Sam-Son Farms; 2, Clayton W L; 3, Canino Michael Werner William and Attfield Roger; 4, Augustin Stable; 5, Schickedanz Bruno; 6, Melnyk Eugene and Bristow Farm; 7, Bradscot Farms; 8, A A C Stables; 9, Kings Lane Farm; 10, Sam-Son Farms; 11, Eaton Hall Farm; 12, Di Giulio Frank and DiGiulio Jr Frank; 13, Mack Earle I; 14, Brandon Brako Stable and Dinkin M; 15, Molinaro Stable; 16, Frankel Gerald

Trainers- 1, Frostad Mark; 2, Clayton W L; 3, Attfield Roger L; 4, Benson MacDonald; 5, Katryan Abraham R; 6, Pletcher Todd A; 7, Barnett Robert E; 8, Bennett Gerald S; 9, Guitard David J; 10, Frostad Mark; 11, Doyle Michael J; 12, Tiller Robert P; 13, Baker Reade; 14, Katryan Abraham R; 15, Armata Vito; 16, Pletcher Todd A

Scratched- Colebrook Lake (21May00 ^{7}WO ^{2})

C ould lightning strike twice? If so, *Dancethruthedawn* was proof positive, a dazzling little filly with feet like teacups and more purple blood than any Canadian-bred could hope for. Winning the 142nd Queen's Plate seemed pre-ordained. Sam-Son Farm, the royal family of thoroughbred racing in Canada at the time, had sold *Scatter the Gold* to Japanese breeding interests before his full-sister, *Dancethruthedawn*, made them dream again. And this time, they were watching a miniature version of their dam, their great race mare, *Dance Smartly*.

Scatter the Gold and *Dancethruthedawn* became the first full-siblings to win the Queen's Plate, much less in back-to-back years. Shades of déjà-vu: *Dance Smartly* had won the Queen's Plate exactly ten years before. *Dancethruthedawn* wasn't as mature or as robust or as accomplished as her famous mother by the time of the $1 million Queen's Plate, but she had that familiar white star on her forehead, and the recognizable slight cock to her head as she charged down the stretch and the

DANCETHRUTHEDAWN AND GARY BOULANGER HIT THE FINISH LINE AHEAD OF *WIN CITY*.

same effortless, ground-eating stride as the greatest mare that ever looked through a Canadian bridle. Like *Scatter the Gold*, *Dancethruthedawn* was by eminent U.S. sire *Mr. Prospector*, which commanded a US$250,000 stud fee. *Dancethruthedawn* was particularly precious to Sam-Son as *Dance Smartly*'s first daughter, a valuable future broodmare prospect. Best of all, she was a Plate winner out of a Plate winner and a sister to a Plate winner. She also became the first filly to win the Queen's Plate since her mother did in 1991, and the thirty-third overall.

Earlier *Dancethruthedawn* had finished twelfth of thirteen in the Kentucky Oaks, but it didn't tell the tale of her. Impatient, rather like her mother, she acted up in the gate after a long wait, got caught behind a wall of horses in the race and shuffled, bumped and finally sustained a cut on her back leg that required a couple of stitches. She followed in the footsteps of her female family by winning the Canadian Oaks, just like *Dance Smartly* had done in 1991, and her granddam, *Classy 'n Smart* had done in 1984. Still, *Dancethruthedawn* and her unheralded entrymate, *Lucky Scarab*, were listed as 2-to-1 second choices behind Plate Trial winner *Win City*, who was noted for his stirring stretch kicks. The filly was the richest of all ten Plate entrants, with earnings of $543,691, but she was facing males for the first time. *Win City*, a gelding, had won his past three starts, all stakes.

Veteran trainer Bob Tiller was surprised that the Sam-Son entry wasn't made a co-favourite with his *Win City*, particularly since she had a five-pound break in the weights. Although a delicate-looking creature, Tiller wasn't fooled by the filly. "Don't judge the book by the cover," he said. "Open a few pages." He was right. *Win City* finished second in the Plate, as the filly pinned him to the rail early behind the pacesetters. She moved up to third place on the backstretch, then made her move approaching the far turn. "She got me in exceptional position," said her rider, Gary Boulanger. "I just had to push the button. She showed today that she is the real package." The early pace was too slow for *Win City* to catch her on a track that was not kind to stretch-kickers. "She just always had the jump on us," said jockey Constant Montpellier. "He kicked in like he has been doing and he just could not go by the filly." She won by only half a length, the margin shrinking with every step. Tiller was obviously disappointed after the race. "I've been trying to win this race for thirty years and I still can't do it," he said. "It's been twenty-six years since I was second (the last time). Check with me in another twenty-six years."

If Tiller was in mourning, Boulanger was experiencing a rebirth of sorts. The Drayton Valley, Alberta-born jockey who had spent most of his career riding in the United States, had finally come home. A year earlier he had been *Scatter the Gold*'s rider, but since Todd Kabel had first call on Sam-Son mounts, he took over the ride, won the Plate and left Boulanger with the leftover, *Strike Smartly*, which finished tenth. This time, however, Boulanger got a chance to deliver a brilliant, cool-headed ride, judging the pace perfectly. "I was screaming and crying and yelling all at the same time," he said after

THE FILLY IS ACCOMPANIED TO THE WINNER'S CIRCLE BY BOULANGER, TAMMY SAMUEL-BALAZ AND MRS. ELIZABETH SAMUEL.

DANCETHRUTHEDAWN | 3-year-old dark bay or brown filly

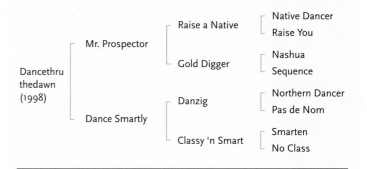

Owner: Sam-Son Farms; *Trainer:* Mark Frostad
Jockey: Gary Boulanger; *Breeder:* Sam-Son Farm (Ont-C)

his journey with the little filly. "My heart was doing ten different things. . . . It's my all-time greatest moment in my riding career." It was even more special because of Boulanger's troubled history. Two years before the Plate, he was physically unstable. His back was a mess. He went in for a four-hour operation and came out after nine-and-a-half hours. He didn't know if he'd ride again. On the way to the winner's circle, Boulanger flung himself onto the filly's neck and the tears fell. He had followed a horrible path to find this kind of happiness. He had fractured a vertebra two years before, but it didn't show up on any X-rays right away. He kept riding. Eventually, he compressed a disc and severed a bunch of nerves. Doctors had to fuse some vertebrae. He was out of action for fifteen months and endured nine-and-a-half months of rehabilitation. "Just to make it back has been a blessing to me," he said. "I thank God for giving me a second chance."

The Prince of Wales was even more dramatic. U.S. trainer James Bond brought in a stunning mystery horse, *Wild Years*—a son of Kinghaven's mare *Lover's Talk*—that had won a maiden race by twenty-two and a half lengths at Belmont Park, widening under wraps. *Wild Years* was actually made the race favourite at 7-to-5. This time, *Dancethruthedawn* hooked up with *Wild Years* early in the hot, humid weather and as she did, Montpellier aboard *Win City* began licking his lips with glee. "The filly was a little closer to the pace, actually fighting with *Wild Years*, and I was right behind those two," he said. "I said to myself: 'You know, I think it's ours today.'" And it was. *Win City*'s late-charging kick gave him the half-length victory down Fort Erie's long stretch. Frostad said she has a tendency to loaf if she finds herself on the lead too early. *Wild Years* finished last with an injury. Neither *Win City* nor *Dancethruthedawn* contested the Breeders' Stakes, with the filly

opting for the $750,000 Alabama Stakes, while *Win City* headed for the Travers at Saratoga. In the Alabama, *Dancethruthedawn* tested heavily favoured *Flute* but the Kentucky Oaks winner went into another gear. She finished fourth, a very tired filly. She was given a rest for the remainder of the year. *Win City* won Horse of the Year honours over *Dancethruthedawn*, who was named three-year-old champion filly.

Dancethruthedawn campaigned in the U.S. as a four-year-old, winning the Doubledogdare Stakes at Keeneland by five-and-a-half lengths and the Grade 1 Go For Wand Stakes at Saratoga by three-and-a-half lengths. She lost a head bob to top U.S. mare *Summer Colony* in the Pimlico Breeders' Cup Distaff Handicap after a furious stretch duel, finished third to *Spain* in the Fleur de Lys Stakes at Churchill Downs, and third in the Grade 1 Personal Ensign Handicap. *Dancethruthedawn* won a total of $1,609,643 during her career, winning seven of sixteen races. Her first foal, *Dance With Doves*, was born in 2004.

NINTH RACE
Woodbine
JUNE 24, 2001

1¼ MILES. QUEEN'S PLATE S. Purse $1,000,000 For Three–Year–Olds, Foaled in Canada. Weight: 126 lbs.

Value of Race: $1,000,000 Winner $600,000; second $200,000; third $110,000; fourth $60,000; fifth $30,000. Mutuel Pool $718,195.00 Exactor Pool $236,541.00 Triactor Pool $340,459.00 Superfecta Pool $70,433.00

Last Raced	Horse	M/Eqt.	A.	Wt	PP	¼	½	¾	1	Str	Fin	Jockey	Odds $1
9Jun01 8WO1	Dancethruthedawn	L b	3	121	10	3hd	31	2hd	1hd	1½	1½	Boulanger G	a- 1.90
2Jun01 7WO1	Win City	L	3	126	7	51	5hd	5hd	31½	31½	23¼	Montpellier C	0.95
2Jun01 7WO3	Brushing Bully	L b	3	126	9	21½	22	11	21	21	3½	Clark D	11.90
5May01 7WO7	Asia	L	3	121	1	6hd	7hd	6hd	4½	45	43¼	Gryder A T	80.95
3Jun01 5WO1	Lucky Scarab	L b	3	126	2	10	10	8hd	7½	51½	55½	Kabel T K	a- 1.90
8Jun01 8WO3	Thatsthebottomline	L bf	3	126	6	4hd	41½	4½	51	61	61½	Sabourin R B	16.75
1Jun01 6WO3	Dawn Watcher	L b	3	126	5	8hd	8hd	10	91	83	7¾	Dos Ramos R A	33.60
2Jun01 7WO2	Millennium Allstar	L f	3	126	3	74	62	71	6hd	7hd	81¾	Landry R C	7.15
2Jun01 7WO5	Highland Legacy	b	3	126	8	93	9hd	9½	10	92	92¾	Husbands P	23.70
3Jun01 10WO6	Sik	L b	3	126	4	1hd	1hd	32½	8½	10	10	David D J	82.30

a–Coupled: Dancethruthedawn and Lucky Scarab.

OFF AT 5:09 Start Good For All But HIGHLAND LEGACY. Won driving. Track fast.
TIME :23², :47¹, 1:12¹, 1:37⁴, 2:03³ (:23.45, :47.32, 1:12.37, 1:37.88, 2:03.78)

$2 Mutuel Prices:

1A– DANCETHRUTHEDAWN (a–entry)	5.80	2.90	2.70
7 – WIN CITY		2.40	2.30
9 – BRUSHING BULLY			4.20

$2 EXACTOR 1–7 PAID $10.90 $2 TRIACTOR 1–7–9 PAID $69.20
$1 SUPERFECTA 1–7–9–2 PAID $528.15

Dk. b or br. f, (Mar), by Mr. Prospector – Dance Smartly , by Danzig . Trainer Frostad Mark. Bred by Sam-Son Farm (Ont–C).

DANCETHRUTHEDAWN stalked the early pace three wide, roused on the turn and assumed command at the quarter pole, opened a length lead in mid stretch and held off a late closing WIN CITY under steady pressure. The latter was allowed to settle outside of rivals, roused five wide on the turn and loomed boldly on the turn, but lost ground while drifting wide in the drive, straightened out in the final furlong and surged at the end under constant right handed urging. BRUSHING BULLY showed good early speed and dueled for the early lead outside of SIK, put that one away on the turn and dueled again briefly with the winner entering the stretch, gave way in the drive, but held gamely for show.

The 143rd Queen's Plate might just go down in history as the wackiest. But lucky for some in a crowd of about twenty thousand sun-baked folk, who were left in shock after lightly raced *T J's Lucky Moon* registered the second biggest upset in the Plate's history, winning by three-quarters of a length. The three-year-old gelding went off at odds of 82-to-1 and paid $166 for a two-dollar win ticket, second only to the $193.35 that *Maternal Pride* paid in winning the race in 1924. For many minutes after the race, people in the crowd who had stood screaming during the stretch drive remained standing, apparently in shock.

Nothing made sense. The race unfolded the way nobody thought it would, except for trainer Vito Armata, who announced at the Queen's Plate breakfast a few days earlier that at the half-mile mark he would like to see *T J's Lucky Moon* in second place. And he was. Nobody bet the race the way everybody thought they would, either. *Shaws Creek* was the morning line favourite, but in the final flash, lightly raced *Ford Every Stream* from the powerful Sam-Son Stable, became the crowd's main hope, going off at 2-to-1. He finished fourth. *Shaws Creek* ended up sixth as the third choice, while *Classic Mike*, the second choice, made a big, bold move around the final turn and then flattened out, finishing eighth in the thirteen-horse field.

Marine Stakes winner *Anglian Prince* finished second with a late charge. "It was kind of disappointing," jockey Jim McAleney said. "The race didn't unfold ideally the way we wanted it to. The pace wasn't as quick as I'd hoped. I had to take him back further than I wanted to just to save a little ground going into the first turn." Jake Barton, riding *Shaws Creek*, said he was disappointed, too. "I got stuck with the decision to either go nine-wide or take a hold. I opted to take a hold and get him in behind. When I did, he didn't really grab onto the bridle like I thought he would." *Forever Grand*, at almost 6-to-1, finished third.

This was a race of lucky moons and superstitions and impossibilities. *Bravely* was scratched the morning before the race after spiking a temperature, leaving only thirteen horses in the field. If that wasn't a warning that presaged a rocky path in the Queen's Plate, what was? Fire alarms went off throughout the grandstand before and after the racing program. They were false. *T J's Lucky Moon* won the one-and-one-quarter-mile race in a sluggish 2:06 4/5, the slowest in sixteen years and the slowest on a track listed as fast since the race was moved to Woodbine in 1956. En route to the winner's circle, he began to stagger from heat exhaustion in thirty-two degree Celsius temperatures. Jockey Steve Bahen jumped off

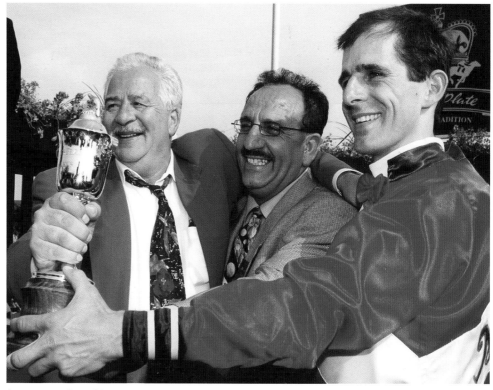

AN ECTASTIC GINO MOLINARO CELEBRATES WITH TRAINER VITO ARMATA AND STEVE BAHEN AFTER *T J'S LUCKY MOON'S* INCREDIBLE UPSET VICTORY AT 82-TO-1 ODDS.

his back and led him to a trackside hose to revive him. In the winner's circle, effusive Italian-born owner Gino Molinaro ignored protocol and greeted Princess Michael of Kent by holding both of her hands, kissing them. He took a timeout to give Bahen a bear hug, then returned to smother royalty with an emotional handshake.

Molinaro, the owner of a frozen food wholesale business, promised before the race that if he won he'd visit the Pope in the Vatican the next day. (A few weeks later Pope Paul came to Toronto and saved Molinaro the trip to Rome.) He also promised to hold the biggest party in history. He'd plunked down fifty dollars across the board on his horse, winning $6,000 on an ornery nag that hadn't won more than $48,000 in his career. The "Lucky Moon" was a son of *Tejabo*, who didn't succeed at stud in Ontario and was sent to British Columbia.

Sicilian-born trainer Vito Armata had entered only one other horse in the Queen's Plate in twenty years. That was *Tricky Hearts*, which finished fifteenth two years before. Armata started to get the hang of it very quickly after that. He entered *T J's Lucky Moon* because he thought the 143rd Queen's Plate was a little weak. "Look at the Belmont [Stakes, won by 70-to-1 shot *Sarava*]," he said. "Anything can happen. That's horse racing." Armata's main Plate hope was *Molly's Wisdom*, but an injury took him out of contention. Molinaro suggested they focus on *T J's Lucky Moon*. Who but he thought it would be a good idea? Armata admitted at times that Molinaro was discouraged with the horse, the winner of only one race in five

STEVE BAHEN AND *T J'S LUCKY MOON* HOLD OFF *ANGLIAN PRINCE* AT THE WIRE.

T J'S LUCKY MOON | 3-year-old dark bay or brown gelding

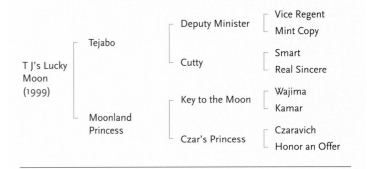

Owner: Molinaro Stable; *Trainer:* Vito Armata
Jockey: Steve Bahen; *Breeder:* Molinaro Stable (Ont-C)

previous starts. The colt had been such a mean sonofabuck the previous season that Armata had him gelded to settle him down, particularly after he kicked a groom in the stomach. This season, he gave the gelding to his best groom. Still, it took *T J's Lucky Moon* a long time to learn anything. Bahen had interesting instructions: not to take hold of the gelding, or big Lucky would run off with him.

In the Plate, *T J's Lucky Moon* didn't get off to the best of starts, stumbling out of the gate after barging against the side of his stall. This didn't seem to worry Bahen, who won his first Plate in seven tries. He didn't care what kind of a long shot the horse was. "Every time you go out, you got a shot to win in your mind," he said. "You ride a 100-to-1 like he's 2-to-1." The long shot was fanned out four-wide heading into the first turn, but Bahen eased him behind horses to the rail. When pace setter *Streakin Rob* lugged out down the backstretch, Bahen pushed his horse through on the rail and took the lead. "The rail is the shortest way around," Bahen said. "I threw the lines at him and let him be happy. Down the lane, I didn't hear anybody coming." Past the wire, Bahen waved his whip in the air. "That's what you ride for," he said. "It's what you want. You want to win the Queen's Plate. Now I've done it. I've won an Oaks too, and there's two other [jewels] and I want to get them."

T J's Lucky Moon was made the morning-line favourite to win the Prince of Wales in a relatively large twelve-horse field (the maximum allowed at Fort Erie) but went off at odds of 8-to-1. Local Fort Erie horse *Le Cinquieme Essai* won the race under local jockey Brian Bochinski. *T J's Lucky Moon* led after a half mile but faded badly in the stretch, finishing tenth. The Breeders' Stakes was overshadowed by a horrific barn fire at Woodbine that killed thirty-two horses a week

before the race. *T J's Lucky Moon* missed the race because he was retired for the rest of the year following an unsatisfactory turf workout a few days before the Breeders' and *Le Cinquieme Essai* was scratched because of a high fever. *Portcullis* won the race, and its owners Sam-Son Farm, decreed that ten per cent of his earnings would go to the Barn Seven fund to help those out that were devastated by the fire.

T J's Lucky Moon was retired in 2004 due to a small tear in his suspensory ligament. He never won another race after his mind-boggling Queen's Plate triumph and finished his career with two wins in ten starts and earnings of $671,505, nearly all of it from his Plate win. In 2003 he raced three times, finishing second once. He took up residence on Molinaro's farm in Acton, Ontario, to live out his days.

NINTH RACE
Woodbine
JUNE 23, 2002

1¼ MILES. QUEEN'S PLATE S. Purse $1,000,000 FOR THREE–YEAR–OLDS, FOALED IN CANADA, WHICH ARE ELIGIBLE AT THE TIME OF THIS NOMINATION FOR THE RENEWAL OF THE 2002 QUEEN'S PLATE. Weight: Colts and Geldings 126 lbs. Fillies 121 lbs. By subscription of $150 each to accompany the nomination by February 1st, 2001 (360 remained eligible); second subscription of $500 by February 1st, 2002 (177 remained eligible, plus 5 supplements); third subscription of $1,000 by May 15th, 2002 (42 remained eligible, plus 4 supplements); and an additional $10,000 when making final entry no later than 8:30 a.m. on Thursday, June 20, 2002.

Value of Race: $1,000,000 Winner $600,000; second $200,000; third $110,000; fourth $60,000; fifth $30,000. Mutuel Pool $926,377.00 Exactor Pool $455,375.00 Triactor Pool $483,506.00 Superfecta Pool $120,971.00

Last Raced	Horse	M/Eqt.	A.	Wt	PP	¼	½	¾	1	Str	Fin	Jockey	Odds $1
25May02 10WO1	T J's Lucky Moon	L	3	126	9	41	2hd	1½	1hd	11	1¾	Bahen S R	82.00
1Jun02 8WO3	Anglian Prince	L bf	3	126	12	10½	10hd	93	71	3hd	21	McAleney J S	11.40
8Jun02 9WO2	Forever Grand	L	3	126	4	21	31	31	21	23	31½	Husbands P	5.60
18May02 10WO3	Ford Every Stream	L b	3	126	10	6hd	7½	7½	4hd	62½	4½	Kabel T K	2.00
29May02 7Del3	Fuzzy Star	L	3	126	1	7hd	4hd	51½	6½	4hd	5¾	Petro N J	60.40
1Jun02 8WO1	Shaws Creek	L	3	126	13	13	13	13	9½	85	6no	Barton J	4.10
8Jun02 9WO3	Barbeau Ruckus	L bf	3	126	6	11½	121½	12hd	10hd	7hd	7nk	Luciani D	45.35
1Jun02 8WO2	Classic Mike	L	3	126	5	8½	61	6½	32½	5½	85½	Jones J	3.35
1Jun02 8WO5	Adjalah	L b	3	126	7	9½	81	8hd	113	101½	9nk	Dos Ramos R A	12.45
1Jun02 3WO2	Twice Bid	L b	3	126	3	12½	11½	11hd	122½	113	102½	Walls M K	26.10
8Jun02 9WO4	Cree Power	L f	3	126	8	31	5½	4hd	5hd	9hd	116	Ramsammy E	50.25
1Jun02 8WO9	Mountain Beacon	L	3	126	11	5hd	9hd	10hd	13	13	12¾	Landry R C	84.65
8Jun02 9WO6	Streakin Rob	L	3	126	2	11	11½	21	81½	124	13	Sutherland C	41.00

OFF AT 5:07 Start Good For All But T J'S LUCKY MOON. Won driving. Track fast.
TIME :23², :48, 1:13, 1:38³, 2:06⁴ (:23.41, :48.07, 1:13.00, 1:38.73, 2:06.88)

	9 – T J'S LUCKY MOON	166.00	54.50	19.10

$2 Mutuel Prices:
9 – T J'S LUCKY MOON 166.00 54.50 19.10
13 – ANGLIAN PRINCE 10.70 6.90
4 – FOREVER GRAND 5.60

$2 EXACTOR 9–13 PAID $2,267.50 $2 TRIACTOR 9–13–4 PAID $15,375.50
$1 SUPERFECTA 9–13–4–10 PAID $29,678.35

Dk. b or br. g, (Mar), by Tejabo – Moonland Princess , by Key to the Moon . Trainer Armata Vito. Bred by Molinaro Stable (Ont–C).

T J'S LUCKY MOON stumbled at the start, but recovered quickly and moved to the rail, stalked the early pace inside of STEAKIN ROB, gained a short lead approaching the three eighths pole, but gave way briefly to FOREVER GRAND midway on the turn, battled back gamely and put that one away in the drive then held the off late charging ANGLIAN PRINCE under steady pressure. The latter was unhurried early between horses, roused four wide on the turn and closed willingly in the drive just missing. FOREVER GRAND stalked the pace three wide, drew even on the second turn and gained a short lead, dueled outside of the winner entering the stretch, but weakened in the late going.

Where is *Wando*? Wonderful *Wando*. Simply *Wando*-ful. Magic *Wando*. *Wando*. *Wando*. *Wando*. The flashy red colt engendered all of these headlines with a most emphatic and popular win in the 144th running of the $1 million Queen's Plate. With his stunning nine-length sashay to the finish wire, a star was born. No horse had sparked the public interest in the way that *Wando* did since the glory days of Canadian racing when *Peteski*, *Izvestia*, *Dance Smartly* and *With Approval* sped to stardom. *Wando* sparked Wandomania, at least in a little corner of the planet called Woodbine.

The characters were all in place to help the mythic story along: the gentlemanly seventy-four-year-old Stetson-crowned owner Gustav Schickedanz, who had bred *Wando*'s grandparents at his farm in Schomberg, Ontario; trainer Mike Keogh, blessed with enough superstition to cut the tag off his underwear after *Woodcarver*'s Plate win in 1999, so he'd know which pair he should wear again to garner good luck; and jockey Patrick Husbands, a Barbadian who honed his early riding skills by tearing around his parents' farm astride the family goats, pigs, sheep, and anything else with four legs.

GROOM AMANDA IRWIN, PATRICK HUSBANDS, *WANDO* AND GUSTAV SCHICKEDANZ.

Wando, the handsome homebred, was a gift in a racing season of many gifts. The nostalgic movie *Seabiscuit* and the down-home allure of *Funny Cide*'s pursuit of the American Triple Crown seemed to shove racing's aura into an upswing. *Wando* helped it along. Named for a river in South Carolina, he attracted attention long before he set foot on the track. Noted U.S. equine artist Richard Stone Reeves saw *Wando* when he was still a foal, and he remarked at how pleasing he was to the eye. Keogh fell under *Wando*'s spell too. At first glance, he thought immediately, "This is the one." He had that effect on people. After he won his first start, a seven-figure offer rolled in. *Wando* went on to win the Vandal Stakes by more than seven lengths, finish second in the Summer Stakes by only a head, and then—most impressively—won the $265,250 Grey Breeders' Cup Stakes, thundering past a talented colt, *Gigawatt*, as if he was standing still. He did this while bleeding profusely from a cut on his right hind ankle. "As soon as he switched leads, he was on top of *Giagwatt* in about three jumps," Keogh said. "He has a really serious turn of foot." The only real smirch to his record was finishing twelfth of thirteen in the Breeders' Cup Juvenile at Chicago. He'd drawn post thirteen in a fourteen-horse field, and was hung out wide with a short run to the first turn.

Schickedanz, who'd had a breeding operation for twenty-five years, finally went big-time several years before *Wando* when he bought an option to breed his best mare (*Sweet Briar Too*) to *Danzig*. The result was *Langfuhr*, and *Langfuhr* begat not only *Wando*, but his stablemate *Mobil*. They were as unlike as night and day: *Mobil* the moody Rottweiler of the stable, *Wando* the pretty gent. *Mobil* and *Wando* made for some great Queen's Plate dramatics. They were never pitted against each other earlier in the season, but Keogh

figured *Mobil* was more apt to get the mile-and-one-quarter distance of the Plate. *Mobil* worked more impressively and won the Queenston Stakes and the Plate Trial. *Wando* stopped hearts with his effort in the Marine Stakes, setting quick fractions, being pressured by two other horses and then exploding for a four-and-a-half-length win. Woodbine's leading rider, Todd Kabel, who rode both, decided to ride *Mobil* in the Plate, even though the colt kicked him in the chest in his final workout. Husbands got to ride *Wando*. He would say later that he'd had his eye on *Wando* from the beginning and was staking the colt out.

Although *Mobil* was the 2-to-1 morning-line favourite, *Wando* became the actual race favourite in the final flash of the odds at 7-to-5. *Wando* jumped to the front at the break, opened up a two-length lead and was never threatened, while *Mobil* finished second. *Wando*'s clocking of 2:02 2/5 was three-fifths seconds slower than *Izvestia*'s Plate record. He ran his final quarter in twenty seconds into a headwind and racked up a Beyer speed figure of 111, the third best in North America so far that season, equal to Wood Memorial winner *Empire Maker*, and a few ticks behind *Funny Cide* (114) winning the Preakness by nine-and-three-quarters lengths. He faced only six rivals in the Prince of Wales as *Mobil* skipped it in search of his own stripes. *Wando* won the Fort Erie classic on the muddy track, not puffing hard enough to blow out a candle. With his regal look he went off at odds of 1-to-4 and won with his ears pricked before seven thousand ecstatic fans.

With a $500,000 Triple Crown bonus on the line and patriotic blood in his veins, Schickedanz opted to run *Wando* in the Breeders' Stakes rather than the $1 million Travers. But *Wando* had become a

AN ECSTATIC PATRICK HUSBANDS CELEBRATES HIS FIRST PLATE VICTORY.

WANDO | 3-year-old chestnut colt

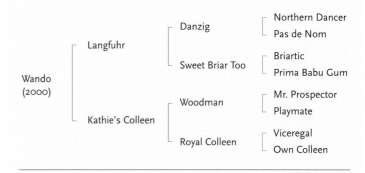

Owner: Gustav Schickedanz; *Trainer:* Michael Keogh
Jockey: Patrick Husbands; *Breeder:* Gustav Schickedanz (Ont-C)

target. Sam-Son Farm entered a tag-team of three horses against the odds-on favourite. One of them, *Parasail*, a speed horse, was obviously meant to soften up *Wando* on the lead. "He kind of got ganged up on pretty good," Keogh said after *Wando* won the Breeders' and became the seventh Triple Crown winner in history. Husbands said it was the toughest race he'd ever ridden in his life. "I had to play so much cat and mouse," he said. *Parasail* took *Wando* six-wide on the first turn. With six furlongs to go in the one-and-a-half mile race, Rob Landry on *Parasail* and Kabel on *Shoal Water* had *Wando* pinned on the rail. When *Wando* tried to speed up, so did his opponents. "We had *Wando* the whole way," Kabel said of himself and Landry. "We had him trapped down in there and he doesn't like to be down in there. *Wando* appeared to be dropping back before the final turn and out of gas and heading for defeat, but it was just Husbands at work, getting out of a jam. The thirty-year-old jockey backed *Wando* off, then sped up again, then "jumped on the brakes" so he could foil the marauders and get around them. It worked. *Wando* went into overdrive when clear and won by one and a half lengths. Kabel was the first to congratulate Husbands afterwards.

With the mantle of greatness settling on him, *Wando* a month later went off as an emotional 3-to-1 favourite in the $1 million Atto Mile, even though he was biting off a huge task, encountering older, international horses on the turf for the first time. He led by a head with a quarter mile remaining, but faltered and settled for fourth, beaten by two and a half lengths. He lost any chance of competing in the Breeders' Cup after fading to third in the Indiana Derby at Hoosier Park in October. Keogh said he suffered some minor cuts on a hind leg in the race. Still he'd done enough. The splendid colt was named Canada's Horse of the Year.

At age four *Wando*'s career took a disappointing turn when he developed a lung infection in mid-season. Keogh said veterinarians at the University of Guelph discovered mould spores in his lungs. He eventually won an allowance at Woodbine and the Mt. Sassafras Stakes at Woodbine. At age five he ran four times and was retired by May. During the US$100,000 Westchester Handicap at Belmont Park *Wando* was bumped on the final turn as two horses bore in on him. He instantly faded to seventh place and Keogh discovered a slight tear in the suspensory ligament of his left hind leg. "The injury wasn't a big deal," Keogh said. "But for a horse like him, it was going to take time to heal and he was going to stand at stud the next year anyway." He retired with earnings of $2,566,060, winning eleven races in twenty-three starts and stood at stud at Lane's End Farm in Versailles, Kentucky. He is part of an impressive roster of stallions that includes his sire, *Langfuhr*.

NINTH RACE
Woodbine
JUNE 22, 2003

1¼ MILES. QUEEN'S PLATE S. Purse $1,000,000 For THREE–YEAR–OLDS, FOALED IN CANADA. Colts and Geldings 126 lbs. Fillies, 121 lbs. Horses not originally nominated may be made eligible by payment of a late nomination fee of $7,500 by February 1st, 2003 or of $15,000 by May 15th, 2003. All monies received from the original nomination and the February 1st, 2003, payments will be divided equally between the gross purses of the Queen's Plate, Prince of Wales and Breeders' Stakes. $300,000 of this purse has been provided through the Thoroughbred Improvement Program and the Canadian Thoroughbred Horse Society. Plus up to $8,730 Breeder Awards.

Value of Race: $1,000,000 Winner $600,000; second $200,000; third $110,000; fourth $60,000; fifth $30,000. Mutuel Pool $978,486.00 Exactor Pool $436,243.00 Triactor Pool $492,285.00 Superfecta Pool $129,916.00

Last Raced	Horse	M/Eqt. A. Wt	PP	¼	½	¾	1	Str	Fin	Jockey	Odds $1
17May03 8WO1	Wando	L	3 126 4	1hd	12½	11	11½	15	19	Husbands P	1.40
31May03 8WO1	Mobil	L	3 126 6	4½	3½	3½	3hd	21	21½	Kabel T K	2.20
31May03 8WO2	Rock Again	L	3 126 9	6hd	6½	72	42½	42½	32½	Coa E M	4.55
30May03 7WO1	Shoal Water	L	3 126 10	21	21	21	21½	3½	42½	Landry R C	17.15
8Jun03 4WO2	Dance Engagement	L	3 126 12	31	41	4½	5hd	5½	5hd	McAleney J S	30.80
31May03 8WO6	Solihull	L	3 126 5	12	12	12	92½	75	63	Luciani D	51.80
31May03 8WO3	Peef	L	3 126 2	8½	7hd	5½	64	61½	72	Bahen S R	62.75
17May03 8WO3	Arco's Gold	L	3 126 8	9½	102	91½	8½	8hd	8¾	Montpellier C	11.20
6Jun03 8WO1	El Gran Maestro	L	3 126 1	117	115	101½	1110	93½	95¾	Jones J	59.70
8Jun03 7WO1	Button Wood	L f	3 126 7	101	9½	8hd	101½	10hd	10½	Sutherland C	29.20
5Jun03 3Bel1	Sircharlesschnabel	L	3 126 3	5½	5½	6hd	71½	1115	1125	Dos Ramos R A	37.15
8Jun03 4WO4	Illusive Force	L	3 126 11	71	8hd	113	12	12	12	Wilson D H	49.20

OFF AT 5:07 Start Good. Won driving. Track fast.
TIME :23, :46³, 1:11⁴, 1:37², 2:02² (:23.04, :46.67, 1:11.93, 1:37.46, 2:02.48)

$2 Mutuel Prices:

4 – WANDO	4.80	3.30	2.80
6 – MOBIL		3.00	2.40
9 – ROCK AGAIN			3.10

$2 EXACTOR 4–6 PAID $14.10 $2 TRIACTOR 4–6–9 PAID $47.30
$1 SUPERFECTA 4–6–9–10 PAID $101.85

Ch. c, (Feb), by Langfuhr – Kathie's Colleen , by Woodman . Trainer Keogh Michael. Bred by Gustav Schickedanz (Ont-C).

WANDO vied for the early lead from off the rail inside of SHOAL WATER, cleared heading into the first turn, was roused passing the quarter pole and started to increase his advantage on the field, was under right handed urging in upper and mid stretch while further increasing his margin, continued to draw off under a strong hand ride for the final sixteenth of a mile as much the best. MOBIL bobbled at the start, stalked the pace three wide the first time through the stretch, moved to a position off the rail on the first turn, advanced on the second turn, gained the place position in upper stretch, and was second best.

JOCKEY ROBERT LANDRY, MARK KREMBIL JOIN CHIEFSWOOD STABLE OWNER ROBERT KREMBIL ADMIRING THE PLATE TROPHY.

The stars were lined up, and Dame Fortune was in full stride, at least for a horse called *Niigon*, on that fateful day of 27 June 2004, when a field of thirteen lined up at the starting gate for the 145th running of the Queen's Plate. *Niigon*'s owners and breeders, Chiefswood Stable, had never won a stakes race and never started a horse in the Plate. The Queen's Plate was only the seventh stakes race the stable contested. Jockey Rob Landry had never won the Plate in thirteen previous tries. *Niigon* left from post thirteen. And although *Niigon* held off race favourite *A Bit O' Gold* by three-quarters of a length to win his first stakes race during the hubbub on Plate day, he never defeated his archrival again. And he never won another stakes race.

If it weren't for *Niigon*, *A Bit O' Gold* would have become another Canadian Triple Crown winner, because he took the Prince of Wales from *Niigon*, and won the Breeders' Stakes on the grass, too. *A Bit O' Gold* became a star, winning year-end honours as Canada's top three-year-old colt, and the following year, Canada's Horse of the Year. He was *Goldie*, owned by the Two Bit Stable, a syndicate that included trainer Catherine Day Phillips and her husband Todd, along with seven others—school teachers, business and financial consultants, a gynecologist and a couple of show jumping folk, who each scraped together $15,000 to buy a share of the $60,000 yearling and another yearling.

Niigon came from a different place, where they think big. While *A Bit O' Gold* came from a mating to a $5,000 stallion, *Niigon* was bred in the purple, a son of 1990 Kentucky Derby winner *Unbridled*—with a stud fee of US$200,000—and *Savethelastdance*, a daughter of *Nureyev*. The name *Niigon* (pronounced knee-gone) is an Ojibway word for "gateway to the future." *Niigon* certainly was that for the Chiefswood Stable. *Niigon* was from only the second crop of homebreds unleashed by Bob Krembil and his son Mark from their state-of-the-art farm near Loretto, Ontario. Krembil had turned his energy toward breeding an international classic winner after the former co-founder and chairman of Trimark Financial Corporation sold out for a reported $2.7 billion in 2000. He started Chiefswood about eight years before *Niigon*'s surprise victory in the Plate, and had invested a tremendous amount in the business, purchasing *Rose of Tara*, a mare in foal to *Storm Cat*, for US$1,950,000.

"What we're trying to do at Chiefswood is have horses race in the classic races in North America," Krembil said. "We really are breeding to race." It was Krembil's idea to breed the stakes-placed *Savethelastdance* to *Unbridled*, but was unable to get a live-foal season. After much persuasion, he bought a no-guarantee season privately. Mark's wife, Stacey, helped to foal *Niigon* at their farm. In early 2002, Krembil hired French-born Eric Coatrieux as the farm's private trainer of twenty-two racehorses. Coatrieux had been to the Kentucky Derby four times, once as an assistant trainer for Roger Attfield with *Talkin Man* in 1995, and three other times as assistant for the powerful Godolphin Stable in Dubai. *Niigon*'s win gave Coatrieux his first stakes victory in his first attempt at the Plate.

Although Krembil always thought *Niigon* was good enough to win the Queen's Plate for him, *Niigon* didn't always oblige. He showed enough promise at age two, when he finished third in the Grey Breeders' Cup Stakes at Woodbine, that Chiefswood considered starting him in the Kentucky Derby, but after three baffling, dismal races at Gulfstream and Keeneland early in the season, they shipped him home. He had trained like a trooper but never ran to his works. As soon as he cleared customs at the Canadian border, *Niigon* was a different horse, more focused. He broke his maiden on 8 May, winning by six and a half lengths in the slop at Woodbine, then finished second to *A Bit O' Gold* in the Plate Trial after some traffic trouble.

But even when *Niigon* was finishing seventh, beaten by twenty-three lengths in his Keeneland start before returning home in April, Landry still had faith in the handsome colt. He knew that his day would come that he would win the Queen's Plate. And his best chance was on *Niigon*. Landry had faced a career of setbacks. One year, he suffered a broken collarbone. In 2001, just before the Plate, a horse reared up and dumped Landry, giving him a nasty elbow injury. He rode the Plate that year, finishing eighth, and didn't ride for a month after that. The day before his ride on *Niigon*, Landry had a juvenile flip over and almost land on him. And in the first race on Plate day he was caught up behind a spill when a horse in front of him broke down after the horses had crossed the finish line.

Landry didn't need any luck in the running of the Plate. His crafty ride aboard *Niigon* made the difference. Jono Jones aboard *A Bit O' Gold*, was shuffled back after being squeezed on the first turn while *Niigon* was forced to run very wide, but made an early move to get to the leaders as Landry planned to get the jump on *A Bit O' Gold*. A long-striding colt, a clear run was what he needed. *A Bit O' Gold* dropped back to seventh, and Jones had to put him into a long, sustained drive at the five-eighths pole, moving earlier than he wanted to. *A Bit O' Gold* tried hard, and passed four horses in a blink, but couldn't get past *Niigon*. Landry, who whipped right-handed more than twenty times down the stretch, said they could have gone around again, and the result would have been no different.

"This is the first piece of evidence that we're on the way," said Krembil, adorned in a Stetson. "It's a very, very big thing for what we're trying to do. It's early days and this isn't it. But it's better to do this than not do this." It meant very much more to Landry. Galloping out after the race, jockey Richard Dos Ramos, who had ridden *Niigon* in the Grey Stakes, reached over and congratulated him. It was Dos Ramos' thirteenth try and he'd never won a Queen's Plate either. Toronto-born Stewart Elliott, who had just won the Kentucky Derby with *Smarty Jones*, finished thirteenth and last with Eugene Melnyk's colt, *Long Pond*, after pressing the pace early. It was Elliott's first Queen's Plate ride.

Niigon was made the overwhelming even-money favourite to win the Prince of Wales Stakes, but the Fort Erie bettors weren't convinced, putting their money on *A Bit O' Gold*. They were rewarded when *A Bit O' Gold* came from three lengths back to nip him by a nose on a sloppy track. *Niigon* skipped the Breeders' Stakes, opting instead for the Jim Dandy Stakes at Saratoga, where his fourth-place finish was upgraded to third after he was bumped by *Eddington* down the stretch. Later *Niigon* finished fourth in the Pennsylvania Derby and was retired for the year.

The following summer in their first rematch since the Prince of Wales, *A Bit O' Gold* won the Dominion Day Stakes. They met again in the Chinese Cultural Stakes. *A Bit O' Gold* won and *Niigon* didn't hit the board. He finished second in the Woodbine Slots Cup, but never found glory again.

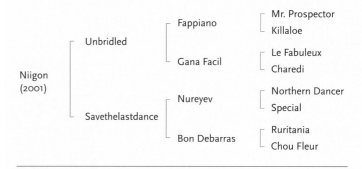

NIIGON | 3-year-old dark bay or brown colt

Niigon (2001)	Unbridled	Fappiano	Mr. Prospector
			Killaloe
		Gana Facil	Le Fabuleux
			Charedi
	Savethelastdance	Nureyev	Northern Dancer
			Special
		Bon Debarras	Ruritania
			Chou Fleur

Owner: Chiefswood Stable; *Trainer:* Eric Coatrieux
Jockey: Robert Landry; *Breeder:* Chiefswood Stable (Ont-C)

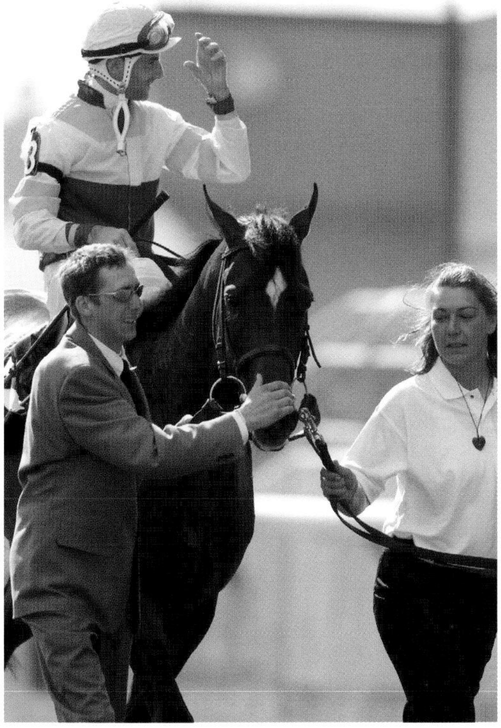

Niigon and jockey Robert Landry are led away by trainer Eric Coatrieux and groom Lorna Carston.

NINTH RACE
Woodbine
JUNE 27, 2004

1¼ MILES. 145TH RUNNING OF THE QUEEN'S PLATE. Purse $1,000,000 FOR THREE-YEAR-OLDS, FOALED IN CANADA. Weight; Colts and Geldings 126 lbs. Fillies, 121 lbs. By subscription of $150 each to accompany the nomination by February 1st, 2003 (417 nominations); second subscription of $500 by February 1st, 2004 (186 remainedeligible plus 4 supplements at $7,500 each); third subscription of $1,000 by May 15th, 2004 (68 remained eligible, plus 4 supplements at $15,000 each); and an additional $10,000 when making final entry no later than June 25, 2004. Horses not originally nominated may be made eligible by payment of a late nomination fee of $7,500 on or before February 1st, 2004 or of $15,000 on or before May 15th, 2004. All monies received from the original nomination (February 1st, 2003) and the February 1st, 2004, payments will be divided equally between the gross purses of the Queen's Plate, Prince of Wales and Breeders' Stakes. $300,000 of this purse has been provided through the Thoroughbred Improvement Program and Canadian Thoroughbred Horse Society.

Value of Race: $1,000,000 Winner $600,000; second $200,000; third $110,000; fourth $60,000; fifth $30,000. Mutuel Pool $658,208.00 Exactor Pool $250,771.00 Triactor Pool $350,036.00 Superfecta Pool $99,355.00

Last Raced	Horse	M/Eqt.	A.	Wt	PP	¼	½	¾	1	Str	Fin	Jockey	Odds $1
6Jun04 8WO2	Niigon	L f	3	126	13	2½	21	1hd	11½	12	1¾	Landry R C	5.90
6Jun04 8WO1	A Bit O'Gold	L	3	126	10	71	5hd	42½	24	28	27¾	Jones J	1.35
5Jun04 5WO1	Will He Crow	L	3	126	3	12½	12hd	12hd	95	41½	31	Bahen S R	30.45
12Jun04 2WO1	Just in Case Jimmy	L	3	126	12	116	9hd	6hd	41	3½	4hd	Dos Ramos R A	23.55
13Jun04 11WO6	His Smoothness	L	3	126	11	8hd	114½	93	71	56	56	McKnight J	45.80
6Jun04 8WO4	Strike Em Hard	L	3	126	5	9hd	7hd	7½	82	72	61	Ramsammy E	46.90
29May04 7WO1	Alleged Ruler	L	3	126	6	101½	10½	81	5hd	6hd	72½	Callaghan S	15.10
5Jun04 9WO1	Silver Ticket	L	3	126	9	11	11	22	32½	84	82½	Kabel T K	5.65
13Jun04 7WO2	Copper Trail	L	3	126	2	13	13	13	105	9hd	93¼	Somsanith N	10.20
21May04 7WO1	Kent Ridge	L b	3	126	8	6hd	8½	3hd	61	1015	1022¾	Husbands P	23.45
21May04 7WO2	Archer Fleet	L b	3	126	4	4hd	3hd	101½	123	121	11no	Husbands S P	33.25
4Jun04 7WO1	Night Sky	L	3	126	7	5hd	62	5hd	115	11½	12no	McAleney J S	11.60
6Jun04 10WO1	Long Pond	L b	3	126	1	3hd	4½	11hd	13	13	13	Elliott S	12.45

OFF AT 5:06 Start Good. Won driving. Track fast.

TIME :23^1, :47^4, 1:12^4, 1:37^4, 2:04^3 (:23.31, :47.83, 1:12.94, 1:37.87, 2:04.72)

$2 Mutuel Prices:				
	13 – NIIGON	**13.80**	**5.10**	**4.10**
	10 – A BIT O'GOLD		**3.10**	**2.90**
	3 – WILL HE CROW			**9.60**

$2 EXACTOR 13–10 PAID $33.80 $2 TRIACTOR 13–10–3 PAID $742.40
$1 SUPERFECTA 13–10–3–12 PAID $5,343.70

Dk. b or br. c, (Mar), by Unbridled – Savethelastdance, by Nureyev. Trainer Coatrieux Eric. Bred by Chiefswood Stables Limited (Ont-C).

NIIGON stalked the pacesetter just to the outside, moved up outside him late backstretch and moved clear quickly early turn, had command to the stretch then held A BIT O'GOLD safe under steady pressure. A BIT O'GOLD rated early in striking range, moved sharply after the leader late backstretch then was determined and gaining gradually to the end. WILL HE CROW was unhurried to the final turn, closed four-wide but never reached contention.

The field that faced the starting gate for the 146h running of the rich Queen's Plate was one of the smallest since the race was held at Woodbine, but full of the most intrigue. Only nine started on 26 June 2005. But all week long the hardboots had been waxing enthusiastic about the quality of the field, about how many more American-owned horses than usual there were (five of them were wholly or partially owned by Americans), about how many Manitoba breds there were (three), and about how *Dance Smartly's* latest son, *Dance With Ravens*, had been disqualified to sixth place from winning the Plate Trial. (Months later his win was reinstated.) And then there was the mystery horse, *Wild Desert*, who proved clearly best of all.

It may have been one of the wildest, slowest, most baffling and rather mysterious Plates in years. To anybody who was paying close attention, the tote board did not lie. Following a dismal eighth-place finish behind *Afleet Alex* in the Arkansas Derby in April, *Wild Desert* had been listed at 6-to-1 in the morning line because of his ten-week absence from the racing wars. Since then, he'd had only one published workout at Monmouth Park, New Jersey, which doesn't require working horses to be identified, and then a slow three-furlong work at Woodbine the previous Friday. Did bettors have a clear understanding of his state of health? During early wagering on a hot, steamy Plate, the odds on *Wild Desert* dropped steadily, from 11-to-1 to 3-to-1 in the final flash. This made the mystery horse the second choice behind *Dance With Ravens*, the royally bred colt that was the thirty-fifth Plate starter for the mighty Sam-Son Farm.

One of those in the know was *Wild Desert's* majority owner Dan Borislow, a forty-three-year-old communications executive from Philadelphia. Borislow made his fortune in telecommunications when he acquired the exclusive rights to sell discounted long distance service to America Online customers in a $100 million deal. He turned Tev-Save Holdings Inc. into a multi billion dollar business, selling it in 1999 for a reported "nine figures." Borislow retired at age thirty-eight to concentrate on buying, breeding and selling racehorses. He is best known for his ownership of *Toccet*, winner of four graded races in 2002, winning the Champagne, Hollywood Futurity, Remsen and Laurel Futurity. *Toccet*, whose name was misspelled at registration, was named after former NHL hockey player Rick Tocchet. In 1999 Borislow made news when he purchased a $1.8 million yearling at Keeneland and named him *Talk Is Money* (in honour of his former business."Every time someone was talking one the phone, I made money.") He also sold broodmare *Beautiful Bid*, who produced Breeders' Cup Distaff Stakes and

WILD DESERT'S PARTNERS—CARL GESSLER JR., LINA TICKNOR, MAJORITY OWNER DAN BORISLOW, KEITH JONES, GOVERNOR GENERAL ADRIENNE CLARKSON AND JOCKEY PATRICK VALENZUELA.

Eclipse Award Winner *Beautiful Pleasure*, for $2.6 million in 2000.

Borislow admitted he won $100,000 wagering at the Woodbine windows on his first Plate horse and claimed he was one of North American's biggest horseplayers. Borislow paid a $7,500 supplementary fee to enter the Plate in Februrary after buying him privately from his initial owner and now partner, Carl Gessler Jr. Gessler paid US$40,000 for the colt as a yearling. Borislow's other partners included New York Yankees' manager Joe Torre and former Philadelphia Flyers player Keith Jones of Brantford, Ontario, who like Torre owned five per cent of the horse. Jones said he wagered $2,000 to win and $2,000 to place on *Wild Desert* and won $13,000.

In the week leading up to the Plate, both Borislow and Jones boasted that *Wild Desert* would be ready for the race. The outspoken Borislow said he'd be very, very disappointed if *Wild Desert* did not win. After the race, Borislow referred all questions about *Wild Desert's* works to the trainer, who was listed as Bobby Frankel, an award-winning trainer from the U.S., who didn't show up for the Plate. He was the colt's third trainer in two-and-a-half months. Borislow had fired trainer Ken McPeek, saying he hadn't prepared the horse properly for the Arkansas Derby, and turned him over to Richard Dutrow Jr., who promptly began serving a sixty-day suspension for a drug medication violation.

Later, after reading newspaper reports on *Wild Desert's* Plate win, racing commissions from New York and New Jersey conducted investigations into *Wild Desert's* whereabouts before the Plate. Although the *Wild Rush* colt had fulfilled all obligations with his three-furlong work at Woodbine just before the race, the Ontario Racing Commission began probing it, too. With the heat rising, Frankel implied only the slightest connection to *Wild Desert* by telling the *Daily Racing Form*: "I don't know anything about it. They asked me to run the horse in my name in Canada. That's what I did. That's all I know."

Eventually, Dutrow served an additional fourteen days and was fined $25,000 by the New York State Wagering Board, which deemed that the trainer was found to have had contact with his barn during his suspension and was therefore actually still the trainer, although Juan Rodriguez had been designated the trainer of record. And finally, more than two years after the Queen's Plate, three Dutrow employees were fined for the mystery surrounding *Wild Desert*'s works in the weeks leading up to the Plate. Rodriguez, Dutrow's assistant, was fined $3,000, although it was reduced to $1,000 and he was put on two years probation. Rodriguez was punished in part for two workout mysteries: according to the board's ruling, *Wild Desert* had worked one day at Aqueduct very early in the morning, before the official clocker showed up. The horse showed no workouts at Aqueduct. Also, Rodriguez obtained a false workout at Monmouth Park on May 29, on a day when the horse had actually worked at Aqueduct. Jockey Rudy Rodriguez was fined $1,000 as the rider who worked *Wild Desert* on both occasions.

In this intriguing Queen's Plate, *Wild Desert* ambled home in 2:07.37, the slowest winning time on a fast track since the Plate returned to its one-and-a-quarter-mile distance in 1957. The colt crawled the final quarter in 27.39 seconds. The only two winning times that had been slower—*Royal Chocolate* in 1973 and *Amber Herod* in 1974—were run on deep, sloppy tracks. Controversial California jockey Pat Valenzuela, riding in his first Plate, bided his time with *Wild Desert* at the back of the field, encountered a bit of traffic on the backstretch, and weaved his way among horses. Meanwhile, flashy Canadian Oaks' winner *Gold Strike*, a Manitoba-bred filly, appeared to have the race in a headlock with her three-length lead at the mile mark. "I really thought no one was going to catch her because she was running so easy," said jockey Jim McAleney. "I honestly said to myself at the half-mile pole, 'It's ours. This is our Plate.' She was running so strong and so well underneath me." But before long, McAleney knew he was in trouble. Apparently the two-week span between the Oaks and the Plate didn't give her enough time to recover. On Plate day she was running in thirty-one-degree Celsius temperatures, and the deep, cuppy track took its toll on her. Although the track was rated fast, many horsemen complained about it being slow and deep, like "a ploughed field."

Wild Desert was bred in Ontario by Windways Farm, who also bred Queen's Plate champion *Victor Cooley*. "I never thought in my wildest dreams that I would win the Queen's Plate," Valenzuela said. "It's an honour to be here and a privilege. The Lord Jesus Christ has blessed us today." One of *Wild Desert*'s shoes fell off in the winner's circle. Borislow said he bought *Wild Desert* specifically to race him in the Queen's Plate. "This is a race we pointed for and this is a race we want."

WILD DESERT | 3-year-old bay colt

Wild Desert (2002)	Wild Rush	Wild Again	Icecapade
			Bushel-n-Peck
		Rose Park	Plugged Nickle
			Hardship
	Desert Radiance	Desert Wine	Damascus
			Anne Campbell
		Handselen	Gummo
			Handi Work

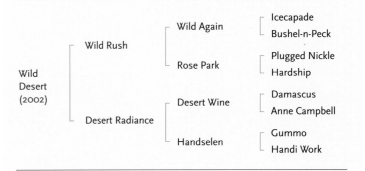

Owner: Borislow, Gessler, Jones, Goldfarb, Dubb, Davis and Diamond Pride
Trainer: Robert Frankel; *Jockey:* Pat Valenzuela
Breeder: Windways Farm Ltd. (Ont-C)

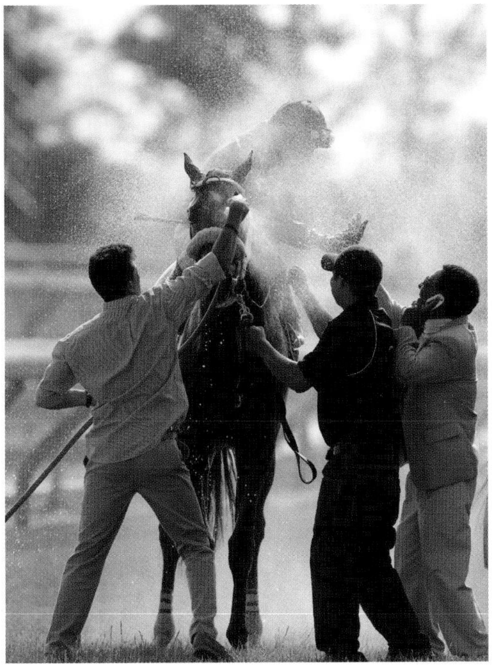

"A hose job?" *Wild Desert* is sprayed down.

NINTH RACE
Woodbine
JUNE 26, 2005

$1\frac{1}{4}$ MILES. 146TH RUNNING OF THE QUEEN'S PLATE. Purse $1,000,000 (plus $1,600 Starters Bonus) (Plus Fifty Guineas, the Gift of Her Majesty the Queen.) For THREE-YEAR-OLDS, FOALED IN CANADA. Weight; Colts and Geldings 126 lbs. Fillies, 121 lbs.

Value of Race: $1,001,600(US $812,700) Winner $600,000 (US $486,840); second $200,000 (US $162,280); third $110,000 (US $89,254); fourth $60,000 (US $48,684); fifth $30,000 (US $24,342); sixth $400 (US $325); seventh $400 (US $325); eighth $400 (US $325); ninth $400 (US $325). Mutuel Pool $893,929.00 Exactor Pool $342,546.00 Triactor Pool $401,816.00 Superfecta Pool $148,718.00

Last Raced	Horse	M/Eqt.	A.	Wt	PP	1/4	1/2	3/4	1	Str	Fin	Jockey	Odds $1
16Apr05 9OP8	Wild Desert	L b	3	126	4	8^{4}	8^{6}	5^{hd}	4^{hd}	$3^{3\frac{1}{2}}$	$1^{\frac{1}{2}}$	Valenzuela P A	3.15
25May05 7CD1	King of Jazz	L	3	126	3	6^{hd}	$5^{\frac{1}{2}}$	6^{hd}	$3^{1\frac{1}{2}}$	2^{hd}	$2^{3\frac{3}{4}}$	Bejarano R	5.55
12Jun05 8WO1	Gold Strike	L b	3	121	6	2^{1}	$2^{1\frac{1}{2}}$	$1^{1\frac{1}{2}}$	1^{3}	$1^{\frac{1}{2}}$	$3^{2\frac{1}{4}}$	McAleney J S	3.45
5Jun05 5WO5	Molinaro Beau	L	3	126	2	9	9	9	9	$7^{3\frac{1}{2}}$	4^{1}	Clark D	53.95
12Jun05 7WO2	Ablo	L b	3	126	5	4^{1}	$3^{\frac{1}{2}}$	4^{1}	$2^{\frac{1}{2}}$	$4^{2\frac{1}{2}}$	$5^{1\frac{1}{4}}$	Olguin G L	27.30
4Jun05 7WO2	Granique	L	3	126	1	1^{hd}	1^{hd}	$3^{\frac{1}{2}}$	$5^{1\frac{1}{2}}$	$5^{1\frac{1}{2}}$	6^{2}	Fraser C	50.60
5Jun05 8WO1	Dance With Ravens	L b	3	126	8	5^{hd}	$6^{\frac{1}{2}}$	8^{5}	6^{2}	6^{hd}	7^{1}	Kabel T K	2.15
5Jun05 8WO3	Get Down	L	3	126	9	$3^{\frac{1}{2}}$	$4^{\frac{1}{2}}$	2^{hd}	7^{2}	$8^{1\frac{1}{2}}$	8^{1}	Migliore R	10.80
5Jun05 8WO2	Three in the Bag	L f	3	126	7	7^{2}	$7^{\frac{1}{2}}$	7^{hd}	8^{hd}	9	9	Landry R C	7.80

OFF AT 5:10 Start Good. Won driving. Track fast.

TIME :23^{4}, :48^{1}, 1:13^{4}, 1:39^{4}, 2:07^{1} (:23.86, :48.36, 1:13.96, 1:39.98, 2:07.37)

$2 Mutuel Prices:				
	5 – WILD DESERT	8.30	4.70	4.50
	4 – KING OF JAZZ		5.90	4.90
	7 – GOLD STRIKE			3.70

$2 EXACTOR 5–4 PAID $40.30 $2 TRIACTOR 5–4–7 PAID $209.20
$1 SUPERFECTA 5–4–7–2 PAID $1,973.60

B. c, (Mar), by Wild Rush – Desert Radiance , by Desert Wine . Trainer Frankel Robert. Bred by Windways Farm Limited (Ont-C).

WILD DESERT rated early in touch with the front runner, closed two-deep late turn, was squeezed by GOLD STRIKE a furlong out then drove to the lead with 70 yards to run. KING OF JAZZ rated early, closed three-deep late turn, bid a furlong out and gained a slight lead but failed to stave off the winner in deep stretch. GOLD STRIKE raced forwardly outside GRANIQUE, moved clear midbackstretch, set a reserved pace and was still in hand on the far turn, was under urging from the top of the stretch, came out near the 1/8 pole bothering WILD DESERT and tired.

Trainer Josie Carroll was always one to brush off any talk of ground-breaking achievements as a female trainer. Yet, the forty-eight-year-old native of Toronto became the first female in the 147-year history of the Queen's Plate to train the winner. And she won the 2006 Plate with style, scoring with 16-to-1 shot *Edenwold*, a two-year-old champion that had been virtually eclipsed in all the pre-race hype.

Other notables had preceded her. Janet Bedford trained the 1984 favourite, *Let's Go Blue*, beaten by only half a length in a bumpy run. Barbara Minshall finished second in 1995 with *Mt. Sassafras* and with *Stephanotis* in 1996. Rita Schnitzler was second with *Brite Adam* in 1993 and third with *Kristy Krunch* in 1996. Catharine Day Phillips was second with *A Bit O' Gold* in 2004. All so close and yet so far. Carroll's history-making exploit all started when she was a nine-year-old schoolgirl, clipping photos of racehorses from newspapers. In 1975, when she took the equine studies program at Humber College, there were only four female trainers licensed in Ontario. "Forget about the gender thing," she said earlier in the week. "My owners have always respected hard work and merit. To play the gender card, I think, is taking away from the other trainers in the race who work equally hard and are very talented." She said she has always been treated as an equal.

The 147th Plate promised to be another year like 2005, when American-based horses dominated the race. This time, *Unification*, a Godolphin Stable colour-bearer that won the Grey Breeders' Cup Stakes as a two-year-old, was made the winterbook favourite, while *Wanna Runner*, trained by Bob Baffert and owned by Mike Pegram (they won the 1998 Kentucky Derby together with *Real Quiet*), was deemed the next best. *Edenwold* was third pick, granted Canada's best chance to defend the country's honour. But in the weeks leading to the Plate few thought this way. First of all there was the question about *Edenwold* getting the distance of the Plate. As a two-year-old he had won three consecutive stakes races, all sprints (*Colin*, *Vandal* and *Simcoe Stakes*) and in his first start going further than a mile—the Coronation Futurity—he finished fourth. However, a horse had run into him, knocked the wind out of him, causing him to stumble. He was flying in the stretch. All along, Carroll maintained *Edenwold* could go the distance.

Wanna Runner, bred by Yvonne Schwabe in Ontario, was the early season dazzler, after having finished third to *Brother Derek*

JIM SAPARA HOISTS QUEEN'S PLATE TROPHY WITH CELEBRANTS—TRAINER JOSIE CARROLL, WIFE ALICE SAPARA, JOCKEY EMILE RAMSAMMY AND WOODBINE CEO DAVID WILLMOT.

and U.S. two-year-old champion *Stevie Wonderboy* in the San Rafael Stakes in California. By the time he headed home to Canada, he was the richest entrant in the Queen's Plate (US$566,950) with wins in the WinStar Derby at Sunland Park, New Mexico, and the Lone Star Derby in Texas. "He looked like *Barbaro* coming down the stretch," quipped Baffert, who was tempted at one time to put the colt on the Kentucky Derby trail. *Wanna Runner* was supplemented to the Plate for $7,500. But on 25 June 2006, *Edenwold*, named after a tiny town in Saskatchewan, bought the Plate home. He ran the race of his life, pushing a sizzling pace all the way, and refused to allow anybody to pass him in the home stretch. He won by three-quarters of a length over *Sterwins* and became the first juvenile champion since *Sound Reason* in 1977 to win the Queen's Plate. He was owned by Jim and Alice Sapara of Edmonton, who had bought him for $100,000 as a yearling in Toronto.

At the draw for post positions three days before the race, Alice had bluntly said that *Edenwold* would win even though he had drawn post position one, which rarely produced a winner in the Plate. So did his jockey, Emile Ramsammy, who was about to win his second Queen's Plate. Ramsammy dyed his hair red and blond to match Sapara's colours just before he left the jock's room. *Malakoff*, owned

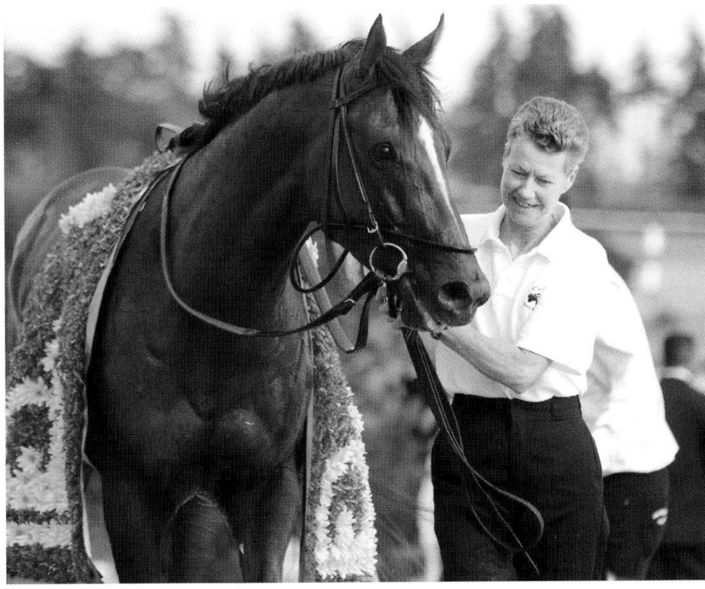

Job over, *Edenwold* and groom Carol Dyer head back to the barn.

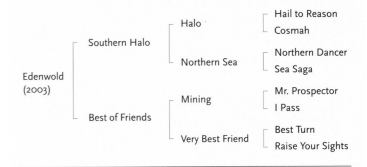

EDENWOLD | 3-year-old chestnut colt

Edenwold (2003)	Southern Halo	Halo	Hail to Reason
			Cosmah
		Northern Sea	Northern Dancer
			Sea Saga
	Best of Friends	Mining	Mr. Prospector
			I Pass
		Very Best Friend	Best Turn
			Raise Your Sights

Owner: James and Alice Sapara; *Trainer:* Josie Carroll
Jockey: Emile Ramsammy; *Breeder:* Gail Wood and W. Diamant (Ont-C)

by Frank Stronach, finished third. *Wanna Runner* finished tenth of thirteen. "It's the first time he's ever thrown a clunker like that," said Baffert, musing that his colt had acted like a horse that might have bled at the five-eighths pole.

It was a gratifying win for the Saparas. Five years earlier a fire destroyed Sapara's manufacturing plant in Alberta, forcing him to sell his Kentucky thoroughbred farm and most of his quality broodmares. Sapara rebuilt his business in ninety days, without laying off any of his three-hundred employees. "That was devastating," Jim Sapara said of the fire. "I lost all enthusiasm about racing when the farm and the horses had to go but Alice said, 'Maybe you should try another one and another one.' You know, this is addictive and it doesn't take much to get me to a horse sale and I never sit on my hands when I get there. That's the big problem." Sapara retired a month after the Plate from his company, Winalta Inc., which produces manufactured and modular housing. He names his horses after small towns in his native Saskatchewan. Afterward, he received a card from school children in *Edenwold*, thanking the Saparas for making the town known across the country.

The story wasn't so happy a few weeks later in Prince of Wales, which turned into the most controversial Canadian Triple Crown race in history. *Malakoff* won the race, impressively, by one and a half lengths, swooping five-wide on the final turn, but stewards disqualified him for bearing in during the final sixteenth and causing a chain reaction that impeded three horses behind him. *Edenwold* got the worst of it, hemmed in and punished on the rail. He finished fifth, but was moved up to fourth on *Malakoff*'s disqualification. The banana-loving *Shillelagh Slew* was elevated to first, giving trainer Mike DePaulo, jockey Dino Luciani and owner David James their first win in the Prince of Wales. James had tried to buy *Edenwold* as a yearling, but empty-handed, he travelled to Kentucky to pick up *Shillelagh Slew* for US$40,000.

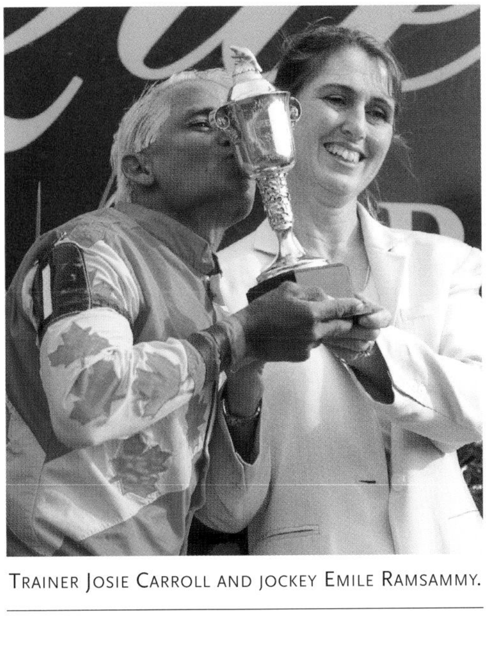

Trainer Josie Carroll and jockey Emile Ramsammy.

TENTH RACE
Woodbine
JUNE 25, 2006

1¼ MILES. 147TH RUNNING OF THE QUEEN'S PLATE. Purse $1,000,000 (plus $3,200 Starters Bonus) PLUS FIFTY GUINEAS, A GIFT OF HER MAJESTY THE QUEEN FOR THREE-YEAR-OLDS, FOALED IN CANADA. Weight; Colts and Geldings 126 lbs. Fillies, 121 lbs.

Value of Race: $1,003,200(US $892,848) Winner $600,000 (US $534,000); second $200,000 (US $178,000); third $110,000 (US $97,900); fourth $60,000 (US $53,400); fifth $30,000 (US $26,700); sixth $400 (US $356); seventh $400 (US $356); eighth $400 (US $356); ninth $400 (US $356); tenth $400 (US $356); eleventh $400 (US $356); twelfth $400 (US $356); thirteenth $400 (US $356). Mutuel Pool $664,429.00

Last Raced	Horse	M/Eqt.	A.	Wt	PP	¼	½	¾	1	Str	Fin	Jockey	Odds $1
4Jun06 ^{8}WO^{3}	Edenwold	L f	3	126	1	3^{hd}	$4^{2\frac{1}{2}}$	2^{1}	1^{hd}	$1^{\frac{1}{2}}$	$1^{\frac{3}{4}}$	Ramsammy E	16.20
10Jun06 ^{7}Mth^{1}	Sterwins	L	3	126	5	1^{1}	$1^{\frac{1}{2}}$	1^{hd}	$2^{1\frac{1}{2}}$	2^{3}	2^{4}	Velazquez J R	4.00
20May06 ^{6}WO^{1}	Malakoff	L	3	126	8	2^{hd}	2^{hd}	$3^{\frac{1}{2}}$	3^{1}	3^{hd}	3no	Kabel T K	4.05
4Jun06 ^{8}WO^{2}	Ascot Bill	L	3	126	6	13	13	11^{2}	9^{7}	$5^{\frac{1}{2}}$	$4^{\frac{1}{2}}$	Stein J	19.10
29Apr06 ^{5}WO^{1}	Shillelagh Slew	L f	3	126	3	7^{hd}	5^{hd}	5^{hd}	$4^{3\frac{1}{2}}$	4^{5}	$5^{6\frac{3}{4}}$	Luciani D	7.55
4Jun06 ^{8}WO^{1}	Pipers Thunder	L	3	126	10	5^{hd}	$7^{1\frac{1}{2}}$	7^{2}	5^{hd}	6^{6}	$6^{15\frac{1}{2}}$	Sabourin R B	10.35
4Jun06 ^{8}WO^{5}	Atlas Shrugs	L	3	126	2	8^{1}	$6^{\frac{1}{2}}$	$6^{1\frac{1}{2}}$	$6^{2\frac{1}{2}}$	$7^{2\frac{1}{2}}$	$7^{1\frac{1}{4}}$	Fraser C	35.30
4Jun06 ^{8}WO^{4}	Cifercat	L	3	126	12	11^{hd}	$10^{\frac{1}{2}}$	$8^{2\frac{1}{2}}$	8^{hd}	8^{3}	8^{1}	Dos Ramos R A	60.30
4Jun06 ^{8}WO^{8}	Hot Deputy	L f	3	126	11	12^{hd}	$12^{\frac{1}{2}}$	13	$11^{1\frac{1}{2}}$	10^{4}	$9^{1\frac{1}{2}}$	Montpellier C	88.45
13May06 ^{8}LS^{1}	Wanna Runner	L bf	3	126	9	4^{1}	$3^{\frac{1}{2}}$	$4^{1\frac{1}{2}}$	7^{hd}	9^{1}	10no	Espinoza V	1.55
4Jun06 ^{8}WO^{6}	Thinking Out Loud	L	3	126	4	$9^{\frac{1}{2}}$	$11^{2\frac{1}{2}}$	10^{1}	10^{hd}	$11^{1\frac{1}{2}}$	$11^{\frac{3}{4}}$	McAleney J S	46.80
2Jun06 ^{3}WO^{3}	Bridgecut	L b	3	126	13	10^{hd}	9^{hd}	12^{3}	13	12^{1}	12^{4}	Wilson E	50.35
4Jun06 ^{8}WO^{7}	Pyramid Park	L b	3	126	7	6^{hd}	$8^{\frac{1}{2}}$	9^{hd}	$12^{\frac{1}{2}}$	13	13	Callaghan S	59.55

OFF AT 6:07 Start Good For All But CIFERCAT. Won driving. Track fast.
TIME :22^{3}, :45^{4}, 1:11^{1}, 1:37^{4}, 2:05^{1} (:22.73, :45.98, 1:11.28, 1:37.99, 2:05.30)

$2 Mutuel Prices:				
	1 – EDENWOLD	34.40	15.90	10.30
	5 – STERWINS		6.60	5.40
	8 – MALAKOFF			4.20

$2 EXACTOR 1–5 PAID $233.60 $2 TRIACTOR 1–5–8 PAID $986.90
$1 SUPERFECTA 1–5–8–6 PAID $5,861.50

Ch. c, (Feb), by Southern Halo – Best of Friends , by Mining . Trainer Carroll Josie. Bred by Gail Wood & W Diamant (Ont–C).

EDENWOLD, prominent early, stalked from the rail, bid inside STERWINS nearing the far turn, dueled then prevailed in the stretch under a steady drive. STERWINS led nearing the first turn, set a reserved pace, was engaged late backstretch, dueled on the far turn then was outfinished in the stretch. MALAKOFF stalked three-wide, chased hard late on the far turn but hung in the stretch. ASCOT BILL, well back early, closed along the rail through the final turn but never reached contention.

On the morning of the 148th Queen's Plate, trainer Ian Black shook the hand of twenty-five-year-old jockey Emma-Jayne Wilson and said: "Let's make history." And so they did. Scrubbing, pumping, pushing and urging long shot *Mike Fox* for all she was worth, Wilson became the first female jockey to win the $1 million Queen's Plate. It was exactly one year after Josie Carroll became the first female trainer to score in the oldest continuously run stakes event in North America. In fact, "Girl Power" carried the year of 2007. Only three weeks before, *Rags to Riches*, a no-nonsense filly with an attitude, had astonished the world by winning the Belmont Stakes against Preakness champ, Curlin, a big, strong colt that was considered a cut above. *Rags to Riches* was the first filly in 102 years to win the Belmont, and only the third in history.

The feminine mystique got off to a rousing start on Plate day when female apprentice jockey Stephanie Fedora won the first race of her career aboard the filly, *Black Tea*, in the first race at Woodbine. Successful apprentice Michelle Rainford also rode in the race. At the time, three of the riders in the top ten were female, with Wilson being the leading money-winning rider in the jockey colony. Wilson's victory came nineteen years after the first female rider in the race's history even got a mount in the race. Julie Krone finished fifth with *No Malice* in 1988. Only two other women had ridden in the Plate since. Francine Villeneuve finished second with the filly *Wilderness Song* in the 1991 Plate, won by another filly, *Dance Smartly*. Villeneuve had another crack at it the next year with *Ragnarok*, but finished twelfth and last. Chantal Sutherland, a two-time Sovereign Award winner as Canada's top apprentice, had had two mounts in the Plate, finishing thirteenth of thirteen with *Streakin Rob* in 2002, and tenth of twelve with *Button Wood* in 2003. Laurie Gulas had been the first female rider to win a Canadian Triple Crown race when she scored with filly *Free Vacation* in the Breeders' Stakes in 1999.

Women in Ontario have won seven of the past nine apprentice jockey awards at the Sovereigns. Wilson had been a firecracker since she started, becoming the first woman and only the third apprentice to win the Woodbine riding title in 2005, her first full year of riding. That year, she won Eclipse Award honours as North America's top apprentice. In 2006, she led Woodbine riders again, earning a second Sovereign Award as Canada's top apprentice. And she got her first Plate mount with *Bridgecut*, a 50-to-1 long shot that finished twelfth of thirteen.

Asked what her reaction would be if she won the Queen's Plate before the race? "I'd be speechless," she said. When it came down to it, Wilson was anything but speechless. "I am just so happy that I can say that I'm the first female [to win the Queen's Plate]," she said, her words tumbling out in high gear. "Girl power, go for it. I'm just so glad it's the last time it'll ever be said. Been there, bought the t-shirt, said and done." After her rousing win, Wilson let out a hoot, raised her arms in the air and hollered all the way back to the winner's circle, where the large crowd at Woodbine gave her a huge

ARMS THRUST SKYWARD, EMMA-JAYNE WILSON ENJOYS HER HISTORICAL MOMENT.

ovation. Black said he had no hesitation in getting Wilson to ride *Mike Fox* in his three previous starts. "She's a wonderful rider, a great rider, as strong as anybody out there. She's a bright, bright girl," he said.

Wilson got her inspiration from a piece of paper that accidentally fell out of a book, *Women in Racing*, that she'd been reading the week of the Queen's Plate. She'd bought the book six years before she became a jockey, when she was working for Park Stud at the Keeneland sales in Kentucky. The piece of paper stated: "*On this day, I, Emma-Jayne Wilson promise, promise to make it as a jockey.*" It was dated 14 September 2001. In the jockey's room before the Plate, Wilson pulled out the piece of paper and used it as a springboard to victory. "It just gave me that inspiration from deep down from when I wanted to be a jockey, to make this happen."

After the break from the gate Wilson was happy to settle *Mike Fox* into a stalking position, just behind the leaders while racing three-wide and four-wide all the way. But she wasn't at all certain, with three-eighths of a mile to go, that she was going to succeed. Going down the backstretch, *Jiggs Coz*, the race favourite and the Plate Trial winner, made a big move around Wilson and *Mike Fox*.

TRAINER IAN BLACK, HUGH GRAHAM, AN EMOTIONAL MORGAN FIRESTONE AND LIEUTENANT GOVERNOR JAMES K. BARTLEMAN.

MIKE FOX | 3-year-old bay colt

Owner: D. Morgan Firestone; *Trainer:* Ian Black
Jockey: Emma-Jayne Wilson; *Breeder:* Firestone Farm Ltd. (Ont-C)

But Wilson started getting a little worried at the three-eighths pole, when *Jiggs Coz* and *Alezzandro*, the pacesetter, started to pull away from them. "I just buried my head and kept on driving," she said. "He dug down so deep. Out of nowhere, I just knew we were flying and the last few jumps were unbelievable." *Mike Fox* defeated seven other horses in the smallest Plate field in thirty years. Canada's top two-year-old of 2006, *Leonnatus Anteas*, was scratched the morning of the race because of injury and missed the entire Triple Crown. *Mike Fox*'s win was gratifying for Oakville businessman Morgan Firestone, who had been involved with horse racing since 1984, and had never won a Plate, although he'd spent plenty on hopefuls at yearling auctions. Ironically, *Mike Fox* was bred by Firestone. *Mike Fox* was Firestone's fourth starter in the Plate. His best effort was an eighth with *San Cielo* in 1991. By the time of the Plate, Firestone had been diagnosed with a rare degenerative disease, similar to Parkinson's, which stripped him of his mobility and his speech. On

Plate day, he rose out of his wheelchair and accepted the Plate trophy, beaming.

Mike Fox's success didn't continue for the rest of the Triple Crown trail. He finished fourth in the Prince of Wales, won by Knob Hill Stables' *Alezzandro*, who gave thirty-one-year-old trainer Kevin Attard his first Triple Crown victory. And on the grass at Woodbine in the Breeders' Stakes *Mike Fox* finished fifth, looming up around the turn, then flattening out. *Marchfield*, who looked hopelessly out of it, twenty lengths in arrears early in the race, made a wicked swoop from last to first for Canada's leading trainer of 2006, Mark Casse. It was the twenty-eighth time in forty-eight years that three different horses won the Triple Crown legs. "You can run these horses every week and you'll have a different winner," said Casse. "There is no standout."

Casse and owner Eugene Melnyk gained belated but richly deserved honours in the year of female domination when *Sealy Hill* won the Royal Tiara, the triple crown for three-year-old fillies in Canada. It was the first time a filly had ever swept the three Triple Crown events—the Canadian Oaks, Bison City and the Wonder Where Stakes since the event was inaugurated in 1999.

HISTORY MAKER EMMA-JAYNE AND PLATE TROPHY.

EIGHTH RACE
Woodbine
JUNE 24, 2007

1¼ MILES. (2.03²) 148TH RUNNING OF THE THE QUEEN'S PLATE. Purse $1,000,000 (plus $1,200 Starters Bonus) FOR THREE–YEAR–OLDS, FOALED IN CANADA. Weight; Colts and Geldings 126 lbs. Fillies, 121 lbs.

Value of Race: $1,001,200(US $936,022) Winner $600,000 (US $560,940); second $200,000 (US $186,980); third $110,000 (US $102,839); fourth $60,000 (US $56,094); fifth $30,000 (US $28,047); sixth $400 (US $374); seventh $400 (US $374); eighth $400 (US $374). Mutuel Pool $815,254.00

Last Raced	Horse	M/Eqt.	A.	Wt	PP	¼	½	¾	1	Str	Fin	Jockey	Odds $1
23May07 ⁷WO¹	Mike Fox	L	3	126	8	3¹	3½	4¹½	3²	33½	1½	Wilson E	15.20
3Jun07 ⁸WO³	Alezzandro	L	3	126	4	1¹	1¹	1¹	11½	12½	2¹¼	Kabel T K	16.65
3Jun07 ⁸WO¹	Jiggs Coz	L	3	126	6	4hd	5hd	3hd	2¹	2²	32½	Clark D	1.25
12May07 ⁴Bel¹	Daaher	L	3	126	2	6½	4hd	5hd	72½	64½	4nk	Garcia Alan	3.50
3Jun07 ⁸WO⁵	Include Us	L bf	3	126	3	8	8	8	6½	4²	51½	Landry R C	36.25
3Jun07 ⁸WO²	Marchfield	L b	3	126	7	5hd	76	6hd	41½	5½	67¾	Husbands P	3.90
23May07 ⁷Bel³	Twilight Meteor	L	3	126	5	2½	2½	2hd	51	74	74	Velazquez J R	4.65
3Jun07 ⁸WO⁴	Cobrador	L	3	126	1	7⁷	6¹	76	8	8	8	Ramsammy E	37.60

OFF AT 4:37 Start Good. Won driving. Track fast.
TIME :23³, :47³, 1:12², 1:37², 2:05² (:23.66, :47.74, 1:12.51, 1:37.48, 2:05.45)

9 – MIKE FOX	32.40	13.10	5.00
$2 Mutuel Prices: 4 – ALEZZANDRO		16.30	5.60
6 – JIGGS COZ			2.40

$2 EXACTOR 9–4 PAID $460.20 $2 TRIACTOR 9–4–6 PAID $1,179.20
$1 SUPERFECTA 9–4–6–2 PAID $3,539.90

B. c, (Jan), by Giant's Causeway – Alexis–Ire , by Alzao . Trainer Black Ian. Bred by Firestone Farm Ltd (Ont–C).

MIKE FOX stalked the pace three-wide to the far turn, was roused along the second path on the far turn, responded smartly in the final furlong and got up late. ALEZZANDRO led early, set a reserved pace, quickened on the far turn, had a clear lead in the stretch but weakened late. JIGGS COZ stalked three-wide, closed into the far turn, chased ALEZZANDRO to deep stretch then hung in the final 70 yards.

Roger Attfield got to the winner's circle of the 149th Queen's Plate the hard way: with a colt nobody (but him) believed could go one-and-one-quarter miles and an impressive truck ride to bypass a picket line manned by the province's lottery commission security personnel.

Attfield, sixty-eight, recovering from a serious heel injury incurred the previous winter, emerged triumphant with *Not Bourbon* in swashbuckling form. It was Attfield's eighth Queen's Plate win, equalling the once seemingly out-of-reach record set by Harry Giddings Jr. that had stood for forty-six years. Attfield had seemed stuck on seven Plates—his previous win came thirteen years earlier when *Regal Discovery* upset the favourites—but then along came *Not Bourbon*, the first Plate winner for diamond explorer/owner Charles Fipke and jockey Jono Jones.

Attfield was an anomaly at this Plate, bringing a hint of the old, golden days in a race that saw many changes and firsts. The grand Sam-Son Farms, which had ruled racing for many years in Ontario and beyond, didn't make it to the starting gate after their sole hope, *Harvest Home*, was scratched the morning of the race. Winless in three starts, his main claim to fame was that he was a son of Sam-Son's own homebred stallion, *Smart Strike*, which the previous year had sired winners of more than $14 million, crushing the previous world record.

Sadly, early in the season, Sam-Son Farms' owners, Liza Samuel and her daughter Tammy Samuel-Balaz, died, leaving the farm with a new generation. And once mighty Windfields was long gone, too, as its owners shut down their commercial breeding operation after seventy-two years. The farm closed its stallion station and returned to a private farm, with a small number of broodmares.

Relatively new to the game was Charles Fipke, a colourful character who also raced *Tale of Ekati* in the Kentucky Derby earlier in the season. *Not Bourbon* was a product of Fipke's breeding acumen. He sent his $600,000 speedball mare, *Bourbon Belle*, to the court of his own unheralded stallion *Not Impossible*, who hardly anybody else but Fipke wanted to breed to. But with Attfield at the helm, nothing was impossible.

"Not many coaches could have done what Roger did with this horse," said Jones. "In the beginning, I had my doubts if [*Not Bourbon*] could get seven-eighths, to be honest."

And although *Not Bourbon* won the one-and-one-eighth-mile Plate Trial in his previous start, Jones still doubted that the chestnut colt would handle the Plate distance because he felt the horse had tired at the end of the prep race.

Not Attfield. He wondered if Jones had already started celebrating his win too soon in the Plate Trial when the maiden *Solitaire* whizzed up the rail, and just fell short of catching him. Many thought *Solitaire* was the coming horse for the Plate, but the James Bond colt had raced only twice before the Plate.

NOT BOURBON'S CONNECTIONS—GROOM SARAH SULLIVAN, JONO JONES, OWNER CHARLES FIPKE AND TRAINER ROGER ATTFIELD.

The other wildcard was filly *Ginger Brew*, winner of the Canadian Oaks two weeks earlier in gritty fashion, ploughing through a tiny hole to win by six lengths for Stronach Stables.

Big, strong *Ginger Brew* was supposed to have stayed on the filly Triple Tiara trail, and leave the Plate game to her male stablemates *Harlem Rocker* and *Jungle Brew*. But the previously undefeated *Harlem Rocker* had finished fourth in the Plate Trial, showing an absolute dislike of the Polytrack surface, and Stronach trainer Brian Lynch changed plans. *Ginger Brew* was such a threat—the richest horse in the race with earnings of $498,295—that the twenty thousand fans that endured sometimes more than an hour wait to get past the numerous picket lines at the track's many entrances, made her the favourite at 9-to-5. In the previous 148 runnings, thirty-three fillies had won the Plate.

Not Bourbon, favoured in the opening morning line, was third best at 9-to-2 at the windows by post time, behind *Solitaire* at 7-to-2. Of the fifteen horses that paid the entry fee, five had never won a race. Another six hadn't won more than one race in their careers. Experience showed, as Attfield could attest. *Ginger Brew* followed *Not Bourbon* just behind the leaders for the first mile. They made their moves on the far turn, fanning out four and five wide, with the filly on the far outside. *Not Bourbon* took the lead with about 330 yards to go, while *Ginger Brew* closed determinedly with every

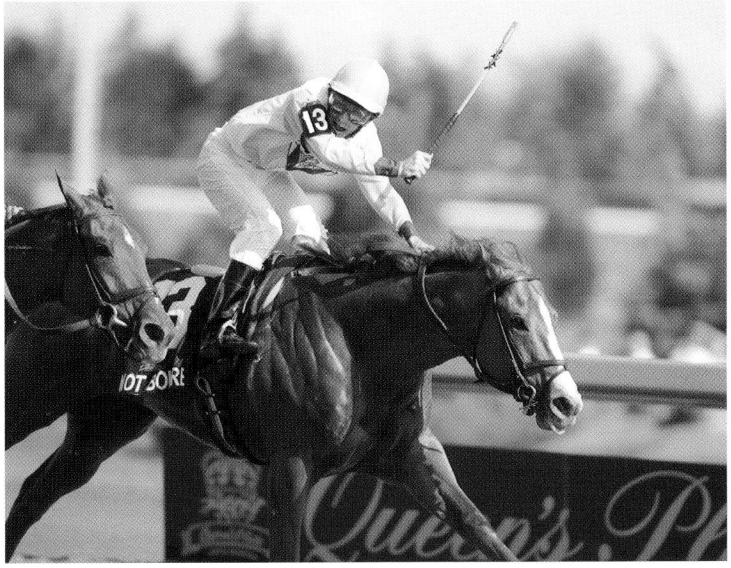

Premature celebration? Jono Jones eyes *Ginger Brew* at the wire.

step to fall short by a diminishing head.

Attfield said the filly never would have gone past *Not Bourbon*. "He's a tough horse to get by, believe me," Attfield said. "He just keeps digging. He gives everything he's got. He ran as hard as he could run." Attfield said that down the backstretch he could see that the normally hot and fiery *Not Bourbon* was relaxed. That gave the trainer confidence. With half a mile to go, he was "super confident." Even with seventy yards to go, he didn't waver.

The trick to *Not Bourbon*'s success, said Attfield, was to get him to relax, and if they could do that, he could run long. He trained him the old-school way, with quick works, saying that you had to train a horse the way the horse was. *Not Bourbon* was naturally fast in the mornings. It helped him relax if he could take the edge off his temperament. "This horse will gallop horses to death," Attfield said. "If there hadn't been any pace at all in this race, we would have gone wire to wire. He's a horse you can't restrain. He's got to run where he wants to run and then he'll relax and he'll stay."

The colt, who had set the track record for six furlongs at Woodbine the previous year, ran the one-and-one-quarter miles in 2:03.59, the fastest Plate in five years. The colt ran his final quarter in a sizzling 24.20 seconds. Of the thirteen-year gap since his previous win, Attfield said: "It's not an easy race to win. It's just been a great thrill. It's always been in my mind, when I won the fifth and the sixth." Attfield said all of his wins have been gratifying, although his first one (*Norcliffe* in 1975) is always special.

Attfield was lucky to be able to walk into the winner's circle on his own power. The previous December, he had been chopping down dead pine trees at his Florida home when he jumped down from a tree and landed on a log. "Totally my fault," he said.

NOT BOURBON | 3-year-old chestnut colt

Not Bourbon (2005)	Not Impossible	Sadlers Wells	Northern Dancer
			Fairy Bridge
		Ball Chairman	Secretariat
			A Status Symbol
	Bourbon Belle	Storm Boot	Storm Cat
			Aliata
		Timeless Girl	Whitesburg
			Timeless Sue

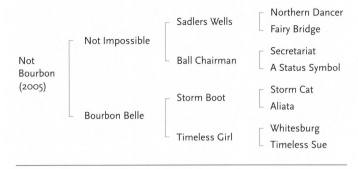

Owner: Charles Fipke; *Trainer:* Roger Attfield
Jockey: Jono Jones; *Breeder:* Charles Fipke (Ont-C)

Alone at the farm, he crawled to the house and got help. At first, doctors diagnosed it as a sprain, but two weeks later X-rays showed a shattered heel that required insertion of a plate with eight screws. The foot later became infected and at one point there was a chance he could lose it. He returned to Canada for treatment.

Only about a month before the Plate, Attfield got back on horseback, with an intravenous bag attached to one hip and a wound treatment pack slung from his other shoulder. The week before the Plate, he got rid of the treatment packs and bags. On Plate day, however, nothing could stop Attfield from rushing to the backstretch to tend to a horse in his barn that was colicking—not even strikers who were holding up traffic outside the track. Attfield steered his four-wheel drive truck over the curb and past the strikers, and got a ticket for his trouble. At sixty-eight, he was not ready to slow down.

NINTH RACE
Woodbine
JUNE 22, 2008

$1\frac{1}{4}$ MILES. (2.03^{2}) 149TH RUNNING OF THE QUEEN'S PLATE. Purse $1,000,000 FOR THREE-YEAR-OLDS, FOALED IN CANADA. Weight: Colts and Geldings: 126 lbs.; Fillies, 121 lbs. By subscription of $500 each to sccompany the nomination by February 2008 (nominations); To continue eligibility the following additional payments must be made: Second subscription of $1,500 by May 2008, (remained eligible). an additional $10,000 when making final entry no later than 8:30 a.m. on Thursday, June 19, 2008.

Value of Race: $1,003,600(US $986,737) Winner $600,000 (US $589,920); second $200,000 (US $196,640); third $110,000 (US $108,152); fourth $60,000 (US $58,992); fifth $30,000 (US $29,496); sixth $400 (US $393); seventh $400 (US $393); eighth $400 (US $393); ninth $400 (US $393); tenth $400 (US $393); eleventh $400 (US $393); twelfth $400 (US $393); thirteenth $400 (US $393); fourteenth $400 (US $393).
Mutuel Pool $784,409.00 Exactor Pool $325,678.00 Triactor Pool $369,755.00 Superfecta Pool $177,584.00

Last Raced	Horse	M/Eqt.	A.	Wt	PP	¼	½	¾	1	Str	Fin	Jockey	Odds $1
1Jun08 ^{7}WO^{1}	Not Bourbon	L	3	126	12	$5^{\frac{1}{2}}$	$4^{\frac{1}{2}}$	$4^{\frac{1}{2}}$	3^{hd}	$1^{1\frac{1}{2}}$	1^{hd}	Jones J	4.65
8Jun08 ^{8}WO^{1}	Ginger Brew	L	3	121	9	6^{1}	$7^{\frac{1}{2}}$	$6^{\frac{1}{2}}$	$5^{1\frac{1}{2}}$	2^{1}	$2^{4\frac{1}{2}}$	Castellano J J	1.90
1Jun08 ^{7}WO^{2}	Solitaire	L	3	126	11	$13^{2\frac{1}{2}}$	13^{hd}	14	$12^{\frac{1}{2}}$	6^{hd}	3^{nk}	Landry R C	3.20
18May08 ^{6}WO^{5}	Deputiformer	L f	3	126	4	7^{hd}	$6^{\frac{1}{2}}$	$5^{\frac{1}{2}}$	$1^{\frac{1}{2}}$	3^{2}	4^{nk}	Baird J	22.30
24May08 ^{7}WO^{2}	Palmers	L	3	126	6	$12^{\frac{1}{2}}$	11^{1}	$10^{\frac{1}{2}}$	8^{hd}	$5^{\frac{1}{2}}$	5^{nk}	Husbands P	23.60
1Jun08 ^{7}WO^{5}	East End Tap	L	3	126	3	11^{hd}	$10^{\frac{1}{2}}$	$11^{\frac{1}{2}}$	6^{hd}	$4^{\frac{1}{2}}$	$6^{1\frac{1}{4}}$	Pizarro T	56.50
4Jun08 ^{2}WO^{1}	Mamma's Knight	L b	3	126	7	14	$12^{\frac{1}{2}}$	$12^{\frac{1}{2}}$	11^{hd}	$9^{1\frac{1}{2}}$	$7^{1\frac{1}{2}}$	Stein J	37.85
18May08 ^{6}WO^{2}	Took the Time	L	3	126	14	4^{hd}	$5^{\frac{1}{2}}$	7^{1}	14	11^{hd}	$8^{3\frac{1}{4}}$	Dominguez R A	13.30
1Jun08 ^{2}WO^{2}	Jungle Brew		3	126	10	9^{1}	14	13^{hd}	13^{hd}	$12^{\frac{1}{2}}$	9^{1}	McAleney J S	9.55
1Jun08 ^{7}WO^{3}	Sebastian's Song	L	3	126	13	$8^{\frac{1}{2}}$	$8^{\frac{1}{2}}$	$9^{\frac{1}{2}}$	$7^{\frac{1}{2}}$	7^{hd}	$10^{1\frac{1}{4}}$	Clark D	21.65
24May08 ^{7}WO^{3}	Shadowless	L b	3	126	8	2^{hd}	3^{1}	3^{2}	2^{hd}	8^{1}	$11^{3\frac{1}{4}}$	Wilson E	23.45
1Jun08 ^{2}WO^{6}	Silver Jag	L b	3	126	5	10^{hd}	$9^{\frac{1}{2}}$	8^{hd}	10^{hd}	$13^{2\frac{1}{2}}$	12^{1}	Callaghan S	59.45
1Jun08 ^{2}WO^{3}	D. Flutie	L	3	126	1	1^{1}	1^{3}	$1^{1\frac{1}{2}}$	$4^{\frac{1}{2}}$	10^{hd}	$13^{\frac{1}{2}}$	Ramsammy E	24.15
24May08 ^{7}WO^{4}	Dylan's Choice	L	3	126	2	3^{1}	2^{hd}	2^{hd}	9^{1}	14	14	Sutherland C	61.85

OFF AT 5:09 Start Good. Won driving. Track fast.

TIME $:23^{2}$, $:47^{3}$, $1:13^{2}$, $1:39^{1}$, $2:03^{2}$ (:23.40, :47.60, 1:13.55, 1:39.30, 2:03.59)

$2 Mutuel Prices:			
13 – **NOT BOURBON**	11.30	5.10	3.40
10 – **GINGER BREW**		3.80	3.00
12 – **SOLITAIRE**			2.90

$2 EXACTOR 13–10 PAID $32.90 $2 TRIACTOR 13–10–12 PAID $83.30
$2 SUPERFECTA 13–10–12–5 PAID $1,914.60

Ch. c, (Mar), by Not Impossible-Ire – Bourbon Belle , by Storm Boot . Trainer Attfield Roger L. Bred by Charles Fipke (Ont-C).

NOT BOURBON, in range, raced three-wide into the far turn, bid four-deep near the 1/4 pole, drove clear upper stretch then held GINGER BREW safe under steady handling. GINGER BREW, well placed early, bid five-wide late on the far turn, was headed at the of the stretch but dug in and rallied determinedly, gaining steadily. SOLITAIRE, unhurried to the far turn, circled the field and rallied seven-wide.

The 150th Queen's Plate bore intriguing echoes of the first. The princely *Eye of the Leopard*—which gave Sam-Son Farms its fifth Plate winner and a hint of glories past—was born a couple of miles from the first winner, *Don Juan*.

John and James White, who bred and owned *Don Juan*, became known as the first family to dominate Canadian thoroughbred racing from their 320-acre farm on the Bronte sideroad near Milton, Ontario. The Whites bred, owned or trained twelve Plate winners. Another similarity of these two great racing stables was their flaming scarlet silks. A century and a half later, the Samuel family, also a first family of racing, was coming to terms with the future of its 200-acre operation, after the deaths of founder Ernie Samuel in 2000 and daughter Tammy Samuel-Balaz, who became the heart and soul of the farm before dying at age forty-seven in January, 2008. Samuel's wife, Elizabeth, died two months later.

That left Tammy's husband, Rick Balaz in charge, although his favourite mode of horsepower had always been with cars, planes and boats. There was never any question that he would continue the Samuel breeding legacy, as a tribute to his wife, and to keep their children, Lisa, seventeen, and Michael, fifteen, connected to it, too. Both of the Balaz children are enthusiastic equestrians.

FRONT AND CENTRE AT THE TOP OF THE STRETCH AS HE BEGINS TO PULL AWAY FROM THE FIELD IS *EYE OF THE LEOPARD* WEARING THE FAMILIAR RED SSF BLINKERS OF SAM-SON FARM.

The 150th Plate brought a rebirth of memories and history for the remaining Samuels: Mark, chairman of the Samuel steel company, and sister Kim Samuel-Johnson who runs the family charitable foundation. Count long-time Sam-Son trainer Mark Frostad in that group as well. He's trained four of their Plate winners.

"We've had a lot of great memories at the track," Mark Samuel said after *Eye of the Leopard*'s determined win. "I don't think I've ever had a more emotional day than today. . . . We had spirits up above cheering that horse home today. It is a special day for the family and we are going to savour this for a long time."

There had been a dry spell for Sam-Son, which hadn't had a horse run in the Plate since 2005. There had been promise, but equal parts of disappointment and injury. The Samuel clan was forced to let the family emotions and affairs of the previous eighteen months settle, before they could move on with any kind of strength. "When you suffer that kind of loss, you need to take stock," Mark Samuel said. "You need some time to grieve, and you need some time to contemplate.

"One thing we know, we had no intention of getting out of racing, or out of breeding. What we knew we needed was a year of status quo to get through that and take stock and see where we were, and then regroup to move forward. We still have the same team we've always had, we've still got the same bloodlines working for us, and we still have the same passion and desire to move forward."

Frostad and Tammy Samuel-Balaz dreamed up the mating of *Eye of the Leopard*, a son of their homebred Woodbine Oaks winner, *Eye of the Sphynx*, with top U.S. sire *A.P. Indy*. *Eye of the Leopard* is the *Sphynx*'s first foal.

"This horse is somewhat of a legacy of the past and branch into the future," Mark Samuel said.

And *Eye of the Leopard* was among the last crop for which matriarch Liza found names. Even the big colt's nickname hearkens to the past. He's "*Lumpy*" on the backstretch. But "*Lumpy*" was also the nickname of one of Ernie Samuel's favourite horses, *Imperial Choice*, second in the 1985 Plate. Indeed, it seemed that on this day, Father's Day, history was repeating itself many times.

But things were changing, too. As the family found its new pulse, a fumbling economy tightened the noose for many businesses, including the steel business. For the first time in its forty-year history, Sam-Son sold a group of yearlings at auction in 2009. A group of five went to the Saratoga select yearling sale in August. Faced with a lot of farm expenses to pay, Sam-Son also shrank its racing stable from thirty-seven in 2008 to twenty-five in 2009. Frostad, long a private trainer for Sam-Son, welcomed some new clients to take up the slack for the first time.

Still, the 150th Queen's Plate acted like it was finding its second wind after an exhausting journey. It felt like one of the glory Plates of old. People jammed a trackside tent for the draw three days before, creating an unmistakable buzz. On the day of the Plate, cars jammed the parking lot, covering the grassy knolls in the far corners. People lined the walking ring six-deep. "I haven't seen anything like this for 30 years," said one hardboot.

And forget the recession. Wagering was brisk on Plate day, with an all sources total of $5,779,982 wagered on the eleven-race card. The only higher handles in Woodbine history came on Queen's Plate day in 2003 and on Breeders' Cup day in 1996.

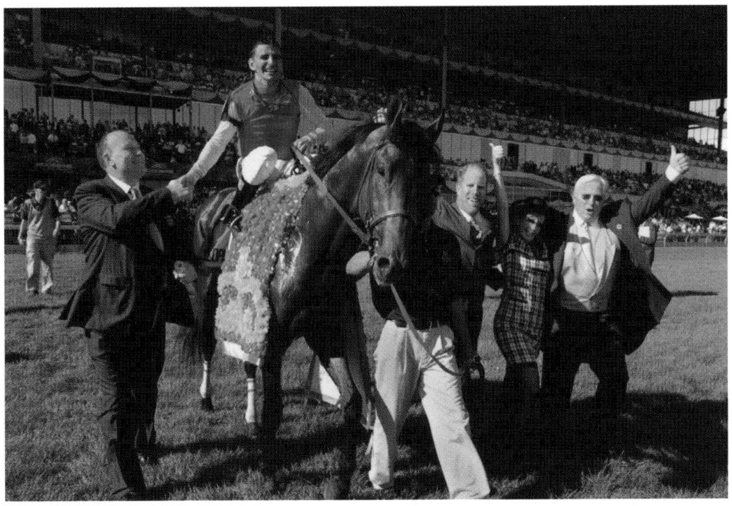

Eye of the Leopard's jockey Eurico Rosa Da Silva and owner Rick Balaz congratulate each other as the exuberant Sam-Sam Farm team crosses the track. Others include groom Cheeco Mendoza on the bridle, Sam-Son's Mark Samuel and Kim Samuel-Johnson and trainer Mark Frostad.

EYE OF THE LEOPARD | 3-year-old bay colt

Eye of the Leopard (2006)	A.P. Indy	Seattle Slew	Bold Reasoning
			My Charmer
		Weekend Surprise	Secretariat
			Lassie Dear
	Eye of the Sphynx	Smart Strike	Mr. Prospector
			Classy 'n Smart
		Queen of Egypt	Vice Regent
			Forelana

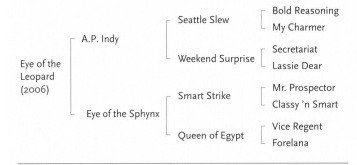

Owner: Sam-Son Farms, Milton, Ont.; *Trainer:* Mark R. Frostad
Jockey: Eurico Rosa Da Silva; *Breeder:* Sam-Son Farm, Ont.

As for the Samuels, they descended as a group of seventeen strong at Woodbine, including some "good old family friends," and some of the farm gang. They came early. "There is no more special day in racing in Canada than Queen's Plate day," Mark Samuel said. "We wanted to spend it together."

The youngsters in the group kept them distracted. The time flew. But by the time of the Plate, they began to feel anxious, so much so, that they were the first to head for the walking ring.

"The emotion was just as strong," Balaz said. "Losing Tammy made it that much more poignant for me and for my kids and I'm sure for Mark and Kim, because we are a close family."

In the months leading up to the Plate, neither Sam-Son nor *Eye of the Leopard* was on anybody's radar. U.S.-based *Square Eddie*, a Kinghaven-bred owned by Paul Reddam, was the winterbook favourite, but sat on the sidelines with injury.

It wasn't until *Eye of the Leopard* broke his maiden at Woodbine six weeks before the Plate, that he began to attract attention.

Reservoir and *Mr. Foricos Two U* set the early pace, while *Eye of the Leopard*, ridden by Brazilian import Eurico Rosa Da Silva, tucked in behind them while going three-wide of the first turn. Da Silva set the Sam-Son colt down for the stretch run, but at first appeared to make no dent on the *Mr. Foricos Two U*'s lead.

Gradually, while bearing out, *Eye of the Leopard* wore down the Catharine Day Phillips colt, a 7-to-1 shot ridden by U.S. Hall of Famer Mike Smith, to win by a neck in 2:03.84. Although Da Silva had been riding at Woodbine for five years, it was his first Plate mount and his first win.

Milwaukee Appeal, with Stewart Elliott aboard, was a closing third, after being blocked at the head of the stretch. Trainer Scott Fairlie felt that with a better trip, she could have won.

True to form, Da Silva exulted all the way to the winner's circle, in tears. He fell onto the horse's neck and patted the big colt. "I'm the happiest man in the world," he exclaimed. "I want to wish everybody good luck.

"I'm working hard and this is only the beginning," said the thirty-three-year-old. "I work much more harder now."

Smith said he didn't expect to make the lead on the backstretch, but *Mr. Foricos Two U* had been very much on his toes. "It was a gallant effort," he said of his horse. "I think that if *Eye of the Leopard* had been on my hip instead of *Milwaukee Appeal*, maybe I would have held him off because he didn't see him way out there."

In the furious fight to the finish, Da Silva whipped his mount twenty-five times with the new Lite Touch whip. Stewards fined both he and Smith for excessive whipping.

"I did use the whip more than I use in another race," Da Silva admitted. "But that whip, I can give for anybody to whip me. That whip don't hurt. Just make noise. I'm very sure I never hurt him."

NINTH RACE
Woodbine
JUNE 21, 2009

1¼ MILES. (2.03^{2}) 150TH RUNNING OF THE QUEEN'S PLATE. Purse $1,000,000 FOR THREE-YEAR-OLDS, FOALED IN CANADA.

Value of Race: $1,003,200(US $883,816) Winner $600,000 (US $528,600); second $200,000 (US $176,200); third $110,000 (US $96,910); fourth $60,000 (US $52,860); fifth $30,000 (US $26,430); sixth $400 (US $352); seventh $400 (US $352); eighth $400 (US $352); ninth $400 (US $352); tenth $400 (US $352); eleventh $400 (US $352); twelfth $400 (US $352); thirteenth $400 (US $352). Mutuel Pool $879,134.00 Exactor Pool $338,920.00 Triactor Pool $394,098.00 Superfecta Pool $198,185.00

Last Raced	Horse	M/Eqt.	A.	Wt	PP	¼	½	¾	1	Str	Fin	Jockey	Odds $1
31May09 ^{8}WO^{1}	Eye of the Leopard	L b	3	126	7	$3^{\frac{1}{2}}$	4^{hd}	4^{hd}	2^{1}	2^{2}	1^{nk}	Da Silva E R	2.35
27May09 ^{7}WO^{1}	Mr. Foricos Two U	L	3	126	5	2^{2}	2^{1}	1^{1}	$1^{\frac{1}{2}}$	$1^{\frac{1}{2}}$	2^{hd}	Smith M E	7.65
7Jun09 ^{9}WO^{1}	Milwaukee Appeal	L b	3	121	4	4^{hd}	5^{1}	$6^{1\frac{1}{2}}$	$4^{\frac{1}{2}}$	$3^{\frac{1}{2}}$	$3^{2\frac{3}{4}}$	Elliott S	4.05
7Jun09 ^{9}WO^{2}	Tasty Temptation	L b	3	121	11	7^{hd}	$8^{\frac{1}{2}}$	3^{hd}	$3^{\frac{1}{2}}$	4^{4}	$4^{2\frac{3}{4}}$	Husbands P	4.85
20May09 ^{1}WO^{3}	Flip for the Coin	L b	3	126	2	$9^{\frac{1}{2}}$	9^{2}	9^{7}	7^{1}	$5^{\frac{1}{2}}$	$5^{\frac{3}{4}}$	Ramsammy E	32.60
31May09 ^{8}WO^{5}	Keino West	L b	3	126	13	$12^{1\frac{1}{2}}$	13	13	12^{1}	8^{1}	6^{2}	Olguin G L	28.35
22May09 ^{4}WO^{3}	Shut It Down	L	3	126	12	11^{3}	$11^{2\frac{1}{2}}$	12^{1}	10^{1}	$6^{\frac{1}{2}}$	$7^{1\frac{1}{4}}$	Baze R A	22.35
31May09 ^{8}WO^{3}	Rapid Release	L	3	126	8	$6^{\frac{1}{2}}$	7^{1}	5^{hd}	6^{1}	$7^{2\frac{1}{2}}$	$8^{4\frac{3}{4}}$	Jones J	10.85
31May09 ^{7}WO^{2}	Stardust Ziggy	L	3	126	10	13	12^{hd}	11^{hd}	11^{2}	10^{1}	$9^{1\frac{1}{2}}$	Baird J	31.00
31May09 ^{8}WO^{6}	Bucephalus	L b	3	126	9	$10^{\frac{1}{2}}$	$10^{1\frac{1}{2}}$	10^{1}	13	13	10^{3}	Pizarro T	37.80
31May09 ^{6}WO^{1}	Reservoir	L b	3	126	6	1^{hd}	$1^{\frac{1}{2}}$	$2^{\frac{1}{2}}$	5^{1}	9^{1}	$11^{4\frac{1}{4}}$	McAleney J S	11.90
31May09 ^{8}WO^{4}	Active Duty	L	3	126	3	$8^{1\frac{1}{2}}$	6^{hd}	$8^{\frac{1}{2}}$	9^{2}	$12^{\frac{1}{2}}$	$12^{1\frac{1}{4}}$	Fraser C	36.65
31May09 ^{8}WO^{9}	El Brujo	L f	3	126	1	5^{1}	$3^{\frac{1}{2}}$	7^{hd}	8^{1}	11^{hd}	13	Wilson E	12.10

OFF AT 5:39 Start Good For All But KEINO WEST. Won driving. Track fast.

TIME :24, :48, $1:12^{4}$, $1:37^{2}$, $2:03^{4}$ (:24.05, :48.11, 1:12.93, 1:37.41, 2:03.84)

$2 Mutuel Prices:				
	7 – EYE OF THE LEOPARD	6.70	4.10	2.90
	5 – MR. FORICOS TWO U		7.20	4.60
	4 – MILWAUKEE APPEAL			3.70

$2 EXACTOR 7–5 PAID $56.10 $2 TRIACTOR 7–5–4 PAID $183.00
$1 SUPERFECTA 7–5–4–11 PAID $344.20

B. c, (Mar), by A.P. Indy – Eye of the Sphynx, by Smart Strike. Trainer Frostad Mark. Bred by Sam-Son Farm (Ont-C).

EYE OF THE LEOPARD stalked the pace up close from the outset, chased three-wide into the stretch, drifted out under left-handed urging a furlong out, straightened away and got up in the final strides. MR. FORICOS TWO U forced the pace then took a short lead entering the backstretch, set a pressured pace, extended his lead a bit on the far turn, battled through the stretch with EYE OF THE LEOPARD and gave way grudgingly in deep stretch. MILWAUKEE APPEAL stalked the pace from between horses, was boxed in at the head of the stretch then rallied determinedly when a pathway opened a furlong out.

Appendices

Plate Starters and Winners

YEAR	HORSE	FINISH	YEAR	HORSE	FINISH	YEAR	HORSE	FINISH
2004	A Bit O' Gold	2nd	2003	Arco's Gold	8th	1951	Bear Field	3rd
2005	Ablo	5th	1980	Arctic Morning	9th	1924	Beau of the West	11th
1940	Abydos	10th	1966	Arctic Troops	8th	1999	Beauty's Boy	17th
1952	Acadian	9th	1956	Argent	2nd	1935	Beechview	9th
1944	**Acara**	**1st**	1962	Argue Around	10th	**1914**	**Beehive**	**1st**
1955	**Ace Marine**	**1st**	2006	Ascot Bill	4th	1970	Bees Wax	15th (Eased)
2000	Ace Of Suedes	9th	2001	Asia	4th	1866	Beeswing	3rd
2009	Active Duty	12th	1989	Askar	15th	1980	Bejilla	5th
2002	Adjalah	9th	1963	Askum	16th	1953	Belflares	4th
1987	Afleet	2nd	1893	Aspinell	5th	1899	Bellcourt	7th
1889	Aide-de-Camp	9th	1929	Assail	6th	1900	Bellcourt	3rd
1890	Aide-de-Camp	5th	1893	Athalo	2nd	1901	Bellcourt	2nd
1892	Aide-de-Camp	15th	1881	Athlete	3rd	**1917**	**Belle Mahone**	**1st**
1997	Air Cool	4th	1883	Athlete	7th	1874	Belle of Ottawa	7th
1929	Airdrome	13th	2006	Atlas Shrugs	7th	1861	Belleville Lass	2nd
1982	Akhtiar	11th	1926	Attack	2nd	1886	Ben Bolt	4th
1981	Al Sarab	4th	2000	Attawapiskat	11th	1887	Ben Bolt	10th
1973	Albert the Consort	4th	1944	Attester	10th	1894	Ben Hur	5th
1892	Albert Victor	14th	1941	Attrisius	3rd	1864	Ben Olcutt	(Unplaced)
1937	Aldwych	6th	1887	Augusta	5th	1992	Benburb	3rd
1938	Aldwych	8th	1885	Aunt Alice	7th	1918	Bencher	10th
2007	Alezzandro	2nd	1886	Aunt Alice	5th	1920	Bencher	8th
1957	Ali's Pride	5th	1887	Aunt Alice	3rd	1955	Bernford	8th
1948	All British	13th	1889	Aunt Alice	7th	1956	Bernmar	10th
1995	All Firmed Up	5th	1983	Autumn Alley	13th	1887	Bessie	13th
1964	All Seasons	8th	1953	Avella	18th	1888	Bessie	7th
1980	Allan Blue	3rd	**1997**	**Awesome Again**	**1st**	1928	Best Bonnet	4th
2004	Alleged Ruler	7th	1984	Axe T.V.	10th	1967	Betemight	6th
2000	Allende	4th	**1930**	**Aymond**	**1st**	1933	Bethankful	9th
1952	Allison Pass	10th	1920	Azrael	6th	1953	Bettergo	17th
1970	**Almoner**	**1st**	1873	Bachelor	7th	1956	Big Berne	5th
1992	**Alydeed**	**1st**	1982	Backwoodsman	15th	1970	Big Blue Bomber	6th
1872	Alzora (late Gaiety)	4th	1955	Baffin Bay	2nd	1968	Big Blunder	2nd
1976	Ambassador B.	9th	1988	Baldski's Prize	11th	1953	Big Heap	6th
1974	**Amber Herod**	**1st**	1953	Ballyray	11th	1966	Big Jive	9th
1912	Amberite	2nd	1972	Barachois	2nd	1928	Bikos	11th
1877	**Amelia**	**1st**	2002	Barbeau Ruckus	7th	1907	Bilberry	3rd
1919	Ammunition	7th	1868	Barbeone (late Venture)	(Unplaced)	1951	Bill Armstrong	11th
2002	Anglian Prince	2nd	1950	Bard of Avon	9th	1907	Billeneer	12th
1920	Anmut	4th	1946	Barefoot Joe	8th	1885	Billie L.	11th
1924	Ann K.	13th	1900	Barley Sugar		1897	Billy Dinmount	9th
1894	Annie D.	9th		(by *Derwentwater)	5th	1955	Birch Hills	11th
1864	Annie Laurie	(Unplaced)	1972	Barley Sugar (by Ambernash)	11th	1963	Black n' Red	12th
1865	Annie Laurie	(Unplaced)	1864	Barney	(Unplaced)	1888	Blackbird	4th
1895	Annie Miller	10th	1892	Baronet	4th	1918	Blackburn	4th
1997	Annihilate	8th	1994	Barron Road	11th	1967	Blenheim Park	5th
1989	Antigonos	13th	**1994**	**Basqueian**	**1st**	1969	Blithe Victor	10th
1920	Antiphon	9th	1967	Battling	9th	1992	Blitzer	7th
1948	Anudona	16th	1872	Bay Boston	5th	1989	Blondeinamotel	4th
1943	Arbor Vita	2nd	1949	Bay Companion	6th	1927	Bloomtip	10th
2004	Archer Fleet	11th	1892	Bay Court	8th	1950	Blue Dance	12th
1998	**Archers Bay**	**1st**	1861	Bay Horse	(Unplaced)	**1961**	**Blue Light**	**1st**
1908	Archie Whyte	8th	**1869**	**Bay Jack**	**1st**	1965	Blue Mel	3rd
1939	**Archworth**	**1st**	**1865**	**Beacon (late Spring)**	**1st (Disq.)**	1953	Blue Scooter	2nd
			1866	**Beacon (late Spring)**	**1st**	1952	Blue Wrack	4th

YEAR	HORSE	FINISH	YEAR	HORSE	FINISH	YEAR	HORSE	FINISH
1946	Bluesweep	3rd	1937	Budron	4th	1992	Change of Fortune	9th
1892	Bob King	11th	1939	Budsis	6th	1974	Changeabout	10th
1860	Bob Marshall	2nd	1919	Bugle March	10th	1904	Chappell Boy	12th
1987	Bodmin Moor	11th	1920	Bugle March	2nd	1873	Charlotte R.	8th
1949	Bolaris	8th	1979	Bull Regent	9th (Eased)	1915	Charon	8th
1979	Bold Agent	2nd	1960	Bulpamiru	7th	1971	Chatty Cavalier	5th
1986	Bold Costume	10th	1990	Bundle Bits	6th	1922	Cheechako	7th
1987	Bold Executive	8th	1949	Bunty Jewel	5th	1923	Cheechako	2nd
2000	Bold n' Fancy	7th	**1938**	**Bunty Lawless**	**1st**	1993	Cheery Knight	2nd
1987	Bold Revenue	7th	1949	Bunty Line	4th	1895	Chickie	5th
1991	Bolulight	6th	1956	Bunty's Flight	6th	1935	Chickpen	2nd
1983	**Bompago**	**1st**	1947	Burboy	2nd	1996	Chief Bearhart	4th
1897	Bon Ino	2nd	1972	Burnt Grass	14th	1965	Chief Brant	10th
1898	**Bon Ino**	**1st**	1904	Butter Ladle	8th	1958	Chomiru	8th
1880	**Bonnie Bird**	**1st**	**1899**	**Butter Scotch**		1957	Chopadette	2nd
1888	Bonnie Boy	6th		**(by *Derwentwater)**	**1st**	1959	Chopayane	6th
1886	Bonnie Duke	6th	1974	Butterbump	5th	1962	Choperion	2nd
1867	**Bonnie Duke**	**1st**	1965	Butterscotch		2006	Cifercat	8th
1889	Bonnie Ino	2nd		(by Canadian Champ)	12th	1993	Circulating	6th
1900	Bonnie Maid	8th	2003	Button Wood	10th	1929	Circulet	14th
1882	Bonnie Vic	6th	1933	By the Sea	20th	2002	Classic Mike	8th
1895	**Bonniefield**	**1st**	1966	Bye and Near	2nd	1982	Cliff House	(Fell)
1928	Bonnington	2nd	1976	Bye Bye Paris	10th	1896	Clipmount	9th
1953	Bonsand	10th	1980	Bye Bye Tony	11th	1925	Cloth Hall	9th
1897	Boston	8th	1925	Byng Boy	15th	1926	Cloth Hall	7th
1997	Bowmore	14th	1997	C.C. On Ice	13th	2007	Cobrador	8th
1896	Bradlaugh	7th	1938	Cabin Gal	3rd	1899	Cocoanut	9th
1885	Braewood	13th	**1958**	**Caledon Beau**	**1st**	1948	Coleraine	15th
1886	Braewood	8th	1912	Calumny	4th	1864	Colleen Bawn	(Unplaced)
1930	Brave Alonzo	10th	1992	Cambridge Champ	11th	**1954**	**Collisteo**	**1st**
1950	Brazen Buz	11th	**1956**	**Canadian Champ**	**1st**	**1889**	**Colonist**	**1st**
1963	Breezy Answer	5th	1958	Canadian Flyer	13th	1978	Colourful Conn	4th
1982	Briar Wind	12th	**1953**	**Canadiana**	**1st**	1973	Combat Day	10th
1953	Briarcrest	13th	1934	Candy Feast	5th	1967	Come by Chance	3rd
1971	Briartic	6th	**1963**	**Canebora**	**1st**	1994	Comet Shine	5th
1993	Briartic Star	9th	1933	Canny Age	13th	1910	Commola	2nd
1868	Brickbat	(Unplaced)	1986	Cap Trinite	6th	1963	Common Market	13th
2006	Bridgecut	12th	1927	Capitol	6th	1904	Con Amore	6th
1979	Bridle Path	6th	1907	Capstan	10th	1895	Confectioner	6th
1992	Bright Feather	8th	1908	Capstan	9th	1976	Confederation	3rd
1966	Bright Monarch	3rd	1917	Captain B.	4th	1974	Conversation	13th
1887	Bright Star	6th	1938	Caracole	5th	1986	Cool Halo	2nd
1929	Brilliant Diamond	17th	1951	Caralita	8th	1971	Cool Moon	4th
1975	Brilliant Sandy	5th	1903	Cardigan	7th	1984	Cool Northerner	5th
1900	Bringloe	14th	1929	Carey	18th (Pulled Up)	2004	Copper Trail	9th
1898	Bristles	7th	1933	Cartwheel	14th	1919	Cora W.	6th
1917	Britannia (by Bannockburn)	9th	1888	Cast Off	3rd	1993	Corporate Runner	8th
1951	Britannia (by Bunty Lawless)	4th	1889	Cast Off	6th	1980	Corvette Chris	15th
1998	Brite Adam	2nd	1884	Castilena	10th	1945	Corvita	8th
1991	British Banker	9th	1959	Castleberry	14th	1951	Corwynt	18th
1931	Bronze	2nd	1999	Catahoula Parish	7th	1942	Cossack Post	2nd
1932	Bronze	7th	1924	Catamaran	(Fell)	1957	Count Teddy	11th
1933	Bronze	17th	1925	Catamaran	5th	1891	Countess	4th
1998	Bronze Shoal	8th	1937	Cease Fire	2nd	1867	Country Maid (see Kate Allan)	2nd
1896	Brother Bob	5th	1928	Cedar Crest	9th	1975	Countryman	8th
1959	Brown Panther	9th	1956	Censor	4th	1979	Coup de Chance	8th
1994	Bruce's Mill	2nd	1959	Chada	17th	1975	Coup de Soleil	13th
1864	**Brunette**	**1st**	1953	Chain Reaction	7th	1967	Courant d'Air	13th
2001	Brushing Bully	3rd	1936	Chalgo	6th	1906	Court Martial	2nd
2009	Bucephalus	10th	1960	Champagne Velvet	3rd	1909	Courtier	5th
1938	Bucharest	13th	1987	Chance For Green	9th	1997	Cowboy Cop	6th
1941	**Budpath**	**1st**	1948	Chance Toss	11th	1990	Cozzene's Prince	8th

YEAR	HORSE	FINISH
2002	Cree Power	11th
1989	Creed	8th
1970	Croquemitaine	10th
1905	Cross of Gold	6th
1996	Crown Attorney	7th
1920	Crown of Gold	7th
1921	Crown of Gold	5th
1985	Crowning Honors	4th
1983	Crushed Ice	9th
1997	Cryptocloser	2nd
1913	Crystiawoga	8th
1929	Cuddle Doon	5th
1944	Cum Laude	5th
1865	Cumberland Maid	(Unplaced)
1866	Cumberland Maid	5th
1899	Curfew Bell	4th
1900	Curfew Bell	12th
1947	Curly J.	14th
1940	Curwen	2nd
1951	Cymro	7th
2008	D.Flutie	13th
1887	D.W.C.	12th
2007	Daaher	4th
1901	Daddy	14th
1968	Dainty Davie	6th
1891	Daisy Deane	10th
1929	Daisy Fair	10th
1899	Dalliance	6th
1897	Dalmoor	4th
1898	Dalmoor	2nd
1899	Dalmoor	2nd
1900	**Dalmoor**	**1st**
1929	Dance Circle	11th
2003	Dance Engagement	5th
1991	**Dance Smartly**	**1st**
1970	Dance to Market	4th
2005	Dance With Ravens	7th
2001	**Dancethruthedawn**	**1st**
1984	Dancing Hare	7th
1914	Dark Rosaleen	2nd
1967	Dauphin Bleu	10th
1985	Dauphin Fabuleux	14th
1999	Dave the Comet	8th
1926	Davenport	4th
1946	David T.	2nd
2001	Dawn Watcher	7th
1969	Day Will Come	14th
1984	Dayspring	9th
1970	Dean of York	9th
1980	Decent Davey	6th
1941	Depositor	8th
1942	Depressor	3rd
2008	Deputiformer	4th
1965	Des Erables	8th
1903	Deseronto	12th
1995	Desert Falcon	14th
1936	Desert Place	11th
1909	Desert Star	4th
1862	Diana	(Unplaced)
1983	Diapason	6th
1894	Dictator	7th
1896	Dictator	3rd
1884	Direction	11th
1947	Dirigo	13th
1995	Disciple	8th
1864	Disdain	(Unplaced)
1974	Doctor McKay	14th (Eased)
1908	Dog of War	7th
1909	Dog of War	6th
1919	Doleful	2nd
1890	Dom Pedro	4th
1892	Dom Pedro	6th
1989	Domasca Dan	3rd
1996	Domasca Dave	13th
1860	**Don Juan**	**1st**
1951	Donstan	14th
1935	Donstick	5th
1902	Doonside	9th
1955	Dorenes Lad	12th
1946	Double Briar	5th
1958	Dr. Em Jay	4th
1899	Dr. Jack	14th
1952	Dress Circle	7th
1884	Driftwood	7th
1882	Driftwood	11th
1980	**Driving Home**	**1st**
1882	Duchess	14th
1925	Duchess (by Simon Square)	2nd
1987	Duckpower	4th
1886	Duke of Wellington	10th
1980	Duns Scotus	10th
1928	Dushka	6th
1929	Dushka	7th
1980	Dusty Old Farmer	4th
2008	Dylan's Choice	14th
1994	Dynamite Stuff	10th
2008	East End Tap	6th
1882	Easter	5th
1932	Easter Dandy	6th
1932	Easter Hatter	5th
1933	Easter Hatter	2nd
1902	Eastern Prince	8th
1881	Echo	5th
1966	Echo Lad	5th
2006	**Edenwold**	**1st**
1961	Edgor's Lane	12th
1864	Edmonton	3rd (Dead heat)
1884	Edmonton (by Stockwood)	5th
1885	Edmonton (by Stockwood)	3rd
1935	Eileen D.	6th
2009	El Brujo	13th
2003	El Gran Maestro	9th
1922	El Jesmar	3rd
1913	Elfain	7th
1866	Eliza C. (late Nora Criena)	(Unplaced)
1927	Eliza Jane	9th
1891	Ella B.	5th
1873	Emily	4th
1874	Emily	2nd
1875	Emma P. (see Sunnyside)	3rd
1939	Ensign Mary	8th
1949	**Epic**	**1st**
1958	Epic Lad	9th
1935	Epicurus	4th
1936	Epicurus	3rd
1952	**Epigram**	**1st**
1952	Eric's Girl	5th
1951	Erindale Kid	(Lost Rider)
1975	Eskimo Bay	11th
1958	Eskimo Flyer	10th
1986	Essa Lad	11th
1967	Ette Rule	12th
1999	Euchre	3rd
1900	Euclaire	6th
1901	Euclaire	5th
1888	Evangeline	2nd
1889	Evangeline	4th
1982	Exclusive Canadian (Placed 5th)	6th
1907	Excuse	11th
1914	Exmer	6th
1878	Exotic	3rd
1993	Explosive Red	5th
2009	**Eye of the Leopard**	**1st**
1971	Fabe Count	2nd
1973	Fabiusand	6th
1948	Face Off	10th
1999	Fadder Ted	14th
1919	Fair and Warmer	12th
1920	Fair and Warmer	11th
1930	Fair Fortune	16th
1945	Fair Jester	4th
1948	Fair Mark	14th
1915	Fair Montague	2nd
1945	Fair Patsy	11th
1955	Fair Shore	15th
1955	Faïrator	16th
1925	**Fairbank**	**1st**
1951	Fairlow	13th
1966	Famous Monarch	11th
1969	Fanfaron	2nd
1970	Fanfreluche	2nd
1889	Fanny Carter	8th
1880	Fanny Wiser	2nd
1882	**Fanny Wiser**	**1st**
1903	Farmer's Foe	11th
1959	Farshore	8th
2000	Fartherthanuthink	13th
1872	**Fearnaught**	**1st**
1897	**Ferdinand**	**1st**
1901	Ferney Tickle	3rd
1902	Ferney Tickle	15th
1945	Ferry Pilot	3rd
1931	Fess	6th
1999	Festive Knight	5th
1983	Feu d'Enfer	7th
1897	Fiddle	5th
1981	**Fiddle Dancer Boy**	**1st**
1972	Fifty Guineas	10th
1985	Fighting Champ	9th
1967	Fils du Nord	11th
1949	Filsis	3rd
1969	Fire n Desire	3rd
1952	Firey Gal	20th
1996	Firm Dancer	5th
1906	First Robber	6th

YEAR	HORSE	FINISH	YEAR	HORSE	FINISH	YEAR	HORSE	FINISH
1885	Fisherman	5th	2002	Fuzzy Star	5th	1938	Grand Dame	4th
1886	Fisherman	9th	1870	Gaiety (seee Alzora)	(Unplaced)	1964	Grand Garcon	3rd
1874	Fisherwoman	3rd	1916	Gala Day	3rd	1992	Grand Hooley	2nd
1875	Fisherwoman	7th	1917	Gala Dress	3rd	1904	Grand Lodge	9th
1876	Fisherwoman	(Unplaced)	1916	Gala Water	2nd	1977	Grand Luxe	7th
1962	**Flaming Page**	**1st**	1943	Gallant Foe	8th	1943	Grandpal	4th
1952	Flareday	19th	1920	Gallant Kitty	5th	2005	Granique	6th
1961	Flashing Top	9th	1917	Galley Head	5th	1930	Granite Rock	14th
1993	Flashy Regent	4th	1919	Galway	8th	1943	Gray Syngo	5th
1921	Flea	9th	1923	Game Scrapper	11th	1949	Graydon Tina	11th
1955	Fleet Brenda	13th	1999	Gandria	2nd	1999	Great Defender	16th
1955	Fleet Countess	14th	1960	Garden Greek	8th	1971	Great Gabe	3rd
1861	Fleeting Moments	3rd	1907	Gay Dora	9th	1982	Great Stake	10th
1993	Fleetward	10th	1921	Gay Kap	6th	1979	Great State	7th
1890	Flip Flap	3rd	1927	Gay Parisian	8th	1955	Great West	(Lost Rider)
2009	Flip for the Coin	5th	1935	Gay Sympathy	3rd	1975	Greek Answer	9th
1945	Floral Gift	12th	1927	Gems to Let	3rd	1986	Grey Classic	8th
1923	Floralia	12th	1872	General Blacksmith	6th	1876	Grey Cloud (ex. Thunder colt)	4th
1947	Florist	10th	1884	General Butler	14th	1988	Grey Skelly	4th
1871	**Floss**	**1st**	1909	Generous Moor	8th	1969	Grey Whiz	6th
1923	**Flowerful**	**1st**	1888	Genesta	5th	1922	Greybourne	8th
1892	Fly	12th	1952	Genthorn	2nd	1928	Grubstake	8th
1965	Flyalong	2nd	1972	Gentleman Conn	3rd	1963	Guiding Wave	19th
1902	Fly-in-Amber	2nd	1959	George Handy	18th	1882	Gwendoline	10th
1903	Fly-in-Amber	(Broke down)	1972	George of Canada	6th	1944	Gypster	12th
1957	Flying Atom	3rd	1999	Geraint	15th	1944	Haggerty	11th
1959	Flying Grey	7th	2005	Get Down	8th	1907	Half a Crown	2nd
1953	Food For Thot	9th	1977	Giboulee	3rd	1908	Half a Crown	3rd
2000	For Our Sake	3rd	1982	Gifted Prince	7th	1905	Half Seas Over	3rd
1995	For Pete's Sake	7th	1930	Gilded Casino	18th	1907	Halfcaste	14th
2002	Ford Every Stream	4th	1967	Gilmore	8th	1990	Halo's Honey	10th
1937	Fore Isus	15th	1871	Gimcrack	4th	1872	Halton (late Chas. Douglas)	3rd
1925	Forecast II	4th	2008	Ginger Brew	2nd	1962	Hammer 'n Tongs	7th
2002	Forever Grand	3rd	1868	Gladiateur (late Dan)	(Unplaced)	1915	Hampton Dame	5th
1873	Forrest colt	9th	1891	Gladstone	7th	1996	Handsome Hansel	12th
1909	Fort Garry	3rd	1892	Gladstone	5th	1987	Hangin On a Star	13th
1972	Fort Myers	15th	1887	Glencairn	11th	1928	Hanna Deebe	3rd
1978	Forty Bye Two	11th	1935	Goggles	12th	**1926**	**Haplite**	**1st**
1989	Forum Fighter	9th	1931	Golader	9th	1958	Happy Harry	5th
1958	Foxy Phil	6th	1912	Gold Bud	6th	1876	Harper Jr.	(Unplaced)
1949	Foxy Rythm	12th	1913	Gold Bud	3rd	1882	Harper Lexington	9th
1932	Fragrant Gift	10th	1914	Gold Bud	5th	1894	Harry A.	8th
1882	Francis L.	12th	1928	Gold Era	10th	1915	Harry Bassett II	9th
1887	Fred B	4th	1939	Gold Fawn	13th (Pulled up)	1887	Harry Cooper	7th
1884	Fred Henry	8th	1918	Gold Galore	5th	**1888**	**Harry Cooper**	**1st**
1885	Fred Henry	2nd	1937	Gold Guard	11th	1989	Harry Laric	10th
1886	Fred Henry	2nd	2005	Gold Strike	3rd	1906	Haruko	3rd
1887	Fred Henry	2nd	**1986**	**Golden Choice**	**1st**	1980	Hasty Rick	8th
1889	Fred Henry	10th	1903	Golden Crest	3rd	1911	Havrock	4th
1995	Freedom Fleet	2nd	1904	Golden Crest	7th	1912	Havrock	7th
1931	Freethinker	8th	1905	Golden Crest	5th	1980	Hawaiian Fighter	12th
1990	French King	12th	1937	Golden Silence	8th	1903	Hawkins	4th
1933	Frigid Frosty	6th	1902	Golden Way	14th	1904	Hawkins	4th
1982	Frigid Lady	14th	1873	Goldfinch	3rd	1928	Head Lad	12th
1940	Frobisher	4th	1925	Goldlands	6th	1933	Heap Good	7th
1914	Froissart	7th	**1937**	**Goldlure**	**1st**	**1913**	**Hearts of Oak**	**1st**
1910	Frolic	6th	1983	Gone to Royalty	4th	1923	Hearts of Rock	9th
1931	**Froth Blower**	**1st**	1908	Good Likeness	12th	1921	Heath Bell	4th
1921	Fuse	8th	1965	Good Old Mort	5th	1892	Heather Bloom	3rd
1922	Fuse	5th	1973	Good Port	13th	1892	Heather Bloom	3rd
1863	Fusilier (late Pluto)	4th	1961	Gramp's Pride	5th	1904	Heather Jock	5th
1985	Fustukian	13th	1988	Granacus	3rd	1865	Hecate	(Pulled up)

YEAR	HORSE	FINISH
1881	Helmbold colt	7th
1944	Hemfox	7th
1919	Hemisphere	11th
1945	Hemjohn	9th
1945	Hemseven	16th
1957	Henry B. Good	4th
1972	Henry Tudor	5th
1954	Heptad	7th
1883	Hercules	8th
1921	**Herendesy**	**1st**
1912	**Heresy**	**1st**
1926	Heretrix	5th
1944	Heulwen	8th
1945	Heydunette	6th
1944	Heysiris	6th
1954	Hi Laude	5th
1960	Hidden Treasure	5th
1952	Hielan Laddie	6th
1983	High Chicago	11th
1978	High Roller	7th
1860	Highflier	(Unplaced)
2001	Highland Legacy	9th
1868	Highland Maid	(Unplaced)
1870	Highland Maid	(Unplaced)
1892	Hindoo	13th
2004	His Smoothness	5th
1925	Hoi Polloi	7th
1966	Holarctic	4th
1957	Holiday Ted	7th
1924	Honey Dear	9th
1923	Honey's Jewel	10th
1919	Hong Kong	3rd
1995	Honky Tonk Tune	11th
1940	Hood	3rd
1976	Hook and Draw	5th
1963	Hop Hop	10th
1934	**Horometer**	**1st**
2006	Hot Deputy	9th
1926	Huckleberry	14th
1875	Hurricane	6th
1877	Hurricane	2nd
1945	Hustling Doom	7th
2000	I And I	2nd
1863	Iago (see Paul Barnes)	3rd
1864	Iago (see Paul Barnes)	(Unplaced)
1995	Ice Agent	13th
1928	Ichitaro	7th
1929	Ichitaro	2nd
1930	Ichitaro	3rd
1982	Icy Circle	4th (Disq. Placed Last)
1926	Ifs and ands	11th
2003	Illusive Force	12th
1993	Imperial Bandit	11th
1985	Imperial Choice	2nd
1922	Impersonator	10th
1951	Impone	17th
1973	Impressive Lady	15th
1985	In My Cap	4th
1986	In The East	7th
1967	In the Ring	14th
2007	Include Us	5th
1905	**Inferno**	**1st**
1973	Ingenious Device	7th
1883	Inspector	6th
1996	Intended Passage	8th
1976	Intrepid Spirit	11th (Eased)
1874	Irish Girl	5th
1929	Irish Sphere	15th
1990	Iskandar Elakbar	3rd
1922	Islander	11th
1937	Isleworth	7th
1924	Isoletta	4th
1989	Ivory Dance	11th
1867	Izeppa	4th
1990	**Izvestia**	**1st**
1884	J.C. Patterson	12th
1884	J.P. Wiser	4th
1903	Jack Canuck	9th
1881	Jack Davis	9th
1872	Jack Vandal	2nd
1869	Jack-on-the-Green	4th
1870	Jack-on-the-Green	2nd
1967	**Jammed Lovely**	**1st**
1961	Jammed Lucky	8th
1969	Jammed Red	4th
1910	Jane Shore	3rd
1911	Jane Shore	3rd
1912	Jane Shore	10th
1993	Janraffole	3rd
1892	Japonica	9th
1942	Jayeffdee	7th
1925	Jean Crest	3rd
1958	Jeansen	14th
1939	Jelwell	5th
1867	Jennie Robinson	(Unplaced)
1898	Jessamine Porter II	5th
1881	Jessie McCulloch	2nd
2007	Jiggs Coz	3rd
1891	Jim Berry	9th
1887	Jim Ferris	14th
1950	Jim's Icra	14th
1912	Joe Gaiety	9th
1894	**Joe Miller**	**1st**
1948	Joey Bomber	3rd
1870	**John Bell**	**1st**
1868	John Collins	3rd
1901	**John Ruskin**	**1st**
1997	John the Magician	10th
1916	Johnnie Austin	6th
1890	Johnny Hunter	6th
1975	Johnny One Step	12th
1867	Johnny Schmoker	(Unplaced)
1958	Jokers Hill	11th
1882	Jonathan Scott	13th
1992	Judge Carson	5th
1936	Judge Pool	13th
1969	**Jumpin Joseph**	**1st**
2008	Jungle Brew	9th
1933	Juniam	12th
1961	Just Don't Shove	2nd
2004	Just In Case Jimmy	4th
1926	Just in Fun	8th
1901	Juvencus	15th
1949	Kan Dis	13th
1947	Kanlee	4th
1946	Kanshore	7th
1901	Kaslo	7th
1869	Kate Allan (late Country Maid)	2nd
1870	Kate Kennett	(Unplaced)
1940	Katie Bud	7th
1992	Keen Falcon	10th
2009	Keino West	6th
1907	Kelpie	7th
1920	Keltie	14th
1907	**Kelvin**	**1st**
1971	**Kennedy Road**	**1st**
2004	Kent Ridge	10th
1990	Key Timing	5th
1984	**Key to the Moon**	**1st**
1946	Khabula	4th
1933	Khaki John	10th
1948	Kid Rumble	8th
1895	Kiltie	8th
1878	King Dodds	5th
1879	King Dodds	2nd
1878	**King George**	**1st**
1962	King Gorm	4th
1893	King Joe	7th
1892	King John	16th
1897	King Ken	10th
1954	King Maple	3rd
1932	King O'Connor	2nd
1933	**King O'Connor**	**1st**
2005	King of Jazz	2nd
1990	King Riviera	13th
1880	King Tom	3rd
1946	**Kingarvie**	**1st**
1970	King's Champion	13th
1922	King's Court	9th
1998	Kinkennie	3rd
1980	Kinsmans Glory	18th (Eased)
1995	Kiridashi	4th
1907	Kirkfield	5th
1931	Kirkland Post	11th
1890	**Kitestring**	**1st**
1864	Kitty Clyde	(Unplaced)
1861	Know Nothing	(Unplaced)
1952	Koofla	14th
1944	Korafloyd	3rd
1996	Kristy Krunch	3rd
1890	La Blanche	2nd
1891	La Blanche	2nd
1985	**La Lorgnette**	**1st**
1973	La Prevoyante	8th
1957	Lad Ator	9th
1917	Ladder of Light	6th
1918	Ladder of Light	2nd
1919	**Ladder of Light**	**1st**
1867	Lady Augusta	(Unplaced)
1963	Lady B. Fast	17th
1901	Lady Berkeley	9th
1902	Lady Bevys	16th
1891	Lady Blair	11th
1860	Lady Carleton	(Unplaced)
1862	Lady Carleton	2nd
1915	Lady Curzon	4th

YEAR	HORSE	FINISH	YEAR	HORSE	FINISH	YEAR	HORSE	FINISH
1885	Lady Dora	12th	1980	Lord Costume	13th	1924	**Maternal Pride**	**1st**
1902	Lady Essex	13th	1880	Lord Dufferin	4th	1913	Mausolus	5th
1878	Lady Harper	6th	1948	Lord Fairmond	2nd	1918	May Bloom	3rd
1902	Lady M.	17th	1952	Lord Strome	8th	1894	May Blossom	10th
1870	Lady May	(Unplaced)	1971	Lord Vancouver	7th	1923	Maypole	5th
1927	Lady McNeil	13th	1996	Lorries Mane Man	11th	1924	Maypole	3rd
1865	**Lady Norfolk**	**1st**	1893	Lou Daly	4th	1918	McCorburn	13th
1895	Lady Sinclair	7th	1894	Lou Daly	3rd	**1950**	**McGill**	**1st**
1898	Lady Sinclair	9th	1868	Louisa	(Unplaced)	1939	McMark	12th
1941	Lady Wales	9th	1997	Love View	5th	1968	McSam	12th
1933	Lady Worthmore	22nd	1974	Lovely Sunrise	7th	1948	Meal Time	6th
1936	Ladymuch	4th	1930	Love's Arrow	13th	1963	Medalia S.	18th
1950	Lady's Lover	8th	1953	Lowmond	8th	1950	Medalofreedom	4th
1976	Laissez-Passer	4th	1955	Loyalist	4th	1893	Mediator	6th
1976	Lake Huron	6th	1978	Lucky Colonel S.	6th	1927	Meeran	11th
1978	L'Alezane	3rd	1988	Lucky J.W.	9th	1868	Meg Merilies	(Unplaced)
1964	Langcrest	2nd	1965	Lucky Marine	6th	1991	Megas Vukefalos	5th
1995	Langfuhr	6th	1973	Lucky Master	9th	1960	Men at Play	4th
1948	**Last Mark**	**1st**	1952	Lucky Pass	16th	1963	Menedict	7th
1915	Last Spark	6th	1969	Lucky Red Patch	8th	1893	Mercury	9th
1916	Last Spark	5th	2001	Lucky Scarab	5th	**1968**	**Merger**	**1st**
1964	Later Mel	6th	1885	Lucy Lightfoot	6th	1955	Merry Life	10th
1952	Latin Lad	3rd	1951	Luscoe's Pride	19th	1894	Merrythought	11th
1962	Lavella	8th	**1902**	**Lyddite**	**1st**	1929	Meteor Sparks	8th
1956	Lawday	7th	**1957**	**Lyford Cay**	**1st**	1924	Mexican Pete	7th
1981	Le Botaniste	9th	1972	Madly Magic	13th	1957	Midi Blue	12th
1982	Le Danseur	3rd	1870	Maggie	(Unplaced)	**1873**	**Mignonette**	**1st**
1976	Le Gaspesien	8th	1886	Maggie May	7th	**2007**	**Mike Fox**	**1st**
1982	Le Grand Argentier	5th (Placed 4th)	1887	Maggie May	9th	1970	Mildenhall	14th
1959	Le Grand Rouge	13th	1900	Magog	4th	1976	Military Bearing	2nd
1981	Le Grand Seigneur	6th	1905	Maid of Barrie	4th	1939	Milius	7th
1981	Le Promeneur	16th	1913	Maid of Frome	2nd	1953	Millbrook (by Flares)	14th
1897	Leading Lady	6th	1961	Maid O'North	11th	1895	Millbrook (by Springfield)	2nd
1898	Leading Lady	6th	**1951**	**Major Factor**	**1st**	**1896**	**Millbrook (by Springfield)**	**1st**
1911	Legislator	7th	1959	Major Flight	2nd	2001	Millennium Allstar	8th
1975	**L'Enjoleur**	**1st**	1963	Major's Choice	9th	1961	Milton Man	7th
1999	Lenny the Lender	4th	2006	Malakoff	3rd	2009	Milwaukee Appeal	3rd
1947	Leonforte	12th	1984	Male Ego	12th	1968	Mink Stole	13th
1984	Let's Go Blue	2nd	2008	Mamma's Knight	7th	1952	Minnedosa	17th
1865	Lettie Brown	(Unplaced)	**1916**	**Mandarin**	**1st**	1885	Minnie A	9th
1881	Lexington	8th	1978	Maple Grove	9th	1884	Minnie Byers	9th
1951	Libertine	2nd	1901	Maple Sugar	4th	1873	Minnie Langley	6th
1869	Liberty (late Nelson)	3rd	1902	Maple Sugar	5th	1862	Mischief	(Unplaced)
1870	Liberty (late Nelson)	(Unplaced)	1903	Maple Sugar	8th	1884	Miss Bruce	15th
1873	Lilly	5th	1950	Maple Wood	6th	1927	Miss Content	12th
1974	Lincoln Fields	6th	1896	Marcella	8th	1900	Miss Dart	9th
1979	Linda's Laughin	5th	2007	Marchfield	6th	1932	Miss Gormley	9th
1929	Lindsay	3rd	1871	Maria Paton	5th	1911	Miss Martimas	8th
1930	Lindsay	7th	1861	Marion	(Lost Rider)	1959	Miss Whiskit	19th
1935	Listaro	10th	1898	Maritana II	3rd	1980	Mister Country	7th
1927	Listerine	15th	**1987**	**Market Control**	**1st**	1984	Mister Lorenzo	8th
1928	Little Margie B.	14th	1882	Marquis	8th	1981	Misty Mogul	12th
1953	Lively Action	3rd	1883	Marquis	4th	1948	Misty Waters	9th
1920	Lively Sleeper	10th	1884	Marquis	2nd	2003	Mobil	2nd
1894	Lochinvar	6th	1903	Marston Moor	13th	1884	Modjeska	3rd
1895	Lochinvar	3rd	1892	Martello	7th	**1947**	**Moldy**	**1st**
1896	Lochinvar	6th	**1893**	**Martello**	**1st**	2005	Molinaro Beau	4th
2000	Lodge Hill	6th	1867	Mary Elliott	(Unplaced)	1921	Moll Cutpurse	3rd
1956	London Calling	3rd	1876	Mary L.	2nd (Disq. Placed last)	1922	Moll Cutpurse	6th
1989	Lone Pine	7th	1970	Mary of Scotland	5th	1938	Mona Bell	2nd
2004	Long Pond	13th	1912	Marybud	8th	1962	Monarch Park	9th
1889	Long Shot	3rd	1929	Master Bobbie	9th	**1936**	**Monsweep**	**1st**

YEAR	HORSE	FINISH	YEAR	HORSE	FINISH	YEAR	HORSE	FINISH
1913	Porcupine	10th	**1988**	**Regal Intention**	**1st**	1936	Samoan	5th
1914	Porcupine	8th	1981	Regal Kapers	15th	1991	San Cielo	8th
1978	Portage Bay	10th	1981	Regal Stafford	5th	1936	Sandalman	8th
1937	Poverty Struck	10th	1949	Regan Lad	7th	1937	Sandalman	12th
1911	Powderman	2nd	1982	Regency Gold	13th	1911	Sanderling	6th
1985	Pre Emptive Strike	3rd	1977	Regent Bird	8th	1910	Sandy Kirkwood	10th
1978	Preacher Joe	5th	1981	Regent Cat	14th	**1904**	**Sapper**	**1st**
1972	Presidial	8th	1993	Regent Runner	7th	1875	Sappho	5th
1951	Prey Seven	10th	1981	Regimen	10th	1899	Sardonyx	8th
1867	Pride of Erin	3rd	1984	Repatriate	14th	1908	Sauce o' Gold	11th
1998	Primaly	10th	1921	Resarf	7th	1909	Sauce o' Gold	7th
1920	Primo	3rd	2009	Reservoir	11th	1902	Saucy Sally	18th
1963	Prince Bubi	6th	1964	Return Trip	4th	1944	Sayonara	4th
1963	Prince Maple	14th	1902	Revelstoke	11th	1951	Scapa Blow	12th
1995	Prince of North	10th	1975	Rex Favor	6th	1918	Scarboro Beach	12th
1863	Prince Patrick	(Unplaced)	1963	Rich	8th	1955	Scarboro Lass	6th
1961	Prince Tour	10th	1868	Ridgeway	(Unplaced)	**2000**	**Scatter the Gold**	**1st**
1883	Princess Louise	3rd	1881	Rienzi	6th	1902	Scotland Yet	6th
1994	Prix de Crouton	8th	1940	Ring Wise	11th (Pulled up)	1939	Sea Cadet	11th
1977	Pro Consul	4th	1917	Ringdove	7th	1982	Sea Chestnut	(Fell)
1991	Professor Rabbit	7th	1983	Rising Young Star	5th	1918	Sea Froth	8th
2006	Pyramid Park	13th	1994	Road Rush	4th	1939	Sea General	2nd
1927	Quartzite	16th	1950	Roanite	13th	1914	Sea Lord	3rd
1926	Quartz-Sinter	10th	1999	Roaring Twenties	9th	1959	Sea Page	16th
1930	Quatra Bras	5th	2003	Rock Again	3rd	1907	Sea Wall	13th
1933	Que Toi	15th	1936	Rock Sure	10th	2008	Sebastian's Song	10th
1860	Queen	4th (Retired)	1983	Rockcliffe	3rd	1983	Second Candy	12th
1892	Queen Mary	2nd	1913	Rockspring	9th	1990	Secret 'n Classy	4th
1954	Queen's Own	2nd	**1883**	**Roddy Pringle**	**1st**	1931	Sedgerose	12th
1961	Queen's Park	6th	1880	Roderick	5th	**1908**	**Seismic**	**1st**
1973	Queen's Splendour	11th	1882	Roderick	4th	1955	Senator Jim	3rd
1932	**Queensway**	**1st**	1992	Rodin	4th	1957	Senor Teddy	10th
1960	Quintain	2nd	1990	Roll the Dice	7th	1932	Serfman	8th
1997	Rabbit in a Hat	9th	1985	Roman Emporer	6th	1924	Seven Oaks	5th
1966	Radiant Colors	10th	1900	Rosa D.	15th	1863	Shadow	
1992	Ragnarok	12th	1890	Rose Maybud	(Broke down)		(late Beauregard)	(Lost Rider)
1991	Rainbows for Life	4th	1940	Rose Mountain	5th	1925	Shadow Dance	12th
1923	Rallim	4th	1866	Rose of Allandale	(Unplaced)	2008	Shadowless	11th
1979	Ram Good	3rd	1868	Rose of Allandale	(Unplaced)	1932	Shady Well	4th
1961	Ramblin Wreck	3rd	1968	Rouletabille	3rd	1875	Sharpcatcher	8th
1949	Ramillion	10th	1949	Royal Bomber	9th	2002	Shaws Creek	6th
1870	Rapid Rain (late Roanoke)	4th	**1973**	**Royal Chocolate**	**1st**	2006	Shillelagh Slew	5th
2009	Rapid Release	8th	1922	Royal Gift	4th	1908	Shimonese	2nd
1974	Rash Move	9th	1932	Royal Guest	11th	**1909**	**Shimonese**	**1st**
1988	Rather Theatrical	8th	1963	Royal Maple	4th	2003	Shoal Water	4th
1868	Rathowen	4th	1986	Royal Treasurer	5th	**1929**	**Shorelint**	**1st**
1870	Rathowen	3rd	1933	Royal Vintage	5th	1991	Shudanz	3rd
1861	Rattler	(Unplaced)	1921	Royal Visitor	2nd	2009	Shut it Down	7th
1989	Rear Admiral	12th	1946	Royal Worth	10th	1926	Siberian	12th
1924	Rebus	10th	1982	Runaway Groom	2nd	2001	Sik	10th
1925	Rebus	14th	2000	Runaway Love	14th	2008	Silver Jag	12th
1926	Rebus	13th	1974	Rushton's Corsair	3rd	1937	Silver Jubilee	3rd
1962	Reckless Rick	12th	1912	Rustling	3rd	1901	Silver Locks	13th
1918	Red Admiral	11th	1973	Rusty Scissors	17th	1955	Silver Spat	9th
1948	Red Bottle	7th	1939	Rye Grass	10th	2004	Silver Ticket	8th
1937	Red Pirate	5th	1985	S. S. Enterprise	11th	1940	Silvos	6th
1938	Red Pirate	10th	1918	Sadducee	7th	1973	Singing Spirit	5th
1970	Regal Admiral	11th	1969	Sailor Conn	7th	1973	Sinister Purpose	2nd
1988	Regal Classic	2nd	**1935**	**Sally Fuller**	**1st**	1947	Sir Achtoi	16th
1983	Regal Decision	14th	1893	Saltpetre	8th	1951	Sir Algahad	15th
1995	**Regal Discovery**	**1st**	1919	Salvo	5th	1959	Sir Chop	10th
1978	**Regal Embrace**	**1st**	1934	Sam Worthy	6th	1876	Sir John	(Unplaced)

1877	Sir John	3rd	2009	Stardust Ziggy	9th	1953	Teddybrook	15th
1983	Sir Khaled	2nd	1940	Star Gaiety	9th	1951	Teddy's Sister	16th
1999	Sir Lloyd	11th	1998	Star On Fire	12th	1961	Tehran's Dan	13th
1950	Sir Strome	2nd	1885	Statesman	10th	1988	Tejabo	6th
2003	Sircharlesschnabel	11th	1986	Steady Effort	3rd	1997	Tempolake	11th
1874	Sister to Vandal	6th	**1979**	**Steady Growth**	**1st**	1984	Ten Gold Pots	3rd
1987	Skate the World	10th	1987	Steady Power	5th	**1942**	**Ten to Ace**	**1st**
1997	Sky and Sea	7th	1987	Steady Zephyr	6th	1899	Terralta	5th
1931	Skygazer	3rd	1989	Stellar Night	6th	1870	Terror	5th
1941	Skyliner	5th	1996	Stephanotis	2nd	1987	That's A Blunder	14th
1939	Skyrunner	3rd	2006	Sterwins	2nd	2001	Thatsthebottomline	6th
1906	**Slaughter**	**1st**	1906	Stock Exchange	5th	1939	The Calf	9th
1997	Sloane Ranger	12th	1985	Stole The Prince	8th	1998	The Fed	6th
1937	Slycat	9th	1958	Stole the Ring	3rd	1999	The Feeber	10th
1938	Slycat	6th	**1865**	**Stone Player**	**1st (Disqualified)**	1966	The Hangman	6th
1915	Smithfield	12th	1940	Storm Light	8th	1959	The Mohawk	15th
1945	Smokey Joe	15th	1986	Storm On The Loose	13th	1900	The Provost	2nd
1977	Social Pleasure	6th	1936	Stormblown	2nd	1957	The Schreiber	8th
1952	Sod Field	12th	1878	Strathmere	4th	1945	The Sheriff	10th
1987	Soggy Sixpense	12th	2002	Streakin Rob	13th	**1874**	**The Swallow**	**1st**
1981	Solar Command	7th	2004	Strike Em Hard	6th	1898	The Tar	4th
1966	Solar Park	7th	2000	Strike Smartly	10th	1959	Theo Geo	11th
1959	Solarway	12th	1958	Stroke O'Twelve	12th	**1903**	**Thessalon**	**1st**
2003	Solihull	6th	1871	Styx	3rd	2006	Thinking Out Loud	11th
2008	Solitaire	3rd	1938	Suffern	9th	1894	Thorncliffe	4th
1968	Solometeor	7th	1972	Suffix	4th	1924	Thorndyke	2nd
1980	Someolio Man	2nd	1962	Sun Dan	5th	1924	Thornton	14th
1963	Son Blue	2nd	1876	Sunbeam	(Unplaced)	1980	Thorny Question	17th
1968	Son Costume	8th	1959	Sunday Sail	4th	2005	Three in the Bag	9th
1982	**Son of Briartic**	**1st**	1953	Sunita	12th	1954	Three Striper	8th
1874	Son of Gilroy	4th	1952	Sunnycrest	21st	1892	Thunder Maid	10th
1875	Son of Gilroy	2nd	1876	Sunnyside (late Emma P.)	3rd	1924	Tiger Tim	6th
1929	Son of Harmony	12th	1965	Super Flow	7th	1937	Tignabruich	16th
1977	**Sound Reason**	**1st**	1907	Supper Dance	15th	1999	Time for Judith	13th
1922	**South Shore**	**1st**	1908	Supper Dance	5th	1973	Time of Plenty	16th
1927	Southern Dawn	14th	1895	Susquehanna	9th	1950	Tinderill	7th
1926	Southern Glow	9th	1947	Sweep Comet	8th	1927	Tippance	7th
1997	Sovereign Storm	3rd	1948	Sweepblu	4th	**1966**	**Titled Hero**	**1st**
1936	Spearman	7th	1943	Sweepgold	7th	**2002**	**T J's Lucky Moon**	**1st**
1949	Speedy Irish	2nd	1988	Sweeping Change	7th	1899	Toddy Ladle	3rd
1971	Speedy Zephyr	8th	1936	Sweepouch	12th	1909	Tollendal	2nd
1932	Spey Crest	3rd	1933	Syndic	8th	1910	Tollendal	7th
1934	Speygold	2nd	1933	Syngo	3rd	1868	Tom Kemble	(Unplaced)
1930	Sphere of Beauty	12th	1939	Syngo Bay	4th	1881	Tom Malone	4th
1996	Spider Wire	10th	1938	Tabhim	11th	1860	Tom Sayers	(Unplaced)
1989	Splashing Success	5th	1908	Table Bay	4th	1972	Tommy Jack	12th
1915	Splutter	7th	1938	Tabmark	7th	2008	Took the Time	8th
1965	Spotted Flyer	11th	1941	Taffrail	4th	1970	Top Call	3rd
1863	Spring (see Beacon)	(Lost Rider)	1994	Tall in the Saddle	7th	1964	Top Ruler	7th
1864	Spring (see Beacon)	3rd (Dead heat)	1958	Tamarind (by *Tournoi)	7th	1965	Top Victory	9th
1899	Spring Blossom	11th	1925	Tamarind (By Ypsilanti II)	11th	1960	Toronto Boy	6th
1896	Springal	2nd	1992	Tannenberg	6th	1864	Toronto Lass	(Unplaced)
1897	Springbok	7th	1917	Tarahera	2nd	2000	Touch of Power	8th
1898	Springbok	8th	1945	Tarian	2nd	1999	Touching	12th
1955	Springhurst	5th	1899	Tartan	13th	1862	Touchstone	3rd
1918	**Springside**	**1st**	1900	Tartan	13th	1863	Touchstone	2nd (Awarded Plate)
1911	**St. Bass**	**1st**	**1915**	**Tartarean**	**1st**	1952	Tour de Force	11th
1920	**St. Paul**	**1st**	2009	Tasty Temptation	4th	1923	Trail Blazer	3rd
1902	St. Rosanna	12th	1926	Taurus	3rd	1982	Transcendent	(Fell)
1954	Staff Reporter	6th	1927	Taurus	5th	1947	Tregaron	9th
1995	Stanley Silver	12th	1935	Tax Free	8th	1962	Tres Suave	6th
1930	Star Crest	8th	1970	Teddikus	7th	2000	Tricky Hearts	15th

YEAR	HORSE	FINISH	YEAR	HORSE	FINISH	YEAR	HORSE	FINISH
1925	Tricky Take Off	10th	1952	Wait on Me	13th	1884	Willie W.	6th
1952	Tring Fair	18th	1862	Wait-a-while	(Unplaced)	**1885**	**Willie W.**	**1st**
1986	Trooper John	12th	1864	Wait-a-while	2nd	**1863**	**Willie Wonder**	**1st (Disq. Placed last)**
1912	Tropaeolum	5th	1868	Wait-a-while	(Unplaced)	1861	Willy Bell	(Unplaced)
1984	Tropare	13th	2000	Wake At Noon	5th	2001	Win City	2nd
1938	Troublemark	12th	1875	Wanderer	(Fell)	1956	Winchester	9th
1927	**Troutlet**	**1st**	**2003**	**Wando**	**1st**	1955	Windermere	7th
1970	True Willie	12th	2006	Wanna Runner	10th	1968	Winning Isle	11th
1975	Trusted Friend	10th	1903	War Medal	6th	1959	Winning Shot	3rd
1990	Truth Squad	11th	1904	War Whoop	3rd	1971	Winter Holiday	9th
1943	Tulachmore	3rd	1948	War Wrack	12th	1953	Winter Lady	16th
1947	Tularch	15th	1941	Warrigan	6th	1983	Wise Strategy	8th
1882	Tullamore	3rd	1963	Warriors Day	3rd	**1989**	**With Approval**	**1st**
1994	Tuxedo Landing	9th	1920	Waska	12th	1986	Wolark	9th
1918	Twelve Bells	9th	1947	Watch Wrack	3rd	**1999**	**Woodcarver**	**1st**
2002	Twice Bid	10th	1989	Wave Wise	14th	1917	Woodruff	8th
2007	Twilight Meteor	7th	1981	Wayover	2nd	1935	Worthing	7th
2000	Twistingbythepool	12th	1962	Welcome Effort	11th	1969	Wyn d'Amour	11th
1908	Two Lips II	13th	1954	Welcome Home	9th	1947	Yellowknife	5th
1862	Tyrant	(Unplaced)	1963	Welcome Pardner	11th	1998	Yodelman	13th
1919	Uncle John	4th	1947	Welsh Man	11th	1970	York Ranger	8th
1941	Undisturbed	2nd	1930	Whale Oil	2nd	1879	Young Blenkiron	3rd
1950	Unionville	3rd	1910	Whaup	4th	1868	Young Jack the Barber	2nd
1975	Upper Shelf	7th	**1965**	**Whistling Sea**	**1st**	**1928**	**Young Kitty**	**1st**
1907	Up-to-Date	8th	1958	White Apache	2nd	**1875**	**Young Trumpeter**	**1st**
1945	**Uttermost**	**1st**	1900	White Clover	7th	1995	Your Majestic	9th
1984	Val Dansant	4th	1928	White Dove	5th	1981	Yours To Command	13th
1982	Valiant Prince	9th	1903	Whiteward	14th	1973	Zaca Spirit	12th
1942	Valkyrian	5th	1969	Wicked Wynnie	12th	1999	Zaha	6th
1910	Valydon	5th	1897	Wicker	3rd	1998	Zap Happy	9th
1930	Varsity	11th	1906	Wicklight	4th	1930	Zarf	15th
1915	Vastatio	10th	1907	Wicklight	4th			
1990	Very Formal	2nd	1908	Wicklight	10th			
1923	Vespra	6th	1938	Wicklow	14th			
1929	Vestip	4th	1907	Wild Flower II	16th			
1930	Vestip	4th	1886	Wild Bruce	3rd			
1931	Vestip	7th	1887	Wild Bruce	8th			
1894	Vicar of Wakefield	2nd	1883	Wild Deer	9th			
1895	Vicar of Wakefield	4th	**2005**	**Wild Desert**	**1st**			
1881	**Vice Chancellor**	**1st**	1860	Wild Irishman	3rd			
1889	Vicino	5th	**1861**	**Wild Irishman**	**1st**			
1996	**Victor Cooley**	**1st**	**1867**	**Wild Rose (by *Lapidist)**	**1st**			
1960	**Victoria Park**	**1st**	1885	Wild Rose (by Princeton)	8th			
1961	Victoria Regina	4th	**1886**	**Wild Rose (by Princeton)**	**1st**			
1972	**Victoria Song**	**1st**	1985	Wild Style	10th			
1973	Victorian Prince	14th	1991	Wilderness Song	2nd			
1891	**Victorious**	**1st**	2004	Will He Crow	3rd			
1947	Victory Chimes	6th	1905	Will King	2nd			
1945	Victory Mark	13th	1946	Willegivit	6th			
1953	Virginia Fair	5th	1882	Williams	2nd			
1904	Virtuoso	13th	1883	Williams	2nd			
1913	Voivode	4th	**1884**	**Williams**	**1st**			
1891	Volga	8th	1951	Willie George	20th			
1994	Von Fleet	6th	**1940**	**Willie the Kid**	**1st**			

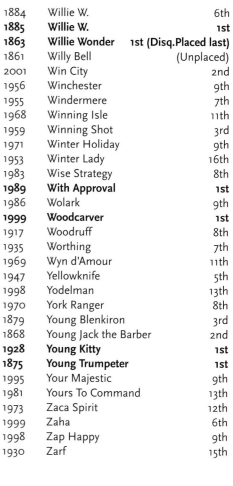

Plate-Winning Jockeys

KENT DESORMEAUX

Year	Horse	Finish
1998	Archers Bay	1st

JOHNNY DEWHURST

Year	Horse	Finish
1955	Silver Spat	9th
1952	Allison Pass	10th
1951	Libertine	2nd
1950	Pine River	10th
1949	Speedy Irish	2nd
1948	Face Off	10th
1947	Mulligan	7th
1946	Kingarvie	1st
1945	Corvita	8th
1944	Sayonara	4th

HUGO DITTFACH

Year	Horse	Finish
1983	High Chicago	11th
1981	Regal Stafford	5th
1980	Somelio Man	2nd
1978	Colourful Conn	4th
1977	Regent Bird	8th
1975	Rex Favor	6th
1974	Muddy York	8th
1973	Impressive Lady	15th
1972	Barley Sugar	11th
1971	Lord Vancouver	7th
1970	Regal Admiral	11th
1969	Sailor Conn	7th
1968	Phelodie	4th
1967	Battling	9th
1966	Arctic Troops	8th
1965	Blue Mel	3rd
1964	Top Ruler	7th
1963	Breezy Answer	5th
1962	King Gorm	4th
1961	Blue Light	1st
1960	Toronto Boy	6th
1959	Sunday Sail	4th

EDDIE DUGAN

Year	Horse	Finish
1911	St. Bass	1st

HENRY ERICKSON

Year	Horse	Finish
1927	Gems to Let	3rd
1926	Haplite	1st
1925	Rebus	14th
1919	Galway	8th

CHARLES FAIRBROTHER

Year	Horse	Finish
1926	Cloth Hall	7th
1908	Seismic	1st

JEFF FELL

Year	Horse	Finish
1986	No Louder	4th
1985	Dauphin Fabuleux	DNF
1984	Axe T.V.	10th
1977	Grand Luxe	7th
1976	Norcliffe	1st
1975	Trusted Friend	10th

ARCHIE FISHER

Year	Horse	Finish
1872	General Blacksmith	6th
1869	Jack-on-the-Green	4th
1868	Nettie	1st

JIM FITZSIMMONS

Year	Horse	Finish
1969	Wicked Wynnie	12th
1968	Big Blunder	2nd
1967	Jammed Lovely	1st
1966	Holarctic	4th
1964	Grand Garcon	2nd
1963	Son Blue	2nd
1962	Flaming Page	1st
1961	Flashing Top	9th

JAMES (JIMMY) FOLEY

Year	Horse	Finish
1919	Bugle March	10th
1909	Sauce o'Gold	7th
1908	Wicklight	10th
1907	Kelvin	1st

JOHN GAGEN

Year	Horse	Finish
1866	Beacon	1st

A.E. (ALLIE) GATES

Year	Horse	Finish
1891	La Blanche	2nd
1890	La Blanche	2nd
1889	Evangeline	4th
1888	Evangeline	2nd
1887	Jim Ferris	14th
1886	Fisherman	9th
1884	Castilena	10th
1883	Williams	2nd
1882	Fanny Wiser	1st
1881	Athlete	3rd
1880	Lord Dufferin	4th
1879	Moss Rose	1st
1878	King George	1st
1876	Fisherwoman	Unplaced

CLIFFORD GILBERT

Year	Horse	Finish
1909	Shimonese	1st

MICHAEL GORMAN

Year	Horse	Finish
1891	Victorious	1st
1890	Flip Flap	3rd

AVELINO GOMEZ

Year	Horse	Finish
1979	Bull Regent	9th
1978	High Roller	7th
1977	Northernette	2nd
1976	Military Bearing	2nd
1973	Zaca Spirit	12th
1972	Henry Tudor	5th
1969	Jumpin Joesph	1st
1967	Pine Point	2nd
1966	Titled Hero	1st
1965	Good Old Mort	5th
1964	Pierlou	5th
1961	Ramblin Wreck	3rd
1960	Victoria Park	1st
1959	Winning Shot	3rd
1957	Lyford Cay	1st
1956	Censor	4th
1955	Senator Jim	3rd

WAYNE HARRIS

Year	Horse	Finish
1968	Merger	1st
1966	Solar Park	7th

BILL HARTACK

Year	Horse	Finish
1964	Northern Dancer	1st
1962	Choperion	2nd

SANDY HAWLEY

Year	Horse	Finish
1997	Annihilate	8th
1996	Chief Bearhart	4th
1995	Honky Tonky Tune	11th
1994	Tall In the Saddle	7th
1993	Flashy Regent	4th
1992	Keen Falcon	10th
1991	British Banker	9th
1990	Very Formal	2nd
1989	Wave Wise	14th
1988	Regal Classic	2nd
1987	Bold Executive	8th
1979	Bold Agent	2nd
1978	Regal Embrace	1st
1976	Laissez-Passer	4th
1975	L'Enjoleur	1st
1974	Native Aid	2nd
1973	Victorian Prince	14th
1971	Kennedy Road	1st
1970	Almoner	1st

JOHN HAZARD

Year	Horse	Finish
1874	The Swallow	1st

FRANCIS (FRANK) HORN

Year	Horse	Finish
1933	Juniam	12th
1927	Troutlet	1st

MR. F. HORTON

Year	Horse	Finish
1892	O'Donohue	1st

PATRICK HUSBANDS

Year	Horse	Finish
2009	Tasty Temptation	4th
2008	Palmers	5th
2007	Marchfield	6th
2004	Kent Ridge	10th
2003	Wando	1st
2002	Forever Grand	3rd
2001	Highland Legacy	9th
2000	Pete's Sake	16th
1999	Sir Lloyd	11th
1998	Bronze Shoal	8th
1995	Prince of North	10th

TAK INOUYE

Year	Horse	Finish
1967	Ette Rule	12th
1965	Whistling Sea	1st

WILLIAM JAMIESON

Year	Horse	Finish
1887	Aunt Alice	3rd
1885	Willie W.	1st
1884	Edmonton	5th
1883	Princess Louise	3rd
1882	Bonnie Vic	6th

JONO JONES

YEAR	HORSE	FINISH
2009	Rapid Release	8th
2008	Not Bourbon	1st
2004	A Bit O'Gold	2nd
2003	El Gran Maestro	9th
2002	Classic Mike	8th

TODD KABEL

YEAR	HORSE	FINISH
2007	Alezzandro	2nd
2006	Malakoff	3rd
2005	Dance With Ravens	7th
2004	Silver Ticket	8th
2003	Mobil	2nd
2002	Ford Every Stream	4th
2001	Lucky Scarab	5th
2000	Scatter the Gold	1st
1999	Lenny the Lender	4th
1998	Primaly	10th
1997	C.C. on Ice	13th
1996	Northface	9th
1995	Regal Discovery	1st
1993	Fleetward	10th
1992	Tannenberg	6th

ROBERT LANDRY

YEAR	HORSE	FINISH
2008	Solitaire	3rd
2007	Include Us	5th
2005	Three in the Bag	9th
2004	Niigon	1st
2003	Shoal Water	4th
2002	Mountain Beacon	12th
2001	Millennium Allstar	8th
2000	For Our Sake	3rd
1999	Catahoula Parish	7th
1998	Pinafore Park	5th
1997	Cowboy Cop	6th
1996	Spider Wire	10th
1995	Ice Agent	13th
1994	Road Rush	4th
1993	Imperial Bandit	11th
1992	Change of Fortune	9th
1989	Ivory Dance	11th

CHARLES (CHIC) LANG

YEAR	HORSE	FINISH
1926	Davenport	4th
1925	Fairbank	1st
1922	El Jesmar	3rd

JACK LAUZON

YEAR	HORSE	FINISH
1999	Time for Judith	13th
1994	Basqueian	1st
1989	Most Valiant	2nd
1988	Regal Intention	1st
1987	Soggy Sixpense	12th
1986	Essa Lad	11th
1985	Wild Style	10th
1984	Male Ego	12th

JAMES LEE

YEAR	HORSE	FINISH
1871	Floss	1st

EDDIE LEGERE

YEAR	HORSE	FINISH
1933	King O'Connor	1st
1932	Shady Well	4th

HARRY LEWIS

YEAR	HORSE	FINISH
1901	Oneiros	11th
1900	Dalmoor	1st
1897	Ferdinand	1st
1896	Millbrook	1st
1891	Pappoose	6th

HERB LINDBERG

YEAR	HORSE	FINISH
1954	King Maple	3rd
1953	Winter Lady	16th
1945	Smokey Joe	15th
1944	Heulwen	8th
1940	Silvos	6th
1939	Gold Fawn	13th (Broke Down)
1938	Mona Bell	2nd
1937	Budron	4th
1935	Sally Fuller	1st

HENRY LITTLE

YEAR	HORSE	FINISH
1930	Aymond	1st
1929	Vestip	4th

CHARLES LITTLEFIELD

YEAR	HORSE	FINISH
1863	Willie Wonder	1st (Disq.)
1862	Palermo	1st
1860	Don Juan	1st

LAWRENCE (LARRY) LYKE

YEAR	HORSE	FINISH
1919	Ladder of Light	1st

FRANK MANN

YEAR	HORSE	FINISH
1948	Red Bottle	7th
1943	Tulachmore	3rd
1936	Judge Pool	13th
1935	Listaro	10th
1934	Horometer	1st
1933	Pepper Prince	19th
1932	Queensway	1st
1931	Froth Blower	1st
1930	Sphere of Beauty	12th
1929	Lindsay	3rd
1928	Hanna Deebe	3rd

MR. A MARTIN

YEAR	HORSE	FINISH
1884	Williams	1st

R.J. MASON

YEAR	HORSE	FINISH
1899	Butter Scotch	1st

COLIN MCDONALD

YEAR	HORSE	FINISH
1947	Moldy	1st
1937	Silver Jubilee	3rd
1936	Spearman	7th
1935	Epicurus	4th

MR. A. MCLAUGHLIN

YEAR	HORSE	FINISH
1867	Wild Rose	1st

LEE MINK

YEAR	HORSE	FINISH
1918	Springside	1st
1917	Tarahera	2nd

JOHN D. MOONEY

YEAR	HORSE	FINISH
1931	Golader	9th
1929	Shorelint	1st
1927	Lady McNeill	13th
1926	Attack	2nd
1925	Forecast II	4th

RONNIE NASH

YEAR	HORSE	FINISH
1952	Acadian	9th
1942	Valkyrian	5th
1940	Willie the Kid	1st
1939	Budsis	6th

CHARLES O'LEARY

YEAR	HORSE	FINISH
1892	Gladstone	5th
1888	Harry Cooper	1st

RICHARD O'LEARY

YEAR	HORSE	FINISH
1889	Colonist	1st
1885	Fisherman	5th
1881	Echo	5th
1880	Bonnie Bird	1st
1874	Fisherwoman	3rd
1873	Charlotte R.	8th
1872	Fearnaught	1st

KEN PARRINGTON

YEAR	HORSE	FINISH
1922	South Shore	1st
1921	Heath Bell	4th

BILL PARSONS

YEAR	HORSE	FINISH
1982	Valiant Prince	8th
1980	Driving Home	1st
1976	Hook and Draw	5th
1975	Mystery Time	3rd

CRAIG PERRET

YEAR	HORSE	FINISH
1998	Nite Dreamer	4th
1994	Bruce's Mill	2nd
1993	Peteski	1st
1992	Alydeed	1st

CHARLES PHAIR

YEAR	HORSE	FINISH
1877	Amelia	1st

H. (KELLY) PHILLIPS

YEAR	HORSE	FINISH
1905	Inferno	1st

LESLIE PICHON

YEAR	HORSE	FINISH
1928	Young Kitty	1st

ARTHUR PICKENS

YEAR	HORSE	FINISH
1916	Mandarin	1st

ROBIN PLATTS

YEAR	HORSE	FINISH
1998	Kinkennie	3rd
1997	Air Cool	4th
1996	Kristy Krunch	3rd
1995	Desert Falcon	14th
1993	Briartic Star	9th
1991	Shudanz	3rd
1990	King Riviera	13th
1988	Baldski's Prize	11th

YEAR	JOCKEY/HORSE	FINISH
1987	Steady Zephyr	6th
1986	Steady Effort	3rd
1985	Preemptive Strike	3rd
1984	**Key to the Moon**	**1st**
1983	Rockcliffe	3rd
1981	Al Sarab	4th
1980	Duns Scotus	10th
1979	Bridle Path	6th
1978	Overskate	2nd
1977	**Sound Reason**	**1st**
1976	Ambassador B.	9th
1975	Coup de Soleil	13th
1974	**Amber Herod**	**1st**
1973	Albert the Consort	4th
1972	**Victoria Song**	**1st**
1970	Mary of Scotland	5th
1968	Dainty Davie	6th

EMILE RAMSAMMY

YEAR	JOCKEY/HORSE	FINISH
2009	Flip for the Coin	5th
2008	D. Flutie	13th
2007	Cobrador	8th
2006	**Edenwold**	**1st**
2004	Strike Em Hard	6th
2002	Cree Power	6th
2000	Fartherthanuthink	13th
1999	Euchre	3rd
1998	Yodelman	13th
1997	Sky and Sea	7th
1996	**Victor Cooley**	**1st**

FRANK REGAN

YEAR	JOCKEY/HORSE	FINISH
1894	**Joe Miller**	**1st**
1892	Bay Court	8th

PAT REMILLARD

YEAR	JOCKEY/HORSE	FINISH
1965	Chief Brant	10th
1962	Argue Around	10th
1960	Champagne Velvet	3rd
1959	Miss Whiskit	19th
1956	Big Berne	5th
1955	Scarboro Lass	6th
1953	Lowmond	8th
1952	Our Omar	15th
1951	Fairlow	13th
1950	Brazen Buz	11th
1948	Chance Toss	11th
1947	Welsh Man	11th
1946	Double Briar	5th
1945	Hemseven	16th
1944	Hemfox	7th
1943	**Paolita**	**1st**
1941	Depositor	8th
1940	Hood	3rd
1939	Milius	7th
1938	Grand Dame	4th
1937	Slycat	9th
1936	Odd Catch	9th
1933	Royal Vintage	5th

GIL ROBILLARD

YEAR	JOCKEY/HORSE	FINISH
1956	London Calling	3rd
1952	**Epigram**	**1st**
1951	Britannia	4th
1950	Jim's Icra	14th
1949	Filsis	3rd

A. ROBINSON JR.

YEAR	JOCKEY/HORSE	FINISH
1881	Jack Davis	9th
1876	Sunbeam	Unplaced
1869	**Bay Jack**	**1st**

FRANK ROBINSON

YEAR	JOCKEY/HORSE	FINISH
1917	**Belle Mahone**	**1st**

CHRIS ROGERS

YEAR	JOCKEY/HORSE	FINISH
1976	Bye Bye Paris	10th
1974	Rash Move	9th
1970	Dance to Market	4th
1969	Wyn d'Amour	11th
1962	Welcome Effort	11th
1959	Theo Geo	11th
1957	Chopadette	2nd
1954	**Collisteo**	**1st**
1952	Sunnycrest	21st
1950	**McGill**	**1st**
1949	**Epic**	**1st**
1948	Coleraine	15th
1947	Sweep Comet	8th
1945	The Sheriff	10th
1944	Heysiris	6th

ROXY ROMANELLI

YEAR	JOCKEY/HORSE	FINISH
1926	Huckleberry	14th
1924	Seven Oaks	5th
1923	Honey's Jewel	10th
1922	Greybourne	8th
1921	Gay Kap	6th
1920	**St. Paul**	**1st**
1904	War Whoop	3rd

DON SEYMOUR

YEAR	JOCKEY/HORSE	FINISH
1994	Von Fleet	6th
1993	Cheery Knight	2nd
1992	Blitzer	7th
1991	Bolulight	6th
1990	**Izvestia**	**1st**
1989	**With Approval**	**1st**
1988	Sweeping Change	7th
1987	Bodmin Moor	11th
1985	Fustukian	13th

KEN SKINNER

YEAR	JOCKEY/HORSE	FINISH
1987	**Market Control**	**1st**

ROBERT SMALL

YEAR	JOCKEY/HORSE	FINISH
1913	Rockspring	9th
1912	**Heresy**	**1st**

WILLIAM SMALL

YEAR	JOCKEY/HORSE	FINISH
1863	**Touchstone**	**1st**

CHARLES W. SMITH

YEAR	JOCKEY/HORSE	FINISH
1943	Gray Syngo	5th
1942	**Ten to Ace**	**1st**
1941	Undisturbed	2nd
1940	Ring Wise	11th

JACOB SMITH

YEAR	JOCKEY/HORSE	FINISH
1883	**Roddy Pringle**	**1st**
1873	**Mignonette**	**1st**

MIKE SMITH

YEAR	JOCKEY/HORSE	FINISH
2009	Mr. Foricos Two U	2nd
1997	**Awesome Again**	**1st**
1995	Freedom Fleet	2nd

JOHN PAUL SOUTER

YEAR	JOCKEY/HORSE	FINISH
1984	Tropare	13th
1982	**Son of Briartic**	**1st**
1981	Le Promeneur	16th
1980	Hasty Rick	8th
1979	Coup de Chance	8th
1978	L'Alezane	3rd

DAVE STEVENSON

YEAR	JOCKEY/HORSE	FINISH
1956	**Canadian Champ**	**1st**
1955	Loyalist	4th
1954	Welcome Home	9th

BRIAN SWATUK

YEAR	JOCKEY/HORSE	FINISH
1992	Bright Feather	8th
1991	Rainbows for Life	4th
1990	Secret 'n Classy	4th
1988	Grey Skelly	4th
1986	Grey Classic	8th
1985	Crowning Honors	4th
1982	Transcendent	DNF
1981	Regal Kapers	15th
1980	Decent Davey	6th
1979	**Steady Growth**	**1st**
1975	New Orient	4th
1970	Big Blue Bomber	6th

J.K. TREUBEL

YEAR	JOCKEY/HORSE	FINISH
1906	**Slaughter**	**1st**

BOBBY USSERY

YEAR	JOCKEY/HORSE	FINISH
1971	Chatty Cavalier	5th
1959	**New Providence**	**1st**

PAT VALENZUELA

YEAR	JOCKEY/HORSE	FINISH
2005	**Wild Desert**	**1st**

HARRY VITITOE

YEAR	JOCKEY/HORSE	FINISH
1901	**John Ruskin**	**1st**

SAM WAINWRIGHT

YEAR	JOCKEY/HORSE	FINISH
1902	**Lyddite**	**1st**

GEORGE WALKER

YEAR	JOCKEY/HORSE	FINISH
1957	Count Teddy	11th
1956	Bunty's Flight	6th
1955	**Ace Marine**	**1st**

GEORGE WALLS

Year	Horse	Finish
1924	**Maternal Pride**	**1st**
1919	Doleful	2nd

MICKEY WALLS

Year	Horse	Finish
2002	Twice Bid	10th
2000	Bold n' Fancy	7th
1999	**Woodcarver**	**1st**
1998	The Fed	6th
1997	Love View	5th
1996	Stephanotis	2nd
1993	Janraffole	3rd
1991	Megas Vukefalos	5th

JIMMY WALSH

Year	Horse	Finish
1905	Half Seas Over	3rd
1904	**Sapper**	**1st**
1903	Perfect Dream	10th

BOBBY WATSON

Year	Horse	Finish
1948	Sweepblu	4th
1947	Kanlee	4th
1946	Bluesweep	3rd
1945	**Uttermost**	**1st**
1944	**Acara**	**1st**
1942	Cossack Post	2nd
1941	**Budpath**	**1st**
1940	Curwen	2nd
1939	Skyrunner	3rd
1937	Red Pirate	5th
1936	Ladymuch	4th
1935	Gay Sympathy	3rd

HARRY WATTS

Year	Horse	Finish
1915	**Tartarean**	**1st**

R. (TINY) WILLIAMS

Year	Horse	Finish
1899	Dalmoor	2nd
1898	**Bon Ino**	**1st**

JOHNNY WILSON

Year	Horse	Finish
1913	**Hearts of Oak**	**1st**
1910	**Parmer**	**1st**

TERRENCE (TERRY) WILLIAMS

Year	Horse	Finish
1927	Eliza Jane	9th
1924	Beau of the West	11th
1923	**Flowerful**	**1st**

EMMA-JAYNE WILSON

Year	Horse	Finish
2009	El Brujo	13th
2008	Shadowless	11th
2007	**Mike Fox**	**1st**
2006	Bridgecut	12th

CHARLES WISE

Year	Horse	Finish
1892	Thunder Maid	10th
1889	Fred Henry	10th
1887	**Bonnie Duke**	**1st**
1886	Ben Bolt	4th
1882	Roderick	4th
1881	Tom Malone	4th
1876	Sunnyside	2nd
1874	Emily	2nd
1873	Emily	4th
1872	Jack Vandal	2nd

MANNY YCAZA

Year	Horse	Finish
1963	Canebora	1st

STERLING YOUNG

Year	Horse	Finish
1947	Victory Chimes	6th
1940	Frobisher	4th
1939	Rye Grass	10th
1937	**Goldlure**	**1st**
1936	Sweepouch	12th
1935	Chickpen	2nd

THE EVENING NEWS. MONDAY.

THE QUEEN'S PLATE.

How the winner would pass the wire if the race were run to-morrow.

Plate-Winning Trainers

BEN ALCOTT

YEAR	TRAINER/HORSE	FINISH
1861	Wild Irishman	1st
1860	Wild Irishman	3rd

A.E. (BERT) ALEXANDRA

YEAR	TRAINER/HORSE	FINISH
1949	Epic	1st
1945	Floral Gift	12th
1944	Korafloyd	3rd
	Gypster	12th
1939	Jelwell	5th
1938	Mona Bell	2nd

JACK ANDERSON

YEAR	TRAINER/HORSE	FINISH
1938	Bunty Lawless	1st

VITO ARMATA

YEAR	TRAINER/HORSE	FINISH
2009	Flip for the Coin	5th
2004	Archer Fleet	11th
2002	T J's Lucky Moon	1st
2000	Tricky Hearts	15th

ROGER ATTFIELD

YEAR	TRAINER/HORSE	FINISH
2009	Rapid Release	8th
2008	Not Bourbon	1st
2007	Include Us	5th
2005	Ablo	5th
2004	Just In Case Jimmy	4th
2002	Twice Bid	10th
2000	For Our Sake	3rd
1998	Pinafore Park	5th
	Primaly	10th
1995	Regal Discovery	1st
	For Pete's Sake	7th
1993	Peteski	1st
	Cheery Knight	2nd
1992	Alydeed	1st
1991	Shudanz	3rd
	Bolulight	6th
1990	Izvestia	1st
	Bundle Bits	6th
1989	With Approval	1st
1988	Sweeping Change	7th
1987	Market Control	1st
	Steady Power	5th
	Bodmin Moor	11th
1986	Steady Effort	3rd
1985	Wild Style	10
1984	Dancing Hare	7th
	Axe T.V.	10th
	Tropare	13th
1983	Rockcliffe	3rd
1982	Akhtiar	10th
1980	Duns Scotus	10th
1976	Norcliffe	1st

R.S. (BOBBY) BATEMAN

YEAR	TRAINER/HORSE	FINISH
1969	Jumpin Joseph	1st
1961	Ramblin Wreck	3rd
1956	Big Berne	5th

MACDONALD (MAC) BENSON

YEAR	TRAINER/HORSE	FINISH
2000	Allende	4th
1985	La Lorgnette	1st
1983	Regal Decision	14th
1982	Cliff House	(Fell)
1979	Bold Agent	2nd
	Bridle Path	6th
1978	Regal Embrace	1st

J.C. (JIM) BENTLEY

YEAR	TRAINER/HORSE	FINISH
1982	Great Stake	9th
1981	Fiddle Dancer Boy	1st
1976	Military Bearing	2nd
1975	New Orient	4th
1971	Kennedy Road	1st
1970	Mildenhall	14th
1967	Betemight	6th
1956	Argent	2nd
1955	Scarboro Lass	6th
	Merry Life	10th
1953	Avella	18th

JAMES BERRY

YEAR	TRAINER/HORSE	FINISH
1869	Bay Jack	1st

IAN BLACK

YEAR	TRAINER/HORSE	FINISH
2007	Mike Fox	1st

HARRY BLAIR

YEAR	TRAINER/HORSE	FINISH
1901	John Ruskin	1st
	Oneiros	11th
	Juvencus	15th
1900	Dalmoor	1st
	Ottoman	11th

STANLEY V. (RIP) BOWDEN

YEAR	TRAINER/HORSE	FINISH
1952	Epigram	1st

CHARLES BOYLE

YEAR	TRAINER/HORSE	FINISH
1908	Table Bay	4th
	Supper Dance	5th
1899	Dalmoor	2nd
	Curfew Bell	4th
	Terralta	5th
	Sardonyx	8th
1898	Bon Ino	1st
	Dalmoor	2nd
	The Tar	4th
1897	Ferdinand	1st
	Bon Ino	2nd
	Dalmoor	4th
1883	Roddy Pringle	1st
1876	Sunnyside	2nd
1874	Emily	2nd
1873	Norlander	2nd
	Emily	4th
1870	Rapid Roan	4th
1862	Palermo	1st

ARTHUR BRENT

YEAR	TRAINER/HORSE	FINISH
1950	Nephisto	5th
	Pine River	10th
1948	War Wrack	12th
	Anudona	16th
1947	Moldy	1st
1946	Kingarvie	1st
1945	Heydunnette	6th
1944	Heysiris	6th
	Heulwen	8th
1940	Star Gaiety	9th
1937	Golden Silence	8th
	Sandalman	12th
	Fore Isus	15th
1936	Sandalman	12th
1930	Brave Alonzo	10th
1929	Cuddle Doon	5th
	Meteor Sparks	8th
	Song of Harmony	12th

W.H. (BILL) BRINGLOE

YEAR	TRAINER/HORSE	FINISH
1937	Goldlure	1st
	Budron	4th
1936	Monsweep	1st
	Sweepouch	12th
1935	Chickpen	2nd
	Donstick	5th
1933	King O'Connor	1st
1932	King O'Connor	2nd
	Shady Well	4th
1930	Pandorus	9th
	Sphere of Beauty	12th
	Gilded Casino	18th
1929	Dance Circle	11th
	Circulet	14th
	Irish Sphere	15th
1928	Young Kitty	1st
	Best Bonnet	4th
1927	Gems to Let	3rd
	Gay Parisian	8th
	Quartzite	16th
1926	Haplite	1st
	Phanariot	6th
	Quartz-Sinter	10th

YEAR	TRAINER/HORSE	FINISH
1925	Duchess	2nd
	Goldlands	6th
	Tamarind	11th
1924	Isoletta	4th
	Beau of the West	11th
1923	**Flowerful**	**1st**
	Pelf	7th
	Floralia	12th
1922	King's Court	9th
	Impersonator	10th
1921	Crown of Gold	5th
1920	Gallant Kitty	5th
	Crown of Gold	7th
1919	Doleful	2nd
	Hong Kong	3rd
	Galway	8th
1918	Gold Galore	5th
	Sea Froth	8th
	Twelve Bells	9th

ERASTUS (RAS) BURGESS

YEAR	TRAINER/HORSE	FINISH
1903	Cardigan	7th
1894	Thorncliffe	4th
1893	Mediator	6th
1889	Cast Off	6th
1887	Fred B	4th
1886	Bonnie Duke	6th
1885	**Willie W.**	**1st**
1884	Willie W.	6th
1883	Princess Louise	3rd
1882	Easter	5th
	Bonnie Vic	6th
1881	**Vice Chancellor**	**1st**
1980	**Bonnie Bird**	**1st**

CHARLES BUTLER

YEAR	TRAINER/HORSE	FINISH
1887	Augusta	5th
	D.W.C.	12th
1886	**Wild Rose**	**1st**
1885	Wild Rose	8th
1884	Marquis	2nd
	J.P. Wiser	4th
1883	Marquis	4th
	Orkney	5th
1882	Williams	2nd
	Marquis	8th

JOHN CARDELLA

YEAR	TRAINER/HORSE	FINISH
1994	Tuxedo	9th
1983	**Bompago**	**1st**

JOSIE CARROLL

YEAR	TRAINER/HORSE	FINISH
2008	Silver Jag	12th
2006	**Edenwold**	**1st**
1997	Sloane Ranger	12th

ERIC COATRIEUX

YEAR	TRAINER/HORSE	FINISH
2006	Pipers Thunder	6th
2004	**Niigon**	**1st**
	Alleged Ruler	7th

M.R. (MARK) COWELL

YEAR	TRAINER/HORSE	FINISH
1939	**Archworth**	**1st**

DANIEL CURTIN

YEAR	TRAINER/HORSE	FINISH
1890	Kitestring	1st
1876	Norah P.	1st

ROBERT DAVIES

YEAR	TRAINER/HORSE	FINISH
1871	Floss	1st
1870	Lady May	Disq.

JAMES E. DAY

YEAR	TRAINER/HORSE	FINISH
2004	His Smoothness	5th
	Copper Trail	9th
2002	Streakin Rob	13th
1994	Comet Shine	5th
1992	Bright Feather	8th
1991	**Dance Smartly**	**1st**
	Wilderness Song	2nd
	Rainbows for Life	4th
1990	Very Formal	2nd
	Secret 'n Classy	4th
1989	Most Valiant	2nd
	Ivory Dance	11th
	Wave Wise	14th
1988	**Regal Intention**	**1st**
	Regal Classic	2nd
1987	Duckpower	4th
	Soggy Sixpence	12th
	Hangin On a Star	13th
1986	No Louder	4th
	Royal Treasurer	5th
	Grey Classic	8th
1985	Imperial Choice	2nd
	In My Cap	4th (DH)
	Dauphin Fabuleux	DNF
1982	Regency Gold	13th
1980	Arctic Morning	9th

JOSEPH H. DOANE

YEAR	TRAINER/HORSE	FINISH
1920	Lively Sleeper	10th
1919	**Ladder of Light**	**1st**
1896	Clipmount	9th

JOHN DYMENT

YEAR	TRAINER/HORSE	FINISH
1909	Fort Garry	3rd
1906	Court Martial	2nd
1905	Will King	2nd
	Maid of Barrie	4th
1904	**Sapper**	**1st**
	Nesto	10th
1903	**Thessalon**	**1st**
	Nesto	2nd
1902	Revelstoke	11th
1901	Bellcourt	2nd
	Lady Berkeley	9th
	Silver Locks	13th
1900	Bellcourt	3rd
	Magog	4th
1899	Bellcourt	7th
1898	Maritana II	3rd
	Jessamine Porter II	5th
1896	Brother Bob	5th
1894	Annie D.	9th

MR. FAGAN

YEAR	TRAINER/HORSE	FINISH
1867	Wild Rose	1st

J.G. (JIM) FAIR

YEAR	TRAINER/HORSE	FINISH
1955	Fairator	16th
1952	Sod Field	12th
1951	Bear Field	3rd
1949	Regan Lad	7th
1948	**Last Mark**	**1st**
	Fair Mark	14th
1945	Victory Mark	13th
1939	McMark	12th
1938	Tabmark	7th
	Tabhim	11th
	Troublemark	12th
1937	Notrouble	13th
1926	Rebus	13th
1925	Rebus	14th

ROBERT FRANKEL

YEAR	TRAINER/HORSE	FINISH
2005	**Wild Desert**	**1st**
1999	Euchre	3rd

MARK FROSTAD

YEAR	TRAINER/HORSE	FINISH
2009	**Eye of the Leopard**	**1st**
2005	Dance With Ravens	7th
2004	Silver Ticket	8th
2003	Shoal Water	4th
2002	Ford Every Stream	4th
	Mountain Beacon	12th
2001	**Dancethruthedawn**	**1st**
	Lucky Scarab	5th
2000	**Scatter The Gold**	**1st**
	Strike Smartly	10th
1997	Cryptocloser	2nd
	Sky and Sea	7th
1996	**Victor Cooley**	**1st**
	Chief Bearhart	4th
1994	Bruce's Mill	2nd

JOHN GAGEN

YEAR	TRAINER/HORSE	FINISH
1866	Beacon	1st

CHARLES N. GATES

YEAR	TRAINER/HORSE	FINISH
1870	John Bell	1st
1868	Highland Maid	Disq.
1867	Ontario Boy	Disq.
1866	Eliza C.	Disq.
1861	Bay Horse	Disq.

LLOYD GENTRY

YEAR	TRAINER/HORSE	FINISH
1941	**Budpath**	**1st**
1940	Curwen	2nd
1933	Easter Hatter	2nd
	Pensweep	11th
1932	Easter Hatter	5th

HARRY GIDDINGS JR.

YEAR	TRAINER/HORSE	FINISH
1948	Lord Fairmond	2nd
1947	Watch Wrack	3rd
1945	Optionor	5th
1943	Tulachmore	3rd
1942	**Ten to Ace**	**1st**

YEAR	TRAINER/HORSE	FINISH
1941	Undistrubed	2nd
1940	Ring Wise	11th
1939	Sea General	2nd
1938	Cabin Gal	3rd
1937	Silver Jubilee	3rd
	Red Pirate	5th
	Pagan King	14th
1936	Epicurus	3rd
	Spearman	7th
1935	Epicurus	4th
	Eileen D.	6th
	Listaro	10th
1934	**Horometer**	**1st**
	Pitchblende	4th
1933	Cartwheel	14th
	Pepper Prince	19th
1932	**Queensway**	**1st**
1931	**Froth Blower**	**1st**
1929	Master Bobbie	9th
1928	Bonnington	2nd
	Bikos	11th
1927	Eliza Jane	9th
1924	Seven Oaks	5th
	Honey Dear	9th
1923	Honey's Jewel	10th
1921	Royal Visitor	2nd
	Heath Bell	4th
1920	**St. Paul**	**1st**
	Primo	3rd
	Bencher	8th
1918	Bencher	10th
1917	Captain B.	4th
1915	Harry Bassett II	9th
1914	**Beehive**	**1st**
1913	**Hearts of Oak**	**1st**
	Ondramida	6th
1911	**St. Bass**	**1st**
1907	Up-To-Date	8th

JACK GIVENS

YEAR	TRAINER/HORSE	FINISH
1930	Ichitaro	3rd
	Lindsay	7th
1929	Ichitaro	2nd
	Lindsay	3rd
	Dushka	7th
1928	Hanna Deebe	3rd
	Dushka	6th
	Ichitaro	7th
1927	Perlapides	4th
1926	Davenport	4th
	Just In Fun	8th
	Siberian	12th
1925	**Fairbank**	**1st**
	Hoi Polloi	7th

LARRY GRANT

YEAR	TRAINER/HORSE	FINISH
1972	**Victoria Song**	**1st**

DR. GEORGE D. MORTON

YEAR	TRAINER/HORSE	FINISH
1873	Goldfinch	3rd
1868	Rose of Allandale	Disq.
1864	**Brunette**	**1st**

W. H. (DOC) HANNON

YEAR	TRAINER/HORSE	FINISH
1874	**The Swallow**	**1st**

DAVID HOFMANS

YEAR	TRAINER/HORSE	FINISH
1997	**Awesome Again**	**1st**

CECIL HOWARD

YEAR	TRAINER/HORSE	FINISH
1948	Sweepblu	4th
1946	Bluesweep	3rd
1945	**Uttermost**	**1st**
	Fair Jester	4th
1944	**Acara**	**1st**
	Ompalo	2nd
	Sayonara	4th
1943	Grandpal	4th
	Sweepgold	7th

JACK HUTTON

YEAR	TRAINER/HORSE	FINISH
1945	Corvita	8th
1939	Rye Grass	10th
1937	Cease Fire	2nd
	Isleworth	7th
1933	Juniam	12th
	Pertoxical	18th
1931	Par Excellence	4th
1930	**Aymond**	**1st**
	Vestip	4th
1929	Vestip	4th

ROY JOHNSON

YEAR	TRAINER/HORSE	FINISH
1976	Confederation	3rd
1969	Wyn d'Amour	11th
	Wicked Wynnie	12th
1968	**Merger**	**1st**
1967	Gilmore	8th
	Dauphin Bleu	10th
1965	**Whistling Sea**	**1st**
	Spotted Flyer	11th
1964	Return Trip	4th
1963	Welcome Pardner	11th
1962	Welcome Effort	11th

P.C. (PETE) KEISER

YEAR	TRAINER/HORSE	FINISH
1955	Springhurst	5th
1953	Sunita	12th
	Briarcrest	13th
1952	Sunnycrest	21st
1950	**McGill**	**1st**
1949	Foxy Rythm	12th

MIKE KEOGH

YEAR	TRAINER/HORSE	FINISH
2008	D. Flutie	13th
2003	**Wando**	**1st**
	Mobil	2nd
1999	**Woodcarver**	**1st**
1998	Kinkennie	3rd
1996	Firm Dancer	5th
1995	Langfuhr	6th

J.G. (JERRY) LAVIGNE

YEAR	TRAINER/HORSE	FINISH
1985	**Old Gun Powder**	12th
1982	**Son of Briartic**	**1st**

YEAR	TRAINER/HORSE	FINISH
1980	Dusty Old Farmer	4th
	Bejilla	5th
1974	Police Car	4th
1973	Fabiusand	6th
	Ingenious Device	7th
	Lucky Master	9th
1972	Nice Dancer	7th
	Parkrangle	9th
1971	Fabe Count	2nd
1970	**Almoner**	**1st**

BARRY T. LITTLEFIELD

YEAR	TRAINER/HORSE	FINISH
1917	**Belle Mahone**	**1st**
	Gala Dress	3rd
	Galley Head	5th
1916	**Mandarin**	**1st**
	Gala Water	2nd
	Gala Day	3rd
1915	Charon	8th
	Vastatio	10th
	Smithfield	12th
1914	Dark Rosaleen	2nd
	Sea Lord	3rd
	Froissart	7th
1913	Maid of Frome	2nd
	Voivode	4th
1912	Rustling	3rd
	Havrock	7th
1911	Jane Shore	3rd
	Havrock	4th
1910	Jane Shore	3rd
	Tollendal	7th
1909	Tollendal	2nd
	Courtier	5th
	Dog of War	6th
1908	**Seismic**	**1st**
	Half a Crown	3rd
	Dog of War	7th
1907	Half a Crown	2nd
	Sea Wall	13th
	Supper Dance	15th
1906	**Slaughter**	**1st**
	Haruko	3rd
1905	**Inferno**	**1st**
	Half Seas Over	3rd
1904	Con Amore	6th
	Virtuoso	13th
1903	War Meal	6th
	Perfect Dream	10th
	Fly-in-Amber	15th
	(Broke down, destroyed)	
1902	Fly-in-Amber	2nd
	Eastern Prince	8th
	Oneiros	10th

HORATIO LURO

YEAR	TRAINER/HORSE	FINISH
1965	Native Victor	4th
1964	**Northern Dancer**	**1st**
1963	Breezy Answer	5th
1962	**Flaming Page**	**1st**
	Choperion	2nd
1960	**Victoria Park**	**1st**

PATRICK MACMURCHY

YEAR	TRAINER/HORSE	FINISH
1966	**Titled Hero**	**1st**
1962	Lavella	8th
1961	**Blue Light**	**1st**
1957	Senor Teddy	10th
1952	Blue Wrack	4th
1947	Yellowknife	5th
	Welsh Man	11th
1942	Jayeffdee	7th

GORDON (PETE) MCCANN

YEAR	TRAINER/HORSE	FINISH
1967	Battling	9th
1966	Arctic Troops	8th
1965	Top Victory	9th
1963	**Canebora**	**1st**
1961	Victoria Regina	4th
	Queen's Park	6th
	Flashing Top	9th
1960	Toronto Boy	6th
1959	**New Providence**	**1st**
	Sea Page	16th
1958	Tamarind	7th
	Epic Lad	9th
1957	**Lyford Cay**	**1st**
	Chopadette	2nd
1956	London Calling	3rd
	Censor	4th
1955	Windermere	7th
1954	Queen's Own	2nd
	Staff Reporter	6th
1953	**Canadiana**	**1st**
	Lively Action	3rd
1952	Dress Circle	7th
	Acadian	9th
1951	**Major Factor**	**1st**
	Britannia	4th
1947	Curly J.	14th
1940	**Willie the Kid**	**1st**

GLENN MAGNUSSON

YEAR	TRAINER/HORSE	FINISH
1987	Skate the World	10th
1982	No No's Boy	7th
1980	**Driving Home**	**1st**
	Mister Country	7th
1974	Rushton's Corsair	3rd
1972	Suffix	4th
1963	Askum	16th
1957	Midi Blue	12th
1955	Silver Spat	9th

A. MARTIN

YEAR	TRAINER/HORSE	FINISH
1884	**Williams**	**1st**

JOHN NIXON

YEAR	TRAINER/HORSE	FINISH
1927	**Troutlet**	**1st**
	Taurus	5th
1926	Taurus	3rd
	Heretrix	5th
1923	Rallim	4th
1920	Bugle March	2nd
1918	McCorburn	13th
1915	**Tartarean**	**1st**

YEAR	TRAINER/HORSE	FINISH
	Fair Montague	2nd
1913	Gold Bud	3rd
1912	**Heresy**	**1st**
	Tropaeolum	5th
1911	Powderman	2nd
	Legislator	7th
1910	**Parmer**	**1st**
	Commola	2nd
	Whaup	4th
1909	**Shimonese**	**1st**
1908	Shimonese	2nd
	Archie Whyte	8th
1907	Kelpie	7th
1904	War Whoop	3rd
1902	Opuntia	3rd
	Parisian Lady	7th

RICHARD O'LEARY

YEAR	TRAINER/HORSE	FINISH
1889	**Colonist**	**1st**
1888	**Harry Cooper**	**1st**
1881	Echo	5th
1878	**King George**	**1st**
1872	**Fearnaught**	**1st**
1870	Terror	5th
1869	Jack-on-the-Green	4th

WILLIAM E. OWEN

YEAR	TRAINER/HORSE	FINISH
1887	**Bonnie Duke**	**1st**
1882	**Fannie Wiser**	**1st**

JOHN PASSERO

YEAR	TRAINER/HORSE	FINISH
1960	Champagne Velvet	3rd
	Hidden Treasure	5th
1958	Happy Harry	5th
	Canadian Flyer	13th
1956	**Canadian Champ**	**1st**
1953	Teddybrook	15th

CHARLES PHAIR

YEAR	TRAINER/HORSE	FINISH
1912	Jane Shore	10th
1911	Placerland	5th
1910	Sandy Kirkwood	10th
1908	Wicklight	10th
1907	**Kelvin**	**1st**
	Halfcaste	14th

TODD PLETCHER

YEAR	TRAINER/HORSE	FINISH
2007	Twilight Meteor	7th
2006	Sterwins	2nd
2000	Lodge Hill	6th
	Pete's Sake	DNF
1998	**Archers Bay**	**1st**

R.R. (RODDY) PRINGLE

YEAR	TRAINER/HORSE	FINISH
1882	Roderick	4th
1880	Roderick	5th
1873	**Mignonette**	**1st**

GIL ROWNTREE

YEAR	TRAINER/HORSE	FINISH
1985	Northern Sister	7th
1984	**Key to the Moon**	**1st**
	Ten Gold Pots	3rd

YEAR	TRAINER/HORSE	FINISH
1982	Exclusive Canadian	5th
1981	Al Sarab	4th
1980	Allan Blue	3rd
1979	Great State	7th
1978	Overskate	2nd
1977	**Sound Reason**	**1st**
1976	Lake Huron	6th
	Ambassador B.	9th
1974	**Amber Herod**	**1st**
1973	**Royal Chocolate**	**1st**
	Good Port	13th
1970	Bees Wax	15th
1961	Tehran's Dan	13th

FRED H. SCHELKE

YEAR	TRAINER/HORSE	FINISH
1943	Pacific Isle	6th
1942	Muckle	6th
1939	Budsis	6th
1938	Aldwych	8th
1937	Aldwych	6th
1935	Beechview	9th
1932	Miss Gormley	9th
1931	Bronze	2nd
	Oil Rite	6th
	Fess	5th
1930	Whale Oil	2nd
	Varsity	11th
1929	**Shorelint**	**1st**
1928	Head Lad	12th
	Mystic Star	13th
1924	Thorndyke	2nd
1923	Trail Blazer	3rd
	Ocean Crest	8th
1922	**South Shore**	**1st**
	Fuse	5th

DANIEL SCHOFF

YEAR	TRAINER/HORSE	FINISH
1875	**Young Trumpeter**	**1st**

JONATHAN SCOTT

YEAR	TRAINER/HORSE	FINISH
1879	**Moss Rose**	**1st**
1878	Moss Rose	2nd
	Exotic	3rd
1876	Grey Cloud	3rd
1875	Emma P.	3rd
	Sappho	5th
	Hurricane	6th
1877	**Amelia**	**1st**
1868	**Nettie**	**1st**

JOHN SHEPPARD

YEAR	TRAINER/HORSE	FINISH
1865	**Lady Norfolk**	**1st**

JOSEPH (YONNIE) STARR

YEAR	TRAINER/HORSE	FINISH
1986	Cap Trinite	6th
1982	Le Grand Argentier	4th
	Briar Wind	11th
1981	Le Grand Seigneur	6th
	Le Promeneur	16th
1979	Coup de Chance	8th
1978	L'Alezane	3rd
1977	Grand Luxe	7th

YEAR	TRAINER/HORSE	FINISH	YEAR	TRAINER/HORSE	FINISH	YEAR	TRAINER/HORSE	FINISH
1976	Le Gaspesien	8th	1952	Epic's Girl	5th		Moorland	4th
1975	**L'Enjoleur**	**1st**		Our Omar	15th	1895	**Bonniefield**	**1st**
1973	La Prevoyante	8th		Tring Fair	18th		Millbrook	2nd
1972	Barachois	2nd	1951	Fairlow	13th		Vicar of Wakefield	4th
1970	Fanfreluche	2nd	1945	Hemseven	16th		Confectioner	5th
	Croquemitaine	10th	1944	Hemfox	7th	1894	**Joe Miller**	**1st**
	Regal Admiral	11th	**1943**	**Paolita**	**1st**		Vicar of Wakefield	2nd
1969	Fanfaron	2nd				1893	**Martello**	**1st**
	Grey Whiz	6th		**RICHARD (DICK) TOWNROW**			Athalo	2nd
1968	Rouletabille	3rd	1962	King Gorm	4th	1892	**O'Donohue**	**1st**
	No Parando	9th		Tres Sauve	6th		Martello	7th
1967	**Jammed Lovely**	**1st**	1959	Winning Shot	3rd	1891	**Victorious**	**1st**
1966	Bye and Near	2nd	**1954**	**Collisteo**	**1st**	1889	Bonnie Ino	2nd
1963	Warrior's Day	3rd		Pancho	4th		Vicino	5th
1961	Just Don't Shove	2nd	1953	Chain Reaction	7th			
	Jammed Lucky	8th	1952	Lord Strome	8th		**JAMES WHITE**	
1960	Men at Play	4th		Allison Pass	10th	1865	Annie Laurie	Disq.
1959	Major Flight	2nd				1864	Annie Laurie	Disq.
	Le Grand Rouge	13th		**DANIEL J. VELLA**		1863	**Touchstone**	**1st**
1958	**Caledon Beau**	**1st**	2004	Night Sky	12th	1862	Touchstone	3rd
	Eskimo Flyer	10th	1998	Platino	11th	1860	**Don Juan**	**1st**
1956	Bunty's Flight	6th		Star on Fire	12th			
1955	**Ace Marine**	**1st**		Yodelman	13th		**ED WHYTE**	
			1997	Cowboy Cop	6th	1918	**Springside**	**1st**
	JOHN TAMMARO			C.C. on Ice	13th	1916	Last Spark	5th
1983	Crushed Ice	9th	1996	Northface	9th	1915	Last Spark	6th
1979	**Steady Growth**	**1st**		Handsome Hansel	12th		Splutter	7th
			1995	Freedom Fleet	2nd	1913	Rockspring	9th
	MIKE TAMMARO			All Firmed Up	5th	1911	Miss Martimas	8th
1986	**Golden Choice**	**1st**		Honky Tonk Tune	11th	1907	Wicklight	4th
			1994	**Basqueian**	**1st**		Kirkfield	5th
	J.J. (JOHNNY) THORPE			Road Rush	4th	1906	Wicklight	4th
1959	Castleberry	14th	1993	Explosive Red	5th	1903	Maple Sugar	8th
1956	Lawday	7th		Circulating	6th		Deseronto	12th
1955	Fair Shore	15th	1992	Rodin	4th	1902	**Lyddite**	**1st**
1954	Three Striper	8th		Blitzer			Maple Sugar	5th
1953	Ballyray	11th	1990	Iskandar Elakbar	3rd		Scotland Yet	6th
1952	Hielan Laddie	6th					Doonside	9th
	Flareday	19th		**GEORGE WALKER**		1901	Ferney Tickle	3rd
1950	Roanite	13th	1922	Paddle	2nd		Maple Sugar	4th
1948	Face Off	10th	**1921**	**Herendesy**	**1st**		Pando	8th
1947	Tregaron	9th		Resarf	7th	1900	The Provost	2nd
1946	Kanshore	7th	1920	Anmut	4th		Barley Sugar	5th
1945	Pattoy	14th	1918	May Bloom	3rd		White Clover	7th
1941	Taffrail	4th		Blackburn	4th	**1899**	**Butter Scotch**	**1st**
1940	Silvos	6th		Sadducee	7th		Toddy Ladle	3rd
1939	Gold Fawn	13th	1917	Tarahera	2nd		Play Fun	10th
1937	Poverty Struck	10th	1915	Lady Curzon	4th	1898	Leading Lady	6th
	Gold Guard	11th	1913	Elfain	7th	1897	Fiddle	5th
1936	Samoan	5th		Crystiawoga	8th		Leading Lady	6th
	Judge Pool	13th				1896	Lochinvar	6th
1935	**Sally Fuller**	**1st**		**JOHN R. WALKER**		1895	Lochinvar	3rd
	Gay Sympathy	3rd	1922	Greybourne	8th		Kiltie	8th
1934	Candy Feast	5th	1919	Pleasure Bent	9th	1894	Lochinvar	6th
				Bugle March	10th	1893	Heather Bloom	3rd
	WILLIE THURNER			Fair and Warmer	12th			
1964	Later Mel	6th	1915	Hampton Dame	5th		**WM. G. (WILLIE) WILSON**	
1963	Son Blue	2nd	1911	Sanderling	6th	1932	Easter Dandy	6th
1962	Sun Dan	5th	1910	Frolic	6th		Royal Guest	11th
1957	Ali's Pride	5th	1904	Perfect Dream	14th	**1924**	**Maternal Pride**	**1st**
1955	Fleet Brenda	13th	**1896**	**Millbrook**	**1st**			
1953	Lowmond	8th		Springal	2nd			

Leading Sires of Plate Winners

CHOP CHOP (4)	Blue Light	1961
	Victoria Park	1960
	Lyford Cay	1957
	Canadiana	1953
HAVOC (4)	Mandarin	1916
	Seismic	1908
	Slaughter	1906
	Inferno	1905
TERROR (4)	Victorious	1891
	Williams	1884
	Fanny Wiser	1882
	Vice Chancellor	1881

**VICTORIA PARK (3)	Victoria Song	1972
	Kennedy Road	1971
	Almoner	1970
*BASSETLAW II (3)	Beehive	1914
	Hearts of Oak	1913
	St. Bass	1911
SPRINGFIELD (3)	Millbrook	1896
	Bonniefield	1895
	Joe Miller	1894
JACK THE BARBER (3)	Fearnaught	1872
	Floss	1871
	John Bell	1870
*LAPIDIST (3)	Wild Rose	1867
	Brunette	1864
	Touchstone	1863

*Imported from England.
**Plate winner.

Winners Who Sired or Foaled Plate Winners

1868	Nettie	Dam of Fanny Wiser (1882)
1902	Lyddite	Dam of Shimonese (1909)
1912	Heresy	Sire of Herendesy (1921)
1922	South Shore	Dam of Shorelint (1929)
		Sally Fuller (1935)
1938	Bunty Lawless	Sire of Epic (1949)
		McGill (1950)
1956	Canadian Champ	Sire of Titled Hero (1966)
		Canebora (1963)

1960	Victoria Park	Sire of Almoner (1970)
		Kennedy Road (1971)
		Victoria Song (1972)
1991	Dance Smartly	Dam of Scatter the Gold (2000)
		Dancethruthedawn (2001)

Evolution of Plate Record Times

On Dirt

HORSE	YEAR	TIME
Izvestia	1990	2:01 4/5
Victoria Park	1960	2:02
Regal Embrace	1978	2:02
Northern Dancer	1964	2:02 1/5
Archers Bay	1998	2:02 1/5
Lyford Cay	1957	2:02 3/5
L'Enjoleur	1975	2:02 3/5
Wando	2003	2:02.48
*Jammed Lovely	1967	2:03
Kennedy Road	1971	2:03
With Approval	1989	2:03

* Filly, 121 lbs. Colts and geldings carried 126 pounds.

On Polytrack

YEAR	HORSE	TIME
2008	Not Bourbon	2:03.59

Plate Attendance and Wagering Handles

YEAR	ATTENDANCE	HANDLE ($)	PLATE HANDLE ($)	YEAR	ATTENDANCE	HANDLE ($)	PLATE HANDLE ($)
1950	34,000*	595,000	(Undisclosed)	1981	30,451	3,628,889	695,956
1951	35,000*	659,000	134,000	1982	33,159	3,980,981	715,302
1952	30,000*	608,297	144,000	1983	30,523	3,528,622	706,546
1953	26,000*	727,006	151,600	1984	32,019	4,244,570	986,644
1954	18,000*	594,082	103,552	1985	31,195	4,222,349	887,026
1955	22,183	840,535	177,413	1986	31,320	4,471,888	919,503
1956	19,120	732,587	128,652	1987	34,335	5,051,838	1,018,715
1957	26,705	1,038,284	209,371	1988	28,812	4,841,031	1,014,019
1958	28,386	1,074,037	188,439	1989	32,485	5,637,603	1,205,271
1959	19,846	863,227	190,777	1990	25,292	5,360,232	958,069
1960	25,052	1,021,852	153,040	1991	26,932	5,459,098	942,768
1961	28,302	1,136,175	214,220	1992	24,101	4,996,880	841,464
1962	32,169	1,228,590	252,290	1993	21,809	4,592,831	807,748
1963	29,308	1,248,373	257,109	1994	18,202	5,320,820	979,386
1964	31,228	1,240,337	240,655	1995	18,279	6,407,132	1,014,059
1965	31,752	1,398,342	292,734	1996	16,025	6,071,718	1,176,882
1966	25,846	1,265,110	236,646	1997		4,083,634	1,076,796
1967	20,507	1,333,927	273,380	1998		4,158,838	1,086,261
1968	32,065	1,534,416	354,049	1999		4,183,900	1,141,237
1969	32,806	1,742,675	421,408	2000		4,218,894	1,441,966
1970	32,170	1,735,362	355,388	2001		4,875,572	1,381,673
1971	30,812	1,658,004	358,422	2002		5,267,545	2,002,940
1972	34,347	2,006,882	471,870	2003		5,814,484	2,054,851
1973	40,137	2,166,056	521,336	2004		4,951,710	1,376,769
1974	32,674	2,328,875	537,108	2005		5,778,542	1,814,061
1975	31,816	2,517,753	533,804	2006		4,967,164	1,475,947
1976	34,877	2,940,813	669,547	2007		5,525,468	1,672,689
1977	32,660	2,784,824	608,154	2008		5,459,862	1,704,944
1978	31,522	3,001,527	751,812	2009		5,779,983	1,843,587
1979	30,690	3,112,009	747,187				
1980	26,598	3,156,777	719,388				

* Estimate only

Note: No attendance figures available from 1997–2009

Plate Presentations

Year	Presenter
1860	Records unavailable
1869	Records unavailable
1870	Premier John Sandfield Macdonald
1871	Records unavailable
1872	Governor General Lord and Lady Lisgar
1873	Miss Mary Morrison
1874	Records unavailable
1880	Records unavailable
1881	Mrs. John Beverley Robinson
1882	Records unavailable
1883	Lieutenant Governor John Beverley Robinson
1884	Lieutenant Governor John Beverley Robinson
1885	Mrs. John Beverley Robinson
1886	Lieutenant Governor John Beverly Robinson
1887	Governor General Lord and Lady Lansdowne
1888	Governor General Sir Alexander Campbell
1889	Miss Marjorie Campbell
1890	Governor General Lord Stanley
1891	Governor General Lord Stanley
1892	Governor General Lord Stanley
1893	Lieutenant Governor Sir George A. Kirkpatrick
1894	Lieutenant Governor Sir George A. Kirkpatrick
1895	Lieutenant Governor Sir George A. Kirkpatrick
1896	Mrs. Lyndhusrt Ogden
1897	Lieutenant Governor Sir George A. Kirkpatrick
1898	Lieutenant Governor Sir George A. Kirkpatrick
1899	Governor General Lord Minto
1900	Governor General Lord and Lady Minto
1901	Mrs. William Hendrie
1902	Robert Davies, Ontario Jockey Club Vice-President
1903	Governor General Lord and Lady Minto
1904	Governor General Lord Minto
1905	Governor General Earl Grey
1906	Governor General Earl and Lady Grey
1907	Lieutenant Governor Sir William Mortimer Clark
1908	Governor General Earl and Lady Grey
1909	Governor General Earl and Lady Grey
1910	Joseph E. Seagram, Ontario Jockey Club President
1911	Governor General Earl Grey
1912	The Governor General, The Duke and Duchess of Connaught
1913	Lieutenant Governor Sir John M. Gibson
1914	The Governor General, The Duke and Duchess of Connaught
1915	Joseph E. Seagram, Ontario Jockey Club President
1916	Lieutenant Governor Sir John S. Hendrie
1917	Lieutenant Governor Sir John S. Hendrie
1918	The Governor General, The Duke of Devonshire
1919	Lieutenant Governor Sir John S. Hendrie
1920	The Governor General, The Duke and Duchess of Devonshire
1921	The Governor General, The Duke and Duchess of Devonshire
1922	Governor General Lord Byng
1923	Governor General Lord and Lady Byng
1924	Lieutenant Governor Henry Cockshutt
1925	Governor General Lord and Lady Byng
1926	Lieutenant Governor Henry Cockshutt
1927	Governor General Lord and Lady Willingdon
1928	Governor General Lord and Lady Willingdon
1929	Lieutenant Governor William Donald Ross
1930	Governor General Lord and Lady Willingdon
1931	Governor General Lord Bessborough
1932	Goveral General Lord and Lady Bessborough
1933	Goveral General Lord and Lady Bessborough
1934	Goveral General Lord and Lady Bessborough
1935	Lady Bessborough
1936	A.E. Dyment, Ontario Jockey Club President
1937	Governor General Lord and Lady Tweedsmuir
1938	Governor General Lord Tweedsmuir
1939	His Majesty King George VI and Queen Elizabeth
1940	Lieutenant Governor Albert Matthews
1941	A.E. Dyment, Ontario Jockey Club President
1942	Lieutenant Governor Albert Matthews
1943	Lieutenant Governor Albert Matthews
1944	Lieutenant Governor Albert Matthews
1945	Lieutenant Governor Albert Matthews
1946	Governor General Viscount and Lady Alexander
1947	Governor General Viscount and Lady Alexander
1948	Lieutenant Governor Ray Lawson
1949	Governor General Vicount Alexander
1950	Governor General Vicount Alexander
1951	Governor General Viscount and Lady Alexander
1952	Premier Leslie M. Frost
1953	Colonel K.R. Marshall, Ontario Jockey Club President
1954	Governor General Vincent Massey
1955	Lieutenant Governor Louis A. Breithaupt
1956	Governor General Vincent Massey
1957	Lieutenant Governor Louis A. Breithaupt
1958	Governor General Vincent Massey
1959	Her Majesty Queen Elizabeth and His Royal Highness The Duke of Edinburgh
1960	Governor General Georges and Madame Vanier
1961	Lieutenant Governor J. Keiller Mackay
1962	Her Majesty Queen Elizabeth, The Queen Mother
1963	Lieutenant Governor Earl Rowe
1964	Lieutenant Governor Earl Rowe
1965	Her Majesty Queen Elizabeth, The Queen Mother
1966	Lieutenant Governor Earl Rowe
1967	Governor General Roland E. Michener
1968	Lieutenant Governor Earl Rowe
1969	Governor General Roland E. Michener
1970	Lieutenant Governor W. Ross Macdonald
1971	Governor General Roland E. Michener
1972	Chief Justice of Canada, J.H. Gerald Fauteux
1973	His Majesty Queen Elizabeth and His Royal Highness The Duke of Edinburgh
1974	Her Majesty Queen Elizabeth, The Queen Mother
1975	The Duke and Duchess of Kent
1976	Governor General Jules and Madame Léger
1977	Lieutenant Governor Pauline McGibbon
1978	The Earl of Westmoreland
1979	Her Majesty Queen Elizabeth, The Queen Mother
1980	Lieutenant Governor Pauline McGibbon
1981	Her Majesty Queen Elizabeth, The Queen Mother
1982	Governor General Edward R. Schreyer
1983	Lieutenant Governor John B. Aird
1984	Lieutenant Governor John B. Aird